Reader's Digest

CREATIVE COOKING

Reader's Digest

Creative Cooking

THE READER'S DIGEST ASSOCIATION (CANADA) LTD.
215 Redfern Avenue, Montreal, Quebec H3Z 2V9

CREATIVE COOKING

The editors wish to express their gratitude for major contributions by the following people:

Chief Editorial Advisers: JAMES A. BEARD, JOSÉ WILSON, ELIZABETH POMEROY
Photographers: ALBERT GOMMI, LYNN ST. JOHN (cover), PHILIP DOWELL
Home Economists: HELEN FEINGOLD, JOY MACHELL
Stylist: KATHY IMMERMAN

Advisers:
Ena Bruinsma
Margaret Coombes
Derek Cooper
Margaret Costa
Denis Curtis
Theodora FitzGibbon
Nina Froud
Jane Grigson
John W. Hearn
Nesta Hollis
Kenneth H. C. Lo
Zena Skinner
Katie Stewart
Marika Hanbury Tenison
Silvino S. Trompetto, M.B.E.
  Maître Chef des Cuisines,
  Savoy Hotel, London
Suzanne Wakelin
Kathie Webber
Harold Wilshaw

Artists:
Color:
Ann Brewster
Roy Coombs
Pauline Ellison
Hargrave Hands
Victor Kalin
Denys Ovenden
Harriet Pertchik
Charles Pickard
Josephine Ranken
Charles Raymond
John Rignall
Rodney Shackell
Faith Shannon
Norman Weaver
John Wilson
Black and white:
David Baird
Brian Delf
Gary Hincks
Richard Jacobs
Rodney Shackell
Michael Vivo
Michael Woods
Sidney Woods
Black-and-white photography:
Michael Newton

The editors also wish to acknowledge the help of the following people and organizations:
Agriculture Canada
  (Food Advisory Div.)
Albrizzi, Inc.
Art Asia, Inc.
Ruth M. Barnes
Christian P. Braun
J. & D. Brauner
  Butcher Blocks
Donna Bright
Terri Bruce
Patricia A. Buckley
Kathryn L. Bull
Canadian Pork Council
Gene Cope
Dominion Stores Ltd.
Nancy Ebbert
Charles L. Edgerly
Virginia Edgerly
Frances B. Fink
Carolyn S. Fulmer
Geoffrey Gale
Richard Ginori
Donna Gisle
Greek Island, Ltd.
Harrods Ltd., London
Elisabeth Helman

Joyce M. Herrick
Sandra J. Hubbell
Erling Hulgaard, Fisheries
  Attaché of Denmark
Georg Jensen
Grace M. Kaufman
Jean Koza
Harriet A. Launier
Susan Lindberg
Leron Linens
Gwen B. Linton
Marguerite A. Mattis
Betsy McCloskey
Edward W. Myers
A. H. Nagelberg
Patricia Orr
Joanne R. O'Toole
Dorothy Trueb Peck
D. Porthault, Inc.
Larry G. Reed
Scandinavian Fishing
  Yearbook A/S
Jeanne A. Schmaltz
R. A. Seelig
Debora Seneca
Ruth L. Sexton

Louis Sherman
Natalie H. Smith
Martha M. Smolich
Alfred E. Tremblay
United Fresh Fruit and
  Vegetable Association
U.S. Livestock
  and Meat Board
U.S. Marine
  Fisheries Service
Helen M. Wacker
Janice White
Joyce D. Wright
Mary Zibelli
Mary Zinsmeister

CONTENTS
OF
CREATIVE
COOKING

To avoid constant repetition of basic information, some technical words and phrases used in this book have been marked with an asterisk [*]. Full information about terms marked in this way will be found by referring to the index.

Each recipe includes a notation for PREPARATION TIME (preparation and mixing of all ingredients) and COOKING TIME (the length of time the dish cooks in the oven or on top of the stove). By adding the two together, the reader can calculate the time required to complete a dish, from initial preparation to serving.

Buying for Quality 8–45

A guide to day-by-day marketing. Comprehensive advice on choosing the finest-quality homegrown and imported fruits and vegetables, freshwater and saltwater fish and shellfish, poultry and game, and meat and variety meats. This section also includes useful information on North American, French, and other imported cheeses.

Twelve Months of Recipes 46–295

More than 600 recipes based on fresh foods in season. These appear under the headings: Soups and First Courses, Fish, Meat, Poultry and Game, Rice and Pasta, Vegetables and Salads, and Desserts. Each month also contains recipes for snacks and supper dishes from leftovers. Recipes for each month are followed by menus for special occasions.

Buying

Tree Fruits

PAGES 10–11

Soft Fruits

PAGES 12–13

Citrus Fruits

PAGES 14–15

Other Fruits and Nuts

PAGES 16–17

Game

PAGE 31

Beef
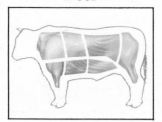
PAGES 32–34

Veal
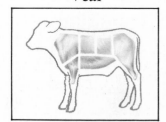
PAGES 34–35

Lamb

PAGES 36–37

for Quality

Vegetables

PAGES 18–23

Freshwater Fish

PAGES 24–25

Saltwater Fish

PAGES 26–27

Shellfish

PAGES 28–29

Poultry

PAGE 30

Pork

PAGES 38–39

Variety Meats

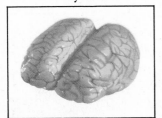

PAGE 40

North American Cheeses

PAGE 41

French Cheeses

PAGES 42–43

Other Imported Cheeses

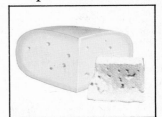

PAGES 44–45

Tree Fruits

Tree fruits include the core fruits, such as apples and pears, and the stone fruits, such as cherries, nectarines, plums, peaches, and nuts. Buy only enough to last a few days because fruit does not keep for long at room temperature. Apples and pears will keep for about two weeks if they are stored in a cool, dry place or in the refrigerator, but all stone fruits, with the exception of plums and nuts, are best eaten on the day of purchase. Remember that fruits are cheaper, more nutritious, and taste best when in season.

McINTOSH
WINESAP
GRANNY SMITH
JONATHAN
DELICIOUS
GOLDEN DELICIOUS
GREENING
ROME BEAUTY

Apples These are divided into eating and cooking apples. Many eating apples are also excellent for cooking, especially if hard. Look for apples that are clean, firm, brightly colored, and free from brownish bruises. Season: all year; peak from September through March.

Fall apples include: **Lobo,** dark red, with juicy, white flesh. Excellent for salads, desserts, and for eating raw. Season: September to November. **Gravenstein,** greenish yellow, with crisp, acid flesh. Good for eating and cooking. Season: September to November.

Winter apples include: **Jonathan,** bright red, with juicy, aromatic, and fairly fine flesh. Excellent for eating raw, and for cooking and baking. Season: October to January. **Cortland,** shiny red, with delicate snow-white flesh. Excellent for salads and fruit cocktails (the flesh does not turn brown from exposure to air). Season: October to February. **Delicious,** brilliant red with fine-grained, juicy flesh. Excellent for salads and for eating raw. Generally not used for cooking. Season: November to February. **Golden Delicious,** bright yellow to gold. Excellent for salads and especially good for cooking and for eating raw. Season: November through March. **McIntosh,** bright red, with very juicy, sweet flesh when ripe. Good for baking and cooking. Cooking time is shorter than for

most other apples. Season: October to April or May. **Newton** (Yellow Newton, Albemarle Pippin), bright yellow to greenish yellow. Flesh is aromatic, crisp, and fairly acid. Excellent for eating raw and good for cooking. Season: January to May. **Northern Spy,** glossy, pinkish red, with very tender and juicy flesh. Excellent for eating and cooking. Season: December to March. **Greening,** bright green to greenish yellow, with rich, fairly acid flesh. Excellent for pies and applesauce; good for baking. Usually not eaten raw. Season: November to February. **Rome Beauty,** bright red, with firm, juicy flesh. Excellent for baking; good for applesauce, pies, and all-purpose cooking. Usually not eaten raw. Season: December through March; some marketed until July. **Golden Russet,** golden brown, with a rough-textured skin. Excellent for desserts. **Winesap,** glossy, bright red, with very firm, coarse, and juicy flesh. Good for all purposes. Keeps well. Season: September to November. **Fameuse** (snow), bright red, with white flesh. Excellent for desserts and baking; good for applesauce. Season: October to December.

Summer apples include: **Yellow Transparent,** with a greenish yellow skin. Good for all purposes; excellent for eating raw. Season: August. **Granny Smith,** bright green skin, hard and crunchy flesh

with a sharp flavor. Good for eating or cooking. These apples are imported from Australia. Season: March through September.

Apricots Small stone fruits with yellow, juicy, sweet flesh. Buy firm, plump apricots with a good orange-golden color. Avoid any that are very firm, mushy, wilted, shriveled, or bruised. Season: May through August; peak in June and July. The Canadian season runs from mid-July to mid-August.

Cherries Most sweet cherries on the market come from the western United States and Canada. Red tart cherries, also called sour or pie cherries, are used mainly in cooked desserts; they have a softer flesh and are

a lighter red. They are usually sold frozen or canned.

Good cherries are bright, glossy, plump, and have fresh-looking stems. Avoid those that are shriveled and any with a dull appearance, leaking flesh, or brown discolorations. Sweet varieties include **Bing, Black Tartarian, Schmidt, Van, Hedelfingen, Napoleon, Lambert, Valera,** and **Windsor.** Season: peak in June and July. Sour varieties include: **English Morello, Northstar, Meteor,** and the widely available **Montmorency.** Season: late July to mid-August.

Nectarines A cross between the peach and the plum, these smooth-skinned stone fruits have sweet, juicy flesh and are usually served as a des-

sert fruit. Like peaches, they are particularly suited for use in fruit salads, ice cream, and pies.

Choose plump fruits with a slight softness along the seam. Most nectarines are orange-yellow with red areas. Avoid dull, hard, or slightly shriveled fruits. Season: late July through September; peak in July and August. Imported from Chile in midwinter.

Peaches The many varieties are customarily classified into two types: freestone and clingstone. Freestone peaches have juicy, soft flesh that comes away easily from the stone; they are good for eating fresh or for freezing. Clingstones have firmer flesh that adheres tightly to the stone; they are mainly used in canning.

NAPOLEON

STANLEY

SANTA ROSA

GREENGAGE

APRICOT

HAZELNUTS

EL DORADO

LARODA

ITALIAN PRUNE

NECTARINE

RIO OSO GEM

WALNUTS

MONTMORENCY

DAMSON

BARTLETT

REDHAVEN

CHESTNUTS

FILBERTS

BOSC

COMICE

Peaches should have a fresh, bright color. Avoid any that are split and those with bruised skins or soft spots. Do not buy very firm or hard peaches that are green; they are probably not mature and will not ripen properly.

Yellow-fleshed clingstones include **Dixired, Redhaven, Babygold 5, Garnet Beauty, Suncling.** Yellow-fleshed freestones include **Envoy, Elberta, Redskin, Loring, Rio Oso Gem,** and **Harbelle.**

Season: late July to late September; peak in July and August.

Pears Bartlett, the most popular variety and the first of the season, is an excellent all-purpose pear. It is ideal for eating raw, for poaching, and for canning. Look for a pale yellow to rich yellow skin with a red blush. Season: August through April. The greenish-yellow **Clapp** is on the market in September.

Fall and winter pears include **Anjou,** greenish yellow; the long-necked **Bosc,** greenish yellow to brownish yellow; **Comice,** greenish yellow to yellow with red; **Seckel,** yellowish brown; and **Keiffer,** yellow. Canadian-grown varieties include **Moonglow, Max-Red Bartlett, Aurora, Magness,** and **Russet Bartlett.**

Pears bruise easily and should be handled with care. They are best bought before fully ripe and left at room temperature for 2 or 3 days. Ripe pears will yield when gently pressed at the stem end and side surfaces. Avoid misshapen, shriveled, bruised, or blackened fruit with dull-looking skin.

Plums and **fresh prunes** Plums vary greatly in appearance, ranging from the yellow-green of the Gages to the dark blue of the Damsons. Popular varieties include **Santa Rosa, Laroda,** and **El Dorado.** Varieties available in Canada include **Greengage, Stanley, Damson, Reine Claude, President,** and **Grand Duke.** Season: August through September.

Only a few types of fresh prunes are on the market. They are all similar in shape and color, ranging from bluish black to purple. Varieties include **Italian, French,** and **Imperial.** Season: July through October.

Plums and fresh prunes are good for use in fruit salads, pies, puddings, preserves, jams, and jellies. Look for firm to slightly soft fruits. Avoid those with skin breaks, punctures, or any that are very hard.

Quinces These bright yellow or greenish-yellow fruits are round or pear shaped. They are indigestible if eaten raw but make excellent jams and jellies. Choose firm but not hard fruits and avoid any with punctures, bruises, or soft spots. Season: October through December.

Chestnuts The shiny brown fruit of the sweet chestnut is enclosed in a fleshy outer covering that breaks open when the nut is ripe. Avoid any that look dry and shriveled. Season: mid-September to March.

Hazelnuts The small, gray-brown nuts grow in clusters partly covered with leafy husks. Ripe, fresh nuts should have firm, not shriveled, husks. Available all year.

Filberts are a variety of hazelnut, but the fruits are more oblong than hazelnuts. Shelled nuts should be crisp and meaty. Avoid any that are shriveled.

Walnuts The shells should have a faint damp sheen. Avoid any that rattle, as they will be dry and shriveled. Shelled walnuts stored covered in the refrigerator or freezer will keep for months. Green or underripe walnuts are sometimes seen in September and October. They can be eaten fresh but are more often used for pickling. Season: all year.

11

Soft Fruits

Strawberries, raspberries, blackberries, and other soft fruits should be used on the day of purchase. They are usually sold in plastic containers. Avoid any badly stained cartons because the fruits might be mushy and often moldy. As soon as possible after buying, tip the berries carefully onto a plate and discard any that are bruised or spoiled. Do not wash the berries or remove the hulls or stems; set them well apart on a tray, uncovered, in the refrigerator. When ready to use, put the berries in a sieve or colander, run cold water over them gently, and drain them thoroughly.

Blackberries These large purple-black berries grow wild but are also cultivated. Because they are extremely soft, they deteriorate quickly and, as fresh dessert berries, must be used as soon as possible after purchase. Delicious when eaten fresh with sugar and cream, they are also excellent for making pies, puddings, jams, jellies, and wines. Avoid containers with too many red and unripe berries. Overripe fruit will usually have a very dull appearance. Stained containers indicate leakage and spoilage. Season: mid-July through August.

Blueberries Originally a wild fruit collected by the Indians during colonial times, blueberries are now grown commercially. The words "huckleberry" and "blueberry" are sometimes used interchangeably, but huckleberries belong to a different genus and are not cultivated.

Blueberries are delicious eaten raw as a breakfast fruit or added to pancakes, waffles, biscuits, and muffins. They also make good pies, cobblers, puddings, sauces, jams, and jellies.

Look for berries that are dark blue and have a silvery bloom, the best sign of quality. The bloom is a natural waxy protective coating. Choose berries that are uniform in size and free from stems and leaves. Avoid damp containers. Season: mid-July through September.

Currants The glossy, sweet-tart **red currants** are eaten raw, in compotes and fruit salads, or made into jams and jellies. Season: in limited quantities from mid-July to early August.

Black Currants are dark, almost black, with fairly tough skin and juicy, slightly acid flesh. Look for containers with large berries and no more than 15 percent dark red and 5 percent green berries turning red.

Black currants can be used in pies, but are best made into jams, jellies, and fruit syrups. Grown in Canada. Season: in limited quantities from June through August; peak in July.

White Currants are eaten raw or used in salads and fruit cups. Grown in Canada. Season: in limited quantities from June through August; peak in July.

Gooseberries When available, these berries usually appear in farmers' markets or through local supplies. They may be green, red, yellow, or white, smooth or hairy, and may grow as large as 1 inch in diameter and 1½ inches long.

Gooseberries taste best when they are cooked and used as fillings for pies and tarts, and in jams, jellies, and preserves. Avoid mushy berries or any that have splits and blemishes on the skin. Season: July.

LOGANBERRIES

RASPBERRIES

BLACKBERRIES

GOOSEBERRIES

SEQUOIA

OZARK BEAUTY

TIOGA

TUFTS

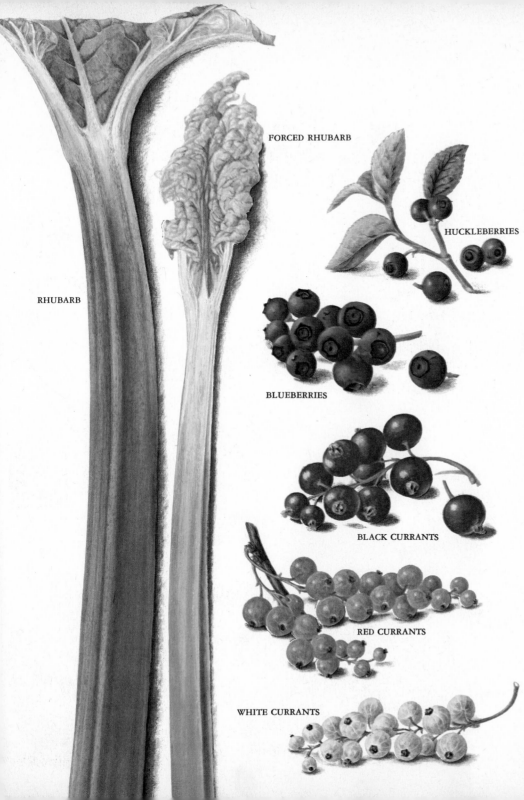

FORCED RHUBARB

RHUBARB

HUCKLEBERRIES

BLUEBERRIES

BLACK CURRANTS

RED CURRANTS

WHITE CURRANTS

Huckleberries These wild berries are usually sold locally because they do not ship well. They are normally smaller and more acid than blueberries, and contain 10 hard seeds. Blueberries have more than twice as many seeds, but these are so small that they are hardly noticeable. Season: in limited quantities from June through August.

Loganberries These tangy, juicy fruits have the shape of blackberries and the color of raspberries, but they are tarter. Highly perishable, the berries are usually sold in cans and are used in making pies, tarts, jams, and preserves or sprinkled on cereals. Season: in limited amounts from late July to early August.

Raspberries These berries grow wild but are also cultivated. They may be red, black, purple, yellow, or amber and are always sold hulled. Avoid any with cracks or pits and any that are very soft or moldy. Wet or stained containers may be a sign of poor quality or spoiled berries. Raspberries are highly perishable and should be eaten as soon as possible after they are purchased.

These fruits are usually served fresh with cream, but they make excellent jams and preserves. Raspberries can be substituted in most recipes calling for strawberries. Season: mid-July to mid-August.

Rhubarb Although technically a vegetable, rhubarb is used as a fruit. It has dark red stalks and coarse green leaves and may need peeling if the rhubarb is tough. Forced, or hothouse, rhubarb has tender, pink, and milder-flavored stalks that do not require peeling. Rhubarb leaves contain large amounts of oxalic acid and should not be eaten.

Because of its extreme acidity, rhubarb should be cooked before eating. It is excellent in pies and is sometimes referred to as a "pie plant." Rhubarb is also used in tarts, puddings, sauces, jams, and jellies. Baked or stewed, it makes a good breakfast food.

Choose crisp, firm, bright red stalks. The hothouse variety is pale pink and has underdeveloped, yellow-green leaves. The condition of the leaves is usually a good guide for determining the freshness of this vegetable. Avoid flabby or wilted stalks. Old rhubarb, rhubarb that has grown too long before harvesting, may be stringy, tough, and pithy. Season: late January to mid-June; peak in early June.

Strawberries The most popular fruit of the berry family, fresh strawberries are served with cream or milk and sugar, used in cakes, pies, and tarts, fruit compotes and salads, ice cream, water ices, and for making jams, jellies, and preserves.

Choose clean, bright berries, free from moisture, with bright green caps. Usually, small to medium strawberries are of better quality than large ones.

Avoid overripe and underripe fruits and those with gray mold. Stained containers indicate spoilage. Berries with large seedy areas have poor flavor and texture.

Among the popular varieties of strawberries planted commercially in Canada and the United States are **Sequoia, Ozark Beauty, Tioga, Tufts, Fresno, Midway, Blakemore, Hood, Florida Ninety, Acadia, Vibrant, Surecrop, Headliner, Guardian,** and **Raritan.** Season: some strawberries available all year; peak in Canada from mid-June through July.

13

Citrus Fruits

Although citrus fruits are frequently used in cooking, they taste best when served fresh. Citrus fruits are available canned, some in syrup and some without sweetening; frozen; and fresh in chilled containers. The extracted pure juices, particularly of oranges and grapefruit, are also sold canned or frozen, with or without added sugar, and in chilled containers.

In general, all fruits should have bright, taut, and slightly moist skins with a definite aroma. Some markets display fruits cut in half to enable customers to gauge the condition of the flesh, the juice content, and the thickness of the skin. When buying citrus fruits, avoid any that are dry-looking, shriveled, or have soft indentations and blemishes on the skin.

Citrus fruits store fairly well. Lemons and grapefruit can be kept in the vegetable compartment of the refrigerator for 1–2 weeks, and other types can be stored in a cool place for about 1 week. However, all citrus fruits should be used before the skins shrivel. Before cutting or serving, the fruits should be rolled firmly between the palms of the hands or back and forth on a flat surface to get an even distribution of juice within the fruit.

All citrus fruits are rich in vitamin C, a vitamin essential for the prevention of scurvy and one that aids normal development of teeth and bones. Eating citrus fruits or drinking their juice is a pleasant way of ensuring that the body has enough of this vitamin.

KUMQUATS

LIME

CLEMENTINE

GRAPEFRUIT

LEMON

Clementines A cross between an orange and a tangerine, the clementine has stiff, orange-red, pebbly skin and slightly acid flesh. Choose fruits that are heavy for their size, with dark orange skins. Season: November to December.

Grapefruit These fruits are squat and round, with pale yellow, bronze, or russet skin. The juicy flesh ranges from pale yellow to pink to red. Usually served fresh as a breakfast dish or as a first course, grapefruit are also good in salads and for making marmalade.

Choose firm fruits, heavy for their size, with thin skins. Grapefruit should feel springy to the touch; avoid puffy or spongy fruits. Grapefruit that are pointed at the stem or have wrinkled or rough skins may have thick skins and too little flesh.

Popular varieties include **Duncan, Marsh** (seedless), **Foster, Thompson** (Pink Marsh), and **Ruby.** Season: all year from California and Arizona; October through June from Florida.

Kumquats These are small, oval, orangelike fruits with bright orange, sweet skin and juicy, slightly bitter flesh. They can be served fresh and eaten with the skin; wash the fruit thoroughly before eating. Available bottled in syrup, kumquats are used for making marmalades and as a garnish for roasts. Sliced thin, they are delicious in fruit salads. Originally cultivated in China and Japan, kumquats are now grown in Florida and California. Choose firm fruits that are heavy for their size and that have no blemishes. Season: November through February.

Lemons Choose plump fruits, heavy for their size and with smooth, oily, deep yellow skins. Those that are rough-skinned and lightweight have less juice, as do those with knobby rather than pointed ends. Season: all year; peak from May through August.

Limes These small fruits are similar to lemons but they have thin, green skin. Most limes on the market are Persian varieties and are the size and shape of lemons, with fine-grained, greenish-yellow pulp. The smaller, yellower round types are Key limes. The rind is smooth, leathery, and very thin.

Avoid limes with dull, dry skins (a sign of aging and loss of flavor) and those with soft spots, skin punctures, and mold. Season: all year; peak from June through August.

Oranges The **Navel** and **Valencia** are the leading varieties from California and Arizona. The seedless Navel, marketed from November until early May, has a thicker, slightly more pebbled skin than the Valencia and is easier to peel and to separate into segments. Navels are especially well suited for eating as whole fruit or for sectioning in salads. The Valencias, in season from late April through October, are good for juicing and slicing in salads, but they have a few seeds.

The oranges from Florida and Texas, grown especially for juice, are the **Parson Browns,** the most important early variety, available from October through November; and the **Hamlins,** in season from October through December. Both these

BLOOD ORANGE

VALENCIA ORANGE

NAVEL ORANGE

JAFFA ORANGE

TANGELO

SEVILLE ORANGE

MANDARIN

TANGERINE

UGLI FRUIT

varieties are pale and thin-skinned. Also abundant in juice are the high-quality **Pineapple** oranges, in the markets from January through February. **Valencias**, in season from April through June, are good for juicing and sectioning. The **Florida Temples**, harvested from early December through March, taper slightly at the stem end. These thick orange-red fruits peel easily, section readily, and have an excellent flavor.

Tangerines, a small type of orange, are distinguished by their loose, bright orange to red skin. Their small, juicy segments contain numerous seeds.

Choose firm tangerines that are heavy for their size, with deep orange to red-orange skins. Avoid any fruits with punctured, cut skins, very soft spots, water-soaked areas, or mold. Season: late November until early March; peak in November through January.

Mandarins are small, round oranges that are easily peeled and segmented; their deep orange flesh contains numerous seeds. They are readily available in cans but in limited quantities when fresh. Season: November through January.

Other less important varieties, available in limited quantities, include **Blood** oranges, noted for their blood-red or crimson flesh; the oval, thick-skinned **Jaffa** oranges—both in season from mid-March to mid-May—and the **Seville** oranges. The latter have too much acid for use in desserts and they are used almost exclusively for making marmalade.

Although not widely available in the United States, the bitter Sevilles are imported from Mexico and the West Indies in February and March; they can be bought in specialty fruit markets and in some Hispanic stores.

Avoid lightweight oranges (less flesh and juice); very rough skin (overly thick skin and less pulp); and dull, dry skin (a result of aging). The color of oranges is not a reliable indication of quality. Green spots or a greenish hue does not mean that the fruit is immature.

Tangelos These are a cross between tangerine and grapefruit, and are usually necked, or drawn out at the stem end. They are very juicy and good for eating as whole fruit or in salads, or squeezed for juice. Season: October through January; peak in November and December.

Ugli Fruits The size of grapefruit, with thick, knobby skin, ugli fruits are usually imported from Jamaica. Small quantities are grown in Florida. The juicy flesh is sweeter than grapefruit and tastes more like an orange. Ugli fruits contain few seeds. Season: October through January.

15

Other Fruits and Nuts

This section describes some of the less familiar fruits as well as some of the better known. Several kinds of fruit are imported and reach the stores in prime condition, though at higher prices than homegrown produce. Most of the fruits are served as fresh dessert fruits. For serving and eating suggestions, see pages 345–348.

Almonds The small, oval, flat nuts in light brown shells are sold in the shell, or shelled blanched or unblanched. Shelled almonds are sold whole or sliced, slivered, or halved. Available all year.

Bananas Normally picked and shipped green, bananas are then stored and sold in varying stages of ripeness. The mealy flesh becomes sweeter as it matures. Choose bananas from a bunch rather than buying them loose. When fully ripe, they should be firm, plump, and golden yellow flecked with brown. Imported mainly from Central and South America. Season: all year.

Brazil Nuts Hard, dark brown, three-edged shells enclose firm, slightly oily nuts. They are sold unshelled or shelled. Avoid any that rattle in the shells. Imported from South America. Available all year.

Chinese Gooseberries (Kiwi Fruit) Egg-shaped or oblong, with brown, hairy skin, these fruits have soft, sweet green flesh, with edible seeds. Avoid any with shriveled skins. Imported from New Zealand. Season: June through February.

Coconuts These large nuts have a hard, dark brown outer shell closely covered with tough fibers. To test for freshness, shake nut to be sure it contains liquid. Imported from Honduras, the Dominican Republic, and Puerto Rico. Season: all year; peak in December.

Cranberries The fruits vary in size, and the color ranges from medium red to blackish red; they have a pleasant but sharp flavor. Select plump, firm berries. Season: September through December.

Dates Fresh dates are plump and shiny, yellow-red to golden brown, with smooth skins and sweet, pulpy flesh. Dried dates should be plump, 1–2 inches long, and shiny; avoid any with a shriveled look or with sugary crystals. Available all year.

Figs These highly perishable fruits are soft when ripe, with greenish-yellow, purple, or black skin. Season: fresh figs from June through October; dried figs, all year.

Grapes Table grapes, such as **Thompson Seedless, Emperor, Tokay,** and **Ribier,** are grown mainly in California and Arizona.

Varieties such as **Catawba, Concord, Delaware,** and **Niagara** are sold for table use in small quantities only; almost all of these grapes are used for making jelly, juice, and wine. The largest producers of these varieties are Ontario, New York, Pennsylvania, and Washington.

When possible, buy in bunches. Choose plump, fresh-looking grapes, firmly attached to their stems. Avoid any that are soft or wrinkled and any with leaking or bleached areas around the stems. Season: table grapes, all year; other Canadian grapes from early September to mid-October.

WATERMELON

HONEYDEW

CRENSHAW

CANTALOUPE

LYCHEES

POMEGRANATE

BANANA

BRAZIL NUTS

BLACK GRAPES

RED GRAPES

GREEN GRAPES

FRESH FIGS

ALMONDS

DRIED DATE

FRESH DATES

DRIED FIG

PASSION FRUIT

PINEAPPLE

PAPAYA

COCONUT

PERSIMMON

MANGO

LOQUAT

PEANUT

CRANBERRIES

PECAN

CHINESE GOOSEBERRIES

Loquats These stone fruits are similar in shape and size to plums, with downy, pale yellow or orange skin. The flesh is slightly tart. Choose firm fruits. Season: April and May.

Lychees or **Litchis** Of Chinese origin, these stone fruits are the size of large cherries, with hard, scaly, red skins that turn brown after picking. The white, pulpy flesh is firm, juicy, and slippery. Buy when skin is red, but avoid any with shriveled skins. Season: mid-June to early July.

Mangoes These large, oval stone fruits come in different shapes and sizes. Some are round; others are long and narrow, either kidney-shaped or pear-shaped. The tough skin is usually green, with red to yellow areas. The flavor of the orange-yellow, juicy flesh is a combination of pineapple and peach. Avoid mushy fruits with a large number of black spots. Season: May through August; peak in June.

Melons These come in many different sizes and shapes.

Cantaloupes may be oval, oblong, or round, and their rind should have a coarse, thick netting, or veining. The skin beneath the netting should be yellow when fully ripe. Look for a smooth, rounded scar at the stem end, indicating maturity. Season: May through September; peak from June through August.

Casabas are sweet, juicy melons, normally pumpkin-shaped but slightly pointed at the stem end. They have shallow ridges running from the stem to the blossom end and range from light green to yellow. Season: July through November; peak in September and October.

Cranshaws, or **Crenshaws**, are large, slightly pointed at the stem

end, and rounded at the blossom end. They have a relatively smooth rind and very shallow furrowing. When ripe, the skin is deep gold and the pale orange flesh is sweet and juicy. Season: July through October; peak in August and September.

Honeyballs are similar to the honeydew but smaller, rounder, and slightly netted over the surface. Season: June through October.

Honeydews are large (5–7 pounds) and oval, with a smooth skin that ranges from creamy yellow to creamy white, depending on its stage of ripeness. The flesh is sweet and fine-grained. Season: all year; peak from June through October.

Persians resemble cantaloupes but are rounder, have a finer netting, and are about the same size as honeydews. The green rind has a yellow tint when ripe. Season: June through October.

Santa Claus, or **Christmas,** melons are oval, with hard, thick, slightly netted gold and green skin and pale green, sweet, mild flesh. Season: December.

Watermelons are oblong or round. The rind is dark green, green with lighter green stripes, or grayish green. When ripe, they should have a relatively smooth surface with filled out ends and a creamy-yellow underside where the melon was in contact with the soil. Season: March through October; peak from June through August.

Papayas Papayas have smooth skins that ripen from green to yellow or orange. The sweet, juicy flesh has a melonlike texture and contains numerous black seeds. Choose medium-size fruits that are at least half yellow. Avoid fruits with bruised or broken skins. Season: all year; slight peak in May and June.

Passion Fruits These fruits are similar in shape and size to large plums. The tough skin is purple and deeply wrinkled when ripe. The aromatic yellow pulp has small, edible seeds. Season: fall.

Peanuts The two major types are the **Virginia** and the **Spanish.** The former has a longer shell, larger nut, and more pronounced flavor. Available in the shell, plain or roasted; or shelled. Season: all year.

Pecans These nuts, native to North America, are grown in the southeastern United States as far north as Indiana, as far west as Texas, and in northern Mexico. Available in the shell. Shelled, they are sold roasted, dry-roasted, salted, or plain. Season: all year; peak from September through November.

Persimmons These deep orange-red fruits have very sweet, orange flesh and may be astringent even when ripe. Choose glossy fruits with stem caps. Season: October through January; peak in November.

Pineapples Imported mainly from Puerto Rico and Hawaii, pineapples are large, oval fruits with hard, knobby skin. Contrary to popular belief, they do not sweeten after harvest, but they may become less acid. Season: all year; peak from March through June.

Pomegranates These fruits are about the size of oranges and vary in color from deep red to purple. They have thin, tough skins and bright red flesh. The seeds, flesh, and juice are edible. Choose fruits that are heavy for their size, with fresh, unbroken skins. Season: September into December; peak in October.

17

Vegetables

Ideally, vegetables should come straight from the field or garden to the kitchen. Although this is seldom possible, there are many clues to their freshness or age. Choose crisp, firm vegetables rather than hard ones. Avoid any that are overly large; they may be coarse and tough. Green beans, peas, zucchini, other squash, and summer vegetables are excellent when very young. This also applies to such root vegetables as carrots, beets, and kohlrabi. Most vegetables are available all year but they are at their best in quality and lowest in price at the peak of their Canadian seasons. They are packed with vitamins and minerals and will be more nutritious, tastier, and retain their crisp texture if they are cooked only long enough to make them tender.

Artichokes, Globe These vegetables are the leafy flower head of the plant. The gray-green, stiff leaves overlap, and the edible parts of the leaves are their fleshy bases. The heart below the leaves has the finest flavor. Buy plump artichokes, heavy for their size, with thick, green, tightly clinging leaves. Season: all year; peak from March through May. See illustration on page 23.

Artichokes, Jerusalem These tubers grow in a mass of twisted knobs and are covered with a thin skin, ranging in color from beige to yellow or brownish red to purple. Select artichokes with a fresh appearance; avoid any that are misshapen or small. Season: October through February.

Asparagus A choice but expensive vegetable, asparagus is sold loose, in bundles, or packaged and graded according to thickness of stem and plumpness of buds. Look for asparagus with tight, well-formed heads. The spears should be a rich green. Avoid asparagus with thin, woody, dry, or shriveled stems. Season: late April to early June.

Avocados These dark green, pear-shaped fruits are usually treated as a vegetable rather than a dessert fruit.

The oily, pale green, soft flesh surrounds a large pit. Avoid avocados with blotched or dry skins. Season: all year. See illustration on page 23.

Beans Comparative newcomers from Europe, the excellent **fava beans,** or **English broad beans,** are similar to lima beans, but their pods are longer, rounder, and thicker. The tough skin on the pods of mature beans should be removed after cooking. Season: mid-April through June.

Most **green beans,** or **snap beans,** are the green-podded varieties and are on the market the year round. The large green **pole beans** and **yellow wax beans** are available only periodically.

Buy slender beans with a bright color. The fresh ones will snap easily when bent. Avoid flabby or wilted vegetables with serious blemishes.

Lima beans, sometimes available shelled, are usually sold in the shell. The shells should be dark green and well filled with beans. Avoid any that are spotted, flabby, or yellow. Season: all year; peak from July through September.

Beets These vegetables are sold by weight without leaves or in bunches with leaves. Choose deep red beets that are firm, round, and smooth. Rough, shriveled, soft, or flabby

JERUSALEM ARTICHOKE

BEETS

SUMMER CABBAGE

SPRING CABBAGE

WINTER CABBAGE

BRUSSELS SPROUTS

WHITE CABBAGE

RED CABBAGE

SAVOY CABBAGE

ENDIVE

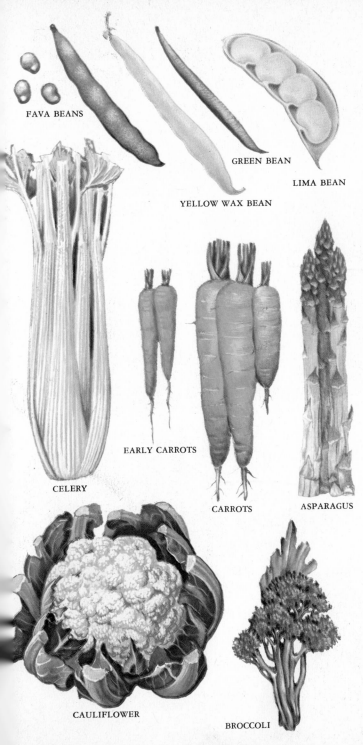

FAVA BEANS

GREEN BEAN

LIMA BEAN

YELLOW WAX BEAN

CELERY

EARLY CARROTS

CARROTS

ASPARAGUS

CAULIFLOWER

BROCCOLI

beets may be tough or woody. Avoid any with soft, wet areas, a sign of decay. Season: mid-June to March.

Beet Tops These greens from the tops of beets are rich in vitamin A. Cook in the same manner as spinach. Season: mid-June to March. See illustration on page 22.

Broccoli While cauliflower, a close relative, has one fused head of curds, broccoli develops thick, fleshy stalks that terminate in small florets. Choose broccoli with firm, compact, green bud clusters; some may be green with a purplish cast. None of the buds should have opened enough to show the yellow flowers (a sign of age). The stems should not be thick or tough. Season: late June to late November.

Brussels Sprouts Aristocrats of the cabbage family, these vegetables should be firm, compact, and bright green. Avoid any that are puffy or have loose, yellow, or wilting leaves. Ragged leaves or holes in the sprouts may indicate worm damage. This is one of the vegetables often ruined by overcooking. Season: late July to December.

Cabbage There are smooth-leaved green cabbages, crinkly-leaved green Savoys, and red cabbages. All varieties are good for any use, although the **red** and **Savoy cabbages** are more popular in salads and slaws. When red cabbage is cooked, an acid, such as vinegar, red wine, or apples, should always be added to retain the cabbage's color.

Summer and **winter cabbages** will have larger, more solid heads than the **spring cabbages. White cabbages,** which have been in storage, are trimmed of their outer leaves and are a lighter green. They are satisfactory if not discolored or wilted.

Chinese, or **celery, cabbage** has some of the characteristics of both cabbage and romaine. The compact stalks range from 10 to 16 inches in length but are normally 4 inches wide. These cabbages are usually eaten in salads but can be cooked like cabbage.

Carrots These root vegetables are among the most inexpensive and nourishing of all vegetables. They are one of the richest sources of vitamin A. Young, slender early carrots are usually sold in bunches with their leaves intact. They are smaller, tenderer, and have a milder flavor and brighter color than carrots harvested for storage. Mature carrots are larger and usually coarser; they are sold packaged without leaves and usually require scraping or peeling. Avoid flabby, wilted, pitted, or broken carrots and any with green areas at the top. Season: late June to late May.

Cauliflower When buying low-calorie cauliflower, choose white to creamy-white, firm, compact heads with bright green leaves. Avoid any with limp leaves or loose, brown, gray, or damaged curds (the white edible portion). Small leaves extending up through the curds do not affect quality. Spreading curds are a sign of age. Season: early June to late October.

Celeriac (celery root, or knob celery) These are the edible roots of a variety of celery. They have fibrous skins and creamy-white flesh with a celery flavor. Look for small, firm roots; large ones may be tough and woody. Season: August through

April; peak from October through April. See illustration on page 23.

Celery The most common variety is the **Pascal** celery. Although usually eaten raw, it is delicious braised, creamed, and in soups and stews. Choose crisp celery with fresh green leaves and a glossy surface. The branches should snap easily. Avoid wilted celery with flabby upper branches. Season: late June through November.

Chicory (curly endive) and **Escarole** The curly, narrow, ragged-edged leaves of **chicory** resemble dandelion leaves. The center of the head has yellowish leaves that have a milder flavor than the dark green outer leaves. **Escarole** has long wavy leaves that are broader and less crinkly than chicory leaves.

Look for crisp, fresh leaves with vivid green outer leaves. Avoid wilted leaves and any yellow or brown discolorations. Season: all year. See illustration on page 21.

Collards Closely related to cabbage and kale, this smooth vegetable is usually cooked with a piece of bacon or salt pork. Choose fresh, crisp leaves. Season: all year; peak from December through April. See illustration on page 22.

Corn The best corn has fresh green husks. Nutritional value and flavor are rapidly lost once the husks have been removed. Make sure the silk ends are free from decay. The stem ends should not be very discolored or dry. The ears should be well filled with plump kernels that exude a milky liquid when punctured. Season: August through October. See illustration on page 22.

19

Vegetables
(*continued*)

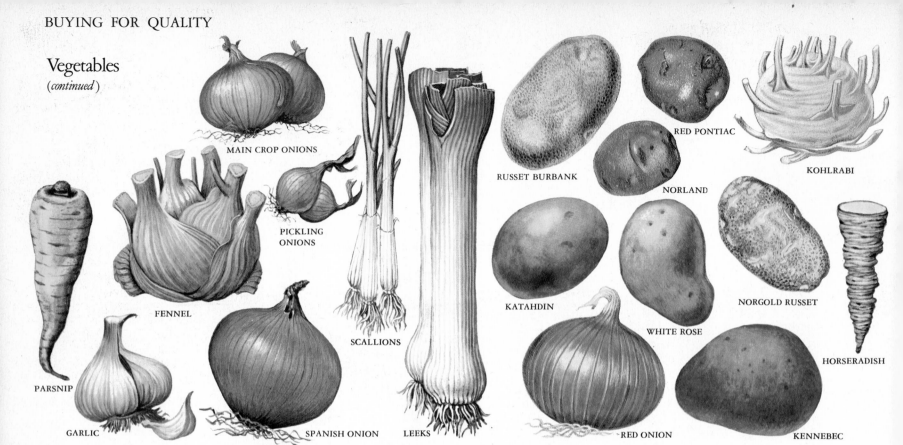

MAIN CROP ONIONS

PICKLING ONIONS

FENNEL

PARSNIP

GARLIC

SPANISH ONION

SCALLIONS

LEEKS

RED ONION

RUSSET BURBANK

NORLAND

KATAHDIN

WHITE ROSE

RED PONTIAC

KOHLRABI

NORGOLD RUSSET

HORSERADISH

KENNEBEC

Cucumbers Choose cucumbers that are firm over their entire length and have fresh green rinds with many small bumps. If the cucumbers are waxed, they should be peeled before use. Avoid any that are large in diameter and those that are turning yellow. Although most cucumbers are grown in fields, there is a large production of greenhouse cucumbers. Season: field from mid-June to late October; hothouse from March to mid-November.

Eggplant A large satin-skinned vegetable that ranges in color from dark purple, to red or yellow, to white; however, those in the markets are usually purple. Prime eggplants should be firm and heavy, with shiny, dark purple skins. Season: August to mid-October. See illustration on page 23.

Endive (Belgian Endive, or Witloof) A member of the chicory family, this expensive vegetable has tightly packed white or pale yellow leaves. Endive is slightly bitter; it is primarily used in salads but is delicious cooked as well. Season: October through May. See illustration on page 18.

Fennel (Anise) Fennel has a globular, swollen stem base, bright green, feathery, dill-like leaves, and a mild licorice flavor. Choose well-rounded bulbs that are pale green to white; avoid deep green bulbs. Season: October through April; peak in November and December.

Garlic The white skin of this bulbous plant encloses small, curved segments known as cloves. These are surrounded by a thin layer of skin that should be peeled. Buy garlic in small quantities; it turns rancid if kept too long. Store in a dry, cool, dark place. Season: all year.

Horseradish The long, strong-flavored root is not used as a vegetable but as an ingredient of cold sauces. It is available fresh as a root, dried, and bottled with vinegar or beet juice. Season: late fall.

Kale The broad leaves vary in color from dark green to purple. They are heavily crimped and have prominent midribs. Avoid kale with yellow, drooping, or damaged leaves. Season: all year; peak from December through February.

Kohlrabi These vegetables have swollen stems with a mild turnip flavor. They are best when young, about 2–3 inches in diameter, and easily pierced with the fingernail. Avoid large vegetables; they may be tough. Season: May through November; peak in June and July.

Leeks These expensive thick-stemmed vegetables have tightly packed layers that branch at the top into dark green leaves. The stems are white, with a faint onion taste. Look for well-shaped, straight leeks, trimmed at the top. Avoid those with yellow leaves. Season: mid-July to mid-December.

Lettuce Four types are generally available: crisphead (usually but incorrectly called iceberg); Cos, or romaine; butterhead; and leaf.

Crisphead is large, solid, and round, with medium green outer leaves and pale green inner leaves.

Romaine, or **Cos,** is long and tapering, with crisp, broad, dark green leaves that are greenish yellow toward the center.

Butterhead includes the most common varieties, **Boston** and **Bibb.** It has a smaller head than crisphead and a slightly flat top. The soft green leaves have a buttery texture and a delicate flavor.

Leaf lettuce does not form heads but has curled or smooth, broad, tender leaves arranged loosely around a stem. It is grown in greenhouses or on truck farms and locally.

Look for signs of freshness; the leaves should have a good, bright color. Crispheads and romaines should be crisp; other types have a softer texture. Usually eaten raw in salads and sandwiches, lettuce is also good braised and used in soups. Season: all year.

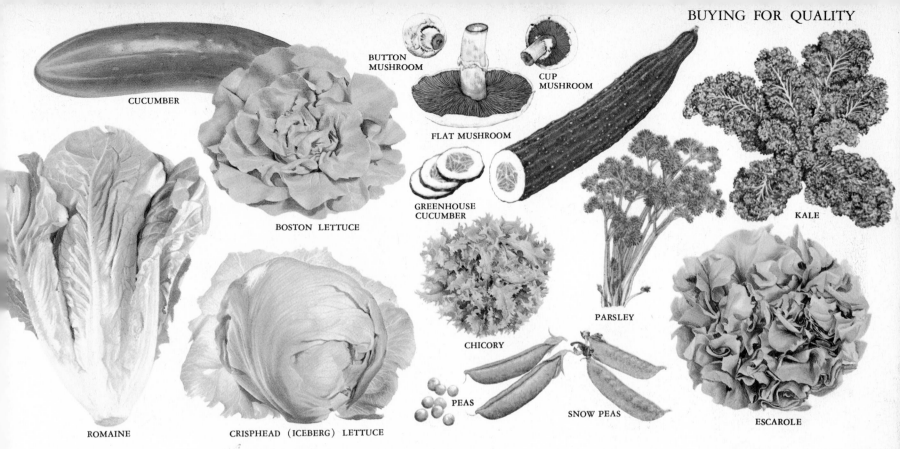

CUCUMBER

BUTTON MUSHROOM

CUP MUSHROOM

FLAT MUSHROOM

GREENHOUSE CUCUMBER

KALE

BOSTON LETTUCE

PARSLEY

CHICORY

PEAS

SNOW PEAS

ESCAROLE

ROMAINE

CRISPHEAD (ICEBERG) LETTUCE

Mushrooms Choose mushrooms carefully, as they turn limp quickly and lose their flavor. Use on the day of purchase. The **cap** and **flat** mushrooms are older and often have a stronger flavor than the more recently harvested **button** mushrooms. Avoid limp, broken mushrooms with a sweaty appearance. Cooked mushrooms have a variety of uses, but raw mushrooms are good eaten in salads. Season: all year; peak in November and December.

Okra These vegetables are curved, generally ribbed seed pods. Select only the small, bright green, tender pods between 2 and 4 inches long. The tips should bend with a slight pressure. Large pods will be tough. Avoid any shriveled pods. Season: all year; peak from June through August. See illustration on page 23.

Onions There are many varieties, but commercially grown onions fall into three general categories.

The **maincrop,** or **globes,** the most common types, are generally yellow, but some have red and white skins. They are round or oval, with a pungent flavor, and are used primarily for cooking.

Bermuda-Granex-Granos, usually yellow-skinned, are milder, less round, and less symmetrical than the globes. They are good for slicing and eating raw, as well as for cooking.

The **Creole** types, such as the **Spanish** onions, are generally much larger than the globes but resemble them in shape. Most types are yellow-skinned, but some are white. Because of their mild flavor, they are ideal for slicing and for salads.

Onions smaller than 1 inch in diameter are called pickling onions or

picklers and may be found among any of the above varieties.

Choose onions that are dry, firm, and regular in shape, with papery skins. Onions with shriveled skins and softness around the neck are immature or decaying. Also avoid any that are beginning to sprout. Onions store well, especially during autumn and winter, if kept in a dry place. Season: early August to July.

Parsley This plant is used mainly for flavoring sauces and as a garnish. Choose bunches of curly or flat-leaf parsley that have fresh green foliage. Avoid any with yellow leaves or tough flowering stems. Season: early June to mid-December.

Parsnips The flavor of these winter vegetables is improved by a

touch of frost, which makes them sweeter. Look for firm, well-formed, small to medium parsnips. They are best when crisp and clean; avoid any with split or dried-up roots or soft brown patches on the crown. Season: September to late June.

Peas These have a delicious sweet flavor when young. Overripe peas will be tough and starchy. Buy bright, crisp, well-filled pods with a velvety texture. Avoid any that have wet pods, or are swollen or pale. Eat one to test for freshness; it should be sweet and tender. Season: all year; peak from February through July.

The expensive **snow peas,** or **sugar peas,** are flat, with edible pods. They are often used in oriental dishes. Season: all year; peak from May through September.

Peppers Most peppers in the markets will be the sweet green variety that turn bright red when they are fully mature. Choose firm, medium to dark green, shiny peppers; avoid any that are misshapen, dull-looking, soft, or flabby. Immature peppers are pale green. Peppers can be stuffed or used in salads. Season: mid-July to late October. See illustration on page 23.

Potatoes These are usually divided into three groups, although the distinctions are not well defined and there is considerable overlapping.

New potatoes is a term most often used to describe those harvested during the late winter and early spring, but the name also applies to freshly dug but not fully matured potatoes. These are best for creaming or boiling. Look for firm,

Vegetables
(continued)

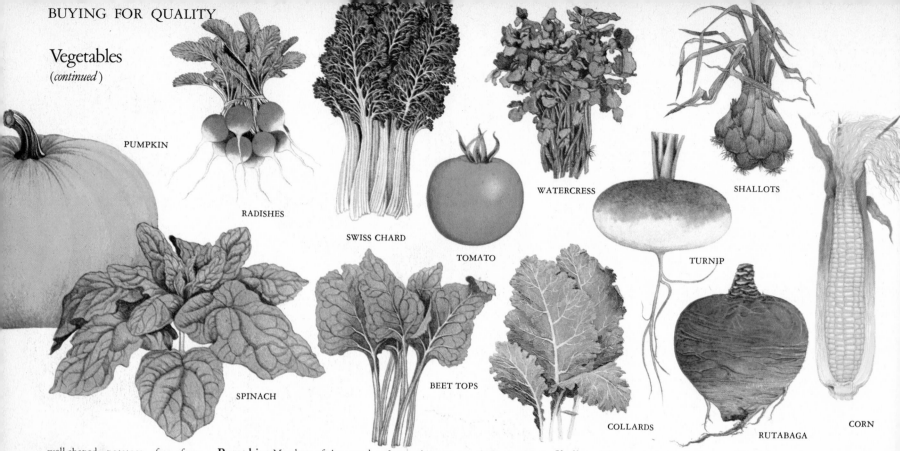

PUMPKIN

RADISHES

SWISS CHARD

TOMATO

WATERCRESS

SHALLOTS

TURNIP

SPINACH

BEET TOPS

COLLARDS

RUTABAGA

CORN

well-shaped potatoes, free from blemishes and light burn (a green skin discoloration).

General-purpose potatoes include the **Katahdin, Kennebec, Norgold Russet, Norland, Red Pontiac,** and **White Rose.** Use for boiling, mashing, frying, and baking. Season: all year.

The area in which baking potatoes are grown, as well as the variety, are important factors that affect the baking quality. The best-known and most widely grown is the **Russet Burbank,** commonly known as the Idaho. Season: all year.

The general-purpose and baking potatoes should be firm, clean, fairly smooth, well-shaped and free from cuts, blemishes, and decay. Avoid any potatoes that have green areas from light burn or any that have sprouted or shriveled.

Pumpkins Members of the gourd family, these vary greatly in size, from very small, about the size of a cantaloupe, to 100 pounds. Choose firm, bright-colored pumpkins, heavy for their size and free from excessive scarring. Season: September through November.

Radishes These small, pungent vegetables are used fresh in salads and for garnishes. They may be round or elongated, bright red, black, white, or purple. Choose small, crisp radishes. Season: mid-April to mid-November.

Rutabagas are relatives of the turnip, but they are larger and have yellow flesh. Some late winter rutabagas are coated with paraffin to prevent shriveling and moisture loss. Remove the paraffin by peeling be-

fore cooking. Choose firm, round or slightly elongated rutabagas, heavy for their size. Avoid any that are cut or bruised. Season: early July to mid-June.

Salsify (oyster plant) Yellowish gray and shaped like a carrot, this root vegetable has a mild, sweet taste resembling the flavor of oysters. Look for young, well-formed roots. Season: June through February.

Scallions (green onions) Known as shallots in Canada, they are used in salads and to flavor other vegetables. Their mild-flavored bulbs have thin skin that peels easily. Choose onions with small bulbs and fresh green tops. Avoid any with wilting leaves. Season: all year; peak from May through July. See illustration on page 20.

Shallots These members of the onion family, often called scallions in Canada, are milder than onions, but they have a slight garlic flavor. Available fresh or dried, shallots are often used to flavor sauces, salads, soups, and meat dishes. Season: October through May; peak in March and April.

Spinach The flat or wrinkled varieties should have large, crisp, dark green leaves, free from blemishes. Avoid leaves that are yellow, wilted, crushed, or decayed. Season: late April to December.

Squash, Summer These vegetables are harvested when they are young and tender.

Yellow Crooknecks, which are widely grown, are moderately warted, have curved, gooselike

necks, and are narrower at the top than at the base. **Straightnecks** are yellow squash that resemble crooknecks but are straighter.

Pattypans (cymlings or scallops) are disk-shaped, with scalloped edges. They are pale green when young and white when mature. These squash are best when no larger than 3 inches in diameter.

Zucchini are straight and cylindrical but slightly larger at the base. Large zucchini can be as long as 10–12 inches but will then be very watery inside. The skin is dark green over a light yellow ground with a greenish-black lacy pattern and dark green stripes. Young zucchini, no more than 6 inches long, are considered the best.

Look for firm, well-developed squash. A tender squash will have glossy skin. Season: all year.

Squash, Winter These squash are marketed when fully mature, with hard shells.

Acorns are small, hard-shelled squash, widely ribbed, and round or slightly conical in shape. Dark green, they turn dull orange mingled with green during storage. The flesh is pale orange. Season: all year.

Buttercups are turban-shaped at the blossom end, with green to dark green skin pockmarked with gray and faintly striped with dull gray. Season: late summer, fall, and winter. Average size of this squash is 6–8 inches in diameter.

Butternuts are cylindrical, with a bulblike base; the skin is light brown or yellow. Average length is 9–12 inches. Season: all year.

Hubbards are huge and globe-shaped with tapered necks and hard, warted, ridged rinds that vary from greenish bronze to grayish blue to reddish orange. Season: late August through March; peak from October through December.

Choose squash with hard, tough skins, indicating full maturity. They should be heavy for their size. Avoid any with sunken or moldy areas.

Sweet Potatoes Two types are available in varying amounts all year.

Moist sweet potatoes, incorrectly called yams, have deep yellow or orange-red flesh. The true yam, the root of a tropical vine, is not grown commercially in North America.

Dry sweet potatoes are low in moisture and have pale yellow flesh that is somewhat mealy when cooked. Not widely cultivated.

Look for smooth-skinned, firm potatoes with an even color. Because they are more perishable than Irish potatoes, select them carefully.

Avoid any with wet, soft decay, dry decay (ends of the potato that are shriveled and discolored), and dry rot (areas on the side of the potato that are sunken and discolored). Season: all year; peak from September through December.

Swiss Chard These have spinach-like, dark green, crisp leaves with prominent white midribs similar to those of celery stalks. The leaves should be cooked like spinach and the stalks like celery. Season: April through November; peak from June through October.

Tomatoes Those with the best flavor are allowed to ripen completely on the vine before being picked. Tomatoes that are shipped for long distances must be harvested when they are green and therefore are not as juicy and flavorful as the home-grown or those from nearby farms.

To ripen tomatoes properly, keep them in a paper bag in a dark place (not the refrigerator). Tomatoes stored in sunny areas may wither and become pulpy. Season: field from early July to September; hothouse from mid-April to July.

Turnips The most popular turnips have purple tops, but some have green tops. These vegetables are sold without leaves or in bunches with leaves. Look for firm, small to medium, round turnips with fresh, crisp tops. Avoid large turnips; they may be fibrous. Season: all year; peak from October through March.

Watercress These peppery, small, round-leaved plants are cultivated but also grow wild by freshwater ponds and streams. Choose bunches of green, crisp leaves; avoid any with yellow or wilted leaves. Season: all year; peak from May through October.

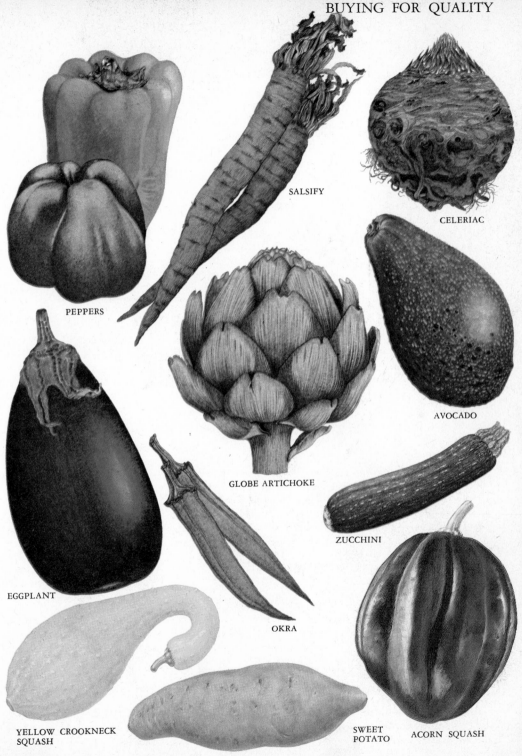

SALSIFY

CELERIAC

PEPPERS

AVOCADO

GLOBE ARTICHOKE

ZUCCHINI

EGGPLANT

OKRA

YELLOW CROOKNECK SQUASH

SWEET POTATO

ACORN SQUASH

Freshwater Fish

When buying freshwater or saltwater fish, make sure that the fish have a fresh, clean smell. Recently caught fish will have no fishy odor. Take a careful look at the eyes; they should be bright and bulging. If they have a sunken or cloudy look, the fish is not fresh. The gills should be bright red and free from slime. As the fish becomes stale, the color of the gills gradually fades to light pink, then gray, then to a greenish or brownish color. The skin of fresh fish has a shiny, iridescent look, and the scales will adhere firmly to the flesh. The flesh is elastic and springs back to its original shape when pressed.

To judge the freshness of steaks and fillets, look for a fresh-cut appearance—firm-textured flesh with no traces of browning around the edges or signs of drying out. The fish will have a fresh, mild smell. Wrapped steaks and fillets are packaged in moistureproof material, with little or no air between the fish and the wrapping.

Frozen fish should be frozen solid, without a brownish tinge or other discoloration in the flesh. The fish should be well centered in the package; if not, it has probably thawed out and been refrozen. Wrappings should be moistureproof and vaporproof, with little or no air between the fish and the wrapping. All frozen cleaned whole fish, if unwrapped, should be covered with a glaze of ice to protect the fish from freezer burn and from drying out.

It is an advantage to have a neighborhood fish dealer. Even though supermarkets sell fish—usually a limited selection—a merchant whose business is fish will know much more and will help the customer to understand how to buy and cook fish.

Fresh and frozen fish are available in various forms in the markets. The following are the best-known cuts:

Whole: fish as it comes from the water. Before cooking, the scales and insides must be removed. Drawn: whole fish with only the insides removed. Dressed or pan-dressed: whole fish with scales, insides, and often the head, tail, and fins removed; ready to cook. Steaks: cross-section slices from large dressed fish; ready to cook. Fillets: sides of fish cut lengthwise; practically boneless and ready to cook. Sticks: elongated pieces of fish cut from frozen blocks of fillets, weighing at least three-fourths of an ounce. Portions: uniformly shaped pieces of boneless fish also cut from frozen fillets but larger than fish sticks.

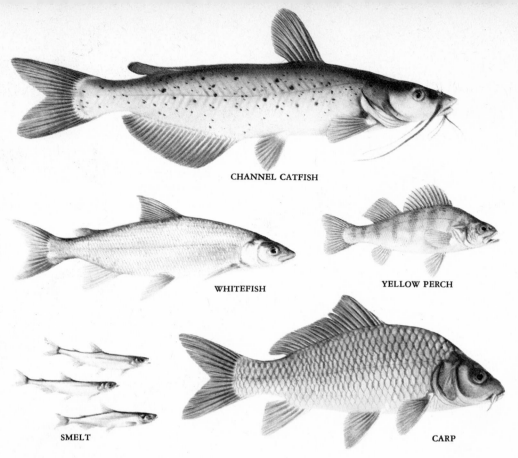

CHANNEL CATFISH

WHITEFISH

YELLOW PERCH

SMELT

CARP

Bass The **largemouth bass** is caught in southern Quebec and Ontario and in B.C. and Manitoba. It weighs about 3 pounds, although much larger sizes have been caught.

The **smallmouth bass** is found in the Great Lakes drainage system. Average weight is 3–4 pounds.

The golden **rock bass**, also called the redeye, is found in the Mississippi Valley, the Great Lakes, and southern Manitoba and Saskatchewan. Average weight of rock bass is 1½ pounds.

The **white,** or **silver, bass,** which is found in the same areas as the rock bass, has a better flavor and texture than rock bass.

The **yellow bass,** about the same size as the white bass, is caught in the eastern part of the United States.

Bass are available whole, as steaks, and as fillets. Bake, broil, poach, or sauté. Season: all year.

Black Crappie (strawberry bass) Black crappie is caught in large numbers in the Mississippi Valley, the Great Lakes, and southern Canada. Average weight is 1–2 pounds. Available whole. Broil or pan-fry. Season: all year.

Buffalo Fish This member of the sucker family is caught in the Mississippi Valley. The average weight of the **redmouth,** or **bigmouth, buffalo** is 2–20 pounds, but it may weigh as much as 70 pounds. The **smallmouth buffalo** weighs up to 45 pounds and is thought to have the finest flavor. Available in the U.S. fresh or smoked; whole, or as steaks and fillets. Bake, poach, or sauté. Season: September to May.

Carp This fish lives in the sluggish rivers, ponds, and lakes of North America. Its average length is 12–20 inches and it weighs from 2 to 8 pounds. The best time to eat carp is from November through March. In summer they tend to take on a muddy taste; this flavor can be eliminated by skinning the fish and soaking it in mildly salted water for 3–4 hours. Available fresh, frozen, or smoked; whole, or as steaks or fillets. Bake, poach, deep-fry, steam, stew, or braise. Season: all year.

Catfish (wolffish) This fish is caught in the Great Lakes, the eastern and central United States, and southern Canada. Some of the common Canadian varieties, ranging in size from 1 to 30 pounds, are the **channel, stonecat, brindled madtom, yellow bullhead** and **spotted.** The spotted catfish is thought to have the best flavor. Available fresh or frozen, whole, or as fillets, steaks, or chunks. Broil, deep-fry, or sauté. Season: all year; peak from March to October.

Freshwater Drum A relative of the sheepshead and croaker, this fish is caught in the Great Lakes and the Mississippi Valley. Average weight is 1½–3 pounds. Available whole. Broil, sauté, or pan-fry. Season: all year; peak in March.

LAKE HERRING

BIGMOUTH BUFFALO

BLACK CRAPPIE

YELLOW WALLEYE

FRESHWATER DRUM

RAINBOW TROUT

LAKE TROUT

LARGEMOUTH BASS

Lake Herring (cisco) A relative of the whitefish, the blue-backed lake herring with silver sides is found in large numbers in the Great Lakes and the upper Mississippi and southern Hudson Bay watersheds. Its average weight is 5 ounces to 1 pound. Available fresh, frozen, smoked, or salted. Broil, deep-fry, or sauté. Season: all year.

Pike The varieties of this popular game fish include the **pickerel, muskellunge,** and the **northern pike.** The latter is gray-blue or green with yellowish or whitish spots. Pikes usually weigh from 1½ to 10 pounds, but some specimens weighing 30 pounds or more have been caught. This fish is found in fresh water from New York to Alaska. Available fresh or frozen; whole if small and as fillets if larger. Bake, broil, braise, or poach. Season: all year; peak in June.

Smelt Members of the salmon family, smelt are olive green with silvery sides and undersides. Smelt are caught along the Atlantic and Pacific coasts, in the Columbia River, the Great Lakes, and in bays from Mexico to Canada. It takes about 10 of these small oily fish to make a pound. If they are fried very crisp, the bones can be left in. Available fresh, frozen, and canned. Broil, deep-fry, or sauté. Season: September to May.

Trout The most widely known varieties of this highly prized food and game fish include the **brook trout** (speckled char), **rainbow trout,**

Kamloops trout, steelhead trout, cutthroat trout, brown trout, and the **Dolly Varden.** Trout are caught in eastern and northern Canada and the United States and in the West from California to British Columbia. The brook trout is considered to be one of the finest-tasting varieties.

The **lake trout,** largest of all the trout, lives in the Great Lakes and in the lakes of Alaska, British Columbia, and the northern United States. This trout varys in color with the season and the lakes from which they are caught, but those found in the markets are usually pale green, with small yellow spots. Market size is about 10 pounds.

Available whole; fresh, frozen, canned, and smoked. Bake, broil, poach, or sauté. Season: all year.

Yellow Perch The range of this species extends from northern Canada south to the Great Lakes, where it is caught in abundance, and as far south as North Carolina. It has been successfully transplanted to the western United States. Its olive-green back merges into golden yellow and becomes lighter toward the stomach. Its sides are marked by 6 or 8 dark vertical stripes. Average weight is 1 pound and length is less than 1 foot. Fish longer than 14 inches tend to be bony, with poor-quality flesh. Available fresh or frozen; whole or as fillets. Broil, deep-fry, or sauté. Season: all year; peak from April to November.

Whitefish This fish, blue-green with silver sides and belly, inhabits lakes from Newfoundland to Brit-

ish Columbia and north to Alaska and the Yukon. The **Rocky Mountain** whitefish, caught as far west as the Pacific Coast, is noted for its excellent flavor and texture. Average weight is 2–6 pounds, but some weigh as much as 15–20 pounds and grow as long as 2 feet. Available fresh or frozen; whole or as fillets; and smoked. Bake, broil, poach, or sauté. Season: all year; peak in May through August.

Yellow Walleye This famous game fish is the largest of the perches. It is caught in great abundance as far west as the Mississippi Valley and north through the Great Lakes to Hudson Bay. Average size is 1½–4 pounds. Available whole or as fillets. Bake, broil, or sauté. Season: all year; peak in June.

25

Saltwater Fish

The normal serving of fish is $\frac{1}{3}-\frac{1}{2}$ pound of edible fish per person. To provide this amount, allow 1 pound of whole or drawn fish (insides removed) per serving; $\frac{1}{2}$ pound of dressed fish (scales, insides, and usually head, tail, and fins removed) per serving; and $\frac{1}{3}-\frac{1}{2}$ pound of fillet or sticks per serving. This rule applies to fresh or frozen fish. Because fillets are 100 percent edible, steaks about 85 percent edible, and whole or drawn fish about 45 percent edible, it may be cheaper to buy fillets, although the price per pound may be higher.

Fresh fish is extremely perishable. If it is not to be cooked immediately, remove it from the wrapper and wrap it with moisture-proof paper, aluminum foil, or transparent plastic wrap, or put it in a tightly covered dish. Store in the coldest part of the refrigerator.

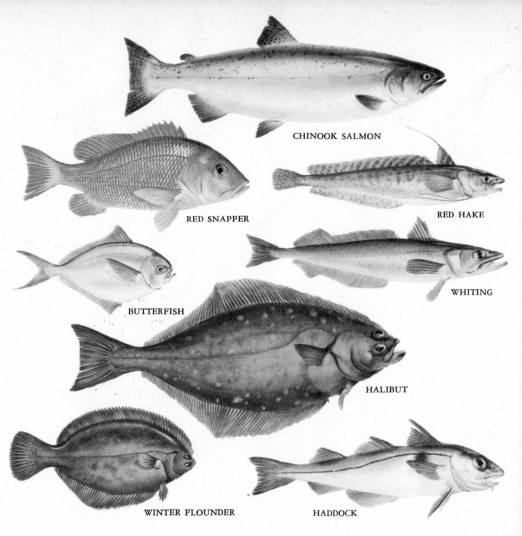

CHINOOK SALMON

RED SNAPPER

RED HAKE

BUTTERFISH

WHITING

HALIBUT

WINTER FLOUNDER

HADDOCK

Bluefish This blue-green fish, found along the Atlantic and U.S. Gulf coasts, weighs up to 10 pounds, but market size is 1–7 pounds. Available fresh or frozen; whole, or as steaks or fillets. Season: all year; greatest quantities in June.

Butterfish Caught off the Atlantic Coast from Nova Scotia to Florida, this delicately flavored fish averages $\frac{1}{2}$ pound. Available whole—fresh, frozen or smoked. Season: all year; peak from April to December.

Cod This important food fish is a native of the North Atlantic and North Pacific, but most of our cod are caught off the Grand Banks of Newfoundland. The mature cod averages 10 pounds in the markets. Available fresh or frozen; whole, or as steaks, fillets, or sticks; and salted, smoked, or pickled. Scrod (young cod) weighs $1\frac{1}{2}-2\frac{1}{2}$ pounds. Season: all year; best months are May to October for Atlantic cod, January to May for Pacific cod.

Flounder The most common type—with a dark gray back and white undersides—is found in the North and South Atlantic, and the South Pacific. The flounder family includes the gray sole, lemon sole, summer flounder, witch flounder, and yellowtail.

The average weight of flounders is $\frac{3}{4}-5$ pounds. Available fresh, frozen, or smoked; whole, or as fillets. Season: all year.

Haddock A close relative of the cod, but smaller ($1\frac{1}{2}-7$ pounds) and marked by a black lateral line, the haddock lives in the North Atlantic from the Strait of Belle Isle to Cape Cod. Available fresh or frozen; whole or as fillets; also smoked. The smoked fish is called finnan haddie. Season: all year; peak is March to July.

Hake This fish lives in the North Atlantic and North Pacific. The average weight is 2–5 pounds. Available fresh. Occasionally sold as deep-sea fillets, but usually whole. Season: all year; peak in September and October.

Halibut This flat fish usually weighs from 5 to 125 pounds, although some may reach 600 pounds. It is a native of the North Atlantic and North Pacific. Chicken halibut, considered the best, weighs 1–9 pounds. Available fresh or frozen; whole, or as steaks or fillets. Season: all year.

Mackerel The long, slender Atlantic mackerel is found near the Continental Shelf from Newfoundland to Cape Cod. Market size is about 2 pounds. Available fresh, frozen, or canned; whole, or as steaks or fillets; and salted or smoked. Season: April through November.

Mullet The many varieties of this fish are natives of the Atlantic Ocean from Cape Cod to North Carolina, the Gulf of Mexico from Florida to Texas, and the Pacific Coast. Average weight is 1–3 pounds. Available frozen, smoked, or salted. Season: all year.

Ocean Perch (rosefish, redfish) A native of the North Atlantic, this fish weighs about 1 pound. Perch is almost always sold as frozen fillets. Season: all year.

Porgy (scup) This fish from the U.S. Atlantic Coast averages 12 inches in length and weighs $\frac{1}{2}-1\frac{1}{2}$ pounds. It is usually sold fresh and whole. Season: January through October.

Red Snapper This superbly flavored fish is considered one of the choicest of the sea. It is caught in the South Atlantic and the Gulf of Mexico. Market size is 2–20

pounds. Available fresh or frozen. Red snapper is sold whole up to 5 pounds, but as fillets or steaks when larger. Season: all year.

Salmon The king of fish inhabits waters off the Atlantic and Pacific coasts of North America. Only one variety of salmon is found in the Atlantic Ocean, but the Pacific Ocean has 5 varieties: spring or chinook salmon (the largest), sockeye salmon, chum salmon, coho salmon, and pink salmon (the smallest). They vary in size from 2 to 30 pounds. Salmon is sold fresh, frozen, or canned; whole or as

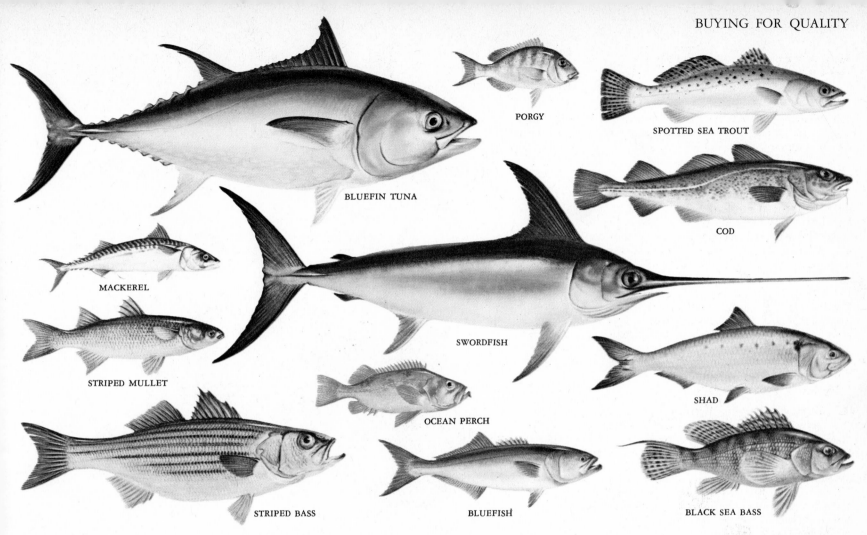

PORGY

SPOTTED SEA TROUT

BLUEFIN TUNA

COD

MACKEREL

SWORDFISH

STRIPED MULLET

SHAD

OCEAN PERCH

STRIPED BASS

BLUEFISH

BLACK SEA BASS

steaks, fillets, or chunks; and smoked or kippered. Season: all year.

Sea Bass The black sea bass (rare in Canada) lives in the Atlantic and Pacific oceans and the white sea bass lives along the Pacific Coast. Available fresh or frozen, usually whole. Season: all year for black bass; May through October for white bass.

Sea Trout Also called weakfish because of its very tender mouth, this species is found in the Atlantic and the Gulf of Mexico. Other

varieties include the spotted sea trout and the white sea trout. Available fresh, frozen, or smoked; whole or as fillets. Season: all year.

Shad This fine-flavored fish, caught in the Atlantic and Pacific oceans, ranges in size from $1\frac{1}{2}$ to 5 pounds. It is usually available fresh and whole. The roe of the shad is considered a delicacy. Season: May and June.

Sole The true sole is not found in North American waters; it inhabits its waters from the Mediterranean Sea to the North Sea. The best is

the Channel (English or Dover) sole. Most so-called sole in the markets is a variety of flounder. It weighs $\frac{3}{4}$–5 pounds. Available fresh or frozen; whole or as fillets. Season: all year.

Striped Bass (rockfish) This delicious fish is found in the Atlantic and Pacific oceans. Market size is usually 2–25 pounds. Available fresh or frozen; whole, or as steaks or fillets. Season: all year.

Swordfish One of the world's great game fish, the swordfish averages about 7 feet in length and

weighs 50–400 pounds. This fish is found in the North and South Atlantic and occasionally in the Pacific Ocean. Swordfish is not sold in Canada; in the U.S. it is available fresh or frozen, usually as steaks. Season: April to September in the Atlantic; September to December in the Pacific.

Tuna A relative of the mackerel and a native of the Atlantic and Pacific oceans, this fish can weigh more than 1,000 pounds. Varieties include the albacore (the only true white-meat tuna), yellowfin, bluefin, and skipjack. Available fresh

or frozen; whole or as steaks. However, most of the catch is canned. Some brands of canned tuna in the United States and Canada bear a seal or code signifying that the tuna has been packed under federal inspection for quality and cleanliness. This does not mean that other brands are unsafe to eat. Season: May through December.

Whiting (silver hake) This member of the cod family is caught off the North Atlantic Coast; it weighs 1–4 pounds. Available fresh or frozen; whole or as fillets; and dry salted. Season: all year.

Shellfish

Shellfish are usually expensive, but they are very nutritious and low in calories. When purchased already shelled, they are even more expensive, but there is no waste.

When buying fresh shrimp, make sure that they have a mild odor and that the meat is firm in texture. The colors of the shell may vary from red to pink to gray, depending on the type; the most common shrimp have gray shells.

Crabs, lobsters, and rock (or spiny) lobsters should be alive when purchased. They should move their legs, and the tail of a live lobster should curl under his body when he is picked up; if it is limp and hangs down, the lobster is probably dead. Frozen rock, or spiny, lobster tails should have clear white meat, no odor, and should be hard-frozen when purchased.

Fresh scallops should have a sweet odor, a firm, white flesh, and should be almost free of liquid when bought in packages.

Live clams, mussels, and oysters in the shell should be tightly closed, or if slightly open, they should close immediately when tapped gently. Gaping shells that do not close indicate that the shellfish is dead and should not be eaten. Do not buy clams or mussels with broken shells. Shucked clams should have little or no liquid. Shucked oysters should be plump, naturally creamy in color, and in clear liquid. Avoid any oysters in containers that have an excessive amount of liquid; there should be no more than 10 percent by weight. Too much liquid indicates poor quality and careless handling.

OYSTER
SHRIMP
LOBSTER
ABALONE
BLUE CRAB

Abalone Found off the coast of British Columbia, these pink or red mollusks are oval-shaped, with a single shell up to 4 inches across, lined with mother-of-pearl. Available in the shell fresh or frozen. Bake or sauté. Season: March to November.

Clams **Soft-shell** clams abound in the waters off Cape Cod, northern New England, and the Atlantic provinces. Smaller sizes are called **steamers,** larger ones are called **in-shells.** Steam, deep-fry, or use in chowders.

Hard-shell clams, sometimes called quahogs, are found from the southern Gulf of St. Lawrence to the Gulf of Mexico. The small clams are known as **littlenecks,** and the medium ones as **cherrystones.** Broil, bake, or eat raw. The larger hard-shell clams are usually made into chowders.

The numerous varieties of clams on the West Coast include the hard-shell **butter, littleneck** (different from the Atlantic Coast variety), **Manila** or **Japanese littleneck,** the giant **goeduck** clam, and the popular soft-shell **razor** clam.

Clams are available fresh, frozen or canned. Season: all year.

Crabs The **blue,** or **common,** hard-shell crabs are found in the North and South Atlantic and Gulf of Mexico. More common in Canada is the **Atlantic snow** (queen) **crab,** found off Newfoundland and Labrador and in the Gulf of St. Lawrence. It weighs an average of 1½ pounds. Available cooked or frozen. Season: all year.

Soft-shell crabs are blue crabs that have shed their old shells; they are not a distinct species. They are caught by fishermen before new, hard shells have formed. Available live or frozen. Deep-fry or sauté. Season: May through September; peak is June through August.

The **Dungeness** crabs from the Pacific Coast and Alaska are larger than the blue crabs, weighing from 1¾ to 3½ pounds. They are usually available live in the shell, frozen, cooked, or canned. These crabs are cooked in the same way as blue crabs. Season: all year.

Alaskan King crabs are the largest edible variety, weighing 6-20 pounds. Available as frozen cooked meat, frozen cooked in the shell, or canned. Broil. Season: all year.

Lobsters **American** lobsters are a mottled, dark greenish blue, tinged with orange-red or brown. When cooked, they turn a vivid red. These lobsters are most abundant around Nova Scotia and Maine, but they range from the Strait of Belle Isle to North Carolina. The 1-pounders (chicken lobsters) and 2-pounders are the most desirable. Available live, cooked in the shell, fresh, frozen, or as canned meat. Broil, bake, steam, or boil. Season: all year.

Rock, or **spiny,** lobsters come from the Caribbean, the Mediterranean, New Zealand, and South Africa. They usually have smaller claws than the American lobster. Available as frozen tails or canned tail meat. Season: all year.

ALASKAN KING CRAB

SEA SCALLOP

MUSSEL

SQUID

HARD-SHELL CLAM

ROCK (SPINY) LOBSTER

DUNGENESS CRAB

Mussels These inexpensive but delicious mollusks have oblong, blue-black shells with "beards," or tufts of hair, that must be removed. Their flesh is orange-pink. They live in shallow waters from Hudson Bay to South Carolina and along the Pacific Coast. Available live in the shell and canned. When cooking mussels, be sure the shells open wide. Any that do not should be discarded. Mussels may be cooked in any of the ways suggested for clams or oysters. Season: all year.

Oysters Atlantic or **eastern** oysters range from the Gulf of St. Lawrence to the Gulf of Mexico and the West Indies. The Canadian catch is sold live in the shell. Grading (federally controlled) is based on shell shape. There are four grades: fancy, choice, standard, and irregular. Bake, broil, or serve raw on a half shell. Season: September through April. **Pacific** oysters grow in waters off British Columbia. They are larger than eastern oysters; market size ranges from 4 to 6 inches. Available fresh, frozen, or canned. Contrary to popular belief, oysters are edible in months lacking an *R*; but because their quality and flavor are so poor after spawning during the summer, they are usually not available. Bake, steam, stew, or deep-fry. Season: all year.

Scallops Sea scallops come from the deep waters off the North Atlantic; the smaller **bay** scallops are found in shallower waters from the Bay of Fundy to the Gulf of Mexico. Bay scallops are tenderer and more delicate-flavored and command a higher price. They are available fresh and frozen. Sea scallops are more readily available and can be bought fresh, frozen, and frozen breaded precooked. Broil, deep-fry, or sauté. Season: all year.

Shrimp These small ten-legged crustaceans are found in the Gulf of Mexico and the South Atlantic and Pacific oceans. Their colors are gray, pale pink, and brown, depending on the variety. It will take 40–50 very small shrimp to make a pound, but only 10–15 large ones. Available fresh, frozen in the shell, frozen shelled, or canned. Broil, boil, sauté, or deep-fry. Season: all year.

Squid These distant relatives of the octopus, usually about 12 inches long, are found in abundance in the Atlantic Ocean from Labrador as far south as Virginia. Available fresh, canned, or dried. Bake, deep-fry, sauté, or stew. Season: all year.

29

Poultry

Poultry, or domestic birds bred specially for the table, includes chicken, turkey, duck, and goose. In Canada all poultry sold must be inspected and graded by Agriculture Canada and must carry Canada A, Canada B, Canada Utility and Canada C grade marks. In the United States, dressed birds that have been inspected and graded by the U.S. Department of Agriculture often carry the official grade mark, although such labeling is not compulsory. Grade A birds are fully fleshed and meaty; Grade B and C birds are less meaty and less attractive in appearance. Grades B and C are seldom printed on poultry labels in the U.S.

Grades do not indicate tenderness: the age of the bird determines this. Young birds are tenderer than old ones, and are best for barbecuing, frying, sautéing, broiling, or roasting. Older birds are more suitable for soups, stews, and other slow-cooked dishes. When buying fresh poultry, check for age by touching the breastbone. In young poultry the tip of the breastbone is soft and flexible; as the bird ages, the breastbone becomes harder and more rigid.

Poultry is also sold frozen or deep-chilled, although these birds may be slightly inferior to fresh poultry in flavor and texture. Frozen birds are quick-frozen at the processing plant and are rock-hard to the touch. Deep-chilled birds are rapidly cooled at the processing plant to 28°–32°F, but not frozen; the flesh can be depressed with the fingers.

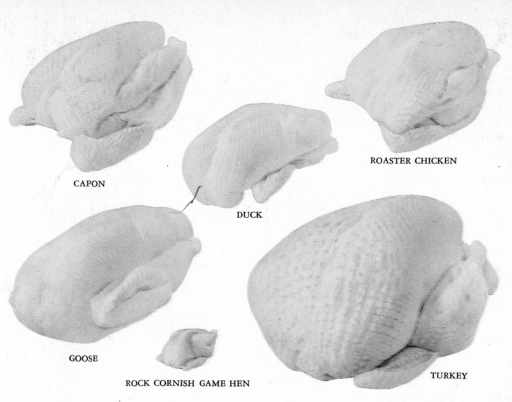

CAPON

ROASTER CHICKEN

DUCK

GOOSE

ROCK CORNISH GAME HEN

TURKEY

Chicken Available throughout the year in Canada and the United States, and sold oven-ready (plucked and drawn) as whole birds, or in halves, quarters, or serving pieces. Chickens are sold under various names, according to their age and weight. **Broiler-Fryers** are 6 to 10 weeks old and weigh up to 4 pounds. Cut up, they are excellent for frying, baking, or broiling; whole, they can be roasted or barbecued. **Roasters,** about 10 weeks to 7 months old, are ideal for roasting, barbecuing, or frying. **Hen, fowl,** or **stewing chicken** is mature and less tender, and weighs 3 pounds or more. Heavier, meatier mature chickens, $4\frac{1}{2}$–6 pounds, are called **Bro-Hens.** These older chickens are best poached or braised, or used in soups, stews, fricassees, chicken pie, and creamed dishes.

Capon A young, desexed male chicken, specially bred to give a high proportion of white, flavorful flesh. Capons, weighing 5–8 pounds, are larger than most chickens. They are exceptionally tender and are most often roasted.

Rock Cornish Game Hen This smallest member of the chicken family, produced by crossing Cornish and White Rock chickens, usually weighs $1\frac{1}{2}$ pounds or less. It is tender and has a meaty, plump breast. Rock Cornish Game Hens are suitable for roasting, baking, broiling, or sautéing. Allow a whole bird for each serving.

Turkey Most turkeys are marketed as deep-chilled or frozen whole birds, ranging from 4 to 25 pounds; the average weight in the markets is 10–14 pounds. Allow 8–12 ounces for each serving.

Young birds are the best buys. Mature turkeys are used in stews, soups, and salads.

Fresh and frozen turkey parts are also available, as are frozen boned rolled turkey roasts. Frozen stuffed turkeys, weighing 6–16 pounds, come already stuffed. Unlike other turkeys, they should not be thawed before roasting.

Duck Ninety percent of the ducks sold on the retail market are frozen and ready to cook when thawed. They are packaged whole or cut up and usually weigh $3\frac{1}{2}$–$5\frac{1}{2}$ pounds.

Ducks are ready for market when 7–8 weeks old, and are labeled as **Duckling** or **Young Duck.** Since they are fatty birds, they are usually roasted, although they may also be broiled or barbecued. Allow $\frac{3}{4}$–1 pound of meat per serving; 1 duck-ling halved or quartered generally serves 2 to 4 people.

Goose Many gourmets consider goose, which is becoming increasingly popular in North America, to be the best tasting poultry. It is a fatty bird with creamy-white flesh that cooks to a light brown and has a slightly gamy flavor.

Geese are sold frozen or deep-chilled and usually weigh 6–12 pounds. Allow 1–$1\frac{1}{2}$ pounds per serving. In some parts of Canada and the United States, fresh geese can be ordered from retail markets during the Christmas season.

Eggs Eggs, rich in protein, iron, vitamin A, and riboflavin, are a staple of the North American diet. Most eggs sold in Canada and the United States are from chickens; eggs from turkeys, ducks, and geese are occasionally available. Government agencies inspect and grade eggs, and the quality and size are indicated on the carton.

Grade Canada A1 and Canada A eggs are best for poaching or frying because of the superior appearance of their bright yolks and firm whites. Grade Canada B eggs are suitable for combining with other ingredients in cooking. All three grades of eggs have the same food value. Shell color—brown or white—does not affect the taste or quality of the egg, but is determined merely by the breed of the hen.

Eggs are marketed as Extra Large (minimum $2\frac{1}{2}$ ounces per egg); Large (minimum 2 ounces per egg); Medium (between $1\frac{3}{4}$ and 2 ounces per egg); Small (between $1\frac{1}{2}$ and $1\frac{3}{4}$ ounces per egg); or Peewee (less than $1\frac{1}{2}$ ounces per egg).

Eggs should always be refrigerated and should be used within a week of purchase for best flavor.

Game

The term "game" is applied to wild animals and birds that are hunted and eaten. In Canada and the United States there are certain seasons, varying from province to province and state to state, in which game can be legally hunted. In season, fresh dressed game is often available in meat markets in large cities; frozen dressed game can be bought the year round in some places, or by mail order. Various small game birds are also sold canned.

Freshly killed game usually must be hung before it is ready for cooking; this tenderizes the flesh and develops the prized gamy flavor. Game birds are hung, unplucked and undrawn, by their beaks in a cool, airy place. They are ready for cooking after about 2 days, when the tail feathers can be pulled out easily. Furred game is eviscerated and hung by the feet for 1–2 weeks. The game is then skinned and cut up—a job that few cooks are willing to do. In most cities, freshly killed game can be taken to a butcher who will hang it and prepare it for cooking.

For roasting or broiling, all game should be young—a condition that is most easily ascertained with unplucked game birds: The beak and feet should be pliable, the plumage soft, and the breast plump.

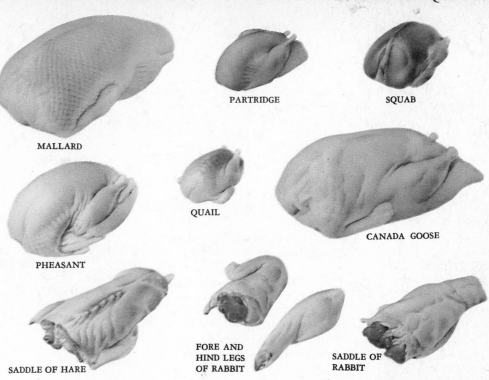

MALLARD

PARTRIDGE

SQUAB

QUAIL

CANADA GOOSE

PHEASANT

SADDLE OF HARE

FORE AND HIND LEGS OF RABBIT

SADDLE OF RABBIT

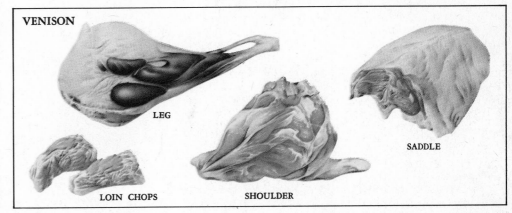

VENISON

LEG

SADDLE

LOIN CHOPS

SHOULDER

GAME BIRDS

Mallard The largest wild duck, with lean, dry flesh. The flight feathers are pointed and the breast is downy in young birds. Hang for one day only. Serve roasted, allowing 1 bird for 2 or 3 persons.

Partridge There are many varieties of partridge in Canada and the U.S. —two are the Gray and the Chukar. Young birds have rounded tips to their feathers, yellow-brown pliable feet, and light-colored, plump flesh. Hang for 3 or 4 days before roasting or broiling; serve 1 bird per person.

Pheasant The delectable pheasant is most prized for roasting. Young birds of both sexes can be recognized by their pliable beaks and feet, and soft, pointed feathers; on cocks the short spurs of the feet are rounded. A hen pheasant, which is considered tenderer and better tasting, will usually serve 3 people; a cock pheasant will serve 4.

Pigeon Wild pigeon, also called wood pigeon, is often tough and is best suited for use in casseroles or other slow-cooked dishes. **Squab** is young domesticated pigeon specially bred for the table, and is generally available in specialty meat markets. It is tender and flavorful, and can be roasted, sautéed, or broiled. Allow 1 bird per serving.

Quail Quail, including the bobwhite, has a less gamy taste than other wild birds. Quail should not be hung, or the delicate flavor will be destroyed. On young birds, the feathers are pointed and the feet soft. Roast, sauté, or broil, serving at least 1 bird per person.

Wild Goose One Canada goose, with an average weight of 7 pounds, will serve 6 persons. On young birds, with lean dark flesh, the flight feathers are pointed and the long dark feet are pliable. Brant geese are smaller, weighing 3–4 pounds.

FURRED GAME

Hare Hare, also known as jackrabbit, is a relative of the rabbit but is larger and has a gamier flavor. A young hare, weighing 6–7 pounds, can be recognized by its small, sharp white teeth, smooth fur, and hidden claws. Hang by the hind legs for about 1 week. Young hares may be roasted whole to serve 4–6 persons; older animals are better casseroled, although the saddle can be roasted.

Rabbit The flesh of wild rabbit has a gamy flavor; domesticated rabbits, sold cut up and frozen, have a flavor similar to chicken. Wild rabbit is cooked in the same way as hare, but is skinned at once after killing and should not be hung.

Venison The best meat comes from the young male deer (buck) at an age of 1½–2 years when the hooves are small and smooth. The lean meat is dark red and close grained, with firm white fat. Hang for at least a week. Venison is sold in roasts, the leg and saddle being the choicest cuts. The loin chops, neck cutlets, and shoulder may be braised.

31

Beef

Wholesale cuts of beef graded by Agriculture Canada are marked with a square brown stamp containing the word Canada, the grade (A-E), and the class (1-4). This stamp and a ribbon stamp running the length of the carcass are found on most meat sold in Canada.

Canada A is the highest quality young beef. It is juicy, bright red, fine-textured, lean, and at least slightly marbled (streaked with fat). Canada B, also from young animals, ranges from bright red to medium dark red. It is often coarse and may not be marbled. Canada C is from young to intermediate animals. C1 usually has less fat than B grade beef; C2 may have a coarse, sinewy texture. Canada D is from mature cows and steers, and generally has a low proportion of lean meat to bone. Canada E, from mature bulls, is used in sausages and other processed meat products. Beef carcasses in Canada are inspected for health and wholesomeness by the Health of Animals Branch of Agriculture Canada.

Wholesale beef cuts graded by the United States Department of Agriculture (USDA) are marked with a purple shield-shaped imprint containing the letters USDA and the name of the grade—prime, choice, good, standard, and commercial. Prime is the highest grade and the most expensive; commercial is flavorful but is one of the less tender grades. The round purple inspection mark—the dye is harmless and need not be removed before cooking—certifies that the meat is clean and healthy and that it has been processed in a plant meeting sanitary regulations. USDA inspection for wholesomeness is also required for all meats sold across state lines.

Cheap cuts of beef are as nutritious as the expensive ones; the only difference is that more time is required to prepare and cook them. Another point to remember is that price is controlled by supply and demand. Because only a given number of steaks can be cut from one animal, steaks are always expensive. In summer, cuts for stewing and braising are not popular, and so should be relatively inexpensive. They are for use in dishes that can be stored in the home freezer.

Because cuts of meat and the names by which they were known differed in various areas of the United States, an identification code was introduced to the U.S. retail meat industry in the mid-1970's. This program eliminates confusion at the meat counter by reducing more than 1,000 retail meat cuts to approximately 300 standard names for all fresh cuts of beef, lamb, veal, and pork. A single cut of meat is no longer known by a number of names, but by one name that has been standardized across the United States.

The cuts of meats illustrated here and on the following pages may not always be available at Canadian supermarkets that specialize in prepacked meats, but a good butcher will supply any cut of meat if he is given a few days' notice.

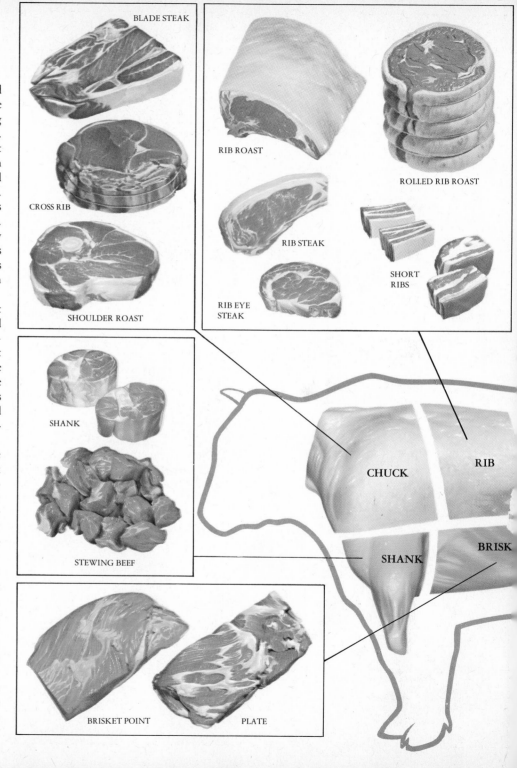

BLADE STEAK

CROSS RIB

SHOULDER ROAST

RIB ROAST

ROLLED RIB ROAST

RIB STEAK

RIB EYE STEAK

SHORT RIBS

SHANK

STEWING BEEF

BRISKET POINT

PLATE

CHUCK

RIB

SHANK

BRISK

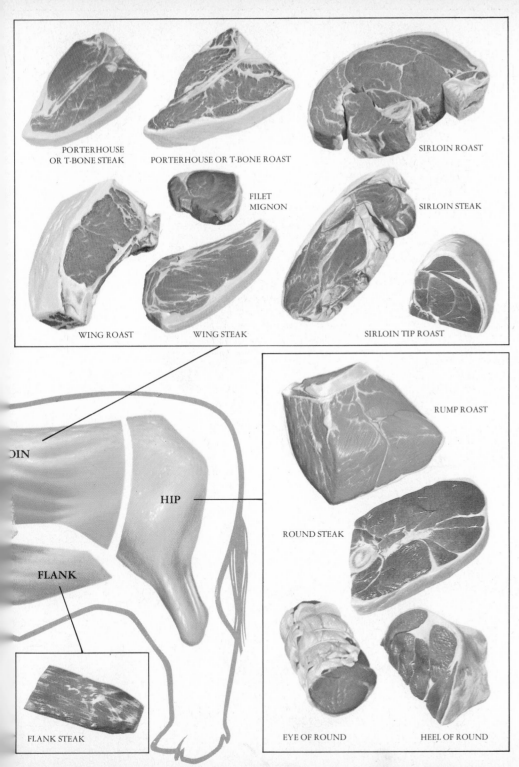

PORTERHOUSE
OR T-BONE STEAK

PORTERHOUSE OR T-BONE ROAST

SIRLOIN ROAST

FILET
MIGNON

SIRLOIN STEAK

WING ROAST

WING STEAK

SIRLOIN TIP ROAST

OIN

HIP

RUMP ROAST

ROUND STEAK

FLANK

EYE OF ROUND

HEEL OF ROUND

FLANK STEAK

CUTS FOR ROASTING

Allow $\frac{3}{4}$–1 pound of rib roast per serving and $\frac{1}{2}$–$\frac{3}{4}$ pound of boneless beef per serving.

From the rib: A **rib roast,** the most tender of all the beef roasts, is a perfect cut for a dinner party. The best section, called the first cut or front cut, is taken from the first three ribs nearest the loin. It is priced slightly higher than the other ribs, but it has less fat and less waste. The center cut, from the two middle ribs, has more fat and waste. The end cut, from the last two ribs closest to the chuck, is likely to be the least tender of the rib roasts. Buy a roast with at least 2 ribs.

The **rolled rib roast** is a rib roast that has been boned, rolled, and tied. Buy at least a 4-pound roast.

The **rib eye roast** is the boneless rib eye. Buy at least a 4-pound roast.

From the loin: The **tenderloin,** although expensive, is excellent company fare. It is always tender, cooks in a short time, and carves easily. A lower grade of tenderloin will have less fat covering and will brown better than a higher grade of meat.

The **sirloin tip roast,** cut from the end of the sirloin, should be of high quality for roasting.

From the hip: The **rump roast** must be of high quality to roast. It is triangular in shape and may be boneless or have the bone in. The rump is juicy and tender and has an excellent flavor.

The **eye of round** should be of high quality for roasting, and fat should be wrapped around it to make it juicy.

STEAKS

Allow $\frac{1}{3}$–$\frac{1}{2}$ pound of boned steak per serving and $\frac{1}{3}$–$\frac{3}{4}$ pound bone-in steak per serving.

From the rib: The fine-flavored **rib steak** is not as tender as the wing steak from the loin but it has more fat and should be less expensive. The best rib steaks come from the section nearest the loin. A 1-inch-thick steak weighs approximately 12–14 ounces and serves 1–2. A rib steak can also be purchased without the bone.

The **rib eye steak,** cut from the eye of the rib roast, is boneless, weighs approximately 8–10 ounces, and serves 1.

From the loin: The **wing steak** is cut from the loin next to the rib end and has no tenderloin. This small steak, averaging about $\frac{1}{2}$–$\frac{3}{4}$ pound, serves 1–2.

The **T-bone steak** from the center section of the short loin is easily identified by the T-shaped bone. It is similar to the porterhouse but smaller in size, and it has less tenderloin and a smaller tail. The average T-bone weighs about $1\frac{1}{2}$–2 pounds and serves 2–3.

The **porterhouse steak** from the larger end of the short loin is one of the most popular steaks because it has a good portion of tenderloin. The tail can be ground for making beef patties. The average cut is about 3 pounds and serves 3–4.

The **boneless wing steak** is not widely available in retail stores. A 1-inch-thick steak weighs about 8–10 ounces and serves 1.

The tenderest steak in the entire carcass is the small, expensive **filet mignon,** cut from the tenderloin. The sizes of the steaks vary because the tenderloin tapers at one end. A 4–6 ounce steak serves 1.

The **sirloin steak** can be identified by the shape of the bone from which it takes its name. Sirloin steaks vary in weight from 3–$4\frac{1}{2}$ pounds and make 4–5 servings.

33

Beef (continued)

The smallest sirloin, called the **pinbone,** is cut from the end of the sirloin nearest the short loin. This steak has a good portion of tenderloin, but a great deal of bone, and is the most wasteful of the sirloins.

The largest, called the **wedge bone,** has the least waste of all the sirloins. It is the least tender because it is closest to the hip.

The cut of beef nearest the rump of the round is usually sold as **boneless sirloin.**

Most Canadian supermarkets offer only a regular **sirloin steak,** which is partly boned and varies in size. However, any good butcher can provide the other sirloin cuts.

From the hip: **Top round,** if of high quality, can be broiled. A $1\frac{1}{2}$–$2\frac{1}{2}$ pound steak serves 4.

From the flank: The tasty **flank steak,** the true London broil, is a thin, boneless, coarse-grained cut about 12–14 inches long, 4–6 inches wide, and 1 inch thick. A 1–2 pound flank steak serves 4. Top-quality steak can be broiled. For best results serve rare. If the steak is cooked until medium or well-done, it may be tough. Carve diagonally across the grain.

CUTS FOR BRAISING

Count on $\frac{1}{4}$–$\frac{1}{3}$ pound of boned meat per serving.

From the chuck: A **blade steak,** from the shoulder, has a blade bone or a round bone (arm), or it may be boneless. A $\frac{1}{2}$-inch-thick piece weighs 8–12 ounces. The **boneless shoulder** from the chuck, and the **short ribs** from the end of the rib roast are good for braising.

From the hip: The **rump steak,** usually boned, is about $\frac{1}{2}$ inch thick and weighs 5–6 ounces.

The popular **round steak,** from the leg, may be cut into top or bottom round. A better quality of **top** round steak will have a good layer of fat and streaks of fat in the lean. A 1-inch-thick steak weighs 2–3 pounds. **Bottom round steak,** less tender than the top round, is usually cut $\frac{1}{2}$ inch thick, but it is available as smaller steaks. Average weight is about 12 ounces.

From the flank: **Flank steak** is normally broiled, but when it is lean and of low quality, it is better braised to make it tender.

From the loin: The **sirloin tip steak,** from the sirloin tip roast, is lean and boneless. A $\frac{1}{2}$-inch-thick steak weighs about 6 ounces.

CUTS FOR POT-ROASTING

Count on $\frac{1}{3}$ pound bone-in meat per serving and about $\frac{1}{4}$ pound boned meat per serving.

The **blade roast** from the chuck, is usually moderately priced but contains 2 or 3 small bones and a larger blade bone.

The **shoulder roast** or **steak** is an ideal cut because its uniform shape cooks evenly throughout.

The **rump roast** is a fine meaty pot roast from the round. It contains a moderate amount of fat and a good deal of connective tissue.

A **sirloin tip roast,** from the loin, makes a good, meaty pot roast, but it lacks fat covering.

Top round, bottom round, cross rib, rolled rib, sirloin, and **eye of round** can be pot-roasted. **Brisket point** and **plate** (often sold rolled) make good pot roasts, but they need long, slow cooking to make them tender. Make sure they are well trimmed of fat.

CUTS FOR STEWING

Stewing beef makes a fine stew with good texture and a rich flavor, but it costs more than other cuts.

Neck, sold boned or bone-in, requires long, slow cooking.

The lean, flavorful **shank** has plenty of connective tissue and must be cooked slowly to ensure tenderness.

The **bottom round** is well flavored, lean, and boneless.

The **heel of round** does not have the fine flavor of chuck, but it is tenderer. The choice grade should be used for stewing.

The **plate** and **brisket point** should be boned; avoid fatty pieces.

Flank steak makes a savory stew, but because it is thinner it takes less time to cook than the other cuts.

GROUND BEEF

Top round is the highest in price of the ground meats, but it has less fat and lacks the fine flavor of chuck.

Ground chuck has slightly more fat than top round and many believe it has the best flavor of all ground beef. It is ideal for hamburgers, meat loaves, and meatballs.

Ground meat loaf blend is a combination of ground beef, veal, and pork. It may also be used for other dishes, such as meatballs.

Tip sirloin, from the end of the sirloin or sides of the round, is lean and has more flavor than the round.

The **flank** is not often available ground, but it has a delicate taste and is different from any of the other kinds of ground beef.

Ground beef or **hamburger,** made up of trimmings from the plate and flank, is sold at the lowest price per pound; but it has more fat than ground chuck and shrinks during cooking.

CORNED BEEF

Corned beef is the rump, plate, or brisket point that has been cured in brine. About 4 pounds will serve 8.

Veal

Veal tends to be dry, with little fat, and therefore requires careful cooking. Its flavor is delicate and somewhat bland, so that sauces, stuffings, and seasonings are often used to provide additional flavor.

With veal cuts and their names far from consistent across the country, Agriculture Canada was preparing a chart of standardized cuts that it hoped to publish in the late 1970s.

When buying veal, look for soft moist flesh that varies in color from off-white to palest pink. The lean should have a fine texture with a thin outside layer of firm, creamy-white fat without any yellow discoloration. Bones should be soft and almost translucent.

Vealers that yield the best veal are usually slaughtered by the age of 3 months. They are raised on milk, which helps to produce the white flesh. Much of the high-quality veal from these calves is sold to hotels and restaurants. However, it can be purchased from specialty butchers.

Old vealers, called calves, are from 14 weeks to 1 year old and weigh about 250 pounds. They provide most of the veal on the market; it is less expensive than milk-fed veal.

CUTS FOR ROASTING

Choose a roast that is at least 3–4 pounds. Allow $\frac{1}{2}$–$\frac{3}{4}$ pound bone-in veal per serving and $\frac{1}{3}$–$\frac{1}{2}$ pound boned veal per serving.

From the shoulder: The **shoulder roast** is boned, rolled, and tied to make carving easier. Extra fat should be added to the exterior of the roast to make it tenderer and juicier. It weighs 4–7 pounds.

From the rib and loin: The **rib** and **loin roasts** make excellent roasts but are rarely available because they are cut into chops. A **crown roast** of veal is 2 or more rib sections that have been tied together to form a circle, which can then be filled with a stuffing or vegetables.

From the sirloin: A **sirloin roast** of 3–4 pounds is a very tender cut. It is sometimes sold boned.

From the leg: The **rump roast,** a good roast for a small family, is a wedge-shaped cut from the upper leg. It weighs 3–5 pounds. It can be boned, rolled, and tied to make the carving easier.

A **leg roast** is a meaty cut with a small bone. A center cut or **round roast** is especially fine. The size of a roast can be 4–6 pounds or larger. This roast may be cut into steaks or cutlets. A **rolled leg** of veal is a center leg roast that has been boned, rolled, and tied for easier carving.

CHOPS AND STEAKS

Allow $\frac{1}{3}$–$\frac{1}{2}$ pound bone-in veal per serving and $\frac{1}{4}$–$\frac{1}{3}$ boned veal per serving. These cuts are tenderer and more succulent if braised.

From the shoulder: The **shoulder steak** has little fat and is usually less expensive than the rib, loin, or leg cuts of veal. The shoulder steak can be left whole or cut into pieces before cooking. A $\frac{3}{4}$- to 1-inch-thick slice serves 2.

The **blade steak** has more bone and less meat than the shoulder steak. It is usually less expensive than the rib, loin, or leg cuts. A $\frac{3}{4}$-inch-thick slice serves 2. If the steak is cut into cubes and made into a stew, it will serve 3.

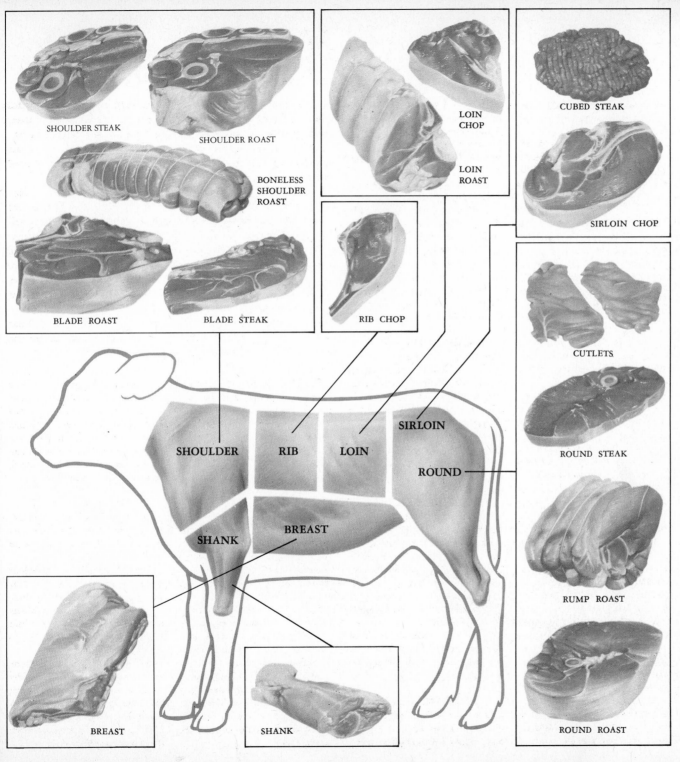

SHOULDER STEAK

SHOULDER ROAST

BONELESS SHOULDER ROAST

BLADE ROAST

BLADE STEAK

RIB CHOP

LOIN CHOP

LOIN ROAST

CUBED STEAK

SIRLOIN CHOP

CUTLETS

ROUND STEAK

RUMP ROAST

ROUND ROAST

SHOULDER

RIB

LOIN

SIRLOIN

ROUND

SHANK

BREAST

BREAST

SHANK

From the rib: The **rib chop** with a rib bone is less meaty than the loin chop and contains no tenderloin. The chops nearest the loin are the best. Those nearest the shoulder have more fat and bone. A $\frac{1}{2}$-inch chop weighs about 4 ounces. Rib chops are also boned.

From the loin: The T-shaped **loin chop** contains part of the tenderloin. It is the best of the chops and the most expensive, although it contains a good deal of bone. A $\frac{3}{4}$-inch-thick chop weighs 6–8 ounces and serves 1. A loin chop containing a portion of the kidney is called a **kidney chop.**

From the sirloin: **Cubed steak** and the **sirloin chop** are cheaper than loin chops. They should be braised to make them tender.

From the leg: **Round steak** looks like a shoulder steak, but is larger. It is perhaps the most widely available of all veal cuts. It has no fat, no waste, and little bone. Cook whole or in serving pieces. A $\frac{1}{2}$-inch-thick steak weighs 1–1$\frac{1}{2}$ pounds.

Cutlets, boneless slices taken from the leg, are often flattened for veal scaloppine. A $\frac{1}{4}$-inch-thick slice weighs 3–4 ounces.

CUTS FOR BRAISING

Allow about $\frac{1}{3}$ pound bone-in veal per serving and about $\frac{1}{4}$ pound boneless veal per serving.

From the shoulder: The **shoulder roast** (4–5 pounds), **blade roast** (4–5 pounds), and a **boneless rolled shoulder** (4–7 pounds) are moderately priced and are ideal cuts of meat for braising.

From the breast: The **breast** of veal can be purchased with or without the bone. It is delicious stuffed with onions, bread crumbs, and herbs. Other veal cuts for braising are the **neck, shank, shank cross cuts,** and **riblets.**

35

Lamb

Most lambs are slaughtered when less than a year old. The spring lamb, however, is ready for the market at 3–5 months, and the baby lamb in 6–8 weeks. Lamb is a delicately flavored meat and a rich source of iron and other important minerals. It is rich in vitamins essential for the release of energy from all foods, good vision, clear eyes, appetite, and for the health of skin and nerve tissues.

The grades of lamb are prime, choice, and good. Prime is the highest quality grade and the most expensive, but it is not widely available in retail markets. It is flavorful, tender, and juicy, with considerable marbling (flecks or streaks of fat within the lean). The choice grade is more widely available, however. This grade is slightly less marbled than the prime, but it is still of high quality. Lamb in Canada is graded Canada A, Canada B and Canada C. Because lamb cuts and their names differ greatly throughout the country, Agriculture Canada was preparing a chart of standardized cuts for publication in the late 1970s.

Lamb varies in color according to the age and breed of the animal. Meat from a young lamb is usually bright pink; red meat comes from an older animal. The fat should be creamy white, not oily or yellow—a yellowish tinge shows excessive age. Lamb roasts should have a good depth of lean meat covered by a moderate layer of fat. The skin should be pliable to the touch, not hard or wrinkled. Legs and shoulder roasts should have a plump, not a flat appearance.

Lamb imported from Australia and New Zealand is frozen and is available in some markets all year long. The meat has a less delicate flavor than the fresh, and the lean is paler. The fat is whiter and crumbles more easily. If the fat looks very brittle, it is a sign that the lamb has been frozen for a long time; it will generally shrink during cooking and some of the flavor will be lost.

Although the choicest cuts of lamb for roasting and broiling come from the rib, loin, leg, and shoulder, do not ignore the cheaper cuts, such as the neck, shank, and breast. These cuts may take more time to prepare, but they can be as tasty as the expensive cuts.

CUTS FOR ROASTING

Buy ½–¾ pound lamb with bone in per serving and ¼–½ pound boned lamb per serving.

From the shoulder: The flavorful **boneless shoulder** is rolled and tied and weighs 3–5 pounds. This tender, juicy roast is easy to carve, but it contains more fat than the leg.

The **square shoulder** is difficult to carve because of its complicated bone structure, but it is usually in-

expensive. Count on a pound of shoulder per serving.

The **cushion shoulder**—a square, flat roast—is boned and tied to make carving easier. One side can be left open for stuffing and then tied. It weighs 2½–4 pounds.

From the rib: The **rib roast,** or rack of lamb, is unsurpassed for tenderness and flavor. It contains very little meat and it is very expensive. A 3-pound rack will serve only 3.

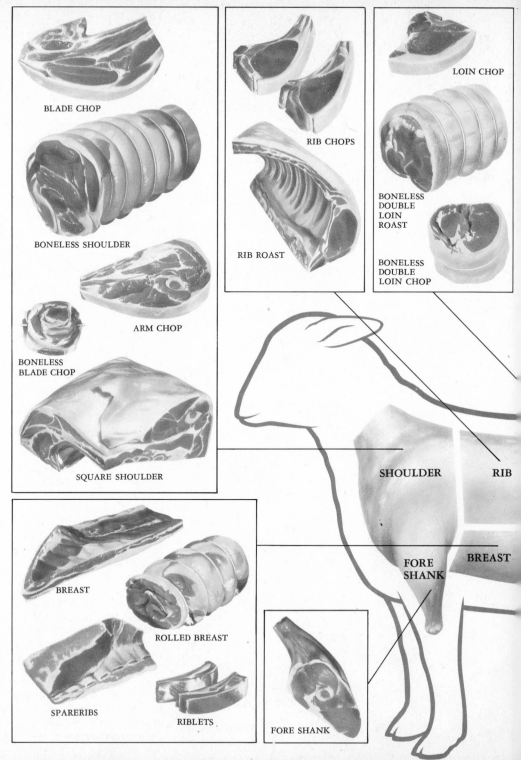

BLADE CHOP

BONELESS SHOULDER

ARM CHOP

BONELESS BLADE CHOP

SQUARE SHOULDER

RIB CHOPS

RIB ROAST

LOIN CHOP

BONELESS DOUBLE LOIN ROAST

BONELESS DOUBLE LOIN CHOP

BREAST

ROLLED BREAST

SPARERIBS

RIBLETS

FORE SHANK

SHOULDER

RIB

FORE SHANK

BREAST

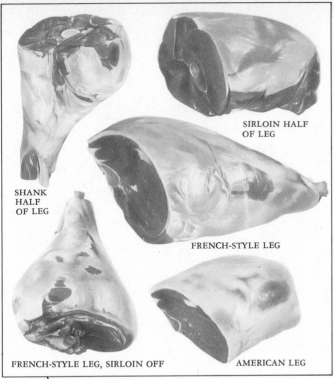

SHANK
HALF
OF LEG

SIRLOIN HALF
OF LEG

FRENCH-STYLE LEG

FRENCH-STYLE LEG, SIRLOIN OFF

AMERICAN LEG

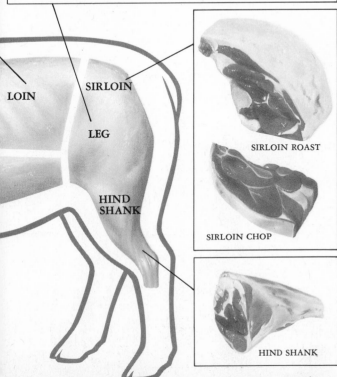

LOIN

SIRLOIN

LEG

SIRLOIN ROAST

HIND
SHANK

SIRLOIN CHOP

HIND SHANK

When two racks are tied together to form a circle, it is called a **crown roast.** The tops of the rib bones are trimmed of meat. This is an elegant roast for a party. Allow 2 ribs per serving. Make sure the chine bone is cracked for easy carving.

From the loin: The expensive **loin roast,** also boned, is not often available in the markets because it is usually cut into loin chops. It has a thin, even layer of fat just below the skin.

From the sirloin: The **sirloin roast** from the upper end of the leg makes a small 2–2½ pound roast.

From the leg: The **whole leg** of lamb, weighing 5–9 pounds, contains the sirloin and the shank. This cut is a good buy for a large family and has little waste. The **French-style leg** has the meat around the end of the leg bone removed. This cut serves 6–8.

(An easy method of carving a whole leg of lamb is to cut the meat parallel to the bone rather than perpendicular to the bone.)

The **round roast,** or shank, is the full leg after the sirloin chops or roast have been removed. When the meat around the end of the leg bone has been removed, it is called the **French-style leg, sirloin off.** When the shank bone is removed and the meat is skewered to the thicker part of the leg, this cut is called an **American leg.**

The **sirloin half of the leg,** serving 4–6, comes from the upper end of the full leg and is more expensive than the shank half. It has more meat than the shank half of the leg and is easier to carve.

The **shank half of the leg,** serving 2–4, is a good buy although it has less meat than the sirloin half of the leg. Ask the butcher to crack the bones to make carving easier.

The **boneless leg** (rolled) is a full leg of lamb that has been boned, rolled, and tied. It weighs 3–6 pounds and serves 5–8.

CHOPS AND STEAKS

Chops and steaks 1–2 inches thick should be broiled. Those cut less than 1 inch should be pan-broiled or braised. Count on ⅓–¾ pound per serving.

From the shoulder: The **blade chop,** boned or bone-in, contains the blade bone and is larger than the loin or rib, but cheaper. It is not as tender as the rib chop. The chops nearest the rib are tenderer. A ¾-inch, 5–8 ounce chop serves 1.

The **arm chop** has an arm bone and a cross section of the rib. It is not as delicately flavored as the blade chop, but it is less expensive.

From the rib: The **rib chop** is smaller than the loin chop and contains the rib bone and no tenderloin. The best and leanest chops are cut nearest the loin. Those cut nearest the shoulder are larger but have less meat and more fat. A 1-inch-thick chop weighs 3–4 ounces. Provide 2 chops per serving.

The **double rib chop** is like the rib chop except that it has 2 ribs and is twice as thick. A chop 2 inches thick weighs about 5–7 ounces and serves 1.

The **Frenched rib chop** of lamb has the meat removed from the end of the bone.

From the loin: The meaty, T-shaped **loin chop** contains tenderloin and is the most expensive of the lamb chops. Be sure that the tough tail of the chop is well trimmed. A 1-inch-thick chop weighs 4–6 ounces. A **double loin chop** is available boned.

In the 2-inch **English chop** from the unsplit loin, the backbone has been removed and the chop skewered together. The kidney may be secured to the center of the chop. It weighs 7–12 ounces.

From the sirloin: The **sirloin chop,** cut nearest the loin end, is the best. Cuts from the rump end have more bone and waste and less meat. A 1-inch-thick chop weighs 4–8 ounces and serves 1.

From the leg: The **leg chop** contains the round leg bone. It is the leanest and has the most meat of all the chops. A 1-inch-thick steak weighs 5–8 ounces.

CUTS FOR BRAISING AND STEWING

Allow ⅓ pound bone-in lamb and ¼–⅓ pound of boned lamb per serving.

From the shoulder: A 6-pound **boneless shoulder** will yield 4 pounds of lean cubes to serve 8.

From the neck: **Neck chops,** inexpensive but flavorful, have a lot of bone and less meat than some other cuts. Three pounds serves 3–4.

From the leg: The **leg chop,** cut from the center of the leg, provides solid meat with a small bone. One and a half pounds made into a stew will serve 4.

The **shank half of leg** from a mature animal is good for moist-cooking. A 5-pound shank half cut into cubes will serve 6–8.

From the shank: The inexpensive but flavorful **shank** contains a lot of bone. One shank will make only a single serving.

From the breast: The **breast** of lamb, weighing about 2 pounds, makes a good budget meal for 2. It is also available boned.

The economical **lamb riblets,** usually 4–6 inches long and 1 inch wide, are thick strips with streaks of fat cut from the breast.

Pork

Prime pork should be well developed, with small bones and without excessive fat. The fat should be firm and a clear milk-white color. Avoid cuts with soft, gray, and oily fat, which leads to excessive weight loss in cooking. The lean should be pale pink, firm, and smooth to the touch, with very little gristle. Freshly cut surfaces should look slightly moist, and the bones should be pinkish-blue.

Pork is highly nutritious. It contains more vitamin B_1, which prevents fatigue and stimulates the appetite, than any other meat. It has more flavor if cooked on the bone, but many roasts are often sold boned and rolled ready for stuffing.

CUTS FOR ROASTING

Buy at least a 3-pound roast. One pound with the bone will serve 2 or 3 people, 3 or 4 if boned.

From the butt shoulder: The **shoulder blade** (butt) **roast** from the upper shoulder is available with the bone in or boned. It weighs 3–8 pounds.

From the loin: The **loin center roast** is meaty from end to end and includes the choice tenderloin. The backbone should be cracked for easier carving. The **loin rib roast** is as tender as the loin center, but it has no tenderloin.

A **crown roast,** an excellent party roast, is made by tying 2 or more center-cut ribs together to form a circle.

The **loin roast boned and rolled** can come from the center or sirloin section of the loin. The **sirloin roast** comes from the back part of the loin, close to the leg. It contains tenderloin, but it is difficult to carve because of the bones.

The **tenderloin** is a 9–12 inch boneless cut that is equivalent to the beef filet and weighs $\frac{3}{4}$–$1\frac{1}{2}$ pounds. It is usually more expensive than other loin cuts. The tenderloin is available sliced or flattened.

From the leg: Because of the high ratio of lean meat to bone, the **leg roast** is an excellent choice for a large family. It weighs 12–16

pounds (bone in) and serves 20 or more. Also available is the **leg roast boned and rolled,** a lean, tender roast that is sold in many sizes.

A leg roast can be cut into two smaller roasts: a shank portion and a loin portion. The full loin portion is perhaps the better buy because it is leaner and meatier. It is harder to carve than the shank portion, however, but the hip (or aitchbone) can be removed. The full shank portion has less meat, but is easier to carve.

From the picnic shoulder: A 5–8 pound **shoulder arm** (picnic) **roast** is not as lean as the loin or leg roast, but it has a great deal of flavor and is good value for the money. A picnic that is boned, rolled, and tied is more attractive and easier to carve. It will take almost a pound of bone-in roast for 1 serving, but a pound of boned pork will serve 2–3.

STEAKS AND CHOPS

Count on $\frac{1}{2}$–$\frac{3}{4}$ pound chops and steaks with bone per serving, and $\frac{1}{3}$–$\frac{1}{2}$ pound boned chops per serving.

Chops have a thick layer of fat running along the outer edge. To prevent chops curling during cooking, use scissors to snip through the fatty layer.

From the shoulder: The **shoulder blade** (butt) **chop** contains a section of the blade bone

and a good deal of fat and gristle, but its cost is low.

The **pork cutlet** or "porklet," from the shoulder butt, is boneless, and cubed for tenderness. The **shoulder arm** (picnic) **chop** is an economical buy, but it is not as tender as the ham steak.

From the loin: The **loin rib chop** differs very little in flavor or quality from the loin chop, but it does not include the tenderloin. A **butterfly chop** is a boned, double-rib chop.

The popular **loin center chop** is the best chop of all because it has more lean meat and less bone and waste.

The **sirloin chop,** from the ham end of the loin, has less lean meat than the center loin.

From the leg: A fresh **ham steak** is lean and tender. Cuts from the shank end are particularly attractive and are uniform in size.

HAMS AND PICNICS

For cooked bone-in hams, allow $\frac{1}{3}$ pound per serving and $\frac{1}{8}$–$\frac{1}{4}$ pound per serving if boned. For uncooked bone-in hams, allow $\frac{1}{2}$–$\frac{3}{4}$ pound per serving and $\frac{1}{3}$ pound if boned. The label on packaged hams should identify them as fully cooked or cook-before-eating hams.

A whole ham roast with the bone is the least wasteful and most prized for flavor of all the hams. For best quality, choose a plump ham with a stubby shank end. A 10–14 pound ham will serve 12–18.

A full **ham loin roast** is a good size to buy for the average family. It is harder to carve than the shank portion, but it is meatier.

The full **ham shank roast** has as much flavor as the loin portion and is easier to carve, but it has less meat and is less expensive.

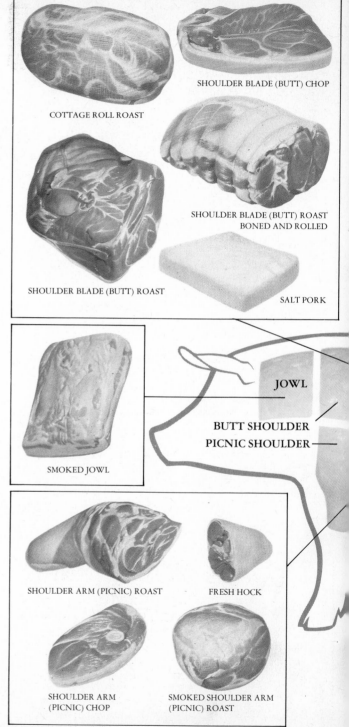

COTTAGE ROLL ROAST

SHOULDER BLADE (BUTT) CHOP

SHOULDER BLADE (BUTT) ROAST BONED AND ROLLED

SHOULDER BLADE (BUTT) ROAST

SALT PORK

SMOKED JOWL

JOWL

BUTT SHOULDER

PICNIC SHOULDER

SHOULDER ARM (PICNIC) ROAST

FRESH HOCK

SHOULDER ARM (PICNIC) CHOP

SMOKED SHOULDER ARM (PICNIC) ROAST

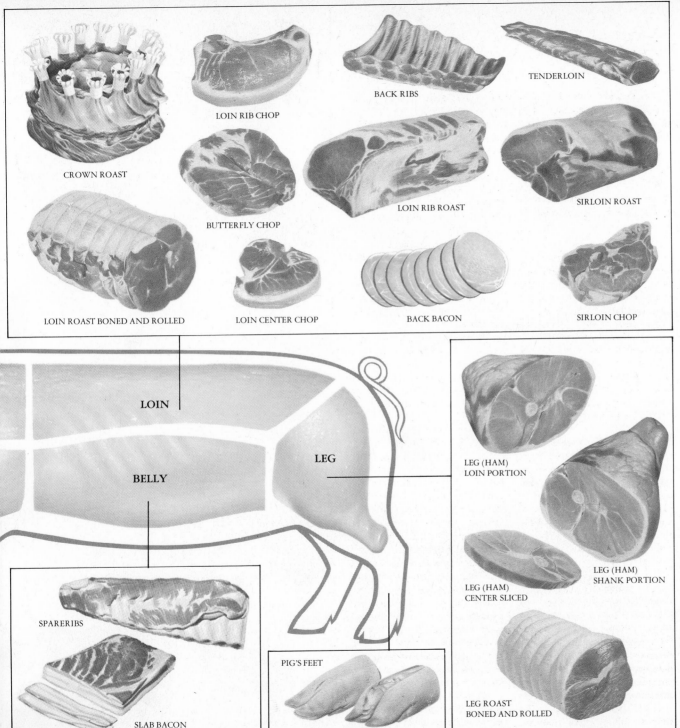

CROWN ROAST

LOIN RIB CHOP

BACK RIBS

TENDERLOIN

BUTTERFLY CHOP

LOIN RIB ROAST

SIRLOIN ROAST

LOIN ROAST BONED AND ROLLED

LOIN CENTER CHOP

BACK BACON

SIRLOIN CHOP

LOIN

BELLY

LEG

SPARERIBS

SLAB BACON

PIG'S FEET

LEG (HAM) LOIN PORTION

LEG (HAM) CENTER SLICED

LEG (HAM) SHANK PORTION

LEG ROAST BONED AND ROLLED

An 8-12 pound **boned, rolled ham** can be purchased in many different shapes, in cans and in airtight wrappers. A boned ham will not have as much flavor as a ham with the bone.

The **smoked shoulder arm** (picnic) **roast** is cheaper than other hams because it has more skin, fat and bone in proportion to lean. It is also difficult to carve. A picnic weighs 5-8 pounds.

The pickled **cottage roll roast** from the neck and shoulder is boneless. It makes a delicious, economical substitute for bacon.

HAM AND PICNIC SLICES
These are available as cook-before-eating slices or as fully cooked slices.

SPARERIBS
Country-style ribs from the shoulder end of the loin contain more meat than the **back ribs** or the **spareribs**. One pound of 2-3 ribs makes 1 serving.

BACON, JOWL, AND SALT PORK
Slab bacon is cheaper than sliced bacon and will keep longer in the refrigerator than sliced. The **smoked jowl** is used like bacon.

Back bacon is an expensive delicacy. It comes from the eye muscle of the loin, is very lean and usually sold sliced.

Salt pork is cured but not smoked and is used to flavor braised dishes and baked beans, or to bard* the dry flesh of game birds.

HOCKS AND PIG'S FEET
Hocks, available fresh or smoked, are good in soups or stews. Allow 1 pound per serving.

Pig's feet are available fresh or pickled in vinegar.

Variety Meats

Variety meats are the parts of slaughtered pigs, cattle, or sheep that are left after the carcass has been cut up. Despite the fact that these meats include some of the most nourishing food available, they have been considered low-priority products by many consumers.

Some variety meats, such as liver, are excellent sources of the minerals and vitamins necessary for good health; however, most of them—particularly brains, kidney, and liver—are high in cholesterol.

Ironically, certain variety meats, such as brains, veal liver, and sweetbreads, are considered gourmet's delicacies and have become expensive for the average family; yet they still compare favorably with other meats in price. Most variety meats seldom require lengthy preparation and cooking. And because they contain no bones and little fat or gristle, waste is cut to a minimum.

Variety meats do not keep well. They should be stored in the refrigerator until ready to be used and should be cooked on the day of purchase. Liver, hearts, sweetbreads, and brains are avilable fresh and frozen.

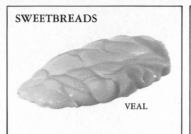

SWEETBREADS

VEAL

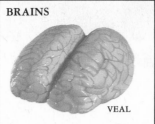

BRAINS

VEAL

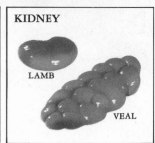

KIDNEY

LAMB

VEAL

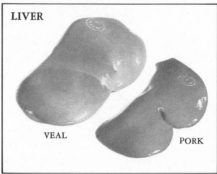

LIVER

VEAL

PORK

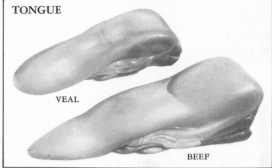

TONGUE

VEAL

BEEF

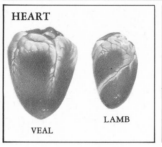

HEART

VEAL

LAMB

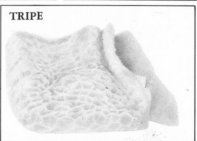

TRIPE

OXTAIL

LIVER

Veal liver is the most expensive, the tenderest, and the mildest-flavored of all the livers. The best quality veal liver is a light reddish-brown color. It is available fresh or frozen in slices. Sauté or broil.

Lamb liver is less expensive than veal liver and is an excellent substitute. Choose liver that is light brown. Avoid any that is dark brown; it is from an older animal.

Pork liver has a stronger flavor than either veal or lamb liver. It is best braised or pan-fried.

Beef liver is coarse and tough but inexpensive. It is not recommended for broiling or sautéing. Soak in milk or lightly salted water for a few hours to mellow the strong flavor. Pan-fry or braise.

Allow 1 pound of beef liver for 4 servings.

KIDNEYS

Lamb and **veal kidneys** are considered best because of their delicate flavor and tenderness. Broil or sauté. The stronger-flavored **pork** and **beef** kidneys are tougher and should be stewed or braised.

Allow 2 lamb kidneys per serving, 1 veal or pork kidney per serving, and 1 beef kidney for 4 servings.

SWEETBREADS

This is the name given to the two portions of the thymus gland, one in the throat and one in the chest cavity. **Veal sweetbreads** are considered a delicacy and are the most readily available of all the sweetbreads. They can be purchased fresh or frozen. Sauté or braise.

Allow 1 pound for 4 servings.

BRAINS

Veal brains have the mildest flavor and are the most popular but they are not always available. **Lamb brains** may be used in any recipe for veal brains. Both types of brains must be soaked in cold water for a couple of hours to remove all blood. **Pork** and **beef brains** are not as delicate in texture and have a stronger flavor.

Allow 1 pound for 4 servings.

HEARTS

Hearts are lower in price than other variety meats and have very little waste. They are flavorful and nutritious but require long, slow cooking. **Veal heart** is the most delicate-flavored, and **lamb heart** is the smallest and the tenderest. Both are best braised. **Pork heart** is larger and less tender than lamb heart and may be stuffed and braised. Choose bright red, firm hearts and avoid any that are gray. The **beef heart** is best if cut into cubes and used in stews and casseroles.

Veal heart makes 3 servings; lamb heart, 1 serving; pork heart, 2 servings; and beef heart, 8–10 servings.

TONGUE

Beef and veal tongue are the most readily available. **Beef tongue** is available fresh, pickled, corned, smoked, and in some areas, ready-to-serve. **Veal tongue** is usually sold fresh. **Lamb** and **pork tongues** are usually precooked and ready to serve. Tongue requires long, slow cooking in liquids to make it tender.

Allow 1 pound for 4–5 servings.

TRIPE

Tripe comes from the inner lining of the stomach of beef. The choicest is **honeycomb tripe** from the second stomach. It should be thick, firm, and white. Avoid any that is slimy and gray or has a flabby appearance.

Tripe is sold partly cooked; ask the butcher how much longer it should be cooked. It can be stewed, broiled, or fried. Tripe is also available pickled or canned.

Allow 1 pound for 4–5 servings.

OXTAIL

Oxtails are the tails of beef cattle and have a great deal of bone and very little meat. The fat should be creamy white, and the meat deep red. Oxtails require long, slow cooking to make them tender and are excellent braised, in casseroles, or as a base for soup.

Allow 2–3 pounds for 4 servings.

North American Cheeses

Cheese is made from milk that has separated into curds (soft, white lumps) and whey (the thin liquid that remains after the curds have been removed). The curds are drained, flavored in any number of ways, pressed into molds, and left to cure through the action of harmless bacteria. They ripen, or grow stronger, with age.

Per capita consumption of cheese in Canada is nearly 16 pounds a year; in the U.S. it is about 12 pounds a year. Natural cheese accounts for about two thirds of consumption in Canada, less than half in the U.S. There is a large demand for process cheese: Bits of natural cheese are mixed together and cooked with preservatives and an emulsifying agent, and sometimes with coloring and flavoring. This pasteurization kills bacteria, halting the ripening process, which in turn arrests the development of flavor. As a result, process cheese tends to be bland.

Among the natural cheeses, Canadian and American versions of Cheddar, which originated in Great Britain, are the most popular. North American manufacturers also produce versions of many European cheeses, such as mozzarella, Münster, and Limburger. Liederkranz and brick, however, are original U.S. creations; Anfrom and Oka are made only in Canada. Fresh (uncured) cheeses are also extremely popular. These include cottage cheese and cream cheese.

The cheeses on this page are among the best and most widely available natural cheeses made in Canada and the United States.

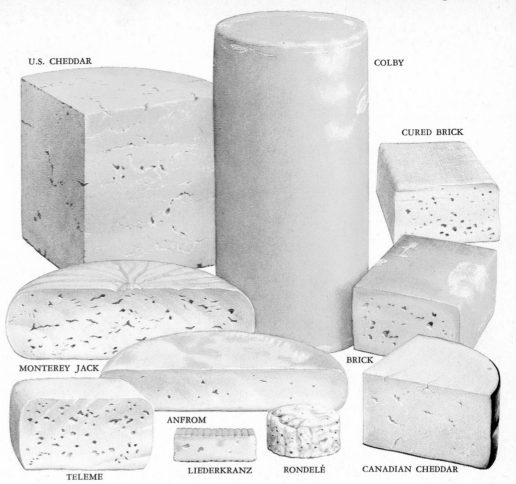

U.S. CHEDDAR   COLBY   CURED BRICK   BRICK   MONTEREY JACK   ANFROM   CANADIAN CHEDDAR   TELEME   LIEDERKRANZ   RONDELÉ

Anfrom A round, flat cheese similar to **Oka,** a Port Salut (p.43) type made by Trappist monks at Oka, Quebec. Anfrom and Oka are more robust and slightly creamier than Port Salut.

Brick This midwestern cheese resembles Cheddar with a light Limburger (p.45) flavor. A wax coating contains its increasingly strong aroma. The cheese is slightly firm and is ideal for slicing.

Canadian Cheddar Made from raw milk, this cheese is slightly nuttier than U.S. Cheddars, and has a sharpness when aged. It is sold under such trade names as Black Diamond and Cherry Hill.

U.S. Cheddars Cheddar is the most widely produced cheese in the United States. When young it is delicate and moist; longer aging results in a sharper taste and a drier, more crumbly texture. In some areas of the country, white Cheddar is preferred, while yellow (orange) Cheddar is favored in others. Color has no effect on taste.

Cheddars made in Wisconsin range from very mild to very sharp, and vary widely in quality; New York Cheddars are of high quality and are more costly; Vermont Cheddar has higher acidity and gives a much sharper taste than age alone will yield. **Tillamook,** a Cheddar made in Oregon, is so popular on the West Coast of the United States that increasing demand has resulted in less aging and, consequently, a milder cheese. **Coon** Cheddar is full-bodied and crumbly.

Colby A variation of Cheddar that is milder, moister, and easier to slice. It is frequently made in the longhorn shape—a cylinder that yields cuts of a half-moon shape.

Cured Brick A smear culture on the outside of this cheese causes it to ripen to a high pungency. It is often sold under the trade names Braumeister and Beerkaese. Cured brick is usually eaten in sandwiches of raw onion and dark bread.

Liederkranz This soft-ripening cheese, which originated in New York and is now made in the midwestern United States, becomes more mellow and aromatic as it ripens. When young it is delicate and semisoft; at maturity it is soft, creamy, and aromatic. Most of the aroma comes from the crust, which is entirely edible but can be removed if considered offensive.

Monterey Jack There are two varieties of this cheese, which originated in Monterey, California: Skim or part-skim Jack is hard and used for grating; high-moisture Jack is semisoft. High-moisture Jack is used in many Mexican dishes, and its smooth creaminess makes it ideal for cooking with a wide range of spices and sauces.

Rondelé A soft spiced cheese flavored with garlic and herbs, of the French Gournay (p.43) type. It is ideal for canapés or as a topping for baked potatoes.

Teleme A creamier member of the Münster (p.43) family, with a subtle, refreshing tartness. The cheese is most popular on the West Coast of the United States but can sometimes be found in specialty shops in other parts of the U.S. and Canada.

French Cheeses

There are hundreds of regional cheeses in France, although only a small proportion is imported into the United States and Canada. These imported cheeses, however, include the best-known varieties that have given France its reputation as producer of many of the world's finest cheeses.

Camembert and Brie are perhaps the most popular, but Roquefort, Pont l'Évêque, Port Salut, and various process and cream cheeses, such as Boursin, Petit-Suisse, and Crème de Gruyère, are also in demand in North America.

Buy Camembert, Brie, and similar soft cheeses in small quantities and eat them without delay. This is necessary because soft cheeses do not keep as well as the hard varieties unless they have been processed. When purchasing a soft-ripening cheese that has already been cut, inspect it to see if it is ripe: An unripe cheese has a white core, or inner layer, with small irregular holes; in ripening, the cheese turns pale yellow toward the top, bottom, and sides, and the holes disappear. A ripe cheese will be smooth, creamy, and pale yellow throughout. If the cheese is a little underripe, store it in the refrigerator and allow it to mature for two or three days.

The edible crusts of Brie and Camembert should remain white when the cheeses are at their peak. The crust of an overripe cheese is mottled with brown spots or bumps. This is not true, however, of double and triple crème cheeses: A strong-smelling brown crust on these soft-ripening cheeses may indicate that the center is at its peak if the cheese is soft to the touch but offers some resiliency.

The blue cheeses, such as Roquefort, taste salty because salt is added to them to slow down the growth of molds on the outside while the inside matures. Unlike most other cheeses, these salty cheeses remain good even when they are slightly overripe.

To store cheese, wrap it tightly in plastic wrap or aluminum foil and place it in the warmest part of the refrigerator (but not near the fans of self-defrosters). Because all cheeses have better flavor and texture when served at room temperature, they should be removed from the refrigerator at least ½ hour before they are to be eaten. Brie, Camembert, and other soft-ripening cheeses should be removed from the refrigerator 3 or more hours before serving in order to attain the proper texture and flavor.

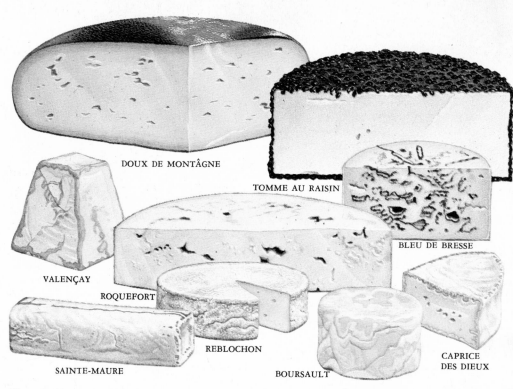

DOUX DE MONTÂGNE

TOMME AU RAISIN

VALENÇAY

BLEU DE BRESSE

ROQUEFORT

REBLOCHON

CAPRICE DES DIEUX

SAINTE-MAURE

BOURSAULT

Banon A white, crumbly cheese formed in 4–4½ ounce cakes and wrapped in chestnut leaves. Banon was originally made from goat's milk, but cow's milk is now widely used. The cheese has a slightly tart, vinous flavor when young. It turns creamy and loses some of its tartness when mature.

Beaumont A round, semisoft cheese from upper Savoy. Its flavor, strengthened with age, suggests a cross between Brie and Port Salut.

Bleu de Bresse A soft, creamy, blue-veined cheese sold in 4-ounce or 8-ounce foil packages. The flavor is delicate and soft, due to added cream. When overripe, the cheese is salty and dry.

Brie A delicate, soft-ripening cheese with an edible white crust. It ripens from the outside toward the center. The large flat wheels are ripe when the firm white core has turned a pale yellow, its small holes have disappeared, and the cheese has a smooth, creamy texture.

Camembert One of the most popular French cheeses, famed since Napoleon named it after a Normandy town. This 8-ounce, round, soft-ripening cheese is stronger than its cousin, Brie. Its reputation for being pungent and ammoniated is based on what it becomes when overripe.

Cantal A hard cow's milk cheese very popular in France. Its flavor is similar to that of Cheddar.

Chèvre (Goat's Milk) France produces several goat's milk cheeses in a variety of shapes and sizes. They are best eaten when they are young (fresh) and have a salty tartness. Specialty shops may carry **Sainte-Maure**, an elongated cylinder, and **Valençay**, a truncated pyramid. **Chevrita**, which contains a small amount of cow's milk, is widely available in Canada.

Comté A dense, nutty cheese made in wheels of 60–90 pounds. It is a French version of Switzerland's Gruyère (p.44).

Coulommiers A 12-ounce, soft-ripening wheel of the Brie-Camembert family. Except for its smaller size, the cheese is virtually indistinguishable from Brie.

Crème de Gruyère A process cheese made from Gruyère, Emmenthal, or a combination of the two. It is sold under many brand names and in many forms. Crème de Gruyère is available with flavorings, including kirsch, orange, garlic, port wine; and with raisins, caraway, almonds, and walnuts.

Double and Triple Crèmes These soft-ripening cheeses usually weigh 4–12 ounces. Because of their high cream content (up to 75 percent butterfat), they have a delicate, buttery flavor. Like Brie and Camembert, they ripen from the outside in, but because of their richness they can be enjoyed before full maturity. For their size they are thicker than Brie, so that the crust may become

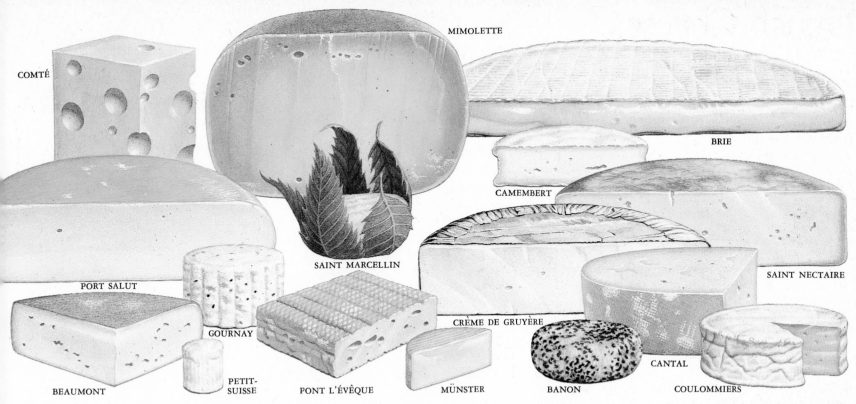

COMTÉ

MIMOLETTE

BRIE

CAMEMBERT

SAINT MARCELLIN

SAINT NECTAIRE

PORT SALUT

GOURNAY

CRÈME DE GRUYÈRE

CANTAL

BEAUMONT

PETIT-SUISSE

PONT L'ÉVÊQUE

MÜNSTER

BANON

COULOMMIERS

strong and ammoniated when the cheese is at its peak; carefully cutting off the top crust will solve this problem. Better-known brand names are **Bellétoile, Boursault, Brillât Savarin, Caprice des Dieux, Fol Amour, Saint Benoît, Semrival,** and **Suprême des Ducs.**

Doux de Montâgne This cheese resembles a large, round loaf of brown bread. It is moist and semisoft, with a delicate, buttery flavor.

Gournay This member of the French Neufchâtel family of soft, fresh cheeses is flavored with either pepper or garlic and herbs, and is sold under such trade names as **Boursin, La Bourse,** and **Tartare Provençal.** It is packed in foil packages weighing about 5 ounces. If kept too long, the cheese becomes bitter. Occasionally a yellow or brownish mold forms around the edge under the foil; it should be gently scraped off with a knife.

French Gruyère Resembles Swiss Emmenthal (p.44). It is studded with large, round holes and has a nut-sweet flavor.

Mimolette A round, firm, orange sphere of the Cheddar family. Cut from 7-pound rounds, the cheese has a smooth texture and is drier than Cheddar. The wax covering retards but does not prevent a frequent dryness in this cheese.

Münster A semisoft, creamy-textured cheese with a reddish rind and a more pungent flavor than its American-made copies. Münster, which comes from the Alsace region of France, is sometimes flavored with cumin or aniseed.

Petit-Suisse A very creamy, fresh, unsalted cheese made from whole milk with cream added. It is very soft and has a faintly sour flavor. Packed with 6 1-ounce cylinders per package, Petit-Suisse is an excellent dessert cheese served with sugar, strawberries, blueberries, or currant preserves.

Pont l'Évêque A square, soft-ripening cheese weighing 8–10 ounces. It is hearty in flavor, though not as strong as its very aromatic crust suggests.

Port Salut A pale yellow, semisoft cheese with a bright orange rind. Historically a strong and aromatic cheese, Port Salut is creamy and fairly mild in its current production. Danish Esrom (p.44) is representative of the character and flavor of the old-style Port Salut.

Reblochon A round 8-ounce cheese produced from the rich cow's milk of upper Savoy. It is a heartier-flavored member of the Port Salut family. Reblochon should be moist. To test for dryness, apply pressure to the edge (not to the top, which has a thin layer of wood veneer under the wrapper). If the cheese is moist, it will yield to the touch.

Roquefort A crumbly blue cheese with a salty but piquant flavor. Roquefort is made from ewe's milk curds sprinkled with bread crumbs; it is specially treated with mold to make the characteristic blue veins. The cheese is ripened in limestone caves.

Saint Marcellin A small, round, crumbly cream cheese made from goat's milk. Saint Marcellin has a mild taste with a touch of saltiness.

Saint Nectaire Made in the Auvergne region since the Middle Ages, Saint Nectaire is a semisoft, pale yellow cheese with a mottled yellow-brown crust. It has a distinctive earthy flavor.

Saint Paulin A semisoft cheese very similar in taste to Port Salut. Saint Paulin is said to be one of the few cheeses made in every province of France.

Tomme au Raisin A Crème de Gruyère (process) cheese originally covered with the pulp and pits left over from wine making. Upon fermentation, the pulp gave a vinous flavor to this creamy, nutty cheese, but it also gave a moldy exterior. Modern production yields a similar flavor but a cleaner rind that is shiny and black. Tomme au Raisin is also known as **La Grappe.**

Other Imported Cheeses

France is the major exporter of cheeses to Canada and the United States, but a number of fine cheeses are imported from other European countries as well. These include Italy, Switzerland, Denmark, Norway, Germany, and Great Britain. Many imported cheeses vary widely in taste and texture from their North American copies, and they are superior in most cases.

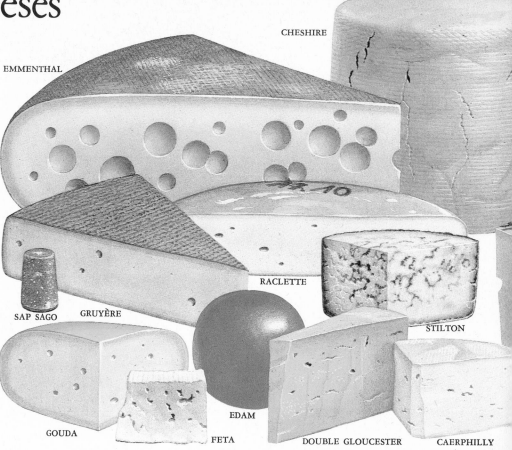

EMMENTHAL

CHESHIRE

RACLETTE

SAP SAGO

GRUYÈRE

STILTON

GOUDA

EDAM

FETA

DOUBLE GLOUCESTER

CAERPHILLY

Bel Paese One of the most famous Italian cheeses, Bel Paese is creamy white, with a yellow wax covering. Soft and compact, the cheese has a delicate, slightly vinous flavor. It is usually served as a dessert cheese, but it may also be used in cooking as a substitute for mozzarella.

Bianco The delicate taste of this German cheese resembles a cross between Bel Paese and Cream Havarti.

Caerphilly Historically a moist and salty cheese, the Caerphilly made in Great Britain today is white, dry, and crumbly, with a refreshing tartness. Grated and melted into a light white sauce, it makes an excellent substitute for Hollandaise sauce.

Cheshire An English cheese, the basis of the original Welsh Rabbit. Cheshire has a slightly tart flavor. Although it is dry, it melts well and is particularly good on bread.

Danish Blue This blue-veined cheese, sold under a variety of names, resembles Roquefort (p.43). Because it is salty and sharp, it is used sparingly—served on crackers, crumbled on salads, or blended with cream cheese, Cheddar, or sour cream for spreads or dips.

Edam This Dutch cheese has a mild flavor when young, and a slightly rubbery consistency. It is always encased in a red wax rind. Edam is similar to its cousin, Gouda, in flavor. Edam, however, is made from partly skimmed milk, while Gouda is made from whole milk.

Emmenthal The original Swiss cheese. Swiss Emmenthal is often imitated, but rarely matched, since legal production requirements are very strict. The cheese is made in 200-pound wheels, and has large holes and a sweet, nutty flavor.

Esrom The Danish version of Port Salut (p.43). When mature, Esrom has a full-bodied flavor close to that of the original French Port Salut. It is made in flat 3-pound loaves and is flecked with tiny holes.

Feta A pickled cheese imported from Greece. Because Feta is made from ewe's milk, its flavor is similar to that of Roquefort (p.43); but, unlike Roquefort, it is unveined and pure white. The cheese is pickled in brine and therefore has a salty flavor. It is used in Greek salads and is served with eggs and fruit.

Fontina Originally made in northern Italy, Fontina is smooth and creamy, with the flavors of Port Salut (p.43) and Gruyère. It is a good table cheese and is also used in cooking. **Danish Fontina** has a softer flavor. The U.S. version of Fontina is unlike the Italian and Danish products; it is hard and sharp, and tastes like a blend of Emmenthal and Parmesan. Fontina sold in Canada comes from Sweden.

Gjetost A whey cheese formed into 9-pound blocks. Gjetost is sweet, with a caramellike flavor. In Norway, where it is made, it is served in wafer-thin slivers on crispbread (a Scandinavian cracker).

Gloucester This English cheese is now called Double Gloucester, since the wheels are twice as thick as they were originally. Double Gloucester resembles Cheddar, but lacks Cheddar's saltiness and sharpness.

Gorgonzola There are two varieties of this Italian cheese: Firm Gorgonzola resembles blue cheese, but has more mold and less sharpness Creamy Gorgonzola, also blue-veined, is less salty and has a delicate flavor when young. As it matures, it becomes more aromatic, sharper, and very soft.

Gouda A smooth, mild cheese from Holland. It has a higher butterfat content than its cousin, Edam. Young Gouda has a red wax rind, while the stronger aged Gouda has a yellow wax rind.

Gruyère This cheese, made in Switzerland, is similar to Emmenthal, but is sharper, denser, and drier, and its nutlike flavor is even more pronounced. Gruyère is excellent when eaten on its own or with fruit, but is also used in making Quiche Lorraine and as a topping for onion soup. When it is past table use, it remains suitable for cooking.

Havarti This Danish version of Tilsit is quite mild when young and develops a heady aroma as it matures. **Cream Havarti**, becoming more popular, contains added cream and has a moist, delicate, buttery flavor.

Jarlsberg This widely sold Norwegian cheese is made in loaves and in 20-pound wheels. It is fine-textured, with a nutty flavor, and is flecked with large holes.

King Christian A Danish cheese spiced with caraway seeds. It is ex-

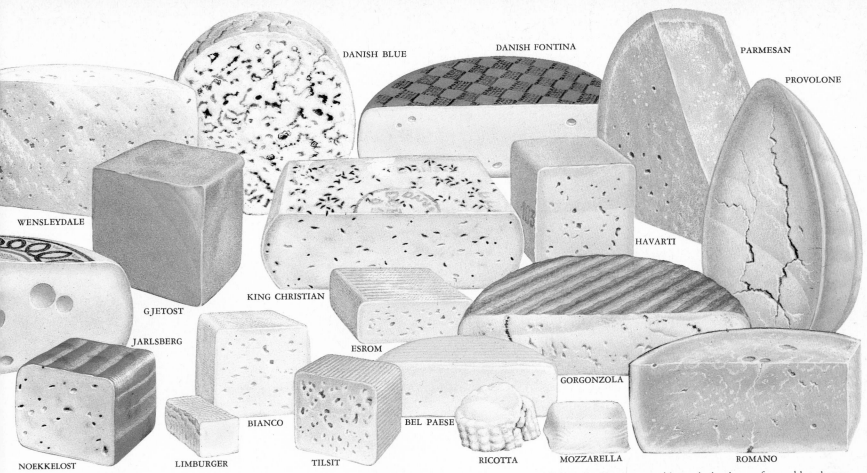

WENSLEYDALE

DANISH BLUE

DANISH FONTINA

PARMESAN

PROVOLONE

GJETOST

KING CHRISTIAN

HAVARTI

JARLSBERG

ESROM

NOEKKELOST

LIMBURGER

BIANCO

TILSIT

BEL PAESE

RICOTTA

GORGONZOLA

MOZZARELLA

ROMANO

cellent for slicing and is particularly good in sandwiches. The caraway flavor is more pronounced when the cheese is grilled.

Limburger Named for the Belgian town where it was first made, Limburger is now imported from Germany. The soft-ripening cheese is made in small loaves; it develops a strong aroma that is not nearly as overwhelming as its reputation suggests. Like any strong cheese, it is best eaten on bread.

Mozzarella A soft, spongy Italian curd cheese with a slightly bland taste. It is used as a staple ingredient in many Italian dishes.

Noekkelost A smooth, semisoft Norwegian cheese spiced with caraway, cumin, and clove.

Parmesan One of the best known Italian hard cheeses. It is strong and fragrant, which makes it excellent for cooking. In grated form, it is one of the staples of the Italian kitchen—used in soups, vegetables, pasta, and meat specialties.

Provolone A hard Italian cheese made in various shapes. The rind is yellow, while the cheese itself is creamy white. Delicate and sweet after ripening for 2 or 3 months, provolone becomes spicy and sharp if kept longer.

Raclette This cheese from Switzerland is named after the dish for which it is used: The cheese is held over a fire until runny, then scraped onto boiled new potatoes and served with dill and onion. Melted raclette can also be served on small squares of dark bread as an hors d'oeuvre and makes an excellent party food.

Romano A hard Italian grating cheese made from sheep's milk, similar to Parmesan in appearance but somewhat stronger in flavor.

Ricotta A soft, bland Italian cheese that is crumbly and dry. Made from sheep's milk and with a low fat content, it is used as a dessert cheese.

Canadian-made ricotta resembles cottage cheese and is used primarily in cooking.

Sap Sago A rock-hard, green grating cheese from Switzerland, sold in 3-ounce cones. It is flavored with mountain herbs. The cheese keeps almost indefinitely and is traditionally grated into melted butter and served on baked potatoes. It also enhances tossed salads and can be mixed with cottage cheese or sour cream for dips or spreads.

Stilton The most prized English cheese. Stilton has a Cheddar base and is blue-veined, with a dry, brown crust. Its flavor is creamy, without

the harshness of many blue cheeses. The cheese is best served on unsalted crackers, accompanied by a glass of port.

Tilsit Originally made by Dutch settlers in East Prussia, this German cheese is also produced in Switzerland and Scandinavia. Tilsit is a savory, straw-colored, aromatic cheese, flecked with small irregular holes.

Wensleydale Crumbly in texture, this English cheese varies in color from white to creamy yellow, but has a consistently mild taste. In northern England it is traditionally served with apple pie. It is also excellent for use in cooking.

45

Twelve Months

JANUARY

FEBRUARY

MARCH

JULY

AUGUST

SEPTEMBER

# of Recipes

APRIL

MAY

PAGES 130–149

JUNE

PAGES 150–171

OCTOBER

PAGES 232–251

NOVEMBER

PAGES 252–271

DECEMBER

PAGES 272–295

January

Now there is frost upon the hill
And no leaf stirring in the wood.

GEORGE O'NEIL

THIS MONTH'S RECIPES

*A well-stocked larder or cellar with strings of onions, trays of apples and parsnips,
and sacks of potatoes, which will last through the winter days.*

49

Food in Season

Although midwinter does not offer the abundance of fruits and vegetables available in the summer and fall, there is a surprising variety of fresh imported food available.

Markets are well stocked with broccoli and Brussels sprouts, which can add a fresh, green touch to winter meals without straining the budget. Broccoli is delicious prepared au gratin (p.65), and Brussels sprouts make an excellent cream soup (p.52). Cauliflower from the United States is also in season, and is especially appetizing when served with almonds (p.63).

Normally expensive avocados are now at their cheapest and make a refreshing first course when served with a tart chili sauce (p.51). California celery is at the peak of its season and can be served at almost every meal, either plain or as an ingredient in hot dishes or green salads (p.64).

The parsnip, a root vegetable that is gaining popularity in North America, is at its most plentiful in January. It is available in most supermarkets and can be used for delectable croquettes (p.63) to serve with meat or poultry.

Oranges and tangerines are also in good supply. Use tangerines to make ice cream (p.66), or serve orange sections baked in a creamy custard (p.65).

Hearty meat stews are ideal main courses for the winter months, and two particularly good ones are included in this section: Lamb and Bean Stew (p.55) and Carbonnades à la Flamande (p.58), a classic Belgian recipe for beef in beer.

SUGGESTED MENUS

Cream of Brussels Sprouts Soup
...
Saddle of Venison
Glazed Onions   Bread Croûtons
...
Iced Tangerines

Smelt with Almonds
...
Carbonnades à la Flamande
Parsnip Croquettes
...
Apple Pie with Cheese Crust

Casserole of Halibut
Fried Rice with Leeks
...
Fig Pie

Fettuccine al Burro
...
Squab with Pâté
...
Flummery

Onions Monégasque
...
Tenderloin of Pork
Broccoli au Gratin   Soufflé Potatoes
...
Apricot Sherbet

Barbecued Stuffed Shrimp
Lettuce and Celery Salad
...
Coconut Cream Pie

Braised Oxtail
Rice with Garlic and Walnuts
...
Fresh Fruit

Savory Fritters
...
Coleslaw with Italian Dressing
Baked Oranges

Soups & First Courses

AVOCADO WITH CHILI SAUCE

The avocado, one of the more expensive fruits, is cheapest in midwinter, when supplies are large. It makes a savory appetizer when flavored with a tart chili sauce.

PREPARATION TIME: *20 minutes*

INGREDIENTS (*for 6*):
3 avocados
2 tablespoons lime juice
4 tablespoons olive oil
½ teaspoon Dijon mustard
2 tablespoons chili sauce
2 tablespoons wine vinegar
½ teaspoon salt
4 drops Tabasco
1 teaspoon Worcestershire sauce

Halve the avocados lengthwise and discard the seeds. Remove and dice the pulp, toss with the lime juice, and set aside. Beat together the remaining ingredients and chill. Just before serving, toss the avocado meat in the sauce and pile this into the avocado shells.

TUNA WITH BEANS

A combination of seasoned tuna and white beans is a good Italian-style beginning for a family meal.

PREPARATION TIME: *10 minutes*

INGREDIENTS (*for 8*):
2 7-ounce cans tuna, packed in olive oil
3 cups cooked flageolet beans
½ cup chopped onion
2 tablespoons chopped parsley
1 teaspoon oregano
2 tablespoons olive oil
1 teaspoon lemon juice
1 teaspoon grated lemon rind
Salt and pepper

Put the tuna and the olive oil from the can into a bowl and break the tuna into small pieces with a fork. Add the remaining ingredients and toss very gently to mix. If made ahead, keep refrigerated and bring to room temperature before serving.

OYSTER PURÉE

An oyster soup made with clam juice and heavy cream laced with cognac is an interesting variation of the well-known oyster stew.

PREPARATION TIME: *10 minutes*
COOKING TIME: *40–45 minutes*

INGREDIENTS (*for 6*):
½ cup uncooked rice
1 quart bottled clam juice
4 tablespoons butter
18 oysters
1½ cups heavy cream
Salt and freshly ground pepper
¼ teaspoon Tabasco
3 tablespoons cognac
GARNISH:
Chopped parsley

Simmer the rice in the clam juice until very soft. Add the butter. Force through a fine sieve or whirl in a blender. Finely chop 12 of the oysters or whirl them in a blender with their liquid. Add to the rice mixture. Stir in the heavy cream. Season to taste with salt, pepper, and Tabasco. Heat just to the boiling point.

Add the 6 whole oysters and heat until they just curl at the edges. Add the cognac and simmer the soup over low heat for 2 minutes.

Ladle into heated cups, putting a whole oyster in each cup. Garnish with chopped parsley and serve with crisp Melba toast.

ONIONS MONÉGASQUE

This excellent, easily prepared first course of baby onions in a wine-flavored sauce is sometimes called Onions Escoffier. It is equally good served as a side dish with a main course of cold meat.

PREPARATION TIME: *20 minutes*
COOKING TIME: *35–40 minutes*

INGREDIENTS (*for 8*):
40 small white onions, about 1 inch in diameter, peeled but with root ends left on
⅔ cup olive oil
⅓ cup wine vinegar
½ cup Madeira or dry vermouth
2 bay leaves
1 teaspoon thyme
1 teaspoon basil
1 tablespoon salt
1 teaspoon freshly ground black pepper
A large pinch of saffron
2 tablespoons tomato paste
¾ cup dark raisins

Put the onions in a deep skillet or saucepan with the oil, vinegar, wine, bay leaves, thyme, basil, salt, pepper, and enough water barely to cover. Bring to a simmer and cook over low heat for 15 minutes. Add a large pinch of saffron and the tomato paste and continue to cook until the onions are tender but still crisp. Then add the raisins and cook until the liquid reduces slightly. Chill in the refrigerator. Serve the onions in the sauce, in soup plates. Garnish with chopped parsley.

SCRAMBLED EGGS WITH SMOKED SALMON

This is an unusual first course for lunch or dinner. It is creamy in texture and its garnish of sliced pepper and whole olives is especially attractive.

PREPARATION TIME: *8 minutes*
COOKING TIME: *25 minutes*

INGREDIENTS (*for 6*):
½ pound unsalted butter
8 ½-inch-thick slices of stale white bread
1 pepper (green or red)
7 eggs
3 tablespoons heavy cream
Black pepper
¼ teaspoon salt
¼ pound shredded smoked salmon
GARNISH:
Red or green pepper
6 parsley sprigs
Watercress
12 pitted black olives

Melt half the butter in a skillet. With a plain or fluted 3-inch pastry or cookie cutter, cut 6 rounds from the bread slices. Cut the other 2 slices into ½-inch fingers. Soak the bread rounds and slices in the melted butter and then place in a preheated 400°F oven for about 20 minutes, or until the rounds are crisp and golden. Remove from the oven and keep warm on a serving dish.

Meanwhile, remove the seeds from the pepper and chop it coarsely. Melt 2 tablespoons of butter in a pan and slowly cook the chopped pepper in it for 15 minutes. Drain on paper towels and keep hot.

Beat the eggs lightly and stir in the cream, freshly ground black pepper, salt, and the salmon. Melt 6 tablespoons of butter in a large,

heavy-bottomed pan over low heat and pour in the egg and salmon mixture. Stir gently and continuously until the eggs begin to form creamy curds. Remove the pan from the heat and quickly arrange the scrambled eggs over the 6 rounds of warm bread.

Scatter the cooked pepper over the eggs and garnish with sprigs of parsley. Decorate the serving dish with thin slices of red or green raw pepper (remove stalk ends and seeds first), small bunches of watercress, and pitted black olives. Serve with the crisp bread fingers.

CREAM OF BRUSSELS SPROUTS SOUP

A generous garnish of toasted almonds gives extra flavor to this interesting green soup. It can be served hot or chilled, and it is also suitable for freezing, in which case the clove of garlic should be omitted.

PREPARATION TIME: *40 minutes*
COOKING TIME: *2 hours*

INGREDIENTS (*for 6–8*):

FOR THE STOCK:
¼ pound salt pork, blanched
1 carrot
1 small turnip
1 clove garlic
1 onion studded with 2 cloves
6 sprigs parsley
1 bouquet garni (p.410)
6 peppercorns
1 bay leaf
2 teaspoons salt

FOR THE SOUP:
2 pounds Brussels sprouts
½ pound potatoes
1 onion
4 tablespoons unsalted butter
1¼ cups milk
Black pepper
½ teaspoon grated nutmeg
½ cup light cream
GARNISH:
1 cup sliced almonds

For the stock, put 5 cups of water into a saucepan and add the blanched* salt pork; cover and bring to a boil. Peel and slice the carrot and turnip, crush the garlic, and add to the stock, along with the clove-studded onion, sprigs of parsley, the bouquet garni, peppercorns, bay leaf, and salt. Bring to a boil again and remove any scum after a minute or so. Cover and simmer for 1½ hours, then strain the liquid through cheesecloth into a measuring cup or bowl. The stock should yield about 4 cups; if less, add boiling water.

Peel the Brussels sprouts and thinly slice the potatoes and onion. Melt the butter in a large skillet and let the onion and potatoes cook in it slowly for 10 minutes, until they have absorbed the butter but not changed color. Toss the Brussels sprouts around with the potatoes and onion, then transfer the contents of the pan to a large saucepan and add the 4 cups of stock and 1¼ cups of milk. Bring this mixture to a boil, cover, and simmer for 20 minutes. Add freshly ground pepper and more salt if necessary.

Allow the soup to cool slightly before puréeing in an electric blender or rubbing it through a sieve. (Place in the freezer at this stage if the soup is to be stored for any length of time.) Stir the nutmeg and cream into the soup; reheat carefully without boiling or chill in the refrigerator for a few hours.

Put the sliced almonds on a baking sheet on the middle shelf of the oven preheated to 350°F; turn the almonds several times until they take on a deep amber color. Remove from the oven and allow them to cool.

Serve the soup hot or chilled and sprinkle generously with the toasted almonds.

Fish

MEDITERRANEAN FISH SOUP

On a cold winter evening this thick Mediterranean soup serves almost as a meal in itself. It can be prepared well in advance and reheated just before serving without losing any of its delicate flavor.

PREPARATION TIME: *35 minutes*
COOKING TIME: *45 minutes*

INGREDIENTS (*for 6–8*):
¾ pound each of fillets of sea bass, flounder, and haddock or cod
1 large onion
6 tablespoons olive oil
1 clove garlic
16-ounce can tomatoes
2 tablespoons tomato paste
1 tablespoon chopped parsley
4 cups fish stock or water
½ cup dry white wine
1 bay leaf
Large piece lemon peel
Salt and black pepper
½ cup heavy cream
GARNISH:
Shrimp
Tomato slices

Cut the fish fillets diagonally into 2-inch pieces. Peel and finely chop the onion. Heat the oil in a heavy-bottomed pan and cook the onion in this until soft but not browned. This will take about 10 minutes. Crush and add the garlic, and sauté for a minute or two before adding the canned tomatoes with their liquid, the tomato paste, and the chopped parsley. Mix and simmer over low heat for 15 minutes. Add the fish, the stock, wine, bay leaf, and lemon peel; bring the mixture back to a simmer, cover with a lid, and cook slowly for 20 minutes. Discard the bay leaf and lemon peel. Season with salt and freshly ground black pepper and allow the soup to cool slightly before proceeding.

Remove 1 piece of fish for each serving, cover the pieces, and keep them warm in a 200°F oven. Put the rest in the blender with the contents of the pan and blend to a smooth, creamy consistency.

Stir in the cream and reheat the soup without bringing it to a boil. Place 1 piece of fish in each bowl and pour the soup over it. For the garnish, float a thin slice of peeled tomato topped with a peeled shrimp in each bowl.

LEEK PIE

This vegetable pie can be served cold as a substantial first course for an otherwise light evening meal, or hot as a main course for lunch. It freezes well and can be left in the freezer for several months.

PREPARATION TIME: *35 minutes*
COOKING TIME: *2 hours*

INGREDIENTS (*for 4–6*):
1 pound leeks
¼ pound back bacon
Black pepper
1–1¼ cups chicken stock
1 bay leaf
1 egg
2 tablespoons heavy cream
Standard pastry (p.354)
GLAZE:
1 egg
½ teaspoon salt

Trim the roots and outer coarse green leaves from the leeks before washing them under running water; pull open the leaf ends to rinse away any hidden dirt. Cut the leeks diagonally into ½-inch slices and put them in a deep 9-inch pie pan. Dice the bacon; mix with the leeks. Pepper well, barely cover with the chicken stock, and add the bay leaf. Put on the center shelf of an oven preheated to 300°F and cook for 1½ hours or until the liquid has almost evaporated. Remove the bay leaf.

Let the leeks cool slightly, then beat the egg and cream together with a fork and stir into the leek mixture. Roll out the pastry ⅛ inch thick on a lightly floured surface and cut it into a circle to fit the pie pan. Moisten the edge of the pie pan and cover the filling with the pastry. Trim the edges, decorate the top with leaves cut from the pastry trimmings, and crimp the edges together firmly to seal them.

(At this stage the pie may be stored in the freezer for later use. The frozen pie can be placed straight in the oven for reheating. There is no need to thaw it first.)

Beat the second egg and the salt together well, and brush over the pastry to give it a golden glaze while cooking. Make a small slit in the top of the pastry to allow the steam to escape. Cook the pie on the center shelf of the oven at 400°F for about 30 minutes or until the crust is golden brown. Allow the pie to cool completely and serve it cut into wedges, accompanied by a tossed green salad.

BARBECUED STUFFED SHRIMP

These zesty stuffed shrimp can be prepared an hour or two ahead of time and refrigerated until shortly before serving.

PREPARATION TIME: *1 hour*
COOKING TIME: *5 minutes*

INGREDIENTS (*for 6–8*):
36 large shrimp
2 tablespoons butter
3 tablespoons finely chopped onion
2 tablespoons finely chopped green pepper
2 tablespoons flour
½ cup light cream
¼ cup cracker crumbs
1 cup cooked crabmeat
1½ teaspoons Worcestershire sauce
1 tablespoon chopped parsley
¼ teaspoon salt
¼ teaspoon black pepper
BARBECUE SAUCE:
1 teaspoon finely chopped onion
2 tablespoons butter
1 tablespoon wine vinegar
1 tablespoon brown sugar
1 tablespoon Worcestershire sauce
½ cup ketchup
3 tablespoons lemon juice
¼ teaspoon salt
¼ teaspoon Tabasco sauce

Shell and devein the shrimp but leave the tails intact. Slit the shrimp down the back, but do not cut in two. Refrigerate.

To make the stuffing, melt the butter in a skillet and sauté the vegetables over low heat for 10 minutes. Add the flour, then the cream, stirring continuously until thick. Add the cracker crumbs, crabmeat, Worcestershire sauce, parsley, salt, and pepper. Mix well.

To stuff the shrimp, put 2 shrimp together back to back with some of the stuffing in between. Press them together and join each stuffed shrimp with toothpicks. Chill.

To make the sauce, sauté the onion in the butter for 5 minutes. Add the remaining ingredients and simmer 5 minutes.

When ready to serve, place the shrimp on a shallow pan. Brush them lightly with the barbecue sauce and broil 2 inches from the heat for about 5 minutes.

SMELT WITH ALMONDS

The delicate flavor of these small saltwater fish is most apparent when they are baked or sautéed.

PREPARATION TIME: *10 minutes*
COOKING TIME: *10 minutes*

INGREDIENTS (*for 6*):
18 smelt
6 tablespoons light cream
Seasoned flour (p.412)
6 tablespoons unsalted butter
1 tablespoon olive oil
1 cup sliced almonds

Lightly wash the smelt in cold water. Split, remove the entrails, and cut off the heads. Dry the cleaned smelt; dip the fish in the cream, and roll in seasoned flour. Melt the butter in a heavy-bottomed skillet, add the olive oil, and gently sauté the smelt for 4 minutes on each side.

Remove the smelt from the pan and keep them warm. Increase the heat slightly and sauté the sliced almonds in the fat in which the fish have been cooked until they turn light brown. Sprinkle the smelt with the almonds and pour in the butter.

FISH CASSEROLE WITH CHEESE CUSTARD

Smoked fish enhances the flavor of this casserole topped with a cheese and tomato custard.

PREPARATION TIME: *35 minutes*
COOKING TIME: *45 minutes*

INGREDIENTS (*for 6*):
1¼ *pounds fresh cod fillet*
6 *ounces smoked cod or haddock*
4 *cups chicken or fish stock*
1 *onion*
3 *cloves*
1 *clove garlic*
Salt and black pepper
1¼ *cups white sauce* (*p.301*)
1 *pound tomatoes*
2 *eggs*
½ *cup grated Parmesan cheese*
1¼ *cups milk*
2 *tablespoons unsalted butter*

Skin the fresh cod* and cut both the fresh and smoked fish into 1-inch-wide slices. Put the fish slices in a deep skillet and cover with the stock. Peel and finely slice the onion and add to the fish, together with the cloves and the crushed garlic. Bring slowly to a boil and season with salt and freshly ground pepper. Simmer for 10 minutes, then remove the fish from the liquid.

Increase the heat and boil the fish liquid rapidly until it has reduced* to 1¼ cups; strain and use it to make the white sauce.

Flake* the fish into a deep 8-inch-wide gratin or baking dish, pour in the hot white sauce, and coat the fish thoroughly. Peel and slice the tomatoes* in a layer over the fish,

and pepper well. Beat the eggs with salt and pepper; beat in the grated cheese and milk. Pour this mixture over the tomatoes and float small pieces of butter on the surface. Bake for 45 minutes, or until golden brown, on the center shelf of an oven preheated to 325°F.

A potato purée or rice, and a green vegetable or salad could be served with the casserole.

MATELOTE OF EELS

A *matelote*—not to be confused with *matelot* ("sailor")—is the French culinary term for a fish stew. In this recipe, eels, mushrooms, and onions are used for a satisfying main course for lunch or supper.

PREPARATION TIME: *20 minutes*
COOKING TIME: *45 minutes*

INGREDIENTS (*for 4-6*):
1½ *pounds eels*
2 *small onions*
6 *tablespoons unsalted butter*
1½ *cups dry white wine*
1 *carrot*
1 *clove garlic*
Bouquet garni (*p.410*)
½ *teaspoon ground mace*
Salt and black pepper
1 *egg yolk*
½ *cup heavy cream*
GARNISH:
12 *button mushrooms*
12 *small white onions*
Sautéed bread triangles

Have the eels skinned and cleaned. Peel and thinly slice the onions; sauté* half in 4 tablespoons of the butter for 5 minutes or until golden. Wash and dry the eels and cut into 2-inch pieces, add to the onion, and continue sautéing gently for about 10 minutes, turning the eels until lightly browned. Pour in the wine and bring to a simmer. Peel, slice, and chop the carrot; peel and crush the garlic; add these to the pan, together with the remaining onion, bouquet garni, mace, and seasoning. Cover with a lid and simmer over low heat for 25 minutes.

Meanwhile, wipe and trim the mushrooms,* peel the onions, and sauté both in the remaining 2 tablespoons of butter; then sauté the bread triangles.* Remove the fish

and keep it warm on a serving dish.

Beat the egg yolk and cream together and add a little of the fish liquid. Blend this into the mixture in the pan and continue gently stirring until the sauce thickens. Pour the sauce over the eels and serve garnished with the mushrooms, onions, and bread triangles.

CASSEROLE OF HALIBUT

This is a highly nutritious, easily prepared dish for lunch or dinner. A garnish of puff pastry crescents adds a touch of sophistication.

PREPARATION TIME: *15 minutes*
COOKING TIME: *50 minutes*

INGREDIENTS (*for 6*):
2 *pounds halibut*
4 *tablespoons unsalted butter*
1 *tablespoon finely chopped onion*
1¼ *cups heavy cream*
Juice of ½ *lemon*
2 *teaspoons paprika*
¼ *pound mushrooms*
¾ *cup peeled shrimp*
GARNISH:
Puff pastry crescents (*p.364*)

Skin the halibut.* Butter an oven-proof casserole, place the halibut in this, and cook for 15 minutes on the middle shelf of an oven preheated to 325°F. Remove from the oven, sprinkle the finely chopped onion over the fish, pour in the cream mixed with the lemon juice, and dust lightly with paprika.

Cover the dish with a lid or foil, return to the oven, and cook for a further 20 minutes, basting* twice with the cooking liquid. Trim and slice the mushrooms,* and sprinkle them, with the shrimp, over the fish; cook for a further 15 minutes, again

Meat

basting twice. Transfer the fish to a warm serving dish and pour the hot liquid over it.

Garnish with puff pastry crescents and serve boiled new potatoes and a green salad with the fish.

PORTUGUESE CODFISH

This Portuguese dish of puréed codfish and potatoes is flavored with garlic and baked in a casserole. It is an interesting dish for luncheon or for Sunday brunch.

SOAKING TIME: *12 hours*
PREPARATION TIME: *1 hour 10 minutes*
COOKING TIME: *35–40 minutes*

INGREDIENTS (*for 8*):
2 pounds dried salt codfish
6–8 medium potatoes
Cream
⅓ cup olive oil
3 cloves garlic, minced
½ cup buttered bread crumbs

Soak the codfish for 12 hours or overnight in cold water. Remove the fish from the bones, pulling it apart into small pieces. Place the fish in a saucepan, cover with cold water, and bring to a boil. Lower the heat and simmer until flaky and tender, or about 5 minutes. Drain well.

When cool enough to handle, shred or chop the fish very fine, or pound in a mortar. Steam the potatoes and mash well, adding just enough cream to moisten them. Add the codfish, olive oil, and minced garlic and beat to make a fluffy mixture. Taste for seasoning.

Turn into a buttered casserole and sprinkle with buttered bread crumbs (p.395). Bake in a 350°F oven until very hot, about 35 minutes.

LAMB AND BEAN STEW

This is one of those hearty, satisfying stews that requires nothing before it and very little afterward.

PREPARATION TIME: *1½ hours*
COOKING TIME: *2 hours*

INGREDIENTS: (*for 6–8*):
½ cup Great Northern beans
6 lamb shoulder chops
Salt and pepper
Flour
2 or more tablespoons oil
2 bay leaves
2 cloves garlic, crushed
½ teaspoon rosemary
½ teaspoon thyme
1 large turnip, quartered
8 carrots, cut in 1-inch lengths
4 medium onions, quartered
6–7 cups beef broth
¼ cup medium pearl barley
⅓ cup lentils
2 large potatoes, diced

Cover the beans with water. Boil for 2 minutes and remove from heat. Soak 1 hour and drain.

Trim any excess fat from the chops. Salt and pepper them, coat lightly with flour, and brown on both sides in the oil. Transfer the chops to a large pot. Add the bay leaves, garlic, rosemary, thyme, the drained beans, vegetables, and enough beef broth to barely cover. Cover and simmer for 1 hour.

Add the barley and lentils. Simmer for ½ hour, add the diced potatoes, and cook for an additional ½ hour. Skim off the fat and taste for seasoning.

Spoon the stew into a warm serving dish. No other vegetables are necessary, but buttered hot biscuits would make a good accompaniment to the stew.

LAMB AND APPLE CASSEROLE

This out-of-the-ordinary combination of lamb, potatoes, and apples makes a delicious one-dish meal. Serve directly from the casserole.

PREPARATION TIME: *30 minutes*
COOKING TIME: *1–1¼ hours*

INGREDIENTS (*for 4–6*):
8 lamb chops
2 pounds potatoes
1 large onion
3 cooking apples
6 tablespoons unsalted butter
1 teaspoon brown sugar
Salt and black pepper
1 cup chicken stock

Peel and thinly slice the potatoes and cover with cold water. Trim excess fat from the lamb chops. Peel and finely chop the onion, and peel, core, and chop the apples. Melt 4 tablespoons of the butter in a pan and sauté the chops until lightly browned on both sides. Sauté the apples and onion in the same fat for about 5 minutes.

Use half the remaining butter to grease the inside of a shallow ovenproof casserole. Dry the sliced potatoes and line the base of the dish with half of them. Arrange the chops on the potato bed and spoon the apple and onion mixture over them. Sprinkle with the sugar, a little salt, and a couple of twists of pepper from the mill. Cover with the rest of the potatoes and pour in the chicken stock. Melt the remaining butter and brush it over the potato layer. Put the dish on the middle shelf of an oven preheated to 350°F and cook for 1 hour, or until the potatoes are tender and golden brown.

Serve straight from the casserole. Brussels sprouts or any other green vegetable could be served also.

TENDERLOIN OF PORK

The tenderloin of pork is a lean cut of meat that should usually be stuffed, marinated,* or larded* to prevent it from drying out.

PREPARATION TIME: *30 minutes*
COOKING TIME: *1½ hours*

INGREDIENTS (*for 6*):
2½–3 pounds pork tenderloin
4 tablespoons unsalted butter
1 clove garlic
STUFFING:
1½–2 cups fine white bread crumbs
¼ cup mixed dried fruits
1 tablespoon finely chopped parsley
1 tablespoon finely chopped onion
1 clove garlic
½ tablespoon chopped tarragon
4 tablespoons melted butter
1 orange
1 egg
Salt and black pepper
SAUCE:
2 cups dried apricots
1 tablespoon brown sugar
Juice of 1 lemon
½ teaspoon curry powder
1 tablespoon kümmel

Prepare the stuffing first: Mix the bread crumbs, the cut-up fruits, parsley, onion, crushed garlic, and tarragon in a bowl. Stir in the melted butter. Add the grated rind of the orange, remove pith and membrane from the flesh, cut the flesh up, and mix it into the stuffing. Beat the egg lightly and use to bind the mixture. Season to taste with salt and freshly ground pepper.

Trim any fat from the tenderloin and remove the transparent skin. Slit the meat lengthwise through half its thickness, open it out, and flatten with the fist or the edge of a cleaver.

Spread the stuffing over the ten-

derloin, roll up tightly from the bottom, and tie with string. Melt the butter in a heavy pan. Peel and slice the garlic and sauté until brown, then remove. Cook the pork for a few minutes in the butter until evenly browned on all sides. Cover the pan with a lid and roast on the center shelf of a preheated oven at 325°F for 1¼–1½ hours (30 minutes to the pound), or until internal temperature registers 175°F on a meat thermometer. Remove the lid for the last 10 minutes to let the meat brown.

To make the sauce, put the apricots in a saucepan with water to cover and stew until tender. Mix in the sugar, lemon juice, and curry powder, and cook for 5 minutes or until thick. Purée the apricots in a blender or food mill before stirring in the kümmel.

Before serving, remove the string and carve the meat into slices. Arrange on a serving dish and spoon over a little of the sauce. Serve the remaining sauce separately with, for example, sautéed potatoes (p.333) and broccoli spears au gratin (p.65) or a purée of spinach.

BRAISED OXTAIL

Oxtail is an inexpensive, nourishing, but fatty meat. This stew is best cooked the day before so that the fat can rise to the top, solidify, and be removed before the stew is reheated.

PREPARATION TIME: *40 minutes*
COOKING TIME: *4¾ hours*

INGREDIENTS (*for 6*):
2 oxtails, cut into 2-inch lengths
Seasoned flour (p.412)
2 onions
3 tablespoons beef drippings
2½ cups red wine or beef stock
Bouquet garni (p.410)
Salt and black pepper
2 bay leaves
1 tablespoon red currant jelly
Rind of ½ lemon and ½ orange
¾ pound carrots
2 small turnips
1 tablespoon lemon juice
1 tablespoon tomato paste
2 cups mushrooms
GARNISH:
3 tablespoons chopped parsley
2 teaspoons grated lemon rind

Coat the 2-inch oxtail pieces lightly with the seasoned flour. Peel and slice the onions.

Melt the drippings in a large skillet and sauté the oxtails in the hot fat for 5 minutes until they glisten, then transfer to a large heavy pot. Sauté the onions in the residue of the fat and, as soon as they begin to color, add them to the oxtail. Pour the wine or beef stock over the oxtail and onions, put the pot over the heat, and bring the wine to a boil. Add the bouquet garni, salt, pepper, bay leaves, jelly, and rind and simmer on top of the stove for 2 hours. Strain the liquid into a wide bowl and set aside to cool.

Peel and slice the carrots and

turnips, and add to the oxtail. Spoon as much fat as possible from the cooled liquid. (If it is thoroughly cold, the fat will have settled in a layer on top and can easily be lifted off.) Pour the liquid over the oxtail. Add the lemon juice and tomato paste, bring to a boil, and place on the lowest shelf of the oven, preheated to 275°F. Cook for 2½ hours. Add the trimmed and sliced mushrooms* to the dish for the last 10 minutes of cooking.

Serve sprinkled with parsley mixed with the lemon peel; rice with leeks (p.62) would also be suitable.

CORNED BEEF AND CARROTS

This version of corned beef omits the customary cabbage, but you may add it if you wish.

PREPARATION TIME: *30 minutes*
SOAKING TIME: *3 hours*
COOKING TIME: *3–4 hours*

INGREDIENTS (*for 6*):
4 pounds corned beef
1 large onion
4 cloves
Bouquet garni (p.410)
6 peppercorns
2 bay leaves
1 slice bacon
10 small carrots
12 small onions
2 small turnips
½ cup dry white wine
½ teaspoon dry mustard
½ teaspoon ground cinnamon

Soak the corned beef in cold water for 3 hours. Remove and wash well in cold water.

Put the corned beef in a large saucepan. Peel the large onion, stud it with the cloves, and add to the beef, together with the bouquet garni, peppercorns, bay leaves, and bacon. Cover with cold water, bring to a boil, and after a few minutes remove the scum with a large spoon; keep the meat on the boil and continue skimming for about 10 minutes. Cover the pan with a tight-fitting lid and reduce the heat, then simmer for 1¾ hours. Remove the pan from the heat and lift out the meat with a slotted spoon; strain the liquid into a bowl.

When the liquid has cooled, remove the congealed fat from the surface. Peel the carrots and onions, and peel and coarsely slice the turnips. Arrange the vegetables in a deep pan, with the beef on top. Pour over the wine and enough strained liquid to cover. Sprinkle in the mustard and cinnamon and cover the pan with a lid. Bring to a boil, then lower the heat and simmer for 1–2 hours more, or until meat is tender when tested with a fork.

Arrange the corned beef in the center of a large serving dish and surround with the vegetables. Cabbage, cut into large chunks, may be added to the simmering meat for the last 20 minutes of cooking.

Serve piping hot, with plain boiled potatoes or buttered noodles and a crisp green salad.

LENTIL CASSOULET

This is a different version of a classic French cassoulet, and it makes an ideal dish for a buffet.

PREPARATION TIME: *about 2½ hours*
COOKING TIME: *2½ hours*

INGREDIENTS (*for 8–10*):
2 pounds lentils
1 tablespoon salt
1 onion, stuck with 2 cloves
3–4 garlic cloves, peeled
1 bay leaf
1 pig's foot, split
1 small leg of lamb, or ½ leg (about 3½ pounds)
3 pounds pork loin or shoulder
½ cup red wine
8–10 Italian sausages
1 cotechino, large saucisson à l'ail, Polish kielbasa, or garlic sausage
4–6 garlic cloves, finely chopped
1½ teaspoons thyme
1 teaspoon ground black pepper
2 tablespoons tomato paste
½ pound salt pork, cut into thin strips
Dry bread crumbs

Pour enough boiling water over the lentils to cover them. Let them stand in the water for 1 hour. While the lentils are soaking, make a broth with 2 quarts of water, salt, onion, peeled garlic cloves, bay leaf, and pig's foot. Drain the lentils and add them to the broth. Bring to a boil, skim off any scum with a spoon, and simmer until the lentils are just tender, about 30 minutes. Do not let them get mushy or overcooked.

While the beans are cooking, salt and pepper the lamb and the pork loin or shoulder, and roast in a 325°F oven for 1½ hours, basting from time to time with the red wine. Allow the

meats to cool, then pour the pan juices into a small bowl and chill in the refrigerator until the fat hardens on top of the juices. Skim off the fat and discard it.

Cut the cooled meats into 2-inch dice, and reserve. Poach the Italian sausages along with one of the other sausages in water to cover for 5 minutes. Cut the large sausage into slices about ½ inch thick.

Blend the chopped garlic cloves with the thyme and black pepper. Remove the pig's foot from the

lentils and cut the skin and meat from the bones. Drain the lentils, reserving the liquid. Discard the bay leaf, onion, and garlic.

Put a layer of lentils in a large earthenware or enameled iron casserole or baking dish, sprinkle with some of the garlic-herb mixture, and strew with some of the diced meats, including skin and meat from the pig's foot and sausages. Repeat layers, ending with a top layer of lentils.

Combine the meat juices, the bean liquid, the remaining red wine, and

the 2 tablespoons of tomato paste. Pour in enough of this liquid to reach almost to the top layer of beans. Top with salt pork. Cover lightly with foil and bake in a 350°F oven for 1 hour.

Remove the foil, sprinkle the top with bread crumbs, and bake 1 more hour, or until the liquid is absorbed, the crumbs browned, and the top glazed. If the liquid is absorbed too quickly during the first hour of cooking, add a little more bean liquid or water.

SPARERIBS IN MARSALA

To many people, pork spareribs are synonymous with Chinese cooking. In this recipe, however, a fortified Italian wine is used to impart a different flavor.

PREPARATION TIME: *40 minutes*
COOKING TIME: *35 minutes*

INGREDIENTS (*for 6*):
6 large pork spareribs
3 tablespoons olive oil
2 cloves garlic
2 tablespoons parsley
1 teaspoon ground fennel
Salt and black pepper
½ cup fresh orange juice
½ cup chicken stock
3 tablespoons Marsala wine
GARNISH:
Orange slices and watercress

Have the meat cut into single rib portions; trim as much fat from the ribs as possible. Heat the oil in a heavy-bottomed pan. Peel and crush the cloves of garlic and rub them over the ribs. Chop the parsley finely and mix with the fennel; rub into the ribs. Put the ribs in the pan, pepper each well, and cook on both sides until pale brown. Pour in the orange juice and stock, add the Marsala, and correct seasoning.

Cook the spareribs on the middle shelf of a preheated oven at 350°F for 35 minutes.

Lift out the ribs and arrange them on a bed of egg noodles.* Skim the fat off the juices and pour these over the meat. Garnish with slices of orange and small bunches of watercress. Broccoli spears au gratin (p.65) or cauliflower with almonds (p.63) could also be served.

HAMBURGER WITH PIZZAIOLA SAUCE

An American tradition, hamburger, is here combined with a classic Italian tomato sauce.

PREPARATION TIME:
Hamburgers, 15 minutes
Sauce, 20 minutes
COOKING TIME:
Hamburgers, 3–7 minutes
Sauce, 35 minutes

INGREDIENTS (*for 4–6*):
2 pounds lean ground sirloin or top round
2 tablespoons unsalted butter
Salt and black pepper
SAUCE:
2 onions
2 cloves garlic
2 green peppers
1 tablespoon olive oil
⅔ cup mushroom caps
1 16-ounce can tomatoes
2 teaspoons oregano or marjoram
Chili sauce
Salt and black pepper

Shape the ground beef into 6 or 8 patties about 1½ inches thick. Avoid overhandling, as this makes them tough. Set the hamburgers aside while preparing the pizzaiola sauce.

Peel and mince the onions and garlic. Remove the stalks and seeds from the peppers and cut them crosswise into thin slices. Heat the oil in a deep, heavy skillet and cook the onions and garlic over gentle heat until they are pale golden. Add the pepper slices and continue cooking for 15 minutes. Wipe the mushrooms,* chop them coarsely, and add to the pan, together with the tomatoes and the oregano or marjoram. Cover and continue cooking the mixture for another 10 minutes. Season to taste with chili sauce, salt, and freshly ground pepper. Leave the pan over low heat while cooking the hamburgers.

Melt the butter in a heavy-bottomed skillet. For rare hamburgers, sauté for 1½ minutes on each side; for pink-rare hamburgers, add another minute each side; for medium, add 2 minutes. Sprinkle with salt and pepper.

Put the hamburgers on a hot serving dish and pour the sauce over them. Serve coleslaw with Italian dressing (p.63) as a side dish.

CARBONNADES À LA FLAMANDE

This is an adaptation of a Belgian recipe for beef in beer. The beer gives the meat a distinctly piquant flavor, heightened by the garlic crust. The dish is best prepared in advance and later reheated.

PREPARATION TIME: *55 minutes*
COOKING TIME: *2¾ hours*

INGREDIENTS (*for 6*):
3 pounds lean beef round or chuck
½ cup drippings or unsalted butter
1 tablespoon olive oil
3 large onions
4 cloves garlic
Salt and black pepper
2 tablespoons flour
1 tablespoon light brown sugar
1¼ cups strong beef stock
2 cups beer
1 tablespoon wine vinegar
Bouquet garni (p.410)
2 bay leaves
GARLIC CRUST:
½ pound unsalted butter
3 cloves garlic
1 loaf French bread

Melt the drippings or butter with the oil in a large skillet on top of the stove. Cut the beef into ½-inch-thick slices, about 3 inches long and 1½ inches wide. Peel and finely slice the onions and crush the 4 cloves of garlic. Quickly brown the beef slices, or *carbonnades,* in the fat, drain, and put to one side. Lower the heat and in the remaining fat cook the onions until golden, then add the garlic. Place the onions and beef in alternate layers in a deep casserole, beginning with the onions and finishing with meat; salt and pepper each layer lightly.

Scrape up the juices in the pan in which the beef and onions were cooked, stir in the flour and sugar, and increase the heat until the mixture forms a roux.* Stir in a little of the stock until the mixture is smooth; bring to a boil. Add the remainder of the stock, the beer, and the vinegar; bring back to a boil and simmer over low heat for a few minutes. Put the bouquet garni and bay leaves in the casserole and pour in enough sauce to just cover the meat. Cover the casserole with a lid and cook on a shelf low in the oven for 2½ hours at 325°F.

The flavor of the carbonnades is improved if the casserole is put aside at this stage and reheated the next day before making the garlic crust.

For the garlic crust, melt the butter in a skillet over low heat. Crush the 3 cloves of garlic and stir into the butter. Cut the French bread into ½-inch-thick slices and soak them in the garlic butter until it is completely absorbed. Put the bread on top of the carbonnades and cook the casserole in a preheated oven at 325°F for 30 minutes. The meat should then be thoroughly heated and the garlic crust should be crisp, with a golden tinge.

Serve from the casserole. Cauliflower with almonds (p.63) could also be served.

Poultry & Game

ROAST PARTRIDGE

Partridge, one of the most delicious of all game birds, makes a superb winter meal. Here, the birds are served on toast, with giblets.

PREPARATION TIME: *20 minutes*
COOKING TIME: *30–35 minutes*

INGREDIENTS (*for* 4):
4 *partridges*
1 *onion, stuck with 2 cloves*
1 *bay leaf*
1 *stick of butter*
4 *thin strips pork fat*
Rosemary
Sage
8 *vine leaves* (*these may be purchased in jars*)

If partridges are not dressed, clean them and take out the livers, gizzards, and hearts. Cook these in a small amount of water for about 20 minutes with the onion and bay leaf. Chop the giblets very fine and reserve them. Put a pat of butter inside each partridge, wrap a piece of pork fat around each one, and sprinkle with a pinch of rosemary and sage. Wrap the partridges with 1 or 2 vine leaves, then tie them with string to hold the leaves firmly in place. Roast the partridges at 425°F for 25–30 minutes. About 5 minutes before the partridges are done, remove the pork fat and the vine leaves and let the partridges brown slightly. While they are cooking, bake 4 pieces of toast until brown, butter them, and spread them with the chopped giblets. Place the partridges on the pieces of toast and pour the pan juices over all.

CHICKEN IN RED WINE

This chicken dish, which includes Beaujolais and brandy, is very similar to the classic French coq au vin.

PREPARATION TIME: *20 minutes*
COOKING TIME: *1 hour*

INGREDIENTS (*for* 4):
3–3½ *pound chicken, disjointed*
¾ *cup diced salt pork*
4 *tablespoons unsalted butter*
Salt and black pepper
16 *small white onions*
6 *tablespoons brandy*
1 *bottle Beaujolais*
½ *cup chicken stock*
Bouquet garni (*p.410*)
2 *cloves garlic*
¼ *pound mushrooms*
SAUCE:
4 *tablespoons flour*
2 *tablespoons unsalted butter*
GARNISH:
Parsley sprigs

Render the salt pork in half of the butter in a deep skillet. Season the chicken pieces to taste with salt and freshly ground pepper. Remove the salt pork from the pan and slowly brown the chicken in the butter over gentle heat.

Peel the onions and add to the pan, together with the rendered pork; turn the onions until they are glazed. Warm the brandy, pour it over the chicken, and set alight. As soon as the flames have died down, pour in the wine and stock; add the bouquet garni and the crushed garlic. Increase the heat to bring the contents of the pan slowly to a boil. Check the seasoning, cover with a lid, and simmer for 30 minutes.

Meanwhile, trim and clean the mushrooms,* sauté them in 2 tablespoons of butter, and drain. Add to

the chicken after it has simmered for 30 minutes. Cover and cook for a further 10 minutes, or until the chicken is tender. Transfer the contents of the pan to a heated serving dish and keep warm.

Turn up the heat and boil the liquid in the pan rapidly until it is re-duced* to about 2 cups. Work the flour and butter together to form a paste; remove the pan from the heat and beat in small balls of the paste until the sauce thickens. Return to the heat and bring slowly to a boil. Pour the sauce over the chicken and garnish with parsley.

Boiled new potatoes tossed in butter and parsley, and young blanched broccoli spears cooked in butter could be served with the chicken as well.

POACHED PARTRIDGE IN VINE LEAVES

Vine leaves impart an unusual flavor to this succulent game bird.

PREPARATION TIME: *25 minutes*
COOKING TIME: *1½ hours*

INGREDIENTS (*for 4*):
2 young partridges
Salt and black pepper
6 lemon slices
4 teaspoons quince jelly
16-ounce jar of vine leaves
¾ pound bacon
1¼ cups dry white wine
4 cups chicken stock
GARNISH:
Watercress
Lemon baskets

Wipe the partridges inside and out, and season with salt and black pepper. Put 3 lemon slices and 2 teaspoons quince jelly inside each bird. Wrap the drained vine leaves around the birds, cover with the bacon slices, and tie firmly with fine string.

Bring the wine and stock to a boil in a large saucepan, together with the partridge giblets. Put the wrapped partridges into the liquid and simmer for 1¼ hours.

Chill the partridges quickly by immersing them in a bowl of ice water until quite cold. Remove from the water, unwrap the bacon and vine leaves, and dry the partridges thoroughly with paper towels.

Serve the partridges whole, on a bed of watercress, garnished with lemon baskets with Cumberland sauce (p.304). A lettuce and celery salad (p.64) would be a suitable light side dish.

CHICKEN WITH ITALIAN SAUSAGES

Chicken goes especially well with Italian sweet sausages when prepared this way.

PREPARATION TIME: *40 minutes*
COOKING TIME: *50 minutes*

INGREDIENTS (*for 4*):
4 tablespoons olive oil
¾ cup finely diced onions
1 clove finely chopped garlic
4 Italian sweet sausages
2–2½ pounds chicken thighs
Salt and pepper
1 cup canned Italian plum tomatoes, drained
Beurre manié (optional)

Sauté the finely diced onion and garlic in 2 tablespoons of the olive oil for 5 minutes. Remove to a small bowl and set aside.

In the same skillet sauté the sausages in the remaining olive oil until they are brown. Remove from the skillet and, when cool, cut them into 2-inch lengths.

Dry the chicken and season well with salt and pepper. Sauté a few pieces of chicken at a time in the olive oil remaining in the skillet and remove them to a platter when browned. Pour off all but 1 tablespoon of the fat.

Add the onions, garlic, sausage, and the tomatoes, and scrape up all the brown bits from the bottom of the skillet. Return the chicken pieces to the pan, turning to coat them with the sauce.

Simmer, covered, for 45 minutes. Season with salt and pepper. Thicken with beurre manié (p.303) if desired. Serve with buttered rice.

CHICKEN BREASTS CHAMPAGNE

Here is an attractive and elegant dish for a dinner party. It is surprisingly easy to prepare.

PREPARATION TIME: *10 minutes*
COOKING TIME: *20 minutes*

INGREDIENTS (*for 6*):
3 whole chicken breasts, halved, skinned, and boned
½ teaspoon lemon juice
½ teaspoon salt
¼ teaspoon white pepper
4 tablespoons butter
2 tablespoons chopped shallots or scallions
2 cups champagne or white wine
1 cup heavy cream
3 egg yolks, beaten
GARNISH:
Chopped parsley

Flatten the chicken breasts slightly with the side of a heavy knife. Rub the breasts with lemon juice, salt, and white pepper.

Melt the butter in a large, heavy skillet. When hot, add the shallots or scallions and the chicken breasts. Sauté the breasts for 3 minutes on each side over moderate heat. Do not overcook the chicken; a minute too long will toughen the meat and dry it out. Remove the chicken to a platter, cover, and keep warm in a 200°F oven.

Pour the champagne into the skillet and reduce* rapidly to ½ cup. Add the cream and cook until the cream thickens slightly. Remove the pan from the heat and let the sauce cool for a moment.

Mix a few tablespoons of the hot sauce into the egg yolks and add this mixture to the pan. Stir and simmer over low heat until the sauce thickens. Do not boil.

Remove the chicken from the oven and pour any juices that have accumulated into the sauce. Stir to blend. Taste carefully for seasoning. Add a few drops of lemon juice if the sauce seems bland. Pour the sauce over the chicken and garnish with chopped parsley.

Serve with buttered spinach or green peas and Rissoto Bianco (p.184), but omit the garlic, olive oil, and cheese in the recipe.

SADDLE OF VENISON

For a special dinner, venison in port is an excellent choice. The saddle should have been hung for at least 3 weeks to ensure a truly succulent roast. A saddle will serve 8 people handsomely, but the recipe is also suitable for a smaller roast.

PREPARATION TIME: *25 minutes*
COOKING TIME: *2¾ hours*

INGREDIENTS (*for 8–10*):
1 saddle of venison, 6–7 pounds
2 carrots
1 Spanish onion
2 stalks celery
Salt and black pepper
¼ pound butter
½ cup olive oil
2 cloves garlic
2 bay leaves
1 sprig or ½ teaspoon powdered thyme
1¼ cups chicken stock
½ bottle port
1 heaping tablespoon flour
4 tablespoons unsalted butter
1 heaping tablespoon red currant jelly

Peel and chop the carrots, onion, and celery. Trim any gristle from the venison, wipe well with a cloth, and season with salt and pepper. Melt the butter and combine with the olive oil in a large roasting pan or skillet; or quickly brown the venison, then remove. Turn up the heat, peel and crush the garlic, and add to the pan together with the bay leaves, thyme, and chopped vegetables. Cook for 5 minutes without browning the vegetables. Return the venison to the pan and cover with foil, making sure it is tightly sealed. Cook for 45 minutes on the bottom shelf of an oven preheated to 375°F; then pour in the boiling stock, reseal the pan, and cook for 1 hour.

Transfer the pan to the top of the stove. Pour the port over the venison and heat until the juices are simmering, then return to the oven; do not reseal. Cook for another hour, basting every 15 minutes. If the roast appears to be cooking too quickly, turn the heat down slightly for the last 30 minutes. Transfer the venison to a dish and keep it hot in the oven while making the sauce.

Strain the liquid from the roasting pan into a saucepan and keep at a fast boil until reduced* by half. Meanwhile, combine the flour and butter to make a paste and use pieces of this to thicken the reduced sauce, stirring continuously. Finally, mix in the red currant jelly and, as soon as this has dissolved, season the sauce with salt and pepper if necessary.

Carve* the venison and arrange the slices on a warmed serving dish. Pour some of the sauce over the meat and surround with glazed onions (p.285), mushroom caps fried in butter, and bread croûtons (p.300). Serve the remainder of the sauce in a sauceboat.

SQUAB WITH PÂTÉ

Young domestic pigeon, called squab, makes an elegant and unusual main course for a dinner party. Here it is stuffed with pâté de foie gras and served on a bed of cabbage garnished with orange wedges.

MARINATING TIME: *overnight*
PREPARATION TIME: *40 minutes*
COOKING TIME: *2 hours 40 minutes*

INGREDIENTS (*for 6*):

6 squabs	STUFFING:	LONG-COOKED
1½ cups dry white wine	*8-ounce can pâté*	CABBAGE:
2 carrots	*1 tablespoon port*	*¼ pound salt pork*
1 onion	*1 egg yolk*	*1 large cabbage*
2 bay leaves	*½ teaspoon allspice*	*6 juniper berries*
4 sprigs parsley	*½ teaspoon light cream*	*4 tablespoons*
2 sprigs thyme	*Salt and black pepper*	*unsalted butter*
Peel of ½ orange	GARNISH:	*Black pepper*
Peel of ½ lemon	*Orange wedges*	*1 teaspoon salt*
4 tablespoons		*½ cup dry white wine*
unsalted butter		*or chicken stock*

Wipe the squabs thoroughly inside and out. Put them in a bowl and pour in the wine; peel and thinly slice the carrots and onion and add to the squabs. Add the bay leaves, parsley, thyme, and orange and lemon peel. Marinate* the birds overnight.

To make the stuffing, stir the pâté smooth, add the port, and stir in the egg yolk. Blend in the allspice and cream, and season to taste with salt and pepper. Remove the squabs from the marinade; drain and dry them. Spoon the stuffing into the birds and sew them up. Salt them lightly and pepper them thoroughly. Melt the butter in a large skillet, brown the birds quickly, then transfer them to a flameproof casserole. Pour in the marinade, bring to a simmer on top of the stove, and adjust seasoning. Cover with a tight-fitting lid and cook in the lower half of the oven at 275°F for 2–2½ hours. The birds are done if the juices run clear when a thigh is pierced.

For the cabbage, dice the salt pork into ½-inch pieces and put in a heavy pan in the oven. When the fat is running freely and the pork is crisping, swirl the fat around the sides of the pan before removing the pork. Core the cabbage, wash, and shred it into the pan of fat.

Push the juniper berries and the pieces of salt pork into the cabbage and dot with butter. Pepper well and sprinkle with salt. Pour in the white wine or chicken stock. Cover the pan tightly with foil. Braise in the oven at 275°F for 2½ hours. Halfway through the cooking, add water if necessary.

Spread the cooked cabbage and pork over the bottom of a serving dish and place the squab on top. Keep warm in a 200°F oven while making the sauce. Strain the liquid, then reduce* it to half the amount over a high flame. Pour this sauce over the squab. Garnish with wedges of orange and serve immediately.

GARDENER'S CHICKEN

A chicken casserole makes a change from roast chicken. Once in the oven, it cooks without supervision.

PREPARATION TIME: *40 minutes*
COOKING TIME: *1½ hours*

INGREDIENTS (*for 4–6*):
1 chicken, approximately 3 pounds
2 slices bacon
2 large onions
2 stalks celery
¼ pound mushrooms
4–6 tablespoons unsalted butter
1 pound small new potatoes
½ pound turnips
16-ounce can tomatoes
Bouquet garni (p.410)
Salt and black pepper
GARNISH:
Fresh parsley and orange rind

Cut the chicken* into 4 or 6 pieces. Chop the bacon. Peel and thinly slice the onions; wash and coarsely chop the celery; clean and slice the mushrooms.* Melt the butter in a large, heavy-bottomed pan and sauté the bacon, onions, mushrooms, and celery for 5 minutes. Tip the pan to drain the butter to one side, remove the vegetables with a slotted spoon, and spread them over the bottom of a large casserole.

Sauté the chicken pieces in the butter residue, adding a little more butter if necessary, until they are golden brown. Remove from the pan and place on the bed of vegetables. Peel the potatoes, peel and slice the turnips, and add these, with the tomatoes and bouquet garni, to the casserole. Season with salt and freshly ground pepper, and cover the casserole with foil before covering with the lid so that no steam can escape. Cook on the middle shelf of a preheated oven at 300°F for about 1½ hours or until tender.

Immediately before serving, sprinkle chopped parsley mixed with the finely chopped rind of ½ orange over the casserole. No additional vegetables are needed.

Rice & Pasta

SPAGHETTI WITH EGGPLANT

In Italy spaghetti frequently forms the main meal of the day. Often oil and garlic are used, but eggplant gives pasta an unusual flavor.

PREPARATION TIME: *1 hour 10 minutes*
COOKING TIME: *15 minutes*

INGREDIENTS (*for 4–6*):
¾ *pound spaghetti*
1 large eggplant
2 tablespoons salt
Seasoned flour (p.412)
6 tablespoons olive oil
Black pepper

Remove the stalk end and wipe the eggplant, cut it into thin round slices, and place these in layers in a colander. Sprinkle salt over each layer and leave for 1 hour to draw out the excess water. Wipe the slices dry on paper towels, cut them into ¼-inch-wide strips, and coat them lightly with seasoned flour.

Heat 4 quarts of water in a large saucepan and, when boiling, add 1 level tablespoon salt and the spaghetti. Stir continuously until the water returns to a boil. Continue boiling, stirring occasionally, for 9 minutes, when the spaghetti should be tender but still slightly undercooked (*al dente*). While the spaghetti is cooking, heat 3–4 tablespoons of olive oil in a skillet and sauté the eggplant until crisp.

Drain the spaghetti, toss it in a colander to remove the last of the water, and pepper well. Warm the remaining olive oil in a saucepan, transfer the spaghetti to a warm serving dish, and pour the oil over it. Toss well and blend the eggplant strips into the spaghetti.

FRIED RICE WITH LEEKS

This unusual rice dish is especially good with slow-cooked meat courses that contain a lot of sauce, such as casseroles and stews.

PREPARATION TIME: *15 minutes*
COOKING TIME: *20 minutes*

INGREDIENTS (*for 4*):
2 pounds leeks
¾ *cup long grain rice*
2 tablespoons salt
4 tablespoons unsalted butter
½ *teaspoon curry powder*
Black pepper

Bring 3 quarts of water to a boil in a large pan for the rice, and boil 2½ cups water in a smaller pan for the leeks. Remove the coarse outer leaves, roots, and tops from the leeks; wash well under cold running water, rinsing away any dirt trapped in the ends; cut into ¼-inch-thick slices. Add a tablespoon of salt to each saucepan of boiling water. Put the leeks in one saucepan and the rice in the other. Stir the rice until it comes back to a boil, cover, and boil for 14 minutes. Meanwhile, simmer the leeks for about 5 minutes, then drain them in a colander. Melt the butter in a skillet and sauté the leeks for about 8 minutes or until just tender.

When it is cooked, turn the rice into a sieve and wash thoroughly under hot running water. Add the drained rice to the leeks in the skillet and blend with the curry powder. Sauté for a few minutes, stirring all the time. Season with freshly ground pepper and serve.

FETTUCCINE AL BURRO

This pasta is a specialty of many Roman restaurants and is ideally made from homemade fettuccine. It may be served as a first course or as a main course for a light lunch.

PREPARATION TIME: *8 minutes*
COOKING TIME: *10–15 minutes*

INGREDIENTS (*for 4–6*):
1 pound fettuccine
1 tablespoon salt
¼ *pound unsalted butter*
6 tablespoons heavy cream
1½ *cups grated Parmesan cheese*
Black pepper

Boil 4 quarts of water in a large saucepan and add the salt and the fettuccine, stirring until the water returns to a boil to prevent the fettuccine from sticking together. Cover and continue to boil for 8 minutes until the fettuccine are tender. Meanwhile beat the softened butter in a bowl until fluffy; gradually beat in the cream and half the cheese. Drain the fettuccine and toss them in a colander to remove the last drops of water.

Put the fettuccine in a hot serving dish, pour in the cheese and cream sauce, and toss to coat thoroughly. Pepper well and serve the remaining cheese in a bowl. A salad of lettuce, sliced fennel, and tomatoes could be served as a side dish.

RICE WITH GARLIC AND WALNUTS

Rice is a good substitute for potatoes and vegetables. Here the rice is given additional flavor that makes it a good choice with goulash, curry, or braised oxtails.

PREPARATION TIME: *15 minutes*
COOKING TIME: *20–25 minutes*

INGREDIENTS (*for 4–6*):
1 cup long grain rice
2 tablespoons finely chopped parsley
2 cloves garlic
¼ *cup shelled walnuts*
½ *cup grated Parmesan cheese*
4 tablespoons olive oil
Salt and black pepper
2 cups chicken stock
1 tablespoon salt
Juice of ½ lemon

Pound the parsley in a mortar with the peeled garlic and nuts until a smooth paste is achieved. Beat in the cheese until the mixture is thick, then gradually beat in 3 tablespoons oil. Season to taste with salt and freshly ground pepper.

Heat 1 tablespoon oil in a heavy pan, add the rice, and stir until coated. Add the chicken stock, salt, and lemon juice. Bring to a boil, cover, reduce heat to a simmer, and cook 20–25 minutes, or until the rice is just tender.

Stir the rice with a fork to separate the grains. Spoon it into a hot serving dish; season with a good grating of pepper. Blend the nut mixture into the rice and serve.

Vegetables & Salads

COLESLAW WITH ITALIAN DRESSING

This quickly made winter salad can be served with cold meat or as a side dish with a plain omelet.

PREPARATION TIME: *10 minutes*

INGREDIENTS (*for 4–6*):
1 cabbage
1 small clove garlic
6 tablespoons olive oil
2 tablespoons white wine vinegar
¼ teaspoon oregano
¼ teaspoon crushed fennel seeds
¼ teaspoon celery salt
Salt and black pepper

Cut away the coarse outer leaves from the cabbage, remove the core, and finely shred the cabbage into a serving bowl. Crush the garlic and put it, with all the other ingredients, into a screw-top jar and shake vigorously. Pour this dressing over the cabbage, toss, and serve.

CAULIFLOWER WITH ALMONDS

Cauliflower is an ideal vegetable to accompany fish or meat in rich sauces. Crisp roasted almonds complement its delicate flavor.

PREPARATION TIME: *10 minutes*
COOKING TIME: *5–8 minutes*

INGREDIENTS (*for 4*):
1 large white cauliflower
Salt
4 tablespoons clarified butter
⅓ cup sliced almonds

Dissolve 2 tablespoons of salt in a large bowl of cold water. Cut away the coarse outer leaves from the cauliflower and break the individual florets from the central stem, leaving

a short stalk on each. Drop the florets in the salted water, together with the inner pale green leaves.

Bring a large pan of salted water to a boil; cook the drained cauliflower, covered, over low heat for 5–8 minutes. Drain in a colander. Meanwhile, sauté the almonds in the clarified butter* over low heat until they turn a deep brown. Put the cauliflower in a dish and spoon the almonds and butter over it.

JERUSALEM ARTICHOKES IN BUTTER

The brown-purple skin of these knobby tubers hides a white, firm and sweet flesh, reminiscent in taste of globe artichokes.

PREPARATION TIME: *30 minutes*
COOKING TIME: *40 minutes*

INGREDIENTS (*for 6*):
1½ pounds Jerusalem artichokes
Juice of 1 lemon
1 tablespoon salt
2 ounces unsalted butter
Seasoned flour (p.412)

Strain the lemon juice into a bowl of cold water. Wash and scrape or thinly peel the artichokes,* cut them into ¼-inch slices, and drop into the water and lemon juice to prevent them from turning gray. Bring a large pan of water to a boil. Drain the artichokes and drop into the boiling water, adding the salt. Boil for 4 minutes, then drain thoroughly in a colander.

Melt the butter in an ovenproof flat dish in an oven preheated to 350°F. Coat the artichokes with the seasoned flour and roll them in the butter. Cook on the middle shelf of the oven for about 40 minutes.

PARSNIP CROQUETTES

Parsnip is an excellent but neglected winter vegetable. These crisp croquettes, which should be prepared in advance, go well with roast meat.

PREPARATION TIME: *30 minutes*
CHILLING TIME: *1 hour*
COOKING TIME: *5 minutes*

INGREDIENTS (*for 4–6*):
2 pounds parsnips
1 tablespoon salt
4 tablespoons unsalted butter
Black pepper
1 teaspoon nutmeg
Fresh white bread crumbs
1 beaten egg, strained
Oil for deep-frying

Bring a large pan of water to a boil and meanwhile peel the parsnips, cutting out the hard centers. Cut the parsnips into thin slices and add, with the salt, to the boiling water. Simmer for 20 minutes, or until the parsnips are tender. Drain thoroughly. Rub the parsnips through a coarse sieve and beat in the butter, pepper, and nutmeg. Allow to cool slightly, then shape into croquettes* about 2½ inches long and 1 inch wide. Roll each croquette in the bread crumbs, then in the strained egg and in the bread crumbs again. Chill in the refrigerator for 1 hour.

Fill a deep-fryer a third of the way up with oil and heat until a cube of bread crisps in it.* Dip the frying basket in and out of the oil, place the croquettes in the basket, and lower them into the oil. Switch off the heat immediately, and in 3 minutes the croquettes should be golden brown.

SOUFFLÉ POTATOES

With just a little extra trouble, plain baked potatoes can be transformed, with the addition of eggs and cream, into light and fluffy individual soufflés. They are ideal to serve with all kinds of meats, particularly steak.

PREPARATION TIME: *15 minutes*
COOKING TIME: *1¼ hours*

INGREDIENTS (*for 6*):

6 large potatoes
4 tablespoons unsalted melted butter
½ cup heavy cream
3 eggs
Salt and black pepper

Wash and dry the potatoes, prick them lightly with a fork, and bake for 1 hour, or until tender, on the middle shelf of a preheated oven at 400°F. Cut a lid lengthwise off the baked potatoes, scoop the flesh out into a bowl, and thoroughly mix in the melted butter and cream. Separate the eggs, beat the yolks lightly, and stir them into the potato mixture. Beat the egg whites with a little salt until stiff and fold into the potato mixture. Season to taste with freshly ground pepper.

Pile this soufflé mixture back into the hollow potato skins, return to the oven, and bake at the same temperature for 15 minutes, or until the soufflés are well risen and beginning to brown lightly.

Serve immediately, before the soufflés have time to collapse.

FASOULIA

In Greece this regional dish of white beans is usually served as a vegetable course on its own. It is particularly good with lamb.

PREPARATION TIME: *8 minutes*
SOAKING TIME: *1 hour*
COOKING TIME: *1¾ hours*

INGREDIENTS (*for 4*):
1 cup white (Great Northern)
   beans
1 large onion
½ cup olive oil
2 cloves garlic
1 bay leaf
½ teaspoon powdered thyme
1 tablespoon tomato paste
Juice of 1 lemon
Salt and black pepper
GARNISH:
Coarsely chopped parsley

Put the beans in a pan containing 2 cups boiling water. Boil for 2 minutes, remove from heat, and leave to soak, covered, for 1 hour. Meanwhile, peel and coarsely chop the onion; sauté it in the olive oil in a deep skillet until it takes color. Drain the beans and add to the onion, together with the peeled and crushed garlic, the bay leaf, thyme, and tomato paste. Cook over moderate heat for 10 minutes, then add boiling water to cover the beans by about 1 inch. Continue cooking at a gentle simmer for 1–1½ hours, or until the beans are quite tender but not mushy. Add the lemon juice and season to taste. Allow the beans to cool in the liquid, which should have the consistency of a thick sauce.

   Serve the cold beans in their liquid, garnished with parsley.

LETTUCE AND CELERY SALAD

Most rich meat dishes, especially those with sweet stuffings, are better accompanied by a salad than by a vegetable dish.

PREPARATION TIME: *10 minutes*

INGREDIENTS (*for 4–6*):
4 lettuce hearts
4 stalks celery
DRESSING:
1 teaspoon Dijon mustard
½ teaspoon salt
½ cup light cream
½ cup olive oil
3 tablespoons tarragon vinegar
GARNISH:
Celery leaves

Cut each lettuce heart into quarters; trim off roots and coarse leaves from the celery. Wash the stalks and chop them coarsely. Place these ingredients in a serving bowl.

   To make the dressing, blend the mustard and salt in a mixing bowl; stir in the cream. Beat in the olive oil, drop by drop, and when all the oil is absorbed, gradually beat in the vinegar until the dressing has the consistency of thick cream. Pour the dressing over the celery and lettuce, toss, and serve garnished with a few celery leaves.

Desserts

BROCCOLI AU GRATIN

Broccoli should be undercooked to preserve its texture and flavor. It can be served tossed in butter or, as here, in a white sauce.

PREPARATION TIME: *10 minutes*
COOKING TIME: *15 minutes*

INGREDIENTS (*for 6*):
1½ *pounds broccoli*
1 *tablespoon salt*
1¼ *cups white sauce (p.301)*
6 *tablespoons unsalted butter*
2–3 *tablespoons fresh white bread crumbs*
Black pepper

Bring a large saucepan of water to a boil. Cut away all coarse leaves from the broccoli* and trim the stalks (tough stalks should be pared). Wash well. Salt the water before adding the broccoli. Bring the water quickly back to a boil and simmer for 5–12 minutes, or until the broccoli is just tender.

Meanwhile, prepare the white sauce and preheat the broiler.

Drain the broccoli well and place in a shallow gratin dish.* Coat with the white sauce. Melt 4 tablespoons of the butter in a small pan, mix in the bread crumbs, and sprinkle them over the broccoli. Dot with the remaining butter, sprinkle with pepper, and place under the broiler for a few minutes until the crumbs are golden brown.

APPLE PIE WITH CHEESE CRUST

A chewy cheese crust adds a new dimension to this old favorite.

PREPARATION TIME: *50 minutes*
COOKING TIME: *55 minutes*

INGREDIENTS (*for 6–8*):
2 *cups all-purpose flour*
½ *teaspoon salt*
1½ *cups finely grated extra-sharp Cheddar cheese*
⅔ *cup shortening*
⅓ *cup ice water*
7–8 *medium apples*
⅔ *cup sugar*
¼ *teaspoon salt*
2 *tablespoons cornstarch*
½ *teaspoon cinnamon*
¼ *teaspoon nutmeg*
3 *tablespoons butter*

Sift the flour with the salt into a bowl. With a pastry blender or 2 knives, cut in the cheese and shortening until it resembles coarse meal. Add enough ice water to hold the mixture together. Shape into a ball, cover, and chill for 30 minutes while preparing the apples.

Preheat the oven to 450°F. Peel, core, and slice the apples. There should be about 7 cups. Combine the sugar, salt, and cornstarch, and sift over the apples. Toss to coat the apples well. Sprinkle with the spices.

Roll out and line a 9-inch pie plate with half the chilled dough. Place the apples in layers in the pie shell. Dot the top with the butter. Roll out the remaining dough and cover the pie. Make a few small slits in the top to allow the steam to escape.

Bake the pie at 450°F for 10 minutes, then lower the heat and bake at 350°F for about 45 minutes, or until the apples are tender but not mushy.

COCONUT CREAM PIE

This is one of the most popular of all custard or cream pies. It looks inviting and tastes delicious.

PREPARATION TIME: *10 minutes*
COOKING TIME: *45 minutes*

INGREDIENTS (*for 6*):
¾ *cup sugar*
7 *tablespoons flour (½ cup minus 1 tablespoon)*
¼ *teaspoon salt*
2 *eggs*
3 *cups milk, scalded*
1 *teaspoon vanilla extract*
½–¾ *cup shredded or flaked coconut*
Baked 8- or 9-inch pastry shell or crumb crust
½ *cup heavy cream, whipped*

Mix together the sugar, flour, salt, and eggs. Slowly add the scalded milk, stirring constantly. Light cream may be used in place of the milk; or part cream and part milk; or, for a rich flavor, use part milk and part evaporated milk.

Return the mixture to low heat and stir constantly until it begins to boil. Reduce the heat to a simmer, continue to stir, and cook 2–3 minutes. Remove the pan from the heat and add the vanilla. Cool to room temperature.

Fold in shredded or flaked coconut, or add layers of coconut as you pour the filling into the shell. Top with whipped cream and sprinkle with coconut; or top with a meringue, sprinkle with coconut, and bake at 350°F for 15–20 minutes.

FLUMMERY

This version of a very old English and Scottish dish makes a pleasant change from the usual dessert.

PREPARATION TIME: *15 minutes*

INGREDIENTS (*for 4–6*):
1 *tablespoon oatmeal*
1¼ *cups heavy cream*
3 *tablespoons clear honey*
4 *tablespoons Scotch whisky*
Juice of ½ lemon

Heat the oatmeal gently in a heavy-bottomed pan until it turns brown, then set aside. Beat the cream until smooth but not stiff. Melt the honey in a saucepan over gentle heat until it runs easily, but do not allow it to boil. Fold the honey into the beaten cream and finally stir in the whisky and lemon juice.

Serve the warm cream and honey mixture in tall individual glasses and sprinkle the brown oatmeal on top.

APRICOT SHERBET

A tart, beautifully flavored sherbet is a perfect dessert after a heavy meal.

PREPARATION TIME: *2½ hours*
FREEZING TIME: *2 hours*

INGREDIENTS (*for 6*):
1 *pound dried apricots*
2 *cups sugar*
2 *tablespoons cognac, apricot liqueur, or kirsch*

Cover the apricots in warm water and soak for 2 hours. Drain. Cook 2 cups sugar in 1 cup water until the mixture boils; boil for 10 minutes. Add the apricots and cook an additional 10 minutes. Put the apricots and the liquid through a food mill or purée them in a blender. Add the cognac, apricot liqueur, or the kirsch.

Pour the mixture into freezer trays and place in the freezer compartment of the refrigerator. When the mixture has become partially frozen, remove it from the refrigerator and turn into a chilled bowl. Beat the sherbet thoroughly with a whisk or heavy fork. The mixture should be almost thin enough to pour; if it is too thick, whisk in a little ice water. Return the mixture to the trays. Freeze until firm but not hard, or freeze packed with ice and coarse salt in a crank freezer until the mixture is frozen but still soft.

BAKED ORANGES

Orange sections are delicious baked in a rich, orange-flavored custard.

MARINATING TIME: *overnight*
PREPARATION TIME: *15 minutes*
COOKING TIME: *50 minutes*

INGREDIENTS (*for 4*):
4 *navel oranges, sectioned*
½ *cup sugar*
4 *tablespoons orange liqueur*
3 *eggs*
⅓ *cup heavy cream*
⅛ *teaspoon salt*

Sprinkle the orange sections with half the sugar and layer them in a rectangular 1½-quart baking dish. Add the liqueur, cover, and refrigerate overnight.

Preheat oven to 350°F. Bake the oranges, covered, for 20 minutes. Drain and save ½ cup of the juice. Beat the eggs with the cream, the remaining sugar, the salt, and the reserved juice. Pour this mixture over the oranges and bake, uncovered, for 25 minutes or until the custard is slightly thickened. Serve warm.

65

ICED TANGERINES

For a special dinner party, this refreshingly tangy and impressive-looking ice cream is a fitting ending. Prepare the ice cream a day ahead.

PREPARATION TIME: *30 minutes*
COOKING TIME: *15 minutes*
FREEZING TIME: *4½ hours*

INGREDIENTS (*for 6*):
8 medium tangerines
¾ cup sugar
1¼ cups water
Juice of ½ lemon
1 egg yolk
1¼ cups heavy cream
GARNISH:
Tangerine slices
Butter shorts or refrigerator cookies
(p.391)

Wipe the tangerines, cut off the tops, and carefully cut out the flesh from both tops and bottoms with a grapefruit knife. Scoop out the remaining pulp with a spoon. Place 6 of the empty tangerine shells in a plastic bag in the refrigerator and set the remaining 2 aside. Squeeze 1¼ cups of juice from the tangerine pulp. Boil the sugar and water in a saucepan over high heat for 10 minutes to make a syrup. Remove and allow to cool. Stir the tangerine and lemon juices into the syrup. Beat the egg yolk and stir into the syrup. Return to the heat and cook gently for 5 minutes, stirring continuously. Cool, pour into a freezing container, cover tightly with a lid, and place in the freezer or the freezer compartment of the refrigerator until lightly set, approximately 1½–2 hours.

Grate the rind of the remaining 2 tangerines and beat the cream until stiff. Break the frozen syrup into a bowl and beat vigorously with a fork until it has an even texture. Beat in

the cream and tangerine rind until the color is uniform and the rind evenly distributed. Spoon this ice cream back into the freezing container, cover with a lid, and freeze 2½ hours longer.

Turn out the mixture, break it down as before, and beat until the texture is even; return to the freezer. One hour before serving, scoop the ice cream into the empty tangerine skins and fix on the lids at an angle.

Brush the outsides of the tangerines with water and place in the freezer. Ten minutes before serving, remove the tangerines from the freezer in order to let the frost on the skins settle.

Serve on a tray decorated with tangerine slices. A dish of butter shorts or refrigerator cookies could be served separately.

FIG PIE

An unusual way of using this familiar dried fruit is as a pie filling.

PREPARATION TIME: *45 minutes*
COOKING TIME: *35 minutes*

INGREDIENTS (*for 6*):
¾ recipe standard pastry (p.354)
½ pound dried figs
Squeeze lemon juice
2 teaspoons cornstarch
½ teaspoon ground allspice
2 tablespoons currants
2 teaspoons molasses or corn syrup

Roll out the pastry* on a floured surface to a thickness of ⅛ inch. Line a deep 8-inch pie plate with the pastry. Cook the dried figs over low heat in water to cover, with a squeeze of lemon juice, until soft.

Drain the figs and retain 1¼ cups of the liquid, adding hot water if necessary. Pour a little of the liquid into a bowl, add the cornstarch, and mix until it resembles a thin, smooth cream. Gradually add the rest of the liquid, stirring well. When well mixed, return it to the saucepan and place over moderate heat. Stir until thickened, then cook for another 2 minutes. Mix in the allspice, currants, and syrup and remove the pan from the heat.

Arrange the figs over the pastry; pour in the thickened fig liquid, making sure that the currants are evenly distributed. Bake the pie for 30–35 minutes on the middle shelf of an oven preheated to 400°F.

Serve hot or cold, with cream or vanilla ice cream (p.342).

PECAN ROLL

This ethereal sponge roll filled with cream is sweet and chewy, and makes an impressive presentation.

PREPARATION TIME: *20 minutes*
COOKING TIME: *15–18 minutes*

INGREDIENTS (*for 8–10*):
1½ tablespoons butter, melted
6 eggs, separated
½ cup sugar
Pinch of salt
1 cup finely ground pecans
1 cup heavy cream
2 tablespoons sugar
½ teaspoon vanilla extract

Preheat oven to 400°F. Brush the melted butter over the bottom of a jelly-roll pan, 15½ by 10½ by 1 inch. Line the pan with waxed paper cut to fit the bottom only. Thoroughly brush the remaining butter over the waxed paper. Do not butter the sides of the pan.

Beat the egg yolks and sugar with a pinch of salt until light and lemon-colored. Fold in the pecans with a rubber spatula. Beat the egg whites until stiff peaks form, and quickly fold them into the egg and sugar mixture.

Gently spread this pecan roll mixture smoothly in the pan and bake for 15–18 minutes. Turn the baked roll out of the pan onto a sheet of waxed paper and peel off the waxed paper that adheres to the top. Allow to cool.

Whip the cream until stiff. Stir in the sugar and vanilla extract. Spread the cream over the cake. Roll up the cake from a narrow end. Cut into 1-inch slices to serve.

Snacks & Supper Dishes

SERENA'S MACARONI AND CHEESE

Bits of ham and fresh tomatoes add color and flavor to plain macaroni and cheese.

PREPARATION TIME: *20 minutes*
COOKING TIME: *20 minutes*

INGREDIENTS (*for 4–6*):
½ *pound macaroni*
4 *cups white sauce (p.301)*
1½ *cups grated Cheddar cheese*
Salt and black pepper
1 *cup cooked diced ham*
4 *large tomatoes, peeled, seeded, and chopped*
2 *tablespoons fresh white bread crumbs*
2 *tablespoons unsalted melted butter*

Cook the macaroni, uncovered, in plenty of boiling salted water for about 15 minutes. Stir 1 cup of the cheese into the white sauce; season to taste with salt and pepper.

Fold the drained macaroni, ham, and tomatoes into the sauce; spoon the mixture into a buttered oven-proof dish. Mix the remaining cheese with the bread crumbs, sprinkle over the macaroni, then pour the melted butter over it. Bake near the top of a preheated oven at 400°F for 20 minutes, or until the top is crisp and golden brown.

PYTT I PANNA

This classic Swedish dish is an excellent way to use up leftover meat and potatoes.

PREPARATION TIME: *10 minutes*
COOKING TIME: *20 minutes*

INGREDIENTS (*for 4*):
4 *cups cooked diced beef or lamb*
5 *potatoes, boiled and chopped*
3 *tablespoons unsalted butter*
1 *tablespoon olive oil*
½ *pound bacon, diced*
1 *large chopped onion*
Salt and black pepper
1 *tablespoon chopped parsley*
1 *teaspoon Worcestershire sauce*
GARNISH:
4 *fried eggs*

Sauté the potatoes in the butter and oil over high heat until golden brown. Drain on paper towels and keep warm. Sauté the meat, bacon, and onion over medium heat until the onion softens and the bacon is cooked. Return the potatoes to the pan, mix the ingredients carefully, and season to taste. Cook for another 5 minutes, shaking the pan to prevent sticking. Stir in the parsley and Worcestershire sauce.

Spoon the mixture into a warm serving dish and top with the lightly fried eggs. Serve at once.

INDIVIDUAL PIZZAS

These pizzas make a good hot snack or cold lunch.

PREPARATION TIME: *15 minutes*
COOKING TIME: *20–25 minutes*

INGREDIENTS (*for 4*):
4 *English muffins*
4 *tablespoons olive oil*
1 *large onion, thinly sliced*
⅔ *cup sliced button mushrooms*
2 *large tomatoes, peeled and sliced*
Salt and black pepper
Basil or marjoram (optional)
8 *thin slices mozzarella or other quick-melting cheese*
8 *anchovy fillets*

Halve the English muffins and brush the surfaces with olive oil, setting 1 tablespoon aside. Cook the onion in the remaining oil until soft; add the mushrooms and cook gently for another 2 minutes.

Arrange the tomato slices on top of the muffin halves, season with salt, pepper, and a little basil or marjoram. Spoon the onion and mushroom mixture on top and cover with the cheese. Halve each anchovy fillet and arrange in a cross pattern on top of the cheese.

Bake in the center of an oven preheated to 350°F for 20–25 minutes.

WINTER SALAD

A crisp salad lunch is welcome even on a winter day. Baked potatoes or crusty French bread make it a complete meal.

PREPARATION TIME: *20 minutes*
CHILLING TIME: *30 minutes*

INGREDIENTS (*for 6*):
2½–3 *cups cooked diced meat or poultry*
½ *small cabbage, shredded*
2 *large grated carrots*
4 *stalks finely chopped celery*
1 *crisp, diced eating apple*
1 *tablespoon white raisins*
Juice of ½ lemon
2 *tablespoons heavy cream*
1¼ *cups mayonnaise*
Salt and black pepper

Mix the meat, all the vegetables, the apple, and the raisins together in a large salad bowl. Whisk the lemon juice and cream into the mayonnaise; season. Add to salad and mix well.

SAVORY FRITTERS

Fritters are made with cooked meat, fresh fruit, or vegetable slices coated in batter and deep-fried.

PREPARATION TIME: *15 minutes*
COOKING TIME: *10 minutes*

INGREDIENTS (*for 6*):
2 *cups cooked diced meat*
1 *large onion, chopped*
½ *green pepper, chopped*
2 *slices bacon, diced*
1 *tablespoon olive oil*
1 *cup flour*
2 *large eggs, separated*
½ *cup milk*
Salt and black pepper
Fat for deep-frying

Cook the onion, pepper, and bacon in the oil until soft; drain thoroughly on paper towels.

Beat the flour, egg yolks, and milk until smooth; season to taste. Stir the meat and the onion mixture into this batter, then carefully fold in the stiffly beaten egg whites.

In a deep-fryer, heat the fat until smoking hot, then drop tablespoons of the mixture into the fat, a few at a time. Cook until puffed up and golden brown, about 1–2 minutes. Drain on paper towels and keep hot.

Serve the fritters with a salad, such as coleslaw (p.63).

New Year's Dinners

A formal dinner for a few guests is a pleasant way to welcome the new year and a nice change of pace from the traditional noisy party. Set the table with colorful dinnerware, as at right, and heighten the festive mood with fresh flowers and candles.

Three-Course Dinner

This easy but elegant menu for four people consists of shrimp salad, duck with orange, new potatoes, and green peas, followed by oeufs à la neige. The appetizer and dessert can be prepared in advance.

La Salade de Crevettes
Le Caneton à l'Orange
Les Pommes Rissolées
Les Petits Pois au Beurre
Les Oeufs à la Neige
WINE: Beaujolais

La Salade de Crevettes
PREPARATION TIME: *20 minutes*

1 pound shelled shrimp
3 tablespoons mayonnaise (p.303)
4 tablespoons heavy cream
Juice of ½ lemon
Salt and black pepper
2 large eating apples, peeled and finely shredded
1 celery heart, shredded
12 shelled walnuts

Blend the mayonnaise with the cream, add the lemon juice, and season with salt and pepper. Fold in the shrimp, apples, and celery.

Spoon the salad into a serving bowl and garnish with the walnuts. Chill the salad in the refrigerator.

Le Caneton à l'Orange
PREPARATION TIME: *45 minutes*
COOKING TIME: *1¾ hours*

2 ducks, 4–5 pounds each
4 oranges
1 tablespoon sugar
½ cup red wine vinegar
1¼ cups giblet stock
Juice of ½ lemon
1 tablespoon arrowroot
3 tablespoons curaçao

Peel the oranges over a plate to catch the juice. Remove all pith and divide the oranges into segments. Cut the rind into strips and boil them for 10 minutes in a little water. Drain them and set aside, with the orange segments, for garnishing.

Preheat the oven to 400°F and place the trussed ducks* on their sides on a rack in a large roasting pan. Cook for 40 minutes, then turn the ducks to the other side and cook for 30 minutes. Finally, place the ducks on their backs and cook for 30 minutes. Baste* frequently.

Boil the sugar and vinegar until reduced* to a light caramel. Add the stock, orange, and the lemon juice and boil for 5 minutes. Thicken the sauce with the arrowroot, thinned with 2 tablespoons water. Strain the sauce, stir in the curaçao, and pour this over the duck.

Les Pommes Rissolées
PREPARATION TIME: *15 minutes*
COOKING TIME: *30 minutes*

1½ pounds small new potatoes
4–6 tablespoons unsalted butter

Cook the peeled potatoes in boiling, lightly salted water for 20–30 minutes. Remove the pan at once and drain the potatoes thoroughly.

Melt the butter in a heavy skillet and cook the potatoes, covered, until golden, shaking the pan occasionally to prevent sticking.

Les Petits Pois au Beurre
PREPARATION TIME: *5 minutes*
COOKING TIME: *8 minutes*

2 packages frozen young peas
2–4 tablespoons unsalted butter

Cook the peas in lightly salted water until just tender. Do not overcook. Drain, and toss the peas in butter.

Les Oeufs à la Neige
PREPARATION TIME: *50 minutes*

4 eggs, separated
Pinch salt
10 tablespoons sugar
2½ cups milk
1 vanilla bean
2 tablespoons brandy

Beat egg whites until stiff, with the salt and 4 tablespoons of the sugar.

Bring 2 cups of the milk to a boil, with the vanilla bean. Spoon the egg whites into 4 oval shapes and poach* them in the slowly simmering milk for 2–3 minutes. Lift them out and leave to drain.

Make a custard (p.341) from the egg yolks, milk, sugar, and the poaching milk. Strain into a dish and stir in the brandy. When cool, top with the poached egg whites.

until the vegetables are tender. Purée in a blender.

Dilute the purée with the remaining $\frac{1}{2}$ cup of milk. Heat for 5 minutes and stir in the butter. Taste for seasoning. Garnish with chopped chives. Serve with 8 thin slices of French bread, trimmed of the crusts and sautéed on both sides in butter until light brown.

Oysters Casino

PREPARATION TIME: *30 minutes*
COOKING TIME: *6 minutes*

24 oysters on the half shell
$\frac{1}{2}$ cup softened butter
$\frac{1}{3}$ cup finely chopped shallots
$\frac{1}{4}$ cup finely chopped parsley
$\frac{1}{4}$ cup finely chopped green pepper
Juice of 1 lemon
2 teaspoons chopped pimiento
4 1-inch squares of partially cooked bacon

Preheat the oven to 450°F. Place the oysters in shallow pans of rock salt (also called ice cream salt). Cream the butter, shallots, parsley, and green pepper. Spoon equal portions of the mixture over the oysters and top with the chopped pimiento and the bacon squares.

Bake until the oysters are heated through and the bacon is brown, about 6 minutes.

over gentle heat for 20 minutes or until tender.

Arrange the chicken on a warm serving dish. Add the shallot to the pan, with the red wine. Bring to a boil and continue boiling for 1 minute. Add the stock and boil briskly until reduced* by half. Stir in the remaining butter, in small pieces, and season to taste.

Just before serving, pour the sauce over the chicken.

Les Pommes Nouvelles

PREPARATION TIME: *5 minutes*
COOKING TIME: *20 minutes*

1 pound new potatoes
3 tablespoons butter

Boil the unpeeled potatoes until tender, then drain and peel. Keep the potatoes warm, sprinkle with salt and pepper, and toss in butter.

Les Haricots Verts au Beurre

PREPARATION TIME: *5 minutes*
COOKING TIME: *10 minutes*

1–1$\frac{1}{2}$ pounds green beans
2–3 tablespoons unsalted butter

Cook the trimmed beans in plenty of boiling water over high heat for about 10 minutes or until just tender. Drain and toss in butter.

Les Pêches Châtelaine

PREPARATION TIME: *20 minutes*
CHILLING TIME: *1–2 hours*

8 canned white peach halves
2 tablespoons brandy
2 tablespoons chestnut purée
$\frac{1}{2}$ cup heavy cream

Put the drained peaches in a dish. Blend the brandy, chestnut purée, and cream. Spoon this over the peaches and chill, covered, in the refrigerator.

Four-Course Dinner

This more elaborate dinner menu for four people can still be prepared in advance. A delicious creamed cauliflower soup is followed by Oysters Casino, and the main course is chicken with new potatoes and green beans. The chilled dessert is white peaches in chestnut-and-brandy-flavored cream. Chablis and Bordeaux wines, followed by vintage port, would suit the menu.

Potage Purée Du Barry
Oysters Casino
WINE: Chablis
Les Suprêmes de Volaille Saint Sylvestre
Les Pommes Nouvelles
Les Haricots Verts au Beurre
WINE: Red Bordeaux
Les Pêches Châtelaine
WINE: Vintage Port

Potage Purée Du Barry

PREPARATION TIME: *10 minutes*
COOKING TIME: *15 minutes*

$\frac{1}{2}$ small cauliflower, separated into florets (about 2 cups)
1 cup sliced raw potatoes
3$\frac{1}{2}$ cups milk
1 teaspoon salt
4 tablespoons softened butter
1 tablespoon chopped chives

Put the cauliflower, potatoes, and salt in 3 cups of the milk and cook

Les Suprêmes de Volaille Saint Sylvestre

PREPARATION TIME: *20 minutes*
COOKING TIME: *25 minutes*

4 boned chicken breasts
10 tablespoons unsalted butter
1 finely chopped shallot
$\frac{1}{2}$ cup red wine
$\frac{1}{2}$ cup chicken stock
Salt and black pepper

Cook the chicken in 4 tablespoons of the butter in a large, heavy skillet

69

February

Old Winter sad, in snow y-clad,
Is making a doleful din. THOMAS NOEL

THIS MONTH'S RECIPES

February is the month when the supply of citrus fruit is at its peak. This is the time to make marmalade, one of the glories of the breakfast table.

Food in Season

Although the supply of fresh vegetables in February is limited, the serious cook can easily get by without resorting to convenience foods. With a little imagination the same few vegetables can be served in enough different ways so that they do not grow tiresome. Leeks, for example, are generally available in winter. They can be served in yogurt sauce, as a side dish (p.83); in a sauce vinaigrette, as a salad (p.82); or they can be combined with chicken in a hearty soup (p.73). Each presentation is substantially different.

Markets are well stocked in February with high-quality imported broccoli, Brussels sprouts, spinach, and green peas. Endive, for crisp winter salads, is also in good supply. Carrots are plentiful and can be put to novel use in a quiche (p.83). Cabbage, too, is available and makes a warming casserole (p.76) on a cold winter night.

Hothouse rhubarb, which will peak in early spring, is beginning to appear in the markets. It can be served with bananas in a superb fruit compote (p.86).

One of the bright spots of winter is the bountiful supply of citrus fruit—firm, juicy oranges, grapefruit, and tangerines. The long days of February are an ideal time for a time-consuming kitchen project, and putting up jars of homemade marmalade (p.88) is one of the most satisfying.

SUGGESTED MENUS

Moules Marinière
...
Pork Tenderloin with Mushrooms
Rice   Tossed Green Salad
...
Candied Oranges Grand Marnier

Steak and Kidney Pie
Boiled Potatoes   Brussels Sprouts
...
Compote of Rhubarb and Bananas

Oeufs en Cocotte
...
Salmi of Duck
Celeriac and Potato Purée
...
Crêpes Suzette

Raie au Beurre Noir
Buttered Potatoes   Green Peas
...
Steamed Jam Pudding

Leeks Vinaigrette
...
Chicken Maryland
French-Fried Potatoes   Celery and Apple Salad
...
Lemon Mousse

Lancashire Hot Pot
Red Cabbage
...
Icebox Cheesecake

Eggs Tonnato
...
Rognons Turbigo
Creamed Potatoes   Broccoli au Gratin
...
Chaussons aux Pommes

Tagliatelle alla Bolognese
...
Stuffed Green Peppers
Chocolate Cake Mousse

Soups & First Courses

MOULES MARINIÈRE

There are several classic versions of this recipe for mussels cooked in white wine in the style of mariners. The following is the most popular and easiest to prepare.

PREPARATION TIME: *30 minutes*
COOKING TIME: *10 minutes*

INGREDIENTS (*for 4*):
2 quarts mussels
1 small onion
3–4 tablespoons dry white wine
2 tablespoons butter
1 teaspoon flour
1 teaspoon chopped parsley

Wash the mussels* in cold water, scrub the shells thoroughly, and rinse several times to remove all grit; pull or scrape away the beards. Discard any mussels with broken shells and any that remain open.

Thoroughly butter the inside of a large saucepan. Peel and finely chop the onion, scatter it over the bottom of the saucepan, and add the wine. Place all the mussels in the pan at once and cover with a lid. Place over high heat and shake the pan for 3–5 minutes, or until the mussels have opened. Take the pan from the heat and lift out the mussels, discarding any that have not opened. Remove the empty half shell from each mussel and place the other half with mussel attached in individual soup plates. Keep hot.

Cream the butter and flour together and blend into the liquid remaining in the pan. Stir this sauce over low heat until it has thickened and is boiling; add the chopped parsley and pour the sauce over the mussels in the plates. Serve at once.

COCK-A-LEEKIE SOUP

Legend has it that this amusingly named Scottish soup originated in the days when cockfighting was popular. The loser was thrown into the stock pot, together with leeks. Prunes were a later addition.

PREPARATION TIME: *10–15 minutes*
COOKING TIME: *1¼ hours*

INGREDIENTS (*for 6*):
1 chicken, about 3 pounds
1 tablespoon salt
6 peppercorns
6 leeks
6 ready-to-eat pitted prunes
GARNISH:
Chopped parsley

Wipe the trussed chicken, rinse the giblets, and place both in a deep saucepan. Pour over enough cold water to cover the chicken (if necessary, split the bird in half so that it remains submerged). Add the salt and peppercorns and bring to a boil. Remove any scum from the surface, cover with a tight-fitting lid, and simmer for about 45 minutes.

Meanwhile, trim the coarse leaves off the leeks to within 2 inches of the top of the white stems and cut off the roots. Split the leeks lengthwise, wash them well under cold running water, then cut them into 1-inch pieces. Skim the soup again and add the leeks and the prunes. Cover the pan and simmer over low heat for another 30 minutes.

Lift the chicken and giblets from the soup; remove skin and bones from the chicken flesh. Reserve the best breast pieces for another recipe and cut the remaining meat into small pieces. Add these to the soup and correct seasoning if necessary.

Just before serving the hot soup, sprinkle it liberally with finely chopped parsley.

EGGS TONNATO

Tuna mayonnaise is the classic sauce for the Italian vitello tonnato. Here it is used on eggs for an hors d'oeuvre or for a light luncheon.

PREPARATION TIME: *20 minutes*
COOKING TIME: *6–8 minutes*

INGREDIENTS (*for 4*):
4 eggs
3½-ounce can of tuna
Juice of ½ lemon
6 anchovy fillets
½ cup mayonnaise (p.303)
Black pepper
4 crisp lettuce leaves
GARNISH:
Finely chopped parsley

Put the eggs in a saucepan, cover with cold water, and bring to a boil. Simmer for 6–8 minutes to hard-cook. Drain the eggs and cover them with cold water immediately to prevent further cooking. Shell the eggs.

Drain the oil from the tuna and mash the fish with the back of a wooden spoon. Blend in the lemon juice, then chop and add 2 of the anchovy fillets. Rub the mixture through a coarse sieve into a bowl and beat until it is a smooth purée.* Add the mayonnaise and blend in well. Season to taste.

Cut the eggs in half lengthwise with a wet knife blade. Arrange the halves in pairs, rounded sides upward, on the lettuce leaves, and coat them with the tuna mayonnaise. Cut the remaining anchovy fillets in half lengthwise and arrange over the eggs. Sprinkle with parsley. Serve with French bread.

Fish

CRÈME DE COQUILLES ST. JACQUES

Scallops—known in France as *coquilles St. Jacques*—are the basis for this creamy soup.

PREPARATION TIME: *10 minutes*
COOKING TIME: *15–20 minutes*

INGREDIENTS (*for 4–6*):
6–8 large sea scallops
1 lemon
6 parsley sprigs
1¼ cups dry white wine
1 small onion
3 tablespoons unsalted butter
¼ cup flour
1¼–2 cups milk
Salt and black pepper
2 egg yolks
3 tablespoons heavy cream
GARNISH:
2 tablespoons chopped parsley
Bread croûtons (p.300)

Cut each scallop into 4 or 5 pieces and put in a saucepan with the sliced lemon and the parsley sprigs. Pour in the wine and bring to a simmer over gentle heat. Cover the pan with a lid and cook the scallops gently for about 15 minutes or until tender. Take the pan off the heat and remove parsley and lemon.

Peel and finely chop the onion. Melt the butter in a large skillet and add the onion; cover and cook gently for about 5 minutes, or until the onion is soft but not brown. Take the pan off the heat. Let the onion cool slightly, then stir in the flour and cook for a few minutes over low heat. Gradually stir in the milk and bring the mixture to a boil, stirring continuously until it is smooth and has thickened. Add the scallops and their liquid; season the mixture to taste and reheat gently.

When ready to serve, blend the egg yolks with the cream; mix in a few spoonfuls of the hot liquid and blend this back into the soup. Serve in individual soup bowls and sprinkle with parsley. Offer a bowl of crisp bread croûtons.

OEUFS EN COCOTTE

This classic French recipe is a compromise between soft-cooked and poached eggs. Each egg is cooked in a small individual flameproof dish with a little cream. Cocotte or ramekin dishes are made for this purpose.

PREPARATION TIME: *5 minutes*
COOKING TIME: *1 minute*

INGREDIENTS (*for 4*):
8 eggs
2 tablespoons butter
Salt and black pepper
8 tablespoons heavy cream

Preheat broiler to very hot. Warm 4 ramekin dishes and butter them thoroughly. Break 2 eggs into each dish, season well with salt and freshly ground pepper, and spoon 2 tablespoons of cream over each egg.

Put the ramekins on a cookie sheet and place them 1 inch below the broiler. Baste every few seconds with the cream.

When cooked (in about 1 minute), the egg whites should be just set, and the yolks still runny. Serve at once. On their own, the eggs make a good first course. As a breakfast or supper dish, serve them with crisp toast points, bacon, sausage links, or chicken livers sautéed in butter.

CELERIAC SALAD WITH PROSCIUTTO

Celery root—or celeriac—in a mustardy mayonnaise is delicious teamed with prosciutto or thinly sliced salami. It makes a novel appetizer.

PREPARATION TIME: *10–15 minutes*
COOKING TIME: *2–3 minutes*

INGREDIENTS (*for 4*):
1 large celeriac
¼ cup mayonnaise (p.303)
¼ teaspoon Dijon mustard
½ pound thinly sliced prosciutto

Peel the celeriac. Cut it into narrow slices and then into matchstick-thin pieces. Add to a pan of boiling salted water and blanch* for 2–3 minutes. Drain in a colander and allow to cool. Blend together the mayonnaise and Dijon mustard and toss the celeriac in this dressing.

Arrange the prosciutto on individual plates, allowing 3 thin slices per person. Divide the celeriac between the portions.

HOT CRAB SOUFFLÉ

The French invented the soufflé, which is basically a thick sauce and a savory or sweet purée* blended with stiffly beaten egg whites. It is a most versatile mixture that can be baked in a variety of ways. This one is the classic version and is flavored with crabmeat and cheese.

PREPARATION TIME: *20 minutes*
COOKING TIME: *35–40 minutes*

INGREDIENTS (*for 4*):
6 ounces crabmeat, fresh, canned, or frozen
2 tablespoons butter
4 tablespoons flour
1¼ cups milk
Salt and black pepper
Cayenne pepper
½ cup grated Cheddar cheese
4 eggs

Melt the butter in a saucepan. Stir in the flour and cook over low heat for a few minutes. Gradually beat in the milk, stirring continuously until the sauce thickens and comes to a boil. Season to taste with salt, freshly ground pepper, and cayenne. Stir in the cheese and allow the sauce to cool for 5 minutes.

Separate the eggs and beat the yolks, one at a time, into the cheese sauce. Flake* the picked over crabmeat finely and blend it into the sauce. Correct seasoning if necessary. Beat the egg whites until stiff, then add to the crab mixture; fold them in gently with a rubber spatula.

Pour the mixture into a buttered 1-quart soufflé dish. Bake in the center of a preheated oven at 375°F for 35–40 minutes, or until the soufflé is well risen and golden brown. Serve immediately. A green salad could also be served.

BRANDADE DE MORUE

This is the original recipe for brandade de morue, made with a mortar and pestle. However, a blender, food mill, or food processor can be used with equal success.

PREPARATION TIME: *soaking (overnight) plus 30 minutes*
COOKING TIME: *20 minutes*

INGREDIENTS (*for 4–6*):
1 pound salt codfish
⅔ cup olive oil
⅓ cup heavy cream
2 cloves garlic
⅓ teaspoon freshly ground black pepper
GARNISH:
Toast triangles fried in olive oil

Cover the codfish with water and soak at least 4 hours or overnight. Drain. Rinse the fish under cold water. Bring it to a boil in cold water to cover. Reduce the heat and simmer for about 10 minutes. Drain the fish and shred it very fine, removing any bits of bone.

Heat the olive oil and the cream separately. Crush the garlic, preferably in a mortar, add the fish, and pound with the pestle until the fish is reduced to a pulp. If a mortar is not available, whirl the garlic and fish in a blender or a food processor, or put it through a food mill twice, using the fine disc. The fish must be very fine; if two grindings do not seem enough, work it with a heavy wooden spoon in a bowl.

When the mixture is almost a paste, put it in a heavy saucepan over very low heat and stir well with a fork. Now gradually add the olive oil and the cream alternately and blend them well. Continue until all the oil and cream are absorbed and the mixture has the consistency of mashed potatoes. Season with freshly ground black pepper, heap the mixture in the center of a serving dish, and surround it with fried toast triangles. For a different texture and a more delicate flavor, beat 2 cups of mashed potatoes into the mixture.

OYSTER SAUSAGES

This old New England recipe is unusual and has a delicious flavor. It is essential to leave the pan uncovered during the poaching period. The sausage casings can be purchased at butcher shops.

PREPARATION TIME: *15–20 minutes*
COOKING TIME: *50 minutes*

INGREDIENTS (8–10 sausages):
2 cups minced oysters
1⅓ cups beef suet, cut into fine shreds
1 cup fresh white bread crumbs
1 teaspoon lemon juice
2 eggs
⅛ teaspoon pepper
⅛ teaspoon allspice
⅛ teaspoon nutmeg
Salt
Oil
Sausage casings

Mix all ingredients together. Taste for seasonings, especially salt. Stuff the mixture into sausage casings and prick each sausage with a fork. Poach, uncovered, in salted water for 45 minutes. Drain. Brown the sausages quickly in hot oil. Serve with lemon butter (p.338) seasoned with chopped parsley.

SCALLOPS IN THE SHELL

In this recipe, scallops are used for a main course. They are served in the deep rounded shells that can be purchased in department stores or gourmet food shops. These shells also make useful hors d'oeuvre dishes.

PREPARATION TIME: *20 minutes*
COOKING TIME: *35 minutes*

INGREDIENTS (*for 2–4*):
4 large sea scallops
¼ pound button mushrooms
¾ cup dry white wine
1 slice lemon
1 bay leaf
1 pound potatoes
2 tablespoons butter
SAUCE:
2 tablespoons butter
2 tablespoons flour
Salt and black pepper
1 egg yolk
2 tablespoons heavy cream
GARNISH:
Chopped parsley

Wash the scallops quickly under cold running water and dry them on paper towels. Cut each scallop into 4–6 slices. Wipe and thinly slice the mushrooms.* Put the scallops and mushrooms in a pan, with 1¼ cups of water, the wine, lemon slice, and bay leaf. Bring to a boil, cover with a lid, and simmer gently for 15–20 minutes. Strain through a colander and set aside 1¼ cups of the fish liquid for the sauce. Remove the lemon slice and bay leaf, and keep the scallops and mushrooms hot.

Meanwhile, put the peeled potatoes on to boil and make the sauce. Melt the butter in a saucepan over low heat, stir in the flour, and cook gently for a few minutes. Gradually mix in the reserved fish liquid, stirring continuously until the sauce is smooth. Bring to a boil and simmer gently for 2–3 minutes. Add the mushrooms and scallops. Season to taste with salt and freshly ground pepper, and reheat gently. Lightly mix the egg yolk and cream, remove the pan from the heat, and stir the egg into the fish mixture.

Mash and season the potatoes. Using a large pastry bag fitted with a rosette tube, pipe a border of mashed potato around the edges of the deep scallop shells. Brush the potato border with 2 tablespoons melted butter and place the shells under a hot broiler for a few minutes until the potatoes are golden brown.

Spoon the scallops into the center of each shell and sprinkle them with chopped parsley. Serve with a tossed green salad for a main course, or as a first course for a dinner party.

Meat

RAIE AU BEURRE NOIR

PREPARATION TIME: *10 minutes*
COOKING TIME: *30 minutes*

INGREDIENTS (*for 4*):
2-pound wing of skate
½ lemon
1 small onion
1 small bay leaf
2-3 peppercorns
3-4 parsley sprigs
½ teaspoon salt
BEURRE NOIR:
6 tablespoons unsalted butter
1 tablespoon white vinegar
1 tablespoon finely chopped parsley

Skate is a flat, ray-shaped fish. Only the wings, which have a delicate and distinctive flavor, are edible. The white flesh is scraped from the prominent bones of the wings with a knife and fork.

Rinse the skate, wipe it dry, and cut into 4 portions. Place in a saucepan with 1¼ cups water. Slice the lemon, peel and slice the onion, and add these to the pan, together with the bay leaf, peppercorns, parsley sprigs, and salt. Bring slowly to a boil, cover with a tight-fitting lid, and simmer gently for 25–30 minutes.

Remove the fish with a slotted spoon and arrange on a hot serving dish. For the sauce, heat the butter in a skillet over low heat until browned, but not scorched. Remove the pan from the heat; stir the vinegar and chopped parsley into the butter and pour it over the skate.

Serve with buttered boiled potatoes and green beans or peas.

STEAK AND KIDNEY PIE

This version of beefsteak and kidney pie, dressed up with a puff pastry crust, is one of the best.

PREPARATION TIME: *3–4 hours*
COOKING TIME: *3 hours*

INGREDIENTS (*for 4*):
2 pounds top round steak
3 veal kidneys
Flour
6 tablespoons butter or oil
2 medium onions, sliced very thin
½ pound mushrooms, sliced
1 teaspoon salt
1 teaspoon freshly ground black
  pepper
1 teaspoon crushed rosemary leaves
1 tablespoon tomato paste
2 ounces cognac
1–2 cups red wine
½ recipe puff pastry (p.363)

Cut the round steak into 2-inch cubes. Trim the fat from the kidneys and cut them into small cubes. Dredge the steak and kidneys in the flour and sear them quickly in the hot butter or oil. Add the thinly sliced onions to the hot fat and let them cook for 2–3 minutes or until just soft.

In a deep baking dish, arrange the meat, onions, and sliced mushrooms. Mix the salt, pepper, rosemary, tomato paste, cognac, and 1 cup of the wine, and pour over the meat. Cover the dish and bake in a 350°F oven for 3 hours, adding more wine if the liquid has cooked away.

Roll the dough into a circle 2 inches larger than the top of the baking dish containing the meat. Place the dough on a cookie or baking sheet and bake at 450°F for 10 minutes. Reduce the heat to 350°F and finish baking until dough is puffed and is a golden brown.

Remove the cover from the meat dish and slip the puff pastry on top. Serve at once, with a green vegetable or tossed salad.

SHREDDED CABBAGE CASSEROLE

This dish, a meal in itself, can be reheated the next day without any loss of flavor.

PREPARATION TIME: *45 minutes*
COOKING TIME: *45 minutes*

INGREDIENTS (*for 6–8*):
MEAT MIXTURE:
½ cup rice
4 tablespoons butter
1 medium onion, chopped
2 cloves garlic, chopped
¼ pound mushrooms, chopped
1 pound ground beef
¼ cup chicken stock
CABBAGE MIXTURE:
2 tablespoons butter
1 medium onion, chopped
1 medium carrot, finely chopped
1 stalk celery, finely chopped
1 cabbage, about 1½ pounds,
  shredded
1½ cups chicken stock
Salt and black pepper

Preheat oven to 350°F. To make the meat mixture, bring 1 cup of salted water to a boil, add the rice, cover, and simmer for 10 minutes.

Heat the butter in a large skillet and sauté the onion and garlic slowly for about 7 minutes, then add the mushrooms and cook for 3 more minutes. Add the ground meat, mix, and sauté over moderate heat 8–10 minutes. Add the stock and rice. Season to taste with salt and pepper. Spoon into a bowl and set aside.

To make the cabbage mixture, heat the butter in the same skillet and sauté the onion, carrot, and celery for 5 minutes. Add the shredded cabbage and 1 cup of the stock. Cover and simmer 10 minutes. Season well with salt and pepper.

In a large casserole, alternate layers of the cabbage mixture and the meat mixture, finishing with the cabbage mixture. Pour over the remaining ½ cup of stock, cover the casserole, and bake for 45 minutes.

Serve with tomato sauce (p.302).

DAUBE DE BOEUF

The French culinary term *daube* describes a braising method of slowly cooking tougher cuts of meat, usually beef, in red wine stock. This method of cooking in a covered casserole tenderizes the meat and prevents it from shrinking.

PREPARATION TIME: *45 minutes*
MARINATING TIME: *3–4 hours*
COOKING TIME: *2 hours*

INGREDIENTS (*for 6*):
2 pounds round steak
¼ pound lean salt pork
1½ cups red wine
1 pound carrots
1 pound onions
6 tablespoons butter
1–2 cloves garlic
Bouquet garni (p.410)
2 cups beef stock
2 tablespoons tomato purée
1 tablespoon chopped parsley
Salt and black pepper

Trim the fat from the beef and cut the meat into 1-inch pieces. Blanch* the lean salt pork, cut off the rind, and dice* it. Put the beef and salt pork in a mixing bowl, pour over the wine, and marinate* for 3–4 hours.

Lift the meat from the marinade (the liquid will be used later). Peel or scrape the carrots and cut them into ¼-inch slices. Peel and finely slice the onions. Using half the butter, sauté the beef and the salt pork in a heavy skillet until they are evenly browned. Lift out the beef and salt pork, then sauté the prepared vegetables in the remainder of the butter. Peel and chop the garlic and add to the vegetables during sautéing.

Cover the bottom of a large casserole with half the vegetables, then add the beef and salt pork and top with the remaining vegetables. Pour the marinade into the casserole and add the bouquet garni.

Deglaze the skillet with the stock. Stir with a wooden spatula or spoon to loosen all sediment, and bring the stock to a boil. Stir in the tomato purée and pour this liquid over the contents in the casserole. Add the chopped parsley, cover with a tight-fitting lid, and cook for 2 hours in the center of an oven preheated to 300°F. Check and if necessary correct the seasoning and remove the bouquet garni. Skim off as much fat as possible from the surface. (This is more easily done if the casserole is allowed to cool completely and is then reheated.)

Serve with creamed potatoes, or with macaroni tossed with butter or olive oil and sharp grated cheese. A crisp green salad is also a good accompaniment.

PORK TENDERLOIN WITH MUSHROOMS

The lean fillet, or tenderloin, of pork usually needs marinating or stuffing to give the meat extra flavor. It can be cooked whole or cut into thick slices for a quick main course.

PREPARATION TIME: *30 minutes*
COOKING TIME: *15 minutes*

INGREDIENTS (*for 6*):
1½ pounds pork tenderloin
2 tablespoons oil
1 tablespoon lemon juice
Black pepper
1 small clove garlic (optional)
SAUCE:
½ pound button mushrooms
1 onion
4 tablespoons unsalted butter
2 tablespoons dry sherry
½ cup heavy cream

Trim away the thin skin, or sinew, and fat from the pork. Cut the meat crosswise into 1-inch-thick slices. Lay the slices between two sheets of waxed paper and beat them flat with a rolling pin. Arrange the slices in a shallow dish. Measure the oil and lemon juice into a bowl and season with black pepper to taste. Peel and crush the garlic, and mix it into the oil and lemon juice. Spoon this marinade* over the pork and leave for about 30 minutes.

Meanwhile, trim and thinly slice the mushrooms.* Peel the onion and chop it finely. Melt the butter in a skillet and gently sauté the onion for 5 minutes until it is soft but not brown. Add the mushrooms and sauté for a few minutes. Lift the veg-etables from the pan and keep them hot. Remove the pork pieces from the marinade and dry them. Sauté slowly in the hot butter for 3–4 minutes, or until cooked through, turning once. Transfer the pork to a hot serving dish and keep it warm.

Add the sherry to the skillet and heat briskly, stirring until it has reduced* to 1 tablespoon. Return the onion and mushrooms to the pan and season with salt and freshly ground pepper. Stir in the cream. Heat gently, stirring until the sauce is almost boiling. Remove from the heat and pour the sauce over the pork. Serve on a bed of rice.

LANCASHIRE HOT POT

The "hot pot" was a tall earthenware pot from which this traditional British dish takes its name.

Mutton chops were stood upright around the inside, and the center was filled with potatoes, carrots, onions, celery, and leeks. It was usual, too, in the days when they were cheap, to put a layer of oysters beneath the potato crust.

PREPARATION TIME: *30 minutes*
COOKING TIME: *2–2½ hours*

INGREDIENTS (*for 4–6*):

2 pounds lamb shoulder
Seasoned flour (p.412)
2 tablespoons drippings
1½ pounds potatoes
2 onions
6–8 carrots
2 stalks celery
1 leek
Salt and black pepper
¼ teaspoon mixed herbs (p.411)
GARNISH:
Chopped parsley

Bone the shoulder of lamb.* Put the bones in a saucepan and cover with cold water. Bring to a boil, and after a few minutes remove the scum; cover with a lid and let the bones simmer over low heat while the vegetables and meat are being prepared.

Trim away any fat and gristle, and cut the meat into small, even pieces. Roll them in seasoned flour before searing in hot drippings until browned and sealed on all sides. Peel the potatoes and cut them into ¼-inch-thick slices. Put aside half the slices for the top and place the remainder in the bottom of a deep buttered casserole.

Peel and coarsely chop the onion. Scrape or peel the carrots and slice them thinly. Wash the celery and chop it finely. Remove the outer coarse leaves and the root of the leek, wash it well, and cut it crosswise into thin slices. Mix all the vegetables together in a deep bowl, season with salt and pepper, and sprinkle the mixed herbs over them. Arrange layers of seasoned vegetables and meat in the casserole, beginning and ending with a layer of vegetables. Top with the remaining potato slices, arranging them neatly in overlapping circles. Strain the liquid from the bones and pour about 2 cups of it into the casserole until it just reaches the upper potato layer. Cover with buttered waxed paper and a tight-fitting lid. Place in the center of an oven preheated to 350°F and cook for 2–2½ hours.

About 30 minutes before serving, remove the lid and paper from the casserole. Brush the potatoes with melted drippings and sprinkle with coarse salt. Raise the oven heat to 400°F and return the uncovered casserole to the oven, placing it above the center so that the potatoes will crisp and brown slightly.

Sprinkle with finely chopped parsley immediately before serving. The hot pot is a meal on its own but is traditionally served with pickled red cabbage.

ROGNONS TURBIGO

This French family dish consists of halved sautéed kidneys supplemented with tiny white onions and small pork sausages.

PREPARATION TIME: *25 minutes*
COOKING TIME: *20–25 minutes*

INGREDIENTS (*for 4*):
6 lamb kidneys
4 small pork sausages
4 tablespoons unsalted butter
8 small white onions
1 tablespoon flour
1¼ cups chicken or beef stock
½ cup dry white wine
1 teaspoon tomato purée
2 tablespoons dry sherry
Salt and black pepper
1 bay leaf
GARNISH:
Chopped parsley and bread croûtons (p.300)

Skin the kidneys,* cut them in half, and snip out the white cores with scissors. Separate the pork sausages, if necessary.

Melt the butter in a large heavy skillet. Gently sauté the kidneys and sausages until brown, then remove from the pan and keep them hot.

Meanwhile, peel the onions, leaving them whole; put them in a saucepan and cover with cold water. Bring to a boil, simmer for 3–5 minutes, then drain.

Stir the flour into the hot fat remaining in the skillet until well blended; cook gently for a few minutes. Gradually add the stock and wine, stirring well until the sauce is smooth. Bring to a boil. Stir in the tomato purée and sherry, and season the mixture to taste with salt and freshly ground pepper.

Put the kidneys, sausages, and onions back into the pan; add the bay leaf, cover with a lid, and simmer gently for 20–25 minutes.

Transfer the sausages, kidneys, and onions to a hot serving dish. Remove the bay leaf, check seasoning, and strain the sauce over the meat. Garnish with crisp bread croû-tons, sprinkle with finely chopped parsley, and serve piping hot.

A rice pilaf, or creamed potatoes, and broccoli go well with this dish.

Poultry

LIVER WITH ONION GRAVY

Liver is one of the most nourishing and digestible variety meats.

PREPARATION TIME: *20 minutes*
COOKING TIME: *25 minutes*

INGREDIENTS (*for 4*):
1 pound lamb's or calf's liver
1 pound onions
10 tablespoons unsalted butter
1 tablespoon flour
1½ cups beef stock
1 teaspoon vinegar
Salt and black pepper
Seasoned flour (p.412)

Peel and thinly slice the onions. Melt 4 tablespoons of the butter in a large skillet, add the onions, and cook over low heat for about 20 minutes or until soft and golden brown. Turn frequently to prevent the onion from sticking to the bottom of the pan. A pinch of sugar may help the onions to brown more quickly.

Blend 2 tablespoons of butter with the flour and add this in small pieces to the hot onions. Stir until melted and blended, then gradually stir in the hot stock. Bring the gravy to a boil, simmer for a moment, then stir in the vinegar and season to taste with salt and ground pepper.

Cut away any skin and gristle from the liver* and cut it into ¼-inch slices. Coat each slice with seasoned flour, making sure both sides are evenly coated.

Melt the remaining 4 tablespoons of butter in a heavy skillet, add the liver slices, and sauté them quickly for about 5 minutes, turning once. Lift them out onto a hot serving dish and pour the onion gravy over them. Creamed or boiled potatoes go well with the liver.

CORNED BEEF HASH

Corned beef hash is one of the rewards of having had corned beef and cabbage for a main course a day or two before. The hash is often served with a poached or fried egg.

PREPARATION TIME: *about 10 minutes*
REFRIGERATION TIME: *overnight*
COOKING TIME: *about 10 minutes*

INGREDIENTS (*for 6*):
1½ cups cooked, finely chopped corned beef
2 cups boiled potatoes
⅓–⅔ cup finely chopped onion
Freshly ground black pepper
½ teaspoon nutmeg
4–6 tablespoons butter or beef drippings
½ cup heavy cream or boiling water

Chop the meat finely with a knife. Do not put it through a meat grinder. Add the potatoes and onion to the meat, as well as a few good grinds of black pepper and the nutmeg. Blend well, cover, and refrigerate for several hours or overnight.

When ready to cook, melt just enough butter or beef drippings in a heavy skillet to cover the bottom (about 4–6 tablespoons). Add the hash and press it down firmly. When the hash develops a crust on the bottom, turn with a spatula so that some of the crust is brought to the top. At this point add the cream or boiling water, which enables the bottom crust to form more quickly. When it has crusted nicely, loosen it with a spatula, fold it once, and turn it out on a platter. Serve with poached eggs and chili sauce.

BROILED TURKEY

To be broiled correctly, turkey should first be placed near the heat, then removed to a lower shelf of the broiler to finish cooking.

PREPARATION TIME: *15 minutes*
COOKING TIME: *45 minutes*

INGREDIENTS (*for 6–8*):
1 turkey, 4–6 pounds
1 stick butter
1–2 shallots, finely chopped
3 tablespoons chopped parsley
1 teaspoon rosemary

Have the butcher split the turkey and remove the backbone. Trim away any bits of bone. Cream the butter until it is fluffy, and beat in the shallots, parsley, and rosemary.

Gently loosen the skin from the breast and slip a few tablespoons of the butter mixture under the skin. With the remaining butter, rub the turkey well on both sides. Extra butter may be needed for basting.

Place the turkey, bone side up, 4 inches from the broiling unit. Broil for 20–25 minutes, watching it carefully to prevent it from browning too much. If it does, remove the turkey to a lower shelf and brush it often with the melted butter.

Turn the turkey with the skin side up toward the broiler and brush it very well with butter. Remove the turkey to a lower shelf of the broiler. Salt and pepper it and continue to broil, watching it constantly and basting occasionally. To test for doneness, pierce one of the thighs. If the juice runs clear, the turkey is done. It should not take more than 40–45 minutes to broil on both sides. If it is not done, and very brown, transfer it to a 350°F oven to finish cooking. Serve with potatoes and a crisp salad.

SALMI OF DUCK

Salmi, a French cooking term, refers to a method of preparing a rich brown stew or casserole of game. It is also a suitable way to make an unusual and delicious party dish out of domestic duck.

PREPARATION TIME: *1 hour*
COOKING TIME: *40–50 minutes*

INGREDIENTS (*for 6*):
2 ducks
3 carrots
2 large onions
1 bay leaf
SAUCE:
2½ cups duck stock
4 tablespoons butter
4 tablespoons flour
1 tablespoon ketchup (optional)
3–4 tablespoons medium-dry sherry or port
Squeeze lemon juice
Salt and black pepper
6–8 pitted green olives

Wipe the ducks inside and out, and rub the skin with coarse salt. Peel and thinly slice a carrot and an onion and put them in a saucepan, together with the duck giblets. Pour over about 4 cups of cold water, cover with a lid, bring to a boil, and simmer over low heat for 30 minutes to make the stock.

Meanwhile, peel and slice the remaining carrots and onions and use them to cover the base of a lightly greased roasting pan. Add the bay leaf, place the ducks on the bed of vegetables, and roast for 30 minutes in the center of the oven preheated to 375°F. Remove and carve each duck* into 4 portions and place in a heavy casserole.

Strain the fat from the roasting pan but retain the vegetables. Pour 2½ cups of strained duck stock into the pan and stir over moderate heat until boiling. Simmer gently until it has reduced* by about a third. Meanwhile, melt the butter in a saucepan over low heat. Stir in the flour and cook gently for 5–10 minutes, stirring occasionally, until the mixture is nutty brown. Remove from the heat and stir in the hot reduced duck stock. Return the pan to the heat; stir until boiling, then add the ketchup (if used), sherry or port, a squeeze of lemon juice, and salt and pepper to taste. Strain the sauce over the ducks in the casserole, cover with a lid, and place in the center of the oven preheated to 350°F. Cook for 40–50 minutes or until the ducks are tender. (If the juices run clear when a poultry skewer is gently pushed into the thigh, the ducks are cooked.) Add the pitted green olives and allow them to heat through for a few moments.

Creamed potatoes and broccoli could be served with the salmi.

CHICKEN MARYLAND

Chicken Maryland, which originated in the American south, is usually accompanied by corn fritters. The bananas and bacon rolls, while not traditional, give an interesting contrast of flavors.

PREPARATION TIME: *25 minutes*
COOKING TIME: *45 minutes*

INGREDIENTS (*for 6*):

3-pound chicken, cut into 8 pieces;
*   or 6 chicken pieces*
Seasoned flour (p.412)
1 egg
1½–2 cups fresh white bread crumbs
8–10 tablespoons unsalted butter
8 lean bacon slices
3 bananas

CORN FRITTERS:
2 tablespoons flour
2 eggs
2 cups whole-kernel corn
Salt and black pepper
1 tablespoon olive oil or corn oil
GARNISH:
Watercress

Remove the skin from the chicken pieces and coat them with seasoned flour. Lightly beat the egg and dip the chicken portions in this before coating them with bread crumbs. Shake off any loose crumbs. Melt about 4 tablespoons of the butter in a large skillet and fry the chicken pieces for about 10 minutes until brown on both sides. Turn down the heat, cover the pan with a lid, and cook gently, turning the chicken once, for 25–30 minutes. (If oven-baked, allow 40 minutes at 400°F.)

Cut the bacon slices in half, roll them up, and thread them on two skewers. Peel and halve the bananas lengthwise, then coat them evenly in seasoned flour.

To make the corn fritters, put the flour, the lightly beaten eggs, corn, 1 teaspoon salt, and ¼ teaspoon freshly ground black pepper in the blender and whirl until thoroughly mixed.

When the chicken pieces are tender, transfer them to a serving dish and keep them warm. Melt 2 tablespoons of butter in the skillet, add the bananas, and sauté them over low heat.

Heat the remaining butter and the oil in a second skillet. When hot, add tablespoons of the corn fritter batter and cook until golden brown on each side. Fry the fritters a few at a time—they take 1–2 minutes to cook. Keep the fritters warm while frying the next batch. While the last fritters are cooking, put the skewers with bacon rolls under a hot broiler for about 2 minutes.

Serve the chicken pieces garnished with the corn fritters, bacon rolls, fried bananas, and sprigs of watercress. A tossed green salad goes well with this dish.

Rice & Pasta

TAGLIATELLE ALLA BOLOGNESE

The paper-thin egg noodles, or *tagliatelle,* are frequently served in Italy with a sauce of ground beef.

PREPARATION TIME: *25 minutes*
COOKING TIME: *45–60 minutes*

INGREDIENTS (*for 4–6*):
$\frac{1}{2}$–$\frac{3}{4}$ *pound tagliatelle*
1 onion
1 clove garlic
1½ cups button mushrooms
2 tablespoons olive oil
1 pound lean ground beef
2 tablespoons flour
16-ounce can tomatoes
1 teaspoon salt
Black pepper
1 teaspoon chopped parsley
¼ level teaspoon mixed herbs
* (p.411)*
2 teaspoons tomato purée
½ cup red wine
1¼ cups beef stock
½–¾ cup Parmesan cheese

Peel and finely chop the onion and the garlic. Wipe and trim the mushrooms;* slice them thinly. Heat the oil in a heavy-bottomed saucepan and add the onion. Cover with a lid and cook gently for about 5 minutes or until the onion is tender. Add the garlic and ground beef, stirring until the meat is thoroughly browned, then add the mushrooms and sauté for a few minutes. Mix in the flour, add the tomatoes and their juice, salt, pepper, parsley, mixed herbs, and tomato purée. Pour in the red wine and stock and bring to a boil. Lower the heat, cover the pan with a lid, and simmer gently for 45 minutes–1 hour.

About 15 minutes before the sauce is ready, put the tagliatelle in a large pan of boiling salted water.

Bring back to a boil and cook for 12 minutes. Drain before piling them on a hot serving dish. Pour the sauce over the noodles and serve with a bowl of grated cheese.

ANDALUSIAN RICE SALAD

This savory dish from southern Spain is served with cold meat.

PREPARATION TIME: *15 minutes*
COOKING TIME: *20 minutes*

INGREDIENTS (*for 4–6*):
1 cup converted rice
1 teaspoon salt
8 tablespoons olive oil
3 tablespoons wine vinegar
1 large clove garlic, minced
1 small onion, minced
Salt and pepper
1 4-ounce jar whole pimientos
2 tablespoons chopped parsley
GARNISH:
Green and black olives
2 tomatoes, quartered

Do not use quick-cooking rice for this dish. Bring 2 cups of water to a boil. Add the salt and converted rice, cover, and cook slowly for 20 minutes or until the rice is just tender.

While the rice is cooking, make a vinaigrette sauce by combining the olive oil, vinegar, garlic, and onion. Season to taste with salt and pepper.

Drain the pimientos. Cut 6 narrow strips and set them aside. Finely chop the remaining pimiento.

Cool the rice slightly. Add the vinaigrette sauce, the chopped pimiento, and parsley. Toss gently.

Spoon the rice into a serving bowl. When cool, cover and chill thoroughly. Decorate the top with the reserved pimiento strips, and the sides with the olives and tomatoes.

HOMEMADE GREEN NOODLES

Making pasta at home takes time and patience, but the results are well worth the effort.

PREPARATION TIME: *25 minutes*
COOKING TIME: *10 minutes*

INGREDIENTS (*for 4*):
⅔ cup all-purpose flour
½ teaspoon salt
1 egg, well beaten
1 tablespoon water
4 tablespoons cooked spinach
Melted butter
Grated Parmesan cheese

Sift the flour and salt onto a pastry board. Make a well in the center and add the egg and water. Work the mixture with the hands, adding more water if necessary, to make a stiff but workable dough.

Squeeze the spinach in the corner of a clean dish towel to extract all of the juices. Chop the spinach very finely, add to the dough, and knead about 10 minutes on a lightly floured board. Cover the dough and let it rest for about 1 hour.

Roll out the dough as thinly as possible. Let it dry about 30 minutes, then roll it up like a scroll and cut on a bias into ⅛-inch-thick strips. Let the noodles dry about 1 hour.

Cook in rapidly boiling salted water 10 minutes or until just tender. Drain. Toss gently with the melted butter and sprinkle with the grated cheese.

Vegetables & Salads

STUFFED GREEN PEPPERS

For this recipe, select squat round peppers that will stand upright. Stuffed peppers are quite filling, and 1 per person is sufficient for a light lunch or supper.

PREPARATION TIME: *20 minutes*
COOKING TIME: *50 minutes*

INGREDIENTS (*for 4*):
4 even-sized green peppers
1 small onion
⅔ cup mushrooms
2 slices lean bacon
2 tablespoons unsalted butter
4–6 chicken livers
1 cup cooked rice
Salt and black pepper
1 teaspoon chopped parsley
1 small egg
¼–½ cup Parmesan cheese
1¼ cups tomato sauce

Cut a circle around the stem end of each pepper to carefully remove the stems and seeds. Place the peppers in a bowl and cover with boiling water. Allow to stand for 5 minutes, then drain thoroughly and set the peppers aside.

Peel the onion, wipe and trim the mushrooms,* and chop both finely. Dice the bacon. Melt the butter in a heavy pan and sauté the bacon, onion, and mushrooms for a few minutes. Add the chicken livers whole, cook for a few minutes over medium heat, then remove the livers and chop them into tiny pieces. Return to the pan. Stir in the cooked rice, salt, pepper, and parsley. Remove the pan from the heat. Lightly beat the egg and use it to bind the rice and liver mixture.

Arrange the peppers, cut surface uppermost, in a buttered baking dish. Spoon the rice mixture into the peppers and sprinkle them with half the grated cheese.

Pour ½ cup hot water into the dish and set it on the upper shelf of an oven preheated to 350°F. Cook for 35–40 minutes.

Immediately before serving, sprinkle the peppers with the remaining cheese. Serve a bowl of hot tomato sauce (p.302) separately.

POTATO GNOCCHI

Served with a tomato sauce, these Italian *gnocchi,* or dumplings, make a good light supper dish. They can also be served with any kind of broiled or sautéed meat.

PREPARATION TIME: *30 minutes*
COOKING TIME: *12–15 minutes*

INGREDIENTS (*for 4*):
1 pound potatoes
Salt and black pepper
¼ teaspoon ground nutmeg
1 cup flour
1 egg
4 tablespoons butter
½ cup Parmesan cheese

Peel the potatoes and cut them into 1-inch pieces. Put in a saucepan, cover with cold salted water, and bring to a boil. Cook over medium heat for 15–20 minutes or until tender. Drain and return the pan to the heat for a few minutes to dry the potatoes thoroughly.

Rub the potatoes through a coarse sieve into a large bowl. Season to taste with salt and freshly ground pepper before mixing in the nutmeg and the flour. Beat the egg and stir it into the potatoes, using a wooden spoon; blend thoroughly until smooth. Turn the mixture out onto a floured working surface and knead lightly. With lightly floured hands, shape the mixture into a roll about 1 inch thick. Cut it into 24 even pieces and shape them into balls.

Bring a large pan of water to a boil. Drop in the gnocchi, a few at a time, and simmer for 5 minutes. When cooked, the gnocchi will rise to the surface; lift them out carefully with a slotted spoon and put in a warm buttered serving dish. While the last of the gnocchi are cooking, melt the 4 tablespoons of butter and pour it over the gnocchi in the dish.

Sprinkle the potato gnocchi with the grated cheese before serving. They can also be served with tomato sauce (p.302).

LEEKS VINAIGRETTE

In place of the inevitable green salad of lettuce and cucumber, try this cold leek salad as a side dish.

PREPARATION TIME: *15 minutes*
COOKING TIME: *30 minutes*

INGREDIENTS (*for 4*):
8 small leeks
1 bay leaf
Salt and black pepper
2 tablespoons wine vinegar
¼ teaspoon Dijon mustard
6–8 tablespoons olive oil
1 tablespoon freshly chopped parsley
GARNISH:
2 hard-cooked eggs

Remove the coarse outer leaves from the leeks; trim off the roots and cut away the green tops, leaving about 4 inches of white stem on each leek. Slice the leeks in half lengthwise, open them carefully, and wash well under cold running water to remove all traces of dirt.

Tie the halved leeks in 4 bundles, put them in a pan of boiling salted water, and add the bay leaf. Bring back to a boil, then lower the heat to a simmer. Cover the pan with a lid and cook the leeks for 30 minutes or until tender. Lift them carefully from the water and place in a colander to drain and cool.

Arrange the cold leeks in a serving dish and prepare the dressing: Put salt and freshly ground pepper in a mixing bowl and add the vinegar and mustard. Blend thoroughly before adding the oil, mixing well. Stir in the chopped parsley and spoon the dressing over the leeks. Marinate* until ready to serve.

Garnish the leeks with slices of hard-cooked egg.

CELERY AND APPLE SALAD

This crisp, easily prepared winter salad is excellent with cold ham for a light lunch or supper. It can also be served as an appetizer preceding a substantial main course.

PREPARATION TIME: *15 minutes*

INGREDIENTS (*for 4*):
1 head celery
4 red eating apples
3 tablespoons French dressing
    (*p.304*)
2 tablespoons mayonnaise (*p.303*)
⅓ cup shelled walnuts
GARNISH:
Watercress

Wash and finely chop the celery stalks. Quarter, core, and dice* the apples. Mix the celery and apples immediately with the French dressing, then fold in the mayonnaise. Chill in the refrigerator.

Just before serving, coarsely chop the walnuts and stir them into the celery and apple. Spoon the salad into a serving dish and garnish with sprigs of watercress.

CARROT QUICHE

This interesting variation of the ever-popular quiche—with a filling of shredded carrots and custard—can be served as a first course, a side dish, or as a light main course for lunch. It goes well with roasts and chicken.

PREPARATION TIME: *45 minutes*
COOKING TIME: *35 minutes for quiche,*
20 minutes for shell

INGREDIENTS (*for 6–8*):

2 cups all-purpose flour
¼ teaspoon salt
¼ pound butter
1 egg
1 tablespoon lemon juice
1 egg yolk for glazing
FILLING:
4–5 carrots, finely shredded
Boiling salted water
4 tablespoons melted butter
1 teaspoon salt
Pinch of marjoram or oregano

2 tablespoons chopped parsley
Dijon mustard
Squeeze lemon juice
4 tablespoons grated Parmesan
    cheese
CUSTARD:
3 egg yolks
2 whole eggs
⅔ cup heavy cream
½ teaspoon salt
Pinch of nutmeg

To make the quiche shell, sift the flour and salt onto a board or into a bowl. Make a well in the center. Add the butter, cut into very small pieces, and the whole egg beaten with lemon juice. Work this mixture thoroughly with the fingertips (or in a mixer with a paddle, not a beater attachment) until the butter is incorporated and the dough stiff. Add a few tablespoons of cold water, if necessary, to hold the dough together. Form into a ball, wrap in waxed paper, and chill for ½ hour.

Roll out the dough between sheets of waxed paper, remove the paper, and line an 8-inch or 9-inch pie pan with the dough. Do not stretch the dough; just lift it up gently and let it settle in the pan. Trim and crimp the edges. Line the dough with a piece of foil and weight it down by filling it with dried beans or rice to prevent pastry from rising during baking.

Bake in a 425°F oven for 15 minutes, then remove the beans or rice and the foil. Brush the inside of the shell with the beaten egg yolk and bake 3 minutes longer. This glaze helps to prevent a soggy crust. Cool slightly before filling.

To make the filling, grate the carrots. Blanch* them in boiling salted water for 1 minute. Drain thoroughly, then mix them with the melted butter, salt, marjoram or oregano, and parsley. Set aside.

To make the custard, beat the egg yolks with whole eggs and blend with cream, salt, and nutmeg.

Brush the baked quiche shell with mustard. Spread the carrot filling evenly over the bottom of the crust. Squeeze a little lemon juice over the filling, then top with Parmesan cheese. Pour in the custard mixture. Bake at 350°F for 35 minutes, or until a knife inserted in the center of the custard comes out clean.

LEEKS IN YOGURT SAUCE

Leeks can be a nice change of pace as a vegetable dish. In this recipe they are served cold and go well with chicken.

PREPARATION TIME: *15 minutes*
COOKING TIME: *30 minutes*

INGREDIENTS (*for 4–6*):
8 slender leeks
Juice of 1 large lemon
¼ teaspoon salt
12 black peppercorns
12 fennel seeds
6 coriander seeds
6 sprigs parsley
2 shallots, peeled and sliced
SAUCE:
1 cup yogurt
3 egg yolks
2 teaspoons lemon juice
Salt and black pepper
Dijon mustard
GARNISH:
Fresh chopped parsley

In a heavy saucepan prepare a broth from 2 cups of water, the lemon juice, salt, spices, parsley, and peeled and sliced shallots. Bring to a boil and cook for 10 minutes.

Meanwhile, trim the leeks, slit them halfway down from the top, and wash them thoroughly under cold running water.

Put the leeks in a skillet wide enough to take them in one layer; pour the strained broth over them. Cover the pan with a lid and simmer the leeks over low heat for 10–15 minutes or until soft. Leave them to cool in the liquid.

For the sauce, beat the yogurt, egg yolks, and lemon juice together in a bowl, and place it over a pan of gently simmering water. Cook the sauce, stirring frequently, until it has thickened, about 15 minutes. Season to taste with salt, pepper, and mustard and set aside.

Before serving, drain the leeks thoroughly and cut each into 2 or 3 diagonal pieces. Arrange them in a warm serving dish, spoon the yogurt sauce over the leeks, and sprinkle with parsley.

Desserts

ICEBOX CHEESECAKE

This cheesecake is not the baked type but the icebox kind, chilled and decorated with fruit.

PREPARATION TIME: *35 minutes*
CHILLING TIME: *3 hours*

INGREDIENTS (*for 6*):
4–6 tablespoons unsalted butter
1½ cups crushed graham cracker crumbs
½ cup sugar
2 envelopes (2 tablespoons) plain gelatin
8 ounces cottage cheese
4 ounces cream cheese
Rind and juice of 1 small lemon
2 eggs
Salt
½ cup heavy cream
GARNISH:
Black grapes and canned mandarin oranges

Melt the butter in a small saucepan over low heat. Remove the pan from the heat and with a fork stir in the graham cracker crumbs and 2 tablespoons of sugar. Press this mixture over the base of an 8-inch cake pan with a removable bottom. Put the pan in the refrigerator to chill while preparing the cheese mixture.

Put ¼ cup of cold water in a small pan and sprinkle the gelatin evenly on the surface. Set aside to soften for 5 minutes. Meanwhile, rub the cottage cheese through a coarse sieve into a large bowl and mix in the cream cheese. Finely grate the lemon rind and mix in well.

Separate the eggs; add 3 tablespoons of sugar and a pinch of salt to the yolks and beat until creamy and light. Gently heat the pan of soaked gelatin, stirring continuously, but do not allow it to boil. Remove from the heat once the gelatin has dissolved, and add the strained lemon juice. Gradually beat this liquid into the egg yolks before blending it all into the cheese mixture. Beat the egg whites until thick, then add in the remaining sugar and beat until stiff. Fold the beaten egg whites and the lightly whipped cream into the cheese mixture. Pour into the prepared chilled cake base and smooth the top until level. Chill in the refrigerator for 2–3 hours or until firm.

When ready to serve, loosen the sides of the cheesecake with a knife blade. Carefully remove the cake from the pan and decorate the top with halved black grapes and mandarin orange segments.

Serve cut into wedges.

CHAUSSONS AUX POMMES

These apple pastries, sold ready-made in most French *boulangeries,* or pastry shops, provide an easily made and delectable dessert.

PREPARATION TIME: *25 minutes*
COOKING TIME: *30 minutes*

INGREDIENTS (*for 4–6*):
2 large cooking apples
1 tablespoon unsalted butter
¼ teaspoon grated lemon rind
¼ cup sugar
1 tablespoon white raisins
Puff pastry (p.363)
1 egg
Confectioners' sugar

Peel, core, and thinly slice the apples. Melt the butter in a saucepan and add the apples and lemon rind. Cover with a lid and cook over low heat until the apples are soft. Beat the apples to a purée* and add sugar and white raisins. Set the mixture aside until cold.

Roll out the puff pastry ¼ inch thick. Using a 3-inch round fluted pastry cutter, cut out circles from the pastry. Gently roll each circle with a rolling pin to form an oval about ⅛ inch thick. Spoon the apple mixture equally over half of each pastry shape. Brush the edges with beaten egg and fold the pastry over. Press the edges firmly to seal. Slash the top of each pastry with a knife, brush with beaten egg, and allow to rest for 15 minutes.

Bake the pastries on wet baking sheets above the center shelf of a preheated oven at 425°F for 10 minutes. Lower to 375°F and continue baking until pastries are golden brown. Dust with sifted confectioners' sugar and serve the pastries warm or cold with cream.

LEMON MOUSSE

Shiny, firm lemons are always plentiful and can be used to make a light mousse to follow a rich main course.

PREPARATION TIME: *30 minutes*
CHILLING TIME: *2 hours*

INGREDIENTS (*for 4*):
Juice and rind of 2 large lemons
1 envelope (1 tablespoon) plain gelatin
3 eggs
½ cup sugar
½ cup heavy cream
GARNISH:
½ cup heavy cream

Sprinkle the gelatin over 2 tablespoons of water in a small saucepan and leave to soak for 5 minutes. Separate the eggs, putting the yolks into a large bowl and the whites into another. Finely grate the rind from the lemons and mix it into the egg yolks, together with the sugar. Squeeze the lemons and strain the juice into the soaked gelatin. Place the saucepan over low heat, stirring continuously. Do not allow to boil, and as soon as the gelatin has dissolved, remove the saucepan from the heat.

Beat the egg yolks and sugar until pale and creamy. Slowly pour in the dissolved gelatin, beating all the time. Continue to beat the mixture until it is cool and beginning to thicken. Lightly beat the heavy cream and fold into the mixture. Beat the egg whites until stiff, then blend them in evenly and lightly.

Pour the mousse into a serving dish or individual dishes and chill until set. Serve a bowl of whipped cream separately or pipe* the whipped cream over the mousse.

TARTE TATIN

This is an upside-down apple tart on a pastry base. Apricots or pineapple can be used in place of apples.

PREPARATION TIME: *30 minutes*
COOKING TIME: *35–40 minutes*

INGREDIENTS (*for 4*):
1 tablespoon unsalted butter
¼–⅓ cup brown sugar
1 pound apples
PASTRY:
1 cup flour
4 tablespoons unsalted butter
2 tablespoons confectioners' sugar
1 egg yolk

Melt the butter and brush it over the inside of a cake pan 7½ or 8 inches in diameter. Line the bottom with waxed paper and brush with melted butter. Sprinkle the brown sugar evenly over the paper and press down with the fingers.

Sift the flour into a bowl. Add the butter, cut into pieces, and rub into the flour. Sift in the confectioners' sugar and stir in the egg yolk and 1 tablespoon of water. Mix to a rough dough in the bowl before kneading it on a floured working surface until smooth. Roll the pastry out to a circle the size of the pan and trim neatly. Set aside.

Peel, core, and thinly slice the apples. Arrange the slices in circles over the brown sugar. Carefully lift the pastry over the top of the apple slices and press down gently. Bake in the center of a preheated oven at 350°F for 35–40 minutes, or until crust is crisp and golden brown.

Cool the tart for about 5 minutes, then turn it out upside down on a serving plate. Remove the waxed paper. Serve the tart hot, with a bowl of whipped cream or pouring cream.

STEAMED JAM PUDDING

Fresh bread crumbs give this delicious English suet pudding a particularly light texture.

PREPARATION TIME: *15 minutes*
COOKING TIME: *2–2½ hours*

INGREDIENTS (*for 4–6*):
1½ cups self-rising flour
1 teaspoon baking powder
Salt
1½ cups fresh white bread crumbs
1 cup shredded beef suet
½ cup sugar
1 egg
Milk to mix
1 tablespoon strawberry jam
SAUCE:
4 tablespoons strawberry jam
½ cup sugar

Sift the flour, baking powder, and a little salt into a mixing bowl; add the bread crumbs, suet, and sugar, and mix well. Lightly beat the egg and stir into the flour, with enough milk to give the dough a soft dropping consistency. Blend thoroughly. Butter a 4–5 cup pudding mold and place 1 tablespoon strawberry jam in the bottom. Spoon in the pudding mixture until the mold is two-thirds full. Cover with a double thickness of buttered waxed paper; fold a pleat in the paper to allow the pudding to expand as it cooks. Secure the paper with string.

Place the pudding in a steamer over a saucepan half-filled with simmering water, or place the dish on an upturned saucer in a saucepan and fill with boiling water two-thirds up the side of the dish. Cover the pan with a tight-fitting lid and steam for 2–2½ hours. Add more boiling water if too much has evaporated before steaming is finished.

About 10 minutes before the pudding is cooked, prepare the sauce: Put the jam, sugar, and 4 tablespoons of water into a pan, stir over low heat to dissolve the sugar, then bring to a boil. Simmer for 2–3 minutes, or until thick and syrupy.

Loosen the sides of the pudding with a knife and turn out onto a hot serving dish. Pour the hot jam sauce into a bowl and serve separately.

CANDIED ORANGES GRAND MARNIER

A tangy dinner-party dessert becomes even more attractive to the hostess when it can be prepared the day before. It should be left to chill in the refrigerator.

PREPARATION TIME: *15 minutes*
COOKING TIME: *45 minutes*
CHILLING TIME: *2–3 hours*

INGREDIENTS (*for 6*):
6 oranges
⅔ cup sugar
Juice of ½ lemon
2 tablespoons Grand Marnier

Cut a slice from the top and bottom of each orange so that it will stand upright. Slice downward through the orange skin, cutting away the peel and all the white pith and leaving only the orange flesh. Cut the oranges crosswise into slices and place them in a serving dish.

Select 6 of the larger pieces of peel and carefully cut away the pith. Shred the peel finely and put it in a saucepan. Cover with cold water, bring to a boil, then drain (this removes the bitter flavor of the peel). Cover the peel with fresh cold water; bring to a boil and simmer for about 30 minutes or until the orange peel is tender. Drain and set aside.

Put the sugar in a heavy-bottomed saucepan, then stir with a wooden spoon over moderate heat until the sugar has melted and turned to caramel. Remove from the heat and add ½ cup of water—it will boil furiously. When the bubbling stops, return the pan to the heat and stir until the caramel has dissolved and a syrup has formed. Add the shredded peel and bring to a boil. Simmer for 2–3 minutes until the peel is glazed. Remove the pan from the heat, cool for a few moments, then add the lemon juice and the Grand Marnier.

Spoon the syrup and candied peel over the oranges. Set aside until cold, basting the oranges occasionally with the syrup. Chill for several hours before serving with scoops of vanilla ice cream.

COMPOTE OF RHUBARB AND BANANAS

Pink tender rhubarb is becoming available early in the year. For a compote, it should be cooked slowly to keep its shape.

PREPARATION TIME: *15 minutes*
COOKING TIME: *35 minutes*
CHILLING TIME: *2 hours*

INGREDIENTS (*for 4*):
1 pound rhubarb
⅔ cup sugar
Juice of 1 orange
1 pound bananas

Trim tops and bottoms off the rhubarb, wash the stalks, and cut them into 1-inch lengths. Place in a casserole or baking dish and add the sugar and strained orange juice. Stir to blend the ingredients thoroughly, and cover with a lid. Bake for 35 minutes in the center of the oven preheated to 325°F. Remove from the oven and leave the casserole to stand, covered, for 5–10 minutes.

Peel and thinly slice the bananas into a serving dish. Pour in the hot rhubarb and the juices. Cool, then chill in the refrigerator. A bowl of cream or vanilla ice cream could be served with the compote.

CRÊPES SUZETTE

For a small dinner party, crêpes Suzette make a spectacular dessert, especially when cooked at the table in a chafing dish.

PREPARATION TIME: *30 minutes*
COOKING TIME: *2–3 minutes*

INGREDIENTS (*for 6*):
12 crêpes (p.343)
2 tablespoons unsalted butter
¼ cup sugar
Juice of 2 oranges
Juice of ½ lemon
2–4 tablespoons orange liqueur

Make the crêpes and keep them hot between two plates over a saucepan of gently simmering water. Melt the butter in a large skillet or crêpes Suzette pan. Stir in the sugar and cook gently until it is a golden-brown caramel. Add the strained orange and lemon juices and stir until the caramel has dissolved and become a thick sauce. Drop a flat crêpe into the pan, fold it in half and then in half again. Push to the side of the pan and add the next crêpe. When all the crêpes are in the hot sauce, add the orange liqueur and set it alight when hot. Shake the pan gently to incorporate the flamed liqueur evenly into the sauce.

Transfer the crêpes to a hot serving dish, pour the sauce from the pan over them, and serve at once.

Snacks & Supper Dishes

SHEPHERD'S PIE

When roast beef graces the Sunday lunch table, this leftover dish follows for Monday's supper.

PREPARATION TIME: *20 minutes*
COOKING TIME: *30 minutes*

INGREDIENTS (*for 4-6*):
2 onions, finely chopped
6 tablespoons unsalted butter
3 cups cooked ground beef or lamb
½ cup beef stock or gravy
1 tablespoon tomato ketchup
¼ teaspoon Worcestershire sauce
Salt and black pepper
2-3 tablespoons milk
1 pound potatoes, boiled and mashed

In a skillet cook the onions in 2 tablespoons of the butter until soft; add the meat and cook until lightly brown. Stir in the stock, ketchup, and Worcestershire sauce. Season with salt and pepper.

Melt the remaining butter and beat it with the milk into the potatoes. Put the meat in a greased baking dish, cover with potato, and ripple the top with a fork. Bake near the top of a preheated oven at 425°F for 30 minutes or until brown.

Serve the pie hot, with a tossed salad or a green vegetable.

WELSH RABBIT

The success of this snack—sometimes called Welsh rarebit—lies in cooking it over low heat until the cheese has melted.

PREPARATION TIME: *5 minutes*
COOKING TIME: *15 minutes*

INGREDIENTS (*for 4*):
2 cups grated Cheddar cheese
2 tablespoons unsalted butter
1 level teaspoon prepared hot mustard
3 tablespoons beer
Salt and black pepper
4 slices buttered toast

Cook the cheese, butter, mustard, and beer in a heavy pan over very low heat; season to taste with salt and freshly ground pepper. Stir occasionally until the mixture is smooth and creamy. Spoon the cheese onto the toast and put under a hot broiler until it bubbles.

EGGS MEDITERRANEAN

This Mediterranean dish of savory scrambled eggs makes a quick lunch or supper snack.

PREPARATION TIME: *15 minutes*
COOKING TIME: *10 minutes*

INGREDIENTS (*for 4*):
1 small onion, finely chopped
4 tablespoons unsalted butter
4 large tomatoes, peeled, seeded and coarsely chopped
1 cup diced ham
4 large eggs
Salt and black pepper
1 tablespoon freshly chopped parsley

Cook the onion in the butter until transparent, add the tomatoes and ham, and cook for a further 2-3 minutes. Stir the lightly beaten eggs into the mixture and season to taste. Continue cooking, stirring occasionally, until the eggs are just set.

Sprinkle the scrambled eggs with parsley and serve at once with crisp toast fingers.

COLCANNON

Irish in origin, this dish of leftover potato and cabbage is excellent with cold roast beef or lamb.

PREPARATION TIME: *10 minutes*
COOKING TIME: *20 minutes*

INGREDIENTS (*for 4*):
1 onion, finely chopped
4 slices lean bacon, diced
3 tablespoons bacon fat or beef drippings
2 cups mashed potatoes
1 cup cooked chopped cabbage
Salt and black pepper

Sauté the onion and bacon in the fat until the onion is soft. Lift them out with a slotted spoon.

Mix the potato and cabbage with the bacon and onion, and season to taste. Shape the mixture into 4 flat cakes, about ½ inch thick. Sauté in the fat until golden brown.

Serve the potato and cabbage cakes topped with a fried egg, or as a vegetable course with cold meat.

CHOCOLATE CAKE MOUSSE

Leftover chocolate cake can be turned into an elegant dessert.

PREPARATION TIME: *20-30 minutes*
CHILLING TIME: *4 hours*

INGREDIENTS (*for 6*):
2-4 thick slices stale chocolate cake
3 ounces semisweet chocolate
3 eggs, separated
⅓ cup sugar
2 tablespoons concentrated frozen orange juice
½ cup heavy cream
2 tablespoons grated chocolate

Melt the chocolate in a bowl set over a pan of simmering water. Beat the egg yolks with the sugar until pale and fluffy, and stir in the melted chocolate. Fold in the orange juice, then the cake, cut in small pieces.

Beat the egg whites and the cream, separately, until thick. Carefully fold both into the chocolate mixture and turn into a serving bowl or individual small dishes. Chill.

Sprinkle with coarsely grated chocolate before serving.

Homemade Marmalade

Marmalade making is time-consuming but economical, and the result, both in flavor and texture, is well worth the trouble. Marmalades from citrus fruits are basically made in the same way as jams and jellies, but the peel, which is an integral part of marmalade, is extremely tough and needs long, slow cooking. Pectin,* which is essential for a good set, exists in the pith (the yellow-white layer beneath the peel and surrounding the fruit pulp) and in the seeds. Both should be tied in cheesecloth and boiled with the chopped peel.

Use a candy thermometer to gauge setting point (220°F), or cook until mixture "sheets" (when two drops of syrup come together and fall as a single drop from the spoon). Commercial pectin may be used to guarantee a thick set; follow the manufacturer's instructions. After skimming the marmalade, leave it to stand for 30 minutes, stirring occasionally. Pour into hot sterilized jars and seal with paraffin, or cover the jars at once with airtight sterilized lids.

LEMON   LIME   DUNDEE

Chunky Orange

PREPARATION TIME: *1¼ hours*
COOKING TIME: *about 2½ hours*

INGREDIENTS (*yield 10 pints*):
3 pounds oranges
Juice of 2 lemons
12 cups water
8 cups sugar

Remove any stem ends from the oranges; scrub and dry them thoroughly. Using a potato peeler or sharp, narrow knife, peel off the rind in thin downward strips, being careful to leave all the white pith behind. Chop or scissor the thin peel into ¼-inch-wide strips and set them aside.

Cut the oranges in half and squeeze out all of the juice, saving the seeds. Cut away the yellow-white pith with a sharp knife, leaving the orange pulp. Chop the pith coarsely and tie it securely in a large piece of cheesecloth, together with the orange seeds.

Cut the orange pulp into small chunks and put them in the preserving pan, with the chopped peel and

the cheesecloth bag. Strain the orange juice into the pan and add the strained lemon juice and the water.

Bring the fruit mixture to a boil over low heat and simmer uncovered for about 2 hours, or until the peel is soft and the contents of the pan have reduced* by half.

For chunky or coarse marmalade, first squeeze the juice from the peeled fruit.

Remove the cheesecloth bag from the pan and add the sugar, stirring continuously until it has dissolved. Turn up the heat and boil the marmalade rapidly until setting point is reached, about 15–20 minutes. Leave the marmalade to cool for about 20 minutes, then remove any scum.

Dundee

PREPARATION TIME: *35 minutes*
COOKING TIME: *about 2½ hours*

INGREDIENTS (*yield 10 pints*):
3 pounds Seville (sour or bitter) oranges
3 lemons
3 Valencia oranges
12 cups water
12 cups sugar
1 tablespoon molasses

Wash the fruit thoroughly, put it in a pan with the water, and cover with a lid. Bring to a boil and cook over low heat for 1½ hours, or until the fruit pierces easily.

Lift out the fruit and leave to cool. Slice the fruit, scraping out all the seeds and adding them to the pan with the cooking liquid. Chop the fruit coarsely.

Boil the fruit juices rapidly for 15 minutes or until reduced* by half. Strain the liquid into a preserving pan, add the chopped fruit, and bring to a boil. Stir in the sugar and molasses and boil until set.

Clear Orange

PREPARATION TIME: *45 minutes*
COOKING TIME: *2¼ hours*

INGREDIENTS (*yield 8 pints*):
3 pounds oranges
12 cups water
Juice of 2 lemons
8 cups sugar

Prepare the oranges as for chunky orange marmalade. Put the finely shredded peel in a pan with half the water and the strained lemon juice. Bring to a boil and simmer, covered, over low heat for 2 hours, or until the peel is tender.

Meanwhile, chop the peeled oranges coarsely and put them in another pan with the remaining water. Bring the mixture to a boil, cover with a tight-fitting lid, and simmer the fruit for 1½ hours.

Strain the liquid from the orange pulp through a fine sieve or cheesecloth into the pan with the soft peel. Bring the mixture to a boil and reduce* slightly before stirring in the sugar. Boil rapidly until set.

CHUNKY ORANGE GRAPEFRUIT THREE-FRUIT CLEAR ORANGE TANGERINE

Grapefruit

PREPARATION TIME: *45 minutes*
COOKING TIME: *2¼ hours*

INGREDIENTS (*yield 10 pints*):
3 pounds grapefruit
½ pound lemons
12 cups water
12 cups sugar

The thick layer of pith beneath the skins of grapefruit ensures a good set with this sweet marmalade.

Grapefruit is more suitable for a jellylike marmalade. Proceed as for clear orange marmalade.

Lemon or Lime

PREPARATION TIME: *1½ hours*
COOKING TIME: *about 2 hours*

INGREDIENTS (*yield 10 pints*):
3 pounds lemons or limes
12 cups water
12 cups sugar

Proceed as for chunky orange marmalade. For a more jellylike marmalade, follow the instructions for clear orange marmalade.

Three-Fruit

PREPARATION TIME: *1 hour*
COOKING TIME: *about 2¼ hours*

INGREDIENTS (*yield 11 pints*):
3 pounds mixed fruit (grapefruit, oranges, and lemons)
12 cups sugar

Slice the quartered grapefruit, oranges, and lemons on a plate to catch the juices for three-fruit marmalade.

Wash and dry the fruit, cut into quarters, then slice thinly, setting the seeds aside. Measure the fruit and juice and put in a bowl, with three times the quantity of cold water.

Tie the seeds in cheesecloth, add to the fruit and water, and let stand for 24 hours.

The thin tough peel on limes is easiest removed in round, not downward, strips. Use scissors to chop the peel.

Bring the mixture to a boil and cook over low heat for about 2 hours. Remove the cheesecloth bag and reserve the fruit pulp and juice (about 12 cups). Return to the pan with the same amount of sugar. Stir until the sugar has dissolved, then boil rapidly until set.

Tangerine

PREPARATION TIME: *1¼ hours*
COOKING TIME: *about 1¾ hours*

INGREDIENTS (*yield 5 pints*):
3 pounds tangerines
6 lemons
10 cups water
6 cups sugar

Cut the clean fruit in half and squeeze out the juice, setting the seeds aside. Remove the membranes with a teaspoon and put them in a bowl, together with the seeds and 1 cup of cold water.

Cut the tangerine peel into narrow strips. Peel the lemons and add their pith to the tangerine seeds.

Leave the peel, the fruit juices, and the remaining water in a large bowl for about 8 hours.

Bring the contents of the bowl to a boil, with the fruit membranes, pith, and peel tied in cheesecloth. Boil steadily for about 1 hour or until reduced* by half, then remove the cheesecloth bag and add the sugar to the fruit. Boil until set.

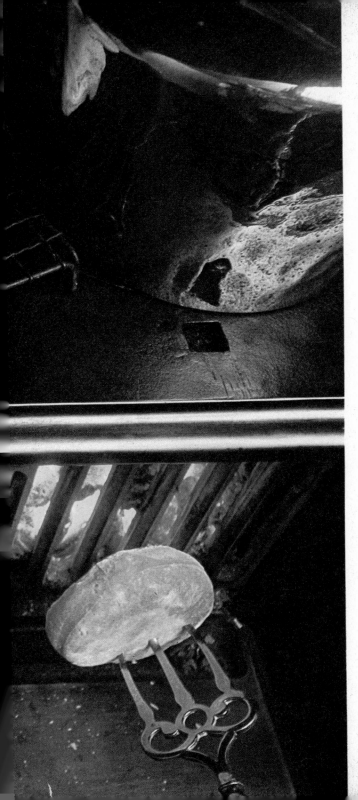

March

With rushing winds and gloomy skies,
The dark and stubborn Winter dies.

BAYARD TAYLOR

THIS MONTH'S RECIPES

The first spring days can be sharp and windy, just right for an afternoon in front of the fire with toasted muffins and homemade jam.

91

Food in Season

Imported leaf vegetables are good buys in March. Spinach and cabbage are at the height of their seasons, as are greens—turnip, mustard, and collard. These vegetables are most easily prepared when simply simmered in a little salted water and served with butter, salt, and pepper. Be careful not to overcook them, however, or they will lose flavor and valuable vitamins.

Spinach is the most versatile of the leaf vegetables: It is delicious when eaten raw as a salad green or creamed as a side dish. It is also used often in Italian dishes, such as Manicotti Stuffed with Spinach (p.101).

Chicory is another imported leaf vegetable at its peak in March. Used raw for salads and as a garnish, it is similar to lettuce but has curly, slightly bitter leaves.

Broccoli, carrots, mushrooms, and Belgian endive are in good supply this month.

Mushrooms can be used in soups, stews, and salads, and also make a rich first course or side dish when cooked in cream (p.103). Belgian endive can be braised in chicken or beef stock (p.102) and served with veal, pork, or duck.

Imported green peas are still available and U.S. artichokes are now beginning to appear in the markets. Perhaps the most important arrival is tender young asparagus; serve it with prosciutto (p.93) as a first course.

Hothouse rhubarb will be abundant for the next few months. It makes a fine dessert when cooked in a cinnamon-flavored tart (p.106).

Oranges and grapefruit are at their most plentiful. Use oranges for luncheon dishes such as Cottage Cheese and Fruit Platter (p.102), or for desserts such as Orange Soufflés (p.104).

SUGGESTED MENUS

Navarin of Lamb
Tossed Green Salad
...
Glazed Lemon Tart

French Onion Soup
...
Goujons of Sole with Tartare Sauce
New Potatoes
Tossed Green Salad
...
Marquise Alice

Champignons à la Crème
...
Leek and Chicken Pie
Glazed Carrots
...
Apple Purée Pudding

Shrimp in Curry Sauce
Boiled Rice
...
Cottage Cheese and Fruit Platter

Danish Liver Pâté
...
Veal Scaloppine
Almond Rice
Lettuce and Tomato Salad
...
Fruits Rafraîchis

Fricadelles
Sugar-Browned Potatoes
Braised Endives
...
Floating Island

Shrimp Provençale
...
Squab with Forcemeat Balls
Creamed Potatoes
Buttered Spinach
...
Charlotte Russe

Soups & First Courses

SHRIMP PROVENÇALE

In cooking, the term *Provençale* implies the use of garlic and tomatoes. This recipe can be used as a first course or as a light lunch or supper dish with a green vegetable.

PREPARATION TIME: *15 minutes*
COOKING TIME: *15 minutes*

INGREDIENTS (*for 4*):
1 pound raw shelled jumbo shrimp
1 onion
1 clove garlic
2 tablespoons oil
16-ounce can tomatoes
3 tablespoons dry white wine
Salt and black pepper
1 teaspoon cornstarch
1 tablespoon chopped parsley

Peel and finely chop the onion and garlic. Heat the oil in a large, heavy-bottomed pan, add the onion, and sauté over low heat for about 5 minutes, or until soft but not browned. Add the garlic and shrimp, and sauté for a further 3 minutes before blending in the tomatoes and the wine. Season to taste with salt and freshly ground pepper, and bring the mixture to a boil. Simmer for about 6 minutes.

Blend the cornstarch with 1 tablespoon of water and stir into the sauce. Cook for a few minutes, stirring until the sauce has thickened. Remove from the heat and add the chopped parsley.

As a first course, the shrimp could be served alone or within a ring of cooked rice. For a lunch or supper dish, buttered green beans would be a good addition.

ASPARAGUS WITH PROSCIUTTO

This interesting first course or luncheon dish is a delightful blend of flavors and an out-of-the-ordinary way to serve asparagus.

PREPARATION TIME:
   approximately 5 minutes
COOKING TIME: *approximately 20 minutes*

INGREDIENTS (*for 1 serving*):
6–8 asparagus
2 thin slices prosciutto
1–2 tablespoons grated Parmesan cheese

Wash the asparagus and remove the tough lower section of the stems. Cook the asparagus spears in salted water to cover until just tender. Drain thoroughly.

On a baking sheet, arrange 1 slice of prosciutto. Top with asparagus spears and cover with the other slice of prosciutto. Sprinkle with freshly grated Parmesan cheese.

Put under a preheated broiler about 3 inches from the heat, just long enough to heat the prosciutto and the cheese.

Transfer to a warm plate with a large spatula or pancake turner and serve at once.

FRENCH ONION SOUP

Although Les Halles in Paris no longer exists, onion soup is permanently associated with that famous market. The porters kept out the cold of a raw winter morning by drinking huge mugs of this traditional soup.

PREPARATION TIME: *20 minutes*
COOKING TIME: *1 hour*

INGREDIENTS (*for 4*):
1 pound onions
4–6 tablespoons unsalted butter
5 cups chicken or beef stock
½ teaspoon salt
4 slices French bread, ½ inch thick
1 cup grated Gruyère cheese

Peel and thinly slice the onions. Melt 2 tablespoons of the butter in a large saucepan; add the onions and stir well. Cover with a lid and cook over low heat for about 15 minutes, or until the onions are soft and transparent. Remove the lid and continue cooking the onions, stirring occasionally, until they are golden brown. Stir in the chicken or beef stock. Taste carefully for salt; if the stock is salty, additional salt may not be necessary. Replace the lid and simmer the soup for 30 minutes.

Meanwhile, spread the remaining butter on both sides of each slice of French bread. Sprinkle half the cheese over one side of the bread slices. Bake the bread on a baking sheet in a preheated oven at 350°F until the bread is crisp and the cheese has melted. Arrange the slices of bread in individual bowls and pour in the hot onion soup.

Serve the remaining grated cheese in a separate bowl.

GOUGÈRE AU FROMAGE

This choux pastry ring with a cheese filling originated in Burgundy. It is often served hot as a first course, but can also be served, thinly sliced, as an appetizer.

PREPARATION TIME: *15 minutes*
COOKING TIME: *30 minutes*

INGREDIENTS (*for 4-6*):
¼ *pound unsalted butter*
1 cup flour
1 teaspoon salt
4 eggs
1 cup grated Gruyère cheese
Egg and milk for glazing

· Put ½ cup of water in a heavy-bottomed saucepan and add the butter, cut into small pieces. Sift the flour and salt. Place the pan of water and butter over gentle heat; as soon as the butter has melted, bring the contents to a brisk boil. Quickly tip in all the flour and, with a wooden spoon, beat for 1 minute over moderate heat until all the ingredients are thoroughly blended. Remove the pan from the heat and continue to beat well for about 5 minutes, or until the mixture leaves the sides of the pan clean.

Beat in the 4 eggs, one at a time, blending each thoroughly before adding the next. When ready, the pastry should be smooth and glossy, and stiff enough to hold its shape when piped. Beat all but ¼ cup of the cheese into the choux pastry.

Grease and lightly flour a baking sheet; trace a circle about 8 inches in diameter on it. Fit a large pastry bag with a 1-inch plain tube and fill the bag with the pastry.

Pipe a circle of the choux pastry onto the tray, following the guideline. If necessary, pipe a second layer on top or alongside the first to use up all the pastry. Brush the surface with a lightly beaten egg mixed with a little milk; sprinkle with the remaining cheese. Place in the center of a preheated oven and bake for 30 minutes at 425°F. Transfer from the baking sheet to a plate and serve hot, cut in slices.

MINESTRONE

This Italian soup, of which there are many regional variations, is substantial enough to serve as a meal in itself. If the soup is served as a first course, increase the amount of stock or use fewer vegetables.

PREPARATION TIME: *15 minutes*
COOKING TIME: *30-35 minutes*

INGREDIENTS (*for 4*):
1-2 carrots
1-2 stalks celery
1 onion
1 small turnip
1 potato
2 tablespoons unsalted butter or 2
tablespoons olive oil
1 clove garlic
4 cups ham or beef stock
2 large tomatoes
1 small leek
1 cup shredded green cabbage
⅔ *cup macaroni*
Salt and black pepper
GARNISH:
½-¾ *cup grated Parmesan cheese*

Peel or scrape the carrot, wash the celery, and chop both finely. Peel and finely chop the onion, turnip, and potato. Heat the butter or oil in a large, heavy-bottomed saucepan and add the prepared vegetables, together with the peeled and crushed garlic. Sauté the vegetables over moderate heat for a few minutes until they begin to soften, then add the hot stock. Cover the pan with a lid and simmer the soup over low heat for 15 minutes, or until the vegetables are almost tender.

Peel the tomatoes,* cut them in half, remove all seeds, and chop the flesh. Trim the roots and coarse outer leaves from the leek, wash thoroughly under cold running water, then shred it finely. Add the toma-toes, the leek, and shredded cabbage to the pan and bring the soup back to a boil. Add the macaroni.

Simmer the soup over low heat—without the lid—for a further 10-15 minutes. Season the soup to taste with salt and freshly ground pepper and serve a bowl of grated Parmesan cheese separately.

DANISH LIVER PÂTÉ

The inexpensive pork liver is not often used for broiling or sautéing, but it is ideal when made into a pâté. This pâté should be left to cool under a heavy weight before being served. It will keep for up to a week in the refrigerator.

PREPARATION TIME: *35 minutes*
COOKING TIME: *2 hours*

INGREDIENTS (*for 6-8*):
1 pound pork liver
1¼ *cups milk*
1 onion
1 bay leaf
6 ounces fresh pork fat from the
pork loin, or fresh ham
6 anchovy fillets
1 teaspoon salt
Black pepper
¼ *teaspoon each of ground nutmeg,*
cloves, and allspice
2 tablespoons unsalted butter
¼ *cup flour*
1 egg, beaten
½ *pound bacon*

Measure the milk into a saucepan. Peel the onion and cut in half. Add the onion and the bay leaf to the milk and bring to a boil over gentle heat. Remove the saucepan from the heat and allow the milk to infuse* for 15 minutes. Strain through a sieve and set the milk aside.

Fish

Remove any skin and sinew from the liver. Put the pork fat, the liver, and anchovy fillets twice through the fine blade of a meat grinder. Blend the mixture thoroughly and season to taste with salt, freshly ground pepper, and the spices.

Melt the butter in a saucepan, add the flour, and cook over low heat for 1 minute. Gradually stir in the milk, beating continuously. Bring the mixture to a boil and cook for 2–3 minutes. Remove from the heat and blend in the liver mixture. Bind with the lightly beaten egg.

Line a 1-pound loaf pan with the bacon slices, allowing the ends to hang over the edges. Spoon the pâté mixture into the pan and fold the ends of the bacon over the top.

Cover the pan with a piece of buttered waxed paper and place in a large roasting pan in 1 inch of cold water. Place in the center of a pre-heated oven and bake for 2 hours at 325°F. The pâté is done when a stainless-steel skewer inserted in the center comes away clean.

Remove the pâté from the heat, cover with aluminum foil, and place a heavy weight that will fit inside the pan on top of the foil. Let the pâté cool, then refrigerate overnight before turning it out. Cut the pâté into thick slices and serve it with hot toast and butter.

SHRIMP IN CURRY SAUCE

Most shellfish are relatively expensive, but when they are combined with a creamy sauce, a small amount will go a long way.

PREPARATION TIME: *10 minutes*
COOKING TIME: *20 minutes*

INGREDIENTS (*for 4*):
½ pound peeled shrimp
2 small onions
1 tablespoon olive oil
1 rounded teaspoon curry powder
1 tablespoon flour
¾ cup fish or chicken stock
1 rounded teaspoon tomato purée
*1 rounded tablespoon mango
   chutney or apricot jam*
Juice of ½ lemon
2 tablespoons unsalted butter
3 tablespoons heavy cream

Peel and finely chop one of the onions. Heat the oil in a saucepan and add the onion. Cover with a lid and sauté over low heat for 2–3 minutes, or until the onion is soft but not brown. Stir in the curry powder and sauté gently for a few minutes. Blend in the flour and cook for 2–3 minutes more. Gradually add the stock and stir until the sauce thickens and comes to a boil. Add the tomato purée, chutney or jam, and lemon juice. Simmer for 5 minutes, then strain the sauce through a sieve.

Rinse the shrimp in cold water and pat them dry on a cloth. Peel and finely chop the remaining onion. Heat the butter in a skillet and sauté the onion until soft, then add the shrimp. Blend in the curry sauce and bring to a boil. Stir in the cream and remove skillet from the heat.

Spoon the shrimp and the sauce into the center of a ring of plain boiled rice.

GOUJONS OF SOLE WITH TARTARE SAUCE

PREPARATION TIME: *20 minutes*
COOKING TIME: *2–3 minutes*

INGREDIENTS (*for 4*):
4 large fillets of sole
Seasoned flour (p.412)
1 large egg
1 tablespoon olive oil
Fine dry bread crumbs
Oil for deep-frying
Salt
TARTARE SAUCE:
¼ cup mayonnaise
1 tablespoon heavy cream
*1 teaspoon each, chopped parsley,
   gherkins, capers*
1½ teaspoons chopped onion
GARNISH:
Lemon wedges

In France the small, smeltlike *goujons,* or gudgeons, are deep-fried and served whole. This recipe is adapted for sole fillets.

Making a slanting cut, slice each of the sole fillets in half and then cut each half lengthwise into 3 or 4 narrow strips.

Coat the fish thoroughly with seasoned flour, shaking off any surplus. Beat the egg lightly and mix in the olive oil. Dip the fish pieces in this mixture before rolling them in the bread crumbs. Refrigerate the fish until it is time to fry them.

For the sauce, mix the mayonnaise (p.303), cream, parsley, gherkins, capers, and onions together. Spoon into a bowl and chill until required.

Heat the oil* in a deep-fryer until a small cube of bread sizzles. Put the fish in the basket and lower it into the hot oil; fry for 2–3 minutes until crisp and golden brown. Remove from the heat and drain the fish on paper towels. Sprinkle with salt and pile the fish onto a hot serving dish. Garnish with wedges of lemon and serve the sauce separately.

A green salad and crusty bread could be served with the fillets.

COULIBIAC

This traditional Russian fish dish, usually served hot with sour cream, is a good choice for a buffet.

PREPARATION TIME: *2 hours*
COOKING TIME: *30 minutes*

INGREDIENTS (*for 8–10*):
2 onions
¾ pound button mushrooms
4 tablespoons unsalted butter
Salt and black pepper
2 slices salmon, each 1 inch thick
1¼ cups dry white wine
3 hard-cooked eggs
6 thin crêpes (p.343)
Puff pastry (p.363)
1 egg for glazing
1 cup sour cream

Peel and finely chop the onions; wipe, trim, and finely chop the mushrooms.* Melt the butter in a large skillet and add the onions. Cover with a lid and cook over low heat for 5 minutes, or until the onions are soft but not brown. Increase the heat and add the chopped mushrooms. Season with salt and freshly ground pepper and cook, stirring continuously, for 5 minutes. Remove the skillet from the heat, correct seasoning if necessary, and let the mixture cool.

Put the salmon in a saucepan with the white wine and a pinch of salt and freshly ground pepper. Simmer the salmon gently for about 10 minutes. Remove the pan from the heat and let the salmon cool in the liquid. Drain thoroughly, remove skin and bones from the salmon, and flake* the flesh with a fork.

When ready to assemble the coulibiac, heat the mushroom mixture slightly. If necessary, warm the crêpes in a pan over boiling water to separate them. Slice the eggs into rounds. Roll out the puff pastry to a rectangle no more than ¼ inch thick and approximately 16 inches long by 9 inches wide. With a pizza wheel or sharp knife, cut the edges straight and reserve the trimmings for decoration. Brush the pastry with the lightly beaten egg to within 1 inch of the edges.

Brush 3 of the crêpes with egg and lay them in a single line down the center of the pastry. Spoon a quarter of the mushroom mixture over the crêpes in a neat strip about 2–3 inches wide and to within 2 inches of the shorter pastry edges. Top with half the flaked salmon and then with another layer of the mushrooms and all of the egg slices. Spoon on half the remaining mushrooms, then the remaining salmon, and then the last of the mushrooms. Top this with the 3 remaining crêpes, brush with the egg, and wrap the crêpes around the filling.

Fold the sides of the pastry up and over the top of the filling so that the edges overlap. Brush thoroughly with egg to seal the edges. Fold the pastry ends over the top and seal with egg. Moisten a baking sheet with cold water. Carefully place the coulibiac on the baking sheet with the sealed edges underneath. Brush the top with egg.

Roll out the pastry trimmings and use for decoration. Cut a small hole in the center of the pastry and insert a small cone of waxed paper.

Place the baking sheet on the center shelf of a preheated oven. Bake at 425°F for about 30 minutes, or until the pastry is golden brown.

Cut the coulibiac in 1½-inch-thick slices and serve immediately with a bowl of sour cream.

SMOKED HADDOCK MOUSSE

A mousse, whether savory or sweet, should be chilled in the refrigerator for several hours before serving. This recipe, suitable for a dinner party or a buffet, can be made several hours or even a day ahead.

PREPARATION TIME: *45 minutes*
CHILLING TIME: *2–3 hours*

INGREDIENTS (*for 6–8*):
2 pounds smoked haddock fillet
1 small onion
2 cups milk
1 bay leaf
3 tablespoons unsalted butter
6 tablespoons flour
Salt and black pepper
Cayenne pepper

2 tablespoons plain gelatin
Juice and rind of 1 lemon
1¼ cups heavy cream
ASPIC:
½ teaspoon plain gelatin
1 tablespoon lemon juice or vinegar
GARNISH:
½ cucumber, unwaxed

Cut the haddock fillet into 8–10 pieces and put them in a saucepan. Peel and slice the onion and add, with the milk and bay leaf, to the fish. Cover the pan with a lid and simmer the fish over low heat for about 10 minutes. Strain the fish through a colander and reserve the milk. Remove all skin and bones, and flake* the haddock finely.

Melt the butter in a saucepan over low heat; stir in the flour and cook for a few minutes until this roux* is light brown. Gradually stir in the milk, beating continuously to get a smooth sauce. Bring this to a boil and cook gently for 2–3 minutes. Season to taste with salt, freshly ground pepper, and cayenne. Pour the sauce into a large bowl, cover with buttered waxed paper, and leave to cool. Measure 4 tablespoons of cold water into a small saucepan and sprinkle in the 2 tablespoons of gelatin. Allow to soak about 5 minutes, then stir the mixture over low heat until the gelatin has dissolved.

Remove the buttered paper and stir the sauce; blend in the fish, melted gelatin, and finely grated rind and juice from the lemon. Correct seasoning if necessary. Whip the cream lightly and fold it into the fish mixture; pour this into a 1½-quart soufflé dish and leave until set.

For the aspic, measure 2 tablespoons of water into a saucepan and sprinkle in the gelatin. Soak for 5 minutes, then stir over low heat until the gelatin has dissolved. Remove the pan from the heat; add 2 tablespoons of water and the lemon juice. Pour a little aspic on top of the mousse. While this is setting slightly, wash and thinly slice the cucumber. Arrange the slices in a circular pattern on the aspic. Spoon over the remaining aspic and chill the mousse in the refrigerator until ready to serve.

Serve with a green salad tossed in French dressing (p.304).

Meat

SAUERBRATEN

This German farmhouse dish of spiced braised beef is marinated for 4–6 days to flavor and tenderize the meat. Sauerbraten is traditionally served with potato dumplings, but buttered noodles or macaroni are less heavy and more suited to Canadian tastes.

PREPARATION TIME: *15 minutes*
MARINATING TIME: *4–6 days*
COOKING TIME: *2 hours*

INGREDIENTS (*for* 4):

2 pounds top round of beef
1 onion
4 peppercorns, crushed
1 clove
1 small bay leaf
Salt and black pepper

1 teaspoon sugar
1 cup wine vinegar
4 tablespoons unsalted butter
1 piece bread crust
2 teaspoons cornstarch

Trim off any fat from the meat. Tie with thin string to maintain its round shape and put it in a large earthenware bowl. Peel and slice the onion and add it to the meat, together with the peppercorns, clove, bay leaf, salt, freshly ground pepper, and the sugar. Pour the vinegar mixed with 2 cups of water over the meat and let it stand, covered, in the refrigerator for 4–6 days, turning it once a day in the marinade.*

Lift the meat from the marinade and pat it thoroughly dry with paper towels. Melt the butter in a deep, heavy-bottomed pan. Add the meat and brown it quickly all over. Season to taste with salt and pour 1½ cups of the strained marinade over the meat. Add the crust of bread. (In Germany a piece of honeycake or gingerbread is sometimes used as well to give extra flavor.) Cover the pan with a lid and simmer over low heat for 1½ hours, or until the meat is tender. Add extra marinade if necessary.

Remove the meat and keep it warm. Strain the liquid through a fine sieve. Measure off 1¼ cups and add more marinade if necessary. Blend the cornstarch with a little water and stir into the liquid; bring to a boil, stirring until smooth. Check and correct flavor and seasoning—the sauce should taste slightly sweet and sour.

Serve the meat cut into slices, with boiled noodles or macaroni; serve the sauce separately. Glazed carrots (p.103) or a green vegetable would also be good side dishes.

NAVARIN OF LAMB

Navarin is a French cooking term applied exclusively to a casserole of lamb and young root vegetables. Loin chops can be used, but rib chops are also suitable.

PREPARATION TIME: *30 minutes*
COOKING TIME: *1¾ hours*

INGREDIENTS (*for* 4):
2 pounds lamb rib chops
Seasoned flour (p.412)
3 tablespoons vegetable oil
1 pound young carrots
1 onion
2 cups chicken or beef stock
1 tablespoon tomato purée
Salt and black pepper ·
Bouquet garni (p.410)
8 small white onions
8 small new potatoes
GARNISH:
Chopped parsley

Trim fat from the meat and coat the pieces with the seasoned flour. Heat the oil in a large skillet and add the meat. Brown as many chops as possible at one time, turning them to color evenly on both sides. Remove from the pan and put them in a large casserole. Scrape and thinly slice the carrots, and peel and coarsely chop the onion. Add these to the casserole. Drain off most of the fat from the skillet. Stir in 1 tablespoon of the seasoned flour; cook over low heat for a few minutes to brown, then gradually stir in the hot chicken or beef stock. Add the tomato purée and bring the sauce to a boil.

Strain the sauce into the casserole; season with salt and freshly ground pepper. Add the bouquet garni. Cover with a lid and place the casserole in the center of a preheated oven at 325°F. Cook for 1¼ hours.

Peel the onions, leaving them whole. Put them in a saucepan and cover with cold water. Bring to a boil, then drain the onions at once. Peel the new potatoes and add, with the onions, to the casserole, placing them on top of the meat. Replace the lid and cook the casserole for a further 30 minutes, or until the vegetables are tender.

Remove the bouquet garni from the casserole, sprinkle with chopped parsley, and serve the navarin from the casserole.

MOUSSAKA

Eggplant is the staple vegetable of the Middle East. It is the basic ingredient in moussaka, which also includes ground beef or lamb.

PREPARATION TIME: *45 minutes*
COOKING TIME: *35–40 minutes*

INGREDIENTS (*for 4*):
4 small or 2 large eggplants
1 large onion
4–6 tablespoons olive oil
1 pound lean ground beef
1 teaspoon salt
2 teaspoons tomato purée
½ cup beef stock or water
Black pepper
2 tablespoons unsalted butter
4 tablespoons flour
1¼ cups milk
1 egg

Peel and finely chop the onion; heat 1 tablespoon of the oil in a heavy-bottomed pan and gently cook the onion for about 5 minutes, covering the pan with a lid. Add the ground beef and sauté until brown and cooked through. Stir in the salt, tomato purée, and stock; season to taste with freshly ground pepper. Bring this mixture to a boil, cover the pan with a lid, and simmer gently for 30 minutes, or until the meat is tender and the liquid is almost absorbed.

Meanwhile, peel and thinly slice the eggplants, arrange them in a layer on a plate, and sprinkle generously with salt; let the eggplants stand for 30 minutes to draw out the bitter juices. Drain, rinse in cold water, and pat thoroughly dry with paper towels. Sauté the eggplant slices in the remaining oil until golden, then drain on paper towels. Arrange a layer of eggplant in the bottom of a large buttered baking

dish or casserole. Cover with a layer of the meat, another layer of eggplant, and so on, until all is used up. Finish with a layer of eggplant.

Melt the butter in a saucepan over low heat and stir in the flour. Cook gently for 1 minute, then gradually blend in the milk, stirring constantly. Bring this sauce to a boil, season with salt and freshly ground pepper, and simmer for 1–2 minutes.

Remove the pan from the heat and beat in the egg; spoon this sauce over the moussaka. Place in the center of a preheated oven and bake at 350°F for 35–40 minutes, or until bubbling hot and browned.

This is a rich and substantial dish, best served straight from the casserole. A tomato and onion salad could be served with it.

VEAL SCALOPPINE

Italian scaloppine are similar to French escalopes, but they are cut against the grain of the meat. Ask the butcher to beat the scaloppine flat and thin.

PREPARATION TIME: *15 minutes*
COOKING TIME: *20 minutes*

INGREDIENTS (*for 4*):
4 veal scallops
Seasoned flour (p.412)
12 tablespoons unsalted butter
1 tablespoon olive oil
½ pound button mushrooms
½ cup Marsala or sweet sherry
1 cup chicken stock

Trim any fat from the scaloppine and coat them thoroughly with seasoned flour. Heat 4 tablespoons of the butter and the oil in a heavy-bottomed pan and sauté the meat over low heat for 3–4 minutes on each side, turning once. Remove the meat from the pan and keep it hot.

Pour all but 1 tablespoon of the hot fat from the pan. Trim and slice the mushrooms* and add to the pan; sauté over medium heat, tossing the mushrooms until coated in the butter, then stirring in the wine and stock. Bring this sauce to a boil and return the scaloppine to the pan. Cover with a lid, lower the heat, and simmer gently for 8–10 minutes. Turn the meat once or twice so that it cooks evenly. Arrange the scaloppine and mushrooms on a serving dish and keep hot. Boil the sauce rapidly until it has reduced by about one-third and has thickened slightly. Beat in the remaining butter and pour the sauce over the veal.

Buttered rice or pasta, and green beans or broccoli, can be served with the scaloppine.

FRICADELLES

These egg-shaped spicy meatballs appear regularly on the family menu in Denmark. They are usually served hot, with a sauce, but are also cut into thin slices and used as toppings for open sandwiches.

PREPARATION TIME: *30 minutes*
COOKING TIME: *30 minutes*

INGREDIENTS (*for 4*):
1 pound lean veal
1 small onion
1 teaspoon chopped parsley
¼ teaspoon dried thyme
1 teaspoon salt
¼ teaspoon ground mace or nutmeg
Black pepper
2 thin slices white bread
1–2 tablespoons milk
1 small egg
2 tablespoons seasoned flour
  (p.412)
1 cup tomato sauce (p.302)
4 tablespoons unsalted butter
GARNISH:
Chopped parsley

Trim fat and sinew from the veal and put the meat through the fine blade of the meat grinder. Peel and finely chop the onion. Put the ground meat in a bowl and add the onion, parsley, thyme, salt, mace (or nutmeg), and a few grinds of pepper.

Trim off the crusts and soak the bread in the milk for a few minutes, then squeeze out the excess liquid. Mash the bread with a fork and add it to the meat, together with the lightly beaten egg. Blend the ingredients thoroughly, using the fingers, until the mixture is firm. Then shape the mixture into 10–12 uniform oblong balls.

Coat the fricadelles with the seasoned flour and set them aside while preparing the tomato sauce. Now

Poultry & Game

RABBIT WITH PRUNES

Rabbit, which can be bought in some butcher shops, makes a pleasant change from chicken. The delicate flesh is enhanced by a flavorful marinade and the fruity contrast of the prunes.

PREPARATION TIME: *45 minutes*
MARINATING TIME: *1 hour*
COOKING TIME: *1½ hours*

INGREDIENTS (*for 4–6*):

2 cut-up rabbits
1 large onion
4 peppercorns, crushed
4 bay leaves
½ cup wine vinegar
Seasoned flour (p.412)
4 tablespoons unsalted butter
2 onions
2½ cups light beer

Juice of 1 lemon
1 sprig thyme
1 teaspoon Dijon mustard
1 tablespoon tarragon vinegar
2–3 tablespoons sugar
Salt and black pepper
8 soaked prunes
2 teaspoons cornstarch

Peel and slice the large onion and add it, with the crushed peppercorns and 2 of the bay leaves, to the rabbit. Mix the wine vinegar with 2 cups of water and pour over the rabbit, covering the pieces completely. Leave the bowl in a cool place to marinate* for about 1 hour, turning the meat occasionally.

Lift the rabbit from the marinade and dry the pieces thoroughly; coat them with seasoned flour. Melt the butter in a large skillet, add the rabbit, and cook until evenly brown all over. Put the pieces of rabbit in a large flameproof casserole. Strain the marinade and pour ½ cup of it over the meat. Peel and finely chop the onions and add to the rabbit, together with the beer, the lemon juice, the other 2 bay leaves, thyme, mustard, vinegar, and sugar. Season

to taste with salt and freshly ground pepper. Bring the mixture to a boil; cover the pan with a lid and leave to simmer gently for 1½ hours, or until rabbit is tender. About 20 minutes before the end of cooking time add the soaked prunes.

When the rabbit is cooked, blend the cornstarch with a little water to a smooth paste. Add some of the hot liquid from the pan and blend thoroughly before stirring it into the liquid. Bring the mixture back to a boil, stirring gently until the sauce has thickened.

Remove the pan from the heat and transfer the pieces of rabbit and the prunes to a hot serving dish. Correct seasoning, if necessary, and pour the sauce over the rabbit. Serve with creamed potatoes (p.333) and a green vegetable.

---

melt the butter in a skillet and sauté the meatballs over high heat until they are evenly brown. Turn the fricadelles once only.

Lift the fricadelles from the pan with a slotted spoon and put them in a baking dish. Pour in the hot tomato sauce, cover the dish with aluminum foil, and cook for 15–20 minutes on the center shelf of an oven preheated to 350°F.

Serve the fricadelles sprinkled with parsley. Boiled potatoes and a green vegetable are usually served with this dish.

STEAK AU POIVRE

A classic peppered steak is always prepared with crushed peppercorns. It is traditionally served with brandy sauce and is ideal for cooking in a chafing dish at the table.

PREPARATION TIME: *15 minutes*
COOKING TIME: *15–20 minutes*

INGREDIENTS (*for 4*):
4 fillet, wing, or rib steaks
2 tablespoons whole black peppercorns
4 tablespoons unsalted butter
1 tablespoon olive oil
2 tablespoons brandy
½ cup heavy cream
Salt

Crush the peppercorns coarsely in a mortar or place them on a board and press them, using a rolling movement, with the bottom of a heavy

pan. With the fingers, press the crushed peppercorns into the surface of the meat on both sides.

Heat the butter and oil in a skillet; sauté the steaks over high heat for 2 minutes, turning them once. This seals the juices and peppercorns in the meat. Lower the heat and cook the steaks for 5 minutes for rare steaks, 8–10 minutes for medium-rare, and 12 minutes for well-done.

Remove the steaks from the pan and arrange on a hot serving dish. Add the brandy to the pan and set it alight when hot. Shake the pan until the flames have died down, then gradually stir the cream into the pan juices. Season the sauce with salt and pour it over the steaks. Freshly cooked broccoli, potato croquettes (p.333), or a green salad go well with these steaks.

SQUAB WITH FORCEMEAT BALLS

Squab, or young domestic pigeons, weigh about a pound. Allow 1 per serving. If not available, substitute 1½–2 chickens or Rock Cornish hens, each of which will serve 2.

PREPARATION TIME: *1 hour*
COOKING TIME: *1¼ hours*

INGREDIENTS (*for 6*):
6 squab
¼ pound lean bacon
2 tablespoons unsalted butter
2 tablespoons plain flour
2 cups hot chicken stock or water
1 teaspoon salt
Black pepper
Bouquet garni (p.410)
12 small white onions
½ pound button mushrooms
FORCEMEAT BALLS:
2 cups fresh white bread crumbs
½ cup shredded beef suet
1 tablespoon finely chopped parsley
Finely grated rind of ½ lemon
Salt and black pepper
1–2 eggs
GARNISH:
Chopped parsley

Dice the bacon. Heat the butter in a deep skillet. Cook the bacon over moderate heat until the fat runs and the bacon pieces are crisp. Remove the bacon from the pan with a slotted spoon and leave to drain on paper towels. Put the squab in the pan to brown them, turning several times. Lift out the squab and put them in a casserole.

Pour away all but 1 tablespoon of the hot fat from the pan; stir in the flour and cook gently for a few minutes until browned. Gradually blend in the hot stock and bring the sauce slowly to a boil. Simmer for a few minutes, then strain the sauce over the squab in the casserole. Add the bacon pieces, the salt, a few twists of pepper, and the bouquet garni. Peel the onions and add them whole to the casserole. Cover the casserole with a tight-fitting lid and place in the center of a preheated oven. Cook for 1 hour at 350°F.

Meanwhile, trim and finely slice the mushrooms.* For the forcemeat balls, measure the bread crumbs, shredded suet, chopped parsley, and lemon rind into a mixing bowl. Season with salt and freshly ground pepper. Beat the eggs lightly and stir them into the mixture with a fork until the forcemeat has a moist but not too wet consistency. Using the tips of the fingers, shape the forcemeat into 8–12 round balls and put these, together with the mushrooms, in the casserole. Replace the lid and continue cooking for 15–20 minutes.

Lift the squab from the casserole and arrange them on a hot serving dish. Surround them with the mushrooms, onions, and forcemeat balls. Remove the bouquet garni before pouring the sauce over the squab. Garnish with chopped parsley and serve with sugar-browned potatoes (p.102).

LEEK AND CHICKEN PIE

Leeks, one of the more subtly flavored vegetables, are excellent combined with chicken. Cook the chicken for this pie well in advance so that it can cool for several hours.

PREPARATION TIME: *1 hour*
COOKING TIME: *1 hour 25 minutes*

INGREDIENTS (*for 6*):
1 chicken, 3½–4 pounds
1 onion
1 bay leaf
½ teaspoon salt
6 parsley stalks
2–3 leeks
Salt and black pepper
Pie pastry (p.354)
Egg and milk for glazing
½ cup heavy cream
GARNISH:
Chopped parsley

Wipe the chicken* inside and out; truss it and put in a large saucepan; cover with cold water. Peel the onion and cut it in half; add the onion, bay leaf, salt, and parsley stalks to the chicken. Cover with a lid, bring to a boil over low heat, then simmer gently for 45 minutes. Remove the pan from the heat and let the chicken cool in the liquid.

Skim the fat from the surface of the stock and take out the chicken. Measure 1¼ cups of stock and set aside (the remainder may be used as the base for a soup). Let the chicken cool. Remove the skin and bones from the chicken and cut the flesh into 1-inch pieces.

Trim the roots from the leeks and trim the green tops to within 1 inch of the white stalks. Slit the leeks in half lengthwise and wash them thoroughly under cold running

Rice & Pasta

water; chop them into ½-inch pieces.

Place a layer of chicken in a buttered 1-quart baking dish, cover with a layer of the chopped leeks, and continue with these layers until all the chicken and leeks are used up. Season each layer with salt and freshly ground pepper, and finally add the reserved chicken stock.

On a floured surface, roll out the pastry to a circle large enough to cover the baking dish. Butter the rim of the dish and line with trimmings of pastry. Lay these from end to end around the rim of the dish and press them firmly into place. Moisten the edges with cold water before covering with the rolled-out pastry dough. Trim and seal the pastry edges together. Make a few slits in the center of the pastry to allow the steam to escape, and decorate the pie with leaves cut from the pastry trimmings. Brush the pie with lightly beaten egg mixed with a few tablespoons of milk.

Bake the pie in the center of a preheated oven for 25 minutes at 375°F. Reduce the heat to 325°F and bake for a further 15 minutes. When ready to serve, cut out a small portion of the pastry and pour in the warmed cream. Replace the pastry, sprinkle the pie with the chopped parsley, and serve.

This pie is substantial and requires no extra vegetables. But young carrots, peas, broccoli, or new potatoes tossed in butter could be served.

CHEESE GNOCCHI

This type of gnocchi is made with semolina, shaped into flat cakes and deep-fried. Farina breakfast cereal is a good quick-cooking substitute for semolina.

PREPARATION TIME: *30 minutes*
COOKING TIME: *5 minutes*
CHILLING TIME: *1½–2 hours*

INGREDIENTS (*for 4*):
3 cups milk
1 small onion
1 clove
1 bay leaf
6 parsley stalks
½ cup semolina or quick-cooking cream of farina
1–1½ cups grated Cheddar cheese
1 tablespoon chopped parsley
Salt and black pepper
Cayenne pepper
1 egg
Fine dry bread crumbs
Oil for deep-frying
GARNISH:
Parsley sprigs

Measure the milk into a saucepan. Peel the onion, leaving it whole, and stick the clove into it. Put the onion, bay leaf, and parsley stalks in the milk. Heat until almost boiling, then remove the pan from the heat, cover with a lid, and leave to infuse* for 15 minutes.

Strain and reheat the milk to the boiling point. Sprinkle in the semolina or cream of farina, stirring continuously. Cook, stirring frequently, for about 3 minutes, or until the mixture is quite thick. Remove the pan from the heat and stir in the grated cheese and chopped parsley. Season to taste with salt, freshly ground pepper, and cayenne pepper. Smooth this gnocchi mixture over a moistened dinner plate, shaping it

into a circle. Chill for 1½–2 hours.

Cut the gnocchi into 8 equal-sized wedge shapes; coat them with the lightly beaten egg and then with the bread crumbs. Shake off any loose crumbs. Place the gnocchi in a frying basket and deep-fry in hot deep oil* until crisp and golden brown, about 1–2 minutes. Drain thoroughly on paper towels before arranging on a hot serving dish. Garnish with a few sprigs of parsley.

Serve with a crisp green salad.

ALMOND RICE

This combination of rice, almonds, and raisins makes a good accompaniment to broiled poultry and ham.

PREPARATION TIME: *5 minutes*
COOKING TIME: *25 minutes*

INGREDIENTS (*for 4*):
¾ cup rice
1 onion
2 tablespoons unsalted butter
3 tablespoons raisins
1½ cups chicken stock
½ teaspoon salt
½ cup toasted sliced almonds
GARNISH:
1 tablespoon chopped parsley

Peel and finely chop the onion. Melt the butter in a saucepan and add the onion; cover the pan with a lid and cook over low heat for about 5 minutes until the onion is soft. Add the rice and toss it with the onion and butter. Stir in the raisins and add the hot stock and the salt. Bring to a boil, lower the heat, and cover the pan with a lid. Simmer the rice for 15–20 minutes or until tender.

When cooked, fluff the rice up with a fork, fold in the almonds, and spoon into a hot serving dish. Sprinkle with parsley.

MANICOTTI STUFFED WITH SPINACH

Manicotti are pasta tubes about 4 inches long and 1 inch in diameter. They are filled with a savory stuffing and served with tomato sauce.

PREPARATION TIME: *45 minutes–1 hour*
COOKING TIME: *20–30 minutes*

INGREDIENTS (*for 4*):
8 manicotti
1 pound fresh spinach
2 tablespoons unsalted butter
¼ cup flour
1 cup milk
Salt and black pepper
2 cups finely diced or minced cooked chicken
2–2½ cups tomato sauce (*p.302*)
¾–1 cup grated Parmesan cheese

Wash the spinach* thoroughly and put it in a large saucepan—no water is needed. Cover with a lid and cook over low heat for about 10 minutes. Drain the spinach through a colander, squeezing firmly with a wooden spoon or in a paper towel to remove all the moisture. Chop the spinach coarsely and set it aside.

Melt the butter in a saucepan and stir in the flour. Cook gently for 1 minute, then gradually blend in the milk, stirring continuously to get a smooth sauce. Bring to a boil and season to taste with salt and freshly ground pepper; simmer gently for 2–3 minutes, or until the sauce has thickened. Take the pan off the heat and stir the spinach and chicken into the sauce; check seasoning.

Put the manicotti in a pan of boiling salted water and boil until the pasta is just tender. Drain and cool for a few minutes before stuffing the tubes with the spinach

and chicken. Using a large pastry bag with a plain tube, pipe the stuffing into the manicotti.

Arrange the manicotti in a buttered baking dish, pour the tomato sauce over them, and sprinkle with half the grated cheese. Place the casserole on the upper shelf of a preheated oven and cook at 350°F for 20–30 minutes or until bubbling hot and brown. Serve the remaining cheese in a bowl.

Vegetables & Salads

SUGAR-BROWNED POTATOES

The Danes traditionally serve these caramelized potatoes with roast pork, duck, and goose and with boiled or baked ham.

PREPARATION TIME: *20 minutes*
COOKING TIME: *10 minutes*

INGREDIENTS (*for* 4):
2 pounds small new potatoes
2 tablespoons sugar
4 tablespoons unsalted butter

Wash the potatoes in cold water and cook them in a pan of boiling salted water for about 10 minutes or until just tender. Drain the potatoes and leave until cool enough to handle, then peel them.

Put the sugar in a skillet over low heat; stir occasionally until the sugar has melted and is a golden caramel color. Add the butter and stir until thoroughly blended with the sugar. Rinse the potatoes in cold water—this makes it easier to coat them with the caramel—before adding them to the caramel in the skillet. Continue cooking over low heat, shaking the pan gently until the potatoes are evenly glazed and golden brown.

Serve the potatoes immediately in a warm serving dish. They can also be used as a garnish with roast meat or whole poultry, or served with slices of baked ham.

BRAISED ENDIVES

The sharp, clean taste of Belgian endives goes particularly well with roast pork, goose, or duck.

PREPARATION TIME: *15 minutes*
COOKING TIME: *50 minutes*

INGREDIENTS (*for* 4):
4 endives
1 small onion
2 tablespoons unsalted butter
Salt and black pepper
⅔ cup chicken or beef stock
GARNISH:
Chopped parsley

Wash and dry the endives, trim off the root ends, and cut each head in half lengthwise. Cut out the small piece of tough core at the base of each heart.

Peel and finely chop the onion. Melt the butter in a flameproof casserole over low heat and sauté the onion in the butter until soft and transparent but not browned. Add the endives, sauté until golden on both sides, then season to taste with salt and freshly ground pepper.

Remove the dish from the heat. Pour the stock over the endives, cover the dish tightly with a lid or foil, and cook in the center of a pre-heated oven at 350°F for 35 minutes.

Serve the braised endives straight from the dish, sprinkled with finely chopped parsley.

COTTAGE CHEESE AND FRUIT PLATTER

A salad of cottage cheese and fruit makes a light and nourishing lunch. Choose seasonal fruit, such as oranges, pineapple, or sliced bananas first tossed in lemon juice.

PREPARATION TIME: *10 minutes*

INGREDIENTS (*for* 4):
1 small head of lettuce
Bunch watercress
2 oranges
4 pineapple rings
8 ounces cottage cheese
French dressing (p.304) or
  mayonnaise (p.303)
GARNISH:
⅓ cup shelled walnuts

Separate the leaves of the lettuce and cut off any coarse stems and damaged leaves; wash the leaves and dry them thoroughly. Remove the lower coarse stems of the watercress and wash and dry the leaves. Cut a slice from the top and bottom of each orange before removing the peel and all white pith; slice the oranges thinly crosswise.

Arrange the lettuce in the center of a platter, with the orange slices and pineapple rings around the edge. Arrange the cottage cheese at one end of the fruit and garnish with sprigs of watercress.

Chop the walnuts coarsely and sprinkle them over the cheese. Mayonnaise or a good French dressing may be served separately, as well as crusty bread and butter.

GLAZED CARROTS

The full flavor of tender young carrots is retained by cooking them in a buttery glaze. Serve them with roast lamb, roast pork, roast chicken, or broiled lamb chops.

PREPARATION TIME: *10 minutes*
COOKING TIME: *20–25 minutes*

INGREDIENTS (*for 4*):
1 pound young carrots
2 tablespoons unsalted butter
Salt and black pepper
1 teaspoon sugar
1 teaspoon chopped parsley

Wash and scrape or peel the carrots and cut them into slices about ¼ inch thick. Melt the 2 tablespoons of butter in a saucepan, add the carrot slices, and season with salt, freshly ground pepper, and the sugar. Add enough cold water to just cover the carrots. Bring quickly to a boil, cover the saucepan with a lid, and simmer gently for 15–20 minutes.

Remove the lid; increase the heat and cook the carrots until all of the liquid has evaporated and only the butter remains—do not allow the carrots to brown. Remove the pan from the heat; add the chopped parsley and toss with the carrots in the butter glaze.

Serve the carrots in a hot dish.

PEPERONATA

This spicy casserole of sweet peppers and tomatoes is of Italian origin. It is served hot as a side dish with meat and with fish, or cold as a salad or as a first course.

PREPARATION TIME: *10 minutes*
COOKING TIME: *30–35 minutes*

INGREDIENTS (*for 4*):
4 large red or green peppers
1 onion
8 large tomatoes
1 clove garlic
Salt and black pepper
2 tablespoons unsalted butter
2 tablespoons olive oil

Peel and finely chop the onion. Wash the peppers, cut them in half lengthwise, and remove the inner ribs and the seeds. Cut the peppers into narrow strips. Peel and seed the tomatoes* and chop them coarsely. Peel the garlic and pound it to a paste in a mortar, adding a little salt.

Heat the butter and oil in a skillet; add the onion and peppers. Cover the pan with a lid and cook the vegetables gently until soft but not brown. Add the tomatoes and garlic and season to taste with freshly ground pepper. Put the lid back on the pan and continue cooking over very low heat, stirring occasionally, for 25–30 minutes. The mixture should now be soft, and the juices from the tomatoes should have evaporated. Correct the seasoning if necessary.

Spoon the mixture into a serving dish and serve hot or cold.

SWISS RÖSTI

This potato cake should be made from potatoes boiled in their skins hours in advance or the day before. It makes an excellent accompaniment for roast meat or poultry.

PREPARATION TIME: *30 minutes*
CHILLING TIME: *overnight*
COOKING TIME: *25 minutes*

INGREDIENTS (*for 4*):
2 pounds potatoes
4–6 tablespoons unsalted butter
1 teaspoon salt
Black pepper

Wash the potatoes and put them in a saucepan of cold water; cover with a lid and bring to a boil. Boil for about 7 minutes until the potatoes are barely tender. Drain, cool, and refrigerate until cold, preferably overnight. Peel the potatoes and grate them coarsely.

Melt the butter in a large, heavy skillet. Add the grated potatoes, sprinkle with the salt, and season to taste with freshly ground pepper. Cook over moderate heat for about 15 minutes, and as the potatoes brown underneath, turn them with a spatula. Towards the end of the cooking time, press down gently on the potato mixture to form a pancake; allow this to become crisp and brown on the underside.

Just before serving, loosen the cake with the spatula, place a round serving plate over the pan, and invert the potato cake.

CHAMPIGNONS À LA CRÈME

For mushrooms in cream sauce, choose small, firm mushrooms that will not break up during cooking. Serve them with broiled meat or chicken, or on buttered toast as a quick snack.

PREPARATION TIME: *10 minutes*
COOKING TIME: *7 minutes*

INGREDIENTS (*for 4*):

1 pound mushrooms
4 tablespoons unsalted butter
Salt and black pepper
Dried mixed herbs (p.411)

1 tablespoon flour
½ cup heavy cream
1 tablespoon chopped parsley
Juice of ½ lemon

Wipe the mushrooms with a damp paper towel. Trim the stalks level with the caps. Melt the butter in a pan and sauté the mushrooms for 1–2 minutes, tossing to coat them evenly with the butter. Season to taste with salt, freshly ground pepper, and the mixed herbs. Cook for a few more minutes to draw out the juices of the mushrooms.

Sprinkle the flour into the pan and stir thoroughly with a wooden spoon to blend the ingredients. Gradually stir in all the cream. Bring the sauce to a boil, stirring continuously until it has thickened. Allow to simmer over low heat for 1–2 minutes, then add the chopped parsley and lemon juice and serve the mushrooms immediately.

Desserts

FLOATING ISLAND

This popular dessert is composed of a meringue, or island, floating in a sea of rich custard. The meringue is layered with crushed almonds and baked. Then the custard is poured around the meringue.

PREPARATION TIME: *1 hour*
COOKING TIME: *30 minutes*

INGREDIENTS (*for 4*):

4 egg whites
1 tablespoon unsalted butter
1 cup sugar
½ cup sugar-coated almonds

CUSTARD:
4 egg yolks
2 tablespoons sugar
1 cup milk
Vanilla extract

Lightly butter the inside of a deep cake pan 6 inches in diameter, and coat it with a little of the sugar. Separate the eggs, setting the yolks aside for the custard. With a rolling pin, coarsely crush the sugared almonds in a dish towel. Beat the egg whites until stiff, then gradually beat in half the sugar; fold the remaining sugar gently into the stiff egg whites. Spread a layer of this meringue mixture over the bottom of the prepared cake pan; follow with a layer of the crushed almonds. Repeat until all the meringue and the almonds are used up, finishing with a layer of meringue.

Set the filled pan in a shallow baking or roasting pan and add boiling water to a depth of 1 inch. Place in the center of the oven and bake for 30 minutes at 350°F. Remove the pan from the oven and leave until cool. As the meringue cools, it will shrink and should be gently eased away from the sides with the fingers.

To make the custard, beat the egg yolks with the sugar, using a wooden spoon. Heat the milk in a saucepan until almost boiling, then stir it into the egg mixture. Blend thoroughly and strain into a bowl. Set this bowl over a saucepan half-filled with simmering water; stir the custard gently until cooked and thickened slightly, about 10 minutes. Remove from the heat, add a few drops of vanilla extract, and allow the custard to cool, stirring occasionally to prevent a skin from forming.

Just before serving, loosen the meringue with the tip of a knife and lift it carefully onto a round deep serving plate. Pour the custard around the meringue, lifting it with a spatula or knife so that the custard runs beneath and around the meringue island.

ORANGE SOUFFLÉS

A light, fluffy soufflé is a good choice for rounding off a meal. These individual soufflés are baked in orange shells and should be served straight from the oven before they collapse.

PREPARATION TIME: *30 minutes*
COOKING TIME: *20 minutes*

INGREDIENTS (*for 4*):
4 large oranges
1 lemon
2 tablespoons unsalted butter
4 tablespoons flour
3 tablespoons sugar
3 eggs
GARNISH:
Confectioners' sugar

Wash the oranges and cut them in half crosswise. Take out all the orange pulp and remove the white pith; set the shells aside.

Squeeze the orange pulp to extract all the juice, and strain it into a bowl together with the strained juice from the lemon. Melt the butter in a saucepan over low heat, stir in the flour, and cook for a few minutes until this roux* is lightly colored. Gradually add the fruit juice, stirring continuously until the mixture has thickened to a smooth sauce. Bring to a boil, simmer for 1–2 minutes, then take the pan off the heat. Stir in the 3 tablespoons of sugar and let the sauce cool slightly.

Separate the eggs and beat 1 yolk at a time into the sauce. (All these preparations can be made in advance.) Beat the egg whites until stiff, then fold them into the sauce carefully but thoroughly, using a rubber spatula. Fill the orange shells with the soufflé mixture. Set the shells on a baking sheet (or in a muffin pan to keep them steady). Bake the orange soufflés in a preheated oven for 20 minutes at 400°F.

Serve the soufflés immediately, dusted generously with sifted confectioners' sugar.

FRUITS RAFRAÎCHIS

An attractive fresh fruit salad is prepared from a selection of fruit whose flavors and colors harmonize. Chill the salad for a few hours so that the flavors can develop.

PREPARATION TIME: *30 minutes*
CHILLING TIME: *2–3 hours*

INGREDIENTS (*for 6*):
2 oranges
½ pound black grapes
½ ripe honeydew melon
2–3 ripe pears
2 bananas
¼ cup sugar
½ cup dry white wine
2 tablespoons kirsch

Choose a deep glass bowl as the serving dish, and place the prepared fruit in layers in the bowl.

With a sharp knife, cut a slice from the top and base of each orange, then cut down each orange in strips to remove the peel and all white pith. Ease out each orange segment and peel off the thin skin. Peel and halve the grapes and remove the seeds. Place in the bowl on top of the oranges and sprinkle with a little of the sugar. Remove the seeds from the melon, cut it in quarters lengthwise, cut away the peel, and dice the flesh. Add the melon to the bowl with another sprinkling of sugar. Quarter, peel, and core the pears, then slice them thinly. Peel the bananas; cut them in half lengthwise before dicing them. Put them in the bowl with the remaining sugar.

Mix the fruit carefully, then pour over the white wine and the kirsch. As the fruit soaks in the liquid, press it down so that it is covered with juice and less likely to discolor.

Chill in the refrigerator for 2–3 hours. A pitcher of cream may be served separately.

ZABAGLIONE

This Italian dish is probably more popular in countries outside Italy. It is quickly made, but care must be taken to prevent it from curdling while cooking.

PREPARATION TIME: *10 minutes*
COOKING TIME: *5 minutes*

INGREDIENTS (*for 4*):
4 egg yolks
¼ cup sugar
4–6 tablespoons Marsala
GARNISH:
Ladyfingers

Put the egg yolks in a mixing bowl, together with the sugar and Marsala wine. Place the bowl in a saucepan half-filled with simmering water. Beat the egg mixture continuously over the heat until thick and fluffy, about 5–7 minutes. On no account must the egg mixture come to a boil.

Remove the bowl from the heat and pour the thickened mixture into warmed serving glasses. Serve at once, garnished with ladyfingers.

MARQUISE ALICE

This French dessert has undergone several changes since its invention by Escoffier, renowned as one of the world's greatest chefs. The classic decoration of whipped cream and red jam has remained unchanged.

PREPARATION TIME: *1 hour*
CHILLING TIME: *1½–2 hours*

INGREDIENTS (*for 6*):
2 tablespoons plain gelatin
4 egg yolks
1 teaspoon instant coffee
¼ cup sugar
2 cups milk
8–10 ladyfingers
1–2 tablespoons rum
½ cup heavy cream
TOPPING:
1 cup heavy cream
2–3 tablespoons sieved strawberry
    jam

Put 4 tablespoons of water in a cup and sprinkle the gelatin over the surface. Leave to soak for about 5 minutes. In a mixing bowl, beat the egg yolks, instant coffee, and sugar with a wooden spoon until the mixture is light and creamy. Heat the milk until almost boiling, then stir it into the eggs. Strain this custard through a coarse sieve into a saucepan, add the soaked gelatin, and stir over low heat for about 2 minutes until the gelatin has completely dissolved. Remove the pan from the heat; pour the custard into a bowl and cool, then refrigerate until it begins to thicken but not set.

Meanwhile, place the ladyfingers in a shallow plate and pour the rum over them. Beat ½ cup of heavy cream until thick and fold it into the thickened custard. Pour half this mixture into a moistened, shallow, round cake pan 8 inches in diameter.

Arrange the ladyfingers like the spokes of a wheel on top. Cover with the remaining custard mixture and leave to chill until firm—about 1 hour in the refrigerator.

When the mixture is firm, loosen the edges inside the pan with the tip of a broad knife. Dip the bottom of the pan in hot water for a few seconds to loosen, then carefully ease the molded custard and cream mixture onto the serving plate. Whip the cream for the topping until thick; spoon half of it into a pastry bag fitted with a rosette tube, and with a metal spatula spread the remainder evenly over the top and sides of the custard. Pipe whorls of the whipped cream at even intervals around the edge of the dessert.

Spoon the sieved jam into a small cone made of waxed paper, snip the end with scissors, and pipe a small blob of jam into the center of each whorl of cream.

Chill until ready to serve.

CHARLOTTE RUSSE

Antonin Carême, the great master of French cuisine, was known as "the cook of kings and the king of cooks." He invented the Charlotte Russe during his brief stay in St. Petersburg in the early 19th century.

PREPARATION TIME: *20 minutes*
CHILLING TIME: *2–3 hours*

INGREDIENTS (*for 6*):
1 3-ounce package ladyfingers, split
⅔ cup apricot jam
1½ teaspoons unflavored gelatin
¼ cup cold water
2½ cups heavy cream
3 tablespoons superfine sugar
3 tablespoons cognac
2 tablespoons sugar
Crystallized flowers (optional)

Line sides and bottom of a Charlotte mold or any 1½-quart mold with the ladyfingers, rounded sides outward. Brush the ladyfingers on the bottom of the mold with some of the apricot jam. Soften the gelatin in the water; dissolve over hot water. Whip 1½ cups of the cream until stiff and add the sugar, cognac, and gelatin, making sure gelatin is evenly distributed throughout. Spoon this mixture into the mold.

Refrigerate for 2–3 hours. Remove from refrigerator and invert on a plate. Brush with more apricot jam to glaze. Whip the remaining cup of cream until stiff, then stir in the sugar. Fill a pastry bag, fitted with a rosette nozzle, with the cream; pipe the cream around the sides of the Russe and make a swirl of cream in the center. Garnish with the optional crystallized flowers. Chill until ready to serve. Note: Crystallized flowers can be purchased in stores specializing in gourmet foods.

GLAZED LEMON TART

The fresh, sharp flavor of this tart is welcome after a rich main course. Preparations for the tart, which can also be served as a pastry with morning coffee, should begin at least 8 hours in advance.

PREPARATION TIME: *1¾ hours*
SOAKING TIME: *8 hours*
COOKING TIME: *25–30 minutes*

INGREDIENTS (*for 6*):

½ *recipe standard pastry (p.354)*
1 tablespoon flour
⅓ *cup ground almonds*
4 tablespoons unsalted butter
4 tablespoons sugar
1 egg

Rind of 1 lemon
TOPPING:
2 small lemons
⅛ *teaspoon vanilla extract*
1 cup sugar

Prepare the topping first: Wash 2 lemons thoroughly in cold water, then cut them into slices about ⅛ inch thick. Remove the seeds carefully and put the slices in a bowl. Cover with boiling water and leave to soak for 8 hours.

Drain the lemon slices, put them in a saucepan, and cover with cold water; bring briskly to a boil. Lower the heat, cover the pan with a lid, and simmer gently for 30 minutes, or until the rinds are soft and the flesh has almost disintegrated. Remove from the heat and let the rinds cool in the liquid.

Roll the pastry out on a lightly floured surface to a circle 9 inches in diameter. Line a 7- or 8-inch flan ring with the pastry and prick the bottom lightly with a fork. Bake the tart shell blind* for 5 minutes, then set it aside while preparing the filling.

Mix the flour and ground almonds. Beat the butter and sugar until soft and light. Beat the egg lightly and blend in the finely grated lemon rind. Gradually stir the egg into the butter mixture, then add the flour and ground almonds. Spread this mixture evenly over the pastry base. Place the tart just above the center of a preheated oven at 375°F and bake for 25–30 minutes, or until the tart has risen and is golden brown and firm to the touch. Remove from the oven and leave to cool completely.

Drain the liquid from the lemon slices, setting aside 1 cup. Add the vanilla extract and the sugar to the lemon liquid and cook in a saucepan over low heat until the sugar has dissolved. Add the lemon slices and simmer gently for about 5 minutes, then transfer the lemon slices onto a plate. Continue to boil the syrup rapidly until the mixture sets*—test by spooning a little onto a cold saucer. Arrange the lemon slices in a circular pattern over the tart. When the syrup is setting, remove the pan from the heat, and as soon as the bubbles have subsided, spoon all the syrup over the lemon slices.

Leave the tart to chill in the refrigerator before serving it cold, cut into wedges.

RHUBARB AND CINNAMON TART

Hothouse rhubarb is now in the markets. In this recipe it is combined with cinnamon, which counteracts the acidity of the fruit. Serve the tart warm or cold, cut into wedges. It can also be frozen.

PREPARATION TIME: *20 minutes*
COOKING TIME: *30 minutes*

INGREDIENTS (*for 6*):

¾ *recipe standard pastry (p.354)*
1 pound rhubarb
¼ *cup sugar*
2 tablespoons flour
½ *teaspoon powdered cinnamon*
½ *cup heavy cream*

On a lightly floured surface, roll out the pastry to a thickness of ⅛ inch and use it to line an 8-inch flan ring set on a greased baking sheet. Trim the rhubarb, wash it, then slice diagonally into ½-inch pieces and arrange over the pastry. Mix the sugar, flour, cinnamon, and cream together and spoon this mixture over the rhubarb. Put the tart on the middle shelf of an oven preheated to 425°F and bake for 30 minutes.

If the tart is to be served warm, let it rest for 10 minutes; otherwise it will be difficult to cut.

Snacks & Supper Dishes

SAVORY POTATO PANCAKES

This is a substantial dish on its own. For a heartier meal, team the potato pancakes with broiled sausages and red cabbage.

PREPARATION TIME: *20 minutes*
COOKING TIME: *15 minutes*

INGREDIENTS (*for 4–6*):
1½ pounds grated potatoes
1 small grated onion
1 cup shredded corned beef
2 slices bacon, diced
Salt and black pepper
1½ tablespoons flour
3 beaten egg yolks
Oil for frying

Wring the grated potatoes in a dish towel to extract excess moisture. Mix together the potatoes, onion, corned beef, and bacon, and season with salt and pepper. Blend the flour into the egg yolks, add to the potato mixture, and stir well.

Heat about ¼ inch of oil* in a skillet until hot. Shape the potato mixture into 6 3-inch-wide cakes. Turn the cakes once, cooking them over high heat until golden brown. Drain them thoroughly on paper towels and keep the first batch warm in the oven while frying the remaining potato pancakes.

SPICED HAM

This is a good way to use leftovers. The ham will keep in a refrigerator for a few days, provided it is sealed with clarified butter (p.337).

PREPARATION TIME: *10 minutes*
COOKING TIME: *5 minutes*

INGREDIENTS (*for 4–6*):
2½–3 cups chopped cooked ham
Pinch each of dried marjoram, thyme, and mace
Salt and black pepper
6 tablespoons unsalted butter

Put the chopped ham through the fine blade of a meat grinder twice. Season the meat to taste with the herbs, salt, and freshly ground pepper. Cook in 4 tablespoons of the butter for about 5 minutes. Pack the meat into an earthenware jar or pot and set aside to cool.

Heat the remaining butter until foaming, strain through cheesecloth, and pour it over the meat. Leave in the refrigerator until set. The spiced meat can be used for sandwich fillings, served as a first course with hot toast fingers, or served as a main course with a salad.

PASTRY PUFFS

With ready-made puff pastry from the freezer, leftover meat can be turned into a quick snack.

PREPARATION TIME: *15 minutes*
COOKING TIME: *10–15 minutes*

INGREDIENTS (*for 4*):
¾ recipe puff pastry (p.363)
2 cups ground cooked meat or liver
4 slices bacon
⅔ cup mushrooms
1 slice white bread
2 sprigs parsley
1 small onion, sliced
3 tablespoons unsalted butter
1 tablespoon tomato ketchup
Salt and black pepper
Fat for deep-frying

Finely mince the bacon, mushrooms, bread, parsley, and onion. Add the meat and cook the mixture in the butter for 5 minutes. Stir in the ketchup and season to taste.

Roll out the pastry to a 12-inch square; cut this into 16 squares and place a heaping tablespoon of the filling in the center of 8 squares. Moisten the edges with water. Cover the filling with the remaining 8 squares and seal the edges firmly.

Cook the pastry in fat,* heated to the smoking point, until the squares are puffed and golden brown. Drain on paper towels and serve at once.

HERBED SCOTCH EGGS

Hard-cooked eggs, wrapped in sausage meat and herbs, make a quick light supper or portable lunch.

PREPARATION TIME: *20 minutes*
COOKING TIME: *5–10 minutes*

INGREDIENTS (*for 4*):
½ pound sausage meat
4 hard-cooked eggs
Flour
1 egg, beaten
1½ cups bread crumbs mixed with ½ teaspoon dried thyme and ½ teaspoon dried parsley
Fat or oil for deep-frying

Divide the sausage meat into 4 equal pieces and shape them into flat rounds about 4 inches wide. Dust the shelled eggs lightly with flour and wrap each one in the sausage meat, pressing the edges firmly together to make a smooth surface. Coat with beaten egg before rolling the eggs in the herbs and crumbs.

Cook the eggs in hot fat* until golden brown. Drain on paper towels and let them cool.

APPLE PURÉE PUDDING

Leftover egg whites can be put to a number of uses other than meringues. Here they are used for a light, fluffy apple dessert.

PREPARATION TIME: *5 minutes*
CHILLING TIME: *2 hours*

INGREDIENTS (*for 4*):
2½ cups applesauce
1 envelope (1 tablespoon) plain gelatin
Juice of 1 lemon
2 stiffly beaten egg whites
½ cup heavy cream, whipped
1 tablespoon sugar
2 drops vanilla extract

Dissolve the gelatin in the lemon juice, placed in a bowl over hot water. Stir it into the applesauce, then fold in the egg whites. Pour into a moistened 4-cup mold and refrigerate for 2 hours until set.

Before serving, unmold the pudding and pipe* on the whipped cream, sweetened with sugar and vanilla extract.

A Gala Dinner Party

Special occasions are often associated with good food and wine shared with close friends. There are engagements and weddings, christenings, exams passed and promotions won, family reunions, or some unexpected stroke of good fortune. These are the times for a grand dinner party when cost is a minor consideration. Even if no particular occasion arises, early spring, with Christmas long forgotten and warm summer days still to come, is an ideal time for a special dinner party.

In the following four-course menu the table is set for twelve for a silver wedding anniversary. The menu is planned so that most of the food can be cooked and prepared early or even the day before.

Menu

Melon and Shrimp Basket
Onion and Anchovy Tartlets
Duck Breasts en Croûte
with Savory Orange Sauce
Orange Pommes Croquettes
Mushroom Caps with
Peas
Braised Celery
Crème Brûlée
Coffee and Petits Fours
WINES: **Chablis, Red Burgundy,**
Champagne
Brandy and Liqueurs

Preparations

The melon and shrimp basket can be prepared during the afternoon and left to chill. Bake the tartlets several days in advance and store them in an airtight tin. Prepare the filling in the morning and spoon it into the tartlets just before putting them in the oven. The cooked tartlets can be wrapped in foil and kept warm by the pilot light in the oven or on top of the stove for at least 1 hour.

The main course of duck breasts en croûte can also be prepared in advance. Roast the ducks and prepare the stuffing in the morning.

Wrap the breasts in pastry in the late afternoon and put them in the oven just before serving the first course.

Prepare the potato croquettes and the sauce in advance. Deep-fry the croquettes while heating the sauce.

Prepare the mushroom caps late in the afternoon and cook them while the sauce is heating. Put the prepared celery on to simmer when the duck is put in the oven.

The crème brulée should be made in the morning, or even the night before. The petits fours* will remain fresh for days if kept airtight.

For the wines, allow 2 bottles of white wine, 3 of red, and 3 of champagne. Serve the white wine and champagne chilled, and the red wine at room temperature.

Duck en croûte, garnished with orange slices, is arranged around potato croquettes. Celery leaves are used to decorate the mushroom caps filled with peas.

The attractively garnished melon

The Table

Give time and thought to setting and decorating the table, as it will be the focal point. A white cloth is the most suitable and should be set with thin-stemmed glasses and silver flatware. The centerpiece, which should be low, may be composed of flowers or fruit. Light the table with candelabra and white candles, or set candles in small flower arrangements.

Small tartlets with radish flowers

White gardenias, used in the centerpiece, also decorate the crème brûlée.

Melon and Shrimp Basket
INGREDIENTS:
1 large melon
French dressing (p.304)
1½ pounds shelled shrimp
6 tablespoons chopped celery
6 tablespoons mayonnaise (p.303)
1 cup sour cream
2 teaspoons curry powder
Grated coconut

Cut the melon* carefully into the shape of a basket. Remove the seeds and scoop the flesh out in well-formed balls. Let them marinate in the French dressing for about 15 minutes.

Set a few shrimp aside for garnishing and blend the remainder, with the celery and drained melon balls, into the mayonnaise mixed with sour cream and curry powder. Spoon this mixture into the melon basket and sprinkle with grated coconut. Chill in the refrigerator.

Onion and Anchovy Tartlets
INGREDIENTS:
¾ recipe standard pastry (p.354)
2 large grated onions
4 tablespoons butter
2 hard-cooked eggs
2 small cans anchovy fillets
½ cup heavy cream

Bake 24 small fluted tartlets from the pie pastry. Cook the coarsely grated onions in the butter until soft and transparent.

Blend the onions with the finely chopped eggs, the drained and chopped anchovies, and the cream. Spoon the mixture into the tartlets and bake in a preheated oven at 350°F for 20–25 minutes.

Duck Breasts en Croûte
INGREDIENTS:
3 ducks
4 tablespoons lean chopped bacon
2 chopped duck livers
4 tablespoons finely chopped onion
Rind of 1 orange
2 tablespoons butter
3 tablespoons chopped green olives
1 tablespoon brandy
Puff pastry (1½ times recipe p.363)
1 large beaten egg

Roast the ducks in the center of the oven for 45–60 minutes at 400°F. Set aside to cool. Sauté the bacon, duck livers, onions, and orange rind in the butter. Add the olives, moistened with the brandy, and cook this mixture over moderate heat for about 5 minutes.

Skin the ducks and carve off the breasts, each in 2 whole slices; cut each breast into 2 equal portions. (Set the duck carcasses aside to make a pâté for an hors d'oeuvre the following day, if desired.) Roll out the puff pastry ¼ inch thick and divide into 12 pieces. Lay a portion of duck breast on each pastry square, spread a little of the bacon and onion mixture over the duck, and wrap the puff pastry around each breast to form an envelope.

Seal the seams with egg and place the envelopes, seams up, on a moistened, floured baking sheet. Brush with egg and bake in a preheated oven at 400°F for about 25 minutes.

Savory Orange Sauce
INGREDIENTS:
1 cup Espagnole sauce (p.302)
Juice of 1 orange
Juice of ½ lemon
4 tablespoons red wine
2 tablespoons red currant jelly
Salt and cayenne pepper

Rub the Espagnole sauce through a fine sieve or whirl in a blender. Add the orange and lemon juices, and the wine and jelly. Heat the sauce through and season to taste with salt and cayenne. Pour into a sauceboat and serve with the duck breasts.

Orange Pommes Croquettes
INGREDIENTS:
2 pounds potatoes
2 egg yolks
1 tablespoon butter
Hot milk
Salt and black pepper
Grated rind of 1 orange
1 beaten egg
¾–1 cup dry white bread crumbs
Oil for deep-frying

Cook the potatoes and drain them thoroughly. Put them back over the heat to dry out completely, then rub them through a sieve or put them through a potato ricer. Beat in the egg yolks, butter, and enough hot milk to make a firm paste. Season to taste with salt and freshly ground pepper and stir in the orange rind. Set the mixture aside until firm.

Shape the potato mixture into croquettes* about 1 inch wide and 1½ inches long. Coat them with beaten egg and bread crumbs and deep-fry in hot oil.*

Mushroom Caps with Peas
INGREDIENTS:
24 large mushroom caps
12 tablespoons unsalted butter
3 10-ounce packages frozen young green peas
4 tablespoons chicken stock
Sugar and salt

Wash the mushrooms. Sauté them in 4 tablespoons of the butter for a few minutes, being careful to retain their shape. Cook the peas according to the package directions. Drain the peas thoroughly and return them to the pan, with the remaining butter and the stock. Season to taste with a pinch of sugar and salt.

Cook the peas over low heat until all the liquid has been absorbed. Spoon over the mushroom caps.

Braised Celery
INGREDIENTS:
6 heads of celery
1 Spanish onion
6 small carrots
1 cup chicken stock
Salt and black pepper
Beurre manié (p.303)
Parsley

Trim the roots from the celery and remove any damaged stalks; wash thoroughly, then cut each stalk in half lengthwise and remove the green leafy tops. Blanch* the celery for 10 minutes in boiling water, drain carefully in a colander, and put in a large baking dish. Cover the celery with the thinly sliced onion and carrots. Pour in the chicken stock and season to taste with salt and freshly ground pepper.

Cover the pan with a lid or foil and simmer the celery over low heat until tender, about 40 minutes. About 5 minutes before the end of cooking time, add small pieces of beurre manié to thicken the stock to desired consistency. Serve the celery sprinkled with chopped parsley.

Crème Brûlée
INGREDIENTS:
6 cups light cream
12 egg yolks
2 tablespoons sugar
3 tablespoons vanilla extract
½ cup brown sugar

Put the cream in the top of a large double boiler or in a bowl over a pan of gently simmering water. Carefully stir the egg yolks, beaten with the sugar and vanilla extract, into the warm cream. Continue cooking gently until the cream has thickened enough to coat the back of a wooden spoon. Strain the cream through a fine sieve into a large soufflé dish or mold and chill for at least 4 hours.

Sprinkle a ¼-inch-thick layer of sifted brown sugar over the chilled cream. Set the dish or mold on a bed of ice cubes on the broiler pan and place under a hot broiler until the sugar has caramelized. Let the mixture cool, then chill it in the refrigerator for 2–3 hours.

DUCK PÂTÉ
Cut the meat from the duck carcasses and grind it coarsely, together with the remaining duck liver. Mix with 2 cups ground veal, 1 cup white bread crumbs, 2 tablespoons finely chopped onion, 1 tablespoon chopped chervil or ½ teaspoon dried chervil, and 3 tablespoons chopped parsley. Season to taste with salt and freshly ground pepper. Stir in the grated rind of an orange and 2 tablespoons brandy or dry sherry. Add 2 lightly beaten eggs to the pâté and mix thoroughly with a wooden spoon.

Spoon the pâté into a buttered terrine and cover with bacon slices. Place in a roasting pan half-filled with boiling water. Bake in the center of the oven at 325°F for 1¼ hours.

April

Once more in misted April
The world is growing green.

BLISS CARMAN

THIS MONTH'S RECIPES

*Exchanging gifts of gaily decorated eggs is
a custom that originated in pre-Christian times.*

Food in Season

Two prized vegetables–artichokes and asparagus–are now available in the supermarkets. Both make superb first courses, but are also used often in early spring as side dishes with roast meat or poultry. Asparagus can be served plain (p.113), chilled and dressed with sauce vinaigrette, or with a bubbling-hot Mornay sauce (p.113). Whole artichokes are usually stuffed or served with melted butter or Hollandaise sauce (p.114); for a more unusual presentation, tender artichoke bottoms can be topped with mushrooms and a garlic dressing (p.123).

Fresh imported green peas are also at their peak, and green leaf vegetables are still in good supply. Rhubarb and grapefruit are plentiful, and strawberries are beginning to appear in the markets. All three make refreshing desserts: Recipes in this section include Rhubarb Crumble (p.125), Grapefruit in Brandy (p.125), and Strawberry Tart (p.126).

Fish and shellfish that can make tasty additions to menus this month are cod, sole, shad, smelts, striped bass, hard-shell clams, and mussels. Try Cod Pie (p.116) or Fish Soufflé (p.116) as change-of-pace seafood dishes.

SUGGESTED MENUS

Avocado and Citrus Salad
...
Lobster Thermidor
Green Salad
...
Grapefruit in Brandy

Artichokes with Hollandaise Sauce
...
Veal with Orange
Sautéed Potatoes
Glazed Onions
...
Sponge Roll with Lemon Cream

Fish Soufflé
Young Peas   Cauliflower
...
Rhubarb Crumble

Chilled Watercress Soup
...
Steak Diane
Baked Potatoes   Fresh Asparagus
...
Banana Fritters

Tomato Ice
...
Chicken Chaud-Froid
Green Salad
New Potatoes
...
French Apple Tart

Ham in Puff Pastry
Apple and Nut Salad
...
Chocolate Mousse

Asparagus in Mornay Sauce
...
Stuffed Flank Steak
Young Peas and Pearl Onions
Duchesse Potatoes
...
Gâteau Saint Honoré

Soups & First Courses

CHILLED WATERCRESS SOUP

Watercress is most often used as a garnish or in salads. It also makes a good basis for a smooth-textured chilled soup. (See picture on p.168.)

PREPARATION TIME: *20 minutes*
COOKING TIME: *45 minutes*
CHILLING TIME: *2 hours*

INGREDIENTS (*for 6–8*):
2 bunches watercress
¾ pound potatoes
1 onion
5 cups brown stock or bouillon
3 tablespoons butter
1 bay leaf
1 clove garlic (optional)
Salt and black pepper
¼ cup heavy cream
GARNISH:
Grated nutmeg (optional)

Wash the watercress thoroughly in cold water and discard any tough stalks and yellow leaves. Peel and thickly slice the potatoes and the onion. Put the potatoes, onion, watercress, stock, butter, bay leaf, and peeled garlic (if used) in a saucepan. Season with salt and pepper.

Bring the soup to a boil, cover the pan with a lid, and simmer until the potatoes and onion are quite soft. Remove the bay leaf and rub the soup through a coarse sieve. Alternatively, let the soup cool a little before puréeing it in the blender.

Return the smooth soup to the pan, stir in the cream, and heat the soup through without boiling. Pour into bowls and allow to cool before chilling in the refrigerator.

Just before serving, sprinkle a little freshly grated nutmeg over the chilled soup. Serve with homemade Melba toast (p.300).

FRESH ASPARAGUS

In April, fresh asparagus from California appears in the markets in abundance. The season lasts through June, as East Coast asparagus supplements the supply. To preserve color and flavor, do not overcook.

PREPARATION TIME: *10 minutes*
COOKING TIME: *20–30 minutes*

INGREDIENTS (*for 4*):

2 pounds asparagus
6–8 ounces melted butter or 8 tablespoons olive oil

2 tablespoons white wine vinegar
Salt and black pepper

Wash the asparagus carefully to remove any traces of sand. Using a vegetable peeler, peel the lower parts of the stalks, away from the tips. If the stalks are woody toward the base, trim off the wood, keeping the stems at a uniform length.

Tie the asparagus in bundles of 10–12, using soft string so as not to damage the stalks. Bring a large pan of lightly salted water to a boil. Place the bundles of asparagus upright in it, with the tips above the water. Time of cooking varies according to the age, size, and length of the asparagus, but as a general rule asparagus is cooked when the tips are soft to the touch.

Untie the asparagus and drain carefully without breaking the tips. Serve the asparagus on individual plates, either warm, with melted butter, or cold, with a mixture of the olive oil and vinegar. Asparagus is most easily eaten with the fingers. Dip the tips in the melted butter or dressing and leave any woody parts of the stems.

ASPARAGUS IN MORNAY SAUCE

Cook the asparagus as described above. Drain them carefully, without breaking the tips, and save 2 tablespoons of the asparagus water for use in the sauce. Make the sauce as follows:

INGREDIENTS (*for 4*):

2 tablespoons butter
4 tablespoons all-purpose flour
1¼ cups milk
2 tablespoons asparagus water

2 tablespoons heavy cream
1 cup grated Cheddar cheese
Salt and black pepper

Melt the butter in a saucepan, add the flour, and cook this roux* for a few minutes until thoroughly blended. Gradually stir in the milk until the sauce is smooth and has thickened. Blend in the asparagus water and cream. Grate the cheese and add all but ¼ cup to the sauce.

Season to taste with salt and freshly ground pepper.

Put the drained asparagus in a buttered ovenproof serving dish and pour the sauce over them. Sprinkle with the remaining cheese and put the dish under a hot broiler until bubbly and brown on top.

MARINATED HERRINGS

In Germany and Scandinavia fresh, smoked, or salted herrings are firm favorites as a first course. They are usually steeped for a few days in a spicy dressing. Small mackerel may be substituted for the herring.

PREPARATION TIME: *35 minutes*
MARINATING TIME: *48 hours*
COOKING TIME: *15–20 minutes*

INGREDIENTS (*for 6*):
6 large herrings
2 cups cider vinegar
3 juniper berries
6 cloves
1 bay leaf
5 peppercorns
2 large onions
6 teaspoons Düsseldorf mustard
2 dill pickles

Put the vinegar, 2 cups of water, juniper berries, cloves, bay leaf, and peppercorns in a saucepan and bring to a boil. Simmer this marinade* for 10 minutes, then leave to cool.

Gut and clean the herrings;* remove the heads and backbones but not the tails. Wash the herrings and dry them thoroughly on paper towels. Peel the onions, slice thinly, and separate the slices into rings. Open the herrings out flat and spread 1 teaspoon of mustard over the inside of each. Cut each pickle into 3 slices lengthwise and place a piece of pickle crosswise at the head end of each herring. Arrange a few of the smaller onion rings down the length of the body and roll each herring from head to tail, securing it with toothpicks.

Arrange the herring rolls in a baking dish and pour the strained marinade over them. Sprinkle with the remaining onion rings. Cover the dish with foil and bake the herrings for 15 minutes in the center of an oven preheated to 350°F. Let them cool in the marinade, then place them in the refrigerator to marinate for 2 days.

Remove the toothpicks and serve the herrings with thin slices of pumpernickel or rye bread.

ARTICHOKES WITH HOLLANDAISE SAUCE

The medium or large California artichokes are perfect for this dish. They could also be served cold, with vinaigrette sauce.

PREPARATION TIME: *30 minutes*
COOKING TIME: *about 45 minutes*

INGREDIENTS (*for 6*):
6 artichokes
1 teaspoon salt
1 cup Hollandaise sauce (p.303)

Wash the artichokes thoroughly under cold running water. Pull off any outer ragged leaves, cut off the top leaves, and snip off the sharp points of the remaining leaves with scissors. Trim the stalks of the artichokes so that they stand level. Bring a large pan of water to a boil, add the salt and the artichokes, and cover with a lid. Cook for 25–45 minutes, depending on size, or until a leaf pulls off easily. Drain the artichokes upside down.

Meanwhile, make the Hollandaise sauce and keep it hot.

Remove the bunch of small undeveloped center leaves and the fuzzy choke from each artichoke. Stand the artichokes on individual serving plates and serve the Hollandaise sauce in a bowl. Provide finger bowls, and side plates for the discarded leaves.

TOMATO ICE

The Italians invented the water ice, or sorbet, which is an iced and sweetened fruit juice. This adaptation of a sorbet makes a refreshing beginning to a meal.

PREPARATION TIME: *10 minutes*
COOKING TIME: *25 minutes*
FREEZING TIME: *4 hours*

INGREDIENTS (*for 6*):
3 pounds ripe tomatoes
1 small onion
2 teaspoons marjoram
1 tablespoon tomato purée
Juice of 1 lemon
1 teaspoon sugar
GARNISH:
Mint, lemon, or cucumber

Wash, dry, and coarsely chop the tomatoes. Peel and coarsely chop the onion. Put the tomatoes, onion, and marjoram in a large saucepan. Bring to a boil, cover with a tight-fitting lid, and simmer over low heat for 25 minutes, or until the tomatoes are soft. Stir occasionally with a wooden spoon to prevent the tomatoes from sticking to the pan. Rub the mixture through a sieve or whirl in a blender. Place in a large bowl and stir in the tomato purée, lemon juice, and sugar. Leave the mixture to cool. Spoon it into ice cube trays and freeze for at least 4 hours or overnight.

Turn the mixture out when frozen solid, crush it with a rolling pin, and pile the tomato crystals into individual serving glasses. Garnish with sprigs of mint, or lemon or cucumber slices.

AVOCADO AND CITRUS SALAD

Slightly overripe avocados mixed with citrus fruit provide a tangy first course. Alternatively, serve the salad with cold ham, chicken, or shellfish.

PREPARATION TIME: *30 minutes*

INGREDIENTS (*for 4–6*):
3 large avocados
Juice of 1 small lemon
1 large grapefruit
1 large orange
Sugar (optional)
GARNISH:
Orange segments
Mint

Peel the avocados with a silver or stainless-steel knife to prevent discoloration of the flesh. Cut them into quarters and remove the pits; cut the flesh into thin sections and pour the lemon juice over them. Cut a slice from the top and bottom of the grapefruit and orange. Peel the fruit, cutting away all the white pith underneath. With a sharp knife, cut between the flesh and segment skins; put the flesh into a large bowl and squeeze the segment skins over the fruit so that no juice is wasted.

Carefully blend the avocado and lemon juice with the citrus fruits; sweeten to taste if necessary. Spoon the mixture into individual serving dishes and garnish with orange segments and sprigs of mint.

Fish

FISH BRAISED IN WHITE WINE

This method of cooking produces a moist fish and a delicious stock for making the rich sauce.

PREPARATION TIME: *20 minutes*
COOKING TIME: *50 minutes*

INGREDIENTS (*for 4–6*):
1 3–4 pound red snapper
2 carrots, diced
1 stalk celery, diced
1 large onion, thinly sliced
6 tablespoons butter
1½ cups dry white wine
1 cup chicken stock
4 tablespoons flour
2 tablespoons dry sherry
3 tablespoons heavy cream
Salt and pepper

Clean the fish and remove the head and tail. Sauté the vegetables in 4 tablespoons of the butter in the bottom of a fish poacher or a roasting pan for 5 minutes. Put the fish on a rack in the poacher or on a sheet of foil (for lifting the fish out easily when done).

Add the wine and stock. Bring to a boil, reduce to a simmer, and cook 5–8 minutes per pound of fish, or until the fish flakes when tested with a fork. When the fish is done, place on a platter and set in a warm oven.

Strain the cooking liquids into a saucepan and discard the vegetables; reduce* the liquid to 2 cups.

Melt the remaining 2 tablespoons of butter in a skillet, add the flour, and cook, stirring, for 2 minutes. Add the 2 cups of reduced liquid to the skillet, and cook, stirring constantly, until thickened. Add the sherry and cream. Season to taste with salt and pepper.

Serve the sauce separately.

LOBSTER THERMIDOR

Lobster is the most expensive of all shellfish but is considered the most delicious. This French recipe for lobster in a rich sauce comes from the famous Café de Paris.

PREPARATION TIME: *50 minutes*
COOKING TIME: *25 minutes*

INGREDIENTS (*for 6*):
3 cooked lobsters, each 1¼–1½ pounds
1 cup fish stock
½ cup dry white wine
1 onion
4 peppercorns
1 bay leaf
1 sprig thyme
Salt and black pepper
2 cups milk
¼ pound unsalted butter
6 tablespoons flour
1 teaspoon Dijon mustard
2 large egg yolks
½ cup light cream
1 teaspoon lemon juice
¾ cup grated Parmesan cheese
1 cup browned bread crumbs
GARNISH:
Lettuce

Pour the fish stock* and white wine into a saucepan, bring to a boil, and boil briskly until the liquid has reduced* to ½ cup. Peel the onion, cut it into quarters, and put it in another saucepan, with the peppercorns, bay leaf, thyme, a pinch of salt, and the milk. Bring to a boil, remove the pan from the heat, cover with a lid, and allow the milk to infuse* for about 30 minutes.

Meanwhile, remove the claws from the lobsters;* split each body in half lengthwise, through the head and tail and along the center line of the shell. Set the shells aside with the feeler claws intact. Discard the gray sac in the head and the black intestinal tube in the body.

Rub any loose coral, or roe, through a fine sieve. Remove the meat from the shells and the claws and cut it carefully into ¾-inch cubes. Melt 4 tablespoons of the butter in a shallow skillet and gently sauté the lobster meat, turning it frequently, for 3–4 minutes. Remove the skillet from the heat and set aside.

Melt the remaining butter in a saucepan, stir in the flour, and cook gently for 2 minutes; remove the pan

from the heat. Strain the infused milk through a fine sieve and gradually stir this and the reduced fish stock into the roux.* Bring this sauce to a boil, stirring continuously, and cook gently for 3 minutes or until the sauce thickens. Allow it to cool for 2 minutes, then stir in the mustard, egg yolks, sieved coral, and the cream. Season with salt and pepper and stir in the lemon juice.

Coat the inside of the empty lobster shells with a little of the sauce. Stir half the remaining sauce into the lobster in the pan and carefully spoon the mixture into the shells. Cover with the remaining sauce; mix the grated cheese with the bread crumbs and sprinkle over the lobsters. Place the shells under a hot broiler and broil until the cheese topping is golden brown.

Serve the lobster on a bed of lettuce with crisp French bread and a tossed green salad.

FISH SOUFFLÉ

Fillets of flounder or cod, fresh or frozen, are delicious when made into pies and soufflés and served with a classic mousseline sauce.

PREPARATION TIME: *30 minutes*
COOKING TIME: *1 hour*

INGREDIENTS (*for 4–6*):
1 pound fresh or frozen fish fillets
Salt and black pepper
1 small bay leaf
Pinch of mace
½ cup milk
6 tablespoons unsalted butter
6 tablespoons flour
Nutmeg
4 large eggs
MOUSSELINE SAUCE:
Juice of ½ large lemon
2 large egg yolks
¼ pound unsalted butter
Salt and black pepper
4 tablespoons heavy cream

Put the fillets into a saucepan and cover with 2 cups cold water. Add ½ teaspoon of salt, the bay leaf, and mace to the fish, and cover the pan with a lid. Bring slowly to a simmer, turn off the heat, and leave the pan to stand for 10 minutes. Lift out the fish with a slotted spoon; set aside 1½ cups of the liquid and add ½ cup of milk to make 2 cups.

Flake* the fish coarsely. Melt 6 tablespoons of the butter in a large saucepan and stir in the flour. Cook this roux* over low heat for 2 minutes, stirring continuously, then gradually stir in the fish and milk liquid. Bring to a boil, still stirring, and cook for 2 minutes or until the mixture is thick and smooth. Season to taste with salt, freshly ground pepper, and nutmeg. Carefully fold the flaked fish into the sauce. Separate the 4 eggs and beat the yolks into the fish mixture, one by one; beat the egg whites until stiff, then gently fold them in as well.

Spoon the mixture into a prepared 1½-quart soufflé dish;* cook in the center of a preheated oven at 400°F for 45 minutes, or until the soufflé is risen and golden brown on top.

For the sauce, put the lemon juice and 1 teaspoon of cold water in a bowl. Beat the egg yolks lightly and stir them into the lemon juice. Stand the bowl over a saucepan of gently simmering water, but do not allow the bottom of the bowl to touch the water. Stir in 1 tablespoon of butter and whisk the mixture until thick.

Remove the bowl from the heat and gradually whisk in the remaining butter, cut into small pieces. Whisk until each piece of butter is completely absorbed before adding the next piece. Season to taste with salt and pepper. Whip the cream and fold it gently into the sauce. Heat the sauce in the top of a double boiler over simmering water, whisking all the time (do not allow the sauce to boil).

Serve the soufflé immediately, with the mousseline sauce served separately in a sauceboat. A green vegetable, such as broccoli, or an endive and beet salad could be served with the soufflé.

HALIBUT AU GRATIN

The delicate flavor of this white-fleshed fish is best retained through simple cooking.

PREPARATION TIME: *15 minutes*
COOKING TIME: *35 minutes*

INGREDIENTS (*for 6*):
1 halibut steak, 1½–2 inches thick
  (about 3 pounds)
1½ cups fish stock (p.298)
2 tablespoons unsalted butter
4 tablespoons flour
½ cup milk
Salt and black pepper
1 large egg yolk
2 tablespoons heavy cream
1 cup grated Cheddar cheese

Put the halibut in a large baking dish. Pour in the fish stock, adding water if necessary, to just cover the fish. Cover the dish with a piece of buttered foil and poach in a pre-heated oven at 350°F for 20 minutes, or until the fish flakes when tested.

Remove the fish from the oven, drain, and arrange on a hot oven-proof serving dish. Strain the fish liquid through cheesecloth. Melt the butter in a saucepan, stir in the flour, and cook for 2 minutes.

Gradually stir in the fish liquid and milk, bring the sauce to a boil, and cook over low heat, stirring continuously, for 2 minutes. Season to taste with salt and freshly ground pepper; remove from the heat. Lightly beat the egg yolk with the cream, blend in a little of the hot sauce, and stir the egg into the sauce; pour it over the fish.

Sprinkle the grated cheese over the sauce and put the dish under a hot broiler for 5–10 minutes, or until the cheese is bubbly brown on top.

Serve the gratin from the dish, with buttered new potatoes and broccoli spears.

COD PIE

This dish makes the most of a small amount of cod. Any other white fish, such as haddock, combines well with the spicy ingredients and pastry.

PREPARATION TIME: *45 minutes*
COOKING TIME: *35 minutes*

INGREDIENTS (*for 4*):
1 pound cod or similar white fish
Salt and black pepper
1 pound tomatoes
1 small clove garlic
1 small green pepper
1 large onion
2 tablespoons oil
1 tablespoon finely chopped parsley
1 bay leaf
½ recipe standard pastry (p.354)
1 small egg, beaten

Put the cod in a saucepan with salt, freshly ground pepper, and enough water to barely cover the fish. Bring to just below a boil and simmer for 10 minutes. Peel and seed the tomatoes* and chop them coarsely. Peel and coarsely chop the garlic. Wash the pepper, remove the stalk end, inner ribs, and all seeds, and chop the flesh into small pieces. Peel and coarsely chop the onion.

Heat the oil in a skillet and sauté the chopped onion and pepper over low heat for 5–10 minutes. Stir in the tomatoes, garlic, parsley, and crumbled bay leaf and cook for a further 5 minutes. Season to taste with salt and freshly ground pepper. Lift the fish from the liquid, remove all skin and bones, and flake* the flesh into the tomato mixture; put it into a deep 8-inch-diameter baking dish.

On a floured surface, roll out the prepared pastry to a circle to fit the dish. Cover the fish with the pastry and make a slit in the center to allow the steam to escape. Use the pastry trimmings to decorate the pie.* Brush the pastry and the decorations with the beaten egg.

Bake the pie in the center of a preheated oven at 425°F for 30–35 minutes or until golden brown. The hot pie can be served by itself, with a tossed green salad, or with a green vegetable.

Meat

BAKED HADDOCK

Haddock can be cooked in the same way as cod, but flavoring is essential.

PREPARATION TIME: *10 minutes*
COOKING TIME: *40 minutes*

INGREDIENTS (*for* 6):
6 haddock fillets
Salt and black pepper
Juice of ½ large lemon
3 tablespoons cooking oil
16-ounce can tomatoes
1 large onion
1 clove garlic
1 small green pepper
Marjoram

Arrange the fillets in a single layer in a large buttered baking dish. Sprinkle them with salt, freshly ground pepper, and the strained lemon juice. Add 1 tablespoon of the cooking oil and cover the dish with buttered foil. Bake in the center of a preheated oven at 350°F for 20 minutes, or until the fish flakes easily when tested with a fork.

Meanwhile, chop the tomatoes; peel and finely chop the onion and the garlic. Wash the pepper, remove the stalk end, ribs, and seeds; chop the flesh into small pieces. Heat 2 tablespoons of the cooking oil in a large skillet. Add the onion, garlic, and pepper and sauté over low heat for 5 minutes. Blend in the tomatoes; season to taste with salt, freshly ground pepper, and marjoram. Simmer for a further 10 minutes. Remove the fish from the oven and drain off most of the liquid. Pour the cooked onion and tomato mixture over the fish and return the dish to the oven for about 10 minutes.

Serve from the dish, with rice and a green vegetable.

VEAL WITH ORANGE

A fruity stuffing and sauce laced with red wine add extra flavor to veal.

PREPARATION TIME: *20 minutes*
COOKING TIME: *2½ hours*

INGREDIENTS (*for* 6):
4–5 pounds boned breast of veal
2 cups fresh white bread crumbs
⅓ cup raisins
⅓ cup black currants
*½ cup shredded or very finely
    chopped beef suet*
Salt and black pepper
Nutmeg
2 large oranges
1 large egg yolk or 2 small yolks
4 tablespoons lard
1 tablespoon cornstarch
6 tablespoons red wine

Prepare the stuffing first by mixing the bread crumbs, raisins, currants, suet, and a pinch each of salt, freshly ground black pepper, and nutmeg together in a bowl. Finely grate the rind from the oranges and add to the stuffing, together with the lightly beaten egg yolk. Stir in enough cold water to bind the mixture.

Spread the stuffing over the boned veal, roll it up, and tie with thin string at 1-inch intervals. Put the meat in a roasting pan, add the lard, and roast the meat for 2½ hours in the center of an oven preheated to 400°F. Baste* occasionally and cover the meat with aluminum foil if it browns too quickly.

Put the meat on a serving dish and keep it warm in the oven. Skim all the fat from the juices in the roasting pan. Pour the juices into a small saucepan and reheat them. Blend the cornstarch with 1 tablespoon of cold water and add to the juices, stirring continuously until the sauce has

thickened. Bring to a boil and season to taste with salt, freshly ground pepper, sugar, and nutmeg. Stir in the red wine and simmer the sauce gently. Remove the white pith from the oranges and cut the flesh into small sections. Add these to the sauce and cook until heated through.

Cut the veal into thick slices and arrange them on a warmed serving dish; serve the sauce separately. A green salad, sautéed potatoes, and small white onions would go well with this roast.

STUFFED FLANK STEAK

Flank steak stuffed with tomatoes, mushrooms, and herbs makes a hearty main course for a family meal.

PREPARATION TIME: *40 minutes*
COOKING TIME: *2 hours*

INGREDIENTS (*for 6*):
1 2-pound flank steak
2 tablespoons butter
1 cup chopped onion
2 cloves garlic, minced
¼ pound mushrooms, chopped
1 cup drained canned tomatoes, chopped
¼ cup chopped parsley
2 cups soft bread crumbs
½ teaspoon oregano
½ teaspoon basil
1 teaspoon salt
½ teaspoon pepper
1 egg, slightly beaten
Vegetable oil
½ cup red wine

Preheat oven to 350°F. Score* the steak on both sides. Melt the butter in a skillet, add the onions and garlic, and cook over low heat for 5 minutes. Add the mushrooms and cook for 3 minutes more. Add the tomatoes, parsley, bread crumbs, seasonings, and egg. Blend well and spread this mixture on the steak. Roll the meat lengthwise, as for a jelly roll, and tie in several places with string.

In a flameproof casserole, brown the meat on both sides in a little oil. Add the wine, cover, and bake for 2 hours. To serve, cut the steak into 1-inch slices and serve with the liquids from the casserole.

PORK AND SPINACH PÂTÉ

This light, colorful pâté can be served hot or cold, as a buffet dish or as an hors d'oeuvre.

PREPARATION TIME: *20 minutes*
COOKING TIME: *1 hour 20 minutes*

INGREDIENTS (*for 8–10*):
2 pounds spinach
2 pounds ground pork shoulder
1 tablespoon salt
1 teaspoon freshly ground black pepper
1 bay leaf
¼ teaspoon ground cloves
¼ teaspoon mace

Wash the spinach well. Bring 2 cups of water to a boil in a large pot. Add the spinach, return to a boil, and cook only until the spinach has wilted, about 5 minutes. Drain and chop the spinach coarsely. Squeeze a small amount of spinach at a time in your hands to extract as much water as possible. Add the ground pork and all seasonings and stir until thoroughly blended.

Place this mixture in a 6–8 cup terrine or bread pan, cover with a piece of buttered paper, and bake at 375°F for 1¼ hours. Do not overcook, or it will become too dry. Slice and serve hot or cold.

TRIPE PROVENÇALE

Tripe is a much-neglected food in this country. The following recipe comes from southern France.

PREPARATION TIME: *20 minutes*
COOKING TIME: *2½ hours*

INGREDIENTS (*for 6*):
2 pounds honeycomb tripe
2½ cups chicken stock (p.298)
Salt and black pepper
1 onion
1 clove garlic
2 tablespoons unsalted butter
1 pound tomatoes
Dried thyme
4 tablespoons dry white wine
1 tablespoon chopped parsley

Wash the tripe thoroughly. Put it in a saucepan and cover with cold water. Bring to a boil. Remove from the heat, drain the tripe, and rinse under cold running water. Cut into 2-inch cubes and return to the saucepan. Pour in the boiling stock and add a pinch of salt. As soon as the stock is boiling again, reduce the heat. Cover the pan with a tight-fitting lid and simmer the tripe for 2 hours or until tender.

Meanwhile, peel and coarsely chop the onion, and peel and crush the garlic. Melt the butter in a skillet and gently sauté the onion and garlic until transparent, about 5 minutes. Peel and seed the tomatoes* and chop them coarsely; add them, with a pinch of dried thyme, the wine, and parsley, to the skillet. Bring this mixture to a boil over gentle heat, cover with a lid, and simmer for 30 minutes. Season to taste with salt and freshly ground black pepper. If the sauce is still thin, remove the lid and boil the sauce over high heat for about 5 minutes until it has reduced* and has thickened slightly.

When the tripe has finished cooking, drain it and stir it into the tomato mixture. Cook over low heat for a further 10 minutes. Arrange the tripe on a hot serving dish and surround it with cooked rice.

LAMB WITH WINE SAUCE

Traditionally, this Russian dish is served with *kasha,* or buckwheat groats, which have a coarse texture and nutty flavor.

PREPARATION TIME: *30 minutes*
COOKING TIME: *3¾ hours*

INGREDIENTS (*for 6*):
3-pound piece of boned leg of lamb
1 large carrot
1 large onion
Salt
5 peppercorns
1 bay leaf
2 tablespoons unsalted butter
4 tablespoons flour
½ teaspoon sugar
Juice of ½ lemon
½ cup dry red wine
1 large egg yolk

Bone the lamb, rinse the bones in cold water, and put them in a large saucepan. Cut the lamb into 6 even slices, trim away as much fat as possible, and add this to the pan. Cover the bones with cold water and bring to a boil. Remove the scum, then cover the pan with a lid and simmer for 2 hours. Strain this stock through a fine sieve or cheesecloth.

Put the lamb slices in a large saucepan and pour in enough of the stock to cover the meat. Bring to a boil, strain the liquid through cheesecloth, and pour it back over the lamb slices. Peel the carrot and the onion and add them whole to the pan. Cover with a lid and simmer the lamb for 1½ hours or until it is tender. Add a pinch of salt, the peppercorns, and bay leaf and simmer for a further 5 minutes.

For the sauce, melt the butter in a saucepan, stir in the flour, and cook for 2 minutes. Gradually add 1¼ cups strained lamb stock, the sugar, lemon juice, and wine. Bring the sauce to a boil, stirring continuously, then simmer for 3 minutes. Let the sauce cool a little, then beat in the egg yolk. Reheat the sauce gently, but do not allow it to boil, or the sauce will curdle. Drain the lamb slices thoroughly and arrange them on a hot serving dish. Pour the wine sauce into a sauceboat and serve it separately.

KIDNEYS IN SAUCE CRÉOLE

Sauce Créole, the classic sauce of the West Indies, is composed mainly of sweet peppers, tomatoes, and fiery Tabasco sauce. It is usually served as a garnish with rice.

PREPARATION TIME: *15 minutes*
COOKING TIME: *20–25 minutes*

INGREDIENTS (*for 4–6*):
1¼ pounds veal or pork kidneys
1 small onion
1 clove garlic
1 small green pepper
2 teaspoons capers
4 tablespoons unsalted butter or 2 tablespoons olive oil
16-ounce can tomatoes
1 teaspoon light brown sugar
1 tablespoon chili sauce
Salt
Tabasco sauce
Lemon juice
6–8 black olives

Peel off the transparent skin surrounding the kidneys and cut them into slices about ¼ inch thick. Snip out the white cores with scissors. Peel and thinly slice the onion. Peel the garlic. Wash the green pepper, remove the stalk and the seeds, and chop the flesh. Chop the capers.

Heat the butter or oil in a heavy-bottomed pan and sauté the onion over moderate heat until soft and transparent. Turn up the heat, add the sliced kidneys, and sauté them for 3–4 minutes or until browned, stirring frequently. Remove the pan from the heat. With a slotted spoon, remove the kidneys to a colander or sieve to drain for about 5 minutes.

Crush the garlic into the pan and add the chopped tomatoes with their juices, the chopped green pepper, and capers. Stir in the sugar and chili sauce, and season to taste with salt, Tabasco, and lemon juice. Return the kidneys to the pan but discard the juices.

Cover the pan with a lid or aluminum foil and simmer over low heat for 10–15 minutes. Meanwhile, halve and pit the olives and add them to the kidneys.

Spoon the kidneys and the créole sauce over noodles tossed in butter. A crisp green salad could be served as a side dish.

HAM IN PUFF PASTRY

A shank end of ham makes an impressive entrée. It serves more people when encased in puff pastry, which keeps the meat moist.

PREPARATION TIME: *30 minutes*
COOKING TIME: *1 hour 10 minutes*

INGREDIENTS (*for 6*):
Shank end of a smoked ham
1 large bay leaf
12 peppercorns
Pinch of mace or nutmeg
4–6 parsley stalks
2 sprigs thyme
1 small onion
Puff pastry (p.363)
1 egg

Ask the butcher to bone part of the ham, leaving the end bone in to make carving easier.

Wash and scrub the ham well and place it in a large kettle. Cover with cold water and add the bay leaf, peppercorns, mace or nutmeg, parsley stalks, thyme, and onion. Bring to a boil, turn down the heat, then cover the pan with a lid and simmer for 20 minutes per pound. Remove the pan from the heat and let the ham cool in the cooking liquid.

Remove the ham from the liquid and carefully remove the skin and excess fat. Roll out the puff pastry to an oblong shape, ⅛ inch thick, and place the ham in the center. Brush the pastry edges with some of the lightly beaten egg; wrap the pastry over the ham and press the edges together to enclose the meat. Seal the edges, pleating the pastry around the bone. Brush with egg.

Cover the bone with a piece of foil to protect it during cooking. Use the pastry trimmings to decorate the crust and carefully transfer the ham to a wet baking sheet. Brush the pastry with the remaining egg.

Bake the ham for 20 minutes in the center of an oven preheated to 450°F; lower the heat to 350°F and continue cooking for another 30 minutes. Cover the crust with buttered waxed paper as soon as the pastry is golden.

Serve hot or cold. A rice salad (p.336), boiled new potatoes, and a purée of spinach are suitable accompaniments to this dish.

LAMB KEBABS

Though lamb kebabs are usually grilled over charcoal, which imparts a delicious flavor to the meat, they are also good broiled.

PREPARATION TIME: *20 minutes*
MARINATING TIME: *30 minutes*
COOKING TIME: *10 minutes*

INGREDIENTS (*for 4*):
1½ pounds boned shoulder of lamb
1-inch piece ginger root
½ cup yogurt
¼ teaspoon ground coriander
¼ teaspoon ground cumin
¼ teaspoon finely chopped fresh or canned green chili
1 clove garlic
Juice of ½ lemon
1 teaspoon salt
GARNISH:
Lemon wedges
Mint

Trim any excess fat from the lamb and cut it into 1-inch cubes. Peel the ginger and chop it coarsely. Put the yogurt in a large bowl and stir in the coriander, cumin, chili, and ginger. Peel the garlic and crush it into the yogurt before adding the lemon juice and salt. Mix the lamb into the yogurt and let it marinate* for at least 30 minutes.

Remove the lamb chunks from the marinade and thread them onto 4 steel skewers, 8–10 inches long, packing the pieces closely together. Put the skewers under a hot broiler and broil, turning from time to time, for 8–10 minutes, or until the lamb is browned on the outside and pink in the center.

Arrange the lamb on skewers on a bed of spiced rice (p.181) garnished with lemon wedges and sprigs of fresh mint.

Poultry

BEEF WITH PEPPERS

The addition of ginger in this dish provides a taste of the Orient.

PREPARATION TIME: *10 minutes*
COOKING TIME: *1¼ hours*

INGREDIENTS (*for 4–6*):
1½ pounds sirloin tip or round of beef
3 tablespoons butter
1 tablespoon vegetable oil
2 medium green peppers
½ pound mushrooms, sliced
2 tablespoons potato starch or cornstarch
1½ cups beef stock
3 tablespoons white vinegar
1 tablespoon sugar
Salt and pepper
¼ teaspoon powdered ginger (optional)

Trim all fat and sinew from the meat and cut it across the grain into strips about ⅛ inch thick and 2 inches long.
Heat 1 tablespoon of the butter and the oil in a heavy skillet and brown half the meat at a time over high heat. Cover with a tight-fitting lid and simmer 40 minutes, or until the meat is tender.
Core, seed, and cut the green peppers into 1-inch strips. Heat the remaining 2 tablespoons of butter in another skillet and sauté the peppers and mushrooms over high heat for 5 minutes, then add to the meat and juices in the skillet.
Blend the cornstarch or potato starch with ¼ cup of cold water. Remove the skillet from the heat and stir this mixture into the meat. Add the beef stock and cook, stirring, until the liquid comes to a boil.
Add the vinegar and sugar. Taste and add more sugar, if desired, but only a teaspoon at a time. Season with salt and pepper and add the powdered ginger, if desired.
Simmer uncovered for about 10 minutes, or until the peppers are tender. Serve with plain boiled rice.

PORK WITH LEMON

In Portugal, where this recipe originates, the quality of pork is generally inferior to that of the dairy-fed pigs in this country. The Portuguese housewife cooks lean pork fillet in a spicy wine sauce.

PREPARATION TIME: *20 minutes*
COOKING TIME: *25–30 minutes*

INGREDIENTS (*for 4–6*):
2 pounds pork fillet
2 tablespoons lard
1 cup dry white wine
4 teaspoons ground cumin
2 cloves garlic
Salt and black pepper
6 slices lemon
2 teaspoons ground coriander

Trim any fat and the thin outer skin from the pork fillet* and cut the meat into 1-inch cubes. Heat the lard in a large skillet and brown the meat, turning it continuously to prevent it from sticking to the pan. Stir in just over ½ cup of the wine and add the cumin. Peel the garlic and crush it over the meat; season to taste with salt and freshly ground pepper. Bring the mixture to a boil, lower the heat, and simmer for about 25 minutes or until tender. Add the remaining wine; cut the lemon slices into quarters and add them to the pan. Continue cooking, stirring, until the sauce thickens slightly. Stir in the coriander.
Spoon the meat and the sauce onto a serving dish. Rice is traditionally served with the pork.

STEAK DIANE

This famous dish originated in Australia, where tender beef fillet is considered obligatory. Prime or choice rump steak may be substituted, however.

PREPARATION TIME: *20 minutes*
COOKING TIME: *10 minutes*

INGREDIENTS (*for 6*):
1½ pounds rump of beef
1 small onion
1 large lemon
12 tablespoons unsalted butter
Worcestershire sauce
1 tablespoon chopped parsley
2 tablespoons brandy

Trim the rump steak and cut it into 6 uniform pieces; beat them flat with a rolling pin until they are no more than ¼ inch thick. Peel and finely chop the onion. Grate the lemon rind finely, squeeze out the juice, strain, and set aside.
Melt 4 tablespoons of the butter in a large, heavy skillet and sauté the onion for about 5 minutes or until soft and transparent. With a slotted spoon, transfer the onion to a plate and keep warm. Sauté 2 steaks at a time over high heat for 1 minute only on each side. Remove the steaks and keep them hot.
Melt another 4 tablespoons of butter until foaming and sauté 2 more steaks; repeat with the remaining meat. Return the onions to the pan, stir in the lemon rind and juice, a few drops of Worcestershire sauce, and the parsley. Cook lightly, then put in the steaks. Pour in the warm brandy and ignite.
Serve the steaks at once on a hot serving dish, with the onion and brandy poured over them. Sautéed potatoes and braised celery (p.109) are suitable vegetables.

CHICKEN PIES

These small pies, with a savory filling, are deep-fried until golden and crisp. They are excellent, hot or cold, for picnics and school lunches.

PREPARATION TIME: *30 minutes*
COOKING TIME: *20 minutes*

INGREDIENTS (*for 10–12 pies*):
½ recipe standard pastry (p.354)
1½ cups skinned, boned, finely diced cooked chicken
1 tablespoon tomato ketchup
1 tablespoon mayonnaise
Worcestershire sauce
Dry mustard
Salt and black pepper
Oil for deep-frying

On a floured surface, roll out the pastry ¼ inch thick and cut out 10–12 circles with a 4-inch round cutter. Mix the chicken with ketchup, mayonnaise, and a few drops of Worcestershire sauce. Season to taste with the dry mustard, salt, and freshly ground pepper.
Spoon the chicken mixture onto half of each pastry round and moisten the edges with water. Fold over the pastry and press the edges tightly together, sealing them with the back of a fork.
Heat the oil* in the deep-fryer and fry the pies, three or more at a time, for 5–10 minutes, or until the pastry is golden brown and crisp. Drain the pies on paper towels.
The pies can be served while still warm, with buttered new potatoes, beans, or peas.

CHICKEN CHAUD-FROID

This is a classic French dish of whole cooked chicken, coated with chaud-froid sauce and elaborately garnished. However, individual chicken breasts are more convenient to serve than a whole chicken.

PREPARATION TIME: *1 hour*
COOKING TIME: *50–55 minutes*

INGREDIENTS (*for 6*):
6 half breasts of chicken
1 large onion
1 sprig thyme
1 small bay leaf
1 small carrot
6 parsley stalks
6 peppercorns
¼ teaspoon salt
1 cup milk
2 tablespoons unsalted butter
2 tablespoons flour
Salt and black pepper
1 envelope plain gelatin
3 tablespoons cold clarified chicken stock
GARNISH:
Cucumber peel
1 large tomato
1 small green pepper
Peel of 1 small lemon
1 cup aspic

Put the chicken breasts in a large saucepan. Peel the onion, cut off a 1-inch slice, and add the larger piece to the pan together with the thyme, bay leaf, and enough cold water to cover the chicken. Bring slowly to a boil, remove the scum, and cover the pan with a lid. Simmer for 20–25 minutes, or until the meat is tender. Lift out the chicken and drain.
Scrape the carrot, leaving it whole, and put it in a saucepan with the onion slice, parsley stalks, peppercorns, salt, and milk. Bring the

Rice & Pasta

mixture slowly to a boil, then turn off the heat and leave the milk to infuse* for 30 minutes.

Melt the butter in a saucepan, stir in the flour, and cook for 2 minutes. Strain the infused milk and gradually stir it into the butter and flour roux.* Bring the sauce to a boil over low heat, stirring continuously, and cook gently for 2 minutes. Season the sauce to taste with salt and freshly ground pepper.

Soften the plain gelatin in the 3 tablespoons cold clear chicken stock, then gradually add it to the white sauce and stir over low heat until completely dissolved.

Remove the skin carefully from the chicken breasts, pat them dry, and place on a wire rack. Cool the

sauce, or stir over cracked ice, until it has thickened slightly and is about to congeal. Coat each chicken breast carefully with the chaud-froid sauce, allowing any excess to run off. Leave for 15 minutes to set.

Cut a 1-inch piece of cucumber peel, the tomato, pepper, and lemon peel into narrow strips. Melt the aspic* in a pan, then stir over a bowl of ice until it starts to thicken. Dip the strips of peel in the aspic and arrange them in decorative patterns on the chicken pieces. Allow the decorations to set before spooning the remaining aspic over the chicken. Leave the chicken in the refrigerator until it has set completely.

Salads or French bread could be served with the chicken.

SHRIMP RING

A small amount of shrimp, lobster, or rock lobster tails can be stretched to make a family meal by combining the shellfish with rice and vegetables.

PREPARATION TIME: *30 minutes*
COOKING TIME: *30 minutes*

INGREDIENTS (*for 4*):
½ *pound shelled cooked shrimp*
2 *tablespoons olive oil*
2 *cups rice*
1½ *chicken bouillon cubes*
3 *tablespoons unsalted butter*
6 *tablespoons flour*
2½ *cups milk*
1 *cup cooked peas*
1 *cup whole-kernel corn*
Salt and pepper
GARNISH:
1 *tablespoon chopped parsley*
Lemon wedges

Heat the oil in a large, deep skillet, add the rice, and sauté for 5 minutes, stirring continuously. Dissolve the bouillon cubes in 4 cups of boiling water and stir into the pan. Bring to a boil, cover, and simmer the rice for 25 minutes or until it is tender and has absorbed all the liquid.

While the rice is cooking, melt the butter in a saucepan, stir in the flour, and cook for 2 minutes. Remove the pan from the heat and gradually stir in the milk until the sauce is smooth.

Return the sauce to the heat and bring to a boil, stirring all the time, until it thickens. Cook gently for 2 minutes more, then stir in the shrimp, peas, and corn; season to taste with salt and freshly ground pepper. Heat this mixture through over low heat without boiling. Butter a ring mold and pack the rice firmly into it. Allow the rice to set, then unmold the ring carefully on a

serving plate. Fill the center with the shrimp mixture and pour any extra over the rice.

Garnish with parsley and lemon wedges and serve the rice ring on its own or with a green salad.

FETTUCCINE IN CREAM

Many Italians eat fettuccine for their midday meal. It is usually served simply, tossed in butter and cheese or in heavy cream.

PREPARATION TIME: *5 minutes*
COOKING TIME: *12 minutes*

INGREDIENTS (*for 6*):
1 *pound fettuccine*
¼ *pound unsalted butter*
1 *cup heavy cream*
Salt and black pepper

Cook the fettuccine for about 12 minutes in plenty of boiling salted water, preferably in 2 or 3 pans, as the pasta needs space to swell. The fettuccine is cooked when a single strand is tender but firm to the bite (*al dente**). Drain the fettuccine in a colander, return it to the saucepan, and toss with the butter and cream until every strand is thoroughly coated. Season to taste with salt and freshly ground pepper. Serve immediately in a hot dish.

ORANGE RICE

Rice cooked with orange goes well with chicken or veal dishes in cream sauce. The rice can also be used cold as the basis for a salad.

PREPARATION TIME: *10 minutes*
COOKING TIME: *40 minutes*

INGREDIENTS (*for 6*):
2 *cups rice*
1 *small onion*
3 *stalks celery*
6 *tablespoons unsalted butter*
2 *large oranges*
½ *teaspoon salt*
2 *sprigs thyme or ½ teaspoon dried thyme*
Black pepper

Peel and finely chop the onion. Wash the celery and cut it into narrow slices. Melt the butter in a large skillet and sauté the onion and celery over low heat for about 5 minutes, until the onion is soft. Finely grate the rind from the oranges; squeeze the flesh and strain the juice. Add 3¾ cups cold water to the pan, together with the orange rind and juice, a pinch of salt, and the thyme. Bring this mixture to a boil.

Add the rice, bring back to a boil, and simmer until the rice is tender and the liquid absorbed, about 25 minutes.

Before serving, remove the thyme and season the rice with freshly ground pepper.

Vegetables & Salads

GNOCCHI ALLA ROMANA

Gnocchi are small dumplings made from a flour, semolina, or potato paste. The Roman gnocchi are made from semolina, but in Canada and the U.S. the semolina breakfast cereal, farina, is more easily found. The paste should be left for several hours to rest. Gnocchi are served with melted butter and plenty of grated Parmesan cheese.

PREPARATION TIME: *30 minutes*
COOKING TIME: *40 minutes*

INGREDIENTS (*for 6*):
4½ cups milk
¾ cup farina
¼ pound unsalted butter
1½ cups grated Parmesan cheese
Salt and black pepper
Grated nutmeg
3 large eggs

Heat the milk to the boiling point, then sprinkle the farina over the milk, stirring continuously. Bring the mixture slowly to a boil, still stirring; cook for 3 minutes. Remove from the heat and stir in 5 tablespoons of butter and 1 cup of the grated cheese; season to taste with salt, pepper, and nutmeg.

Lightly beat the eggs and gradually beat them into the farina mixture. Pour this paste into a buttered jelly-roll pan and spread it evenly until ½ inch thick.

Set the paste aside for several hours until it is firm and cold.

Cut the paste into 1½-inch squares with a cold, wet knife. Roll the pieces to the size and shape of walnuts (if necessary, roll them in a little farina to make shaping easier). Place them in a buttered baking dish. Sprinkle with salt and pepper. Melt the remaining butter in a saucepan and pour it over the gnocchi; sprinkle with the remaining cheese. Cook in the center of a preheated oven at 350°F for 30 minutes, or until the gnocchi are pale golden in color. Serve at once.

RATATOUILLE

Eggplant casserole or stew appears under various names in the Mediterranean countries. It is called moussaka in Greece and the Balkans and ratatouille in France.

PREPARATION TIME: *30 minutes*
COOKING TIME: *1¼ hours*

INGREDIENTS (*for 4*):
2 large zucchini
2 large eggplants
5 large tomatoes
1 large green pepper
1 small red pepper
1 large onion
2 cloves garlic
4 tablespoons olive oil
Salt and black pepper

Trim the zucchini and eggplants but do not peel them. Wash well and cut them crosswise into ¼-inch-thick slices. Put them in a colander, cover with a plate, and weight the plate down; leave for 1 hour to press out excessive moisture. Peel and seed the tomatoes* and chop them coarsely. Wash the peppers, remove the white inner ribs and all seeds, and dice the flesh. Peel and coarsely chop the onion and garlic.

Heat the olive oil in a deep flame-proof casserole and sauté the onion and garlic for 5 minutes over low heat until transparent. Add the peppers, cook for a further 10 minutes, then add the remaining ingredients and season to taste with salt and freshly ground pepper. Cover the pan with a tight-fitting lid and cook the mixture over low heat, stirring from time to time, for 1 hour, or until the vegetables are soft and the mixture thick and well blended. If the mixture is still too liquid, remove the lid and cook it down over high heat. Correct the seasoning, if necessary, with additional salt and pepper.

Serve the ratatouille hot with roast leg of lamb or broiled lamb chops, or cold with olive oil and lemon juice, as an appetizer.

ONION QUICHE

The recipe for this rich, creamy quiche comes from Alsace in France. It can be served hot or cold with a green salad for a main course, or cut into small wedges for a first course.

PREPARATION TIME: *45 minutes*
COOKING TIME: *40 minutes*

INGREDIENTS (*for 4–6*):
1 pound onions
4 tablespoons unsalted butter
1 bay leaf
Salt and pepper
¾ recipe standard pastry (p.354)
2 large eggs
Grated nutmeg
1¼ cups light cream

Peel the onions and slice them thinly. Melt the butter in a skillet and add the onions and bay leaf. Season with salt and pepper and cover the onions with a piece of buttered waxed paper. Cover the pan with a tight-fitting lid and cook the onions over low heat for 30 minutes, or until they are soft and golden. Shake the pan occasionally to prevent the onions from sticking.

Prepare the pastry and roll it out ¼ inch thick on a lightly floured surface. Line an 8–9 inch flan ring, set on a baking sheet, with the pastry. Trim the edge and prick the pastry base with a fork. Beat the eggs lightly in a large bowl and season with salt, pepper, and nutmeg. Stir in the cream. Drain the cooked onions in a colander, remove the bay leaf, and spread the onions over the pastry shell. Strain the egg mixture through a sieve over the onions.

Bake the quiche in the center of a preheated oven at 400°F for 40 minutes. When cooked, the pastry should be golden and the filling should be set; it will sink slightly as the quiche cools.

SAUTÉED LEEKS

This dish can be served hot with any lean broiled or roast meat. It can also be served as a side dish or salad with cold ham and chicken.

PREPARATION TIME: *10 minutes*
COOKING TIME: *25 minutes*

INGREDIENTS (*for 4–6*):
2 pounds leeks
4 tomatoes
6 tablespoons olive oil
2 cloves garlic
1 bay leaf
Salt and black pepper
Juice of ½ lemon

Cut away the roots and any damaged green leaves from the leeks, slice them in half lengthwise, and wash under cold running water to remove all traces of sand. Cut into 1-inch slices. Peel and seed the tomatoes.* Heat half the oil in a large skillet and add the leeks. Peel the garlic cloves and crush them over the leeks, then add the bay leaf. Season to taste with salt and freshly ground pepper.

Cover the pan with a tight-fitting lid and cook over low heat for 20 minutes. Chop the tomatoes, add them to the pan with the rest of the oil, and cook for a further 5 minutes. Remove the bay leaf. Spoon the leeks into a serving dish and sprinkle the lemon juice over them.

APPLE AND NUT SALAD

Sour cream is a refreshing dressing, less rich than mayonnaise. It is here combined with apples, raisins, nuts, and vegetables in a crisp salad to serve with cold meat.

PREPARATION TIME: *30 minutes*

INGREDIENTS (*for 4–5*):
4 crisp eating apples
3 teaspoons lemon juice
¾ cup shelled walnuts
½ cup sour cream
¼ head of a red cabbage
3 stalks celery
12 large radishes
⅓ cup raisins
Salt and black pepper

Wash and core the apples and chop them into rough chunks. Put them in a bowl and sprinkle the lemon juice over them to prevent the apples from turning brown. Chop the walnuts coarsely and set aside about ¼ cup for garnish. Pour the sour cream into a bowl and stir in the chopped apples and walnuts.

Remove any damaged and coarse outer leaves from the cabbage, wash it, and cut out the thick center stalk. Shred it finely, first one way and then the other. Wash and thinly slice the celery. Wash and trim the radishes and slice them evenly. Cut the raisins in half.

Stir all these ingredients into the sour cream and season to taste with salt and freshly ground pepper. Spoon the salad into a serving dish and garnish the top with the remaining walnuts.

ARTICHOKES WITH MUSHROOMS

Artichoke bottoms topped with mushrooms and with garlic dressing make an unusual salad to serve with cold meats and poultry. This dish can also be served as a first course.

PREPARATION TIME: *25 minutes*
COOKING TIME: *1 hour*

INGREDIENTS (*for 6*):
6 large artichokes
12 large mushrooms
6 tablespoons olive oil
3 tablespoons white wine vinegar
1 clove garlic
Salt and black pepper

Trim off the stems and rinse the artichokes* thoroughly under cold running water. Put them in a large saucepan of boiling water, cover with a lid, and boil until a leaf pulls away easily. Remove the artichokes, drain them upside down, and leave them to cool completely.

Wipe and trim the mushrooms;* cut them into slices, discarding the stalks. Pour the oil into a small bowl. Add the vinegar and peeled and crushed garlic; season to taste with salt and freshly ground pepper.

Pull off and discard all the leaves and the choke from the base of the artichokes. Set the artichoke bottoms on individual serving plates and arrange the mushroom slices on top; pour over the garlic dressing.

Desserts

IMAM BAYILDI

This Turkish dish takes its name from the *Imam*, or Muslim holy man. He is said to have swooned with pleasure after being served this delectable combination of eggplant, tomatoes, and onions.

PREPARATION TIME: *30 minutes*
COOKING TIME: *40 minutes*

INGREDIENTS (*for 6*):
3 large eggplants
Salt and black pepper
Olive oil
3 large onions
¾ pound tomatoes
1 clove garlic
½ teaspoon ground cinnamon
1 teaspoon sugar
1 tablespoon chopped parsley
1 tablespoon finely chopped pine nuts (optional)

Cut the leafy ends from the eggplants, wipe them, and put them in a large saucepan. Add boiling water and cover with a lid; cook the eggplants for 10 minutes. Drain the eggplants, plunge them into cold water, and leave for 5 minutes. Cut them in half lengthwise and scoop out most of the flesh, leaving a ½-inch-thick shell. Set aside the scooped-out flesh. Arrange the shells in a buttered baking dish and sprinkle them with a little salt and freshly ground pepper. Pour 4 teaspoons of olive oil into each shell and cook the eggplant shells, uncovered, in the center of a preheated oven at 350°F for 30 minutes.

While the shells are cooking, peel and finely chop the onions. Peel and seed the tomatoes* and chop them. Peel and crush the garlic. Heat 2 tablespoons of oil in a skillet, add the onions and garlic, and sauté gently for 5 minutes. Then add the toma-

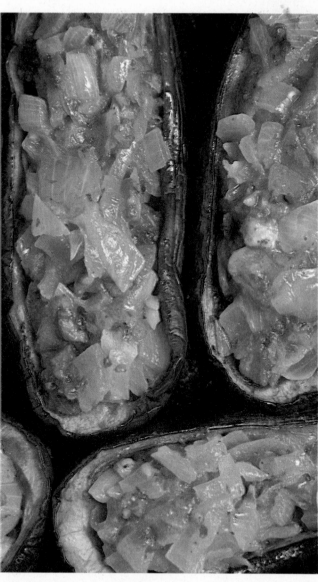

toes, cinnamon, sugar, and parsley; season to taste with salt and pepper. Continue simmering this mixture until the liquid has reduced* by half, about 20 minutes. Chop the eggplant flesh and add it to the skillet,

with the chopped pine nuts, if used, and cook for a further 10 minutes.

Remove the eggplant shells from the oven. Stuff them with the tomato mixture. Serve hot or cold, alone or with roast or broiled meat.

FRENCH APPLE TART

The open *flans,* or tarts, prepared with a sweet filling of fruit or jam, originated in the Alsace region of France. Remove the metal flan ring that holds the pastry in shape before serving the tart.

PREPARATION TIME: *1 hour*
CHILLING TIME: *30 minutes*
COOKING TIME: *45 minutes*

INGREDIENTS (*for 4–6*):
2 pounds cooking apples
2 red eating apples
1½ cups flour
Salt
¼ pound unsalted butter
¾ cup sugar
1 large egg yolk
Juice of 1 lemon
1 tablespoon apricot preserves

Sift the flour and a pinch of salt into a mixing bowl. Cut 6 tablespoons of the butter into small pieces and rub it into the flour until the mixture resembles coarse crumbs. Mix in 1 tablespoon sugar. Make a well in the center of the flour, drop in the egg yolk, and mix to a stiff dough with a little cold water.

Wrap the pastry in waxed paper and chill for 30 minutes. Meanwhile, peel and core the cooking apples and cut them up coarsely. Melt the remaining butter in a saucepan and add the apple pieces and 7 tablespoons of sugar. Cover with a lid and cook gently for 10 minutes. Strain the apples, saving the juice. Rub the cooked apples through a coarse sieve, then allow this purée* to cool. Wash the eating apples; core them before cutting them into ¼-inch rings. Sprinkle with a little lemon juice to prevent them from turning brown.

Roll out the pastry ⅛ inch thick on

a floured surface and use it to line a 7-inch flan ring set on a greased baking sheet. Trim the pastry edges and prick the bottom with a fork. Spoon the apple purée over the pastry and smooth the top. Arrange the apple rings in an overlapping pattern on the purée.

Put the apple juice, 2 tablespoons lemon juice, preserves, and remaining sugar in a saucepan. Cook over low heat until the sugar has dissolved, then bring to a boil and boil briskly for 4 minutes. Brush a little of this glaze* over the apple slices.

Bake the tart for 45 minutes in the center of a preheated oven at 400°F. If the apple slices brown too quickly, cover the top with foil. Remove the tart from the oven, brush with the remaining glaze, and serve it hot or cold, with whipped cream.

CHOCOLATE MOUSSE

Chocolate mousse is one of the most popular desserts, and is easy and quick to make.

PREPARATION TIME: *20–30 minutes*
CHILLING TIME: *1 hour*

INGREDIENTS (*for 6*):
12 ounces sweet cooking chocolate
4 tablespoons strong coffee
1 tablespoon unsalted butter
1 tablespoon Cointreau
4 large eggs

Break the chocolate into squares and put them in a bowl with 4 tablespoons of strong coffee. Set the bowl over a pan of gently simmering water and leave the chocolate to melt, stirring it occasionally. Remove the bowl from the water and stir in the butter and Cointreau.

Separate the eggs and beat the whites until stiff. Beat the yolks into the slightly cooled chocolate mixture, then gently fold in the whites. Spoon the mousse into individual glasses and leave to set in the refrigerator for about 1 hour.

RHUBARB CRUMBLE

The tart flavor of young spring rhubarb blends well with a sweet, crumbly topping.

PREPARATION TIME: *20 minutes*
COOKING TIME: *40 minutes*

INGREDIENTS (*for 4–6*):
2 pounds rhubarb
¾ cup sugar
1½ cups flour
6 tablespoons unsalted butter
½ cup heavy cream
1 piece preserved ginger, chopped
1 teaspoon ginger syrup

Wash the rhubarb stalks* and trim off the ends. Chop the stalks into ½-inch sections. Put the rhubarb in a deep baking dish, sprinkle over half the sugar, and add 2 tablespoons of cold water. Sift the flour and rub the butter in until it forms a crumbly mixture; blend in the remaining sugar. Cover the rhubarb with this crumble, patting it down well. Bake in the center of a preheated oven at 375°F for about 40 minutes or until crisp and golden on top.

Whip the cream until it stands in soft peaks; flavor with chopped ginger and the syrup.

Serve the rhubarb crumble warm or cold and offer the whipped cream separately.

SPONGE ROLL WITH LEMON CREAM

The lemon cream in this recipe can also be used for a cake filling.

PREPARATION TIME: *35 minutes*
COOKING TIME: *35 minutes*

INGREDIENTS (*for 6*):
4 eggs, separated
¼ cup sugar
¼ cup flour, sifted
¼ cup cornstarch
½ teaspoon vanilla extract
½ teaspoon grated lemon rind
LEMON CREAM:
¼ pound butter
Grated rind of 1 lemon
Juice of 3 large lemons
¼ teaspoon salt
1½ cups sugar
3 whole eggs plus 3 egg yolks
1 cup heavy cream
1 cup unsalted pistachio nuts
Confectioners' sugar

Beat the egg whites until soft peaks form, then gradually add the sugar and beat until stiff. Beat the egg yolks slightly. Stir 1 cup of egg whites into the yolks. Pour this over the remaining egg whites. Fold in the flour, cornstarch, vanilla extract, and lemon rind. Pour into a jelly-roll pan lined with waxed paper. Bake at 400°F for 10 minutes. Cool slightly. Turn out on a towel sprinkled with confectioners' sugar. Trim edges of the cake. Cool.

To make the lemon cream, melt the butter in the top of a double boiler. Add the rind, juice, salt, sugar, and eggs. Cook over hot water, whisking until thick. Cool. Whip the cream and fold into the filling. Spread on the sponge roll and sprinkle with the nuts. Roll up from a short end. Sprinkle with confectioners' sugar. Serve in slices.

GRAPEFRUIT IN BRANDY

PREPARATION TIME: *12 minutes*
COOKING TIME: *8 minutes*

INGREDIENTS (*for 6*):
4 large grapefruit
½ cup sugar
1 teaspoon cinnamon
4 tablespoons brandy

The slightly acid flavor of grapefruit is equally refreshing before or after a rich main course. Slices of grapefruit, poached in a light syrup and sprinkled with brandy, clear the palate. The dish can be served hot or cold.

Cut off all the peel and pith from the grapefruit and carefully poke out the pithy core with the little finger. Slice the fruit into 1-inch-thick rounds. Put the sugar in a large saucepan with ½ cup cold water and the cinnamon. Cook over low heat, stirring frequently, until the sugar has dissolved, then boil for 2 minutes. Lower the heat, add the grapefruit slices, and poach* them for 6 minutes, turning once.

Arrange the grapefruit slices on a serving dish, pour the brandy over them, and serve hot or chilled.

GÂTEAU SAINT HONORÉ

This cake is a Parisian specialty, named after Saint Honoré, the patron saint of pastrycooks. It is a case of short and choux pastries, filled with vanilla-flavored cream.

PREPARATION TIME: *1 hour*
COOKING TIME: *25 minutes*

INGREDIENTS (*for 4–6*):
1½ cups flour
Salt
4 tablespoons unsalted butter
2 tablespoons lard
1 large egg
Vanilla extract
3 tablespoons sugar
2 cups heavy cream
4 tablespoons vanilla sugar
GARNISH:
Candied cherries
Angelica

Sift 1 cup of the flour and a pinch of salt into a bowl, and rub in half the butter and all the lard until the mixture has a crumbly texture. Mix to a stiff dough with cold water. On a floured surface, roll out this short pastry to a circle 6 inches in diameter and trim the edge, using a plate as a guide. Place the pastry on a greased baking sheet.

Sift the remaining flour and a pinch of salt into a bowl. Put the remaining butter and ½ cup water in a saucepan and bring to a boil. Remove the pan from the heat and add the flour all at once; beat the dough until smooth.

Allow this choux pastry* to cool, then beat in the egg and a few drops of vanilla extract. Spoon the pastry into a pastry bag fitted with a large plain tube. Pipe small puffs about 1 inch in diameter closely around the edge of the short pastry. Pipe the remaining choux pastry into the same-sized puffs on a separate greased baking sheet. Bake the pastries for 15–20 minutes, or until golden brown, in the center of an oven preheated to 400°F. Remove from the oven and allow the pastries to cool.

Heat the sugar with 3 tablespoons of cold water in a small pan until the sugar has dissolved. Bring to a boil, but remove from the heat immediately when the mixture begins to thicken or turns a pale golden color. Dip the individual choux puffs in this caramel and arrange them on top of the puffs on the pastry base to form a double layer.

Whip the cream until stiff, stir in the vanilla sugar,* and spoon into the center of the gâteau. Garnish with whole candied cherries and strips of angelica.*

STRAWBERRY TART

This tart is very good but easy to make. Other berries and fruit, such as blackberries or blueberries, may be substituted for the strawberries. If the dessert is refrigerated, bring it to room temperature before serving.

PREPARATION TIME: *30 minutes*
COOKING TIME: *15–20 minutes*

INGREDIENTS (*for 4–6*):
1 cup all-purpose flour
Pinch of salt
6 tablespoons butter, cut into small pieces
1 egg yolk
4 tablespoons confectioners' sugar
1 teaspoon vanilla extract
¼ teaspoon grated lemon rind
½ cup red currant jelly
1 pint strawberries
1 cup heavy cream

Sift the flour and salt onto a board or into a bowl. Make a well in the center. Add the butter, egg yolk, confectioners' sugar, vanilla extract, and lemon rind. Work the ingredients in the center, drawing in the flour until the dough is smooth.

Pat out the dough onto the bottom and sides of an 8-inch cake pan. Prick the bottom and sides of the dough with a fork.

Bake in a preheated 375°F oven for 15–20 minutes, or until pastry is a light golden brown. Cool.

To make the glaze, put the currant jelly in a small saucepan. Melt it slowly over low heat. Cool slightly and brush the glaze over the bottom of the pastry.

Wash and hull the strawberries and arrange them, points up, over the bottom of the pastry. Brush the strawberries with the remaining currant glaze.

Just before serving, whip the cream until light and fluffy but not stiff; sweeten it to taste with a little superfine sugar or vanilla sugar and spoon it around the edge of the tart. Cut tart into wedges and serve.

BANANA FRITTERS

Crisp fruit fritters are a simple, delicious, and economical dessert. Rosewater, nutmeg, or almond extract flavorings can be added to the whipped cream.

PREPARATION TIME: *20 minutes*
COOKING TIME: *8–12 minutes*

INGREDIENTS (*for 6*):
6 small bananas
1 cup flour
Pinch of salt
1 large egg
½ cup milk or milk and water
Oil for deep-frying
Sugar
Whipped cream

Sift the flour with the salt into a mixing bowl. Make a well in the center and break in the egg. Add half the liquid and beat the batter* mixture with a wooden spoon until smooth. Gradually add the rest of the liquid and beat until the batter is blended and has the consistency of heavy cream. If time permits, let the batter stand for 1 hour.

Peel the bananas and cut them in half lengthwise. Dip them in the batter. Heat a deep-fryer with about 1½ inches of oil* to 375°F. With a slotted spoon, lower 3 banana halves into the hot oil and deep-fry until crisp and golden, about 2–3 minutes. Drain the fritters on paper towels and keep them warm.

Serve the fritters on a warmed dish and sprinkle sugar over them. Serve a bowl of whipped cream separately.

Snacks & Supper Dishes

BEEF DIABLE

Strong and spicy sauce diable, made from vinegar, mustard, and beef stock, adds an unusual flavor to leftover meat.

PREPARATION TIME: *5 minutes*
COOKING TIME: *35 minutes*

INGREDIENTS (*for 4*):
8–10 slices roast beef or pot roast
1 tablespoon olive oil
2 onions, finely chopped
1 crushed clove garlic
1 tablespoon flour
1 tablespoon Dijon mustard
1 tablespoon white wine vinegar
¾ cup beef stock
2 teaspoons brown sugar
¼ teaspoon Worcestershire sauce
1 teaspoon chopped capers
1 bay leaf
Salt and black pepper
3–4 tablespoons browned bread crumbs
3 tablespoons melted butter

Heat the oil over medium heat and cook the onions and garlic until golden. Blend in the flour. Add mustard and vinegar and gradually stir in the stock. Bring this sauce to a boil and stir until thick and smooth. Add the sugar, Worcestershire sauce, capers, and bay leaf and season with salt and pepper. Simmer for 5–10 minutes, stirring frequently.

Put the sliced beef in a lightly buttered baking dish. Pour over the sauce, first removing the bay leaf. Sprinkle with the bread crumbs and pour over the melted butter. Bake in the center of a preheated oven at 375°F for about 20 minutes or until golden brown. Serve hot, with buttered rice.

CHICKEN AND CHEESE TOASTS

A few mushrooms and a little cheese turn scraps of cooked chicken into a delicious light meal.

PREPARATION TIME: *10 minutes*
COOKING TIME: *15 minutes*

INGREDIENTS (*for 4*):
2 cups cooked diced chicken
1 cup thick white sauce (p.301)
Salt, black pepper, and cayenne
1 teaspoon hot mustard
⅔ cup thinly sliced button mushrooms
4 slices buttered toast
½ cup grated Cheddar cheese

Season the white sauce with salt, pepper, and cayenne to taste and blend in the mustard. Stir the chicken and mushrooms into the sauce and simmer over low heat until heated through.

Spoon the chicken mixture onto the toast and sprinkle with the cheese. Broil until the cheese is brown and bubbling. A tomato and onion salad or a green vegetable goes well with this.

FRIED RICE

A small amount of leftover beef, ham, or chicken can be used for this version of Chinese fried rice.

PREPARATION TIME: *10 minutes*
COOKING TIME: *10 minutes*

INGREDIENTS (*for 4–6*):
4 cups cooked rice
2 tablespoons olive oil
3 beaten eggs
1½ cups cooked meat, cut into matchstick strips
2 shredded lettuce leaves
4 chopped scallions
⅔ cup thinly sliced button mushrooms
1 tablespoon soy sauce

Heat the oil in a large, heavy-bottomed pan over medium heat. Pour in the eggs and cook, stirring with a fork, until the eggs are beginning to set. Stir in the rice, meat, vegetables, and soy sauce. Cook, stirring constantly, until all the ingredients are heated through.

Serve hot, accompanied by green peas or beans.

KIDNEY SCRAMBLE

Sautéed kidneys and scrambled eggs make a quick but substantial snack.

PREPARATION TIME: *10 minutes*
COOKING TIME: *10–15 minutes*

INGREDIENTS (*for 4*):
4 chopped lamb kidneys
2 tablespoons unsalted butter
¼ teaspoon Worcestershire sauce
1 teaspoon tomato ketchup
¼ teaspoon hot mustard
Salt and black pepper
6 eggs
4 tablespoons light cream
4 slices buttered toast

Sauté the kidneys over high heat in half the butter until lightly browned. Stir in the sauces and mustard; season with salt and pepper and cook over moderate heat for 2 minutes more. Keep the kidneys warm.

Lightly beat the eggs with the cream and season with salt and pepper. Melt the remaining butter in a pan and cook the eggs over low heat, stirring occasionally, until just beginning to set. Spoon the eggs onto the toast and top with the kidneys. Serve at once.

CLUB SANDWICHES

This triple-decker sandwich is one of the most popular culinary inventions of all time.

PREPARATION TIME: *15 minutes*
COOKING TIME: *5 minutes*

INGREDIENTS (*for 4*):
12 slices white bread
4 tablespoons unsalted butter
4 small sliced tomatoes
8 slices cooked bacon
8 small lettuce leaves
8 thin slices cooked chicken or turkey
4 tablespoons mayonnaise (p.303)

Toast the bread and remove the crusts; butter 8 slices on one side, the remaining 4 slices on both sides. Cover 4 slices with tomato; top with the bacon; put those slices buttered on both sides on top, and cover with lettuce and chicken or turkey. Spread mayonnaise over the meat and cover with the last 4 slices of toast. Press the sandwiches firmly together and quarter them; spear each with a cocktail pick and serve.

Easter Customs

Easter is one of the holiest festivals in the Christian year, although many of its customs are pre-Christian in origin. The custom of giving eggs goes back to the times when eggs, as a symbol of renewed life, were exchanged at spring festivals.

Hot cross buns possibly stem from the small wheat cakes eaten at the spring festivals in honor of Astarte, the Phoenician fertility goddess. The cross on the buns, however, is of Christian origin.

The rich simnel cake, made with butter and fruit and decorated with almond icing, is baked for Easter in Great Britain. Most other countries also have their special Easter fare. The Russian housewife bakes a yeast cake, known as *Kulich,* which she wraps in a spotless napkin to take to church for the priest's blessing. In Portugal the traditional dessert is made of fine strands of egg yolk called angel's hair. The Italians bake *Colomba,* which is similar to the Russian *Kulich,* and the Sicilians make *Cassata alla Siciliana*—layers of cake and ice cream covered with chocolate icing. In Poland the Easter fare is a huge buffet. The place of honor goes to the Easter lamb, made of butter or white sugar, a symbolic representation of Christ.

Good Friday

On Good Friday, the most solemn penitential day of the Christian calendar, fish has traditionally been the main course. Recipes for this menu serving 8—except for the sole cushions—are on pages 113, 114, 124, and 333.

Avocado and Citrus Salad
Sole Cushions with
Hollandaise Sauce
Fresh Asparagus
Sautéed Potatoes
Chocolate Mousse

Sole Cushions
INGREDIENTS:
8 large sole fillets
Butter
1 finely chopped onion
¼ pound button mushrooms
1 tablespoon chopped parsley
Salt and black pepper
¾ cup dry white wine
½ recipe puff pastry (p.363)
1 egg yolk

Butter a shallow ovenproof dish and spread the onion over the bottom. Cover with the thinly sliced mushrooms and parsley. Fold each sole fillet in thirds and arrange them over the mushrooms. Season with salt and freshly ground pepper and pour over the wine.

Cover the dish with buttered waxed paper and bake in the center of the oven at 350°F for 10 minutes. Remove the dish and allow to cool.

Roll out the puff pastry ⅛ inch thick and divide it into 16 squares. Spoon the mushroom mixture over half the squares, and top with a sole fillet. Moisten the pastry edges with water, cover each square with the remaining pastry, and seal the edges firmly with the fingers.

Brush the cushions with the beaten egg yolk and bake them for 15–20 minutes in the center of a preheated oven at 400°F.

Serve the sole cushions hot, with a bowl of Hollandaise sauce (p.303).

Decorating Eggs

Use only white-shelled eggs for decorating. Hard-cooked in spinach water, they take on a green color, and those boiled with raw beets turn red. Onion or shallot skins wrapped around the eggs and wound with cotton thread give an orange-brown mottled effect. Flower petals can be placed on damp eggs, covered with onion skin, and kept in place with string or tape. The boiled eggs will then bear the imprint of both petals and onion skins.

Alternatively, add a few drops of vegetable dye or food coloring to the water to dye the eggs carmine, blue, green, or yellow, or use one of the small egg-dying kits sold at supermarkets during the Easter season. Narrow strips of masking tape can be stuck onto the eggs in geometric patterns. Peeling off the tapes afterwards will reveal white patterns on a colored background. Polish all boiled eggs with a little olive oil.

The eggs can be boiled before being decorated with crayons, vegetable dyes, or watercolors. Trace complicated designs on uncooked eggs, first dipped in vegetable dye.

Easter Sunday

Young spring lamb and stuffed eggs are traditional at Easter.

Stuffed Eggs
Saddle of Lamb with Wine Sauce
Green Beans with Sauce
Vinaigrette
Carrot and Potato Purée
Grapefruit in Brandy (p.125)

Stuffed Eggs
INGREDIENTS:
8 hard-cooked eggs
1–2 small cans anchovy fillets
2 teaspoons capers
6 tablespoons olive oil
2 tablespoons lemon juice
Dijon mustard
Black pepper
Lettuce leaves

Halve the eggs lengthwise and mash the yolks with the other ingredients. Arrange the whites on lettuce and fill with the yolk mixture.

Saddle of Lamb
INGREDIENTS:
6-pound saddle of lamb
3½ cups red wine
4 tablespoons medium-dry sherry
4 tablespoons brandy
4 tablespoons melted butter
1 teaspoon rosemary
Arrowroot
MARINADE:
1 finely chopped carrot
2 finely chopped onions
3 parsley sprigs
½ teaspoon thyme
1 bay leaf
6 peppercorns
2 cloves
¼ teaspoon mace or nutmeg
4 tablespoons wine vinegar

Put the marinade* ingredients in a pan with ¾ cup of water. Boil for 30 minutes; blend in the wines and brandy. Marinate lamb for 12 hours.

Place the lamb in a roasting pan. Brush it with the melted butter and sprinkle with the rosemary. Cook in the center of a preheated oven at 350°F for 2½ hours.

Boil the marinade briskly until reduced* to 2½ cups. Strain. Return to a boil; thicken with arrowroot diluted with water. Correct seasoning.

The Ukrainians are famous for their beautifully decorated eggs, which resemble miniature mosaics. The complicated designs are carefully traced on uncooked eggs that are dipped, at various stages, in different vegetable dyes. Only a small part of the egg is colored at a time, the other areas being masked with beeswax or adhesive tape.

Children will delight in a chocolate egg within a chicken egg. Carefully pierce the broad end of a raw egg with a small skewer; shake out the white and yolk. Let the eggshell dry out. Pour melted chocolate through a small funnel into the egg.

Green Beans with Sauce Vinaigrette
INGREDIENTS:
3 pounds green beans
6 tablespoons vegetable oil
2 tablespoons wine vinegar
2 teaspoons finely chopped chives
Salt and black pepper

Trim and wash the beans, but leave them whole. Boil the beans in salted water 5–10 minutes, or until the beans are tender. Drain well.

Put the oil and vinegar in a bowl or in a screw-top jar. Beat with a fork or shake vigorously before seasoning to taste with chives, salt, and pepper. Add to the beans, reheat slowly, and serve immediately.

Carrot and Potato Purée
INGREDIENTS:
4–6 carrots
4–6 potatoes
½ cup light or heavy cream
4 tablespoons butter
Salt
Freshly ground black pepper

Peel the carrots* and potatoes;* boil them in separate pots until tender. Purée the carrots and mash the potatoes. Combine the two vegetables. Add the heavy cream, butter, salt, and pepper to taste. Mix thoroughly. Add more cream, if necessary, to make the purée fluffier; add more butter, if desired. Heat in a double boiler and serve.

Easter Cakes

Simnel Cake
INGREDIENTS:
½ pound unsalted butter
Grated rind of 2 large lemons
1 cup sugar
4 large eggs
1 cup chopped mixed candied fruit
1 cup raisins
3 cups black currants
3½ cups all-purpose flour
Salt
Pinch of baking powder
1 teaspoon allspice
⅔ cup ground almonds
1 cup confectioners' sugar
½ cup superfine sugar
1 large egg, lightly beaten
Lemon extract
3 tablespoons lemon juice

Cream the butter with the lemon rind and the sugar. Beat in the eggs, one at a time, and stir in the fruit. Add the flour, a little salt, baking powder, and allspice. Fold into the creamed mixture.

Grease and line a 7-inch round deep cake pan. Spoon the cake mixture into the pan and level off the top. Bake in the center of a preheated oven at 325°F for 3–3½ hours.

Mix together the almonds and all the sugar. Add half the lightly beaten egg, a few drops of lemon extract, and the lemon juice. Knead until the almond paste is smooth.

Roll two-thirds of the almond paste out to a 7-inch round and place on top of cooled cake. Shape remaining paste into 11 balls—to represent the Apostles, excluding Judas—and set around the edge.

Hot Cross Buns
INGREDIENTS:
4 cups all-purpose flour
1 teaspoon sugar
1 tablespoon active dry yeast
¾ cup lukewarm milk
¼ cup warm water
1 teaspoon each salt and allspice
½ cup sugar
4 tablespoons melted butter
1 beaten egg
2 tablespoons currants
2–4 tablespoons chopped mixed candied fruit

Sift 1 cup of the flour with 1 teaspoon sugar. Add the yeast and stir in the milk and water. Let stand 20–30 minutes. Sift the remaining flour with the salt and allspice. Add ½ cup sugar. Stir the melted butter, together with the egg, into the risen yeast mixture. Fold in the flour, currants, and fruit.

On a floured surface, knead the dough until perfectly smooth. Divide into 12 pieces and shape into buns. Set the buns well apart on greased and floured baking sheets and let them rise in a warm place until doubled in size.

Make two slashes on top of each bun to form a cross. Bake just above the center of a preheated oven at 375°F for 15–20 minutes.

Let the buns cool on a wire rack; while still warm, brush them with a glaze made from ¼ cup sugar and 2 tablespoons water.

Polish Easter Cake
INGREDIENTS:
½ cup butter
½ cup sugar
6 egg yolks
1 package active dry yeast
¼ cup warm water (110°–115°F)
Grated rind of 1 lemon
Grated rind of 1 orange
1 teaspoon salt
1 teaspoon cinnamon
1 cup lukewarm milk
4 cups all-purpose flour
1 cup golden seedless raisins
¼ cup sliced almonds
ICING:
2 cups confectioners' sugar, sifted
¼ cup cold water
Grated rind of 1 lemon
2 teaspoons lemon juice

In a large bowl, cream the butter and sugar until light and fluffy. Add 5 of the egg yolks, one at a time, beating well after each addition.

Soften the yeast in the warm water. Add this to the mixture, with the lemon and orange rinds, salt, and cinnamon. Add the lukewarm milk and only enough flour to make a soft dough. Stir in the raisins. Knead the dough about 10 minutes. Cover; let the dough rise until it has doubled in bulk, about 2 hours.

Butter a 3-quart bundt pan* and shape the dough to fit it. Cover and let rise until doubled in bulk. Beat the remaining egg yolk with 2 tablespoons of cold water. Brush the dough generously with this mixture and sprinkle with the sliced almonds. Bake in a preheated oven at 350°F for 30 minutes.

Mix the sugar, water, lemon rind, and juice. Pour over the cake.

129

May

Here's to the day when it is May
And care as light as a feather.

BLISS CARMAN

THIS MONTH'S RECIPES

Slim fresh river trout such as these make the finest eating.
Trout living in lakes tend to be larger and less delicate in flavor.

Food in Season

Although few seasonal foods are at their peak this month, many are making their first appearance in the markets and will grow less expensive as June approaches. May sees the arrival of the succulent fruits that signal the first hot days of summer—juicy cherries, peaches, watermelons, and ripe, golden apricots (delicious in Croûtes aux Abricots, (p.146). Rhubarb, strawberries, mangoes, and pineapples are also plentiful.

Imported green peas and radishes are relatively inexpensive in May. Radishes are usually confined to salads or used as garnishes. Green peas, however, are extremely versatile: They can be prepared as a side dish with butter or cream sauce, used in soups or stews, or served in cold vegetable salads. An out-of-the-ordinary way to prepare fresh green peas is with eggs and spices (p.142).

U.S. asparagus is still of the highest quality and is becoming cheaper. An economical way of using the stems and cooking liquid left over from asparagus with new potatoes (p.142) is to make a soup (p.142). Asparagus can also be puréed to prepare a classic French dish, Lamb Argenteuil (p.138).

Imported cucumbers, tomatoes, and sweet corn are improving in quality and are becoming more plentiful. Try Savory Cucumbers (p.144) as an unusual hot snack or hors d'oeuvre.

Soups & First Courses

CREAM OF SPINACH SOUP

This velvety soup can be puréed in a blender. Serve it hot or cold.

PREPARATION TIME: *15 minutes*
COOKING TIME: *25 minutes*

INGREDIENTS (*for 6*):
5 cups washed, chopped fresh
spinach
3 tablespoons butter
⅓ cup chopped scallions, white part
only
½ teaspoon salt
⅛ teaspoon nutmeg
⅛ teaspoon black pepper
2 tablespoons flour
4 cups chicken stock
3 egg yolks, lightly beaten
1 cup heavy cream
GARNISH:
2 tablespoons chopped egg white
2 tablespoons chopped scallions,
green part only

Melt the butter in a heavy stainless steel or enameled saucepan and sauté the scallions over moderate heat for 5 minutes. Add the spinach and cook gently for 3 minutes, stirring occasionally. Stir in the salt, nutmeg, freshly ground pepper, and flour. Cook 2 minutes. Add the chicken stock, stir, bring slowly to a boil, and simmer 5 minutes.

Mix the egg yolks with the cream. Add a few tablespoons of the hot stock to the egg mixture, then return to the saucepan and heat, stirring, until the soup thickens. Do not boil, or the soup will curdle. Garnish with chopped egg white and the green scallions.

GRAVAD LAX

The traditional version of this Scandinavian dish uses fresh dill, but it can also be made with dried dill. The pickling adds a subtle flavor to fresh salmon.

PREPARATION TIME: *30 minutes*

INGREDIENTS (*for 6*):
1½ pounds salmon, middle cut
PICKLE:
2 tablespoons sea salt
1½ tablespoons granulated sugar
1 teaspoon crushed black
peppercorns
1 tablespoon brandy (optional)
2 tablespoons chopped fresh dill or 1
tablespoon dried dill
SAUCE:
2 tablespoons German mustard
1 tablespoon sugar
1 large egg yolk
7 tablespoons olive oil
2 tablespoons wine vinegar
1 tablespoon chopped fresh dill or 1
teaspoon dried dill
Salt and white pepper

Ask the fish dealer to cut the salmon into 2 fillets. Mix all the pickling ingredients. Lay the first piece of salmon, skin down, over one fourth of the mixture and rub half of the pickle over the cut side. Spread the flesh side of the second piece of salmon with the remaining mixture, rubbing it well into the flesh. Place the second piece of salmon, skin side up, over the first. Cover the salmon with a piece of aluminum foil and a small, heavy board weighed down with 2 cans. Leave the salmon to press in a cool place or in the refrigerator for up to 5 days, but not less than 12 hours, turning the salmon once a day.

Before serving, scrape off the pickle and dry the salmon thor-

oughly on paper towels. Slice the fish thinly with a sharp knife, either parallel to the skin, as with smoked salmon, or obliquely to the skin.

For the sauce, beat the mustard with the sugar and egg yolk until smooth. Gradually add the oil and vinegar, mixing well between each addition. Season the mixture to taste with dill, salt, and white pepper.

Arrange the chilled slices of salmon on individual plates and garnish with a sprig of fresh dill, if desired. Serve buttered rye bread and the sauce separately.

CANAPÉS À LA CRÈME

This is a quickly prepared appetizer. The combination of hot crisp bread, salty anchovies, and cold sour cream makes an unusual contrast of tastes and textures.

PREPARATION TIME: *8 minutes*
COOKING TIME: *10–12 minutes*

INGREDIENTS (*for 4*):
8 slices white bread
12 anchovy fillets
½ cup clarified butter
4 tablespoons sour cream
GARNISH:
Parsley sprigs

Cut a round from each slice of bread with a 3-inch plain or fluted pastry cutter. Drain the anchovy fillets and cut each in half lengthwise. Melt the clarified butter* in a skillet and sauté the bread until golden brown. Keep the slices warm in the oven on a hot serving dish.

When all the bread has been sautéed, quickly arrange 3 anchovy fillets on each slice, spoon on the chilled sour cream, and garnish with a small sprig of parsley.

Serve immediately, before the cream melts into the hot bread.

CHICKEN LIVER PÂTÉ

This pâté should be allowed to mature for 2 days, and will store well in the freezer.

PREPARATION TIME: *30 minutes*
COOKING TIME: *45 minutes*

INGREDIENTS (*for 6*):
½ pound chicken livers
6 ounces sausage meat
1 egg
Salt and black pepper
Ground thyme and marjoram
1 tablespoon brandy
2–3 tablespoons Madeira or medium-dry sherry
¼ pound pork or bacon fat
1 bay leaf

Remove any stringy bits and discolored parts from the chicken livers; chop them finely or put them in the blender to make a purée.* Mix the liver purée with the sausage meat and stir in the egg. Season to taste with salt, pepper, thyme, and marjoram, and finally stir in the brandy and Madeira or sherry.

Fry a spoonful of the pâté in a little butter to test seasoning; taste, and adjust if necessary. Put the pâté mixture into a 3-cup terrine or ovenproof glass loaf pan. Cut the pork or bacon fat into narrow strips and place them on top of the pâté in a decorative pattern. Set the bay leaf in the center. Stand the terrine in a roasting pan and pour in enough boiling water to come halfway up the dish. Bake in the center of the oven at 400°F for 45 minutes.

Leave the pâté to cool, then cover with a lid or foil and store in the refrigerator for about 2 days to give the flavors time to develop fully.

Serve the pâté cold, with hot, crisp toast or home-baked bread.

ELIZA ACTON'S APPLE SOUP

In 1845 Eliza Acton published her *Modern Cookery,* the first important English cookbook. It included this recipe for a tart apple soup. Miss Acton gives Burgundy as the place of origin, but a similar soup was known in medieval Britain.

PREPARATION TIME: *10 minutes*
COOKING TIME: *30 minutes*

INGREDIENTS (*for 6*):
2 pints brown stock (p.298)
¾ pound cooking apples
½ teaspoon ground ginger
Salt and black pepper
4 tablespoons rice

Remove all fat from the surface of the prepared cool stock. Wash the apples and chop them coarsely without removing peel or core. Bring the stock to a boil in a large pan, add the apples, and cover the pan with a lid. Simmer the soup over low heat until the apples are tender.

Pour the soup through a sieve, rubbing through as much of the fruit pulp as possible. Stir in the ginger and season with salt and ground pepper. Reheat the soup and remove any scum from the surface.

While the soup is cooking, boil the rice in plenty of salted water. Drain thoroughly through a sieve and keep the rice warm.

Spoon the soup into bowls and serve the rice separately.

FRENCH TURNIP SOUP

The French frequently use flavorful and inexpensive white turnips as the basis for a creamy soup.

PREPARATION TIME: *20 minutes*
COOKING TIME: *45 minutes*

INGREDIENTS (*for 6–8*):
¾ pound small white turnips
½ pound potatoes
1 leek
1 onion
4 tablespoons butter
4 tablespoons flour
8 cups vegetable stock (p.298)
Salt and black pepper
2 large egg yolks
3 tablespoons heavy cream
GARNISH:
Bread croûtons (p.300)

Peel and dice the turnips and potatoes; rinse them in cold water. Remove the roots and coarse outer leaves from the leek, cut in half, and rinse thoroughly under cold running water to remove all traces of dirt. Chop the leek coarsely. Peel and coarsely chop the onion.

Melt the butter in a large pan and add the vegetables. Cover the pan with a lid and cook the vegetables over low heat for about 10 minutes without browning them. Add the flour and cook for a few minutes, stirring continuously. Gradually blend in the stock and season to taste with salt and freshly ground pepper. Simmer the soup over low heat for about 30 minutes, or until the vegetables are cooked.

Let the soup cool a little before puréeing it in a blender or food mill, or rubbing it through a fine sieve. Return the soup to the pan and reheat over low heat.

Beat the egg yolks with the cream

Fish

in a small bowl, blend in a little of the hot soup, and then stir it all back into the soup. Stir over low heat for a few minutes, without allowing the soup to boil. Taste for seasoning.

Serve the soup at once, with a separate bowl of bread croûtons.

FRICASSEE OF EGGS

Nowadays "fricassee" describes poultry or eggs prepared in a white sauce, though the term originally meant a white stew of meat, fish, or vegetables. This fricassee of eggs makes a good first course when served in small dishes or in tartlet shells of pastry.

PREPARATION TIME: *20 minutes*
COOKING TIME: *15 minutes*

INGREDIENTS (*for 6*):
6 large eggs
6 parsley sprigs
6 tarragon sprigs (optional)
¼ pound unsalted butter
¾ cup heavy cream
Salt and black pepper
Lemon juice

Hard-cook the eggs for about 10 minutes, then plunge them into cold water for a few minutes to prevent further cooking. Shell the eggs, quarter them, and set aside. Chop the herbs finely.

Melt the butter in a skillet, stir in the cream, and let the mixture bubble until it has thickened to the consistency of a sauce. Add the herbs and season to taste with salt, freshly ground pepper, and lemon juice.

Reheat the quartered eggs carefully in the sauce and spoon the mixture into individual serving dishes or tartlet shells.

CLAM PIE

This dish was developed from an old New England recipe.

PREPARATION TIME: *40 minutes*
COOKING TIME: *1 hour*

INGREDIENTS (*for 6*):
2 quarts clams in their shells
1 cup dry white wine
1 carrot, chopped
1 medium onion, chopped
1 bay leaf
1 teaspoon freshly ground pepper
VELOUTÉ SAUCE:
4 tablespoons butter
4 tablespoons flour
1 cup milk
½ pound mushrooms, sliced
5 tablespoons butter
Salt and pepper
3 tablespoons sherry
Flaky pastry (p.362)

Scrub the clams thoroughly under cold running water and place them in a large pot (not aluminum). Add the white wine, carrot, onion, bay leaf, and pepper. Cover tightly and steam until the clams open. Discard any that do not open. Remove the meat from the shells and chop the clams. Strain the broth through cheesecloth and reserve 1 cup.

For the velouté sauce, melt the butter and stir in the flour. Cook until slightly browned, stirring constantly. Gradually stir in the reserved broth and milk; stir until thick. Cook 10 minutes and season to taste.

Sauté the mushrooms quickly in the butter and season to taste with salt and pepper. Combine the mushrooms, clams, sauce, and sherry.

Pour into a deep 1½-quart baking dish and top with pie crust rolled ¼ inch thick. Bake at 450°F for 15 minutes. Reduce the heat to 350°F and bake until the crust is golden.

TROUT WITH MUSHROOMS

This recipe from the Pyrénées combines fresh river trout with button mushrooms and a Pernod sauce. Frozen rainbow trout can be used if fresh ones are not available.

PREPARATION TIME: *10 minutes*
COOKING TIME: *15 minutes*

INGREDIENTS (*for 4*):
4 cleaned trout, each weighing 6–8 ounces
Seasoned flour (p.412)
½ cup clarified butter
½ pound button mushrooms
1 clove garlic
2–3 tablespoons Pernod or Ricard
½ cup heavy cream
Salt and black pepper

Coat each trout with seasoned flour, shaking off any excess. Melt the clarified butter* in a large, heavy skillet and sauté the trout over moderate heat for 5 minutes on each side, or until the skin is golden brown and crisp.

Meanwhile, wash and trim the mushrooms* and slice them thinly. Peel and crush the garlic clove. Transfer the trout to a serving dish and keep them warm in the oven, turned to its lowest setting. Sauté the mushrooms and garlic in the trout juices, over low heat, for 3–4 minutes. Stir in the Pernod or Ricard* and let the liquid bubble rapidly for a few minutes. Add the cream, stirring continuously until the sauce has reduced* to the consistency of thick cream. Season the mixture to taste with salt, freshly-ground pepper, and a little more Pernod if necessary. Pour the sauce over the trout.

Serve immediately, with boiled buttered potatoes and a crisp green salad or green vegetable.

Meat

WHITING WITH ORANGE SAUCE

Fish with orange was as popular in the 18th century as fish with lemon is today. Originally, sharp Seville oranges were used, but the mixture of orange and lemon in this French recipe is equally good.

PREPARATION TIME: *10 minutes*
COOKING TIME: *30 minutes*

INGREDIENTS (*for 6*):
6 whiting
Salt and black pepper
1 lemon
1 orange
5 tablespoons heavy cream
½ cup plus 2 tablespoons dry white
  wine
3 large egg yolks
Cayenne pepper
¼ pound unsalted butter
Seasoned flour (p.412)
GARNISH:
1 orange, cut into wedges
Chopped parsley

Clean and wash the whiting and fillet each into two. Dry the fillets thoroughly on absorbent paper tow-els and season with salt and black pepper; sprinkle with the juice of ½ lemon. Set aside. Grate the rind from the orange and set aside; squeeze the juice of the orange and remaining ½ lemon into a double boiler.

For the sauce, stir the cream, wine, and egg yolks into the fruit juices and set over simmering water. Whisk the sauce mixture continu-ously until it has the consistency of thin cream. Season to taste with salt, pepper, and cayenne and blend in the orange rind. Cut half the butter into small pieces and beat them one by one into the sauce. Keep the sauce hot, but do not allow it to boil.

Coat the whiting fillets with sea-soned flour. Melt the remaining butter in a skillet and sauté the fillets until they are golden brown on both sides.

Garnish the fillets with orange wedges and chopped parsley. The sauce can be served separately or poured over the fish. Offer French bread for mopping up the sauce.

SOLES AUX CRÊPES

The combination of buttered fillets of sole with featherlight strips of crêpe is a specialty of the town of Bayeux in northern France.

PREPARATION TIME: *15 minutes*
COOKING TIME: *25 minutes*

INGREDIENTS (*for 6*):
12 fillets of sole
Seasoned flour (p.412)
½ cup clarified butter
6 tablespoons unsalted butter
1 heaping tablespoon chopped
  parsley
BATTER:
½ cup all-purpose flour
¼ teaspoon salt
1 egg
5 tablespoons milk
GARNISH:
Lemon wedges

Begin by making the batter, so that it can rest while the fillets are being sautéed. Sift the flour and salt into a bowl, make a well in the center, and add the lightly beaten egg. Mix thoroughly and add 5 tablespoons water and the milk gradually, beat-ing well until the batter is free from lumps and has the consistency of light cream. Add more water to the batter if necessary.

Wipe the sole fillets on a damp cloth, coat them with seasoned flour, and shake off any surplus. Melt the clarified butter* in a large pan and sauté the fillets over moderate heat until golden brown on both sides, turning once. Arrange the fillets on a serving dish and keep them warm.

Butter a hot crêpe pan and make 3 or 4 crêpes from the batter. Roll the crêpes up and cut them crosswise into ½-inch strips. Melt the remaining butter and reheat the crêpe ribbons, turning them until they are hot and golden. Blend in the chopped parsley and pile the crêpe strips over and among the sole fillets. Garnish with wedges of lemon.

A rice salad with fennel (p.284) would be a tasty side dish.

SALMON STEAKS WITH CREAM

Fresh salmon is the king of fish, and its delicate flavor should never be smothered by a rich sauce or mayon-naise. This recipe is a simple but suc-cessful way of cooking salmon steaks so that they retain their flavor.

PREPARATION TIME: *5 minutes*
COOKING TIME: *20 minutes*

INGREDIENTS (*for 6*):
6 salmon steaks, each 1 inch thick
Salt and black pepper
4 tablespoons butter
2–2½ cups light cream
Small bay leaf
GARNISH:
Lemon wedges

Wipe the steaks with a damp cloth and season them with salt and freshly ground pepper. Butter an ovenproof serving dish large enough to accom-modate the salmon steaks in a single layer. Pour over enough cream to cover the fish. Lay the bay leaf on top and cover the dish with a sheet of aluminum foil.

Bake the steaks in the center of a preheated oven at 375°F for 20 minutes, basting with a little extra cream if necessary.

Serve the salmon in the cooking dish and garnish with wedges of lemon. Buttered new potatoes with parsley, and a crisp salad of lettuce and cucumber, are traditional ac-companiments to salmon.

BEEF STEW WITH OLIVES

Shank of beef is an inexpensive cut and excellent for stewing. The gelat-inous part holding the nuggets of meat together adds a good texture to the sauce and prevents the meat from becoming stringy during cooking.

PREPARATION TIME: *20 minutes*
COOKING TIME: *3¼ hours*

INGREDIENTS:
2½–3 pounds of beef shank
Seasoned flour (p.412)
1 large onion
1 large carrot
2 cloves garlic
Vegetable oil
½ cup plus 2 tablespoons red wine
2½ cups brown stock (p.298)
Bouquet garni (p.410)
1 teaspoon anchovy paste
Salt and black pepper
¾–1 cup black or green olives
GARNISH:
Chopped parsley

Remove any large lumps of fat from the beef. Cut the meat into 1–1½ inch chunks and coat with seasoned flour. Peel and finely slice the onion, car-rot, and garlic. Pour a thin layer of oil into a large skillet; when hot, sauté the meat and vegetables until brown. Transfer the contents of the pan to a casserole dish.

Pour the wine and a little stock into the skillet. Boil these juices rap-idly while scraping up all the residue. Pour into the casserole, adding enough stock to cover the meat. Tuck in the bouquet garni and stir in the anchovy paste and plenty of freshly ground pepper. Cover with a lid or foil. Simmer the casserole in the center of a preheated oven at 300°F for 2–3 hours, or until the meat is tender.

Transfer the cooked meat and vegetables to a shallow warm serving dish and sprinkle with a little salt. Boil the liquid in the casserole rapidly until it has reduced* and thickened to a rich sauce. Remove the bouquet garni. Add the olives and simmer for 5 minutes. Correct seasoning if necessary. Pour some of the sauce over the meat and serve the remainder in a sauceboat.

Garnish the meat with parsley and surround with triangles of toast or boiled potatoes.

SWEETBREADS À LA CASTILLANE

Calf's sweetbreads are combined with a fruit purée in this classic recipe from Tours in France.

PREPARATION TIME: *25 minutes*
COOKING TIME: *30 minutes*

INGREDIENTS (*for 6*):
1½–2 pounds sweetbreads
2–2½ cups chicken stock
2 teaspoons lemon juice or white wine vinegar
4 dessert apples
¼ pound butter
4 ripe bananas
Superfine sugar
Seasoned flour (p.412)
5 tablespoons brandy
½ cup heavy cream
Salt and black pepper

Put the sweetbreads in a bowl with 1 teaspoon of salt and enough tepid water to cover. Leave to soak for 1 hour, then drain.

Put the sweetbreads in a saucepan and cover with chicken stock; add the lemon juice or vinegar. Bring to a boil over low heat, then simmer for 10 minutes. Drain the sweetbreads through a layer of cheesecloth and

set the liquid aside for the sauce.

When the sweetbreads have cooled, carefully cut off any fibers, pieces of tube, or discolored parts, but leave the thin skin around the sweetbreads intact.

Wash the apples, but do not peel or core them. Cut them into large pieces and put them in a pan with 4 tablespoons butter. Cover with a lid and cook over low heat until quite soft. Rub the apples through a sieve or whirl in a blender to make a fine purée.* Peel and mash the bananas and blend them into the apple purée. Add sugar and lemon juice to taste. Spoon the purée over the bottom of a serving dish and keep it warm.

Cut the sweetbreads into ½-inch-thick slices and toss them in seasoned flour. Brown them lightly in the remaining butter in a heavy skillet over moderate heat. Add ½ cup of the reserved liquid and continue cooking the sweetbreads until the liquid has reduced* to a syrupy coating consistency. Turn the sweetbreads over from time to time. If the liquid reduces too quickly before the sweetbreads are cooked, after about 25 minutes, add a little more stock. Lift the sweetbreads from the pan and arrange them on top of the purée.

Add the brandy to the pan juices, stirring well, before blending in the cream. Cook the sauce over low heat for a few minutes until it is thick.

Pour the sauce over the sweetbreads or serve it in a sauceboat. Buttered rice and a green salad go well with this meal.

PORK WITH PISTACHIO NUTS

A loin of pork is particularly suitable as a main dish for a cold buffet. Leave it to season for 2 or 3 days in saltpeter, which gives a pink glow to cold pork. If saltpeter is unobtainable, pieces of salt pork placed down the middle of the pork can be used to impart a similar flavor and color.

PREPARATION TIME: *20 minutes*
COOKING TIME: *2½ hours*

INGREDIENTS (*for 8–10*):
4–5 pound loin of pork
¼ teaspoon saltpeter
1½ tablespoons salt
4 teaspoons brown sugar
2 tablespoons shelled pistachio nuts
Black pepper
½ cup dry white wine

Buy the pork 2 or 3 days before it is wanted and ask the butcher to bone the meat and to give you the bones. Mix together the saltpeter, salt, and brown sugar; rub it into the pork, particularly on the boned side. Place

the pork, boned side down, in a deep dish, cover with foil, and leave in the refrigerator for 2–3 days.

Before cooking, pat the meat dry with a clean cloth. Make small incisions with a sharp knife in the fat and press in the shelled pistachio nuts. Sprinkle the meat with plenty of freshly ground black pepper; roll it neatly and tie the meat securely with string.

For the cooking, use a deep ovenproof pot into which the meat fits snugly with the bones tucked around the sides. Pour the dry white wine and 2 cups of water over it. Add a little more water if the meat does not fit tightly into the dish. Cook, uncovered, in a preheated oven at 350°F for 30 minutes until the fat has colored. Then cover with a double layer of aluminum foil; reduce the oven temperature to 300°F and continue cooking the pork for another 2 hours.

When the pork is cooked, remove the bones and leave the meat to cook in the juice, which will set to a jelly. Remove the jelly when set and chop it up finely. If you wish to serve the fat, scrape it from the top of the meat and put it on a small serving dish. Carve the cold pork into ¼-inch-thick slices and arrange them on a dish garnished with the chopped jelly.

Serve with whole wheat bread and the dish of pork fat. The pistachio nuts give the pork a distinctive flavor and an attractive appearance—their green color contrasts with the pink and white of the pork. A green salad tossed in a French dressing (p.304) would go well with the cold pork.

LAMB ARGENTEUIL

In its classic form, this recipe uses asparagus from the district of Argenteuil in France. Tender domestic asparagus gives an equally delicate flavor to the dish.

PREPARATION TIME: *30 minutes*
COOKING TIME: *1 hour*

INGREDIENTS (*for 6*):
2 pounds asparagus
2-pound boned shoulder of lamb
4 small onions
4 tablespoons butter
1½ tablespoons seasoned flour
  (p.412)
½ cup heavy cream
Salt and black pepper
Lemon juice

Wash and scrape the asparagus,* but do not trim. Tie in 3 or 4 bundles with soft string and cook in a large pan of lightly salted water. When the asparagus are tender, after 15–20 minutes, drain well and set the cooking liquid aside. Cut off the asparagus tips about 3 inches down the stems and put the tips aside. Whirl the stems in a blender, then put them through a sieve to make a purée,* discarding any tough or stringy parts.

Trim as much fat as possible off the lamb and cut the meat into 2-inch pieces. Toss them in the seasoned flour to coat evenly. Peel and coarsely chop the onions. Melt the butter in a deep skillet and cook the meat and onions until brown. Gradually blend in about 1¼ cups of the asparagus liquid, stirring continuously until the sauce is smooth and creamy. Simmer until the meat is tender (about 50 minutes), stirring occasionally and removing any fat that rises to the surface. If the liquid evaporates too quickly, cover the pan with a lid.

When the meat is cooked, stir the asparagus purée and cream into the sauce. Season to taste with salt, freshly ground pepper, and a few drops of lemon juice. The sauce should be fairly thick.

Arrange the asparagus tips around the edge of a warm serving dish and spoon the meat and sauce into the center. Boiled new potatoes are all that is needed with the meat.

GRATIN OF HAM

The Morvan region of Burgundy is famous for its cured hams. These are often served with a cream sauce, as in the following recipe. Virginia ham makes a delicious substitute.

PREPARATION TIME: *15 minutes*
COOKING TIME: *45 minutes*

INGREDIENTS (*for 6*):
12 slices baked ham (approximately
  1½ pounds)
¼ pound button mushrooms
2 tablespoons butter
1 onion
3 shallots
½ cup dry white wine
1–1¼ cups canned tomatoes
1¼ cups heavy cream
Salt and black pepper
¼ cup grated Parmesan cheese

Arrange the slices of ham, overlapping each other, in a large, shallow flameproof dish.

Trim the mushrooms* and slice them thinly. Melt the butter in a small skillet and cook the mushrooms for about 8 minutes over low heat. Spoon them, with the butter, over the ham. Peel and finely chop the onion and shallots and put them in a small pan with the wine. Bring to a boil and continue boiling over high heat until the wine has reduced* to about 1½ tablespoons.

Chop the tomatoes coarsely and add to the onions. Cover the pan and simmer over low heat for 10 minutes. Rub the onion and tomato mixture through a fine sieve, and put the resulting purée in a clean pan.

Blend the cream into the purée and bring this sauce to a boil. Season to taste with salt and freshly ground pepper. Pour the sauce over the ham and mushrooms and sprinkle the cheese on top. Bake the ham gratin near the top of the oven, preheated to 450°F, for 10 minutes or until bubbling and brown on top.

Serve the gratin while still bubbling hot, with buttered rice and a tossed green salad.

BEEF PAUPIETTES

Paupiettes are thin slices of meat, usually beef, that are stuffed and rolled into cork shapes which the French call *alouettes sans têtes* ("larks without heads"). The meat should be cut very thinly: Ask the butcher to cut it on the meat slicer.

PREPARATION TIME: *45 minutes*
COOKING TIME: *1½ hours*

INGREDIENTS (*for 4*):
1½ pounds top round of beef, cut in
  thin slices
2½ teaspoons Dijon mustard
Salt and black pepper
STUFFING:
3 ounces lean salt pork
1 cup diced cooked chicken or pork
1 shallot
1 large clove garlic
3 tablespoons butter
1 cup fine white bread crumbs
1 egg
4 teaspoons chopped parsley
½ teaspoon chopped thyme
5 tablespoons brandy
SAUCE:
1 pound mixed vegetables (onions,
  carrots, turnips, peas, green
  beans, parsnips)
3 tablespoons beef drippings or lard
1¼ cups beef stock
½ cup red wine
Beurre manié (p.303)

Pound the beef slices wafer-thin between two pieces of waxed paper; each slice should measure about 4 square inches. Spread a little mustard over each slice; season with salt and ground pepper.

Remove the rind and chop the salt pork finely. Dice the chicken or pork. Peel and finely chop the shallot and garlic. Melt the butter in a small skillet over moderate heat and cook the shallot and garlic until soft and transparent.

In a mixing bowl, blend together the salt pork, chicken, shallot, and garlic. Add the bread crumbs and the lightly beaten egg. Stir in the chopped thyme and parsley, and season the stuffing with salt and black pepper; add the brandy.

Spoon the stuffing equally on the beef slices; roll up each slice and tuck the ends over to keep the stuffing in place. Tie each paupiette securely in several places with thin string. Set the meat aside.

To make the sauce, peel and finely chop the onion, then brown it lightly over moderate heat in the lard or drippings. Wash and prepare the vegetables, then chop them finely. Add these to the onion and cook for a few minutes to brown slightly. Spoon the vegetables into a large shallow casserole and put the paupiettes on top in a single layer. Pour the stock and wine into the pan in which the vegetables were cooked, scraping up all the residue.

Pour the pan juices over the meat, cover the casserole with a lid, and cook in the center of the oven, preheated to 325°F, for 1½ hours. Remove the lid after 20 minutes. Turn the meat once during cooking.

Lift the paupiettes from the casserole, remove the string, and arrange the meat on a warm serving dish. Surround the paupiettes with the vegetables. Pour the cooking liquid into a small saucepan and boil rapidly to reduce* the sauce by a third. Thicken the sauce with beurre manié and heat it through. Spoon a little of the sauce over the meat and serve the rest in a sauceboat.

Serve with buttered noodles or creamed potatoes.

PORK NOISETTES WITH PRUNES

This is a specialty from Tours in the Loire district, where some of the finest French pork and wine are produced. It is an easily prepared dish, but the prunes—large California ones—should be soaked overnight.

PREPARATION TIME: *15 minutes*
COOKING TIME: *40 minutes*

INGREDIENTS (*for 6*):
6 slices pork tenderloin, each 1 inch
  thick, or 6 boned loin chops
1 pound large California prunes
½ bottle dry white wine
Seasoned flour (p.412)
4 tablespoons unsalted butter
4 teaspoons red currant jelly
2 cups heavy cream
Salt and black pepper
Lemon juice

Leave the prunes in a bowl to soak in the wine overnight. Put the prunes and wine in a saucepan and gently simmer, covered, for 20–30 minutes or until tender.

While the prunes are cooking, trim any excess fat off the pork tenderloin or chops. Coat them with seasoned flour, shaking off any surplus. Melt the butter in a heavy-bottomed pan and brown the meat lightly over gentle heat, turning it once only. Cover the pan with a tight-fitting lid and simmer the pork for 30 minutes.

When the meat is nearly done, pour the prune liquid into the pan. Increase the heat and boil rapidly for a few minutes until the liquid has reduced* slightly. Lift the meat onto an ovenproof serving dish and arrange the prunes around it. Keep the meat and prunes warm in the oven while making the sauce.

Stir the red currant jelly into the juices in the pan and boil this sauce over high heat until it has the consistency of syrup. Lower flame slightly and gradually blend in the cream, stirring continuously until the sauce is smooth and thick. Season to taste with salt, pepper, and lemon juice.

Pour the sauce over the meat and serve at once. Traditionally, the pork noisettes are served with boiled potatoes as the only side dish.

TRIPE FRITTERS

Tripe is always sold blanched and usually partially cooked, but make sure to ask the butcher how much longer it should be cooked. The additional cooking time can vary from 30 minutes to 2 hours.

PREPARATION TIME: *20 minutes*
COOKING TIME: *1–2½ hours*

INGREDIENTS (*for 6*):
2 pounds tripe
Bouquet garni (p.410)
2 onions
2 carrots
2 leeks
1 celery stalk
12 black peppercorns
1–2 teaspoons salt
1¼ cups fritter batter (p.344)
Oil for deep-frying
GARNISH:
6 lemon wedges

Put the tripe in a large pan, cover with water, and add the bouquet garni. Cover the pan with a lid and bring the tripe slowly to a boil. Meanwhile, peel and thinly slice the onions and carrots; wash the leeks and the celery thoroughly and cut them into thin slices. Add the vegetables, peppercorns, and 1 teaspoon of the salt to the pan; reduce the heat and simmer the tripe until it is very tender.

While the tripe is cooking, make up the fritter batter. Leave it to rest for 1 hour, adding the egg white just before coating the fritters.

Drain the cooked tripe thoroughly in a colander; the stock can be used as base for a soup or casserole for another meal. Let the tripe cool slightly, then cut it into strips about 1 inch by 1½ inches. Fold the beaten egg white into the fritter batter and coat the tripe strips thoroughly, a few at a time. Heat the oil* in the deep-fryer and cook the fritters until golden brown and crisp. When the fritters are ready, lift them out with a slotted spoon onto a baking sheet covered with a few layers of crumpled paper towels. Keep the fritters warm in the oven (200°F) while deep-frying the next batches of tripe.

Serve the fritters garnished with lemon wedges. A tossed green salad or tomatoes and onions in a French dressing (p.304) would be suitable side dishes.

BRAINS IN CURRY SAUCE

Brains, like any other variety meat, require careful cleaning, and soaking for at least 1 hour. But they are so flavorful and nourishing that they are worth a little trouble.

PREPARATION TIME: *1¼ hours*
COOKING TIME: *30–35 minutes*

INGREDIENTS (*for 4–6*):
2 pounds calf's brains
2½ cups milk
1 onion
1 clove garlic
4 tablespoons butter
1½ tablespoons all-purpose flour
1½ teaspoons curry powder
1¼ cups chicken stock
½–¾ pound green seedless grapes
½ cup heavy cream (optional)
Salt and black pepper

Cover the brains with cold water, add 2 tablespoons of salt, and leave to soak for 1 hour. Rinse them thoroughly under cold running water and remove the fine skin that covers the brains. Cut away any fibers and discolored parts and put the brains in a pan with enough milk to cover.

Bring to a simmer and cook gently for 10 minutes or until the brains are firm. Drain and set the milk aside. Cut the brains into ½-inch slices and arrange them on a serving dish; cover with foil and keep warm.

Peel and finely chop the onion and garlic. Melt the butter in a saucepan and cook the onion and garlic over gentle heat for 5 minutes. Stir in the flour and curry powder, mixing well. Gradually add the chicken stock and ½ cup of the milk in which the brains were cooked; blend thoroughly. Simmer this sauce until it has reduced* to the consistency of thick cream.

While the sauce is cooking, add the grapes and simmer for a further 5 minutes. Stir in the cream and season to taste with salt and freshly ground pepper.

Pour the sauce over the brains and serve with plain boiled rice and triangles of toast.

Poultry

CHICKEN LIVERS WITH GRAPES

Chicken livers are available in the supermarket, either fresh or frozen, and usually at bargain prices. They make a good lunch or supper dish, especially when prepared with a wine sauce delicately flavored with green grapes.

PREPARATION TIME: *25 minutes*
COOKING TIME: *15 minutes*

INGREDIENTS (*for 6*):
1½ pounds chicken livers
Salt and black pepper
¾ pound seedless green grapes
6 slices white bread
1½ sticks butter
2 tablespoons vegetable oil
⅓–½ cup Madeira, port, or sweet sherry

Rinse the chicken livers quickly in cold water and pat them dry. Cut away all the white, stringy pieces and any discolored parts that may have been in contact with the gallbladder—they add a bitter flavor if left on. Season the livers to taste with salt and freshly ground pepper and set them aside.

Remove the crusts from the bread slices. Melt 4 ounces of the butter in a pan, together with the oil; when hot, sauté the bread golden brown on both sides. Put the sautéed bread on a baking sheet and keep warm in the oven while the livers are cooking.

Melt the remaining butter and sauté the livers for 3–5 minutes on each side. Do not overcook; they should be slightly pink in the center. Remove the livers from the pan and keep warm. Stir the wine into the pan juices and reduce* by rapid boiling until the sauce has thickened to a syrupy consistency. Add the grapes to the sauce and let them heat through.

To serve, arrange the sautéed hot bread on a serving dish, top with chicken livers, and spoon the grapes and sauce over them. Serve the livers immediately, before the sauce soaks into the sautéed bread.

CHICKEN BREASTS WITH SAGE

In Italy, where this dish originated, chicken breasts (*petto di pollo*) are usually cooked with a strong flavoring of herbs.

PREPARATION TIME: *30 minutes*
COOKING TIME: *45 minutes*

INGREDIENTS (*for 6*):
3 whole chicken breasts
Seasoned flour (p.412)
1 tablespoon olive oil
1 tablespoon butter
2 thin slices ham
½ cup dry white wine
½ cup chicken stock
12 fresh sage leaves
Salt and black pepper

Skin and bone the breasts* and cut each one in half lengthwise. Coat the chicken with seasoned flour. Heat the oil and butter in a skillet over moderate heat and lightly brown the chicken.

Cut the ham into narrow strips and add to the chicken. When the chicken is golden brown, pour in the white wine and enough stock to almost cover the chicken breasts. Then add the coarsely chopped sage.

Cover the pan with a lid and simmer the chicken over moderate heat for 15–20 minutes. Remove to a serving dish and keep it warm. Increase the heat and rapidly boil the liquid until it has reduced* to a thin coating consistency. Season to taste with salt and pepper.

Pour the sauce over the chicken and serve at once with French bread and a green vegetable.

PEKING DUCK

Several local variations are combined in this version of the classic Chinese recipe. It did not, in fact, originate in Peking, but in Inner Mongolia, and became famous in Peking restaurants only in the last century. Serving and eating Peking duck are matters for some ceremony; the crackling skin is sliced off and served with sliced duck meat, to be wrapped in pancakes with scallions and a spicy sauce.

PREPARATION TIME: *2 hours*
COOKING TIME: *1½ hours*

INGREDIENTS (*for 4–6*):
1 large duck, approximately 5–6 pounds
2 tablespoons brandy, vodka, or gin (optional)
18 scallions
PANCAKES:
4 cups all-purpose flour
2 tablespoons sesame seed oil
TABLE SAUCE:
5 tablespoons Hoisin, or plum, sauce
2 teaspoons sugar
2 teaspoons sesame seed oil
BASTING SAUCE:
4 tablespoons soy sauce
1½ tablespoons superfine sugar

The essence of Peking duck is its crisp skin, which is stripped off the cooked duck and served separately. The skin of the uncooked duck should be thoroughly dried. Wipe and dry the duck and pass a length of string under the wings so that it can be suspended from a rod or broom handle placed across the seats of two chairs. Set a plate under the duck to catch any drips. Rubbing the skin with the brandy, vodka, or gin aids the drying process. Direct a blast of air at the duck from an electric fan and let it dry for at least 3–4 hours. Alternatively, hang the duck for 8 hours or overnight in a drafty place.

Remove roots and blemished leaves from the scallions, trimming them to a length of 3–4 inches. Wash them thoroughly. Use a sharp knife to make two cuts ½–¾ inch long at the bulb end of each scallion, then make two similar cuts at right angles to the first cuts. Put the scallions in a large bowl of iced water and leave in the refrigerator until required. The cut ends of each scallion will fan out to resemble a brush.

To make the pancakes, sift the flour into a bowl. Bring 2½ cups of water to a boil and, mixing all the time, gradually add only enough of the boiling water to make a soft dough that leaves the sides of the bowl clean. Knead the dough for 10 minutes on a lightly floured surface until it becomes rubbery. Cover with a cloth and leave for 20 minutes. Roll the dough out, ¼ inch thick, and cut it into rounds with a plain 2-inch cookie cutter. Brush the top of half the rounds with sesame seed oil and place an unbrushed round on top. Roll out each pair of pancakes (about 14), as thinly as possible, to a diameter of about 6 inches.

Heat an ungreased griddle or heavy skillet for 30 seconds, then lower the heat. Put in the first pair of pancakes, turning when bubbles appear on the surface and the underside is flecked with brown and looks floury. Cook all the pancakes in this way (they may puff up into balloons), and allow them to cool. Wrap the cooked pancakes in several foil packages and store them in the refrigerator until needed.

Mix the table sauce ingredients together in a small pan, add 1 tablespoon of cold water, and bring the sauce to a boil; stir over low heat for 2–3 minutes. Pour the sauce into a serving bowl.

Rice & Pasta

RISOTTO ALLA MILANESE

There are several versions of Milanese risotto, some made with chicken broth, others with white wine or Marsala. The classic flavoring of saffron, however, is always included in this dish. The rice can be served as a course on its own, and is also the traditional accompaniment to Osso Buco (p.180).

PREPARATION TIME: *20 minutes*
COOKING TIME: *20 minutes*

INGREDIENTS (*for 6*):
2 cups Italian or short grain rice
1 marrow bone
1 small onion
6 tablespoons unsalted butter
½ cup dry white wine
5 cups boiling beef stock
½ teaspoon powdered saffron
¾ cup grated Parmesan cheese

Ask the butcher to chop the bone into several pieces, so that the marrow can be easily extracted with a skewer—it should yield about ⅓ cup. Peel and finely chop the onion.

Melt half the butter in a large, heavy-bottomed pan, add the onion and sauté over moderate heat until translucent. Add the marrow. Pour the wine over the onion and boil briskly until reduced* by half. Add the rice and sauté it, stirring until it begins to change color.

Stir the boiling stock, a cupful at a time, into the rice until completely absorbed. Blend in all the stock and, finally, stir in the saffron. The rice should be tender after 15–20 minutes. If necessary, add a little hot water to the pan to prevent the rice from drying out.

Stir the remaining butter and grated Parmesan cheese into the rice and serve at once.

SPAGHETTI ALL'UOVA

Known as poor man's spaghetti, this pasta dish has no meat sauce, but is served only with eggs and Romano cheese. This cheese, made from sheep's milk, is a specialty from the Sabine district.

PREPARATION TIME: *10 minutes*
COOKING TIME: *10–15 minutes*

INGREDIENTS (*for 6*):
1¼ pounds spaghetti
Salt
2–3 ounces Romano or Parmesan cheese
6 eggs
½ pound butter

Bring a large pot of lightly salted water to a boil, add the spaghetti, and cook, uncovered, for 10–12 minutes or until *al dente.**

Meanwhile, grate the cheese into a serving bowl. Break the eggs into a large bowl and beat them lightly with a fork. Put half the butter on a serving dish and cut the remainder into small pieces.

Drain the cooked spaghetti in a colander and put it into a large hot serving bowl. Stir in the eggs quickly, tossing the spaghetti and eggs thoroughly with two spoons until the eggs have set.

Dot the spaghetti and egg mixture with the pieces of butter and serve at once. Serve on the side the grated cheese and remaining butter.

Mix the ingredients for the basting sauce with ½ cup of cold water, and brush the sauce all over the duck. Place the duck, breast upwards, on a wire rack in a roasting pan. Pour in enough boiling water to reach ¼ inch up the sides of the pan. Roast the duck in the lower part of a preheated oven at 400°F for 1¼ hours. Brush with the basting sauce every 15 or 20 minutes. After 45 minutes turn up the heat to 450°F. Then put the packages of prepared

pancakes into the oven to reheat.

To assemble the final dish, cut off the duck skin with scissors or a sharp knife, in 1–2 inch squares; place on a serving dish and keep warm. Carve the meat into long thin slivers and arrange on another dish to keep warm. Pile the pancakes on a hot dish and cover with a napkin or folded cloth to keep them warm. Put the scallion brushes in a bowl or dish and arrange all these dishes, with the table sauce, on the table.

To eat, carefully pull the two halves of a pancake apart, starting where the seam can be seen quite clearly. Dip a scallion brush in the sauce and brush it liberally onto the soft moist side of the open pancake. Top with pieces of the duck skin and the slivers of meat; carefully fold and roll up the pancake.

The Chinese use chopsticks to eat the rolled pancakes, but fingers and a fork are just as effective. Fingerbowls are useful.

Vegetables & Salads

RICE CAKES

In central and northern Italy these small sweet cakes are often deep-fried and sold piping hot on street corners. This recipe is for a slightly more elaborate version that could be served as a snack or as a dessert.

PREPARATION TIME: *10 minutes*
COOKING TIME: *30 minutes*

INGREDIENTS (*for 6*):
⅔ *cup short or long grain rice*
1¼ *cups milk*
Salt
½ *cup superfine sugar*
3 tablespoons butter
1 lemon
½ *cup plus 1 tablespoon all-purpose flour*
3 eggs
1 tablespoon rum
Vegetable oil
2½ *teaspoons powdered cinnamon*

Bring a large pan of water to a boil, add the rice, and boil steadily for 7 minutes. Drain the rice in a sieve, rinse under cold running water, and return to the pan with the milk.

Simmer over moderate heat for about 10 minutes, or until the milk is almost completely absorbed.

Remove the pan from the heat and stir in a good pinch of salt, 2 teaspoons of the sugar, and the butter. Grate the rind from the lemon into the rice and then cut the lemon into wedges. Allow the rice to cool until tepid; stir in the flour. Separate the eggs. Beat the yolks thoroughly and then add them to the rice, together with the rum.

Whip the egg whites until stiff and dry, then fold them carefully into the rice mixture. Heat sufficient oil to half fill the basket in the deep-fryer; when hot, drop tablespoons of rice mixture into the oil, a few at a time. Cook until the rice cakes are delicately golden brown, then remove and drain on crumpled paper towels. Do not overcook, as this hardens the outer layer of rice.

Serve with the wedges of lemon and a bowl of the remaining sugar mixed with the cinnamon.

ASPARAGUS WITH NEW POTATOES

With the leftover stems and liquid from this recipe, one can make an asparagus soup for another meal.

PREPARATION TIME: *45 minutes*
COOKING TIME: *30 minutes*

INGREDIENTS (*for 6*):
2 pounds asparagus
2 pounds new potatoes
½ *teaspoon salt*
6 thin slices prosciutto
½ *pound unsalted butter*
Lemon juice
GARNISH:
1 tablespoon fresh chopped parsley

Wash the asparagus* carefully and lightly scrape the spears away from the tips. Cut off the lower 2 or 3 inches of each spear where the white stalk begins and set these pieces aside. Tie the asparagus in bundles with soft string.

Wash and scrape the potatoes and put them in a large saucepan with the reserved pieces of asparagus. Cover with plenty of cold water, then add the salt and bring the water to a boil. Stand the bundles of asparagus upright in the pan and cover with a lid (if the pan is not deep enough, cover with foil). Cook over moderate heat for about 10–12 minutes, or until the asparagus tips are tender to the touch.

Remove the asparagus bundles from the pan, but leave the potatoes to cook until tender. Untie the asparagus and divide into 6 equal portions. Wrap a slice of prosciutto around each portion and arrange them neatly around the edge of a serving dish.

Lift the cooked potatoes from the pan and drain them (setting aside the liquid and asparagus pieces for the soup). Put the potatoes in the center of the serving dish. Melt the butter over low heat, pour a little over the potatoes, and serve the remainder, seasoned with a little lemon juice, in a sauceboat.

Sprinkle the chopped parsley over the potatoes and serve the dish warm rather than hot.

ASPARAGUS SOUP

Use the asparagus water and stem sections from the previous recipe, together with:

1 large onion
1 small clove garlic
4 tablespoons butter
1½ *tablespoons all-purpose flour*
Milk
Salt and black pepper
½ *cup light or heavy cream*
GARNISH:
Chopped chervil or parsley

Peel and finely chop the onion and garlic. Melt the butter in a large saucepan and cook the onion and garlic in this until soft and transparent. Stir in the flour and cook for a few minutes, before gradually blending in the asparagus water. Add the asparagus stalk sections and cook the soup for 10 minutes.

Take the pan off the heat, leave the soup to cool slightly, then put it first through a blender and then through a sieve to make a purée.* Add milk to the desired soup consistency and season to taste with salt and freshly ground pepper. Reheat the soup and blend in the light or heavy cream, without letting the soup boil.

Serve the soup in individual bowls and sprinkle the chopped chervil or parsley on top.

JEWISH EGGS AND PEAS

Fresh or even frozen green peas are excellent for this adaptation of an 18th-century European recipe. It can be served as a first course or as a supper dish on its own.

PREPARATION TIME: *20 minutes*
COOKING TIME: *15–20 minutes*

INGREDIENTS (*for 6*):
2½ *pounds green peas*
6 tablespoons olive oil
¼ *teaspoon nutmeg*
¼ *teaspoon mace*
Cayenne pepper
Salt and black pepper
7 eggs
½ *cup light cream*

This dish should be cooked in a shallow, flameproof casserole which can be brought straight to the table. Shell the peas (they should now measure 3–4 cups) and put them in the casserole with ¼ cup of water, the oil, spices, a few twists of freshly ground pepper, and about ¼ teaspoon salt. Cover the pan with a lid and simmer until the peas are half-cooked, after about 8 minutes. Correct seasoning if necessary.

Remove the casserole from the heat and make 6 depressions in the peas with a large spoon. Break 6 eggs, one at a time, into a saucer and slip an egg into each depression. Return the casserole to the heat, cover with a lid, and cook for a further 8–10 minutes, or until the whites have set.

Beat the remaining egg with the cream. Pour this mixture over the cooked eggs and place the dish under a hot broiler for 2–3 minutes to set. Serve with crusty bread and butter.

PISSALADIÈRE

This strongly flavored tart is a specialty of the region around Nice. It is somewhat similar to the Italian pizza, but the pastry crust is of lighter texture. Pissaladière makes a substantial lunch or supper dish when served with a green salad.

PREPARATION TIME: *20 minutes*
COOKING TIME: *1¼ hours*

INGREDIENTS (*for 6–8*):
1½ cups all-purpose flour
1 teaspoon cinnamon
6 tablespoons unsalted butter
1 egg
2 pounds onions
3 cloves garlic
7–8 tablespoons olive oil
2 cups canned tomatoes
1 tablespoon tomato paste
1 teaspoon sugar
Bouquet garni (p.410)
Salt and black pepper
¾ cup black olives
2 2-ounce cans anchovy fillets

Sift together the flour and cinnamon into a mixing bowl; cut up the but-

ter and rub it into the flour until the mixture resembles bread crumbs. Add the lightly beaten egg and enough cold water to make the pastry come cleanly away from the sides of the bowl.

Knead the pastry lightly on a floured board and then roll it out ¼ inch thick. Line a 10- or 11-inch-diameter tart or pie pan with the pastry; prick the base lightly with the prongs of a fork. Bake the tart blind* in the center of an oven preheated to 400°F for about 15 minutes, or until the pastry is set but not brown.

Peel the onions and slice them thinly; peel and finely chop the garlic. Heat the olive oil in a large, heavy-bottomed pan and cook the onions and garlic over low heat until they are soft and transparent, after about 40 minutes.

Chop the tomatoes coarsely and put them in a separate pan with the tomato paste, sugar, and bouquet garni; boil rapidly to reduce* the mixture to about 6 tablespoons. Remove the bouquet garni and stir the tomatoes into the cooked onions. Season to taste with pepper and a little salt, bearing in mind the saltiness of the anchovies and olives.

Spoon the onion and tomato mixture into the pastry crust and arrange the anchovy fillets in a criss-cross pattern on top; decorate with the black olives. Bake the tart in the center of an oven, preheated to 400°F, for 20 minutes; brush the top with a little olive oil after the tart has cooked for 10 minutes.

Pissaladière is best served hot as soon as baked. Cut it into wedges like a pie.

NAPOLEON'S BEAN SALAD

In exile on St. Helena, Napoleon was still emperor at his own table. This white bean salad is said to have been a favorite of his and was served every day at lunchtime. Soak beans for about 8 hours before cooking.

PREPARATION TIME: *10 minutes*
COOKING TIME: *2–3 hours*
CHILLING TIME: *1 hour*

INGREDIENTS (*for 6*):
½ pound (1 cup) flageolet beans
1 onion
1 carrot
Bouquet garni (p.410)
Salt and black pepper
½ cup finely chopped parsley,
*   chervil, tarragon, chives, or*
*   scallions*
⅓ cup olive oil
1½ tablespoons tarragon vinegar
1½ teaspoons Dijon mustard
½ teaspoon superfine sugar

Drop the beans into 1 quart rapidly boiling water. Bring rapidly back to a boil. Boil for 2 minutes. Remove pan from heat and let the beans soak in the water for 1 hour. Drain the beans and put them in a large pan or casserole. Peel and quarter the onion and carrot, and add them, with the bouquet garni and plenty of black pepper, to the beans. Pour over enough water to cover the beans by ½ inch. Put a lid on the pan and cook in the center of a preheated oven at 275°–300°F for 3 hours, or on top of the stove at simmering point for 2 hours. If necessary, add water to cover during cooking so that the beans do not dry out.

Season the cooked beans to taste with salt and cook for another 5 minutes. Drain the beans in a colander, remove the onion, carrot,

and bouquet garni, and put the beans in a large serving bowl. Add the chopped herbs, oil, vinegar, mustard, and sugar to the beans. Stir to blend the ingredients thoroughly and leave to chill in the refrigerator for about 1 hour.

LIMOGES POTATO PIE

In spring the country around Limoges in France can be wet and cold. Consequently, the regional food tends to be warm and filling. This potato pie can be served as a supper dish on its own or as a first course.

PREPARATION TIME: *35 minutes*
COOKING TIME: *35 minutes*

INGREDIENTS (*for 6*):
Puff pastry (p.363)
1½ pounds new potatoes
1 medium onion
3–4 cloves garlic
Salt and black pepper
Nutmeg
4 tablespoons butter
⅓ cup light cream
⅓ cup heavy cream
1 egg
Bunch of fresh parsley, chives, and
*   chervil*

Prepare the recipe for puff pastry as directed on p.363. Roll out half the pastry on a lightly floured board and use to line a 10-inch flan ring or shallow cake pan. Wash and peel the potatoes. Slice the potatoes very thinly and put them in a bowl of cold water to prevent them from turning brown.

Bring a pan of lightly salted water to a boil, put in the sliced potatoes, and cook for 2 minutes only, after the water has returned to a boil. Drain the potatoes thoroughly

in a colander. Peel and finely chop the onion and garlic.

Put a layer of potato slices on top of the pastry crust, sprinkle with the onion and garlic, and season with a little salt, nutmeg, and freshly ground pepper. Repeat these layers, seasoning each, until all the vegetables are used up, finishing with a layer of potato. Dot the vegetables with the butter, cut into small pieces. Mix the creams together and pour about half over the potatoes.

Roll out the remaining pastry and cover the pie, sealing the edges firmly. Make a small hole in the center of the pastry crust for the steam to escape. Beat the egg into the remaining cream and brush a little of this mixture over the pastry to glaze it while cooking. Score the pastry lightly into sections with a sharp knife—this makes it easier to cut the finished pie into portions.

Bake the pie near the top of a preheated oven at 450°F for 30 minutes. Protect the pastry with a piece of buttered paper if the pastry browns too quickly.

Chop the fresh herbs finely and blend them into the remaining egg and cream mixture. When the pie is cooked, pour the egg and cream mixture into the center hole, using a small kitchen funnel. Do this slowly in case there is not room for all the cream. Return the pie to the oven for 5 minutes, then serve at once.

SAVORY CUCUMBERS

Cucumber is most often used raw in salads or for garnishing, and rarely appears as a cooked main course. In this French recipe, stuffed cucumbers are served hot as a savory snack.

PREPARATION TIME: *10 minutes*
COOKING TIME: *50 minutes*

INGREDIENTS (*for 6*):
3 cucumbers, unwaxed
$\frac{3}{4}$ cup long grain rice
1 large onion
9 tablespoons butter
$\frac{1}{2}$ pound mushrooms
4 lean slices bacon
Salt and black pepper
3 eggs
GARNISH:
Chopped parsley

Wash, but do not peel, the unwaxed cucumbers. Cut each in half crosswise, then cut each half in 2 lengthwise. Scrape out the seeds with the point of a teaspoon and discard. Cook the cucumbers for 10 minutes in boiling, lightly salted water. Drain, cover with a lid, and keep them warm in the oven at its lowest setting.

Cook the rice slowly in a covered saucepan in 2 cups boiling salted water for 25–30 minutes. While the rice is cooking, peel and chop the onion, and cook over gentle heat in 4 tablespoons of the butter until translucent but not brown.

Trim and thinly slice the mushrooms;* add to the onions. Cut the bacon into narrow strips; add to the mixture in the pan and season with salt and freshly ground pepper. When the rice is cooked, drain in a sieve and rinse under cold running water. Stir it into the onion mixture, adding 4 tablespoons of butter. Cook over low heat, stirring occasionally, for 5–10 minutes.

Lightly beat the eggs and season with salt and pepper. Cook 2 or 3 small omelets (p.335) in the remaining butter. Roll the omelets up and cut them into strips about $\frac{1}{2}$ inch wide. Add these strips to the rice mixture.

To serve, arrange the cucumber boats on a hot dish and fill them with the rice mixture. Sprinkle with chopped parsley.

Desserts

CHERRY-NUT CAKE

Rich with cherries, walnuts, and whisky, this cake needs no frosting and keeps well for days. It is best made the day before serving.

PREPARATION TIME: *35 minutes*
COOKING TIME: *1 hour*

INGREDIENTS (*for 8–10*):
1 8-ounce jar maraschino cherries
$1\frac{1}{2}$–2 cups walnut meats
$1\frac{1}{2}$ cups all-purpose flour
$1\frac{1}{4}$ teaspoons double-acting baking powder
$\frac{1}{2}$ teaspoon salt
2 teaspoons nutmeg
$\frac{1}{2}$ cup good rye or bourbon whisky
3 eggs
1 cup sugar
1 stick soft butter
2 tablespoons confectioners' sugar (optional)

Drain and chop the cherries and dry on paper towels. Chop the walnuts and mix with the cherries and $\frac{1}{2}$ cup of the sifted flour in a small bowl. In another bowl, sift the remaining cup of flour with the baking powder and the salt. In a third bowl, combine the nutmeg and whisky.

Separate eggs* and set the yolks aside. Beat the egg whites with an egg beater or with an electric mixer at high speed until stiff; gradually add $\frac{1}{3}$ cup of the sugar, beating until very stiff. Set aside.

In a large mixing bowl beat the butter, the remaining $\frac{2}{3}$ cup sugar, and the egg yolks for about 5 minutes or until fluffy. Slowly beat in the whisky and the flour mixtures, alternately and a little at a time, and beat only until the batter is smooth. With a rubber spatula fold in the cherries and walnuts, then fold in the stiffly beaten egg whites. Turn the mixture into a 9-inch tube pan, greased and lined with wax paper cut to fit the bottom.

Bake in the center of a preheated oven at 325°F for 1 hour, or until a cake tester inserted in the middle of the cake comes out clean. Cool in the pan on a wire rack for 30 minutes. Remove the cake from the pan and peel off the paper. When completely cool, dust the top with confectioners' sugar, if desired.

GOOSEBERRY TART

In May gooseberries are occasionally available in the markets. This dessert is based on an English recipe from the 18th century when puréed, wine-flavored fruits were popular.

PREPARATION TIME: *1 hour*
COOKING TIME: *15 minutes*

INGREDIENTS (*for 6*):
$1\frac{1}{2}$ pounds gooseberries
1 cup all-purpose flour
4 teaspoons confectioners' sugar
11 tablespoons unsalted butter
1 large egg yolk
Superfine sugar
3 large eggs
1 tablespoon orange-flower water or 2 tablespoons white muscatel

Sift together the flour and confectioners' sugar into a large bowl. Cut up 5 tablespoons of the butter and rub into the flour until the mixture resembles fine bread crumbs. Add one egg yolk and enough water to bind the pastry.

Roll the pastry out on a lightly floured surface to $\frac{1}{4}$-inch thickness and use to line a buttered 7-inch-diameter, loose-bottomed pie plate. Prick the pastry with a fork and bake it blind* in the center of a preheated oven at 350°F for 15 minutes.

Wash and drain the gooseberries. Put them in a large saucepan with 5 tablespoons of water. Cover the pan with a lid and cook over low heat for 10 minutes, then increase the heat and cook until the gooseberries have burst and are soft.

Rub the gooseberries through a sieve and sweeten this purée* with superfine sugar to taste. Put the purée in a clean pan. Stir over low heat, adding the remaining 6 tablespoons of butter in small pieces.

Remove the pan from the heat. Beat the 3 eggs and stir them into the purée. Return the pan to the heat and cook, stirring continuously, until the purée thickens. It should not be allowed to boil. Cool slightly, then add orange-flower water or wine to taste.

If necessary, reheat the pastry shell. Spoon the gooseberry purée into the pastry shell and serve it warm, with cream.

CHILLED ALMOND SOUFFLÉ

This rich soufflé with a crunchy topping makes an excellent dessert for a dinner party.

PREPARATION TIME: *25–30 minutes*
COOKING TIME: *5–10 minutes*
CHILLING TIME: *3–4 hours*

INGREDIENTS (*for 6*):
$\frac{1}{4}$ pound whole shelled almonds
1 cup sugar
$1\frac{1}{4}$ cups milk
$\frac{1}{2}$ vanilla bean
3 large eggs, separated
1 envelope gelatin
$1\frac{1}{4}$ cups heavy cream
1 tablespoon confectioners' sugar
GARNISH:
$\frac{1}{2}$ cup blanched almonds
8 graham crackers

Split the unblanched almonds in half. Put 8 tablespoons of sugar and 2 tablespoons of cold water into a small pan and cook over low heat, stirring until the sugar dissolves. Bring this syrup to a boil and continue cooking, without stirring, until the syrup turns golden brown. Stir in the almonds. Remove the pan from the heat and spread the mixture to cool on an oiled cookie sheet. When it is cool and set, break it into large pieces and crush it to a fine powder in a blender or with a rolling pin.

To make the soufflé, bring the milk, vanilla bean, and remaining sugar to a boil over low heat. Put the egg yolks in the top of a double boiler and gradually pour in the hot milk, beating all the time to prevent curdling. Put this pan over barely simmering water and beat until the custard thickens slightly. Take the bowl from the heat and remove the vanilla bean. Dissolve the gelatin in 5 tablespoons of hot water, allow it to cool a little, then add to the custard. Stir well and strain into a bowl.

When the mixture is cool but not set, whip the cream with the confectioners' sugar until thick, and fold into the custard. Beat the egg whites until stiff and fold them in. Blend in the almond mixture.

Tie foil around a straight-sided 1-pint soufflé dish so that it extends by about 1 inch around the top. Pour in the soufflé mixture and refrigerate for 3–4 hours.

For the garnish, toast the blanched almonds under the broiler until lightly browned, then grind them finely. Crush the graham crackers with a rolling pin and blend with the almonds. Before serving, remove the foil collar and press the almond mixture into the soufflé's sides and over the top.

GÂTEAU DE PITHIVIERS FEUILLETÉ

This splendid French puff pastry cake is a specialty of Pithiviers, a small town just south of Paris.

PREPARATION TIME: *2 hours*
COOKING TIME: *50 minutes*

INGREDIENTS (*for 6*):
Puff pastry (p.363)
1 egg for glazing
1 tablespoon confectioners' sugar
ALMOND CAKE:
7 tablespoons butter, softened
8 tablespoons sugar
¾ cup finely ground almonds
1 whole egg plus 1 egg yolk
1½ tablespoons kirsch

Prepare the puff pastry as directed on p.363. Divide the pastry in half and place one half in refrigerator. Roll the other half out ⅛ inch thick on a floured surface. Using an inverted 10-inch cake pan as a guide, cut a disk 10 inches in diameter. This will be the bottom layer. Roll up the pastry disk on the rolling pin and unroll top side down on a baking sheet moistened with cold water. Refrigerate 30 minutes or more.

Take the other half of the pastry out of the refrigerator, roll out ⅛ inch thick, and cut another disk 10 inches in diameter. Roll up this disk on the rolling pin and unroll it on a baking sheet covered with waxed paper. This will be the top layer. Refrigerate 30 minutes or more.

To make the almond cake, beat the soft butter and the sugar until fluffy. Add the other ingredients and mix briefly. Set in the refrigerator 1–2 hours or in the freezer 30–40 minutes to harden. Using your hands, shape the mixture into a patty 5 inches in diameter, wrap in waxed paper, and return it to the refrigerator to chill until ready to use.

Remove the bottom layer of pastry from the refrigerator and set the almond cake on its center. Brush the area around the almond cake lightly with ice water.

Remove the other disk from the refrigerator and quickly, with the palms of the hands, press down on the dough to enlarge the disk to about 10½ inches in diameter. Unroll it over the almond cake, and press firmly with lightly floured fingers all around the edges. Invert a 9-inch cake pan, center it on the cake and press down firmly to seal the two circles. With a sharp knife, make a nick every 1½ inches around the top edge of the pastry. Cut shallow scallops from one nick to the next, cutting both layers of pastry at once. Refrigerate for 20 minutes and preheat oven to 425°F.

Remove the cake from the refrigerator. With a small knife, make a ½-inch hole in the center of the top and insert a buttered aluminum foil chimney. Beat the egg lightly with 1 teaspoon of water and brush it over the top of the pastry to glaze it. Do not brush the vertical edges with this mixture, as this may keep the pastry from rising properly. With the point of a small knife, cut curved lines ⅛ inch deep from the center of the pastry to the edge of each scallop to represent flower petals. Reduce oven heat to 400°F and bake for 50 minutes, or until sides are lightly browned.

Remove from the oven and sift confectioners' sugar over the cake. Place it under the broiler for a few minutes to melt the sugar. Slide onto a rack to cool. Serve warm or cold at the table, cut into wedges like a pie.

A portion of croûtes aux abricots, topped with whipped cream and garnished with chopped angelica. A perfect dessert after a rich main course.

Biscuit Tortoni is an impressive dessert. Victor Hugo, who often dined at the Tortoni restaurant, is said to have been extremely fond of this ice cream.

CROÛTES AUX ABRICOTS

A croûte is a classic French garnish of bread. For a dessert, the croûtes should be sweet bread, and brioches are the most suitable.

PREPARATION TIME: *10 minutes*
COOKING TIME: *20 minutes*

INGREDIENTS (*for 6*):
12 ripe apricots
¾ cup sugar
3 brioches
¾–1 cup clarified butter
½ cup heavy cream
1 tablespoon kirsch (optional)
GARNISH:
Angelica*

Cut the apricots in half and remove the pits. Bring the sugar and 2 tablespoons of cold water to a boil in a saucepan, then add the apricots and poach them gently for 6–8 minutes; they should be tender and retain their shape. Carefully lift out the apricots and keep them warm. Turn up the heat and boil the liquid rapidly until it has reduced* to a thick syrup. Do not allow it to turn brown and caramelize. Let the syrup cool.

Trim the crusts from the brioches and cut into 6 slices, ½ inch thick; sauté them in clarified butter* on both sides until golden brown. Keep warm. Whip the cream lightly and flavor it to taste with the apricot syrup and kirsch (if used).

To serve, arrange the fried brioche slices on a dish and put 4 apricot halves on each slice. Top with a swirl of cream and garnish with finely chopped angelica.

BISCUIT TORTONI

During the 19th century, Tortoni's restaurant in Paris was famous for its buffet table, patronized by many great writers. This dessert was one of its best-known creations.

PREPARATION TIME: *15 minutes*
FREEZING TIME: *3 hours*

INGREDIENTS (*for 6–8*):
1¼ cups heavy cream
½ cup plus 2 tablespoons light cream
½ cup confectioners' sugar
Salt
12 macaroons
6 tablespoons cream sherry
GARNISH:
Gaufrettes (French wafers) or almond cookies

About 1 hour before beginning preparations, turn the freezer to its coldest setting.

Whip the creams together with the sugar and a pinch of salt until the mixture is firm but not stiff. Spoon into a 9-inch loaf pan or plastic box, cover with a lid or a double layer of foil, and freeze the cream until nearly solid.

Put the macaroons into a plastic or brown paper bag and crush them to fine crumbs with a rolling pin, or in a blender. Set aside a third of the crumbs for decoration.

Break up the frozen cream mixture into a bowl and blend in the sherry and remaining macaroon crumbs with a whisk. The mixture should stay light; add a little more sugar and sherry if necessary. Spoon the mixture into the washed and dried container, cover, and return to the freezer.

When the cream has frozen quite firm again, remove it from the refrigerator and invert the container on a serving plate. Rub the container with a cloth wrung out in very hot water until the ice cream drops out. Press the macaroon crumbs lightly into the top and sides of the ice cream with a broad-bladed spatula and serve at once.

AVOCADO FOOL

The origin of the word "fool" to describe a purée of fruit mixed with cream or custard goes back to 16th-century England. It was then a synonym for a trifling thing of small consequence. This avocado fool is an unusual, refreshing dessert, best flavored with lime.

PREPARATION TIME: *20 minutes*
CHILLING TIME: *2 hours*

INGREDIENTS (*for 6*):
3 large avocados
2 limes or 1 large lemon
1½ tablespoons confectioners' sugar
½ cup heavy cream

Peel the avocados* and remove the pits. Dice the avocado flesh finely. Cut a thin slice from the middle of one lime or the lemon and divide the slice into 6 small wedges; set them aside. Squeeze the juice from the fruit into a blender and then add the confectioners' sugar.

Blend for 30 seconds. Add the diced avocado and blend until the mixture has become a smooth purée.* Whip the cream and fold it into the purée, adding more sugar and fruit juice to taste.

Spoon into 6 individual glasses and chill in the refrigerator for at least 2 hours. Garnish with the reserved lime or lemon wedges, and serve with ladyfingers.

Snacks & Supper Dishes

PASTIES

The pasty was the midday meal of miners in Michigan's copper country, and it is still eaten there. The pastry envelope contains a filling of vegetables, meat, or poultry.

PREPARATION TIME: *20–30 minutes*
COOKING TIME: *40 minutes*

INGREDIENTS (*for 4*):
Standard pastry (p.354)
½ pound stewing beef
2 coarsely grated potatoes
1 small turnip, coarsely grated
1 finely chopped onion
Salt and black pepper
1 tablespoon unsalted butter
1 egg, lightly beaten

Trim any excess fat from the beef and cut the meat into paper-thin slices with a sharp knife. Mix the meat with the vegetables.

Roll out the pastry,* about ¼ inch thick, on a lightly floured board and, using a large saucer as a guide, cut out 4 circles. Pile the filling in the center of each pastry circle. Season with salt and pepper, and top with a piece of butter. Dampen the pastry edges with cold water and carefully draw up 2 edges to meet on top of the filling. Pinch and twist the pastry firmly together to form a neat fluted and curved pattern. Cut a small air vent in the side of each pasty.

Brush the pasties with the lightly beaten egg and place them on a greased baking sheet. Bake in the center of a preheated oven at 425°F for 10 minutes. Reduce the heat to 350°F for 30 minutes.

BARBECUED SAUSAGES

A spicy basting sauce, more often used with foods cooked on outdoor grills, adds tang to these oven-baked pork sausages.

PREPARATION TIME: *10 minutes*
MARINATING TIME: *1 hour*
COOKING TIME: *20 minutes*

INGREDIENTS (*for 4*):
1 pound pork sausages
2 tablespoons olive oil
2 tablespoons tomato ketchup
2 teaspoons Dijon mustard
½ teaspoon Worcestershire sauce
Salt and black pepper

Pierce the skin of the sausages with the prongs of a fork. Arrange them in one layer in a roasting pan or ovenproof dish. Mix together the oil, ketchup, mustard, and Worcestershire sauce. Season with salt and pepper and pour this marinade over the sausages. Set the sausages aside for at least an hour, turning them occasionally.

Bake in the center of a hot oven, preheated to 400°F, for 20 minutes, basting frequently, until the sausages are well browned.

Serve hot with creamy mashed potatoes and broiled tomatoes, or cold in buttered rolls.

SALMON DREAMS

Golden fried salmon sandwiches provide a quick snack. For a light lunch or supper, a tossed salad or a green vegetable may be served with them.

PREPARATION TIME: *15 minutes*
COOKING TIME: *8–10 minutes*

INGREDIENTS (*for 4*):
16 slices white bread
4 tablespoons unsalted butter
7¾-ounce can salmon
2 ounces cream cheese
1 tablespoon grated Cheddar cheese
Salt and black pepper
1 egg
1 tablespoon milk
Paprika
Fat or oil for frying

Using a 2–3 inch biscuit cutter, cut 16 circles from the bread, and butter each circle. Drain the salmon and remove any skin and bone. Mash the flesh with a fork; stir in the cream cheese and grated cheese. Season with pepper and a little salt. Spread the mixture thickly on half the bread circles, top with remaining slices, and sandwich firmly together.

Beat together the egg and milk. Season with salt, pepper, and paprika. Dip the sandwiches in the beaten egg and sauté them on both sides in hot fat until crisp and golden. Drain on crumpled paper towels and serve at once.

LAMPLE PIE

The name of this unusual dish is an 18th-century corruption of "lamb and apple pie." The herbs add a fresh taste to leftover meat.

PREPARATION TIME: *20 minutes*
COOKING TIME: *35 minutes*

INGREDIENTS (*for 4-6*):
1½-2 cups finely chopped cooked lamb
1-1½ cups finely chopped cooked ham
½ pound cooking apples (peeled, cored, and sliced)
1 large thinly sliced onion
Salt and black pepper
¼ teaspoon each, rosemary and sage
1⅛-1¾ cups chicken stock
1 tablespoon tomato paste
Standard pastry (p.354)
1 beaten egg

Arrange the chopped lamb and ham in layers with the apple and onion in an 8-inch buttered baking dish. Sprinkle each layer with a little salt, pepper, and herbs. Mix the stock with the tomato paste and pour it over the pie. Cover the pie with rolled-out pastry, sealing the edges firmly; cut an air vent in the center of the pastry for the steam to escape. Brush the pastry with the lightly beaten egg.

Bake in the center of the oven, preheated to 450°F, for 10 minutes, then lower the heat to 350°F and cook for a further 25 minutes. Serve hot or cold with a crisp green salad and beer.

SPANISH CAKE DESSERT

Stale sponge or fruit cake and a little leftover fruit salad are here transformed into a delicious warm dessert with a custard sauce.

PREPARATION TIME: *10 minutes*
COOKING TIME: *15 minutes*

INGREDIENTS (*for 4-6*):
4 large slices stale sponge or fruit cake
1 cup fruit, fresh or canned
½ cup fresh or frozen orange juice
1 tablespoon rum
1 teaspoon cornstarch
1¼ cups light cream
2 egg yolks
4 tablespoons sugar
Salt
Vanilla extract

Arrange the sponge or fruit cake in a lightly buttered ovenproof dish and top with fruit. Pour over the orange juice and rum, and bake in the center of a preheated oven at 375°F for 10-15 minutes.

Mix the cornstarch with a little cream. Beat the egg yolks with the remaining cream and stir in the cornstarch mixture, sugar, and a pinch of salt. Cook this custard over low heat, stirring continuously until smooth. Whisk for a further 3 minutes, or until the custard is thick and glossy. Add vanilla extract to taste, pour the custard over the warm cake and fruit, and serve at once.

A Southwestern Dinner

The Mexican-influenced cooking of Texas, New Mexico, Arizona, and southern California has grown in favor throughout Canada and the United States in recent years. Popularly known as "Mexican food," it is indeed Mexican-inspired, and some foods, such as the tortilla, have remained unchanged since being introduced from Mexico. But most dishes have been adapted to North American tastes and use more meat and cheese than are common in true Mexican cooking. The most famous dish of the area, chili con carne—though Mexican in spirit—comes from Texas.

The staple of southwestern cooking is the tortilla, a thin cake made from *masa harina* (finely ground corn flour). Tortillas are served as bread and also form the basis of several dishes: The taco, for example, is a folded tortilla fried crisp and stuffed with a savory filling; enchiladas are rolled tortillas filled with meat or cheese and baked in spicy sauce. (For making tortillas at home, a small metal tortilla press, available at specialty shops, is almost a necessity. Alternatively, some brands of frozen tortillas are surprisingly good.)

The menu on these pages is a Texas-style Mexican dinner (or, as it is known in the Southwest, "Tex-Mex" food). The chili con carne and frijoles refritos can be made a day or two ahead; chili is always better the second day, after the flavors have blended and developed.

Arguments persist in the Southwest over what constitutes authentic chili. Some cooks insist that the beef must be cubed, not ground; purists say that tomatoes are a recent and unnecessary addition; many cooks use freshly ground chili peppers instead of commercial chili powder. But on one point all agree: Real Texas chili never contains beans. Beans are best served as a side dish.

The most popular southwestern bean dish is frijoles refritos, or refried beans. Pinto beans (mottled kidney beans) are mashed and fried with fat and seasonings. Some cooks purée the beans in a blender; others mash them with a fork for a coarser consistency.

Guacamole, a chilled purée of avocado, is an ideal, cooling contrast to the heaviness of chili. It can be served atop shredded lettuce as a salad, spooned into avocado halves, or served as a dip with deep-fried tortilla chips. As a dessert, sopaipillas—puffed-up squares of deep-fried pastry coated with cinnamon and sugar or honey—are light and sweet. Nachos, crisp tortilla pieces topped with cheese and fiery jalapeño peppers, are usually served as an hors d'oeuvre.

Southwestern dinners are hearty and informal. The food is most attractive when served in rustic earthenware or brightly painted pottery, and beer and iced tea make far more appropriate accompaniments than wine or mixed drinks.

Nachos

PREPARATION TIME: *15 minutes*
COOKING TIME: *3 minutes*

INGREDIENTS (*for 4 dozen*):
6 *tortillas*
½ *cup vegetable oil*
¾ *pound mild, semisoft cheese*
  (*preferably Monterey Jack*)
8 *jalapeño peppers, sliced*

Cut each tortilla into eighths and deep-fry in the vegetable oil over high heat until golden and just crisp. Drain on paper towels. Thinly slice the cheese into wedges that are slightly smaller than the tortilla pieces. Place a wedge of cheese on each piece of tortilla and top each with a small sliver of jalapeño pepper. (Keep in mind that the peppers are extremely hot.)

Arrange the tortillas on a baking sheet and place under a preheated broiler until the cheese is bubbly. Pile the nachos on a tray and serve immediately.

Chili Con Carne

PREPARATION TIME: *15 minutes*
COOKING TIME: *3 hours*

INGREDIENTS (*for 6–8*):
2 *large onions, chopped*
4 *tablespoons bacon fat or corn oil*
½ *pound beef suet,* finely chopped*
3 *pounds top round or rump of beef, cut into small cubes*
2 *cloves garlic*
1 *tablespoon salt*
3 *tablespoons chili powder*
1 *tablespoon cumin seeds*
Dash of Tabasco
Beef stock (or water and bouillon cubes), heated to boiling

Sauté the onions in fat or oil until soft. Add the beef suet (available at most supermarkets) and cook very slowly until the suet is completely rendered* and the onion is almost melted into the fat.

Add the meat, garlic, and salt. Brown the meat cubes well on all sides, stirring frequently to mix the meat with the fat and onions.

Mix the chili powder, cumin, and Tabasco with the meat and cover with boiling stock. Simmer over low heat, covered, for 2½ hours, stirring occasionally to prevent the mixture from sticking. Taste for seasoning and add more salt and chili powder if desired. The meat should be very tender and almost shredded. Spoon it into warm bowls.

Serve the chili con carne with bowls of sharp grated cheese, peeled, seeded, and chopped tomatoes, and chopped onions as garnish.

Frijoles Refritos
(Refried Beans)

PREPARATION TIME: *8 hours, or overnight*
COOKING TIME: *3–3½ hours*

INGREDIENTS (*for 4*):
1 *pound dried pinto beans*
Water
2 *cloves garlic, crushed*
1 *tablespoon sugar*
½ *tablespoon salt*
½ *pound finely diced salt pork*
½ *cup lard or bacon fat (or more), melted*

Soak the beans in water to cover 8 hours or overnight. Drain. Add the garlic and sugar and cover with water. Bring to a boil, reduce the heat, and simmer. Add the salt and salt pork after the beans have cooked for ½ hour. Continue to simmer very slowly until the beans are tender, about 3 hours or more.

Melt ¼ cup of the lard or bacon fat in a heavy skillet. Add a few beans at a time to the skillet and mash them until they are well blended with the fat. Continue to add the fat and beans gradually until all the fat and beans are used. Cook slowly, mashing the beans occasionally so that they become rather crisp at the edges. The beans must be very hot, crisp, and creamy.

Serve the beans on individual salad plates, alongside guacamole. They can be spread on crisp tortilla pieces or eaten with a fork.

Guacamole

PREPARATION TIME: *20 minutes*

INGREDIENTS:
2 medium-sized avocados
1 or 2 chopped green chilies (canned peeled green chilies)
2 tablespoons lime juice
1–1½ teaspoons salt

Buy avocados that are soft enough to mash but not so soft that they have turned dark. Mash well with a fork. Add green chilies, removing the tiny seeds unless a hot, zesty flavor is desired. Mix in the lime juice and salt to taste; amounts will depend on the size of the avocados. If the guacamole is not used immediately, put the avocado pit in the mixture and cover tightly with plastic wrap to prevent it from darkening.

For a very spicy guacamole, use one very finely chopped jalapeño or serrano chili instead of the green chilies. The dish can be varied by adding the traditional peeled, seeded, and chopped ripe tomatoes and finely chopped onion. Not so traditional but very good additions are crumbled crisp bacon, chopped roasted peanuts, coarsely chopped toasted filberts, or paper-thin strips of flavorful ham. Serve atop shredded lettuce, or spooned into avocado halves, or as a dip.

Sopaipillas

PREPARATION TIME: *30 minutes*
COOKING TIME: *30 minutes*

INGREDIENTS (*for 3 dozen*):
3 cups unsifted all-purpose flour
2½ teaspoons baking powder
1 teaspoon salt
3 tablespoons butter or shortening
3 eggs
¼ cup sugar
⅓ cup water
Oil for deep-frying
Honey or ½ cup sugar mixed with 1 teaspoon cinnamon

Sift the flour, baking powder, and salt into a bowl. Cut in the butter or shortening with a pastry blender until mixture resembles coarse meal. Beat the eggs and sugar together very well and add to the dry ingredients with enough water (about ⅓ cup) to make a soft dough. Knead on a floured board until smooth and elastic, about 10 minutes. Cover with a towel and let stand for 30 minutes or longer.

Roll out the dough to a ⅛-inch thickness and cut it into 3-inch squares. Deep-fry, 2 or 3 at a time, in the oil (heated to 360°F) for 2½–3 minutes, turning often to brown evenly. Drain on paper towels. Serve with honey or dip in the cinnamon-sugar mixture.

Tortillas

PREPARATION TIME: *10 minutes*
COOKING TIME: *25 minutes*

INGREDIENTS (*for 12 tortillas*):
2⅓ cups masa harina (corn flour)
1½ cups warm water
1 teaspoon salt

Mix the *masa harina* (available in specialty stores and some supermarkets) with the salt and add 1 cup of the warm water gradually, stirring constantly. Knead the dough on a lightly floured board, adding enough of the remaining water by tablespoonfuls until the dough becomes smooth and firm and no longer sticks to the fingers.

Divide the dough into 12 equal portions and form these into balls. Use a tortilla press or roll the balls between oiled waxed paper into very thin, round pancakes about 5 inches in diameter.

Cook one tortilla at a time on a moderately hot ungreased griddle or skillet, about 2 minutes on each side, turning once with a spatula when the bottom is very lightly browned. As the tortillas are cooked, stack them on a large sheet of aluminum foil. When all are done, wrap the foil over the stack and warm in a 300°F oven for 5 minutes. Wrap the warmed tortillas in a napkin and serve in a covered dish.

June

'Long about knee-deep in June,
Bout the time strawberries melts
On the vine . . .   JAMES WHITCOMB RILEY

THIS MONTH'S RECIPES

A nostalgic summer menu: tea on the lawn
with cucumber sandwiches and strawberries and cream

Food in Season

June heralds the season for sunny lunches on the terrace and carefree barbecues in the backyard. It is the time for warm-weather foods—for homemade ice cream, savory cold soups, crisp salads, and succulent chilled vegetables in sauce vinaigrette; for white wines and rosés, and tall pitchers of minted iced tea and sangría. The food is lighter, the style more relaxed. And fresh garden vegetables are becoming less expensive. Some of the best bargains are to be found at rural roadside stands that sell home-grown produce.

Cucumbers are abundant. Use them often in green salads, and, for an unusual dish, combine them with strawberries in Salad Elona (p.163). Cucumbers need not be restricted to salads, of course; they are just as delicious when used as an ingredient in hot poultry or fish dishes, as in Mackerel with Cucumber (p.155).

By June tomatoes are growing redder, juicier, and less expensive. Serve them simply with salt and pepper—in season they are so flavorful they do not need a dressing. For a main course, cook them with veal (p.156). Fresh green beans and tasty corn can be served hot, as a side dish, or cold, in vegetable salads.

A number of fruits make their first appearance in the markets in June. Apricots are far cheaper than at any other time of year, and make a superb stuffing for baked ham (p.159). Mangoes are at their peak, as are cherries and California grapefruit. Strawberries are plentiful and inexpensive, and other berries, too, now begin to appear in the markets. Blueberries make an excellent deep-dish pie (p.165), and Blackberry Swiss Charlotte (p.165) can be an elegant ending for a summer dinner.

SUGGESTED MENUS

Cold Broccoli Soup
...
Salmon en Croûte
Buttered New Potatoes
Cucumber Salad
...
Strawberry Ice Cream

Cold Crab Tart
...
Lamb in Red Wine
Roast Potatoes
Buttered Carrots
...
Deep-Dish Blueberry Pie

Pork Chops with Apples
...
Creamed Potatoes
Peas and Scallions
...
Berry-Lemon Pudding

Stuffed Anchovy Eggs
...
Baked Ham with Apricot Stuffing
Baked Potatoes
Creamed Spinach
Tomato Salad
Zucchini and Chive Salad
...
Strawberry Ice

Curries: Hot Chili Fish Curry,
Madras Beef Curry, Vindaloo of Eggs
Boiled Rice
...
Peach Melba

Blini with Caviar
...
Poulet Sauté Marengo
Buttered Noodles
Green Salad with Sauce Vinaigrette
...
Blackberry Swiss Charlotte

Soups & First Courses

COLD BROCCOLI SOUP

This appealing pale green soup makes a delicious beginning for a summer meal. It can be prepared early in the day or even a day ahead.

PREPARATION TIME: *25 minutes*
COOKING TIME: *20 minutes*
CHILLING TIME: *4 hours*

INGREDIENTS (*for 6*):
1 small onion
1 stalk celery
1 carrot
2 tablespoons butter
1 pound or 3 large stalks of
    broccoli
3 cups chicken broth
1½ cups light cream
Salt
Pepper

Chop the onion, celery, and carrot. In a large pot sauté them in the butter over medium heat for about 5 minutes or until golden, stirring occasionally. Wash the broccoli thoroughly, cut off the buds, peel the stalks, and coarsely chop them.

Put the chopped stalks in the pot with the sautéed vegetables and add the chicken broth. Bring to a boil. Reduce the heat and simmer for 15 minutes. Add the broccoli buds. Cook for 5 minutes more, or until the buds are just tender. With a slotted spoon, remove about half of the buds and set them aside for garnishing the soup.

Purée the soup in a blender, about 2 cups at a time, or put the soup through a food mill. Cool uncovered. Add the cream. Chill in the refrigerator for 4 hours or more. Season with salt and pepper to taste.

Serve garnished with a few broccoli buds in each bowl. This soup is also good served piping hot.

BLINI WITH CAVIAR

In Russia, where this hors d'oeuvre originated, *blini*—crisp, light, yeast-raised pancakes—are traditionally served with caviar, sour cream, and coarsely chopped raw onions.

PREPARATION TIME: *2 hours*
COOKING TIME: *20 minutes*

INGREDIENTS (*for 6*):
1 package active dry yeast
3 cups all-purpose flour
2 large onions
1 cup sour cream
2 3½-ounce jars Danish black
    lumpfish caviar
1 large lemon
2 tablespoons unsalted butter
2 large eggs
1 tablespoon sugar
Salt
1¼ cups milk
Oil for sautéing

Measure 1½ cups of lukewarm water (110°–115°) into a bowl. Sprinkle the yeast on the surface and leave the bowl in a warm place for 15 minutes, or until the mixture froths. Sift half the flour into a large mixing bowl and gradually add the yeast mixture. Beat to a smooth batter, cover the bowl with a clean cloth, and leave the batter to rise in a warm place for about 30 minutes, or until it has doubled in volume.

Meanwhile, peel and coarsely chop the onions, and put them in a serving bowl. Spoon the sour cream and caviar into 2 individual serving bowls. Wash the lemon, cut it into 6 wedges, and arrange these in another bowl. Chill the condiments until serving time.

Melt butter in a small saucepan and allow it to cool slightly. Separate the eggs. Gradually add the remain-

ing flour to the risen batter, then the melted butter, egg yolks, sugar, and a pinch of salt. Beat the mixture until smooth. Warm the milk, but do not boil, and gradually add it to the batter, whisking continuously. Cover the batter again and set aside to double as before.

Beat the egg whites until they stand in soft peaks, and fold them into the risen batter. Cover the batter and leave to rise for the third time.

Heat a little oil in a large heavy skillet over high heat. Put 2 tablespoons of batter in the pan at a time to make two blini, each about 4 inches wide. If the batter is too thick it can be thinned with a little warm water. Cook the blini for about 1 minute on each side or until they are golden brown. Keep them hot on a wire rack in the oven until all the batter is used—it should make 20–24 pancakes.

Serve the blini, 2 or 3 to each plate, and pass bowls of onions, cream, caviar, and lemon wedges.

153

Fish

AVOCADOS BRISTOL FASHION

Scarlet lobster and green avocados make an attractive first course for a special occasion. Avocados should always be prepared at the last minute; otherwise the delicate green flesh turns brown.

PREPARATION TIME: *25 minutes*

INGREDIENTS (*for 4*):
2 large avocados
1½-pound boiled lobster
6 tablespoons heavy cream
2 teaspoons lemon juice
Cayenne pepper
Salt
Paprika

Ask the fish dealer to split the cooked lobster in half lengthwise. Remove the gray sac in each half of the head and the black intestinal vein. Remove all the lobster meat from the body, tail, and claws. Set the thinner scarlet crawler claws aside for garnish.

Chop the lobster meat finely, put it in a bowl, and stir in the cream and lemon juice. Season to taste with cayenne pepper.

Cut the avocados in half lengthwise and remove the pits. Using a silver teaspoon, scoop out some of the avocado flesh, leaving a ½-inch lining to hold the shape of each half shell. Dice the flesh finely and fold it into the lobster mixture. Season with salt if necessary.

Pile the lobster mixture into the avocado shells and sprinkle with a little paprika. Arrange the claws on top in a decorative pattern.

BRAINS IN BLACK BUTTER

Calf's brains are traditionally used in this classic French recipe. Lamb brains are equally good.

PREPARATION TIME: *30 minutes*
COOKING TIME: *35 minutes*

INGREDIENTS (*for 4*):
1 pound brains
1 bay leaf
Salt and black pepper
6 ounces unsalted butter
2 teaspoons caper liquid
1 tablespoon capers

Soak the brains in a bowl of cold, lightly salted water for at least 30 minutes to remove all blood. Drain the brains and peel off the outer transparent membrane. Rinse the brains again in cold water and carefully divide each brain into 2, making 4 pieces.

Put the brains in a saucepan and cover with cold, lightly salted water. Bring to a boil over moderate heat, and carefully remove any scum. Lower the heat, add the bay leaf, and cover the pan with a lid. Cook the brains gently for 20 minutes. (Lamb brains will take only 15 minutes.) Drain well and transfer the brains to a warmed serving dish. Sprinkle with salt and freshly ground pepper.

Melt the butter in a small pan over moderate heat and let the butter brown without burning it. Stir in the capers and liquid and pour this sauce over the brains immediately.

Serve the brains with crusty bread to mop up the butter.

SAUTÉED SCALLOPS WITH GARLIC

The pungent taste of garlic contrasts with the freshness of parsley to make this a delicious way to serve tender bay scallops.

PREPARATION TIME: *5 minutes*
COOKING TIME: *5–10 minutes*

INGREDIENTS (*for 4*):
1½ pounds bay scallops
Flour
6 tablespoons olive oil
2 or 3 cloves garlic, peeled and finely chopped
Salt and pepper
½ cup chopped parsley

Wash and dry the scallops and roll them in flour. Heat the olive oil in a large skillet. Add the scallops and cook them very quickly, tossing them lightly in the hot oil and shaking the pan so that the scallops do not stick. While they are cooking, add the chopped garlic and mix it in well. Then season the scallops with salt and pepper to taste.

Just before removing the skillet from the heat, add the chopped parsley and toss only enough to coat the scallops. Serve in large scallop shells for an unusually attractive dish. Garnish with lemon wedges.

HADDOCK BARRIE

Fresh haddock and shrimp are here combined in a cheese sauce and finished off as a gratin.

PREPARATION TIME: *15 minutes*
COOKING TIME: *30 minutes*

INGREDIENTS (*for 4*):
4 fresh haddock fillets, each approximately 6 ounces
12 shelled cooked shrimp
Seasoned flour (p.412)
4 tablespoons butter
3 tablespoons all-purpose flour
1¼ cups milk
2 ounces Cheddar cheese
1 small onion
Salt and cayenne pepper
6 tablespoons heavy cream

Wash the fillets and pat them dry on paper towels. Coat each fillet lightly with seasoned flour. Use half the butter to grease a shallow ovenproof dish and arrange the fillets in a single layer in this.

Melt the remaining butter in a small pan, stir in the flour, cook for a few minutes, then gradually add the milk to make a white sauce (p.301). Grate the cheese and blend it into the sauce, together with the peeled and finely chopped onion. Chop the shrimp coarsely and stir them into the sauce. Season to taste with salt and pepper, and stir in the heavy cream.

Pour the sauce over the fish and bake in the center of an oven, preheated to 400°F, for 20 minutes. If by that time the top has not browned, put the dish under a hot broiler for a few minutes.

Serve the fillets at once. Plain boiled rice or new potatoes and a green vegetable, such as spinach, go well with this dish.

SALMON EN CROÛTE

June is one of the peak months for salmon. This recipe combines salmon and a purée of fresh asparagus that are wrapped in featherlight puff pastry. The dish makes a perfect main course for a dinner party. It can be served hot or even prepared a few hours in advance and served cold.

PREPARATION TIME: *45 minutes*
COOKING TIME: *40 minutes*

INGREDIENTS (*for 4–6*):

2 fillets skinned salmon
  (*approximate weight 1½ pounds
  each*)
1 pound asparagus
2 tablespoons heavy cream
½ teaspoon chopped dill
Salt and black pepper
½ recipe puff pastry (*p.363*)
3 thin slices boiled ham
1 egg yolk
1 tablespoon milk
GARNISH:
Lemon wedges

Wash and trim the asparagus,* tie in a bundle, and cook upright in a pan of lightly salted water for 10–15 minutes, or until the tips are soft to the touch. Drain the asparagus thoroughly and cut off the soft tips (the stems can be used in an omelet); rub the tips through a coarse sieve or purée in a blender. Blend the cream and dill into this asparagus purée and season to taste with freshly ground pepper.

Spread the asparagus purée over one salmon fillet, and cover with the other. (Any remaining purée can be spread on top of the second fillet.) Wrap the ham slices around the salmon and set it aside.

Roll out the puff pastry on a floured surface to a rectangle about 12 inches by 10 inches. Place the salmon in the center of the pastry and wrap the pastry over the fish.

Beat the egg yolk lightly with the milk and brush the edges of the pastry. Seal the long edge firmly with more egg. Tuck in the short ends of the pastry neatly and seal with egg.

Place the salmon on a wet baking sheet with the seam beneath. Cut 1 or 2 holes in the pastry for the steam to escape, and decorate the top with leaves made from the pastry trimmings. Brush with the remaining egg and milk. Bake in the center of an oven, preheated to 425°F, for 20 minutes; then lower the heat to 375°F and bake for a further 20–25 minutes, or until the pastry has turned a golden brown.

Serve the salmon, hot or cold, cut in slices and garnished with lemon wedges. New potatoes tossed in butter and dill, and a cucumber salad, are traditional side dishes.

MACKEREL WITH CUCUMBER

The cool, pale green look of young cucumber heralds summer. Its clean taste suits oily fish, such as mackerel and trout. This dish can be served hot or cold.

PREPARATION TIME: *25 minutes*
COOKING TIME: *35 minutes*

INGREDIENTS (*for 4*):
4 mackerel, about ½ pound each
6 tablespoons butter
1 small unwaxed cucumber
Salt and black pepper
2 tablespoons white wine vinegar or
  dry white wine

Ask the fish store to gut and clean the mackerel and cut off the heads. Wash the fish and pat them dry on paper towels. Grease a large, shallow ovenproof dish with 2 tablespoons of the butter. Wash and dry the cucumber and slice it thinly; put a layer of cucumber slices over the bottom of the dish. Place the mackerel on top and cover with the remaining cucumber slices. Season to taste with salt and freshly ground black pepper.

Sprinkle the vinegar or wine over the fish and cucumber, and dot with 2 tablespoons butter cut into small pieces. Cover the dish and bake the fish on the center shelf of an oven, preheated to 425°F, for 20 minutes.

Remove the dish from the oven and transfer the fish and cucumber to a serving dish. Keep it warm if the mackerel is to be served hot. Strain the juices from the fish through a fine sieve into a saucepan. Bring to a boil and continue boiling briskly, adding the remaining butter in bits and stirring occasionally. When the liquid has reduced* by about half and resembles a glaze,* pour it over the mackerel and serve at once, or leave to cool.

For a hot main course, serve with potatoes tossed in butter and chopped parsley, and with young peas. Served cold, a green salad and garlic potatoes (p.287) could complement the dish.

COD GOURMET

Cod is a popular and inexpensive fish and can be cooked in a number of ways. This recipe for poaching it in white wine, mushrooms, and shallots is ideal for a light summer meal.

PREPARATION TIME: *15 minutes*
COOKING TIME: *20 minutes*

INGREDIENTS (*for 4*):
4 cod fillets, approximately 5
  ounces each
2–3 tablespoons all-purpose flour
6 tablespoons unsalted butter
3 shallots
¼ pound mushrooms
Salt and black pepper
2 tablespoons dry white wine
2 teaspoons lemon juice
GARNISH:
1 tablespoon chopped parsley

Wash and skin the cod fillets. Pat them dry on paper towels and coat with a little flour. Grease a large, shallow ovenproof dish with 2 tablespoons of the butter and arrange the fillets in this. Peel and finely chop the shallots. Melt the remaining butter in a pan and sauté the shallots over low heat for 2–3 minutes, or until translucent. Wipe and trim the mushrooms,* slice them thinly, and add to the shallots. Cook for a further 2 minutes, then season to taste with salt and freshly ground pepper.

Spoon the shallot and mushroom mixture over the cod fillets and pour over the wine. Cover the dish with a lid or foil and bake the fish for 15 minutes in the center of an oven preheated to 425°F.

Serve the fish straight from the dish. Sprinkle with lemon juice and garnish with parsley.

Meta

MONTE CARLO HADDOCK

Win or lose, a night at the casino can take its toll in exhaustion. The restaurants along the coast at Monte Carlo used to specialize in breakfasts that would leave a gambler refreshed. Haddock with eggs was one such meal.

PREPARATION TIME: *10 minutes*
COOKING TIME: *20–30 minutes*

INGREDIENTS (*for 4*):
1 pound smoked haddock fillet
2½ cups milk
1 bay leaf
4 tablespoons butter
¼ cup all-purpose flour
Salt and cayenne pepper
¾ cup grated Cheddar cheese
4 eggs

Wash and dry the haddock fillet before putting it in a large pan with the milk and bay leaf. Poach* the fillet, uncovered, over moderate heat for about 10 minutes. Carefully lift out the fish with a slotted spoon, remove the skin, and divide the fillet into 4 portions. Arrange these in a warm ovenproof dish and keep hot in the oven.

Strain the milk and use it, with the butter and flour, to make a white sauce (p.301). Season to taste with salt and cayenne pepper. Stir in the grated cheese.

Poach the eggs* in a pan of lightly salted, simmering water until they are just set. Lift the eggs out with a slotted spoon and place one egg on each haddock portion. Pour over the sauce and place the dish under a hot broiler for 2–3 minutes, until the sauce is lightly browned.

Serve the haddock with creamed spinach (p.162).

CRAB TART

Most savory tarts are baked blind— that is, the pastry is partly cooked before the filling is added. They are ideal for summer fare, since they are quick to make and equally good served hot or cold.

PREPARATION TIME: *20–30 minutes*
COOKING TIME: *30 minutes*

INGREDIENTS (*for 4-6*):

PASTRY:
2 cups all-purpose flour
¼ teaspoon salt
¼ teaspoon cayenne pepper
4 tablespoons butter
4 tablespoons lard
¼ cup grated Cheddar cheese
1 egg yolk

FILLING:
½–¾ pound crabmeat
3 eggs
2 teaspoons lemon juice
½ teaspoon Worcestershire sauce
½ cup heavy cream
Salt

For the pastry, sift the flour, salt, and cayenne pepper into a mixing bowl. Rub in the butter and lard, cut into pieces, until the mixture is crumbly. Add the cheese; bind the pastry with the egg yolk and a little cold water. Set aside for 30 minutes.

Roll the pastry out on a lightly floured surface and use it to line a flan ring 9 inches in diameter. Prick the pastry at the bottom and bake it blind in a preheated oven at 400°F for 10 minutes or until golden.

Flake the crabmeat* finely into a bowl. Beat the eggs with the lemon juice and Worcestershire sauce, and stir it into the crabmeat. Blend in the cream. Add salt to taste.

Spoon into the pastry-crust lining. Bake in a preheated oven at 375°F for 25–30 minutes.

Serve the tart hot or cold.

BEEF WITH GREEN PEAS

Top round of beef is usually stewed or braised. It can, however, be made into a succulent pot roast by cooking it slowly in a casserole.

PREPARATION TIME: *10 minutes*
COOKING TIME: *1½–2 hours*

INGREDIENTS (*for 6*):
1 clove garlic (optional)
2½–3 pounds lean top round of beef
1 teaspoon salt
½ teaspoon black pepper
4 tablespoons unsalted butter
1½ pounds fresh green peas

If the garlic is used, cut it into slivers, make several shallow incisions in various places in the meat, and insert the garlic slivers. Season the meat with the salt and freshly ground pepper. Melt half the butter in a heavy skillet over medium heat and brown the beef in it on all sides to seal in the juices.

Put the meat in an ovenproof casserole into which it will fit fairly closely. Shell the peas and put them around the sides of the beef. Melt the remaining butter and pour it over the meat. Cover the casserole with a lid and cook in the center of a preheated oven at 325°F for 1½ hours. At this stage the meat should be rare. Allow another 30 minutes for well-done meat.

Lift out the beef, carve into thin slices, and arrange them on a warmed serving dish, surrounded by the peas. Serve the liquids in a separate dish. Boiled new potatoes with a little chopped mint are ideal for this dish.

VEAL WITH TOMATOES

Shoulder of veal, which is cut from the top of the foreleg and boned, is best cooked in a casserole.

PREPARATION TIME: *20 minutes*
COOKING TIME: *1½–2 hours*

INGREDIENTS (*for 6*):
2½-pound boned shoulder of veal
Salt
4 tablespoons unsalted butter
1½ pounds tomatoes
2 onions
6–8 black peppercorns
Sprig fresh or ½ teaspoon dried tarragon

Tie the veal shoulder neatly with string to keep its shape during cooking. Season lightly with salt. Melt half the butter in an ovenproof casserole over moderate heat and brown the meat on all sides to seal in the juices.

Peel, seed, and coarsely chop the tomatoes.* Peel and finely chop the onions. Melt the remaining butter in a pan and sauté the tomatoes and onions over moderate heat for 3–4 minutes. Crush the peppercorns and add them to the tomato mixture, add the tarragon, and pour it all over the meat in the casserole. Cover and bake in the center of a preheated oven at 300°F for 1½–2 hours.

Remove the string and serve the veal hot, cut into thick slices, with the tomato sauce spooned over them. Plain spaghetti tossed in butter would make this a substantial meal.

PORK CHOPS WITH APPLES

Tart cooking apples are traditionally served with pork to counteract the fattiness of the meat. They appear as stuffings and sauces with roasts, and can also, as here, be used with oven-cooked chops.

PREPARATION TIME: *15 minutes*
COOKING TIME: *1 hour 10 minutes*

INGREDIENTS (*for 4*):
4 thick pork chops
2–4 tablespoons unsalted butter
Salt and black pepper
3–4 large cooking apples
Juice of 1 lemon

Trim any excess fat from the chops and put them in a buttered oven-proof dish. Season to taste with salt and freshly ground pepper. Peel, core, and thinly slice the apples, and arrange over the chops to cover them completely. Melt the remaining butter and brush some of it over the apple slices. Sprinkle with lemon juice and cover the dish tightly with a lid or foil.

Cook the chops in the center of a preheated oven at 325°F for 1 hour. Remove the foil, brush the apples with the remaining butter, and cook for a further 10 minutes, or until the apples are lightly browned but not dry, and the chops are tender.

Serve the chops from the cooking dish or on a warmed serving plate. Small new potatoes and braised Belgian endive (p.102) go well with the sharp apple taste.

TERRINE DE CAMPAGNE

The French word *terrine* originally meant an earthenware dish, but by extension it now also refers to the contents of the dish, whether fish, meat, or poultry. This farmhouse-style terrine of calf's liver and veal is a good choice for a picnic lunch or supper. It should, like all other terrines, be served cold.

PREPARATION TIME: *20 minutes*
COOKING TIME: *2 hours*

INGREDIENTS (*for 6–8*):
¾ pound thin bacon slices
¾ pound calf's liver
1½ pounds ground veal
1 large onion
2 cloves garlic
1 tablespoon tomato purée
¼ teaspoon summer savory or sage
¼ teaspoon oregano
8 tablespoons butter
½–⅔ cup dry red wine
Salt and black pepper
4 bay leaves

Stretch the bacon with the flat blade of a knife. Line a 5-cup terrine* or soufflé dish with the bacon, allowing the ends to hang over the edges.

Clean the liver, removing any tough tissue, and put the meat through the coarse disk of a meat grinder. Peel the onion and chop it finely. Mix together the liver, onion, and veal in a large bowl. Peel the garlic and crush over the meat in a press. Stir in the tomato purée, savory, and oregano. Melt the butter and stir into the terrine mixture together with enough wine to give a moist but not wet consistency. Season to taste with salt and freshly ground pepper.

Spoon the mixture into the dish, over the bacon. Arrange the bay leaves on top and fold over the ends of the bacon.

Cover the dish with a lid or tight-fitting foil. Cook the terrine for 2 hours on the middle shelf of an oven preheated to 350°F.

When cooked, remove the lid from the dish; cover with fresh foil and a flat board that will just fit into the terrine. Place a heavy weight on the board and leave the dish to cool. Then chill, still weighted down.

Serve straight from the terrine, or turn out onto a serving dish and cut into wedges. Crusty bread and a tossed green salad make this terrine a substantial main course.

LAMB IN RED WINE

Leg of lamb makes a good choice for a large gathering. Spices and wine give a fresh summer taste.

PREPARATION TIME: *15 minutes*
COOKING TIME: *1¾–2 hours*

INGREDIENTS (*for 6–8*):
5-pound leg of lamb
2 cloves garlic
1 tablespoon oil
Salt and black pepper
Ground ginger
2 onions
2 carrots
4 tablespoons unsalted butter
3–4 sprigs of thyme
1¼ cups dry red wine

Remove the thin membrane (fell) and excess fat from the lamb. Peel the garlic and cut each clove into 3 or 4 slivers. With the point of a sharp knife, make small incisions in the meat and press the garlic into these. Rub the lamb with the oil, a little salt and freshly ground pepper, and dust with ginger. Peel the onions and carrots and chop them coarsely.

Melt the butter in a roasting pan and quickly brown the meat over moderate heat to seal in the juices. Remove the meat from the pan and cook the onions and carrots for a few minutes in the butter until golden. Spoon the vegetable mixture into a large ovenproof dish, add the thyme, and place the meat on top; cover with a lid or foil.

Cook the meat in the center of an oven preheated to 425°F for 25 minutes, then pour in the wine and lower the heat to 350°F for a further 1–1¼ hours. Baste* 2 or 3 times with the wine.

Remove the lamb and keep it warm on a serving dish in the oven. Strain the cooking juices and boil them briskly until they have reduced* by about ⅓. Remove any fat by drawing paper towels over the surface, or skim off the fat with a spoon. Heat the juices through and correct seasoning.

Serve roast potatoes and young carrots, tossed in chopped parsley, with the lamb. Pour the pan juices into a sauceboat and serve separately as a gravy.

CURRIES

It is a popular misconception in the Western world that a curry consists of pieces of meat or poultry in a curry-flavored sauce. A proper curry, as served daily in India, Pakistan, and Malaysia, is an array of fish, meat, poultry, and vegetable dishes, each flavored with a compound of spices that is usually sold in the United States and Canada as curry powder.

The following selections, which should be served together for 6–8 people, have been adapted to Western eating habits. The dishes are all fairly hot, and it is advisable to experiment with the amount of curry powder used, adding too little at first rather than too much. Meat curries benefit from being made a day in advance to allow the flavors to blend.

HOT CHILI FISH CURRY

PREPARATION TIME: *15 minutes*
COOKING TIME: *1 hour 10 minutes*

INGREDIENTS:
½ pound shelled cooked shrimp or 1 pound cooked diced fish fillets
2 onions
1 clove garlic
2 tablespoons unsalted butter
1–2 tablespoons curry powder
½ teaspoon chili powder
2½ cups chicken stock
2 tablespoons tomato purée
Juice of 1 lemon
2 teaspoons honey
1 star anise (optional)
Salt and black pepper

Peel and coarsely chop the onions, and peel and crush the garlic. Melt the butter in a heavy pan and sauté the curry and chili powder over low heat for about 1 minute. Add the onions and garlic and cook for a further 2–3 minutes. Gradually stir in the stock and add the tomato purée, lemon juice, and honey. Add the star anise, * if used, and simmer this sauce, covered with a lid, for about 1 hour. The sauce will now be quite thick.

Remove the anise, stir in the shrimp or fish, and cook for about 10 minutes. Season to taste with salt and freshly ground pepper.

MADRAS BEEF CURRY

PREPARATION TIME: *20 minutes*
COOKING TIME: *2½ hours*

INGREDIENTS:
1½ pounds chuck steak
1 large onion
2 cloves garlic
6 tablespoons lard or beef drippings
2 tablespoons curry powder
5 cups beef stock
Juice of ½ lemon
2 bay leaves
Salt and black pepper
1 tablespoon brown sugar
2 tablespoons tomato purée

Peel and finely chop the onion and garlic. Melt half the lard in a heavy pan. Stir in 1 heaping tablespoon of curry powder and sauté over low heat, stirring continuously, for 1 minute. Add the onion and garlic, and sauté for a further 2 minutes. Pour in the stock and lemon juice, and add the bay leaves. Bring this to a boil, cover, and simmer over low heat for 45 minutes.

Meanwhile, trim any fat and gristle from the meat and cut it into 1-inch pieces. Season the meat with salt and freshly ground pepper, and dust with the remaining curry powder. Melt the rest of the lard in a heavy pan and sauté the meat for 2–3 minutes over high heat, until it is brown on all sides.

Strain the curry stock through a coarse sieve over the meat; stir in the sugar and tomato purée. Cover the pan with a lid and simmer the meat for about 1½ hours or until tender. By this time the stock will have reduced* and become a thick sauce. At this stage, more curry powder may be added; it should be lightly sautéed for a moment in a little fat before being added to the sauce.

Set the beef curry aside to cool completely. Skim off any fat that has risen to the surface before reheating the curry.

VINDALOO OF EGGS

PREPARATION TIME: *15 minutes*
COOKING TIME: *1½ hours*

INGREDIENTS:
8 eggs
2 onions
2 tablespoons unsalted butter
2 teaspoons curry powder
½ teaspoon chili powder
1½ tablespoons all-purpose flour
½ cup white wine vinegar
2 cups chicken, beef, or veal stock
1 bay leaf
1 sprig thyme
Salt and black pepper

Hard-cook the eggs for 8 minutes, then plunge them into cold water. Remove the shells and set the eggs aside to cool. Peel and finely chop the onions. Melt the butter in a heavy pan and sauté the curry and chili powders for 1–2 minutes over low heat. Blend in the flour to make a thick paste. Add the onions and cook for about 2 minutes, stirring all the time. Gradually stir in the vinegar and stock until the sauce is quite smooth. Add the bay leaf and thyme, and season to taste with salt and freshly ground pepper.

Simmer the sauce, covered, for about 1 hour, stirring occasionally. Cut the hard-cooked eggs in half lengthwise and arrange them in 1 layer in an ovenproof serving dish; strain the curry sauce through a coarse sieve over the eggs.

Leave the eggs to steep in the sauce for 2–3 hours. Cover the dish with a lid or foil and heat it through in the oven at a temperature of 400°F for about 30 minutes. Serve hot from the dish.

Serve the 3 hot curry dishes together, with a bowl of plain boiled rice. Provide small dishes of spicy pickles and chutneys, such as lime-and-mango, sweet pepper, and tomato chutneys.

Grated coconut, thin onion rings, sliced bananas in a little lemon juice, and diced cucumber in sweetened wine vinegar also make refreshing side dishes. A bowl of plain yogurt is cooling and also helps in digesting spicy curries.

Chapatis—small griddle cakes of unleavened bread—are served with curries in India. Poppadoms, which are more popular in Malaysia, are wafer-thin pancakes, deep-fried until crisp and golden.

BAKED HAM WITH APRICOT STUFFING

Baked stuffed hams are ideal for large parties. Leftover ham makes delicious casseroles, croquettes, hash, salads, and sandwiches.

PREPARATION TIME: *15 minutes*
MARINATING TIME: *6 hours*
COOKING TIME: *2¼ hours*

INGREDIENTS (*for 10–12*):
6-pound piece of ham, boned
1 cup red wine
2 bay leaves
½ pound apricots
½ teaspoon arrowroot (optional)
Cloves
2–3 tablespoons brown sugar

Ask the butcher to bone the ham, leaving plenty of room for the stuffing. Put the meat in a large bowl, add the wine and bay leaves, and leave to marinate* for at least 6 hours; turn the meat frequently.

Wash and dry the apricots, cut them in half, and remove the pits. Lift the meat from the marinade. Put the wine marinade in a saucepan, add the apricots, and bring to a boil over low heat. Simmer for about 10 minutes, or until the apricots are soft and the wine has been absorbed. Remove the bay leaves. Let the apricots cool slightly and purée them.

Dry the ham thoroughly. Stuff with as much of the apricot purée as possible and tie securely. (Any surplus purée can be boiled up with extra wine and thickened with a little arrowroot to make a sauce.) Wrap the stuffed ham tightly in a double layer of foil and make a small slit in the center of the foil for the steam to escape. Place on a baking sheet and

cook in the center of the oven, preheated to 350°F, for 2 hours.

Remove the ham from the oven, unwrap the foil, and let the meat cool slightly. With a sharp knife, slit the skin lengthwise and remove it entirely, leaving a layer of fat no more than ⅛ inch thick over the meat.

Make shallow diagonal cuts, ¾ inch apart, through the fat to form a pattern of diamond shapes, and insert a whole clove at each intersection. Pat the brown sugar firmly over the fat and transfer to a roasting pan.

Glaze* the ham in the oven, preheated to 425°F, for about 15

minutes or until the sugar has melted and turned golden brown.

Serve the ham hot or cold, cut into thin slices. Creamed spinach (p.162) and baked potatoes would be suitable for a hot ham, and salads ideal with the cold meat.

Poultry

DUCK PAPRIKA

The Hungarians traditionally flavor many of their poultry and meat dishes with paprika. This recipe makes a change from plain roast duck and is a good main course for a dinner party.

PREPARATION TIME: *15 minutes*
COOKING TIME: *1¼–1½ hours*

INGREDIENTS (*for 4–6*):
1 5-pound duck
2 onions
1 clove garlic
3 tablespoons unsalted butter
2 tablespoons all-purpose flour
2 teaspoons paprika
1 cup red wine
Salt and black pepper
4–5 tomatoes
Chicken or duck stock
1 teaspoon arrowroot

Wipe the duck inside and out with a damp cloth, pat it thoroughly dry, and truss* it neatly. Peel and finely chop the onions and garlic. Melt the butter in a large flameproof casserole or skillet, and cook the onions and garlic for a few minutes until translucent. Add the duck and brown it on all sides. Lift the duck from the pan, sprinkle in the flour and paprika, and cook for a few minutes. Pour in the wine and stir until it becomes a smooth sauce. Season to taste with salt and freshly ground pepper. Return the duck to the pan.

Peel, seed, and coarsely chop the tomatoes* and add them to the duck, thinning the sauce with a little stock if necessary.

Cover the dish with a lid and simmer over low heat for about 1¼ hours, or until the duck is tender. It may be necessary to add more stock.

When cooked, remove the duck and carve it into 6–8 portions; arrange these on a serving dish and keep hot. Skim all fat off the sauce; if necessary, blend a little arrowroot with cold water and stir into the sauce to thicken it. Spoon the sauce over the duck and serve with boiled rice (p.336).

POULET SAUTÉ MARENGO

According to legend, this now classic dish was invented by Napoleon's chef after the Battle of Marengo in 1800. The ingredients, which then included freshwater crawfish, were apparently at hand in the devastated countryside.

PREPARATION TIME: *45 minutes*
COOKING TIME: *1 hour*

INGREDIENTS (*for 6*):
1 chicken, approximately 4½ pounds, or 8 chicken parts
2 onions
1 clove garlic
4 tablespoons unsalted butter
3 tablespoons olive oil
4 tablespoons all-purpose flour
½ cup chicken stock
1¼ cups Marsala wine
6 tomatoes
12 mushrooms
1 white truffle (optional)
Salt and black pepper
1 tablespoon brandy

Wipe the chicken or the parts thoroughly with a clean damp cloth. (Cut a whole chicken* into 8 neat pieces.) Peel the onions and garlic; coarsely chop the onions and crush the garlic. Heat the butter and oil in a large skillet over moderate heat, and sauté the onions, garlic, and chicken pieces until golden. Sprinkle over the flour and cook, stirring, until all the fat is absorbed and the flour is slightly browned. Gradually stir in the stock and Marsala, and bring the mixture to a boil. Lower the heat and let the chicken simmer in the sauce.

Peel, seed, and coarsely chop the tomatoes.* Trim the mushrooms* and slice them finely. Chop the truffle finely, if used. Add the toma-toes, mushrooms, and truffle to the pan. Season to taste with salt and freshly ground pepper. Cover the pan with a lid or foil and simmer over low heat for about 1 hour, or until the chicken is tender. Stir occasionally to prevent the sauce from sticking. About 10 minutes before the end of cooking time, stir the brandy into the sauce.

Serve hot, with boiled new potatoes or with plain buttered noodles. Crawfish, placed around the chicken, were the traditional garnish.

CHICKEN IN MUSHROOM SAUCE

This method of cooking chicken produces a light, easily digested meal. Any chicken and mushroom sauce left over can be made into a creamed soup.

PREPARATION TIME: *25 minutes*
COOKING TIME: *1½ hours*

INGREDIENTS (*for 6*):
1 chicken, approximately 3½ pounds
2 onions
2 celery stalks
3 tablespoons unsalted butter
Salt and black pepper
1 bay leaf
12–16 mushrooms
Worcestershire sauce
1 tablespoon all-purpose flour
5 tablespoons heavy cream
GARNISH:
1 tablespoon finely chopped parsley

Peel and finely chop the onions. Wash the celery and chop finely. Melt 2 tablespoons of the butter in a large heavy pan over low heat; cook the onion and celery until soft and just beginning to change color. Do not brown.

Meanwhile, wipe the chicken inside and out, and truss* it. Clean the giblets and liver. Put the chicken, giblets, and liver in the pan with the onion and celery, with enough water to cover the chicken. Bring to a boil, remove any scum, and add salt, freshly ground pepper, and the bay leaf. Cover the pan with a lid and simmer gently for 1–1½ hours, or until the chicken is tender. Do not overcook. Lift the chicken onto a warm dish and keep it hot. Strain the cooking liquid and set aside for making the sauce.

Trim and thinly slice the mushrooms.* Melt the remaining butter in a small pan and cook the mushrooms over low heat for 2–3 minutes. Add a few drops of Worcestershire sauce and sprinkle the flour over the mushrooms. Cook, stirring continuously, until all the fat has been absorbed into the flour. Gradually blend in about ½ cup of the strained chicken stock to make a smooth sauce. Correct seasoning if necessary. Stir in the cream and heat the sauce through.

Carve the chicken* and arrange the slices and pieces in a deep serving dish. Pour the mushroom sauce over it and garnish with chopped parsley. Serve with broccoli spears and boiled potatoes, or buttered rice.

Rice & Pasta

CHICKEN PILAF

A pilaf is basically an Eastern method of cooking rice with various spices. It can be served plain to replace potatoes, but is more often mixed with cooked meat, chicken, or fish.

PREPARATION TIME: *20 minutes*
COOKING TIME: *1 hour*

INGREDIENTS (*for 6*):
3 cups skinned and coarsely chopped
    cooked chicken
2 onions
1 clove garlic
¼ pound unsalted butter
1¼ cups long grain rice
3¾ cups chicken stock
16 mushrooms
Saffron
Salt and black pepper
3 tomatoes

Peel and finely chop the onions and garlic. Melt the butter in a large flameproof casserole and sauté the onion and garlic until soft but not brown. Add the rice and continue to sauté, stirring continuously, until the rice is transparent. Pour the chicken stock over the rice.

Trim the mushrooms* and chop them coarsely. Add them to the rice with a pinch of saffron and season with salt and freshly ground pepper. Bring the mixture quickly to a boil and stir it thoroughly before covering the casserole.

Cook the rice in the center of the oven, preheated to 350°F, for 40 minutes. Meanwhile, peel, seed, and chop the tomatoes.* Blend the chicken and tomatoes thoroughly into the rice and return it to the oven. Continue cooking at the same temperature for about 20 minutes longer, or until the rice has absorbed all the liquid. If the rice dries up too quickly, add a little more of the chicken stock—the pilaf should be slightly moist.

Serve the pilaf at once. A plain tossed green salad could be served with this dish.

SPAGHETTI ALLE VONGOLE

Spaghetti with clams (*vongole*) is a regular dish on the dinner menu in southern Italy. Cheese is never served with this spaghetti recipe.

PREPARATION TIME: *15 minutes*
COOKING TIME: *20 minutes*

INGREDIENTS (*for 4–6*):
1 pound spaghetti
Salt
3 tablespoons butter
4 cloves garlic
1 tablespoon olive oil
6 tablespoons white wine
10½-ounce can minced clams

Cook the spaghetti, uncovered, in plenty of boiling salted water for 10 minutes or until just tender. Drain the spaghetti thoroughly in a colander, and put it in a warmed serving dish. Add the butter and toss the spaghetti in this.

While the spaghetti is cooking, peel and finely chop the garlic. Heat the oil in a small skillet and sauté the garlic for 2–3 minutes over moderate heat. Pour the wine over the garlic and increase the heat to the boiling point to reduce* the wine a little. Add the clams with 2–3 tablespoons of their liquid, and remove the pan from heat.

Just before serving, heat the clam sauce through and pour over the spaghetti. Serve with crusty bread and a tomato salad.

RAVIOLI WITH CHEESE

Ravioli is one of the most popular Italian pastas. It can be served with butter and grated cheese, rather than a heavy tomato sauce, to preserve its subtle flavor.

PREPARATION TIME: *1 hour*
COOKING TIME: *10 minutes*

INGREDIENTS (*for 6–8*):
2 cups sifted flour
6 egg yolks
¾ teaspoon salt
½ cup warm water
1 pound ricotta cheese
1 cup grated Parmesan cheese
2 tablespoons grated onion

Sift the flour onto a board; make a well in the center, and place 3 of the egg yolks in the well. Add ¼ teaspoon of the salt and 3 tablespoons of the water. Work it into the flour and knead until a stiff dough is formed, adding a little more warm water if necessary. Knead until smooth and elastic. Cover the dough and let it stand for 15 minutes.

Divide the dough in half, and roll out 1 of the halves as thinly as possible. In a mixing bowl, mix the remaining egg yolks, the ricotta cheese, Parmesan cheese, onion, and remaining salt until well blended. Place 1 teaspoonful of the mixture on the center of the dough; repeat, spacing teaspoonfuls 2 inches apart in each direction.

Roll out the remaining half of the dough and carefully position it as a top layer, brushing the outside edges lightly with water to seal the layers. Press the 2 layers of dough together around each mound of the cheese mixture.

Cut into squares with a pastry wheel or a sharp knife. Drop into boiling salted water, and simmer for 10 minutes. Drain well. Serve with melted butter and additional grated Parmesan cheese.

Vegetables & Salads

MANICOTTI WITH CREAMED HADDOCK

The pasta tubes known as manicotti are usually served with a creamed stuffing of meat or chicken. For a summer meal, fish makes a lighter filling. This dish is excellent for lunch or supper.

PREPARATION TIME: *30 minutes*
COOKING TIME: *45 minutes*

INGREDIENTS (*for 4–6*):

1 pound smoked haddock fillet
2½ cups milk
2 bay leaves
12 manicotti tubes
6 tablespoons heavy cream
Salt and black pepper
4 tablespoons unsalted butter
4 tablespoons all-purpose flour
1 cup grated Cheddar cheese

Wash and dry the haddock; put it in a wide pan with the milk and the bay leaves. Bring the milk slowly to a simmer and poach* the haddock over low heat for about 10 minutes. Remove the pan from the heat, lift out the haddock with a slotted spoon, and leave to cool. Strain the milk through a fine sieve and set it aside to cool.

Bring a large pan of water to a boil, add 2 teaspoons salt and the manicotti. Boil, uncovered, for about 15 minutes or until the pasta is just tender. Drain the manicotti in a colander and rinse under cold water. Leave it to drain completely on layers of paper towels.

While the manicotti is cooking, remove the skin and bones from the haddock and flake the flesh into a bowl. Pound with a pestle or mash with a fork until smooth, and gradually work in the cream. Season to taste with salt and freshly ground black pepper.

Fit a pastry bag with a plain tube, fill it with the haddock mixture, and pipe it into the manicotti tubes. Arrange the tubes in one layer in an ovenproof dish greased with 1 tablespoon of butter.

Make a thick white sauce (p.301) from the remaining butter, the flour, and strained milk. Stir ¾ cup of the grated cheese into the sauce. Cook for a few minutes over low heat, then pour it over the manicotti.

Sprinkle the remaining cheese over the sauce and put the dish in a preheated oven at 375°F for 25 minutes, or until the cheese is bubbly and golden brown on top.

Serve the manicotti in the sauce while still hot. Crusty bread and a salad of cucumber and celery in a vinaigrette sauce (p.304) could be served with the pasta.

CREAMED SPINACH

Young crisp spinach leaves should be cooked as soon as possible after buying or picking them. This dish goes well with most roast meats, particularly with ham.

PREPARATION TIME: *10 minutes*
COOKING TIME: *10–15 minutes*

INGREDIENTS (*for 4*):

2 pounds spinach
½ teaspoon salt
2 tablespoons butter
¼ teaspoon grated nutmeg
6 tablespoons heavy cream

Remove the stalks and coarse midribs from the spinach and throw away any bruised leaves. Wash the spinach thoroughly several times in lots of cold water to get rid of all sand and grit. Put the spinach in a large saucepan with only the water clinging to the leaves. Cook over low heat, shaking the pan, until the spinach has reduced in volume and made its own liquid. Add the salt and cover the pan with a lid.

Cook gently for 5–8 minutes, then drain the spinach thoroughly in a fine sieve, squeezing out as much liquid as possible.

Chop the spinach coarsely on a board. Melt the butter in the saucepan, add the spinach and nutmeg, and heat through before stirring in the cream. Serve in a hot dish.

TOMATO SALAD

In most areas the first locally grown tomatoes should be in the markets in June. They make a refreshing start to a meal, and can be served as a side dish with cold meats.

PREPARATION TIME: *20 minutes*
CHILLING TIME: *1 hour*

INGREDIENTS (*for 6*):
12 tomatoes
1–2 teaspoons superfine sugar
Salt and black pepper
5 tablespoons olive or corn oil
4 teaspoons white wine vinegar
1 tablespoon chopped chives or
  tarragon

Peel and thinly slice the tomatoes and place them in a shallow serving dish. Sprinkle with the sugar, and season to taste with salt and freshly ground pepper. Mix the olive or corn oil and the white wine vinegar together and sprinkle this over the tomatoes. Add chopped chives or tarragon and leave the salad to chill in the refrigerator for at least 1 hour before serving. Turn the tomato slices once or twice to coat them with the dressing.

MUSHROOM SALAD

Mushrooms should be used as soon as possible after purchase. They tend to go limp and brown when stored in the refrigerator.

PREPARATION TIME: *15 minutes*
STANDING TIME: *1 hour*

INGREDIENTS (*for 4–6*):
1 pound large mushrooms
Salt and black pepper
2 teaspoons Worcestershire sauce
1 tablespoon soy sauce

Wipe and trim the mushrooms,*
and slice them, as thinly as possible,
into a deep serving dish. Season to
taste with salt and freshly ground
pepper, and sprinkle the Worcestershire and soy sauces over them. Mix
the salad well and set aside for about
1 hour, turning the mushroom slices
from time to time in the dressing.

The mushrooms will have made
quite a lot of juice by the time they
are ready for serving; this is an essential part of the dressing and should
not be drained off.

ZUCCHINI AND CHIVE SALAD

Zucchini, while increasingly popular
as a vegetable, are also suitable for a
fresh chilled salad to serve with cold
meat and poultry.

PREPARATION TIME: *10 minutes*
COOKING TIME: *5 minutes*
CHILLING TIME: *1 hour*

INGREDIENTS (*for 4*):
¾ pound zucchini
2 tablespoons olive or corn oil
Juice of ½ lemon
Salt and black pepper
1 heaping tablespoon chopped chives

Clean the zucchini thoroughly with
a vegetable brush and trim them.
Bring a large pan of lightly salted
water to a boil and drop in the zucchini. Bring the water back to a
boil and cook for 5 minutes to soften
the zucchini slightly and reduce the
bitterness of the skin. Drain
them immediately in a colander and
rinse in cold water.

Cut the drained zucchini crosswise into ½-inch-thick slices and put
them in a shallow serving dish. Make
a dressing from the oil and lemon
juice, season with salt and freshly

ground pepper, and pour over the
zucchini. Add the chopped chives
and blend thoroughly before chilling
the salad in the refrigerator.

SALAD ELONA

This unusual salad of cucumber and
strawberries is an ideal side dish to
serve with cold chicken and turkey,
or with delicately flavored fish, such
as salmon.

PREPARATION TIME: *15 minutes*
CHILLING TIME: *1 hour*

INGREDIENTS (*for 4–6*):
1 small cucumber
12 large, tart strawberries
Salt and black pepper
1–2 tablespoons dry white wine or
  white wine vinegar

Peel the cucumber and slice it thinly.
Wash and hull* the strawberries,
drain them in a colander, then
cut them into thin, even slices. Arrange the slices in a decorative pattern in a shallow serving dish—an
outer circle of cucumber slightly
overlapped by a circle of strawberries,
then more cucumber, finishing with
a center of strawberry slices. Season
lightly with salt and freshly ground
pepper. Sprinkle the wine or vinegar
over the salad and chill in the refrigerator before serving.

*This selection of summer salads
shows, from top to bottom,
Zucchini with Chives, Mushroom
Salad, Tomato Salad, and
Salad Elona.*

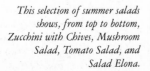

163

Desserts

PEAS AND SCALLIONS

It is a happy coincidence that scallions and young garden peas are available in June. They make an excellent combination to serve with roast lamb or chicken.

PREPARATION TIME: *15–20 minutes*
COOKING TIME: *20–30 minutes*

INGREDIENTS (*for 4–6*):
2½ pounds fresh green peas
10–12 scallions
1¼ cups chicken stock
Beurre manié (p.303)
Salt and black pepper

Shell the peas. Trim the roots and outer leaves from the scallions; wash them and cut the stems off, leaving about 1 inch of green on each bulb. Put the scallions in a pan with the stock and bring slowly to the simmering point. Cook gently until they begin to soften, then add the peas and continue to cook over low heat until the peas are tender (about 20 minutes).

When the peas are just cooked, gradually crumble the beurre manié into the mixture and stir carefully, so that the peas do not break up, until the stock has thickened enough to make a sauce. Season to taste with salt and freshly ground pepper. Serve immediately.

EGGPLANT AND TOMATO RAGOÛT

This unusual vegetable casserole is particularly good with broiled and sautéed meats. Select firm, shiny, and unblemished eggplants and extract the bitter juices before cooking.

PREPARATION TIME: *40 minutes*
COOKING TIME: *30–35 minutes*

INGREDIENTS (*for 4*):
2 large or 3 small eggplants
Salt and black pepper
1 large onion
2 tablespoons unsalted butter
16-ounce can of tomatoes
1 teaspoon sugar

Peel the eggplants and cut them into ½-inch slices crosswise. Arrange the slices on a large plate and sprinkle with salt. Leave them to stand for 30 minutes to draw out the bitter juices. Drain the slices, rinse under cold water, and pat them thoroughly dry on paper towels.

Peel and thinly slice the onion. Melt the butter in a saucepan, add the onion, and cook over low heat for about 5 minutes, or until soft but not brown. Add the eggplant slices, mixing them with the onion. Stir in the tomatoes with their juice, and season with freshly ground pepper and the sugar. Cover the pan with a lid and simmer gently for 30 minutes. Correct seasoning if necessary, and serve from the casserole.

LETTUCE AND GREEN PEAS

Young peas are sometimes cooked with fresh mint. Here, additional flavor is given by adding lettuce leaves to provide an unusual vegetable combination for meat or poultry dishes, such as lamb or duckling.

PREPARATION TIME: *15 minutes*
COOKING TIME: *25 minutes*

INGREDIENTS (*for 4–6*):
10 outer romaine lettuce leaves
2 pounds fresh green peas
1 teaspoon chopped mint
2 tablespoons butter
1 teaspoon sugar
Salt and black pepper

Wash the lettuce leaves thoroughly, but do not dry them. Use half to line the base of a heavy saucepan. Shell the peas and put them with the mint on top of the lettuce. Add the butter, cut into small pieces, and the sugar. Sprinkle with salt and freshly ground pepper, and lay the remaining lettuce leaves on top of the peas.

Cover the pan with a lid and cook over gentle heat for about 25 minutes or until the peas are tender, shaking the pan occasionally to prevent sticking.

Carefully spoon the lettuce and peas, with all of the cooking liquid, into a deep warm dish and serve immediately.

PEACH MELBA

Except for the frozen raspberries, this is the classic dish that Escoffier created for Dame Nellie Melba, the famed Australian soprano.

PREPARATION TIME: *15 minutes*
COOKING TIME: *10 minutes, plus time for cooling*

INGREDIENTS (*for 6*):
1 cup sugar
1½ cups water
1 teaspoon vanilla extract
6 peaches
1 package frozen raspberries, thawed, or 2 cups fresh raspberries and ½ cup sugar
6 scoops vanilla ice cream

Combine the sugar, water, and the vanilla extract in a saucepan. Bring the mixture to a simmer, stirring until the sugar is dissolved.

Meanwhile, put the peaches in a bowl and cover with boiling water. Leave the peaches for no more than 1 minute, then drain and peel them. Cut the peaches in half and carefully remove the stones.

Add the peach halves to the sugar-water mixture and simmer until just tender. Drain the peaches on a rack until cool. Chill in the refrigerator. Force the raspberries through a sieve. If fresh raspberries are used, stir ½ cup of sugar into the purée. Arrange the peaches on scoops of vanilla ice cream and top with the raspberry purée.

BLACKBERRY SWISS CHARLOTTE

The classic Charlotte, which probably originated in France, is a cold dessert of cooked fruit set in a mold of ladyfingers. In this version, cultivated blackberries are used, but raspberries are equally suitable. The Swiss meringue topping, flavored with blackberry syrup, should be crisp on top with a soft marshmallow texture underneath.

PREPARATION TIME: *40 minutes*
COOKING TIME: *25 minutes*

INGREDIENTS (*for 4–6*):

1 pound cultivated blackberries
½ cup superfine sugar
4 teaspoons cornstarch
2 small egg yolks
5 tablespoons heavy cream
Lemon juice

¼ pound ladyfingers
MERINGUE TOPPING:
2 small egg whites
4 ounces confectioners' sugar
5 tablespoons blackberry syrup

Hull* the blackberries and set aside a dozen large berries for decoration. Simmer the superfine sugar and 1¼ cups water in a pan over low heat until the sugar has dissolved to a syrup. Add the blackberries to the syrup and cook over very low heat for 10 minutes, or until tender but still whole. Drain the syrup into a measuring cup and set the blackberries aside.

Put the cornstarch into a small pan and gradually blend in 1¼ cups of the blackberry syrup; cook over low heat for 3–4 minutes, stirring constantly, until the mixture is clear and beginning to thicken. Remove from the heat and set aside.

Separate the eggs, setting the whites aside for the meringue. Beat together the yolks and cream, and gradually stir this into the thick syrup mixture. Sharpen and sweeten to taste with lemon juice and superfine sugar.

Cut one rounded end off each ladyfinger. Put a ½-inch layer of the blackberry cream in the base of a 2½-cup soufflé dish. Stand the ladyfingers, cut edge downward, close together around the inside of the dish to make a casing. Put a single layer of blackberries over the cream, followed by another layer of the cream, and so on, finishing with a layer of the blackberry cream.

For the meringue topping, put the egg whites in a mixing bowl with the confectioners' sugar and 5 tablespoons of blackberry syrup. Place the bowl over a pan of boiling water and whisk the mixture steadily until it stands in soft peaks. Remove the bowl from the pan and continue whisking until the meringue is cool. Swirl or pipe the meringue over the blackberry cream.

Bake the Charlotte in the center of a preheated oven at 300°F for 20 minutes or until the meringue topping is delicately colored. Serve the dessert cold, decorated with the reserved fresh blackberries.

DEEP-DISH BLUEBERRY PIE

PREPARATION TIME: *30 minutes*
CHILLING TIME: *1 hour*
COOKING TIME: *45 minutes*

INGREDIENTS (*for 6*):
PASTRY:
2¼ cups flour
½ teaspoon salt
½ cup butter
¼ cup vegetable shortening
Ice water
FILLING:
2–2½ quarts blueberries
3 tablespoons flour
Sugar to taste (about 1 cup)
6 tablespoons butter
1 egg yolk, beaten

This truly American pie is an all-time favorite. It is sometimes served warm with ice cream, at other times with a pitcher of heavy cream.

Sift the flour and salt into a mound on a mixing board or marble slab. Add the two fats and quickly rub it into the flour with the fingers. Then add just enough ice water to hold the pastry together (3–4 tablespoons). Pull off small bits, flatten with the heel of your hand, and form these pieces into one ball. Chill in refrigerator for 1 hour.

Butter a deep-dish pie plate lightly. Pour in the blueberries, mounding them slightly in the center. Sprinkle them with the flour, then add the sugar and dot with butter. Roll out the crust and place it over the berries. Flute the edges and cut a vent in the top. Brush the crust with the beaten egg yolk. Bake at 450°F for 10 minutes, then lower heat to 350°F and continue to bake until the crust is browned. Serve warm with maple or vanilla ice cream, or a pitcher of heavy cream.

165

STRAWBERRY ICE CREAM

PREPARATION TIME: *15–20 minutes*
FREEZING TIME: *12 hours*

INGREDIENTS (*for 6*):
1 pint strawberries
¾ cup confectioners' sugar
Squeeze lemon juice
¾ cup heavy cream
½ cup light cream
GARNISH:
6–8 large strawberries

This ever-popular dessert, perfect for a warm summer's evening, makes a little fruit go a long way. It is best if prepared the day before.

Hull* and wash the strawberries in a colander, drain them thoroughly, and cut them into small pieces. Put them in the blender with the sieved sugar and lemon juice. (If you have no blender, use a large spoon to rub the strawberries through a fine sieve, and add the sugar and lemon juice to the purée.*)

Combine the two creams and whip until thick but not stiff; blend into the strawberry purée.

Spoon the strawberry mixture into a plastic freezer container, cover with the lid, and put in the freezer for 12 hours. One or 2 hours before serving, remove the ice cream from the freezer and thaw slightly in the refrigerator.

Scoop the ice cream into individual dessert bowls and decorate with slices of fresh strawberries.

STRAWBERRY ICE

Ices are both easy and economical to make. They are refreshing at any time of day and make a perfect summer dessert after a rich main course. If you make the ices in the freezing compartment of the refrigerator, turn the dial to its coldest setting before freezing them.

PREPARATION TIME: *10 minutes*
FREEZING TIME: *minimum 3 hours*

INGREDIENTS (*for 4–6*):
1 pint strawberries
¼ cup confectioners' sugar
2 cups lemonade
2 egg whites

Wash and hull* the strawberries, drain them thoroughly in a small colander, then cut them into small pieces. Rub the strawberries through a sieve and stir the sugar into the purée.* (Alternatively, put the fruit and sugar in a blender to purée.) Add enough lemonade to the strawberry purée to make 2 cups liquid. Spoon the mixture into an ice cube tray or a plastic freezer container, cover with foil or a lid, and put in the freezer or the freezing compartment of the refrigerator.

When the mixture begins to freeze around the sides of the container, remove from the freezer. Scrape the frozen bits into the center of the container with a fork to break up any ice crystals. Whip the egg whites until stiff, but not dry, and fold them into the strawberry mixture. Return to the freezer, either in the original container or spooned into small molds. Cover and freeze the ice until set.

Serve the water ice spooned into dessert bowls or in the molds.

BERRY-LEMON PUDDING

Blackberries go well with the lemon flavor of this pudding, which can be eaten hot or cold.

PREPARATION TIME: *25 minutes*
COOKING TIME: *45 minutes*

INGREDIENTS (*for 4*):
½ pound blackberries
2 tablespoons unsalted butter
½ cup sugar
1 lemon
2 eggs
½ cup milk
¼ cup flour
½ cup heavy cream, whipped

Cream together the butter and 2 tablespoons of the sugar in a mixing bowl. Wash the lemon and finely grate the rind into this mixture. Squeeze the juice from the lemon and strain it in. Beat thoroughly.

Separate the eggs and beat the milk into the yolks. Add this, little by little, to the butter mixture, alternating with the sifted flour and remaining sugar. Beat until thoroughly blended. Beat the egg whites until stiff but still moist, and fold them into the mixture.

Hull* the berries. Set a few large ones aside for decoration. Put the remaining berries in the base of a 2½-cup soufflé dish. Pour the creamed mixture over the berries and set the dish in a roasting pan containing 1 inch of hot water. Bake in a preheated oven at 375°F for 40–45 minutes or until the top is golden brown and set. Test by pressing the top with a finger—the pudding is cooked if there is no imprint.

Sprinkle the pudding with sugar and add the remaining berries. Serve hot or cold, with whipped cream.

Snacks & Supper Dishes

OMELET ALPHONSE

The owner-chefs of small French bistros are experts at turning leftover meat and vegetables into savory omelets. Here is one good example.

PREPARATION TIME: *10 minutes*
COOKING TIME: *10 minutes*

INGREDIENTS (*for 3–4*):
6 eggs
4 tablespoons heavy cream
½ cup cooked diced ham
½ cup cooked peas
½ cup cooked chopped carrots
Salt and black pepper
2 tablespoons unsalted butter
½ cup grated Cheddar cheese

Beat the eggs briskly with a fork for about 30 seconds and stir in half the cream. Fold in the ham, peas, and carrots. Season with salt and pepper.

Melt the butter in a large omelet pan and cook the egg mixture over moderate heat for about 6 minutes, poking through the mixture once or twice with a knife to release air. When the omelet is just set, fold it neatly in half and slide onto an ovenproof serving dish. Mix the cheese with the remaining cream and pour over the omelet. Place under a hot broiler until browned. Serve with a tomato or mushroom salad.

QUICK CHICKEN PÂTÉ

Pâté is a popular start to a meal, but it usually takes a long time to make. This recipe quickly transforms a little leftover chicken into a well-flavored pâté.

PREPARATION TIME: *10 minutes*
COOKING TIME: *5 minutes*
CHILLING TIME: *30 minutes*

INGREDIENTS (*for 4*):
2 slices bacon, diced
4 ounces liverwurst or
    braunschweiger
1 cup cooked, finely chopped chicken
1 crushed clove garlic
1 teaspoon finely chopped parsley
1 teaspoon finely chopped chives
Salt and black pepper

Fry the bacon, without extra fat, for about 5 minutes over medium heat. Pour off the fat and blend it with the liver sausage. Add the bacon, chicken, garlic, parsley, and chives. Season this mixture with salt and pepper. Blend well.

Pack the pâté in a small earthenware dish, cover, and chill for at least 30 minutes in the refrigerator.

Serve with hot toast.

MIDSUMMER SALAD

Leftover cold meat and salad vegetables can be combined into an eye-catching, refreshing salad.

PREPARATION TIME: *20 minutes*
CHILLING TIME: *30 minutes*

INGREDIENTS (*for 4*):
12 small or 6 large sliced
    mushrooms
2 large or 4 small grated carrots
Salt and black pepper
½ bunch watercress
½ peeled cucumber, thinly sliced
1 head shredded lettuce
12 thin slices cold meat or poultry
Sauce vinaigrette (p.304)
4 tablespoons heavy cream

Gently toss the mushrooms and carrots and pile them in the center of a shallow serving dish. Surround with rings of watercress, shredded lettuce, cucumber, and meat.

Chill the salad in the refrigerator. Just before serving, mix the sauce vinaigrette with the cream and spoon the sauce evenly over the mushroom-carrot mixture.

STUFFED ANCHOVY EGGS

Eggs are often served as an appetizer with cocktails. They can also be served as a hot supper or luncheon dish, with creamed spinach (p.162).

PREPARATION TIME: *20 minutes*
COOKING TIME: *15 minutes*

INGREDIENTS (*for 4*):
8 hard-cooked eggs
2-ounce can anchovy fillets
2 tablespoons tomato ketchup
2 tablespoons heavy cream
Salt and black pepper
½ cup grated Cheddar cheese
1¼ cups white sauce (p.301)
½ teaspoon paprika

Cut the shelled eggs in half lengthwise and take out the yolks. Mash the drained anchovy fillets with a fork, and mix in the egg yolks. Pound to a smooth paste with a pestle or wooden spoon. Blend in the ketchup and cream, and season to taste with salt and pepper.

Fill the egg whites with the yolk mixture and arrange them, cut side down, in a buttered ovenproof dish. Stir half the cheese into the white sauce and pour this over the eggs. Sprinkle with the remaining cheese and dust lightly with paprika. Put the dish under a hot broiler to brown the sauce lightly.

FRENCH TOAST WITH FRUIT SAUCE

Fried fritters of stale bread—a version of French toast—can make a delicious quick dessert.

PREPARATION TIME: *10 minutes*
COOKING TIME: *10 minutes*

INGREDIENTS (*for 6*):
8 thick slices stale white bread
⅓ cup milk
2 eggs
4 tablespoons sugar
¼ teaspoon vanilla extract
8¾-ounce can of apricots
Juice of ½ lemon
2–4 tablespoons unsalted butter

Remove the crusts from the bread and cut each slice into 3 fingers. Whisk the milk and eggs, and stir in the sugar and vanilla extract.

Make a purée from the apricots and their syrup by rubbing them through a coarse sieve or putting them in a blender. Stir in the lemon juice and heat the purée over moderate heat. Keep warm.

Dip the bread fingers in the milk and egg mixture and fry them in the butter until golden brown. Drain on paper towels and arrange on a warm dish. Pour the purée over them before serving. A pitcher of cream may be offered as well.

Summer Wedding Receptions

Holding a wedding reception at home may appear to be a formidable undertaking, but it has several advantages which make the idea well worth considering. The main advantage, of course, is that it saves a great deal of money and, in addition, the food can be more original than that supplied by most catering companies and hotels for these functions. With careful planning, a reception held in familiar surroundings, imaginatively transformed for the occasion, will make a wedding day to remember.

The following menus offer a choice between a full-scale wedding breakfast for 12 people and a buffet for 50. The breakfast will give few problems on the day itself, since all the food can be made 24 hours earlier. The buffet, however, requires more careful planning. First, measure the room where the reception is to be held. There should be at least 4 square feet per person. Remember, too, that some furniture, such as tables for food and drink and chairs for elderly guests, is essential. Three reception rooms, approximately 10 feet by 12 feet, or the equivalent, would be ideal; arrange the food in one room and wine in another so that the guests will circulate. A very pleasant alternative, if there is a lawn big enough, is to rent a tent and arrange the buffet on tables inside it. The tent should measure at least 25 feet by 30 feet.

Tableware for this many guests can be a problem and is best borrowed from friends. It can be rented from catering firms, but this is usually expensive. Glasses, however, are an exception and can be rented at a nominal cost.

Wedding Breakfast for Twelve

Chilled Watercress Soup
Cold Poached Salmon
Potato Salad with Chives
Salad Elona
Green Salad with French Dressing
Raspberries with Cream
Cheese and Crackers
Fruit
Coffee

Bavarian Cup   Champagne

Chilled Watercress Soup

Double the quantities for the recipe shown on p.113. Cook the soup the night before and leave to chill in the refrigerator until just before serving.

Poached Salmon

A 6–7 pound salmon will be sufficient. Poach* it the day before in a court bouillon* and leave it to cool before skimming it. Fillet the salmon,* leaving it whole, and refrigerate it overnight. Garnish the salmon next morning. Lay alternate thin slices of cucumber and hard-cooked eggs down the center and cover them with a little aspic. Decorate the dish with watercress, shrimp in their shells, and radish flowers.* Cover the dish and refrigerate until needed. Serve with mayonnaise or herbed mayonnaise (p.303).

Set the table for the wedding breakfast around a low flower arrangement. On the table (top) are bowls of watercress soup, garnished with tiny leaves, and Italian bread sticks (grissini) in a tall glass. To garnish the poached salmon, arrange a collar of thin cucumber slices below the head to hide the gills.

Salads

For the potato salad, allow 4 pounds small new potatoes, $1\frac{1}{2}$ cups mayonnaise (p.303) mixed with $\frac{1}{2}$ cup sour cream, and a small bunch of chopped chives. Boil the potatoes the night before and peel them. In the morning, dress the potatoes with the mayonnaise and sprinkle with the chives. Set the salad aside.

For Salad Elona, double the quantities given on p.163.

The green salad requires 2 large heads of romaine, 2 bunches of watercress, and 1 large bunch of celery. Prepare the salad in the morning, mix the French dressing, and store both in the refrigerator. Dress the salad just before serving it.

Raspberries with Cream

These must be prepared on the morning of the wedding. Allow 3 quarts raspberries, a serving bowl of sifted confectioners' sugar, and 3 cups heavy cream. Wash the raspberries carefully, drain, and put in a serving dish. Chill. Just before serving, whip the cream lightly and pour it into a serving bowl.

Cheese Board

This might include a soft cream cheese, a Camembert, Cheddar, and blue cheese. Offer a selection of crackers and serve with fresh fruit, such as peaches, grapes, and bananas.

Wines

Welcome the guests with dry sherry—2 bottles will be ample. During the meal serve refreshing Bavarian cup and toast the bride and groom with champagne. Allow 3 bottles of champagne, each of which will provide 8 glasses, for the toast.

Bavarian Cup

Four pitchers of this barely alcoholic drink will be required for 12 guests. In each pitcher, slice 10–12 large strawberries and pour a miniature bottle of Grand Marnier (or other orange-based liqueur) over them. Leave the strawberries to infuse for at least 30 minutes, then add a tray of ice cubes. To each pitcher add 1 bottle of a good chilled Riesling wine to the strawberries soaking in Grand Marnier; fill each pitcher with half as much again of cold soda water, and stir. Serve immediately.

Serve the Bavarian cup from pitchers or from bowls, and ladle a few strawberry slices into each glass.

Buffet Menu for Fifty Guests

**Chicken and Mushroom
Vol-au-vents**
Shrimp Vol-au-vents
Roast Stuffed Turkey
Whole Baked Glazed Ham
Mixed Green Salad
**Tomato, Mushroom, and
Potato Salads**
CHEESES: **Blue, Cheddar, Brie,
Camembert, Bel Paese**
French Bread and Butter
Radishes, Celery
Trifles
Fruit Salad
Coffee

Preparations

As these are somewhat more time-consuming for a large-scale buffet, the wise hostess will ask a couple of friends to help her both with the advance preparations and on the day itself. The hard work can be finished the day before: the chicken for the vol-au-vents poached, the turkey roasted, and the ham glazed. The trifles and the fruit salad can be made and stored in the refrigerator until the next day.

On the wedding day itself, arrange the food, plates, flatware, glasses, and cake on the buffet. Decorate the trifles and fruit salad, assemble the cheese boards, and set the wine to chill in a bath of ice cubes. Fix paper frills around the turkey legs and ham bone. Leave the carving to the host or a guest; this can be done during the buffet as required.

Vol-au-vents

Order 10 dozen vol-au-vent cases (patty shells) from a good bakery, giving at least a week's notice. For the fillings, simmer a chicken (approximately 5 pounds) in water with 2 onions, 2 celery stalks, 1 bay leaf, a sprig of tarragon, salt, and pepper. Leave the cooked chicken to cool. Reduce* the stock to 5 cups. Strain the stock and use it for a thick white sauce (p.301). Blend ½ cup heavy cream into the sauce. Skin the

chicken, chop the meat finely, and mix with half the sauce. Blend in ½ pound lightly sautéed mushrooms and spoon the filling into half the vol-au-vent shells.

Blend enough tomato purée into the remaining sauce to color it delicately. Sharpen with the juice of half a lemon. Stir in ¾ pound. finely chopped cooked shrimp and fill the remaining vol-au-vent shells.

Heat the vol-au-vents on baking sheets in the oven at 350°F for 15 minutes before serving.

Roast Stuffed Turkey

Order a turkey weighing 22 pounds. Use a forcemeat stuffing (p.320) for the body cavity and stuff the neck

cavity with chestnut and potato purée (p.246). Cook the turkey, wrapped in foil, at a temperature of 350°F for 5 hours. Remove foil and cook for an additional 30 minutes at 400°F so that the turkey will brown.

Glazed Ham

A good meat market will supply the ham cooked at no extra charge, or it may be ordered from a delicatessen. Score the top of the ham into a diamond pattern and brush it with a glaze of honey and light brown sugar. Set the ham for 30 minutes in the center of a preheated oven at 450°F. Garnish with halved candied cherries spiked with whole cloves.

Salads

For the green salad, allow 8 heads of Boston and 8 heads of romaine lettuce, with 6 bunches of watercress. Make the tomato salad from 7 pounds of tomatoes, and for the mushroom salad (p.162) use 3

pounds of mushrooms. For the potato salad, use 6 pounds small new potatoes, 2½ cups mayonnaise (p.303) blended with 1¼ cups heavy cream, and several tablespoons of finely chopped chives.

Cheese Boards

Make up at least two cheese boards from 7 pounds of assorted cheeses. Allow 8 long French loaves and 2½ pounds of butter.

Desserts and Fruit Salad

Make 5 large sherry trifles (p.341) and decorate them on the day of the party with piped whirls of whipped cream. For the fruit salad, choose 6 large cans of different fruits and mix with 1½ pounds eating apples, 1 large fresh pineapple, 2 quarts strawberries, 1 pound seedless grapes, 8 large oranges, and 8 large pears. Heat, but do not boil, ½ bottle medium-dry white wine with 3–4 tablespoons superfine sugar. Pour

this syrup over the bowls of fruit salad and set aside to cool. Sprinkle with Angostura bitters.

Wines

The toast should traditionally be drunk with sparkling wine—champagne for preference, but German Rhine or Moselle wines, Italian Spumanti, French Vouvray, and white Burgundy are all cheaper and make good substitutes. Each bottle provides 8 glasses.

A glass of sherry on arrival and a choice of inexpensive red or white wines are perfectly adequate. Alternatively, serve pitchers of Bavarian cup and make pitchers of fruit juice for the children.

July

This is July of the bountiful heat,
Month of wild roses, and berries,
and wheat.   ALBERT D. WATSON

THIS MONTH'S RECIPES

*Midsummer brings an abundance of fruit and vegetables,
and they are far more delicious fresh from the garden.*

173

Food in Season

Mouth-watering fresh vegetables are inexpensive in midsummer. Cooked until just crisp, and seasoned with butter, salt, and pepper, they are nourishing, easy to prepare, and vastly superior in taste to their frozen or canned counterparts.

Green beans are abundant this month and can be cooked in any number of ways: Green Beans Mimosa (p.184) is a refreshing summer salad, while Beans in Sour Cream (p.185) makes a good side dish for meat or poultry. Markets are well stocked with garden-fresh tomatoes and with inexpensive beets, carrots, lettuce, and green peppers. Eggplant and yellow squash have also become more plentiful.

By July, fresh herbs are more often seen in vegetable markets, gourmet shops, and some supermarkets. Most herbs—particularly basil, sage, and rosemary—are far better when used fresh rather than dried; it is worth the trouble to look for them in shops or to grow them in a sunny corner of the garden.

Summer desserts can make imaginative use of the wide variety of fruit available. Raspberries can be combined with yogurt to make an unusual sherbet (p.187) or mixed with other berries in a Summer Pudding (p.188). Cherries are at their cheapest and can be used in Clafouti Limousin (p.187). Fresh peaches make a superb baked dessert (p.187).

Shellfish—especially crabs, clams, and lobsters—are plentiful along the seacoasts in midsummer and are less expensive than at any other time of year.

SUGGESTED MENUS

Lettuce Soup
...
Spiced Brisket of Beef
Tomatoes with Horseradish Mayonnaise
Clafouti Limousin

Stuffed Eggs Provençale
...
Truites Jurassienne
Mushrooms and Shrimp
...
Raspberry-Yogurt Sherbet

Shrimp and Mushrooms Flambé
...
Rock Cornish Hens with Olives
Brown Tom
...
Coeur à la Crème

Crab Quiche
...
Turkey Scallops Cordon Bleu
Green Beans Mimosa
...
Cold Caramel Soufflés

Smoked Trout Mousse
...
Sesame Chicken with Spiced Rice
Cucumber au Gratin
...
Summer Pudding

Cucumber Cups with Shrimp
...
Osso Buco
Risotto Bianco
...
Baked Stuffed Peaches

Lebanese Cucumber Soup
...
Luxury Pizza
Crisp Salad with French Dressing
...
Fresh Fruits

Soups & First Courses

SHRIMP AND MUSHROOMS FLAMBÉ

This is a light and easily made first course for a dinner party.

PREPARATION TIME: *10 minutes*
COOKING TIME: *10 minutes*

INGREDIENTS (*for 4*):
½ pound small cooked shrimp
½ pound mushrooms
3 tablespoons unsalted butter
Pinch nutmeg
Black pepper
4 slices whole wheat bread
2 tablespoons brandy

Trim and wipe the mushrooms;* slice them thinly. Melt the butter in a small skillet and cook the mushrooms for 2–3 minutes, or until they are slightly softened. Add the shrimp to the pan and stir over moderate heat until they are heated through. Season to taste with a little nutmeg and a few twists of freshly ground pepper.

Toast the bread slices and arrange them on individual warmed serving plates; keep warm.

Warm the brandy in a small pan, pour over the shrimp, and set alight. As soon as the flames have died down, spoon the shrimp and mushroom mixture onto the hot toast and serve immediately.

LEBANESE CUCUMBER SOUP

There are many variations of this popular Middle Eastern cucumber soup. It can only be served cold, but is refreshing in hot weather and looks tempting with a few pink shrimp floating on top. It is extremely easy to prepare and would be an unusual first course for a roast leg of lamb dinner.

PREPARATION TIME: *15 minutes*
CHILLING TIME: *about 1 hour*

INGREDIENTS (*for 4–6*):
1 large or 2 small cucumbers
1¼ cups light cream
⅔ cup yogurt
1 clove garlic
2 tablespoons tarragon vinegar
Salt and black pepper
2 tablespoons finely chopped fresh mint
GARNISH:
1 tablespoon finely chopped gherkins
Sprigs of mint
18 shrimp (optional)

Wash and dry the cucumber. Do not peel it unless it is waxed, but grate it coarsely into a bowl. Stir in the cream and the yogurt. Peel and crush the garlic and add it to the cucumber, together with the vinegar. Season to taste with salt and freshly ground pepper. Stir in the chopped mint. Chill the soup in the refrigerator for at least 1 hour.

Serve the pale green soup in individual bowls.

For a summery look, garnish each bowl with a thin cucumber slice, chopped parsley, chives, gherkins, or a sprig of fresh mint. On special occasions, float a few shelled cooked shrimp on top of the soup instead of the green garnish.

HERRING SALAD

This hearty, unusual delicacy has graced Swedish smorgasbords and central European buffets for generations. It is best prepared the day before serving, so that the various flavors have time to blend. This colorful salad can serve as a main course, as a luncheon dish, or as a principal item for a cold buffet.

PREPARATION TIME: *5–10 minutes*
CHILLING TIME: *1 hour or more*

INGREDIENTS (*for 8*):
1½ cups cooked diced potatoes
1½ cups cooked diced veal
1½ cups raw diced apples
1½ cups cooked diced beets
1½ cups diced marinated herring
2 tablespoons capers, drained
¾ cup finely chopped onion
Mayonnaise

Combine all ingredients except the mayonnaise and toss well. Chill in the refrigerator for several hours or overnight. Toss with mayonnaise. Arrange in a large salad bowl lined with salad greens. Garnish the salad with one or more of the following: mayonnaise, chopped hard-cooked egg whites and yolks, dill pickle slices, or black and green olives.

SMOKED TROUT MOUSSE

This fish mousse, which has a creamy texture and smoky flavor, makes an attractive beginning to a meal. It can be prepared a day in advance and kept in the refrigerator until serving time.

PREPARATION TIME: *15 minutes*
CHILLING TIME: *1 hour*

INGREDIENTS (*for 4–6*):
¾-*pound smoked trout*
⅓ *cup cottage cheese*
⅓ *cup sour cream*
Juice of ½ lemon
Salt and black pepper
GARNISH:
Finely chopped parsley

Remove the skin and bones from the flesh of the trout and flake* the meat into a blender. Add the cottage cheese and the sour cream to the flaked fish. Blend the mixture until smooth. If you have no blender, pound the flaked fish to a smooth paste with a mortar and pestle before mixing in the sieved cottage cheese and sour cream. Season to taste with the lemon juice, salt, and pepper. Spoon the mousse into individual ramekins and chill in the refrigerator for 1 hour or more.

Sprinkle finely chopped parsley in a neat border around the edge of each dish. Serve with fingers or triangles of hot toast and butter.

STUFFED EGGS PROVENÇALE

Stuffed eggs are always popular—as a first course, with cocktails, or at picnics and cold buffets. This is one of the many versions of the classic French recipe.

PREPARATION TIME: *40 minutes*
COOKING TIME: *15 minutes*

INGREDIENTS (*for 4–6*):
6 eggs
1 cup pitted black olives
¼ *cup flaked canned tuna*
6 anchovy fillets
2 tablespoons capers
1 teaspoon Dijon mustard
5–6 tablespoons olive oil
2 teaspoons brandy
Black pepper
Lemon juice
GARNISH:
Lettuce or watercress

Hard-cook the eggs and plunge them into cold water. When cold, shell the eggs, halve them lengthwise with a sharp knife, and carefully remove the yolks. Set aside. Using a mortar and pestle, pound the olives to a smooth paste. Add the tuna, anchovy fillets, and capers, and continue pounding until the mixture is perfectly smooth. Blend in the mustard and gradually work in the olive oil and brandy until the mixture is creamy and thick.

Season to taste with freshly ground pepper and a little lemon juice. Press the egg yolks through a coarse sieve and blend them into the fish mixture.

Pile the stuffing into the hollow egg whites or pipe it through a pastry bag fitted with a rosette tube. Arrange the stuffed eggs on a bed of lettuce or watercress, and serve with crusty bread and butter.

LETTUCE SOUP

A surplus of home-grown lettuce, or heads not quite crisp enough for a salad, can be used for an economical soup. The pale green, light-textured soup is ideal on a summer day.

PREPARATION TIME: *10 minutes*
COOKING TIME: *15 minutes*

INGREDIENTS (*for 4–6*):
1 head Boston lettuce
Salt
1 small onion
3 tablespoons butter
2 cups chicken stock
Black pepper, sugar, grated nutmeg
2 cups milk
1–2 egg yolks
2 tablespoons heavy cream
GARNISH:
Bread croûtons (*p.300*)

Wash the lettuce leaves thoroughly and blanch* them for 5 minutes in boiling salted water. Drain and rinse in cold water. Chop the leaves; peel and finely chop the onion.

Melt the butter in a saucepan and sauté the onion in it for 5 minutes or until soft. Add the lettuce shreds, setting a few aside. Pour the stock over the onions and lettuce and bring the soup to a boil. Season to taste with salt, freshly ground pepper, sugar, and a little nutmeg.

Allow the soup to cool slightly before blending it or rubbing it through a sieve. Add the milk to the soup and reheat gently; simmer for about 5 minutes.

Lightly beat together the egg yolks and cream. Spoon a little of the hot, but not boiling, soup into this and blend thoroughly. Pour the egg mixture into the soup and simmer gently until the soup thickens. On no account should it reach the boiling point, or the eggs will curdle.

Just before serving, add the rest of the lettuce shreds. Ladle the soup into plates and serve with a bowl of crisp bread croûtons.

TARAMASALATA

A Greek hors d'oeuvre (*mézé*) nearly always includes a dish of creamy pâté made from the dried, salted, and pressed roe of the gray mullet. Red caviar is a good substitute.

PREPARATION TIME: *30 minutes*
CHILLING TIME: *45 minutes*

INGREDIENTS (*for 4–6*):
1 onion
1–2 cloves garlic (optional)
4 slices white bread, each ¾ *inch thick*
5 tablespoons milk or water
1 8-ounce jar red caviar
6–8 tablespoons olive oil
Juice of 1 large lemon
Black pepper

Peel and grate the onion and squeeze to remove the water. Peel and crush the garlic if used. Remove the crusts and soak the bread in the milk.

Add the onion, and garlic, if used, to the caviar and beat thoroughly with a wooden spoon until quite smooth. Squeeze the bread dry and beat it into the caviar mixture. Add the olive oil alternately with the lemon juice, little by little, as for making a mayonnaise. Beat vigorously after each addition until the mixture is a creamy purée.

Season to taste with freshly ground pepper and pack into a pot or individual ramekins. Cover and chill lightly.

Serve with hot crisp toast, softened unsalted butter, black olives, and lemon wedges.

Fish

SMOKED HADDOCK SOUFFLÉ

Warm, sunny days call for light, delicate meals. This haddock soufflé is delicious and easy to prepare. It can constitute the main course, or it can be made in small individual soufflé dishes and served as a first course.

PREPARATION TIME: *30 minutes*
COOKING TIME: *30 minutes*

INGREDIENTS (*for 4–6*):
¾ *pound smoked haddock fillet*
1¼ *cups milk*
5 *tablespoons unsalted butter*
4 *tablespoons all-purpose flour*
Grated rind of ½ lemon
2 *tablespoons grated Parmesan cheese*
Cayenne pepper
4 *eggs*
1 *tablespoon finely chopped parsley*

Wash the haddock fillet and pat it dry with paper towels. Put it in a large shallow pan and pour over the milk with 1 tablespoon of water. Bring slowly to a boil, then remove the pan from the heat. Lift out the fish with a slotted spoon and allow to cool slightly; set the cooking liquid aside and flake* the flesh of the haddock into a mixing bowl. Mash it finely with a fork.

Melt 4 tablespoons of the butter in a small pan and blend in the flour; remove from the heat and gradually add the haddock liquid, stirring continuously. Return the pan to the heat and simmer, stirring, until the sauce thickens to a creamy consistency. Flavor the sauce with the lemon rind, cheese, and cayenne; stir in the haddock.

Separate the eggs and beat the yolks into the mixture one at a time. Beat the egg whites until stiff but not dry, and fold them carefully into the fish mixture. Butter a 1½–2 pint prepared soufflé dish* or 6 small soufflé dishes; sprinkle over the chopped parsley.

Spoon the haddock mixture into the dish and bake it in the center of a preheated oven at 400°F for 30 minutes, or until it is well risen and golden.

Plain buttered potatoes and a green vegetable could accompany the soufflé for a main course.

FILLETS OF SOLE DUGLÉRÉ

A famous French chef, Adolphe Dugléré, invented this now-classic dish in the 19th century.

PREPARATION TIME: *20–30 minutes*
COOKING TIME: *25 minutes*

INGREDIENTS (*for 4*):
8 *fillets of sole*
2–3 *shallots*
4 *large tomatoes*
4 *tablespoons unsalted butter*
½ *small clove garlic*
Salt and black pepper
½ *cup fish stock*
½ *cup dry white wine*
1–1¼ *cups heavy cream*
Beurre manié (*p.303*)
1 *teaspoon chopped fresh tarragon (optional)*
1 *egg yolk*
Lemon juice
Tabasco
GARNISH:
Chopped parsley

Peel and finely chop the shallots. Peel, seed, and chop the tomatoes. Use 1 tablespoon of butter to thoroughly grease a shallow, flameproof dish. Peel and cut the garlic and rub it lightly around the dish. Arrange the sole fillets in a single layer in the dish and season with salt and freshly ground pepper.

Sprinkle the shallots over the fish and top with the tomatoes. Pour in the stock and the wine, and cover the dish with buttered waxed paper. Bring the contents of the dish to the simmering point on top of the stove, then lower the heat. Poach* the sole gently for about 7 minutes or until cooked but still firm. Alternatively, bake the fish in the center of a preheated oven at 350°F for about 15 minutes.

When cooked, put a cover over the fish and drain it. Keep the fish warm. Bring the cooking liquid, with the shallots and tomatoes, to a boil and reduce* by at least a quarter. Take the pan from the heat and stir in the cream; add the beurre manié, piece by piece, and whisk until completely absorbed. Blend in the tarragon if used. Melt the remaining butter and beat with the egg yolk; blend this into the cream sauce. Correct seasoning.

Just before serving, arrange the sole fillets on a large flat heated dish and sprinkle them with a little lemon juice. Stir a few drops of Tabasco into the sauce. Coat the fillets with the sauce and sprinkle with parsley.

This rich dish needs no more than a plain green salad and perhaps a few boiled potatoes to complement it.

MACKEREL WITH TOMATOES

Mackerel is sometimes known as the poor man's trout—unjustly so, for although both are oily fish, their flavors are quite distinct. Mackerel is most plentiful in summer, and makes an excellent main course.

PREPARATION TIME: *30 minutes*
COOKING TIME: *20 minutes*

INGREDIENTS (*for 4–6*):
6 *medium mackerel*
Seasoned flour (*p.412*)
4 *tablespoons vegetable or olive oil*
1 *onion*
8 *small mushrooms*
1 *clove garlic*
¾ *pound firm tomatoes*
2 *tablespoons butter*
Salt and black pepper
1 *teaspoon chopped parsley*
2 *teaspoons wine vinegar*

Clean and fillet the mackerel.* Wash the fillets, wipe them dry on a clean cloth, and coat them with seasoned flour, shaking off any surplus. Heat 3 tablespoons of the oil in a heavy skillet and, when hot, sauté the fillets for about 10 minutes or until golden brown, turning once.

While the mackerel is sautéing, peel the onion and garlic, and wipe and trim the mushrooms.* Finely chop the onion and mushrooms and crush the garlic. Peel the tomatoes* and slice them thinly. Heat the remaining oil in a clean pan and sauté the onion for a few minutes over moderate heat. Add the mushrooms and garlic, and cook very slowly for a further 5 minutes. Season to taste with salt and freshly ground pepper, and stir in the parsley and vinegar. Cook the tomato slices for 3 minutes in the butter, using a separate pan over gentle heat.

To serve, arrange the warm mackerel fillets on a serving dish, put the tomatoes between them, and spoon a little of the onion mixture onto each fillet. Serve with new potatoes and a tossed green salad.

Meat

SALMON KEDGEREE

Kedgeree—an East Indian dish of fish and rice—makes a good light lunch or supper dish.

PREPARATION TIME: *5 minutes*
COOKING TIME: *30 minutes*

INGREDIENTS (*for 4–6*):
½ pound cooked salmon
Salt, black pepper, and cayenne
¾ cup long grain rice
1 onion
4 tablespoons butter
2 hard-cooked eggs
GARNISH:
Chopped parsley

Remove any skin and bones from the salmon and flake* it carefully. Bring 1½ cups of water to a boil in a large saucepan, adding a pinch each of salt, pepper, and cayenne. Add the rice, cover tightly with a lid or foil, and cook over low heat for about 25 minutes, or until all the water is absorbed and the rice is fluffy.

While the rice is cooking, peel and finely chop the onion. Melt a little of the butter in a pan and sauté the onion until soft and transparent. Set aside. Chop the whites of the hard-cooked eggs coarsely and press the yolks through a sieve.

Cut the remaining butter into small pieces and stir into the cooked rice, with the flaked salmon, onion, and egg whites. Season to taste and heat the mixture through gently.

To serve, pile the kedgeree upon a warmed flat dish and decorate with the sieved egg yolks, arranged in a star or cross pattern. Sprinkle generously with chopped parsley and serve with hot buttered toast fingers.

TRUITES JURASSIENNE

The sauce for this trout dish comes from the Jura region in France.

PREPARATION TIME: *15 minutes*
COOKING TIME: *35–45 minutes*

INGREDIENTS (*for 6*):
6 medium trout
4 tablespoons unsalted butter
2 shallots or 1 small onion
1¼ cups rosé wine
½ cup Hollandaise sauce (p.303)
1 tablespoon heavy cream
Salt and black pepper
GARNISH:
Bread croûtons (p.300) and
  chopped parsley

Lay the trout side by side in a buttered ovenproof dish. Peel and finely chop the shallots and sprinkle them over the fish. Pour in the wine and cover the dish with buttered waxed paper or foil. Cook the trout in the center of a preheated oven at 300°F for 25 minutes.

Meanwhile, prepare the Hollandaise sauce and heat without boiling. When the trout are cooked, lift them carefully onto a dish towel and remove the skins. Keep warm on a serving dish.

Strain the cooking liquid and reduce* it by fast boiling until there are only 2–3 tablespoons left. Let this cool slightly, then stir it into the warm Hollandaise sauce. Finally, stir in the cream. Adjust the seasoning.

To serve, pour the sauce over the fish. Garnish with fried bread croûtons and a sprinkling of chopped parsley. Boiled potatoes and mushrooms cooked in a little butter go well with the trout.

LAMB KIDNEYS EPICURE

Nutritious lamb kidneys make an excellent main course.

PREPARATION TIME: *15 minutes*
COOKING TIME: *15 minutes*

INGREDIENTS (*for 4*):
8 lamb kidneys, approximately 1¼
  pounds
2 tablespoons butter
1 small shallot
1½ tablespoons all-purpose flour
1¼ cups beef stock
Salt and black pepper
1 tablespoon Dijon mustard
2 teaspoons red currant jelly
2 tablespoons heavy cream
1 tablespoon port

Remove any fat from the kidneys* and slice them in half lengthwise. Put them in a bowl and cover with boiling water; leave for 2 minutes. Drain and dry the kidneys; remove the skin and snip out the cores with scissors. Cut each half into 3 or 4 slices. Melt the butter in a skillet and cook the kidneys over moderate heat for 3–4 minutes until they are lightly browned.

Remove the kidneys from the pan and keep them warm. Peel and finely chop the shallot and cook in the pan juices until softened. Blend in the flour and gradually add the stock. Simmer the sauce, stirring frequently, until smooth and creamy. Season to taste with salt and freshly ground pepper. Blend in the mustard, red currant jelly, cream, and port. Reheat the kidneys in the sauce over low heat, but do not let the sauce reach the boiling point or it will separate.

Pile the kidneys and the sauce over a bed of rice. Sautéed mushrooms could be an extra vegetable.

SWEETBREADS WITH BEURRE NOISETTE

Ideally, this lunch or supper dish should be made with fresh, not frozen, veal sweetbreads. Sweetbreads should be soaked before cooking.

PREPARATION TIME: *30 minutes*
COOKING TIME: *40 minutes*

INGREDIENTS (*for 4–6*):
1¼ pounds sweetbreads
4 tablespoons white wine vinegar
1 carrot
1 stalk celery
2 cups chicken or veal stock
½ bay leaf
1 sprig thyme
6 peppercorns
¾ cup clarified butter
Salt and black pepper
Seasoned flour (p.412)
3 tablespoons unsalted butter
1 tablespoon olive oil
GARNISH:
Chopped fresh parsley
Lemon wedges

Soak the sweetbreads for 1 hour in several changes of cold water to remove all traces of blood. For the last ½ hour, soak the sweetbreads in fresh cold water with 1 tablespoon of vinegar. Put them in a pan with fresh cold water and bring slowly to a boil. Take the pan off the heat, drain the sweetbreads, and cool them under running water. Remove the black veins and pull off as much of the thin skin around them as possible without tearing the sweetbreads. Wrap them in cheesecloth and let cool in the refrigerator between two weighted plates or wooden boards to flatten them. Meanwhile, scrape, wash, and slice the carrot and celery.

Put the sweetbreads in a pan, cover them with the stock by about 1 inch, and add the carrot, celery, bay leaf, thyme, and peppercorns. Put the pan over low heat and bring slowly to the simmering point; cook for 10 minutes, uncovered. Remove the sweetbreads from the pan with a slotted spoon, strain the stock through a fine sieve, and return the sweetbreads to the stock until they are cool enough to handle.

Remove the sweetbreads from the stock and dry them on a dish towel. Heat the remaining vinegar in a small pan and boil until it has reduced* by two-thirds. In a separate pan, heat the clarified butter* gently and, when light brown, stir in the vinegar. Season to taste with salt and freshly ground pepper.

Cut the sweetbreads into thick slices and coat them lightly with the seasoned flour. Melt the unsalted butter and the olive oil together in a heavy skillet over moderate heat and cook the sweetbreads for about 3 minutes on each side, or until they are lightly browned. Remove the sweetbread slices to a heated serving dish and pour the brown butter over them.

Sprinkle with chopped parsley and serve at once. Garnish the sweetbreads with wedges of lemon. Boiled rice and cucumber au gratin (p.185) make good side dishes.

SPICED BRISKET OF BEEF

INGREDIENTS (*for 8–10*):
4-pound lean boned brisket of beef
2 cups Kosher salt
2 shallots
3 bay leaves
1 teaspoon potassium nitrate
  (saltpeter)
1 teaspoon allspice
4 tablespoons brown sugar
1 teaspoon powdered cloves
1 teaspoon powdered mace
½ teaspoon crushed black peppercorns
½ teaspoon dried thyme

PREPARATION TIME: *20 minutes*
COOKING TIME: *4–5 hours*

This makes a perfect dish for summer, ideal for a buffet or a large dinner party. The beef should be left to steep in spices for 8 days before being cooked and pressed.

Wipe the boned but not rolled meat with a clean damp towel and put it in a large bowl. Rub the meat well on all sides with 1½ cups of the salt. Cover the bowl with cheesecloth and leave for 24 hours in the lower part of the refrigerator or in a cool place.

Peel and finely chop the shallots and the bay leaves. Put these in a bowl with the remainder of the salt and the rest of the ingredients and mix together. Each day, rub this mixture well into the salted meat, pouring off any liquid that may have accumulated in the bowl. All the spicing mixture should have been absorbed after 7 days.

Roll the spiced meat neatly and tie it securely with string. Put the meat in a heavy pot just large enough to hold it. Cover the meat with warm water. Simmer, covered, over low heat for 4–5 hours or until meat is tender when stuck with a fork. Let the meat cool in the liquid, then lift it out. Place it between two plates with a heavy weight on top and leave it to press for 8 hours.

Serve the spiced brisket cold, sliced, and accompanied by baked potatoes, a selection of salads, pickled beets, and gherkins.

OSSO BUCO

PREPARATION TIME: *30 minutes*
COOKING TIME: *1¾–2 hours*

INGREDIENTS (*for* 6):
2½-pound veal shank
Seasoned flour (p.412)
3 carrots
2 stalks celery
1 onion
2 cloves garlic
4 tablespoons butter
1 cup dry white wine
1 cup chicken or veal stock
16-ounce can of tomatoes
Salt and black pepper
Sugar
1 sprig or ½ teaspoon dried rosemary
GARNISH:
4 tablespoons finely chopped parsley
Finely grated rind of 2 large lemons
2–3 cloves finely chopped garlic

Italy is the homeland of this appetizing, inexpensive stew of veal shank with marrow. The traditional Milanese garnish, known as gremolata, gives a colorful look to the finished dish.

Ask the butcher to saw the veal shank into pieces about 1½ inches thick. Coat the veal pieces with seasoned flour. Clean the vegetables and chop them finely.

Melt the butter in a heavy pan large enough to take all the meat in one layer. Brown the meat and the vegetables. When the meat is lightly browned, stand each piece upright to prevent the marrow falling out during cooking. Pour in the wine and stock and add the tomatoes with their juice. Season to taste with salt, freshly ground pepper, and sugar. Then add the rosemary. Simmer,

covered, over low heat for 1½ hours, or until the meat is tender.

While the veal is cooking, mix the ingredients for the garnish.

Pour the sauce over the meat and sprinkle with the garnish. The marrow is usually left in the bones, but it can also be extracted and spread on toast. In Italy, osso buco is served with Risotto alla Milanese (p.141), but buttered egg noodles are more suitable for a summer meal.

VITELLO TONNATO

In Italy this cold terrine of veal in tuna sauce is a standby for hot summer days. The classic version uses boiled veal, but in some regions the meat is roasted instead. It should be made the day before and left to chill in the refrigerator overnight.

PREPARATION TIME: *30 minutes*
COOKING TIME: *1¾ hours*

INGREDIENTS (*for* 6):
2½ pounds leg or loin of veal
1 carrot
1 onion
1 stalk celery
4 peppercorns
1 teaspoon salt
3½-ounce can of tuna
4 anchovy fillets
½ cup olive oil
2 egg yolks
Black pepper
2 tablespoons lemon juice
GARNISH:
Capers
Gherkins
Fresh tarragon (if available)

Ask the butcher to bone the leg or loin of veal, tie it in a neat roll, and give you the bones.

Scrape and wash the carrot and peel the onion; quarter both. Clean

and chop the celery. Put the meat into a large saucepan together with the bones. Add the vegetables, peppercorns, salt, and enough water to cover the meat. Bring the water quickly to a boil, turn down the heat, cover the pan with a lid, and simmer for about 1¾ hours, or until the meat is tender. Lift the meat carefully out of the pan and set aside to cool. Reduce* the cooking liquid by fast boiling, strain through cheesecloth, and set aside.

To make the sauce, drain the tuna and anchovy and put in a bowl with 1 tablespoon of the olive oil. Mash with a fork until thoroughly mixed. Blend in the egg yolks and season with pepper. Rub this paste through a sieve into a small bowl. Stir in half the lemon juice, then add the remaining oil, little by little, beating well after each addition. When the sauce has become thick and shiny, add some lemon juice to taste. Stir in about 2 tablespoons of the veal liquid to give the sauce the consistency of thin cream.

Cut the cold veal into thin slices and arrange them in a terrine. Cover the meat completely with the sauce, then wrap the dish closely in foil and leave overnight to marinate.*

Before serving, garnish the dish with capers and a few sliced gherkins, or with a sprig of tarragon. Cold rice salad (p.336) or a tossed lettuce and tomato salad could complement the meat.

NOISETTES OF LAMB SHREWSBURY

These little round fillets, or noisettes, are cut from the loin or rib of lamb. They are excellent as the main course for a dinner party, especially since the time-consuming sauce can be made well in advance.

PREPARATION TIME: *15–25 minutes*
COOKING TIME: *2 hours for sauce, 12 minutes for the noisettes*

INGREDIENTS (*for* 4–6):
8–12 noisettes of lamb
5 tablespoons unsalted butter
1 tablespoon olive oil
SAUCE:
1 small carrot
1 small onion
2 stalks celery
1 slice lean bacon
3 tablespoons butter
Lamb trimmings
4 tablespoons all-purpose flour
2½ cups brown stock
1¼ cups dry white or red wine
2 teaspoons tomato purée
Bouquet garni (p.410)
1 sprig or ½ teaspoon dried rosemary
2–3 tablespoons red currant jelly
Salt and black pepper

The noisettes (2–3 ounces each) can be cut from chops from the loin or the rib; the latter are smaller, but have a more delicate flavor. Most good meat markets will prepare the noisettes on request, but ask for the trimmings to be included with the order. Alternatively, buy 8–12 chops, remove the bone from each, and shape the meat into neat rounds about 2 inches across. Tie them firmly with string.

Prepare the sauce first. Scrape the carrot, peel the onion, and clean the celery; dice these vegetables. Dice

Poultry

SESAME CHICKEN WITH SPICED RICE

Sesame seeds and oil are used throughout the Far East, particularly in Japan, to impart a mildly spicy flavor to meat and poultry. This chicken dish is served on a bed of spiced rice that also goes well, hot or cold, with a number of other chicken or meat dishes.

PREPARATION TIME: *50 minutes*
COOKING TIME: *25 minutes*

INGREDIENTS (*for 4*):
2 chickens, each about 3 pounds
¾ cup long grain rice
¾ cup all-purpose flour
Salt and black pepper
1 teaspoon powdered sesame seed or
  1 level tablespoon sesame seeds
6 tablespoons butter
1 teaspoon olive oil
1¼ cups chicken stock
3 tablespoons dry white wine
½ teaspoon ground coriander
¼ teaspoon ground ginger
Chili powder
1¼ cups heavy cream

For this dish, use only the chicken breasts, and reserve the legs for another recipe.

Skin the chickens,* and with a sharp knife carefully carve each breast away from the bone in one piece. Remove the legs. Use the skin, the wings, and the carcasses to make a strong chicken stock. Strain the stock through cheesecloth and reduce* it by fast boiling to 1¼ cups.

Before cooking the chicken, cook the rice in a large pan of boiling salted water. Season the flour with salt, freshly ground pepper, and the sesame powder or seeds, and coat the chicken breasts evenly with the seasoned flour. Melt 4 tablespoons of the butter in a heavy pan, add the olive oil, and sauté the chicken over moderate heat for about 3 minutes on each side, or until lightly golden. Drain off the butter and pour the stock and wine over the chicken. Cover the pan with a lid and simmer over low heat for 10–15 minutes, or until the chicken is tender.

Stir the remaining butter into the cooked rice. Season to taste with salt and pepper, and blend in the coriander, ginger, and a pinch of chili powder. Pile the spiced rice onto a warm serving dish and keep it hot.

Lift the chicken breasts from the pan and arrange them on the rice. Stir the cream into the liquid in the pan and simmer, stirring continuously, until the mixture is a thick and creamy sauce. Pour over the chicken and serve.

ROCK CORNISH HENS WITH OLIVES

These delicious small birds may be prepared in a great variety of ways. This version has a particularly savory appeal. Usually, one Rock Cornish hen is served per person.

PREPARATION TIME: *15 minutes*
COOKING TIME: *1¼–1¾ hours*

INGREDIENTS (*for 2*):
2 small Rock Cornish hens
1 large onion
1 carrot
1 green pepper
3 stalks celery
6 sprigs of parsley
Salt and pepper
1 cup white wine
24 small green olives

Put the giblets, wing tips, and neck into a small saucepan with 2 cups of water and cook, covered, for 45 minutes. Strain and set the broth aside. Peel the onion and carrot and remove the seeds from the green pepper. Chop these and the celery and parsley, all rather coarsely. Arrange the chopped vegetables on the bottom of a baking dish.

Rub the hens with salt and pepper and place them on top of the vegetables. Add the white wine to the strained broth and pour this over all. Roast in a 325°F oven for 1½–1¾ hours, or until the hens are brown and crisp. To prevent the birds from drying out, baste about every 20 minutes with the broth in the pan during the roasting.

When the hens are done, remove them to a hot platter and keep them warm by placing them in the turned-off oven with the door open while making the sauce. Rub the vegetables and broth through a fine sieve with a large spoon, put them through a fine disc of a food mill, or use an electric blender to liquefy the vegetables thoroughly.

Reheat the sauce, skim off excess fat, and taste for seasoning. Add the olives and heat them through. Serve the sauce in a sauceboat with the hens. Accompany the dish with small new potatoes cooked in their jackets in salted water, or peeled steamed potatoes seasoned with butter and garnished with parsley; and tiny green peas.

the bacon and blanch* for a few minutes. Melt the butter in a heavy pan over moderate heat. Sauté the diced vegetables, chopped lamb trimmings, and bacon in this for 10 minutes. Remove the pan from the heat and stir in the flour; return the pan to a low heat and cook for a further 10 minutes, stirring continuously, until the mixture is light brown. Take the pan off the heat.

Bring the stock and wine to a boil in a separate pan; whisk this into the vegetable mixture. Stir in the tomato purée and add the bouquet garni with the fresh rosemary, if used. Simmer the sauce, partly covered, over gentle heat for at least 2 hours, stirring occasionally to prevent sticking. Remove any scum from time to time. When the sauce is thick enough to coat the back of a spoon, remove it from the heat.

Strain the sauce through a coarse sieve and remove any fat that rises to the top.

About 30 minutes before serving, reheat the sauce gently. Stir in the red currant jelly and powdered rosemary (if used); simmer until the jelly has melted. Season to taste with salt and pepper and keep warm.

Heat the butter and oil in a heavy pan and sauté the prepared noisettes over moderate heat for 4–6 minutes on each side, depending on the size. They should be well browned, and slightly pink inside.

Serve the noisettes with the thick dark brown sauce poured over them. Boiled new potatoes and zucchini or green beans are suitable vegetables.

TURKEY SCALLOPS CORDON BLEU

Turkey makes a good main course for a dinner party, especially as scallops can now be bought precut.

PREPARATION TIME: *20 minutes*
COOKING TIME: *25 minutes*

INGREDIENTS (*for 4*):
4 turkey scallops
4 slices lean boiled ham
4 thin slices Fontina, Bel Paese, or
*   Gruyère cheese*
4–6 ounces mushrooms
6 tablespoons unsalted butter
Seasoned flour (p.412)
1 tablespoon olive oil
Black pepper
1–2 tablespoons chopped parsley
4–6 tablespoons hot chicken stock
*   (p.298)*
GARNISH (*optional*):
Watercress

Buy the turkey scallops or cut them from an uncooked turkey breast. The white breast meat should give 5 slices from each side. Before slicing the breast, cut down slantwise behind the wishbone and remove this to give another scallop. Wrap tightly in foil and store the surplus scallops in the freezer.

Cut the ham and cheese slices to fit the scallops. Trim the mushrooms* and slice them thinly; cook until soft in 1 tablespoon of the butter and set them aside. Coat the turkey scallops evenly, but not too thickly, with the seasoned flour.

Melt the remaining butter and the oil in a large skillet over moderate heat. Sauté the scallops for about 5 minutes on each side. Place a slice of ham on each scallop, spoon over a

thin layer of mushrooms, and season lightly with freshly ground pepper. Sprinkle a little of the parsley over the mushrooms and cover with a slice of cheese. Pour the hot stock over the scallops. Cover the pan closely with a lid or foil and cook over low heat for about 10 minutes or until the cheese has melted.

Lift out the scallops and arrange on a hot serving dish; sprinkle over the remaining parsley or garnish with sprigs of watercress. The richness of the scallops is best offset by a dish of buttered ribbon noodles and a tossed green salad.

POULET À LA CRÈME

This recipe for a casserole of chicken in a rich cream and calvados sauce comes from Normandy. It loses none of its flavor if any leftovers are reheated the next day. Just warm it in a double boiler.

PREPARATION TIME: *10 minutes*
COOKING TIME: *1¼–1½ hours*

INGREDIENTS (*for 4–6*):

1 3–4 pound chicken
1 Spanish onion
2 slices cooked ham or lean bacon
Salt and black pepper
5 tablespoons butter
4 tablespoons calvados or brandy
2 teaspoons finely chopped celery
*   leaves*
1¼ cups dry cider or unsweetened
*   apple juice*
2 large egg yolks
½ cup heavy cream
GARNISH:
2 eating apples
2 tablespoons unsalted butter

Peel and finely chop the onion, and dice the ham or bacon. Wipe the trussed chicken inside and out with a clean damp cloth and set the giblets aside. Season the chicken well with salt and pepper.

Melt the butter in a pan over moderate heat and cook the onion until soft and transparent. Stir in the ham or bacon and cook for another 2–3 minutes. Brown the chicken lightly all over in the butter. Warm the calvados or brandy in a small pan and set alight (calvados will produce a fair amount of flame). While the liquor is still flaming, pour it over the chicken. Shake the pan gently until the flames die out.

Add the chicken neck, gizzard, and heart to the pan, but omit the liver. Sprinkle with the chopped celery leaves and pour in the cider or apple juice; let it come to a boil, then simmer for a few minutes. Turn the chicken on its side and cover the pan closely with foil and then a lid. Cook over low heat. (Alternatively, put the contents in a casserole and cook

at 325°F in the center of the oven.)

After 20–25 minutes, turn the chicken over on the other side and cook for a similar period, still covered. Finally, turn the chicken breast upwards, cover, and cook for a further 10 minutes.

While the chicken is cooking, peel and core the apples for the garnish. Cut them, without breaking, into ¼-inch-thick rings. Melt the butter in a small pan and sauté the apple rings until golden brown, turning once.

Lift the chicken onto a warm serving dish and keep hot. Strain the liquid and reduce* slightly by fast boiling. Remove the pan from the heat. Beat together the egg yolks and the cream; add a few spoonfuls of the warm liquid from the pan and whisk back into the pan juices. Stir over low* heat until the sauce has thickened.

Just before serving, pour the hot sauce over the chicken and garnish with the apple slices. Little more than a green salad is needed, but boiled potatoes could also be served.

Rice & Pasta

LUXURY PIZZA

The classic Italian pizza comes from Naples and consists of a light yeast dough with a savory filling. The cheese should by tradition be mozzarella, but any quick-melting cheese, such as Gruyère, is suitable.

PREPARATION TIME: 1¾ *hours*
COOKING TIME: 20–25 *minutes*

INGREDIENTS (*for* 6):

2 *cups all-purpose flour*
1 *teaspoon salt*
5 *tablespoons milk*
½ *cake fresh or 1 package active dry yeast*
1 *teaspoon sugar*
3 *tablespoons melted unsalted butter*
1 *large egg*
FILLING:
2 *large onions*
2 *small cloves garlic*

1 *pound tomatoes*
2 *tablespoons olive oil*
1 *tablespoon chopped fresh marjoram or ½ teaspoon dried oregano*
Salt and black pepper
6 *ounces quick-melting cheese*
GARNISH:
2-*ounce can anchovy fillets*
½–¾ *cup black olives*

Sift the flour and salt into a warm bowl and make a well in the center. Heat the milk until tepid (110°–115°) and use a few drops to cream together the fresh yeast and sugar. (If using active dry yeast, proof in all the tepid milk and the sugar.) Pour the yeast mixture and all the milk into the flour, together with the melted butter and beaten egg. Work the dough with the hands until it is smooth and leaves the sides of the bowl clean. Shape the dough into a ball and put it into an oiled plastic bag. Leave it in a warm place until it has doubled in bulk.

Meanwhile, prepare the filling: Peel and coarsely chop the onions and garlic. Peel and seed the tomatoes* and chop them coarsely. Heat the olive oil in a heavy pan and cook the onion and garlic over moderate heat until soft and transparent. Add the tomatoes to the pan. Cook for about 10 minutes, then stir in the marjoram or oregano. Season to

taste. Set the filling aside. Cut the cheese into thin wedge-shaped slices and drain the anchovy fillets.

When the dough has risen, knead it lightly with the fingertips for 1–2 minutes. Shape it into a circle 12 inches across. Put it on a greased and floured baking sheet. Cover the dough with the onion and tomato mixture to within 1 inch of the outer edge. Arrange the cheese on top in a fanlike pattern, slightly overlapping the slices. Decorate the cheese with the anchovies and dot with olives.

Bake the pizza near the top of a preheated oven at 425°F for 20–25 minutes, or until the cheese has melted and browned slightly and the dough is well risen.

Pizza is best served straight from the oven, but it can also be served cold or reheated in the oven at low heat. A crisp green salad tossed in a French dressing (p.304) would be ideal with the pizza for a main course.

GNOCCHI VERDI

The Italians take infinite trouble over their pasta dishes, and these spinach dumplings require both patience and practice. However, they are so light and delicious that they are worth mastering. The quantities are sufficient for a light main course for 4 or for a first course for 6.

PREPARATION TIME: 20 *minutes*
CHILLING TIME: 2 *hours*
COOKING TIME: 15–20 *minutes*

INGREDIENTS (*for* 4–6):
1 *pound fresh spinach*
¼ *pound butter*
¾ *cup cottage or cream cheese*
2 *eggs*
2 *tablespoons heavy cream*
4 *tablespoons all-purpose flour*
¾ *cup grated Parmesan cheese*
Salt and black pepper
Nutmeg

Wash the spinach thoroughly several times in lots of cold water. Put the spinach in a large pan with a closely fitting lid. Cook, without extra water, over moderate heat for about 5 minutes or until the spinach is just soft. Drain thoroughly in a sieve, pressing out all moisture. Chop the spinach finely.

Melt 4 tablespoons of the butter in a pan, add the spinach, and cook, stirring constantly, for about 2 minutes or until all moisture has evaporated; if necessary squeeze the spinach in a sieve again. Rub the cottage cheese through a sieve, add to the spinach, and cook for a further 3–4 minutes, stirring all the time. Remove the pan from the heat. Fold the lightly beaten eggs into the spinach. Stir in the cream, flour, and ¼ cup of Parmesan cheese. Season to taste

with salt, freshly ground pepper, and grated nutmeg. Turn the gnocchi into a flat dish and chill for 2 hours or until firm.

Bring a large pan of lightly salted water to the simmering point. Between floured hands, shape the gnocchi into small balls no more than ¾ inch wide. Drop the balls into the simmering water, a few at a time. As soon as they puff up and rise to the surface, remove them carefully with a slotted spoon.

Arrange the gnocchi in a buttered ovenproof dish, melt the remaining butter, and pour it over them. Sprinkle with the remaining cheese and put the dish under a hot broiler until the cheese has melted and browned.

Serve at once.

Vegetables & Salads

RISOTTO BIANCO

Rice is the staple food in northern Italy, as pasta is in the south. An Italian risotto is always served as a meal on its own—usually plain, with just butter and cheese.

PREPARATION TIME: *10 minutes*
COOKING TIME: *20–25 minutes*

INGREDIENTS (*for 4–6*):
1 cup rice, preferably Italian
 Arborio
1 small onion
1 small clove garlic
6 tablespoons butter
2 teaspoons olive oil
3½–4 cups white stock (p.298)
Salt and black pepper
1 cup grated Parmesan cheese

Peel and finely chop the onion and garlic. Heat 4 tablespoons of the butter with the oil in a deep skillet and cook the onion and garlic until soft and just beginning to color. Add the rice to the pan. Cook over low heat, stirring continuously, until the rice is yellow and shiny.

Add a third of the hot stock to the rice; bring to a boil, stir, then cover the pan with a lid. Cook over moderate heat until all the liquid is absorbed, then gradually stir in the remaining stock. Cover the pan again and simmer the rice, stirring occasionally, until all the stock has been absorbed, usually after 15 minutes. The rice should then be creamy and firm. Watch the risotto carefully while cooking to see that it does not dry out or burn.

Season the risotto to taste with salt and freshly ground pepper. Gently stir in the remaining butter and half the cheese. Spoon the risotto into a warm shallow dish, stir lightly with a fork, and sprinkle with the rest of the cheese.

GREEN BEANS MIMOSA

A green salad need not be composed of the ubiquitous lettuce and cucumber. Crisp cooked green beans, seasoned with olive oil and lemon juice, make a refreshing change in warm summer months.

PREPARATION TIME: *10 minutes*
COOKING TIME: *3–4 minutes*

INGREDIENTS (*for 4–6*):

1 pound young green beans
Salt
6 tablespoons olive oil

2 tablespoons lemon juice
GARNISH:
1 large hard-cooked egg

Trim and wash the beans,* leaving them whole. Cook them in salted water for 3–4 minutes. They should stay crisp. Drain the beans and arrange them radiating from the center of a round, shallow serving dish.

Pour the olive oil, mixed with the lemon juice, over the still-warm beans. Add more salt if necessary, and set the beans aside to cool.

Separate the white and yolk of the hard-cooked egg. Chop the white finely and rub the yolk through a coarse sieve.

Before serving, decorate by arranging the egg white in the center of the dish. Scatter the yolk among the beans to resemble mimosa.

SPINACH WITH MUSHROOMS

This dish of spinach purée and mushrooms in a cheese sauce is best served on its own. It makes a light lunch or supper dish.

PREPARATION TIME: *20 minutes*
COOKING TIME: *20 minutes*

INGREDIENTS (*for 4–6*):
2 pounds fresh spinach
6 tablespoons butter
Salt and black pepper
Grated nutmeg
½ pound mushrooms
4 tablespoons all-purpose flour
2 cups milk
1 cup grated Cheddar cheese

Remove any stalks and coarse midribs from the spinach, and wash the leaves thoroughly several times in lots of cold water. Put the spinach into a large pan, salt lightly, and cook, covered with a lid, over moderate heat for 5–7 minutes or until the spinach has softened. Drain thoroughly in a colander, squeezing out all moisture. Rub the spinach through a coarse sieve, put it through a fine disc of a food mill, or purée it in a blender.

Melt 2 tablespoons of the butter in a pan and reheat the purée gently. Season to taste with salt, freshly ground pepper, and nutmeg. Spread the purée over the bottom of a buttered ovenproof dish. Trim the mushrooms,* removing the stalks. Arrange the mushrooms on top of the spinach, rounded side up, and place the dish under, but not too close to, the broiler.

Use the remaining butter, the flour, and milk to make a smooth white sauce (p.301). Season to taste and continue cooking until the sauce thickens. Add the grated Cheddar cheese and simmer for a few minutes.

Pour the hot sauce over the spinach and mushrooms and put under the broiler until the sauce is bubbly and brown. Serve immediately.

EGGPLANT WITH HAM

The increasing popularity of eggplant has occasioned a number of new recipes, apart from such well-known classics as moussaka and ratatouille. For this hot lunch or supper dish, the eggplants are filled with a ham stuffing.

PREPARATION TIME: *25 minutes*
COOKING TIME: *20 minutes*

INGREDIENTS (*for 4*):
4 small or 2 large eggplants
6 ounces ham in ¼-inch-thick dice
½ cup olive oil
4 tablespoons unsalted butter
1½ tablespoons flour
1¼ cups milk
Salt and black pepper
Juice of ½ lemon
1–1½ cups dry white bread crumbs

Remove the stalk ends from the eggplants* and wipe them with a damp cloth. Cut each in half lengthwise with a sharp knife, and carefully scoop out the flesh without breaking the skin. Finely dice the eggplant flesh and the ham.

Heat the oil in a heavy pan over moderate heat and sauté the eggplant shells until brown, turning them over with a metal spatula. Remove and drain on paper towels. Cook the diced eggplant flesh in the oil in the pan and, when softened and lightly browned, remove from the pan and drain. Melt half the butter in another pan and sauté the ham until brown.

Sprinkle the flour into the pan in which the eggplant was cooked and blend until the oil is absorbed. Gradually add enough milk to make a thick white sauce (p.301), stirring all the time. Mix in the cooked ham and eggplant meat, add lemon juice, and season to taste.

Spoon this mixture into the eggplant shells and set them in a buttered baking dish. Sprinkle bread crumbs over the stuffing and dot with the remaining butter. Bake near the top of the oven, preheated to 400°F, until brown. Serve at once.

CUCUMBER AU GRATIN

Firm cucumber with a crisp finish of cheese makes a good accompaniment to broiled fish or chicken.

PREPARATION TIME: *15–20 minutes*
COOKING TIME: *30 minutes*

INGREDIENTS (*for 4–6*):
2 cucumbers
1½ cups grated Gruyère cheese
Salt and black pepper
3–4 tablespoons butter

Peel the cucumbers and cut them into 3-inch pieces. Slice each piece in half lengthwise and remove the seeds. Cook the cucumber in boiling salted water for 10 minutes, then drain and dry.

Arrange a layer of cucumber in the base of a buttered ovenproof dish. Sprinkle with a third of the cheese, and season with salt and freshly ground pepper. Repeat these layers, finishing with cheese. Dot the top with butter.

Bake the cucumber gratin in the center of a preheated oven at 400°F for 30 minutes.

MUSHROOMS AND SHRIMP

This is a refreshing salad for a hot day. It can be served as a light lunch with thin whole wheat bread and butter, or as a first course.

PREPARATION TIME: *15 minutes*
STANDING TIME: *1 hour*

INGREDIENTS (*for 4*):
½ pound large mushrooms
½ cup olive oil
2 tablespoons lemon juice
1–2 cloves garlic
Salt and black pepper
¼ pound small cooked shrimp
GARNISH:
3 tablespoons chopped parsley

Wipe and trim the mushrooms;* slice thinly into a shallow salad dish. Mix together the oil and lemon juice in a small bowl. Season with the peeled, crushed garlic and freshly ground pepper (do not add salt yet). Pour this dressing over the mushrooms and turn the slices several times so that they are well coated. Let the mushrooms stand for about 1 hour in the refrigerator.

The mushrooms absorb a lot of oil while standing; if necessary add a little more oil just before serving. Add the shrimp and sprinkle lightly with salt. Garnish the dish with the chopped parsley.

TOMATOES WITH HORSERADISH MAYONNAISE

For this dish choose large, firm tomatoes of even size. Serve them chilled as a side dish with cold meat or with broiled steaks and chops.

PREPARATION TIME: *20 minutes*
CHILLING TIME: *2 hours*

INGREDIENTS (*for 4–6*):
8 firm tomatoes
½ cup mayonnaise (p.303)
Salt
½ cup heavy cream
Lemon juice
2 tablespoons fresh grated horseradish
GARNISH:
Chopped chives, chervil, basil, or parsley

First, prepare the mayonnaise and set it aside. Peel the tomatoes* and slice off the tops with a serrated knife. Carefully scoop out the seeds and juice with a teaspoon, without breaking the flesh. Sprinkle the inside of the tomato cups with salt, stand them upside down on a plate to drain, and chill them in the coldest part of the refrigerator for at least 2 hours.

Lightly whip the cream and mix it into the mayonnaise; add lemon juice to taste and stir in the grated horseradish (the tomato caps may also be chopped and stirred into the mayonnaise). Cover and chill on the bottom shelf of the refrigerator for about 1 hour.

Just before serving, spoon the horseradish mayonnaise evenly into the tomato cups and sprinkle with chopped herbs.

BEANS IN SOUR CREAM

In summer, locally grown green beans are plentiful and excellent. Preserve their crispness and flavor by cooking them for a few minutes only, and finish them off in an unusual cream dressing. Serve with roast or broiled meat and poultry.

PREPARATION TIME: *15 minutes*
COOKING TIME: *15–20 minutes*

INGREDIENTS (*for 4–6*):
1 pound green beans
½ cup sour cream
Salt and black pepper
Grated nutmeg
½ teaspoon caraway or dill seeds (optional)
4 tablespoons butter
¾ cup coarse, fresh white bread crumbs

Trim the beans and slice them crosswise into 1-inch pieces. Cook the beans in a pan of boiling salted water for 5 minutes, then drain thoroughly. Season the sour cream to taste with salt, freshly ground pepper, and nutmeg, and add the caraway or dill seeds if used. Toss the beans in this dressing to coat them thoroughly.

Use 1 tablespoon of the butter to grease an ovenproof dish. Melt the remaining butter and toss the bread crumbs in it. Put the beans in the dish and top with the bread crumbs. Bake the beans in the center of a preheated oven at 350°F for 15–20 minutes, or until the topping is crisp and brown.

Serve the beans at once.

Desserts

BROWN TOM

The name of this dish describes a casserole of fresh tomatoes with a crumble of bacon and whole wheat bread crumbs. Serve it on its own or with sausages for lunch or supper.

PREPARATION TIME: *20 minutes*
COOKING TIME: *30–35 minutes*

INGREDIENTS (*for 4*):
1 pound tomatoes
1 large onion
2 slices lean bacon
4 large slices whole wheat bread
1 tablespoon chopped parsley
1½ teaspoons chopped fresh basil
3 tablespoons butter
Salt and black pepper
Sugar

Peel and coarsely chop the onion; chop the bacon into pieces. Put the onion and bacon through the fine blade of the meat grinder. Remove the crust and crumble the bread into the bacon and onion mixture. Now add the herbs. Peel and thinly slice the tomatoes.

Put a layer of the bacon mixture in the bottom of a buttered shallow ovenproof dish. Cover this with a layer of tomatoes and season with salt, freshly ground pepper, and a little sugar. Repeat these layers until all the ingredients are used up, finishing with a layer of bacon crumbs.

Dot with the remaining butter and bake near the top of the oven at 400°F for 30–35 minutes or until brown and bubbling. Serve at once.

PEPPER, ANCHOVY, AND TOMATO SALAD

This unusual salad goes perfectly with broiled chops and with most chicken dishes. It can also be served as a light beginning to a substantial meal.

PREPARATION TIME: *35 minutes*
CHILLING TIME: *30 minutes*

INGREDIENTS (*for 4*):
2 large sweet red peppers
3 large tomatoes
2 2-ounce cans anchovy fillets
1 clove garlic
3–4 tablespoons olive oil
Juice of ½ lemon
Salt and black pepper

Put the peppers under a hot broiler or impale them on a fork and hold over a gas flame, turning them frequently until the skins are charred and black all over. The black outer skin then rubs off easily under cold running water. Remove the stalk ends and seeds from the peppers and cut out any white pith. Cut the flesh into wide strips. Peel the tomatoes,* cut them into slices, and remove the seeds. Drain the anchovy fillets and rinse them in cold water to remove excess oil and salt; ease them carefully apart.

Arrange the pepper strips on a flat serving dish with the sliced tomatoes, and lay the anchovy fillets on top in a lattice pattern.

Peel and crush the garlic and mix with the oil. Pour this dressing over the salad and sprinkle with lemon juice, salt, and very little freshly ground pepper. Chill for at least 30 minutes before serving.

CLAFOUTI LIMOUSIN

A clafouti is a sweet batter baked with fresh fruit. In the Limousin region of France, where the pudding originated, it is traditionally made with black cherries.

PREPARATION TIME: *15 minutes*
COOKING TIME: *30 minutes*

INGREDIENTS (*for 6*):
1½ pounds black cherries, pitted
3 eggs
4 tablespoons all-purpose flour
Salt
6 tablespoons sugar
2 cups milk
1 tablespoon dark rum (optional)
2–3 tablespoons unsalted butter

Beat the eggs lightly together in a bowl. Sift the flour and blend in. Add a pinch of salt and 4 tablespoons of sugar. Heat the milk until lukewarm and gradually pour it into the egg mixture, stirring continuously. Add the rum if used.

Butter a wide shallow ovenproof dish thoroughly. Put in the cherries, pour the batter over them, and dot with the remaining butter. Bake in the center of a preheated oven at 425°F for 25–30 minutes. When the dish is cooked, the cherries will have risen to the top and the batter will have set like a baked custard.

Sprinkle the pudding with the remaining 2 tablespoons of sugar and serve lukewarm.

RASPBERRY-YOGURT SHERBET

A sherbet will be welcome on a hot summer's evening. One of the most delicious is made from fresh raspberries, which are plentiful in July. Adding yogurt to this dessert enhances its flavor.

PREPARATION TIME: *15 minutes*
FREEZING TIME: *2–3 hours*

INGREDIENTS (*for 6*):
1½ cups raspberries
4–6 tablespoons sugar
1¼ cups yogurt
Juice of ½ lemon
1 tablespoon (1 envelope) gelatin
2 egg whites

Make a thick purée from the raspberries by rubbing them through a sieve and into a bowl. Sweeten to taste with the sugar. Stir the yogurt and the lemon juice into the sweetened purée.

Place 4 tablespoons of cold water in a small bowl and sprinkle the gelatin over it. Leave the gelatin to stand for 5 minutes and then set the bowl over a pan of hot water. Stir until the gelatin has dissolved and the liquid is clear.

Add the liquid gelatin to the raspberry purée. In a separate bowl, beat the egg whites until stiff but not dry, and then fold them into the purée.

Spoon the mixture into a container, cover with a lid, and set in the freezer or the freezing compartment of the refrigerator. When almost frozen, beat the purée with a rotary beater. Then allow the mixture to freeze firmly.

COEUR À LA CRÈME

This is a classic French summer dessert made from cheese and cream. Traditionally it is set in little heart-shaped molds of wicker or porcelain (available at department stores or gourmet food shops) and served with cream and strawberries or raspberries.

PREPARATION TIME: *20 minutes*
CHILLING TIME: *12 hours*

INGREDIENTS (*for 4–6*):
8 ounces cream cheese or cottage cheese
1¼ cups heavy cream
4 teaspoons sugar
2 egg whites
1½ cups raspberries
½ cup light cream

Rub or press the cheese through a fine sieve and mix with the heavy cream before stirring in the sugar. (Cream cheese makes a richer, denser mixture than cottage cheese.) Beat the egg whites until stiff but not dry, and fold them into the cheese and cream mixture.

Line the heart-shaped molds with cheesecloth to make unmolding easier. Alternatively, line a fine-mesh sieve with cheesecloth and use it as a mold.

Spoon the cheese and cream mixture into the prepared molds and place them on a wide plate. Leave in the refrigerator overnight to drain and chill.

Just before serving, unmold the cream cheese onto a serving plate. Pour the light cream over it and serve with fresh raspberries, strawberries, other fresh fruit, or with a sweetened fruit sauce.

BAKED STUFFED PEACHES

Traditionally this delectable Italian dessert is made with *amaretti*—tiny, crisp macaroons made from apricot kernels or small almonds. These cookies can often be purchased in Italian markets.

PREPARATION TIME: *20 minutes*
COOKING TIME: *20–30 minutes*

INGREDIENTS (*for 4–6*):

4 large peaches
4 teaspoons sugar
1 tablespoon unsalted butter
1 egg yolk
½ cup crushed amaretti

Cream together the sugar, butter, and egg yolk in a small bowl. Add the crushed amaretti to the creamed mixture and stir well.

Pour boiling water over the peaches and leave for 2–3 minutes. Peel and halve the peaches and remove the pits. Enlarge the cavities slightly by scooping out some of the flesh with a pointed teaspoon. Add the peach pulp to the egg mixture and blend well.

Pile the stuffing into the peach halves and arrange them in a buttered ovenproof dish. Bake on the center shelf of a preheated oven at 350°F for 20–30 minutes, or until the peaches are soft but still shapely. Serve the peaches warm, with a bowl of whipped cream.

COLD CARAMEL SOUFFLÉS

The bittersweet taste of caramel makes a refreshing end to a summer meal. It can be made hours ahead.

PREPARATION TIME: *35 minutes*
SETTING TIME: *2½ hours*

INGREDIENTS (*for 4*):
½ cup plus 2 tablespoons sugar
1 envelope (1 tablespoon) gelatin
Juice of 1 lemon
2 eggs plus 1 egg yolk
½ cup heavy cream

To make the caramel, put ½ cup of sugar with 1¼ cups of water in a small, heavy pan over low heat. Cook without stirring until the sugar has dissolved. Increase the heat and boil the syrup rapidly until it is pale golden brown. Remove the pan from the heat and stand it on a cold surface. Add 4 tablespoons of hot water, stir, and pour the caramel into a warm bowl.

Soak the gelatin in 3 tablespoons of warm water to which the lemon juice has been added. Separate the eggs and beat the 3 egg yolks with 2 tablespoons of sugar in a bowl. Place the bowl over a pan of hot water and beat the egg mixture until it thickens. Remove the bowl and let the egg mixture cool.

Dissolve the gelatin over hot water. Blend the caramel and the gelatin thoroughly into the egg mixture. Leave to cool.

Beat the 2 egg whites until stiff but not dry, and lightly whip the cream. When the soufflé mixture is cold, but not completely set, fold in the cream and egg whites.

Spoon the mixture into individual soufflé dishes to set. Chill for at least 30 minutes.

SUMMER PUDDING

The origin of this classic English dessert, a composition of fresh summer berries, is unknown. But as early as the 18th century this pudding was served to hospital patients who were not allowed rich cakes and pastries. It is far from a bland dessert, however, and is unusually colorful and appetizing.

PREPARATION TIME: *30–40 minutes*
CHILLING TIME: *8 hours*

INGREDIENTS (*for 6*):
6–8 slices stale, crustless white
  bread, ½ inch thick
1½ pounds mixed berries
½ cup sugar

Strawberries, raspberries, red currants, as well as black cherries, are all suitable for this dish, and can be mixed according to taste and availability. The more varied the fruits, the better the result.

Line the bottom of a 4-cup soufflé dish with enough bread to cover the base completely. Line the sides of the dish with more bread slices; if necessary, cut to shape, so that the bread will fit closely together.

Hull* and carefully wash the fruit, and remove the pits from the cherries. Put the fruit in a wide heavy-bottomed pan and sprinkle the sugar over it. Bring to a boil over very low heat and cook for 2–3 minutes only, until the sugar melts and the juices begin to run. Remove the pan from the heat and set aside 1–2 tablespoons of the fruit juices. Spoon the fruit and the remaining juice into the bread-lined soufflé dish and cover the surface completely with the rest of the bread.

Put a plate that fits the inside of the dish on top of the pudding and

weight it down with a heavy object, such as a can or jar. Place the pudding in the refrigerator and leave to chill for 8 hours.

Before serving the pudding, re-move the weight and plate. Cover the dish with the serving plate; hold the plate firmly against the dish and turn upside down to unmold the pudding. Use the reserved fruit juice to pour over any parts of the bread that have not been soaked through and colored by the fruit juices.

Serve the pudding with a bowl of cream or whipped cream.

Snacks & Supper Dishes

CREAM CHEESE AND BACON PIE

This is a quick and delicious variation of a French quiche, suitable for a supper or a picnic.

PREPARATION TIME: *25 minutes*
COOKING TIME: *30 minutes*

INGREDIENTS (*for 4–6*):
¾ recipe standard pastry (p.354)
4 slices bacon
1 egg
3 egg yolks
1 8-ounce package cream cheese
½ cup plus 2 tablespoons heavy cream
Salt and black pepper
3 small tomatoes, peeled and sliced
GARNISH:
Bacon rolls

Line an 8-inch flan ring or pie pan with the rolled-out pastry. Cut the bacon slices crosswise into ¼-inch strips; fry, without extra fat, over moderate heat for 5 minutes or until golden brown. Drain on paper towels, then arrange in the bottom of the pastry shell.

Beat the egg and egg yolks, add the softened cream cheese, and continue beating until the mixture is smooth. Gradually beat in the cream. Season with salt and pepper, and pour the mixture over the bacon. Arrange the tomatoes on top.

Bake the pie in the center of a preheated oven at 400°F for 20 minutes, then lower the heat to 350°F and bake for a further 10 minutes, or until set.

Serve the pie garnished with bacon rolls.* Cut it into wedge shapes and serve it hot with a green vegetable, or cold with a green salad.

CHICKEN AND HAM LOAF

This dish makes good use of leftover chicken. It is excellent for picnics and packed lunches and also stores well in the freezer.

PREPARATION TIME: *1¼ hours*
COOKING TIME: *1 hour*

INGREDIENTS (*for 6–8*):
2 cups cooked skinned and diced chicken
1 large loaf of unsliced bread
6 tablespoons butter
2 finely chopped onions
½ pound thinly sliced mushrooms
1 tablespoon chopped parsley
Salt and black pepper
½ pound sausage meat
6 slices lean bacon, diced
2 cups cooked diced ham
2 tablespoons dry sherry (optional)
¼ teaspoon each sage and thyme

Cut a ½-inch slice off the top of the loaf and carefully pull out the soft bread inside (use for making bread crumbs). Leave ½-inch inner lining of bread to preserve the shape. Melt 4 tablespoons of the butter and brush this onto the loaf, inside and out.

Replace the lid and put the loaf on a baking sheet in the center of a preheated oven at 400°F. Bake for 5–10 minutes or until crisp and golden. Leave to cool.

Cook the onions in the remaining butter until soft, add the mushrooms, and cook for a further 2 minutes. Stir in the chopped parsley and season with salt and pepper.

Mix together the sausage meat, bacon, ham, and 3 heaping tablespoons of bread crumbs; stir in the sherry and herbs, and season to taste. Press half the sausage mixture well down into the loaf case; cover with half the onion and mushroom mixture. Arrange the chicken on top and cover with the onion and a final layer of sausage meat. Replace the breadcrust lid and wrap the loaf in aluminum foil. Bake in the center of the oven at 375°F for 1 hour.

Serve the loaf hot or cold, cut into thick slices.

CUCUMBER CUPS WITH SHRIMP

For a cool first course, few ingredients combine so well for flavor and eye appeal as cucumber and shellfish.

PREPARATION TIME: *15 minutes*
CHILLING TIME: *30 minutes*

INGREDIENTS (*for 8*):
2 large unwaxed cucumbers
½ pound small raw shrimp
1½ cups plain yogurt
1 tablespoon chopped fresh mint or 1 teaspoon dried mint leaves
2 canned pimientos, drained and chopped
Salt and pepper

Cut the ends off the cucumbers and cut each cucumber into 4 equal crosswise pieces. Hollow out the centers to form cup shapes, leaving a shell ¼ inch thick. With a sharp knife remove ½-inch-wide strips of skin at ½-inch intervals to make vertical stripes. Cook shrimp, shell and devein them. Reserve 8 of the shrimp for decoration. Chop remaining shrimp. Mix the yogurt, shrimp, mint, and pimiento. Season to taste with salt and pepper. Spoon mixture into the well-drained cucumber cups. Top with the reserved shrimp. Chill for 30 minutes. Garnish with fresh mint. Serve with thin slices of whole wheat bread.

PROSCIUTTO AND GORGONZOLA SANDWICH

This quick Italian-style snack is an interesting variation of the traditional ham and cheese sandwich.

PREPARATION TIME: *10 minutes*

INGREDIENTS (*for 1*):
2 slices sandwich bread
2–3 very thin slices prosciutto
2–3 thin slices soft Gorgonzola cheese

Place the prosciutto and cheese between the bread slices. Trim the edges. Spread both sides with butter and sauté sandwich over low heat until crisp and brown. Cut in half or thirds before serving. The cheese should melt and hold the sandwich together.

Summer Barbecues

That great North American pastime, the barbecue or cookout, too often is centered around the same boring fare—hamburgers, hot dogs, steaks, or chicken—when the possibilities for imaginative dishes are almost unlimited. Fish, pork, lamb, and veal, as well as vegetables and fruit, take on a subtle new flavor when cooked on an outdoor grill, and can be prepared in any number of ways.

The grill on which the food is cooked may be as simple as a small, inexpensive hibachi—which many cooks find adequate—or an elaborate affair complete with electrically operated spit, warming oven, and detachable hood. Charcoal briquets make the best fuel. To start the fire, build a pyramid of 30–40 briquets in the firebox of the grill. Pour ½ cup of odorless starter fluid over the top of the pile and let it soak in for 2 or 3 minutes before lighting. Half an hour after the fire is lit, the coals should be giving out intense heat and should be covered with a thin layer of white ash. The fire is now ready. Spread the burning coals evenly over the firebox to make an area of coals greater than the surface area of the food to be grilled. Add extra briquets at the edges of the burning coals to be raked in when more fuel is needed.

For most charcoal broiling, a grill-level temperature from 275° to 375°F—usually around 350°—is best. Although the temperature of the fire can be controlled only by spreading the coals or by dousing a too-hot fire with water, most barbecues have grills or fire baskets that can be lowered or raised according to the amount of heat needed. A common fault in outdoor cooking is putting too much fuel on the fire (it is always easier to add than to subtract). Another mistake is neglecting to trim the meat of fat, which melts and drops onto the hot coals, causing a flareup. Always keep a water-filled sprinkler bottle handy to douse flames from any dripping fat.

Have ready 2 or 3 pairs of long-handled tongs for turning and lifting the food. Use long-handled brushes for basting. For extra aroma, keep a few fresh sprigs of thyme or rosemary handy to throw on the coals during the last stages of cooking.

Marinades and Basting Sauces

Marinades add flavor and tenderize tougher cuts of meat and poultry.

Red wine marinade: Combine 2 cups of red wine; ¼ cup each of chopped onion and carrot; a few peppercorns; and an herb bouquet of bay leaf, parsley, and thyme. Use as a marinade for rabbit, game, and less tender cuts of beef and lamb. For basting, add 1 cup of oil.

White wine marinade: Make as above, substituting white wine for red, and marjoram for thyme. Use for poultry, game birds, and veal.

Soy sauce marinade and baste: Combine equal parts of soy sauce, dry sherry or sake, and vegetable oil, with chopped garlic and grated fresh ginger to taste. Use for poultry, shellfish, pork, veal, and beef.

Barbecue marinade and baste: To make a highly seasoned sauce for meat and poultry, combine an 8-ounce can of tomato sauce; ½ cup of

red wine; 1 teaspoon each of dry mustard, sugar, and salt; 1 tablespoon each of vinegar and Worcestershire sauce; 1 pressed or grated garlic clove; and Tabasco to taste. Simmer 10 minutes and strain. For basting, add ½ cup of oil.

Meat

All meats are good candidates for the barbecue, although very lean or less tender cuts benefit from being marinated first. Steaks and hamburgers are favorite choices, but lamb, pork, and veal are just as good. Try broiling racks of lamb, trimmed of fat and well massaged with a mixture of oil, crushed garlic, and crushed rosemary. Or try lamb shoulder steaks, lamb chops, or butterflied leg of lamb. Pork steaks, ham steaks, and pork chops grill well, and so do spareribs. Young veal loin chops may be broiled, provided they are well coated with oil and are cooked slowly over low heat.

Poultry

Chicken, turkey, duck, and squab are excellent when broiled. The trick is to avoid overcooking, which can render them dry and almost tasteless. Split broilers, with the backbone removed for easier cutting, may be rubbed with melted butter or oil combined with chopped fresh herbs and seasonings, or with lemon juice or soy sauce, or prepared with a soy sauce marinade. Whole chickens or turkeys may be spit-roasted.

Fish

Fish can be delectable grilled over charcoal, but it is delicate and must be handled carefully. Always have the grill hot and well greased, or use one of the specially designed fish-shaped hinged grills to hold and turn the fish. Whole fish of any size are suitable for grilling. First, sprinkle the inside of the cleaned fish with salt, pepper, and lemon juice. Put it on a greased grill or in a greased hinged grill and brown carefully on both sides, basting with melted butter and white wine, or melted butter flavored with lemon juice and tarragon, or with a soy sauce baste. Whole fish can also be wrapped in a double thickness of oiled aluminum foil and cooked right on the coals.

Fish steaks and fillets can be broiled in the same way as whole fish. Shellfish, such as lobsters, crabs, and shrimp, are delicious broiled. For extra flavor, marinate the shrimp first, in or out of the shells.

Kebabs

This popular form of charcoal cooking combines on skewers various meats, poultry, and vegetables, and sometimes fruit and fish. The ingredients should be cut into cubes or pieces of equal size and threaded on the skewers, allowing 2 skewers per person. Some of the foods that can be used are: lean leg of lamb; beef rump, round, or chuck; ham; pork; duck; squares of chicken; frankfurters, cut in thirds; bacon-wrapped kidneys; marinated shrimp and scallops; large pieces of lobster; and many vegetables–mushrooms, small white onions, cherry tomatoes, green pepper squares, eggplant cubes, chunks of zucchini, chunks of parboiled yam or sweet potato.

The best fruits to use as kebabs are the firm ones—pineapple chunks, quartered apples, orange sections, peach and apricot halves, and bananas cut in thirds. Sprigs of fresh herbs add flavor to the kebab combinations.

An unusual way to broil duck is as a kebab: Cut the duck into 8 portions, let it steep in a marinade, and then arrange each piece of duck on a large skewer with thick slices of orange and onion interspersed with button mushrooms. Brush with oil, salt, and pepper, and grill the duck over hot coals.

Marinate meats and poultry for kebabs in advance, if desired. According to the foods used, grill kebabs 15–20 minutes, turning them to brown all sides and basting frequently. Fish and shellfish will probably take even less time.

Vegetables

Vegetables cooked over, or in, the coals gain a delicious new flavor. Corn, with the silk removed, and soaked in water for half an hour, can be grilled in its own husks; or it may be husked, brushed with butter, wrapped in heavy-duty aluminum foil, and grilled. Whole onions, beets, and potatoes may be wrapped in a double thickness of heavy foil and cooked in the coals.

Some vegetables are firm enough to go directly on the grill—boiled whole carrots, dipped in butter; unpeeled slices of eggplant, brushed with oil; large mushroom caps, brushed with butter; artichoke bottoms or quartered green or red peppers, dipped in oil. Others, such as tomato slices, are easier to handle if done in a hinged grill. Combinations of vegetables can be cut in pieces or chunks and cooked on the grill in aluminum foil packages, with butter and seasonings. Whole vegetables—among them potatoes, sweet potatoes, eggplant, onions, green peppers, and acorn squash—can also be cooked on the spit, if it is not being used for meat or poultry.

Fruit

Many fruits lend themselves to grilling. Firm peaches, peeled and halved, can be grilled. Brush the halves with butter and broil cut side down; then turn, put a little butter, brown sugar, and rum in the cavities, and finish broiling. Serve with ham or turkey, or as a dessert. Broiled pineapple slices, brushed with butter, are good with pork, ham, and poultry.

Thickly sliced, unpeeled oranges dipped in melted butter and cooked quickly in a hinged grill are delicious with duck and chicken. Thick apple rings can also be dipped in butter and cooked in the hinged grill. Sprinkle them generously with sugar before serving. Apples and bananas can be roasted in their skins: Wrap in heavy-duty foil and put them at the edge of the coals, turning once or twice until they are fork-tender. Apples take about 30 minutes, bananas 10 to 15. Serve the apples with pork, duck, or goose. Serve the bananas with chicken or meat, or with rum sauce as a dessert.

With barbecued food, serve salads such as tomatoes with onion rings, chicory or romaine lettuce with watercress and avocado, and diced apple and celery.

191

August

Sing a song of Summer,
    the world is nearly still,
The mill-pond has gone to sleep,
    and so has the mill.   W. C. MONKHOUSE

THIS MONTH'S RECIPES

*Picnic fare for a warm day in August: Tarte Basquaise is served with rice salad
and tomatoes with horseradish mayonnaise; in the background, melons with raspberries.*

193

Food in Season

The long, warm days of August call for picnics, barbecues, and casual meals on the patio. Many of the recipes in this chapter—particularly Gazpacho Andaluz and Salade Niçoise (p.195), and Melon Ice Cream (p.208)—are ideally suited for such alfresco dining and make imaginative use of the many fruits and vegetables that are abundant and inexpensive.

Plums are at their peak this month and can be served in wine sauce (p.206) as an elegant dessert. Prunes, pears, cantaloupes, peaches, nectarines, and watermelons are available in great quantities. Stuffed Watermelon with Kirsch (p.208) makes a particularly attractive presentation for a large gathering.

Eggplant is now at the height of its season, and there are good supplies of corn, beets, and peppers in the markets. The summer staples, tomatoes and cucumbers, can be prepared in new ways: Tomatoes can be baked with eggs (p.196), and cucumbers can be served with shrimp and mushrooms (p.196) as a first course.

Take advantage of plentiful fresh squash and green beans in August. Zucchini in Hollandaise Cheese Sauce (p.205) is a delectable accompaniment for roast chicken or lean roast meats, while Green Beans with Sabayon Sauce (p.206) is unusually good with broiled fish.

SUGGESTED MENUS

Cucumber with Shrimp and Mushrooms
...
Veal Scallops with Ginger Wine
Ragoût of Lettuce and Peas
...
Granita al Caffè

Gazpacho Andaluz
...
Sole with Oranges
Tossed Green Salad
Buttered New Potatoes
...
Plums in Wine

Chilled Carrot Soup
...
Salmi of Partridge
Fried Bread Crumbs or Bread Sauce
...
Peaches with Sour Cream

Yogurt Soup
...
Boeuf à la Mode en Gelée
Cucumber in Sour Cream
...
Melon Ice Cream

Eggs Baked in Tomatoes
...
Baked Picnic Ham
Carrots Paysanne
...
Bananas à l'Archestrate

Kipper Pâté and Toast
...
Pork Cooked in Milk
Tossed Green Salad
...
Danish Layer Cake

Salade Niçoise
...
Spaghetti with Tuna Sauce
...
Lemon Syllabub

Soups & First Courses

CHILLED MULLIGATAWNY SOUP

Mulligatawny soup is made with a rich meat stock strongly flavored with curry. This version transforms the traditional soup into a cool summer delight.

PREPARATION TIME: *20 minutes*
COOKING TIME: *30 minutes*
CHILLING TIME: *1½–2 hours*

INGREDIENTS (*for* 6):
1 onion
1 carrot
4 tablespoons unsalted butter
3 tablespoons flour
1 tablespoon curry powder
6 cups beef stock
2 tablespoons canned mango nectar or 1 tablespoon syrup drained from mango chutney
GARNISH:
Cauliflower florets

Peel and finely chop the onion and carrot. Melt the butter in a large pan over moderate heat and cook the vegetables until the onion is transparent. Sift the flour and curry powder together and stir into the vegetables. Continue cooking over moderate heat, stirring constantly until the mixture is a deep brown color. Gradually stir in the hot stock and bring the soup to a boil. Simmer over low heat for 30 minutes, then set aside to cool slightly.

Put the soup through a coarse sieve, or whirl in a blender for 1–2 minutes, then stir in the mango nectar or syrup. Chill in the refrigerator for at least 1½ hours.

Before serving, remove any fat from the surface of the soup. Pour into bowls and garnish with tiny florets of raw cauliflower.

SALADE NIÇOISE

There are numerous versions of this Provençal hors d'oeuvre, but all have in common the basic ingredients of lettuce, eggs, anchovy fillets, black olives, and tomatoes.

PREPARATION TIME: *25 minutes*

INGREDIENTS (*for* 6):
2 eggs
½ pound green beans
¾ pound firm tomatoes
½ onion
1 head lettuce
½ green pepper
½ cup garlic-flavored French dressing (p.304)
7-ounce can of tuna
2-ounce can anchovy fillets
½ cup small black olives

Hard-cook the eggs for 8–10 minutes, then plunge them into cold water. Shell and quarter them, and set aside to cool. Trim the beans, wash them, and cook in boiling salted water for 5–8 minutes; drain and set aside to cool.

Peel the tomatoes* and cut into quarters. Peel and thinly slice the onion; break it into individual rings. Wash and dry the lettuce. Wash the pepper, cut out the core and seeds, and slice it thinly.

Put half the French dressing in a shallow bowl and toss the shredded lettuce and beans in it. Drain and flake* the tuna and arrange it, with the drained anchovy fillets, olives, green pepper, and onion rings, on top of the lettuce and beans. Surround with the quartered tomatoes and hard-cooked eggs. Sprinkle with the remaining dressing and serve the salad immediately.

GAZPACHO ANDALUZ

On a hot summer day a chilled soup is particularly welcome. This Andalusian salad soup is also decorative, served with several crisp, colorful garnishes. In Spain ice cubes are usually added to each soup bowl before serving.

PREPARATION TIME: *35 minutes*
CHILLING TIME: *1–2 hours*

INGREDIENTS (*for* 6):
1½ pounds tomatoes
4 large, ½-inch-thick slices stale white bread
2 large garlic cloves
4 teaspoons herb or red wine vinegar
4 tablespoons olive oil
2 cups canned tomato juice
2 canned pimientos
1 large Spanish onion
1 small cucumber
Salt and black pepper
2 tablespoons mayonnaise (optional)
2 cups ice water
GARNISH:
1 small cucumber
2 small peppers
4 large tomatoes
Bread croûtons (p.300)
Raw onion rings
Black olives, hard-cooked eggs (optional)

Peel the tomatoes,* remove the seeds, and chop the flesh finely. Cut the crusts off the bread and crumble it finely into a large bowl. Peel and crush the garlic and add to the bowl. Stir in the vinegar and gradually add as much olive oil as the crumbs will absorb. Stir in the tomatoes and canned juice and mix thoroughly. Chop the pimientos finely, peel and grate the onion and cucumber, and stir all 3 into the tomato mixture. Season to taste with salt and freshly ground pepper. Whirl the mixture in a blender until smooth, or rub it through a fine sieve.

The soup should be perfectly smooth—it can be made creamier by the addition of mayonnaise. Dilute the soup with ice water until it has the consistency of thin cream. Adjust the seasoning. Chill the soup in the refrigerator until serving time.

The garnishes are traditionally served in separate small bowls, and the contents stirred into the soup until it is nearly solid. Peel and dice the cucumber; chop the prepared peppers and the peeled tomatoes. Sauté the bread croûtons, and peel and thinly slice the onion. Small pitted black olives and sliced hard-cooked eggs can also be served.

EGGS BAKED IN TOMATOES

This light and colorful first course can also be served as a snack.

PREPARATION TIME: *40 minutes*
COOKING TIME: *20 minutes*

INGREDIENTS (*for 4*):
4 large firm tomatoes
Salt and black pepper
1 clove garlic
4 eggs
2 teaspoons tomato purée
2 tablespoons heavy cream
1 tablespoon grated Parmesan cheese
4 slices bread
2 tablespoons unsalted butter
2 teaspoons olive oil

Wash the tomatoes, wipe them dry, and slice off the tops with a sharp knife. Carefully scoop out the pulp with a spoon and sprinkle the inside of the shells with salt and the peeled and finely chopped garlic. Turn the tomato shells upside down to drain for 30 minutes.

Break an egg carefully into each tomato shell, keeping back as much as possible of the white. Season with salt and freshly ground pepper. Blend the tomato purée with the cream and spoon gently over the eggs. Sprinkle each with a little grated Parmesan cheese. Put the tomatoes in an ovenproof dish and bake near the top of a preheated oven at 350°F for 15–20 minutes or until the eggs have just set.

Meanwhile, cut the bread into rounds with a fluted pastry cutter. Heat the butter and oil in a pan and sauté the bread until crisp and golden brown on both sides.

As soon as the eggs are set, arrange 1 tomato on each round of bread and serve at once.

YOGURT SOUP

In the Middle East, yogurt is used instead of cream in many dishes. It gives a refreshing tang to a soup.

PREPARATION TIME: *15 minutes*
COOKING TIME: *20 minutes*

INGREDIENTS (*for 6*):
1 pint yogurt
1½ teaspoons cornstarch
4 cups chicken stock
5 egg yolks
3 tablespoons ground almonds
Salt and black pepper
2 tablespoons chopped mint
1 tablespoon unsalted butter

Stabilize the yogurt before cooking by blending the cornstarch with a little water and gradually beating it into the yogurt. Pour the mixture into a saucepan and bring it slowly to a boil over moderate heat, stirring continuously. Simmer the yogurt gently for 10 minutes or until it has thickened.

Meanwhile, bring the chicken stock to a boil in another pan. Remove from the heat; let it cool slightly while lightly beating the egg yolks. Spoon a little of the stock into the eggs and blend thoroughly before stirring this mixture into the stock. Heat over low heat until just simmering—if brought to the boiling point, the eggs will curdle—stirring all the time until the stock has thickened. Gradually stir the yogurt into the stock.

Blend the ground almonds into the soup and correct the seasoning if necessary. Sauté* the chopped mint for 1–2 minutes in the tablespoon of butter and blend into the soup just before serving.

CUCUMBER WITH SHRIMP AND MUSHROOMS

Cucumber is usually served raw in salads or sandwiches, but it loses none of its flavor or freshness by being cooked. This quick little hors d'oeuvre has something of the delicate taste of Chinese food.

PREPARATION TIME: *15 minutes*
COOKING TIME: *15 minutes*

INGREDIENTS (*for 4*):
1 large or 2 small cucumbers, unwaxed if possible
Salt and black pepper
¼ pound button mushrooms
3 tablespoons butter
1 teaspoon flour
5 tablespoons chicken stock
5 tablespoons light cream
Soy sauce (optional)
½ pound shelled shrimp
GARNISH:
Finely chopped chives, basil, or dill
Cucumber twists

Wash the cucumber, but do not peel it unless it is waxed. Cut it into ½-inch pieces and cook for 3–4 minutes in boiling, lightly salted water. Rinse the cucumber in cold water and drain thoroughly in a colander. Trim the mushrooms* and cut them into ¼-inch-thick slices.

Melt the butter in a small pan and cook the mushrooms for 2–3 minutes, or until lightly browned. Add the diced cucumber and simmer, covered, for 2–3 minutes over low heat. Sprinkle in the flour and blend thoroughly. Gradually add the stock and cream, stirring the mixture until smooth. Bring gently to a boil and season to taste with salt, freshly ground pepper, and a few drops of soy sauce. Simmer gently for another 2–3 minutes, then stir in the shrimp and heat through, but do not boil.

Spoon into a warmed serving dish or individual deep scallop shells. Sprinkle with the herbs and decorate with thin twists of cucumber. Serve the cucumber mixture immediately with thinly sliced whole wheat bread and butter, or crisp toast fingers.

CHILLED CARROT SOUP

As young home-grown carrots become more plentiful, it is well worth trying this soup. It can be served hot, but the subtle creamy flavor is more pronounced if the soup is chilled.

PREPARATION TIME: *20 minutes*
COOKING TIME: *45 minutes*
CHILLING TIME: *1 hour*

INGREDIENTS (*for 6*):
1¼ pound carrots
1 onion
3–4 cloves garlic
2 tablespoons butter
5 cups beef stock
1 cup heavy cream
Salt and black pepper
GARNISH:
Finely chopped parsley

Peel and thinly slice the onion; peel and crush the garlic. Melt the butter in a heavy pan, and cook the onion and garlic gently over low heat. Keep the pan covered with a lid until the onion is soft and transparent but not golden. Meanwhile, trim and scrape the carrots, and then chop them coarsely. Add these to the onion and continue cooking, covered, for about 8 minutes. Bring the beef stock to a boil and pour it over the vegetables. Bring the contents of the pan to simmering point and maintain this over lowest possible heat for about 30 minutes.

Fish

Remove the soup from the heat and allow to cool slightly before whirling in a blender until smooth. Alternatively, rub the soup through a fine sieve into a bowl.

In a separate bowl, lightly whip half of the cream until it holds its shape. Stir the whipped cream into the soup and season to taste with salt and freshly ground pepper. Chill the soup in the refrigerator for at least 1 hour.

Serve the soup in individual bowls, trickling into each a good tablespoon of the remaining cream. Sprinkle the finely chopped parsley over each bowl of soup.

STUFFED MUSHROOMS

For this dish select large mushrooms, fairly uniform in size. Crabmeat, shrimp, or chicken may be substituted for the ham.

PREPARATION TIME: *20 minutes*
COOKING TIME: *15 minutes*

INGREDIENTS (*for 4*):
12 mushrooms
3 tablespoons butter
¼ cup finely chopped onion
1 cup soft bread crumbs
½ cup chopped cooked ham
2 tablespoons sherry
½ teaspoon tarragon
Salt and pepper to taste

Preheat the oven to 375°F. Remove and chop the mushroom stems. Sauté them with the onion in 1 tablespoon of the butter for 2 minutes. Add the crumbs, ham, sherry, and seasonings. Stuff the mushrooms with this mixture and dot the tops with the remaining butter. Bake about 15 minutes, or until browned and tender.

SOLE WITH ORANGES

Cold poached sole fillets coated in mayonnaise make a quick and simple meal on a hot day. The richness of the sauce is balanced by an orange garnish in a sharp French dressing.

PREPARATION TIME: *20 minutes*
COOKING TIME: *20 minutes*

INGREDIENTS (*for 4–6*):
12 fillets of sole
Juice of ½ lemon
3 oranges
Salt and black pepper
3 tablespoons butter
½ cup mayonnaise (p.303)
Paprika
2-ounce can anchovy fillets
2 tablespoons French dressing (p.304)

Sprinkle the sole fillets with the lemon juice and the juice of half an orange, then season with salt and freshly ground pepper. Finely grate the rind from an orange and sprinkle over the fish. Roll up the fillets, beginning at the wide end, and secure with wooden cocktail picks or toothpicks. Lay the rolled fillets in a buttered ovenproof dish.

Squeeze the juice of half an orange over the fish. Dot with small pieces of butter and cover the dish with buttered waxed paper or foil. Bake in the center of a preheated oven at 425°F for about 12 minutes, or until the fillets are tender but still firm. Remove the dish from the oven and leave to cool.

Lift the cold fillets carefully onto a shallow serving dish and remove the toothpicks. Add the juice and grated rind of half an orange, drop by drop, to the mayonnaise and coat the fillets with it. Sprinkle with paprika and arrange two halved anchovies over each fillet.

Peel the remaining oranges, removing all pith, and cut them into thin round slices with a sharp serrated knife. Dip the orange slices in the French dressing and serve separately or as a garnish for the fillets.

Serve with a salad of blanched, sliced zucchini, strips of red and green pepper, and onion rings.

SALMON IN ASPIC

This makes an excellent and attractive centerpiece for a special dinner or a cold buffet. It can be prepared several hours in advance, which is an advantage.

PREPARATION TIME: *30 minutes*
COOKING TIME: *1–1½ hours*

INGREDIENTS (*for 8*):
1 small Coho salmon,
  approximately 2½–3 pounds
1 envelope (1 tablespoon) gelatin
1 tablespoon white wine vinegar
6 tablespoons dry sherry
2 egg whites
STOCK:
1 carrot
1 onion
Bouquet garni (p.410)
4 peppercorns
1½ tablespoons wine vinegar
½ teaspoon salt
GARNISH:
¼ pound peeled cooked shrimp
Watercress

Begin by making the stock, putting all the ingredients, with 2½ cups of water, in a pan. Bring to a boil, cover the pan with a lid, and simmer for 20 minutes. Strain the stock through cheesecloth.

Remove the fins and gills from the salmon and cut a 1-inch-deep inverted V out of the tail to make it resemble a mermaid's tail. Wash the fish thoroughly to remove all traces of blood, and put it in a fish poacher, or a large flameproof dish. Pour the warm stock over it and cover with a lid or foil. Cook the fish for 25–30 minutes on top of the stove; or bake for 50 minutes in the oven, preheated to 350°F, basting with the stock.

Remove the fish from the broth and allow to cool on a rack or plate.

When quite cold, snip the skin near the head with a pair of scissors and peel the skin off carefully, leaving the head and tail intact. Split the fish along the entire length of the backbone with a sharp knife and snip the bone below the head and above the tail. Ease the backbone out carefully without breaking the salmon.

Strain the fish liquid through cheesecloth into a saucepan. Dissolve the gelatin in a cupful of the liquid and heat the remainder over moderate heat, whisking steadily until the liquid is hot. Stir in the dissolved gelatin, the vinegar, sherry, and the egg whites; whisk steadily until the mixture comes to a boil. Remove the pan from the heat at once and leave the liquid to settle for 5 minutes. Bring to a boil again, remove from the heat, and leave it to settle once more. The liquid should now look clear; otherwise, repeat the boiling process again. Strain the liquid through a clean cloth wrung out in cold water and set aside to cool.

Spoon a little of the cool aspic over the bottom of a serving dish and leave it to set. Arrange the salmon carefully on top of the aspic. Garnish the fish with the shrimp and spoon a little of the aspic over it. When the shrimp have set, spoon aspic over the whole salmon and leave to set.

Serve the salmon garnished with sprigs of watercress and the remaining chopped aspic. Serve with a dish of mustard mayonnaise (p.303) or horseradish mayonnaise (p.303).

SWEET-SOUR SALMON

In German cookery a sweet-sour sauce is frequently served with fish and with braised meat. Sweet-sour salmon is often served hot, but the sweet-tangy flavor is more pronounced when this dish is chilled.

PREPARATION TIME: *10 minutes*
COOKING TIME: *35–40 minutes*
CHILLING TIME: *2–3 hours*

INGREDIENTS (*for 4*):
4 salmon steaks, 1 inch thick
Salt and black pepper
2 large onions
2 tablespoons white wine vinegar
2 tablespoons light brown sugar
Juice of 2 lemons
2 egg yolks
GARNISH:
Cucumber slices

Season the salmon steaks with salt and freshly ground pepper and arrange in a shallow ovenproof dish. Cover with peeled and sliced onions.

Pour boiling, lightly salted water over the fish to barely cover it. Seal the dish with foil and bake in the center of a preheated oven at 325°F for 20–25 minutes. When done, the central bone can be removed without bringing any flesh with it. Lift the salmon steaks carefully out of the dish with a slotted spoon and arrange them on a serving dish.

Strain the cooking liquid through cheesecloth and measure 1¼ cups into a saucepan; add the vinegar, brown sugar, and lemon juice. Simmer over low heat until the liquid has reduced* slightly. Beat the egg yolks in the top of a double boiler and stir in a tablespoonful of the reduced liquid; blend thoroughly, and gradually add all the liquid. Set the bowl over simmering water and stir the sauce continuously until it thickens to a coating consistency.

Pour the sauce over the salmon and cool it before chilling for at least 2 hours in the refrigerator.

Garnish the salmon steaks with thin unpeeled slices of unwaxed cucumber and serve with boiled potatoes and a crisp green salad.

TROUT WITH BRETON SAUCE

Breton sauce is reminiscent of mayonnaise, but is easier to make and less oily. The sharp flavor of the sauce makes it a perfect foil for cold trout or mackerel.

PREPARATION TIME: *25 minutes*
COOKING TIME: *25–30 minutes*

INGREDIENTS (*for 4–6*):
4 large trout
1 tablespoon olive oil
SAUCE:
2 tablespoons Dijon mustard
2 egg yolks
2 teaspoons wine, cider, or tarragon
*   vinegar*
Salt and black pepper
6 tablespoons unsalted butter
2 tablespoons chopped fresh parsley
*   and chives*
GARNISH:
½ cucumber

Wash and clean the trout thoroughly; cut off the heads and dry the fish. Wrap each trout in a piece of oiled aluminum foil and put them in an ovenproof dish. Bake in the center of a preheated oven at 425°F for 15–18 minutes.

Remove the dish from the oven and open the foil packages to allow the trout to cool slightly. Split each fish along the belly, and with a pointed knife carefully loosen the backbone. Ease the backbone out gently so that most of the small bones come away with it. Set the trout aside to cool.

To make the sauce, beat the mustard, egg yolks, and vinegar together until well blended; season to taste with salt and freshly ground pepper. Put the butter in a bowl over a pan of hot water and stir until it has softened but not melted. Gradually add the butter to the egg mixture, beating all the time, until the sauce has the consistency of thick cream. Stir in the finely chopped herbs.

Before serving, gently peel the skin from the cold trout, cut each into 2 fillets, and arrange on a serving dish. Pour the sauce over the fillets. Peel the cucumber, cut it in half lengthwise, and scrape out the seeds with a pointed teaspoon. Dice the flesh and sprinkle it evenly over the trout.

Serve with crusty bread and butter as a main course or, in small quantities, as a first course.

CRAB MOUSSE

On a hot day a light and fluffy cold mousse is the perfect meal. The mousse can be made in advance from fresh, frozen, or canned crabmeat.

PREPARATION TIME: *45 minutes*
CHILLING TIME: *3 hours*

INGREDIENTS (*for 6*):
1 pound crabmeat
2 tablespoons grated Parmesan
*   cheese*
½ cup heavy cream
1½ tablespoons unflavored gelatin
½ cup cold water
½ cup bottled clam broth
Salt and black pepper
Cayenne pepper
Juice of 1 lemon
4 egg whites
GARNISH:
Cucumber slices

Pick over the crabmeat carefully, removing all bits of shell. Finely flake* the crabmeat into a bowl. Add the cheese and pound thoroughly. Alternatively, whirl the meat and cheese in a blender with the cream at a medium speed for 1–2 minutes.

Soak the gelatin in the water for 5 minutes, then dissolve it over hot water. Add the clam broth. Stir this mixture into the crab mixture and add the cream (if not already used). Season to taste with salt, freshly ground black pepper, a pinch of cayenne, and lemon juice. Put the mixture in the refrigerator and leave until cold and thick.

Beat the egg whites until stiff but not dry, then fold them into the crab mixture. Turn the mousse into a soufflé dish and leave to set in the refrigerator for at least 3 hours.

Dip the soufflé dish in very hot water for 5 seconds and unmold the mousse on a chilled round platter.

Garnish the mousse with thin cucumber slices. A potato and chive salad or a tossed green salad would be suitable accompaniments.

SOLE VÉRONIQUE

The French culinary term *véronique* describes a dish, usually fish, served in a sauce made from white wine and cream. The traditional garnish is muscat grapes, but white seedless grapes may be used.

PREPARATION TIME: *20 minutes*
COOKING TIME: *20 minutes*

INGREDIENTS (*for 4–6*):
8 fillets of sole
2 shallots
3 button mushrooms
1 sprig parsley
1 bay leaf
Salt and black pepper
3 teaspoons lemon juice
½ cup medium-dry white wine
1½ tablespoons unsalted butter
2 tablespoons flour
½ cup milk
½ cup heavy cream
6 ounces white seedless grapes

Meat

Arrange the fillets in a lightly buttered ovenproof dish. Peel and finely chop the shallots; trim the mushrooms* and slice them thinly. Sprinkle both over the fish and add the parsley and bay leaf. Season with salt, freshly ground pepper, and 2 teaspoons of lemon juice.

Pour the wine over the fish, adding sufficient water to barely cover the fillets. Seal the dish closely with foil, and bake in the center of a preheated oven at 425°F for 10–12 minutes, or until tender.

Remove the dish from the oven; carefully lift out the fillets and keep them warm. Strain the liquid into a small saucepan. Boil rapidly over high heat until it has reduced* by about half. Melt the butter in a separate saucepan and stir in the flour; blend well and cook over moderate heat for 2 minutes.

Add the milk to the reduced liquid to make 1¼ cups, and gradually add it to the butter and flour mixture, stirring continuously. Simmer over low heat until the sauce has the consistency of thick cream. Stir in the cream and the remaining lemon juice and bring the sauce back to boiling point. Remove from the heat, correct seasoning, and fold in two-thirds of the grapes.

Fold the fillets in half and arrange them on an ovenproof serving dish. Pour the sauce over the fish and brown under a hot broiler. Arrange the remaining grapes at either end of the dish and serve at once. Green beans mimosa (p.184) and buttered potatoes would go well with the fish.

BOEUF À LA MODE EN GELÉE

Most classic recipes for cold jellied beef use the expensive fillet, but top round poached slowly until very tender makes an excellent alternative. The dish is ideal for buffet entertaining and should be prepared a day in advance.

PREPARATION TIME: *30 minutes*
MARINATING TIME: *4 hours*
COOKING TIME: *4½–5 hours*

INGREDIENTS (*for 6–8*):
3 pounds top round or rump of beef
¼ pound salt pork
1 calf's foot or pig's foot
1¼ cups dry red wine
2 cloves garlic
Salt and black pepper
1–2 tablespoons beef drippings
2 tablespoons brandy
2 shallots
2 bay leaves
1¼ cups beef stock or water
15 small onions
10 young carrots

Ask the butcher to lard the beef with the salt pork and chop the calf's or pig's foot into pieces. If the meat is not larded, cut the salt pork into strips narrow enough to fit into the eye of a larding needle, and long enough to be threaded through the meat. Pull the fat strips through the meat and trim them off at each end.

Put the meat in a deep bowl and pour in the wine. Cover and marinate* for about 4 hours, turning the meat frequently.

Peel the garlic, cut it into small strips, and push them into the meat with the point of a knife. Season with salt and pepper.

Bring a large saucepan of salted water to a boil and blanch* the calf's or pig's foot pieces for 10 minutes.

Drain in a colander, then set aside.

Melt half the drippings in a heavy-bottomed deep pan over high heat, and brown the meat all over to seal in the juices. Reduce the heat. Pour the brandy over the meat, let it warm through slightly, then set it alight. When the flames have died down, add the calf's or pig's foot pieces.

Peel and finely chop the shallots and add them with the bay leaves to the pan. Heat the stock or water in a separate pan, blend in the wine, and pour it over the meat. Bring this liquid to a boil and cover the pan tightly with both foil and the lid.

Cook in the center of a preheated oven at 300°F for about 3 hours.

Meanwhile, peel the onions, leaving them whole. Wash and scrape the carrots and split them in half lengthwise. Heat the remaining drippings in a small pan and lightly brown the vegetables. Add them to the meat after 3 hours' cooking and simmer for a further 1–1½ hours.

Lift the meat onto a dish and remove the vegetables with a slotted spoon. Let the liquid cool, then strain it through cheesecloth into a bowl. Leave the liquid in the refrigerator overnight to set to a jelly.

The next day, carefully scrape the surface fat from the jelly with a spoon dipped in hot water. Cut the meat into neat thin slices and arrange them in a deep serving dish together with the carrots and onions. Melt the jelly in a saucepan over low heat, then pour it carefully over the meat and vegetables. Leave the dish in a cool place to allow the jelly to reset.

Serve the jellied beef with a selection of salads, such as a crisp green salad tossed in a sharp French dressing (p.304), a tomato salad, and a cold potato salad.

VEAL SCALLOPS WITH GINGER WINE

These thin cuts from the leg of veal are usually served with a creamy sauce, frequently made from white wine or Marsala. The ginger wine in this recipe adds an unusual, slightly spicy flavor.

PREPARATION TIME: *10 minutes*
COOKING TIME: *15 minutes*

INGREDIENTS (*for 4*):

4 veal scallops, each ¼ inch thick and weighing about 3 ounces
Seasoned flour (p.412)
4 tablespoons unsalted butter
1 teaspoon olive oil
6 tablespoons imported ginger wine

2 teaspoons lemon juice
4 tablespoons heavy cream
Salt and black pepper
GARNISH:
4 lemon twists
1 tablespoon chopped parsley

Cut any fat off the scallops and trim them into neat shapes. Dust them lightly with the seasoned flour. Heat the butter and oil in a heavy-bottomed pan over moderate heat and sauté the veal until golden brown on both sides. Lift the slices onto a serving dish and keep them warm.

Add the ginger wine to the pan and bring it gently to a boil, scraping up the pan juices with a rubber spatula. Reduce the heat and simmer slowly for 5 minutes, or until the wine is syrupy. Stir in the lemon juice and the cream, and simmer for a further 2–3 minutes, or until the sauce is a pale coffee color. Season to taste with salt and freshly ground pepper. Pour the sauce over the meat and garnish each scallop with a lemon twist sprinkled with the chopped parsley.

Serve the scallops with plain boiled potatoes and green beans.

BAKED PICNIC HAM

Picnic ham, from the shoulder, is one of the most economical cuts of pork and is ideal for a family meal, providing plenty of leftover meat to serve cold or in sandwiches.

PREPARATION TIME: *20 minutes*
COOKING TIME: *2–2¼ hours*

INGREDIENTS (*for 8*):
5-pound smoked picnic ham
8 peppercorns
3 cloves
Bouquet garni (p.410)
¼–⅓ cup light brown sugar
½ cup imported dry cider or unsweetened apple juice
4 peaches
6 tablespoons unsalted butter
3 tablespoons honey or dark brown sugar
Cinnamon

Put the picnic ham in a heavy pan just large enough to hold the ham, and add sufficient cold water to cover it completely. Add the peppercorns, cloves, and bouquet garni. Bring to a boil over moderate heat, remove any scum from the surface, and cover the pan with a lid. Reduce the heat and simmer the ham for 1½ hours.

Lift the meat from the pan and leave it to cool and set. Score the fat in a diamond pattern, at ½-inch intervals, and press the light brown sugar firmly all over the fat. Put the ham in a roasting pan, heat the cider or apple juice, and pour it over the meat. Baste* the ham a few times without disturbing the sugar coating.

Drop the peaches in boiling water for 10 seconds, then peel the peaches, cut them in half, and remove the pits. Enlarge the cavities slightly by scraping them with a pointed teaspoon. Blend the butter, honey (or sugar), and a pinch of cinnamon until creamy. Spoon this mixture into the peach halves.

Bake the picnic ham in the center of a preheated oven at 350°F for ½ hour, basting frequently with the juice. Place the peaches around the ham, raise the oven temperature to 400°F, and bake for a further 15 minutes, or until the top of the ham is golden brown and shiny.

Serve the picnic ham whole or sliced, garnished with the baked peaches. Plain boiled potatoes and a tossed green salad, or carrots paysanne (p.206) and buttered green beans would make good vegetable side dishes.

PORK COOKED IN MILK

The Italians frequently pot-roast meat and chicken in milk. This method of cooking produces a delicious, tender dish. For this recipe, choose boned leg of pork or, more economically, pork shoulder. It can be served hot or cold.

PREPARATION TIME: *10 minutes*
COOKING TIME: *2 hours*

INGREDIENTS (*for 6*):
2½ pounds boned rolled pork
Salt and black pepper
1 clove garlic
12 coriander seeds
2 onions
2 slices cooked ham
1 tablespoon olive oil
4 cups milk

Ask the butcher to bone the meat and to trim part of the fat off the pork before rolling it. Rub it all over with salt and freshly ground pepper. Peel the garlic and cut it lengthwise into small strips. Make small incisions in the meat with the point of a knife and push in the garlic strips and coriander seeds.

Peel and finely chop the onions; dice the ham. Heat the oil in a heavy-bottomed pan or flameproof dish into which the meat will fit closely. Sauté the onions and ham in the oil for a few minutes until they begin to color. Put in the meat and brown it lightly all over. In a separate pan bring the milk to a boil, then pour it over the pork so that it reaches ½ inch over the meat.

Cook the pork, uncovered, over low heat (set the pan on an asbestos mat, if available) for about 1 hour. The milk should be kept barely at simmering point during cooking and will form a cobwebby skin that gradually turns pale golden brown. After 1 hour break the milk skin and turn the meat over, scraping all the skin from the sides toward the center of the pan.

Continue cooking the meat slowly for a another 45 minutes, or until the milk has reduced* to a cupful of thick sauce.

Lift the meat carefully with a large spatula onto a warm serving dish and pour the sauce with the bits of onion and ham over it.

Serve the pork hot or cold, with boiled potatoes and a crisp salad or green vegetable.

LIVER WITH DUBONNET AND ORANGE

Lamb's or calf's liver is most suitable for this recipe. The fruity, sweet sauce, made from wine and oranges, blends surprisingly well with juicy, slightly undercooked liver.

PREPARATION TIME: *15 minutes*
COOKING TIME: *10–15 minutes*

INGREDIENTS (*for 6*):
1 pound liver
Seasoned flour (p.412)
2 small onions
1 clove garlic
1 tablespoon olive oil
3 tablespoons butter
SAUCE:
1 tablespoon orange juice
8 tablespoons red Dubonnet
2 tablespoons fresh chopped parsley
Rind of 1 orange, coarsely grated
1 teaspoon finely grated lemon rind

Trim off any tough and discolored parts of the liver, cut into slices ½ inch thick, and coat them with seasoned flour.

Peel and finely chop the onions and garlic. Heat the oil and butter in a large, heavy pan over moderate heat and cook the onions and garlic, covered, until soft and beginning to turn golden.

Add the liver slices to the onions in a single layer and cook over low heat. As soon as the blood begins to run, turn the liver over and cook the other side for a slightly shorter time.

When cooked, arrange the liver on a warm serving dish. Cover with the onions, lifted from the pan with a slotted spoon. Keep the dish hot.

To make the sauce, stir the orange juice and Dubonnet into the pan juices. Boil rapidly until the liquid has reduced* by half. Remove the pan from the heat and stir in most of the chopped parsley and the grated orange and lemon rind, reserving a little of each for garnish.

Pour the sauce over the liver; sprinkle with the remaining parsley and orange and lemon rind. Serve at once with creamed potatoes and a green vegetable.

BRAISED SHOULDER OF LAMB

This recipe comes from New Zealand and is ideal for the frozen lamb imported from there. The boned shoulder is rolled around a savory apricot stuffing.

PREPARATION TIME: *30 minutes*
COOKING TIME: *2⅓ hours*

INGREDIENTS: (*for 6*):
4-pound boned shoulder of lamb
Salt and black pepper
2½ cups stock
6 carrots
6 stalks celery
6 turnips
2 large onions
STUFFING:
½ cup dried apricots
2 tablespoons butter
1 tablespoon chopped onion
4 tablespoons fine white bread crumbs
1 teaspoon chopped parsley
1–2 tablespoons milk

Put the dried apricots in cold water and soak overnight. Drain and chop them finely.

To make the stuffing, melt the butter in a skillet over moderate heat and cook the onions until soft and transparent. Remove from the heat and add the bread crumbs and the parsley; season to taste. Stir in enough milk to give a soft consistency, and add the apricots.

Sprinkle the cut surface of the lamb with salt and pepper. Spread the stuffing over the meat, roll it up, and tie with string. Place the meat in an ovenproof casserole.

Put the casserole in a preheated oven set at 450°F and cook for 15 minutes, uncovered. Pour in half the stock and reduce the heat to 350°F. Cover the casserole with a lid and cook for 45 minutes. Meanwhile, coarsely chop the carrots, celery, turnips, and onions.

Arrange the vegetables around the meat and add the remaining stock. Cover and cook for another 1¼ hours.

Remove the casserole from the oven, and lift the meat and the vegetables onto a serving dish.

Skim the fat from the pan juices and boil to reduce* them by half. Pour this gravy into a sauceboat and serve separately.

JAMBON À LA CRÈME

The classic French recipe for a whole ham, cooked and then dressed in a cream sauce, can easily be adapted for a small family meal.

PREPARATION TIME: *20 minutes*
COOKING TIME: *20 minutes*

INGREDIENTS (*for 4–6*):
8 thick slices baked ham
½ pound mushrooms
1 cup dry white wine
3–4 shallots
1 pound tomatoes
5 tablespoons butter
1½ tablespoons flour
1 cup heavy cream
Salt and white pepper
½ cup grated Parmesan cheese

Trim the mushrooms* and slice them thickly. Cook them in a shallow pan, with the wine, until the wine has reduced* to about 3 tablespoons. Lift the mushrooms from the pan with a slotted spoon and set them aside.

Peel and finely chop the shallots, add them to the wine in the pan, and cook over medium heat until virtually all the wine has evaporated. Peel the tomatoes,* remove the seeds, and chop the flesh coarsely.

In a separate pan, melt 4 tablespoons of the butter, stir in the flour, and cook for 2 minutes. Gradually stir in the cream to make a smooth sauce. Season to taste with salt and pepper. Stir in the cooked shallots and the chopped tomatoes. Bring the sauce to a boil, then lower the heat and simmer gently for 5–6 minutes, stirring occasionally to prevent sticking.

Arrange the ham in a lightly buttered flameproof dish, sprinkle with the mushrooms, and pour in the cream sauce. Sprinkle the cheese evenly over the sauce and dot with the remaining butter. Put the dish under the broiler until the ham is heated through and the cheese is lightly browned and bubbly. (Or cook the dish in the center of a preheated oven at 400°F until the cheese is browned.)

Buttered noodles and a tossed green salad, or boiled potatoes and creamed spinach (p.162) would be suitable side dishes.

Poultry & Game

KIDNEYS IN SHERRY

Lamb or veal kidneys are suitable for this Spanish family dish. Other fortified wines, such as port or Madeira, may be substituted for the sherry. Do not overcook kidneys; they should be pink at the centers.

PREPARATION TIME: *20 minutes*
COOKING TIME: *15 minutes*

INGREDIENTS (*for 4*):

10–12 *lamb kidneys*
1 *onion*
1 *small clove garlic*
3 *tablespoons olive oil*
1 *small bay leaf*
1 *tablespoon flour*
4 *tablespoons beef stock*
1½ *tablespoons chopped parsley*
Salt and black pepper
5 *tablespoons dry sherry*
GARNISH:
Chopped parsley

Remove the fat and the outer membranes from the kidneys,* cut them in half lengthwise, and snip out the cores with scissors. Cut each half into 3 or 4 slices.

Peel and finely chop the onion and garlic. Heat half the oil in a small skillet over moderate heat and add the onion, garlic, and bay leaf. Cook, stirring frequently, for about 5 minutes, or until the onion is soft and transparent. Stir in the flour and blend thoroughly. Gradually add the stock and cook over high heat, stirring all the time, until the mixture thickens and comes to a boil. Blend in the parsley, reduce the heat, and simmer the mixture over low heat for 3 minutes, then remove the bay leaf. Set the mixture aside.

Heat the remaining oil in a large skillet. Season the kidneys with salt and a little pepper and sauté in the oil over moderate heat for about 5 minutes, turning them frequently to brown quickly on all sides without burning. Lift the kidneys onto a plate and pour the oil from the pan before adding the sherry. Bring the sherry to a boil, scraping in the brown sediment at the bottom of the pan. Blend the onion mixture into the sherry, and add the kidneys. Bring to boiling point, and simmer for 2–3 minutes. Adjust seasoning.

Serve the kidneys in the sauce on a bed of fluffy saffron-flavored rice garnished with parsley. Sautéed mushroom caps or halved broiled tomatoes would also be suitable.

MUSTARD RABBIT

Originally wild rabbit was used in this French farmhouse stew. Today the rabbits sold in markets are bred for the table and are often found cut up and frozen. In this dish, chicken may be substituted for the rabbit, but it will take less time to cook.

PREPARATION TIME: *15 minutes*
COOKING TIME: *1¼ hours*

INGREDIENTS (*for 4–6*):

2½–3 *pound rabbit or 6 rabbit*
    parts
4 *tablespoons Dijon mustard*
Seasoned flour (p.412)
4 *tablespoons unsalted butter*
1 *thick slice salt pork*
1 *onion*
1 *clove garlic*
1¼ *cups heavy cream*
GARNISH:
Chopped chervil or parsley
Bread croûtons (p.300)

Cut the rabbit into 6 or 8 neat pieces and put them in a large bowl. Cover with cold salted water and leave to soak for 1–2 hours. Drain and dry thoroughly. Coat the rabbit pieces evenly with mustard and leave them in the refrigerator overnight, covered with cheesecloth.

The following day dust the rabbit lightly with seasoned flour, shaking off any surplus. Melt the butter in a flameproof casserole and lightly brown the pieces on both sides; lift them out and set aside. Remove the rind and coarsely chop the salt pork. Peel and finely chop the onion and garlic. Sauté the salt pork for 2–3 minutes in the butter, then add the onion and garlic and cook over low heat until the onion is soft.

Return the rabbit to the casserole, cover tightly with a lid or foil, and simmer over low heat for 30 minutes. Remove the casserole from the heat and stir in the cream. Cover again and cook over low heat on top of the stove, or in an oven preheated to 325°F, for about 45 minutes, or until the rabbit is tender. Gently stir once or twice.

Serve the rabbit straight from the casserole, sprinkled with the fresh herbs and garnished with bread croûtons. Buttered noodles or boiled potatoes can be served with the rabbit, together with a green vegetable.

DUCK WITH APRICOTS

Oranges are a classic flavoring and garnish with duck. This recipe provides the sharper tang of fresh apricots, now at the end of their season. Canned apricots may also be used.

PREPARATION TIME: *10 minutes*
COOKING TIME: *2–2½ hours*

INGREDIENTS (*for 4*):

1 *duck, approximately 5 pounds*
Salt and black pepper
1¼ *cups veal or chicken stock*
½ *cup medium-dry white wine*
1 *pound fresh apricots*
Juice of ½ orange
1 *tablespoon apricot brandy*
2 *tablespoons brandy*
GARNISH:
Apricot slices

Rub the skin with salt and freshly ground pepper. Place the duck on a rack over a shallow roasting pan. Prick well and place in a preheated 450°F oven for 30–40 minutes, until the skin is well browned and the fat has drained into the pan. Then transfer the duck to a large ovenproof casserole.

Add the stock and wine to the roasting pan, heat until the liquid reaches boiling point, then pour it over the duck. Cover the casserole with a lid or foil and cook the duck in the center of a preheated oven at 325°F for 1½ hours.

Wash and dry the apricots, cut them in half, and remove the pits.

Rice & Pasta

Put half the apricots around the duck after 45 minutes.

Lift the cooked duck onto a serving dish and keep it warm. Strain the cooking liquid and skim off as much fat as possible. Rub the cooked apricots through a sieve, or whirl in a blender, and reserve the purée.* Pour the strained liquid back into the casserole and boil it briskly until it has reduced* by a third. Add the orange juice and thicken this sauce with the apricot purée.

Arrange the remaining fresh apricot halves around the duck. Warm the brandies, pour them over the duck, and set alight. Serve at once, with brown rice and a green salad. Offer the sauce separately.

SALMI OF PARTRIDGE

Young partridges are usually roasted whole and served, one per person, on a slice of bread. But unless quite young and tender, the birds are better used in a salmi—a cooking method of partly roasting the birds, braising them in game stock, and serving them in a wine sauce.

PREPARATION TIME: *10 minutes*
COOKING TIME: *1½ hours*

INGREDIENTS (*for 2–4*):
2 partridges
1 onion
Salt and black pepper
¼ pound mushrooms
½ cup red wine
12 juniper berries or ¼ cup gin
1 tablespoon unsalted butter
1 tablespoon flour
GARNISH:
Chopped parsley

Have the partridges trussed and barded,* and ask for the giblets. Put the partridges, breast side down, in a roasting pan and cook them for 15 minutes in the center of a preheated oven at 375°F. Remove them from the oven, cut off the barding fat around each bird, and carve the breasts off neatly. Slice each breast piece in half and set aside.

Put the carcasses in a pan, cover with cold water, and simmer with the peeled and chopped onion for about 30 minutes. Strain this stock through cheesecloth and season with salt and freshly ground pepper.

Trim the mushrooms* and slice them thickly.

Put the breasts in a wide shallow pan; add the mushrooms and enough stock to cover the contents. Put a lid on the pan and simmer over low heat for about 30 minutes.

Meanwhile, blend the wine into the remaining stock; add the giblets and the mashed livers. Crush the juniper berries lightly and add them (or the gin) to the wine stock. Bring the mixture to a boil and simmer for 10–15 minutes.

Lift the cooked partridge breasts from the pan and arrange them on a serving dish. Keep it warm in the oven and pour the liquid into the wine stock. Blend the butter and flour together, and add, in small pieces, to the stock. Stir continuously, over low heat, until it thickens to a sauce. Simmer for a few minutes; adjust seasoning.

Pour the sauce over the partridge breasts and sprinkle with finely chopped parsley. Partridges are usually served with shoestring potatoes or Saratoga chips (p.333), fried bread crumbs or bread sauce (p.304), and sprigs of watercress.

ARANCINI SICILIANI

"Sicilian oranges".is the literal translation of this lunch or supper dish. The "oranges" are crisp rice balls with a filling of cheese and ham.

PREPARATION TIME: *45 minutes*
COOKING TIME: *30 minutes*

INGREDIENTS (*for 6*):
1 cup Italian or short grain rice
½ cup grated Parmesan cheese
2 small eggs
1¼ cups thick tomato sauce (p.302)
Salt and black pepper
½ cup finely diced Bel Paese cheese
½ cup finely diced cooked ham,
   chicken, or salami
½–¾ cup fine fresh bread crumbs
Oil for deep frying
2–3 tablespoons light cream
   (optional)
GARNISH:
Fresh mint or basil leaves

Bring a large pan of salted water to a boil, add the Italian or short grain rice, and cook rapidly until just tender, about 15–20 minutes. Rinse with cold water and drain the rice thoroughly.

Put the rice in a bowl and stir in the Parmesan cheese, the lightly beaten eggs, 1 tablespoon of the tomato sauce, and a little salt. Blend the ingredients thoroughly, then set aside until cold.

Put the Bel Paese cheese and the diced meat in a bowl. Stir in 2 tablespoons of the tomato sauce and season to taste with salt and pepper.

Take 2 teaspoons of the cold rice and mold it in the well-floured palm of the hand; put a teaspoon of the cheese and meat mixture into the hollow, top with a little more rice, and shape it all into a ball about 1½ inches wide. When all the balls (about 12) have been shaped, coat them thickly with bread crumbs.

In a deep-fat fryer, heat the oil* until hot, and fry the rice balls, two or three at a time, until golden brown. Drain on paper towels and keep the rice balls hot.

Just before serving, garnish each "orange" with a fresh mint or basil leaf. The remaining tomato sauce can be thinned with a little cream, heated through without boiling, and served separately.

ANCHOVY EGGS WITH FETTUCCINE

Savory stuffed eggs are often served as an hors d'oeuvre, but they can also form the basis for an economical and quick lunch or supper dish.

PREPARATION TIME: *20 minutes*
COOKING TIME: *15 minutes*

INGREDIENTS (*for 6*):
1 pound fettuccine
2 cups medium white sauce (p.301)
¾–1 cup grated Parmesan cheese
12 eggs
3 tablespoons anchovy paste
6 tablespoons unsalted butter
½ cup heavy cream
Salt and white pepper

Prepare the white sauce first, then stir the grated cheese into it and keep it warm. Put the eggs in a large pan of cold water and bring to a rolling boil. Turn off the heat and let the eggs stand 12–15 minutes. Plunge into cold water.

Shell the eggs under cold running water. Cut them in half lengthwise and carefully remove the yolks. Warm the whites in a bowl of hot water. Rub the egg yolks through a sieve into a bowl and blend in 4 tablespoons of softened butter, the anchovy paste, and the cream. Season to taste with freshly ground white pepper.

Spoon the yolk mixture into a pastry bag fitted with a rosette tube and pipe it into the egg whites. Arrange the filled eggs, rounded side down, in a lightly buttered ovenproof dish. Cover with foil and heat through in the center of a preheated oven at 300°F for about 8 minutes.

Meanwhile, cook the fettuccine in a large pan of boiling salted water until just tender, about 8–10 minutes. Drain thoroughly, set aside, and keep warm.

Remove the eggs from the oven, pour the hot cheese sauce carefully over them, and put the dish under a hot broiler for 2 minutes until the sauce is brown and bubbly.

Toss the fettuccine in the remaining butter, season with salt and pepper, and turn into a warm serving dish. Serve the anchovy eggs separately, and offer a side salad of tomatoes or crisp romaine lettuce.

Vegetables & Salads

SPAGHETTI WITH TUNA SAUCE

Lighter and more summery than spaghetti with a tomato or meat sauce, this dish makes a good family meal. Serve it with crusty bread and a crisp green salad tossed in French dressing (p.304).

PREPARATION TIME: *10 minutes*
COOKING TIME: *15 minutes*

INGREDIENTS (*for 4–6*):
1 pound spaghetti
1 clove garlic (optional)
2 tablespoons olive oil
4 tablespoons butter
1 cup chicken stock
3 tablespoons dry white wine or
vermouth
7-ounce can of tuna
Salt and black pepper
GARNISH:
2 tablespoons finely chopped parsley

Bring a large pan of salted water to a boil, add the spaghetti, and bring back to a boil. Cook for 7–12 minutes or until the spaghetti is just resistant to the bite (*al dente**). Stir occasionally with a wooden spoon.

Peel and finely chop the garlic. Heat the oil and half the butter, and sauté the garlic for 1–2 minutes, then stir in the stock and wine. Boil briskly over high heat until the liquid has reduced* to about $\frac{1}{2}$ cup. Drain the oil from the tuna, flake* the fish, and add it to the stock. Season with salt and pepper.

When the spaghetti is cooked, drain it thoroughly in a colander and toss it in the remaining butter. Put the spaghetti in a warm serving dish, pour over the hot tuna sauce, and sprinkle with the chopped parsley. Serve at once.

SPINACH ROLL

Late summer spinach or even the frozen variety is ideal for this Yugoslavian puff pastry dish. It will serve as a light meal on its own, or it can be part of a lunch.

PREPARATION TIME: *45 minutes*
COOKING TIME: *30 minutes*

INGREDIENTS (*for 4*):
2 pounds fresh spinach
¾ recipe prepared puff pastry
(p.363)
½ cup cottage cheese or ricotta cheese
3 eggs
¼ cup grated Parmesan cheese
Salt and black pepper
1 egg yolk

Roll the prepared puff pastry out on a floured surface to a rectangle 12 inches long by 8 inches wide and $\frac{1}{4}$ inch thick. Lightly grease and flour a baking sheet.

Wash the spinach thoroughly, discarding any stalks and tough midribs. Put it, still wet, in a large saucepan. Cover with a lid and cook over low heat for 5–7 minutes or until just tender. Drain in a colander, chop it finely, and drain again (do not squeeze completely dry).

Rub the cottage cheese through a sieve. Separate the 3 eggs. Lightly beat the 3 yolks and add them to the spinach in a mixing bowl. Blend in the cottage or ricotta and the Parmesan cheeses; season with salt and freshly ground pepper. Beat the egg whites until stiff and fold into the mixture.

Moisten the edges of the pastry with cold water and spoon the spinach mixture down the center of the rectangle and to within 1 inch of the shorter edges. Quickly fold the pastry over the spinach, close the edges tightly, and seal all three sides firmly with the lightly beaten extra egg yolk. Roll out the pastry trimmings and use them to decorate the top of the roll. Brush with the remaining egg yolk to glaze.

Make 2 or 3 slits in the top of the pastry for the steam to escape. Carefully lift the pastry roll onto the baking sheet.

Bake in the center of a preheated oven at 450°F for 20 minutes, then reduce the temperature to 350°F for another 10 minutes, or until the pastry is well risen and golden brown. Serve the roll, hot or cold, cut into thick slices.

POTATOES IN BEEF BOUILLON

Potatoes baked this way are delectable with all types of roasts, including chicken and turkey.

PREPARATION TIME: *30 minutes*
COOKING TIME: *1¼ hours*

INGREDIENTS (*for 6*):
6 tablespoons butter
2 pounds potatoes
1 teaspoon salt
¼ teaspoon pepper
1 cup grated Swiss cheese
1¼ cup beef bouillon

Grease the bottom of a 10-inch ovenproof baking dish with 1 tablespoon of the butter. Wash, peel, and slice the potatoes about $\frac{1}{8}$ inch thick. Arrange the potatoes in layers, sprinkling each layer with salt, pepper, and cheese. Sprinkle a few tablespoons of cheese on top and dot with remaining butter.

Warm the bouillon and pour it over the potatoes. Set the baking dish over heat and bring to simmer. Bake in the center of a 425°F oven for 20–30 minutes until the potatoes are tender and slightly browned.

BEETS WITH ORANGE

In this recipe cooked beets are combined with orange marmalade. The two flavors blend surprisingly well and make a good side dish with any strong game, goose, or duck.

PREPARATION TIME: *5 minutes*
COOKING TIME: *10 minutes*

INGREDIENTS (*for 4*):
1 pound cooked beets
2 tablespoons unsalted butter
1 tablespoon marmalade
Juice of ½ orange
GARNISH:
Slice of orange

Peel and dice the cooked beets. Measure the butter, marmalade, and orange juice into a saucepan, heat until the butter melts, then add the beets. Simmer gently, stirring occasionally, for about 10 minutes, until the liquid has evaporated and the beets are evenly glazed.

Spoon the beets into a hot serving dish. Cut towards the center of a thin orange slice, twist the two halves in opposite directions, and place on top as a garnish.

RAGOÛT OF LETTUCE AND PEAS

Peas that are no longer quite young are the main component of this French vegetable stew. It makes a filling dish on its own, but can also be served as an accompaniment to roast meat and poultry.

PREPARATION TIME: *25 minutes*
COOKING TIME: *45 minutes*

INGREDIENTS (*for 4*):
2 large heads of Boston lettuce
2 pounds fresh peas
12–16 large scallions
6 ounces lean cooked ham
6 tablespoons butter
Salt and black pepper
½–1 teaspoon sugar
GARNISH:
Fried bread triangles

Shell the peas, setting aside about a dozen of the smaller pods. Remove the coarse outer leaves from the lettuce and cut the heads into quarters lengthwise; wash and drain thoroughly. Trim the roots and stems from the scallions. Cut the ham into ½-inch cubes.

Melt 5 tablespoons of the butter in a large heavy-bottomed pan over moderate heat. Put the lettuce, peas, pea pods, and scallions into the pan and coat them carefully in the melted butter. Season to taste with salt and freshly ground pepper. Add the cooked ham and 3 tablespoons of hot water; cover the pan with a tight-fitting lid.

Cook over very low heat for 10–20 minutes depending on the age of the peas. Test often; the peas should be tender but not mushy when cooked. Shake the pan from time to time to prevent sticking.

Before serving, remove the pea pods and stir in the sugar and remaining butter, being careful not to mash the peas.

Serve the ragoût hot, garnished with triangles of fried bread.

CORN ON THE COB

Corn on the cob should be freshly picked, with soft, tender kernels. Serve the ears as a separate vegetable course.

PREPARATION TIME: *10 minutes*
COOKING TIME: *5 minutes*

INGREDIENTS (*for 4*):
4 ears of corn
4 tablespoons butter
Salt and black pepper
2 teaspoons sugar

Pepper butter, to be served with the corn, should be made well in advance so that it can be chilled. Stir the butter until smooth and season highly with freshly ground pepper and extra salt to taste. Shape the butter into an oblong roll and wrap it in foil or waxed paper. Chill in the refrigerator until firm.

Remove the husks and cornsilk from the ears and put them, with the sugar, in a shallow pan holding just enough boiling water to cover them. Keep the water boiling and cook the corn for no more than 5 minutes.

Drain the corn and serve it at once, with the butter cut into ¼-inch-thick slices on a separate plate. Insert special corn holders, small skewers, or strong toothpicks at either end of each ear by which to hold it.

ZUCCHINI IN HOLLANDAISE CHEESE SAUCE

The delicate flavor of young zucchini is best preserved when paired with melted butter or a simple sauce.

PREPARATION TIME: *30 minutes*
COOKING TIME: *30 minutes*

INGREDIENTS (*for 6*):
½ pound zucchini
2 tablespoons unsalted butter
Salt and black pepper
Juice of ½ lemon
SAUCE:
½ pound unsalted butter
3 egg yolks
1–2 tablespoons lemon juice
1 tablespoon water or dry white wine
Salt and black pepper
3 tablespoons grated Parmesan cheese

Wash and trim the zucchini; blanch* in boiling water for 1–2 minutes. Drain, wipe dry, and cut the zucchini in half lengthwise. With a pointed teaspoon, scoop out a shallow groove in each half.

Arrange the zucchini, cut side up, in a large, shallow, lightly buttered ovenproof dish. Sprinkle with salt, freshly ground pepper, and the lemon juice. Cut the remaining butter into small pieces over the zucchini and cover the dish tightly. Bake in the center of a preheated oven at 350°F for 25 minutes.

Meanwhile, cut all but 2 tablespoons of the butter into small pieces and let it melt slowly in a small, heavy-bottomed pan over low heat. As soon as the butter has melted, remove the pan from the heat and pour the butter into a measuring cup. Put the 3 egg yolks into the same pan and beat thoroughly with a wire whisk. Add 1 tablespoon of lemon juice and 1 of water (or wine), with a good pinch of salt; beat again. Add 1 tablespoon of cold butter to the egg yolk mixture and put the pan over low heat on an asbestos mat. Cook, whisking steadily, until the egg yolks are creamy and beginning to thicken enough to coat the wires of the whisk. Remove the pan from the heat and beat in the remaining tablespoon of butter.

Add the melted butter to the egg mixture, drop by drop, whisking continuously. As the mixture thickens, the butter may be added more rapidly. When the sauce has the consistency of thick cream, season to taste with salt, pepper, and lemon juice. If the sauce is too thick, it can be thinned with 3–4 teaspoons of water or light cream. Finally, stir in 2 tablespoons of cheese.

Spoon the sauce into the grooves of the cooked zucchini and sprinkle with the remaining cheese. Put the dish under a hot broiler until the cheese is lightly browned. Serve at once, as a side dish to roast chicken or lean roast meat.

Desserts

CARROTS PAYSANNE

In cooking, *paysanne* refers to vegetables cooked in butter and used to garnish meat and poultry. Young carrots make a good accompaniment to broiled meat.

PREPARATION TIME: *15 minutes*
COOKING TIME: *30 minutes*

INGREDIENTS (*for 4–6*):
1 pound small carrots
1 large onion
2 slices lean bacon
5 tablespoons unsalted butter
½–1 cup chicken stock or water
1 teaspoon sugar
4 tablespoons heavy cream
Salt
GARNISH:
Finely chopped parsley

Trim the tops and roots from the carrots, scrape them, and wash thoroughly. Blanch* the carrots for 5 minutes in boiling salted water, then drain in a colander.

Peel and thinly slice the onion. Dice the bacon. Melt the butter in a wide shallow pan over low heat, and cook the onion and bacon until just soft and beginning to color.

Add the carrots to the bacon and onion, and pour over enough stock or water to barely cover the vegetables. Cover the pan with a lid and cook over moderate heat until the carrots are tender. Lift out the carrots with a slotted spoon; set them aside and keep them hot.

Boil the liquid over high heat until it has reduced* to a few tablespoons. Add the sugar and cream, and season to taste with salt. Simmer the liquid, uncovered, until the sauce has thickened slightly.

Pour the cream sauce over the carrots and sprinkle with parsley.

GREEN BEANS WITH SABAYON SAUCE

In Tuscany, where this recipe originates, the sauce is traditionally made with muscatel grape juice. *Sabayon* is a French corruption of the Italian *zabaglione,* and the sauce should have the same fluffy consistency.

PREPARATION TIME: *15 minutes*
COOKING TIME: *15–20 minutes*

INGREDIENTS (*for 6*):
1½ pounds green beans
Salt
SAUCE:
2 egg yolks
2 tablespoons dry white wine
* sweetened with 1 tablespoon*
* sugar*
1 tablespoon white wine vinegar

Trim and wash beans. Bring a pan of salted water to a boil and cook the beans for 4–6 minutes or until just tender; do not overcook. Drain the beans through a colander and put them in a shallow serving dish; cover the dish with aluminum foil and keep warm in a 250°F oven.

Meanwhile, put all the sauce ingredients in the top of a double boiler. Mix lightly with a fork and place over simmering water. Whisk the sauce until it is thick and frothy, and rises in the pan.

Pour the sauce over the beans and serve at once. This dish goes well with broiled fish or meat.

CUCUMBER IN SOUR CREAM

This unusual salad, in a refreshing summery dressing, goes well with both hot and cold meats. It is an especially good accompaniment to roast beef, veal, or chicken.

PREPARATION TIME: *15–20 minutes*
CHILLING TIME: *2 hours*

INGREDIENTS (*for 4*):
2 large or 4 small cucumbers
1½ tablespoons flour
½ teaspoon each of salt, sugar, and
* dry mustard*
2 tablespoons tarragon or white
* wine vinegar*
2 egg yolks
4 tablespoons olive oil
½ cup sour cream
2 tablespoons finely chopped chives

Put the flour, salt, sugar, and mustard in a small, heavy-bottomed pan with 1 tablespoon of water. Cook over low heat, stirring until the ingredients are thoroughly blended. Gradually add the vinegar and 2 tablespoons of water. Continue cooking until the mixture has thickened to a smooth sauce. Bring this quickly to a boil, then simmer over low heat for 2–3 minutes.

Remove the pan from the heat and beat the egg yolks into the sauce, one at a time. Add the oil, a few drops at a time. Chill the sauce in the refrigerator.

About an hour before serving, stir the sour cream and the chopped chives into the sauce. Return it to the refrigerator.

Wash and peel the cucumber (remove the seeds if necessary) and cut it into ½-inch cubes. Just before serving, stir the cucumber into the sour cream sauce.

PLUMS IN WINE

The flavor of plums is brought out deliciously by poaching them in a syrupy wine and serving them warm.

PREPARATION TIME: *5 minutes*
COOKING TIME: *30 minutes*

INGREDIENTS (*for 6*):
1½–2 pounds firm red-fleshed plums
½ cup sugar
1¼ cups tawny port, medium-dry
* sherry, or Madeira*
2 tablespoons sliced almonds

Dissolve the sugar in 1¼ cups of water and simmer for 10 minutes. Stir in the wine and bring the syrup to simmering point again.

Remove any stems from the plums; wash and dry them. Add the plums, one at a time, to the simmering syrup. Cover the pan with a lid and remove from the heat. Leave the plums in the syrup for 10 minutes.

Lift out the plums with a slotted spoon and put them in a serving dish. Cover the dish with a plate or foil, and leave in a warm place. Boil the syrup over high heat until it has reduced* by about one-third and thickened slightly. Pour it over the poached plums.

Meanwhile, toast the sliced almonds for about 5 minutes in the oven until golden. Scatter these over the plums and serve at once, with a pitcher of cream.

GRANITA AL CAFFÈ

Strong, bitter black coffee, preferably a continental roast, should be used for this Italian water ice. It is sometimes served with whipped cream.

PREPARATION TIME: *10 minutes*
CHILLING TIME: *3–4 hours*

INGREDIENTS (*for 4*):
2 cups strong black coffee
5 tablespoons sugar
½ cup heavy cream

Turn the refrigerator to its coldest setting 1 hour before beginning preparations. Melt 4 tablespoons of sugar in ½ cup of water over moderate heat, stirring until the sugar has completely dissolved. Bring this syrup to a boil and boil steadily for 5 minutes. Remove from the heat and leave the syrup to cool.

Stir the coffee into the cold syrup, and pour the mixture into ice cube trays. For the best texture, the dividers should be left in the trays so that the ice will set in cubes. Put the trays into the freezing compartment for at least 3 hours. Stir the ice occasionally with a fork to scrape the frozen crystals around the edges into the center.

Turn the frozen cubes into a bowl and crush them lightly with a pestle or break them up with a fork. Spoon the ice into individual glasses and serve at once with a separate bowl of whipped cream sweetened with the remaining sugar.

PEACHES WITH SOUR CREAM

Golden firm peaches make refreshing summer desserts—served uncooked, poached in white wine, or baked in a pie crust. Here poached peaches are served chilled with a sour cream and toasted almond topping.

PREPARATION TIME: *35 minutes*
CHILLING TIME: *30 minutes*

INGREDIENTS (*for 6*):
6 large peaches
1 cup vanilla sugar (or 1 cup sugar and 2 teaspoons vanilla extract)
Superfine sugar
1 cup sour cream
GARNISH:
¼ cup toasted sliced almonds

Mix the vanilla sugar* or the sugar and the vanilla extract in 1¼ cups of water in a small pan and cook over moderate heat. Simmer this syrup for 5 minutes.

Wash and dry the peaches thoroughly, then poach* them lightly in the syrup for 5–10 minutes, depending on the ripeness of the fruit.

Lift the peaches from the syrup, allow to cool slightly, then peel off the skins and cut the peaches in half. Remove the pits, and slice the peaches into a serving bowl, one layer at a time, sprinkling each layer with a little superfine sugar. Strain the syrup and keep for another use.

Cover the top of the peaches with a thick layer of sour cream and chill in the refrigerator for 30 minutes. Just before serving, sprinkle the top with the toasted almonds.

DANISH LAYER CAKE

There are many versions of the Danish layer cake, ranging from simple to complex. The most traditional recipes use a combination of sponge cakes, cream, and fruit.

PREPARATION TIME: *45 minutes*
COOKING TIME: *25 minutes*
CHILLING TIME: *1 hour*

INGREDIENTS (*for 6–8*):
4 eggs
Rind and juice of ½ lemon
1¼ cups confectioners' sugar
¾ cup all-purpose flour
2 tablespoons cornstarch
½ teaspoon baking powder
FILLING:
1 envelope (1 tablespoon) gelatin
2½ cups heavy cream
6 teaspoons vanilla sugar (or 6 tablespoons sugar and 1 teaspoon vanilla extract)
5 slices fresh pineapple cut ¼ inch thick, or 5 slices canned pineapple
1½ ounces dark unsweetened chocolate squares

Separate the eggs and put the yolks in a large bowl, together with the lemon rind and juice. Sift the confectioners' sugar into the yolks and beat until fluffy and pale cream in color. Beat the egg whites in a separate bowl until they stand in soft peaks, then fold them carefully into the yolk mixture. Sift the flour, cornstarch, and baking powder together and blend well into the sponge mixture.

Butter a round cake pan 8 inches in diameter and line with buttered waxed paper. Spoon the sponge mixture into the pan, smoothing it level around the sides. Bake in the center of a preheated oven at 350°F for 25 minutes or until the sponge is golden and well risen.

Loosen the edges of the sponge cake with a sharp knife and turn it out on a wire rack to cool. Remove the waxed paper. When completely cold, cut the cake into 3 thin layers and sandwich with the filling.

Dissolve the gelatin in 4 table-spoons of warm water, then melt it over hot water. Cool slightly. Whip the cream, setting one-third aside for the topping. Fold the cooled gelatin into the remaining cream and add the vanilla sugar* or the sugar and vanilla extract. Peel and trim the pineapple slices (or drain thoroughly if using canned pineapple); set one slice aside and chop the other four finely. Grate the chocolate and blend into the cream with the chopped pineapple. Leave the filling to set.

Spread half the filling between the sponge layers. Cover the top and sides with remaining filling. Pipe the reserved whipped cream through a narrow rosette tube around the edge and down the sides of the cake. Garnish the top with the reserved pineapple, cut into small chunks.

Chill the layer cake in the refrigerator for about 1 hour and serve it cut into wedges.

207

MELON ICE CREAM

The Italians introduced water ices, or sorbets, to Europe at least two centuries before cream ices became known. Today, virtually any sweetened fruit juice can be made into ice cream with the addition of egg custard and cream.

PREPARATION TIME: *30–40 minutes*
CHILLING TIME: *3 hours*

INGREDIENTS (*for 4*):
1 large ripe melon (cantaloupe, Persian, or cranshaw)
½ cup sugar
4 egg yolks
5 tablespoons imported ginger wine
2 tablespoons lemon juice
2 cups heavy cream

A few hours before preparing the ice cream, set the refrigerator to its coldest setting.

Slice about 1½ inches off the top of the melon; remove the seeds and fibers with a small spoon. Scoop all the melon pulp into a small saucepan, taking care not to pierce the shell. Add the sugar and place the pan over low heat until the sugar has melted into the melon and the mixture is a soft pulp. Mash with a fork.

Beat the egg yolks until light and creamy, and add them to the melon pulp, stirring well. Continue cooking and whisking over very low heat, so that the eggs will not curdle, until the mixture has the consistency of thin cream.

Pour the melon mixture into a bowl and allow it to cool completely. Stir in the ginger wine and lemon juice, mix thoroughly, then fold in the lightly whipped cream. Cover the bowl with foil and chill for 30 minutes.

Spoon the melon cream into a freezing tray or container, cover with foil or the lid, and freeze for 2–3 hours. Stir the ice cream several times during freezing to prevent crystals from forming.

Pile the ice cream into glasses or the chilled melon shell and serve at once. Any surplus ice cream can be stored for several months in plastic containers in the freezer.

STUFFED WATERMELON WITH KIRSCH

Kirsch, a colorless brandy made from cherries, adds a delectable flavor to fruit. Here it is mixed with melon, pineapple, and strawberries to make an attractive summer dessert.

PREPARATION TIME: *1½ hours*
CHILLING TIME: *3 hours*

INGREDIENTS (*for 20*):
1 good-sized, oblong-shaped watermelon
1 cantaloupe
1 honeydew or cranshaw melon
1 fresh pineapple or 1 20-ounce can of pineapple chunks
1 quart strawberries
Sugar
⅔ cup kirsch or bourbon, or more or less of kirsch or bourbon to taste

Remove a slice from the top third of the watermelon. Using a melon-ball cutter, remove as much of the watermelon in nicely formed balls as possible. Place these in a large bowl. Scoop out remainder of the watermelon and save for another use. Keep the melon shell chilled until time for filling.

Cut the other melons in half, remove seeds, and scoop out as many well-shaped balls as possible. Place these with the watermelon balls.

Peel and cut the pineapple into cubes, or cut the canned pineapple into small wedges, and combine with melon balls.

Hull the strawberries but leave them whole, and blend them with the pineapple and the melon balls. Add sugar to taste, if necessary. Add the kirsch or the bourbon.

Chill the fruit for several hours in the refrigerator. With a large spoon fill the watermelon shell with the melon balls and the other fruit so that the different colors of the fruit are reasonably interspersed throughout. Chill again. Serve, set in crushed ice in a larger bowl to keep it chilled, and add sprigs of fresh mint for decoration.

LEMON SYLLABUB

Syllabub is a frothy drink or dessert made with cream and wine. It was a favorite in Elizabethan England.

PREPARATION TIME: *20 minutes*
STANDING TIME: *6 hours*
CHILLING TIME: *3 hours*

INGREDIENTS (*for 6*):
1 lemon
3–4 tablespoons brandy
6 tablespoons sugar
1¼ cups heavy cream
½ cup sweet white wine
GARNISH:
Rind of 1 lemon

Peel the lemon thinly with a potato peeler. Squeeze out the juice into a small bowl and add enough brandy to make 5 tablespoons of liquid. Add the peeled lemon rind and let stand for at least 6 hours.

Strain the liquid through a fine sieve and stir in the sugar until it has dissolved completely. Whip the cream until it holds its shape. Mix the wine into the lemon and brandy, then add this liquid to the cream, a little at a time, whisking continuously. The cream should absorb all the liquid and still stand in soft peaks. Pile the mixture into individual glasses and chill for several hours.

For the garnish, cut the lemon rind into very narrow strips about 1½ inches long; blanch* for 2–3 minutes in boiling water. Serve the syllabub with a cluster of lemon strips.

Snacks & Supper Dishes

SUNDANCER EGGS

Baked eggs are one of the classic quick snacks, equally welcome at breakfast or at midnight.

PREPARATION TIME: *10 minutes*
COOKING TIME: *8–10 minutes*

INGREDIENTS (*for 4*):
8 eggs
8 thin slices lean bacon, diced
4 tablespoons butter
¼ pound finely chopped button mushrooms
Salt and black pepper
4 tablespoons heavy cream
Chervil
4 slices white bread
Oil for frying

Sauté the bacon in the butter over moderate heat for 3 minutes. Add the mushrooms and cook for a further 2 minutes. Season with salt and pepper. Spoon this mixture into eight small ramekin dishes, and break an egg into each dish. Top with cream and sprinkle with a little freshly chopped chervil.

Bake in the center of a preheated oven at 350°F for 8–10 minutes or until the egg whites are just set.

Meanwhile, cut the crust off the bread and slice it into rectangles. Deep-fry in hot oil until crisp and golden. Serve 2 ramekins per person and offer the bread separately.

KIPPER PÂTÉ

This rich, smoky fish pâté keeps well in the refrigerator. It is excellent as a sandwich filling or as a first course served with toast.

PREPARATION TIME: *20 minutes*

INGREDIENTS (*for 4*):
2 boned kippers
1 tablespoon heavy cream
6–8 tablespoons softened butter
1 tablespoon lemon juice
Cayenne pepper
¼ teaspoon ground mace

Place the kippers, head down, in a pitcher, pour in enough boiling water to cover all but the tails, and let stand for 5 minutes. Pour off the water and remove all skin and any small bones from the kippers. Set aside to cool.

Pound the kippers until smooth, then blend in the cream and butter, add the lemon juice, and season with cayenne and mace. (This may also be done in a food processor.) Store the pâté in an earthenware jar, in the refrigerator.

BANANAS À L'ARCHESTRATE

This delicious dessert is quick and easy enough to make as a snack, yet elegant enough for a dinner party. Its sweet topping of bananas and cognac is served warm.

PREPARATION TIME: *5 minutes*
COOKING TIME: *2 minutes*

INGREDIENTS (*for 6–8*):
6–8 firm, ripe bananas
2 tablespoons butter
½ cup dark brown sugar, packed
⅓ cup cognac
Ice cream

Peel and slice the bananas about ⅛–¼ inch thick. Heat the butter in a large skillet. Add the bananas, sprinkle the brown sugar over them, and sauté quickly, about 30 seconds, tossing them gently with a rubber spatula as they cook. Be careful not to mash the bananas.

Pour the warm cognac into a ladle, ignite the cognac, and pour it over the bananas. Serve immediately over ice cream. Vanilla is the best choice, although other flavors can be used as well.

BAKED TOMATOES

A little leftover meat and rice can be made into a savory filling for tomatoes. Serve them with boiled potatoes and green beans.

PREPARATION TIME: *20 minutes*
COOKING TIME: *35 minutes*

INGREDIENTS (*for 6*):
12 large firm tomatoes
1 finely chopped onion
1½ cups cooked minced meat
1 cup cooked rice
3–4 tablespoons butter
2–3 tablespoons stock
1 tablespoon light cream
2 teaspoons Worcestershire sauce
2 tablespoons chopped parsley
Pepper
2 ounces (½ cup) grated American cheese
1 tablespoon bread crumbs

Cut a thin slice from the top of each tomato and scoop out the pulp. Cook the onion in the butter until soft. Add the meat, rice, stock, cream, Worcestershire sauce, and parsley. Season with pepper and cook for 3 minutes.

Fill the tomatoes with the meat mixture and put them in a lightly buttered ovenproof dish. Sprinkle with the grated cheese and bread crumbs, and bake in a preheated oven at 375°F for 15–20 minutes.

RARE ROAST BEEF SALAD

Cold roast beef marinated in a piquant dressing is here transformed into a complete main course for a hot summer day.

PREPARATION TIME: *15 minutes*
CHILLING TIME: *1¼ hours*

INGREDIENTS (*for 4*):
½–¾ pound cold rare roast beef
½ cup olive oil
2 tablespoons wine vinegar
1 teaspoon dry English mustard
4 finely chopped anchovy fillets
2 teaspoons finely chopped capers
1 tablespoon chopped chives
3 tablespoons finely chopped parsley
Black pepper
8 cooked, thinly sliced potatoes
2 hard-cooked eggs

Cut the beef into matchstick strips. Blend the oil, vinegar, and mustard thoroughly. (Put aside half of this mixture for the sliced potatoes.) Add the anchovy fillets, capers, chives, and half of the parsley; season with pepper. Marinate* the meat in this dressing for at least 1 hour. Marinate the potatoes in a separate bowl in the remaining dressing.

Pile the meat salad in the center of a serving dish and garnish with chopped hard-cooked eggs. Arrange the potato slices around the edge of the dish. Sprinkle with the remaining parsley. Chill before serving.

Eating out of Doors

There is something irresistibly festive about eating out of doors, and with a little planning and imagination, a family picnic can become a feast to remember.

Containers for the food are important. Picnic chests, bowls, and flasks of plastic are available everywhere, and although insulated picnic bags and wide-necked vacuum bottles are more expensive, they do ensure crisp salads and chilled— or hot—drinks and soups.

Pack chilled or hot soups in vacuum bottles and take along a carton of cream to trickle into the soup, and a garnish of chopped lettuce, chervil, or watercress packed separately in a small plastic box. A mousse or pâté can be packed in the dishes in which they were prepared or cooked. A whole tongue, ham, spiced brisket of beef, or cold stuffed loin of pork is easiest carried whole, wrapped in foil, and carved at the picnic. Small pieces of chicken, lamb chops, sausages, and hard-cooked stuffed eggs can be packed in individual plastic bags.

Pour sauces and salad dressings into screw-top glass or plastic jars, closed tightly to prevent leakage. Pack washed salad ingredients separately in individual plastic bags so that guests can make their own salads. Rice salads and potato salads, both dressed while still hot with mayonnaise (p.303) and a sprinkling of chopped herbs, are best packed in rigid containers so that they cannot be mashed.

Thirst-quenching drinks are the most suitable for a picnic; well-chilled white or rosé wines and beer are preferable to heavy red wines. Take fruit juice, lemonade, or milk for the children, and plenty of iced coffee for everyone. Plastic bags of crushed ice are available at most drive-in markets and some service stations.

A hamper packed with cold pizza, and cream cheese and bacon pie. Bread crumb ice cream is packed with fresh pears.

Family Picnics

For a simple family picnic, foods that are easy to eat with the fingers cannot be surpassed.

A strongly flavored soup, such as mulligatawny (p.195), makes an excellent beginning and can be served hot or cold.

For the main course, choose from veal terrine de campagne (p.157), pizza (p.183), cream cheese and bacon pie (p.189), or pasties (p.147). Good alternatives would be club sandwiches (p.127). Bring along in separate containers sliced chicken, crisp bacon, lettuce, tomatoes, and mayonnaise. Let everyone make his own favorite sandwich. Salads might include lettuce, watercress, and tomatoes, with a separate French dressing (p.304).

Ice creams make ideal picnic desserts but need careful packing. Spoon crunchy bread crumb ice cream straight into a wide-necked vacuum bottle, and pack any spaces with sliced peaches or pears.

Bread Crumb Ice Cream

PREPARATION TIME: *20 minutes*
FREEZING TIME: *2–3 hours*

INGREDIENTS (*for* 6):
1¼ *cups heavy cream*
2 *tablespoons vanilla sugar*
3 *thick slices stale, crustless whole wheat bread*
½ *cup dark brown sugar*

An hour before preparing the ice cream turn the refrigerator to its coldest setting. Blend the cream and vanilla sugar* in a bowl and beat until fluffy. Spoon the mixture into shallow ice trays or a plastic container, cover with foil or the lid, and put into the freezing compartment of the refrigerator. When the mixture has begun to set around the edges, take it out of the freezer and stir the sides into the middle to prevent ice crystals forming. Repeat this twice during freezing.

Reduce the bread to fine crumbs and mix with the brown sugar. Spread the crumbs on a lightly oiled baking sheet and put this into the center of an oven preheated to 400°F. Leave until the sugar caramelizes and the crumbs are golden brown; stir them occasionally. Allow the mixture to cool, then thoroughly break up into crumbs again with a fork.

When the ice cream is nearly set, turn it into a chilled bowl, beat with an eggbeater and stir in the crumbs. Spoon the mixture into the ice trays and return them, covered, to the refrigerator. Freeze until firm, about 2 hours.

Children's Picnic Boxes

Children prefer simple food and often need to be catered to separately. Surprise boxes are a good idea to encourage finicky young eaters to join in the fun.

Pack an individual lunch or plastic refrigerator box for each child, labeling it with the owner's name. Fill it with a choice of savory and sweet items, all separately wrapped. These could include a small pasty (p.147), a hollowed-out soft roll filled with creamy scrambled egg or chopped hard-cooked egg and tomato. Pack a hard-cooked egg in waxed paper with an individual twist of salt. Fill a 3-inch piece of celery with cream cheese, or make a plain cheese sandwich interesting by cutting it out in the shape of the child's initial.

A gelatin dessert or rice pudding can be set in individual molds and wrapped in plastic wrap. A gingerbread figure decorated with colored frosting, or a frosted cupcake or cookie make attractive desserts. Include an apple, a plastic cup and spoon, and drinking straws wrapped in a paper napkin.

A Romantic Picnic for Two

A picnic can be a very romantic occasion deserving a careful choice of menu (see picture on p.192). Chilled carrot soup (p.196) is a perfect beginning, followed by Tarte Basquaise. Accompany the tart with lettuce, green onions, and tomato cups filled with horseradish mayonnaise (p.185).

Tarte Basquaise
PREPARATION TIME: *30 minutes*
COOKING TIME: *40 minutes*

INGREDIENTS (*for 2*):
½ recipe standard pastry (p.354)
1 small onion, finely chopped
1 clove garlic, finely chopped
1 tablespoon butter
1 egg
1 egg yolk
½ cup heavy cream
½ cup fresh white bread crumbs
4 peeled, seeded, and chopped
    tomatoes
1 diced red pepper
Salt and black pepper
Grated Parmesan cheese

Roll the prepared pastry out, ¼ inch thick. Use it to line a 6-inch flan ring set on a greased baking sheet. Cook the onion and garlic in the butter until soft, then set aside.

Beat the egg and the egg yolk with the cream and pour over the bread crumbs in a bowl. Stir in the tomatoes and red pepper, and season the mixture to taste with salt, pepper, and cheese.

Spoon the onion mixture over the pie crust and top with the egg and cream. Bake in the center of the oven at 375°F for 40 minutes.

For dessert, chilled fruit is ideal on a warm day. Cut a small melon in half and pile fresh raspberries into the two hollows. Wrap each half in plastic wrap and chill thoroughly before packing.

A Formal Picnic Party

This menu, composed for outdoor entertaining, features elegant but simple food. For a first course serve crab mousse (p.198) made in individual soufflé dishes, which can be wrapped in foil and stacked in the hamper. Veal stuffed with kidneys is easily carved and makes a good main course for a formal picnic party.

Veal Stuffed with Kidneys
PREPARATION TIME: *25 minutes*
COOKING TIME: *3 hours*

INGREDIENTS (*for 8*):
5-pound loin of veal
½ pound veal kidneys
Salt and black pepper
2 cloves garlic
2–3 sprigs marjoram or thyme
1 small onion
2 carrots
½ cup dry white wine
GARNISH:
Watercress

Ask the butcher to bone the loin and to give you the bones. Trim the fat from the kidneys* and remove the outer skin; snip out the cores with scissors. Lay the boned veal flat on a board and spread the kidneys over the cut side. Season with salt and freshly ground pepper. Peel and finely chop the garlic and herbs; sprinkle them evenly over the kidneys. Carefully roll up the meat and tie it securely with string at 1–2 inch intervals.

Rub the outside of the meat thoroughly with salt and pepper, place it in a roasting pan, and surround with the veal bones. Peel and coarsely chop the onion; scrape and finely chop the carrots. Arrange the vegetables around the meat. Heat the wine, with ½ cup of water, in a small pan and pour over the meat. Cover the pan with foil or a lid and cook in the center of the oven, preheated to 350°F, for 2¼ hours.

Turn the meat over halfway through cooking and add a little more wine and water if necessary. Remove the covering for the last 30 minutes to brown the meat.

Lift the meat from the pan and set it aside to cool. Pour the pan juices, bones, and vegetables into a pan and simmer over low heat for 45 minutes. Strain the liquid into a bowl and leave until cool. Let the liquid set to a jelly in the refrigerator before removing any fat that settles on the top.

Serve the stuffed veal with the cold chopped jelly, romaine lettuce, sliced tomatoes, cucumber in sour cream (p.206), and boiled new potatoes dressed in mayonnaise.

For dessert, chill strawberries and blueberries and pack in a wide-necked vacuum bottle, to be served with Coeur à la Crème (p.187). A selection of cheeses, with crackers and butter, completes the meal.

211

September

All-cheering Plenty, with her flowing horn,
Led yellow Autumn, wreath'd with nodding corn.

ROBERT BURNS

THIS MONTH'S RECIPES

*The harvest begins: Autumn's fruits and crops—pumpkins,
squash, apples, and corn—are at their most bountiful.*

Food in Season

After the carefree months of summer entertaining, the first chilly days of a changing season arouse a renewed interest in working in the kitchen. It is the time of the harvest, and markets are overflowing with fruit—mouth-watering grapes, honeydews, and pears, all abundant in September. The succulent honeydew, sliced and wrapped with smoky ham (p.215) makes a superb beginning for a rich meal, while pears flambéed with brandy (p.227) are a dramatic ending for one.

Apples fill the markets during the fall season and are the basis for a delicious pudding with almonds (p.227). Coconuts, used freshly grated in cakes, pies, and other desserts, have been scarce all summer, but are now becoming more plentiful.

Eggplants and squash are at their least expensive, and the markets are also well stocked with beans, beets, cabbage, peppers, sweet potatoes, and cauliflower. One of the simplest yet most elegant ways to prepare cauliflower is with buttered bread crumbs and hard-cooked egg yolks (p.224).

September is the last month of the year in which to take advantage of abundant and low-priced corn, nectarines, peaches, and plums. By October they will be in short supply.

Hearty soups are in order as the weather turns cooler. Two especially good ones are borscht (p.215) and Potage Paysanne (p.216).

At the fish market, lake trout, eels, and hard-shell crabs are readily available, and there are also large quantities of mackerel, red snapper, chub, lake herring, whitefish, yellow pike, soft-shell crabs, and sea scallops. For unusual seafood dishes, try Mackerel in Cider (p.217) and delicate Crab Puffs (p.217).

SUGGESTED MENUS

Spinach Ramekins
...
Baked Stuffed Shoulder of Veal
Zucchini Gratiné
...
Poires Flambées

Tarte Ricotto
...
Pescado a la Marina
Buttered Green Beans
Crisp Green Salad
...
Brandy-Apricot Trifle

Melon and Ham Gondolas
...
Teriyaki Chicken
Buttered Broccoli
Creamed Potatoes
...
Quiche Reine-Claude

Borscht
...
Wild Duck with Bigarade Sauce
Tomatoes with Green Peas
...
Hazelnut Gantois

Egg Cocktail
...
Beef Jardinière
Buttered Cabbage
...
Rice Pudding

Potage Paysanne
...
Épigrammes d'Agneau
French-Fried Cabbage
...
Apple and Almond Paradise Pudding

Paella Valenciana
Green Salad with Sauce Vinaigrette
...
Fruit Gâteau

Soups & First Courses

LAMB AND LEMON SOUP

This Greek soup is a thick and meaty broth, and almost a meal in itself.

PREPARATION TIME: *15 minutes*
COOKING TIME: *3¼ hours*

INGREDIENTS (*for 6*):
2 pounds neck of lamb, chopped
2 carrots
1–2 turnips
2 onions
2 leeks
1 stalk celery
1 sprig parsley
2 bay leaves
½ teaspoon dried oregano or thyme
½ teaspoon dried marjoram
¼ cup pearl barley or long grain rice
Salt and black pepper
Juice of 1 lemon
2 egg yolks
GARNISH:
1 lettuce heart

Trim as much fat as possible off the lamb. Put the meat into a large saucepan with 5 cups of water and bring to a boil. Meanwhile, wash and scrape the carrots and turnips and chop them coarsely; peel and coarsely chop the onions. Trim the leeks and wash them under cold running water. Wash the celery and chop this and the leeks coarsely.

Remove any scum from the broth. Add the vegetables to the lamb, together with the herbs and barley (if using rice, add this 1 hour later). Season with salt and freshly ground pepper. Cover the saucepan and simmer for 2–2½ hours, or until the meat comes away from the bones.

Remove the bay leaves and parsley and lift out the meat. Pick the meat off the bones while the soup continues to simmer. Chop up the lamb and return it to the pan.

Remove the broth from the heat and allow it to get cold (if possible, let it stand overnight). Lift off the fat that has solidified in a layer on top of the broth. Bring the soup back to a boil and, just before serving, beat the lemon juice and the egg yolks together in a small bowl. Mix in 3–4 tablespoons of the hot broth and add this mixture to the pan; heat the broth through without boiling, stirring occasionally.

Serve the soup sprinkled with finely shredded lettuce heart.

BORSCHT

There are numerous variations of this famous Russian soup, but beets and sour cream are traditional in every borscht, whether it is served hot or cold. It can be made with almost any kind of stock, including beef, chicken, or duck.

PREPARATION TIME: *25 minutes*
COOKING TIME: *1 hour 20 minutes*

INGREDIENTS (*for 6*):
1 pound uncooked beets
1 onion
1 leek
1 carrot
1 turnip
1 large potato
1 stalk celery
5 cups strong beef, chicken, or duck stock
1 bay leaf
1 tablespoon chopped parsley
Salt and black pepper
1 tablespoon tomato purée
1 teaspoon sugar
1 tablespoon lemon juice
½ cup sour cream
GARNISH:
3 tablespoons chopped mint, dill, or chives

Peel the beets, set aside one quarter of them, and dice the remainder finely. Peel and thinly slice the onion; trim the roots and coarse outer leaves from the leek, wash it thoroughly under cold running water, and chop it finely. Wash and peel the carrot and turnip and shred into very thin strips. Wash, peel, and dice the potato. Wash the celery and chop it finely.

Put the prepared vegetables in a large pan with the stock, bay leaf, parsley, and a good seasoning of salt and freshly ground pepper. Cover the pan with a lid and simmer the soup for 30 minutes. Mix together the tomato purée, sugar, and lemon juice in a small bowl and add to the soup. Continue cooking the soup over low heat, stirring occasionally, for a further 30 minutes or until the root vegetables are tender.

Ten minutes before serving, grate the reserved beets and add to the soup. Thin with a little more stock if necessary. Serve the soup piping hot with a dollop of sour cream and a sprinkling of chopped chives.

To serve the borscht cold (*borscht givrée*) chill the soup thoroughly before adding the sour cream. The soup can be puréed,* if preferred. Before serving, add a little more lemon juice. Pour the soup into individual bowls, and top with a swirl of sour cream. Finely chopped green onion, hard-cooked egg, and grated cucumber can also be sprinkled on the top as a garnish.

MELON AND HAM GONDOLAS

Sweet, ripe melon combines perfectly with Italian raw smoked ham, known as *prosciutto,* or with the Westphalian variety from Germany. Any type of well-ripened fig is also delicious with ham.

PREPARATION TIME: *12 minutes*

INGREDIENTS (*for 6*):
½ large ripe honeydew melon
6 wafer-thin slices smoked ham
Juice of 1 lemon
Black pepper
GARNISH:
Lemon wedges

Chill the melon thoroughly. Cut it into 6 long slices, scoop out the seeds, and cut the skin away. Place 1 piece of melon on each slice of ham and wrap the ham neatly around the melon. Sprinkle the fruit with lemon juice and pepper.

Serve each of the melon and ham gondolas garnished with a wedge of lemon.

SPINACH RAMEKINS

This unusual appetizer is a creamy pâté of spinach, sardines, and eggs. Serve it with plenty of *grissini* (breadsticks) or Melba toast (p.300).

PREPARATION TIME: *10–15 minutes*
CHILLING TIME: *30 minutes– 1 hour*

INGREDIENTS (*for.4*):
1 pound spinach
1 onion
½ teaspoon dried tarragon
1½ tablespoons finely chopped parsley
1 hard-cooked egg
4 sardines
2 tablespoons heavy cream
Salt and black pepper
GARNISH:
1 hard-cooked egg
4 anchovy fillets

Pull the spinach leaves off the stalks and wash in several changes of cold water to remove all traces of sand. Peel and finely chop the onion. Put the wet spinach in a large saucepan with the onion, tarragon, and parsley; cover with a lid. Cook over low heat for 7–10 minutes or until softened, then drain thoroughly.

Chop one hard-cooked egg and the boned sardines and blend with the spinach. Rub the mixture through a coarse sieve, or put in a blender and reduce it to a purée.* Stir in the cream and season to taste with salt and freshly ground pepper. Spoon the creamed spinach into individual ramekins or small serving dishes and chill in the refrigerator until the spinach has set.

For the garnish, separate the white and yolk of the hard-cooked egg; chop the white finely and sieve the yolk. Decorate each ramekin with alternate rows of the egg white and yolk. Split the anchovy fillets in half lengthwise and lay them on top in a crisscross pattern.

TARTE RICOTTO

Quick and easy to prepare, this can be made as one large pie and served cut into wedges. It is more attractive made in small tartlet molds and is equally good when served with cocktails or as a first course.

PREPARATION TIME: *15 minutes*
COOKING TIME: *15–20 minutes*

INGREDIENTS (*for 6*):
¾ recipe standard pastry (p.354)
½ pound cream cheese
Salt and black pepper
2 eggs
2 slices smoked salmon or ham
2 teaspoons grated lemon rind or chopped parsley
2 ounces Gruyère cheese
GARNISH:
Watercress
Black olives

Roll out the prepared pastry, ¼ inch thick, on a lightly floured surface. Line a greased 8-inch flan ring or 6 greased individual tartlet molds with the pastry.

Stir the cream cheese until smooth in a bowl, and season to taste with salt and freshly ground pepper. Beat the eggs lightly with a fork and gradually stir them into the cream cheese. Shred the smoked salmon or ham and add to the cream cheese, together with the grated lemon rind or chopped parsley. Spoon the cream mixture into the flan ring or individual tart shells and smooth it level with the edge of the pastry crust. Using a cheese slicer or a very sharp knife, cut the Gruyère cheese into thin slivers; lay them on top of the cream filling.

Bake the pie or tartlets in the center of a preheated oven at 400°F for 15–20 minutes, or until the cheese filling is well risen and the top of the pie is golden brown.

Serve the Tarte Ricotto as soon as it comes out of the oven. Garnish with several sprigs of watercress and whole black olives.

POTAGE PAYSANNE

This farmhouse vegetable soup makes a substantial meal. Select vegetables according to availability and choice—the quantities in the recipe are merely a guide. Peas, green beans, and watercress may be added after the soup comes to a boil.

PREPARATION TIME: *30 minutes*
COOKING TIME: *1 hour*

INGREDIENTS (*for 6*):
2–3 carrots
1–2 turnips
2–3 parsnips
1–2 leeks
½ small head of celery
1 large onion
6 mushrooms
2 slices bacon
½ pound tomatoes
4 tablespoons butter
2 tablespoons flour
½ cup milk
4 cups white stock
Salt and black pepper
Lemon juice
Mixed herbs (p.411)
GARNISH:
2 teaspoons chopped mint or parsley
Bread croûtons (p.300)

Wash and peel the carrots, turnips, and parsnips; dice them finely. Remove the roots and outer coarse leaves from the leeks, wash them thoroughly under cold running water, and chop coarsely. Wash the celery and slice the stalks finely; peel and coarsely chop the onion. Trim and thinly slice the mushrooms.*

Dice the bacon. Peel, seed, and coarsely chop the tomatoes.*

Melt the butter in a large heavy pan and sauté the bacon, onion, celery, and mushrooms over moderate heat until soft but not browned. Add the prepared carrots, turnips, parsnips, and leeks and sauté them lightly. Remove the pan from the heat and stir in enough flour to absorb the remaining fat. Gradually blend in the milk. Return the pan to the heat, stir in the hot stock, and bring the soup to a boil, stirring continuously. Add the tomatoes, stir well, and bring the soup to the simmering point.

If necessary, thin the soup with water or more milk. Season to taste with salt, freshly ground pepper, lemon juice, and a pinch of mixed dried herbs. Cover the pan with a lid and simmer the soup over very low heat until the root vegetables are tender (about 45 minutes).

Serve the soup hot, garnished with mint or parsley and crisp bread croûtons. Garlic bread* or a separate bowl of grated cheese would make the soup even more substantial.

Any leftover soup can be sieved or puréed in the blender, and thinned to taste with milk or tomato juice. Before serving, stir a little cream into each bowl and garnish as before.

Fish

CRAB PUFFS

These little crab-stuffed pastry puffs may be served hot or cold as a main course or buffet dish, allowing 2 per person. For a first course, 1 per person is sufficient.

PREPARATION TIME: *40 minutes*
COOKING TIME: *15 minutes*

INGREDIENTS (*for 4*):
¼ pound crabmeat
6 mushrooms
2 tablespoons unsalted butter
2 tablespoons chopped watercress
2–3 teaspoons flour
¼–½ cup light cream
1 tablespoon dry sherry
Salt and black pepper
1–2 teaspoons lemon juice
½ recipe puff pastry (p.363)
1 egg
GARNISH:
Lemon wedges
Watercress sprigs

Trim and thinly slice the mushrooms.* Melt the butter in a pan over low heat and sauté the mushrooms and flaked crabmeat for a few minutes. Mix in the chopped watercress. Remove the pan from the heat and stir in enough flour to absorb all the butter. Stir in the cream and return the pan to the heat, cooking gently for 4–5 minutes. Re-move from the heat, add the sherry, and season to taste with salt, freshly ground pepper, and lemon juice. Set aside to cool.

Roll out the puff pastry, on a lightly floured surface, to a rectangle 16 inches by 8 inches. Cut the pastry into 8 4-inch squares with a sharp knife. Put 2 teaspoons of the crab mixture into the center of each square. Brush the pastry edges with a little beaten egg, and fold each square into a triangle. Press the edges firmly together, completely sealing in the filling. Crimp the edges with a fork and brush the top of each puff with beaten egg. Make 2 or 3 slits in the top of each puff to allow the steam to escape.

Place the puffs on a damp baking sheet. Bake just above the center of a preheated oven at 450°F for 10–15 minutes, or until the puffs have risen and are golden brown.

Serve the crab puffs hot or cold, garnished with lemon wedges and sprigs of watercress. A tossed green salad would be a suitable side dish for a main course.

MACKEREL IN CIDER

Because mackerel is a very oily fish, it deteriorates quickly; it should be cooked as soon as possible after purchase. The recipe given here comes from Somerset, England.

PREPARATION TIME: *20 minutes*
COOKING TIME: *35 minutes*

INGREDIENTS (*for 4*):
4 mackerel
Salt and black pepper
2 eating apples
1 small onion
½ pound Cheddar cheese
4–6 tablespoons melted butter
1 cup fresh white bread crumbs
3–4 tablespoons dry cider or dry white wine
GARNISH:
Lemon wedges
Freshly chopped parsley

Have the fish market cut off the heads, slit the fish down the belly, and gut the mackerel. Clean thoroughly in cold water. The backbones may be removed from the mackerel, but this is not essential. Dry the mackerel thoroughly on paper towels and season them lightly with salt and pepper.

Peel and coarsely grate the apples, onion, and about half of the cheese. Melt the butter in a small pan over low heat. Mix the grated apple, onion, cheese, and the bread crumbs together in a bowl and bind with 1 tablespoon of the melted butter. Stuff the mackerel with this mixture and secure the opening of each with 2 or 3 wooden skewers.

Grate the remaining cheese finely. Place the mackerel side by side in an ovenproof dish and sprinkle 1 tablespoon of grated cheese over each. Pour over the remaining melted butter and sufficient cider or wine to cover the bottom of the dish. Lay a piece of buttered foil or waxed paper loosely over the dish and place in the center of a preheated oven at 350°F. Bake for 25–35 minutes, or until the mackerel are cooked through and golden brown.

Serve the mackerel straight from the dish, garnished with lemon wedges and parsley.

Potatoes in their jackets make a perfect addition to this dish.

PESCADO A LA MARINA

The South Americans, even more than the French, are great believers in marinating meat and fish before cooking them. The marinade, made with olive oil, lemon juice, onion, and garlic, imparts an unusual flavor to fish fillets. It is then cooked with white wine and egg yolks to make the sauce.

PREPARATION TIME: *20 minutes*
MARINATING TIME: *1 hour*
COOKING TIME: *15 minutes*

INGREDIENTS (*for 4*):
1½-pound haddock or cod fillet
1 egg
1½–2 cups fresh white bread crumbs
Oil for sautéing
MARINADE:
4 tablespoons olive oil
2 tablespoons lemon juice
1 small onion
1 clove garlic
1–2 bay leaves
1 teaspoon salt
Black pepper and ground nutmeg
MARINA SAUCE:
½ cup dry white wine
2 egg yolks
GARNISH:
1 tablespoon finely chopped parsley

Make the marinade* first: Blend to-gether the olive oil and lemon juice. Peel and finely chop the onion and garlic, and add to the oil and lemon mixture, together with the bay leaves, salt, freshly ground pepper, and a pinch of nutmeg.

Wash the fish fillet and divide it into 4 or 6 pieces. Place them in a shallow dish and pour the prepared marinade over them. Leave to marinate for about 1 hour, turning the fish from time to time.

Lift out the fish, setting the marinade aside. Dry the fillets thoroughly on paper towels. Lightly beat the egg and brush it over the fish before coating with bread crumbs. Press the crumbs well in and shake off any surplus. Leave the coating to harden while making the sauce.

Bring the marinade to a boil, then strain it through a fine sieve into a bowl. Add the wine. Beat the egg yolks together in a separate bowl and gradually stir in the wine and marinade. Place the bowl over a saucepan of gently simmering water and stir continuously with a wooden spoon until the sauce thickens sufficiently to coat the back of the spoon. If the sauce shows signs of curdling, add a tablespoon of cold water and immediately remove the bowl from the heat.

Heat the oil in a heavy-bottomed pan and sauté the fish until golden brown on both sides, turning once. Drain on paper towels.

Serve the fish hot, sprinkled with parsley. Serve the marina sauce separately and offer creamed potatoes and green beans. The fillets can also be served cold with a tartare sauce (p.303) and a crisp green salad with sauce vinaigrette (p.304).

217

MOULES À LA POULETTE

In France the mussels in this classic dish, made with white wine and cream, are served in their half shells and eaten with the fingers. The sauce is mopped up with bread. Alternatively, remove the mussels entirely from the shells and serve them in the sauce as a soup.

PREPARATION TIME: *30 minutes*
COOKING TIME: *10 minutes*

INGREDIENTS (*for 4–6*):
4 quarts mussels
1 bay leaf
1 parsley sprig
1 shallot
6 black peppercorns
2 cups dry white wine
½ cup heavy cream
2 egg yolks
2 tablespoons chopped parsley
Black pepper
Lemon juice

Clean the mussels* thoroughly, discarding any with broken or open shells. Scrape away all grit and remove the beards (the tough, hairlike filaments that protrude from between the two shells). Put the mussels in a large, heavy saucepan with the bay leaf, parsley, peeled and finely chopped shallot, and the peppercorns. Pour in the white wine, cover the pan with a tight-fitting lid, and cook the mussels over high heat just until the shells open.

As the shells open, remove the mussels from the pan, throw away the empty top halves, and place the mussels in their half shells in a warmed casserole. Cover them with a dish towel to prevent them from drying out and to keep them warm. Strain the warm cooking liquid through cheesecloth.

Mix the cream and egg yolks to-gether in a bowl and blend in a few tablespoons of the mussel liquid. Add to the remaining liquid, together with the chopped parsley. Season to taste with freshly ground pepper and lemon juice. Reheat the liquid, without boiling, until it has thickened slightly.

Serve the mussels in individual deep soup plates, with the sauce poured over them. Set a finger bowl with a slice of lemon by each plate. Offer plenty of crusty bread and provide an extra bowl or plates for the empty mussel shells.

Meat

BAKED STUFFED SHOULDER OF VEAL

Braising veal rather than roasting it preserves the juices and combines them with the stock to make a very good gravy. Make the stock the day before, if possible, since it takes about 3 hours to cook.

PREPARATION TIME: *35 minutes*
COOKING TIME: *1¾ hours*

INGREDIENTS (*for 6*):

3 pounds boned shoulder of veal
4 tablespoons butter
½ cup dry white wine
½–1 cup stock
STOCK:
1 large onion
2 carrots
1 stalk celery
Bouquet garni (p.410)
STUFFING:
2 cups stock

½ cup long grain rice
Pinch saffron
1 bunch watercress
½ cup shelled walnuts
1 lemon
4 slices bacon
Salt and freshly ground black
* pepper*
1 egg
GARNISH:
Watercress

Ask the butcher to bone the shoulder of veal and to chop the bones. Put the bones, together with the cleaned and chopped stock vegetables, in a saucepan and cover with cold water. Add the bouquet garni and season well with salt and black pepper. Cook this stock for about 3 hours. Strain and set aside.

With a sharp knife, open the cavities in the meat to make pockets for the stuffing. Cook the rice, with the saffron, in 2 cups of the reserved veal stock for 12–14 minutes or until tender.

Wash and chop the watercress, chop the walnuts finely, and grate the rind from the lemon. Cook the bacon in a little of the butter over low heat until crisp. Remove the bacon from the pan; drain and chop it coarsely.

Put the drained rice in a mixing bowl and add the bacon fat from the pan, the bacon, watercress, walnuts, and lemon rind. Season to taste with salt and pepper. Bind the stuffing with the lightly beaten egg.

Spread the stuffing evenly into the pockets of the veal. Roll up the meat and tie with string.

Brown the veal briskly in the remaining butter in a roasting pan. Pour over the wine and roast the veal in the center of a preheated oven at 350°F for about 1½ hours. Baste* frequently with the wine, adding a little stock if necessary.

Put the veal on a warmed serving dish and remove the string. Add ½ cup of stock to the roasting pan. Boil over high heat until the liquid is light brown and has reduced* by about half. Pour the gravy into a warm sauceboat.

Serve the sliced veal garnished with sprigs of watercress. Roast potatoes go well with the meat; so does zucchini gratiné (p.226).

MEAT ROLL EN CROÛTE

Golden crisp puff pastry is often used to make a covering for such expensive dishes as fillet of beef, boned poultry, or salmon. However, the same delicious crust can be used to encase ground meats.

PREPARATION TIME: *25 minutes*
COOKING TIME: *1¾ hours*

INGREDIENTS (*for 6*):

2 pounds lean ground pork
1 onion
1 clove garlic
2 tablespoons chopped parsley
Salt and black pepper
2 teaspoons Worcestershire sauce

3 eggs
¼ pound Bel Paese or Gouda cheese
18 mushrooms
½ recipe puff pastry (p.363)
½ cup stock or bouillon
GARNISH:
Watercress

Peel and finely chop the onion and crush the garlic. Mix together the pork, onion, garlic, and parsley in a large bowl; season to taste with salt and freshly ground pepper. Beat the Worcestershire sauce with 2 of the eggs and stir into the meat mixture. Butter a large loaf pan thoroughly and press in half the meat mixture in an even layer. Dice the cheese finely, trim and chop the mushrooms,* and put both on top of the meat; cover with the remaining pork, leveling off the surface smoothly. Cover the pan with buttered foil or waxed paper.

Place the pan in a roasting pan containing about ½ inch of water, and bake in the center of a preheated oven at 375°F for 1¼ hours. Remove the pan from the oven. Carefully pour off the liquid around the meat in the pan and set it aside for gravy. Leave the meat in the pan to cool and shrink slightly.

Raise the oven heat to 450°F. Roll out the puff pastry on a lightly floured surface to a thin rectangle measuring roughly 12 inches by 8 inches. Turn the meat out of the pan and place it in the center of the pastry; wrap the pastry over and around the meat, sealing the edges with lightly beaten egg.

Put the pastry-wrapped meat loaf, seam underneath, on a damp baking sheet, and brush the top with beaten egg. Decorate the loaf with the pastry trimmings, and cut 2 or 3 slits in the pastry for the steam to escape. Bake in the oven for 20–25 minutes, or until the pastry is well risen and golden brown.

Skim the fat from the reserved gravy and put it, with the stock, in a small saucepan. Boil rapidly until it has reduced* slightly. Season to taste and pour into a warm sauceboat.

Serve the crusty meat roll hot, garnished with sprigs of watercress and surrounded with halved broiled tomatoes, sautéed mushroom caps, and boiled buttered potatoes.

HUNGARIAN GOULASH

This internationally famous stew is usually made from beef, though pork, veal, or chicken may also be used. Different regions of Hungary have their own favorite goulash recipes. Some use fresh tomatoes, others caraway seeds, garlic, or marjoram. But whatever else goes into a goulash, it always contains paprika.

PREPARATION TIME: *35 minutes*
COOKING TIME: *about 2 hours*

INGREDIENTS (*for 4*):
1¼ pounds chuck steak
1 pound onions
4 tablespoons vegetable oil
3¾ cups beef stock or water
Salt
4 tablespoons tomato purée
3–4 teaspoons paprika
2 teaspoons sugar
2 tablespoons flour
½ cup sour cream

Cut the meat into 1½-inch cubes. Peel and thinly slice the onions. Add the oil to a deep, heavy-bottomed skillet and sauté the meat and onions over moderate heat until the onions are golden. Add the hot stock, season with salt, and bring to simmering point over medium heat.

Meanwhile, blend the tomato purée, paprika, sugar, and flour in a bowl until smooth. Stir in a few tablespoons of the hot stew liquid.

Remove the pan with the onions and meat from the heat and stir in the tomato purée mixture, blending thoroughly. Return to the heat and bring back to a simmer. Cover and cook the stew over gentle heat for 2 hours or until the meat is tender. Stir occasionally.

Before serving, skim the fat, stir in the sour cream, and adjust seasoning.

ROAST PORK WITH APPLE AND NUT STUFFING

Shoulder of pork is a good cut for roasting because the meat is tender. When boned and stuffed it is easily carved even by the unskilled.

PREPARATION TIME: *20 minutes*
COOKING TIME: *2 hours*

INGREDIENTS (*for 6*):
3½-pound shoulder of pork, boned
1 small onion
½ cup cashew nuts or peanuts
2 thick slices white crustless bread
1 cooking apple
1 stalk celery
1 tablespoon chopped parsley
2 tablespoons butter
Salt and black pepper
½ teaspoon dried summer savory
Lemon juice
2–3 tablespoons vegetable oil
½ cup dry white wine

Peel and finely chop the onion and coarsely chop the nuts. Dice the crustless bread; peel, core, and dice the apple. Wash and finely chop the celery and the parsley.

Melt the butter in a small pan over moderate heat and sauté the onion and nuts until they are just turning color. Add the bread, apple, celery, and parsley to the onion and nuts, and continue cooking until the apple has softened. Season to taste with salt, pepper, summer savory, and lemon juice.

Open up the pocket in the pork and spread the stuffing evenly. Roll up and tie securely with string at regular intervals.

Place the pork in an oiled roasting pan; brush with oil and sprinkle with salt. Roast for 20–30 minutes above the center of an oven preheated to 400°F. Move to a shelf just

below the center and reduce the temperature to 350°F. Cook for a further 1½ hours, or until the juice comes out amber-colored when a skewer is pushed into the meat.

Put the pork on a serving plate and keep it warm. Leave the residue in the roasting pan to settle, then carefully skim or pour off the fat. Add the wine to the pan juices and bring to a boil over moderate heat, scraping in all the residue. When the gravy has colored, season to taste and pour it into a warm sauceboat.

A purée of potatoes, buttered cabbage, or green beans are ideal with this tasty pork roast.

ÉPIGRAMMES D'AGNEAU

This classic French recipe is an unusual way of cooking breast of lamb. It is also an economical dish, for the stock can be used as the basis for a lamb and lemon soup (p.215). The intriguing title is credited to an 18th-century marquise. Unaware of the meaning of the word *épigramme*, overheard in a conversation, she ordered her chef to produce a dish of épigrammes! This is the result.

PREPARATION TIME: *30 minutes*
COOKING TIME: *2 hours*
STANDING TIME: *3 hours*

INGREDIENTS (*for 4–6*):
*2 breasts of lamb, unboned and
    weighing about 3 pounds
1 onion
2 leeks
1–2 stalks celery
3–4 carrots
Bouquet garni (p.410)
2 teaspoons salt
6 peppercorns
1 large egg
¾–1 cup dry white bread crumbs
4 tablespoons unsalted butter
2 tablespoons corn oil*
GARNISH:
*Watercress sprigs
Lemon wedges*

Peel and slice the onion. Cut the roots and coarse outer leaves from the leeks, wash thoroughly under cold running water, and chop them coarsely. Wash the celery and peel the carrots; chop both coarsely.

Trim as much fat as possible from the breasts of lamb and put them in a large pan with the prepared vegetables, the bouquet garni, salt, and peppercorns. Cover with cold water and bring to a boil. Remove any scum from the surface, then cover the pan with a lid and simmer gently for 1½ hours. Remove the meat from the pan, allow to cool slightly, then carefully pull out and discard all the bones. Strain the cooking liquid through a fine sieve and keep it to use as the basis for a soup.

Lay the meat flat between two boards and place a heavy weight on top. Leave until quite cold. Trim off any remaining fat and cut the meat into 2-inch squares. Dip the meat in the lightly beaten egg and coat evenly with the bread crumbs. Set the meat aside until the coating has hardened.

Heat the butter and oil in a heavy-bottomed pan and sauté the meat squares until crisp and golden on both sides (about 20 minutes). Drain on paper towels.

Serve the épigrammes on a warmed dish, garnished with sprigs of watercress and lemon wedges. Sautéed potatoes,* broccoli spears, and a Béarnaise sauce (p.303) or tartare sauce (p.303) would go well with the épigrammes.

CHATEAUBRIAND

This famous dish is named after the 18th-century French writer Chateaubriand. Because it is a double fillet steak cut from the thick end of the fillet of beef, it serves at least two persons.

PREPARATION TIME: *5 minutes*
COOKING TIME: *8–10 minutes*

INGREDIENTS (*for 2*):
*12–14 ounce chateaubriand
1 tablespoon melted butter
Black pepper*
GARNISH:
*Watercress
Maître d'hôtel butter (p.338)*

Trim the chateaubriand and if necessary flatten it slightly—it should be 1½–2 inches thick. Brush one side with melted butter and season with freshly ground pepper. Do not add salt, as this will extract the juices.

Put the steak, buttered and seasoned side up, under a hot broiler and cook 4–5 minutes under high heat to brown the surface and seal in the juices. Turn the steak over, brush with the remaining melted butter, and season with pepper. Turn the heat down and broil the steak for a further 4–5 minutes, turning it once only. The steak should be cooked through but remain pink inside.

Lift the steak onto a board and carve it, at a slight angle, into 6 even slices. Remove the sliced steak, in one movement, to a warmed serving dish and garnish with sprigs of watercress and slices of maître d'hôtel butter.

Traditionally, a chateaubriand is served with château potatoes (p.333) and a Béarnaise sauce (p.303). A tossed green salad makes an excellent side dish.

HAM SLICES IN MADEIRA SAUCE

Ham slices with a flavorful Madeira sauce make an appetizing dish.

PREPARATION TIME: *20 minutes*
COOKING TIME: *20–25 minutes*

INGREDIENTS (*for 4*):
*4 ham slices, each ½–¾ inch thick
12–18 mushrooms
1 large onion
4 large tomatoes
4 tablespoons butter
¼ teaspoon dried basil
¼ teaspoon dried marjoram
¼ cup Madeira or sweet sherry
½ cup ham stock or bouillon
Salt and black pepper
1 teaspoon sugar
Lemon juice*

Slash the fat on the ham slices at 1-inch intervals to prevent them from curling while cooking. Wipe the mushrooms; remove the stalks and chop them coarsely, leaving the caps whole. Peel and thinly slice the onion; peel and seed the tomatoes* and chop them coarsely.

Heat the butter in a heavy-bottomed pan over moderate heat until it stops bubbling. Sauté the ham slowly until golden on both sides, about 8 minutes, turning several times. Remove the ham from the pan and keep it warm in the oven.

Sauté the onion and mushroom caps and stalks lightly in the pan juices until softened; add the tomatoes, basil, and marjoram. Cover the pan with a lid or foil and simmer for about 5 minutes, shaking the pan from time to time.

Return the ham to the pan and add the Madeira or sherry, with enough stock to almost cover the meat. Season to taste with salt, freshly ground pepper, sugar, and lemon juice. Cover and continue cooking over low heat for 10 minutes or until the ham is tender.

Arrange the slices on a hot serving dish with the sauce poured over them. Baby Brussels sprouts, tossed in butter, and creamed potatoes or fluffy boiled rice would be suitable side dishes.

SWEET AND SOUR PORK CHOPS

These flavorful chops take only 5 minutes to prepare for the oven.

PREPARATION TIME: *5 minutes*
COOKING TIME: *1½ hours*

INGREDIENTS (*for 6*):
*6 pork loin chops, 1 inch thick
Salt and pepper
1 tablespoon Dijon mustard
1 cup water
½ cup ketchup or chili sauce
3 tablespoons dark brown sugar
4 tablespoons white vinegar
1 tablespoon Worcestershire sauce*

Preheat oven to 350°F. Salt and pepper the chops. Place them in 1 layer in a large baking dish. Mix the remaining ingredients and pour over the chops. Bake uncovered 1½ hours. Do not baste. Skim the fat from the sauce. Serve with mashed potatoes and a watercress salad.

BEEF JARDINIÈRE

Some cuts of beef, such as top round, bottom round, and brisket, are not tender enough to oven-roast successfully. They do, however, make excellent pot roasts, cooked in liquid with fresh vegetables (*jardinière*). Top and bottom round are lean cuts, but brisket of beef usually needs some of the fat trimmed off before being rolled and tied.

PREPARATION TIME: *25 minutes*
COOKING TIME: *2½–3 hours*

INGREDIENTS (*for 6*):

3 pounds rolled top or bottom round
    or brisket of beef
8 small onions
½ pound small carrots
2 young turnips
4 tablespoons beef drippings
½ cup dry red wine

2 bay leaves
½ teaspoon mixed herbs (p.411)
6 peppercorns
1 teaspoon salt
½ pound young green beans or fresh
    peas
1 pound potatoes (optional)

Peel the onions, leaving them whole. Scrape or peel the carrots, and peel and quarter the turnips. Melt the drippings over high heat in a large heavy pan or flameproof casserole. Brown the meat quickly on all sides in the fat to seal in the juices. Add the onions and sauté until golden. Put the carrots, turnips, and wine into the pan, together with the bay leaves, mixed herbs, peppercorns, and the teaspoon of salt.

Cover the pan with a close-fitting lid or foil and simmer over low heat on top of the stove or in the center of an oven preheated to 300°F for 2½–3 hours or until the meat is tender. If the liquid evaporates during cooking, add a little beef stock or water.

Trim the beans and cut them into 1-inch pieces (or shell the peas). Cook them in lightly salted boiling water for 10 minutes or until just tender.

Remove the meat from the pan, carve it, and arrange the slices on a hot serving dish. Surround the meat with the vegetables and garnish with the beans. Remove the bay leaves from the pan juices; skim off the fat or soak it off the surface with paper towels. Season the gravy to taste with salt and freshly ground pepper and pour it into a warm sauceboat.

Potatoes may be added to the meat for the last hour of cooking or served separately.

CHINESE PANCAKES

Deep-fried pancake, or crêpe, rolls with a savory filling are found on almost every Chinese menu. There are many fillings—this one contains pork and shrimp—but bean sprouts are an essential ingredient.

PREPARATION TIME: *45 minutes*
COOKING TIME: *15 minutes*

INGREDIENTS (*for 4*):

8 thin crêpes (p.343)
1 scallion
1 stalk celery
6 button mushrooms
6–8 canned water chestnuts
½ cup fresh or canned bean sprouts
½ cup chopped cooked lean pork
½ cup chopped cooked shrimp
1 tablespoon vegetable oil
2 teaspoons soy sauce
1 tablespoon dry sherry
2 teaspoons cornstarch
2 tablespoons chestnut liquid
1 egg
Oil for deep-frying

Trim the root tips and the tops of the leaves from the scallion, leaving on it most of the green; chop the scallion finely. Wash the celery, trim the mushrooms,* and chop both finely. Thinly slice the water chestnuts. If fresh bean sprouts are used, trim any damaged ends from the sprouts and blanch* in boiling water for 5 minutes. Drain the sprouts well and chop coarsely.

Make 8 very thin crêpes and pile them on top of each other, between sheets of waxed paper, to keep them soft and pliable while preparing the filling.

Heat the vegetable oil in a skillet over low heat and stir-fry the scallion, celery, and mushrooms until soft. Add the pork and shrimp and stir-fry lightly. Stir in the water chestnuts, bean sprouts, soy sauce, and sherry.

Blend the cornstarch to a smooth paste with the chestnut liquid in a small bowl, and stir this mixture into the pan. Continue cooking, stirring thoroughly, for 3–5 minutes, or until the cornstarch is cooked and all the ingredients are well glazed.

Spoon equal portions of the filling in the center of each crêpe. Brush the edges with lightly beaten egg and fold two sides of each crêpe over the filling. Fold the opposite sides over to make a small neat package and seal the edges with beaten egg. Turn the crêpes upside down to firm the seams, and set them aside for 10–15 minutes.

Heat the frying oil,* with the frying basket in the pan, to 375°F and fry the crêpe packages, 2 or 3 at a time, until they are crisp and golden. As each batch is finished, lift the crêpes carefully onto paper towels to drain.

Keep the crêpes hot while frying the next batch. Serve at once, with boiled rice and a crisp lettuce and celery salad (p.64).

Poultry & Game

WILD DUCK WITH BIGARADE SAUCE

Wild duck (mallard or teal) has less fat than the domestic variety, but a stuffing of fresh oranges imparts both moisture and flavor. The rich sauce is traditionally made with bitter oranges (bigarade oranges), but a good variation can be achieved by using sweet oranges sharpened with a little lemon juice.

PREPARATION TIME: *25 minutes*
COOKING TIME: *45–55 minutes*

INGREDIENTS (*for 4*):
1 large or 2 small wild ducks
1–2 oranges
Poultry drippings or cooking fat
Bouquet garni (p.410)
Salt and black pepper
BIGARADE SAUCE:
1 large onion
1 stalk celery
6 small mushrooms
2 slices bacon
¼ pound carrots
2 small or 1 large orange
1 small or ½ large lemon
4 tablespoons drippings
2–2½ tablespoons flour
½ cup red wine
½ cup tomato juice
½ cup giblet stock
½ teaspoon dried mixed herbs
  (p.411)
Salt and black pepper
4 teaspoons red currant jelly
¼ cup port

When buying the duck, ask for the neck and giblets. Wipe the duck inside and out with a clean damp cloth. Peel and quarter the orange and put it inside the duck. Spread the duck breast with drippings or fat and place the bird in a greased roasting pan. Cover the pan with foil and roast 45 minutes or longer, according to size, just above the center of an oven preheated to 400°F. The duck is cooked when a skewer inserted in the thigh lets out colorless juices. Remove the foil from the duck after 30 minutes' roasting.

While the duck is cooking, chop the liver coarsely and set it aside. Put the neck and giblets in a pan with 1¼ cups of water, the bouquet garni, and a seasoning of salt and freshly ground pepper. Cover the pan with a tight-fitting lid and simmer the stock for 15–20 minutes.

For the sauce, peel and finely chop the onion, wash and chop the celery, and trim the mushrooms* before slicing them. Chop the bacon finely.

Scrape or peel the carrots and chop them finely. Grate the rind from the orange and lemon, squeeze the juices, and set both aside. Melt the drippings in a heavy-bottomed pan and sauté the onion, celery, mushrooms, and bacon until soft. Add the carrots to the pan and continue cooking over medium heat until the onion begins to color.

Stir in enough flour to absorb all the fat and cook, stirring continuously, until the mixture is a pale caramel color. Remove the pan from the heat and gradually blend in the wine, tomato juice, duck liver, and ½ cup of strained giblet stock. Stir until smooth, then return the pan to the heat and bring the sauce slowly to a boil, stirring all the time. Add the mixed herbs and salt and pepper to taste; blend in the orange and lemon rind and juices.

Cover the pan with a lid and simmer the sauce over low heat for about 30 minutes or until the vegetables are tender. If necessary, thin the sauce with more giblet stock.

When the duck is cooked, lift it carefully from the roasting pan tail downward so that the orange juice

TERIYAKI CHICKEN

PREPARATION TIME: *2½ hours*
COOKING TIME: *25–35 minutes*

INGREDIENTS (*for 4*):
1 3–3½ pound chicken, split or cut
  into serving pieces
¼ cup sake or sherry
¼ cup oil
¼ cup soy sauce
1 clove garlic, crushed
1 teaspoon ground ginger
1–1½ tablespoons sesame seeds

This poultry dish, inspired by the Orient, blends soy sauce with garlic and spices. A sesame-seed coating makes it particularly delicious.

Mix the sake or sherry, oil, soy sauce, garlic, and ginger. Pour over the chicken and marinate for 2 hours. Turn the chicken over occasionally during this period to keep the pieces well coated with the marinade.

Broil 5–6 inches from the flame, basting frequently with the marinade and turning the chicken every 5–10 minutes. When almost done, dip each piece of chicken in the marinade, roll thoroughly in sesame seeds, and return to the broiler to brown. Watch the chicken carefully to make sure that the sesame seeds do not burn.

Rice & Pasta

runs back into the pan. Put the duck on a serving dish and keep it warm. Pour the fat slowly from the pan and add enough giblet stock to cover the bottom of the pan. Boil rapidly on top of the stove, scraping in all the brown residue from the bottom and sides of the pan. Cook until the liquid is lightly colored, then stir it into the bigarade sauce. Stir in the red currant jelly and port, and continue cooking over low heat until the jelly has dissolved. Adjust seasoning to taste.

Carve the duck and arrange the slices on a warm serving dish; spoon over a little of the sauce and serve the remainder in a sauceboat. A border of duchesse potatoes (p.333) can be piped* around the duck, and fresh young Brussels sprouts would also be a good accompaniment.

RABBIT SAUTÉED WITH TARRAGON

In some sections of the country young rabbits are available frozen. They are cut up, ready to cook, and are surprisingly good. A chicken of comparable size may be substituted for the rabbit in this recipe, but it will take less time to cook.

PREPARATION TIME: *10 minutes*
COOKING TIME: *¾–1 hour*

INGREDIENTS (*for 4–6*):
1 young rabbit, 3–3½ pounds, or 1 frozen rabbit
½ cup flour
1 teaspoon salt
1½ teaspoons dried tarragon
½ teaspoon freshly ground black pepper
4 tablespoons butter
4 tablespoons vegetable oil
¾–1 cup dry white wine
¼ cup chopped parsley

Ask the butcher to cut the rabbit into 12 serving pieces. If the rabbit is frozen, thaw the cut-up pieces completely before cooking.

Place the flour, salt, dried tarragon, and pepper in a plastic bag. Add a few of the pieces of rabbit at a time and shake well. Remove the pieces to a plate and let them stand at room temperature for 30 minutes.

In a large skillet melt the butter, add the vegetable oil, and sauté a few pieces of the rabbit at a time over medium heat, turning carefully with tongs. When the pieces are nicely browned, remove them to a plate and keep them warm. Then sauté the remaining pieces.

Return all of the rabbit to the skillet, add ½ cup of the wine, cover tightly, and reduce the heat to a simmer. Cook the rabbit over low heat for 15 minutes.

Remove the cover, turn the pieces, cover tightly, and simmer 30–45 minutes until tender. Remove the rabbit to a heated platter.

Add the remaining wine to the skillet and increase the heat. Add additional tarragon to taste and the chopped parsley. Bring to a boil, shake the skillet well, and pour the sauce over the rabbit. Serve with crisp sautéed potatoes and a lettuce and tomato salad.

PAELLA VALENCIANA

Probably the most famous of all Spanish dishes, paella has many local variations. All, however, contain the basic ingredients of chicken, onion, and saffron-flavored rice. In Spain paella is cooked in and served straight from a large two-handled iron pan (*paella*) from which the dish takes its name.

PREPARATION TIME: *1 hour*
COOKING TIME: *1 hour*

INGREDIENTS (*for 6*):
1 chicken, about 2½ pounds
3 parsley sprigs
1 bay leaf
1 sprig marjoram
Salt and black pepper
½ pound ripe tomatoes
1–2 red or green peppers
½ pound peas or green beans
1 14-ounce can artichoke hearts (optional)
1 pint mussels
1 onion
4 tablespoons olive oil
1½ cups long grain rice
½ pound large shelled shrimp
¼ pound chorizo sausage, cooked
Powdered saffron
GARNISH:
6 large unshelled shrimp
6 lemon wedges

Cut the legs and wings off the chicken before severing the whole breast section from the lower carcass. Divide the breast section in half lengthwise along the breast bone. Leave the flesh on the bone to prevent shrinkage during cooking.

Put the remaining carcass and the giblets in a large pan, add the parsley, bay leaf, marjoram, and enough cold water to cover. Season thoroughly with salt and freshly ground pepper.

Bring the stock to a boil, then cover with a lid and simmer for about 30 minutes. Strain the stock through a fine sieve and set aside.

While the stock is cooking, prepare the vegetables and shellfish. Peel and seed the tomatoes* and chop them coarsely. Wash the peppers, cut off the stalk bases, remove the seeds, and cut the flesh into narrow slices or strips. Shell the peas or trim the green beans and cut into 2-inch lengths. Drain and halve the artichokes if used. Clean the mussels,* and peel and finely slice the onion.

Heat the oil in a paella dish or a large, heavy-bottomed pan over moderate heat. Sauté the chicken pieces until golden on both sides; remove from the pan and divide each into smaller pieces. Sauté the onion in the oil, stirring constantly, until onion becomes transparent, then add the rice and sauté until it is a pale golden color. Return the chicken pieces to the pan, together with the prepared vegetables, the mussels, and the large shelled shrimp.

Pour over enough chicken stock to cover all the ingredients. Cover with foil or a lid and simmer for 20 minutes or until the stock is absorbed and the rice is just tender. Stir occasionally while cooking and add more stock, if necessary, until the rice is cooked but not mushy.

Lift the mussels from the pan and keep them warm. Slice the sausage thinly and add to the mixture in the pan, together with the artichokes and a pinch of saffron—just enough to give the rice a golden color. Stir thoroughly and season to taste with salt and freshly ground pepper.

Remove the top shells from the mussels. Arrange the bottom shells with the mussels on top of the rice.

Serve the paella in the pan, garnished with the unshelled shrimp and wedges of lemon. A bowl of green salad, dressed with a sauce vinaigrette (p.304), can be served as a side dish, but the paella is a substantial meal in itself.

Vegetables

LUMACHINE CON COZZE

This is an Italian dish of snail-shaped egg pasta shells (*lumachine*) and mussels. Young fresh mussels are best, but canned mussels, without their brine, can be used instead.

PREPARATION TIME: *30 minutes*
COOKING TIME: *25 minutes*

INGREDIENTS (*for 4*):
1 quart fresh mussels
1 pound ripe tomatoes
1 clove garlic
1½ tablespoons olive oil
1 tablespoon chopped parsley
½ teaspoon each, dried marjoram and basil
½ pound small lumachine shells
Salt and black pepper
Lemon juice

Scrub and clean the mussels* thoroughly. Remove the beards (the tough, hairlike filaments that protrude from between the shells) and discard any mussels with broken or open shells.

Peel and seed the tomatoes* and chop them coarsely. Peel and finely chop the garlic. Heat the oil in a skillet and lightly sauté the garlic. Add the tomatoes, parsley, and herbs and bring this mixture to the simmering point.

Put the cleaned mussels in a large saucepan and cover with a lid. Cook over moderate heat, shaking the pan occasionally, until the mussels open. Remove the mussels from their shells and set them aside. Strain the cooking liquid through cheesecloth to remove any sandy sediment, then add the tomato mixture. Simmer over low heat for 20 minutes.

While the tomatoes are cooking, bring a large pan of water to a boil, add 2-3 teaspoons of salt, and cook the pasta shells for 12 minutes, or until tender but not soft. Drain in a colander and cover with a clean cloth to keep the pasta warm.

Add the mussels to the tomato sauce and heat through. Season to taste with freshly ground pepper, adding salt only if necessary, and sharpen with lemon juice. Put the pasta shells in a warmed deep serving dish and pour the mussels and sauce over them. Serve at once, with crusty French or Italian bread.

GREEK RICE RING

Particularly attractive when molded in a ring, this spicy rice dish, served hot or cold, makes a light main course. Kebabs, shellfish, or chicken make it even more substantial.

PREPARATION TIME: *20 minutes*
COOKING TIME: *35-40 minutes*
SETTING TIME: *1 hour*

INGREDIENTS (*for 6*):
1 cup long grain rice
Salt and black pepper
Lemon juice
2 large ripe tomatoes
1 tablespoon finely chopped chives
1 tablespoon finely chopped parsley
8 green olives
½ teaspoon each, dried basil and marjoram
1 red pepper
4 tablespoons olive oil
2 tablespoons tarragon vinegar
GARNISH:
Black olives, red pepper strips

Cook the rice in a large pan of boiling salted water with a teaspoon of lemon juice for about 15 minutes, or until the rice is just tender. Thoroughly drain the rice in a colander and cover with a dry cloth to absorb the steam and keep the rice fluffy.

While the rice is cooking, peel and seed the tomatoes.* Chop them finely and put them in a large bowl together with the chives, parsley, and finely chopped green olives. Blend in the dried herbs. Scald the pepper in boiling water for 5 minutes, then cut off the stalk end and remove the seeds. Cut the red pepper into narrow strips; set 8 strips aside and chop the remainder finely. Add them to the tomato mixture.

Add the still-warm rice to the tomato mixture. Blend the oil and vinegar together in a small bowl and season to taste with salt and freshly ground pepper. Pour enough of this dressing over the rice to moisten it thoroughly, adjust seasoning, and sharpen to taste with lemon juice. Press the rice firmly into a ring mold and allow to set in a cool place for at least 1 hour.

To serve hot, cover the rice mold with buttered foil or waxed paper and place it in a roasting pan containing about ½ inch of boiling water. Heat on top of the stove for 15-20 minutes, then remove the covering and place the serving dish over the mold. Turn it upside down and give a sharp shake to ease the rice out. Garnish with black olives and strips of red pepper.

Invert half a grapefruit in the center of the ring and skewer grilled lamb kebabs* in a fan arrangement in the grapefruit.

For a cold lunch, unmold the rice ring as already described, without reheating it. For a more substantial meal, fill the center with cooked chicken, shrimp, or lobster, all dressed in mousseline sauce (see Fish Soufflé, p.116).

CAULIFLOWER POLONAISE

Plainly cooked cauliflower is an excellent accompaniment to meat or poultry that is served in a rich sauce. The attractive garnish makes the dish particularly appetizing.

PREPARATION TIME: *15 minutes*
COOKING TIME: *20 minutes*

INGREDIENTS (*for 4-6*):
1 cauliflower
2 hard-cooked eggs
4 tablespoons butter
¾ cup dry bread crumbs
2 tablespoons chopped parsley
Salt and black pepper
Lemon juice

Cut off the tough outer leaves and thick stalk base of the cauliflower. Wash thoroughly. Cook the cauliflower whole in boiling salted water for 10-15 minutes or until just tender. Drain in a colander and cover with a dry cloth to keep warm.

Meanwhile, shell the eggs; remove the yolks and rub them through a sieve; chop the whites finely with a stainless-steel knife. Melt the butter in a small pan and sauté the bread crumbs until crisp. Remove the pan from the heat, stir in the parsley, and season to taste with salt, freshly ground pepper, and lemon juice.

Place the cauliflower in a warm serving dish, sprinkle evenly with the fried bread crumbs, and garnish with the chopped egg yolks and whites in an attractive pattern.

TOMATOES WITH GREEN PEAS

Stuffed large firm tomatoes are an ideal side dish to serve with broiled or roast meats. They can also be served as a hot first course, allowing 1 tomato per person. The stuffings used in this month's recipes for cucumbers and peppers can also be used—in fact all three of these stuffings are interchangeable.

PREPARATION TIME: *20 minutes*
COOKING TIME: *15 minutes*

INGREDIENTS (*for 6*):
6 large firm tomatoes
1 small onion
3 tablespoons butter
1 cup cooked peas
2 teaspoons chopped fresh mint
Salt and black pepper
1 egg yolk
GARNISH:
Black olives

Wash and dry the tomatoes thoroughly. Slice off the top of each with a sharp serrated knife and carefully take out the core and seeds with a pointed teaspoon. Turn the tomatoes upside down to drain thoroughly while making the stuffing.

Peel and finely chop the onion. Melt 2 tablespoons of the butter in a small heavy-bottomed pan and cook the onion over moderate heat until soft but not colored. Add the cooked peas and chopped mint to the onion. Cook the mixture for 3 minutes, stirring all the time. Allow the mixture to cool slightly, then rub it through a coarse sieve or purée it in a blender.

Return the purée to the pan and season to taste with salt and freshly ground pepper. Beat the egg yolk lightly, then add it to the peas and onions. Stir over low heat until the mixture thickens. Remove from the heat and set the stuffing aside to cool and stiffen slightly.

Season the inside of the drained tomatoes with salt and pepper and spoon in the prepared stuffing. Replace the tomato lids and secure each with a wooden cocktail pick.

Arrange the tomatoes in a well-buttered ovenproof dish and cover tightly with foil. Bake for 15 minutes in an oven preheated to 375°F until the tomatoes are just tender but still retain their shape.

Serve the tomatoes hot, garnished with an olive skewered on each cocktail pick.

STUFFED GREEN PEPPERS

Large, squat green peppers filled with a flavorful meat stuffing make a light lunch or supper dish. They can also be included in cold buffet or picnic fare.

PREPARATION TIME: *20 minutes*
COOKING TIME: *30 minutes*

INGREDIENTS (*for 4*):
4 large green peppers
1 onion
1½ tablespoons olive oil
½ pound ground beef or pork
1 thick slice white bread
1 egg
Salt and black pepper
Summer savory
2 tablespoons chopped parsley

Wash and dry the peppers.* Use a sharp knife to cut off the stalk ends with a small circle of pepper attached to each. Set the stalks aside and remove the seeds and ribs carefully from the peppers without breaking the skins. Scald the peppers for 5 minutes in a saucepan of boiling lightly salted water. Lift out the peppers and drain upside down.

Peel and finely chop the onion and cook it until transparent in 1 tablespoon of the oil in a heavy-bottomed pan. Add the meat, stirring continuously until it has browned and separated into grains. Remove the pan from the heat and discard any fat that has accumulated.

Remove the crust from the bread and soak it in the lightly beaten egg. Mash the bread and egg with a fork and stir it into the meat; season with salt, freshly ground pepper, and summer savory. Add the parsley and blend thoroughly until the stuffing is firm but still moist.

Brush the inside of an ovenproof dish with oil. Spoon the stuffing loosely into the peppers and place them upright in the dish. Brush the skins lightly with oil and put 2 or 3 tablespoons of water in the bottom of the dish. Cover the peppers tightly with aluminum foil and a lid and bake them in the center of a preheated oven at 375°F for 30 minutes or until the peppers are tender.

Arrange the peppers on a warmed serving dish and replace the stalk caps at an angle so that a little of the stuffing shows. Serve with hot, crusty French bread and a tomato sauce (p.302) flavored with paprika and sour cream.

FRENCH-FRIED CABBAGE

Use firm white cabbage for this recipe. The deep-fried, crisp but feather-light shreds make an excellent accompaniment to broiled fish or meat. Serve the cabbage immediately while still crisp.

PREPARATION TIME: *5 minutes*
COOKING TIME: *10 minutes*

INGREDIENTS (*for 4*):
½ medium white cabbage
½ cup milk
½ cup flour
Oil for deep-frying
Salt

Discard any dark or damaged outer leaves, wash the cabbage, and cut out the hard central stalk. Shred the cabbage finely.

Dip a few cabbage shreds at a time in the milk, then toss them in the flour on a sheet of waxed paper.

Heat the oil to 375°F in a deep-fryer; put a few shreds of coated cabbage into the frying basket and deep-fry for 1–2 minutes until crisp and golden. Drain on paper towels and keep hot until all the shreds have been cooked.

Sprinkle the cabbage with salt and serve at once.

Desserts

STUFFED CUCUMBER RINGS

These stuffed and baked cucumbers are good as a light lunch or supper dish. They can also be served as a side dish with roast veal or veal chops, or with sautéed, broiled, or roast chicken.

PREPARATION TIME: *25 minutes*
COOKING TIME: *45 minutes*

INGREDIENTS (*for 2–4*):

2 pounds short thick cucumbers
6 tablespoons butter
⅔ cup mushrooms
¼ pound lean cooked ham
1 tablespoon chopped parsley
¼ teaspoon dried summer savory
Salt and black pepper
2–3 tablespoons fresh white bread crumbs

Peel the cucumbers and cut into rings 1½–2 inches thick. Scoop out the seeds. Butter a large ovenproof dish and arrange the cucumber rings in this in a single layer.

Trim the mushrooms* and chop them coarsely. Dice the ham. Heat 2 tablespoons of the butter in a pan and lightly sauté the mushrooms and ham for 2–3 minutes. Add the parsley and savory, and season to taste with salt and pepper. Stir in enough bread crumbs to bind the stuffing.

Lightly sprinkle the cucumber rings with salt and pepper before filling them with the stuffing. Dot the tops of the cucumber rings with the remaining butter and cover the dish tightly with foil so that the cucumbers will cook in their own steam. Bake in the center of a preheated oven at 375°F for 45 minutes or until the rings are just tender. They should be slightly crisp.

Serve the rings with a hot cheese (p.301) or tomato sauce (p.302).

ZUCCHINI GRATINÉ

The subtle flavor and light consistency of zucchini make them an excellent accompaniment to delicately flavored fish, chicken, or veal dishes.

PREPARATION TIME: *5 minutes*
COOKING TIME: *25–30 minutes*

INGREDIENTS (*for 4*):
6 zucchini
4 tablespoons butter
Salt and black pepper
⅓ cup grated Cheddar cheese
*4 tablespoons heavy cream
(optional)*

Wash and dry the zucchini; do not peel them but cut off the stalk ends. Slice each zucchini in half lengthwise with a sharp knife.

Melt the butter in a shallow flameproof dish and sauté the zucchini, cut side downward, until light golden. Turn the zucchini over, season them with salt and freshly ground pepper, and sprinkle the grated cheese over them.

Cover the dish with a lid or foil and bake for 20 minutes in the center of a preheated oven at 375°F.

If cream is used, heat in a pan over moderate heat; do not let it boil. Pour it over the baked zucchini and cheese just before serving.

FRUIT GÂTEAU

This elegant dessert consists of a sponge cake filled with fresh berries and cream. It can be assembled to look like a jewel box by setting the sponge lid at an angle and letting the berries appear over the edge.

PREPARATION TIME: *50–60 minutes*
COOKING TIME: *15 minutes*

INGREDIENTS (*for 6–8*):

4 eggs
½ cup sugar
1 cup self-rising flour
¼ teaspoon salt
*½–¾ pound mixed berries
(strawberries, raspberries, red currants)*
1¼ cups heavy cream
¾ cup confectioners' sugar

Lightly butter and flour a rectangular cake pan approximately 14 inches by 8 inches. Put the eggs and sugar into a deep mixing bowl and beat with a whisk until the eggs are pale and thick enough for the whisk to leave a trail. Sift the flour and salt together, and fold gently into the creamed egg mixture.

Spoon this sponge-cake mixture into the prepared pan, spreading it evenly and making sure the corners are filled. Bake just above the center of a preheated oven at 375°F for 15 minutes, or until the sponge cake is golden and firm to the touch.

Turn the sponge cake out onto a wire rack and allow to cool completely, preferably overnight. Meanwhile, wash the berries and drain thoroughly on paper towels. Whip the cream until it is fluffy.

Carefully cut the sponge cake in half crosswise with a sharp knife. Spread a little more than half of the whipped cream over one cake half. Cut an oblong out of the other cake half, leaving an outer, unbroken edge, like a picture frame, 1 inch wide all around.

Carefully lift this frame onto the cream-covered base and fill the box, or cavity, with the fruit, reserving a few berries for decoration. Sprinkle the sifted confectioners' sugar over the fruit, and cover the box with the lid set at a slight angle. Pipe* the remaining cream onto the lid and decorate with the reserved fruit.

The cake will keep for 2–3 hours in the refrigerator. It should not be assembled too far in advance, however, or the fruit will become mushy and stain the cream.

BRANDY-APRICOT TRIFLE

Fresh apricots are sometimes available at this time of year. They form the basis of this rich dessert, suitable for a dinner party.

PREPARATION TIME: *20 minutes*
COOKING TIME: *30 minutes*
CHILLING TIME: *2 hours*

INGREDIENTS (*for 4–6*):
2½ cups custard sauce (p.341)
1 pound fresh apricots
½ cup white wine
4 tablespoons sugar
6 tablespoons brandy
½ pound ladyfingers
½ cup heavy cream

Prepare the custard and set aside to cool. Wash and dry the apricots, cut them in halves, and remove the pits. Put the wine and sugar in a pan and bring slowly to a boil. When the sugar has dissolved, add the apricot halves and cook them in this syrup over low heat until softened; set aside to cool.

Put the apricots in a glass bowl or serving dish and pour the syrup and brandy over them. Set aside 6–8 ladyfingers for decoration and break the remainder into small pieces. Sprinkle them over the apricots and brandy, stirring carefully to let the ladyfingers absorb the liquid. Spoon the custard, which should now be almost at setting point, over the apricots and chill the trifle in the refrigerator for about 2 hours.

Just before serving, whip the cream until stiff and pipe* it in swirls over the trifle. Decorate the top with the remaining ladyfingers.

POIRES FLAMBÉES

This French recipe for pears in brandy is an ideal dessert to cook in a chafing dish at the table. Fresh, firm peaches and apricots are also excellent cooked in this way.

PREPARATION TIME: *15 minutes*
COOKING TIME: *10 minutes*

INGREDIENTS (*for 4*):
4 ripe firm dessert pears
2 tablespoons unsalted butter
2 tablespoons brandy
8 ⅛-inch slices fresh ginger
1–2 tablespoons ginger syrup
2 tablespoons heavy cream

Peel the pears thinly, cut them in half, and carefully scoop out the cores with a pointed teaspoon.

Heat the butter in a chafing dish, a shallow flameproof dish, or a skillet over moderate heat. Sauté the pears, cut side down, until golden brown. Turn the pears over and sauté the other side. Fill a warmed tablespoon with brandy, set it alight, and pour it over the pears. Repeat with the remaining brandy.

Arrange the pears on individual plates, placing 2 ginger pieces in each cavity. Add the ginger syrup and cream to the pan juices and stir over gentle heat until well blended and heated through. Spoon a little sauce over each portion and serve immediately.

APPLE AND ALMOND PARADISE PUDDING

The combination of creamed rice, fruit, and crisp topping makes this dessert a great favorite with children. Pears or other fall fruit can be used instead of apples.

PREPARATION TIME: *30 minutes*
COOKING TIME: *35 minutes*

INGREDIENTS (*for 4*):
⅓ cup long grain rice
1¾ cups milk
¼ teaspoon vanilla extract
1½ pounds cooking apples
8–10 tablespoons sugar
6 tablespoons heavy cream
3–4 tablespoons apricot jam
TOPPING:
1 large egg white
2 tablespoons ground almonds
2 tablespoons sugar
2 tablespoons sliced almonds

Put the rice and milk in a heavy-bottomed saucepan and bring slowly to simmering point. Cover with a lid and cook over low heat for about 25 minutes, or until the rice is cooked but still slightly nutty in texture. Stir frequently during cooking to prevent sticking. Sweeten the rice to taste with vanilla extract and a little sugar. Leave to cool.

Peel, core, and slice the apples. Put 8 tablespoons of sugar with 1¼ cups of water in a saucepan over low heat and stir until all the sugar has dissolved. Bring this syrup to simmering point, then add the apple slices. Cook gently for 5 minutes or until just tender; they should retain their shape. Lift the slices carefully into a colander to drain and cool.

Whip the cream lightly and fold it into the cooled rice. Spread the apricot jam over the base of a shallow, 7-inch-diameter ovenproof dish or pie plate. Cover the jam with apple slices and spoon the creamed rice over them.

Beat the egg white for the topping until stiff. Mix together the ground almonds and sugar and fold in the egg white. Spoon this mixture over the rice and scatter the sliced almonds on top. Put the dish under a hot broiler for a few minutes until the almonds are crisp and golden. Serve at once.

HAZELNUT GANTOIS

A *gantois,* or Flemish pastry, consists of crunchy cookie dough layered with fresh fruit and whipped cream. The dessert is topped with crisp golden caramel.

PREPARATION TIME: *1 hour*
CHILLING TIME: *30 minutes*
COOKING TIME: *25–30 minutes*

INGREDIENTS (*for 4–6*):
¼ *pound shelled hazelnuts or filberts*
1 *cup plus 2 tablespoons flour*
4½ *tablespoons sugar*
6 *tablespoons unsalted butter*
3 *cups raspberries or 6–8 peaches*
1¼ *cups heavy cream*
CARAMEL TOPPING:
6 *tablespoons sugar*

Put the hazelnuts or filberts in the broiler pan and broil under medium heat, shaking the pan frequently, until the nuts are toasted. Rub them in a colander with a dry cloth to remove the skins. Take one quarter of the nuts, chop them coarsely, and set aside. Chop the remainder of the nuts very finely.

Sift the flour into a mixing bowl and add the ground hazelnuts or filberts and the sugar. Rub in the butter until the mixture resembles fine bread crumbs, then knead lightly for a few minutes. Chill the dough in a refrigerator for at least 30 minutes or until the dough is firm.

Meanwhile, pick over the raspberries, removing any spoiled or moldy ones, or peel the peaches* and cut them into thin slices.

Shape the firm dough into a thick sausage, on a lightly floured board. Divide the dough into 4 equal pieces and roll each piece out to a 7-inch circle about ⅛ inch thick. Lift the circles carefully onto greased

baking sheets. Bake in the center of a preheated oven at 350°F for 15 minutes, or until the cookies are golden brown and firm. Remove to a wire rack and leave them to cool.

For the caramel topping, put the 6 tablespoons of sugar and 2 tablespoons of water in a small pan over low heat. Stir until the sugar has completely dissolved. Turn up the heat and boil the syrup, without stirring, until it is caramel-colored.

Pour enough of the caramel over one baked circle to cover it, spreading it evenly with an oiled knife. Sprinkle the coarsely chopped nuts around the edge and arrange some of the raspberries or peach slices in the center. Trickle over the remaining caramel or pull this into thin threads to make a spun-sugar* veil on top of the baked circle.

Whip the cream with a pinch of salt until stiff, and sweeten to taste with a little sugar. Assemble the cake by spreading the cream in equal layers over the remaining 3 circles; arrange the fruit evenly on each layer. Put the circles on top of each other, finishing with the caramel-topped circle. Serve the gantois at once, cut into pie-shaped wedges.

QUICHE REINE-CLAUDE

Lorraine is the land of quiches, and Alsace of guiches. Both are names for an open tart with a cream filling combined with sweet or savory ingredients, such as bacon, cheese, vegetables, or seafood. This version uses greengage plums (*reine-claudes*) and is served with a pastry cream.

PREPARATION TIME: *40 minutes*
COOKING TIME: *30 minutes*

INGREDIENTS (*for 6*):

1 *flan shell*
½ *pound greengage plums*
4 *tablespoons greengage jam*
1 *tablespoon lemon juice*
½ *cup heavy cream*

PASTRY CREAM:
2 *eggs*
¼ *cup sugar*
¼ *cup flour*
1¼ *cups milk*
½ *teaspoon vanilla extract or 1 tablespoon lemon juice*

Bake a 7-inch flan shell made from enriched pastry (p.355) or pâte sucrée (p.365). Let the baked shell cool completely before assembling the dessert.

Make the pastry cream next, as this too should not be used until quite cold: Put 1 whole egg and 1 egg yolk in a mixing bowl (set aside the remaining egg white). Whisk the sugar with the eggs until creamy and nearly white, then whisk the sifted flour into the eggs and gradually add the milk. Pour the mixture into a small saucepan and bring to a boil, whisking continuously.

Simmer this pastry cream over very low heat for 2–3 minutes to cook the flour. Flavor to taste with vanilla extract or lemon juice and pour the cream into a shallow dish to cool. Stir from time to time to prevent a skin from forming.

Spread the cold pastry cream over the base of the flan shell. Cut the greengage plums in half, remove the pits, and arrange the fruit evenly over the cream.

Put the greengage jam in a small heavy-bottomed pan with 3 tablespoons of water and the lemon juice. Cook over low heat, stirring until the jam has dissolved and the mixture is clear. Increase the heat and boil rapidly to form a glaze.* Do not overboil—the glaze is ready when it will coat the back of the spoon and falls off in heavy drops. Rub the glaze through a coarse sieve.

Spoon the glaze over the greengage plums, covering them completely; brush the top edge of the tart with the remaining glaze to give a smooth finish. Set the tart in a cool place until the glaze has set.

Just before serving, whip the remaining egg white until stiff but still moist. Whip the cream into soft peaks, and fold in the egg white. Sweeten the mixture to taste with a little sugar and serve in a separate bowl to accompany the quiche.

Snacks & Supper Dishes

CROUSTADES WITH CREAM SAUCE FILLING

Crisp bread shells are quick to prepare and make good substitutes for pastry shells and vol-au-vents.

PREPARATION TIME: *20 minutes*
COOKING TIME: *15 minutes*

INGREDIENTS (*for 4*):
16 thin slices white bread
3-4 tablespoons olive oil
1 small, finely chopped onion
1 tablespoon butter
1½ cups finely chopped cooked ham or poultry
½ cup cooked, diced vegetables
½ cup medium white sauce (p. 301)
Salt and black pepper

Cut circles from the bread slices with a 3-inch pastry cutter; brush them on both sides with olive oil and press them into muffin pans or custard cups. Bake in the center of the oven preheated to 400°F for 8-10 minutes or until crisp and golden brown. Remove from the pans and set aside to cool.

Sauté the chopped onion in the butter until soft, then add the meat and vegetables.

While the onions are cooking, make the white sauce and season it with salt and pepper. Stir in the vegetables and meat, and spoon the mixture into the croustades. Bake the croustades in a preheated oven at 375°F for 5 minutes.

Serve the hot croustades on their own as an appetizer, or with vegetables as a main course.

CHICKEN SALAD

Leftover chicken and potatoes form the basis for this substantial lunch or supper dish.

PREPARATION TIME: *25 minutes*
CHILLING TIME: *30 minutes*

INGREDIENTS (*for 4*):
1-1½ cups cooked, diced chicken
2 cooked, diced potatoes
½ small peeled and diced cucumber
2 thinly sliced scallions
2 stalks celery, chopped
½ cup French dressing (p. 304)
1 crushed clove garlic
1 teaspoon paprika
1 small head of lettuce
4 hard-cooked eggs
2 tablespoons mayonnaise
2 tablespoons tomato ketchup

Put the chicken, potatoes, cucumber, scallions, and celery in a bowl. Pour over the French dressing, to which has been added the crushed garlic and paprika. Toss the salad ingredients well.

Arrange the washed and dried lettuce leaves on a large flat serving dish and pile the salad in the center. Halve the eggs lengthwise and arrange them around the chicken. Mix the tomato ketchup and mayonnaise together and pipe* or spoon over the eggs. Chill the salad in the refrigerator for at least 30 minutes.

EGG COCKTAIL

This quickly made appetizer is also excellent as a sandwich filling.

PREPARATION TIME: *20 minutes*
COOKING TIME: *8 minutes*

INGREDIENTS (*for 4-6*):
5 hard-cooked eggs
1½ cups mayonnaise
1 teaspoon grated onion
1 tablespoon chopped green pepper
1 tablespoon tomato ketchup
1 tablespoon heavy cream
Salt and black pepper
2 chopped scallions
6 black olives, pitted and chopped
3 shredded lettuce leaves
GARNISH:
Lemon slices

Mix the mayonnaise, onion, green pepper, tomato ketchup, and cream together; season with salt and pepper. Fold in the coarsely chopped eggs, scallions, and olives.

Arrange the lettuce shreds in individual sherbet glasses and pile the egg mixture on top. Garnish each with a thin lemon slice and serve with hot buttered toast.

For a sandwich filling, the shredded lettuce can be mixed into the egg cocktail and spread thickly on white or whole wheat bread.

VEGETABLE AND CHEESE SOUFFLÉ

Cooked vegetables are incorporated into a cheese soufflé to make this light supper dish.

PREPARATION TIME: *20 minutes*
COOKING TIME: *25-30 minutes*

INGREDIENTS (*for 4*):
1 cup cooked, diced vegetables
3 tablespoons unsalted butter
1 tablespoon flour
½ cup milk
3 eggs
½ cup grated Cheddar cheese
Salt and cayenne pepper

Melt 2 tablespoons of the butter over moderate heat. Blend in the flour and cook the roux* over low heat for 1 minute. Gradually add the milk, stirring continuously until the sauce has thickened.

Separate the eggs, and beat the yolks, one at a time, into the sauce. Stir in the vegetables and cheese, and season with salt and cayenne pepper. Whip the egg whites until stiff but not dry, and fold them carefully into the cheese and vegetable sauce.

Turn the mixture into a buttered 1½-2 pint soufflé dish and bake in the center of a preheated oven at 375°F for 25-30 minutes, or until the soufflé is well risen.

RICE PUDDING

Rice puddings vary greatly in flavor, preparation, and finished texture. This is a rather different approach that yields extremely good results. The rice is washed, dried, and cooked a few moments in butter before it is added to the milk.

PREPARATION TIME: *45 minutes*
COOKING TIME: *1½ hours*

INGREDIENTS (*for 4-6*):
⅓ cup rice
2 tablespoons butter
4 cups milk
3 tablespoons sugar
⅛ teaspoon salt
Nutmeg

Wash the rice in several changes of cold water. Drain the grains and dry between sheets of paper towels. In a heavy 1½-quart casserole, melt the butter over low heat. Add the rice and heat it, stirring constantly, until the grains whiten. Do not let them brown. In a saucepan, combine the milk with the sugar and salt, and heat it to just below the boiling point. Add it to the rice, stirring just long enough to blend. Let the milk bubble over the heat for a few seconds. Remove the casserole from the heat and sprinkle the top of the rice and milk with nutmeg. Set the casserole uncovered in an oven preheated to 300°F. Bake the pudding for 2 hours, stirring every half hour for the first 1½ hours. Serve warm or cold.

A Birthday Party for Young Children

Most mothers would agree that the most exhausting of all parties are those for children's birthdays. But proper planning and a few hours of advance preparation can take much of the strain out of coping with a handful of boisterous children. Issue proper invitations to the young guests that clearly state the times when the party will start and finish. A birthday party for 6- to 8-year-olds usually should not last longer than 2–2½ hours.

Most young children are fussy about their food and shy away from unfamiliar and elaborate concoctions. They are fond of snack food—such as potato chips, pigs-in-blankets, and mild cheese—and prefer gelatin and ice cream desserts. The favorite treat of the party is, of course, the birthday cake. For drinks, serve a fresh-fruit punch, orange juice, lemonade, or flavored milk shakes, with plenty of colored drinking straws.

Serve the food toward the end of the party when the children have come to know one another. Keep the various food portions small enough to be eaten with the fingers or small plastic spoons and arrange all the food on the table at the same time so that the children can choose for themselves.

Protect the dining table against the inevitable overturned drinks and spilled food. A paper or plastic tablecloth provides a gay background for the food, and a paper cloth can simply be thrown out afterward. As an extra precaution, cover the table with a large piece of clear plastic before putting on the paper cloth. Plastic or heavy-duty paper plates eliminate much of the dishwashing.

In fine weather a backyard party is usually the most successful; certainly it makes cleaning up easier and eliminates worries about soiled furniture and breakage. Arrange the food on a picnic table and borrow folding lawn chairs, if necessary, for seating.

Provide colorful paper hats for the young guests and decorate the party room with balloons and crêpe paper. Children usually expect a small party favor, such as a bag of candy or an inexpensive toy. Small plastic cars, colored pencils or crayons, coloring books, and paper dolls need not strain the budget.

On the right is a section of a birthday table showing food popular with young children. Reading from left to right and from top: potato chips, and a "hedgehog" of Vienna sausages; below these are a soft roll with cream cheese and pineapple filling, pigs-in-blankets (small pastry-wrapped sausages), and a checkerboard of white and yellow cheese squares. Other soft rolls contain a tuna salad filling. Also popular are crackers and breadsticks. Sandwiches are cut into fancy shapes after being spread with red jelly.

Sandwiches & Snacks

Cut small sandwiches of white bread in round, oval, or other geometric shapes, or as letters of the alphabet. Butter the sandwiches lightly and spread them with a variety of fillings, such as soft cream cheese mixed with finely grated cucumber, or egg salad flavored with chopped watercress. Non-runny jelly and bananas sweetened with brown sugar make a good filling. Split small soft rolls in half, spread them with butter, and top with, for example, tuna or salmon salad, or with softened cream cheese blended with finely chopped pineapple.

Heat Vienna sausages and leave them to cool before skewering them on wooden cocktail picks. Vienna sausages or small wieners can also be used to make pigs-in-blankets: simply wrap the sausages in biscuit dough and bake until the dough is risen and golden brown.

Have plenty of potato chips and flavored crackers on hand, as well as fruit juice and soft drinks.

Desserts

Make these desserts in small individual portions and provide the children with small plastic spoons with which to eat them.

Orange baskets Cut firm oranges in half and scoop out the flesh carefully without breaking the skins. Press the flesh through a strainer and use the juice as the base for orange drinks. Fill the empty orange halves with fresh or canned fruit salad, and before serving top with scoops of vanilla ice cream.

Bunnies on the lawn Dissolve a packet of lime gelatin as directed on the package. Pour the gelatin over the bottom of a large shallow dish and chill to set. Place thoroughly drained pear halves, rounded sides up, on the gelatin. Pipe* fluffy tails from thick cream at one end of each pear and use toasted almonds to represent the ears. Small chocolate chips or raisins become the eyes, and pieces of candied cherries the tongues.

Strawberry boats These are popular with children and are easy for them to handle. Bake the pastry in advance and keep in a container until required. It may also be frozen.

Sift 1½ cups all-purpose flour with a pinch of salt and rub in 5 tablespoons butter and 1½ tablespoons lard. Knead into a dough with a little cold water. Leave the dough in a cool place for 30 minutes, then roll it out thinly and use it to line small well-greased boat-shaped molds (barquettes). Prick the pastry boats all over with a fork before baking blind* for about 10 minutes in the center of a preheated oven at 400°F.

Spread a thin layer of custard sauce (p.341) or strawberry jelly over the bottom of the cooled boats and top with halved strawberries or any other seasonal fruit.

Cookies & Cakes

Small frosted cupcakes and cookies are more appealing to children than large sponge cakes, except for the birthday cake. Cupcakes are easily made from a genoise sponge-cake mixture (p.388); bake the cakes in small paper cups and when cold cover them with colored frosting. Before the frosting has set, decorate the cakes with small candies.

A clock cake is a different kind of birthday cake. It can be made in advance or frozen for several days and decorated on the day of the party.

Cream ¾ cup unsalted butter with ¾ cup sugar and the grated rind and juice of a lemon. Add 3 egg yolks, one at a time, beating thoroughly after each addition, then fold in 1½ cups self-rising flour and a pinch of salt. Beat the three egg whites until stiff but not dry and carefully fold them into the sponge-cake mixture. Spoon this into a buttered and floured round cake pan, 9 inches in diameter. Bake in the center of a preheated oven at 375°F for 40–50 minutes. To test for doneness, insert a toothpick into the cake. If it is clean when removed, the cake is done. Cool on a wire rack and remove from the pan onto a serving plate.

Cover the cooled cake with apricot glaze (p.394) and leave until the glaze has set.

For the decoration, sift 1 pound confectioners' sugar into a bowl and set it over a pan of simmering water. This heating of the sugar helps to destroy the raw taste of the cornstarch filler. Add 4 tablespoons warm water and a squeeze of lemon juice to the sugar. Beat thoroughly for 1 minute, then add food coloring and beat until the sugar has dissolved. Spread the frosting evenly over the top and sides of the cake.

Place 12 chocolate dinner mints or cookies around the edge of the cake. Color the remaining frosting a different shade and spoon it into a pastry bag fitted with a fine plain round tube. Pipe two circles on top of the cake to represent the clock rim, then pipe numerals 1–12 onto the mints or cookies and pipe on the clock hands. The minute hand should point to 12 and the hour hand to the age of the birthday child. Set birthday candles inside the clock rim or around the appropriate number.

October

And close at hand, the basket stood
With nuts from brown October's wood.

JOHN GREENLEAF WHITTIER

THIS MONTH'S RECIPES

A feast of pheasants, served with Saratoga chips, roasted chestnuts, and bread sauce, makes a sumptuous main course for a festive October dinner.

Food in Season

Cold weather calls for meals that are hearty and sustaining—thick stews and succulent roasts, hot vegetable dishes, and warming drinks sipped by the fire.

Despite the onset of the first frosts, fresh fruit and vegetables are still available in October. Apples and pears are at their best, while eggplants and melons are at the end of their seasons. Nuts are becoming more plentiful and remain in good supply through Christmas.

Crisp fall apples are delicious eaten on their own but can also be used in cooking; combined with raisins, they make a good German-style stuffing for roast goose (p.242). Pears, stuffed with walnuts and cherries and coated with chocolate (p.248), are a spectacular dessert for a dinner party. Firm cooking pears, such as Anjou, can be mixed with green beans (p.245) and served hot as a side dish for meat or poultry.

Fresh game, dressed and ready to cook, is available at many butcher's shops in the fall. Venison or any game bird can be used to make a rich soup with port wine (p.235). One of the most prized game birds, pheasant, is a sumptuous main course; serve it roasted, on a bed of cabbage, accompanied by boiled potatoes (p.243).

Red snapper is readily available this month. Stuffed with almonds, cucumbers, and onions (p.237), it is an attractive main course for a dinner party. Oysters are at their least expensive and can be served raw with cocktail sauce as a first course, or mixed with shrimp and ham in a magnificent Creole jambalaya (p.238).

SUGGESTED MENUS

Honeydew Cups
...
Pork Chops in Cider
Chickpea Patties
Baked Cabbage
...
Shoe-Fly Pie with Raisins

Game Soup with Port Wine
...
Finnan-Filled Crêpes
Broccoli with Poulette Sauce
...
Fresh Fruit

Avocado, Pear, and Nut Salad
...
Pheasant with Cabbage
...
Delices de Poires au Chocolat

Seafood en Brochette
...
Veal Rolls with Frittata Filling
Buttered Green Beans
Duchesse Potatoes
...
Hungarian Hazelnut Torte

Broiled Flank Steak
Scalloped Potatoes
Tossed Green Salad
...
Vanilla Pots de Crème

Rillettes of Pork
...
Carré d'Agneau Dordonnaise
Turkish Fried Carrots
...
Compote of Dried Fruits

Jambalaya
Tossed Green Salad
...
Fresh Figs and Yogurt

Soups & First Courses

AVOCADO, PEAR, AND NUT SALAD

Avocados and pears discolor quickly when peeled. For this salad it is essential to mix the dressing first and sprinkle the diced pears generously with lemon juice before blending them quickly into the dressing.

PREPARATION TIME: *15 minutes*
CHILLING TIME: *1 hour*

INGREDIENTS (*for 6*):
3 avocados
1 cup sour cream
2 teaspoons tarragon vinegar
Salt and black pepper
Dijon mustard or Worcestershire sauce
Sugar
Juice of 1 lemon
1 large or 2 small pears
3 tablespoons salted almonds or peanuts
GARNISH:
Chopped chives

Put the sour cream in a mixing bowl and stir in the tarragon vinegar. Season to taste with salt, freshly ground pepper, mustard or Worcestershire sauce, and a little sugar. Mix thoroughly.

Cut the avocados in half, remove the pits, and carefully scoop out the flesh with a silver teaspoon. Leave a narrow inner lining of flesh in the avocado shells and set them aside. Dice the flesh and put the pieces in a bowl. Sprinkle with lemon juice. Peel, core, and dice the pear, add to the avocado, and sprinkle with the remaining lemon juice.

Chop the salted almonds coarsely and set a little aside for garnishing. Mix the remainder with the avocado and pears. Add the dressing and blend thoroughly. Pile the salad into the avocado shells and wrap each of the shells in foil. Chill for 1 hour.

Just before serving, unwrap the avocado shells, arrange them on small plates, and garnish with the chopped almonds and chives.

GAME SOUP WITH PORT WINE

This is a rich, sustaining soup for cold autumn days. It can be made from neck of venison or from any game bird, such as pheasant or partridge, that is too tough for roasting.

PREPARATION TIME: *55 minutes*
COOKING TIME: *2½–3 hours*

INGREDIENTS (*for 6*):
1 pound venison or a 2-pound game bird
1 large onion
1 parsnip or turnip
1 carrot
1 leek
3 stalks celery
½ pound mushrooms
¼ pound butter
1 bay leaf
Thyme, marjoram, and basil
Salt and black pepper
1–2 cloves garlic
½ cup flour
½ cup port or Burgundy
GARNISH:
Bread croûtons (p.300)

Cut the venison into 2–3 inch chunks, trimming off any gristle. If a game bird is being used, chop it, through the bone, into small portions; clean thoroughly. Peel and coarsely chop the onion, parsnip, and carrot. Wash the leek and celery well under cold running water and chop them coarsely also. Trim and thinly slice the mushrooms.*

Melt half the butter in a large pan over moderate heat and sauté the meat, turning it frequently, until it begins to color. Add the onion, leek, and celery to the pan and brown evenly. Put the parsnip, carrot, and bay leaf, together with a pinch of thyme, marjoram, and basil, into the pan. Season with salt, freshly ground pepper, and the crushed garlic. Pour in 7–8 cups water, or enough to cover the contents in the pan; bring to a boil over high heat.

Remove any scum that rises to the surface, then add the sliced mushrooms. Cover the pan with a lid and simmer over low heat for about 2 hours, or until the meat is perfectly tender.

Strain the stock through a fine sieve and leave to cool slightly. Remove the bay leaf and all bones, then put the meat and vegetables in the blender with a little of the soup to make a thick purée.*

Melt the remaining butter in a large pan over moderate heat; blend in the flour and cook, stirring continuously, until the roux* is caramel-colored. Take the pan off the heat and gradually blend in the port and about 1¼ cups of stock. Return the pan to the heat, bring to simmering point, stirring all the time, then blend in the meat and vegetable purée and about 4 cups of stock to make a thick soup. Heat the soup through over low heat for about 15 minutes and correct seasoning if necessary.

Serve the soup in individual bowls, garnished with small bread croûtons.

CHILI, BEEF, AND BEAN SOUP

This is the kind of winter soup that is a meal in itself—spicy, hearty, and filling. The ingredients include red kidney beans and chickpeas, which can be bought canned. The soup is even better when prepared a day in advance.

PREPARATION TIME: *10 minutes*
COOKING TIME: *45 minutes*

INGREDIENTS (*for 4*):
1 large onion
1 green or red pepper
4 tablespoons bacon fat or butter
½ pound ground beef
16-ounce can tomatoes
2 cups canned red kidney beans
1 cup canned chickpeas
2 cups stock or bouillon
1 teaspoon chili powder
Salt
GARNISH:
Lettuce

Peel and finely chop the onion; cut off the stalk base of the pepper, remove the seeds, and chop the pepper finely. Melt the fat in a large heavy-bottomed pan and sauté the onion until it begins to color. Add the meat and continue to cook over medium heat until it is well browned.

Add the tomatoes with their juice, the drained beans, drained chickpeas, and chopped pepper. Stir in the stock or bouillon, mixing thoroughly. Season to taste with chili powder and a little salt. Cover the pan and simmer the soup for 30 minutes. Allow to cool, then purée in a blender or rub it through a coarse sieve.

Reheat the thick soup before serving. Garnish with finely shredded lettuce and serve with tortillas (p.149) or hot garlic bread.

Fish

RILLETTES OF PORK

In France most country towns have their own versions of rillettes—a coarse-textured terrine of pork and pork fat. It makes a pleasant change from smooth pâtés.

PREPARATION TIME: *30 minutes*
COOKING TIME: *4 hours*

INGREDIENTS (*for 6*):
2 pounds pork shoulder
¾ pound fresh pork kidney fat (leaf lard)
Salt and black pepper
1 clove garlic
1 bay leaf
1 sprig parsley
1 sprig thyme or rosemary

Have the shoulder of pork boned. Cut it into narrow strips. Dice the pork fat finely and season the meat and fat with salt, freshly ground pepper, and the peeled crushed garlic. Pack the meat and fat into a casserole or terrine. Push the herbs down into the center of the meat and pour about ½ cup of water over it. Cover the casserole with a lid or foil.

Bake for 4 hours in the center of the oven preheated to 275°F. Stir the contents of the casserole occasionally to prevent a crusty top forming. When the meat is tender, turn the contents of the casserole into a sieve placed over a mixing bowl; leave until the fat has dripped through the sieve and into the bowl. Remove the herbs and shred the meat with 2 forks or put it in a blender for a few moments to make a coarse purée.* Adjust seasoning if necessary.

Pack the meat firmly into one large earthenware pot or several small ones. Pour enough liquid fat into the pot to cover the meat by ¼ inch. Leave in the refrigerator until the fat on the surface has set solid.

Serve the terrine with crusty French bread for a first course, or with a watercress salad tossed with Sauce Vinaigrette (p.304).

HONEYDEW CUPS

A well-chilled melon salad is a good choice before a rich main course.

PREPARATION TIME: *40 minutes*
CHILLING TIME: *1 hour*

INGREDIENTS (*for 6*):
1 honeydew or cantaloupe melon
1 cucumber
Salt
6 tomatoes
DRESSING:
1–2 tablespoons sugar
3 tablespoons lemon juice or tarragon vinegar
6 tablespoons salad oil
GARNISH:
2 teaspoons each, chopped mint, chives, and chervil or parsley

Peel the cucumber and cut it into ½-inch pieces; sprinkle with salt and allow to stand for 30 minutes. Cut the melon in half crosswise and remove the seeds. Carefully scoop out the flesh in small balls or cut it into small wedges. Peel the tomatoes,* cut them in half, and remove cores and seeds. Chop the tomato flesh coarsely and set aside.

Mix the ingredients for the dressing, adding the oil last of all. Rinse the cucumber in cold water and pat dry on paper towels.

Put the melon, tomato, and cucumber in a large bowl, pour over the dressing, and mix well. Chill the salad in the refrigerator for at least 1 hour, stirring occasionally.

Serve the salad in individual glass bowls and sprinkle with the mixed chopped herbs.

FISH MOUSSE WITH BERCY SAUCE

This mousse is prepared like a soufflé, but as it is steamed in the oven instead of baked, it can be kept waiting for tardy guests without collapsing. It is here served as a main course with a classic Bercy sauce, but can also be served in small individual molds as a first course.

PREPARATION TIME: *30 minutes*
COOKING TIME: *1½ hours*

INGREDIENTS (*for 4–6*):
1 pound haddock or cod fillets
4 cups court bouillon (p.308)
2 tablespoons butter
4 tablespoons flour
5 tablespoons milk
2 eggs
5 tablespoons heavy cream
1½ tablespoons chopped parsley
1–2 teaspoons anchovy essence or paste
Lemon juice
Salt and black pepper
3–4 tablespoons bread crumbs
BERCY SAUCE:
1 small onion
4 tablespoons unsalted butter
½ cup dry white wine
1¼ cups fish stock
1½ tablespoons flour
5 tablespoons heavy cream
Salt and black pepper
GARNISH:
Lemon slices
Parsley sprigs

Bring the court bouillon to a boil. Simmer the fish, uncovered, over low heat in the bouillon for 8–10 minutes or until tender. Lift the fish out of the pan with a slotted spoon and set the liquid aside. Remove the skin and any bones from the fish and flake* it finely into a bowl. Then mash the flesh with a fork or turn it into a coarse purée* in the blender.

Melt the butter in a saucepan over moderate heat, stir in the flour, and cook this roux* for 2 minutes, without coloring. Add enough fish liquid to the milk to make ½ cup, and gradually blend this into the roux to make a thick white sauce. Cook the sauce for 3–5 minutes, stirring continuously and adding a little more fish liquid if the sauce gets too thick. Mix in the fish purée. Separate the eggs and beat the yolks with the cream; add them to the fish mixture, together with the chopped parsley. Season to taste with anchovy essence or paste, lemon juice, salt, and freshly ground pepper.

Whisk the egg whites in a bowl until stiff but still moist. Fold them into the fish mixture. Toast the bread crumbs on a baking sheet in a warm oven and meanwhile brush a 2½-cup charlotte mold or cake pan with oil and line it evenly with the crumbs.

Spoon the fish mixture into the mold—it should be three-quarters full. Cover the top with a piece of buttered foil and place the mold in a roasting pan with ½ inch of water in the bottom. Bake in the center of a preheated oven at 325°F for 1–1¼ hours, or until the mousse is well risen and set.

About 30 minutes before the mousse is ready, prepare the sauce. Peel the onion and chop it finely. Sauté it over low heat in half the butter until soft, then add the wine and fish stock. Increase the heat and rapidly boil the liquid, uncovered, until it has reduced* by half. Knead the flour with the remaining butter to a beurre manié (p.303); shape it into small balls and drop them, one at a time, into the liquid. Stir this sauce over gentle heat until it thickens, then stir in the cream. Do not let the sauce reach boiling point or it will curdle. Season to taste with salt and freshly ground pepper.

Unmold the mousse onto a warm serving dish and garnish with lemon slices and sprigs of parsley. The sauce can be poured over the mousse or into a separate sauceboat. Buttered spinach or broccoli au gratin (p.65) would be suitable vegetables with the mousse.

STUFFED RED SNAPPER

This superb fish adapts well to baking. The stuffing is a novel combination of onions, cucumbers, and almonds.

PREPARATION TIME: *20 minutes*
COOKING TIME: *40–45 minutes*

INGREDIENTS (*for 4–5*):
1 4–5 pound red snapper
Salt and pepper
Soft butter
½ cup chopped almonds
1 cup chopped onions
1 clove garlic, minced
4 cups dry bread crumbs
1 cup minced cucumber
1 teaspoon dried thyme
Dry sherry

Ask your fish dealer to bone the fish and prepare it for stuffing. Rub the inside with salt, pepper, and butter. Toast the almonds.* Sauté the onion and garlic in butter until soft. Combine them with the bread crumbs, cucumbers, and toasted almonds. Season with salt, pepper, and thyme and moisten with a little sherry. Stuff the fish and close the opening with toothpicks. Salt and pepper the fish and bake in a well-greased dish at 350°F for 40–45 minutes, or until the fish flakes when tested with a fork. Baste with the pan juices.

DEVILED CRAB

Deviled dishes originated in England early in the 19th century. The main ingredient, which may be meat, poultry, or fish, is cooked in a sharp hot sauce, topped with bread crumbs, and finished off under the broiler or in the oven.

PREPARATION TIME: *20 minutes*
COOKING TIME: *5–10 minutes*

INGREDIENTS (*for 4*):
1 pound fresh crabmeat
½ cup heavy cream
1 teaspoon Dijon mustard
1–2 teaspoons anchovy essence or paste
1 teaspoon Worcestershire sauce
1–1½ tablespoons lemon juice
Pinch cayenne pepper
Salt and black pepper
4 tablespoons toasted bread crumbs
4 tablespoons grated Cheddar cheese
GARNISH:
Lemon wedges

Mix the cream, mustard, anchovy essence or paste, and Worcestershire sauce together in a saucepan. Season to taste with lemon juice, cayenne, salt, and freshly ground black pepper. Stir the crabmeat into the cream mixture and heat through over moderate heat without boiling.

Spoon the crab mixture into 4 individual baking dishes and cover with a topping of bread crumbs and grated cheese. Put the dishes on a baking sheet in the center of a preheated oven at 400°F, or under a hot broiler, until the cheese is brown and bubbly on top.

Serve as a first course, garnished with lemon wedges.

FINNAN-FILLED CRÊPES

Cured haddock from Findon in Scotland, known as finnan haddie, is cleaned and split before being smoked. This dish can be served as a main course, allowing 2 crêpes per person; as a first course 1 crêpe will be enough.

PREPARATION TIME: *20 minutes*
COOKING TIME: *30 minutes*

INGREDIENTS (*for 4*):
½ pound poached smoked haddock fillet
1¼ cups crêpe batter (p.343)
1 small onion
2 tablespoons chopped celery
¼ pound mushrooms
7 tablespoons unsalted butter
16-ounce can tomatoes
Salt and black pepper
Lemon juice
3–4 tablespoons grated Cheddar or Gruyère cheese
GARNISH:
Lemon wedges
Parsley sprigs

Make 8 small thin crêpes from the batter and set them aside. Peel and finely chop the onion and prepare the celery. Trim and thinly slice the mushrooms.*

Melt 3 tablespoons of the butter and sauté the onion, celery, and mushrooms until soft. Add the tomatoes, and season with salt and freshly ground pepper. Simmer the contents of the pan, uncovered, until it has reduced* to a thick purée.*

Meanwhile, remove the skin from the haddock and flake* the flesh. Add the haddock to the onion and tomato mixture, sharpen it to taste with the lemon juice, and carefully adjust the seasoning.

Spoon 2 tablespoons of the filling down the center of each crêpe and fold the sides over to form an envelope. Arrange the stuffed crêpes side by side in a shallow baking dish. Melt the remaining butter and pour it over the crêpes. Sprinkle generously with grated cheese and set the dish under a hot preheated broiler or in the oven until the cheese has melted and is bubbly brown.

Garnish the crêpes with lemon wedges and parsley sprigs and serve immediately. Buttered peas make a nice accompaniment.

JAMBALAYA

This classic Creole dish from New Orleans combines shellfish with spicy sausage and country ham.

PREPARATION TIME: *25 minutes*
COOKING TIME: *1½ hours*

INGREDIENTS (*for 6*):
*1 tablespoon bacon fat or rendered
   ham fat
2 medium onions, chopped
6 pork link sausages, highly
   seasoned
1 tablespoon flour
1½–2 cups diced country-style ham
3 medium tomatoes, peeled, seeded,
   and chopped
1 cup uncooked rice
1 large garlic clove, minced
2 cups chicken stock
1 ½-inch piece of dried red pepper
   pod, crushed, or ¼ (or more)
   teaspoon Creole or cayenne pepper
½ teaspoon dried thyme
1 medium green pepper, diced
3 tablespoons minced parsley
1½ pounds raw shrimp, shelled
1½ pounds raw oysters, shucked*

Melt the fat in a heavy pot with a tight-fitting cover. Add the onions and sausages, and stir over moderate heat until sausages brown slightly and onions are translucent. Add flour and cook slowly, stirring constantly, until the mixture turns a light brown.

Add the ham and tomatoes and cover tightly, simmering over low heat for about 30 minutes. Add the rice, garlic, stock, seasoning, green pepper, and parsley. Cover tightly and simmer over very low heat for 40 minutes or more until rice is cooked but not mushy. Do not stir.

Add shrimp and cook for 2 minutes. Add oysters and cook for 3 minutes. Adjust seasoning and serve.

SEAFOOD EN BROCHETTE

PREPARATION TIME: *20 minutes*
COOKING TIME: *8 minutes*

INGREDIENTS (*for 2*):
*4 slices bacon, cut into 1-inch
   pieces
4 large uncooked shelled shrimp
4 sea scallops
2 chunks lobster tail
Salt
Pepper
Dried tarragon
4 tablespoons butter, melted
1 lemon, quartered*

Skewers, or kabobs, of various seafoods can be grilled outdoors or broiled in the kitchen, and are always an elegant addition to any menu. Serve the seafood on small skewers for a first course, or on large skewers for a main course.

Broil or bake the bacon in a 350°F oven until firm but not crisp. Arrange the seafood and the bacon pieces alternately on two skewers. Salt and pepper them well and crumble a little dried tarragon over them. Brush the seafood well with melted butter.

Broil about 3 inches from the heat or over charcoal 3–4 minutes, only long enough to cook through and crisp the bacon. Turn the skewers often and baste them with additional melted butter. Add more salt and pepper if needed. Serve with lemon wedges, and, if the seafood is cooked indoors, with fried parsley (p.397–398).

Meat

SAUTÉED KIDNEYS

Lamb kidneys make a quick and savory main course for lunch.

PREPARATION TIME: *25 minutes*
COOKING TIME: *20 minutes*

INGREDIENTS (*for 6*):
*12 lamb kidneys
2 large onions
4 tablespoons unsalted butter
1½ cups button mushrooms
1 tablespoon tomato purée
¼ cup port or dry sherry
Salt and black pepper*
GARNISH:
Parsley

Peel and thinly slice the onions. Melt the butter in a large skillet and add the onions. Cover the pan with a lid and cook over low heat for 7 minutes. Remove the skin around the kidneys,* cut them in half, and snip out the white cores with scissors. Rinse the kidneys, pat them dry on paper towels, then cut them into 1-inch chunks. Trim and halve the mushrooms;* add them with the kidneys to the skillet and sauté briskly for 3 minutes.

Blend the tomato purée with the port or sherry. Add to the kidneys and season to taste with salt and freshly ground pepper. Reduce the heat and simmer the kidneys for 7–10 minutes or until tender.

Arrange the kidneys and sauce on a hot serving dish and garnish with sprigs of parsley. Rice or buttered noodles go well with the kidneys.

PORK CHOPS IN CIDER

With the onset of cool fall weather, casseroles give a warm and welcoming glow to the evening meal. Shoulder chops of pork are ideal for this easily prepared dish; but veal chops may be cooked in the same way with equal success.

PREPARATION TIME: *25 minutes*
COOKING TIME: *45 minutes*

INGREDIENTS (*for 6*):
6 pork shoulder chops
½ pound mushrooms
1 large onion
6 tablespoons butter
1 teaspoon dried savory
Salt and black pepper
*½–⅔ cup imported dry cider or dry
    white wine*
1 cup grated Cheddar cheese
6 tablespoons toasted bread crumbs
GARNISH:
Parsley sprigs

Wipe and trim the mushrooms.* Set 6 or 7 caps aside and slice the remainder thinly. Peel the onion and chop it finely. Grease a shallow ovenproof dish with a little of the butter and arrange the sliced mushrooms over the bottom. Scatter the onion and savory over the mushrooms, and season with salt and freshly ground pepper.

Trim most of the fat off the chops and lay them on top of the vegetables. Pour over enough cider or wine to come just level with the meat and push the mushroom caps, dark side up, between the chops.

Mix the cheese with the bread crumbs. Spread this mixture evenly over the chops and the mushroom caps, and dot with the remaining butter. Bake in the center of a preheated oven at 400°F for 45 minutes,

or until the shoulder chops are tender and the topping is crisp and golden brown.

Serve the chops straight from the dish, and garnish each mushroom cap with a small sprig of parsley. Green beans and baked potatoes dressed with sour cream and chopped chives are ideal side dishes for this pork dish.

CARRÉ D'AGNEAU DORDONNAISE

Walnuts and liver pâté are an integral part of many dishes from the Dordogne region of France. They are both used in this recipe, which transforms rack of lamb into a spectacular party dish.

PREPARATION TIME: *30 minutes*
COOKING TIME: *1¼ hours*

INGREDIENTS (*for 4–6*):
2 racks of lamb
½ cup shelled walnuts
½ small onion
4 ounces pâté with truffles
*4 tablespoons fresh white bread
    crumbs*
2 tablespoons finely chopped parsley
Salt and black pepper
Lemon juice
2 tablespoons cooking oil
¼ cup dry white wine
1 teaspoon powdered rosemary

Have the racks of lamb boned and ask the butcher to give you the bones. Trim any excess fat off the meat. Chop the walnuts finely by hand or in a blender. Peel and grate the onion. Stir the pâté until it is smooth, and beat in the walnuts and onion. Mix the bread crumbs and chopped parsley into the stuffing, and season with salt, pepper, and lemon juice.

Spread the underside of each rack with the stuffing. Roll the meat neatly and tie with string at 2-inch intervals. Put the 2 meat rolls in an oiled roasting pan and brush them with oil. Cook in the center of the oven preheated to 400°F for about 20 minutes, or until the meat is golden brown. Reduce the heat to 375°F and cook for a further 20–25 minutes, or until the lamb is tender and pink in the center.

Meanwhile, put the lamb bones in a large saucepan with salt and pepper. Cover the bones with cold water, bring to a boil, and simmer the stock for 30–40 minutes.

Remove the meat from the roasting pan and allow it to cool and set slightly before removing the string. Put the meat back in the turned-off oven to keep warm. Carefully pour off the fat in the roasting pan and add the wine to the meat juices. Bring to a boil on top of the stove; add about 1¼ cups of strained stock and the rosemary. Cook this gravy over high heat until it has reduced* slightly. Correct seasoning and strain the gravy into a warm sauceboat.

Serve the lamb, cut into thick slices, on a warm serving dish. Rissolé potatoes (p.68), Brussels sprouts, and halved broiled tomatoes could be arranged around the meat as colorful side dishes.

STEAK TARTARE

This highly spiced mixture of raw beef and eggs was originally served as a hangover cure; today it is an international favorite as a luncheon or supper dish.

PREPARATION TIME: *25 minutes*

INGREDIENTS (*for 8*):
*2 pounds freshly ground lean beef
    put through the grinder twice
    (top or bottom round, or top
    sirloin)*
12 anchovy fillets
1 medium onion, very finely chopped
2 teaspoons or more Dijon mustard
3 raw egg yolks
2 teaspoons salt or to taste
1 teaspoon freshly ground pepper
4 tablespoons cognac
Parsley
Chives

Spread the meat on a chopping board in a rectangle. Chop the anchovies very finely. Blend them into the meat with 2 heavy-bladed

knives, using a spreading stroke with one hand and a chopping stroke with the other. Fold the meat in from the edges to the center and then spread it out as before.

Add the onion, mustard, and egg yolks and spread and chop. Fold in again from the edges to the center. Spread and chop until the meat is a rectangle once more. Add the salt and freshly ground pepper and the cognac. Tabasco and Worcestershire sauce may be added to taste, if desired. Spread and chop, this time very well, and again bring in the edges to form a large patty.

Place in a bowl and cover with chopped parsley and chives, or form a large patty and arrange on a board or platter. Garnish with chopped parsley. Serve with rye or pumpernickel bread. Steak tartare may also be shaped into small balls, rolled in chopped parsley or finely chopped nuts, and served on toothpicks as an hors d'oeuvre.

239

DOLMAS

In Turkey one of the most popular main course dishes is fresh grape leaves stuffed with rice and ground lamb and served with yogurt. Young cabbage leaves or imported bottled grape leaves make excellent, flavorful substitutes.

PREPARATION TIME: *40 minutes*
COOKING TIME: *1 hour*

INGREDIENTS (*for 4–6*):
12 fresh grape or cabbage leaves, or
  bottled grape leaves
1 onion
½ cup long grain rice
6 tablespoons butter
4 cups white stock (p.298)
1 pound lean ground lamb
2 teaspoons chopped fresh mint or
  parsley
1 teaspoon powdered rosemary
Salt and black pepper
Juice of ½ lemon
½ cup yogurt

Peel the onion and chop it finely. Melt 2 tablespoons of the butter in a large heavy-bottomed pan and sauté onion and rice until lightly colored. Add enough stock to cover the rice and cook over low heat until tender. Stir frequently and add more white stock if necessary.

Leave the rice and onion to cool and set. Stir in the ground lamb, the mint or parsley, and rosemary, and mix thoroughly. Season to taste with salt and freshly ground pepper. Blanch* the fresh grape or cabbage leaves for a few minutes in boiling water, then remove the coarse stalks. If using bottled grape leaves, unravel carefully without breaking them.

Spread out the leaves and put a spoonful of the lamb and rice filling on each; fold the leaves over to make small, neat packages. Pack them closely in layers in a flameproof casserole or skillet. Add enough stock to cover, and sprinkle with the lemon juice; dot with the remaining butter. Put a plate on top of the dolmas to keep them submerged in the liquid while they are cooking.

Cover with a lid or foil and simmer over low heat for about 1 hour. Lift out the dolmas with a slotted spoon and arrange them on a warm serving dish. Serve the yogurt in a separate bowl.

VEAL AND HAM PIE

Veal pies became popular during the 18th century and were often made into jellied molds. This recipe is a simpler farmhouse version.

PREPARATION TIME: *2½ hours*
COOKING TIME: *2½ hours*

INGREDIENTS (*for 4–6*):
2 pounds stewing veal
1 veal shank bone
4–5 cups chicken stock
2 bay leaves
Bouquet garni (p.410)
1 tablespoon chopped parsley
6 black peppercorns
Salt and black pepper
½-pound piece cooked ham
3 hard-cooked eggs
Rind from 1 lemon
Flaky pastry (p.362)
1 egg
1 teaspoon olive oil

Ask the butcher to saw the shank bone into pieces. Place the veal and the shank bone in a large pan and cover with stock. Add the bay leaves, bouquet garni, parsley, and peppercorns. Bring to a boil, cover, and simmer for 2 hours. Cool slightly, then remove the meat and cut it into small pieces. Strain the liquid, season to taste with salt and freshly ground pepper, and set it aside.

Cut the ham into narrow strips and mix with the veal. Shell the hard-cooked eggs, place them in the center of a 5-cup pie dish, and pack the veal and ham around them. Grate the lemon rind and sprinkle it over the top. Pour the liquid over the pie filling to just cover it.

Roll out the flaky pastry ¼ inch thick. Cover the pie with the pastry and make a slit in the center. Beat the egg, mix it with the olive oil, and brush over the pastry. Bake the pie for 10 minutes in the center of an oven preheated to 450°F. Reduce the heat to 400°F and bake for another 20 minutes, or until the pastry is golden brown. Give the pie a half turn halfway through cooking. Pour in more stock, if necessary, through the pastry slit.

Serve the pie hot with boiled potatoes and a green vegetable, or, ideally, cold with a tossed salad.

PIG'S KNUCKLES AND SAUERKRAUT

This hearty dish is a delight on a crisp fall night. A mug of beer makes an ideal accompaniment.

PREPARATION TIME: *30 minutes*
COOKING TIME: *3–3½ hours*

INGREDIENTS (*for 6*):
3 pounds sauerkraut
6 pig's knuckles
1 onion stuck with 2 cloves
1½ teaspoons freshly ground pepper
1 tablespoon caraway seeds
1 pint or more of broth, beer, or
  white wine
12 frankfurters

Place half of the sauerkraut in a layer on the bottom of a large kettle. Add the knuckles and the onion, pepper, and caraway seeds. Then add the rest of the sauerkraut in a layer. Pour the broth, beer, or white wine over the sauerkraut and cover. Bring to a boil; lower the heat and simmer gently until the knuckles are thoroughly tender, about 3–3½ hours. Add the frankfurters 10 minutes before the dish is done.

Serve the knuckles on a bed of sauerkraut with the frankfurters as a garnish. Boiled potatoes are a must as a side dish; also serve plenty of good mustard or horseradish, and perhaps some pickles.

BROILED FLANK STEAK

A preliminary marinade helps to tenderize this steak and gives it added flavor and color.

PREPARATION TIME: *10 minutes*
MARINATING TIME: *30 minutes or*
  more
COOKING TIME: *6 minutes*

INGREDIENTS (*for 4*):
1 2-pound flank steak
3 tablespoons minced onion
1 garlic clove, minced
2 tablespoons vegetable oil
2 tablespoons soy sauce
½ teaspoon dried thyme
Juice of ½ lemon

Score* the steak on both sides and lay it flat in a broiling pan. Mix the remaining ingredients and pour them over the steak. Turn the steak over in the marinade a few times to coat it well. Cover and refrigerate at least 30 minutes or overnight. Preheat broiler for 15 minutes. Broil the steak 3 minutes on each side. The steak should be rare. To serve, cut the steak across the grain and at a sharp angle into very thin slices.

VEAL ROLLS WITH FRITTATA FILLING

A *frittata* is an Italian cross between an omelet and a pancake. It is a traditional filling for rolled veal and is first cooked like a thin pancake until golden brown and then placed over the meat. In Italy the frittatas are often served as a garnish with veal scallops as well.

PREPARATION TIME: *30 minutes*
COOKING TIME: *1½ hours*

INGREDIENTS (*for 4*):

8 veal scallops, about 3 ounces
  each
2 eggs
½ cup chopped mortadella sausage or
  lean ham
1 tablespoon chopped fresh parsley
1–2 tablespoons grated Parmesan
  cheese
6 tablespoons butter

¼ pound button mushrooms
1 onion
1–2 tablespoons flour
½ cup milk
½–1 cup stock or bouillon
Salt and black pepper
Lemon juice
Dried mixed herbs (p.411)

Beat the veal scallops thin between sheets of waxed paper. Trim them neatly and set aside. Beat the eggs lightly and stir in the chopped sausage, parsley, and grated cheese.

Melt a little butter in a small omelet pan and, when hot, spoon in enough of the egg mixture to thinly cover the bottom of the pan. Cook the frittata until golden brown, then turn it and cook the other side. Cook the remaining mixture, to make 8 frittatas in all.

Cover each veal scallop with a frittata, trimming these to the shape of the meat. Roll up each scallop and tie at intervals with fine string.

Trim the mushrooms* and cut them in half if large. Peel the onion and slice it thinly. Melt the remaining butter in a heavy-bottomed pan and sauté the veal rolls over high heat until golden brown. Lift the rolls from the pan. Sauté the mushrooms and onion in the remaining butter in the pan until soft, then take the pan off the heat. Blend in enough flour to absorb all the fat, and gradually stir in the milk and ½ cup of stock. Lower the heat and bring the sauce to a simmer, stirring continuously. Cook for 5 minutes, then season with salt, pepper, lemon juice, and dried herbs.

Add the veal rolls to the sauce, thinning it with a little more stock if necessary (the sauce should cover the rolls completely). Cover pan and simmer for about 1 hour or until the meat is tender.

Lift out the veal rolls, remove the string, and arrange them on a hot serving dish. Spoon a little of the sauce over the meat and serve the remainder in a sauceboat. Duchesse potatoes (p.333) and buttered broccoli or green beans would be good accompaniments.

TOURNEDOS EN CROÛTE

The small, thick slices—or *tournedos*—cut from the fillet of beef are among the most expensive cuts of meat. But for a special occasion, tournedos can be encased in a light puff pastry, and 4 ounces of meat will then be sufficient for each person.

PREPARATION TIME: *30 minutes*
COOKING TIME: *40 minutes*

INGREDIENTS (*for 6*):
6 tournedos
4 tablespoons unsalted butter
½ recipe puff pastry (p.363)
4 ounces pâté with truffles
1 egg
1 onion
½ cup red wine
1¼ cups beef stock
Salt and black pepper
GARNISH:
Watercress

Trim any excess fat off the tournedos. Heat the butter in a heavy-bottomed pan and brown the meat quickly on both sides to seal in the juices. Set aside to cool.

Roll out the puff pastry on a floured surface to a rectangle ⅛ inch thick. Divide the pastry into 6 equal squares, each large enough to wrap around a tournedos. Spread one side of each tournedos with pâté and place it, pâté side down, on a pastry square. Brush the edges of the pastry with cold water and draw them together over the meat to form a neat package. Seal the edges of the pastry carefully with the fingers.

Place the pastry packages, with the seams underneath, on a wet baking sheet. Lightly beat the egg and brush over the pastry. Make 2 or 3 slits in each package for the steam to escape, and decorate with leaves cut from the pastry trimmings. Brush with beaten egg.

Bake the tournedos in the center of a preheated oven at 425°F for 15–20 minutes. At this point the pastry should be well risen and golden brown, and the meat will be rosy-pink in the middle. For well-done steaks, lower the heat to 350°F and cook for another 10 minutes.

Make the sauce while the tournedos are cooking. Peel and finely chop the onion and sauté until just colored in the butter left in the pan. Add the wine and let it bubble over moderate heat for 2–3 minutes, stirring up the residue from the pan. Blend in the stock and simmer for a further 5 minutes. Season with salt and freshly ground pepper.

Arrange the tournedos on a warm serving dish garnished with several sprigs of watercress. Pour the sauce into a sauceboat and serve with scalloped potatoes and Turkish fried carrots (p.246).

241

Poultry & Game

ROAST GOOSE WITH GERMAN-STYLE SWEET STUFFING

Goose is a much-neglected bird, yet it has endless possibilities. It is not only an excellent choice for holidays but makes a festive dinner any time of the year.

PREPARATION TIME: *30 minutes*
COOKING TIME: *2½–3 hours*

INGREDIENTS (*for 6–8*):
1 goose, fresh or frozen, 8–10 pounds
STUFFING:
6 cups day-old bread, cut into cubes
3 cups chopped apples
1 cup raisins
½ cup sugar
1 teaspoon salt
1 teaspoon cinnamon
½ teaspoon allspice
½ cup water
¼ cup melted butter

If the goose is frozen, place it, still in its original wrap, on a tray in the refrigerator for 1–1½ days to thaw. The goose may be thawed in 4 or 5 hours if it is placed, unwrapped, in a sink with cool or cold water. Change the water often to hasten thawing. To thaw at room temperature in 6–10 hours, leave the goose in its original wrap and place it in a brown paper bag, or wrap in 2 or 3 layers of newspaper and place on a tray.

Cook immediately after thawing, or refrigerate until ready to cook. Remove the neck and giblets from the body cavity; cook them immediately in enough salted water to cover and reserve for another use. Remove the excess fat from the body cavity and neck skin. Reserve this fat and render it (p.412) for use in other cooking. Rinse bird inside and out, and drain well.

The wings may be removed at the second joint or tied flat against the body with a cord around each wing and across the back. If 2 end pieces of wings are removed, cook them with the neck and giblets.

To make the stuffing, combine the bread cubes, apples, and raisins in a large bowl. Mix the sugar with the salt, cinnamon, and allspice; sprinkle this over the bread mixture and toss well. Stir in water and butter. Fill the neck and the body cavity loosely with the stuffing. Fasten the neck skin to the back of the goose with a skewer. Tie the legs together with string, or tuck the legs in the band of skin at the tail, if it is present. It is not necessary to truss the bird.

Place the goose, breast side up, on a rack in a roasting pan. Insert a meat thermometer deep into inside thigh muscle without touching the bone. Roast, uncovered, for 1 hour in a preheated 400°F oven. It is not necessary to baste. During roasting, spoon or siphon off accumulated fat and reserve it for use as a shortening in other cooking. This should be done at half-hour intervals so that the fat will not brown excessively.

After roasting for 1 hour, reduce the oven temperature to 325°F and continue cooking for 1½–2 hours, or until thermometer registers 180°–185°F. Stuffing temperature should also be checked and should register 165°F. If a thermometer is not used, press the meaty part of the leg between protected fingers. It should feel very soft. Also, prick the thigh with a fork. The juices running out should be beige in color, not pink.

COUNTRY CAPTAIN

Tradition holds that an East Indian officer gave this chicken dish to a sea captain who carried the recipe to the United States.

PREPARATION TIME: *40 minutes*
COOKING TIME: *25–30 minutes*

INGREDIENTS (*for 4*):
1 3-pound frying chicken
⅓ cup flour
1 teaspoon salt
¼ teaspoon black pepper
¼ cup butter
½ cup finely diced onion
½ cup finely diced green pepper
1 clove garlic, minced
1½ teaspoons curry powder
½ teaspoon dried thyme
2 cups canned stewed tomatoes
3 tablespoons dried currants
¼ cup blanched toasted almonds

Cut the chicken into serving pieces; wash and dry them thoroughly, and coat them with a mixture of the flour, salt, and pepper.

Heat the butter in a large skillet and brown the chicken. Remove the chicken and add the onion, green pepper, garlic, curry powder, thyme, and the stewed tomatoes to the skillet. Stir to loosen the browned particles on the bottom of the skillet.

Return the chicken to the skillet, cover, and cook slowly 25–30 minutes or until tender. Stir the currants into the sauce and garnish with the toasted almonds.* Serve the chicken with boiled rice and chutney.

CHICKEN KIEV

This classic recipe of deep-fried chicken fillets stuffed with flavored butter comes from Russia. The initial preparation of the dish should be done well in advance to allow time for chilling.

PREPARATION TIME: *40 minutes*
CHILLING TIME: *2 hours*
COOKING TIME: *15 minutes*

INGREDIENTS (*for 4*):
2 whole chicken breasts
¼ pound unsalted butter
Grated rind and juice of 1 small lemon
2 tablespoons fresh chopped tarragon or parsley
Ground nutmeg (optional)
Salt and black pepper
1 large egg
2 cups fresh white bread crumbs
Fat or oil for deep-frying
GARNISH:
Watercress

Cream the butter in a bowl with the lemon rind, tarragon or parsley, and a pinch of nutmeg. Season to taste with salt, freshly ground pepper, and a little lemon juice. Shape the butter into a rectangular block, wrap it in foil, and leave in the freezer until solid.

Meanwhile, skin and bone the breasts, removing each half breast in one complete piece. Lay the breast pieces between sheets of waxed paper and beat them flat.

Cut the frozen butter into 4 finger-length pieces and place one in the center of each chicken piece. Fold the edges over neatly and roll up tightly, completely enveloping the butter. Beat the egg lightly and brush over the chicken rolls before coating them evenly with bread crumbs; press the crumbs in thoroughly. The chicken rolls may be coated a second time for a crisper finish, patting the egg with a brush so as not to disturb the first coating. Roll again in crumbs. Leave the rolls in the refrigerator until the coating has set, about 1 hour.

Heat the fat or oil* to 375°F in a deep-fryer. Fry the chicken rolls in 2 batches until golden brown, about 6 minutes. Do not allow the fat to get too hot, or the chicken will brown before it is cooked. Drain the rolls on paper towels.

Arrange the chicken rolls on a warmed serving dish and garnish with small bunches of watercress. New potatoes and sliced zucchini cooked in butter make good side dishes with the chicken.

CHICKEN FRICASSEE

This dish probably has a French origin, but chicken fricassee in its many versions has become a North American favorite.

PREPARATION TIME: 1¼ hours
COOKING TIME: 1 hour

INGREDIENTS (for 4–6):
1 4-pound chicken, cut into serving pieces
6 cups water
1 small veal bone
Salt
1 onion
1 sprig parsley
1 sprig thyme
1 bay leaf
1–2 cloves
3 tablespoons butter or margarine
3 tablespoons flour
1 cup milk or cream
Salt, pepper, nutmeg
Chopped parsley

To make the broth, stew the neck, wing tips, and giblets in 6 cups of water with a small veal bone for 1 hour. Salt to taste. Strain the hot broth and pour it over the chicken in a large kettle. Add the onion, parsley, thyme, bay leaf, and cloves. Simmer, covered, until chicken is tender. This should take about 1 hour; but may vary, depending on the age of the chicken.

In a skillet melt the butter, add the flour, and blend well. Add 2 cups of chicken broth and stir until it begins to thicken. Add the milk or cream gradually, stirring until the mixture is thoroughly blended. Season with salt, pepper, and nutmeg.

Arrange the pieces of chicken on a warm serving platter. Surround with boiled rice or buttered noodles and pour the sauce over all. Sprinkle with finely chopped parsley.

PHEASANT WITH CABBAGE

This has long been a favorite of pheasant lovers and makes a satisfying meal on a cool fall evening. However, if pheasant is unavailable or too expensive, the dish may be prepared with chicken.

PREPARATION TIME: 15 minutes
COOKING TIME: about 1 hour

INGREDIENTS (for 4):
2 young pheasants
Salt and white pepper
6 tablespoons bacon fat or butter
4 slices bacon
1 medium head green cabbage
1 cup heavy cream
12 juniper berries
Paprika

Sprinkle the pheasants inside and out with salt and pepper. Brown the pheasants in hot bacon fat or butter on all sides in a large casserole or Dutch oven. Top the breasts with bacon slices and secure the bacon with toothpicks. Reduce the heat, cover, and simmer 1 hour until almost tender. Remove the pheasants and set aside.

While the pheasants are cooking, shred the cabbage and parboil in salted water for 10 minutes. Drain.

Place the cabbage in a casserole, cover, and cook slowly for 10 minutes. Season with salt and white pepper. Add the pheasants to the cabbage, pour the cream over them, and add the juniper berries. Simmer, covered, for 5 minutes. Before serving, sprinkle the birds and cabbage with a little paprika.

Serve on a warm platter with boiled new potatoes.

243

Rice & Pasta

SCHINKENFLECKERL

Most pasta dishes are of Italian origin, but this recipe for lasagne with ham is traditional both in Austria and Switzerland.

PREPARATION TIME: *15 minutes*
COOKING TIME: *40–45 minutes*

INGREDIENTS (*for 4*):
½ *pound lasagne*
1–1½ *tablespoons olive oil*
2 *tablespoons toasted bread crumbs*
½ *pound lean ham*
2 *shallots or 1 small onion*
4 *tablespoons butter*
1 *cup sour cream*
2 *eggs*
Salt and black pepper
½ *cup grated Gruyère or Cheddar cheese*
GARNISH:
1 *small green pepper*

Grease a round 6-inch-diameter cake pan with the oil and coat it evenly with the bread crumbs.

Bring a large pot of salted water to a boil and add the lasagne. Bring back to a boil and cook over high heat for 10–15 minutes, or until the lasagne is al dente.* Drain thoroughly in a colander and cut the lasagne strips into squares. Put squares in a large bowl.

While the pasta is cooking, dice the ham, and peel and finely chop the shallots or the onion. Melt the butter in a small skillet and cook the shallots over moderate heat for 5 minutes or until soft and transparent. Blend the contents of the pan into the pasta.

Blend the sour cream and eggs in a small bowl, stir in the ham and grated cheese, and add this mixture to the pasta. Blend thoroughly and season to taste with salt and freshly ground pepper.

Spoon the pasta mixture into the prepared cake pan and place it in a roasting pan with enough cold water to reach 1 inch up the sides of the cake pan. Bake in the center of a preheated oven at 400°F for 30 minutes, or until the mixture has set and is light brown on top.

Remove the pan from the oven and allow the mixture to cool and shrink slightly before unmolding it onto a warmed serving dish. Garnish with wedges or small squares of lightly broiled green pepper. Halved tomatoes and mushroom caps, put under a hot broiler for a few minutes, would also be an attractive garnish. Place them on top and around the sides of the schinkenfleckerl.

Serve with a tossed green salad with French dressing (p.304).

SPAGHETTINI ESTIVI

A combination of hot and cold ingredients makes this an unusual variation of the ever-popular pasta.

PREPARATION TIME: *20 minutes*
COOKING TIME: *10–12 minutes*

INGREDIENTS (*for 2–4*):
3 *medium tomatoes, peeled and sliced*
1 *medium onion, thinly sliced*
1 *tablespoon chopped fresh basil or ½ teaspoon dried basil*
6 *tablespoons olive oil*
1½–2 *tablespoons wine vinegar*
Salt
Freshly ground black pepper
1 *pound very thin spaghetti*
GARNISH:
Parsley, chopped

Combine the sliced tomatoes, onion, and basil. Mix the olive oil, vinegar, salt, and freshly ground pepper to taste. Chill until very cold.

Cook the spaghetti in boiling salted water until just tender to the bite—do not overcook. Drain it well. Toss the hot spaghetti with the tomato salad. Sprinkle with a little chopped parsley.

ITALIAN SUPPLÌ

Rice balls, or *supplì*, are popular in Italy, both as a light lunch or as a first course. The risotto may be flavored with saffron instead of tomato juice, which is used in this recipe, and chopped ham or salami may be substituted for the shrimp. The cheese must be soft, like mozzarella or Bel Paese, so that it will pull into threads when the rice balls are broken open. The Italians call it *supplì al telefono*.

PREPARATION TIME: *30 minutes*
CHILLING TIME: *45 minutes*
COOKING TIME: *15 minutes*

INGREDIENTS (*for 6*):
1 *cup Italian short grain rice*
1 *onion*
4 *tablespoons butter*
1¾ *cups tomato juice*
½ *cup chicken stock or water*
1–2 *tablespoons grated Parmesan cheese*
Salt and black pepper
Paprika
2 *large eggs*
½ *pound mozzarella or Bel Paese cheese*
¼ *pound cooked tiny shrimp or cubed ham*
1½ *cups fresh white bread crumbs*
Oil for deep-frying

Peel and finely chop the onion. Melt the butter in a large heavy-bottomed pan and cook the onion until transparent. Add the rice and sauté it in the butter, stirring continuously until it is just starting to color. Pour in the tomato juice, cover the pan with a lid, and cook over low heat until the liquid is absorbed and the rice is just tender. Stir frequently and add a little chicken stock or water if the tomato juice is absorbed before the rice is cooked.

Take the pan off the heat and stir in the grated Parmesan cheese; season to taste with salt, freshly ground pepper, and a little paprika. Beat the eggs lightly and blend into the risotto mixture. Turn it into a bowl and leave in the refrigerator to cool and stiffen.

Cut the mozzarella or Bel Paese cheese into ½-inch cubes. Put a level tablespoon of the cold risotto in the palm of the hand. Press a shrimp or ham cube and a cube of cheese into the center; cover with another spoonful of risotto. Press and shape the mixture into a ball. Continue until all the risotto, shrimp, and cheese are used—the mixture will make 12–14 balls.

Roll the rice balls in the bread crumbs. Heat the cooking oil* in a deep-fryer to 375°F and fry the rice balls in batches until crisp and golden, about 4 minutes to each batch. Drain the rice balls on paper towels while frying the next batch.

Serve the supplì hot as it is, or with a crisp celery salad or with a mixed green salad tossed in French dressing (p.304).

SICILIAN PASTA

This interesting and pungent pasta dish also has the virtue of being easy to prepare.

PREPARATION TIME: *5 minutes*
COOKING TIME: *10–12 minutes*

INGREDIENTS (*for 4*):
1 *pound very thin spaghetti*
½ *cup olive oil*
4 *garlic cloves, peeled and finely minced*
½ *cup raisins, soaked in Marsala*
18 *anchovy fillets, finely chopped*
½ *cup pine nuts*
¼–½ *cup chopped parsley*

Cook the spaghetti in boiling salted water until just tender to the bite. Do not overcook. Drain it well and keep hot.

Sauté the garlic in the oil for 1–2 minutes. Add the remaining ingredients and toss quickly to just heat through. Serve this sauce on the hot spaghetti, without cheese.

Vegetables

BROCCOLI WITH POULETTE SAUCE

In this recipe the broccoli is served with a classic French vegetable sauce whose creamy-white color contrasts well with the dark green vegetable.

PREPARATION TIME: *10 minutes*
COOKING TIME: *30 minutes*

INGREDIENTS (*for 4–6*):
2 pounds broccoli
Salt and black pepper
4 tablespoons butter
1 tablespoon flour
1 egg yolk
Juice of ½ lemon
2 tablespoons heavy cream

Trim the tough stalks and leaves off the broccoli. Wash thoroughly in cold water. Put the broccoli in a large pan of boiling salted water. Cover the pan with a lid and simmer over low heat for about 15 minutes or until just tender. Lift the broccoli carefully into a colander to drain; set the liquid aside and keep it warm.

Melt the butter in a small saucepan, then take the pan off the heat. Stir in the flour to make a roux,* and gradually blend in 1¼ cups of the broccoli liquid. Bring this sauce to a boil over low heat and simmer for about 10 minutes. Beat the egg yolk with 1 tablespoon of lemon juice and 2 tablespoons of the hot sauce. Remove the sauce from the heat and blend in the egg mixture.

Stir in the cream. Keep the sauce warm, but do not allow it to boil, or the egg and cream will curdle. Season to taste with salt, freshly ground pepper, and more lemon juice. Put the broccoli in a warm deep serving dish and pour over the sauce.

WESTPHALIAN BEANS AND PEARS

A blending of sweet and sharp flavors is characteristic of German cookery. This recipe for green beans makes an appetizing vegetable dish with roast pork or ham.

PREPARATION TIME: *15 minutes*
COOKING TIME: *30 minutes*

INGREDIENTS (*for 4–6*):
1 pound young, tender green beans
4 large, firm, slightly underripe cooking pears
2 cups stock or bouillon
Lemon rind
4 slices bacon
2 tablespoons light brown sugar
1 tablespoon tarragon vinegar

Peel the pears and cut them in half lengthwise. Remove cores and cut each half across into 3–4 pieces. Bring the stock to a boil and drop in a piece of lemon rind and the pears. Simmer, uncovered, over low heat for 10 minutes.

Meanwhile, trim and wash the beans and add them to the pears. Continue cooking over low heat.

Cut the bacon slices crosswise into ½-inch-wide strips. Sauté the bacon strips, with no additional fat, in a skillet over low heat until the fat runs and the bacon becomes crisp. Remove the bacon from the pan with a slotted spoon and keep it warm. Stir the sugar into the fat in the skillet; blend in the vinegar and 2 tablespoons pear and bean liquid. Mix thoroughly, then add to the pan containing the pears and beans. Simmer, uncovered, until the liquid has reduced* to a syrupy sauce and the beans are tender. Remove the lemon. Spoon the beans, pears, and liquid into a hot serving dish and sprinkle with the bacon.

CHICKPEA PATTIES

These patties can also be made from split peas or lentils. Serve the patties with boiled or baked ham, or with broiled bacon.

PREPARATION TIME: *50 minutes*
COOKING TIME: *2¼ hours*

INGREDIENTS (*for 4*):
½ pound chickpeas
1 onion
2½ cups ham stock
2 tablespoons butter
2 tablespoons chopped parsley
Salt and black pepper
1 large egg
¼ cup bacon fat or drippings

Soak the dried chickpeas in a bowl of water for 8 hours or overnight. Drain the chickpeas and put them in a saucepan with the stock. Bring to a boil, cover the pan with a lid, and simmer for about 2 hours or until tender (if they are very hard, this may take as long as 5 hours).

Drain the chickpeas and make them into a coarse purée* in a blender or a food mill. Peel and finely chop the onion. Sauté the onion in the butter over low heat about 5 minutes.

Blend the cooked onion into the chickpea purée, together with the finely chopped parsley. Season to taste with salt and pepper; bind the purée with beaten egg. Spread the mixture on a flat plate and divide it into 8 equal portions. Roll each portion into a ball between floured hands, then flatten it into a round patty shape. Chill the patties for about 30 minutes or until set.

Heat the fat in a heavy-bottomed pan over moderate heat and sauté the patties until golden brown on both sides, turning once. Drain the patties on paper towels.

PARSNIP PURÉE

A vegetable that is too often overlooked, the parsnip can make a delicious accompaniment to game, turkey or chicken, or a roast.

PREPARATION TIME: *40 minutes*
COOKING TIME: *25–30 minutes*

INGREDIENTS (*for 6*):
3 pounds parsnips
1 teaspoon salt
1 teaspoon sugar
¼ pound (½ cup) butter, melted
4 tablespoons heavy cream
¼ cup or more Madeira
Buttered bread crumbs

Put the parsnips in enough boiling salted water to cover and cook for 20–40 minutes or until tender. Do not overcook. Drain the parsnips and plunge them into cold water to cool so they can be peeled easily.

Remove the skins and put the parsnips through a food mill or through the purée attachment of an electric mixer. Combine the purée with the salt, sugar, butter, cream, and Madeira. Whip with a large spoon or electric mixer and spoon into a 1-quart baking dish. Dot with additional butter, sprinkle with buttered bread crumbs (p.395), and bake at 350°F for 25–30 minutes.

TURKISH FRIED CARROTS

In Turkey cold or warm yogurt is often used to dress vegetables and salads. These fried carrots are especially suited to broiled or roast lamb.

PREPARATION TIME: *15 minutes*
COOKING TIME: *20 minutes*

INGREDIENTS (*for 4*):
1 pound carrots
1 tablespoon seasoned flour (p.412)
2 tablespoons olive oil
Salt and black pepper
1¼ cups yogurt
GARNISH:
1 tablespoon chopped mint or 1
teaspoon caraway seeds

Peel or scrape the carrots and wash them. Cut them crosswise into ¼-inch-thick slices. Bring a pan of salted water to a boil and cook the carrots for about 10 minutes or until nearly tender. Drain in a colander, then spread the carrots on paper towels to dry thoroughly.

Toss the carrots in seasoned flour, shaking off any surplus. Heat the oil in a heavy-bottomed pan and sauté the carrots over moderate heat until golden brown. Season to taste with salt and freshly ground pepper. Put the yogurt in a separate pan over low heat and let it warm through. Be careful not to let it reach the boiling point or it will curdle.

Spoon the carrots into a hot serving dish, pour over the yogurt, and sprinkle with mint or caraway seeds.

CHESTNUT AND POTATO PURÉE

Chestnuts are traditionally served as stuffing or as garnishes with game birds. This purée of potato and chestnuts is an excellent vegetable to serve with all kinds of game, turkey, or roast ham.

PREPARATION TIME: *20 minutes*
COOKING TIME: *30 minutes*

INGREDIENTS (*for 6–8*):
¾ pound fresh chestnuts or ½ pound
canned chestnut purée
2½ cups stock or bouillon
2 cups mashed potatoes
4 tablespoons butter
4–5 tablespoons light cream
Salt
Ground nutmeg or black pepper
4 tablespoons chopped celery heart

Make a small cut on the flat side of each chestnut and roast them on a baking sheet near the top of an oven heated to 400°F. After 5–10 minutes the skins will crack. Peel the two layers of skin from the chestnuts while they are still warm.

Put the stock in a saucepan, add the peeled chestnuts, and cover the pan with a lid. Bring to a boil, then simmer the chestnuts for 20 minutes or until tender. Drain the chestnuts and rub them through a coarse sieve.

Blend the chestnut purée with the mashed potato, stir in the butter, and heat the mixture through over low heat. Blend in enough cream to give the purée a fluffy texture, and season with salt and ground nutmeg or freshly ground pepper.

Blend in the chopped celery just before serving.

SCALLOPED POTATOES

For this recipe, choose firm, waxy potatoes that will not break up during long, slow cooking. The dish can be served with any type of broiled or roast meat, or it can be made into a main dish by adding ground ham or flaked cooked fish between the potato layers.

PREPARATION TIME: *15–20 minutes*
COOKING TIME: *1½ hours*

INGREDIENTS (*for 6*):
1½ pounds potatoes
1 onion
¼ pound Cheddar cheese
4 tablespoons butter
Salt and black pepper
1 egg
1¼ cups milk

Peel and wash the potatoes and cut them into thin slices. Peel and finely chop the onion and grate the cheese. Use a little of the butter to grease a shallow baking dish. Arrange the potato slices in layers in the dish, sprinkling each layer with onion, cheese, salt, and freshly ground pepper. Finish with a thick layer of cheese and dot the top with the remaining butter.

Beat the egg and milk together and pour this mixture carefully over the potatoes. Cover the dish with buttered waxed paper or foil. Bake in the center of a preheated oven at 350°F for 1½ hours, or until the potatoes are tender and the topping is golden. If cooked too quickly, the egg and milk will curdle.

BAKED CABBAGE

Cabbage is one of the least expensive vegetables. Baked in a cheese sauce, it goes well with sausages and ham.

PREPARATION TIME: *30 minutes*
COOKING TIME: *15 minutes*

INGREDIENTS (*for 6*):
1½ pounds cabbage
3 tablespoons butter
3 tablespoons flour
1 cup milk
Salt and black pepper
Ground mace or nutmeg
1 cup salted chopped peanuts
½–1 cup grated Cheddar cheese

Discard any damaged outer leaves and cut the cabbage into quarters. Cut out the center stalk and shred the cabbage finely.

Heat ½ inch of water in a large heavy saucepan and add 1 teaspoon of salt. Put in the washed cabbage, a handful or two at a time, seasoning each of the layers with freshly ground black pepper.

Cover the pan with a lid and cook over low heat for about 10 minutes, or until the cabbage is cooked but still crisp.

Meanwhile, make a thick white sauce (p.301) from the butter, flour, and milk. Season to taste with salt, pepper, and mace (or nutmeg).

Butter an ovenproof dish lightly and arrange a layer of cabbage over the bottom. Cover with some of the sauce and sprinkle with nuts and cheese. Fill the dish with layers of cabbage, sauce, nuts, and cheese, finishing with cheese. Bake in the center of a preheated oven at 425°F for 15 minutes, or until the cheese is golden brown.

Serve the cabbage at once.

Desserts

FRESH FIGS AND YOGURT

Purple, black, and green figs are generally available for a short season – August through October – and should be used while they are most plentiful and least expensive.

PREPARATION TIME: *15 minutes*
CHILLING TIME: *2 hours*

INGREDIENTS (*for 4*):
8 fresh figs
½ cup heavy cream
½ cup yogurt
3–4 tablespoons light brown sugar

Submerge the figs in hot water for 1 minute. Drain, peel, and quarter each fig. Beat the cream lightly and blend it into the yogurt. Spoon a little of the cream mixture into 4 sherbet glasses. Top with a layer of figs, followed by more cream and figs, and finish with a layer of cream mixture. Sprinkle each layer with brown sugar.

Chill in the refrigerator for at least 2 hours to allow the sugar to melt into the cream.

Fresh figs are usually available from August through October.

COMPOTE OF DRIED FRUITS

A blend of dried fruits is a welcome change from other desserts at any time of the year.

PREPARATION TIME: *10 minutes*
COOKING TIME: *40 minutes*

INGREDIENTS (*for 12*):
½ pound each, dried prunes, apricots, and peaches
¼ pound dried pears
1½–2 cups water
3 slices lemon
¾–1 cup sugar
Bourbon, cognac, or rum

Cover the fruit with water in a large saucepan and bring it just to a boil. Add the lemon slices and the sugar. Simmer for 15–20 minutes or until the fruit is puffed.

Add the cognac, bourbon, or rum to taste. Let fruit stand in the pan for a few minutes after it has stopped simmering.

Transfer the fruit to a serving dish and allow it to cool slightly. Serve with heavy cream or whipped cream.

CLAFOUTI WITH PLUMS

Clafouti, a baked pudding, should be served warm with either whipped cream or pouring cream.

PREPARATION TIME: *20 minutes*
COOKING TIME: *40 minutes*

INGREDIENTS (*for 6–8*):
1 pound firm, ripe purple plums
2 teaspoons lemon juice
3 tablespoons kirsch
½ cup butter
½ cup and 1 tablespoon granulated sugar
1 teaspoon grated lemon peel
¼ teaspoon nutmeg
3 eggs
1 cup unsifted all-purpose flour
Powdered sugar

Drop plums in boiling water for 10 seconds. Remove from the water; peel and slice, or leave them whole but remove the pits. Combine the lemon juice and the kirsch with the plums and marinate 30 minutes, stirring occasionally.

Cream the butter with ½ cup of the sugar, lemon peel, and nutmeg until fluffy, then beat in the eggs, one at a time. Mix in the flour until the batter is smooth. Spread this batter in a greased and floured 9- or 10-inch cheesecake pan with a removable bottom or springform sides, or in a 10-inch pie plate.

Remove the plums from the marinade with a slotted spoon and distribute the plums evenly over the batter. Mix the remaining tablespoon of sugar with the marinating liquid and drizzle this over the fruit. Bake in a 375°F oven for 40 minutes, or until cake around fruit springs back firmly when lightly touched.

Serve slightly warm, lightly dusted with powdered sugar.

SHOO-FLY PIE WITH RAISINS

This dessert, a Pennsylvania Dutch specialty, takes its unusual name from its extreme sweetness. It is said that flies are so attracted to the pie that it is necessary to shoo them away while it is cooling.

PREPARATION TIME: *30 minutes*
COOKING TIME: *35 minutes*

INGREDIENTS (*for 6*):
½ recipe standard pastry (p.354)
⅔ cup raisins
⅓ cup molasses
¼ teaspoon baking soda
TOPPING:
¾ cup sifted flour
½ teaspoon cinnamon
¼ teaspoon ground nutmeg
¼ teaspoon ground ginger
4 tablespoons unsalted butter
⅓ cup light brown sugar, firmly packed

Prepare the standard pastry and roll it out thinly on a lightly floured board. Line an 8-inch flan ring or shallow pie plate with the pastry. Crimp* the edges between finger and thumb for a decorative finish. Prick the bottom of the pastry all over with a fork and cover with the raisins. Mix the molasses with 5 tablespoons of hot water and the baking soda; pour over the raisins.

For the topping, sift together the flour and spices. Cut the butter into small pieces and rub them into the flour until the mixture resembles fine bread crumbs. Stir in the brown sugar and sprinkle over the filling.

Bake the pie on the shelf above the center of a preheated oven at 425°F for 10 minutes, or until the pie begins to brown. Reduce the heat to 325°F and bake for a further 15 minutes, or until the topping has just set.

Cut the pie into wedges and serve it warm or cold. If desired, serve with ice cream or whipped cream.

DELICES DE POIRES AU CHOCOLAT

Large ripe winter pears, such as Comice, are ideal for this attractive dessert of chocolate-covered pears. It makes a good choice for a dinner party, as it can be prepared a day in advance and left in the refrigerator.

PREPARATION TIME: *20 minutes*
COOKING TIME: *20 minutes*
CHILLING TIME: *2–3 hours*

INGREDIENTS (*for 4*):
4 ripe dessert pears
1½ tablespoons shelled walnuts
2 tablespoons candied cherries
4 ounces unsweetened chocolate
2 tablespoons cold black coffee
2 tablespoons unsalted butter
1–2 tablespoons rum
2 eggs
GARNISH:
Angelica, or whipped cream and chopped pistachio nuts

Peel the pears thinly and cut out the cores from the base of the fruit, leaving the stem and top intact. Cut a small sliver from the base of each pear so that it will stand upright. Coarsely chop and mix together the walnuts and cherries and press a little of this mixture into the core cavities of the pears. Stand the pears upright in 1 large or 4 small shallow serving dishes.

Break up the chocolate and put it in a bowl with the coffee. Stand the bowl over a saucepan of boiling water and stir occasionally until the chocolate has melted. Remove the bowl from the heat and stir in first the butter and then the rum. Separate the eggs and beat the yolks, one at a time, into the chocolate mixture. Whisk the egg whites until stiff but still moist, and fold them carefully into the chocolate. The consistency

should be similar to that of a mousse.

Spoon the chocolate mixture over the pears until they are evenly coated. Soften the angelica strips in hot water; cut into ½-inch lengths and slice them crosswise into 8 diamond shapes. Make a small slit on either side of each pear stalk and in-

sert an angelica diamond, twisting them to resemble small leaves.

Chill the chocolate pears in the refrigerator for at least 2–3 hours or overnight.

Whipped cream, piped* around the pears, and chopped pistachio nuts are also attractive garnishes.

HUNGARIAN HAZELNUT TORTE·

Hungarian dessert cakes—or tortes —are internationally famous, and several of them were perfected by Dobos, a 19th-century Hungarian confectioner. This classic hazelnut torte has a chocolate cream filling and a caramel topping. It will improve somewhat in flavor if kept cool for a day or two in a completely airtight container.

PREPARATION TIME: *30 minutes*
COOKING TIME: *30–40 minutes*

INGREDIENTS (*for 6*):

⅔ cup unblanched hazelnuts
4 eggs
10 tablespoons sugar
FILLING:
4 tablespoons unsalted butter
½ cup confectioners' sugar

2 teaspoons Dutch cocoa
1 teaspoon instant coffee
TOPPING:
6 tablespoons sugar
12 hazelnuts

Grease 2 round 8-inch cake pans. Line bottoms of pans with waxed paper cut to fit. Grease the waxed paper. Grind the unblanched hazelnuts finely in a blender or coffee grinder. Separate the eggs and beat the whites until stiff but still moist. Whisk the egg yolks with 10 tablespoons of sugar until they are pale lemon in color and the mixture trails off the beater in ribbons.

Fold the ground nuts and egg whites alternately into the egg yolks. Divide the mixture equally between the 2 cake pans and bake in the center of an oven preheated to 350°F for 30 minutes or until set. Test by pressing the top of the cakes with a finger—it should leave no impression. Remove the cakes from the oven and allow them to shrink slightly before turning them out to cool on a wire rack.

Meanwhile, prepare the filling: cream the butter until fluffy and sift

the confectioners' sugar, cocoa, and coffee together; beat this gradually into the butter. When the cakes are cool, sandwich them together with the filling. Set the torte aside while preparing the caramel topping.

Put 2 tablespoons of water and 6 tablespoons of sugar in a small, heavy-bottomed saucepan. Stir the contents over low heat until dissolved into a clear syrup. Increase the heat and boil the syrup rapidly, without stirring, until it is a rich golden color.

Remove the pan from the heat immediately and pour most of the caramel over the top of the cake. Spread it evenly with an oiled knife and mark the topping into portions with the tip of a knife. Garnish the top quickly with the whole nuts before the caramel hardens. The remaining caramel can then be trickled over the nuts.

Snacks & Supper Dishes

FRIDAY NIGHT SPECIAL

Store-bought fish cakes usually provide a speedy if uninspired meal. But served with cheese, tomato sauce, and a tossed green salad, they become a family treat.

PREPARATION TIME: *5 minutes*
COOKING TIME: *15 minutes*

INGREDIENTS (*for 4–6*):
12 fish cakes
1 tablespoon olive oil
1 clove garlic, finely chopped
1 small, finely chopped onion
2 cups canned tomatoes
1 tablespoon tomato purée
½ teaspoon sugar
¼ teaspoon sage
Salt and black pepper
Fat or oil for sautéing
12 thin slices Cheddar cheese

Heat the oil in a pan and cook the garlic and onion over medium heat until the onion is transparent. Add the tomatoes with their juice, the tomato purée, sugar, and sage. Season with salt and freshly ground pepper. Bring to a boil, then simmer for 5 minutes.

Heat the fat in a heavy skillet and sauté the fish cakes until crisp on both sides. Top the drained fish cakes with cheese and broil until the cheese has melted. Arrange on a serving dish, and pour the sauce over them.

ALPINE FONDUE

Ideally, this cheese fondue should be cooked in the Swiss earthenware caquelon,* but a heavy-bottomed saucepan may be used instead.

PREPARATION TIME: *5 minutes*
COOKING TIME: *15–20 minutes*

INGREDIENTS (*for 4–6*):
2 peeled cloves garlic
¾ pound diced Gruyère cheese
½ cup milk
2 cups dry white wine
1 tablespoon kirsch
Salt and white pepper
1 loaf French bread

Rub the sliced garlic around the sides and base of the cooking pan. Cook the cheese and milk over very low heat, stirring continuously with a wooden spoon, until the cheese melts and the mixture becomes smooth and creamy. Gradually blend in the wine and kirsch; season with salt and pepper. Do not boil.

Heat the French bread in the oven until crisp. Cut it into 1-inch cubes. Use forks or skewers for dipping the bread into the cheese.

EGGS BENEDICT

This dish of ham and eggs makes a delicious snack or supper dish.

PREPARATION TIME: *5 minutes*
COOKING TIME: *15–25 minutes*

INGREDIENTS (*for 4*):
½–¾ cup Hollandaise sauce (p.303)
½ teaspoon dry mustard
Cayenne pepper
Mixed herbs (p.411)
4 slices cooked ham or back bacon
4 tablespoons unsalted butter
4 eggs
4 slices thick white bread or halved English muffins

Season the Hollandaise sauce with the mustard, a little cayenne, and mixed herbs. Keep it warm. Trim the ham to fit the bread, or cook the bacon in a little butter. Meanwhile, poach the eggs* in salted water and toast the bread or muffins.

Warm the ham or bacon. Butter the toast or muffins; cover each piece with ham or bacon and top with an egg. Pour the warm sauce over them.

MUSHROOMS WITH BACON

Crisp bacon and fresh or canned mushrooms are convenient ingredients for snacks or quick meals.

PREPARATION TIME: *10 minutes*
COOKING TIME: *20 minutes*

INGREDIENTS (*for 4*):
¼ pound sliced button mushrooms
1 tablespoon butter
8 slices bacon
1¼ cups white sauce (p.301)
¼ teaspoon mixed herbs (p.411)
Cayenne, salt, black pepper
4 slices buttered white toast

Sauté the mushrooms in the butter over low heat for 3 minutes. In another pan, fry the bacon until crisp–do not use any fat–then drain on paper towels and crumble the bacon into small pieces.

Make the white sauce, add the mixed herbs, and season with salt, freshly ground pepper, and cayenne. Gently fold the mushrooms and bacon into the sauce; heat through. Serve on buttered toast.

VANILLA POTS DE CRÈME

This easily made, delicately rich dessert is universally popular. Serve it with thin, crisp cookies.

PREPARATION TIME: *20 minutes*
COOKING TIME: *approximately 15 minutes*

INGREDIENTS (*for 6*):
6 egg yolks
½ cup sugar
2 cups heavy cream, scalded
1 teaspoon vanilla extract

Preheat the oven to 300°F. Beat the egg yolks until thick. Beat in the sugar and gradually add the cream, stirring constantly. Stir in the vanilla. Strain through a sieve and pour into 6 custard cups. Place the filled cups in a pan of warm water and cover the cups with a sheet of aluminum foil. Bake 15 minutes or until a knife inserted in the center of the custard comes out almost clean. Chill the pots de crème in the refrigerator for several hours.

Southern Cooking

The popular concept of American Southern cooking is of limited, ordinary fare centered around fried chicken, hominy grits, and low-cost, overcooked vegetables. Nothing could be further from the truth. The cooking of the region is more varied than that of any other part of the United States, with traditions imported from the British Isles, France, Spain, and Africa. It ranges from the elegant dishes of antebellum plantation society to the simple and satisfying "soul food" that has become fashionable in recent years.

Flavorful cured or smoked meats, such as Virginia ham or pit-barbecued beef, figure prominently in Southern cooking, as do the excellent shrimp, crabs, and oysters from the Atlantic Ocean and the Gulf of Mexico. Corn, sweet potatoes, and butter beans are favored vegetables, along with a variety of greens—collard, turnip, and mustard—that are usually cooked with salt pork. Hot breads, notably cornbread, hush puppies, or biscuits, are always served with meals, and the warm climate makes tall glasses of minted iced tea the most popular beverage. Desserts include ambrosia, sweet layer cakes, chess (custard) pies, and cobblers. The recipes on these pages are among the more traditional of the South.

Crab Cakes

PREPARATION TIME: *10 minutes*
COOKING TIME: *15 minutes*

INGREDIENTS (*for 6*):
1 pound cooked fresh crabmeat
4 tablespoons butter or oil
1 medium onion, chopped
1 cup dry bread crumbs
3 eggs
1 teaspoon salt
1 teaspoon dry mustard
¼ cup chopped parsley
Heavy cream
Flour

Carefully pick over the crabmeat, removing all bits of shell. Melt the butter in a skillet and cook the onion over low heat until just transparent. Add the bread crumbs and blend well. Stir in the crabmeat, the beaten eggs, and the seasonings. Add just enough heavy cream to make the mixture hold together.

Shape into 6 flat cakes. Roll each cake in flour and sauté in butter or oil until nicely browned on both sides and heated through. Serve with tartare sauce (p.303) or with lemon butter (p.338).

Cornbread

PREPARATION TIME: *10 minutes*
COOKING TIME: *18–20 minutes*

INGREDIENTS (*for 8*):
½ cup sifted all-purpose flour
1½ cups yellow cornmeal
1 teaspoon salt
1 teaspoon sugar
3 teaspoons baking powder
3 eggs, well beaten
1 cup milk
¼ cup light cream
⅓ cup melted butter

Sift dry ingredients together into a mixing bowl. Add eggs and milk and beat with a wooden spoon. Beat in the cream and melted butter.

Pour into an 8½-by-11-inch well-buttered pan and bake at 400°F approximately 15–18 minutes. Cut into squares while still hot and fold into a napkin before serving.

Hopping John

PREPARATION TIME: *15 minutes*
COOKING TIME: *35 minutes*

INGREDIENTS (*for 6*):
2 10-ounce packages frozen black-eyed peas
3 cups boiling water
1 piece lean slab bacon, about ½ pound, cut into 1-inch cubes
1 yellow onion, peeled and coarsely chopped
3 cups cooked rice
2 tablespoons bacon drippings, butter, or margarine
2 teaspoons salt
⅛–¼ teaspoon crushed hot red chili peppers
⅛ teaspoon black pepper

Put the frozen black-eyed peas, water, bacon, and onion in a large saucepan. Cover and simmer 30-35 minutes, or until peas are tender. Remove the bacon. Mix in remaining ingredients lightly and serve.

This dish is traditionally served on New Year's Day in the South.

Baked Glazed Ham

PREPARATION TIME: *5 minutes*
COOKING TIME: *3½–4 hours*

INGREDIENTS (*about 24 servings*):
1 10-12 pound, bone-in uncooked ham
Whole cloves
½ cup orange marmalade
½ cup firmly packed brown sugar
½ teaspoon ground cloves

Follow the baking instructions on the wrapper exactly. If the ham has no directions, preheat the oven to 325°F and place the ham, fat side up, on a rack in a shallow roasting pan. Insert a meat thermometer in the center of the thickest part of the ham. Do not touch the bone.

Bake until the thermometer registers 160°F, or 18-20 minutes per pound. Do not baste or cover the pan. Cooking time will be approximately 3½-4 hours.

Thirty minutes before the ham is done, remove it from the oven and carefully remove the rind with a sharp knife. Score the fat in a diamond pattern by making shallow cuts, about ⅛ inch deep and 1 inch apart, diagonally across the fat. Repeat this procedure at a different angle. Insert a whole clove in the center of each diamond.

Mix the orange marmalade, the brown sugar, and the cloves and spread this over the ham. Return the ham to the oven and continue to bake until the meat thermometer registers 160°F.

Brunswick Stew

PREPARATION TIME: *30 minutes*
COOKING TIME: *3½ hours*

INGREDIENTS (*for 8*):
1 pound chuck, cubed
1 pound lean pork
1 pound chicken parts
1 pound onions
1 1-pound 13-ounce can tomatoes
Juice of 1½ lemons
2 tablespoons Worcestershire sauce, or more to taste
1 pound potatoes
1 cup corn
1 cup lima beans
½ cup butter
Tabasco
Salt and pepper to taste

Place the meat in a heavy pot and add water to cover. Cover the pot and cook over low heat until the meat is very tender, 2 hours or more.

Remove the meat from the pot and save the broth. Let the meat cool, then pull it apart into shreds. Discard the bones. Return the meat to the liquid in the pot.

Dice the onions and add them, with the tomatoes, lemon juice, and Worcestershire sauce, to the meat. Bring to a boil, reduce the heat, and simmer gently for 1 hour.

Finely dice the potatoes and add them, with the corn, lima beans, and butter, to the pot. Cook slowly for 30

minutes. Stir the mixture with a wooden spoon until it is almost the consistency of mush. Season to taste with Tabasco, salt, and pepper.

Serve the stew piping hot with cornbread or biscuits and coleslaw.

Brunswick stew was traditionally made with game. If desired, substitute one pound of squirrel meat for the chicken.

Collards

PREPARATION TIME: *15 minutes*
COOKING TIME: *2 hours*

INGREDIENTS (*for 6-8*):
4 pounds fresh collards
1½ pounds slab bacon, or a meaty country-style ham bone
Water
Salt
Pepper

Trim and discard any large stems. Wash the collards in several changes of cold water to remove any sand. Cut the leaves into coarse strips.

Combine them with either the bacon or the ham bone. Cover with water, bring to a boil, and simmer for 1-2 hours. Taste for salt and add freshly ground pepper to taste.

Chop up the bacon, or scrape off the pieces of meat from the ham bone and discard the bone. Drain the collards. Mix the meat with collards and serve. Collards are especially good with pork or game.

Ambrosia

PREPARATION TIME: *20 minutes*

INGREDIENTS (*for 6*):
4 large seedless oranges
3 ripe bananas
¼ cup sugar or to taste
1½ cups grated fresh coconut

Peel the oranges, removing all white fiber. Section the oranges carefully so that the sections keep their shape. Peel the bananas and cut them into ¼-inch slices. Sprinkle with the sugar and coconut and toss lightly. Cover and refrigerate for 2 hours and serve.

Sweet Potato Pie

PREPARATION TIME: *30 minutes*
COOKING TIME: *45-55 minutes*

INGREDIENTS (*for a 9- or 10-inch pie or 2 8-inch pies*):
Standard pastry (p.354)
3 eggs
2 cups cooked, sieved sweet potatoes
1 cup brown sugar or ¾ cup white sugar
¼ teaspoon salt
¼–½ teaspoon ginger
½–1 teaspoon cinnamon
⅛–¼ teaspoon cloves
½–1 teaspoon nutmeg
1–1½ cups evaporated milk or light cream
Grated rind of 1 orange (optional)
1 tablespoon molasses (optional)

Preheat the oven to 450°F. Line a 9- or 10-inch pie plate or 2 8-inch pie plates with the pastry.

Break the eggs into a mixing bowl and beat with a rotary beater until the yolks and whites are combined. Add the sweet potatoes, sugar, salt, spices, milk or cream, and the orange rind and molasses, if desired, and stir to combine thoroughly. Ladle the mixture into the pie shell or shells.

Bake the 9- or 10-inch pie for 15 minutes; bake the 8-inch pies for 10 minutes; then reduce the heat to 325°F and bake about 30 minutes longer, or until the filling appears set except for about 2 inches at the center when the pie or pies are shaken very gently.

Alternately, bake 10 or 15 minutes at 450°F, depending on the size of the pie, then turn the oven off. Do not open the oven door. Leave the 10-inch pie in the oven 40-50 minutes; 8-inch pies for 35 minutes. The filling should be set when removed. This latter method will work only with a well-insulated oven. Cool the pie or pies on a rack.

This pie is an excellent, richer substitute for pumpkin pie on Thanksgiving Day.

November

Come, ye thankful people, come,
Raise the song of Harvest-home!

HENRY ALFORD

THIS MONTH'S RECIPES

November's cornucopia overflows with apples, walnuts, and cranberries while Indian corn and gourds brighten the first gray days of winter.

Food in Season

November feasting encompasses the full harvest of autumn fruits and vegetables and the bounty of fresh game. Apples and squash are still plentiful, and two seasonal fruits, cranberries and persimmons, are also in the markets. There are also large supplies of pears, grapefruit, and tangerines; broccoli, Chinese cabbage, sweet potatoes, turnips, and Brussels sprouts are abundant.

Venison and game birds are available in many markets and are no more difficult to prepare than any other fresh meat or poultry. Try venison chops with a whisky sauce (p.263), or cube the meat and bake it in a savory game pie (p.262).

Nuts are a tasty accompaniment to fall dishes. They can be used in desserts, as in Apple and Nut Strudel (p.268), and even in a hearty chicken soup (p.256).

Two little-used vegetables—leeks and celeriac—should not be overlooked. Leeks, prepared with tomatoes and garlic, can be served hot as a side dish or cold as a salad (p.265). Celeriac, the knobby, turnip-shaped root of the celery plant, is delicious when puréed with potatoes and served as a side dish to game (p.265).

SUGGESTED MENUS

Smoked Herring with Horseradish Cream
...
Coeur Coriandre
Creamed Potatoes
...
Crêpes Georgette

Chicken and Almond Soup
...
Halibut Plaki
Galette Lyonnaise
...
Bourbon Coffee Chiffon Pie

Smoked Eel Smetana
...
Savory Game Pie
Celeriac and Potato Purée
...
Linzertorte

Petits Royales au Parmesan
...
Crown Roast of Pork
Green Beans, Tuscany Style
...
Apple and Nut Strudel

Lamb Casserole
Roasted Onions
...
Bread and Butter Pudding

Shrimp Cocktail
...
Orange-Glazed Lamb Roast
Buttered Brussels Sprouts
...
Meringue Mont Blanc

Leeks à la Niçoise
...
Lasagne Verdi al Forno
Green Salad with Sauce Vinaigrette
...
Crème Caramel à l'Orange

Soups & First Courses

SHRIMP COCKTAIL

This recipe for the popular shrimp cocktail calls for a dressing of mayonnaise and garlic, rather than the traditional tomato-based sauce.

PREPARATION TIME: *25 minutes*

INGREDIENTS (*for 6*):
36 cooked shrimp of medium size
  or 3 cups tiny bay shrimp
1 cup mayonnaise (p.303)
4 tablespoons chili sauce
2 tablespoons finely chopped garlic
2 tablespoons Dijon mustard
2 tablespoons chopped parsley
GARNISH:
6 lemon slices
6 sprigs watercress

Arrange the shrimp in 6 chilled cocktail glasses. Mix the mayonnaise with the chili, garlic, mustard, and parsley and spoon over shrimp.
  Garnish with lemon slices and sprigs of watercress.

NEW ENGLAND FISH CHOWDER

Fish chowder is a New England dish that has many variations. This cream-based version is simple, easy to prepare, and offers excellent results.

PREPARATION TIME: *15 minutes*
COOKING TIME: *40 minutes*

INGREDIENTS (*for 4*):
¼ cup diced salt pork
¼ cup sliced onions
2 cups diced potatoes
2 cups hot water
1½ pounds fillet of haddock, cod, or
  ocean perch
Salt and freshly ground black
  pepper
2 cups light cream
Butter

Sauté the salt pork in a skillet over low heat until it is nicely browned. Add the onions and sauté gently. Add the potatoes and hot water and cook a few minutes, or until the potatoes are partly done. Then add the fish fillets and cook until they are easily flaked with a fork.
  Season to taste with salt and pepper. Add the cream and let it heat through. Serve the chowder in bowls and top each serving with a generous pat of butter.

SMOKED EEL SMETANA

This quick appetizer is reputed to have been a favorite of Smetana, the Czech composer. For a special occasion it makes a nice change from smoked trout or salmon.

PREPARATION TIME: *15 minutes*

INGREDIENTS (*for 4*):
½ pound smoked eel fillets
2 hard-cooked eggs
1 teaspoon Dijon mustard
3 tablespoons olive oil
1 tablespoon tarragon vinegar
3 tablespoons sour cream
Salt and black pepper
2 tablespoons chopped beets

Peel off skin and arrange the fillets on 4 individual serving plates. Cut the eggs in half and rub the yolks through a coarse sieve; chop the whites finely. Mix together the yolks, mustard, oil, vinegar, and sour cream. Season to taste with salt and freshly ground pepper, and add the beets to the dressing.
  Arrange the dressing along one side of the eel fillets and sprinkle with the chopped egg white. Serve with thin slices of whole wheat bread and butter or Melba toast.

SMOKED HERRING WITH HORSERADISH CREAM

PREPARATION TIME: *15 minutes*
COOKING TIME: *30 minutes*

INGREDIENTS (*for 4*):
4 smoked herring fillets
4 tablespoons heavy cream
2–3 teaspoons lemon juice
2 teaspoons grated horseradish
1 teaspoon tarragon vinegar
Salt and black pepper
½ cucumber
GARNISH:
Lemon slices

Smoked herrings are inexpensive appetizers. They look particularly attractive served in deep scallop shells, and can be prepared several hours in advance.

If the herring is heavily smoked, soak the fillets in water for several hours. Drain, dry, remove the skin, and break the fillets into bite-sized pieces.
  Blend the heavy cream with the lemon juice, grated horseradish, and vinegar, and season to taste with salt and freshly ground pepper.
  Cut the unpeeled cucumber into thin slices and use to line 4 deep scallop shells or individual shallow serving dishes. Mix the herring carefully into the dressing and pile the mixture into the center of the shells.
  Top each portion with a lemon slice and serve with thin slices of buttered whole wheat bread or Melba toast.

Fish

CHICKEN AND ALMOND SOUP

In this delicate soup, bread crumbs are added for thickening, and ground almonds for flavoring.

PREPARATION TIME: *30 minutes*
COOKING TIME: *about 3½ hours*

INGREDIENTS (*for 6*):
1 4–5 pound stewing chicken
1 pound mixed root vegetables (onions, carrots, and turnips)
3 stalks celery
10 black peppercorns
½ teaspoon salt
Bouquet garni (p.410)
⅓ cup ground almonds
3 tablespoons fresh white bread crumbs
½ cup heavy cream
GARNISH:
Chopped parsley or chives
Bread croûtons (p.300)

Peel and coarsely chop the vegetables. Put the chicken in a large saucepan, together with the vegetables, peppercorns, salt, and bouquet garni. Cover with cold water and bring to a boil over high heat. Remove any scum from the surface, lower the heat, and cover the pan with a lid. Simmer for 2–3 hours or until the fowl is tender.

Lift the chicken from the stock; let it cool slightly before removing the skin and cutting all the flesh off the carcass. Put the meat in the blender with the vegetables.

Put the purée in a large pan, mix in the almonds and bread crumbs, and stir in about 5 cups of the chicken stock, strained through a sieve. Bring the soup to a boil and simmer over low heat for 30 minutes, stirring frequently.

Before serving, blend half a cup of hot soup with the cream and stir this mixture back into the soup. Correct seasoning and serve the soup garnished with finely chopped parsley or chives and with bread croûtons.

PETITS ROYALES AU PARMESAN

This unusual first course is a molded custard, delicately flavored with Parmesan cheese.

PREPARATION TIME: *20 minutes*
COOKING TIME: *35 minutes*
CHILLING TIME: *3 hours*

INGREDIENTS (*for 4*):
2 eggs plus 3 egg yolks
1¼ cups chicken consommé
2 teaspoons chopped parsley or chervil
2 teaspoons chopped chives
1 teaspoon powdered thyme or oregano
½ cup heavy cream
¼ cup grated Parmesan cheese
1–½ cup grated Gruyère or Emmenthal cheese
GARNISH:
Watercress sandwiches

Beat the eggs and egg yolks together. Bring the consommé to a boil over low heat, together with the parsley (or chervil), chives, and thyme (or oregano). Simmer, uncovered, for 5 minutes. Gradually strain the consommé into the eggs, stirring all the time. Blend in 2 tablespoons of cream.

Butter 4 dariole molds* or custard cups and pour the consommé mixture into them. Set them in a roasting pan containing ½ inch of water; cover the molds with a piece of buttered waxed paper. Bake in the center of an oven, preheated to 350°F, for about 15 minutes or until set. Remove the molds from the oven and allow them to cool completely before chilling in the refrigerator for a few hours.

About 20 minutes before serving, preheat the oven to 400°F. Unmold the custards onto a buttered ovenproof dish. Pour over the remaining cream, cover with grated Parmesan, and sprinkle generously with Gruyère cheese. Place the dish near the top of the oven and bake until the cheese melts and turns golden.

Serve at once, with a separate plate of thin sandwiches of buttered whole wheat bread and finely chopped watercress.

AVOCADO CUPS

The bland flavors of avocado, smoky bacon, and tart dressing make this a delectable combination for a first course or for lunch.

PREPARATION TIME: *20 minutes*

INGREDIENTS (*for 4*):
4 slices bacon
2 tablespoons red-wine vinegar
6 tablespoons vegetable oil
1 teaspoon salt
Freshly ground pepper
2 teaspoons minced shallots or onion
6–8 ripe cherry tomatoes
2 chilled, ripe avocados

Fry the bacon until crisp, then crumble and set aside. Beat together the wine, oil, salt, pepper, and the shallots or onion.

Cut the avocados in half lengthwise, discard the seeds, and scoop out the pulp. Save the shells. Dice the pulp and cut the tomatoes in half if large or leave whole if small. Pour the dressing over the avocado pieces and tomato halves, and toss gently. Heap into the shells and serve while still cold.

POACHED BASS

Striped bass, sometimes called rockfish, is among the most prized fish of North America. This dish is delicious served hot or cold.

PREPARATION TIME: *30 minutes*
COOKING TIME: *10 minutes per inch measured thickness of fish*

INGREDIENTS:
1 6-pound striped bass
COURT BOUILLON:
1 carrot, chopped
1 onion stuck with 2 cloves
3 garlic cloves
1 tablespoon freshly ground pepper
2 cups white wine
1 lemon, sliced
Water
GARNISH:
Watercress or parsley
Lemon wedges
Hollandaise sauce (p.303) or melted butter

Measure thickness of fish at the thickest point. Arrange the fish in a piece of cheesecloth or foil with the ends protruding from the poacher or pan, so that the fish can be easily lifted out when done. Put all the ingredients for the court bouillon in a fish poacher or long pan and bring to a boil. Reduce heat and simmer 10 minutes. Lower the fish into the simmering bouillon. Add water, if necessary, to cover the fish. When it returns to a simmer, cook about 10 minutes per measured inch. Remove from broth and carefully remove the cheesecloth. Arrange the fish on a platter. Add watercress or parsley and lemon wedges. Serve the poached fish with Hollandaise sauce (p.303) or melted butter.

FRITTO MISTO MARE

PREPARATION TIME: *30 minutes*
COOKING TIME: *35 minutes*

INGREDIENTS (*for 6*):
½ *pound smelts*
3 *small whiting,*
    cut in half
½ *pound raw shrimp*
Oil for deep-frying
BATTER:
4 *teaspoons vegetable oil*
1 *cup flour*
Salt
1 *egg white*
GARNISH:
Parsley sprigs, lemon wedges

The Mediterranean abounds with small fish which the local people mix together and deep-fry (*fritto misto*) until crisp and golden. They can be deep-fried in a light, almost transparent batter or simply dusted with flour before deep-frying—in that case, shrimp should be deep-fried in their shells, and the heads need not be removed from the small fish.

Make the batter* first so that it has time to rest while the fish is being prepared. Blend the oil with 1¼ cups of tepid water and gradually stir it into the flour sifted with a pinch of salt. Beat the batter until quite smooth. Just before using it, fold the stiffly beaten but still moist egg white into the batter.

Cut the heads off the fish and shell the shrimp. Heat the oil* to 375°F (a cube of bread will crisp in 1 minute when the oil is hot enough). Dip the fish and the shrimp, one at a time, in the batter, using either tongs or a small slotted spoon. Hold them over the bowl for a moment to allow the surplus batter to drip off, then put them into the basket in the hot oil and deep-fry for 5–6 minutes until crisp. Cook the fish in small batches and drain them well on paper towels.

Serve the fish on a heated dish, garnished with parsley sprigs, lightly fried in the oil, and lemon wedges. A tartare sauce (p.303) and crusty bread are also suitable.

HALIBUT DUGLÉRÉ

This French seafood dish can be made with halibut steaks or thick fillets of sole, which should be folded over in two, lengthwise. For a first course, only half quantities are necessary. The fish should be flaked, mixed with dugléré sauce (tomato, cream, and parsley), and served in small heated dishes.

PREPARATION TIME: *15 minutes*
COOKING TIME: *35 minutes*

INGREDIENTS (*for 4*):
4 *halibut steaks or thick sole fillets*
Fish bones
2 *tablespoons butter*
Juice of 1 lemon
Salt and black pepper
½ *cup dry white wine*
SAUCE:
2–3 *tomatoes*
2 *tablespoons butter*
2–3 *tablespoons flour*
1 *tablespoon fresh chopped parsley*
5 *tablespoons heavy cream*
GARNISH:
Lemon twists and parsley sprigs

Wash and trim the halibut steaks and put the fish bones in a saucepan of cold water to make a court bouillon (p.308).

Butter a shallow ovenproof dish thoroughly. Rub the steaks with lemon juice, place them in the dish, and season with salt and freshly ground pepper. Add the wine and sufficient court bouillon to come to the top of the fish without covering it. Place a piece of buttered foil or waxed paper, cut to fit, over the fish and cook in the center of a preheated oven at 375°F for 25 minutes, or until the fish flakes easily when tested with a fork.

Lift the fish onto a warm serving dish and strain the cooking liquid.

While the fish is cooking, peel the tomatoes.* Remove the pulp in the center of the tomatoes with a teaspoon and rub it through a sieve to remove the seeds. Set the tomato liquid aside and cut the tomato shells into thin strips.

Melt the butter for the sauce in a small pan, remove from the heat, and stir in enough flour to absorb all the butter. Blend in the tomato liquid and about 1 cup of the reserved fish liquid. Return the pan to the heat and bring the sauce to the simmering point, stirring continuously. Cook over low heat for 3–5 minutes. Add the tomato strips and the parsley, and then stir in the cream; do not let the sauce boil again. Adjust seasoning with salt, freshly ground pepper, and lemon juice and pour the sauce over the fish.

Garnish the halibut with lemon twists* and sprigs of parsley. Serve with duchesse potatoes (p.333) or with small molds (timbales*) of boiled and buttered rice.

Meat

WINTER GARDEN FLOUNDER

The distinctive flavor of Jerusalem artichokes blended with leeks is an excellent combination with flounder or other white fish. If Jerusalem artichokes are not available, use potatoes and reduce the cooking time.

PREPARATION TIME: *25 minutes*
COOKING TIME: *50 minutes*

INGREDIENTS (*for 4*):
2 flounders, each 1¼ pounds
1 pound Jerusalem artichokes
½ pound leeks
4 tablespoons butter
½ cup cider or white wine
1 lemon
Salt and black pepper
½ cup heavy cream

Ask the fish dealer to fillet each fish into 4 pieces. Use the trimmings to make a court bouillon (p.308).

Peel and thinly slice the artichokes; wash and trim the leeks and slice them thinly. Melt the butter in a shallow flameproof casserole, add the vegetables, cover with a lid, and cook gently for 5 minutes. Add the cider or wine, the juice of half the lemon, and strain in enough court bouillon to just cover the vegetables. Cover again and simmer gently for 30 minutes, or until the artichokes are just tender.

Season the fillets with salt, freshly ground pepper, and lemon juice; fold them in half and place on top of the vegetables. Cover and cook over low heat for 10 minutes. Remove the fish to a warm plate; reduce* the liquid in the pan slightly, then stir in the cream. Adjust seasoning and replace the fish; heat through.

Serve the flounder in the casserole, with buttered peas.

IRISH STEW

Irish stew is one of the most popular luncheon dishes served in restaurants in North America. It has universal appeal and is often found on French menus as well.

PREPARATION TIME: *3 hours*
COOKING TIME: *1–1½ hours*

INGREDIENTS (*for 6*):
3–3½ pounds lamb shoulder
1 pound neck of lamb
2 quarts water
1 medium onion stuck with 2 cloves
1 large bay leaf
2 large garlic cloves
1 tablespoon salt
½ teaspoon freshly ground black pepper
½ teaspoon thyme
1 sprig parsley
3 thinly sliced medium onions
3 leeks, split in half, washed, and diced
1 bay leaf
¼ teaspoon nutmeg
½ teaspoon thyme
4 medium potatoes, finely diced
Additional salt, pepper, nutmeg
2 tablespoons finely chopped parsley
Slices of toast, or hot biscuits
¾ pound chopped spinach (optional)

Have a butcher bone the shoulder, or do it yourself; in any case, keep the bones. Put the bones and neck in a deep saucepan with water to cover. Bring to a boil and cook 5–6 minutes, skimming the scum from the surface. Add the onion, bay leaf, garlic cloves, salt, pepper, thyme, and the sprig of parsley.

Bring to a boil again, reduce the heat, and simmer 2½ hours to make a strong broth. Strain; cool the broth and put it in the refrigerator overnight. Next day, skim off the solidified fat from the top of the broth.

HALIBUT PLAKI

PREPARATION TIME: *20 minutes*
COOKING TIME: *10–12 minutes*

INGREDIENTS (*for 4*):
2–2½ pounds of halibut, cut into 1-inch-thick slices
¼ cup olive oil
2 large onions, thinly sliced
4 cloves garlic, peeled
1-pound can Italian plum tomatoes
Juice of ½ lemon
1 large bunch parsley, chopped
2 bay leaves
Pinch of rosemary (optional)
Pinch of thyme (optional)
Salt
Black pepper
White wine
GARNISH:
Lemon wedges

This is an unusual way to cook firm fish, such as halibut, gray mullet, cod, and haddock. Plaki is a favorite dish in Greece and the Middle East.

Heat the olive oil in a heavy skillet and sauté a few of the halibut slices at a time very briefly on each side to sear them. As they are seared, transfer them to an ovenproof baking dish large enough to hold the slices in one layer. Add the sliced onions and the garlic cloves to the skillet. Sauté them for about 10 minutes or until they are soft and slightly colored.

Add the plum tomatoes, lemon juice, chopped parsley, bay leaves, and the rosemary and thyme (if used). Season generously with salt and freshly ground pepper. Stir well, then simmer very gently for about 10 minutes. If the mixture gets too thick as it cooks, add a little white wine or water.

Pour this sauce over the fish and bake in a 425°F oven for 10–12 minutes. Cover the top with a piece of cooking parchment or aluminum foil after the first 5 minutes of cooking time. Garnish with lemon wedges. Plaki is also good served warm, rather than hot.

258

Remove all fat from the lamb shoulder and discard. Cut the meat into pieces 1 inch wide and 2 inches long. Put the meat in a heavy pan with the sliced onions, diced leeks, bay leaf, nutmeg, thyme, and enough of the lamb broth to come 1 inch above the meat.

Bring to a boil, skim off any scum that rises to the surface of the liquid, reduce the heat, and simmer, covered, for 1 hour; then test the meat for tenderness.

If the meat still seems a bit tough, cook it another 15 minutes or until the meat can be pierced easily with a fork. Then add the finely diced potatoes. Cook for 30 minutes, until the stew is slightly thickened by the potatoes. Taste for seasoning; if necessary, add 1–2 tablespoons of salt, a few grinds of pepper, and a touch of nutmeg. Cook a few minutes longer to blend the flavorings with the stew, then add the finely chopped parsley and cook about 1 minute more.

Serve the stew in bowls or soup plates with slices of buttered toast or hot biscuits, and eat with a spoon and a fork. The stew will have a fine color and even better flavor if ¾ pound coarsely chopped spinach is added about 15 minutes before the end of the cooking time.

VEAL CHOPS MAGYAR

Paprika is the commonest spicing in Hungarian dishes. It varies considerably in strength according to its place of origin; a paprika sauce should be tasted after it has been cooked for a while.

PREPARATION TIME: *20 minutes*
COOKING TIME: *1¼ hours*

INGREDIENTS (*for 4*):

4 large veal chops
Seasoned flour (p.412)
½ pound mushrooms
1 onion
2 tablespoons butter
1 tablespoon oil
2–3 tablespoons flour
1¼ cups milk
1¼ cups veal stock or chicken bouillon
Salt
Juice of 1 small lemon
3 tablespoons tomato paste
3–4 teaspoons paprika
2 teaspoons sugar
½ cup light cream
GARNISH:
Rice
6–8 mushroom caps
Paprika
1 tablespoon chopped parsley

Trim the fat off the chops and coat them with seasoned flour. Trim the mushrooms* and, if large, cut them into quarters or halves. Peel and thinly slice the onion. Heat the butter and oil in a flameproof casserole, pat the loose flour off the chops, and sauté them over high heat until golden brown, turning once. Remove the chops from the pan and sauté the mushrooms and onion for a few minutes until soft.

Remove the casserole from the heat and stir in enough flour to absorb the fat. Gradually blend in the milk and then the stock, stirring continuously. Bring to simmering point and cook for 3 minutes, or until the sauce has thickened. Season to taste with salt and lemon juice. Mix the tomato paste, paprika, sugar, and light cream together in a small bowl. Blend in 3 or 4 tablespoons of this hot sauce and pour the mixture back into the main sauce, stirring thoroughly.

Return the veal chops to the casserole. They should be completely covered by the sauce, so add a little more stock if necessary. Cover the casserole with a lid and cook over low heat for 45 minutes or until the veal is tender, stirring from time to time to prevent sticking. Do not allow to reach the boiling point, or the sauce will separate.

Adjust seasoning and arrange the chops in the center of a serving dish with the sauce spooned over them. Surround with a border of fluffy rice, garnished with the whole mushroom caps sautéed in a little butter. Set the mushrooms, dark side uppermost, on the rice, and dust the center of each mushroom with paprika. Sprinkle chopped parsley between the mushrooms.

CROWN ROAST OF PORK

This is an impressive main course for a large dinner party. The crown, which should be ordered in advance, cannot be constructed from less than 12 chops. The butcher should carefully trim off the excess fat so that the meat will crisp when filled with the stuffing.

PREPARATION TIME: *35 minutes*
COOKING TIME: *2⅓ hours*

INGREDIENTS (*for 10–12*):

1 crown roast of pork (12 chops)
Vegetable oil
1 bouillon cube
STUFFING:
1 large onion
2 stalks celery
3 medium carrots
6 canned pineapple slices
2 tablespoons corn oil
½ cup cooked rice
1½ tablespoons chopped fresh parsley
1 teaspoon dried savory
1–2 teaspoons paprika
½ cup white raisins
Salt and black pepper
Lemon juice
GARNISH:
6 canned pineapple slices
Watercress

Prepare the stuffing first. Peel and finely chop the onion, celery, and carrots. Finely chop 6 pineapple slices and reserve the liquid.

Heat the corn oil in a pan over moderate heat and sauté the onion and celery until just turning color. Add the rice, carrots, and parsley, together with the savory, paprika, pineapple, and white raisins. Mix all the ingredients thoroughly and heat through. Season to taste with salt, freshly ground pepper, and lemon juice. Set the stuffing aside to cool.

Stand the crown of pork in a greased roasting pan and rub the meat thoroughly with oil. Spoon the stuffing into the center of the crown and cover it with a piece of foil. Wrap foil around each chop bone to prevent it from charring. Roast the crown in the center of a preheated oven at 375°F for 2¼ hours, or until amber-colored juice runs out when a skewer is inserted in the meat. Lift out the crown and keep it warm on a serving dish in the oven.

Sauté the pineapple slices used for garnishing in the hot fat in the roasting pan for about 4 minutes, or until golden brown on both sides. Slit one side of each pineapple slice and arrange in a curling twist around the crown of pork.

Carefully pour off the fat from the roasting pan and add the pineapple liquid to the residue in the pan. Crumble the bouillon cube into the juices and bring the liquid to the boiling point. Cook over high heat until the liquid is brown and has reduced* slightly. Pour into a warm sauceboat or small bowl.

Remove the foil from the tips of the chops and replace with paper frills. Garnish with small sprigs of watercress between the pineapple twists. Serve the crown with roast or rissolé potatoes (p.68) and with green beans.

259

COEUR CORIANDRE

Hearts are usually stuffed and braised slowly for several hours, as they tend to be dry. In this French farmhouse recipe they are marinated in lemon juice before being braised in an apple and cider sauce with an unusual spicing of coriander.

PREPARATION TIME: *30 minutes*
COOKING TIME: *1–1½ hours*

INGREDIENTS (*for 4*):
4 lamb or 2 veal hearts
Juice of 1 lemon
3 medium onions
2 medium cooking apples
2–3 tablespoons flour
3 tablespoons butter
Salt and black pepper
2 bay leaves
½ cup imported dry cider or white wine
1 teaspoon crushed coriander seeds
1 teaspoon sugar
2 thin slices unpeeled lemon

Cut the hearts into slices about ½ inch thick and remove all fat, gristle, and blood vessels. Put the slices in a bowl with the lemon juice and leave to marinate* for 30 minutes. Meanwhile, peel and slice the onions, and peel, core, and slice the apples.

Drain the heart slices and coat them with flour, then sauté them quickly in the butter in a flameproof casserole. Add the onions and continue sautéing the heart slices until pale golden. Season well with salt and freshly ground pepper. Add the bay leaves and the cider or wine. Cover the heart slices with the apple and sprinkle them with coriander seeds and sugar. Lay the lemon slices on top of the apples.

Put the lid on the casserole and simmer over low heat on top of the stove, or in a preheated oven at 300°F, for about 1 hour or until tender. When cooked, remove the lemon slices and bay leaves, and stir the apple slices into the sauce.

Serve with creamed potatoes.

TOURNEDOS ROSSINI

The Italian composer Rossini (1792–1868) enjoyed a great reputation not only as a musician, but also as a creator of gourmet dishes. The following is one of his best-known culinary masterpieces. It was traditionally garnished with truffles or mushrooms.

PREPARATION TIME: *15 minutes*
COOKING TIME: *20 minutes*

INGREDIENTS (*for 6*):
6 tournedos of beef
6 slices firm white bread
8–10 tablespoons unsalted butter
1 tablespoon vegetable oil
¼ cup Madeira, Marsala, or cream sherry
½ cup Espagnole sauce (p.302)
½ cup brown stock
Salt and black pepper
GARNISH:
6 slices pâté de foie gras
6 slices truffle or 6 large flat mushroom caps

Ask the butcher to trim the tournedos and tie them neatly. Cut 6 circles from the bread slices to fit the tournedos exactly.

Heat 4 tablespoons of butter and the oil in a large skillet over medium heat and sauté the bread until crisp and golden. Drain on paper towels and keep hot.

Heat 3 tablespoons butter in the skillet and sauté the tournedos over high heat, turning once, for 1½–2 minutes on each side. They should be a rich brown on the outside and rosy pink inside. Lift out and keep warm. Add the wine to the skillet, stirring to scrape up all the residue in the pan. Cook until the juices have reduced,* about 2 minutes. Blend in the prepared Espagnole sauce and the stock, and let the sauce cook, uncovered, until it has thickened.

Meanwhile, heat the remaining butter in another skillet and sauté the slices of foie gras over high heat until golden. Lift out and keep warm. Lightly sauté the truffles or mushrooms in the remaining butter.

To serve, arrange the bread circles on a warmed dish, set a tournedos on each, and top with a slice of foie gras and truffle or mushroom cap.

Correct the seasoning of the sauce, pour enough sauce around the bread to cover the bottom of the dish, and spoon the remainder into a warm sauceboat or bowl. Serve with matchstick potatoes (p.333) and buttered spinach or broccoli.

LAMB CASSEROLE

This French country-style casserole is made from one of the least expensive cuts of lamb.

PREPARATION TIME: *35 minutes*
COOKING TIME: *1¾ hours*

INGREDIENTS (*for 4–6*):
3 pounds shoulder of lamb, cut in serving-sized pieces
3 leeks
6 fresh tomatoes or 16-ounce can tomatoes
½ pound carrots
2 cloves garlic
2 tablespoons oil
1 tablespoon sugar
Salt and black pepper
1½ tablespoons flour
2 cups stock or bouillon
1 bay leaf
½ teaspoon powdered thyme
½ pound green beans

Preheat the oven to 450°F. Trim the roots and coarse outer leaves off the leeks, wash thoroughly under running water, and chop them. Peel and seed the tomatoes.* Peel or scrape the carrots, but leave them whole, and peel the garlic cloves.

Heat the oil in a flameproof casserole on top of the stove and quickly brown the lamb pieces on both sides. Sprinkle with sugar. Lower the heat and toss the contents until the sugar caramelizes slightly. Season with salt and freshly ground pepper, and sprinkle in half the flour.

Place the casserole, uncovered, in the hot oven for 5 minutes. Turn the meat over, season again, and sprinkle with the remaining flour. Bake for a further 5 minutes. Reduce the oven heat to 325°F. Remove the casserole, lift out the meat, and lightly sauté the leeks in the casserole on top of the stove. Add the stock and bring to a boil, scraping up any residue on the bottom of the casserole. Return the meat to the casserole; add the tomatoes, carrots, bay leaf, thyme, and crushed garlic. Cover with a lid and bring to a simmer. The sauce should almost cover the meat; add a little more stock if necessary.

Return the casserole to the center of the oven and cook for 1½ hours, or until the meat is tender. Trim the beans and cut them into ½-inch pieces. Cook in boiling salted water for 10 minutes or until just tender. Drain, add the beans to the casserole, and cook them in the sauce for a further 5 minutes.

Serve the lamb from the casserole with baked potatoes.

SCALOPPINE WITH ARTICHOKES AND LEMON SAUCE

For this easily prepared dish, choose small veal scaloppine, ¼ inch thick. Be sure to buy *fonds* (bottoms) of artichokes, not the hearts.

PREPARATION TIME: *15 minutes*
COOKING TIME: *25 minutes*

INGREDIENTS (*for 4*):
8 veal scaloppine (about 1 pound)
Seasoned flour (p.412)
4 tablespoons butter
1 tablespoon finely chopped shallot or onion
14-ounce jar or can artichoke bottoms
½ cup dry white wine
1¼ cups chicken stock or bouillon
2 small lemons
½ cup heavy cream
Salt and black pepper

Trim any fat from the scaloppine and coat them in seasoned flour. Heat the butter in a heavy-bottomed pan over medium heat and sauté the scaloppine for a few minutes until golden brown, turning once.

Add the chopped shallot and drained artichoke bottoms, and pour in the white wine. Bring the mixture to a simmer, then reduce the heat. Add enough stock or bouillon to cover the veal completely. Grate the rind from the lemons and set aside; add the squeezed lemon juice to the sauce. Cover the pan with a tight-fitting lid and cook over low heat for 20 minutes, or until the veal is tender.

Stir in the cream and simmer the sauce for a further 5–6 minutes, uncovered, until the sauce has a creamy texture. Adjust seasoning with salt and freshly ground pepper.

Arrange the scaloppine in the center of a warmed serving dish and surround with a border of buttered noodles or fluffy rice. Pour the sauce over the meat and top with a scattering of grated lemon rind.

ORANGE-GLAZED LAMB ROAST

A fruit-flavored glaze and stuffing transform a leg of lamb into a dish fit for a special occasion. Have the lamb boned but not rolled.

PREPARATION TIME: *20 minutes*
COOKING TIME: *2¼ hours*

INGREDIENTS (*for 6–8*):
5-pound leg of lamb, boned
1 large onion
Grated rind of 2 oranges
2 tablespoons butter
1½ cups fresh white bread crumbs
⅓ cup white raisins
⅓ cup dark raisins
⅓ cup dried currants
½ teaspoon dried rosemary
½ teaspoon dried thyme
Salt and black pepper
Juice of 1 orange
GLAZE:
½ cup light brown sugar
Juice of ½ lemon
Juice of 1 orange
2 tablespoons Worcestershire sauce
SAUCE:
½ cup red wine
1¼ cups beef bouillon
GARNISH:
Orange slices
Watercress

Prepare the stuffing for the lamb first. Peel and finely chop the onion and grate the rind from 2 oranges. Melt the butter in a pan over medium heat and sauté onion for 3 minutes. Mix together in a bowl the bread crumbs, raisins, currants, and the onion. Blend in the orange rind, rosemary, and thyme, and season to taste with salt and freshly ground pepper. Bind the stuffing with the squeezed juice of 1 orange.

Pack the stuffing into the lamb. Tie the meat into a neat shape, securing it with string. Put it in a greased baking pan.

Place the glaze ingredients in a small pan and cook over low heat for 1 minute, then spoon the glaze over the meat. Roast in the center of a preheated oven at 375°F for 2 hours, or until internal temperature registers 145°F on a meat thermometer. Baste frequently.

Remove the lamb to a warm serving dish and keep it hot in a 250°F oven while making the sauce. Stir into the pan the wine and bouillon for the sauce, and boil over high heat, scraping in all the residue from the glaze. Continue boiling briskly until the sauce has reduced* and thickened slightly. Correct seasoning if necessary.

Remove the string and serve the lamb garnished with thin orange twists* and sprigs of watercress. Pour the sauce into a warm sauceboat or small bowl. Galette Lyonnaise (p.265) and buttered salsify (p.23) or green beans would go well with the lamb.

Veal scaloppine and artichoke bottoms are arranged on a bed of buttered noodles.

Glazed leg of lamb is garnished with orange twists and watercress.

Poultry & Game

FLAMED PORK TENDERLOIN WITH APRICOTS

This quick and easy dish can be cooked in a chafing dish at the table, once all the ingredients have been prepared. Prunes may be used instead of dried apricots; either fruit should be soaked in water for 3-4 hours.

PREPARATION TIME: *25 minutes*
COOKING TIME: *15 minutes*

INGREDIENTS (*for 4*):
1¼ *pounds pork tenderloin*
½ *cup dried apricots, soaked in water*
2 *tablespoons dry sherry*
Seasoned flour (*p.412*)
2 *tablespoons unsalted butter*
2 *tablespoons brandy*
5 *tablespoons sour cream*
Salt and black pepper
Lemon juice

Put the apricots and the water in which they were soaking into a saucepan, add the sherry, and cook over low heat for 15 minutes. Trim any fat off the pork tenderloin, cut it into 1½-inch-thick slices, and toss them in the seasoned flour.

Heat the butter in a skillet or chafing dish over medium heat and sauté the pork on both sides until golden and tender, turning once only. Pour off any surplus fat. Heat the brandy, set it alight, and pour it over the pork. Add the drained apricots and stir until the brandy flames have burned out.

Mix the sour cream with the apricot liquid and pour it into the pan. Simmer for a few minutes, then season to taste with salt, freshly ground pepper, and lemon juice. Serve with fluffy boiled rice.

DUCK WITH TANGERINES

This dish is cooked in a way not usually associated with roast duck: The bird is roasted continental style, with liquid in the pan, and is served with a smooth tangerine-flavored sauce laced with port. The recipe can also be prepared very successfully with wild duck.

PREPARATION TIME: *35-40 minutes*
COOKING TIME: *1¼ hours*

INGREDIENTS (*for 3-4*):

1 *4-5 pound duck*
Bouquet garni (*p.410*)
1 *cup cooked noodles*
1 *onion*
2 *teaspoons fresh chopped parsley*
½ *teaspoon dried thyme*
Pinch nutmeg
2½ *tablespoons honey*
2 *tablespoons beer*
2 *egg yolks*
¼ *cup heavy cream*
3 *tangerines*
4 *tablespoons port*
Lemon juice
Salt and black pepper
GARNISH:
Tangerine slices and watercress

Put the duck giblets in a saucepan with water to cover; add salt, freshly ground pepper, and the bouquet garni. Cover the pan with a lid and cook for about 25 minutes or until the giblets are tender. Strain and set the cooking liquid aside. Skin the gizzard and chop this, the heart, and the liver finely.

Chop the drained noodles coarsely and mix in the giblets, chopped onion, herbs, and nutmeg. Mix half the honey and half the beer with the egg yolks and cream and stir this into the noodle mixture. Open the vent and remove any pieces of fat from the duck, spoon in the stuffing, and close the opening.

Put the duck in a roasting pan, breast downwards, and pour water into the pan to a depth of ½ inch. Roast in the center of a preheated oven at 375°F for 20 minutes, basting* occasionally. Remove the duck from the roasting pan, put in a wire rack, and replace the duck, breast upwards. Pour the remaining honey and beer over the duck and continue roasting for a further 30 minutes, or until the duck is crisp and golden and the legs are tender when tested with a skewer.

Meanwhile, grate the rind from the tangerines and set aside. Having first removed the pith and seeds, put the fruit in a blender.

When the duck is ready, lift it onto a warm serving dish. Add the tangerine pulp and rind to the pan, together with the port and 2¼ cups of the reserved giblet stock. Boil on top of the stove over high heat until the gravy has reduced* and thickened slightly. Sharpen with lemon juice and adjust seasoning. Strain the gravy into a warm sauceboat.

Garnish the duck with watercress sprigs and thin slices of unpeeled tangerine. Serve with roast or duchesse potatoes (p.333) and buttered green beans.

SAVORY GAME PIE

A traditional game pie is usually cooked under a covering of puff or suet pastry. The pastry for this pie is less trouble than a puff pastry and richer and lighter than suet pastry. The pie filling may be venison, game bird, or a less tender cut of beef, all of which should be marinated to give them flavor and tenderness.

PREPARATION TIME: *45 minutes*
MARINATING TIME: *8 hours*
COOKING TIME: *approximately 2½ hours*

INGREDIENTS (*for 6*):
1½-*pound leg or shoulder of venison, or rump of beef*
2 *ounces salt pork, blanched and well drained*
½ *pound mushrooms*
2 *tablespoons butter*
1-2 *tablespoons flour*
Salt and black pepper
MARINADE:
1 *onion*
1 *stalk celery*
7 *coriander seeds*
7 *whole allspice or juniper berries*
2 *bay leaves*
2 *sprigs parsley*
Pinch marjoram
1 *cup red wine*
5 *tablespoons olive oil*
PASTRY:
2 *cups all-purpose flour*
½ *teaspoon salt*
¼ *pound butter*
3 *tablespoons lard*
2 *egg yolks*
1 *egg*

Cut the venison or beef into 1-inch cubes, removing all gristle. Prepare the vegetables and spices for the marinade: peel and finely chop the onion, wash the celery and chop it finely, and crush the coriander seeds and allspice or juniper berries.

Put the venison in a large bowl in layers with the prepared vegetables and crushed spices. Add the bay leaves, parsley sprigs, and marjoram, and pour in the wine mixed with the oil. Cover the bowl with plastic wrap and allow the meat to marinate in the refrigerator for at least 8 hours.

Precook the pie filling to avoid overbaking the pastry. Dice the blanched salt pork and sauté it over low heat to extract all the fat. Add the butter to the pan, together with the trimmed and sliced mushrooms.* Blend in enough flour to absorb all the fat, and cook this roux* for about 3 minutes.

Lift the meat from the marinade and strain this through a sieve. Gradually blend the marinade liquid into the roux, add the venison, and bring the sauce to a boil. Thin with a little water if necessary, and season to taste with salt and freshly ground pepper. Cover the pan with a tight-fitting lid and simmer over low heat for 1½ hours. Adjust seasoning and leave the meat to cool while making the pastry.

Sift the flour and salt into a mixing bowl. Rub in the butter and lard until the mixture has the consistency of bread crumbs. Beat the egg yolks with 2 tablespoons of cold water and blend into the flour. Knead the pastry dough until it leaves the sides of the bowl clean, adding more water if necessary. Cover the kneaded dough with waxed paper and refrigerate for at least 1 hour.

Spoon the cooled meat and sauce into a deep pie dish or baking dish, setting a pastry funnel or inverted egg cup in the center. Roll out the pastry on a floured surface to a thickness of ¼ inch. Cut off ½-inch-wide pastry strips and place them on the moistened rim of the pie dish. Brush with water before covering the filling with the remaining pastry. Seal the pastry edges and trim them with a knife. Scallop the edges and brush the pastry with lightly beaten egg; decorate with leaves cut from the pastry trimmings and brush the leaves with more egg. Make a few small slits in the top of the pastry for the steam to escape.

Bake the pie in the center of a preheated oven at 425°F for 20 minutes, then reduce the heat to 375°F and bake for a further 30 minutes, or until the pie is golden brown.

Serve the game pie hot, with creamed celeriac (celery root) and potato purée (p.265).

POULE AU POT

This has been a standard dish of French cuisine for generations. It is good served cold for a picnic and can be reheated successfully. If stewing chicken is hard to find, substitute a large roasting chicken and reduce the cooking time to 1½–2 hours.

PREPARATION TIME: *40 minutes*
COOKING TIME: *3–3½ hours*

INGREDIENTS (*for 6*):
1 6–7 pound stewing chicken
8 large onions
1 cup leftover cooked ham or pork,
  or ½ pound pork butt
3–4 parsley sprigs
4 tablespoons butter
3 cups dry bread crumbs
1 teaspoon thyme
2 eggs, well beaten
1 ham butt or 3–4 pounds beef
  (short ribs, rump, or brisket)
1 onion stuck with 2 cloves
8 carrots
1½ tablespoons salt
6 turnips, peeled

Clean the stewing chicken of all inside fat and remove the neck, leaving the surrounding skin. Grind 2 of the onions with the leftover ham or pork, or the pork butt, and the parsley. Sauté the mixture slowly in 4 tablespoons of the butter and combine with the bread crumbs, thyme, and the beaten eggs. Mix well. Stuff the chicken loosely with this mixture. Put a piece of aluminum foil in the vent to make it watertight. Sew up the vent with string and tie it tightly.

Place the chicken in a large, heavy pot with the ham butt or beef, onion stuck with the 2 cloves, 2 of the carrots, the salt, and just enough water to cover. Bring to a boil. Skim off the scum, reduce the heat, and simmer, covered, for 3½ hours or until the meat and chicken are tender. If the meat takes longer to cook, remove the chicken carefully, cover it with aluminum foil, and keep it warm in a 250°F oven. Add the remaining onions, carrots, and turnips 1 hour before serving.

Serve the broth in soup bowls as the first course. Follow with sliced chicken, the stuffing, and the vegetables. Add the sliced meat if desired. The meat may be reheated slowly in some of the broth the next day for another meal.

VENISON CHOPS

For this dish, chops from a young deer are preferable; otherwise they will take a long time to cook and would require marinating for 24 hours. The whisky sauce lends a distinctive flavor to the game.

PREPARATION TIME: *20 minutes*
COOKING TIME: *1¾–2 hours*

INGREDIENTS (*for 6*):
6 venison neck chops
2 slices lean bacon
1 onion
2 carrots
2 stalks celery
Juice of 1 lemon
12 juniper berries
1 teaspoon dried marjoram or
  thyme
Salt and black pepper
3 tablespoons butter
3 tablespoons all-purpose flour
¾–1¼ cups stock or water
2 tablespoons Scotch whisky
2 tablespoons cranberry sauce
Juice of 1 small orange
GARNISH:
Bread croûtons (p.300)
Whole cranberries or orange wedges

Trim the venison chops and beat them lightly to flatten them. Chop the bacon coarsely. Peel and finely chop the onion, carrots, and celery.

Rub the chops with lemon juice and crush the juniper berries in a mortar or with the blade of a knife. Mix with the marjoram or thyme and add a few twists of ground pepper; rub this mixture into both sides of each chop.

Heat the butter in a flameproof casserole and sauté the bacon over low heat until the fat runs. Turn up the heat and brown the chops briskly on both sides, then remove from the casserole. Sauté the onion, carrots, and celery until lightly colored; season with salt. Sprinkle the flour over the vegetables and cook over low heat until the mixture is light brown. Blend in the stock and the whisky, and bring the sauce to a simmer. Put the chops back in the sauce, making sure that it just covers the top of the meat. If necessary add a little more stock.

Cover the dish with a lid and cook in the center of a preheated oven at 325°F for about 1½ hours, or until the meat is tender. Remove the chops from the dish and keep them warm. Add the cranberry sauce and orange juice to the sauce, adjust seasoning, and add lemon juice to taste.

Arrange the chops upright around a mound of celeriac (celery root) or chestnut and potato purée (p.246). Intersperse the chops with sautéed bread croûtons and garnish with whole cranberries or peeled orange wedges. Paper frills may be placed over the ends of the chops. Pour the sauce into a warmed sauceboat and serve separately.

Rice & Pasta

SPICED CHICKEN AND RICE

This is one of the great dishes from the famous Indonesian *rijsttafel* ("rice table"). It makes an attractive centerpiece for a buffet, surrounded by small dishes of colorful fresh vegetables and fruit to which guests help themselves.

PREPARATION TIME: *35 minutes*
COOKING TIME: *2 hours*

INGREDIENTS (*for 6–8*):
1 small chicken, approximately 3½
  pounds
1 pound onions
1 bay leaf
1 sprig parsley
Salt and black pepper
2 cups long grain rice
3 tablespoons olive or vegetable oil
2 tablespoons peanut butter
1 teaspoon chili powder
¼ pound peeled shrimp
¼ pound diced cooked ham
1 teaspoon cumin seeds
1½ teaspoons coriander seeds
1 clove garlic
Pinch ground mace
GARNISH:
½ cucumber
2 hard-cooked eggs
8–12 unshelled shrimp

Put the chicken in a large pan, with one whole peeled onion, the bay leaf, and parsley sprig. Add a seasoning of salt and freshly ground pepper, and enough cold water to cover the chicken. Bring to a boil, remove any scum from the surface, then reduce the heat. Cover the pan with a lid and simmer for about 1 hour or until the chicken is tender.

Lift out the chicken and leave to cool slightly. Strain the stock through a fine sieve and use 4 cups of it to cook the rice until just tender.

Drain the rice thoroughly in a colander and cover with a dry cloth.

Remove the skin from the chicken and cut the meat into small pieces. Peel and thinly slice the remaining onions. Heat the oil in a large pan and sauté the onions over low heat until they begin to color. Stir in the peanut butter and chili powder. Add the shelled shrimp, diced ham, the chicken, and finally the rice, which should now be dry and fluffy. Continue to sauté over low heat, stirring frequently, until the rice is slightly brown. Crush the cumin and coriander seeds and the peeled garlic, and stir them, with the mace, into the rice. Season the mixture to taste with salt.

Pile the rice and chicken mixture

on a hot serving dish and garnish with thin slices of unpeeled cucumber, wedges of hard-cooked egg, and large shrimp.

Arrange a number of small side dishes or bowls around the chicken. A suitable selection might include apricot-and-mango chutney; sliced tomatoes, dressed with sugar and lemon juice; peeled, sliced oranges; and sliced green and red pepper with raw onion rings, both in a vinaigrette sauce (p.304). Other bowls might contain small wedges of fresh pineapple, fried sliced bananas with lemon juice, and fresh shredded and toasted coconut. Shelled almonds or cashew nuts sautéed a few minutes in a little butter are also frequently served with a rijsttafel.

LASAGNE VERDI AL FORNO

The district around Bologna in Italy is famous for its lasagne—often made with spinach (*lasagne verdi*). The pasta is usually baked in the oven with a Bolognese *ragú*, or meat and vegetable sauce, and alternating layers of thick Béchamel sauce. This dish is an ideal main course for a small party, as all the preparations can be done well in advance of cooking. Lasagne can be successfully frozen for several weeks.

PREPARATION TIME: *1 hour*
COOKING TIME: *20 minutes*

INGREDIENTS (*for 6*):
½ pound green lasagne
2 slices bacon
1 small onion
1 carrot
⅔ cup button mushrooms
2 tablespoons butter
1½ cups ground beef
2–3 chicken livers (optional)
1 tablespoon tomato paste
½ cup dry white wine
1¼ cups beef stock or bouillon
1 teaspoon sugar
Salt
2 cups Béchamel sauce (p.301)
½ cup grated Parmesan cheese

Chop the bacon. Peel and finely chop the onion and carrot, and trim the mushrooms* before cutting them into thin slices.

Melt half the butter in a large heavy-bottomed pan over low heat and cook the bacon until the fat runs, then add the vegetables and sauté them lightly. Crumble in the ground beef and add the cleaned and chopped chicken livers, if used. Blend in the tomato paste. Continue cooking and stir continuously until the meat has browned. Add the wine and let the mixture bubble for a few minutes before adding the stock. Season to taste with sugar and add salt if stock is used. Cover the pan with a lid and simmer over low heat for 30–40 minutes. Meanwhile, make a thick Béchamel sauce.

Cook the lasagne in a large pan of boiling salted water for 10–15 minutes or until just tender, stirring occasionally. Drain the pasta in a colander and rinse with cold water to prevent it from sticking together.

Thoroughly butter a shallow baking dish, about 10 inches by 8 inches. Cover the bottom with a thin layer of the meat mixture, then Béchamel sauce, and lastly the drained lasagne. Repeat these layers until all the ingredients are used up, finishing with Béchamel sauce. Sprinkle the top with the grated Parmesan cheese.

Bake in the center of the oven, preheated to 400°F, for about 15–20 minutes or until the top is crisp and bubbly. Serve from the dish accompanied by a tossed green salad.

Vegetables

TAGLIATELLE ALLA CARBONARA

Many Italian pastas, such as *tagliatelle* (flat egg noodles), spaghetti, and macaroni, were formerly cooked over a charcoal burner (*alla carbonara*). By extension the term now covers a pasta dish made with bacon, eggs, and cheese.

PREPARATION TIME: *10 minutes*
COOKING TIME: *15 minutes*

INGREDIENTS (*for 6*):
½ *pound tagliatelle*
2 tablespoons butter
1 tablespoon olive oil
2 slices bacon, coarsely chopped
½ *cup diced cooked ham*
4 eggs
½ *cup grated Cheddar cheese*
¼ *cup grated Parmesan cheese*
Salt and black pepper

Cook the tagliatelle in plenty of well-salted boiling water for 10–15 minutes or until just tender. Drain thoroughly in a colander.

While the tagliatelle is cooking, heat the butter and oil in a pan over moderate heat and cook the bacon and ham until they are crisp. Beat the eggs and cheeses together in a bowl.

Add the drained pasta to the bacon and ham and stir carefully until evenly coated with fat. Pour in the beaten eggs and cheese and continue stirring over gentle heat until the eggs thicken slightly. Be sure to remove the pan from the heat before the eggs are scrambled.

Spoon the mixture into a warm dish and serve at once with a bowl of grated Parmesan cheese and with a crisp green salad.

LEEKS À LA NIÇOISE

French vegetable dishes or salads prepared *à la niçoise* imply the addition of tomatoes and, usually, a garlic flavoring. This dish can be served hot with broiled fish, meat, or chicken, or cold as an hors d'oeuvre.

PREPARATION TIME: *15 minutes*
COOKING TIME: *20 minutes*

INGREDIENTS (*for 4*):
2 pounds young leeks
½ *pound tomatoes*
3–4 tablespoons olive oil
Salt and black pepper
1 large clove garlic
1 tablespoon fresh chopped parsley
Lemon juice

Cut the roots and most of the green tops off the leeks so that they are of even length. Rinse them thoroughly under cold running water and dry them on paper towels.

Peel and seed the tomatoes* and chop them coarsely.

Heat the oil in a flameproof casserole over medium heat and put in the leeks side by side. Sauté until lightly colored underneath, then turn them over and season with salt and freshly ground pepper. Cover the casserole with a lid and cook the leeks over gentle heat for 10 minutes, or until the thick white part is tender. Lift out the leeks and keep them warm.

Add the tomatoes, crushed garlic, and parsley to the casserole and cook briskly for 2–3 minutes, stirring continuously. Adjust seasoning and sharpen to taste with lemon juice. Put the leeks back into the sauce and serve hot or cold.

GALETTE LYONNAISE

This savory potato dish, with its classic Lyonnaise flavoring of onion and cheese, is excellent with either fish or meat. Extra cheese may be mixed with the potato as well as sprinkled over the top.

PREPARATION TIME: *35 minutes*
COOKING TIME: *25 minutes*

INGREDIENTS (*for 4*):
1 pound potatoes
½ *pound onions*
5 tablespoons butter
1 egg, beaten
Salt and black pepper
Pinch nutmeg
2 tablespoons grated Cheddar or Parmesan cheese
GARNISH:
Parsley sprigs

Peel the potatoes, cut them into even pieces, and boil them in lightly salted water. Rub the potatoes through a coarse sieve. Peel and finely chop the onions. Heat 4 tablespoons of butter and cook the onions over low heat until they are soft and golden. Stir the contents of the pan into the potatoes. Add the beaten egg and season to taste with salt, freshly ground pepper, and nutmeg.

Spoon the potato mixture into a greased, shallow baking dish; smooth the top, sprinkle over the grated cheese, and dot with the remaining butter. Bake the potatoes in the center of a preheated oven at 400°F for about 20 minutes or until golden brown on top.

Serve the potatoes from the dish, garnished with sprigs of parsley.

CELERIAC AND POTATO PURÉE

Celeriac, or celery root, is a turnip-shaped, knobby root vegetable with a strong celery flavor. As a purée, it is especially good with game or roast duck and goose.

PREPARATION TIME: *10 minutes*
COOKING TIME: *45 minutes*

INGREDIENTS (*for 4–6*):
1 pound celeriac
1½ *cups cooked mashed potatoes*
3 tablespoons butter
¼ *cup heavy cream*
Salt and black pepper

Scrub the celeriac thoroughly in cold water to remove all traces of dirt. Put it in a pan of boiling water and cook, unpeeled, for 35–40 minutes or until

quite tender. Leave to cool slightly, then peel the celeriac and chop it finely. Purée* it through a sieve or in a blender.

Blend the celeriac purée with the mashed potatoes, add the butter and the heavy cream, and season to taste with salt and freshly ground pepper. Heat the purée through over low heat before serving.

ROASTED ONIONS

The sweet flavor of large Spanish onions is particularly enhanced by roasting them whole in their skins.

PREPARATION TIME: *5 minutes*
COOKING TIME: *2–2½ hours*

INGREDIENTS (*for 6*):
6 large Spanish onions
4–6 tablespoons butter
Coarse salt
GARNISH:
Paprika
Parsley sprigs

Line a deep roasting pan with foil to prevent the sugar contained in the onions from sticking to the pan. Cut the roots from the unpeeled onions and stand them upright in the roasting pan. Bake in the center of the oven, preheated to 350°F, for 2

hours, or until the onions are tender when they are tested with a skewer or small knife.

Remove from the oven, carefully peel off the onion skins, and set the onions on a hot serving dish. Open the tops slightly with a pointed knife blade and push a small piece of butter into each. Sprinkle the onions with salt and top each with a sprinkling of paprika or parsley.

Desserts

AUSTRIAN CABBAGE WITH SOUR CREAM

Most classic Austrian cooking belongs to the period of the Austro-Hungarian Empire and includes Hungarian, Yugoslavian, and Czech dishes. Sour cream and paprika are characteristic of both Hungarian and Austrian recipes. They are combined in this vegetable dish, which goes well with roast veal and pork.

PREPARATION TIME: *20 minutes*
COOKING TIME: *30 minutes*

INGREDIENTS (*for* 4):
1 small green cabbage
1 small onion
2–4 tablespoons butter or bacon fat
½ cup sour cream
Salt and black pepper
½ teaspoon paprika

Remove any discolored or coarse outer leaves and cut the cabbage into quarters. Cut out the stalk and shred the cabbage. Wash and drain it thoroughly in a colander. Peel and finely chop the onion.

Heat the butter or fat in a flameproof casserole over moderate heat and cook the onion lightly until softened. Add the cabbage and sauté until it is thoroughly coated with the butter or fat. Stir in the sour cream and season to taste with salt, pepper, and paprika.

Cover the dish with a tight-fitting lid and bake on the lower shelf of an oven, preheated to 325°F, for about 30 minutes. It is essential to bake the cabbage at low heat or the cream will separate.

Serve the cabbage at once from the casserole.

GREEN BEANS TUSCANY STYLE

This Italian method of cooking beans is an unusual way to prepare this popular vegetable. The beans go well with roast or broiled meat and poultry.

PREPARATION TIME: *10 minutes*
COOKING TIME: *15 minutes*

INGREDIENTS (*for* 4):
1 pound green beans
4 tablespoons butter
1 tablespoon olive oil
2 teaspoons chopped fresh sage or 1 tablespoon chopped fresh parsley
1 large clove garlic
Salt and black pepper
1 tablespoon grated Parmesan cheese

Trim the beans. Cut them into 2-inch pieces. Cook the beans in boiling salted water over low heat until just tender. Drain the beans thoroughly and cover them with a cloth to keep warm.

Heat the butter and oil over moderate heat; stir in half the sage or parsley and the peeled and crushed garlic. Sauté for 1 minute, then add the beans. Season to taste with salt and freshly ground pepper, and stir over low heat for 5 minutes.

Mix in the Parmesan cheese and serve the beans at once, sprinkled with the remaining herbs.

BOURBON COFFEE CHIFFON PIE

This combination of whisky, coffee, and cream makes a good dessert that can be prepared hours ahead.

PREPARATION TIME: *35 minutes*
CHILLING TIME: *5 hours*

INGREDIENTS (*for* 8):
1¼ cups graham cracker crumbs
¼ cup sugar
¼ cup butter, melted
½ teaspoon nutmeg
3 eggs
1 envelope unflavored gelatin
½ cup cold strong coffee
⅔ cup sugar
Pinch of salt
5 tablespoons bourbon
4 tablespoons coffee liqueur
1 cup heavy cream

Preheat the oven to 350°F. To make the crust, mix the crumbs, sugar, melted butter, and nutmeg, and spoon into a 9-inch pie plate. Press the crumbs evenly over the bottom and against the sides. Bake 5 minutes. Cool thoroughly.

To make the filling, separate the eggs and set aside. Sprinkle the gelatin over the coffee in a saucepan. Add ⅓ cup of the sugar, salt, and the egg yolks. Stir thoroughly. Cook over low heat only until the gelatin is dissolved. Do not boil.

Remove the mixture from the heat. Add the bourbon and the liqueur. Chill until it starts to thicken but do not let it jell.

Beat egg whites until stiff, adding the remaining sugar gradually. Fold them into the gelatin mixture.

Whip the cream and fold it into the mixture. Spoon this into the crust and chill for 5 hours. Garnish with more whipped cream if desired.

CHINESE PEARS

Despite its name, this unusual and aromatic dessert is French in origin. It is sweet and rich, suitable for a dinner party. Bartlett, Comice, or other squat dessert pears are excellent for this recipe.

PREPARATION TIME: *35 minutes*
COOKING TIME: *35 minutes*

INGREDIENTS (*for* 6):
6 large ripe pears
½ cup white raisins
⅓ cup pine nuts
6 teaspoons honey
2 tablespoons unsalted butter
½–¾ cup dry white wine
6 teaspoons ginger syrup
½ cup red currant jelly

Peel the pears thinly and cut a small slice from the base of each so that it will stand upright. Remove a ¾–1 inch lid from the top of each pear and scoop out the core and seeds. Coarsely chop the raisins and pine nuts, mix with the honey, and spoon the mixture into the pear cavities. Replace the lids.

Grease an ovenproof dish with the butter and stand the pears in the dish together with any remaining stuffing. Pour in the white wine and cover the dish with foil. Bake the pears in the center of an oven, preheated to 350–375°F, for about 30 minutes or until tender—the time varies according to the type and ripeness of the pears.

When cooked, place the pears in individual serving bowls and keep them warm in the oven. Pour the cooking juices into a small saucepan and add the ginger syrup and red currant jelly. Boil over moderate heat until the jelly has dissolved. Pour this sauce over the pears and serve at once.

CRÈME CARAMEL À L'ORANGE

Caramel custard is a favorite international dessert, especially after a rich or spicy main course. In this Spanish recipe the caramel custard is given additional flavor by fresh or frozen orange juice.

PREPARATION TIME: *30–35 minutes*
COOKING TIME: *30 minutes*
CHILLING TIME: *2 hours*

INGREDIENTS (*for 4*):
Rind of 1 orange
1 cup fresh or frozen orange juice
3 eggs plus 3 egg yolks
2 tablespoons sugar
CARAMEL:
½ cup sugar

Finely grate the orange rind and leave it to steep in the orange juice.

Meanwhile, warm but do not grease four dariole molds* or custard cups and make the caramel: Put the ½ cup sugar and 2 tablespoons of cold water in a small heavy-bottomed pan over low heat; stir gently until the syrup is clear. Turn up the heat and boil briskly, without stirring, until the syrup turns a golden caramel color. Pour a little caramel into each dariole mold or custard cup. Twist the molds quickly until they are evenly coated with the caramel (use thick oven mitts to handle the molds, as they will be very hot).

Heat the orange juice and grated rind in a pan over low heat. Whisk the whole eggs, egg yolks, and 2 tablespoons of sugar until creamy. When the orange juice is on the point of boiling, strain it into the eggs, stirring briskly. Pour the orange cream into the prepared molds and set them in a roasting pan containing 1 inch of hot water.

Cover the molds with buttered waxed paper and bake in the center of a preheated oven at 350°F for about 30 minutes or until completely set.

Remove the molds from the oven, allow them to cool, and then chill in the refrigerator for at least 2 hours. Just before serving, unmold the caramel custards on individual plates and serve with a pitcher of cream.

CRÊPES GEORGETTE

These crêpes, with a rum-flavored pineapple filling, are said to have been created for Georgette Leblanc, close friend of the Belgian poet Maeterlinck.

PREPARATION TIME: *30 minutes*
COOKING TIME: *5 minutes*

INGREDIENTS (*for 6*):
1 cup crêpe batter (p.343)
6 canned pineapple slices
1 cup vanilla-flavored pâtissière cream (see Quiche Reine-Claude, p.228)
3–4 tablespoons rum
¼ cup melted butter
Confectioners' sugar

Prepare the crêpe batter and use it to make 12 very thin crêpes. Drain and finely chop the pineapple slices. Make the pâtissière cream next and flavor it with 1 tablespoon rum. Mix the chopped pineapple into the cream. Put a good tablespoon of the warm cream mixture in the center of each crêpe and fold the 2 sides over it so that they overlap.

Place the stuffed crêpes side by side in a well-buttered, warmed baking dish. Brush them with the melted butter and dredge generously with sifted confectioners' sugar. Heat a metal skewer and press the

length of it onto the sugar to make a crisscross pattern.

Set the dish under a hot broiler for about 5 minutes to glaze the sugar topping. Just before serving, warm the remaining rum, set it alight, and pour it over the crêpes.

MERINGUE MONT BLANC

In the original recipe by Escoffier, Mont Blanc aux Marrons, cooked chestnuts were rubbed through a sieve into a peak shape and capped with whipped cream. In this version, a shell made of meringue is filled with sherry-flavored chestnut purée and whipped cream. The meringue and filling can be made in advance, but the dessert should not be assembled until just before serving.

PREPARATION TIME: *35 minutes*
COOKING TIME: *1 hour*

INGREDIENTS (*for 6*):
2 teaspoons corn oil
2 egg whites
½ cup superfine sugar
FILLING:
4 tablespoons unsalted butter
4 tablespoons sugar
1 cup canned sweetened chestnut purée
2 tablespoons dry sherry
Lemon juice
1¼ cups whipped cream
GARNISH:
¼ cup blanched pistachio nuts

Line a large baking sheet with waxed paper or cooking parchment and on it draw 2 7-inch pencil circles, using a saucepan lid or bowl as a guide. Brush the paper lightly with the corn oil.

Beat the egg whites until dry, add 2 tablespoons of the superfine sugar,

and beat again until stiff. Lightly fold in the remaining sifted sugar. Put this meringue mixture into a pastry bag fitted with a large rosette tube. Pipe* a ring of meringue inside one of the marked circles and spread the other circle completely with meringue, about ¼ inch thick. Pipe the remaining meringue into 8 small rosettes of equal size.

Bake the meringues in the center of a preheated oven at 275°F for about 1 hour, or until the meringues are crisp, dry, and lightly browned. Lift the rosettes off the paper, turn the paper upside down, and carefully peel it off the meringue ring and the flat base. Leave meringues on a wire rack until they are cool.

For the filling, cream together the butter and sugar; beat the chestnut purée until smooth and beat it into

the creamed butter and sugar, little by little. Flavor to taste with sherry and lemon juice.

To assemble, place the meringue base on a flat serving plate. With a pastry bag with a plain tube, pipe a little of the whipped cream around the edge of the meringue base. Set the ring on top. Fill the center of the shell with the chestnut purée mixture, piling it up into a mound. Pipe a little of the whipped cream on the bottom of each rosette and arrange them on top of the meringue ring. Pipe the remaining cream over the chestnut mound to resemble snow, and scatter the blanched, chopped pistachio nuts over the purée.

APPLE AND NUT STRUDEL

Austria (particularly around Vienna) is renowned for its rich pastries and cakes. The strudel recipe is probably the most popular of them all, in spite of the fact that it takes practice to get a true strudel dough really thin. This famous pastry should be almost transparent, or, as the Austrians say, "thin enough to read your love letters through."

PREPARATION TIME: *1 hour*
COOKING TIME: *40 minutes*

INGREDIENTS (*for 6*):
1 cup all-purpose flour
3½ tablespoons corn oil
Flour for rolling out
4 tablespoons melted unsalted butter
FILLING:
4 tablespoons unsalted butter
1½ cups fresh white bread crumbs
½ cup hazelnuts or walnuts
1 pound cooking apples
1 teaspoon ground cinnamon
¼ cup sugar
⅓ cup white raisins
Grated rind of ½ lemon
Confectioners' sugar

Sift the flour into a warmed bowl; make a well in the center and stir in the vegetable oil mixed with 2 tablespoons warm water. Work the mixture into a soft dough, adding more warm water as required. Knead the dough thoroughly on a lightly floured surface, then roll it into a long sausage shape. Pick up the strudel dough by one end and hit it against the pastry board. Repeat this lifting and hitting process, picking up the dough by alternate ends, for about 10 minutes.

Knead the elastic strudel dough into a ball and leave it to rest on a plate for about 30 minutes, covered

by an inverted warm mixing bowl.

Meanwhile, heat the butter for the filling and gently sauté the bread crumbs until golden. Chop the nuts coarsely. Peel, core, and coarsely chop the apples.

Spread a large clean cloth over the countertop and sprinkle it evenly with flour. Roll out the strudel dough on the cloth, as thinly as possible, and brush it with a little warm corn oil to keep it pliable. Place the hands under the dough and stretch it over the backs of the hands by pulling them away from each other until the dough is paper-thin. Work on one area at a time until all the dough is nearly transparent.

When the dough is thin enough, trim off the uneven edges with a sharp knife or scissors. Brush the melted butter over all the dough; spread the sautéed bread crumbs on

top. Cover these with the chopped apples to within 2 inches of the edges. Mix the cinnamon and sugar, and sprinkle over the apples, together with the chopped nuts, white raisins, and grated lemon rind. Fold the lower edge of the dough over the filling, then lift the edge of the cloth and roll the strudel up like a jelly roll. Seal the seam with water and tuck under the ends.

Lift the strudel and roll it off the sheet onto a greased baking sheet, seam underneath. Curve the strudel into a horseshoe shape and brush the top with the remaining melted butter. Bake in the center of a preheated oven at 425°F for 10 minutes, then lower the heat to 400°F and bake for about 30 minutes, or until the pastry has turned golden brown.

Serve hot or cold, dusted with sifted confectioners' sugar.

LINZERTORTE

This Austrian torte, named after the town of Linz, is popular both as a dessert and as an accompaniment to morning or afternoon coffee. It is traditionally served with *schlagsahne*.

(This consists of ½ cup of sweetened whipped cream into which a stiffly beaten egg white is folded just before serving.) The dessert should be cut into thin wedges.

PREPARATION TIME: *30 minutes*
CHILLING TIME: *1½ hours*
COOKING TIME: *50 minutes*

INGREDIENTS (*for 6*):

¾ cup flour
½ teaspoon ground cinnamon
6 tablespoons sugar
½ cup unblanched ground almonds or hazelnuts
Grated rind of ½ lemon
¼ pound unsalted butter

2 egg yolks
¼ teaspoon vanilla extract
12-ounce jar thick raspberry jam
GLAZE:
1 egg yolk
1 tablespoon heavy cream

Sift the flour, cinnamon, and sugar into a mixing bowl. Add the ground almonds and finely grated lemon rind; blend thoroughly and then rub in the butter until the mixture resembles bread crumbs.

Beat the egg yolks with the vanilla and stir into the flour and almond mixture. Using a wooden spoon, work it into a soft dough. Wrap in waxed paper or foil and chill for 1 hour in the refrigerator.

Butter a cake pan with removable bottom, 9 inches in diameter by 1½ inches deep. (If you do not have a 9-inch cake pan with a removable bottom, use a regular 9-inch pie plate and do not unmold the torte.) Knead the dough to soften it slightly, then press it with the fingers over the bottom of the pan and up the sides. The lining should be not more than ¼ inch thick, and the surplus dough should be pushed up over the top edge and trimmed off neatly with a knife. Spread the jam evenly over the bottom of the torte, using about three-fourths of the jar.

Knead the pastry trimmings together and roll them out on a well-floured board to a rectangle 9 inches by 3 inches. Cut this into 6 strips, each ½ inch wide. Lift the strips, one at a time, with a metal spatula and lay them across the raspberry filling in a lattice pattern. Press the ends of the strips into the pastry lining. Run a sharp knife around the top of the pan to loosen the pastry that extends above the lattice pattern, then fold it inwards and down onto the strips to make a ½-inch-wide border.

For the glaze, beat the egg yolk and cream together and brush this over the lattice and border. Chill the torte for 30 minutes in the refrigerator, then bake it in the center of a preheated oven at 350°F for 50 minutes or until lightly browned.

Leave the torte to cool and shrink slightly, then loosen the edge with a knife. Place the cake pan on a jar or can and gently push down the rim. Slide the torte onto a serving plate and serve it warm or cold with a bowl of schlagsahne.

Snacks & Supper Dishes

STUFFED CABBAGE LEAVES

The outer leaves of cabbage can be used to encase leftover meat. Baked potatoes and a tomato sauce make this a good main course.

PREPARATION TIME: *15 minutes*
COOKING TIME: *30 minutes*

INGREDIENTS (*for 4*):
8 large cabbage leaves
2 tablespoons olive oil
2 finely chopped onions
2 cups ground cooked chicken or ham
2 teaspoons chopped parsley
2 tablespoons packaged poultry stuffing
2 teaspoons tomato purée
1 tablespoon butter
1 cup canned tomatoes
Salt, black pepper, and cumin

Trim the cabbage leaves into squares or rectangles; blanch* them in boiling salted water for 3 minutes. Drain thoroughly and leave to cool.

Heat the oil in a heavy-bottomed pan; add the onions and cook over low heat until transparent. Stir in the meat, parsley, stuffing, tomato purée, 3 tablespoons of boiling water, butter, and tomatoes. Season with salt, pepper, and cumin. Bring to a boil and simmer for 5 minutes.

Spread out the cabbage leaves; spoon the filling onto each leaf in equal portions and roll the leaves into neat packages. Put them in a lightly buttered baking dish, seams downward; cover the dish with foil or a lid and bake for 25 minutes in the oven at 350°F.

Serve the cabbage leaves with a thick tomato sauce (p.302).

CHEESE AND CHUTNEY DIP

This savory, curry-flavored dip, to be served with cocktails, can be created very quickly.

PREPARATION TIME: *10 minutes*
CHILLING TIME: *30 minutes*

INGREDIENTS (*for 6*):
½ pound cream cheese
2 tablespoons heavy cream
2 teaspoons curry powder
1 tablespoon ketchup
2 teaspoons lemon juice
4 tablespoons finely chopped chutney or sweet pickle
GARNISH:
Celery leaves

Blend the softened cream cheese with the cream until smooth. Stir the curry powder into the ketchup, with the lemon juice, and add to the cheese, together with the chutney or sweet pickle. Mix well before piling into a serving dish. Chill the dip for about 30 minutes.

Serve the dip with crisp crackers, Melba rounds, or potato chips. Alternatively, offer strips of fresh carrots, celery, green pepper, and cauliflower florets, and garnish the cheese dip with celery leaves.

COUNTRYSIDE POTATOES

Day-old baked potatoes are here transformed into a light main course when served with a tomato salad or tossed green salad.

PREPARATION TIME: *10 minutes*
COOKING TIME: *20 minutes*

INGREDIENTS (*for 4*):
4 large baked potatoes
2 slices bacon
¼ pound softened cream cheese
1–2 tablespoons light cream
2 teaspoons chopped parsley
Salt and black pepper
½ cup grated Cheddar cheese

Cut the potatoes in half, scoop out the pulp, and mash it finely. Quickly cook the bacon, without any added fat, until crisp; drain on paper towels and crumble the bacon into the mashed potato. Blend in the softened cream cheese, the cream, and parsley. Mix thoroughly and season with salt and freshly ground pepper.

Pile the mixture back into the potato skins and sprinkle with the grated cheese. Bake in the center of a preheated oven at 400°F for about 20 minutes.

FISHERMAN'S PIE

Leftover cooked fish forms the basis for this economical dish.

PREPARATION TIME: *25 minutes*
COOKING TIME: *25–30 minutes*

INGREDIENTS (*for 4–6*):
½ pound cooked whitefish
½ pound cooked smoked haddock
Juice of 1 lemon
2 tablespoons chopped parsley
½ small chopped green pepper
2 hard-cooked eggs, chopped
2 cups white sauce (p.301)
Salt and black pepper
1½ cups self-rising flour
3 tablespoons butter
2 teaspoons dry mustard
½–¾ cup grated Cheddar cheese
½ cup milk

Fold the skinned and flaked* fish, the lemon juice, parsley, green pepper, and eggs into the white sauce. Season with salt and pepper. Spoon the mixture into a 5-cup baking dish.

Sift the flour into a bowl and rub in the butter. Add the mustard and cheese and sufficient milk to make a soft pliable pastry dough. Knead this lightly on a floured surface, and roll out to a circle ¾ inch thick and large enough to cover the dish. Cut the pastry into 8 triangles and place over the fish so that the points meet in the center. Brush with milk and bake at 425°F for 25 minutes or until golden.

ORANGE UPSIDE-DOWN BISCUITS

These sweet biscuits with a sticky orange coating are a favorite with children. They can be made successfully with a biscuit mix.

PREPARATION TIME: *30 minutes*
COOKING TIME: *30–40 minutes*

INGREDIENTS (*for 8*):
½ cup orange juice
½ cup plus 1 tablespoon sugar
½ cup butter
Baking powder biscuit dough (p.381)
1 teaspoon cinnamon
1 teaspoon grated orange rind

Preheat the oven to 400°F. Combine the orange juice, ½ cup sugar, and half of the butter. Cook over low heat until the butter has melted. Pour into a round 9-inch cake pan.

Roll out the biscuit dough into a square about ¼ inch thick. Melt the remaining butter and brush it over the dough. Sprinkle with 1 tablespoon of sugar, the cinnamon, and grated orange rind.

Roll the dough up like a jelly roll and cut into 1½-inch slices. Place the slices in the orange mixture and brush them with 1 tablespoon of melted butter.

Bake 30–40 minutes or until the tops are crusty brown. Turn the biscuits upside down on a plate.

Breakfasts and Brunches

The North American breakfast is a varied meal. It ranges from a hasty gulp of orange juice and coffee on the way to the office to a leisurely family feast of fruit and cereal followed by sausages and pancakes with maple syrup; eggs and bacon with hashed brown potatoes; and regional specialties such as scrapple, codfish cakes, and country-style ham with cornbread. Eggs are enduringly popular, as are waffles, coffee cakes, and French toast. Brunch is the entertaining face of breakfast, usually held on a weekend day at noon so that it can serve either as breakfast for late risers or lunch for others. A brunch party is a comparatively relaxed way to entertain with a flexible menu that is not tied to a rigid time schedule but can be cooked on the spot or kept warm in chafing dishes. Brunch also provides an opportunity to serve dishes that do not quite fit other patterns of entertaining. These range from old favorites, such as eggs Benedict, corned beef hash, and chicken à la king, to more exotic dishes drawn from the world's cuisines, such as kedgeree, deviled kidneys, and huevos rancheros.

Breakfast

Frosted Oranges

PREPARATION TIME: *1 hour*
CHILLING TIME: *1 hour*

INGREDIENTS (*for 4*): *6 large oranges; 1 grapefruit; ½ cup white seedless grapes; 1 cup sweetened canned or packaged coconut; light rum (optional); 1 egg white, slightly beaten; ¼–½ cup sugar*

Cut the tops off 4 of the oranges evenly or in a sawtoothed pattern and remove most of the pulp with a grapefruit knife. Scoop out the remaining pulp with a spoon. Save the pulp for a snack the next day.

With a sharp knife, peel the remaining 2 oranges and the grapefruit, cutting away all the white skin beneath the peel. Remove the pulp in sections by cutting down through the membranes. Add the grapes, coconut, and rum if desired, and toss gently. Refrigerate for 1 hour.

To frost the orange shells, brush them very lightly, only enough to dampen them, with the egg white. Roll the shells in the sugar. Set the shells aside to dry for 15 minutes.

Pile the fruit in the shells, making sure that some of the grapes show around the top for color.

Hangtown Fry

PREPARATION TIME: *5 minutes*
COOKING TIME: *10 minutes*

INGREDIENTS (*for 4*): *8 oysters, well drained; 1 beaten egg; cracker crumbs; butter; 6 eggs; 2 tablespoons water; salt and pepper; crisp bacon*

Dip the oysters in the beaten egg, then in the cracker crumbs, and fry in plenty of butter until golden brown. Beat 6 eggs well with the water, salt, and pepper to taste. Pour the eggs over the oysters and cook as for an omelet (p.335). Roll the omelet onto a hot platter and garnish with strips of crisp bacon.

Moravian Sugar Cake with Pecans

PREPARATION TIME: *30 minutes*
RISING TIME: *2 hours*
COOKING TIME: *20–25 minutes*

INGREDIENTS (*for 27 3-inch squares*): *2 packages active dry yeast; 1 cup warm water (110°F); ¾ cup sugar; 1 teaspoon salt; 2 large eggs, well beaten; 1 cup butter, melted; 1 cup warm mashed potatoes; 5–6 cups all-purpose flour; 1 cup chopped pecans.* TOPPING: *1 cup packed dark brown sugar; 3 teaspoons cinnamon; ½ cup butter, melted*

Dissolve the yeast in the water. Mix the sugar, salt, eggs, and 1 cup of melted butter in a large bowl. Gradually beat in the potatoes. Beat in 1 cup of the flour until smooth.

Stir in the yeast mixture, then beat in only enough of the remaining flour to form a light, soft dough. Put the dough in a greased bowl. Cover. Let rise in a warm place until doubled in bulk (about 2 hours).

Punch down the dough and divide it into 3 pieces. Press them evenly into 3 buttered 9-inch square pans. Sprinkle the pecans over the dough. Cover and let rise until doubled in bulk.

Mix the brown sugar and cinnamon. Make indentations about 1 inch apart in the dough in each pan and spoon some of the sugar mixture into each depression. Drizzle ½ cup of melted butter over the top.

Bake at 350°F about 20 minutes or until cakes are golden brown. Cool. Cut into squares.

Buttery Baked Pancake

PREPARATION TIME: *10 minutes*
COOKING TIME: *15–20 minutes*

INGREDIENTS (*for 2*): *2 eggs; ½ cup flour; ½ cup milk; ¼ teaspoon nutmeg; 5 tablespoons butter; 2 tablespoons sifted confectioners' sugar; juice of ½ lemon*

Preheat oven to 425°F. Beat eggs slightly, then mix in the flour, milk, and nutmeg. Leave the batter slightly lumpy.

Melt butter in a 12-inch skillet with a heatproof handle. When the butter is hot, pour in the batter.

Bake 15–20 minutes or until golden brown. Sprinkle with the sugar and return to the oven for 1 or 2 minutes. Sprinkle with the lemon juice.

Cut into wedges and serve with jelly, jam, or marmalade. Note: The pancake will puff while it is baking, but it will fall when removed from the oven.

Oeufs en Cocotte (p.74)

Creamed Chipped Beef and Mushrooms

PREPARATION TIME: *15 minutes*
COOKING TIME: *15 minutes*

INGREDIENTS (*for 4–6*): *5 ounces chipped beef; 4 tablespoons butter; ½ pound mushrooms, thinly sliced; 2 teaspoons Worcestershire sauce; freshly ground black pepper; 2 cups Béchamel sauce (p.301)*

Pour boiling water over the chipped beef and let it stand for 5 minutes. Drain and cut into 1-inch strips. Heat the butter in a skillet. Add the mushrooms and sauté over medium heat. Season with the Worcestershire sauce and pepper to taste. Cook for 5 minutes, add the chipped beef, and remove from heat. Stir in the Béchamel sauce, combine well, and taste to adjust seasoning. Heat through and spoon over toast or rice.

Brunch

Eggs Suzette

PREPARATION TIME: *20 minutes*
COOKING TIME: *1–1¼ hours*

INGREDIENTS (*for 6*): *6 large potatoes; 6 tablespoons butter; 3 tablespoons sour cream; 1 tablespoon chopped chives; 1 tablespoon crisp, crumbled bacon; 2 teaspoons salt; 1 teaspoon freshly ground black pepper; 6 eggs; ½ cup or more Cheddar cheese, grated*

Bake the potatoes.* Scoop out the pulp and blend well with the butter, sour cream, chives, bacon, and salt and pepper. Mix thoroughly and spoon back into the shells. Make a hollow in the top of each potato and drop into it a raw egg. Sprinkle lavishly with the grated cheese and bake in a 350°F oven just long enough to cook the eggs and melt the cheese.

Chicken Hash

PREPARATION TIME: *10 minutes*
COOKING TIME: *20 minutes*

INGREDIENTS (*for 4*): *4 tablespoons chicken fat or butter; 1 large onion, finely chopped; 5 small boiled potatoes, cooled; rosemary, salt, and pepper; 2½ cups diced dark and white meat of cooked chicken; ¼ cup chicken gravy (optional); ½ cup heavy cream; ½ cup chopped parsley*

Melt the chicken fat or butter in a skillet and sauté the onion until limp and golden. Dice the potatoes and add them to the skillet. Season with a little crushed rosemary, salt, and pepper to taste. Mix in the diced chicken and the optional chicken gravy. Mix well together and cook gently for 5 minutes. Pour in the heavy cream and cook down for a few minutes. Quickly fold in the chopped parsley. Serve immediately. Top each serving with a poached egg, if desired.

Pineapple with Crème Fraîche and Ginger

PREPARATION TIME: *20 minutes*
CHILLING TIME: *1 hour*

INGREDIENTS (*for 4–6*): *1 large pineapple; 1 cup crème fraîche (p.305) or sour cream; 1 tablespoon honey; ½ teaspoon cinnamon; ½ cup preserved candied ginger or ginger marmalade*

With a long narrow knife, cut off the top and bottom of a large pineapple. Cut out the core. Cut between the fruit and the skin. Push out the fruit and the core. Slice the fruit about ½ inch thick and replace it in the shell. Chill for 1 hour. Place on a plate and decorate with lemon leaves and flowers, if desired.

Sour cream may be used as an accompaniment to the pineapple, but the crème fraîche is much better. Flavor the crème fraîche or sour cream with the honey. Spoon into a small serving bowl. Sprinkle the top with the cinnamon. Put the ginger in another small serving bowl. Let the guests help themselves.

Bread and Butter Pudding

PREPARATION TIME: *20 minutes*
COOKING TIME: *55 minutes*

INGREDIENTS (*for 6–8*): *10–12 ½-inch slices French bread; 3 tablespoons butter; 4 whole eggs; 4 egg yolks; 1 cup sugar; ¼ teaspoon salt; 4 cups milk; 1 cup heavy cream; 2 teaspoons vanilla extract. APRICOT SAUCE: 2 cups apricot jam; 1 cup water; 2 tablespoons sugar; 3 tablespoons brandy*

Preheat oven to 375°F. Trim the crust from the bread, and butter each slice on one side. Beat the eggs, sugar, and salt until well blended.

In a saucepan stir in the milk and cream and bring just to a boil. Stir this mixture very gradually into the egg mixture. Add the vanilla extract.

Arrange the bread slices, buttered side up, in a 2-quart baking dish and strain the custard mixture over them. Set the dish in a roasting pan. Fill the roasting pan with hot water to a depth of 1 inch.

Bake for 45 minutes, or until a knife inserted in the center of the pudding comes out clean. If the top has not browned, slide the pudding under a hot broiler for a few seconds.

Serve warm with apricot sauce made by cooking the jam, water, and sugar together over low heat for 10 minutes, stirring occasionally. Force the mixture through a sieve and stir in the brandy.

Popovers (p.344)

Huevos Rancheros
(Mexican-Style Eggs)

PREPARATION TIME: *25 minutes*
COOKING TIME: *25 minutes*

INGREDIENTS (*for 4*): *3 cups drained, canned tomatoes; 1 small hot green pepper or 1 canned jalapeño pepper; 2 cloves garlic, peeled and chopped; 4 tablespoons peanut oil; ½ cup onions, finely chopped; 1 sweet green pepper, finely chopped; ½ teaspoon cumin; 2 teaspoons chili powder; ¼ teaspoon oregano; ½ teaspoon salt, or to taste. Additional peanut oil for frying the tortillas and the eggs; 8 small tortillas (p.149); 8 eggs; 1 cup finely grated Monterey Jack cheese*

Whirl the tomatoes, the hot green or jalapeño pepper, and the garlic in a blender until just smooth.

Sauté the onion and sweet green pepper in the oil until soft, but not brown. Add the blended ingredients and the salt. Cook over moderately high heat for about 5 minutes until slightly thickened. Add the cumin, chili powder, and the oregano. Taste for salt. Set the sauce aside.

Brush a large skillet lightly with oil and fry the tortillas lightly on both sides. Cover with aluminum foil and keep warm.

Warm the sauce. Fry the eggs briefly on one side only in oil. Lay the tortillas in a large platter. Place an egg on each tortilla. Cover the eggs with the sauce. Sprinkle the cheese evenly over the eggs and place under a very hot broiler until cheese begins to melt. This should take only a few seconds. Serve immediately.

The better brands of frozen or canned tortillas, available in most supermarkets, can be used in this recipe in place of homemade ones.

December

Cheese, apples and nuts, joly Carols to heare,
as then in the countrie is counted good cheare.

THOMAS TUSSER

THIS MONTH'S RECIPES

*A wassail bowl filled with warm ale, wine, and spices, and with fruit
floating on top, brings a touch of Merrie England to the Christmas table.*

Food in Season

Hospitality is as much a part of December as are carols, mistletoe, and the brightly decorated tree. It is time for welcoming friends and for sharing the delightful food and drink of the holiday season.

Recipes this month make use of avocados, coconuts, tangelos, tangerines, celery, and fennel. The licorice-flavored fennel, growing in popularity each year, can be cooked like celery or eaten raw. It is especially good in a salad with rice and mayonnaise (p.284).

Many root vegetables—carrots, sweet potatoes, turnips, rutabagas, parsnips, and Jerusalem artichokes—are good buys this month. Cream of Jerusalem artichoke soup (p.275) makes a fine beginning to a winter meal, while sweet potatoes with apples (p.285) or a parsnip casserole (p.286) go exceptionally well with a pork roast, suckling pig (p.294), or pork chops with cream (p.280).

Other vegetables available in December include broccoli, mushrooms, Belgian endive, leeks, and Brussels sprouts. One of the best ways to cook leeks is as a Crème Vichyssoise (p.276). And for a refreshing change from green salads, try endive with oranges (p.285).

December is the last month that fresh cranberries will be on the market until next fall. Roast lamb with cranberry stuffing (p.281) is a festive party dish for this time of year. Persimmons are still available, and oranges, grapefruits, and apples will be plentiful throughout the winter. Apples make a good stuffing for duck and goose (p.292) and a quick but delicious dessert when combined with macaroons and rum (p.287).

SUGGESTED MENUS

Cream of Jerusalem Artichoke Soup
...
Meat Loaf
Brussels Sprouts with Sour Cream
Garlic Potatoes
...
Fresh Fruit

Crème Vichyssoise
...
Halibut with Corn
Broccoli au Gratin
...
Paris–Brest

Pears in Tarragon Cream
Goose in Cider
Red Cabbage
...
Meringue à la Reine

Eggs Mollet in Pâté
...
Filet de Boeuf en Croûte
Baked Cauliflower in Cheese Sauce
...
Champagne Charlie

Eggs in Provençale Sauce
Mackerel with White Wine Sauce
Buttered Spinach
Sautéed Potatoes
...
Sour Cream Tart

Shrimp Baked in Sour Cream
...
Lamb à la Greque
Endive and Orange Salad
...
Apple-Rum Meringue

Spaghettini with Mussel Sauce
Waldorf Salad
...
Orange Chiffon Cream

Soups & First Courses

SHRIMP BAKED IN SOUR CREAM

This easily made appetizer can be prepared well in advance and then baked just before serving.

PREPARATION TIME: *10 minutes*
COOKING TIME: *10 minutes*

INGREDIENTS (*for 4*):
½ *pound cooked peeled shrimp*
Black pepper
½ *cup sour cream*
Fresh white bread crumbs
4 tablespoons unsalted butter
GARNISH:
Parsley sprigs

Butter 4 small ovenproof dishes and divide the shrimp between them. Season thoroughly with freshly ground pepper and cover with sour cream.

Sprinkle a thin layer of fine bread crumbs over the sour cream and dot with pieces of butter. Bake in the center of a preheated oven at 375°F for 10 minutes. Finish the shrimp under a hot broiler for 1–2 minutes or until the bread crumbs are golden brown on top.

Garnish each dish with a sprig of parsley and serve immediately with thin slices of French or Italian bread and butter.

CREAM OF JERUSALEM ARTICHOKE SOUP

Sweet-flavored Jerusalem artichokes are the basis for this cream soup. It freezes well.

PREPARATION TIME: *30 minutes*
COOKING TIME: *45 minutes*

INGREDIENTS (*for 8*):
1½ *pounds Jerusalem artichokes*
Juice of 1 lemon
1 onion
¼ *cucumber*
4 tablespoons butter
4 cups chicken stock
1¼ *cups dry white wine (optional)*
6 parsley stalks
Salt and black pepper
1¼ *cups heavy cream*
GARNISH:
½ *cup yogurt*
3 tablespoons fresh chopped parsley

Peel the Jerusalem artichokes,* cut them into ½-inch pieces, and leave them in a bowl of cold water to which the strained lemon juice has been added. Peel and thinly slice the onion; wipe and slice the cucumber unless it is waxed, in which case peel before slicing.

Drain the Jerusalem artichokes and dry them. Melt the butter in a large skillet and add the Jerusalem artichokes, the onion, and cucumber. Cook the vegetables in the butter for 5 minutes over low heat—do not allow them to color. Pour over the stock and wine. Bring the soup to a boil and add the parsley stalks. Season with salt and freshly ground pepper. Cover the pan with a lid and reduce the heat.

Simmer the soup for about 20 minutes, or until the vegetables are soft. Remove the pan from the heat and allow the soup to cool slightly.

Purée it in the blender or rub it through a sieve. Correct seasoning. Stir in the cream just before serving, but do not allow the soup to boil.

Serve the soup in individual bowls. Trail a little yogurt over the surface of each bowl and sprinkle with finely chopped parsley.

PEARS IN TARRAGON CREAM

For this simple first course, choose firm but ripe squat pears, such as Bartletts. They are served with a classic French tarragon cream.

PREPARATION TIME: *10 minutes*
CHILLING TIME: *1 hour*

INGREDIENTS (*for 6*):
6 dessert pears
1¼ *cups heavy cream*
2 tablespoons tarragon vinegar
Sugar
Salt and black pepper

Chill the pears in the refrigerator. Beat the cream and vinegar together until thick but not too stiff. Season to taste with sugar, salt, and freshly ground pepper. Peel and halve the pears and scoop out the center cores with a teaspoon.

Serve the pears rounded side up on individual small plates, with the tarragon cream spooned over them.

EGGS MOLLET IN PÂTÉ

The creamy texture of *eggs mollet*—eggs boiled until the whites are firm but the yolks still soft—blends well with pâté and aspic, and makes an unusual first course.

PREPARATION TIME: *30 minutes*
CHILLING TIME: *2 hours*

INGREDIENTS (*for 6*):
10½-*ounce can beef bouillon*
⅔ *envelope (2 teaspoons) plain gelatin*
6 small eggs
6 ounces pâté de foie gras
24 pitted black olives
GARNISH:
Parsley

Sprinkle gelatin onto ¼ cup of the cold bouillon and let it soften. Combine with remaining bouillon in a saucepan and cook over moderate heat, stirring continuously until the gelatin has dissolved. Remove from the heat and leave the aspic to cool while cooking the eggs.

Put the eggs into a pan of boiling water and cook them gently for 6 minutes. Lift out the eggs and plunge them into cold water. Shell the eggs carefully and put them in a bowl of cold water.

Brush 6 shallow ramekin dishes with oil. Divide the pâté into 6 equal portions and spread it over the bottom and up the sides of the ramekins. Nest a drained and dried egg in the pâté and surround it with 4 olives. Spoon the aspic over the eggs and olives and leave to set in the refrigerator for about 2 hours. Remove the ramekins 30 minutes before serving and decorate them with sprigs of parsley.

Serve the eggs with hot French bread and butter.

Fish

EGGS IN PROVENÇALE SAUCE

The fragrant spicy sauce in which these eggs are baked is typical of Provençale cuisine. The classic tomato sauce takes some time to prepare and cook; but, as it stores well in the freezer, double or triple quantities can be made. Do not add the garlic if the sauce is to be stored for longer than 1 month.

PREPARATION TIME: *30 minutes*
COOKING TIME: *1 hour*

INGREDIENTS (*for 6*):
2 pounds ripe tomatoes
1 large onion
2 cloves garlic
2 tablespoons olive oil
¼ teaspoon chopped basil
1 bay leaf
Bouquet garni (p.410)
Small piece lemon peel
1 tablespoon tomato paste
Sugar
Salt and black pepper
6 eggs

Peel the tomatoes* and cut them in half crosswise. Remove the seeds with a teaspoon and coarsely chop the pulp. Peel and finely chop the onion and garlic. Heat the oil in a heavy-bottomed pan and cook the onion over low heat for 10 minutes. Add the garlic, the tomato pulp, basil, bay leaf, bouquet garni, chopped lemon peel, and tomato paste. Season to taste with sugar and salt. Stir the ingredients thoroughly and simmer for 30 minutes, or until the contents have reduced* to a thick purée.* Remove the bouquet garni and bay leaf.

Put 2 tablespoons of the sauce into each of 6 ramekin dishes. Make a hollow in the center of the sauce and break an egg carefully into each. Sprinkle the eggs with salt and freshly ground pepper. Bake the eggs for about 10 minutes, or until just set, in the center of an oven preheated to 375°F.

Serve at once, with warm, crusty French bread.

BARBECUED SPARERIBS

This is a substantial first course, prepared in the Chinese style—that is, baked in a sauce. The racks of pork spareribs should be cut into 12 individual ribs for easy eating with the fingers.

PREPARATION TIME: *15 minutes*
COOKING TIME: *45 minutes*

INGREDIENTS (*for 4*):
12 single pork spareribs
4 tablespoons clear honey
3 tablespoons soy sauce
3 tablespoons tomato ketchup
Tabasco sauce
1 small clove garlic
Dry mustard
Paprika
Salt and black pepper
Juice of 1 small orange
4 tablespoons wine vinegar

Broil the ribs for 10–15 minutes under a preheated broiler until they are brown, turning them several times. Arrange them in a single layer in a large roasting pan and pour in the pan juices.

Put the honey, soy sauce, tomato ketchup, and a few drops of Tabasco sauce into a bowl; peel the garlic; crush it with the side of a knife and add it to the bowl. Season to taste with the dry mustard, paprika, salt, and freshly ground pepper, then add the orange juice and wine vinegar.

Mix, then pour over the spareribs.

Cook, uncovered, in the center of a preheated oven at 350°F for 30 minutes. Serve the ribs piping hot in the sauce. Provide a finger bowl at each place setting.

CRÈME VICHYSSOISE

This soup was created by Louis Diat when he was chef of a New York hotel in 1910. It has since become universally famous. It should be served chilled.

PREPARATION TIME: *30 minutes*
COOKING TIME: *35–40 minutes*
CHILLING TIME: *2–3 hours*

INGREDIENTS (*for 6*):
2 pounds leeks
1 pound potatoes
4 tablespoons butter
1 stalk celery
2½ cups chicken stock
2½ cups milk
Salt and black pepper
Freshly grated nutmeg
1¼ cups heavy cream
GARNISH:
Chopped chives

Trim the roots and coarse outer leaves from the leeks and wash them thoroughly in cold water. Slice the leeks diagonally into ¼-inch pieces. Peel and coarsely dice the potatoes. Melt the butter in a large skillet and add the leeks and potatoes. Cook the vegetables over moderate heat for 7 minutes, stirring continuously. Add the coarsely chopped celery to the pan. Pour in the chicken stock and milk, and bring the soup slowly to a boil. Season with salt, freshly ground pepper, and nutmeg. Simmer the soup for 25 minutes, or until the vegetables are tender.

Allow the soup to cool slightly before puréeing in the blender or rubbing it through a sieve. Correct seasoning and stir in the cream.

Chill the soup in the refrigerator for 2–3 hours. Serve in chilled individual bowls, garnished with chopped chives.

CABBAGE SOUP WITH KNOCKWURST

This hearty soup, served with dark pumpernickel bread and beer, is an ideal lunch for a wintry day.

PREPARATION TIME: *20 minutes*
COOKING TIME: *45 minutes*

INGREDIENTS (*for 6–8*):
2 pounds cabbage
3 tablespoons butter
1½ cups chopped onions
2 large potatoes
1 large clove garlic, chopped
2 quarts water
1½ teaspoons salt
1 teaspoon caraway seeds
2 knockwursts

Shred the cabbage coarsely and set aside. Heat the butter in a Dutch oven. Add the onions and sauté slowly for 5 minutes.

While the onions are cooking, peel and cube the potatoes. Add the cabbage, garlic and potatoes to the onions and cook over low heat for 10 minutes, stirring frequently.

Add the water, salt, and the caraway seeds. Bring to a boil, reduce the heat, and simmer for 20 minutes or until the vegetables are almost done.

Cut the knockwursts into ¼-inch slices and add these to the soup. Cook for 10 minutes. Serve in large bowls with plenty of pumpernickel bread, butter, and cold beer.

SCALLOPED CLAMS

This dish is a pleasant change from the familiar scalloped oysters. For a perfect lunch, serve the scalloped clams with a tossed green or mixed salad and fruit for dessert.

PREPARATION TIME: *15 minutes*
COOKING TIME: *20–25 minutes*

INGREDIENTS (*for 4*):
7 tablespoons butter
½ cup toasted bread crumbs
1 cup cracker crumbs
Salt and pepper
¼ teaspoon paprika
2 cups finely chopped clams
2 tablespoons minced shallots or scallions
3 tablespoons minced parsley
½ cup light cream

Mix 6 tablespoons of the butter with the bread crumbs and cracker crumbs. Add the salt and pepper to taste and the paprika. Put aside ⅓ cup of this mixture for the top. Combine the remaining mixture with the clams, shallots or scallions, and parsley. Spoon into a buttered baking dish and sprinkle the top with the ⅓ cup of the crumb mixture. Pour in the light cream and dot the top with the remaining tablespoon butter. Bake at 375°F for 20–25 minutes.

MACKEREL WITH WHITE WINE SAUCE

Mackerel, one of the most flavorful of fish, would be more highly prized if it were more expensive. Here, a creamy white wine sauce lifts it a few rungs up the status ladder.

PREPARATION TIME: *20 minutes*
COOKING TIME: *30 minutes*

INGREDIENTS (*for 4*):
4 small or 2 large mackerel
Seasoned flour (p.412)
4 tablespoons unsalted butter
Juice of ½ lemon
SAUCE:
½ cup fish stock
½ cup dry white wine
½ cup heavy cream
Salt and black pepper
1 egg yolk
GARNISH:
Finely chopped parsley

Clean and fillet each mackerel* into two. Rinse under cold water, dry, and coat each fillet with seasoned flour.

Make the wine sauce before sautéing the fillets. Bring the stock (made from the fish bones) and the white wine to a boil. Simmer over low heat for about 15 minutes or until it has reduced* by half. Stir in the cream, heat the sauce through, and season to taste with salt and freshly ground pepper. Beat the egg yolk in a bowl; stir a little of the warm sauce into the egg. Add the egg yolk to the sauce and return the pan to the heat for 1 minute. Keep the sauce warm, but do not let it boil, or it will curdle.

Melt the butter in a skillet, put the fillets into the pan, and sauté over low heat for 5–6 minutes; turn the fish over and cook the other side for the same length of time. Remove the fillets from the pan and keep warm on a serving dish. Add the lemon juice to the butter in the pan and pour the mixture over the fillets.

Serve the mackerel sprinkled with parsley and pour the sauce into a warm sauceboat. Buttered spinach and sautéed potatoes can accompany the mackerel as a main course.

CIOPPINO

This seafood dish from the West Coast of the United States has been attributed to Portuguese, Italian, and French settlers. No one really knows who started cooking cioppino, or the origin of the name, but it is without doubt one of the most delicious of seafood creations.

PREPARATION TIME: *45 minutes*
COOKING TIME: *40 minutes*

INGREDIENTS (*for 6*):
1 2–3 pound sea bass or striped bass
1 pound shrimp
1 quart clams or mussels
¼ pound dried mushrooms (Italian variety)
1 Dungeness crab or a 1-pound lobster
3–4 tomatoes
1 green pepper
½ cup olive oil
1 large onion, chopped
2 cloves garlic, chopped
3 tablespoons chopped parsley
⅓ cup tomato purée
2 cups red wine
Salt and pepper

Cut the raw fish into serving pieces. Shell the shrimp, leaving the tails intact. Clean the mussels or clams with a stiff brush under cold running water. If mussels are used, with a sharp knife cut off the tuft of hairs, or beard, that clings to the shell. Put the mussels or clams in a heavy pot, add about ½ inch of water, and steam them until they open. Save the liquid. Soak the mushrooms in cold water. Break the crab apart,* or if lobster is used, cut it into several pieces. Peel and coarsely chop the tomatoes* and the green pepper.

Place the olive oil in a deep pot. When it is hot, add the onion, garlic, parsley, mushrooms, and green pepper and cook for 3 minutes. Next, add the tomatoes and the purée, the wine, and the liquid from the clams or mussels. Salt and pepper to taste, cover, and simmer for 30 minutes.

Add the cut-up fish, the shrimp, and the crab or lobster, and cook until done. Add the clams or mussels to reheat them for a minute. Serve with red wine and garlic bread.

Meat

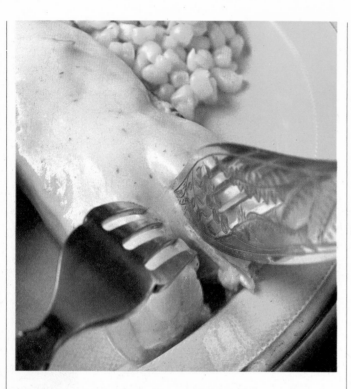

HALIBUT WITH CORN

The delicate flavor of halibut should not be impaired by strong sauces and garnishes. In this recipe, the baked fish is complemented by whole-kernel corn and a Béarnaise sauce.

PREPARATION TIME: *15 minutes*
COOKING TIME: *25 minutes*

INGREDIENTS (*for 6*):
6 halibut steaks or fillets, 4–6
* ounces each*
2 teaspoons lemon juice
Black pepper
¼ pound unsalted butter
7-ounce can whole-kernel corn
1¼ cups Béarnaise sauce (p.303)

Butter 2 large sheets of aluminum foil and place the fish steaks on one sheet. Sprinkle with lemon juice, grind over a little pepper, and dot the fish with pieces of butter. Cover with the second piece of foil and seal tightly to form a loose package. Bake for 25 minutes in the center of an oven preheated to 350°F.

Heat the drained corn over moderate heat, then stir 4 tablespoons of butter into it. Season with freshly ground pepper and spread the corn over the bottom of a shallow serving dish. Arrange the halibut on the corn, pour in the juices from the foil package, and coat each steak with Béarnaise sauce.

Serve with broccoli spears au gratin (p.65).

CRAB WITH MUSHROOMS

This combination of mushrooms and crabmeat makes a good main course. The dish can also be served as a first course, and shrimp can be substituted for crab.

PREPARATION TIME: *10 minutes*
CHILLING TIME: *1 hour*

INGREDIENTS (*for 4*):
½ pound fresh or frozen crabmeat
½ pound button mushrooms
2 cloves garlic
Juice of ½ lemon
Tabasco sauce
6 tablespoons olive oil
Salt and black pepper
½ cup heavy cream
GARNISH:
¾ cup black olives
Chopped parsley

Trim and finely slice the mushrooms* into a mixing bowl. Crush the garlic and add to the mushrooms, the strained lemon juice, a few drops of Tabasco, and the olive oil. Season to taste with salt and freshly ground pepper. Blend all the ingredients thoroughly and spoon them into a shallow serving dish; leave to chill for 1 hour.

Just before serving, blend the flaked crabmeat with the cream and stir this into the mushrooms.

Garnish the crab and mushrooms with olives and finely chopped parsley. Serve with warm crusty bread and butter. A salad of green peppers, endive, and fennel tossed in an Italian dressing (see Lettuce and Celery Salad, p.64) would also go well with this crab dish.

FILET DE BOEUF EN CROÛTE

Whole fillet of beef in puff pastry is a classic, if highly extravagant, French dish. For a special occasion, however, the time and expense involved are well worth the effort.

PREPARATION TIME: *1 hour*
CHILLING TIME: *1 hour*
COOKING TIME: *1½ hours*

INGREDIENTS (*for 8*):
4 pounds fillet of beef
½ clove garlic (optional)
2 tablespoons unsalted butter
½ recipe puff pastry (p.363)
2 ounces pâté de foie gras
½ teaspoon ground thyme
1 egg
1 tablespoon olive oil
CUCUMBER SAUCE:
½ cucumber
¼ cup heavy cream
½ cup yogurt
½ teaspoon ground ginger
3 teaspoons lemon juice
Salt
MUSHROOM SAUCE:
1 small onion
½ pound mushrooms
1¼ cups chicken stock
2 tablespoons unsalted butter
1 tablespoon flour
½ cup milk
Salt and black pepper
2 tablespoons Madeira (optional)
1 egg yolk
GARNISH:
Watercress

Trim any fat from the fillet, roll it into a neat shape, and tie it at intervals with fine string.

Cut the garlic into slivers and insert them into the beef with the point of a sharp knife. Spread softened butter over the top of the fillet. Cook the meat for 10 minutes on a rack in a roasting pan on the center shelf of an oven preheated to 425°F. Remove the beef from the oven and leave to cool. When the beef is quite cold, remove the string.

Roll out the prepared puff pastry, ⅛ inch thick, to an oblong 3½ times the width of the fillet and 7 inches longer. Spread the pâté over the top of the fillet, place the meat, pâté side down, in the center of the pastry, and sprinkle with the thyme. Fold the pastry over and under the meat, brushing the seams with water and sealing them thoroughly. Turn the pastry over so that the seam is underneath; prick the top with a fork and decorate with leaves cut from the pastry trimmings. Cover the pastry with a cloth or plastic wrap and leave it in the refrigerator for at least 1 hour.

Meanwhile, prepare the cucumber and mushroom sauces. For the cucumber sauce, peel and coarsely grate the chilled cucumber. Just before serving, mix it with the heavy cream, yogurt, ground ginger, and lemon juice. Season the mixture to taste with salt.

To make the mushroom sauce, peel and finely chop the onion and the trimmed mushrooms.* Put these ingredients in a saucepan with the chicken stock and bring slowly to a boil. Lower the heat and simmer the mixture for 30 minutes. Cool slightly, then purée the mixture in a blender.

Melt the butter in a pan, stir in the flour, and cook the roux* for 3 minutes, stirring continuously. Gradually blend in the milk and bring the sauce to a boil over low heat. Mix in the mushroom purée, season with salt and freshly ground pepper, and stir in the Madeira, if used. Simmer for a further 10 minutes, then remove from the heat and allow to cool slightly. Stir the beaten egg yolk into the sauce just before serving.

Beat the egg with the oil and brush it over the pastry to glaze it during cooking. Set the pastry roll on a wet baking sheet and bake in the center of an oven, preheated to 425°F, for 35 minutes. The pastry should then be golden brown, and the beef rosy-pink inside.

Place the beef in its pastry on a bed of watercress and serve with broccoli spears au gratin (p.65) and the cucumber and mushroom sauces in separate sauceboats.

MEAT LOAF

This easy-to-make dish is always a favorite. Serve it hot with tomato sauce or cold, cut into thin slices. It makes superb sandwiches.

PREPARATION TIME: *15 minutes*
COOKING TIME: *1¾ hours*

INGREDIENTS (*for 8–10*):
2 pounds ground beef
1 pound ground pork
2 garlic cloves, finely chopped
1 fairly large onion, finely chopped
1 teaspoon salt
1 teaspoon freshly ground black
  pepper
1 crumbled bay leaf
½ teaspoon crumbled thyme leaves
1 teaspoon freshly chopped green
  pepper
½ cup dry bread crumbs
2 eggs
Bacon or salt pork

Mix all ingredients in a large bowl, except the bacon or salt pork, and knead with the fingers until the mixture is thoroughly blended. Arrange enough slices of bacon or salt pork on the bottom of a baking

dish to form a base for the meat loaf. Form the meat into a long loaf or round cake. Brush the loaf with butter and cross the top of the loaf with 2–4 additional slices of bacon. Roast at 325°F, basting occasionally, for 1½–1¾ hours, or until the meat is cooked through.

Frequent basting with the juices makes a moister loaf. If the meat loaf is served hot, let it stand on a hot platter for 10–15 minutes before carving it, to settle the juices. It is even more delicious served at room temperature with a green salad tossed in vinaigrette sauce.

While the meat loaf is cooking, prepare the tomato sauce.

TOMATO SAUCE:
1 small onion, diced
3 cups fresh or canned Italian
  tomatoes
½ teaspoon sugar
½ bay leaf
½ teaspoon oregano
1 tablespoon butter
Salt and pepper

Sauté the onion over low heat for 5 minutes. Add the tomatoes, sugar, bay leaf, and oregano. Cook about 20 minutes. Add the butter and stir to mix. Press the mixture through a sieve or whirl in a blender. Season with salt and pepper.

LAMB À LA GREQUE

Greek cooking is characterized by its use of eggplant, tomatoes, herbs, and the invaluable lemon. Lamb is the meat most commonly used in Greece, but it is often lean and stringy and more suitable for casserole dishes than for roasting.

PREPARATION TIME: *1–1½ hours*
COOKING TIME: *1¼ hours*

INGREDIENTS (*for 6*):
3 pounds boned shoulder of lamb
½ pound eggplant
Salt
4 tablespoons olive oil
2 large onions
16-ounce can tomatoes
6-ounce can tomato paste
4 bay leaves
¼ teaspoon crushed coriander seeds
¼ teaspoon grated nutmeg
1 tablespoon chopped parsley
Salt and pepper
Juice of 1 lemon
3½ cups chicken stock
17-ounce can apricots, drained
4 tablespoons unsalted butter
1 cup long grain rice
GARNISH:
¾ cup pitted black olives
Orange peel

Remove the stalk ends and wash the eggplant* but do not peel it; cut lengthwise into ¼-inch-thick slices. Place the slices in a bowl and sprinkle them generously with salt to draw out the excess water. Mix thoroughly and leave for 45 minutes. Drain the eggplant slices and dry them on paper towels.

Heat the olive oil in a heavy pan and sauté the eggplant slices just until golden, then drain them thoroughly on paper towels.

Trim any excess fat from the lamb,

cut the meat into 1-inch cubes, and cook it over low heat in a dry skillet, turning the meat frequently, until the fat runs and the meat turns a light brown.

Peel and finely chop the onions, add them to the lamb, and continue cooking until the onions are transparent. Add the chopped tomatoes with their liquid, the tomato paste, bay leaves, coriander seeds, nutmeg, chopped parsley, salt, freshly ground pepper, and lemon juice. Pour 1½ cups chicken stock over the lamb and bring the mixture to a boil.

Line a large buttered casserole with the eggplant slices and spoon in the lamb mixture. Cover the casserole tightly with foil and the lid. Cook for 1 hour in the center of an oven preheated to 350°F. Remove the covering from the casserole, lay the drained apricots over the lamb, and return the casserole to the oven while preparing the rice.

Melt 1 tablespoon butter in a heavy pan, add the rice, and stir until

golden. Pour in 2 cups chicken stock, season with salt and pepper, and bring to a boil. Reduce heat, cover, and simmer until done (about 20 minutes).

Melt the remaining butter and stir into the rice. Spoon the rice in a ring onto a warm serving dish and fill the center with the lamb and eggplant. Garnish the rice with black olives, the apricots, and narrow strips of orange peel.

Serve the lamb with a lettuce and tomato salad tossed in a dressing made with salad oil, orange juice, and a few drops of lemon juice seasoned with salt.

279

ROLLATINE DE MANZO AL FORNO

The name of this Italian dish means, quite simply, "beef rolls cooked in the oven." Wafer-thin slices of beef and ham are rolled around a stuffing and cooked in wine.

PREPARATION TIME: *45 minutes*
COOKING TIME: *1 hour*

INGREDIENTS (*for 6*):
12 thin slices top round or rump of
   beef, each approximately 4
   inches by 3 inches by ¼ inch
12 wafer-thin slices cooked ham
3 cloves garlic
12 thin slices salami
4 hard-cooked eggs
¾ cup raisins
½ cup grated Parmesan cheese
8 tablespoons finely chopped parsley
½ teaspoon grated nutmeg
½ teaspoon oregano
Salt and black pepper
2 tablespoons unsalted butter
1¼ cups beef stock
1¼ cups dry white wine
4 bay leaves
6 cloves
2 tablespoons Marsala

Place each slice of beef between sheets of waxed paper and flatten it with a rolling pin. Cover the beef slices with ham, trimmed to fit, and spread the slices with peeled and crushed garlic.

Finely chop the skinned salami, the hard-cooked eggs, and raisins, and put them in a bowl. Blend in the cheese, parsley, nutmeg, and oregano, and season with salt and freshly ground pepper.

Divide this mixture equally over the beef and ham slices. Fold over the short sides to keep the stuffing in place and roll the slices up. Tie the rolls with fine string.

Place the rolls in a buttered ovenproof dish. Pour the beef stock and white wine over them and cook for 30 minutes in the center of the oven, preheated to 375°F. Add the bay leaves, cloves, and Marsala and cook for a further 30 minutes.

Serve the beef rolls with fettuccine al burro (p.62) and cauliflower with almonds (p.63).

PORK CHOPS WITH CREAM

Pork chops are coated with egg and bread crumbs and cooked with cream in this delectable 19th-century farmhouse dish.

PREPARATION TIME: *10 minutes*
COOKING TIME: *30–35 minutes*

INGREDIENTS (*for 4*):
4 large or 8 small pork chops
4 strips of bacon
Flour
1 or 2 eggs, lightly beaten
Fine bread crumbs
Salt and black pepper
1 cup heavy cream

Wipe the chops with a damp cloth and slash the fat around the edges at 1-inch intervals to keep them from curling during cooking. In a large skillet, fry the bacon strips until crisp, then place them on absorbent paper to drain. Dip the chops in flour and then in the egg. Roll the chops in the crumbs. Brown them quickly in the hot bacon fat, turning them with a spatula or pancake turner and being careful not to loosen the crumbs. When the chops are browned on both sides, add half the cream and season to taste with the salt and pepper. Reduce the heat, cover the pan, and simmer gently for 20–25 minutes, or until the pork chops are tender.

Remove the meat to a hot platter and keep warm. Add the remaining cream to the pan. Scrape up all the bits of brown from the skillet and stir them thoroughly into the sauce. Pour this sauce over the chops. Crumble the bacon and sprinkle it evenly over the top of the sauce. Serve immediately.

VIENNESE VEAL CUTLETS

The influence of Hungarian cooking—with its emphasis on sour cream and paprika—is evident in this Austrian recipe. The veal cutlets for this dish should be thick, not thin, and long slow cooking blends the flavors of the herbs, spices, wine, and sour cream.

PREPARATION TIME: *10 minutes*
COOKING TIME: *1 hour*

INGREDIENTS (*for 4*):
4 veal cutlets, each 1 inch thick
   and approximately 6 ounces
½ teaspoon rosemary leaves
4 tablespoons unsalted butter
1 tablespoon olive oil
1 clove garlic
Seasoned flour (p.412)
2 cups mushrooms
6 tablespoons dry white wine
½ cup sour cream
Tabasco sauce
Salt and black pepper
1 teaspoon paprika
GARNISH:
Chopped parsley or paprika

Trim the veal cutlets. Make small incisions in them with the point of a knife and insert small spiky rosemary leaves. Heat the butter and oil in a heavy-bottomed pan over low heat. Peel the garlic and sauté it until brown, then discard.

Coat the veal cutlets lightly with seasoned flour, shake off any surplus, and sauté them in the butter and oil until brown, turning them once.

Cover the pan with a lid and cook the cutlets over low heat for a further 12 minutes. Add the trimmed and sliced mushrooms* to the cutlets. Turn the mushrooms until they have absorbed most of the fat. Pour the wine into the pan and blend well. Increase the heat, then add the sour cream. Do not let it boil, or it will separate. Season to taste with salt, freshly ground pepper, a touch of Tabasco, and the paprika. Turn down the heat and simmer the veal, uncovered, for a further 30 minutes.

Lift out the veal and, if necessary, reduce* the sauce to the desired consistency by cooking down.

Pour the sauce over the veal and serve at once, sprinkled with parsley or a little paprika. A parsnip casserole (p.286) would go well with the veal cutlets.

CROWN ROAST OF LAMB

The crown is made by joining a double rack of lamb to form a circle, and the center is stuffed with a savory cranberry filling. The bones are frequently decorated with paper frills, but small glazed onions make an unusual and edible garnish for this attractive meat dish.

PREPARATION TIME: *45 minutes*
COOKING TIME: *2 hours*

INGREDIENTS (*for 6*):

Crown roast of lamb
½ cup beef drippings
STUFFING:
½ pound cranberries
½ cup chicken stock
2 tablespoons sugar
1 onion
¼ pound mushrooms
2 tablespoons butter

1 clove garlic
4 tablespoons chopped parsley
1½ teaspoons ground thyme
2 cups fresh white bread crumbs
1 egg
Salt and black pepper
GARNISH:
Glazed onions

For the stuffing, put the cranberries, stock, and sugar in a saucepan; if necessary, add enough water to cover the fruit. Bring the cranberries to a boil and cook over high heat until they burst open and the liquid has reduced* to a thick sauce.

Peel and finely chop the onion; trim and coarsely chop the mushrooms.* Melt the butter in a pan and sauté the onion until soft but not colored. Add the peeled and crushed garlic and cook for 1 minute. Add the mushrooms, turning them in the butter until they are lightly colored. In a bowl, combine the cranberries and the onion and mushroom mixture with the parsley, thyme, and bread crumbs. Beat the egg lightly and mix it thoroughly with the stuffing. Season to taste with salt and freshly ground black pepper.

Spoon the stuffing into the hollow crown. Wrap foil around the bones to protect them during roasting. Melt the drippings in a roasting pan and place the stuffed crown in it. Roast on a low shelf in a preheated oven at 375°F for 10 minutes. Reduce the heat to 350°F and continue roasting. Allow 15–16 minutes to the pound, and baste* frequently with the drippings.

Remove the crown roast and keep it warm. Skim off as much fat as possible; then boil the pan juices and stir to make a gravy. Pour it into a warm sauceboat.

Serve the crown roast with garlic potatoes and an endive and orange salad (p.285). Spike a glazed onion (p.285) on each bone.

Poultry

TURKEY MAYONNAISE

Turkey mayonnaise can be made with leftover turkey and is ideal as a picnic or party dish. For a large party, simply roast or poach a whole turkey breast and double or triple the ingredients in this recipe.

PREPARATION TIME: *40 minutes*

INGREDIENTS (*for 4*):
½ *cup walnuts, toasted*
½ *cup shredded tart apples*
1 *teaspoon lemon juice*
2 *cups cooked turkey breast, cut in*
   1–1½ *inch cubes*
1–1½ *cups mayonnaise (p.303)*
1–2 *tablespoons Dijon mustard*
Watercress
Bibb lettuce
GARNISH:
Capers and mayonnaise

To toast the walnuts, spread them in a single layer on a cookie sheet and place in a preheated 350°F oven for about 15 minutes. Stir occasionally to brown them evenly. Cool.

Toss the apples with the lemon juice to prevent them from darkening. Toss the cubed turkey well with the walnuts and the apples. Combine the mayonnaise with the Dijon mustard, add to the turkey mixture, and toss very lightly. Mound the salad on a bed of watercress and Bibb lettuce. Garnish with additional mayonnaise and a few capers.

This salad is equally successful when made with chicken, duck, or goose. Follow the same instructions and increase the number of walnuts, if desired. Peanut oil can be substituted for the olive oil when making the mayonnaise.

CHICKEN WITH FORTY CLOVES OF GARLIC

Garlic lovers find this one of the most appetizing of chicken dishes. After long cooking, the garlic taste is strong but not overpowering.

PREPARATION TIME: *15 minutes*
COOKING TIME: *1½ hours*

INGREDIENTS (*for 8*):
8 *chicken legs and thighs*
40 *cloves garlic*
4 *stalks celery*
⅔ *cup olive oil*
6 *sprigs parsley*
1 *tablespoon dried tarragon*
½ *cup dry vermouth*
¼ *teaspoon pepper*
Dash of nutmeg
2½ *teaspoons salt*

Rinse the chicken in cold water and pat dry with paper towels. Peel the garlic, leaving the cloves whole. Cut the celery into thin slices.

Pour the oil into a shallow dish or a plate and turn all the chicken pieces in the oil so that they are coated on all sides. Put the celery slices in the bottom of a heavy casserole with a tight-fitting cover. Add the parsley and tarragon. Lay the chicken pieces on top and sprinkle with the vermouth, pepper, nutmeg, and 1 teaspoon of the salt.

Pour the remaining oil in the plate into the casserole. Add the garlic cloves and sprinkle with the remaining salt. Over the top of the casserole lay a piece of aluminum foil large enough to extend 1 inch over the edge all around. Cover with the lid of the casserole to make a tight seal. Alternatively, make a thick flour and water paste and spread it with the fingers all around the edge of the casserole where the cover and casse-role meet, to make an airtight seal. Put a layer of foil around the lid to cover the circle of flour paste.

Bake in a 375°F oven for 1½ hours. Do not remove the lid during the cooking period. Serve from the casserole, with hot toast or thin slices of pumpernickel on which to spread the softened garlic cloves.

ROAST CHICKEN WITH WATERCRESS STUFFING

A combination of watercress, onions, and celery is a welcome change from the usual stuffings for poultry. Roasting the chicken at a high heat and basting it frequently gives the skin a rich brown color.

PREPARATION TIME: *40 minutes*
COOKING TIME: *1¼ hours*

INGREDIENTS (*for 4*):
¾ *cup finely chopped onion*
¾ *cup finely chopped celery*
¾ *cup butter*
1 *bunch watercress, washed, dried,*
   and finely chopped
2 *cups diced, day-old white bread*
3½-*pound roasting chicken*

Sauté the onion and celery in ¼ cup of the butter until soft. Add the watercress and cook until all the liquids have evaporated. In another skillet sauté the bread in ¼ cup of the butter until lightly browned, and add to the vegetable mixture.

Stuff the chicken with this mixture. Truss* the chicken, sprinkle it with salt and pepper, and rub it all over with the remaining ¼ cup of butter. Place the chicken on its side in a roasting pan in a preheated 425°F oven and roast 20 minutes, basting once with the drippings. Turn the chicken on its other side and roast for another 20 minutes, basting once. Turn it on its back and continue to roast about 35 minutes more, basting about every 5 minutes. When chicken is done, the juices will run clear at the thigh when it is pierced with the point of a knife.

BLANQUETTE OF TURKEY

After Christmas Day, cold turkey tends to lose its charm; even so, the leftovers may be turned into a delicious main course, and an excellent stock can be made from the carcass.

PREPARATION TIME: *20 minutes*
COOKING TIME: *30 minutes*

INGREDIENTS (*for 4–6*):
6 *cups diced cooked turkey meat*
1 *large onion*
6 *tablespoons unsalted butter*
6 *tablespoons flour*
2½ *cups turkey or chicken stock*
1 *small can pimientos*
⅔ *cup button mushrooms*
1 *clove garlic*
Salt and black pepper
Pinch each of powdered mace and
   nutmeg
2 *egg yolks*
4 *tablespoons heavy cream*
1 *tablespoon lemon juice*

Peel and thinly slice the onion. Melt the butter in a large skillet and cook the onion over low heat until soft and transparent. Mix in the flour and cook this roux* for 3 minutes. Gradually stir in the stock and simmer the sauce until it thickens.

Meanwhile, slice the drained pimientos thinly, trim and slice the mushrooms,* and peel and crush the garlic. Add these ingredients to the sauce, with the turkey; season to taste with salt, freshly ground pep-per, mace, and nutmeg. Heat the mixture through and then remove from the heat. Beat the egg yolks, cream, and lemon juice until the mixture has the consistency of thin cream. Blend this slowly into the turkey mixture and return the pan to the heat. Heat through over low heat, but do not let the mixture boil.

Spoon the blanquette of turkey into a warm serving dish and serve with buttered green beans, broccoli, or Brussels sprouts.

DUCK WITH CHERRIES

Duck cooked this way requires little attention, and as carving is done beforehand, it presents no problems when brought to the table. The finished dish can also be frozen.

PREPARATION TIME: *20 minutes*
COOKING TIME: *1¼ hours*

INGREDIENTS (*for 4*):
1 *duck, approximately 5 pounds*
Salt and black pepper
2 *tablespoons unsalted butter*
½ *cup Madeira or sherry*
2 *cups canned black cherries with*
   their juice
Lemon juice
½ *cup port*
1 *tablespoon cornstarch*
GARNISH:
3 *tablespoons chopped parsley*

Cut the duck* into 4 equal portions and prick the skin thoroughly with a heavy needle. Season with salt and freshly ground pepper. Melt the butter in a large skillet and sauté the duck over low heat for about 20 minutes or until brown all over. Drain the fat from the pan and pour the Madeira, the juice from the cherries, and a few drops of lemon juice over the duck. Bring the contents to a simmer, cover the pan tightly with a lid, and continue simmering the duck for 45–55 minutes.

Lift the duck pieces from the pan, drain thoroughly on paper towels, and keep them warm.

Skim as much fat as possible from the pan juices and stir in the port. Mix the cornstarch with 2 tablespoons of cold water and stir into the pan juices until thickened. Bring to a boil and adjust seasoning; add the cherries and heat through.

Arrange the pieces of duck, coated with the sauce, on a dish. Sprinkle with parsley and serve with Jerusalem artichokes in butter (p.63) or shoestring potatoes (p.333).

GOOSE IN CIDER

Fresh geese are found in many markets in November and December. They are superior in texture and flavor to their frozen counterparts, which are available the year round.

PREPARATION TIME: *15 minutes*
COOKING TIME: *3¾ hours*

INGREDIENTS (*for 4–6*):
8-pound goose
1¼ cups stock (p.298)
1 onion
6 cloves
½ orange
Salt and black pepper
2½ cups dry cider or white wine
2 tablespoons calvados (optional)
GARNISH:
Saratoga chips
Thick slices of bacon
Watercress
Oranges

Wipe the goose thoroughly inside and out with a damp cloth. Use the giblets to make stock.

Put the peeled onion, stuck with the cloves, and ½ orange inside the goose. Sew up the vent or secure it with small skewers. Rub the skin with salt and freshly ground pepper and prick the breast with a fork so that the fat can drain out.

Place the goose, breast side up, in a large roasting pan. Pour in half the cider and all the stock and roast the goose in the lower half of a preheated oven at 450°F for 15 minutes. Baste* with more cider and reduce the heat to 350°F. Continue roasting for about 3 hours, removing fat as it accumulates in the pan. Baste occasionally with cider.

Remove the roasting pan from the oven and skim as much fat as possible from the pan juices. Pour the warmed calvados over the goose and set it alight. As soon as the flames die down, transfer the goose to a serving dish and keep it warm while making the gravy.

Pour the pan juices into a saucepan and boil them briskly until they have reduced* to a thin gravy.

Serve the goose garnished with Saratoga chips (p.333), thick slices of bacon, cooked crisp, sprigs of watercress, and small halved oranges. Red cabbage cooked with apple and vinegar is an excellent accompaniment. Serve the gravy separately.

Rice & Pasta

SPAGHETTINI WITH MUSSEL SAUCE

The fine thin strands of spaghetti, known as *spaghettini,* make a lighter-than-usual pasta dish. Here spaghettini is served with a shellfish sauce, as a main course.

PREPARATION TIME: *1 hour*
COOKING TIME: *15 minutes*

INGREDIENTS (*for 4–6*):
1 pound spaghettini
4 pints mussels
2 tablespoons salt
8 tablespoons olive oil
3 cloves garlic
½ cup fish stock (p.298)
Black pepper
1 tablespoon finely chopped parsley

Wash the mussels* under cold running water, scrubbing the shells and scraping off the beards. Leave the mussels in a pail of cold water to which has been added about 2 tablespoons of salt.

Set a large pan of lightly salted water to boil. Meanwhile, heat 3 tablespoons oil in a large skillet. Add 2 peeled and crushed cloves of garlic and sauté in the oil until brown. Remove the garlic. Put the mussels in the pan, place over high heat, cover with a lid, and shake the pan for 5 minutes or until the shells have opened. Remove the pan from the heat and discard any mussels that remain closed. Turn the contents of the pan into a bowl, cool slightly, and ease the mussels from the shells, retaining the liquid.

Put the spaghettini into the pan of boiling salted water, stirring until the water boils again. Cook the spaghettini for 7–10 minutes, stirring occasionally, until just tender. Drain thoroughly in a colander.

Heat the remaining oil in the skillet over low heat. Peel and crush the remaining garlic and sauté until golden. Pour half the contents of the pan over the spaghettini and toss until it gleams. Return the mussels and their liquid to the skillet and heat through gently. Add the fish stock and continue cooking for 1–2 minutes until thoroughly heated. Pepper well and stir in the parsley.

Spoon the mussels and liquid over the spaghettini, toss, and serve at once, with slices of warm French or Italian bread.

RICE SALAD WITH FENNEL

The sweet aniseed flavor of bulbous fennel blends well with rice and Pernod-flavored mayonnaise. The salad is usually served as an accompaniment to cold meat or fish.

PREPARATION TIME: *30 minutes*
COOKING TIME: *20 minutes*
CHILLING TIME: *30 minutes*

INGREDIENTS (*for 4–6*):
¾ cup long grain rice
2 fennel roots
7-ounce can tuna
¾ cup pitted black olives
1 tablespoon Pernod
½ cup mayonnaise (p.303)
GARNISH:
6 scallions
3 hard-cooked eggs

Bring a large pan of lightly salted water to a boil and cook the rice for 20 minutes. Rinse the rice with cold water and drain it. Cool.

Trim the fennel,* wash the roots in cold running water, then cut them into thin slices. Drain the oil from the tuna and break the flesh up with a fork. Mix the rice, fennel, tuna, and olives together in a salad bowl. Stir the Pernod into the mayonnaise and fold this dressing into the salad.

Trim the scallions and cut them in half lengthwise. Shell and quarter the eggs. Garnish the salad with the scallions and eggs and leave it to chill in the refrigerator for 30 minutes.

RICE AND CHEESE CROQUETTES

These small, crisp rice cakes go well with fish, lamb, and veal dishes. They can also be served on their own, with an apricot sauce. Brown rice may be used, but this requires boiling for 45 minutes.

PREPARATION TIME: *10 minutes*
STANDING TIME: *1 hour*
COOKING TIME: *5 minutes*

INGREDIENTS (*for 4–6*):
3 cups cooked long grain rice
1 cup grated Emmenthal cheese
2 tablespoons softened butter
Black pepper
2 eggs
2 cups fresh white bread crumbs
Oil for deep-frying

Put the rice in a mixing bowl, stir in the cheese and butter, a few twists of freshly ground black pepper, and 1 lightly beaten egg.

Shape the rice mixture into 3-inch-long croquettes,* roll them in the bread crumbs, then dip them in lightly beaten egg. Roll the croquettes in the bread crumbs again, then leave them on a plate to set in the refrigerator for 1 hour.

Heat enough oil in a large pan to come no more than one-third up the sides. The oil is hot enough for deep-frying (375°F) when a cube of bread rises to the surface and is golden

Vegetables & Salads

brown in 30 seconds. Arrange the croquettes in the frying basket and lower it carefully into the hot oil; turn off the heat immediately. After 3–5 minutes the croquettes should have risen to the surface and be golden brown and crisp.

Remove them from the oil, drain on paper towels, and serve at once.

PASTA WITH ANCHOVY SAUCE

This recipe for noodles in a pungent sauce comes from the district of Calabria in southern Italy.

PREPARATION TIME: *5 minutes*
COOKING TIME: *15 minutes*

INGREDIENTS (*for 6*):
1¼ pounds noodles
2-ounce can anchovy fillets
1¼ cups olive oil
2½ cups fresh white bread crumbs
Chili powder

Cook the noodles in salted water until just tender. While the noodles are cooking, drain the anchovies and chop and mash them finely. Cook them in half the olive oil until dissolved into a smooth paste. Heat the remaining oil in a separate pan, sauté the bread crumbs until golden brown, and season them with chili powder to taste.

Drain the noodles and mix in the anchovy paste. Serve the bread crumbs in a separate bowl.

WALDORF SALAD

This famous salad was created at the Waldorf-Astoria Hotel in New York. The tart combination of apple and celery makes it an excellent counterbalance to rich meats, such as duck and pork.

PREPARATION TIME: *45 minutes*
STANDING TIME: *30 minutes*

INGREDIENTS (*for 6*):
1 pound tart red eating apples
2 tablespoons lemon juice
½ head celery, thinly sliced
½ cup coarsely chopped walnuts
*½ cup mayonnaise (p.303), seasoned
    with Dijon mustard*
1 head lettuce

Wash and core the apples; slice 1 apple finely for use as a garnish, and dice the remainder. Dip the apple slices in the lemon juice to prevent them from discoloring. Set aside.

Add the celery and walnuts to the diced apple and mix with the mayonnaise. Line a serving bowl with the cleaned and chilled lettuce leaves, pile the salad into the center, and garnish with the apple slices.

GLAZED ONIONS

These small buttered onions are appetizing and decorative with elaborate meat dishes, such as fillet of beef en croûte (p.278) or crown roast of lamb (p.281).

PREPARATION TIME: *15 minutes*
COOKING TIME: *20 minutes*

INGREDIENTS (*for 4*):
1 pound small white onions
4 tablespoons unsalted butter
2 tablespoons sugar

Fill a large saucepan with water, bring to a boil, and put in the onions. Cook over low heat for 7 minutes, then drain and peel the onions.

Melt the butter in the saucepan, add the onions, and toss them over low heat for 3 minutes. Sprinkle over the sugar and continue tossing the onions for a further 4 minutes until they are evenly glazed and tender. Serve the onions with the glaze.

ENDIVE AND ORANGE SALAD

This slightly sharp, refreshing salad goes well with most kinds of game, cold meats, or roast duck.

PREPARATION TIME: *20 minutes*

INGREDIENTS (*for 6*):
4 endives
3 oranges
French dressing (p.304)

Remove any brown outer leaves and the root ends from the endives. Wash and drain thoroughly, then cut the endives into thin slices crosswise. Peel the oranges with a sharp knife, removing all the white pith with the peel. Slice the oranges thinly crosswise and remove the seeds. If the oranges are large, cut each slice in two.

Mix the endive and orange slices in a serving bowl and pour over the French dressing (made with orange juice instead of vinegar, if desired). Toss and serve.

SWEET POTATOES WITH APPLES

This delicious mixture of sweet potatoes and tart apples can be served by itself as a vegetable casserole, or with roast pork.

PREPARATION TIME: *20 minutes*
COOKING TIME: *40 minutes*

INGREDIENTS (*for 6*):
1 pound sweet potatoes
1¼ pounds cooking apples
6 tablespoons butter
1 teaspoon salt
½–¾ cup brown sugar
1 teaspoon nutmeg
1 tablespoon lemon juice

Peel and thinly slice the sweet potatoes; peel, core, and thinly slice the apples. Butter a casserole and in it arrange alternate layers of sweet potatoes and apples, starting and finishing with sweet potatoes. Sprinkle each layer with salt, sugar, nutmeg, and lemon juice and dot with the remaining butter.

Set the casserole on the lowest shelf of a preheated oven and cook at 400°F for about 40 minutes or until the potatoes are tender. Serve from the casserole.

PARSNIP CASSEROLE

This vegetable casserole is an unusual combination of parsnips, tomatoes, cheese, and cream. It goes well with roast lamb and pork.

PREPARATION TIME: *40 minutes*
COOKING TIME: *40 minutes*

INGREDIENTS (*for 6*):
2 pounds parsnips
1 pound tomatoes
5 tablespoons oil
6 tablespoons butter
2 teaspoons brown sugar
Salt and black pepper
1½ cups grated Gruyère cheese
1¼ cups light or heavy cream
4 tablespoons fresh white bread crumbs

Peel the parsnips; cut away and discard any hard central cores. Slice the parsnips thinly. Peel the tomatoes,* remove the seeds, and cut the flesh into medium slices. Heat the oil in a skillet and lightly sauté the parsnips for about 4 minutes.

Grease a 5-cup casserole with half the butter and place a layer of parsnips over the bottom. Sprinkle with a little sugar, salt, and freshly ground pepper, and add a little cream before covering with a layer of tomatoes. Spread a little more cream and cheese over the tomatoes and repeat these layers until all the ingredients are used up, finishing off with cream and cheese. Top with the bread crumbs and dot with the remaining butter.

Cook the parsnip casserole for 40 minutes, or until bubbly, in the center of a preheated oven at 325°F. Serve from the casserole.

BAKED CAULIFLOWER IN CHEESE SAUCE

The strong, smooth flavor of Gruyère cheese contrasts well with crisp cauliflower. This dish can be served with broiled or roasted meats.

PREPARATION TIME: *20 minutes*
COOKING TIME: *50 minutes*

INGREDIENTS (*for 6*):
1 large cauliflower
1 onion
4 tablespoons unsalted butter
1½ cups fresh white bread crumbs
1¼ cups milk
½ cup grated Gruyère cheese
Salt and black pepper
Ground nutmeg
5 beaten eggs

Cut away the coarse outer leaves from the cauliflower and break off the florets. Bring a large pan of lightly salted water to a boil. Add the florets, cover the pan with a lid, and boil gently for 5–8 minutes. Drain.

Meanwhile, finely chop the onion. Melt 2 tablespoons of butter and sauté the onion for 10 minutes. Butter the inside of a 6-cup baking dish and line it evenly with ½ cup of bread crumbs.

In a saucepan, bring the milk to a boil and add the Gruyère cheese and the remaining butter. Season to taste with salt, pepper, and a little nutmeg. Stir in the remaining bread crumbs and the onion. Remove from the heat and blend in the beaten eggs. Fold the cauliflower into the sauce and spoon the mixture into the baking dish.

Bake on the lower shelf of a preheated oven at 325°F for 50 minutes or until firm.

POMMES DE TERRE NOISETTE

Small golden balls of sautéed potatoes make an attractive garnish for broiled steaks, chops, or sautéed meat. They should be left to soak in cold water for a few hours to remove excess starch. The cooked potatoes can be tossed in beef drippings and sprinkled with chopped parsley. They are then known as *pommes de terre à la parisienne*.

PREPARATION TIME: *20 minutes*
COOKING TIME: *10 minutes*

INGREDIENTS (*for 6*):
2 pounds potatoes
3 tablespoons salt
6 tablespoons unsalted butter

Peel the potatoes and let them soak for 2 hours in cold water in which 2 tablespoons salt have been dissolved. Drain and dry the potatoes. Using a melon ball scoop, take out small balls, about the size of walnuts, from the potatoes. (Use the leftover potatoes in a soup.)

Bring a pan of water to a boil, add 1 tablespoon salt, and cook the potato balls over low heat for 3 minutes. Drain thoroughly in a colander and dry on a cloth.

Melt the butter over gentle heat in a skillet. Toss the potatoes in the butter for about 5 minutes until golden and cooked through.

Using a slotted spoon, lift the potato balls into a warm serving dish, sprinkle with a little salt, and serve.

Desserts

GARLIC POTATOES

Mashed or creamed potatoes are given additional flavor by garlic. The bitterness of garlic is reduced if the cloves are boiled for a few minutes before using.

PREPARATION TIME: *20 minutes*
COOKING TIME: *1½ hours*

INGREDIENTS (*for* 6):
3 pounds baking potatoes
20 cloves garlic
¼ pound unsalted butter
2 tablespoons flour
1¼ cups milk
1 teaspoon salt
Black pepper
3 tablespoons heavy cream
3 tablespoons finely chopped parsley

Wash and dry the potatoes, prick them with a fork, and bake on the center shelf of an oven preheated to 400°F for 1 hour or until tender.

Put the garlic in a small pan and cover with water; boil for 2 minutes, then drain and peel. Melt 4 tablespoons butter in a heavy-bottomed saucepan and add the garlic. Cover the pan and cook the garlic gently for 10 minutes or until tender. Remove the garlic. Stir the flour into the butter in the pan and cook over low heat for 2 minutes. Gradually blend in the milk, stirring constantly until the sauce is smooth and thick. Add the salt, a few twists of pepper, and the garlic. Boil for 2 minutes.

Whirl the sauce in the blender or rub it through a fine sieve, then return it to the saucepan and heat through. Set aside.

Scoop the flesh from the baked potatoes, rub it through a sieve, and beat in the remaining butter, a little at a time. Season to taste with salt and pepper. Stir the cream into the garlic purée, then beat the mixture into the potatoes. Stir in the parsley.

Heat the mashed potato and garlic mixture through if necessary, pile it back into the warm potato skins, and serve immediately.

BRUSSELS SPROUTS WITH SOUR CREAM

Brussels sprouts are an excellent winter vegetable but, like cabbage, they are too often overcooked to a tasteless mass. Properly cooked sprouts should be just soft to the bite. A dressing of sour cream and nutmeg gives the vegetable an unusual flavor.

PREPARATION TIME: *10 minutes*
COOKING TIME: *15 minutes*

INGREDIENTS (*for* 6):
1½ pounds Brussels sprouts
1 tablespoon salt
½–1 teaspoon freshly grated nutmeg
½ cup sour cream

Peel and wash the sprouts. Bring a large pan of water to a boil and add the salt and the sprouts. Bring back to a boil and cook for 5 minutes until the sprouts are just tender. Drain well in a colander. Stir the nutmeg into the sour cream.

Return the sprouts to the saucepan and toss over moderate heat for a few minutes to dry them out completely. Pour in the sour cream, toss the sprouts over gentle heat for 1 minute, and serve.

APPLE-RUM MERINGUE

Meringue is a favorite topping for many desserts. In this recipe it covers tart cooking apples over rum-soaked *amaretti*, the tiny Italian macaroons. Ladyfingers can be used if amaretti are not readily available.

PREPARATION TIME: *30 minutes*
COOKING TIME: *15 minutes*

INGREDIENTS (*for* 6):
¼ pound amaretti
4 tablespoons light rum
1½ pounds cooking apples
2 tablespoons unsalted butter
½ teaspoon cinnamon
½ cup brown sugar
3 egg whites
¼ teaspoon salt
⅓ cup granulated sugar
⅓ cup superfine sugar

Cover the bottom of a china flan dish with the amaretti and pour the rum over them. Peel, core, and thinly slice the apples into a saucepan; add the butter, cinnamon, brown sugar, and 2–3 tablespoons water. Simmer for 10–15 minutes, or until the apples are just cooked. Leave to cool, then spoon the apples over the amaretti.

Beat the egg whites with the salt until stiff but not dry. Stir in the granulated sugar and beat for about 2 minutes or until the meringue mixture is smooth and glossy. Fold in the superfine sugar and immediately spoon the meringue over the apples. Swirl the meringue into soft peaks with a spatula.

Bake for 10–15 minutes in the center of a preheated oven at 350°F until the meringue is pale beige. Serve hot or cold, with a bowl of fresh cream.

PARIS–BREST

In the late 19th century this pastry dessert was created in honor of a famous bicycle race that was run on a circular route from Paris to Brest and back again. It is a concoction of choux pastry and Chantilly cream.

PREPARATION TIME: *30 minutes*
COOKING TIME: *30 minutes*

INGREDIENTS (*for* 4):
2 tablespoons unsalted butter
1 teaspoon sugar
½ cup milk
1 cup flour, sifted
3 eggs
⅓ cup sliced almonds
CHANTILLY CREAM:
1 cup heavy cream
3 tablespoons confectioners' sugar
1 egg white

For the choux pastry,* put the butter, sugar, and milk into a saucepan over moderate heat and bring to a boil. Stir in the sifted flour, remove the pan from the heat, and beat vigorously with a wooden spoon until the dough leaves the sides of the pan clean. Beat 2 eggs, one by one, into the choux. Then add the yolk of the third egg, beating vigorously until the dough is smooth and shiny. If the dough seems too thick, beat in the remaining egg white.

Spoon the dough into a pastry bag fitted with a large plain nozzle. Pipe a ring about 1½ inches wide and 8 inches in diameter onto a greased baking sheet. Sprinkle the almonds over the dough and bake in the middle of a preheated oven at 425°F for 30 minutes or until dark brown.

Cool the choux ring on a wire rack, then split it in half horizontally with a sharp knife.

For the Chantilly cream, whip together the heavy cream, 2 tablespoons sifted confectioners' sugar, and an egg white until light and fluffy. Spoon the cream into the hollow bottom half of the ring. Cover with the top half and dust with the remaining confectioners' sugar.

ORANGE CHIFFON CREAM

The taste of fresh oranges is predominant in this pastry shell filled with a fluffy mixture of eggs and cream. For a more elaborate dessert, cover the chilled tart with whipped cream before garnishing.

PREPARATION TIME: *45 minutes*
COOKING TIME: *30 minutes*
CHILLING TIME: *1 hour*

INGREDIENTS (*for 6*):
¾ recipe standard pastry (p.354)
1 tablespoon plain gelatin
4 eggs
5 tablespoons sugar
½ cup fresh orange juice
1 tablespoon lemon juice
Grated rind of 1 orange
½ cup heavy cream
GARNISH:
Dark sweet chocolate
Orange rind matchsticks

Roll out the prepared pastry ⅛ inch thick and use it to line an 8–9 inch flan ring. Prick the bottom with a fork and bake blind* for 10 minutes in the center of the oven, preheated to 400°F. Reduce the heat to 375°F and bake 20 minutes longer. Cool the pastry on a wire rack.

Sprinkle the gelatin over 5 tablespoons of cold water in a small bowl. Set aside. Separate the eggs and, with a wire whisk, beat the yolks with the sugar until they are pale yellow and thick. Beat in the orange and lemon juices.

Pour the creamed egg mixture into a double boiler or set the bowl over a pan of barely simmering water. Cook over low heat, stirring continuously with a wooden spoon, until the mixture thickens. Remove from the heat and mix in the orange rind and the dissolved gelatin. Blend

thoroughly and leave to cool slightly. Beat the cream and egg whites in separate bowls until stiff, and carefully fold first the cream, then the egg whites, into the orange mixture.

Spoon the mixture into the pastry shell and chill in the refrigerator for at least 1 hour.

Just before serving, grate the chocolate over the cream and garnish with orange rind matchsticks.

CHAMPAGNE CHARLIE

George Leybourne, star of the English music hall of the 1890's, often ordered champagne for his audiences, a gesture that earned him the nickname of Champagne Charlie. This ice cream, named after him, is a superb dessert.

PREPARATION TIME: *10 minutes*
COOKING TIME: *10 minutes*
FREEZING TIME: *5 hours*

INGREDIENTS (*for 6*):
¾ cup sugar
2 oranges and 2 lemons
2½ cups chilled champagne
2½ cups heavy cream
¾ cup brandy
36 amaretti
GARNISH:
Amaretti
Lemon peel

Put the sugar in a pan with ½ cup of water. Bring to a boil and boil rapidly for 6 minutes to make a light syrup. Do not stir. Meanwhile, grate the rind from 1 orange and squeeze the juice from the oranges and lemons. Add the rind and the strained juice to the syrup and leave to cool. When cool, stir in the 2½ cups of chilled champagne.

Pour the mixture into a plastic container and cover with the lid or a double layer of foil. Freeze for 1½–2 hours, or until frozen around the edges. Scoop the mixture into a chilled bowl and whip with a wire whisk until smooth. In a separate bowl, beat the cream until stiff and blend it slowly into the champagne syrup until the mixture is smooth and uniform in color. Blend in 2 tablespoons of brandy. Spoon the ice cream into the container, cover, and freeze for about 3 hours.

About 30 minutes before serving, place 6 amaretti in the bottom of each champagne glass. Pour a tablespoon of brandy over the amaretti and leave them to soak. Scoop the ice cream into the glasses. Hang a thin spiral of lemon peel from the rim of each glass and pour a teaspoon of brandy over each portion. Serve the ice cream immediately, with a separate plate of amaretti.

MERINGUE À LA REINE

These small meringue boats with a cream filling were first served at the French court in the 18th century. It is said that Queen Marie Antoinette was so fond of them that she even made them with her own hands.

PREPARATION TIME: *15 minutes*
COOKING TIME: *2 hours*

INGREDIENTS (*for 6*):
3 egg whites
Salt
6 tablespoons granulated sugar
6 tablespoons superfine sugar
¼ cup lightly toasted chopped
  almonds
1 cup heavy cream
3 tablespoons sweet sherry
Juice of 1 orange
GARNISH:
Crystallized fruit

In a warm dry bowl, beat the egg whites, with a pinch of salt, until stiff but not dry. Add the granulated sugar and continue beating for 2 minutes until the meringue mixture is smooth and glossy. Gently fold in the superfine sugar and almonds.

Spoon the meringue into a pastry bag fitted with a ½-inch-wide rosette tube. Pipe out 3-inch-long oval shapes (or *barquettes*) onto a lightly floured baking sheet. Bake the meringues in the center of a preheated oven at 275°F for 1½–2 hours. The meringues should then have a faint tint of beige. Leave the barquettes on a wire rack to cool.

Whip the cream and beat in the sherry and strained orange juice. Fill the hollows in the barquettes with the cream mixture and garnish with crystallized fruit.

SOUR CREAM TART

This tart, whose texture is reminiscent of cheesecake, makes a good family dessert and may be served hot or cold. For a more elaborate menu, a chilled apricot purée could be served as a topping.

PREPARATION TIME: *40 minutes*
COOKING TIME: *40 minutes*

INGREDIENTS (*for 6*):
¾ recipe standard pastry (p.354)
3 eggs
⅔ cup sugar
1⅓ cups white raisins
½ teaspoon ground cinnamon
¼ teaspoon ground cloves
¼ teaspoon salt
⅔ cup sour cream
Grated rind of 1 lemon

On a floured surface, roll out the prepared pastry ⅛ inch thick. Line a 9-inch flan ring with the pastry. Prick the bottom with a fork and put the pastry in the refrigerator.

Separate the eggs and beat the yolks thoroughly with the sugar until pale yellow and thick enough to leave a trail, or ribbon, on the surface of the mixture. Finely chop the white raisins and beat them into the eggs, together with the cinnamon, cloves, salt, sour cream, and lemon rind. Beat the egg whites in a separate bowl until stiff but not dry. Fold the egg whites carefully and evenly into the yolk mixture and spoon it into the pastry shell. Bake for 15 minutes on a shelf low in a preheated oven at 425°F, then reduce the heat to 350°F and bake 25 minutes longer.

Let the tart cool for about 10 minutes before removing the ring and cutting the tart into wedges.

Snacks & Supper Dishes

RED FLANNEL HASH

A breakfast favorite, this colorful and flavorful hash is often served with poached or fried eggs.

PREPARATION TIME: *15 minutes*
COOKING TIME: *15–20 minutes*

INGREDIENTS (*for* 4):
1 finely chopped onion
2 tablespoons beef drippings
3 cups finely chopped baked potato
1–¾ cup cooked diced beets
1½ cups finely chopped corned beef
2 tablespoons finely chopped parsley
2 tablespoons heavy cream
Salt and black pepper

Sauté the onion in the beef drippings for about 2 minutes or until the onion is transparent. Mix in the finely chopped potatoes, beets, corned beef, parsley, and cream. Season the hash with salt and freshly ground black pepper.

Press the hash mixture down firmly and evenly with a spatula. Cook over high heat for 15 minutes or until it is well browned and crisp on the bottom. Turn the hash out upside down onto a warmed dish and serve immediately.

CROQUE MONSIEUR

This hot sautéed sandwich, a specialty of France, may be served either as a snack, an hors d'oeuvre, or as a luncheon dish with a green salad.

PREPARATION TIME: *10 minutes*
COOKING TIME: *10 minutes*

INGREDIENTS (*for* 4):
8 square slices white bread, ⅓ inch thick
6 tablespoons butter
4 slices lean ham
1 cup grated Cheddar cheese
Butter for sautéing

Butter the bread and cover 4 slices with the ham and cheese. Top with the remaining bread and press the sandwiches firmly together. Trim off the crusts and cut each sandwich into 3 fingers. Sauté the bread fingers in hot butter until golden brown on both sides. Drain on paper towels before serving.

BACON PANCAKE

This simple, inexpensive dish makes a good cold-weather meal. For a touch of color, serve the pancake with broiled tomatoes.

PREPARATION TIME: *15 minutes*
COOKING TIME: *30 minutes*

INGREDIENTS (*for* 4):
¾ cup flour
1 cup milk
2 eggs
Salt and black pepper
1½ teaspoons mixed herbs (p.411)
½ pound lean bacon

Sift the flour into a bowl and stir in half the milk. Add the eggs and remaining milk and beat until the batter is smooth and light. Season with salt and ground pepper and mix in the herbs.

Cut the bacon into ½-inch-wide strips. Pan-fry over medium heat for 3–4 minutes. Measure 2 tablespoons of the fat into a baking dish, add the drained bacon, and pour in the pancake batter. Bake in the center of a preheated oven at 350°F for 30 minutes or until set.

TURKEY OR CHICKEN TOASTS

This quick recipe solves the problem of what to do with Christmas leftovers from turkey and from cooked vegetables, such as cauliflower, carrots, beans, or broccoli.

PREPARATION TIME: *15 minutes*
COOKING TIME: *5 minutes*

INGREDIENTS (*for* 4):
8 thin slices turkey or chicken, skinned
½ cup thick white sauce (p.301)
Salt and black pepper
Dried tarragon
4 slices white bread
Butter
2 cups cooked chopped vegetables
½ cup grated Cheddar cheese

Make the white sauce and season with salt, pepper, and tarragon. Toast the bread, trim off the crusts, and spread with butter. Arrange the turkey on the toast, cover with vegetables, and spoon on the sauce.

Sprinkle the toasts with the cheese and brown under a hot broiler until the cheese has melted and is golden brown on top. Serve at once.

CHRISTMAS PUDDING WITH DESTINY SAUCE

A Christmas pudding can be a sorry sight the next day; but served with a light creamy sauce, it becomes a mouth-watering new dessert.

PREPARATION TIME: *5–10 minutes*
COOKING TIME: *5 minutes*

INGREDIENTS (*for* 4–6):
8 thin slices Christmas pudding
½ cup heavy cream
1 tablespoon sifted confectioners' sugar
2 tablespoons port
3 tablespoons unsalted butter
2 tablespoons superfine sugar

Beat the cream until thick, then blend in the confectioners' sugar and port. Chill in the refrigerator.

Sauté the Christmas pudding in the butter over medium heat for 4 minutes, turning once. Arrange the slices on a warm serving dish, dust with the superfine sugar, and serve the chilled cream in a separate bowl.

In the Midst of Winter

Much of December is devoted to preparing the delightful seasonal food of the holidays—fruitcakes and candies, punches and Christmas cookies, and special meals for Christmas Eve and Christmas Day. December is one of the busiest times of the year for entertaining, and hospitality finds its most festive expression in a well-stocked table.

At a Christmas party, wassail punch and a Christmas pudding bring a touch of merry England to the scene, and fruitcakes are almost essential for the Christmas table. Two recipes are included on this page—one for an American white fruitcake, and another for an English Christmas cake decorated with almond paste and icing.

On the following pages are recipes for a Christmas Eve dinner of boeuf bourguignon, with a first course of lobster Newburg. The center of the Christmas Day feast is, of course, the turkey. A selection of stuffings and sauces are given on page 292.

White Fruitcake

PREPARATION TIME: *40 minutes*
SOAKING TIME: *overnight*
COOKING TIME: *4 hours*

INGREDIENTS:
1½ cups white raisins
1½ cups candied cherries
1½ cups chopped candied pineapple
½ cup candied citron, ground
½ cup candied orange peel, ground
½ cup candied lemon peel, ground
2–2½ cups pecans, coarsely chopped
2 cups almonds, halved
1 cup white port
4 eggs
½ cup butter
½ cup sugar
1 cup flour
2 teaspoons lemon extract
⅓ cup bourbon or rye whisky

To remove the preservatives from the candied fruit, place the fruit in a large bowl and cover with boiling water. Stir, let stand 30 seconds, and drain the fruit well.

Put the fruit and nuts in a large flat dish and add the port. Cover with a sheet of aluminum foil or plastic wrap and soak overnight in the refrigerator. Allow the mixture to reach room temperature before preparing the cake.

Separate the eggs and beat the whites until stiff. In a large bowl, cream the butter and sugar with a wooden spoon, then beat in the egg yolks and flour alternately. Add the lemon extract and the bourbon or rye; fold in the beaten egg whites with a rubber spatula. Fold in the fruit and nuts and any port remaining in the dish.

Spoon the mixture into a tube pan that has been buttered and lined on the bottom and sides with brown paper cut to fit. Bake the cake at 250°F for about 4 hours, or until a wire cake tester inserted into the cake comes out clean.

When done, wrap the pan in aluminum foil and cover with a towel until the cake is cool. Remove the cake from the pan and discard the brown paper. Store the cake in an airtight container.

This cake improves with age. It tastes best and is more easily sliced when prepared a month in advance.

To decorate a Christmas cake: Ten days before Christmas, double the recipe for almond paste. Brush the cake with apricot glaze and, when nearly set, cover the top and sides with the rolled-out almond paste. Three days later, make the royal icing, spread it over the top and sides, and leave to set. The cake can be decorated in a simple trellis pattern. For a Christmas scene, as depicted on this cake, color almond paste with food coloring and roll it out thinly. Trace the design on thin cardboard and cut the paste from these shapes. Set the decoration with royal icing.

Christmas Cake

PREPARATION TIME: *2½ hours*
COOKING TIME: *about 5 hours*

INGREDIENTS:
3 cups self-rising flour
½ teaspoon salt
2 teaspoons allspice
1 teaspoon ground nutmeg
1 teaspoon ground cinnamon
½ teaspoon ground cloves
⅔ cup ground almonds
1 pound black currants
1 pound dark raisins
1 pound white raisins
1½ cups candied cherries
1 cup blanched almonds
1½ cups whole mixed candied citrus peel
¼ cup angelica (optional)
1½ cups unsalted butter
1¼ cups dark brown sugar
Grated rind and juice of 1 lemon
8–9 large eggs
8 tablespoons brandy
Double recipe almond paste (p.394)
Royal icing (p.393)

Butter a 10-inch-wide, round or square cake pan thoroughly; line it with a double layer of waxed paper brushed with melted butter. Tie a double layer of brown paper around the outside of the pan well above the rim—this prevents the Christmas cake from burning.

Mix the dry ingredients—flour, seasoning, spices, and ground almonds—together in a large bowl. Mix in the finely chopped fruits and chopped blanched almonds.

In a separate bowl, cream together the sugar, butter, and grated lemon rind until fluffy. Beat in 8 eggs, one at a time. Stir them into the flour and fruit mixture, followed by the lemon juice and 4 tablespoons brandy. The mixture should be soft and moist. If necessary, add the remaining egg beaten with a little milk.

Spoon the cake mixture into the prepared pan, level off the top, and bake the cake on the shelf below the center of a preheated oven at 300°F for 1½ hours. Reduce the heat to 250°F and bake for a further 3–3½ hours. The cake is done when it begins to shrink from the sides. Cover the cake with brown paper during the last 2 hours to prevent burning.

Remove the cake from the oven. Allow it to cool slightly before turning it out onto a wire rack to cool. When completely cold, wrap the cake in foil, seal tightly, and store until 6 weeks before Christmas. Then make holes with a skewer in the bottom of the cake and, using a funnel, pour in 4 tablespoons brandy. Reseal the cake and leave until needed for icing.

Christmas Pudding

PREPARATION TIME: *1¼ hours*
COOKING TIME: *10 hours*

INGREDIENTS (*for 2 large puddings*):
1 pound dark raisins
½ cup mixed candied citrus peel
½ cup blanched almonds
1½ cups currants
1½ cups white raisins
1 cup flour
½ teaspoon ground nutmeg
½ teaspoon ground allspice
½ teaspoon ground cinnamon
1 teaspoon salt
⅓ cup ground almonds
4 cups shredded suet
4 cups fresh white bread crumbs
½ cup dark brown sugar
6 large eggs
4 tablespoons brandy
1 cup milk
2 tablespoons unsalted butter

Chop the raisins, candied peel, and blanched almonds. In a large bowl mix together all the fruits, the sifted flour, spices, salt, and ground almonds. Blend thoroughly until all the fruit is well coated (this is easiest when done with the hands). Work in the suet, bread crumbs, and sugar. Beat the eggs lightly with a fork and stir them into the pudding mixture. Add the brandy and milk, stirring until the pudding has a soft dropping consistency.

Butter well 2 1-quart pudding molds, spoon in the pudding, and cover each mold with a pleated double layer of buttered waxed paper.

Set the pudding molds in 1 or 2 large pans of boiling water that reaches two-thirds up the sides of the molds. Boil steadily for 6 hours and add more boiling water as necessary. Remove the puddings, leave them to cool, then cover them with fresh waxed paper or aluminum foil, then with clean cloths. Store the puddings in a cool place.

On Christmas Day boil the puddings for a further 4 hours. Turn them out of the molds and garnish each pudding with a sprig of holly. Pour warmed brandy over them and set alight. Serve with brandy sauce.

Brandy Sauce

6 tablespoons unsalted butter
6 tablespoons sugar
Grated rind of ½ orange
2–3 tablespoons brandy

Cream the butter until soft and pale. Beat in the sugar and orange rind. Gradually beat in the brandy until the mixture is frothy. Chill in the refrigerator for 2–3 hours or until solid. The brandy sauce will melt on the hot pudding.

Oatmeal Cookies

PREPARATION TIME: *15 minutes*
COOKING TIME: *20–25 minutes*

INGREDIENTS (*for 24 cookies*):
¾ cup all-purpose flour
½ teaspoon baking soda
6 tablespoons light brown sugar
1 cup rolled oats
6 tablespoons unsalted butter
1 tablespoon rum
1 tablespoon light corn syrup

Sift the flour and baking soda into a bowl; add the sugar and the oatmeal, blending thoroughly. Heat the butter with the rum and syrup in a small pan until the butter has just melted. Pour into the flour mixture and blend well with a wooden spoon.

Between floured hands, shape the dough into balls 1 inch in diameter. Set the balls well apart on buttered baking sheets. Bake in the center of a preheated oven at 325°F for 20–25 minutes or until golden brown.

Cool on a wire rack.

Wassail Bowl

PREPARATION TIME: *5 minutes*
COOKING TIME: *20 minutes*

INGREDIENTS:
3 quarts ale or beer
1 pound light brown sugar
1 large stick cinnamon
1 teaspoon grated nutmeg
½ teaspoon ground ginger
2 lemons, thinly sliced
1 bottle medium-dry sherry

Pour 1 quart of the ale into a large pan. Add the sugar and cinnamon stick and simmer the mixture slowly over low heat until the sugar has dissolved. Add the spices and lemon slices, the sherry, and remaining ale.

Before serving the punch, remove the lemon slices.

The traditional British wassail bowl, becoming more popular in North America, can be garnished not only with lemon slices but also with baked apples. The apples are baked in a moderate oven until tender, and floated in the punch.

Christmas Eve Dinner

Lobster Newburg

PREPARATION TIME: *15 minutes*
COOKING TIME: *30 minutes*

INGREDIENTS:
1½ pounds cooked lobster
4 slices white bread
¼ pound unsalted butter
Salt and black pepper
½ cup sherry or Madeira
1 tablespoon brandy (optional)
3 egg yolks
1 cup heavy cream
Paprika

Carefully extract the meat from the tail and claws of the lobster* and cut it into 1½–2 inch pieces.

Trim 4 circles from the white bread and leave to soak in 6 tablespoons melted butter until it is absorbed. Bake the butter-soaked bread on a baking sheet in the center of the oven for 25 minutes at 300°F.

Meanwhile, melt the remaining 2 tablespoons butter in a heavy-bottomed saucepan. Add the lobster meat and season with salt and freshly ground black pepper. Heat through over very low heat for 5 minutes, then pour in the sherry or Madeira and the brandy. Continue cooking the mixture over very low heat until the wine has reduced* by half, about 10 minutes. While the lobster is cooking, beat the egg yolks and stir in the heavy cream.

Remove the pan from the heat and pour the egg and cream mixture over the lobster. Shake the pan until the cream has mixed thoroughly with the wine, then move it gently to and fro over gentle heat until the sauce has the consistency of thick cream. Do not stir, or the meat will disintegrate and the sauce will curdle. After about 3 minutes the lobster should be ready. Adjust seasoning and spoon the lobster and sauce on the bread rounds. Sprinkle the lobster with a little paprika and serve.

Boeuf Bourguignon

PREPARATION TIME: *30 minutes*
COOKING TIME: *2 hours 40 minutes*

INGREDIENTS:
2 pounds top round of beef, cut into 2-inch cubes
¼ pound unsalted butter
1 tablespoon olive oil
1 finely sliced onion
1 tablespoon flour
3 tablespoons brandy
2 cloves garlic
Bouquet garni (p.410)
Salt and black pepper
1 bottle red wine
½ pound lean salt pork, blanched and diced
20 small white onions
½ pound button mushrooms
Finely chopped parsley

Dry the meat thoroughly on paper towels. It will not brown if it is too damp. Melt 6 tablespoons butter in a large flameproof casserole. Add the oil and then the meat. Cook over high heat until the meat is browned, then add the sliced onion. Cook until the onion is transparent, sprinkle in the flour, and toss the meat to coat it with the flour. Continue cooking for a few minutes. Pour in the warmed brandy and ignite it.

Add the crushed garlic, the bouquet garni, salt, and plenty of freshly ground black pepper. Pour in enough red wine to cover the meat. Bring the mixture to a simmer, cover the casserole with a lid, and cook in the center of a preheated oven at 300°F for 2 hours.

Meanwhile, sauté the salt pork in the remaining butter until crisp, add the onions, and cook until golden. Stir the contents of the pan into the casserole and continue cooking for a further 30 minutes. Sauté the mushrooms in the fat remaining in the pan and add to the casserole. Cook for another 10 minutes.

Remove the bouquet garni, sprinkle generously with parsley, and serve from the casserole.

Stuffings and Sauces

Chestnut stuffing for turkey

INGREDIENTS: *4 tablespoons unsalted butter; 1 peeled and chopped onion; turkey heart and liver, chopped; 1½ cups sliced mushrooms; 8 ounces chestnut purée; 1 small can pâté de foie gras; 1 stalk celery, chopped; ¼ pound chopped, blanched salt pork; 1 tablespoon chopped parsley; salt and black pepper; 1 cup bread crumbs (optional)*

Sauté the onion, turkey heart, and liver in the butter until the butter has been absorbed. In a large bowl, mix the chestnut purée with the pâté and blend in the contents of the pan, together with the celery, salt pork, and parsley. Season to taste and, if necessary, add enough bread crumbs to bind the stuffing. Fill the breast end of the turkey with the chestnut stuffing and fill the body cavity with sausage stuffing.

Sausage stuffing

INGREDIENTS: *1½ pounds pork sausage meat; 2 cups fresh white bread crumbs; 2 chopped shallots; ¼ pound ground pork; 1 beaten egg; salt and black pepper*

In a large bowl, work the bread crumbs and the shallots into the sausage meat, together with the ground pork. Bind the stuffing with the egg and season to taste.

Forcemeat stuffing for goose

INGREDIENTS: *¼ pound veal; ¼ pound lean pork; 1 goose liver; 1 small onion; 1 tablespoon butter; 2 large slices crustless white bread; 1 tablespoon chopped parsley; 1 tablespoon chopped thyme; ¼ cup red wine; 1 large egg; salt and black pepper*

Put the veal, pork, goose liver, and peeled onion through the fine blade of a meat grinder. Sauté this mixture in the butter until golden brown. Remove from the heat and stir in the bread, soaked in a little milk and squeezed dry. Add the herbs and wine, and use the beaten egg to bind the stuffing before seasoning to taste.

Apricot stuffing for goose and duck

INGREDIENTS: *1½ cups dried apricots; juice of 1 lemon; 1 tablespoon brown sugar; 1 large green pepper, finely chopped; 1 large cooking apple, peeled, cored, and diced; 4 stalks chopped celery; 2 cups fresh white bread crumbs; 6 tablespoons melted butter; grated rind of 1 orange; 2 beaten eggs; salt and black pepper*

Put the apricots in a pan with water to cover, the lemon juice, and the sugar; bring to a boil and simmer for 10 minutes. Set aside to cool. Drain the apricots, chop them coarsely, and mix with the pepper, apple, and celery. Stir in the bread crumbs, melted butter, orange rind, and the beaten eggs. Season to taste with salt and freshly ground black pepper and bind the stuffing with about 6 tablespoons of the apricot juice.

Prune and apple stuffing for goose and duck

INGREDIENTS: *20 prunes; juice and rind of ½ lemon; 1 tablespoon brown sugar; ½ cup cooked rice; 2 large cooking apples, peeled, cored, and coarsely chopped; goose liver; 1 stalk celery, chopped; ½ teaspoon ground mace; 1 tablespoon chopped parsley; salt and black pepper; 1 beaten egg*

Soak the prunes in cold water for ½ hour. Put them, with the water, lemon juice, and sugar into a pan; bring to a boil and simmer for 10 minutes. Set aside to cool, then remove the pits and quarter the prunes. Mix the prunes with all the remaining ingredients, adding the egg last. Stir in as much of the prune juice as the stuffing will absorb and pour the remainder into the bird before stuffing it.

Spiced cranberry sauce

INGREDIENTS: *1 pound cranberries; 1-inch piece ginger root; 1 whole cinnamon stick; 2 teaspoons whole allspice; 6 cloves; 1 cup cider vinegar; 1 cup brown sugar*

Put the cranberries in a pan with all the spices tied in a cheesecloth bag. Pour in the vinegar and bring to a boil. Simmer the cranberries until they are soft and the skins begin to pop, after about 25 minutes. Add the sugar and simmer for a further 20 minutes. Remove the spices and store the preserve in small jars. Serve cold with roast turkey.

Bacon rolls

INGREDIENTS: *½ pound bacon*

Cut each bacon slice across into 2 pieces. Fry the pieces until crisp. While it is still warm, roll up each piece and secure each with a toothpick. Remove the sticks when the bacon has cooled and become hard.

Port wine sauce

INGREDIENTS: *1 cup port; 1 tablespoon red currant jelly; 1 cup rich beef gravy (or melt 2 tablespoons butter in a skillet, add 2 tablespoons flour, and cook 2 minutes; stir in 1 cup cold beef stock and cook until thickened); salt and black pepper*

Combine the port and red currant jelly with the beef gravy in a saucepan. Bring the mixture to a boil, season to taste with salt and freshly ground black pepper, and pour into a warm sauceboat.

A succulent stuffed turkey with its trimmings is the highlight of a traditional Christmas dinner

Christmas in Europe

Italy

Traditional Christmas fare varies considerably between northern and southern Italy, but stuffed roasted capon is enjoyed throughout the country. Ham, too, is popular, and is often served in a pastry crust with candied fruits in a mustard syrup (*Mostarda di Frutta*).

Prosciutto in Crosta

SOAKING TIME: *2 hours*
PREPARATION TIME: *1 hour*
COOKING TIME: *3¾ hours*

INGREDIENTS (*for 8–10*): *1 ham, approximately 6 pounds; 1 chopped onion; 1 large chopped carrot; 1 stalk chopped celery; 1 clove; 1 bottle dry Spumanti; 2½ cups stock; puff pastry (p.363); 1 beaten egg; 3 tablespoons butter; 5 tablespoons flour; 3 teaspoons Dijon mustard; salt and black pepper; 14-ounce can or jar Mostarda di Frutta*

Soak the ham for 2 hours in cold water, then cut away the skin. Put the prepared vegetables in a large pan, add the ham, clove, wine, and stock. Cook the ham, covered, over moderate heat for 3 hours, then let it cool in the liquid.

Remove the fat from the ham. Roll out the puff pastry ¼ inch thick. Place the ham in the center and wrap the pastry over it, sealing the edges firmly. Decorate with pastry leaves and brush with egg. Set the ham on a damp baking sheet and cook in the center of a preheated oven at 425°F for 35 minutes.

Make a white sauce (p.301) from the butter, flour, and 2½ cups of the strained cooking liquid. Stir in the mustard and season. Decorate the ham with the Mostarda di Frutta. Serve the sauce separately.

Germany

Traditionally, the Christmas dinner in Germany includes roast goose or pork with red cabbage, and game such as hare, venison, and pheasant. *Christstollen*, which are fruity yeast cakes, are traditional, and in many households the main dish on Christmas Eve is still carp cooked in beer.

Karpfen in Bier

PREPARATION TIME: *35 minutes*
COOKING TIME: *1¾ hours*

INGREDIENTS (*for 6*): *1 carp, approximately 3–4 pounds; 3 tablespoons white wine vinegar; 2 chopped carrots; 1 chopped leek; 1 chopped onion; 1 bay leaf; 1 clove; salt and black pepper; 1½ cups cubed gingerbread; 4 cups beer or ale; juice and rind of 1 lemon*

Clean the carp and leave it to soak for 1 hour in cold water and the vinegar. Put the chopped vegetables, bay leaf, clove, salt, and pepper into a pan large enough to hold the carp. Add 2½ cups of water. Simmer this stock, covered, for 1 hour. Soak the gingerbread in 1 cup of ale.

Put the carp into the stock, with the lemon juice and remaining beer or ale. Cook over low heat for 20 minutes or until the carp is tender. Lift out the fish and keep it warm. Strain the liquid, add the gingerbread, and boil this mixture rapidly until it has reduced* by half.

Strain the sauce over the carp and garnish with lemon rind.

Rumania

In the countryside, where old traditions die hard, Christmas centers around folk singing and dancing, churchgoing, and feasting. Pork is the favorite meat and comes in a great variety of smoked hams and sausages, and as stuffings for cabbage (*sarmale*). Suckling pig and lamb are spit-roasted over an open fire and are traditionally served with roasted eggplant. In Rumania holiday feasting continues until New Year's Day and is then followed by a short period of strict fasting that continues until January 6.

Suckling Pig

PREPARATION TIME: *20 minutes*
COOKING TIME: *4–4½ hours*

INGREDIENTS (*for 6–8*): *1 3-week-old suckling pig, approximately 10 pounds; 1¼ cups rum; 1¼ cups olive oil; 2 tablespoons salt*

If oven space permits, truss the prepared piglet with the legs stretched out; otherwise, fold them underneath the belly. Insert a wooden plug in the mouth and protect the tail and ears with foil.

Mix the rum and oil and brush it all over the piglet. Rub the salt into the skin. Place the piglet on a rack in a large roasting pan and cook on the lower shelf of a preheated oven at 325°F. Allow 25 minutes to each pound. Baste every 15 minutes with more rum and oil.

When the piglet is cooked, remove the foil from its mouth and replace the wooden plug with a bright red apple. To carve, cut off the head and the forelegs, and then the rear portion and legs. Slit along and through the backbone, remove the rib cage, and carve the meat and skin into narrow slices. Carve the shoulder and legs in wide slices.

Spain

The Christmas symbol is the crèche, a miniature representation in wood and ceramic of the manger scene. In towns, international Christmas fare is usually turkey and suckling pig, while the mountain districts favor less festive dishes, usually with lamb. This dish of lamb with red bell pepper and tomatoes comes from Navarre. Every confectionery shop displays its own version of *turron*, a sweetmeat cake based on nougat. New Year's Eve is also a festive occasion, and it is not until Epiphany, January 6, that gifts are exchanged and distributed to children by the "Three Wise Men."

Cordero a la Chilindron
PREPARATION TIME: *20 minutes*
COOKING TIME: *50 minutes*

INGREDIENTS (*for 6*): *2 pounds boned leg or shoulder of lamb; 1 red bell pepper; salt and black pepper; 2 tablespoons olive oil; 2 chopped cloves garlic; 1 finely chopped onion; $\frac{1}{4}$ pound diced prosciutto; 16-ounce can tomatoes*

Put the red bell pepper under a hot broiler. Turn it frequently with tongs until it is charred all over, then gently rub the skin off under cold water. Remove the stalk end of the charred pepper and the seeds and cut the flesh into long, thin strips.

Cut the lamb into $1\frac{1}{2}$–2 inch cubes, removing any excess fat. Season to taste with salt and freshly ground black pepper. Heat the olive oil in a large, heavy-bottomed pan and sauté the chopped garlic until golden. Add the finely chopped onion, the lamb, and diced prosciutto and cook over moderate heat for about 10 minutes, or until the lamb is browned. Stir the pepper strips and tomatoes, with their juice, into the pan.

Simmer the lamb, uncovered, over low heat for about 40 minutes or until tender.

Serve with buttered rice, French or Italian bread, and a green salad.

France

The main Christmas meal, the *réveillon,* is served after midnight mass on Christmas Eve. The menu for this family occasion may include pâté de foie gras, oysters, or other shellfish. Game, roast goose, or turkey stuffed with chestnuts and truffles are also traditional. But whatever the glories of the Christmas spread, the *réveillon* must include a dish of blood sausage. The following dish, which comes from the Normandy region, combines the traditional ingredients: goose and blood sausage served on a bed of apple purée and garnished with small red apples.

Oie à la Normande
PREPARATION TIME: *25 minutes*
COOKING TIME: *2$\frac{3}{4}$ hours*

INGREDIENTS (*for 6–8*): *1 goose, approximately 10 pounds; 1 pound blood sausage; 1 crushed garlic clove; 2 large eating apples, peeled and grated; $\frac{1}{3}$ cup port; salt and black pepper*

Skin the blood sausage and pound it smooth with the goose liver and garlic. Blend in the apples and bind the stuffing with the port. Stuff the goose with this mixture. Prick the skin all over with a skewer and rub it thoroughly with salt and pepper.

Place the goose in a roasting pan and cover with aluminum foil. Roast on the lowest shelf of an oven preheated to 400°F, allowing 15 minutes to the pound plus 15 minutes. After 1 hour, drain the fat from the pan and pour $\frac{1}{2}$ cup cold water over the goose. Remove the foil about 30 minutes before cooking is complete and baste the goose every 10 minutes with the pan juices.

Serve the goose on a thick bed of unsweetened apple purée and garnish with polished apples set on cocktail picks.

Scandinavia

It is the Scandinavians who most joyously celebrate Christmas. From December 13, St. Lucia's Day, until well into the New Year, the tables are laden with traditional Christmas fare. This includes rich cakes and biscuits and a smorgasbord of cold pickled fish, meats, salads, and cheeses. The Christmas meal is served on Christmas Eve and may include roast goose or duck, or the popular leg of pork, which has a crisp skin and is flavored with bay leaves and cloves.

Roast Leg of Pork
PREPARATION TIME: *15 minutes*
COOKING TIME: *3$\frac{1}{4}$ hours*

INGREDIENTS (*for 8*): *6-pound leg of pork; 4 tablespoons butter; coarse salt; 6 cloves; 12 small bay leaves*

Ask the butcher for a leg of pork with the skin on. Score the skin by cutting with the tip of a sharp knife through to the fat beneath; make parallel diagonal cuts at $\frac{1}{2}$-inch intervals. Repeat at an angle to make diamonds or squares.

For a very crisp skin, place the leg, skin side down, in a roasting pan and pour in boiling water to a depth of 1 inch. Set the pan just below the center of an oven preheated to 450°F. Cook for 15 minutes. Remove the pan from the oven and remove the pork from the pan. Pour off the liquid and set it aside for basting.

Grease the pan with butter and rub the skin of the leg well with coarse salt. Insert the cloves and bay leaves in the score marks. Roast the pork, skin side up, at 350°F, allowing 30 minutes to the pound. Baste the pork every 30 minutes with the reserved liquid.

Serve the leg of pork garnished with cored, roasted apple halves filled with red currant jelly. Traditionally, this dish is accompanied by sugar-browned potatoes (p.102) and long-cooked red cabbage (see Squab with Pâté, p.61).

Basic Cooking Methods

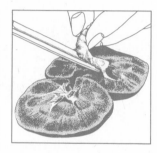

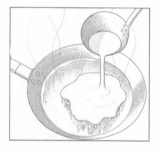

The Cook's Workshop

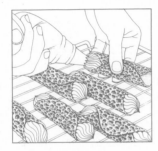

Stocks and Soups

The basis for all soups is good fresh stock made from the bones and flesh of fish, meat, or poultry, with added vegetables and herbs. The stock ingredients should harmonize with those of the soup.

There are five basic stocks: brown, white, fish, vegetable, and poultry or game stock. Brown stock can be used for most soups, although fish, vegetables, and game soups all gain in flavor when prepared with their own type of stock.

Fresh bones and meat are essential ingredients for brown and white stocks. Use marrow bone and shank of beef for brown stock, and knuckle of veal for a white stock. Ask the butcher to chop the bones into manageable pieces; the chopped bones release gelatin while cooking, which gives body to the stock.

Vegetables give additional flavor; avoid potatoes, however, which make the stock cloudy. Strong-flavored vegetables, such as turnips and parsnips, should be used sparingly.

STOCKS

Brown Stock

PREPARATION TIME: *15 minutes*
COOKING TIME: *5 hours*

INGREDIENTS (*for 3 quarts*):
1 pound marrow bones
2–3 pounds shank of beef
3 tablespoons butter or beef drippings
1–2 leeks
1 large onion
1–2 stalks celery
2–3 carrots
2 bouquets garnis (p.410)
Salt and crushed black peppercorns

Blanch* the bones for 10 minutes in boiling water, then put them, with the chopped meat and butter or drippings, in a roasting pan. Brown the bones in the center of a 425°F oven for 30–40 minutes. Turn them over occasionally to brown them evenly. Put the roasted bones in a large pan, add the cleaned and sliced vegetables, the bouquets garnis, and the crushed peppercorns. Cover with cold water to which ½ teaspoon salt has been added.

Bring the contents slowly to a boil, remove any scum from the surface, and cover the pan with a tight-fitting lid. Simmer the stock over lowest possible heat for about 4 hours to extract all flavor from the bones. Add hot water if the level of the liquid should fall below the other ingredients.

Strain the stock through a fine sieve or cheesecloth into a large bowl. Leave the stock to settle for a few minutes, then remove the fat from the surface by drawing paper towels over it. If the stock is not required immediately, let the fat settle in a surface layer, which can then be easily lifted off.

Once the fat has been removed, correct seasoning if necessary.

White Stock

This is made like brown stock, but the blanched veal bones are not browned. Place all the ingredients in a large pan of water and proceed as for brown stock.

Fish Stock

The basis for this stock is bones and trimmings, such as the head and the skin. Any white fish, such as cod, halibut, or sole, can be used.

PREPARATION TIME: *5–10 minutes*
COOKING TIME: *30 minutes*

INGREDIENTS (*for 1 pint*):
1 pound fish trimmings
Salt
1 onion
Bouquet garni (p.410), or 1 large leek and 1 stalk celery

Wash the trimmings thoroughly in cold water and put them in a large pan with 2½ cups lightly salted water. Bring to a boil over low heat and remove any surface scum. Meanwhile, peel and finely chop the onion and add to the stock, with the bouquet garni or the cleaned and chopped leek and celery. Cover the pan with a lid and simmer over low heat for 30 minutes. Strain the stock through a sieve or cheesecloth. Store, covered, in the refrigerator.

Fish stock does not keep well and should be used the day it is made.

Chicken, Turkey, or Game Stock

The ingredients for this stock can be the carcass of a chicken, turkey, or game bird, together with the scalded feet of the bird, if available, and the cleaned giblets. Cook as for white stock, simmering for 2–3 hours. Strain, then remove the fat.

Vegetable Stock

This inexpensive but quick and tasty stock is made from uncooked vegetables. The ingredients may include the outer leaves of cabbage, lettuce and other greens, cauliflower stalks, and peelings from carrots, leeks, and parsnips. Chop these trimmings coarsely, put them in a pan, and cover with lightly salted water. Put the lid on the pan and simmer the stock over low heat. A bouquet garni (p.410) and 6–8 crushed peppercorns may be added for extra flavor. Strain the stock through cheesecloth.

Cooking stock in a pressure cooker

Place the stock ingredients with lightly salted water in the pressure cooker—it must not be more than two-thirds full. Bring to a boil and remove the scum from the surface before fixing the lid. Lower the heat

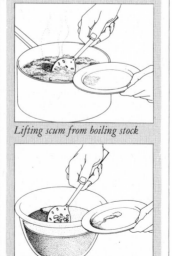

SKIMMING STOCK

Lifting scum from boiling stock

Removing surface fat

and bring to 15 pounds pressure. Reduce the heat quickly and cook steadily for 1 hour. Strain the stock and remove the fat.

Storing stocks

If not required for immediate use, prepared stocks can be stored in the refrigerator. After the fat has been removed, pour the cooled stock into a container and cover with a lid. It will keep for 3 or 4 days, but to ensure absolute freshness, boil the stock every 2 days. Fish and vegetable stocks spoil quickly and should be made and used on the same day. If refrigerated they will keep for 2 days.

Freezing stocks

Stocks can be stored satisfactorily in a freezer, where they will keep for up to 2 months. Boil the prepared stock over high heat to reduce* it by half. Pour the concentrated cooled stock into ice cube trays, freeze quickly, and transfer the stock cubes to plastic bags. Alternatively, pour the cooled stock into ½- or 1-pint freezing containers, leaving a 1-inch space at the top.

To use frozen stock, let it thaw at room temperature or simply turn it into a saucepan and heat over low heat, stirring occasionally. Add 2 tablespoons water to every cube of concentrated stock.

Ready-made stocks

Many ready-made stock preparations are available, usually in the form of canned broths, bouillon cubes, meat extracts, and meat-and-vegetable extracts. In an emergency these preparations are acceptable replacements for homemade stocks, but they have a sameness of flavor and lack body and jelling qualities. Since they are highly seasoned, be careful about extra flavorings until the soup has been tasted.

SOUPS

There is an enormous variety of classic and international soups. These fall into two distinct categories, according to their consistency: thin soups and thick soups.

Thin soups are divided into consommés and broths; and thick soups into purées and cream soups. Thick soups also include classic French velouté soups, which are based on a velouté sauce. These are seldom made today, however.

Thin soups
(consommé and broth)
A consommé is a clear soup made from clarified stock and meat, poultry, fish, or vegetables. The basic stock must be accentuated by the main ingredient, so that a beef consommé is made from brown stock and lean beef, and a chicken consommé from chicken stock and chicken flesh.

Consommés are particularly suitable for party menus and may be served hot or as a chilled jellied soup with various garnishes.

Beef Consommé
PREPARATION TIME: *15 minutes*
COOKING TIME: *2 hours*

INGREDIENTS (*for 6*):
½ pound lean beef
1 small carrot
1 small onion or leek
7–8 cups brown stock
Bouquet garni (p.410)
1 egg white

Shred the meat finely and peel and chop the vegetables. Put all the ingredients in a large pan, adding the egg white last. Heat gently, beating continuously with a wire whisk, until a thick froth forms on the surface. Cease beating, reduce the heat immediately, and simmer the consommé very slowly for 1½–2 hours. Do not let the liquid reach a boil, as the foam layer will break up and cloud the consommé.

Carefully strain the consommé into a bowl through a double layer of cheesecloth or a scalded jelly bag. Strain the consommé again through the egg foam in the cheesecloth—the soup should now be perfectly clear and sparkling.

Reheat the consommé, correct the seasoning if necessary, and serve hot or cold. If chilled in the refrigerator, the soup will jell.

CLEARING CONSOMMÉ

Whisking consommé to a froth

Straining cooked consommé

Broths
These semiclear soups are made from water in which meat, poultry, fish, vegetables, and seasonings have been cooked. Barley and rice are sometimes added as thickeners. Broths are often a by-product of the main course, such as the classic pot-au-feu. Vegetables can be cooked and braised in broths. Some of these soups, such as beef and chicken, can be made richer by long simmering.

Scotch Broth
This nourishing, easily prepared soup of lamb, barley, and vegetables is a complete meal in itself.

PREPARATION TIME: *30 minutes*
COOKING TIME: *2–3 hours*

INGREDIENTS (*for 8*):
1 pound neck of lamb
½ cup pearl barley
2 onions
¼ pound carrots
¼ pound turnips
3 leeks
Salt and black pepper
Finely chopped parsley

Ask the butcher to chop the meat into small pieces. Put the meat with 3 quarts of water in a large pot. Bring to a boil and remove any scum from the surface. Reduce the heat, add the barley, and simmer gently for 20–30 minutes.

Meanwhile, peel and finely chop the onions, carrots, and turnips. Trim and thoroughly wash the leeks, then cut them into thin rounds. Add all the vegetables to the pot, with 1 teaspoon salt and several twists of black pepper. Cover the pot and simmer over low heat for 2 hours. Lift out the bones. Strip off as much meat as possible and stir this back into the broth. Adjust seasoning and serve sprinkled with parsley.

Pot-au-feu
PREPARATION TIME: *20 minutes*
COOKING TIME: *2½ hours*

INGREDIENTS (*for 6–8*):
2 pounds top round of beef
2½ quarts brown stock
2 large carrots
1 turnip
2 large onions
2–3 leeks
1 stalk celery
1 small cabbage
1 set of chicken giblets

Tie the meat firmly with string so that its shape is retained during cooking. Put it in a large deep pan or

casserole and add the cold stock. Cover the pan with a tight-fitting lid and bring the stock slowly to a boil. Remove any scum.

Meanwhile, peel the carrots, turnip, and onions and cut them into even chunks. Remove the roots and outer coarse leaves from the leeks and cut the white part into rounds. Clean and coarsely chop the celery; wash and quarter the cabbage. Add all the vegetables except the cabbage to the pan and simmer gently for 1½ hours. Add the cleaned chicken giblets and continue simmering for another 30 minutes before adding the cabbage. Cook until the cabbage is tender, about 15–20 minutes.

Lift out the meat and vegetables and keep them hot. Remove the string and slice the meat. Serve with the vegetables, a horseradish sauce (p.304), and boiled potatoes.

Serve the soup the following day, with rice, pasta, or bread croûtons (p.300), or with any leftover meat and vegetables stirred in.

Thick soups
This group includes puréed soups thickened with starchy ingredients, such as flour, cereals, and potatoes. Cream soups are thickened with butter, cream, and egg yolks.

The thickening agents, known as liaisons, also enrich the texture of a soup and change its color. Liaisons must be added in correct proportions to the liquid; otherwise the soup may curdle or become too starchy.

Liaison to liquids

For soups rich in starch:
  1–2 tablespoons flour
  2½ cups liquid

For soups with little starch:
  2–3 tablespoons flour
  2½ cups liquid

For cream soups:
  1–2 egg yolks or 10
    tablespoons cream
  2½ cups liquid

Puréed soups
For these soups, the main ingredients are rubbed through a sieve or puréed in a blender or food processor. The soup is further thickened with a starchy liaison. Puréed soups are usually made from vegetables, but can also be prepared from meat, poultry, game, fish, and even fruit.

A purée made from starchy vegetables, such as dried peas, split peas, dried beans, or potatoes, will produce a thick soup that needs little or no additional starch. It can be adjusted to soup consistency by adding a little stock or water.

A thin purée from spinach, watercress, or other leafy vegetables will need thickening with flour. The addition of flour also prevents the purée from sinking to the bottom of the pan. Mix the correct liaison of flour with a few tablespoons of cold water, then stir this mixture into the soup and bring to the boiling point over gentle heat.

MAKING PURÉED SOUPS

Sieving cooked vegetables

Scraping purée off the sieve

Potato Soup

PREPARATION TIME: *15–20 minutes*
COOKING TIME: *20 minutes*

INGREDIENTS (*for 4–6*):
2 leeks
1 pound potatoes
3 tablespoons butter
5 cups white stock (p.298)
Salt and black pepper

Wash and finely chop the leeks and peel and coarsely chop the potatoes. Cook the leeks in 2 tablespoons of butter in a large pan until soft but not colored. Add the potatoes and pour in the stock. Season lightly with salt and freshly ground pepper. Bring the ingredients to a boil, cover with a lid, and simmer until the potatoes are quite tender.

Remove the soup from the heat and leave it to cool slightly. Rub the soup through a sieve or purée it in a blender, a little at a time. Reheat the puréed soup over low heat, adjust the seasoning, and then stir in the remaining butter.

Tomato Soup

PREPARATION TIME: *25 minutes*
COOKING TIME: *30 minutes*

INGREDIENTS (*for 6*):
1 pound ripe tomatoes
1 onion
2 tablespoons butter
Salt and black pepper
⅓ cup long grain rice
5 cups white stock (p.298)
Bouquet garni (p.410)

Peel and finely chop the onion. Peel the tomatoes,* cut them in half, and remove the seeds with a teaspoon. Chop the tomato flesh coarsely. Melt the butter in a large heavy-bottomed pan and cook the onion over low heat until transparent. Add the chopped tomato flesh and season with salt and freshly ground black pepper. Blend in the rice and stock, and add the bouquet garni. Bring the soup to a boil and cover the pan with a lid. Reduce the heat and simmer the soup for 15–20 minutes, or until the rice is tender. Remove the bouquet garni.

Rub the purée through a fine sieve—a blender will not get rid of any remaining tomato seeds. Reheat the soup over low heat and adjust the seasoning.

Cream soups

These thick soups are a combination of a puréed soup and Béchamel sauce (p.301). They are usually thickened and enriched with cream, egg yolks, or both.

Most cream soups are based on a vegetable purée, but chicken or fish can also be used as the main ingredient. For creamed chicken soup, the meat is cooked separately in white stock. It is then minced finely, added to a Béchamel sauce, and thinned down with stock, if necessary, to the required consistency.

Cream soups take little time to prepare and keep well in the freezer.

Care is required when thickening with cream or egg yolks to prevent the soup from curdling. Put the cream or yolks in a small bowl and beat in a little hot soup until the liaison has the same temperature as the soup. Blend the liaison slowly into the hot soup, stirring continuously, but do not let the soup reach a boil. The soup can also be reheated in the top of a double boiler.

Ladle a little of the hot soup into a bowl of cream or egg yolks.

Cream of Vegetable Soup

PREPARATION TIME: *20 minutes*
COOKING TIME: *15–20 minutes*

INGREDIENTS (*for 4*):
1 pound mixed vegetables (carrots, celery, leeks, cabbage)
4 tablespoons butter
2½ cups Béchamel sauce (p.301)
Salt and black pepper
1¼–2 cups milk
½ cup light cream

Peel or scrape and wash the vegetables before chopping them finely. Blanch* the vegetables for 2 minutes in boiling water, then drain thoroughly in a colander.

Melt the butter in a heavy-bottomed saucepan over low heat and cook the vegetables, covered, for 5–10 minutes or until soft. Blend in the Béchamel sauce and simmer gently for 15 minutes, or until the vegetables are tender.

Rub the thick mixture through a sieve or whirl it in a blender to make a smooth purée. Reheat the soup over low heat without boiling, thinning with milk to the desired consistency. Correct the seasoning and blend in the cream just prior to serving the soup.

SOUP GARNISHES

Garnishes are added to soups either as an embellishment to improve the flavor or to provide a contrasting texture or color.

Consommé julienne, for example, is garnished with julienne strips of carrot, celery, leek, and turnip. These strips are boiled in lightly salted water until soft, then rinsed in cold water and added to hot consommé just before serving.

Consommé royale is garnished with firm savory egg custard cut into tiny fancy shapes. Beat 1 egg with 1 tablespoon of cleared stock and pour into a small bowl or dariole* molds. Bake the molds in a pan of water placed in the center of a preheated oven at 350°F for 20 minutes or until the custard is firm.

Bread croûtons are cubes of bread sautéed in butter or baked until crisp and golden. They are a classic garnish with thick soups. Serve them in a separate dish or sprinkled over the soup.

Cheese makes a pleasant accompaniment to most vegetable soups. Choose a well-flavored hard cheese, such as Parmesan, Romano, or Sap Sago, and serve it finely grated in a separate dish or sprinkled over the soup. Finely chopped fresh herbs may be mixed with the cheese.

Dumplings are ideal for turning a meat or vegetable soup into a substantial family meal. Mix 1 cup self-rising flour with ½ cup shredded suet and a sprinkling of salt and freshly ground black pepper. Finely chopped herbs, such as parsley or sage, can also be added. Bind the mixture with enough cold water to make a soft dough. Shape the dough into 16 balls and drop them into the simmering soup for the last 15–20 minutes of cooking.

Melba toast is made by toasting thin slices of white bread, carefully splitting them through the middle, and toasting the uncooked surfaces under a hot broiler. Alternatively, cut stale bread into very thin slices, place them on a baking sheet, and dry them in the bottom of a 250°F oven until they are crisp and curling at the edges.

Pasta is used to garnish many thin soups. Macaroni, tagliatelle, and spaghetti can be broken into short pieces and added to puréed soups for the last 20 minutes of cooking. For hot consommés, cook the pasta separately so that the starch will not cloud the soup.

Vegetable and fruit garnishes add color to plain cream soups. Celery leaves, watercress, and parsley should be trimmed and washed before they are floated on the soup.

Cucumber can be cut into julienne strips as a garnish for chilled soups. For hot soups, sauté cucumber strips or thin rounds of leeks in a little butter.

Thin slices of lemon or orange make an attractive garnish for clear soups and tomato soup.

A garnish of thinly sliced mushrooms lends additional texture and flavor to cream soups. Sauté the sliced mushrooms in a little butter until soft but not browned. Drain thoroughly before spooning them over the soup.

Thin onion rings add more flavor to soups. They can be sautéed like cucumber strips and leek rounds; alternatively, coat them in a little milk and flour, and deep-fry them until crisp and golden.

SOUP GARNISHES

Julienne strips

Cutouts for consommé royale

Cutting bread croûtons

Slicing Melba toast

Sauces, Gravies and Dressings

Sauces first came into widespread use in the Middle Ages, to disguise the flavor of long-stored meat that had been inadequately cured. Today they are used to add flavor, color, and moisture to many foods.

There are two main groups of sauces: savory and dessert. The first group includes white, brown, and egg-based sauces, and the cold sauces and salad dressings. French chefs have created most of the hundreds of variations on the basic savory sauces. However, most of the dessert sauces, the second group, originated in North America and England. Horseradish, apple, and other puréed fruit sauces are savory sauces, but they do not belong in any particular subgroup.

The main ingredient of all sauces is the basic liquid, which may be milk, wine, stock, or vegetable or fruit juices. These are thickened with fat, flour, arrowroot, eggs, or cream, or they may be boiled down (reduced) to the desired consistency.

BASIC WHITE SAUCE

This is prepared either by the roux or the blending method:

Roux method

A roux is composed of equal amounts of butter and flour combined with milk to obtain the required consistency. Melt the butter in a saucepan, blend in the flour, and cook over low heat for 2–3 minutes, stirring constantly so that the roux bubbles but does not brown.

Gradually add the warm or cold liquid to the roux, which will at first thicken to a nearly solid mass. Beat vigorously until the mixture leaves the sides of the pan clean, then add a little more milk. Allow the mixture to thicken and boil between each addition of milk. Continuous beating is essential to obtain a smooth sauce. When all the milk has been added, bring the sauce to a boil. Let it simmer for about 5 minutes and add the seasoning.

A basic white sauce can also be made by putting the basic ingredients (fat, flour, and liquid) into a pan at the same time. Cook over low heat, beating with a whisk until thickened. Boil 3 minutes.

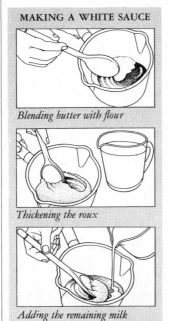

MAKING A WHITE SAUCE

Blending butter with flour

Thickening the roux

Adding the remaining milk

Blending method

For this method the thickening agent is mixed to a paste with a little cold milk. Mix 2 tablespoons flour (or 2 teaspoons cornstarch) with a few tablespoons taken from 1¼ cups of cold milk. Blend to a smooth paste in a bowl and bring the remaining milk to a boil.

Pour the hot milk over the paste and return the mixture to the pan. Bring to a boil over low heat, stirring continuously with a wooden spoon. Simmer the sauce for 2–3 minutes until thick. Add a pat of butter and a little salt and white pepper. Cook for 5 minutes.

A basic white sauce can be made into other savory sauces. Delicately flavored rich sauces, such as the classic French Béchamel and velouté, have evolved from the basic white sauce. These sauces are, in turn, the main components for the compound white sauces.

Béchamel Sauce

PREPARATION TIME: *20 minutes*
COOKING TIME: *5–10 minutes*

INGREDIENTS (*1 cup*):
1 cup milk
½ small bay leaf
Sprig of thyme
½ small onion
¼ teaspoon grated nutmeg
2 tablespoons butter
2 tablespoons flour
Salt and black pepper
2–3 tablespoons cream (optional)

Put the milk, with the bay leaf, thyme, onion, and nutmeg in a pan and bring slowly to a boil. Remove from the heat, cover with a lid, and leave the milk to infuse for 15 minutes. In a heavy-bottomed pan, melt the butter, stir in the flour, and cook the roux for 3 minutes.

Strain the milk through a fine sieve and gradually blend it into the roux. Bring to a boil, stirring continuously, then simmer for 2–3 minutes. Adjust seasoning and stir in light or heavy cream, if desired.

SIMPLE WHITE SAUCES

	Pouring sauce	Other ingredients	Method of preparation	Serving suggestions
Butter sauce	1 cup white sauce (use lightly salted water instead of milk)	*1 egg yolk* / *1 tablespoon water* / *6 tablespoons butter*	Beat the egg yolk with water and blend into the sauce with the butter cut into pieces.	*Fish or vegetables*
Caper sauce	1 cup white sauce (use half milk and half white or fish stock)	*1 tablespoon caper juice or lemon juice* / *1 tablespoon capers*	Add caper juice or lemon juice to the stock before making the sauce. Add the finely chopped capers to the sauce just before serving.	*Poached fish*
Cheese sauce	1 cup white sauce	*½ cup grated sharp Cheddar cheese* / *½ teaspoon dry mustard* / *Pinch cayenne*	Beat the grated cheese into the sauce until smooth. Season with mustard and cayenne.	*Eggs, fish, pasta, and vegetables*
Egg sauce	1 cup white sauce	*1 hard-cooked egg* / *2 tablespoons chopped chives*	Finely chop the egg and the chives and add to the sauce.	*Poached or steamed fish*
Fish sauce	1 cup white sauce (made from half milk and half fish stock, simmered with bay leaf, rind of ⅓ lemon, then strained)	*⅓ cup shrimp or* / *1 teaspoon anchovy paste*	Peel and chop the shrimp. Before seasoning the sauce, add the shrimp or anchovy.	*Poached or steamed fish*
Mushroom sauce	1 cup white sauce	*⅔ cup mushrooms* / *1 tablespoon butter* / *Squeeze lemon juice*	Trim and slice the mushrooms. Sauté in butter and lemon juice until tender. Drain before folding into the sauce.	*Fish, meat, poultry*
Parsley sauce	1 cup white sauce	*2 tablespoons parsley*	Finely chop the parsley; add to sauce before serving.	*Poached or steamed fish, and vegetables*

SAUCE CONSISTENCIES

Consistency	Uses	Ingredients	
		Butter, Flour	Milk
Thin sauce	Basis for soups	*1 tablespoon each*	*1 cup*
Pouring sauce (*medium*)	For accompanying sauces	*1½ tablespoons each*	*1 cup*
Coating sauce (*medium thick*)	For coating sauces	*2 tablespoons each*	*1 cup*
Panada sauce (*very thick*)	For binding croquettes and as basis for soufflés	*3 tablespoons each*	*1 cup*

COMPOUND WHITE SAUCES

	Ingredients	Method of preparation	Serving suggestions
Allemande sauce	1 cup Velouté sauce 2 egg yolks ½ cup white stock 3 tablespoons butter	Beat the egg yolks with the stock and blend into the sauce. Simmer gently, stirring until thick, smooth, and reduced by one-third. Stir in the butter, cut into pieces, and adjust seasoning.	*Chicken, eggs, fish, vegetables*
Aurora sauce	1 cup Velouté sauce 4 tablespoons tomato purée or 1 tablespoon concentrated tomato paste 3 tablespoons butter	Blend the tomato purée or tomato paste into the sauce. Stir in the butter, cut into pieces, and correct the seasoning.	*Eggs, poultry, sweetbreads, fish, vegetables*
Chantilly sauce	1 cup Suprême sauce ½ cup heavy cream	Whip the cream until light and fluffy. Fold into the Suprême sauce.	*Serve immediately with poultry.*
Chaud-froid sauce	1 cup Velouté sauce 1 cup jellied white stock 4 tablespoons light cream	Add the stock and cream to the sauce. Cook over gentle heat until reduced to coating consistency. Adjust seasoning.	*Cold, as a coating for chicken, eggs, and fish*
Hungarian sauce	1 cup Velouté sauce 1 onion 2 tablespoons butter Bouquet garni ¼ teaspoon paprika 6 tablespoons white wine	Sauté the finely chopped onion in the butter until clear. Add the rest of the ingredients. Bring to a boil and reduce by half. Strain through a sieve before adding to the sauce.	*Fish and veal*
Mornay sauce	1 cup Béchamel sauce ½ cup grated Parmesan or Gruyère cheese	Blend the cheese into the sauce. Do not reheat.	*Chicken, eggs, veal, fish, vegetables, and pasta*
Suprême sauce	1 cup Velouté sauce 2 egg yolks 2 tablespoons heavy cream 2 tablespoons butter	Beat the egg yolks and cream together. Blend into the sauce and heat without boiling. Stir in the butter (cut into pieces).	*Serve immediately with eggs, poultry, and vegetables.*

COMPOUND BROWN SAUCES

	Ingredients	Method of preparation	Serving suggestions
Demi-glace sauce	1 cup Espagnole sauce ½ cup jellied brown stock	Add the jellied stock to the Espagnole sauce. Bring to a boil and cook until the sauce is shiny and thick enough to coat the back of a spoon.	*Game: add 3 tablespoons Madeira to finished sauce.* *Poultry: add 1½ cups mushrooms and 1 tablespoon Madeira.*
Devil sauce	1 cup Espagnole sauce 1 small onion 1 cup white wine 1 tablespoon wine vinegar Sprig of thyme Small bay leaf 1 tablespoon parsley Cayenne	Finely chop the onion and mix with the wine, vinegar, thyme, and bay leaf. Bring to a boil and reduce by half. Strain and add to the Espagnole sauce. Boil for a few minutes and add the chopped parsley and cayenne to taste.	*Chicken*
Red wine sauce	1 cup Espagnole sauce ½ onion 4 tablespoons butter 1 cup red wine Bouquet garni	Sauté the finely chopped onion in 2 tablespoons butter until clear. Add the rest of the ingredients and boil to reduce by half. Strain and add to Espagnole sauce. Cook until reduced by one-third. Stir in 2 tablespoons butter.	*Game*
Robert sauce	1 cup Espagnole sauce 1 onion 1 tablespoon butter 8 tablespoons red wine 1 teaspoon mustard	Sauté the chopped onion in butter. Add the red wine and boil until reduced by half. Strain and add to the Espagnole sauce. Heat gently and stir in 1 teaspoon mustard.	*Roast pork*
Tomato sauce	1 cup Espagnole sauce (made from tomato juice instead of brown stock) ¼ pound ham	Dice the ham and add to the finished sauce.	*Serve with broiled chicken, meat leftovers, chops, pasta, meat patties.*

Velouté Sauce

PREPARATION TIME: *5–10 minutes*
COOKING TIME: *1 hour*

INGREDIENTS (*1 cup*):
2 tablespoons butter
2 tablespoons flour
2 cups white stock
Salt and black pepper
1–2 tablespoons light or heavy cream (optional)

Make the roux with the butter and flour. Gradually stir in the hot stock until the sauce is quite smooth. Bring to a boil, lower the heat, and let the sauce simmer for about 1 hour until reduced by half. Stir occasionally. Strain and season to taste. Stir in light or heavy cream, if desired.

BROWN SAUCES

A basic brown sauce is made by the roux method, using the same proportions of flour, fat, and liquid (brown stock) as for a basic white sauce. Melt the fat in a pan and stir in the flour. Cook the roux over low heat, stirring continuously with a wooden spoon, until the roux is light brown in color. Gradually stir in the brown stock and proceed as for a white sauce.

Espagnole Sauce

This classic sauce, made from a brown roux, is the basis of many compound brown sauces.

PREPARATION TIME: *10 minutes*
COOKING TIME: *1¼ hours*

INGREDIENTS (*approximately 1 cup*):
1 carrot
1 onion
2 ounces lean salt pork, blanched
2 tablespoons butter
2 tablespoons flour
2 cups brown stock
Bouquet garni (p.410)
2 tablespoons tomato paste
Salt and black pepper

Peel and dice the carrot and onion. Dice the salt pork after removing the rind. Melt the butter in a heavy-bottomed saucepan and cook the carrot, onion, and salt pork over low heat for 10 minutes, or until the vegetables and pork are light brown.

Blend in the flour, stirring the roux until it is light brown. Gradually blend in 1 cup of brown stock, stirring constantly until the mixture has cooked through and has thickened. Add the bouquet garni, cover with a lid, and place an asbestos mat between the burner and the pan. Simmer the sauce for 30 minutes. Add the remaining stock and the tomato paste. Cover the pan again and continue cooking for 30 minutes, stirring frequently. Strain the sauce through a sieve, skim off fat, and adjust seasoning.

MAKING ESPAGNOLE SAUCE

Blending in the flour

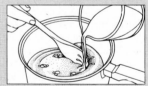
Stirring in the stock

Straining the sauce

Gravies
The most frequently used and most easily prepared brown sauce is gravy, made by boiling the pan residues of roasted meat with brown stock. Gravies may be thick or thin.

Thick gravy

Pour off most of the fat from the roasting pan, leaving about 2 tablespoons of the sediment. Stir in 1 tablespoon flour and blend thoroughly with the fat. Stir constantly with a wooden spoon, cooking until the gravy thickens and browns. Gradually blend in 1 cup hot brown stock or vegetable liquid. Boil for 2–3 minutes. Season to taste and strain. Serve with a roast.

Thin gravy

Pour all the fat from the pan, leaving only the pan residues. Add 1 cup hot vegetable liquid or brown stock (this may be made from a bouillon cube). Stir the mixture well. Boil for 2–3 minutes to reduce* slightly. This gravy is traditional with roast beef.

Thickening agents for sauces

Basic white and brown sauces can be thickened or enriched with cornstarch or arrowroot and water; *beurre manié* (kneaded butter and flour); or egg yolks and cream.

Cornstarch and arrowroot

To thicken 1 cup of liquid to a sauce of coating consistency, stir 1 tablespoon cornstarch with 3 tablespoons cold water and mix into a smooth paste. Blend a little of the hot liquid into the liaison, then return this to the sauce. Bring the sauce to a boil, stirring constantly for 2–3 minutes to allow the starch to cook through.

Arrowroot is best used to thicken clear sauces that are to be served at once. To thicken 1 cup sauce, use 2 teaspoons arrowroot mixed to a paste with water. The sauce should not be reheated; this may cause the sauce to thin out.

Beurre manié

This liaison is ideal for thickening sauces and stews at the end of cooking. Knead 2 tablespoons of butter and 4 tablespoons flour into a paste. Add small pieces of the beurre manié

to the hot liquid. Stir or whisk continuously to dissolve the butter and disperse the flour. Simmer the sauce until it is thick and smooth and has lost the starchy taste of raw flour. Do not boil, or sauce may separate.

Egg yolks and cream

These are used when enriching a basic white sauce. Mix 1 egg yolk with 2–3 tablespoons cream in a bowl. Blend in a little of the hot sauce until the liaison has the same temperature. Remove the sauce from the heat and stir in the liaison with a wooden spoon. Return the pan to the heat and simmer the sauce over low heat without boiling. Overheating causes the sauce to curdle.

EGG-BASED SAUCES

Care and practice is required to prevent these rich sauces from curdling. They are made from egg yolks and a high proportion of butter. Through continuous beating, these two main ingredients are emulsified to a thick and creamy consistency.

Hollandaise Sauce
PREPARATION AND COOKING
TIME: *20 minutes*

INGREDIENTS (*1 cup*):
3 tablespoons white wine vinegar
1 tablespoon water
6 black peppercorns
1 bay leaf
3 egg yolks
12 tablespoons (1½ sticks) soft butter
Salt and black pepper

Boil the white wine vinegar and water with the black peppercorns and the bay leaf in a small saucepan until the mixture has reduced* to 1 tablespoon. Leave to cool. Cream the egg yolks with 1 tablespoon butter and a pinch of salt. Strain the vinegar into the egg yolks and set the bowl over a pan of simmering water. Turn off the heat. With a wire whisk, beat in the remaining butter, 1 tablespoon at a time, until the sauce is shiny and has the consistency of thick cream. Season with salt and freshly ground black pepper.

A Hollandaise sauce may curdle because the heat is too sudden or too high, or because the butter has been

added too quickly. If the sauce separates, it can often be saved by removing from the heat and beating in 1 tablespoon of cold water.

Béarnaise Sauce

This sauce is similar to Hollandaise sauce but has a sharper flavor. It is served with broiled meat and fish.

PREPARATION AND COOKING
TIME: *20 minutes*

INGREDIENTS (*1 cup*):
4 tablespoons wine vinegar
4 tablespoons white wine
1 tablespoon minced onion or shallot
¼ teaspoon black pepper
3 egg yolks
8 tablespoons butter
Salt and black pepper
1 teaspoon dried tarragon

Put the vinegar, wine, the minced onion or shallot, and pepper in a small saucepan; boil steadily until reduced* to 2 tablespoons. Strain and set aside to cool.

Follow the method used for making Hollandaise sauce, then add 1 teaspoon of dried tarragon.

COLD SAUCES

Mayonnaise and its variations are the most widely used of savory cold sauces. They are served with hors d'oeuvres, salads, cold meat, poultry, and vegetable dishes. Mayonnaise, like Hollandaise and Béarnaise sauce, is based on eggs and fat, but oil is used instead of butter.

It is essential that ingredients and equipment are at room temperature. Assemble the bowl, egg, and oil at least 1 hour before using.

Mayonnaise
PREPARATION TIME: *20 minutes*

INGREDIENTS (*½ cup*):
1 egg yolk
¼ teaspoon salt
½ teaspoon dry mustard
Black pepper
½ cup olive or salad oil
1 tablespoon white wine vinegar or lemon juice

Beat the egg yolk until thick. Beat in the salt, mustard, and a few twists of pepper. Add the oil, drop by drop, beating vigorously with a whisk between each addition of oil so that it is absorbed completely before the next drop. As the mayonnaise thickens and becomes shiny, the oil may be added in a thin stream. Finally, blend in the vinegar.

The flavor of mayonnaise can be varied by using a tarragon, garlic, or chili pepper vinegar, or by substituting lemon juice for vinegar. Chopped parsley, chives, or crushed garlic can also be added when the mayonnaise is finished. Alternatively, fold ½ cup of whipped cream into the finished mayonnaise.

A mayonnaise may curdle if the oil was cold or was added too quickly, or if the egg yolk was stale. To save a curdled mayonnaise, beat a fresh yolk in a clean bowl and gradually beat in the curdled mayonnaise. Alternatively, beat in a teaspoon of tepid water until the mayonnaise is thick and shiny.

MAYONNAISE SAUCES

	Ingredients	Method of preparation	Serving suggestions
Anchovy mayonnaise	1 cup mayonnaise *2 teaspoons anchovy paste*	Mix the anchovy paste thoroughly into the finished mayonnaise.	*Fish and vegetable salads*
Herbed mayonnaise (Sauce verte)	1 cup mayonnaise *½ cup finely chopped mixed green herbs: parsley, chives, watercress, spinach*	Mix the chopped herbs into the mayonnaise.	*Cold salmon*
Horseradish mayonnaise	1 cup mayonnaise *1 tablespoon grated fresh horseradish or drained bottled horseradish*	Mix the horseradish into the mayonnaise.	*Fish and meat salads; salmon in aspic*
Mustard mayonnaise	1 cup mayonnaise *1 tablespoon Dijon mustard*	Mix the mustard into the mayonnaise.	*Fish, beef, and vegetable salads; salmon in aspic*
Orange mayonnaise	1 cup mayonnaise *Rind of 1 orange* *1–2 tablespoons whipped cream*	Fold the grated orange rind and lightly whipped cream into the mayonnaise.	*Salads*
Remoulade sauce	1 cup mayonnaise *1 teaspoon each, chopped capers, chervil, gherkins, parsley, tarragon, onion*	Mix the finely chopped herbs and vegetables and blend into the mayonnaise.	*Cold shellfish and egg dishes*
Tartare sauce	1 cup mayonnaise *2 teaspoons capers* *3 small sour gherkins* *1 teaspoon chives* *1 tablespoon heavy cream*	Finely chop the gherkins and chives. Add all the ingredients to the mayonnaise.	*Sautéed or broiled fish*

SALAD DRESSINGS

A good dressing is essential to a salad, but it must be varied according to the salad ingredients. A plain vinaigrette sauce is probably best for a green salad, but egg, fish, meat, and vegetable salads nearly always benefit from additional flavors. For a mixed fruit and green salad, vinaigrette sauce might be too sharp.

There are no hard rules for making salad dressings, but a fine olive or salad oil is very important. Dry the greens and never add the dressing until just before serving.

Sauce Vinaigrette

PREPARATION TIME: *3 minutes*

INGREDIENTS ($\frac{1}{2}$–$\frac{3}{4}$ *cup*):
6–8 tablespoons oil
2 tablespoons vinegar
Salt and black pepper
1 tablespoon finely chopped herbs, such as basil, chives, parsley, tarragon; or $\frac{1}{4}$ teaspoon dried herbs (optional)

Put the oil and vinegar in a bowl or in a screw-top jar. Beat with a fork or shake. Season to taste with salt and freshly ground pepper. For an herbed vinaigrette, add the herbs.

French Dressing

PREPARATION TIME: *3 minutes*

INGREDIENTS ($\frac{1}{2}$–$\frac{3}{4}$ *cup*):
8 tablespoons oil
2 tablespoons vinegar
2 teaspoons Dijon mustard
$\frac{1}{2}$ teaspoon each salt and black pepper

Beat or shake all the dressing ingredients together. Any of the following ingredients can be added to taste: 1–2 crushed garlic cloves; 2 tablespoons chopped fresh tarragon or chives; 1 tablespoon tomato paste and a pinch of paprika; 2 tablespoons each finely chopped parsley and chopped or grated onion; 1 teaspoon anchovy paste (for cold fish or cold cooked vegetable salads).

MISCELLANEOUS SAUCES

Bread Sauce

PREPARATION TIME: *20 minutes*
COOKING TIME: *15 minutes*

INGREDIENTS (*1 pint*):
1 onion
1–2 cloves
1 bay leaf
2 cups milk
1$\frac{1}{2}$ cups fresh white bread crumbs
2 tablespoons butter
Salt and black pepper

Peel the onion and stick the cloves into it. Put the onion, bay leaf, and milk into a pan and bring to a boil. Remove the pan from the heat, cover with a lid, and leave to infuse* for 15 minutes. Add the bread crumbs and the butter. Cook, uncovered, over lowest possible heat for 15 minutes, then remove the onion and bay leaf. Season to taste with salt and pepper. Serve with chicken or turkey.

Horseradish Sauce

PREPARATION TIME: *10 minutes*

INGREDIENTS (*about* $\frac{3}{4}$ *cup*):
3 tablespoons fresh grated horseradish
$\frac{1}{2}$ cup sour cream
Salt and black pepper
Pinch of dry mustard

Fold the horseradish into the sour cream and season to taste with salt, freshly ground pepper, and mustard. Serve with roast beef.

Mint Sauce

PREPARATION TIME: *10 minutes*
RESTING TIME: *30 minutes*

INGREDIENTS (*about* $\frac{1}{2}$ *cup*):
Small handful of mint leaves
1–2 teaspoons sugar
2 tablespoons vinegar

Wash and dry the mint leaves. Put them on a board, sprinkle with the sugar, and chop them finely. Place the chopped mint in a bowl and stir in 2 tablespoons boiling water. Add

the vinegar and leave the sauce to stand for 30 minutes.

Alternatively, add the chopped mint to 3–4 tablespoons finely chopped red currant jelly. Blend in the finely grated rind of an orange and mix thoroughly.

Serve with roast lamb.

Applesauce

PREPARATION TIME: *10 minutes*

INGREDIENTS (*1 cup*):
1 pound cooking apples
2 tablespoons unsalted butter
Sugar (optional)

Peel, core, and slice the apples. Put them in a pan with 2–3 tablespoons of water and cook over low heat for about 10 minutes. Rub the cooked apples through a coarse sieve or purée them in a blender. Stir in butter and add sugar if necessary.

For a pungent horseradish applesauce, add 1$\frac{1}{2}$ tablespoons freshly grated horseradish.

Serve the applesauce with roast pork, goose, or duck.

Cranberry Sauce: See page 292.

DESSERT SAUCES

The sweet dessert sauces are mainly of North American and British origin. They are most often served warm with baked and steamed puddings, stewed and poached fruit, and with ice cream.

Apricot Sauce

PREPARATION TIME: *5 minutes*
COOKING TIME: *6 minutes*

INGREDIENTS (*1 cup*):
4 tablespoons apricot preserves
Juice and rind of $\frac{1}{2}$ lemon
1$\frac{1}{2}$ teaspoons arrowroot
2 tablespoons sugar (optional)

Pare the rind from the lemon, leaving behind the white pith. Squeeze out the juice. Blend the arrowroot with $\frac{1}{2}$ cup water in a small pan and

stir in the preserves. Cook over low heat until the preserves melt, then stir in the lemon rind and juice.

Bring the sauce to a boil and cook for 2 minutes, stirring continuously. Strain the sauce through a sieve, return it to the pan, and reheat; sweeten to taste.

Serve apricot sauce hot with steamed or baked puddings. It can also be served cold with ice cream, in which case the arrowroot should be reduced to 1 teaspoon.

Brandy Sauce

PREPARATION AND COOKING TIME: *10–12 minutes*

INGREDIENTS (*1 cup*):
2 tablespoons brandy
1 tablespoon cornstarch
1 cup milk
1 tablespoon sugar

In a bowl, blend the cornstarch to a smooth paste with 1 tablespoon of the milk. Bring the remaining milk to a boil; pour it over the cornstarch, stirring well. Return the sauce to the pan, add the sugar and brandy, and cook over low heat for 2–3 minutes.

Serve the sauce hot with steamed fruit puddings, Christmas pudding, or mince pies.

Butterscotch Sauce

PREPARATION AND COOKING TIME: *25 minutes*

INGREDIENTS (*1 cup*):
6 tablespoons granulated sugar
1$\frac{1}{2}$ teaspoons arrowroot
2 tablespoons unsalted butter

Heat the sugar over gentle heat in a heavy-bottomed pan until dissolved. Increase the heat and let the sugar bubble until it caramelizes to a golden brown. Remove the pan from the heat, add (without stirring) 6 tablespoons of boiling water, and return the pan to the heat. Simmer the caramel for a few minutes, stirring all the time, until dissolved.

Blend the arrowroot with 4 tablespoons water and stir into the cara-

mel. Bring the mixture to a boil over low heat. Add the butter, cut into small pieces, and cook the sauce until thick and clear, stirring all the time to prevent the sauce from burning.

Serve the sauce warm with ice cream or baked apples.

Chocolate Sauce I

PREPARATION AND COOKING TIME: *15 minutes*

INGREDIENTS (*1 cup*):
2 ounces unsweetened chocolate
2 level teaspoons cornstarch
$\frac{3}{4}$ cup plus 1 tablespoon water
4 tablespoons unsalted butter
6 tablespoons sugar
1 teaspoon vanilla extract

Break the chocolate into small pieces. Blend the cornstarch with 2 tablespoons of the measured water in a small bowl or cup. Put the chocolate in a small pan, add the rest of the water, and cook over low heat until dissolved and smooth. Do not allow the chocolate mixture to boil. With a wooden spoon, stir the blended cornstarch quickly into the chocolate and add the butter and sugar.

Cook the chocolate sauce for a few minutes, stirring continuously, then add vanilla extract to taste.

Serve the sauce hot with unfrosted cake, ice cream, or poached pears.

Chocolate Sauce II

PREPARATION AND COOKING TIME: *10 minutes*

INGREDIENTS ($\frac{3}{4}$ *cup*):
4 ounces semisweet chocolate
1 tablespoon unsalted butter
2 tablespoons water
2 tablespoons clear honey
1 teaspoon vanilla extract (optional)

Break the chocolate into pieces and put them in a small pan with the butter, water, and honey. Cook over low heat until the chocolate has melted, then stir in the vanilla.

Serve hot, with vanilla ice cream, or warm, over profiteroles.

Honey Sauce

PREPARATION AND COOKING
TIME: *8 minutes*

INGREDIENTS (½ *cup*):
4 tablespoons unsalted butter
1½ teaspoons cornstarch
½–¾ cup thin clear honey

Melt the butter in a small pan over low heat, without browning it; stir in the cornstarch.

Gradually blend in the honey and bring the sauce to a boil, stirring all the time. Heat for 2–3 minutes to cook the cornstarch.

Serve the sauce warm with vanilla ice cream or banana splits.

Sauce Sabayon

PREPARATION TIME: *7 minutes*
COOKING TIME: *5 minutes*

INGREDIENTS (1 *cup*):
2 egg yolks
4 tablespoons sugar
¼ teaspoon arrowroot
5 tablespoons sherry, white wine, fruit juice, or strong black coffee

In a deep bowl, beat the egg yolks and sugar until thick, creamy, and pale in color. Blend the arrowroot to a paste with a little of the liquid, then beat it, with the rest of the liquid, into the eggs. Place the bowl over a pan of gently simmering water and beat the sauce with a whisk until thick and frothy.

Serve at once with fruit puddings or apple pie.

Sour Cream Sauce

PREPARATION TIME: *10 minutes*

CHILLING TIME: *30 minutes*
INGREDIENTS (1 *cup*):
½ cup heavy cream
½ cup sour cream
1 teaspoon sugar

Beat the cream until it just holds its shape, then fold in the sour cream and the sugar. Refrigerate the sauce for about 30 minutes.

Serve with cooked fruit, fruit pies, mince pies, or fruit salads.

Crème Fraîche

PREPARATION TIME: *2 minutes*

STANDING TIME: *8 hours*
INGREDIENTS (1 *cup*):
1 cup heavy cream
2 teaspoons buttermilk, yogurt, or sour cream

Put the heavy cream in a jar. Add the buttermilk, yogurt, or commercial sour cream. Shake to mix. Cover loosely and place in an oven with a pilot light for 8 hours or overnight, or let stand at a room temperature of 85°F. (At a lower temperature the cream must stand from 24 to 36 hours.) Stir, cover, and refrigerate. When cold, the crème will be thick and ready to use.

Serve with fruit, desserts, or use in cooking as a substitute for sour cream. Unlike sour cream, crème fraîche will not curdle when boiled.

Syrup Sauce

PREPARATION AND COOKING
TIME: *8 minutes*

INGREDIENTS (¾ *cup*):
4 tablespoons light corn syrup
2 teaspoons arrowroot
2 tablespoons lemon juice

Blend the arrowroot to a smooth paste with ½ cup of water in a small pan. Add the syrup and lemon juice. Bring the sauce to a boil over low heat, stirring all the time, and cook until thick. Serve warm with ice cream, pancakes, or waffles.

Fish

Fish are sold fresh, frozen, salted from the barrel, smoked, pickled, or canned. Flat fish, such as sole and flounder, are sold whole or filleted. Whole round fish, such as cod and haddock, are also sold as steaks.

Many shellfish are sold already boiled. However, mussels, clams, and oysters in their shells must always be bought live.

Cook fish on the day it is bought, and for a main course allow ½ pound of dressed fish per person, or 1 good-sized fillet or steak. A medium mackerel or trout will serve 1 person. If the fish course is to be followed by several other courses, halve the fish quantities suggested for a main course. However, it is better to err on the generous side, and cold fish can easily be made into fish cakes or a salad.

PREPARATION OF FISH

Fish markets will usually clean and fillet fish ready for cooking. But if this has not been done, a few simple preparations are necessary. Unwrap the fish as soon as possible and if it has to be stored in the refrigerator for any length of time, wrap it in plastic wrap or foil to prevent its smell from spreading to other food.

Preparation includes scaling, cleaning, skinning, and filleting.

Scaling

Cover a wooden board with several sheets of newspaper. Lay the fish on the paper and, holding it by the tail with paper towels, scrape away the scales from the tail toward the head, using the blunt edge of a knife. Rinse the scales under cold running water. Alternatively, cook the fish without removing the scales, and skin it before serving.

Cleaning

Once scaled, the fish must be cleaned, or gutted. The method of cleaning is determined by the shape of the fish—in round fish the entrails lie in the belly, but in flat fish, such as flounder, they are found in a cavity behind the head.

Round fish

(including cod, bluefish, mackerel, and trout). With a sharp knife, slit the fish along the belly from behind the gills to just above the tail. Scrape out and discard the entrails. Rinse the fish under cold running water and, with a little salt, gently rub away any black skin inside the cavity.

The head and tail may be left on the fish if it is to be cooked whole. Use a sharp knife or scissors to cut off the lower fins on either side of the body and the gills below the head. Alternatively, cut the head off with a sharp knife just below the gills and slice off the tail.

Small round fish, such as smelt, need less preparation. Wipe the fish with a damp cloth. Cut off the heads just below the gills, leaving the tails intact. Squeeze out the entrails. Fresh eels are sold live; the fish dealer will cut off the heads and may also skin the fish.

Flat fish

(including sole and flounder). Make a semicircular slit just behind the head on the dark-skinned side. This opens up the cavity that contains the entrails. Scrape the entrails out and wash the fish thoroughly. Cut off the fins with a sharp knife and cook the fish whole.

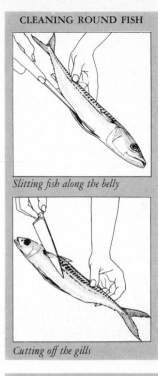

CLEANING ROUND FISH

Slitting fish along the belly

Cutting off the gills

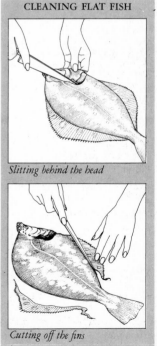

CLEANING FLAT FISH

Slitting behind the head

Cutting off the fins

Skinning

Again, the method varies according to the type of fish.

Round fish

These are usually cooked with the skin on, but it is also possible to remove the skin before cooking. Cut away a thin strip of skin along the backbone. Using a sharp knife, loosen the skin around the head, then gently draw it down toward the tail. Cut it off. Repeat on the other side of the fish.

Flat fish

Lay the fish, dark skin uppermost, on the board. Make a slit across the skin just above the tail. Slip the thumb into the slit and gently loosen the skin. Holding the fish firmly by the tail, pull the skin quickly toward the head (dip the fingers in a little salt to get a better grip). Cut the skin off. The white skin on the other side may be removed in the same way, but it is usually left on.

Filleting and boning

The fish can now be cut into serving portions. Fillets of both round and flat fish are popular, as they provide a solid piece of fish without any bones.

Round fish

To fillet a large fish, such as haddock, cut the head off the cleaned fish and then cut along the backbone, working toward the tail. Insert the knife blade at a slight angle to the bone and, keeping the sharp edge toward the tail, gently ease the flesh from the bone with slicing movements.

Continue cutting in line with the backbone until the whole fillet is freed and can be lifted off. With the tip of the knife, ease off the backbone to reveal the other fillet, and cut off the tail. If the fish is large, the fillets can be cut into serving portions.

Boning large round fish
(salmon and lake trout)

Using a sharp knife or scissors, cut the fins and gills off the cleaned fish. Wash the fish under cold running water to remove all traces of blood, then place it in a fish cooker and poach it in court bouillon (p.308).

Lift the poached fish onto a board, and with a sharp knife or scissors snip the skin just below the head and above the tail. Carefully peel off the skin, leaving head and tail intact. Snip the backbone below the head and above the tail. Then, with the blade of a sharp knife, split the fish along the backbone. Ease the bone out from the back without breaking the fish in two.

Boning small round fish

Smaller round fish, such as trout and mackerel, can be filleted as already described but are more often boned and cooked whole or with a stuffing.

To bone a cleaned mackerel, cut off the head, tail, and fins. Open out the split fish and spread it flat, skin side up. Press firmly along the center back of the fish to loosen the backbone, then turn the fish over. Starting at the head, ease away the backbone with the tip of a knife, removing at the same time as many of the small bones as possible. The fish can now be folded back into its original shape or cut with a sharp knife into 2 long fillets.

Steaks

Large round fish are often sold cut into thick steaks from the middle of the fish or from the tail end. These should be cleaned, but not skinned, before cooking. The small central bone is best removed after cooking. If it is removed before cooking, the center of the steak should be filled with a stuffing.

Filleting flat fish

A large sole or flounder will yield 4 small fillets, 2 from each side. Lay the fish, dark skin up, on the board and cut off the fins with a sharp knife. Make the first cut along the backbone, working from the head toward the tail. Then make a semicircular cut just below the head, through half the thickness of the fish. Slant the knife against the backbone, and with short, sharp strokes of the knife, separate the left fillet from the bone. Make a thick cut just above the tail and remove the fillet. Turn the fish around and remove the right fillet in the same way. Turn the fish over and remove the fillets on the other side.

COOKING METHODS

A number of basic cooking methods are suitable for all fish, whether they are whole, filleted, or cut into steaks. But whatever cooking method is chosen, fish should be cooked for a short time only. Prolonged cooking time toughens the flesh and destroys the flavor. The best and simplest rule to go by, worked out by the Canadian Department of Fisheries, is to measure the thickness of the fish at its thickest point (from underside to upperside) and give it 10 minutes cooking time per measured inch, whatever the cooking method. A whole salmon 4 inches thick in the center would take 40 minutes poaching; a $\frac{1}{2}$-inch-thick fillet, 5 minutes poaching or sautéing; and a 2-inch-thick swordfish steak, 10 minutes sautéing on each side. Double the cooking time if using fish that has been frozen.

Baking

This method is suitable for small whole fish and for individual cuts, such as fillets and steaks.

Brush the prepared fish with melted butter and season with lemon juice, salt, and freshly ground pepper. Make 3 or 4 diagonal score marks on each side of whole round fish so that they will keep their shape. Lay the fish in a well-buttered, shallow baking dish. Bake in the

SKINNING A ROUND FISH

Cutting skin from the backbone

Drawing skin toward the tail

SKINNING A FLAT FISH

Slitting skin above the tail

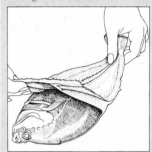

Drawing skin toward the head

CUTTING A ROUND FISH INTO TWO FILLETS

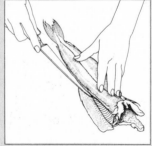

1 *Cutting along the backbone*

2 *Easing the flesh from the bone*

3 *Freeing the backbone*

4 *Cutting off the tail*

BONING A COOKED SALMON

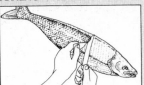

Peeling skin toward the tail

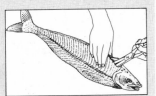

Snipping the backbone

Easing backbone from the fish

BONING A MACKEREL

Slitting fish along the belly

Pressing along the backbone

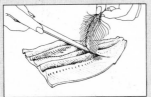

Easing away the backbone

REMOVING THE FOUR FILLETS FROM A FLAT FISH

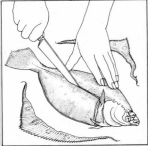

1 *Cutting down the backbone*

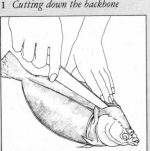

2 *Slitting just below the head*

3 *Separating fillet from the bone*

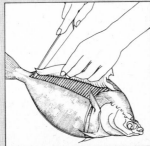

4 *Removing the fillet*

center of a preheated oven at 400°F, following the timing given under Cooking Methods.

During baking, baste* the fish frequently—this is particularly important with white fish. Or lay slices of bacon over the fish to provide basting during cooking.

Before baking, fish may be stuffed with a filling of fine bread crumbs seasoned with salt, pepper, herbs, or parsley and bound with a little melted butter. Spoon the filling loosely into the cavity, as it tends to swell during cooking. Close the opening on round fish securely with toothpicks.

For individual stuffed fillets, spread the mixture over the fillet, roll it up, and secure with toothpicks.

Baking can also be done in aluminum foil, which is excellent for sealing in flavor and aroma. It also cuts down on oven cleaning. Place the prepared fish on buttered foil and sprinkle with lemon juice, salt, and pepper. Wrap the foil loosely over the fish, place in a baking dish, and cook in the center of a preheated oven at 450°F.

Braising

Large fish, such as halibut and salmon, can be cooked by this method. Peel and finely chop 2 carrots, 1 onion, and 1 leek or parsnip. Sauté these vegetables in a little butter and spread them over the bottom of a large baking dish. Lay the prepared fish on top and sprinkle with salt and freshly ground pepper. Add a few sprigs of fresh herbs, such as parsley and thyme, or a bay leaf. Pour over enough fish stock or white wine to come just level with the fish.

Cover the dish and cook in the center of a preheated oven at 350°F until the fish flakes when tested with a fork. Lift out the fish carefully and strain the cooking liquid. This may be used as a sauce and can be thickened with egg yolks or cream, or by fast boiling until it has reduced* to the desired consistency.

Sautéing

This is one of the most popular cooking methods. It is suitable for steaks and fillets of cod, haddock, hake, and flounder, as well as for small whole fish such as sardines, mackerel, smelts, catfish, and trout. Coat the prepared fish in seasoned flour (p.412) or dip them first in lightly beaten egg, then in dry bread crumbs, shaking off any surplus. Heat an equal amount of butter and cooking oil in a skillet over moderate heat. Put in the fish and sauté until brown on one side; turn it over with a wide spatula. Allow approximately 10 minutes cooking time, depending on the thickness of the fish. Remove the fish from the pan and drain thoroughly on paper towels.

Deep-frying
(fillets, catfish, whitebait)

A deep pan, ideally one fitted with a wire frying basket, is essential. The frying medium is vegetable oil or vegetable fat. The deep-fryer should be no more than half-filled with oil and heated over moderate heat to 375°F. A cooking thermometer will give the accurate temperature; if a thermometer is not available, test by dropping a 1-inch cube of day-old bread in the oil. If the bread browns in 60 seconds, the oil has reached the correct temperature.

Because of the high temperature required for deep-frying, the fish must be coated with batter or egg and bread crumbs.

After frying fish, strain the fat or oil, using a fine mesh strainer. The food particles left in unstrained fat will cause the fat to decompose during storage. The strained oil should be stored in sealed bottles and used only for frying fish. The oil can be used again and again, provided it is always strained.

Coating Batter

PREPARATION TIME: *10 minutes*

INGREDIENTS:
1 cup flour
Salt
1 egg
½ cup milk, approximately

Sift the flour and a pinch of salt into a large mixing bowl. Make a hollow in the center of the flour and break the egg into it. Beat these ingredients thoroughly with a wooden spoon and gradually mix in the milk. Beat steadily until the batter is smooth and free of lumps.

For a lighter coating batter, which gives a crisper finish to the fried fish, add 1 tablespoon olive oil to the sifted flour and salt. Beat in the yolk of the egg and 3–4 tablespoons milk until the batter is smooth. Just before using the batter, beat the egg white until stiff and fold it into the batter. The prepared fish should first be dipped in seasoned flour (p.412), then in batter.

Egg and bread crumb coating

Roll the prepared fish in seasoned flour (p.412), then dip it in beaten egg. Coat with dry bread crumbs, pressing them in well and shaking off any surplus.

Before frying, check the temperature of the oil in the deep-fryer. Use the frying basket only for fish coated with egg and bread crumbs—batter-coated fish will stick to the basket. Fry only a few pieces at a time, as overcrowding the pan lowers the temperature of the oil and ruins the coating. Fry the fish for 5–10 minutes until the egg and bread crumb coating is crisp and golden.

Wait until the oil returns to the required temperature before frying another batch of fish; if the oil is not hot enough to form a crust, the fish will be grease-soaked.

As soon as the fish is fried, lift it out with a slotted spoon and leave to drain on paper towels.

Fish

Broiling

This quick cooking method is suitable for small whole fish, fillets, and steaks. Whole fish should be scored with 3 or 4 diagonal cuts of a sharp knife on each side of the body. This allows the heat to penetrate more evenly and prevents the fish from splitting while cooking.

Brush the fish with melted butter or oil and sprinkle them with lemon juice. Baste* several times during broiling to prevent the flesh from drying out.

Broil all fish under a preheated hot broiler. Put fish on a well-oiled rack or on oiled aluminum foil. The fish is cooked when the flesh separates easily into flakes when tested with a knife or fork.

During broiling, whole fish and thick steaks should be turned over once to ensure that both sides are evenly cooked. Thin fish steaks and fillets, however, need to be cooked on one side only.

Poaching

This is ideal for all types of fish, whether whole, filleted, or cut into steaks. Poaching—slow simmering in liquid—can be done in a large saucepan or fish cooker on top of the stove, or in a shallow covered dish in the oven at 350°F. For easy removal after poaching, tie a large fish loosely in cheesecloth or place it on a buttered wire rack.

Cover the fish completely with lightly salted water (1½ teaspoons salt to 5 cups of water). Add to the pan a few parsley or mushroom stalks, a good squeeze of lemon juice, a slice each of onion and carrot, together with a bay leaf and 6 peppercorns. For fish fillets, use a poaching liquid of equal amounts of milk and water, lightly seasoned with salt, freshly ground black pepper, and 1 bay leaf.

Bring the liquid to a boil over moderate heat, then cover the pan and lower the heat. Simmer the fish until it flakes when tested with a fork. Lift out the cooked fish with a large spatula and use the poaching liquid as the base for a sauce.

Whole fish, such as salmon, trout, and striped bass, are usually poached in a classic preparation of fish stock made with white wine and seasonings, known as court bouillon.

Court Bouillon

PREPARATION TIME: *10 minutes*
COOKING TIME: *20 minutes*

INGREDIENTS:
2 carrots
1 onion
2 stalks celery
2 shallots
1 bay leaf
3 parsley sprigs
2 sprigs thyme
2 tablespoons lemon juice
1 cup dry white wine
Salt and black pepper

Peel and finely chop the vegetables. Put them in a large saucepan with all the other ingredients and 4 cups of water. Bring to a boil, cover with a lid, and simmer over low heat for 15 minutes. Allow the court bouillon to cool slightly, then strain and pour it over the fish to be poached.

Salmon Mousse

PREPARATION TIME: *35 minutes*
COOKING TIME: *20 minutes*
CHILLING TIME: *3–4 hours*

INGREDIENTS (*for 6–8*):
1 pound fresh salmon
2½ cups hot court bouillon
1¼ cups cream, lightly whipped
4 tablespoons softened butter
½ cup dry sherry
2 tablespoons lemon juice
Salt and cayenne pepper
2 tablespoons gelatin

GARNISH: *Twists of cucumber and lemon*

Wipe the salmon with a damp cloth and put it in a buttered ovenproof dish; pour in the hot court bouillon. Cover with foil and poach in the oven at 350°F for 20 minutes. Let the salmon cool in the liquid, then remove skin and bones. Pound the salmon until smooth, then fold in the lightly whipped cream. (Alternatively, purée the salmon and cream in a blender until smooth.) Stir in the softened butter, the sherry, and lemon juice; blend thoroughly and season to taste with salt and a little cayenne pepper.

Measure 6 tablespoons of the hot court bouillon into the top half of a double boiler and sprinkle the gelatin on top. Set over simmering water until the gelatin has dissolved. Let the mixture cool slightly, then beat it into the mousse.

Spoon the mousse into a lightly oiled mold or 1-pound loaf pan; chill it in the refrigerator for 3–4 hours or overnight.

To serve, invert the mousse onto a serving dish and garnish with twists of cucumber and lemon.* Pipe* mayonnaise, colored green with a few drops of food coloring if desired, around the edges.

Steaming

Fillets and thin cuts of fish cooked in this manner are easily digestible and are ideal for invalids, older people, and young children.

Roll the fillets or lay them flat in a perforated steamer and sprinkle lightly with salt and freshly ground pepper. Set the steamer over a pan of boiling water and cook the fish for 10–15 minutes or until tender when tested with a fork.

If a steamer is not available, place the fish on a buttered deep plate. Cover with a piece of buttered waxed paper and another plate or a lid from a saucepan. Set the plate over a pan of boiling water, cover, and steam for about 15 minutes.

SHELLFISH

Small shellfish are served as hors d'oeuvres, and in soups and sauces. Large shellfish, such as crabs and lobsters, can be served either as a first or a main course.

All fresh shellfish must be boiled before being served. Oysters and clams, which are usually eaten raw, are the exception. Shellfish require little cooking time, and overboiling makes them tough and fibrous.

Most shellfish have indigestible or unwholesome parts, such as the beard of the mussel and the "dead men's fingers," or gills, under the shells of crabs and lobsters. These parts, as well as the stomach sac and the intestinal veins, must be removed during preparation.

Shellfish are often served with a wedge of lemon, with mayonnaise, or with a sharp sauce.

Clams

Clams are of two types: hard-shell and soft-shell. Hard-shell clams are usually served raw. Soft-shell clams are steamed. Allow 12 clams per person. Smoked and canned clams are also available.

Clam Fritters

PREPARATION TIME: *25 minutes*
COOKING TIME: *10 minutes*

INGREDIENTS (*for 6*):
2 cups sifted all-purpose flour
2 teaspoons baking powder
1 teaspoon salt
¼ teaspoon pepper
2 cups shucked raw hard-shell clams
Milk
Juice of ½ lemon
2 eggs, beaten
2 teaspoons grated onion
½ teaspoon Worcestershire sauce
1 tablespoon melted butter
Fat for deep-frying

Sift the flour, baking powder, salt, and freshly ground pepper together.

Chop the clams, drain, and save the liquid. Add enough milk to the clam liquid to make ¾ cup, then add the lemon juice, eggs, grated onion, and Worcestershire sauce. Stir in the flour mixture and beat well. Stir in the clams and butter.

Drop the mixture by tablespoons into deep, hot fat (375°F on a frying thermometer). Fry until crisp and golden brown.

Drain the fritters on crumpled paper towels and serve with tomato sauce (p.302), if desired.

Manhattan Clam Chowder

PREPARATION TIME: *15 minutes*
COOKING TIME: *1 hour 10 minutes*

INGREDIENTS (*for 6*):
2 dozen shucked raw hard-shell clams
4 slices bacon or salt pork, diced
1 cup sliced onions
½ cup diced celery
½ cup diced carrots
3 cups peeled, seeded, and chopped tomatoes or 3 cups drained, chopped canned tomatoes
3 cups water
½ teaspoon salt
¼ teaspoon pepper
½ teaspoon dried rosemary
3 cups peeled raw potatoes, cut into ¼-inch dice
1 tablespoon chopped parsley

Drain the clams and save the liquid. Chop the clams, discarding all the black parts, and set aside. Sauté the bacon or salt pork in a large saucepan until crisp. Pour off all but 2 tablespoons of the fat. Add the onions, celery, and carrots. Cook this mixture slowly for 5 minutes.

Add the reserved clam liquid, the tomatoes, water, salt, pepper, and rosemary. Simmer for 45 minutes.

Add the potatoes and simmer about 12 minutes more. Stir in the chopped clams and simmer 2–3 minutes longer. Season to taste with additional salt if necessary. Finely chopped parsley sprinkled over the chowder will add color and flavor.

Crabs

Crabs are often available cooked and prepared by the fish market. When buying a fresh crab, make certain that it has both claws and that it is heavy for its size. The edible parts of a crab are the meat in the claws and in the body shell. Allow 8–10 ounces prepared crab per person.

Wash the crab and put it in a large saucepan with plenty of cold water seasoned with 1 tablespoon lemon juice, a few parsley stalks, 1 bay leaf, a little salt, and a few peppercorns. Cover the pan with a lid and bring the water slowly to a boil. Cooking time is short—a 2½–3 pound crab about 8 inches across the body shell should be boiled for only 15–20 minutes. Let the crab cool in the cooking liquid. To remove the meat, place the cooked crab on a board and twist off the legs and the two large claws. Twist off the pincers and crack each claw open with a nutcracker, or by a sharp blow with a hammer or the handle of a heavy knife.

Empty the meat into a bowl and use a pick or sharp pointed knife to remove all the meat from the crevices in the claws. Set the small legs aside for decoration or, if they are large, crack them open with a hammer and extract the meat with a skewer.

Remove the back and the spongy parts under the crab's shell. Then remove the apron from the underside of the body.

Using a spoon, gently scrape the meat from the shell and put it in another bowl until required.

Cut the body in two and pick out the meat left in the leg sockets.

Crabmeat Casserole

PREPARATION TIME: *30 minutes*
COOKING TIME: *40 minutes*

INGREDIENTS (*for 6*):
1 pound cooked crabmeat
2 tablespoons butter
¼ cup finely chopped green pepper
¼ cup finely chopped onion
1 tablespoon flour
1 cup light cream or milk
1 egg
1 tablespoon sherry
1 teaspoon Dijon mustard
⅓ cup mayonnaise
Salt and pepper
TOPPING:
3-ounce package cream cheese
1 cup grated sharp Cheddar cheese
2 tablespoons butter
½ teaspoon Worcestershire sauce
1 tablespoon light cream or milk
1 egg

Remove all bits of shell from the crabmeat and set aside.

Heat the butter in a large skillet and sauté the green pepper and onion until soft, about 10 minutes. Add the flour and cook, stirring, for 1 minute. Stir in the cream or milk and then the crabmeat.

Beat the egg, sherry, mustard, and mayonnaise together. Combine with the crabmeat mixture. Season to taste with salt and pepper.

Spoon into a buttered 1½-quart casserole. Beat together all the ingredients for the topping and spoon over the crabmeat mixture.

Bake at 350° for 40 minutes. Let cool 10 minutes. Serve the casserole with a green salad.

Lobsters

Lobsters are often sold ready-cooked, but ideally they should be purchased alive. The shells turn bright red during cooking. A 1½-pound lobster will serve 1 person.

Rinse the lobster under cold running water. Grip it firmly from behind around the body and drop it into a large pan of boiling salted water. Cover with a lid and bring back to a boil. Simmer over low heat, allowing 5 minutes for a 1-pound lobster and 3 minutes for each additional pound.

Broiled lobster

To prepare a lobster for broiling, kill the lobster by inserting the point of a heavy knife between the head and the tail to sever the spinal cord. Turn the lobster over on its back and cut down through the entire length of the lobster, leaving the back shell intact. Spread the lobster open and remove the dark intestinal vein that runs down the center and take out the stomach, or sac, about 2 inches below the head. The green liver, or tomalley, and the coral, only in the female lobster, is edible and need not be removed. Crack the large claws with a hammer or mallet.

Place the lobster on a broiler pan, shell side down, and brush generously with melted butter. Broil 3 inches from the heat for 15–20 minutes, depending on size, and baste occasionally with melted butter. Serve the lobster with melted butter and lemon wedges.

Cold lobster

Twist the claws off the boiled lobster. Using a hammer or a lobster cracker, crack open the large and small claws and carefully extract the meat. Remove the thin membrane from the center of each large claw.

Place the lobster on a board, back upward, and split in half along its entire length with a sharp knife. Open out the two halves and remove the gills, the dark intestinal vein that runs down the tail, and the small stomach sac, about 2 inches long, that lies just below the head. The green creamy liver, or tomalley, in the head is a delicacy and should not be discarded. The coral, or roe, in a female lobster should also be kept; it is bright coral red. It is usually added to the accompanying sauce.

Extract the meat from the tail in one piece, and with a small lobster pick take out the meat from the feeler claws or set them aside for decoration. Wash and polish the empty half shells and put all the meat back in them. Garnish with the claws and serve with homemade mayonnaise (p.303).

Boiled lobster may also be served hot, in which case each person removes the meat himself.

DRESSING A COOKED LOBSTER

1 *Cracking open the claws*

2 *Splitting the lobster*

3 *Removing intestines*

INTESTINAL VEIN

GILLS

LIVER (TOMALLEY)

STOMACH SAC

4 *Cleaned half lobster*

5 *Half lobster ready to serve*

Fish

Mussels

Mussels must always be bought alive and absolutely fresh. As soon as possible, put them into a pail of cold salted water and throw away any mussels with open or broken shells. If time allows, add about ⅓ cup oatmeal or flour for every 2 quarts of water. Let the mussels soak an hour or more. The live mussels will feed on the oatmeal and excrete their dirt. Throw away any mussels that float to the surface.

Scrub the shells with a stiff brush to remove all grit. With a sharp knife, scrape away the beard, or seaweedlike strands protruding from each shell, and also scrape off the barnacles growing on the shells. Rinse the mussels in several changes of cold water to remove any grit that remains on the shells.

Put the cleaned mussels in a large, heavy-bottomed pan containing chopped parsley, shallots or onions, and ½ inch of water or white wine. Cover the pan with a lid and steam the mussels over low heat. As soon as the shells open, take the pan off the heat and, if desired, remove a half shell from each. Keep the mussels warm under a dry cloth and strain the cooking liquid through cheesecloth. Serve the mussels on a deep warmed platter with the liquid poured over them.

Oysters

Until the 19th century, oysters were everyday fare, but they are now expensive and something of a luxury. They are delicious served raw as an hors d'oeuvre; 6 oysters per person should be allowed.

Scrub the tightly closed shells with a stiff brush to remove all sand. Open the shells over a fine strainer set in a bowl to catch the oyster juice. Hold the oyster in one hand, with the deep shell in the palm, and insert the tip of an oyster knife, or a knife with a short strong blade, into the hinge. Twist the knife to pry the hinge open and cut the two muscles that lie above and below the oyster. Run the knife blade between the shells to open them, and discard the rounded shell. After opening the shell, cut away the oyster cleanly with a sharp knife.

Serve the oysters in their flat shells on a bed of cracked ice. They are traditionally garnished with lemon wedges and are often accompanied by a tomato-based cocktail sauce.

Shrimp

These shellfish are available all year round and are sold both raw and ready-cooked, and often shelled. Live shrimp are gray, pink, or brown but turn red during cooking. Drop the shrimp into a pan of boiling salted water, cover with a tight-fitting lid, and boil for 2–4 minutes, according to size.

To shell cooked shrimp, hold the fish between two fingers, then gently peel away the soft body shell and the small crawler claws.

These shellfish are served hot or cold, as an hors d'oeuvre or in seafood cocktails, salads, curries, soups, and sauces. The large, or jumbo, shrimp may be broiled or coated in batter or in beaten egg and bread crumbs and then deep-fried.

Shrimp in Coconut Cream

PREPARATION TIME: *1 hour*
COOKING TIME: *20 minutes*

INGREDIENTS (*for 4*):
1 fresh coconut or 1 package
 unsweetened shredded coconut
½ cup boiling water
2 large onions, finely chopped
3 tablespoons butter
1 teaspoon curry powder
1 medium green pepper, sliced
12 large cooked shrimp, shelled and
 deveined

First make the coconut cream: Punch holes in the eyes at the top of the coconut; drain and save the colorless liquid. Break open the coconut with a hammer. Remove the meat and the dark skin. Shred the coconut finely, or use the packaged coconut and pour in ½ cup of boiling water. Steep for 20 minutes, then squeeze through cheesecloth to produce the cream. Set aside 1¼ cups of the cream.

Sauté the onions over low heat in the butter until soft and pale golden. Add the curry powder and cook for a further 2–3 minutes. Add the pepper slices. Cover and simmer for 10 minutes. Add the shrimp, season with salt, and simmer for 1 more minute.

Keep the heat as low as possible. Stir in the coconut cream and simmer until shrimp and sauce are heated through. Do not let the sauce boil. Serve with plain boiled rice.

Scallops

Fresh bay scallops and the larger sea scallops are sold already cleaned and removed from their shells.

Put the scallops in a pan of cold water. Bring to a boil, remove any scum, and simmer the scallops for 5–10 minutes, being careful not to overcook them.

Scallops can also be baked, sautéed, deep-fried, broiled, or served in a cheese or mushroom sauce.

Scallops with Tomatoes and Paprika

PREPARATION TIME: *15 minutes*
COOKING TIME: *15 minutes*

INGREDIENTS (*for 2–3*):
1 cup finely chopped tomatoes
1 pound sea scallops
4 tablespoons butter
¼ cup white wine
1 teaspoon paprika
1 clove garlic, minced
½ teaspoon dried basil
Salt and pepper
3 tablespoons freshly grated
 Parmesan cheese

Cook the tomatoes until reduced* to about ½ cup; this should take about 10 minutes. Set aside.

Preheat the oven to 425°F. Wash the scallops in cold water to free them of all sand, and pat them dry with paper towels. Cut them into ½-inch crosswise slices.

Heat 2 tablespoons of the butter in a large skillet. Add the sliced scallops and sauté them for 2 minutes, tossing occasionally with a spatula. Add the wine, the cooked tomatoes, paprika, garlic, and basil. Bring to a simmer and cook 3 additional minutes. Season to taste with salt and freshly ground pepper.

Spoon the scallop mixture into a 1½-quart rectangular baking dish. Sprinkle the cheese over the top and dot with the remaining butter. Bake for 10 minutes.

Serve over boiled rice.

Scallops Seviche

PREPARATION TIME: *10 minutes*
MARINATING TIME: *3 hours*

INGREDIENTS (*for 4*):
½ pound bay scallops
Juice of 4 limes
2 tablespoons finely chopped onion
¼ teaspoon minced garlic
2 tablespoons finely chopped green
 chili peppers or green bell peppers
1 tablespoon chopped parsley
3 tablespoons olive oil
Salt and pepper

Place the scallops in a large bowl and cover them with the lime juice. Chill in the refrigerator 3 hours or more.

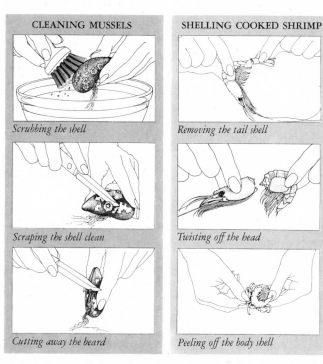

CLEANING MUSSELS

Scrubbing the shell

Scraping the shell clean

Cutting away the beard

SHELLING COOKED SHRIMP

Removing the tail shell

Twisting off the head

Peeling off the body shell

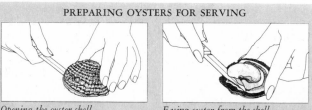

PREPARING OYSTERS FOR SERVING

Opening the oyster shell

Easing oyster from the shell

Drain well in a colander. Add remaining ingredients except salt and pepper and toss well. Season to taste with salt and pepper.

Serve as a first course or as a main course for a summer lunch.

SMOKED AND PRESERVED FISH

A small group of fish is preserved or cured by salting, brining, or smoking. There are two methods of smoking—cold and hot. Cold-smoked fish require cooking, but hot-smoked fish are ready for the table because they have been cooked during smoking.

Cod, smoked
Cold-smoked; poach, bake, or broil as for smoked haddock.

Cod roe, smoked
Ready to eat; serve as an hors d'oeuvre or first course on lettuce leaves with lemon wedges and crisp fingers of toast.

Eel, smoked
Hot-smoked; available whole or in fillets to serve as an hors d'oeuvre.

Haddock, smoked
Cold-smoked. Poach* fillets on top of the stove in a pan of milk or milk and water, allowing 8 minutes per pound. Alternatively, put the haddock in a buttered baking dish, dot with butter, and add a few tablespoons of milk. Cover the dish and bake in the center of a preheated oven at 350°F for about 15 minutes. Smoked haddock is also suitable for broiling.

Herrings, smoked
These include bucklings and kippers. Bucklings are hot-smoked and ready to eat. Serve as an hors d'oeuvre, with a sharp sauce.

Kippers can be bought with the bone in, or filleted and packed in vacuum-sealed bags ready for cooking. Cook kippers under a hot broiler for 5 minutes. Cook vacuum-packed fillets according to the instructions on the package.

Herrings, salted
These include rollmops and Bismarck herrings. Both are boned herring fillets preserved in spiced vinegar. Rollmops are rolled around a stuffing of onions, gherkins, and peppercorns. Bismarck herrings are flat fillets. Both are ready for serving as an appetizer.

Mackerel, smoked
Hot-smoked, ready for serving. Use for hors d'oeuvres or as a main course with a light sour cream dressing and new potatoes.

Sablefish, smoked
Known on the West Coast as black cod, this is usually steamed and served with drawn butter.

Salmon, smoked
Hot-smoked, ready to eat. Serve in very thin slices, with lemon wedges. Lox is a less expensive but saltier type of smoked salmon.

Sturgeon, smoked
Hot-smoked, ready to eat. This very delicate fish should be sliced very thin and served as an hors d'oeuvre.

Trout, smoked
Hot-smoked and ready for serving cold as a first or a main course. Either sharp or mild horseradish, sour cream, or whipped cream sauce may be served with filleted smoked trout.

Whitefish, smoked
Hot-smoked, ready to eat. This tender, light-textured fish is usually sold whole except for larger fish, which are sold in pieces. It should be skinned and filleted, and is usually served as an hors d'oeuvre.

Meat

Meat is the most popular food in the North American diet. The average Canadian eats 160 pounds of meat a year, of which beef represents about 95 pounds. Next comes pork, then veal and lamb.

Meat will keep for 2–3 days in the refrigerator. Remove the wrapping paper as soon as possible after purchase. Place the meat on a clean plate, wrap it loosely in plastic wrap, and, leaving the ends open to allow the air to circulate, store in the refrigerator.

Ground meat and variety meats do not keep well and should preferably be used on the day of purchase. Once meat has been cooked, it should be cooled as quickly as possible before storing. For a detailed guide to cuts of meat, see pages 32–40.

COOKING METHODS

There are no set rules for cooking meat, as each cut lends itself to preparation, cooking, and presentation in several different ways. In general, however, the tender cuts are roasted or broiled, while the tougher cuts are more suitable for pot-roasting, boiling, braising, and stewing.

Roasting
This is the traditional method for cooking large pieces of meat. It can be done in several ways, oven-roasting being the most common, and again there are two methods. With quick-roasting, the meat is cooked at a high temperature that quickly seals in the juices, thus preserving the full flavor. At the same time, however, the meat shrinks.

Slow-roasting is done at a lower oven temperature over a long period. This method of cooking reduces shrinkage of the meat and usually produces a roast that is tenderer than quick-roasted meat.

Whichever roasting method is used, the meat must first be weighed, and the cooking time calculated. Place the meat, fat side up, on a wire rack in a shallow roasting pan. Rub a lean roast with butter, vegetable oil, or olive oil. Do not add water to the roasting pan and do not cover pan.

Place the pan in the center of the oven. During roasting, the melting fat bastes* the meat; if there is little fat, spoon the pan juices over the meat occasionally.

Roasting times and temperatures
The size and shape of a roast and the way in which it has been prepared influence cooking times. Large roasts require less roasting time per pound than small ones, and roasts on the bone cook more quickly than boned ones because bones are a conductor of heat. A roast with the bone in is thought to have a better flavor than a boned roast.

Rolled roasts with a wide diameter take less cooking time than roasts with a narrow diameter, although they may weigh the same. Roasts that weigh less than 3 pounds should always be slow-roasted for at least 1½ hours. Smaller roasts are unsatisfactory for oven roasting, as they shrink and dry out.

Meat thermometer
A meat thermometer, which registers the internal temperature of meat, is useful for assessing roasting times. Before cooking, insert the thermometer into the thickest part of the meat, but make certain that it does not touch bone or fat. When the thermometer registers the required internal temperature, the roast will be cooked. This type of thermometer is particularly useful for cooking beef when wider margins of doneness are dictated by personal preference. A new, improved meat thermometer, more accurate than the kind that can be used in the oven, is inserted in the meat near the end of the roasting time and gives a fast temperature reading. As it registers from 0° to 220°F, the thermometer can also be used to determine the internal temperature before the meat is put in the oven.

Spit-roasting
This traditional roasting method has been revived by the invention of the electric rotisserie. This device is attached to a grill or built into an oven and consists of a horizontal revolving shaft or spit strong enough to hold large roasts, whole game or poultry, and kebabs.

For even roasting, the roast must have a uniform shape. Rolled and stuffed roasts must be tied firmly or skewered to keep their shape.

Thread the meat on the spit so that the weight is evenly distributed. Place on the rotisserie and operate it according to the manufacturer's instructions. While the meat revolves, it is basted with its own juices and cooks evenly.

Foil-roasting
Roasting in foil is becoming increasingly popular, mainly because it saves the oven from being spattered with the roasting juices. Wrap the meat loosely in foil, sealing the edges firmly; basting is unnecessary, but remove the foil for the last 20–30 minutes of cooking to brown the meat. Foil wrapping is particularly recommended for slightly tough cuts, as the moist heat tenderizes the meat. The meat, however, steams rather than roasts and will have a

different flavor and texture than meat roasted by dry heat. At the same time, aluminum foil deflects heat, and the oven temperature should therefore be raised.

Pot-roasting and braising

These allied methods are particularly suitable for smaller and slightly tougher cuts, such as brisket, round, chuck, and rump of beef. Melt enough fat to cover the bottom of a deep, heavy-bottomed pan, put in the meat, and brown it over moderately high heat. This should take about 15 minutes. Do not rush this procedure; the browner the meat, the richer the sauce will be. Lift out the meat, put a bed of chopped root vegetables, such as carrots and onions, in the bottom of the pan. Replace the meat and add 1 cup liquid (beef stock, red wine, water, or tomato juice).

Cover the pan with a tight-fitting lid and cook over low heat until the meat is tender; allow 25–30 minutes per pound. Turn the meat often.

Alternatively, put the browned meat in a deep baking dish, cover it tightly, and cook in the center of a preheated oven at 325°F, using the same timing. Lift out the cooked meat. Drain off the fat and use the juices for gravy or sauce.

To braise, coat the meat with seasoned flour (p.412) and brown it evenly in hot fat. Put the meat on a bed of diced, lightly sautéed root vegetables in a casserole or heavy pan. Pour in enough water or stock and tomato purée to cover the vegetables; add herbs and seasonings.

Cover the casserole with a tight-fitting lid and cook on the stove or in the center of a preheated oven at 325°F until tender, about 2–3 hours. Add more liquid if necessary.

ROASTING TIMES FOR MEAT

Cut	Weight in Pounds	Oven Temperature	Meat Thermometer Temperature	Approximate Minutes Per Pound
BEEF				
Rib	6–8	300°–325°F	140°F (rare)	23–25
			160°F (medium)	27–30
			170°F (well)	32–35
	4–6	300°–325°F	140°F (rare)	26–32
			160°F (medium)	34–38
			170°F (well)	40–42
Rolled rib	5–7	300°–325°F	140°F (rare)	32
			160°F (medium)	38
			170°F (well)	48
Rib eye	4–6	350°F	140°F (rare)	18–20
			160°F (medium)	20–22
			170°F (well)	22–24
Boneless rolled rump (high quality)	4–6	300°–325°F	150°–170°F	25–30
Sirloin tip	3½–4	300°–325°F	140°–170°F	35–40
	4–6	300°–325°F	140°–170°F	30–35
VEAL				
Leg	5–8	300°–325°F	170°F	25–35
Loin	4–6	300°–325°F	170°F	30–35
Boneless shoulder	4–6	300°–325°F	170°F	40–45
LAMB				
Leg	5–8	300°–325°F	165°F (well)	20–25
Shoulder	4–6	300°–325°F	165°F (well)	20–25
Boneless	3–5	300°–325°F	165°F (well)	30–35
Cushion	3–5	300°–325°F	165°F (well)	20–25
PORK, FRESH				
Loin				
Center	3–5	300°–325°F	170°F	30–35
Half	5–7	300°–325°F	170°F	35–40
Crown	4–6	300°–325°F	170°F	35–40
Shoulder arm (picnic) roast				
Bone in	5–8	300°–325°F	170°F	30–35
Rolled	3–5	300°–325°F	170°F	35–40
Shoulder butt	4–6	300°–325°F	170°F	40–45
Leg (fresh ham)				
Whole (bone in)	12–16	300°–325°F	170°F	22–26
Boneless top	10–14	300°–325°F	170°F	24–28
Half (bone in)	5–8	300°–325°F	170°F	35–40
Tenderloin	½–1	300°–325°F	170°F	45–60
PORK, SMOKED				
Ham (cook-before-eating)				
Whole	10–14	300°–325°F	160°F	18–20
Half	5–7	300°–325°F	160°F	22–25
Shank or loin portion	3–4	300°–325°F	160°F	35–40
Ham (fully cooked)*				
Half	5–7	300°–325°F	140°F	18–24
Shoulder arm (picnic) roast (fully cooked)	5–8	300°–325°F	140°F	25–30

*Allow approximately 15 minutes per pound for fully cooked whole hams
Adapted from PORK © 1975 Canadian Pork Council and from the U.S. National Livestock and Meat Board chart

Stewing

This long slow-cooking method is suitable for the tougher cuts of meat. Cut the meat into 1½–2 inch cubes, coat them evenly in seasoned flour (p.412), and brown them quickly in very hot fat.

Lift the meat onto a plate and sauté a few sliced carrots and onions in the fat until golden. Sprinkle in 1–2 tablespoons of flour, or enough to absorb all the fat; sauté until the mixture is pale brown. Stir in enough warm stock to give a pouring consistency. Season with salt, pepper, and herbs and bring the sauce to a boil.

Put the meat in a casserole, pour in the sauce and vegetables, and cover with a tight-fitting lid. Simmer the stew on top of the stove or in an oven at 325°F until tender, about 1½–3 hours.

Boiling

Suitable for tough cuts of beef, tongue, and corned beef. Bring a pan of water, in which the meat will fit snugly, to a boil. Use just enough water to barely cover the meat. The greater the volume of water, the less flavorful the meat will be. Add salt (2 teaspoons to each pound of meat), a bouquet garni (p.410), a large onion studded with cloves, and the meat. Bring the contents of the pan to a boil, remove any scum from the surface with a spoon, then cover the pan with a tight-fitting lid and lower the heat.

Simmer the meat over very low heat until tender. Add a selection of chopped root vegetables to the pan for the last 45 minutes of cooking if the meat is to be served hot. For cold boiled meat, let the meat cool in the cooking liquid. Drain the meat thoroughly before serving.

Corned beef should be placed in cold water and brought quickly to a boil. Drain the meat and proceed as already described. A very salty piece should be soaked in water for several hours before being boiled.

Broiling

This quick-cooking method is suitable for small tender cuts of meat, such as steaks and chops, and for sausages, liver, kidneys, and ham steaks.

Brush drier meats with oil or melted butter. On pork chops, snip the outer layer of fat or rind at 1-inch intervals to prevent curling and shrinkage during broiling.

Grease the broiler rack with oil or butter to prevent the meat from sticking. Put the meat on the rack and set it under a preheated broiler. Turn the meat once only during broiling and baste with the pan juices if the meat begins to dry out.

Pan-broiling and frying

Pan-broiling is another quick-cooking method for the same types of meat as suggested for broiling.

Melt just enough butter or oil to cover the bottom of a skillet (drippings may be used for beef). Heat the butter quickly. Put the meat in the pan and cook it over moderately high heat, turning once only. For thicker cuts, lower the heat after the meat has browned and continue cooking until tender.

Lift out and drain the meat and keep it warm while making the gravy. Pour the fat from the pan and stir a little stock or wine into the pan juices. Bring to a boil, correct seasoning, and pour the gravy into a warm sauceboat.

Bacon needs little or no extra fat for frying. Arrange the slices so that the lean parts overlap the fat in a cool pan, then fry over moderate heat, turning once, until the slices are brown and crisp.

Sausages are often pricked with a fork before frying to prevent the skins from bursting. This is unnecessary if they are fried over low heat for 20 minutes.

BEEF

Allow ¾–1 pound of beef per person from a roast on the bone, and ½–¾ pound per person from boned cuts. For average portions, allow an 8-ounce steak per person.

Roasting

The best beef cuts for roasting include sirloin, rib roasts, and whole fillet. Rump, too, may be slow-roasted, but it is usually more suitable for pot-roasting.

Sirloin and rib roasts are sold on the bone or as rolled roasts. Boning and rolling can also be done at home without a lot of trouble.

Boning and rolling (sirloin)

Lay the meat, bones down, on a steady board. Using a sharp, broad knife, cut the meat across the grain at the thick bone at the top of the meat (chine bone). Insert the knife at the top where the meat has been loosened and move it downward in sawing movements, following the bones carefully, until the meat comes away from the bones in one piece. Use the bones for stock or a soup.

Lay the boned meat on the board, skin side up, and roll it tightly from the thickest end. Tie it securely with a piece of string to hold its shape. Cut 2-inch strips of pork fat and tie them, slightly overlapping, around the meat. A wider strip of fat may be tied with string over the top of the rolled sirloin to provide extra fat during roasting.

Larding (fillet)

A whole piece of fillet is an excellent, if expensive, cut for roasting. As it has no fat, this must be added in some form to prevent the meat from drying out during roasting. First trim any skin or sinews from the fillet, then cut salt pork into strips narrow enough to be threaded through the eye of a larding needle. Thread short lengths of the fat about

---

BONING AND ROLLING SIRLOIN

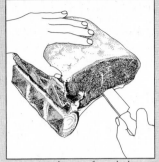

1 *Severing the meat from the bone*

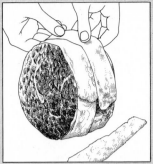

3 *Laying pork fat around the roast*

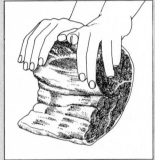

2 *Rolling up the boned meat*

4 *Rolled roast with fat tied on top*

½ inch deep at intervals on all four sides of the fillet.

Alternatively, wrap thin bacon slices, slightly overlapping, around the fillet and secure with thin string in several places along the fillet. (Bacon also adds extra flavor.) Fillet should be quick-roasted until the internal temperature reaches 125°F.

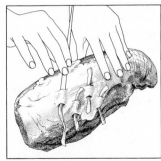

Lard beef fillet by threading short lengths of fat through the meat.

Pot-roasting and braising

Flank, brisket point, top round, rump, chuck, and bottom round are the best cuts for pot-roasting or braising; to cook these cuts, follow directions given under Meat.

Boiling

Plate, brisket point, and short ribs are ideal for slow simmering with vegetables. Plate and brisket point can often be bought corned.

Salting or pickling (plate, brisket point)

Put 1 gallon cold water with 1½ pounds salt, 1 ounce saltpeter, and ¾ cup brown sugar in a large pan. Bring to a boil and boil for 20 minutes. Strain the liquid through cheesecloth into a large earthenware bowl and allow liquid to cool. Put the meat in the liquid and keep it submerged by covering it with a

---

weighted plate. Leave the meat in the salting liquid for 5–10 days, depending on thickness. Soak in cold water for about 1 hour before boiling.

Broiling and pan-broiling

These cooking methods are suitable for all steaks—fillet, sirloin, rump, porterhouse, and T-bone. Follow the general directions. Fillet steak is also used for the classic Russian dish, Beef Stroganoff.

Beef Stroganoff

PREPARATION TIME: *10 minutes*
COOKING TIME: *25 minutes*

INGREDIENTS (*for 4–6*):
1¼–1½ *pounds fillet steak*
1 *onion*
¼ *pound mushrooms*
4 *tablespoons unsalted butter*
1 *tablespoon tomato purée*
1–1½ *tablespoons flour*
¼ *cup sour cream*
Salt and black pepper
Lemon juice

Trim the steak. Beat it flat between two sheets of waxed paper and cut it into narrow short strips. Peel and finely chop the onion and trim and slice the mushrooms.* Heat 2 tablespoons of the butter and sauté the vegetables over low heat until soft and just beginning to color. Stir in the tomato purée and enough flour to absorb the fat. Continue cooking over very low heat for 2–3 minutes, then carefully blend in the sour cream. Do not boil, or the sour cream will curdle.

Heat the remaining butter in a second pan and sauté the meat over high heat until brown all over; blend it into the sauce. Season to taste with salt, freshly ground pepper, and lemon juice. Serve immediately with fluffy boiled rice and green beans.

Stewing

This slow-cooking method is ideal for all the tougher cuts of beef, such as hip, chuck and shank. Stews are ideal for winter meals, they store

---

well in the freezer, and many people consider them best if cooked a day in advance. A precooked stew, however, must be heated through thoroughly before being served.

The Hungarian stews, or *gulyas*, are internationally famous and differ from the average stew in their sweet and spicy flavor. They are ideally made from chuck steak, but lean boned shoulder of lamb or pork may also be used for variety.

VEAL

The flavor of veal is delicate, and the flesh tends to be dry unless carefully cooked. It does not keep well and should be used on the day of purchase. Allow ½–¾ pound per person of veal on the bone and about ⅓–½ pound per person of boneless veal.

Roasting

This method is suitable for large cuts, such as shoulder, rump, leg, and the double loin, or saddle. The shoulder is often boned and stuffed. As the meat is fairly dry, it must be basted* frequently. Boned breast is the most economical veal cut. It is ideal for stuffing—allow 1 pound of stuffing to a 6-pound breast. Use the slow-roasting method rather than the quick-roasting one.

Pot-roasting and braising

Boned and rolled shoulder of veal can be pot-roasted or braised. Stuffed breast of veal is also recommended for braising.

Boiling and stewing

Veal sold for stews usually comes from the shoulder, breast, shank, and the neck. These contain a large amount of bone. If bought on the bone, allow at least ⅓ pound per serving; allow ¼ pound if boneless. Round, rump, and sirloin can be used, but these cuts tend to be dry after they are cooked.

Broiling and sautéing

Chops from the loin or rib of veal are suitable for sautéing and braising. Broiling, however, is usually less successful, since the meat has a tendency to dry out and toughen when cooked this way.

For sautéing, the most popular and most widely available veal cuts are scallops—thin slices, usually cut from the top of the leg.

Veal scallops should be thinned and tenderized by pounding before they are cooked. Purchase ¼-inch-thick slices from the butcher. Place them between sheets of waxed paper and beat them flat with a meat pounder or rolling pin until they are no less than ⅛ inch thick. Before cooking, dip the scallops in beaten egg, then coat them with fresh white bread crumbs. Sauté in a little hot butter and oil for 5 minutes, turning once. Garnish with lemon slices and chopped parsley.

PREPARING VEAL SCALLOPS

Placing scallop between paper

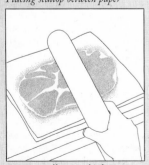

Beating scallop out thinly

LAMB

Lamb is a rather fatty meat, and the fat that rises to the surface from stewed, boiled, or braised lamb should be skimmed off.

Allow ½–¾ pound of lamb on the bone per person and ¼–½ pound of boned lamb per serving.

Roasting

The double loin, or saddle, with the kidneys attached, can be roasted whole and makes an attractive dish.

Whole leg and shoulder of lamb are among the most popular cuts. They are usually sold on the bone but can also be purchased boned for stuffing and rolling. Give the butcher 1–2 days notice.

Rack of lamb, from the rib section, is one of the most popular roasts, quick-cooking and small enough to serve 2–3 people. Two racks can be sewn together for the classic crown roast.

Roast Leg of Lamb

PREPARATION TIME: *5 minutes*
COOKING TIME: *1 hour 40 minutes*

INGREDIENTS (*for 8*):
1 clove garlic, finely chopped
1 teaspoon dried basil
1 teaspoon salt
½ teaspoon pepper
4 tablespoons Dijon mustard
2 tablespoons soft butter
5-pound leg of lamb
1 cup beef broth

Mix the garlic, basil, salt, pepper, mustard, and butter, and brush over the lamb. Leave the lamb at room temperature for 2 hours.

Roast at 325°F until medium rare (15–20 minutes per pound).

Remove the meat to a platter. Place the pan over direct heat; add the beef broth and scrape up all the brown bits on the bottom of the pan. Bring to a boil. Cook for a moment, skim off the fat, and strain the sauce into a sauceboat.

Crown roast

Many butchers will prepare a crown roast if given a few days notice, but if this is not possible, buy two matching racks of lamb, each containing 7–8 rib chops.

Trim as much fat as possible from the thick part of each rack, and with a sharp knife cut the top 1½–2 inch layer of meat from the thin end of the bones. Scrape off all fat and meat to leave the bone ends clean. When both pieces of meat have been prepared, sew them together with a trussing needle and fine string, using the thick ends of the meat as the base of the crown.

Slit the lower half of the formed crown between each bone, about 1–2 inches up from the base and, if necessary, tie a piece of string around the middle. Wrap foil around the ends of the scraped bones to protect them during the roasting. Fill the cavity of the crown with a stuffing of vegetables, rice, or chestnuts before or after roasting.

Butchers who sell prepared crown roasts often put the trimmings into the hollow crown. These should be removed before stuffing and roasting. (They can be saved and used later for stock.)

To carve a crown roast, remove the foil from the bones. Pierce one side of the meat with a fork to steady it. Then, with a knife held in the other hand, slice down between the ribs, removing one rib at a time to a dinner plate. Depending on its consistency, the stuffing in the center of the crown can either be removed with a spoon or carved and served with the meat.

Guard of honor

This is also prepared from two racks, but the bones are trimmed clean for about 2½–3 inches. The two pieces of meat are then joined and sewn together, skin side up, along the bottom meaty part of the joints. Fold the meat together, skin outside, so that the cleaned bones meet and

PREPARING A CROWN ROAST

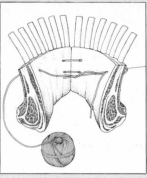

1 Trimming meat from bones

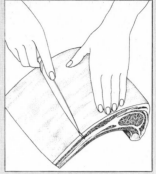

2 Scraping bone ends clean

3 Sewing prepared racks together

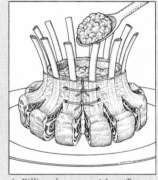

4 Filling the crown with stuffing

crisscross on top. Cover these with foil to prevent them from discoloring while cooking. Fill the cavity with a savory stuffing, such as bread crumbs and herbs, and tie the roast at intervals to keep its shape during slow-roasting.

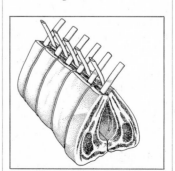

Join together two racks of lamb to make a guard of honor.

Braising

The best cuts for braising are the shoulder, breast, and shank. The shoulder or breast can be boned and rolled, but make sure to trim most of the fat off.

Stewing and boiling

Breast of lamb, shoulder, and neck are the best and most economical cuts for stews and casseroles. As they are all fatty, they should be trimmed of as much fat as possible before being cooked.

Broiling and pan-broiling

Lamb rib chops, which have a high proportion of bone, may be broiled or pan-broiled. Chops from the loin are meatier than rib chops. Shoulder chops are less expensive and also less

BONING AND ROLLING RACK OF LAMB

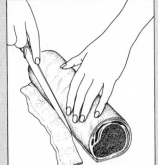

1 *Easing out rib bones*

3 *Trimming off excess fat*

2 *Rolling up the boned rack*

4 *Cutting meat into noisettes*

tender, but can be very tasty when pan-broiled. Noisettes are neatly trimmed round slices taken from the rack. Cut off the thick chine bone at the thick end of the rack and trim away all excess fat from the meat. Using a sharp pointed knife, cut along either side of each rib bone and ease it out. Roll up the boned rack lengthwise and tie it with fine string at ½-inch intervals. Cut the rolled rack into 2-inch-thick slices and sauté or broil for about 6 minutes on each side.

PORK

A good-quality pork roast should have a moderate amount of fat—lean pork is generally lacking in flavor, and fatty pork is wasteful. Allow ½–¾ pound of pork on the bone or ⅓–½ pound of boned meat per serving.

Pork must be thoroughly cooked to be digestible, and underdone pork can be dangerous because of disease-producing organisms in the meat. It was formerly recommended that pork be cooked to an internal temperature of 185°F; research has now proved that pork is safe at a temperature of 170°F.

Roasting
The pork cuts considered most suitable for roasting, on or off the bone, are the leg, the loin, and the more

reasonably priced pork shoulder.

Leg and loin are often boned, stuffed, and rolled before roasting; shoulder of pork, which is an awkward cut to carve because of the position of the bone, should also be boned and rolled.

Pork Loin Stuffed with Prunes
A prune stuffing, plus marinating in red wine, make this pork roast a particularly attractive and unusual main course for a dinner party.

MARINATING TIME: *24 hours*
PREPARATION TIME: *30 minutes*
COOKING TIME: *2½ hours*

INGREDIENTS (*for 6*):
1 box pitted prunes
¼ cup cognac
5–6 pounds pork loin roast
2 large yellow onions, sliced
2 stalks celery, sliced
2 carrots, sliced
5 bay leaves
8 peppercorns
2–3 cups dry red wine
⅓ cup butter
2 tablespoons flour
1 cup cream
Salt and pepper

Soak the prunes in the cognac for 24 hours, turning them occasionally. Ask the butcher to bone the roast but save the bones. Roast the bones in the same pan with the loin; they make a tasty leftover for the cook. They can also be used for making soup or stock.

With a larding needle or a knife, make a small hole the entire length of the meat (or ask the butcher to do this). Stuff the hole with the prunes, pushing them in with the handle of a wooden spoon. Tie the roast securely with string in several places. Put the meat in a deep bowl and add the onions, celery, carrots, bay leaves, peppercorns, and the wine.

Marinate the meat in this mixture for 24 hours if possible. Drain, dry with paper towels, and brown the

roast on all sides in butter. Put it on a rack in a roasting pan, baste well with the strained marinade, and roast in a preheated 450°F oven for 15 minutes. Reduce the heat to 350°F and cook until the roast is done, about 2 hours, basting from time to time with the marinade.

Make a gravy to accompany the roast by skimming the fat from the pan juices; add about 2 tablespoons of flour to the remaining juices. Then pour in the cream and cook, stirring constantly with a wire whisk or wooden spoon, over low heat until thickened. Season to taste with salt and pepper. Let the roast stand for 15 minutes before carving. Serve the gravy separately.

Sautéing and broiling
Pork chops are better sautéed than broiled, as the lean meat has a tendency to dry out and toughen while cooking. Large pork loin chops often have a thick strip of fat around the outer edge, which tends to curl during cooking. To prevent this, snip the fat with scissors or make cuts with a sharp knife at 1-inch intervals.

Pork spareribs, which are cut from the lower rib section of the belly, are usually roasted or broiled and are excellent when barbecued outdoors over charcoal.

Slices of lean pork tenderloin may be sautéed, but the whole tenderloin or fillet of pork is usually cooked by roasting or broiling.

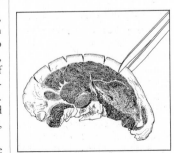

Snipping the fatty edge of a loin chop to prevent it from curling

HAM
Hams are sold whole, halved, or cut into thick slices. They are suitable for all cooking methods—boiling, baking, broiling, braising, and sautéing.

Cooking methods
Whole hams, unless they are the tenderized and ready-to-bake type, should be soaked in cold water to remove excess salt. They are then boiled or parboiled before being roasted, braised, or baked.

Put the ham in a large pan, cover with cold water, and bring slowly to a boil. Cover the pan with a lid and reduce the heat so that the meat is cooked at a slow simmer. Fast boiling hardens the tissue and causes shrinkage of the meat. Cook for 20 minutes per pound.

Lift out the ham, allow it to cool and set slightly, then peel off the skin with the fingers.

To roast or bake a ham, place in a roasting pan, fat side up, and brush with a glaze. Then wrap the ham in foil and bake in the center of a preheated oven at 300°F for 45 minutes–1 hour until well glazed and heated through.

If desired, score a diamond pattern in the exposed fat, insert whole cloves in the intersections, and pat brown sugar over the top of the ham to glaze it. Return the ham to the oven and roast at 425°F for the last 30 minutes. Honey can be used for glazing instead of brown sugar.

Aged and country-style hams are sold with cooking instructions printed on the package that vary according to the curing methods. Follow the manufacturer's instructions carefully.

Country-style ham
To prepare a country-style ham, soak the ham in cold water to cover for 24–36 hours. Drain. If mold remains, scrub well with a vegetable brush and a mild unscented soap. Rinse thoroughly, making sure that

no trace of soap residue remains on the meat.

Place the ham in a large pot of simmering water to cover. Simmer over low heat, allowing 25-30 minutes per pound. Take the ham from the pot. Remove the skin from the ham while it is still warm.

If desired, score the fat with a sharp knife, making diagonal cuts about ⅛ inch deep and 1 inch apart across the fat. Repeat the cuts at an angle to make diamonds or squares. Stud each intersection with a clove, or glaze with the following:

Mix 1 cup light brown sugar with 2 teaspoons dry or Dijon mustard and ½ teaspoon ground cloves. Add some of the rendered fat from the cooking liquid to make a stiff paste and brush this evenly over the ham.

Bake the ham at 425°F for 30 minutes. Serve it hot or cold, cut into very thin slices.

PREPARING HAM

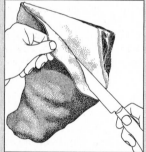

Skinning a ham

Studding the fat with cloves

VARIETY MEATS

Some of the internal organs of beef, veal, lamb, and pork are edible. These organs include the hearts, kidneys, livers, brains, tongues, and sweetbreads. Also classed as variety meats are beef and veal marrow bones, oxtail, and pig's head and feet, as well as pork sausages and blood pudding. These meats are rich in vitamins, minerals, and proteins. They are easily digestible, and, in some cases, priced low.

Brains

Veal, lamb, and pork brains may all be prepared and cooked in the same manner. Soak the brains in lightly salted cold water to remove all traces of blood. Remove the thin covering membrane. Put the brains in a pan of well-flavored stock, bring to a boil, and simmer over low heat for about 20 minutes. Drain thoroughly, then allow the brains to cool and press them under a weight.

Cut the cold brains into ½-inch slices, coat them in beaten egg and bread crumbs, and sauté in butter until golden brown. Alternatively, coat the slices in batter (p.307) and deep-fry them. Garnish with lemon slices and parsley. Allow 2 sets of brains per person.

Hearts

Beef, veal, and lamb hearts are particularly nutritious. They are usually stuffed and pot-roasted, braised, or stewed. Beef heart, however, because it is very tough and muscular, is better chopped and slow-cooked in casseroles. Veal and lamb hearts are tenderer and have a more delicate flavor. Allow 1 heart per person.

Rinse off all the blood under cold running water and snip out the stumps from the arteries and the tendons with scissors. Stuff the hearts with an onion or bread stuffing and sew up the opening. Pot-roast or braise the hearts for 1½-2 hours or until tender.

STUFFING A HEART

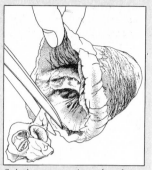

Snipping out arteries and tendons

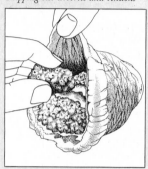

Stuffing the heart

Kidneys

Beef kidneys have a strong flavor and are used, chopped, for braising or in pies. Veal, lamb, and pork kidneys are all suitable for broiling and sautéing, although pork kidneys are less tender than calf and lamb. Allow 2-3 kidneys per person.

Any kidney fat and the thin transparent skin surrounding the kidneys must be peeled off. Cut the kidneys in half lengthwise and snip out the central cores.

Brush the kidneys with melted butter, sprinkle with salt and freshly ground black pepper, and broil or sauté them for not more than 6 minutes, turning them once only.

Fat from beef kidneys is sold as suet and, after rendering down, is suitable for deep-frying. Suet is also used in recipes for a number of pastries and puddings, and in such meat dishes as chili con carne.

TRIMMING KIDNEYS

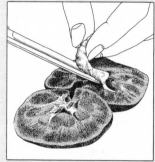

Removing kidney membranes

Snipping away the core

Livers

Beef liver, which is slightly coarse and tough, should be soaked for at least 1 hour in cold water to remove excess blood and improve the flavor. It is best braised, although it can be sautéed like veal, lamb, and pork liver.

Cut beef liver into ¼-inch slices, coat with seasoned flour (p.412), and brown in butter, together with thinly sliced onion and a few slices of bacon. Put the liver slices in a casserole, with the onion and bacon; cover with brown or white stock or tomato sauce. Put the lid on the dish and cook in the center of a preheated oven at 350°F for 45 minutes or until the liver is tender.

For broiling and sautéing, veal or lamb liver is preferable. Cut off any gristly portions and remove any central cores with a knife or scissors. Wash and dry the liver thoroughly,

PREPARING LIVER

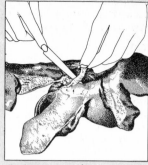

Cutting away gristle

Cutting into slices

then cut into ¼-inch-thick slices. Brush the liver slices well with melted butter and sprinkle with salt and freshly ground black pepper before broiling them.

Alternatively, coat the slices in seasoned flour (p.412) and sauté in butter over gentle heat. Avoid overcooking liver, as this toughens it—as soon as blood begins to run, turn over the slices and cook the other side for a shorter time.

Pork liver, which has a stronger flavor, may be prepared and cooked in the same way as veal and lamb liver. It is also used as an ingredient in pâtés, stews, and casseroles.

Liver Baked in Red Wine

PREPARATION TIME: *30 minutes*
COOKING TIME: *45 minutes*

INGREDIENTS (*for 6*):
6 ½-inch slices beef or veal liver
Seasoned flour (p.412)
½ cup chopped onion
3 tablespoons butter
1 cup beef consommé (p.299)
1 cup red wine
½ teaspoon dried thyme
2 tablespoons flour
Salt

Be sure to remove the skin from the liver. Dust the liver thoroughly with seasoned flour and sauté, with the onion, in the butter until the liver is light brown.

Arrange the liver slices in a large baking dish. The slices may overlap. Combine the consommé with the wine and thyme and pour over the liver. Cover with foil and bake at 350°F for 45 minutes.

Pour the liquid from the baking dish into a saucepan. Mix 2 tablespoons of flour with 3 tablespoons cold water and stir into the liquid. Simmer and stir 2-3 minutes until the sauce has thickened. Taste, and season with salt if necessary. Pour the sauce over the liver.

Serve with mashed potatoes (p.333) and a green salad.

Sweetbreads

Veal and lamb sweetbreads are prepared in the same way. One pair of sweetbreads will serve 2 people. First, soak the sweetbreads in cold water for 1-2 hours to remove all blood. Then drain well and cover again with cold water.

Bring to a boil and drain off the liquid immediately; cover the sweetbreads with cold salted water and bring them to a boil again over low heat. As soon as boiling point is reached, lift out the sweetbreads and rinse under cold running water. Remove the black veins that run through the sweetbreads and as much as possible of the thin membranes that cover them.

Put the sweetbreads in a pan, barely cover with white stock, and add a tablespoon of butter and a squeeze of lemon juice. Bring to a boil, cover the pan with a lid, and simmer gently for 15-20 minutes. Leave the sweetbreads to cool in the liquid, then drain. Coat with seasoned flour, beaten egg, and bread crumbs and sauté in butter until golden brown. Serve with a creamy sauce and sautéed mushrooms. Sweetbreads can also be used as a filling for vol-au-vents.

Tongues

Beef tongue is the largest, weighing 4-6 pounds. It can be purchased pickled, smoked, canned, or fresh and is cooked whole. Soak a pickled tongue overnight in cold water, drain, and put in a large pan. Cover with cold water, bring to a boil, then drain thoroughly. Return the tongue to the pan, cover with fresh cold water, and add 6 peppercorns, 1 bouquet garni (p.410), and a sliced onion. Bring to a boil, cover with a lid, and simmer for 2-3 hours or until tender. (Cook a fresh tongue for 5-6 hours.)

Plunge the cooked tongue into cold water, then peel off the skin by slitting it on the underside, starting from the tip end. Remove bones and gristle from the root end and trim the tongue neatly.

Lamb tongues are much smaller, weighing only about 8 ounces each.

Peel the skin away from a cooked tongue, starting at the tip.

Soak them for 1-2 hours in lightly salted water. Boil the tongues, with 1 sliced onion, 1 bouquet garni, a few peppercorns, and enough water to cover, for about 2 hours. Peel the tongues and serve them hot. Alternatively, slice and serve cold.

Tripe

There are three kinds of tripe—honeycomb, pocket, and smooth. Honeycomb is the most widely available. This is sold blanched and partly cooked. Fresh, ready-to-cook tripe needs only 2 hours of cooking time.

Tripe Lyonnaise

PREPARATION TIME: *10 minutes*
COOKING TIME: *about 2¼ hours*

INGREDIENTS (*for 4*):
1 pound ready-to-cook honeycomb tripe
4 tablespoons unsalted butter
2 medium onions, thinly sliced
2 tablespoons white wine vinegar
Salt and black pepper
2 teaspoons chopped parsley

Wash the tripe in cold water. Put in a saucepan with water to cover, bring to a boil, reduce heat, cover, and simmer for 2 hours or until tender.

Drain the tripe, pat dry with paper towels, and cut into strips ½-1 inch wide. Melt 2 tablespoons butter in a skillet and sauté the onions until lightly browned.

Heat the remaining butter in a second skillet and gently sauté the tripe strips until golden brown.

Combine the onions and tripe and cook together for 10 minutes, tossing constantly. Add the vinegar to the pan, season to taste with salt and pepper, and sprinkle with the parsley. Serve with mashed potatoes.

Marrow bones

The marrow contained in the large beef thigh bones and shoulder bones is considered a delicacy. Have the bones sawn into manageable lengths; scrape and wash them before sealing the ends with a flour-

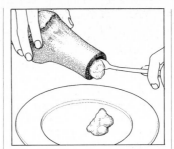

Scoop cooked marrow from the bone, using a small pointed teaspoon.

and-water paste. Tie each bone in a piece of cheesecloth and simmer gently in a court bouillon (p.308) for 1½-2 hours. Drain, then extract the marrow with a pointed teaspoon and spread on toast.

Veal bones

The bones of young calves contain a large quantity of gelatin, which sets to jelly after boiling. Calf's head and feet are ideal for jellied stocks; they are scarce, however, and pig's feet, which also contain gelatin, may be used instead.

Oxtail

This is sold skinned and cut into approximately 2-inch pieces and is ideal for rich stews. As oxtail has a high percentage of fat and bone, allow 1 oxtail for 3-4 servings.

PREPARATION TIME: *25 minutes*
COOKING TIME: *3-3½ hours*

INGREDIENTS (*for 4*):
1 oxtail, about 2 pounds
¼ cup seasoned flour (p.412)
4 tablespoons beef drippings or oil
2 onions
½ pound carrots
2 stalks celery
1½ cups brown stock
Bouquet garni (p.410)

Trim as much fat as possible from the pieces of oxtail and toss them in seasoned flour. Heat the fat in a heavy-bottomed pan and brown the oxtail over high heat. Lift out the oxtail and put in a casserole. Sauté the sliced onions, carrots, and celery in the fat until lightly browned, sprinkle in the remaining seasoned flour, and cook until it has absorbed all the fat. Stir in the stock gradually, then pour this sauce over the oxtail. Add the bouquet garni, cover the casserole tightly with a lid, and cook on a shelf low in the oven at 300°F for about 3 hours or until tender. Add more stock during cooking if the oxtail is drying out.

Pig's head

This is often used for making head cheese. It must be soaked for at least 24 hours in cold salted water before being boiled. Calf's head, too, makes an excellent head cheese but is now rarely obtainable except from specialty butchers.

Sausages

Pork sausages are easily made at home. They consist of equal amounts of lean minced meat and fat, seasoned with salt, pepper, and herbs. This mixture is stuffed into the blanched intestines (obtainable from some butchers) with the aid of a sausage funnel attached to a meat grinder. Twist the filled intestines every 3-4 inches.

Blood pudding

Blood pudding is made from seasoned pig's blood and suet stuffed into blanched pig intestines and slowly poached before being marketed. Sauté blood pudding in hot butter and serve with apple purée and mashed potatoes.

Pig's feet

Pig's feet cooked in liquid can be served hot or cold or used to produce jellied stock.

Carving Meat

Boned and rolled roasts of beef, pork, lamb, and veal generally present no real carving problems, since the bones have already been removed by the butcher. But for many people, carving meat with the bone in can be a perplexing and messy task. Carving is made considerably easier when the carver knows the positions of the bones in the roasts.

When carving, it is essential to use a good sharp knife and a two-pronged carving fork with a thumb guard. With this equipment, the carver can produce neat slices that leave the unused portion of the roast looking neat enough to serve cold at a later time. Most meats—whether beef, pork, lamb, or veal—should be carved across the grain because this makes it tenderer. Beef blade roasts and rib roasts should be sliced thin; whole hams, rump and shank halves of ham, shoulder arm (picnic) roasts, pork roasts, and veal roasts should be sliced slightly thicker than beef. A leg of lamb should be cut fairly thick; it can be carved with the grain into horizontal slices, but the slices should be cut thin to ensure tenderness.

LEG OF LAMB

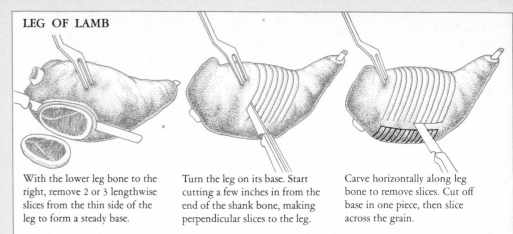

With the lower leg bone to the right, remove 2 or 3 lengthwise slices from the thin side of the leg to form a steady base.

Turn the leg on its base. Start cutting a few inches in from the end of the shank bone, making perpendicular slices to the leg.

Carve horizontally along leg bone to remove slices. Cut off base in one piece, then slice across the grain.

BEEF RIB ROAST

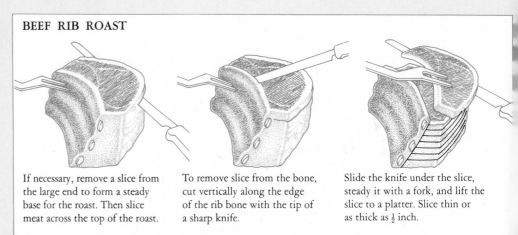

If necessary, remove a slice from the large end to form a steady base for the roast. Then slice meat across the top of the roast.

To remove slice from the bone, cut vertically along the edge of the rib bone with the tip of a sharp knife.

Slide the knife under the slice, steady it with a fork, and lift the slice to a platter. Slice thin or as thick as ½ inch.

PORK LOIN ROAST

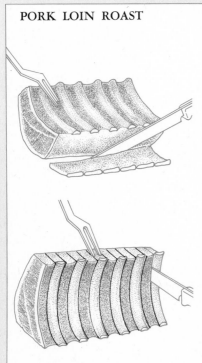

If the backbone has not been removed by the butcher, cut it off before bringing the roast to the table: Insert a fork between the rib bones. Insert the tip of a knife between the backbone and the meat and cut away the backbone, leaving as little meat on the bone as possible.

Place the meat on a platter on its broad end, with the curved rib side facing the carver. Slice vertically between each rib, allowing 1 chop per serving. To make thinner slices, cut as close as possible along each side of the rib bone. One slice will be boneless; the next will contain the rib bone.

BEEF BLADE ROAST

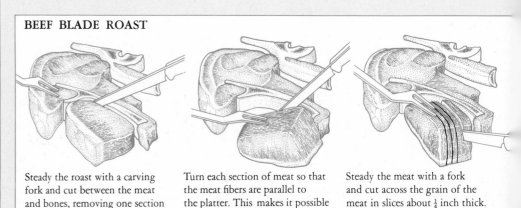

Steady the roast with a carving fork and cut between the meat and bones, removing one section of the roast at a time.

Turn each section of meat so that the meat fibers are parallel to the platter. This makes it possible to carve against the grain.

Steady the meat with a fork and cut across the grain of the meat in slices about ¼ inch thick. Lift onto a platter.

WHOLE HAM

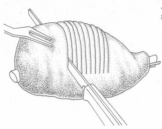

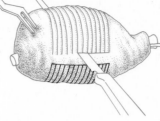

Place ham fat side up, shank end to the right. Remove the first 2 or 3 slices from the thin side of the ham to form a base.

Turn ham on base. Cut thin, perpendicular slices to the leg bone, or lift off in one piece and slice as for shoulder arm (picnic) roast.

Remove all slices by cutting along leg bone. If more meat is needed, remove the base in one piece, then cut across the grain.

SHANK HALF OF HAM

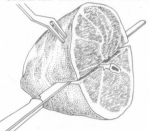

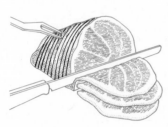

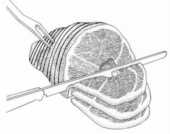

Place the shank end at the left; turn the ham so that the thickest portion is up. Steady shank with a fork and cut along the bone.

Place the section just removed, with the freshly cut side down, on a carving board and make thin, vertical slices.

To slice the lower part, remove the bone with the tip of the knife, turn the thickest part down, and slice as for upper portion.

LOIN HALF OF HAM

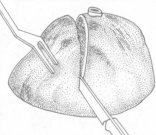

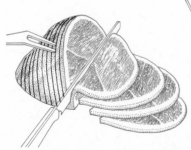

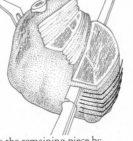

Place ham, cut side down, on a platter. Cut down the length of the interior bone and remove the boneless piece.

Place the boneless piece, with the freshly cut side down, on another platter. Carve into thin slices across the grain.

Carve the remaining piece by cutting horizontal slices to the bone. Remove each slice from the bone with tip of knife.

SHOULDER ARM (PICNIC) ROAST

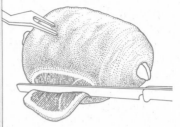

Carving is the same for a roasted smoked picnic and a roasted fresh picnic. First, remove a few lengthwise slices from the smaller side of the shoulder to form a steady base.

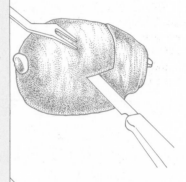

Turn the roast on its base. Starting on the left side of the elbow point, cut down to the arm bone, turn the knife, and cut along the bone to remove the upper portion of the shoulder.

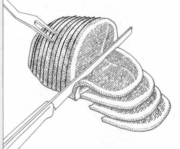

Steady this portion with a carving fork and cut the boneless portion into thin perpendicular slices, slicing across the grain of the meat with a very sharp knife.

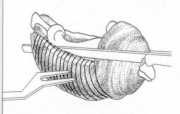

Remove the remaining meat of the shoulder from both sides of the arm bone and cut it into thin perpendicular slices across the grain, as for the upper portion.

319

Poultry and Game

As with many foods that were once seasonal, poultry and game are now available all year because of the widespread use of freezing. Even so, freshly killed poultry is superior in taste to frozen birds, and game is at its best when it is in season, which generally lasts from early fall through the winter.

PREPARATION OF POULTRY

Most poultry is sold ready for cooking—that is, hung, plucked, drawn, and trussed. Oven-ready frozen poultry must be thawed slowly before cooking. It should be left in its wrapping and placed in a refrigerator for 24–48 hours, according to size, to thaw. It should never be thawed in hot or warm water.

Fresh poultry that is not sold ready for cooking must be prepared in the following way:

Hanging

After killing, poultry should be hung head downward in a cool, airy place. The length of time each bird is hung depends on the weather and the age of the bird. Chickens should be hung for about 24 hours, geese and ducks for 1–2 days, turkeys for 3–5 days. Older birds should be hung a few days longer.

Plucking

Pluck the feathers before hanging and just after killing because they are most easily removed while the bird is still warm. Hold the bird firmly on a large sheet of butcher's paper and begin plucking at the top of the breast. Take out two or three feathers at a time, pulling them down toward the head.

After plucking, singe the remaining down and hairs from the bird with a lighted taper, wipe the bird with a clean cloth, and remove any remaining quills with tweezers.

Drawing

Lay the bird on its back and cut off the head, leaving about 3 inches of neck. Slit the skin along the underside of the neck and loosen it; pull the skin toward the body. Cut or twist off the neck close to the body; remove the crop, windpipe, and any fat present.

Put the fingers of the right hand into the neck opening, palm downward. Keeping the fingers high under the breastbone, dislodge the entrails gently but do not attempt to remove them.

Using a knife, make a slit at the vent end, and with the left hand pull out the entrails and any excess fat. Cut the gall bladder away from the liver and set the heart, liver, gizzard, and neck aside for stock or gravy.

Wipe the bird thoroughly, inside and out, first with a damp cloth and then with half a lemon.

Make a slit in the skin around the knee joint at the base of each drumstick to expose the four or five tendons. Using a skewer, pull out one tendon at a time, leaving them attached to the foot. Bend the shank backward until the skin is taut, then twist the bone to dislocate it. Cut off the foot and discard it.

Stuffing

After drawing, poultry is trussed ready for cooking, but it is usually stuffed first. A stuffing improves the flavor and appearance of poultry, and it also makes the meat go further.

Stuffings are based on bread crumbs made from day-old bread,

meat, and rice to which melted butter is added, together with herbs and seasonings. Because a stuffing expands during cooking, it is necessary to stuff the bird loosely; a basic 2-cup stuffing or forcemeat mixture is enough for a 3½-pound chicken.

Basic Forcemeat Stuffing

PREPARATION TIME: *15 minutes*

INGREDIENTS:
2 cups fresh white bread crumbs
2 tablespoons butter, melted
1 small onion
Salt and black pepper
1 egg
Stock or water

Put the bread crumbs in a bowl and stir in the melted butter. Peel and finely chop the onion and blend into the bread crumbs. Season with salt and pepper. Beat the egg lightly and mix into the bread crumbs. Add enough stock or water to give a moist but firm consistency.

Using a small spoon, fill the cavity of the bird with the stuffing. Chicken, duck, and goose are stuffed from the vent end. Turkey is sometimes stuffed from the neck end as well as from the vent end.

The basic stuffing can be mixed with 2 tablespoons finely chopped parsley or 1 teaspoon chopped sage.

Celery stuffing

Chop 3 celery stalks finely and sauté them in a little butter for a few minutes. Stir the celery into the basic stuffing. This mixture may be flavored further by adding about ¾ cup finely chopped dried apricots.

Apple stuffing

Chop 2 medium cooking apples finely. For the butter in the basic stuffing, substitute 1 tablespoon bacon fat or 1 slice finely chopped bacon, then blend in the apples.

PLUCKING POULTRY AND GAME

1 Begin plucking at the breast.

2 Singe off hairs with lighted taper.

DRAWING POULTRY

1 Pull neck skin toward the body.

5 Pull out entrails and fat.

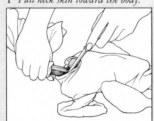
2 Cut off neck close to the body.

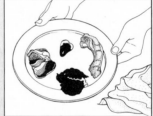
6 Set the giblets aside.

3 Dislodge entrails by hand.

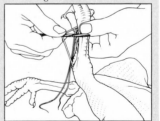
7 Pull out leg tendons.

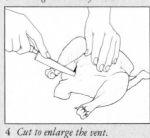
4 Cut to enlarge the vent.

8 Twist and break the bone.

Mushroom stuffing

Trim and chop 4 ounces of fresh, firm white mushrooms* and sauté them in the melted butter for the basic stuffing. Mix the mushrooms with the bread crumbs, onion, egg, and seasonings.

Rice stuffing

Melt 2 tablespoons of butter and lightly sauté 1 small finely chopped onion until transparent. Add ½ cup long grain rice and sauté with the onion for 2–3 minutes. Season with salt and freshly ground black pepper, and pour 1 cup stock or water over the rice. Bring the mixture to a boil, then cover the pan with a tight-fitting lid. Cook over low heat until all the liquid has been absorbed and the rice grains are tender.

Sausage stuffing

A meaty stuffing helps to keep the flesh of a large bird moist. Make up the basic stuffing and mix it with ½ pound sausage meat. Alternatively, melt 2–4 tablespoons of butter and lightly sauté 1 finely chopped onion and 1 pound of sausage meat for 2–3 minutes. Turn the mixture into a bowl and add ½ cup white bread crumbs, salt and pepper to taste, and 1 beaten egg and water to bind. Allow the mixture to cool before stuffing the bird.

Trussing

Once stuffed, the bird should be trussed so that it will keep its shape during cooking. Trussed poultry also looks more attractive when it reaches the table. To tie up a bird, use a trussing needle that has an eye large enough to take a piece of fine string. If a trussing needle is not available, use poultry skewers and string to secure the bird.

Using a trussing needle

Place the chicken on a board, breast down. Fold the loose neck skin over the back, closing the neck opening. Fold the wing tips over the body so

TRUSSING POULTRY WITH A NEEDLE

1 Fold loose neck skin over back.

2 Fold wing tips to hold neck skin.

3 Slit the skin above the vent.

4 Push tail through slit.

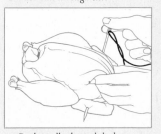

5 Push needle through body.

6 Insert needle in first joint.

7 Tie string securely on wings.

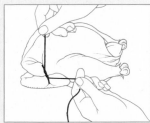

8 Truss through right side of tail.

9 Loop string around legs.

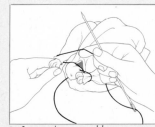

10 Pull legs closely together.

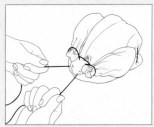

TRUSSING WITH A SKEWER

Insert skewer below thighs.

Cross string over back of bird.

Loop string around drumsticks.

as to hold the neck skin in position. Turn the chicken breast side up.

Make a slit in the skin above the opening at the vent of the body and put the tail through this.

Thread the trussing needle with string. Insert the needle through the second joint of the right wing; push it through the body and out through the corresponding joint on the left side. Insert the needle through the first joint, where the wing is attached to the body, on the left side. Pass the needle through the body again and out through the corresponding joint on the right side. Tie the ends of the string securely.

To truss the legs, press them close to the body; thread the needle again and pass it through the right side of the tail. Loop the string first around the right leg and then around the left leg. Pass the needle through the left side of the tail, pull the string tightly to draw legs together. Tie the ends.

Trussing with a skewer

Fold the neck skin and wing tips over the back of the bird as already explained, and pull the tail through the slit above the vent.

Lay the bird on its back and, pushing the legs up toward the neck, insert a poultry skewer just below the thigh bone. Push the skewer all the way through the body so that it comes out below the thigh bone on the other side.

Turn the bird on its breast. Pass a piece of string over the wing tips and beneath and up over the ends of the skewer. Cross the string over the back of the bird.

Turn the bird onto its back again, loop the string around the drumsticks and tail, then tie the ends of the string securely.

Barding

After trussing, the bird is ready for cooking. If it is to be roasted, the lean breast flesh should be protected to prevent it from drying out. This is known as barding and consists of covering the breast with bacon.

Barding is not necessary for duck or goose. However, chicken, turkey, and game birds have drier flesh and benefit from barding.

During cooking, the fat from the bacon melts and bastes the flesh, thus keeping it moist. The bacon also adds extra flavor to the poultry. About 20 minutes before the end of cooking time, remove the crisp bacon slices from the breast and return the bird to the oven so that the breast will brown.

Cover the breast with bacon and secure with string.

Poultry and Game

Disjointing

A chicken or duck can be cooked whole or cut into serving pieces. A small bird can be halved by placing it, back down, on a board and cutting lengthwise down and through the breastbone and then through the backbone. Use a very sharp knife.

Each half of the bird can also be divided into two. Tuck the blade of the knife underneath the leg joint and slice the leg away from the wing portion, holding the knife at an angle of 45 degrees.

To disjoint a chicken, pull the chicken leg away from the body and slice down to where the thigh joins the carcass. Break the joint and cut the whole leg away with a knife. The leg can be divided into the drumstick and thigh. Next, cut down through the wing joint, severing the wing from the body. Cut along the natural break in the rib cage to separate the top of the breast from the lower carcass. Pry open until the back cracks. Leave the breast in 1 piece or cut into 2 or 3 pieces. The remaining carcass can be frozen and used at a later time for making stock.

Boning

For a classic galantine of chicken, the bird must be boned whole. Lay the drawn bird on its breast on a board and remove the wings at the second joint. The feet and first joint of the legs should have been removed when the bird was drawn.

Using a small sharp knife, make a cut down the center of the back, starting at the neck end. Cut the flesh away from the rib cage down to the wing joints. Sever the sinews where the wings join the carcass.

Holding the exposed wing bone in one hand, scrape the flesh away along the wing bone. Cut off the sinews at the end of the bone and pull the bone from the flesh. The flesh has now been pulled inside out. Repeat with the other wing.

Cut along and down the carcass until the leg joint is reached. Sever the sinews between the ball-and-socket joint. Pulling at the end of the leg bone with one hand, scrape along the bone until the next joint in the leg is reached. Sever the sinews around this joint and pull the bone from the flesh, scraping down with the knife. The legs are also turned inside out as the bone is pulled away. Repeat with the other leg, then continue working down either side of the breastbone, being careful not to puncture the skin. Finally, work the flesh away from the tip of the breastbone and remove the carcass.

COOKING METHODS

Roasting is the most popular method of cooking whole chicken, duck, goose, guinea hen, and turkey. With the exception of duck and goose, which are fatty birds, all poultry should be barded or generously brushed with butter or oil before roasting.

Poaching and steaming are suitable methods for cooking older birds and poultry parts. The cooked flesh is mainly used in other dishes, such as fricassees. Braising and casseroling are ideal, though slow, ways to cook older birds or poultry parts.

Broiling or sautéing is reserved for split small and young birds, and for cooking chicken parts.

CHICKEN

Poaching

Rub the surface of a whole chicken with lemon juice to preserve the color, and place it in a pan. Add a bouquet garni (p.410), a peeled carrot and onion, and enough water to just cover the bird. For every pound of poultry add ½ teaspoon salt. Bring the water to a boil and remove any scum from the surface. Reduce the heat to a gentle simmer, then cover with a lid and cook until the bird is tender, about 1–3 hours, depending on age and tenderness. Chicken parts need only 15–20 minutes. Lift the chicken from the pan and serve hot, with a Béchamel sauce, or cold. Use the cooking liquid to make sauce or as the basis for a soup.

Braising and casseroling

Lightly sauté a whole bird or parts in a little butter until golden. Remove the bird from the pan and sauté about 1 pound of cleaned, coarsely chopped vegetables, such as carrots, onions, celery, and turnips, in the butter. Replace the poultry on the bed of vegetables and cover the pan tightly with a lid. Cook over low heat on top of the stove or in a 325°F oven until tender. Braising is a slow process, taking up to 2 hours, but cooking time depends on the size and age of the bird.

For a chicken casserole, sauté the parts in butter until golden, then put them in a flameproof casserole. Pour stock, wine, or a mixture of both over the bottom of the dish to a depth of 1 inch. Add salt and pepper, chopped herbs, or a bouquet garni, and cover the dish with a lid. Cook as for braising, on top of the stove or

---

DISJOINTING A CHICKEN OR DUCK

1 Cut off legs.

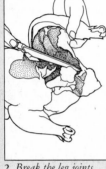

2 Break the leg joints.

3 Slice toward wing joint.

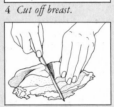

4 Cut off breast.

5 Cut breast in half.

BONING A CHICKEN OR SMALL GAME BIRD

1 Remove wing at second joint.

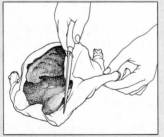

2 Sever sinews at wing joint.

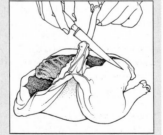

3 Scrape flesh along wing bone.

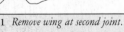
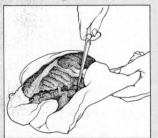

4 Cut through leg joint.

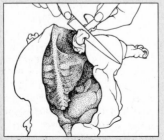

5 Sever sinews at leg joint.

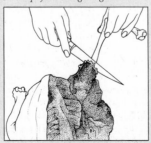

6 Turn leg inside out.

in the oven, for 1–1½ hours or until tender. A selection of lightly sautéed vegetables, such as small white onions, mushrooms, baby carrots, and small new potatoes, may be added halfway through cooking.

Broiling and sautéing

Tiny squab chickens and small broilers are excellent for broiling. One average bird (about 1½ pounds) will serve 2 persons. To prepare a whole bird for broiling, place it on its breast, cut through the backbone, and open the bird out. Flatten the bird with a meat pounder, breaking the joints where necessary.

Brush the bird all over with melted butter and season lightly with salt and freshly ground black pepper. Cook the bird on the broiler pan under moderate heat for 20–30 minutes, turning it frequently.

Before frying chicken parts, coat them with seasoned flour (p.412) or with beaten egg and bread crumbs. For sautéing, brown the chicken pieces quickly in hot fat, then lower the heat, cover, and cook gently until the meat is tender, about 20 minutes. For deep-frying, heat the oil to 375°F and cook the coated chicken pieces for 10–15 minutes or until tender and crisp on the outside.

Roasting

A roasting chicken weighing 3½–4 pounds will serve 3–4 persons. Place the barded or well-buttered chicken on a rack on its side in a roasting pan in the center of an oven preheated to 375°F. Allow 20 minutes on each side plus 20 minutes on its back. Baste well. A chicken weighing 4–6 pounds will give 4–6 servings. It should be roasted at 325°F, allowing 25 minutes on each side plus 25 minutes on the back. A capon with an average weight of 6–8 pounds provides 8–10 portions; it should be roasted at 325°F.

Alternatively, loosely wrap the chicken in foil and roast at 400°–425°F, allowing 20 minutes per pound plus an extra 20 minutes. Open the foil 20 minutes before cooking is complete to allow the bird to brown. Use a skewer to test the bird for doneness. Insert the skewer through the thickest part of the thigh; if clear juices run out, the bird is cooked.

Stuffed Chicken East Indian Style

PREPARATION TIME: *30 minutes*
COOKING TIME: *35–40 minutes*

INGREDIENTS (*for 6*):
2 small roasting chickens
Salt
2 medium onions, finely chopped
½ cup clarified butter (p.337)
1 teaspoon ground cardamom
1 teaspoon black peppercorns
¼ pound chicken livers, chopped
¾ cup fresh white bread crumbs
Vegetable oil

Wipe the chickens thoroughly and rub them inside with salt. Sauté the onions gently in 3 tablespoons butter until soft. Add the cardamom and ground peppercorns; reduce the heat and continue cooking the onions 6–7 minutes. Add the chopped chicken livers and cook until brown. Season with salt.

Simmer the mixture for 7–8 minutes, then remove from the heat and stir in the bread crumbs. Stuff the chickens with this spicy filling. Brush them with oil and arrange the chicken on a rack in the roasting pan. Roast the chickens in the center of a preheated oven at 400°F for 35–40 minutes, basting with the remaining butter.

Steaming

Place the trussed but unstuffed chicken on a wire rack over a deep pot of boiling water. Cover chicken with foil and steam for 3–4 hours, adding more water when necessary. Let the chicken cool. Remove the skin from the cooked chicken and use the flesh in low-calorie diets or in various recipes.

Galantine of Chicken

PREPARATION TIME: *1½–2 hours*
COOKING TIME: *1½ hours*

INGREDIENTS (*for 6*):
1 chicken, approximately 4 pounds
½ pound minced veal
½ pound minced lean pork
1 small onion, finely chopped
Salt and black pepper
Mixed herbs (p.411)
Juice and rind of 1 lemon
¼ pound mushrooms, finely chopped
1 egg, beaten
Chicken stock (p.298)
¼ pound lean ham, cut into ½-inch strips
8 olives, pitted

Clean and bone the chicken as directed. Make a stock with the carcass, bones, and giblets.

For the stuffing, finely chop the chicken liver. Put the veal and pork in a bowl, mix in the onion and chicken liver, and season to taste with salt, pepper, and mixed herbs (p.411). Add the lemon juice and rind, and mushrooms. Stir the beaten egg into the stuffing, with enough chicken stock to moisten.

Lay the chicken on a board, skin side down, and spread over it half the stuffing to within ½ inch of the edges. Top with the ham and the olives. Cover with the remaining stuffing. Draw the long sides of the chicken over the stuffing and sew it together with string.

Wrap the chicken in a double layer of cheesecloth and tie the ends securely. Tie 1 or 2 pieces of string around the chicken to keep it in shape. Put it in a large pan and cover with stock. Cover the pan and simmer for about 1½ hours.

When done, lift out the chicken and press it between two plates with a heavy weight on top. Leave until nearly cold, then remove the string and cheesecloth and return the chicken to press until cold.

Remove the thread from the cold galantine, then decorate and serve it as chicken chaud-froid (p.120).

Roast boned chicken

Proceed as for galantine of chicken but do not tie the stuffed chicken in cheesecloth. Instead, place it with the sewn seam downward in a greased roasting pan; brush the top generously with melted butter or oil and sprinkle with salt and pepper.

Cover the chicken with buttered waxed paper and roast in the center of a preheated oven at 400°F for 1¼–1½ hours. Remove the paper after 1 hour to allow the skin to brown.

Serve the boned chicken hot or cold, cut into slices.

Coq au Vin

PREPARATION TIME: *40 minutes*
COOKING TIME: *about 1¼ hours*

INGREDIENTS (*for 4*):
1 3–3½ pound chicken
Bouquet garni (p.410)
Salt and black pepper
1½ cups chicken broth
¼ pound lean salt pork or bacon
2 tablespoons brandy
1½ cups Burgundy or other red wine
4 small white onions, peeled
¼ pound button mushrooms, sliced
1 large clove garlic, peeled
Beurre manié (p.303)
GARNISH:
4 small white onions, glazed
⅔ cup button mushrooms
1 tablespoon chopped parsley

Clean and truss the bird. To make a stock, add the giblets, the bouquet garni, and a little salt and pepper to the broth. Cover with a tight-fitting lid and simmer over low heat for 1 hour. Dice the salt pork or bacon and simmer it in 2 quarts of water for 10 minutes. Drain and dry.

In a 3-quart flameproof casserole or pan, cook the pork or bacon until it is lightly browned. Remove the pork or bacon and set aside. Pour off all but 3 tablespoons of the fat. Brown the bird all over in the hot fat. Warm the brandy in a small pan, ignite it, and pour the flaming brandy over the bird. As soon as the flames subside, pour in the wine and add the pork, onions, mushrooms, and crushed garlic. Pour in enough stock to come halfway up the bird. Cover with a lid and cook over low heat on top of the stove or in an oven at 300°F for 1 hour or until the bird is tender.

Remove the bird and divide it into serving pieces; keep these warm. Lift out the onions, bacon, and mushrooms with a slotted spoon and arrange them over the chicken. Reduce* the cooking liquid by brisk boiling, then lower the heat and gradually beat in pieces of beurre manié until the sauce has thickened. Correct seasoning and pour the sauce over the chicken.

Serve garnished with glazed small white onions (p.285), sautéed button mushrooms, and freshly chopped parsley.

Chicken Liver Pâté

PREPARATION TIME: *15 minutes*
COOKING TIME: *10 minutes*
CHILLING TIME: *2–3 hours*

INGREDIENTS (*for 6*):
1 pound chicken livers
4 tablespoons butter
1 small onion
2 bay leaves
Dried thyme
Salt and black pepper
2 tablespoons brandy

Melt the butter and sauté the peeled and finely chopped onion, the bay leaves, and a good pinch of thyme for 2–3 minutes. Trim away any green bits of gall bladder and cut the chicken livers into small pieces; add to the pan. Cook over low heat for 5 minutes or until the livers are cooked. Discard the bay leaves and purée the liver mixture in a blender or grind twice in a meat grinder.

Season to taste with salt and freshly ground black pepper, and stir in the brandy. Press the pâté into a jar and chill for several hours.

DUCK

Duck is prepared for roasting in the same way as chicken. Because duck is a fatty bird, it does not need barding or brushing with butter before cooking, but the skin should be pricked all over with a needle to allow the fat to run out of the bird during cooking. Season the duck with salt and freshly ground pepper and cook in a moderately hot oven, about 400°F, allowing 12–15 minutes per pound.

Duck can also be disjointed and braised for about 1 hour in a preheated 350°F oven.

Because the meat is very rich, duck is best served with sharply flavored sauces and fruit, such as oranges, peaches, or cherries. Allow 1 pound of duck per person.

GOOSE

Goose is fattier than chicken and therefore does not need to be brushed with melted butter before cooking. Before roasting a young bird, stuff it from the vent end, sprinkle with salt, and bard the bird with any fat taken from its body cavity. Loosely cover the bird with a piece of foil and roast at 400°F, allowing 15 minutes per pound plus an extra 15 minutes. Alternatively, slow-roast the goose near the bottom of the oven at 350°F, allowing 25 minutes per pound. Allow ¾ pound of goose for each person.

GUINEA HEN

All the methods of cooking chicken, particularly braising, can be applied to guinea hen. When roasting the bird, bard the lean breast meat well with bacon; otherwise the flesh will dry out. A small guinea hen will serve 1–2 people.

TURKEY

A drawn turkey is usually filled with two different stuffings. The neck end can be stuffed with chestnut or veal forcemeat, and the body cavity filled with a sausage stuffing (p.321). An average turkey weighing 10–12 pounds will require a sausage stuffing made from at least 2 pounds of sausage meat.

Veal Forcemeat

PREPARATION TIME: *20 minutes*

INGREDIENTS:
1½ cups white bread crumbs
2 tablespoons butter, melted
1 small onion
¼ pound lean veal
2 slices lean bacon
Salt and black pepper
1 egg
Stock or water

Mix the bread crumbs with the butter and blend in the finely chopped onion. Put the veal and bacon through the fine blade of a meat grinder and add to the bread crumbs. Season the mixture to taste with salt and freshly ground black pepper, then add the lightly beaten egg and enough white or chicken stock (or water) to bind the stuffing.

Chestnut Stuffing

PREPARATION TIME: *20 minutes*

INGREDIENTS:
Basic veal forcemeat stuffing
2 tablespoons chopped parsley
2 slices bacon
8 ounces chestnut purée
Grated rind of 1 lemon

Make up the basic veal forcemeat stuffing and blend in the finely chopped parsley. Chop the bacon finely; fry it in a skillet without any extra fat for 2–3 minutes or until crisp. Mix the drained bacon thoroughly into the stuffing, together with the chestnut purée and the finely grated rind of 1 lemon.

Roasting

Before roasting the stuffed and trussed turkey, the bird should be generously coated with softened butter and barded* with fat bacon strips or thinly sliced salt pork. Barding helps keep the turkey from drying out during roasting.

Roasting methods for turkey depend on the size of the bird and the time available. At low oven temperature, the turkey must be frequently basted with its own juices, even if it is barded. At a higher temperature, wrap the bird loosely in aluminum foil to prevent the flesh from drying out. About ½ hour before cooking is complete, open the foil to allow the skin of the bird to become brown and crisp.

When buying turkey, allow ¾ pound oven-ready weight per person, and 1 pound if the bird is not drawn and trussed. Boned and rolled turkey roasts are also available.

GAME BIRDS

All game birds should be hung before plucking and drawing to allow the flavor to develop and the flesh to become tender. Most game birds are bought already hung, plucked, and trussed (and sometimes barded). Freshly killed birds should be hung by their feet in a cool, airy place. The period of hanging depends on the age of the bird, the weather, and individual taste. Young game is hung for a shorter time than old game; and warm, damp weather causes the flesh to decompose more quickly than cold, dry weather. On the average, hang game birds for 7–10 days, or until the soft breast feathers can be plucked out easily.

After hanging, game birds are plucked, drawn, and trussed in the same way as poultry, but the feet are left on. They are best cooked quite simply, and young birds are excellent for roasting; they do not require stuffing. Older and tougher birds are better braised or casseroled.

Braising

Older birds and those of uncertain age are best cooked by this method to make them moist and tender. Before cooking, cut the bird into serving pieces, coat with seasoned flour (p.412), and sauté in a skillet in hot fat until brown. Remove the browned game from the pan and place in a casserole. Rinse the pan with ½ cup dry red wine or game stock. Add the liquid to the casserole, cover tightly with a lid, and cook in the center of a preheated oven at 325°F for 1 hour, or until the meat is tender.

Broiling

Small, tender birds, such as grouse, partridge, and quail, can be broiled. With a sharp knife, split them through lengthwise along the breastbone and flatten the bird; brush generously with melted butter. Place the bird under a hot broiler and cook for 25–30 minutes, basting continuously and turning frequently until it is browned.

Roasting

Before roasting, game birds must be barded with strips of fat pork or bacon. Sprinkle the inside with salt and pepper and put a large chunk of butter inside the bird to keep it moist. Place the prepared game bird on a rack in the roasting pan. Baste frequently during cooking and remove the fat strips for the last 10–15 minutes. Sprinkle the breast lightly with flour and continue cooking until brown.

Serving roast game

Small birds, such as grouse, partridge, plover, quail, snipe, and woodcock, are usually served whole on buttered toast and garnished with watercress. One bird should be allowed per person. Larger birds, such as pheasant, are split lengthwise with a knife or poultry shears to give 2 portions per bird.

ROASTING TIMES FOR TURKEY

Weight	Method 1 (325°F)	Method 2 (450°F)
6–8 pounds	3–3½ hours	2¼–2½ hours
8–10 pounds	3½–3¾ hours	2½–2¾ hours
10–14 pounds	3¾–4¼ hours	2¾–3 hours
14–18 pounds	4¼–4¾ hours	3–3½ hours
18–20 pounds	4¾–5¼ hours	3½–3¾ hours
20–24 pounds	5¼–6 hours	3¾–4¼ hours

ROASTING TIMES FOR GAME BIRDS

Bird	Temperature	Time
Grouse	400°F	30–45 minutes
Partridge	400°F	30–45 minutes
Pheasant	425°F	Allow 20 minutes per pound
Pigeon and Dove	425°F	Allow 20 minutes per pound
Quail	425°F	20 minutes
Snipe	425°F	20 minutes
Woodcock	425°F	20 minutes

WILD DUCK

These game birds, which include mallard, teal, and canvasbacks, should be hung for only 2–3 days. After hanging, the birds are plucked, drawn, and trussed as other game.

Wild duck should not be overcooked. Coat the bird with softened butter and roast at 425°F, allowing 20 minutes for teal and 30 minutes for mallard. For extra flavor, baste the bird frequently with a little orange juice or port.

Serve with wild rice and onion-and-orange salad.

WILD GOOSE

This can be prepared and roasted in the same way as the domestic kind but, as the flesh is dry, it should be barded thoroughly with several strips of bacon first.

FURRED GAME

This includes hare, which is a true game animal, and rabbit, which is now specially bred for the table.

Rabbit is eaten when 3–3½ months old. Fresh or frozen prepared rabbits are sold cleaned and skinned. If necessary, rabbit can be prepared at home. However, it should never be hung, but skinned and cleaned as soon as it has been killed.

Always wear rubber gloves when dressing rabbit or any wild meat. Although the danger of tularemia infection is not great, it can be transmitted by hares, rabbits, and other animals to man through cuts and scratches on the hands and arms. Take care to see that all wild meat is thoroughly cooked.

Skinning a rabbit

Lay the rabbit on several pieces of paper and begin by cutting off the feet at the first joint with a sharp knife. Follow the six step-by-step

SKINNING A RABBIT

1 *Cut off feet at the first joint.*

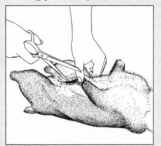

2 *Slit the skin along the belly.*

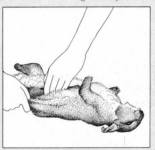

3 *Ease skin away from the flesh.*

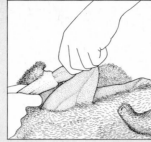

4 *Pull the skin over the hind legs.*

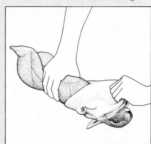

5 *Pull the skin toward the head.*

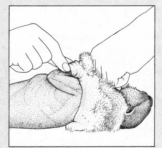

6 *Ease skin off forelegs and head.*

CLEANING A RABBIT

Cut open the belly with scissors.

Remove all internal organs.

instructions illustrated at left. In preparing a rabbit to be roasted whole, the head may be left on but the eyes should be removed. If the head is removed, cut it off directly behind the ears.

Cleaning and trussing

Slit the belly from the hind legs toward the head with a pair of scissors. Draw out all the internal organs. The kidneys, liver, and the heart can be kept and used for sauce. Take care not to break the gall bladder, as it imparts a bitter taste. Discard all the other organs. Catch any blood in a large bowl. Wipe out the inside of the rabbit with a damp cloth.

If the animal is to be roasted whole, cut the sinews of the hind legs at the thighs so that the legs can be brought forward. Press the legs close to the body and secure them with skewers or a trussing needle and string. Tuck the forelegs up and close to the body and truss them in the same way as the hind legs.

Disjointing

A rabbit is stewed or braised more often than it is roasted whole. Cut the skinned and cleaned animal into 8 serving pieces. With a sharp knife, first cut off the skin flaps below the rib cage and discard them. Divide the carcass in half lengthwise along the backbone, then cut off the hind legs at the top of the thigh, breaking the bone. Cut off the forelegs around the shoulder bones, then cut each half of the carcass into 2 pieces with a sharp knife.

If the saddle of the rabbit—the section between the hind legs and forelegs—is to be roasted whole, cut off the skin flaps below the rib cage, hind legs, and forelegs as already described, but do not slit the rabbit through the backbone.

DISJOINTING A RABBIT

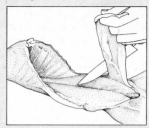

Remove skin flaps below the rib cage.

Divide the carcass in half.

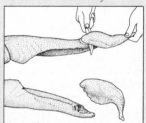

Cut off hind legs at the thighs.

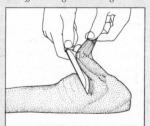

Remove the forelegs.

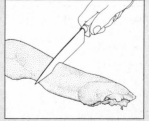

Divide remaining carcass.

COOKING RABBIT

Braising

This is a suitable method for cooking a disjointed rabbit. Coat the pieces in seasoned flour (p.412) and brown them in hot fat in a pan. Remove the pieces from the pan and place in a casserole. Rinse the pan with 1 cup red wine or game stock, scraping up the pan residues. Pour this liquid over the rabbit, cover tightly with a lid, and cook at 325°F for about 2 hours or until the meat is tender. Add a little more stock or wine, if necessary, and thicken the juices in the casserole with a little of the reserved blood and sour cream or beurre manié (p.303) before serving.

Roasting

Fill the body cavity of the animal with forcemeat stuffing (p.320) and sew the flesh together. Lay slices of fat bacon over the back and add 4 tablespoons of drippings to the pan. Place rabbit, breast down, in pan. Roast at 350°F for 1½–2 hours. Frequent basting is necessary. The bacon should be removed about 15 minutes before cooking is completed to allow the rabbit to brown.

Rabbit with Herbs

PREPARATION TIME: *20 minutes*
COOKING TIME: *1 hour*

INGREDIENTS (*for 4*):
1 2½–3 pound domestic rabbit,
    ready-to-cook, fresh, or frozen
3 tablespoons olive oil
6 shallots, finely chopped
2 medium onions, finely chopped
2 cloves garlic, finely chopped
¼ teaspoon each of parsley, chervil,
    tarragon, savory, basil, and
    thyme
Salt and pepper
2 tablespoons tomato paste
½ cup beef bouillon

If the rabbit is fresh, cut it into serving pieces. If frozen and cut up, thaw completely. Dry the rabbit thoroughly on paper towels.

In a large skillet, sauté the rabbit in the hot olive oil until brown. Pour off all but 2 tablespoons of the fat. Add the chopped shallots, onions, garlic, herbs, salt, and freshly ground pepper.

Cover the skillet, lower the heat, and continue to cook for 40 minutes or until the rabbit is tender.

Mix the tomato paste with the bouillon and stir it into the liquids in the skillet. Cook, uncovered, for about 5 minutes more. Then thicken the sauce with a beurre manié (p.303), if desired.

VENISON

Venison must be hung in a cool, airy place for 2–3 weeks, or until it is slightly high in flavor. Using a clean, damp cloth, wipe away any moisture as it accumulates on the flesh during the hanging period.

Meat from a young deer is delicate and can usually be cooked without marinating, but the flesh of an older animal is considerably tougher and is usually steeped in a marinade for 12–48 hours before cooking.

COOKING METHODS

Sautéing

Chops or steaks taken from the loin of venison are suitable for sautéing. Trim any surplus fat and gristle from the steaks or chops and flatten them slightly with a meat cleaver. Season lightly with salt and freshly ground pepper and sauté the steaks in oil or butter over high heat for about 12 minutes or until tender, turning them once only.

The fillet, cut into 2-inch-thick slices, can also be sautéed. Flatten the slices a little, then pan-fry over high heat, without fat, for 1 minute on each side to seal the meat. Add butter and reduce the heat; continue cooking for about 8 minutes, turning the slices once.

Roasting

Leg, loin, and saddle of venison are large cuts that are suitable for roasting after marinating. Cover the roast with a thick paste of flour and water, to keep the meat moist, before roasting just below the center of the oven at 375°F; allow 35 minutes per pound. Remove the paste for the last 20 minutes of cooking to allow the meat to brown.

Alternatively, brush the meat generously with oil, then wrap it in foil before roasting.

Marinade 1

PREPARATION TIME: *10 minutes*

INGREDIENTS:
1 large onion, chopped
1 carrot, chopped
1 stalk celery, chopped
1–2 cloves garlic, crushed
Bouquet garni (p.410)
6 black peppercorns
4 cups red wine
1 cup olive or vegetable oil

Mix the ingredients thoroughly and pour over the venison in a shallow dish. Leave the bowl, covered, in the refrigerator for 1–3 days. Turn the meat frequently.

Marinade 2

PREPARATION TIME: *10 minutes*

INGREDIENTS:
3 cups dry white wine
1¼ cups olive oil
2 onions, chopped
2 carrots, chopped
2 cloves garlic, crushed
1 teaspoon salt
1 bay leaf
2 tablespoons chopped parsley
¼ teaspoon thyme
8 black peppercorns
1 clove
6 coriander seeds
6 juniper berries, crushed

Mix the ingredients and pour into a bowl just large enough to hold the venison. Marinate in the refrigerator for 1–3 days, turning occasionally.

Venison Stew

Meat from the shoulder, neck, and upper loin is slightly tough and is best used for stews. It should be cut into 1-inch cubes and marinated.

MARINATING TIME: *4 hours*
PREPARATION TIME: *30 minutes*
COOKING TIME: *about 1½ hours*

INGREDIENTS (*for 4*):
2 pounds venison
½ pound bacon
4 tablespoons butter
2 onions
2 tablespoons flour
1¼ cups red wine
1 clove garlic, crushed
Bouquet garni (p.410)
Salt and black pepper
MARINADE:
1 finely chopped onion
Salt and black pepper
Sprig of thyme
1 bay leaf
6 tablespoons oil
2 tablespoons brandy

Mix the marinade ingredients together and steep the meat for 4 hours, then lift it out, drain thoroughly, and wipe dry.

Chop the bacon. Cook in a heavy-bottomed pan over moderate heat until the fat runs. Add the butter and the peeled, coarsely chopped onions; cook until transparent. Sprinkle in the flour and let this roux* brown, stirring continuously with a wooden spoon. Add the marinated and dried venison.

Cook the venison until brown on all sides, stirring occasionally. Add the red wine until the sauce just covers the meat. Mix in the crushed garlic, add the bouquet garni, and cover the pan with a tight-fitting lid. Cook the venison over low heat for 45 minutes–1 hour, then stir in the strained marinade and continue cooking, covered, until meat is tender; this will take about 45 minutes.

Remove the bouquet garni and correct seasoning with salt and freshly ground pepper.

CARVING POULTRY AND GAME

The technique for carving poultry follows certain basic steps. First, remove the legs and wings and then carve the breast meat downward in thick or thin slices. Serve each person white meat from the breast and dark meat from the body or legs.

Chicken and large game birds are carved in the same way as turkey. Small game birds are either served whole, 1 per person, or they can be cut in half in the same way as duckling to serve 2 people.

To carve a saddle of lamb or venison, cut across the base of the loin and at a right angle down the center of the saddle, forming a T shape. Cut thin slices down the length of the saddle. Carve each side of the loin end, slanting the slices toward the middle. Turn the saddle over and slice the fillet lengthwise.

DUCKLING

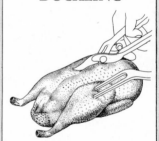

Small duckling and some larger game birds are often split after cooking, and half a bird is served to each person. Remove the trussing string or skewers from the roast duckling, then split the bird in half with a carving knife, a pair of poultry shears, or strong kitchen scissors. Insert the scissors in the neck end and cut along the center of the breastbone to the vent; split the bird in half by cutting all the way through the backbone.

DUCK

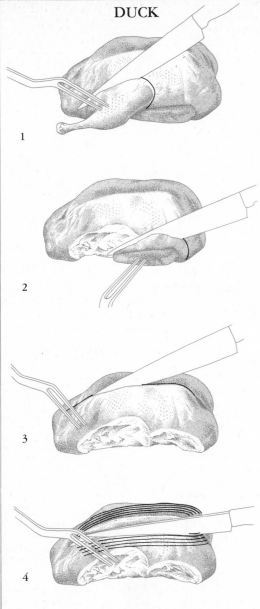

1 Cut off both legs. 2 Remove the wings on either side of the breast and detach the wishbone from the neck end. 3 Slice down the center of the breast. 4 To carve the meat from the breast, hold the blade of a sharp knife at an angle of 45 degrees to the breast, then cut fairly thick, slightly wedge-shaped slices. The cuts should be parallel to the first cut along the breastbone.

GOOSE

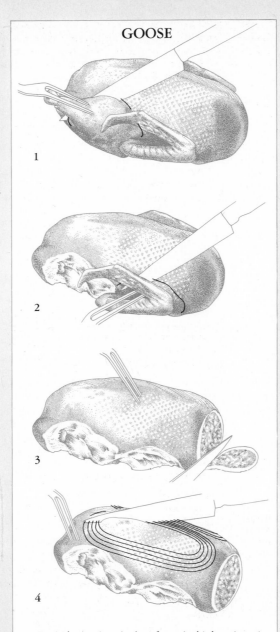

1 Begin by cutting the legs from the bird at the point where the thigh bones meet the body. 2 Remove both wings. 3 Cut thick slices across the neck end with the stuffing. 4 Fairly thick and even slices are then taken from both sides of the breastbone along the whole length of the bird. To remove these slices, carve downward, with the knife blade held almost flat.

TURKEY

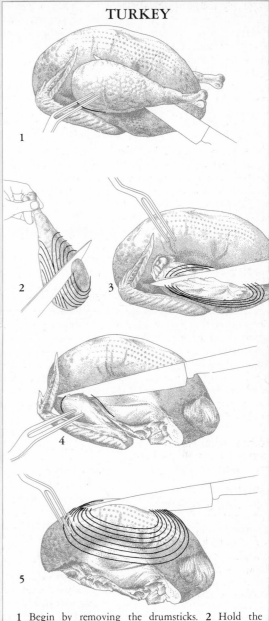

1 Begin by removing the drumsticks. 2 Hold the knuckle end of the drumstick in one hand and slice the meat downward, following the direction of the bone. Rotate the drumstick and carve until all meat is removed. 3 Slice the meat from the thigh bones. 4 Remove the wings. 5 Cut the breast meat in thin downward slices from either side of the breastbone.

Vegetables

Vegetables yield the most food value and flavor when they are fresh. But if they have to be stored, keep them in a cool, airy place or in the vegetable compartment of the refrigerator. However, certain fruits and vegetables should not be stored together. Carrots stored next to apples will take on a bitter taste; and potatoes will quickly spoil if they are stored with onions. Cut the leaves from root vegetables before storing to prevent the sap from rising from the roots, thus depriving the vegetables of some of their food value.

Choose vegetables that are crisp and firm rather than hard. The size is sometimes an indication of age and quality; overlarge vegetables may be old, and therefore coarse.

Prepare vegetables immediately before cooking by thorough washing and, if necessary, scrubbing with a brush. But do not soak vegetables at any stage during preparation because their mineral salts and vitamins are soluble in water. Since the most nutritious part of root vegetables and onions lies just under the skin, only a thin outer layer should be peeled away. If the vegetables are young, just scrape them lightly.

Vegetables can be used whole or can be cut up for quicker cooking. To cut vegetables, use a sharp cook's knife. When slicing, do not lift the point of the knife from the chopping board but use it as a pivot. Keep the wrist flexible and raise the knife just above the vegetables before chopping down again. Guide the knife with a forefinger placed on the back of the blade.

Some vegetables—cabbages, for example—may be merely halved and quartered before cooking; but most can be prepared by the following five methods:

Slicing
Cut the vegetables into narrow rounds or slices and divide these into strips. Fine matchlike sticks, known as julienne strips, are used to garnish soups.

Dicing
Slice the vegetables lengthwise into sticks; then cut these across into small cubes.

Shredding
Cut thin slivers from the sides of a vegetable, such as cabbage, that has been quartered. Slice evenly and rhythmically, always bringing the knife just above the vegetable before pressing down again.

Rounds
Cut the vegetable crosswise to get thick, round slices.

Chopping
Cut the vegetables finely or coarsely as required by the recipe.

COOKING METHODS

After preparing vegetables, do not soak them. Only peeled potatoes need to be kept in water; otherwise they turn brown.

Boiling
Use only a minimum of salted water, and for each cup of water add ½ teaspoon of salt. Root vegetables are put into cold salted water, and all other vegetables into boiling water.

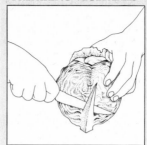

Removing stalk from cabbage

Shredding quartered cabbage

Slicing turnips into rounds

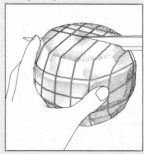

Cutting slices into dice

Bring the water to a boil. Add the prepared vegetables, cover the pan, and quickly return to a boil. Reduce the heat and boil at moderate heat until the vegetables are tender but firm. The vegetable liquid can be used to make stock, sauce, or gravy.

Steaming
Method 1—Place the prepared vegetables in a steamer above rapidly boiling water. Sprinkle with salt, allowing 1 teaspoon to each pound of prepared vegetables. Cover the steamer with a tight-fitting lid and steam until just tender, usually 3–5 minutes longer than the vegetables would take to boil.
Method 2—Use a wide shallow pan. Melt 2–4 tablespoons butter in the pan and add the prepared vegetables. Cover the pan with a tight-fitting lid and place over moderate heat until steam forms. Reduce the heat and cook until the vegetables are tender, shaking the pan occasionally to prevent sticking.

Sautéing
This method is suitable for very tender vegetables such as eggplants, zucchini, and tomatoes, or for onion slices. Cook these vegetables in butter in an uncovered pan over moderate heat. Stir occasionally with a wooden spoon.

Most other vegetables must be precooked or parboiled before sautéing. Heat butter, oil, or other fat in a heavy-bottomed pan, add the prepared and thoroughly drained precooked vegetables, and sauté until tender and golden brown.

Deep-frying
Potatoes are often deep-fried, but this method can be used to cook other vegetables, such as thick slices of onion, which are usually coated with flour, batter, or egg and bread crumbs before frying.

Heat the fat or oil in a deep, heavy-bottomed pan to 375°F. To check the temperature, drop a cube of bread in the heated fat or oil; if it browns in 40–50 seconds, the correct temperature has been reached.

Before placing the vegetables in the fat, dry them on paper towels or a clean dish towel. Place a few pieces of vegetable at a time in the fat; cook until crisp.

Braising
This method is suitable for root vegetables and onions. After preparing the vegetables, blanch them by plunging them into a large pan of rapidly boiling water for 2–3 minutes. Then flush them with cold water to stop the cooking process and to set the color.

Lightly sauté the drained vegetables in butter in a pan. Then add ½–1 cup of stock to each pound of prepared vegetables. Season lightly, add a chunk of butter, and cover with a tight-fitting lid. Cook the vegetables until just tender.

Lift the vegetables out of the pan and reduce the juices by boiling them rapidly.

Baking
Brush the prepared vegetables (cucumbers, zucchini, cherry tomatoes) with melted butter or oil and cook in a 400°F oven until tender.

Roasting
This method is applied to roots and tubers, usually cooked around a roast. Place the prepared vegetables in the hot fat and cook at 425°F for 45 minutes–1 hour. Alternatively, parboil the vegetables for 10 minutes, drain, then add to the hot fat. Roast for 20–30 minutes only.

PREPARING AND COOKING VEGETABLES

Artichokes, Globe

PREPARATION:
Cut off stalk and, using scissors, trim off point from each outer leaf; rinse and drain. Rub cut surfaces with lemon to prevent darkening. Chokes can be removed before or after cooking. Spread top leaves apart and pull inside leaves out to reveal hairy choke. Using a teaspoon, scrape away hairs to expose the base, or fond. Remaining leaves around the base can also be stripped away, leaving the fond.

COOKING METHODS:
Boiling Whole artichokes: 40–45 minutes in salted water. Without chokes: 15–20 minutes. Drain artichokes upside down.
Braising Blanch for 5 minutes. Refresh in cold water. Place on a bed of sautéed vegetables, moistened with wine or stock, and add a bouquet garni (p.410). Cover and cook for 1 hour.
Steaming Whole artichokes: Method 1 for 50–55 minutes. Without chokes: Method 1 for 20–25 minutes. Stuffed artichokes: Method 1 for 30–35 minutes.

SERVING SUGGESTIONS:
Hot: with melted butter or Hollandaise sauce (p.303). To eat, pull out one leaf at a time and dip edible base of leaf in accompanying sauce. Scrape off fleshy base of leaf between the teeth. When all leaves are removed, eat artichoke base with knife and fork.
Cold: with mayonnaise, vinaigrette sauce (p.304), or tartare sauce (p.303).

Artichokes, Jerusalem

PREPARATION:
Scrub and thinly peel under running water; place in acidulated water.*

COOKING METHODS:
Boiling For 25–30 minutes in salted acidulated water. Drain. Jerusalem artichokes can also be boiled in their skins and then peeled.
Steaming Whole artichokes: Method 1 for 35–40 minutes. Quartered: Method 2 for 30 minutes.
Deep-frying Parboil for 20 minutes, dry, cut in thick slices, dip in a light batter; deep-fry 3–4 minutes.

SERVING SUGGESTIONS:
Boiled or steamed with melted butter, Hollandaise (p.303), Béchamel, or cheese sauce (p.301).

Asparagus

PREPARATION:
Cut off woody parts from ends of stalks. Using knife, scrape white part of stalks downward. Tie asparagus in bundles, all heads together.

COOKING METHOD:
Boiling For 11–14 minutes in salted water that comes to just below the asparagus tips.

SERVING SUGGESTIONS:
Serve 8–10 stalks per portion; an average bundle gives 3–4 portions. Hot: with melted butter, Mornay sauce (p.302), or Hollandaise sauce (p.303). Cold: with vinaigrette sauce (p.304) or mayonnaise (p.303).

Avocados

PREPARATION:
Just before servng, slice in half lengthwise around the pit, using a stainless steel or silver knife to prevent discoloration of the flesh. Leave the skins on if avocados are to be served as a first course with a filling or dressing. The flesh can also be carefully scooped out with a spoon and mixed with salad vegetables or seafood.
   If avocado is to be left for any length of time, toss the flesh in lemon juice to prevent discoloration.

COOKING METHOD:
Baking Peel off skin from halved avocados, slice thinly, place in buttered baking dish, sprinkle with lemon juice and seasoning; cover with slices of chicken breast, white sauce, crumbs, and butter. Bake at 375°F for 45 minutes.

SERVING SUGGESTIONS:
Often served fresh as a dip or a mousse, with sauce vinaigrette (p.304).

Beans, Fava

PREPARATION:
Young and tender beans: wash, trim, and cook in their pods. Mature beans: remove from pods. Large beans: remove from their skin after cooking and make into a purée.

COOKING METHODS:
Boiling For 15–20 minutes, whether in or out of their pods. Mature beans: up to 30 minutes.
Steaming Method 1 for 10–15 minutes.

SERVING SUGGESTIONS:
Serve small beans shelled or in their pods, tossed in butter and sprinkled with finely chopped parsley or summer savory. Serve older beans with a cream sauce.

Beans, Green

PREPARATION:
Wash and trim; leave whole or cut into 1½–2 inch lengths.

COOKING METHODS:
Boiling For 5–10 minutes in salted water. Refresh with cold water. Drain well, then reheat with butter and herbs.
Steaming Method 1 for 10–15 minutes.

SERVING SUGGESTIONS:
Dress with garlic, anchovy, or herb butters (p.338).

Beans, Lima

PREPARATION:
Wash the pods. Shell the beans just before cooking.

COOKING METHOD:
Boiling For 20–25 minutes, covered, in 1 inch of salted water until just tender.

SERVING SUGGESTION:
Toss with butter.

Beets

PREPARATION:
Cut off leaf stalks 1–2 inches above the root, but do not trim off tapering root. Wash well.

COOKING METHODS:
Boiling Depending on the size, for 1–2 hours in salted water. Slide off the skins when beets are cooked.
Steaming Method 1 for about 2 hours.
Baking Wrap beets in buttered foil. Bake at 325°F for 30 minutes–1 hour.

SERVING SUGGESTIONS:
Cold cooked beets can be served sliced or diced in salads.

Broccoli

PREPARATION:
Wash the broccoli thoroughly in cold water; drain well in a colander. Remove any coarse outer leaves and tough parts of the stalks.

COOKING METHODS:
Boiling For 15–20 minutes in salted water.
Steaming Method 1 for 20–25 minutes.

SERVING SUGGESTION:
With Béarnaise sauce (p.303).

Brussels Sprouts

PREPARATION:
Wash: trim off damaged outer leaves. Make an X cut in base of stems.

COOKING METHODS:
Boiling For about 10 minutes in minimum of salted water.
Braising Parboil in salted water for 5 minutes. Drain and keep warm. Sauté thinly sliced onion rings. Add a little stock and seasoning. Simmer 5 minutes. Add sprouts; simmer for another 5 minutes, basting occasionally.
Steaming Method 1 for about 15 minutes.

SERVING SUGGESTION:
Tossed with butter, or sour cream, and seasoning.

Cabbage

PREPARATION:
Remove the coarse outer leaves; cut cabbage into quarters and remove hard center core. Wash thoroughly, drain in a colander, and cook either in wedges or finely shredded.

COOKING METHODS:
Boiling Shredded cabbage: cook in salted water for 5–8 minutes. Cabbage wedges: for 10–15 minutes.
Braising Parboil cabbage wedges in salted water for 10 minutes. Refresh in cold water. Place on a bed of sautéed vegetables. Add a bouquet garni (p.410) and enough stock to cover. Bake for 1 hour at 350°–375°F. Red cabbage: braise shredded cabbage in butter, add chopped apples, vinegar, and sugar to taste. Simmer, covered, for 1 hour.
Steaming Shredded cabbage: Method 1 for 10 minutes. Cabbage wedges: Method 1 for 20 minutes.

SERVING SUGGESTION:
Toss boiled cabbage gently with butter and season with salt and freshly ground pepper.

Carrots

PREPARATION:
Trim; wash in cold running water. Scrape young carrots; peel old ones with a potato peeler. Small carrots can be left whole; large ones can be cut into any shape desired: quarters, rings, sticks, or cubes.

COOKING METHODS:
Boiling For 10–30 minutes in salted water or stock.
Steaming Method 1 for 15–40 minutes, depending on age of carrots and size of pieces.

SERVING SUGGESTIONS:
Toss boiled carrots with butter, chopped parsley, or mint; or serve with a Béchamel sauce (p.301).

Cauliflower

PREPARATION:
Cut off damaged outer leaves. If cauliflower is to be cooked whole, cut an X in base of stalk. Alternatively, separate cauliflower by breaking it into individual florets. Wash well in cold water.

COOKING METHODS:
Boiling For 12–15 minutes in salted, acidulated water, partially covered with saucepan lid.
Steaming Method 1 for 15–25 minutes.
Frying Parboil florets for 10 minutes. Drain and cool; dip in egg and bread crumbs, then deep-fry for 3 minutes.

SERVING SUGGESTIONS:
With white or cheese sauce. Serve deep-fried florets with tartare sauce (p.303).

Celeriac

PREPARATION:
Wash and slice; then peel, dice, or cut into matchstick strips.

COOKING METHODS:
Boiling for 25–30 minutes in salted, acidulated water* with lid on. Drain.
Steaming Method 1 for 35 minutes.
Sautéing Sauté matchstick celeriac strips in butter for 30 minutes.

SERVING SUGGESTIONS:
Boiled celeriac with Béchamel or Hollandaise sauce (p.303). Celeriac can also be puréed in a blender, or grated fresh as a salad vegetable.

PREPARING AND COOKING VEGETABLES

Celery

PREPARATION:
Trim away root end and remove damaged outer stalks and green tops. Separate the stalks and wash them in cold water. Remove any coarse fibers and cut the stalks into even lengths: 2–2½ inches for boiling, 3–4 inches for braising or steaming.

COOKING METHODS:
Boiling For 15–20 minutes in salted water, covered with a lid.
Braising Blanch halved or whole heads of celery for 10 minutes. Sauté diced bacon, sliced onions, and carrots in a buttered casserole. Add celery and enough stock to cover. Bring to a boil, cover, and simmer 1½–1¾ hours.
Steaming Method 1, for 20–30 minutes.
Au gratin Sprinkle with grated cheese or bread crumbs and bake or broil.

SERVING SUGGESTIONS:
Boiled and steamed with cheese sauce (p.301) made from half the cooking liquid and the same quantity of milk. Fresh, as a salad vegetable.

Chicory

PREPARATION:
Discard damaged outer leaves. For salads, separate remaining leaves and wash thoroughly in cold water. Leave vegetable whole for braising.

COOKING METHOD:
Braising As for lettuce.

SERVING SUGGESTIONS:
Fresh, as a salad vegetable.

Corn

PREPARATION:
Strip the husks and remove the silks with a brush under cold running water.

COOKING METHODS:
Boiling Cook ears in water for 5–10 minutes. Add salt halfway through cooking time.
Steaming Method 1, for 10–15 minutes.

SERVING SUGGESTIONS:
With butter, salt, and pepper.

Cress

PREPARATION:
With scissors, snip the cress from its bed into a colander or sieve; rinse thoroughly in cold water and dry well with paper towels.

SERVING SUGGESTIONS:
Use in salads, sandwiches, or as a garnish for savory dishes.

Cucumbers

PREPARATION:
Peel and seed cucumber; cut into strips; slice or dice. If the cucumber is to be stuffed, cut it in half lengthwise and scoop out seeds.

COOKING METHODS:
Boiling For 10 minutes in salted water.
Steaming Method 1, for 20 minutes. Method 2, for 10–20 minutes.
Baking Peel, slice thickly, and dot with butter and freshly chopped herbs. Bake at 375°F for 30 minutes.

SERVING SUGGESTIONS:
Boiled cucumber with a cream sauce flavored with dill, tarragon, or celery seeds. Cucumbers are also used as a raw salad vegetable or garnish.

Eggplants

PREPARATION:
Wipe, trim both ends, and peel if necessary. Slice, dice, or halve. Sprinkle cut surfaces with salt and let stand for 30 minutes. Rinse and dry.

COOKING METHODS:
Sautéing Coat prepared slices in seasoned flour or leave plain. Sauté in butter or vegetable oil.
Broiling or baking Brush eggplant slices with melted butter or oil.
Stuffing and baking Cut eggplant in half lengthwise. Scoop out the pulp, leaving a ¾-inch-thick shell. A savory mixture, including the pulp and other ingredients, is piled back into the shells, then baked at 325°F for 20–30 minutes. Other recipes include moussaka (p.98) and ratatouille (p.122).

SERVING SUGGESTIONS:
Sautéed or broiled, with meat; stuffed with Parmesan cheese topping, or served with tomato or cheese sauce.

Endives

PREPARATION:
Trim away outside damaged or wilted leaves. Separate them into spears or slice them across.

COOKING METHODS:
Boiling For 15–20 minutes in salted, acidulated water.*

Braising Scoop out the hard core at the base and leave endives whole. Blanch, if necessary, and drain. Butter casserole, arrange endives on the bottom, and dot with more butter. Add 2–3 tablespoons water and sprinkle endives with a little lemon juice and salt. Cover and bake for 1–1¼ hours at 350°F.

SERVING SUGGESTIONS:
Serve boiled endives with cheese, Béchamel sauce (p.301), or tomato sauce (p.302).

Fennel

PREPARATION:
Trim off top stems and slice off the bottom. Wash well in cold water.

COOKING METHOD:
Braising As for celery.

SERVING SUGGESTIONS:
Thinly sliced, as a salad vegetable or garnish. Also good with cheese sauce.

Kale

PREPARATION:
Separate leaves from stems and remove midrib from leaves. Wash thoroughly in cold water. Cut leaves in pieces.

COOKING METHODS:
Boiling For 8–10 minutes in salted water.
Steaming Method 1, for about 15 minutes.

SERVING SUGGESTION:
Toss with butter, salt, and pepper.

Kohlrabi

PREPARATION:
Cut off leaves around bulb and trim off tapering roots. Wash in cold water, then peel thickly. Small globes can be left whole. Slice or dice large ones.

COOKING METHODS:
Boiling Depending on size, for 30–60 minutes in salted water. Drain.
Braising Parboil in salted water for 5 minutes. Braise with a little chopped onion and bacon; moisten with white wine or stock. Cook for 1 hour or until tender, depending on size.
Steaming Method 1, for about 1 hour.

SERVING SUGGESTIONS:
Kohlrabi can be mashed, puréed, or baked. Toss boiled kohlrabi in melted butter and finely chopped herbs, or serve with a white sauce (p.301).

Leeks

PREPARATION:
Cut off roots and green tops; remove coarse outer leaves if necessary. Cut down through the white part and wash carefully to remove dirt from leaves. Leeks can be left whole or halved, or sliced into thick rings or 2-inch lengths.

COOKING METHODS:
Boiling Boil 2-inch pieces of leeks in salted water for 15 minutes; sliced rings for 10 minutes; whole, for 20 minutes.
Braising Blanch leeks in boiling salted water for 5 minutes. Drain; sauté in butter for 5 minutes. Add stock or water to cover and a bouquet garni (p.410). Cover and cook for 1 hour.
Steaming Method 1, for about 25 minutes, depending on the size of leeks. Leeks cut in rings: Method 2, for about 10–15 minutes.
Deep-frying Prepared leeks can be blanched for 5 minutes, drained, and marinated in lemon juice. Dip in a light batter before deep-frying.

SERVING SUGGESTIONS:
Boiled, with a Béchamel sauce (p.301) or Mornay sauce (p.302). Use young leeks as a salad vegetable.

Lettuce

PREPARATION:
Trim off bottom and remove any damaged outer leaves. Separate the leaves; wash; drain and dry well for a salad. Leave whole if braised.

COOKING METHODS:
Boiling For 10 minutes in salted water. Drain thoroughly and chop finely. Heat butter in a pan and add a little chopped onion, garlic, and cream. Stir in chopped lettuce and season.
Braising Blanch 5–6 minutes. Refresh under cold running water and drain thoroughly. In a casserole, melt butter and sauté a little chopped bacon, carrot, and onion. Fold tops of lettuce to make a neat shape and lay on top of the vegetables. Add stock to a depth of ½ inch, cover, and bake 40–45 minutes at 325°–350°F. Pour the reduced* pan juices over the lettuce.

SERVING SUGGESTIONS:
Boiled with Mornay sauce (p.302) or Hollandaise sauce (p.303). Fresh in green salads. Also for garnish.

Mushrooms

PREPARATION:
Trim the base of the stalks; wipe with a damp cloth or rinse mushrooms in cold water; dry well. Peel wild mushrooms.

COOKING METHODS:
Steaming Cover and cook in the top of a double boiler with a little butter and salt for 20 minutes or until tender.
Sautéing and broiling Flat cultivated mushrooms are suitable for sautéing and broiling. Button mushrooms can be dipped in fritter batter and deep-fried or sautéed. Sauté sliced mushrooms in butter for 3–5 minutes. Serve with the juices. Brush whole mushrooms with butter or oil and broil under moderate heat for 6–8 minutes, turning once.

SERVING SUGGESTIONS:
Sautéed with pan juices, cream, and thyme. Button mushrooms as garnish or fresh in salads.

Okra

PREPARATION:
Wash thoroughly but do not remove the stems.

COOKING METHODS:
Boiling For 7–15 minutes in salted water. Alternatively, parboil for 5 minutes, then finish cooking in butter.
Braising Parboil okra in boiling salted water for 5 minutes; braise for a further 30–45 minutes.

SERVING SUGGESTIONS:
Toss in melted butter or serve with Hollandaise sauce (p.303).

Onions

PREPARATION:
Trim roots and peel away papery skins. Onions can be left whole, or chopped, sliced, or diced. Green onions, or scallions, need the root removed and the green tops trimmed.

COOKING METHODS:
Boiling Cook in salted water for 20–30 minutes, depending on size.
Baking Parboil large onions for 15–20 minutes. Remove the centers of the onions and fill the cavities with a savory mixture. Bake for 45–60 minutes at 350°–375°F.
Sautéing Cut onions in thin slices and sauté gently in hot fat.
Deep-frying Slice onions thickly. Dip in

PREPARING AND COOKING VEGETABLES

milk and seasoned flour (p.412) before deep-frying for about 3 minutes.
SERVING SUGGESTIONS:
Boiled, with butter or with a white or cheese sauce (p.301).

Parsnips
PREPARATION:
Cut off roots and tops. Peel. If young, cut in thick slices; if mature, cut in quarters and remove the hard core.
COOKING METHODS:
Boiling For 30–40 minutes in salted water.
Roasting Parboil for 5 minutes. Drain and roast with meat, or braise in butter with a little stock.
Steaming Method 1, for about 35 minutes for young parsnips.
Puréeing Parsnips can be boiled, then puréed with a little butter and nutmeg.
Deep-frying Cut parsnips into thin slivers and deep-fry.
SERVING SUGGESTIONS:
Tossed with butter and parsley.

Peas
PREPARATION:
Shell fresh peas. (Snow peas, however, are cooked, pods and all, in the same way as green beans.)
COOKING METHODS:
Boiling Gently for 15–20 minutes in salted water with a sprig of mint and 1 teaspoon of sugar. A little lemon juice helps to preserve the color.
Steaming Method 1, for about 25 minutes.
SERVING SUGGESTION:
Tossed with butter and chopped mint.

Peppers
PREPARATION:
Wash, cut in half lengthwise, and remove the stalk, seeds, and whitish membrane around the sides. Slice or dice as required. If peppers are to be filled with a savory mixture, cut around the stalk and lift away the core. Scoop out membrane and seeds.
COOKING METHOD:
Baking Parboil in salted water for 10 minutes. Drain, then fill with a savory meat or vegetable filling. Place in pan, add a little stock, and bake at 350°F for 25–30 minutes.

SERVING SUGGESTIONS:
Hot, with cheese sauce (p.301) or tomato sauce (p.302). Cold, with vinaigrette sauce or French dressing.

Potatoes See page 333.

Pulses (dried peas, beans, lentils)
PREPARATION:
If bought loose, pick over and wash the pulses under running water. Place in a large bowl and cover with boiling water; soak for 2 hours. For packaged and quick-cooking types, follow the directions on the package.
COOKING METHODS:
Boiling Put in a saucepan and add salt—1 teaspoon for ½ pound of pulses. Bring to a boil, cover, and simmer until tender. Pulses can also be soaked overnight in cold water, drained, and placed in a saucepan with fresh water and salt. Bring to a boil and simmer until tender. Follow package directions for no-soaking types.
SERVING SUGGESTIONS:
Hot, puréed with butter, salt, and pepper. Cold, tossed in garlic-flavored French dressing (p.304).

Pumpkins
PREPARATION:
Wash and cut pumpkin into bite-size pieces. Peel off skin and remove pith and seeds.
COOKING METHODS:
Boiling For 20–30 minutes in salted water.
Steaming Method 1, for 35–40 minutes.
Roasting For 45–50 minutes.
SERVING SUGGESTION:
With a cheese sauce (p.301).

Radishes
PREPARATION:
If eaten whole, cut off the tops, leaving ⅓ inch of stalk, and remove the tapering root. Wash well in cold water.
COOKING METHOD:
Boiling Cook large radishes whole in salted water for about 10 minutes.
SERVING SUGGESTIONS:
As a raw salad vegetable or as a garnish for savory dishes. Serve boiled radishes with a well-seasoned cream sauce.

Rutabagas
PREPARATION:
Trim stalk and root ends, peel thickly, and cut in ½–1 inch cubes.
COOKING METHOD:
Boiling For 30–40 minutes in salted water. Drain and dry the rutabagas over gentle heat.
SERVING SUGGESTIONS:
Toss with melted butter, salt, and pepper; or mash with butter, nutmeg, and salt. Use in stews and casseroles.

Salsify
PREPARATION:
Scrub well in cold water; cut off top and tapering root end. Scrape off skin and cut into 1–2 inch lengths. Plunge immediately into cold, acidulated water.*
COOKING METHOD:
Boiling For 45 minutes in salted water.
SERVING SUGGESTIONS:
With butter, white sauce (p.301), or Béarnaise sauce (p.303). Use leaves in salads or cooked as a green vegetable.

Shallots
PREPARATION:
Prepare and cook as for onions.
SERVING SUGGESTIONS:
Used to flavor stocks and soups.

Spinach
PREPARATION:
Wash spinach several times in cold water to remove dirt and grit. Do not dry, but place in a saucepan with no extra water.
COOKING METHOD:
Boiling Sprinkle leaves with a little salt; cover and cook gently, shaking the pan occasionally, for about 10 minutes. Drain thoroughly.
SERVING SUGGESTIONS:
Reheat with cream, salt, and pepper. Chop finely or make into a purée.

Squash, Summer (straightneck, crookneck, and pattypan)
Wash, but do not peel. Trim both ends. Slice, cube, or leave whole.
COOKING METHODS:
Boiling For 10–15 minutes, or until just tender, in a small amount of salted water.

Steaming Whole squash: Method 1, for 15–20 minutes. Sliced: Method 2, for about 10 minutes.
SERVING SUGGESTIONS:
Toss in butter or serve with white sauce (p.301) or cheese sauce (p.301).

Squash, Winter (Hubbard, acorn, and butternut)
Scrub well. Cut butternut and Hubbard into serving pieces. Remove seeds and fibers. Cut acorn squash in half crosswise; remove seeds and fibers.
COOKING METHODS:
Boiling Cook butternut for 25–30 minutes in salted water, then peel.
Baking Cook Hubbard at 400°F for 1 hour or until tender. Cook acorn squash, cut side down, for 25 minutes. Then turn cut side up, season with butter, salt, and pepper, and cook for 30–35 minutes longer.

Sweet Potatoes
PREPARATION:
Scrub well and peel if necessary.
COOKING METHODS:
Boiling Cook in the skins in salted water, covered, for about 25 minutes. If peeled, cook uncovered for 15 minutes.
Baking Bake in jackets in a 425°F oven for 1 hour.
SERVING SUGGESTIONS:
As for potatoes.

Swiss Chard
PREPARATION:
Wash; cut off white stalks. Prepare and cook green leaves like spinach.
COOKING METHOD FOR STALKS:
Boiling For 15 minutes in salted acidulated water.* Drain.
SERVING SUGGESTIONS:
With butter, Béchamel sauce (p.301), or cheese sauce (p.301).

Tomatoes
PREPARATION:
Remove stalk if necessary. To skin, see illustrations on page 332.
COOKING METHODS:
Broiling Cut tomato in half, top with a small pat of butter, and season. Broil under moderate heat for 5–10 minutes.
Baking Prepare tomatoes as above or leave whole. Arrange in a shallow

buttered baking dish. Bake at 350°F for 15 minutes. Whole tomatoes should be placed stalk end down, cut crosswise on top, and brushed with vegetable oil or olive oil before baking.
SERVING SUGGESTIONS:
Hot: as a first course or accompaniment to savory dishes. Cold: sliced, with vinaigrette and chopped parsley, or quartered in salads, and as a garnish.

Turnips
PREPARATION:
Wash; trim stalk ends and tapering roots. Peel thickly. Small young turnips can be left whole; large ones should be quartered or cut into eighths.
COOKING METHODS:
Boiling For 25–30 minutes in salted water.
Steaming Method 1, for 30–40 minutes.
SERVING SUGGESTIONS:
Toss in parsley and butter or serve with a white sauce (p.301).

Watercress
PREPARATION:
Wash thoroughly in cold water and drain and dry well.
SERVING SUGGESTIONS:
Watercress is used in salads or as a garnish for savory dishes. Chopped watercress can be mixed with salad vegetables or mixed into sauces and mayonnaise.

Zucchini
PREPARATION:
Scrub with a vegetable brush under cold running water; trim both ends. Cook without peeling, either whole, sliced in rounds, or halved with the centers scooped out before filling.
COOKING METHODS:
Boiling For 10–15 minutes in salted water.
Steaming Whole zucchini: Method 1, for 15–20 minutes. Sliced: Method 2, for about 10 minutes.
Baking Parboil hollowed-out zucchini for 5 minutes. Drain, cut side down. Brush with butter and season. Bake at 375°F for 25 minutes.
SERVING SUGGESTIONS:
Sprinkled with tarragon, paprika, or chopped parsley.

Vegetables

PREPARING GLOBE ARTICHOKES FOR COOKING

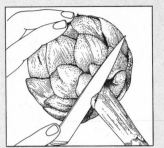

1 *Cutting stalk off artichoke*

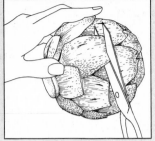

3 *Trimming points off leaves*

2 *Slicing off top leaves*

4 *Removing choke from fond*

ENDIVE

Cutting out the white bitter root at the base of blanched endive

CORN ON THE COB

Scrub corn under running water with a brush to remove the silks.

TWO WAYS OF PEELING FRESH TOMATOES

1 *Put in hot water for 1 minute.*

1 *Hold tomato over open gas flame.*

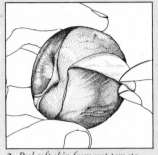

2 *Peel soft skin from wet tomato.*

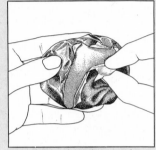

2 *Peel away charred tomato skin.*

ASPARAGUS

Tying a bundle with fine string

Cooking the bundle upright

CUCUMBER

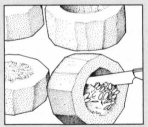

Scraping out the seeds from peeled cucumber slices

WILD MUSHROOMS

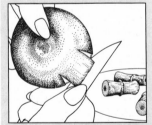

Trim by removing stalks and peeling ragged skin.

PEPPERS

Slicing peppers from which stalk and seeds have been removed

CAULIFLOWER

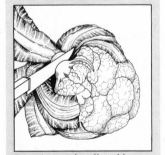

Removing tough stalk and leaves

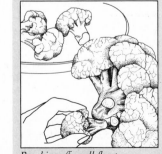

Breaking off small florets

PEELING, SLICING, AND CHOPPING ONION

Peel off skin and trim root. Cut onion in half, through the root, then cut downward in slices. To chop, turn the onion and slice across the first cuts. To dice, chop again across these cuts.

332

POTATOES

Potatoes fall into two main categories: the waxy boiling type and the mealy baking variety.

Waxy potatoes are best boiled, French-fried, roasted, or used in salads. Mealy potatoes can be baked, roasted, or French-fried.

PREPARING POTATOES

New potatoes need only be washed, scraped lightly, and washed again. They may also be boiled in their skins and peeled before serving to save scraping time. Cut a small band of skin from around the center to prevent the skin from bursting. Old potatoes should be washed well, peeled thinly with a vegetable peeler, and then cut into even-sized pieces and cooked as soon as possible to prevent discoloration.

A pound of old potatoes gives about 3 portions; a pound of new ones about 4 portions.

COOKING METHODS

Boiling
If the potatoes are large, cut into even-sized pieces and put into cold salted water. Bring to a boil and simmer covered about 15–20 minutes for new potatoes and about 20 minutes for old potatoes. Small potatoes may be cooked whole.

Steaming
Whole, halved, or quartered potatoes, peeled or unpeeled, can be steamed over boiling water until just pierceable with a knife point.

Mashing
Boil old potatoes. Drain well, and dry the potatoes in the pan over low heat. Using a potato masher or a fork, mash the potatoes in the pan until free of lumps. Alternatively,

rub the potatoes through a sieve or put them through a potato ricer.

Creaming
Put mashed potatoes in a clean saucepan. To each pound of potatoes add 2 tablespoons of butter, a little milk, salt, and freshly ground pepper; then put the pan over gentle heat. Beat the mixture until light and fluffy. For a smoother mixture, beat in 1 egg.

Duchesse potatoes
Beat an egg, mix it into creamed potatoes, and put the mixture in a pastry bag. Pipe into mounds, about 2 inches high, on a lightly greased baking sheet. Or pipe the potatoes into a border around a shallow baking dish. Bake near the top of the oven at 400°F for about 25 minutes, or until the potatoes are golden.

Potato croquettes
Prepare creamed potatoes. Roll the mixture into small balls and coat thickly with egg and bread crumbs. In a skillet heat the fat to 375°F—at this temperature a cube of bread dropped into the fat should brown in 40–50 seconds. Fry the croquettes for 2–3 minutes, drain thoroughly, and fry again at the same temperature for 2–3 minutes.

Sautéing
Boil potatoes until they are almost cooked and cut them into slices about ¼ inch thick. Sauté in hot fat, turning them until crisp and golden brown on both sides.

French-frying
Peel old potatoes and cut them into ¼–½ inch slices. Cut these slices into strips ¼–½ inch wide. Soak in cold water. Drain well and dry thoroughly before using. Put some fat into a fryer (or a deep saucepan) and heat to 385°F. When a strip dropped in the fat rises to the surface, surrounded by bubbles, the fat is hot enough for frying. Place a layer of

potato strips in a wire basket and lower into the fryer; cook for 4–6 minutes or until golden. Drain well on paper towels. Just before serving, fry the potatoes again for 1–2 minutes. Drain the potatoes on paper towels, salt lightly, and serve.

Shoestring potatoes
Peel old potatoes and cut them into very small, thin strips, about the size of matchsticks. Cook in the same way as French fries, allowing a shorter cooking time—about 3 minutes for the first frying.

Saratoga chips
Peel and wash the potatoes. Cut into thin rounds. Soak in cold water, dry, and fry in hot fat in the same way as French fries. For the first frying, allow only 3 minutes.

Baking
Wash and dry Idaho-type potatoes. Bake at 400°F about 1 hour.

Château potatoes
Cut potatoes into 1½–2-inch ovals. Coat with melted butter. Cook, covered, on top of the stove for 30–35 minutes. Shake occasionally.

Anna potatoes
Peel old or new potatoes and slice them thinly. Arrange the slices in layers in a well-greased baking dish. Sprinkle each layer with salt, pepper, and melted butter. Cover the dish lightly with buttered waxed paper or foil and bake for 1 hour in the center of the oven at 375°F. Serve at once.

Roasting
Peel and cut into even-sized pieces. Parboil for 5 minutes, then drain. Place in a roasting pan with melted beef drippings, and roast near the top of the oven at 425°F for 40 minutes, turning once. When brown, drain on paper towels.

Alternatively, put the cut potatoes around a roast for the last 50–60 minutes of cooking time.

HERBS AND THEIR USES

Fresh and dried herbs are much used in cooking to impart additional flavor to a dish. The choice of herb is entirely personal, but certain herbs go particularly well with certain foods. Fresh herbs are superior in taste to dried herbs, but are not as strong. If a recipe calls for dried herbs and fresh herbs are being substituted, triple the amount.

Basil Use with oily fish and in vegetable dishes, especially with tomato.

Bay leaf Use in bouquet garni (p.410) and with oily fish, pork, veal, goose, and in pâtés and terrines.

Chervil As garnish to soups, and with delicate fish and shellfish. Also in fines herbes omelets, salads, and herb butters.

Dill Use to flavor sauces, salad dressings, and mayonnaise. As garnish to fish soups, fish, tiny boiled potatoes, and to flavor lamb stews.

Fennel Use with roast lamb, oily fish, and to flavor sauces. Fennel seeds are ideal for flavoring roast pork and chicken.

Garlic The most widely used flavoring, particularly with tomato and meat dishes.

Marjoram Ideal with strong-flavored oily fish, also with roast lamb, pork, veal, chicken, duck, and partridge. A favorite herb with tomato dishes. Marjoram may be used as a substitute for oregano.

Mint Use to flavor cooked peas, new potatoes, cucumbers, and carrots.

Oregano Use in sauces for pasta and in Italian dishes with tomato or cheese.

Parsley The traditional garnish with fish and many soups. Used to flavor sauces and vegetable dishes. A necessary ingredient of bouquet garni (p.410) and maître d'hôtel butter (p.338).

Rosemary A favorite herb with oily grilled fish; also used to flavor roast lamb and pork.

Sage Mainly used in stuffings for pork, chicken, turkey, and duck.

Savory Summer savory has a more delicate mint flavor than winter savory. Both are used to flavor salads, soups, broiled fish, and egg dishes. Superb with green beans.

Tarragon Use to flavor white wine vinegar and in salad dressings and mayonnaise. Excellent with oily fish, roast or sautéed chicken, in omelets, and for herb butters.

Thyme The traditional ingredient of a bouquet garni (p.410). Use to flavor oily fish, soups and stews, stuffings, marinades, roast pork, veal, and poultry.

Eggs

Eggs are probably the most useful of all foods. There is no waste on them apart from the shell. They are rich in vitamin B_2, fairly rich in protein, and low in calories: a 2-ounce egg contains only 90 calories--fewer than 1 ounce of cheese. Eggs can be boiled, fried, baked, poached, or scrambled, and used for meringues. Added to other foods, they act as a raising agent in soufflés, cakes, and pastry and as an emulsifying agent in mayonnaise and salad dressings. They are used to thicken soups and sauces, to bind stuffings and croquette mixtures, and as a crisp coating for fried food.

Freshness

Test an egg for freshness by lowering it into a bowl of water. If it lies on its side, it is quite fresh. If it stands on end it is less fresh, and if it floats to the top it is stale and possibly bad. When broken, a fresh egg smells pleasant, the yolk is round and firm, and the white evenly distributed. A stale egg usually has a slight smell and spreads out thinly when broken.

Storing eggs

Eggs stored in the refrigerator will keep for as long as 2 months. Remove the eggs from the refrigerator at least 45 minutes before using.

Separated eggs should be stored in the refrigerator in separate covered containers. Pour a thin layer of milk or water over the yolks to prevent them from hardening. Yolks can be stored for 4 days, but whites should not be kept for more than 2-3 days.

Separating eggs

Knock the egg sharply against the rim of a bowl or cup to break the shell in half. Carefully transfer the yolk from one half shell to the other until all the white has drained into the bowl, then slide the yolk into another bowl.

Beating eggs

Whole eggs should be beaten vigorously, turning them over with upward movements, using a fork, spoon, whisk, or electric hand beater or electric mixer. Beating the eggs in this manner draws in air and so increases the volume of the eggs; the biggest volume is obtained from eggs beaten in a warm room at a temperature of 75°F. Use beaten eggs immediately.

When mixing egg yolks and sugar, beat the yolks first, then add the sugar and continue beating until the mixture drops in broad ribbons.

Egg whites beaten to a stiff but not dry foam are used for soufflés or meringues. Use a spotlessly clean and dry bowl, preferably of unlined copper, of a shape that keeps the whisk in constant contact with the egg whites as they are beaten.

Folding in egg whites

Pile the beaten egg whites on top of the mixture, and with a rubber spatula draw part of the mixture from the bottom of the bowl over the whites. Incorporate all the whites carefully so that they do not lose their air content. Egg whites can also be folded in with the hands.

Baked eggs (eggs en cocotte)

For each serving, melt 1 tablespoon of butter in a small ovenproof dish; break an egg into a cup and slide it into the dish. Season lightly with salt and freshly ground pepper. Bake the egg in the center of a preheated oven at 350°F for approximately 8 minutes, or until the white is just set.

Alternatively, spoon 2 tablespoons of heavy cream over the seasoned egg and set the ovenproof dish in a pan containing an inch of hot water. Bake as before.

Boiled eggs

Boiled eggs can be soft-cooked (softly set white, with a runny yolk), medium-cooked for eggs mollet

COOKING TIMES FOR EGGS

Soft-cooked

Extra large eggs	4½ minutes
Large eggs	3-3½ minutes
Medium eggs	2½-3 minutes

Medium-cooked

Extra-large eggs	6½ minutes
Large eggs	4-5 minutes
Medium eggs	3½-4½ minutes

Hard-cooked

Extra-large eggs	12 minutes
Large eggs	10 minutes
Medium eggs	9 minutes

(firm white, with a just-soft yolk), or hard-cooked (with a firm white and dry, solid yolk).

Soft-cooked eggs Bring a pan of cold water to a boil over gentle heat and, with a spoon, carefully lower each egg into the water. To cook a large number of eggs, put them in a wire basket or egg holder so that all the eggs can be immersed in the water at the same time and can be removed all at once.

Medium-cooked eggs Put the eggs in a saucepan and cover them with cold water; bring the water to a boil over low heat. As soon as water boils, remove the saucepan from the heat, cover it with a lid, and leave the eggs to stand in the pan for the length of time indicated on the egg-cooking chart on this page.

Hard-cooked eggs Cook the eggs in boiling water for 10-12 minutes. Plunge them immediately in cold water to prevent further cooking and to make shelling easier. Tap the eggs around the middle with the back of a knife and pull away the two half shells. Shelled eggs should not be exposed for long to air, as they become tough. Put eggs to be served cold in ice water.

Fried eggs

Melt butter (2-4 tablespoons is enough for 4 eggs) or equal amounts of oil and butter, in a skillet* over low heat. Break the eggs, one by one, onto a saucer and slide them into the fat. Reduce the heat immediately and baste* the eggs with the butter to ensure even cooking. Fry the eggs for 3-5 minutes, or until the whites are firm.

Poached eggs

Fill a heavy-bottomed skillet with cold water to a depth of 1 inch, add a pinch of salt, and bring to a boil. Reduce the heat and keep the water just simmering. Break the eggs, one by one, onto a saucer and slide them carefully into the gently simmering water. Using 2 spoons, quickly gather the whites over and around the yolks. Cover the skillet with a lid and simmer the eggs for 4-5 minutes, or just until the yolks are set and the whites are firm.

For more regularly shaped poached eggs, round pastry cutters can be set in the pan and the eggs slid inside them. Alternatively, an egg poacher can be used: Half fill the pan of the poacher with water, bring to a boil, then reduce the heat and keep the water simmering. Melt a pat of butter or margarine in each egg container and break an egg into them. Season lightly with salt and freshly ground pepper. Cover the pan with the lid and cook the eggs for 2 minutes or until they just set.

For poached eggs, gather the egg whites around the yolks.

Scrambled eggs

Use 2 large eggs per person, and for each egg allow 1 tablespoon butter. Beat the eggs with a little salt and freshly ground pepper in a bowl. Melt the butter in a heavy-bottomed pan or in the top of a double boiler, pour in the egg mixture, and cook over low heat. As the egg mixture begins to thicken, stir it continuously until it is soft.

Omelets

There are two types of omelets—plain and fluffy (soufflé). Plain omelets are served as an entrée, while fluffy omelets may be entrées or desserts. Cook omelets in a special omelet pan or small skillet that is never washed, only wiped.

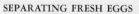

Break the shell in half.

Drain egg white from shells.

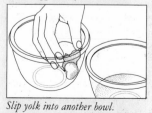

Slip yolk into another bowl.

Plain Omelet

PREPARATION TIME: *3 minutes*
COOKING TIME: *1½–2 minutes*

INGREDIENTS (*for 1*):
2 eggs
1 tablespoon water
¼ teaspoon salt
Freshly ground pepper
1 tablespoon butter

Break the eggs into a bowl. Add the water, salt, and pepper; beat until blended but not foamy. Get the pan very hot, add the butter, which should immediately sizzle and melt, and pour in the egg mixture. Holding the pan handle with one hand, shake the pan while stirring rapidly with a fork for a minute or two. When the omelet is almost set but still slightly runny on top, gather it at the far edge of the pan with the back of a fork and quickly turn it out onto a warm plate. Serve the omelet at once.

MAKING AN OMELET

Stirring the eggs with a fork

Gathering the eggs at edge of pan

Turning omelet onto a plate

Savory omelets

Many ingredients can be added to the omelet mixture before cooking, or they can be cooked separately and spread on the omelet before folding.

Cheese: add ¼ cup finely grated cheese to mixture before cooking.

Ham: sprinkle 1 tablespoon of finely chopped ham over the omelet before folding.

Spanish: Sauté 1 chopped medium onion and 1 chopped green pepper in 3 tablespoons of butter or bacon fat until soft. Add 1 cup canned, drained tomatoes, 1 teaspoon salt, ¼ teaspoon black pepper, and ½ teaspoon dried basil. Simmer, stirring occasionally, for about 25 minutes. Spoon on the omelet before folding. Enough for 2 omelets.

Fluffy omelets

These can be filled with savory ingredients or served as a dessert.

PREPARATION TIME: *15 minutes*
COOKING TIME: *3–5 minutes*

INGREDIENTS (*for 2*):
2 eggs
¼ teaspoon salt
Black pepper
1 tablespoon butter

Separate the eggs and beat the whites until stiff, then beat in the salt and a few grinds of pepper. Beat yolks with 2 tablespoons of water until thick, and fold them into egg whites.

Melt the butter in an omelet pan and spoon in the egg mixture. Cook over moderate heat until the underside is golden. Place under a hot broiler for a moment to brown the top lightly. Add any savory filling and fold the omelet in half.

For a sweet omelet, omit salt and pepper and beat the egg whites with 2 tablespoons sugar. Add a few drops of vanilla extract to the creamed egg yolks, then cook the omelet as already described. Spread with a thin layer of warm preserves or fruit purée before folding it in half. Sprinkle with sugar before serving.

Soufflés

These light, airy egg dishes may be sweet or savory and are served hot or cold. Hot soufflés are based on a thick white sauce to which egg yolks are added before the beaten whites are folded in. To allow even rising during baking, always use a straight-sided buttered soufflé dish and let the soufflé mixture come no more than three-quarters up the sides. It is not necessary to prepare a hot soufflé with a paper collar but it is vitally important to serve it the moment it is taken from the oven, or it will collapse.

Ham Soufflé

PREPARATION TIME: *20 minutes*
COOKING TIME: *45 minutes*

INGREDIENTS (*for 4–6*):
3 eggs
1¼ cups thick white sauce (p.301)
Salt and black pepper
¾ cup cooked chopped ham
1 egg white

Butter a 7-inch, 1½-quart soufflé dish and tie a paper collar around it. Separate the eggs and prepare the white sauce. Cool it slightly, then stir in the chopped ham. Beat the egg yolks, one at a time, into the basic sauce, and beat the whites in a bowl until stiff. Fold the whites carefully into the soufflé mixture and spoon it into the dish.

Set the prepared soufflé dish in a pan of hot water and bake in the center, or just above, of a preheated oven at 350°F for 40–45 minutes, or until the soufflé is well risen and has turned golden brown.

Hot soufflé variations

Caramel: omit salt and pepper from the white sauce. Heat 3 tablespoons of sugar until melted and brown; stir into sauce before adding eggs.

Cheese: blend 1 cup finely grated aged Cheddar cheese into the sauce.

Chocolate: omit salt and pepper from the sauce and blend in 2 ounces melted sweet chocolate.

Corn: blend ½ cup whole-kernel corn and 2 slices bacon, cooked and crumbled, into the sauce.

Fish: add ¾ cup cooked, finely flaked haddock to the sauce.

Cold soufflés

These sweet soufflés are made with whipped cream and gelatin. As they are not baked but left to set in the refrigerator, they cannot rise. To achieve the characteristic risen look of a soufflé, the dish is prepared with a paper collar extending above the rim. Cut a band 3 inches deeper than the dish from a double layer of waxed paper; aluminum foil will work equally well. Fold up 1 inch along one of the long edges. Wrap the band around the dish, the folded edge level with the bottom and the upper edge extending beyond the rim by 2 inches. Tie the band securely in place with string or hold it on with a rubber band. Spoon the prepared soufflé mixture into the dish until it reaches almost to the top of the collar.

When the soufflé has set, remove the paper collar. This is most easily done by running a long, narrow warmed knife blade between the set soufflé and the paper.

Lemon Soufflé

PREPARATION TIME: *25 minutes*
CHILLING TIME: *1–2 hours*

INGREDIENTS (*for 4*):
2 lemons
3 eggs
⅓ cup sugar
2 teaspoons gelatin
½ cup heavy cream

Grate the rind from the lemons and squeeze out the juice. Separate the egg yolks from the whites and beat the yolks, sugar, lemon rind, and juice in a bowl until thick.

In a small bowl, mix the gelatin with 2 tablespoons of cold water and set the bowl in a pan of hot water until the gelatin has completely dissolved and is clear.

Allow the gelatin to cool slightly, then pour it into the lemon mixture and blend thoroughly.

Beat the heavy cream until it just holds its shape, then fold it into the lemon mixture.

Beat the egg whites until stiff and fold them carefully into the mixture when it has nearly set. Spoon the lemon soufflé into a prepared 6-inch or 4-cup soufflé dish and chill in the refrigerator until set.

Cold sweet soufflé variations

Chocolate: melt 2–3 ounces sweet chocolate and stir it into the yolk mixture; then add 1 tablespoon brandy or rum.

Coffee: add 4–5 tablespoons strong black coffee and 1 tablespoon Tia Maria or curaçao liqueur to the yolk mixture.

Orange: add the grated rind of a large orange and 4 tablespoons orange juice to the yolk mixture.

MAKING A SOUFFLÉ COLLAR

Wrapping paper band around dish

Securing band with string

335

Rice and Pasta

These foodstuffs are cereals that form the basic diet in many countries. Because these cereals are rather bland in themselves, they combine well with many other types of food. Both can replace vegetables with a main course.

RICE

There are several varieties of rice—white polished rice, brown unpolished rice, and wild rice. In addition, parboiled rice and precooked rice are widely available.

White and brown rice

White and brown rice come in two grain sizes—long and short grain.

Long grain rice is suitable for making savory dishes, such as curries, salads, paellas, stuffings, croquettes, and rice molds.

Short grain rice is best used for puddings, risottos, and molds.

Parboiled rice

Because it is steamed by a special process before milling, parboiled or partially cooked rice retains much of its food value and flavor.

Precooked rice

This has been fully cooked, then dehydrated before packaging. It is prepared by soaking in hot water for 5 minutes. Precooked rice can be used for quick sweet or savory rice dishes.

Wild rice

This is not a cereal but long seeds from a grass growing wild in parts of Canada and the northern United States. It has a unique flavor, but is expensive.

Cooking white rice

Wash rice before cooking it by putting it in a strainer and rinsing it under cold running water. (This is not necessary with packaged North American rice.) Allow 2 ounces uncooked rice per person. During cooking, rice almost triples in bulk.

After cooking, rice should be dry and slightly fluffy, separated into individual grains. To obtain this result, cook rice by boiling or by the absorption methods described below.

Boiling white rice

Use 8 cups of water and 1 teaspoon salt to each cup of rice. Measure the water into a large pan and bring to a boil; add the salt and rice. Boil the rice rapidly for 12–15 minutes, or until soft but not mushy. To test the rice, squeeze a grain between thumb and forefinger. When cooked, the center will be just soft.

Drain the rice in a sieve and rinse it under hot water. Return it to the pan, with a chunk of soft butter, and toss the rice to coat it evenly with the butter.

Cover the pan with a lid and leave for 10 minutes to dry the rice. Shake the pan occasionally to prevent the grains from sticking together.

Alternatively, put the drained rice in a shallow, buttered baking dish, cover it tightly, and allow it to dry in the center of a preheated oven at 325°F for 10 minutes.

Absorption

Method 1 This is an easy cooking method that ensures tender separate grains. For each cup of rice (enough for 3 servings), use 2 cups of water or clear stock and ½ teaspoon salt. Bring the liquid to a boil in a large pan, then add the salt and rice, stirring for a few minutes.

As soon as the water boils again, cover with a tight-fitting lid. Cook the rice over low heat for 15–20 minutes and do not at any time uncover the pan.

At the end of 15–20 minutes, all the water should be absorbed and the rice should be dry and tender. Remove the pan from the heat and separate the grains with a fork. Serve immediately.

Method 2 Rice can also be cooked by absorption in the oven. Use the same measurements as in the first method and put the rice in a casserole dish. Pour in boiling salted liquid, stir thoroughly, and cover the dish tightly with foil and a lid. Cook the rice in the center of a preheated oven at 350°F for 30–45 minutes, or until all the liquid is completely absorbed and the grains are soft.

Cooking brown rice

Brown rice can be cooked in the same way as white rice but needs a longer time. For boiled rice, allow about 25 minutes; with the absorption method, simmer the rice for 45 minutes. Brown rice cooked in the oven needs about 1 hour.

Cooking wild rice

Wash 1 cup wild rice in 3 or 4 changes of cold water, then cook in 4 cups salted boiling water for about 25–30 minutes until done but not mushy. Drain and serve with butter.

Rice Pilaff

PREPARATION TIME: *5 minutes*
COOKING TIME: *30 minutes*

INGREDIENTS (*for 4*):
½ cup long grain rice
1 onion
2 tablespoons butter or oil
1 cup boiling chicken stock
Salt and black pepper

Peel and finely chop the onion. Melt the butter and sauté the onion until pale golden. Add the rice and sauté until the rice is faintly colored. Pour the boiling stock over the rice and add ½ teaspoon salt and freshly ground pepper to taste. Cover the saucepan with a tight-fitting lid and cook over low heat until all the liquid is absorbed, about 20 minutes.

Rice mold

Cold cooked rice can be made into an attractive hot or cold main course. Heat a garlic-flavored sauce vinaigrette (p.304) and toss the rice in this. Cooked peas may also be added. Pack the dressed rice and peas loosely into a ring mold and smooth the top with a spatula.

If the rice is to be served warm, set the ring mold in a roasting pan containing 1 inch of boiling water. Cover the mold with foil and simmer on top of the stove for 10–15 minutes. Place a serving dish on top of the mold and turn it upside down. The center of the mold can be filled with chopped chicken, flaked fish, or shrimp, in a creamed or curry sauce. Creamed or buttered vegetables are also good.

If the rice is to be served cold, let the rice cool, cover with foil, then put the mold in the refrigerator for about 1 hour or until firm. Hold a serving dish over the mold, turn the mold upside down, and fill the center with seafood bound with a lemony mayonnaise (p.303).

RICE MOLD

Filling the buttered ring mold

Turning out the set rice

Rice salads

Cold leftover rice makes a good basis for a variety of salads. Toss the rice in a well-flavored sauce vinaigrette (p.304) or a thinned-down mayonnaise (p.303), and serve with cold meat, fish, or poultry. For a more substantial course, mix the dressed rice with chopped ham or chicken, flaked fish, such as tuna, and chopped pimientos and add cooked peas and whole-kernel corn. Fresh herbs, such as finely chopped parsley, chives, and tarragon, can also be mixed with a rice salad.

PASTA

Pasta dishes include macaroni, spaghetti, tagliatelle, lasagne, ravioli, cannelloni, vermicelli, and many others. The basis of pasta is flour made from a hard durum wheat. The flour is mixed with oil and water, and sometimes spinach purée and egg, to a paste. This is rolled and cut or shaped into long threads, tubes, strips, and other different shapes that sometimes enclose a stuffing or filling. Pasta is dried before being sold.

Pasta can be served as a main dish, as a side dish (instead of potatoes, for example), as a first course, or as a garnish with soups. As a first or main course, pasta is usually served with a savory sauce or filling, often with grated Parmesan cheese.

Cooking and serving pasta

All pasta is boiled, but cooking times vary according to the shape, size, and freshness of the different kinds. Pasta should be cooked in plenty of boiling salted water until it is just firm to the bite (*al dente*). Overcooking turns pasta into a soft and soggy mass. Allow about 3 ounces of uncooked pasta for each person.

Bring a large pan of salted water to a rolling boil and add a couple of drops of oil and the pasta. The long strands of spaghetti should not be broken up. Hold the spaghetti at one end and lower the other into the boiling water. As the spaghetti softens and curls around in the water, push the rest of the spaghetti down.

Keep the pasta at a steady boil, uncovered, until just tender. Stir occasionally to prevent the pasta from sticking to the pan. To test, try a piece between the teeth; it should be just soft to the bite. Drain thoroughly in a colander, then return the pasta to the pan with a large chunk of butter or a tablespoon of olive oil. Toss the pasta thoroughly and season with salt and pepper.

Types of pasta

There are many different types of pasta on sale in supermarkets and Italian groceries. The more available are shown in the illustration opposite. Reading from top to bottom are five types of straight spaghetti, from the threadlike capellini, followed by fedelini, spaghettini, spaghetti, and the thicker mezzani. Below is fusilli, a spindle-shaped spaghetti, followed by a ribbon pasta, mafalde, and the large tubular manicotti, suitable for filling with savory mixtures such as meat or cheese. Tagliatelle, a flat and narrow ribbon noodle, is available as yellow and green (*verde*) pasta. Below tagliatelle are two tubes of the familiar macaroni.

Pasta in fancy shapes, all of which are served with a savory sauce or butter and Parmesan cheese, includes elbow macaroni, butterfly farfalle, wheel-shaped ruote, shell pasta known as conchiglie, corkscrew tortiglioni, and the small hat-shaped cappelletti.

Pasta used for soup garnishes comes in many small and decorative forms, such as nocchette, followed by conchigliette, the tiny rings known as anellini, and the grainlike semini. Last is the smallest of all, acini di pepe.

Spaghetti with Oil and Garlic

PREPARATION TIME: *10 minutes*
COOKING TIME: *about 7 minutes*

INGREDIENTS (*for 4*):
1 pound spaghetti
½ cup olive oil
2 teaspoons minced garlic
½ cup grated Parmesan cheese

Cook the spaghetti in 6 quarts of boiling salted water until just tender; drain. Warm the olive oil and garlic in a saucepan. Toss spaghetti quickly with the oil and garlic. Serve the cheese separately.

Linguine with Clam Sauce

PREPARATION TIME: *30 minutes*
COOKING TIME: *about 7 minutes*

INGREDIENTS (*for 4–6*):
24 cherrystone clams
6 quarts water
2 tablespoons salt
1 pound linguine
1 cup heavy cream
½ cup butter
1 tablespoon finely chopped garlic
¼ cup finely chopped parsley
3 tablespoons finely chopped fresh basil or 1 teaspoon dried basil
½ teaspoon dried thyme
Pepper
½ cup freshly grated Parmesan cheese

Open the clams and save the juice. Chop the clams coarsely.

Bring the water to a boil and add the salt and linguine. While the linguine is cooking, heat the heavy cream in a saucepan just to a boil.

Meanwhile, melt half the butter in another saucepan and add the chopped clams, their juice, garlic, parsley, basil, thyme, freshly ground pepper to taste, and the hot cream. Remove the saucepan from the heat.

When the linguine is done, drain it quickly in a colander. Pour the linguine onto a large heated platter, add the sauce, and toss. Add the remaining butter, cheese, and salt to taste. Toss again. Serve immediately.

Do not break spaghetti, but curl the strands gradually into boiling water.

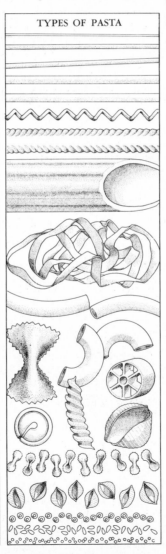

TYPES OF PASTA

Fats and Oils

Fats and oils play an important part in cooking, as they enhance or sometimes alter the flavor of food, especially during sautéing or deep-frying.

FATS

These are derived from animal foods, such as meat, dairy products, and oily fish, and from nuts or vegetables. Cooking fats include butter, blended and hydrogenated fats, drippings, lard, margarine, and suet.

Bacon fat

Rendered bacon fat can be used for sautéing meats and vegetables.

Butter

This is made from the fatty substances skimmed from full cream milk. It is churned and then pressed to squeeze out water. It is used as the cooking medium for egg dishes, for sautéed vegetables and other foods, and in baking cakes.

Clarified butter

This is sometimes used in recipes for sautéing and broiling. It is an expensive cooking medium, as 8 ounces of butter produce only about 5 ounces of clarified butter. Melt 8 ounces of unsalted butter in a small pan over gentle heat until the butter begins to foam. Cook until the foaming stops. Remove the pan from the heat and let it stand until the milky deposits have sunk to the bottom, leaving a clear yellow liquid. Pour this liquid carefully through cheesecloth into a bowl.

Melted butter

Usually served as a sauce with poached fish and boiled vegetables. Melt over low heat and season with salt, freshly ground pepper, and drops of lemon juice.

Beurre noisette

This is melted butter allowed to brown lightly before being seasoned. It is served with eggs, brains, poached skate, fish roe, and boiled vegetables, such as Brussels sprouts.

Beurre noir

Melted butter heated until it becomes nut-brown, but not black. Add 2 tablespoons of finely chopped parsley, 1 tablespoon of wine vinegar, and 1 tablespoon of chopped capers to every 4 ounces of butter. Serve with the same types of food as beurre noisette.

Meunière butter

This sauce is made from the butter in which fish has been sautéed. Add a little extra butter to the pan juices and cook until light brown. Blend in a squeeze of lemon juice and a little chopped parsley.

Savory butters

These are used to garnish meat, fish, and vegetable dishes, or they can be added to sauces. Softened butter is flavored with varying ingredients according to the dish it is meant to garnish. On average, allow 2 tablespoons of butter per person.

Soften the butter in a bowl before blending in the flavoring ingredient. Herbs and vegetables must be finely chopped, pounded, or thoroughly crushed. A mortar and pestle are ideal for this purpose. When all the ingredients are combined, roll the butter flat between two sheets of damp waxed paper. Chill in the refrigerator before cutting into small fancy shapes.

SAVORY BUTTERS

Butter (4 ounces)	Flavoring	Preparation	Serving suggestions
FISH BUTTERS			
Anchovy butter	*6 anchovy fillets*	Rinse the anchovies in cold water to remove salt and oil. Dry. Rub through a sieve and blend with the butter.	*Broiled meat or fish. As a garnish for cold hors d'oeuvres, or added to a white sauce*
Crab or shrimp butter	*4 ounces crabmeat or 4 ounces cooked shrimp*	Rub the crabmeat or shrimp through a sieve and blend with the butter.	*As garnish for cold hors d'oeuvres or cold fish, or added to fish sauces*
FRUIT BUTTERS			
Lemon butter	*Grated rind of ½ lemon Salt and black pepper*	Blend the rind with the butter. Season to taste with salt and pepper.	*As garnish for cold hors d'oeuvres*
Tomato butter	*2 tablespoons tomato paste*	Blend the tomato paste with the butter.	*Broiled meat or fish, as garnish for cold hors d'oeuvres, or added to sauces*
HERB BUTTERS			
Chive butter	*8 tablespoons chopped chives*	Blanch and drain the chives. Mince and pound to a paste. Blend into the butter.	*Broiled meat or fish*
Chivry (ravigote) butter	*1 teaspoon each chervil, chives, parsley, and tarragon 1 tablespoon chopped shallot*	Wrap the herbs in cheesecloth and blanch in scalding-hot water for 3 minutes. Drain, dip the bag in cold water, drain again, and wring dry. Blanch the shallots and pound, with the herbs, to a paste. Blend with the butter.	*As garnish for cold hors d'oeuvres, or added to white sauces*
Maître d'hôtel butter	*1 tablespoon minced parsley Salt and black pepper Lemon juice*	Blend the parsley with the butter and season to taste with salt, ground pepper, and a few drops of lemon juice.	*Broiled meat or fish, boiled vegetables, and coated fried fish*
Tarragon butter	*¼ cup fresh tarragon leaves*	Blanch the tarragon in scalding-hot water, drain, and dry. Pound to a paste and blend with the butter.	*As garnish for cold hors d'oeuvres*
Nut butter	*¼ cup blanched almonds, walnuts, or pistachio nuts*	Crush the nuts to a fine paste: add a few drops of water to prevent the paste from becoming oily. Blend with the butter.	*As garnish for cold hors d'oeuvres, or added to sauces and soups*
VEGETABLE BUTTERS			
Garlic butter	*4 cloves garlic*	Peel and crush the garlic and blend with the butter.	*As garnish for cold hors d'oeuvres, or added to white sauces*
Green butter	*4 ounces spinach*	Blanch the spinach, drain, and wring out as much moisture as possible. Pound until smooth, then blend with the butter.	*Added to white sauces or used as garnish for cold fish*
Horseradish butter	*4 tablespoons grated horseradish*	Pound the horseradish smooth in a mortar, with the butter.	*As garnish for cold hors d'oeuvres, or added to white sauces*
Mushroom butter	*4 ounces button mushrooms 2 tablespoons butter Salt and black pepper*	Chop the mushrooms finely, cook lightly in butter, and season to taste. Pound until smooth, then blend with the butter.	*As garnish for cold hors d'oeuvres, or added to white sauces*
Shallot butter	*4 ounces shallots*	Blanch the shallots in scalding-hot water and drain. Peel and chop finely. Pound to a paste, then blend into the butter.	*Broiled meat or fish*
MISCELLANEOUS BUTTERS			
Mustard butter	*1 tablespoon Dijon mustard*	Blend the mustard thoroughly with the softened butter.	*Broiled meat or fish*
Snail butter	*1 tablespoon chopped shallot 1 teaspoon chopped parsley 1 clove garlic Salt and black pepper*	Chop the shallot and parsley finely. Peel and crush the garlic. Blend with the butter and season with salt and pepper.	*Stuffed into snail shells*

Drippings

This is the rendered fat from meat, chiefly beef or pork.

The fat can be used for deep-frying, but as it has a fairly high water content, it tends to spatter as it cooks and is better used for roasting and sautéing.

Lard

This is processed from pure pork fat and is excellent for both sautéing and deep-frying. It can be used in pie pastries and in some cakes. Leaf lard, or pork kidney fat, is even purer.

Margarine

Made from vegetable oils and fats blended with milk or cream and vitamins, margarine is interchangeable with butter for baking purposes. It is not suitable for deep-frying because of its high water content.

Poultry fats

Rendered fat from the cavities or under the skins of chicken, goose, duck, and turkey is excellent for sautéing and as an ingredient in certain dishes.

Suet

The fat deposits from the loins and around the kidneys of beef or sheep. It is sold fresh for grating or chopping. Suet is used in some pastries, in mincemeat, Christmas puddings, and stuffings.

Vegetable shortening

Those sold under various brand names in cans are usually composed of oils, such as soybean, corn, or peanut, made solid by incorporating hydrogen into them, which also improves their keeping qualities. Some are combinations of vegetable and animal or dairy fats. Hydrogenated lard and shortening can be kept in a cool place, unrefrigerated, for 2–3 months; they keep even longer in the refrigerator. Use for sautéing, deep-frying, and for making pastry, cakes, and biscuits.

OILS

Edible oils are liquid forms of fat derived from fish, vegetables, cereals, fruits, nuts, and seeds. Oils vary in color and flavor, and choice is a matter of individual taste. Most oils are suitable for sautéing and sometimes for baking, but for mayonnaise and salad dressing, olive oil is best.

Cooking with oil

Vegetable oils (and lard) or oil in combination with butter can be used for sautéing. They are, however, more frequently used for deep-frying. Good-quality oils or lard can be heated to the high temperatures that are necessary to seal and crisp food on the outside without being absorbed into the food.

Deep-frying

For deep-frying, use a deep, heavy-bottomed saucepan or a special deep-fryer fitted with a wire basket for easy removal of foods. Fill the pan no more than one-third with oil, vegetable shortening, or melted lard, and heat over moderate heat. The temperature of 375°F is suitable for most deep-frying.

Fritters and croquettes are fried at 375°F, while French fries can be fried at 385°F. The higher heat is necessary because the water content of potatoes lowers the temperature of the oil. However, for best results, deep-fry potatoes twice at 375°F. Fry them for 2–3 minutes to extract the water, drain, and reheat the oil before frying the second time.

Frying times vary according to the size and type of food. For foods made from previously cooked ingredients, such as croquettes, allow only 2–3 minutes. Fritters need 3–5 minutes; French fries, 4–6 minutes.

Oil, vegetable shortening, and lard can be used several times for deep-frying. After cooking, let the oil cool completely, then strain it into a jar. Store, covered, in the refrigerator for up to 3 months.

Desserts

A dessert is the high point of a meal. Choose it carefully so that the entire meal is well balanced. If the main course is rich, the dessert should be simple and light. After a vegetable luncheon, serve a protein dessert made with cream, milk, eggs, or cheese. A menu short of rice, potatoes, or pasta can be topped off with a cake, rice pudding, or other starchy dessert.

STEAMED, BOILED, AND BAKED PUDDINGS

Puddings can be steamed in a large saucepan. Stand the pudding on a rack to raise it. Pour water into the pan until it reaches halfway up the basin or mold. Keep at least a 1-inch space around the basin.

The water in the pan must be kept gently boiling throughout cooking. Add more boiling water at intervals as it boils away.

Preparing a pudding basin or mold

Butter the basin or mold lightly and cut and butter a round of cooking parchment or waxed paper to fit the bottom; this prevents the pudding from sticking when it is turned out. Fill the basin no more than two-thirds with pudding mixture. Butter a piece of waxed paper thoroughly and make a 1-inch pleat in the center to allow for the pudding to rise. Lay the paper over the top of the basin and cover it with a piece of pleated foil. Tie the paper and foil covering securely with string below the lip of the basin. Make a string handle to lift the pudding out.

Turning out a pudding

Lift the pudding from the pan and remove the covering. Allow it to cool and shrink slightly, then loosen the pudding at one side of the basin to let in the air. Place a dish over the basin and turn it upside down.

Baked puddings

Apart from steaming, puddings can also be baked in the oven. The pudding mixture should be a little softer than for steamed puddings to give a crisp surface.

To prevent jam-based puddings from caramelizing, set the dish in a shallow pan of water. Bake in a preheated oven at 350°–375°F.

Apple Crumble

PREPARATION TIME: *25 minutes*
COOKING TIME: *45 minutes*

INGREDIENTS (*for 4–6*):
1½ pounds cooking apples
2 tablespoons sugar
Grated rind of ½ lemon
TOPPING:
1½ cups flour
6 tablespoons margarine
4 tablespoons granulated sugar
1 tablespoon brown sugar

Peel, core, and slice the apples thinly. Put them into a 1½-quart baking dish and sprinkle with the 2 tablespoons sugar. Top the apples with the grated lemon rind.

For the topping, sift the flour into a mixing bowl; cut up the margarine into small pieces and rub it lightly into the flour with the tips of the fingers. Mix in the granulated sugar. Spoon the crumble mixture evenly over the apples and press it down lightly. Sprinkle the brown sugar evenly over the top.

Place the dish on a baking tray and bake in the center of the oven at 400°F for 45 minutes.

Blueberry Grunt

This is an easy dish to make. Other fruits, such as apples, peaches, or apricots, can be substituted for the blueberries.

PREPARATION TIME: *20 minutes*
COOKING TIME: *25–30 minutes*

INGREDIENTS (*for 6*):
3 cups blueberries
⅓ cup sugar
¼ teaspoon cinnamon
¼ teaspoon nutmeg
¼ teaspoon cloves
¼ cup molasses
2 tablespoons lemon juice
BISCUIT CRUST:
1 cup flour
1½ teaspoons baking powder
¼ teaspoon salt
3 tablespoons butter
1 tablespoon vegetable shortening
1 egg, lightly beaten
⅓–½ cup milk
HARD SAUCE:
1 cup confectioners' sugar, sifted
½ cup butter, softened
Pinch of salt
1 tablespoon brandy or rum

Pick over the berries, removing any stems, twigs, and leaves. Wash, drain, and spread them in a deep 9-inch pie pan. Combine the sugar and spices and sift the mixture over the berries. Dribble the molasses over the berries and sprinkle them with lemon juice. Bake the berries at 375°F for 5 minutes, or just until they begin to render juice. Remove the pan from the oven. Increase the heat to 425°F.

To make the crust, sift the flour with the baking powder and salt and blend in the butter and shortening. Stir in the beaten egg and as much of the milk as is needed to produce a soft dough. Drop the dough by tablespoons over the berries and spread it evenly to cover them. Bake 20 minutes, or until the biscuit dough is well browned.

To make the hard sauce, beat the confectioners' sugar gradually into the softened butter. Add the salt and the brandy or rum. Blend. Chill thoroughly. Serve the dessert with this sauce on the side, or with heavy cream from a pitcher.

Lemon Pudding

PREPARATION TIME: *15 minutes*
COOKING TIME: *40 minutes*

INGREDIENTS (*for 4–6*):
3 egg yolks
3 tablespoons all-purpose flour
1 cup sugar
½ teaspoon salt
1½ tablespoons melted butter
6 tablespoons lemon juice
1 tablespoon grated lemon rind
1¼ cups milk
3 egg whites

Preheat the oven to 350°F. Beat the egg yolks well. Sift the dry ingredients and combine with the egg yolks. Add the melted butter, lemon juice, lemon rind, and milk. Beat the egg whites until stiff and fold them into the mixture.

Pour into a 2-quart baking dish and bake for 40 minutes or until firm. This pudding separates into a cake on top and a custard on the bottom. Serve with whipped cream.

Chocolate Mocha Pudding

PREPARATION TIME: *10 minutes*
COOKING TIME: *20 minutes*

INGREDIENTS (*for 4–6*):
2 squares (2 ounces) unsweetened chocolate
1 cup strong coffee
⅔ cup sugar
¼ cup all-purpose flour
¼ teaspoon salt
1 cup milk
3 egg yolks, beaten
2 tablespoons butter
2 teaspoons vanilla extract

Heat the chocolate and coffee together over low heat until the chocolate is melted. Stir to blend.

Combine the sugar, flour, and salt in the top of a double boiler. Stir in the milk. Gradually stir in the hot coffee-chocolate mixture. Bring rapidly to a boil, stirring constantly. Cook for 2 minutes.

Blend a small amount of the hot mixture into the beaten egg yolks, then stir into the mixture in the double boiler. Cook over simmering water for 5 minutes, stirring constantly, until thickened.

Remove from the simmering water and stir in the butter and the vanilla extract. Spoon into individual bowls and chill thoroughly before serving.

Peach and Almond Pudding

PREPARATION TIME: *20 minutes*
COOKING TIME: *45 minutes*

INGREDIENTS (*for 8*):
¼ cup light brown sugar, firmly packed
¼ teaspoon cinnamon
¼ cup chopped almonds
3 cups sliced peaches
1½ cups sifted all-purpose flour
2 teaspoons baking powder
¾ teaspoon salt
¼ cup butter
½ cup sugar
1 egg
½ cup milk
½ teaspoon vanilla extract
1 cup heavy cream, whipped

Butter the bottom of an 8-inch square baking dish and sprinkle with the brown sugar, cinnamon, and chopped almonds. Place the sliced peaches in the dish.

Sift together the flour, baking powder, and salt. Cream the butter and sugar until light and fluffy. Beat in the egg, then the dry ingredients alternately. Add the milk mixed with the vanilla extract.

Spoon the batter over the fruit. Bake at 350°F for about 45 minutes. Serve with the whipped cream.

JELLIES, MOLDS, AND MOUSSES

These cold desserts are all made with unflavored gelatin, an extract from animal bones, tendons, and skin. Gelatin is available in granular and sheet form.

Some fresh fruit—pineapple, for example—contains enzymes that prevent the jelling action from taking place. However, these enzymes are destroyed if canned fruit is used or if the fruit is cooked before being combined with the gelatin.

Setting gelatin

Jellied mixtures left to set in a refrigerator need less gelatin than those setting at normal room temperature. Desserts made in individual glasses need less gelatin than a dessert made in a mold for turning out later. Jellied mixtures tend to toughen if kept too long in a refrigerator. They are best eaten on the day they are made.

Directions for using granular gelatin are given on the package. In general, 1 ¼-ounce package (1 tablespoon) will set 2 cups of liquid placed in a mold in the refrigerator, and 2 teaspoons will set the same amount of liquid if it is spooned into serving glasses. Fruit purées and ingredients of a similar consistency, such as molds and mousses, need 1 teaspoon gelatin to jell 1 cup for setting in glasses.

For coating and glazing with jelly, for whipped jellies, and for setting fruit decorations, use the jelly when it has set to the consistency of unbeaten egg white.

Sheet gelatin

Sheet gelatin must be washed in cold water and then soaked in a bowl of cold water until soft, about 15–20 minutes. Squeeze the softened gelatin lightly to extract surplus water, and place it in a bowl with the measured amount of liquid used in the recipe. Place the bowl in a pan of hot water and heat, without boiling, over low heat until dissolved. Six sheets of gelatin equal 1 ounce of granular gelatin.

Grape Mold

PREPARATION TIME: *40 minutes*
SETTING TIME: *about 3 hours*

INGREDIENTS (*for 4*):
1¼ pounds large green grapes
2 tablespoons sugar
4 tablespoons water
1½ teaspoons unflavored gelatin
Juice of 2 oranges
Juice of 1 lemon
½ cup light cream

Dissolve the sugar with 2 tablespoons of water in a small pan over low heat, and dissolve the gelatin in a cup with the remaining water. Stir the hot sugar liquid into the gelatin, blend thoroughly, and stir it all into the fruit juices. The liquid should now measure 1 cup; add cold water if necessary. Leave the mixture to cool until it has jelled to the consistency of unbeaten egg white.

Peel and seed the grapes;* this is most easily done by dipping the whole bunch in boiling water for 30 seconds, then stripping off the skins and extracting the seeds from the stalk ends. Strain the fruit juices into a measuring cup.

Divide the grapes equally between 4 sundae glasses and spoon the jelly over them. Leave in the refrigerator until set, and just before serving float a thin layer of cream on top of each.

Honeycomb Mold

PREPARATION TIME: *45 minutes*
SETTING TIME: *3 hours*

INGREDIENTS (*for 6*):
Rind of 1 lemon
2 cups milk
2 eggs
¼ cup sugar
1 envelope (1 tablespoon) gelatin
2 tablespoons water

Peel the rind from the lemon as thinly as possible, using a vegetable peeler. Put the milk in a saucepan with the lemon rind and heat over very low heat for about 10 minutes.

Meanwhile, separate the eggs and beat the yolks with the sugar until thick and creamy. Strain the hot, not boiling, milk into the egg mixture and stir thoroughly. Return this custard to the pan and cook over low heat, stirring constantly, until it begins to thicken. Do not let it boil. Remove the pan from the heat.

Dissolve the gelatin in the water, then stir it into the custard. Put aside until it begins to set. Beat the egg whites until stiff, then fold them into the custard.

Rinse a 1-quart mold with cold water and spoon the mixture into the mold. Leave in the refrigerator until set. To turn out, dip the mold in hot water for 5 seconds, place a serving dish over the mold, and turn upside down.

Raspberry Mousse

PREPARATION TIME: *45 minutes*
SETTING TIME: *2 hours*

INGREDIENTS (*for 6*):
2 cups raspberries
3 whole eggs plus 2 egg yolks
½ cup sugar
1 envelope (1 tablespoon) gelatin
3 tablespoons water
1 cup heavy cream
Grated chocolate

Set 8 raspberries aside for garnish. Put the remainder (cleaned and washed) in a pan and simmer for about 5 minutes until soft. Rub the raspberries through a sieve—the purée should measure about 1 cup.

Put the whole eggs and the egg yolks in a bowl, together with the sugar. Place the bowl over a pan of hot water and beat the eggs until thick and fluffy. Take the bowl from the pan and set in a bowl of chilled water or ice cubes. Beat the egg mixture until cool.

Dissolve the gelatin in the water, stir it quickly into the raspberry purée, then beat this into the egg mixture. Whip the cream lightly and fold it into the raspberry mixture as it begins to set. Spoon the mousse into an attractive serving dish and leave in the refrigerator for 3 or more hours until set.

Just before serving, sprinkle coarsely grated chocolate over the mousse and decorate with the whole raspberries.

The texture of this mousse is light and creamy. For a firmer set, increase the gelatin to 4 teaspoons.

Honey Mousse

PREPARATION TIME: *45 minutes*
SETTING TIME: *3 hours*

INGREDIENTS (*for 6–8*):
¾ cup honey
Juice and grated rind of 1 lemon
4 eggs
1 teaspoon orange liqueur
2 cups heavy cream, whipped

Heat the honey, lemon juice, and rind in the top of a double boiler. Beat the eggs in a bowl, then slowly beat in the hot honey. Return the mixture to the double boiler. Stir over boiling water until thickened. Pour into a large bowl, cool, cover, then chill until cold. Add the liqueur and fold in the whipped cream. Turn into a serving dish; chill 3 hours.

SYLLABUBS AND TRIFLES

Syllabubs, which date back to Elizabethan times in the 16th century, were originally a drink consisting of a bubbling wine, called *Sill* or *Sille,* mixed with frothy cream. They later developed into a rich dessert with the addition of brandy, sherry, cream, and sugar. The trifle, developed from the syllabub in the 18th century, was made more substantial by the addition of such ingredients as sponge cake and preserves.

Syllabubs are ideal desserts for dinner parties, as they can be prepared well in advance.

Syllabub

PREPARATION TIME: *30 minutes*
RESTING TIME: *8 hours*

INGREDIENTS (*for 4*):
1 lemon
6 tablespoons white wine or sherry
2 tablespoons brandy
⅓ cup superfine sugar
1 cup heavy cream

Peel the lemon thinly, leaving all the white pith behind, and squeeze out the juice. Put the rind and 4 tablespoons of lemon juice in a bowl, add the wine (or sherry) and brandy, and leave the mixture to stand, covered, for several hours or overnight.

Strain the liquid into a clean bowl, add the sugar, and stir until dissolved. Pour the cream slowly into the liquid, stirring all the time. Beat the syllabub until it stands in soft peaks, then spoon it into small individual glasses or custard cups. Keep the syllabub in a cool place, but not in a refrigerator, until serving time. Serve with ladyfingers or small crisp cookies.

Separated Syllabub

PREPARATION TIME: *20 minutes*
RESTING TIME: *8 hours*

INGREDIENTS (*for 4*):
2 egg whites
½ cup superfine sugar
Juice of ½ lemon
½ cup sweet white wine
1 cup heavy cream

Beat the egg whites in a deep bowl until they form stiff peaks. Fold in the sugar, lemon juice, and wine with a rubber spatula. In another bowl, beat the heavy cream until it just holds its shape, then fold it into the egg whites.

Spoon the syllabub into tall, slim glasses and leave overnight or for several hours in a cool place. Serve with small macaroons.

Sherry Trifle

PREPARATION TIME: *30 minutes*
CHILLING TIME: *30 minutes*

INGREDIENTS (*for 6–8*):
8 ladyfingers
½ cup strawberry or other red jam
29-ounce can sliced peaches
4 tablespoons dry sherry
4 tablespoons peach juice
Custard sauce
2 tablespoons sliced almonds
1 cup heavy cream
8 small macaroons

Split the ladyfingers in half length-wise, spread them with a layer of jam, and sandwich them together. Cut the ladyfingers into ½-inch cross-wise slices and arrange them over the bottom of a shallow glass dish. Drain the peach slices, set a dozen aside for decoration, and arrange the remaining slices upright around the sides of the dish. Sprinkle the sherry and peach juice over the ladyfingers. Prepare the custard sauce.

Scatter the sliced almonds over the ladyfingers and peaches, and spoon the warm custard over them. Let stand at room temperature until completely cool. Beat the heavy cream until it just holds its shape (do not beat until stiff). Spoon it over the custard. Swirl the cream with a knife and decorate with peach slices and macaroons. Chill thoroughly in the refrigerator.

Syllabub Trifle

PREPARATION TIME: *30 minutes*
RESTING TIME: *4 hours*

INGREDIENTS (*for 6–8*):
1 quart strawberries
½ pound seedless green grapes
2 dozen small macaroons
3 egg whites
¾ cup superfine sugar
½ cup dry white wine
Juice of ½ lemon
2 tablespoons brandy
1 cup heavy cream

Hull,* wash, and drain the strawberries. Set 6–8 strawberries aside and arrange half the remainder together with half the grapes over the bottom of a glass dish. Set 8 macaroons aside and lay half of the remainder over the fruit. Cover the macaroons with the rest of the strawberries and grapes and place the last macaroons over them.

Beat the egg whites with half the sugar until stiff but not dry, then fold in the remaining sugar with a rubber spatula. Mix the wine, lemon juice, and brandy and blend it carefully into the egg whites. Beat the cream until it just holds its shape, set a little aside for decoration, and fold the egg white mixture into the remaining cream.

Spoon the cream over the macaroons and leave the trifle in the refrigerator until it is chilled but not cold.

Decorate the trifle with the reserved strawberries and macaroons sandwiched with cream.

EGG CUSTARDS

There are two basic types of egg custard: baked or steamed, and the softer pouring custard that is used as a sauce for cakes and puddings.

Egg whites set a baked custard, and the yolks give it its creamy consistency. However, because the yolks thicken at a higher temperature (149°F) than the egg whites (144°F), it is important to cook custards at the correct heat. Too much heat, especially direct heat, will cause an egg custard to curdle. Use a double boiler for making a pouring custard and stand a baked custard in a shallow container with about 1 inch cold water. If a double boiler is not available for cooking the pouring custard, use a heavy saucepan over very gentle heat.

For baked custards, 2 whole eggs plus 2 egg yolks will set 2 cups of milk. For a pouring custard, use 4 egg yolks—the whites cause curdling—to every 2 cups of milk.

Custard Sauce

PREPARATION AND COOKING TIME: *20 minutes*

INGREDIENTS (*for 1 pint*):
2 cups milk
½ vanilla bean
4 egg yolks
2 tablespoons sugar

Put the milk in a saucepan with the vanilla bean and heat over very gentle heat without boiling. Remove the pan from the heat, cover, and leave to infuse for 10 minutes. Remove the vanilla bean.

Beat the yolks in a bowl, add the sugar, and gradually stir in the hot milk. Strain the custard back into the pan or into the top of a double boiler with hot, not boiling, water in the bottom. Stir the custard continuously over very low heat until it is creamy and thick enough to coat the back of a wooden spoon. If the custard is to be used cold, pour it into a bowl and sprinkle with sugar to stop a skin from forming.

A curdled custard (one that has become too hot) can often be rescued by turning the custard into a cold bowl and beating it.

Baked Custard Pudding

PREPARATION TIME: *15 minutes*
COOKING TIME: *35 minutes*

INGREDIENTS (*for 4*):
2 cups milk
1–2 tablespoons butter
Strip of lemon rind
2 whole eggs plus 2 egg yolks
2 tablespoons sugar
Grated nutmeg

Butter the inside of a 4-cup glass casserole or baking dish. In a saucepan, bring the milk and lemon rind (free of all pith) to just below boiling point, then remove from the heat. Beat the eggs and yolks in a bowl, using a fork, until well mixed but not frothy. Beat in the sugar. Pour the milk over the eggs, then stir and strain the custard into the dish. Dot the custard with tiny flakes of butter and sprinkle the surface with grated nutmeg.

Set the dish in a shallow baking or roasting pan with about 1 inch of cold water. Bake the custard in the center of a preheated oven at 350°F for about 35 minutes, or until the custard is set and the top golden brown. Serve the custard pudding warm or cold.

Baked custard variations

Coconut: add ½ cup shredded coconut to the strained custard.

Macaroon: crumble 6 macaroons and add them and ½ teaspoon grated lemon or orange rind to the strained custard, blending thoroughly.

Maple: add ¼ cup maple syrup to the strained custard.

MERINGUES

Meringue, with its crisp outer texture and aerated inside, forms the basis for many desserts: Shells and baskets can be filled with cream or fresh fruit. Meringue is also a favorite topping for pies and tarts and is a must for the famous French custard, Oeufs à la Neige.

Meringue is quite easy to make provided a few points are observed. The whisk and bowl must be absolutely clean and dry, and the egg whites quite free from any particles of yolk. Ideally, use 2- to 3-day-old eggs. The shapes of whisk and bowl also influence a good meringue; a balloon whisk gives greater volume. An electric mixer will beat the egg whites more quickly but gives less volume. Choose a wide bowl when using a balloon whisk.

The sugar for a meringue must be fine. Superfine sugar is generally used, but equal quantities of superfine and confectioners' sugar produce meringue with a pure white color and a crisp, melting texture. Do not use granulated sugar, as the coarse crystals break down the egg albumen, thus reducing the volume.

Basic Meringue

INGREDIENTS:
2 egg whites
½ cup superfine sugar

Put the egg whites in a bowl and beat with a whisk until they are fairly stiff but not dry. Tip in half the sugar and continue beating the stiff whites until the texture is smooth and firm and the whites stand in stiff peaks when the whisk is lifted. Lightly but evenly fold in the remaining sugar with a rubber spatula.

Meringue shells

Line a baking sheet with baking parchment or aluminum foil. Using 2 tablespoons, set the meringue in 6–8 small mounds on the sheet or foil and shape them into ovals with the spoons.

Alternatively, spoon the meringue mixture into a pastry bag fitted with a ½-inch-wide plain or rosette tube. Turn the top of the bag down over the hand to form a cuff, then fill the bag, using a rubber spatula. Ease the meringue down toward the tube by twisting the top of the bag. Pipe 6–8 meringue whirls onto the baking sheet.

Sprinkle the meringues lightly with superfine sugar and set the baking sheet in the coolest part of the oven—this is usually the lowest shelf. Dry the meringues in a preheated oven at the lowest possible heat for 2–3 hours. This slow cooking will prevent the meringues from becoming tough.

Halfway through drying, the meringues can be taken out and the bottom of the shells can be pressed in lightly to make more space for cream filling. Return the shells, placed on their sides, to the oven until completely dry.

Cool the meringues on a wire rack. Unfilled, they will keep for about a week in an airtight container. To serve, fill the hollows of the meringues with sweetened cream, ice cream, or fruit.

Meringue Cuite

This is made with confectioners' sugar and has a firmer texture than basic meringue; it is ideal for making hollow basket shapes, to be filled with cream or fruit.

INGREDIENTS (*for 6 baskets*):
2¼–2½ *cups confectioners' sugar*
4 egg whites
Vanilla extract

Sift the confectioners' sugar onto a sheet of waxed paper. Beat the egg whites until frothy with a hand rotary beater or electric beater. Beat in the sugar, a little at a time, then flavor the whites with a few drops of vanilla extract.

Set the bowl over a pan half-filled with simmering water and beat the meringue until it holds its shape and leaves a thick trail when the whisk is lifted out.

Meringue baskets

Line 1 or 2 baking sheets with baking parchment. Pencil 6 circles 3 inches wide a little apart on the paper. Spread about half the prepared meringue cuite evenly over the penciled circles to form the bases for the baskets, and spoon the remaining meringue into a pastry bag fitted with a 6- to 8-point rosette tube. Pipe 2 layers, one on top of the other, around the edge of each basket base. Place the meringues in the bottom of a cool oven set at 275°–300°F; dry them for about 45 minutes, or until the baskets come easily away. Cool on a wire rack.

Serve the basket filled with Chantilly cream (p.397) or vanilla ice cream topped with fresh fruit or canned and drained fruit.

ICE CREAMS AND WATER ICES

Homemade ice creams and water ices are quite different in texture and flavor from the commercial varieties. It is as easy to make these at home as it is to make an egg custard or sugar syrup. Indeed, a basic ice cream is more often than not based on a custard enriched with heavy cream. The basis of a water ice is a sugar syrup flavored with fruit juice or purée.

Pointers to success

1 The amount of sugar in the mixture is important: if too much, the ice cream will not freeze, and if too little, it will be hard and tasteless. Freezing does, however, take the edge off the sweetness, and this must be kept in mind when tasting. In sherbets or water ices it is even more important to have the correct amount of sugar because the soft yet firm consistency depends on the sugar content.
2 Some recipes recommend milk instead of cream, especially for strongly flavored ice cream. The milk must be evaporated, not homogenized, milk.
3 Use maximum freezing power. Whichever freezing method is used, the cream will have a better texture if it is frozen as quickly as possible. Chill the equipment as well as the ingredients thoroughly in the freezing compartment of the refrigerator before starting the recipe.
4 Once the ice cream is frozen, it should be transferred to a shelf in the refrigerator for a little while before serving. Rock-hard ice creams and water ices are never pleasant and lose much of their flavor.
5 Ice cream can be stored in the freezer for up to 3 months.

Making ice cream in a refrigerator

Set the dial of the refrigerator at the coldest setting 1 hour before the ice cream mixture is to be frozen.

Make up the mixture according to the recipe. Remove the dividers and pour the mixture into empty ice-cube trays or any other suitable freezing container, such as fancy molds, loaf pans, or strong plastic or stainless-steel containers. Cover containers with aluminum foil or lids and place in the freezing compartment of the refrigerator.

To obtain a smooth texture, the ice crystals must be broken down as they form and the ice cream mixture should be beaten at intervals until partly frozen and slushy. Remove the tray from the freezing compartment. With a large spoon, scrape the ice crystals that have formed on the sides and bottom toward the center of the tray. Beat the mixture with a fork until just smooth but not melted and return the tray, covered, to the freezing compartment. Thereafter, leave the ice cream undisturbed in the refrigerator until it has become completely firm, after 2–3 hours.

Freezing time varies with different refrigerators, but several hours are necessary in every case. When freezing and ripening of the ice cream is complete, return the dial to its normal temperature setting, or other food in the refrigerator may be ruined by exposure to such cold temperatures.

MAKING ICE CREAM

Beating the egg yolks

Breaking up ice crystals

Making ice cream in a freezer

Set dial to coldest setting 1 hour before ice cream is to be frozen.

Prepare the ice cream mixture according to the recipe, place it in a stainless-steel mixing bowl in the freezer, and leave it until mushy.

Remove the bowl from the freezer and beat the mixture thoroughly with a rotary beater. Pour the ice cream into empty ice cube trays or rigid plastic containers, and freeze until firm. Set the dial of the freezer to its normal temperature. If the ice cream is to be stored for any length of time, the container should be sealed or wrapped and labeled.

Making ice cream in an electric or hand-operated ice cream freezer

Prepare the ice cream mixture according to the recipe. Pour the mixture into the freezer can with the dasher, cover tightly, and lower into the freezer, packed with alternating layers of cracked ice and rock salt in the proportion of approximately 1 cup salt to 6 cups ice. (Kosher salt can be substituted for rock salt.) Connect the dasher with the crank mechanism and turn by hand or by electricity. When the ice cream is frozen, remove the can and wipe off all salt. Remove dasher, press the ice cream down, and cover the can again. Drain off the salt water, return the can to the freezer, and repack it with ice and salt until ready to serve. (A sherbet should be turned only until softly frozen, then served immediately on chilled plates.)

Vanilla Ice Cream

PREPARATION TIME: *25 minutes*
FREEZING TIME: *about 3 hours*

INGREDIENTS (*for 6*):
1 cup milk
Vanilla bean
1 whole egg plus 2 egg yolks
6 tablespoons sugar
1 cup heavy cream

Bring the milk almost to a boil with the vanilla bean, then remove from the heat and allow it to infuse for about 15 minutes. Remove the vanilla bean. Cream the whole egg, egg yolks, and sugar until pale. Stir in the vanilla-flavored milk and strain this mixture through a sieve into a clean pan. Heat the custard mixture slowly over gentle heat, stirring all the time, until the mixture thickens enough to just coat the back of a wooden spoon. Pour the custard into a bowl and leave to cool.

Whip the cream lightly and fold it carefully and thoroughly into the cooled custard. Spoon into ice cube trays or a suitable freezing container, cover, and set in the freezing compartment until half-frozen. Beat the ice cream thoroughly, then freeze until firm.

For a praline ice cream, quickly stir in ½ cup of finely crushed praline, nut brittle, or toasted hazelnuts to the beaten, half-frozen ice cream before returning it to the freezing compartment.

For coffee ice cream, add 2 tablespoons very strong coffee to the cooled custard mixture.

Canned, drained pineapple, thoroughly crushed, may be added to the ice cream at the half-frozen stage.

Rich Chocolate Ice Cream

PREPARATION TIME: *20 minutes*
FREEZING TIME: *4 hours*

INGREDIENTS (*for 6*):
6 tablespoons sugar
4 egg yolks
2 cups light cream
Vanilla bean
7 ounces semisweet chocolate

Put the sugar with 6 tablespoons of water in a small pan and heat gently until the sugar has dissolved completely. Bring to a boil and continue boiling until the sugar has reached the thread stage,* about 220°F. Beat the egg yolks lightly in a mixing bowl, then pour in the syrup in a thin stream, beating all the time.

Put the cream, vanilla bean, and chocolate, broken into small pieces, in a pan and cook over low heat until just below boiling point. Remove the vanilla bean and pour the chocolate cream into the egg mixture, beating until it is thoroughly mixed. Cool and freeze.

Lemon Granita

A true Italian *granita* is a coarse-textured water ice flavored with fruit or coffee.

PREPARATION TIME: *15 minutes*
FREEZING TIME: *3–4 hours*

INGREDIENTS (*for 4*):
½ cup sugar
1 cup fresh lemon juice
Finely grated rind of 2 lemons

Put the sugar in a pan with 1 cup of cold water. Bring to a boil over gentle heat, stirring occasionally, until the sugar has dissolved, then continue boiling, without stirring, for 5 minutes. Remove the syrup from the heat and leave it to cool.

Stir the fruit juice and rind into the cooled syrup and pour the mixture into ice-cube trays with the dividers left in. Set the trays in the freezing compartment and freeze until mushy. Remove the trays and scrape the ice crystals with a fork from the sides toward the center. Repeat twice at 30-minute intervals, then return the trays to the freezing compartment and leave them to freeze until solid.

Remove the frozen cubes from the trays—this is most easily done by rubbing a cloth wrung out in hot water over the bottom and sides of the trays. Shake the cubes into a bowl. Crush the cubes coarsely with a pestle and spoon them into glasses. Serve the granita immediately.

Batters

Batters provide the basis for a large number of dishes, from breakfast pancakes and waffles to Russian blini, stuffed crêpes for hors d'oeuvres, and French crêpes Suzette.

Batter is a mixture of flour, salt, egg, and milk or other liquid. The proportions vary, depending on the consistency required. Crêpes, for instance, need a thin, creamlike batter, while fritters need a thick coating batter. For crisp coating batters, 1 tablespoon of oil can be used with ½ cup of water, or the liquid can be a combination of half milk and half water.

Batters do not, as some people think, need to stand for a while before being cooked, although this may be done for practical reasons. Batter can be left, covered, at room temperature for as long as 4 hours, or for 24 hours if the mixture is stored in a refrigerator. It may be necessary to add a little more milk or other liquid to restore the batter to its original consistency.

Basic Crêpe Batter

PREPARATION TIME: *20 minutes*

INGREDIENTS (*for 16–18 crêpes*):
⅞ cup all-purpose flour
Pinch of salt
3 eggs
2 tablespoons melted butter
1–1½ cups milk

Sift the flour and salt into a large bowl. Using a wooden spoon, make a hollow in the center of the flour and drop in the lightly beaten eggs. Slowly pour half the milk into the flour, gradually working the flour into the milk with the spoon. When all the flour is incorporated, beat the mixture vigorously with a wooden spoon, whisk, or hand or electric beater until it becomes smooth and is completely free of lumps. Allow this mixture to stand for a few minutes. Then add enough of the remaining milk, beating continuously, to make a thin batter with the consistency of light cream.

For dessert crêpes, sift 1 tablespoon sugar with the flour and salt and add 1 teaspoon of vanilla extract to the batter. Liqueur can be substituted for the vanilla extract.

Basic Coating Batter

PREPARATION TIME: *20 minutes*

INGREDIENTS:
1 cup all-purpose flour
Pinch of salt
1 egg, beaten
½ cup milk

Follow recipe for basic crêpe batter.

Pancakes

PREPARATION TIME: *15 minutes*
COOKING TIME: *5 minutes*

INGREDIENTS (*for 14 4-inch pancakes*):
1½ cups sifted all-purpose flour
1 teaspoon salt
2 tablespoons sugar
2 teaspoons baking powder
1 egg
3 tablespoons melted butter
1½ cups milk

Resift the flour with the salt, sugar, and baking powder into a pitcher. In a small bowl, beat the egg and add the butter and milk. Stir into the flour mixture. Pour the batter onto a hot griddle. Cook about 2–3 minutes, turn only once, and continue to cook until the other side is done.

Crêpes

PREPARATION TIME: *20 minutes*
COOKING TIME: *25 minutes*

INGREDIENTS (*for 8–10 crêpes*):
1 cup basic crêpe batter
Melted butter for frying

To make crêpes, use a 6-inch heavy-bottomed shallow crêpe pan or a skillet with sloping sides. Heat well and brush with just enough melted butter to gloss the pan to prevent the batter from sticking. Moderately high heat is necessary, and the pan should be hot before the batter is poured in.

Pour in just enough batter, about 1½ tablespoons, to flow in a thin film over the bottom; tilt the pan in all directions to distribute the batter evenly. Use a ladle for pouring in the batter. The heat is right if the underside of the crêpe becomes golden in 1 minute; adjust the heat to achieve this. Grasp the crêpe with the fingers of both hands and invert it, or flip the crêpe over with a metal spatula, or toss by flicking the wrist and lifting the pan away from the body. The other side of the crêpe should also be done in about 1 minute but will not be as brown.

Slide the crêpe out onto a plate. Alternatively, invert pan over a plate; the crêpe will fall out. When all are made, fill with desired filling.

To store crêpes for a day or two, put oiled waxed paper between each crêpe, stack them, and wrap the whole pile in foil. Store in the refrigerator or in the freezer.

To reheat crêpes, wrap 3 or 4 crêpes in foil and heat through in the oven at 300°F. Alternatively, brush a flat baking pan with melted butter, arrange overlapping crêpes on it, brush with butter, and put into a hot oven for 4–5 minutes.

For savory stuffed crêpes, fill them with a freshly made filling, place in a baking dish, top with a sauce or grated cheese, and heat through under the broiler or in a preheated oven at 375°F for about 30 minutes.

COOKING CRÊPES

Pour batter into buttered pan.

Flip over the half-cooked crêpe.

Straighten crêpe with a spatula.

Slide crêpe onto a plate.

343

Batters

Sausages in Batter

PREPARATION TIME: *20 minutes*
COOKING TIME: *45 minutes*

INGREDIENTS (*for 4*):
1 pound pork sausages
1 cup crêpe batter made with milk

Put sausages, in a buttered 10-by-12-inch pan, in a preheated oven at 425°F for 10 minutes until fat from sausages is sizzling. Remove pan, pour batter over sausages, and cook for 35–45 minutes until batter is well risen and golden. Serve at once.

Yorkshire Pudding

PREPARATION TIME: *20 minutes*
COOKING TIME: *35–40 minutes*

INGREDIENTS (*for 4*):
1 cup basic crêpe batter
2 tablespoons beef drippings or lard

Heat the drippings in a small baking pan near the top of a preheated oven at 425°F until smoking hot. Pour in the prepared batter and bake for 35–40 minutes.

A Yorkshire pudding can also be cooked underneath a roast of beef. Place the meat on a rack so that the fat and meat juices will drip down into the pudding.

Popovers

PREPARATION TIME: *10 minutes*
COOKING TIME: *40 minutes*

INGREDIENTS (*for 8–12 popovers*):
1 cup sifted all-purpose flour
½ teaspoon salt
1 cup milk
1 tablespoon melted butter
2 eggs

Preheat oven to 450°F. Butter aluminum muffin tins and set aside. Put all ingredients into a small bowl and beat until just smooth. Do not overbeat. Fill each muffin tin one-third full. Bake 20 minutes. Reduce heat to 350°F and bake 20 minutes longer. Do not open the oven door to check for doneness until 35 minutes have passed. Serve at once.

Waffles

PREPARATION TIME: *12 minutes*
COOKING TIME: *20 minutes*

INGREDIENTS (*for 20 waffles*):
1½ cups all-purpose flour
Pinch of salt
1 tablespoon baking powder
2 tablespoons sugar
2 eggs, separated
1 cup milk
4 tablespoons melted butter
Few drops of vanilla extract

Sift the flour, salt, and baking powder into a bowl and stir in the sugar. Make a well in the center and drop in the egg yolks; mix thoroughly, then gradually beat in the milk and butter alternately. Add vanilla extract. Beat egg whites and fold into batter.

Heat the well-greased waffle iron until it is hot. Brush the waffle iron with melted butter, pour in a little batter, and cook for about 30 seconds. Serve with butter or syrup.

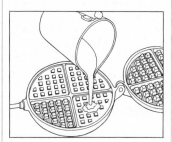
Waffles: pouring batter into the iron

Yeast-Raised Waffles

PREPARATION TIME: *15 minutes*
RESTING TIME: *8 hours or overnight*
COOKING TIME: *20 minutes*

INGREDIENTS (*for 6–8 waffles*):
½ cup lukewarm water (110°F)
1 package active dry yeast
2 cups lukewarm milk (110°F)
½ cup melted butter or margarine
1 teaspoon salt
1 teaspoon sugar
2 cups flour
2 eggs
Pinch of baking soda

In a large bowl mix together the lukewarm water and the yeast. Let this mixture stand for 5 minutes.

Add the lukewarm milk, butter or margarine, salt, and sugar. Then beat in the flour.

Cover the bowl and let stand 8 hours or overnight at room temperature. Do not refrigerate.

When time to cook the waffles, add the eggs and the baking soda and beat well. The batter will be thin.

Pour the batter into a waffle iron and cook as the manufacturer directs. Serve with melted butter, honey, or syrup.

Fritter Batter

PREPARATION TIME: *5 minutes*
RESTING TIME: *1 hour*

INGREDIENTS:
1 cup all-purpose flour
Pinch of salt
1 tablespoon corn oil
½ cup water
1 egg white

Sift the flour and salt together into a bowl. Make a well in the center, add the oil and water, beating until smooth. Allow the batter to rest for 1 hour.

Beat the egg white until stiff but not dry, then fold it evenly into the batter with a rubber spatula.

Kromeski

PREPARATION TIME: *30 minutes*
RESTING TIME: *1½ hours*
COOKING TIME: *15 minutes*

INGREDIENTS (*for 12 kromeski*):
½ cup fritter batter
2 tablespoons butter
2 tablespoons flour
½ cup milk
1 small egg yolk
Salt and black pepper
1 small green pepper
2 cups finely chopped cooked chicken

Prepare the batter and leave to stand for 1 hour. Meanwhile, melt the butter in a small pan. Remove the pan from the heat and stir in the

PREPARING KROMESKI
Molding mixture into cork shapes

Kromeski wrapped in bacon

flour with a wooden spoon. Return the pan to the heat and cook the roux* for a few minutes without coloring, then gradually stir in the milk and simmer gently. Cook the sauce, stirring all the time, for 3–5 minutes until it is thick and smooth. Remove from the heat and beat in the egg yolk. Season to taste with salt and freshly ground pepper.

Cut the stalk from the pepper, remove the seeds and the midribs, and dice the flesh finely. Blanch* the diced pepper in boiling water for 1 minute. Drain and cool quickly in cold water, then drain again. Blend the chicken and pepper into the white sauce and set aside to cool.

On a floured board, divide the cooled mixture into 12 equal portions. Mold each portion into a cork shape, using a knife and the fingers. Refrigerate for about 30 minutes.

Dip the kromeski in the batter. In a large pan, fry a few kromeski at a time for about 5 minutes in deep fat heated to 375°F. Lift the kromeski out with a slotted spoon and drain on paper towels. Serve hot.

Fruit Fritters

PREPARATION TIME: *15 minutes*
COOKING TIME: *12 minutes*

INGREDIENTS:
½ cup fritter batter
1¼ pounds canned peach halves, pineapple rings, or 1½ pounds bananas, or 3 cooking apples
1 egg white
Superfine sugar

Prepare the basic fritter batter and allow it to rest. Fill a deep-fryer halfway up with corn oil and heat slowly to 375°F. While the oil is heating, prepare the fruit: Drain the syrup from the canned peaches and pineapple and dry the pieces thoroughly on paper towels.

If using bananas, remove the skins and cut the bananas into 3 or 4 diagonal chunks; peel, core, and cut the apples in slices about ½ inch thick.

Beat the egg white until stiff but not dry, and fold it evenly into the prepared batter.

Dip the chosen fruit into the batter. Allow any excess to drain off, and fry the fruit in the hot oil for 2–3 minutes, turning the fruit halfway through cooking. Fry only a few pieces at a time. Drain on paper towels. Keep the fried fritters warm in the oven at 300°F until all are cooked. Serve dredged with the superfine sugar.

FRYING FRUIT FRITTERS
Draining batter from fritter

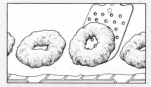
Draining fried fritters

Fruit

Fresh fruit makes delicious eating on its own, in fruit salads, or with cheese. In this section will be found recipes and suggestions on how to stew, poach, and bake fruit, and on how to prepare fresh fruit salads and fruit purées to be used in ice creams and sherbets or as filling for pies and puddings. Fruit is also used for jams and jellies, pickles, and chutneys. For a detailed buying guide see pages 10–17.

With crop spraying so widespread in modern fruit farming, it is essential that all fruit should be washed in running water before serving, especially if it is to be eaten fresh. Apart from soft fruits, such as berries, most fruit will keep in good condition for as long as a week if stored in a refrigerator.

Apples

Both cooking and eating apples are used for desserts. They can be baked, stewed, puréed (1 pound makes 1 cup purée) or used as fillings for pastry, puddings, cream-based foods, and mousses. Both types are also used for making jams, jellies, pickles and chutneys. Sliced apples for decoration should be dipped in lemon juice to prevent discoloration.

Apricots

Perfect ripe apricots are excellent served as a dessert fruit. They can also be poached in sugar syrup or used in pie fillings sweetened with vanilla sugar. Pit apricots by cutting them in half with a sharp knife, following the slight indentation line. Twist the two halves in opposite directions to separate them, and remove the pit.

Bananas

These are usually served raw or used fresh in fruit salads. They can also be baked, or sautéed in butter.

Slice bananas as close to serving time as possible, or leave them in fresh citrus fruit juice to prevent discoloration.

Blackberries

These berries are used in pie fillings, fruit puddings, jams, and jellies.

Blackberries are especially good when combined with apples. Hull* the berries before use.

Blueberries

The large cultivated blueberries are good for fruit salads and compotes and to eat with sour or heavy cream. The smaller wild blueberries are best for pies and preserves. Both types should be eaten soon after purchase.

CUTTING APRICOTS IN HALF

Split the fruit lengthwise.

Separate the two halves.

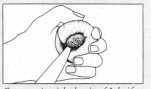
Remove pit with the tip of a knife.

Cherries

Both light and dark sweet cherries are served as a dessert fruit. For cooking in pies, puddings, compotes, and jams, choose the tart Montmorency and Morello cherries. Strip them of the stalks; ideally, push out the pits with the special tool known as a cherry pitter.

Chinese Gooseberries (Kiwi Fruit)

Serve these as a dessert fruit. Cut them in half crosswise and scoop out the flesh with a spoon. They can also be used to make jams and jellies.

Cranberries

These small, tart red berries, traditional with the Thanksgiving turkey, can be used for pies, preserves, relishes and sherbet.

Currants

Red currants can be eaten fresh or in a sugar frosting (see Garnishes, p.396). Red currants are also suitable for compotes, fruit salads, pastries, jams, and jellies.

Custard Apples

Serve this dessert fruit on its own or with sugar and cream.

Dates, fresh

Serve these as a dessert fruit or use in fresh fruit salads. Squeeze the stem end to remove the date from its slightly tough skin.

Figs, fresh

This dessert fruit is served fresh; peel figs and eat them with a knife and fork. Cream may be served with them. They are also delicious with prosciutto.

Gooseberries

Gooseberries, available in North America in midsummer, are usually cooked. They can be used for such desserts as gooseberry tart, and in pies, puddings, jams, and jellies. Trim with a knife or with scissors.

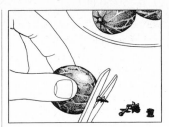
Trim gooseberries by snipping off stalk and flower ends.

Grapes

This delicious fruit, available in either regular or seedless varieties, is served for dessert, plain or in a sugar frosting (see Garnishes, p.396). Grapes also make a good addition to fresh fruit salads. Table varieties are not cooked, except for the classic garnish known as à la Véronique. Those used for grape jelly and pie filling are the slipskin variety, usually Concord. Most grapes are easily peeled, away from the stem end, using the fingernails. If the skins are difficult to remove, dip a few grapes at a time in boiling water for 30 seconds, then plunge them immediately into cold water.

Remove the seeds from whole grapes by digging the rounded end of a clean new bobby pin into the stem end of the grape; scoop out the seeds. Alternatively, make a small cut down the length of the grape, being careful not to cut completely through, and ease out the seeds with the tip of the knife.

Remove seeds from grapes by inserting a bobby pin into the stalk end.

Grapefruit

This popular citrus fruit is usually served fresh as a breakfast dish or a first course. To prepare a grapefruit, cut the fruit in half crosswise and, ideally, use a curved saw-edged grapefruit knife to cut around inside the skin to loosen the flesh. Make deep cuts between the grapefruit pieces close to the membranes dividing them. Flip out any seeds with the point of the knife. The central core of the fruit can be cut away, but this is not essential.

For hot grapefruit, sprinkle the halves with a little sherry and light brown sugar, and put under a hot broiler for a few minutes to glaze.

Empty half-grapefruit shells look attractive as serving "dishes." Use kitchen scissors to cut out a series of small V's around the edge of the half shells. (This is known as vandyking.) Fill the shells half with orange and half with grapefruit segments, adding a mint-leaf garnish.

PREPARING GRAPEFRUIT

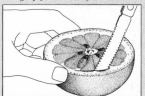
Cut grapefruit in half crosswise.

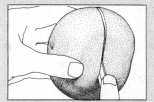
Loosen flesh from skin.

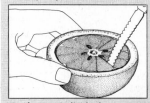
Cut between individual segments.

Fruit

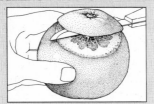

PEELING WHOLE GRAPEFRUIT

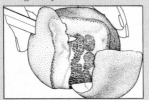

Cut off slice from stalk end.

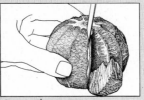

Remove strips of pith and peel.

Cut out the segments.

To peel and section a whole grapefruit, hold the fruit firmly with the tips of the fingers and cut a thin slice from the stem end of the fruit until the flesh just shows. Place the grapefruit, cut side down, on a plate; with a sawing action cut the peel and pith off in strips to reveal the flesh. Trim off any remaining pith. Carefully cut out each segment of fruit by placing the knife close to the membrane and cutting through to the

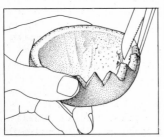

To make vandyke grapefruit, snip small V shapes from empty half shells.

center; then gently work the knife around under the segment and up against the adjoining membrane to release the segment.

Kumquats

These bitter fruits are eaten whole, with the skin, and are also used fresh as a garnish for duck. They can be preserved whole in syrup or brandy and served with cream. Kumquats are also used in marmalades.

Lemons

Lemons are among the most useful fruits in the kitchen, and the rind and juice are used in a great many dishes. They make an attractive garnish for food and long drinks. Rub sugar lumps over the skin of a lemon until they are well colored, then use the lumps whole or crushed as a flavorful and decorative addition to iced drinks.

Lemon juice can be substituted for vinegar in any recipe except pickling, and can be used to sour fresh or evaporated milk or fresh cream: Add 1 tablespoon juice to $\frac{1}{2}$ cup cream. Store lemons in the refrigerator and, if cut, cover with plastic wrap.

Limes

These are used in a similar way to lemons, and lime juice is particularly good squeezed over melon wedges. It also gives a fresh, tangy flavor to salad dressings.

Lychees (litchis)

Lychees, sweet subtropical fruits grown in Florida and Hawaii, are served as dessert fruits on their own or added to fruit salad. Pinch the parchmentlike outer skin to crack it, then peel it off.

Mangoes

These tropical fruits should not be cut until just before serving. Cut them lengthwise into 3 slices, above and below the stone. However, this allows the aroma to escape; ideally,

SERVING MANGOES

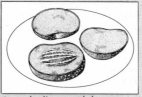

Cut three horizontal slices.

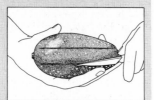

Serve the slices unpeeled.

fresh mangoes should be served whole with only the skin cut. Peel the skin back lengthwise with a knife and scoop out the pulp with a spoon. Mangoes are also made into chutney, jams, and jellies and served as a side dish with curries.

Melons

Cool ripe melon is served as a first or last course, with a squeeze of fresh lemon or lime juice. Refrigerate melon only long enough to chill it, or the delicate flavor will be lost.

To prepare a large melon, such as honeydew, cut it in half lengthwise with a sharp knife. Cut each half lengthwise into slices and scoop out the seeds with a spoon or fork. A fully ripe melon slice can be served with the skin attached, or the skin can be loosened by running the knife blade between flesh and skin. Leave the skin underneath the melon slice as a container for the fruit.

A small melon, such as cantaloupe, usually only serves 2 persons. Cut it in half crosswise and scoop out the seeds with a teaspoon.

To shape a large melon, such as a watermelon, into a basket, first cut a thin slice from the bottom so that the melon will stand upright. From the top, make 1 vertical cut $\frac{1}{2}$ inch

PREPARING MELON

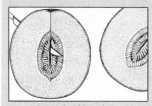

Cut melon in half lengthwise.

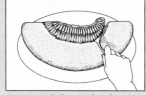

Remove seeds from melon slices.

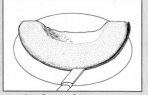

Cut skin from melon.

from the center to halfway down the melon; make a similar cut $\frac{1}{2}$ inch to the other side. Cut the melon horizontally, stopping at the downward cuts, and lift out the two sections, leaving a 1-inch-wide handle. Remove the seeds from the melon and scoop out the flesh with a small ball scoop; fill the cavity with the melon balls and other fruits.

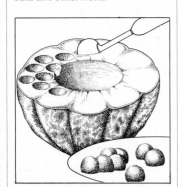

To scoop out melon balls, use a small semicircular ball scoop.

Nectarines

These tender dessert fruits need no peeling. Serve with dessert knives and forks, cut the fruits in half, and slip out the pits.

Oranges

The most widely available citrus fruit, oranges are served fresh on their own and in fruit salad. They are often used in cooking, especially in sauces and stuffings, and provide the essential ingredient for marmalades.

Peel and cut oranges as described under grapefruit. Alternatively, peel oranges in round strips, remove all pith, and cut the oranges into slices across the grain. If oranges do not peel easily, chill them in the refrigerator for about 1 hour or cover them with boiling water and leave for a few minutes.

Papayas

Tropical fruits with sweet, smooth yellow flesh, papayas can be eaten like melons, after removing the black seeds. They can be diced or used in fruit salads and sherbets.

Passion Fruit

The sharp, tangy juice of these tropical fruits is used to flavor cocktails, punches, or fresh fruit cups, as well as fruit pies. They can also be served as a dessert (the flesh is scooped out with a spoon).

Peaches

Peaches are usually served whole as a dessert, but are also excellent in fruit salads, open-faced tarts, and pies. Peach purée can be used as a basis for ice creams, soufflés, and other recipes. To peel fresh peaches, dip them in a bowl of boiling water, count to 10, then drain and put the peaches at once in a bowl of cold water. Peel off the skin in downward strips with a small knife.

Pears

Really ripe dessert pears can be eaten on their own or served in fruit salads. They can also be poached* and served chilled with a raspberry or hot chocolate sauce (p.304). To prepare pears for poaching, cut them in half lengthwise with a sharp knife. Fresh pears discolor quickly, and stainless steel or silver tools should be used in the preparation. Scoop out the core and seeds with a pointed spoon. Poach the pears at once before they turn brown.

Persimmons

For serving fresh, wash and lightly chill the fruit and serve with a pointed spoon to dig the juicy flesh out of the skin. A squeeze of lemon or lime may be added, and the skin can be marked in quarters and peeled back for an attractive presentation. The pulp can be used as a basis for ice creams, jellies, and sauces.

Pineapples

A ripe pineapple is best served as a dessert fruit. Slice off the leaf and the stem ends, and cut the pineapple across into ½-inch-thick slices. Using a sharp knife, cut off the skin and the woody "eyes" in the flesh of each slice. Remove the tough center core with a small plain pastry cutter or an apple corer. Arrange the slices on a flat dish and sprinkle with granulated or light brown sugar and 2 tablespoons of liqueur, such as kirsch or Cointreau. Leave to marinate* for about 2 hours before serving.

For a spectacular party dessert, slice off the leaf end only and, without splitting the skin, cut around the edge of the pineapple between the flesh and skin, loosening it at the base as well. Extract the flesh, remove the core, and cut the flesh into wedge-shaped pieces. Set the shell on a serving dish, replace the wedges, and cover with the top. Pineapple shells also make attractive containers for fruit salad, pineapple sherbet, ice cream, and fruit punch.

PREPARING PINEAPPLE

Slice off leafy top.

Remove skin from pineapple slices.

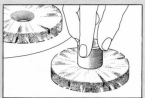

Stamp out center woody cores.

Plums

A few varieties, such as greengages, are excellent as dessert fruits. All types are also suitable for making pies, fruit salads, puddings, jams, chutneys, and pickles.

The small, very firm-fleshed damson plums are used not only for making preserves, but also in a variety of pies and puddings.

Pomegranates

These fruits are served fresh as a dessert. Serve them with the tops sliced off and dislodge the large seeds with a nut pick or spoon; suck the flesh from the seeds. The deep red seeds also make an attractive garnish.

Quinces

Quinces are only served cooked, usually in the form of jam, jelly, or in preserves. They are also combined in small amounts with apple for making pie filling.

Raspberries

Like other berries, ripe raspberries should be used as soon as possible after purchase or picking. If it is necessary to wash them, put them in a colander and let water flow gently through them. Drain and use the berries at once.

To make raspberry purée, rub the fruit through a nylon sieve, pressing it with a wooden spoon, or use a blender and strain the purée to remove the seeds—2 cups fresh raspberries will give 1 cup purée.

Rhubarb

Particularly suited for pie fillings and blends especially well with strawberries and apples. In baked puddings, tarts, and jams, rhubarb blends well with many other flavors, such as grated orange rind, ginger, mace, and cinnamon. Hothouse tender rhubarb needs little preparation other than cutting off the root ends and the leaves. Older rhubarb is somewhat coarser, and tough strings of skin must be peeled off. Wash and drain the rhubarb thoroughly before using it in a recipe.

Cooked rhubarb makes a quick and tasty dessert when served with a pitcher of heavy cream. Wash and cut the trimmed rhubarb into 1-inch pieces and layer them with ⅓–½ cup sugar in an ovenproof dish. Sprinkle the fruit with the juice and grated rind of an orange. Cover and cook in the center of a preheated oven at 350°F for about 35 minutes until the rhubarb is just tender.

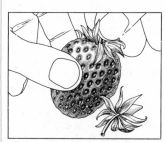

To hull strawberries, remove the green leaves and soft center stems.

Strawberries

Like raspberries, these soft fruits must be eaten soon after picking. The calyxes at the stalk ends are sometimes left on the berries for decoration, but strawberries are usually hulled.* Serve whole or sliced (use a stainless-steel knife to prevent discoloration). Strawberry purée is made in the same way as raspberry purée and yields the same amount.

Ugli Fruit

Ugli fruit is a cross between the tangerine and the grapefruit. It can be prepared and served in the same way as grapefruit halves.

Fresh Fruit Salad

PREPARATION TIME: *30 minutes*
STANDING TIME: *1–2 hours*

INGREDIENTS (*for 6*):
½ cup granulated sugar
2 tablespoons lemon juice
1 tablespoon orange liqueur or kirsch
½ pound seedless green grapes
2 eating apples
2 ripe pears
2 oranges
2 bananas

Put the sugar, with ½ cup of water, in a small pan. Heat gently to dissolve the sugar, then bring to a boil for 2–3 minutes. Set aside until cold, then add the lemon juice and liqueur and pour into a large serving bowl.

Add the grapes to the sugar syrup in the bowl. Wipe the apples, quarter them, discard the cores, and thinly slice the apple quarters into the bowl. Halve and peel the pears, remove the cores, and cut the pears into chunks. Add to the bowl. Peel and cut oranges into segments and squeeze the juice from the orange membranes into the bowl. Peel and slice the bananas and add, with the orange segments, to the bowl. Turn the fruit in the syrup. Cover and leave in a cool place, preferably not the refrigerator, for 1–2 hours to develop the flavors.

Strawberries, pitted cherries, plums, halved apricots, sliced peaches, and red currants are also good in fresh fruit salads, as are pineapples, grapefruits, and melons.

Pineapple in Kirsch

PREPARATION TIME: *20 minutes*
CHILLING TIME: *1 hour*

INGREDIENTS (*for 8*):
1 small pineapple
2 large oranges
2 tablespoons superfine sugar
2 tablespoons kirsch

Cut all the skin from the pineapple;* slice the flesh into 8 rounds and remove the cores. Slice the peel and white pith from the oranges and cut each orange crosswise into 8 slices. Arrange 1 slice of pineapple and 2 of orange on individual dessert plates. Dissolve the sugar in 2 tablespoons of water in a small pan over gentle heat, add the kirsch, and spoon the syrup over the pineapple.

Chill and serve with a pitcher of chilled cream.

Pineapple Romanoff

PREPARATION TIME: *20 minutes*
CHILLING TIME: *2 hours*

INGREDIENTS (*for 6–8*):
1 large pineapple
½ cup confectioners' sugar
3 tablespoons Cointreau
3 tablespoons rum
1 cup heavy cream
3 tablespoons kirsch
Grated rind of 1 orange

Slice and peel the pineapple,* cut into segments, and place them in a serving dish. Toss with half the sugar. Add the Cointreau and rum and chill for 2 hours.

One hour before serving, whip the cream and add the remaining sugar and the kirsch. Spoon the whipped cream mixture over the pineapple segments and toss them gently to coat all the segments well. Sprinkle the top with the grated orange rind and serve.

Baked Pears in Cream and Kirsch

PREPARATION TIME: *10 minutes*
COOKING TIME: *40 minutes*

INGREDIENTS (*for* 4):
4 tablespoons butter
6 tablespoons sugar
4 pears
½ cup heavy cream
Pinch of salt
½ teaspoon vanilla extract
2 tablespoons kirsch

Preheat oven to 475°F. Melt half the butter and pour into an 8- or 9-inch pie plate. Sprinkle half the sugar over the butter.

Peel the pears, cut them in half lengthwise, and core. Place the pears, cut side down, in the pie plate. Sprinkle with the remaining sugar and dot with the remaining butter. Bake, uncovered, about 20 minutes.

Mix the cream, salt, vanilla extract, and kirsch. Pour this over the pears. Bake, uncovered, for another 20 minutes or until the cream is just slightly thickened. Remove and place on a rack. Serve warm.

Pears in Red Wine

PREPARATION TIME: *10 minutes*
COOKING TIME: *about 1 hour*

INGREDIENTS (*for* 4):
4 firm pears
¼ cup light brown sugar
1 cup red wine

Halve the pears lengthwise, scoop out the cores, and peel the pears. Lay them in a single layer in a baking dish and sprinkle with the sugar. Mix the wine with 1 cup of water and pour it over the pears. Cover the dish with foil and cook in the center of a preheated oven at 350°F for about 50 minutes or until tender.

Lift the pears out with a slotted spoon and set them in a serving dish. Boil the cooking liquid briskly until it has reduced by half, then spoon it over the pears. Serve the pears hot or cold, with a bowl of cream or Chantilly cream (p.397).

Peaches in Wine

PREPARATION TIME: *20 minutes*
CHILLING TIME: *20 minutes*

INGREDIENTS (*for* 4):
4 ripe peaches
4 teaspoons superfine sugar
6–8 tablespoons sweet white wine

Peel the peaches, cut them in half, and remove the pits. Slice the peaches into individual serving glasses. Sprinkle with sugar and spoon the wine over them. Chill.

Peaches with Ginger

PREPARATION TIME: *15 minutes*
CHILLING TIME: *3 hours*

INGREDIENTS (*for* 4):
½ cup freshly squeezed orange juice
2 tablespoons honey
Pinch of salt
4 cups peeled, sliced peaches
2 tablespoons finely chopped candied
    ginger
Flaked coconut
Mint sprigs

Mix the orange juice, honey, and salt. Add the peach slices and ginger. Toss gently to mix. Cover and chill 3 hours. Spoon into sherbet glasses. Sprinkle with coconut and garnish with mint sprigs.

Poached Apricots

PREPARATION TIME: *10 minutes*
COOKING TIME: *10 minutes*

INGREDIENTS (*for* 4):
1 pound fresh apricots
⅓–½ cup granulated sugar
Lemon rind or cinnamon stick

Wash and dry the apricots. Put the sugar, 1 cup of water, and the thinly pared lemon rind or cinnamon in a saucepan and place over low heat until the sugar has dissolved. Bring to a boil and cook for 2 minutes. Strain this syrup through a sieve.

Cut the apricots in half with a small sharp knife. Twist the two halves to separate them. Discard the pits. Return the syrup to the pan; place the apricot halves, rounded side

down, in the syrup and bring slowly to a boil. Reduce the heat, cover the pan, and simmer gently until the fruit is tender, about 10 minutes. Leave to cool.

Baked Fruit Flambé

PREPARATION TIME: *30 minutes*
COOKING TIME: *20 minutes*

INGREDIENTS (*for* 6):
1 medium pineapple
1 pound plums
4 tablespoons orange marmalade
Grated rind and juice of 1 lemon
½ teaspoon ground cinnamon
½ cup dark brown sugar
4 tablespoons unsalted butter
4 tablespoons white rum

Peel, core, and slice the pineapple. Cut the slices in half. Cut the plums in half and remove the pits. Place the pineapple and plums in a wide shallow casserole. In a small pan, heat together the marmalade, lemon rind and juice, cinnamon, sugar, and butter. Stir well and pour the mixture over the fruit. Cover and cook in a preheated oven at 400°F for about 20 minutes. Just before serving, place the rum in a warm ladle, ignite with a match, and pour it flaming over the fruit. Serve with a pitcher of cream.

Brown Sugar Apples

PREPARATION TIME: *15 minutes*
COOKING TIME: *30 minutes*

INGREDIENTS (*for* 4):
1½ pounds cooking apples
2 tablespoons butter
Grated rind and juice of 1 lemon
½–⅔ cup light brown sugar

Peel and core the apples and cut them into even, thin slices. Butter a deep baking dish and arrange the fruit in layers, sprinkling each layer with the lemon rind, lemon juice, and sugar. Dot the top layer of apples with flakes of butter.

Bake in the center of a preheated oven at 375°F for 30 minutes or until tender. Serve with heavy cream.

Baked Apples

PREPARATION TIME: *10 minutes*
COOKING TIME: *30–45 minutes*

INGREDIENTS (*for* 4):
4 large cooking apples
5 tablespoons dark brown sugar
5 tablespoons butter
Grated rind and juice of 1 lemon
1 cup candied cherries
1 tablespoon brandy

Wash the apples and remove the cores, using a sharp knife or apple corer. Make a cut in the skin around the middle of each apple. Place the apples in a baking dish. Fill the cavity of each apple with a teaspoon of sugar and a small piece of butter. Bake in the center of a preheated oven at 350°F for about 30 minutes, basting occasionally with the apple juices in the dish.

Meanwhile, grate the lemon rind and squeeze out the juice. Melt the remaining butter and sugar in a small saucepan. When the sugar has dissolved, boil gently to a rich caramel color. Add the lemon rind and juice, cherries, and brandy to the pan and blend thoroughly, using a wooden spoon to loosen the caramel and work it into the mixture. Simmer for 1–2 minutes. Spoon over the baked apples and serve hot.

Cherries Jubilee

PREPARATION TIME: *5 minutes*
COOKING TIME: *5 minutes*

INGREDIENTS (*for* 8):
1 cup sugar
⅛ teaspoon salt
2 tablespoons cornstarch
2 cups water
2 pounds pitted Bing cherries
6–8 tablespoons kirsch or cognac
2 pints vanilla ice cream

Combine the sugar, salt, cornstarch, and water. Add the pitted cherries and cook until thickened, stirring constantly. Pour the kirsch or cognac over the top and ignite. Spoon immediately over individual servings of very hard vanilla ice cream.

Strawberries with Raspberry Sauce

PREPARATION TIME: *15 minutes*
CHILLING TIME: *5 hours*

INGREDIENTS (*for* 6):
2 pints fresh strawberries
1 pint fresh raspberries
½–¾ cup sugar
⅓ cup kirsch, preferably imported
Whipped cream (optional)

Hull the strawberries. Wash the strawberries and raspberries separately. Drain them on paper towels. Put the raspberries, ½ cup of the sugar, and kirsch in a blender; purée about 30 seconds. Taste the purée for sweetness and add the remaining ¼ cup of sugar if needed.

Pour the purée over the strawberries, cover, and refrigerate for 5 hours. Gently toss the strawberries occasionally to coat them with the sauce. Serve cold, with slightly sweetened whipped cream if desired.

Macédoine of Fruit

PREPARATION TIME: *30 minutes*
CHILLING TIME: *3 hours*

INGREDIENTS (*for* 8):
¼ cup brandy
¼ cup Cointreau
1 small pineapple
1 apple
2 peaches
1 banana
1 cup strawberries
1 cup Bing cherries
1 cup blueberries
¼ cup almond slices
Sugar

Combine the brandy and Cointreau in a large bowl. Peel and dice the pineapple and the apple. Peel and slice the peaches and banana. Hull the strawberries and remove the pits from the cherries. Remove the stems from the blueberries.

Add all the fruit to the bowl. Add the almonds and sugar and stir gently to mix all ingredients.

Chill for 3 hours and stir gently before serving.

Preserving

Fruit can be made into jams, jellies, pickles, and chutneys, or it may be canned. The most suitable methods of preserving depend on the type of fruit and its quality and ripeness. Only the finest-quality fruit should be used for canning and freezing, while bruised and underripe fruit can be used to make jams and jellies. Overripe fruit is ideal for syrups and chutneys.

Recipes for marmalades are on pages 88–89.

JAMS AND JELLIES

Jams and jellies are a combination of fresh fruit, sugar, and water; the latter are boiled together until setting point is reached. A good set depends on the presence of pectin, acid, and sugar in correct proportions. Pectin, which is found in the fruit cells, reacts with the sugar to give a gel, and acid speeds the release of the pectin.

Fruits have natural pectin and acid in varying quantities. Apples, cranberries, Concord grapes, damson plums, and gooseberries are rich in pectin and acid and are therefore excellent for jams and jellies. Fruits such as apricots, greengage plums, pineapple, and strawberries are less rich in pectin and acid. They make good jams but set less firmly than pectin-rich fruit.

Fruits low in pectin and acid include nectarines, peaches, pears, and raspberries. These do not give a good set on their own, and pectin and acid must be supplemented.

Testing for pectin
Put 1 tablespoon of the cooked but unsweetened strained fruit juice in a glass and leave to cool. Add 1 tablespoon 190° proof grain alcohol and shake gently. If a large clot forms, the fruit has enough pectin for the jam to set; if there are numerous small clots, the pectin content in the juice is too low.

Missing pectin can be supplemented by adding lemon juice, which is rich both in pectin and acid content. Allow 2 tablespoons of lemon juice to each 4 pounds of fruit. Alternatively, add ½ teaspoon of citric or tartaric acid to the fruit before cooking.

Commercial powdered or bottled pectin can also be used. Follow the manufacturer's directions. The more pectin present, the more sugar it will set, but too much pectin flavor spoils the taste of the fruit.

Sugar
Use granulated sugar because it dissolves quickly. The sugar should be warmed in the oven before being used in a recipe.

Sugar has a hardening effect on fruit; it should therefore only be added to thoroughly softened fruit. Strawberries, which quickly lose their shape during cooking, are the exception. They are best sprinkled with sugar and left to stand overnight before cooking.

Preserving pans
Choose a large, heavy-bottomed pan made from aluminum or stainless steel. Copper or brass preserving pans can be used to make jams, jellies, and marmalades, but should not be used for pickles and chutneys because the vinegar in these preserves reacts adversely with the metal. The pan should be wide in proportion to its depth to allow for rapid evaporation of water and other liquids before the sugar is added, and for quick boiling afterwards.

Preparing the fruit
Select fresh, slightly underripe fruit and cut out any bruised or damaged parts. Berries should be hulled,* and gooseberries should be trimmed. No more than 3–4 quarts of any type of fruit should be cooked at one time.

Wash and drain the fruit carefully. Berries are most easily cleaned by placing them in a sieve or colander and immersing it in cold water several times. Large fruit, such as apples, should be chopped, and fruits with pits should be halved or quartered and the pits removed. Do not let the fruit stand in cold water.

Cooking the fruit
Put the prepared fruit in the preserving pan and add water if specified in the recipe. Bring the fruit and water to a simmer over very gentle heat. Simmering softens the skin and breaks down the flesh while releasing the pectin. When the fruit has been reduced* to a pulp and the volume has decreased by one-third, remove the pan from the heat and add the warmed sugar. Stir thoroughly until the sugar has completely dissolved. One tablespoon of glycerine added after the sugar has dissolved prevents scum from forming on the top of the jam or jelly.

Return the pan to the heat and boil rapidly until setting point is reached. This varies from 3 minutes to 20 minutes, according to the type and quantity of the fruit. If fruit is overboiled, the jam becomes sticky and flavorless and its color darkens; if boiled too little, it fails to set.

Setting point
The most accurate method of testing for setting is with a candy thermometer. Jams and jellies have generally reached setting point when the thermometer registers 220°F, which is 8 degrees above boiling point.

Alternatively, use the saucer test. Put a teaspoon of jam on a cold saucer. As the jam cools, a skin forms. If the skin crinkles when pushed with a finger, the jam has set.

Yet another method is the sheet test. Stir the jam with a wooden spoon and hold it flat so that the jam in the bowl of the spoon can cool. Turn the spoon on its side and allow the jam to drop. If the jam sets partly on the spoon and the drops come together and fall away in a sheet rather than separate drops, setting point has been reached.

Filling and covering
As soon as setting point is reached, remove the pan from the heat. Let the jam stand for 15 minutes before removing any scum from the top with a slotted spoon. Pour the jam into hot, carefully sterilized jars or jelly glasses.

Pour an ⅛-inch layer of melted hot paraffin over the surface of the jam so that wax touches the glass on all sides. A thin layer of paraffin, which can expand or contract readily, makes a better seal than a thick layer or 2 thin layers. Puncture any air bubbles in the paraffin with a knife point. Wipe the rim of the jar with a clean damp cloth. Leave until the paraffin cools and hardens, then cover with metal lids.

Leave the filled jars to cool completely before labeling them. Store in a cool, dark place.

MAKING JAMS AND JELLIES

1 Cook fruit in heavy-bottomed pan.

4 Saucer test for setting point.

2 Add warmed sugar.

5 Remove scum from finished jam.

3 Sheet test for setting point.

6 Pour jam into hot jars.

JAMS

Apple
YIELD: *5 quarts*

INGREDIENTS:
6 pounds cooking apples
5 cups water
Rind and juice of 4 lemons
1/3 cup ground ginger (optional)
14 cups sugar

Peel, core, and chop the apples. Tie the peel and core in cheesecloth and put with the apples and water into the preserving pan. Add the finely grated lemon rind and the juice, together with the ginger, if used. Cook until pulpy, then squeeze out and discard the cheesecloth bag. Stir in the sugar and boil until set.

Apricot
YIELD: *2½ quarts*

INGREDIENTS:
3 pounds apricots
Juice of 1 lemon
2 cups water
7 cups sugar

Quarter the washed and pitted apricots and put them, with the lemon juice and water, into a large saucepan. Crack about 12 of the pits with a hammer, remove the kernels, and blanch* in boiling water for 5 minutes before splitting them in half. Add the kernels to pan. Simmer until the fruit is pulpy, stir in the sugar, and boil rapidly until set.

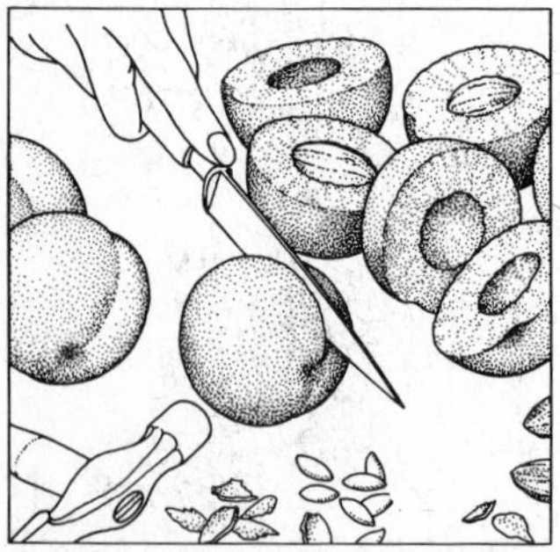

To prepare apricots for jam, cut them in half and remove pits and kernels.

Blackberry
YIELD: *5 quarts*

INGREDIENTS:
16 cups blackberries
½ cup water
Rind and juice of 2 lemons
14 cups sugar

Put the cleaned fruit, the water, and lemon rind and juice in the pan. Simmer until the fruit is soft. Stir in the sugar and boil rapidly until setting point is reached.

Blueberry
YIELD: *3 quarts*

INGREDIENTS:
3 pounds blueberries
3 cups water
14 cups sugar

Put the cleaned fruit in the preserving pan with the water. Bring to a boil and simmer until the fruit is soft. Stir in the sugar and boil rapidly until set.

Cherry
YIELD: *3½ quarts*

INGREDIENTS:
6½ pounds dark cherries
Juice of 3 lemons
8¼ cups sugar

Pit the cherries and tie the pits in cheesecloth. Put them in the pan with the cherries and lemon juice. Simmer over low heat until the juices begin to run and the fruit is tender. Remove the cheesecloth bag, stir in the sugar, and proceed in the usual way.

Gooseberry
YIELD: *3 quarts*

INGREDIENTS:
3 pounds gooseberries
2½ cups water
9¼ cups sugar

Bring the cleaned gooseberries and water to a boil and simmer until tender. Stir in the sugar and proceed in the usual way.

Plum
YIELD: *5 quarts*

INGREDIENTS:
6 pounds plums
2½ cups water
14 cups sugar

Follow the instructions given for apricot jam.

Raspberry
YIELD: *5 quarts*

INGREDIENTS:
16 cups raspberries
14 cups sugar

Put the cleaned fruit in the pan, without any water, and heat gently until the fruit begins to break up and the juices run. Simmer until reduced by a third, stir in the sugar, and proceed as usual.

Rhubarb
YIELD: *2½ quarts*

INGREDIENTS:
4½ pounds rhubarb
Juice of 3 lemons
7 cups sugar

Wipe and trim the rhubarb and cut the stems into 1-inch pieces. (Prepared weight should be 3 pounds.) Layer with sugar in a large bowl and add the lemon juice. Leave overnight. Put the contents of the bowl into a pan, bring to a boil, and boil rapidly until setting point is reached.

Strawberry
YIELD: *3¾ quarts*

INGREDIENTS:
4 pounds strawberries
9½ cups sugar

Hull,* wash, and drain the strawberries. Layer with the sugar in a large bowl. Cover with a cloth and leave in a cool place for 24 hours. Bring the contents of the bowl to a boil in a pan and boil for 5 minutes. Leave the strawberries in the bowl for 48 hours, then boil for 20 minutes or until setting point is reached.

JELLIES

Fruit jellies should be bright and clear, with a good flavor, and not too firmly set. Jellies, like jams, are best when they are made from fruit rich in pectin and acid.

Prepare the fruit as for jams, then simmer it in water—the amount depends on the hardness of the fruit. Cook the fruit slowly for 45 minutes–1 hour, or until quite tender, then strain it through a scalded jelly bag, letting it drip for at least 1 hour. Do not squeeze the bag, as this makes the jelly cloudy.

Measure the quantity of strained juice and add sugar. Bring the juice and sugar to a boil and boil rapidly for about 10 minutes or until setting point is reached. Take the pan off the heat and remove any scum.

The amount of sugar used depends on the pectin content of the fruit. Test as for jam and allow 2½–2¾ cups of sugar to each 2½ cups of juice rich in pectin. For juice of lower pectin content, allow 2 cups of sugar to each 2½ cups. Yield depends on the ripeness of the fruit and the number of extracts taken.

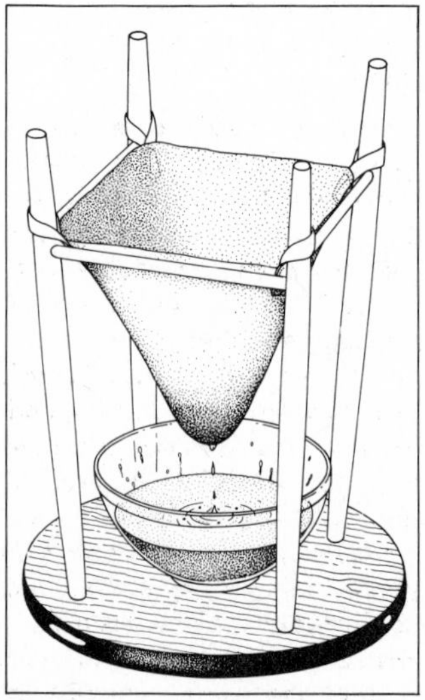

Upend a stool to strain fruit juice through a scalded jelly bag.

Fruit particularly rich in pectin can be boiled a second time to yield another extract: Allow the cooked fruit to drip for only 15 minutes, then return the fruit pulp to the pan with half the quantity of water used initially. Simmer for 30 minutes. Strain and allow to drip for 1 hour. Mix the two extracts together, add sugar, and finish cooking.

Pour the juice into warm jars and cover as for jams.

Blackberry
11 cups blackberries
2½ cups water
Juice of 2 lemons
Sugar

Simmer the fruit with the water and lemon juice until quite tender. Strain once through a jelly bag and measure the juice. Allow 2½ cups of sugar to each pint of juice, then follow general instructions.

Crab Apple
4 pounds crab apples
7½ cups water
Sugar

Simmer the washed and chopped fruit with the water until the apples have cooked to a pulp and the liquid has reduced by one-third. Strain. Allow 2½ cups of sugar to each 2½ cups of juice.

Cranberry
4 cups cranberries
3 cups water
Sugar

Wash the cranberries thoroughly and pick over them, removing any stems and leaves. Drain. Put the cranberries in a saucepan with the water and simmer them until soft. This should take about 20 minutes. Strain through a jelly bag or rub through a fine sieve, and measure the juice. For each cup of juice, add ¾ cup of sugar. Boil until the sugar has dissolved, then boil 5 minutes more and proceed as usual.

Damson Plum

6 pounds damson plums
7½ cups water
Sugar

Simmer the plums with all the water to take one extract. Each 2½ cups of juice will require 2½ cups of sugar to reach setting point.

Gooseberry

4 pounds gooseberries
5–7½ cups water
Sugar

For jelly, there is no need to remove the ends from the gooseberries. Simmer the fruit with 5 cups of water for the first extract. Return the strained pulp with 2½ cups of water for the second extract. If only one extract is taken, use 7½ cups of water. Allow 2½–2¾ cups of sugar to 2 cups of juice.

Grape

3 pounds Concord grapes
¾ cup water
Sugar

Mash the grapes and simmer with the water for 15 minutes. Strain through a jelly bag and measure the juice. For each cup of juice add ¾ cup of sugar, then follow the general directions for making jelly.

Quince

2 pounds quinces
7½ cups water
1 tablespoon citric acid
Sugar

Chop or mince the fruit. Take two extracts, following the general instructions. Use 5 cups of water and the citric acid for the first extract, 2½ cups of water for the second. Allow 2–2½ cups of sugar to 2 cups of juice.

FRUIT BUTTERS AND CHEESES

In making fruit butters, the pulp of ripe fruit, such as apples, pears, plums, and peaches, is simmered with sugar or honey until it becomes thick and dense. The so-called cheese, firmer and more solid than fruit butter, is made from plums, quinces, or similar fruit.

As a large quantity of fruit is needed to give a small amount of preserve, butters and cheeses are practical to make only when there is a glut of fruit. Fruit cheese should be left to mature for at least 2 months.

Lemon butter, also known as lemon curd and lemon cheese, is made with eggs, which diminishes its keeping quality. Lemon butter has a soft, spreading consistency and can be used on toast, like a preserve, or as a filling for tartlets and jelly rolls. Lemon butter should be made in small quantities, refrigerated, and used within a month.

Damson Cheese

APPROXIMATE YIELD: *5–6 pounds*

INGREDIENTS:
6 pounds damson plums
1¼ cups water
Sugar

Remove any stalks and leaves from the fruit; wash thoroughly. Put the damsons and the water in a heavy-bottomed pan and cover with a lid. Simmer over gentle heat until the fruit is quite soft, then rub it through a fine sieve.

Weigh the fruit pulp and return it to a clean, dry pan. Boil rapidly until the pulp is thick and has reduced by about one-third. Add the sugar, allowing 1 pound (2⅓ cups) to 1 pound of pulp. Continue cooking the mixture, stirring all the time, until a spoon drawn across the bottom of the pan leaves a firm line.

Pour into small, straight-sided pots brushed with glycerine. Cover as for jelly.

Lemon Butter

APPROXIMATE YIELD: *2 cups*

INGREDIENTS:
3 eggs
Grated rind and juice of 2 large lemons
¼ pound butter
1 cup sugar

Beat the eggs lightly with a fork and mix in the grated lemon rind and juice, butter, and sugar. Place this mixture in the top of a double boiler or in a bowl over hot water. Heat gently, stirring occasionally until the sugar has dissolved and the curd thickens. Pour the lemon butter into small sterilized jars and cover immediately as for jelly.

Mincemeat

This preserve can be made in a short time. It is steeped in brandy or rum and left to mature for about 1 month. Mincemeat can be used either as a garnish or in desserts.

APPROXIMATE YIELD: *2–2½ quarts*

INGREDIENTS:
½ pound cooking apples, such as Spartan or Rome beauty
1⅓ cups currants
1⅓ cups dark raisins
1⅓ cups white raisins
⅔ cup candied cherries
½ cup chopped mixed peel
¾ cup shelled walnuts
2 cups shredded suet
1 pound light brown sugar
2 teaspoons allspice
⅓–¼ cup brandy or rum

Peel, core, and chop the apples. Chop the dried fruits; mix in a large bowl with the nuts and apples. Blend in the shredded suet, brown sugar, and allspice. Add enough brandy or rum to give a moist mixture. Cover the bowl with a cloth or plastic wrap and leave for 48 hours to allow the fruit to swell.

Stir well. Put the mincemeat into sterilized jars and cover.

FRUIT SYRUPS AND WINES

Syrups are made from the sweetened juices of berries, such as blackberries, raspberries, and strawberries. Syrup is a useful way of preserving ripe fruit.

Wash and drain the fruit thoroughly. Put in a pan and cook over gentle heat until the juices run freely. Most fruits require no additional water, but blackberries need 1 cup of water to each 6 pounds of fruit. Use a wooden spoon to crush whole fruit. Bring the fruit rapidly to a boil, then boil for 1 minute and remove the pan from the heat.

Strain through a scalded jelly bag and leave to drain overnight. Press the pulp in the bag to squeeze out any remaining juices.

Measure the quantity of extracted juice and allow 2 cups sugar to each 2½ cups of juice. Cook the mixture over very gentle heat until the sugar has dissolved completely; stir, and strain the mixture through several layers of cheesecloth. Pour the syrup into sterilized bottles to within 1½ inches of the top; seal with scalded screw caps or corks.

Corks and stoppers should be boiled for 15 minutes before using. Secure the corks with insulating tape to prevent them from blowing off during processing.

Place the filled bottles of syrup on a trivet or rack in a deep pan. Fill a large pan with water to within 1 inch of the top of the bottles. Heat the water to 170°F and hold it at this temperature for 30 minutes. Alternatively, bring the water to the simmering point and hold; simmer for 20 minutes.

Lift out the bottles, tighten the screw caps or press in the corks, and leave to cool. When the corks are dry, brush the top of each bottle with melted paraffin wax, covering the corks and ½ inch of the neck.

To serve, dilute 1 part syrup with 5 parts water and mix thoroughly with a wooden spoon.

Fermented syrups

These are made from the same types of berries as fruit syrups, but no heat is applied and a fuller fruit flavor is thus obtained.

Place the fruit, without any water, in a large earthenware bowl or jar and crush it well. Cover the bowl with a cloth and leave the fruit to ferment. When bubbles appear on the surface of the crushed fruit, fermentation is complete. Most fruits ferment within 24 hours if kept in a warm place.

Strain the fermented fruit through a jelly bag and leave to drip overnight; then squeeze the bag to obtain any remaining juice. Add 2½ cups of sugar to each 2½ cups of juice, stir until dissolved, then strain the syrup through cheesecloth. Pour into clean bottles and seal with sterilized caps or corks.

Fermented syrups can be processed by heating the sealed bottles as for fruit syrups. Alternatively, a chemical preservative, such as sulphur dioxide, can be added to the syrups. Allow 1 fruit-preserving tablet dissolved in 1 tablespoon of water to each 2½ cups of juice. Stir

MAKING FRUIT SYRUPS

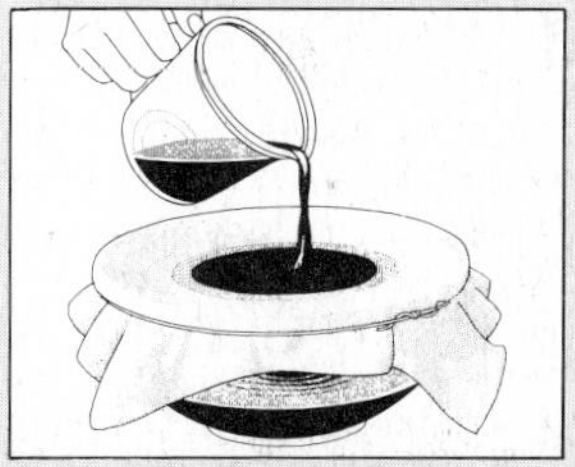

Strain the fermented syrup.

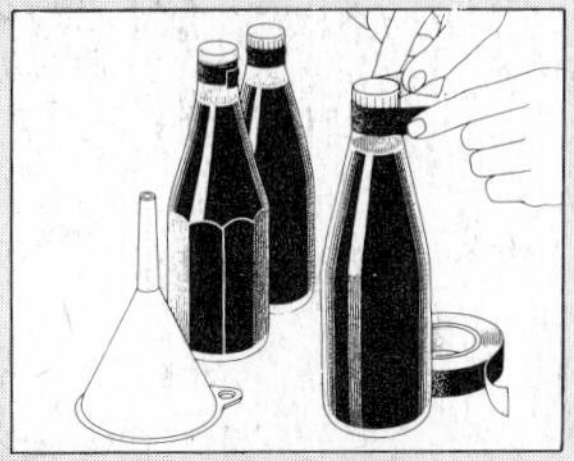

Seal caps on bottled syrup.

into the strained syrup before bottling and sealing.

Fermented strawberry syrup has little acid and requires citric acid in the proportions of 3 tablespoons to each 10 cups of juice. Add the citric acid with the sugar.

HOMEMADE WINES

These are made on the same principle as fermented syrups but require careful control to produce a good wine. Boiling water is added to the fruit, and this mixture, known as must, is left to ferment for a specified time. The strained juice is mixed with fresh yeast or wine yeast tablets before the sugar is added.

Wine-making equipment, obtainable at hardware stores, farmer's supply stores, or from mail-order sources for wine-making supplies, is necessary for the successful preparation of wines. Follow the manufacturer's instructions carefully.

Homemade wine should be left to mature for 6–9 months; it is then siphoned into clean bottles, corked tightly, and left for up to 1 year before it is drunk.

CANNING

This preserving method involves sterilization of fruit. It must be of the finest quality—fresh and ripe but not mushy. The fruit should be free of all blemishes and rotten areas; these may spoil the entire contents of the container.

All types of fruit are suitable for canning. Berries should be carefully cleaned—stalks, stems, and leaves removed. Gooseberries should be trimmed, and rhubarb cut into even lengths. Apples, pears, and quinces should be peeled, cored, and quartered or sliced, while peeled apricots and peaches can be canned whole or in halves, with the pits removed. Plums are usually canned whole.

Syrup and jars for canning

Fruit can be preserved in water, but the flavor and color is improved when the fruit is canned in a syrup made with proportions of 1 cup of sugar to 2 cups of water.

Pack the prepared fruit into sterilized canning jars. Do not dry the insides of the jars; the fruit slips more easily into place when jars are wet. Pack the fruit as closely as possible without squashing it and pour the syrup over it. Release any air bubbles by inserting a sterilized knife blade down the side of the jar or by jerking the filled jar. Add a little more syrup if necessary.

Seal the jars with glass or metal lids and with clamps or screw-on rings. If using rings, screw on the ring and then give a quarter turn to loosen. This allows steam to escape from the jars during processing and prevents them from bursting. Canning jars, clamps, and rings can be used again, but new rubber rings and self-sealing lids must be bought every time.

Methods of canning

Fruit can be processed either in a water bath or a pressure cooker or a canner.

For the water-bath method, place the filled jars on a rack in a large pan, making sure that the jars do not touch each other. Pour in enough hot water to immerse the jars by at least 1 inch, cover the pot with its lid, and bring to a boil over moderate heat. Boil for the recommended time. Processing time varies according to the size and type of fruit and the size of the jars.

When the fruit has been processed, remove the jars from the pan of water with tongs or a jar lifter; place on a dry, warm surface. Tighten the screw rings immediately and leave the jars undisturbed overnight.

Pressure canning or cooking is the only method recommended for nonacid fruits and vegetables. When

CANNING FRUIT

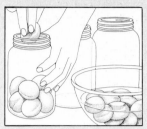

Pack fruit firmly into jar.

Pour sugar syrup over fruit.

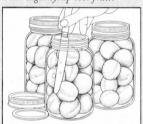

Release air bubbles from filled jars.

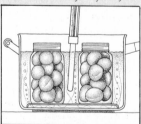

Can fruit in boiling water.

Maintain 5-pound pressure.

using a pressure cooker, make sure that it is deep enough to take the canning jars and that there is a reliable control to maintain a steady pressure of 5 pounds or more. Cover the bottom of the pan with water to a depth of 1 inch, put in the rack, and set the prepared jars on top. Cover the cooker but leave the vent open; heat until the steam flows—this should take 5–10 minutes.

Close the vent, and process at the necessary pressure for the recommended time, following the manufacturer's instructions carefully. Remove the pan from the heat and leave it to cool for 10 minutes before releasing the pressure. Open the pressure cooker, remove the jars, and tighten the screw rings.

Canning tomatoes

Tomatoes can be canned on their own or in brine. Use small or medium peeled tomatoes and pack them tightly so that no liquid is needed. Sprinkle 1 teaspoon salt and $\frac{1}{2}$ teaspoon sugar over each pound of tomatoes. Process the jars in a boiling water bath, 35 minutes for pints and 45 minutes for quarts.

Alternatively, pack the tomatoes in jars and cover with brine made from 1 tablespoon salt to 1 quart of water. Process in a boiling water bath for 45 minutes.

Tomato Purée
6 pounds ripe tomatoes

Wash and quarter the tomatoes. Cook them over low heat in an aluminum or stainless-steel pan until the juices run and the tomatoes have reduced to a pulp. Rub through a nylon sieve. Return the purée to a boil, then pour it into hot jars. Seal the jars as for canning and process in a boiling water bath for 20 minutes.

PICKLING

Pickles are fresh vegetables or fruits preserved in vinegar. Good-quality vinegar, with an acetic acid content of at least 5 percent, is essential for pickling. White vinegar shows off the color and texture of pickles, but cider vinegar gives a better flavor. Whichever vinegar is chosen, it is usually flavored with spices.

See illustration on page 374.

Preparing spiced vinegar

To make spiced vinegar, add 2 tablespoons each of whole allspice, cloves, and white peppercorns; 2 pieces stick cinnamon; and a 1-inch piece whole bruised ginger root to 1 quart of vinegar. Steep the spices in the vinegar for 1–2 months and shake the bottle occasionally. Strain before use.

For immediate use, spiced vinegar can be prepared by a quicker method. Put the spices and vinegar into a bowl, cover, and stand it in a pan of cold water. Bring the water to a boil, remove the pan from the heat, and leave the spices in the warm vinegar for about 2 hours. Keep the bowl covered so that no flavor is lost. Strain the vinegar before use.

Methods of pickling

Wash and prepare the vegetables or fruit according to the recipe. Vegetables must be liberally sprinkled with coarse salt to draw out excess water, which would otherwise dilute the vinegar. Put the vegetables in layers with the salt or immerse them completely in a brine solution of 1 pound coarse pickling salt or kosher salt to 1 gallon of water.

Leave the vegetables to steep in the salt for 24–48 hours, then rinse in cold water and drain thoroughly. Do not use metal sieves or colanders.

Pack the vegetables into sterilized dry canning jars to within 1 inch of the top. Pour over enough spiced vinegar to come $\frac{1}{2}$ inch above the vegetables. Seal the jars tightly with self-sealing lids and rings. It is essential that the jars are sealed airtight, otherwise the vinegar will evaporate and the pickle will dry out.

The number of jars needed depends on the size of the pickled vegetable and how tightly they are packed. In general, 1 pound of solid ingredients will fill a 1-pint jar.

Label and date the jars. Store in a cool, dry place for at least a month.

Sweet pickles

For sweet pickles, omit the peppercorns when preparing the spiced vinegar and use this as a base for a syrup, allowing 5 cups of sugar to each 2½ cups of spiced vinegar. Simmer the fruit in the syrup until just tender. Pack the fruit or vegetables in jars, pour over the syrup, and seal.

When pickling whole fruit, prick lightly to prevent shrinkage.

Pickled Beets

3 pounds uncooked beets
2½ cups spiced vinegar, approximately

Wash the beets carefully without damaging the skins. Cook in lightly salted water until tender, about 2 hours. Peel and cut the beets into small dice or slices. Pack into jars and cover with cold spiced vinegar.

Pickled Cucumber

3 large cucumbers
4 large onions
4 tablespoons coarse salt
2½ cups distilled white vinegar
¾ cup granulated sugar
1 teaspoon celery seeds
1 teaspoon mustard seeds

Wash, dry, and thinly slice the cucumbers. Peel and slice the onions. Mix the two ingredients together in a bowl and sprinkle with the salt. Leave 2 hours. Rinse and drain.

Bring the vinegar, sugar, and spices to a boil and simmer for 3 minutes. Pack the drained cucumbers and onions loosely in warm jars. Cover with the spiced vinegar and seal immediately.

Pickled Cauliflower

2 pounds cauliflower
2 sweet red peppers
¼ teaspoon black pepper
¼ tablespoon marjoram
¼ teaspoon garlic powder
¼ cup white wine vinegar
2 cups vegetable oil

Break cauliflower into florets. Bring to a boil and simmer 5 minutes in water to cover. Drain. Pack in 3 hot, sterilized pint jars. Cut peppers into thin rings. Mix with remaining ingredients. Put in jars and seal at once.

Pickled Peaches

4 pounds peaches
2½ cups spiced vinegar syrup

Peel the peaches.* Cut away any discolored parts, then halve and quarter them. Poach* in the vinegar syrup for 10 minutes or until tender.

Pack the fruit tightly into warm jars. Boil the syrup for 2–3 minutes, remove any scum, and pour the syrup over the fruit. Seal at once.

Pickled Onions

6 pounds small white pickling onions
5 cups spiced vinegar

Select small, uniform onions and put them, unpeeled, in brine. Leave for 12 hours, then peel the onions and immerse them in fresh brine for a further 24–36 hours. Remove from the brine, rinse, and drain thoroughly. Pack into sterilized jars and cover with cold spiced vinegar. Seal. Leave for 2–3 months before using.

Pickled Red Cabbage

1 large red cabbage
7–8 cups spiced vinegar

Select a firm, bright-colored cabbage. Remove the outer leaves and center stalk. Shred the cabbage finely and layer it with salt in a large bowl. Leave for 24 hours, then drain and rinse thoroughly. Pack loosely into jars, cover with cold spiced vinegar, and seal. Use within 3 months.

Piccalilli

6 pounds prepared vegetables (cucumber, red and green bell peppers, small onions, cauliflower, beans)
7½ cups white vinegar
6 teaspoons dry mustard
2 teaspoons ground ginger
1¼ cups granulated sugar
6 tablespoons flour
4 teaspoons turmeric

Clean and prepare the vegetables: Cut the cucumber into 1-inch cubes; chop the peppers coarsely; peel the onions; break the cauliflower into florets; and cut the beans into 1-inch lengths. Immerse the vegetables in brine and leave overnight.

Spice the vinegar with mustard and ginger, and add the sugar.

Rinse and drain the vegetables thoroughly. Put them in a pan, pour in the hot vinegar syrup, and simmer for 20 minutes. Lift the vegetables out with a slotted spoon and pack into warm jars.

Mix the flour and turmeric to a smooth paste with a little vinegar. Stir this into the hot syrup. Boil for 2 minutes, then pour over the vegetables and seal.

Tomato Sauce

6 pounds ripe tomatoes
1¼ cups granulated sugar
1¼ cups spiced vinegar
1 teaspoon paprika
2 teaspoons salt
Cayenne pepper

Wash and quarter the tomatoes. Cook them over gentle heat until the juices run, then increase the heat and boil rapidly until reduced to a pulp. Rub through a nylon sieve and return the purée to a clean pan. Stir in the sugar, vinegar, paprika, salt, and a pinch of cayenne. Bring to a boil and cook until the mixture has the consistency of a sauce.

Pour the tomato sauce into sterilized bottles and seal. Process the bottles for 30 minutes. (See instructions for Fruit Syrups, p.351).

CHUTNEYS

Chutneys are usually made from fruit, such as apples, mangoes, gooseberries, plums, and tomatoes. Flavorings are added in the form of spices, onions, garlic, and salt, and the preserve is sweetened with sugar, or sugar and dried fruits. Chutneys require long, slow cooking in an aluminum or stainless-steel pan. The preserve should be smooth and pulpy, with a mellow flavor. Pour the chutney into warm, sterilized jars and seal. Leave for 2–3 months before using.

See illustration on page 374.

Apple Chutney

4 pounds cooking apples
2½ cups vinegar
2–3 cloves garlic
3¾ cups brown sugar
1 cup crystallized ginger or 2 teaspoons ground ginger
½ teaspoon allspice
Cayenne pepper
½ teaspoon salt

Peel, core, and chop the apples. Cook with 1¼ cups of vinegar and the crushed garlic until thick and pulpy. Add the remaining vinegar, the sugar, ginger, allspice, a good pinch of cayenne, and salt. Continue cooking for a further 20 minutes or until thick. Put in sterilized jars and seal.

Apple Mint Chutney

4 pounds cooking apples
1 pound ripe tomatoes
2½ cups vinegar
2½ cups brown sugar
1 cup crystallized ginger or 2 teaspoons ground ginger
½ teaspoon allspice
Pinch cayenne pepper
½ teaspoon salt
2¾ cups seedless raisins
1½ cups well-packed mint leaves, finely chopped

Peel, core, and chop the apples, and peel, seed, and chop the tomatoes.* Cook the apples with 1¼ cups of vin-

egar until thick and pulpy, then stir in the remaining vinegar, the sugar, ginger, allspice, cayenne pepper, salt, and raisins.

Cook for a further 15 minutes, then stir in the mint and cook for 5 more minutes or until thick. Put in sterilized jars and seal.

Mango Chutney

2 teaspoons pickling spices
2 pounds very ripe mangoes
1 pound cooking apples
3 medium onions
2 cups white or brown malt vinegar
2¼ cups firmly packed light brown sugar

Tie the pickling spices in a piece of cheesecloth. Cut the mangoes into 2-inch pieces. Discard the seeds. Peel and chop the apples finely and chop the onions.

Put the bag of spices, the fruits, and onions into a large saucepan. Add ½ cup of the vinegar. Cook until the mixture is soft, adding a little more vinegar if the mixture becomes too stiff.

Stir in the sugar and remaining vinegar. Boil until chutney has the consistency of thick jam. Put in sterilized jars and seal.

Tomato Chutney

6 pounds ripe tomatoes
½ pound onions
4 teaspoons whole allspice
1 teaspoon cayenne pepper
1 tablespoon salt
1¼ cups vinegar
2 cups brown sugar

Peel and quarter the tomatoes* and put them in a large pan, together with the peeled and thinly sliced onions. Add the allspice, tied in cheesecloth, and the cayenne and salt. Cook over gentle heat until the mixture is pulpy, then stir in the remaining ingredients. Simmer until thick. Put in sterilized jars and seal.

Pastry

The many different kinds of pastry made today have evolved over the centuries from a crude flour and water dough mixture invented by the Romans. The paste was wrapped around meat and game before roasting and was not intended to be eaten. It served only to retain the meat juices and aroma.

As time passed, the paste was enriched with fat and milk and began vaguely to resemble pie pastry. By medieval times, pastry making was well established, and rich pastry crusts, known as coffers, became as important as the contents of the huge fruit, fish, meat, and game pies they covered.

As different areas and localities developed their own puddings and pies, many pastry variations emerged from the basic fat, flour, and water recipe. One was the 14th-century raised hot-water crust. This was indigenous to Britain and was used with meat and game pies. It was molded from the inside with a clenched fist and then filled and baked until crisp and brown.

By the 17th century both flaky and puff pastries were being used for elaborate pies, and the decorations and intricate patterns on the finished pies were works of art. Later still, continental pastry making added to the ever-growing number of recipes. Yet today, the basic art of pastry making is much as it has been for centuries.

Pastry is no longer used principally to retain the juices of the filling it covers. Its chief purpose is to complement the flavor of the filling and at the same time to provide a convenient shell in which anything from a quiche to a lemon meringue pie can be cooked. It also helps to stretch a limited serving of meat, fish, game, or fruit.

Although much mystique surrounds pastry making, there are no great secrets to guarantee instant success, for pastry making is an art that is mastered by care, patience, and practice. There are, however, a few essentials that must be observed before good results can be achieved. The kitchen, working surface, and utensils should be cool, and the recipe must always be strictly adhered to, especially in regard to measurements. Pastry should be made as quickly as possible, and handling kept to a minimum. Cutting in the flour and shortening with a pastry blender will usually produce a light and tender pastry. A vigorous stirring motion, on the other hand, will develop the gluten in the flour, making the pastry tough.

Pie crust is probably the best-known and most commonly used pastry. The standard pie crust recipe is given in this section, along with a number of variations including one-stage (fork), oil, enriched, stirred, and cheese crusts. An uncooked crumb crust for cream pie or chiffon pie is also included, as are suet and hot-water pastries.

The light pastries, so prized in France, are used not only for desserts but also for savory dishes. These include choux, flaky pastry, and the puff pastries; all are harder to make than standard pie crust.

PIE PASTRY

This popular and versatile pastry is used for savory and sweet pies, tarts, and tartlets. It is usually made by the rubbing-in method, but there are several other ways of making pie pastry. All-purpose flour is recommended. The fat should be lard or a white vegetable shortening; ideally, use equal amounts of lard and butter or firm margarine. Margarine alone, no matter how high the quality, produces a yellow, firm pastry.

The standard recipe is for 8 ounces pastry, which always means 2 cups ($\frac{1}{2}$ pound) flour to $\frac{1}{2}$ cup ($\frac{1}{4}$ pound) fat. The amount of flour may be doubled or halved, but the ratio of flour to fat should remain the same.

The standard recipe yields enough pastry to cover a 2-pint pie or baking dish, or a 9-inch flan ring, or to line and cover a 7-inch pie plate.

The following basic pie pastries can be used for either savory or sweet pies. Enriched pastry, however, is mainly used for lining flan rings.

Pie pastries are usually baked in the center of a preheated oven at 400°F. They are sometimes baked blind—that is, partially cooked—if their fillings require less cooking; they are cooked completely if the filling requires no further cooking.

Standard Pastry
PREPARATION TIME: *15 minutes*

INGREDIENTS:
2 cups all-purpose flour
½ teaspoon salt
4 tablespoons lard
4 tablespoons margarine or butter
2–3 tablespoons cold water

Sift the flour and salt into a wide bowl. Cut up the firm fats and rub them into the flour, using the tips of the fingers or a pastry blender, until the mixture resembles fine bread crumbs. Lift the dry mixture well out of the bowl and let it trickle back through the fingers to keep the pastry cool and light. Gradually add the water, sprinkling it evenly over the surface of the dry ingredients (un-even addition of the water may cause blistering when the pastry is cooked). Mix the dough lightly with a round-bladed knife until it forms large lumps.

Gather the dough together with the fingers until it leaves the sides of the bowl clean. Form it into a disk rather than a ball. Do not knead or pat the dough. Wrap in waxed paper, plastic wrap, or aluminum foil and chill in the refrigerator for at least 30 minutes or until ready to use.

Roll the pastry out, using short, light strokes, and rotate it regularly to keep it an even shape.

One-Stage (Fork) Pastry
Margarine gives this easily prepared pastry a yellow-tinted crust with a smooth appearance and soft crumb. Stick margarine yields better results than soft margarine.

PREPARATION TIME: *10 minutes*

INGREDIENTS:
10 tablespoons margarine
2 cups all-purpose flour
2 tablespoons water

Put the margarine with 2 tablespoons of flour and the water in a deep mixing bowl. Cream these ingredients with a fork until well mixed. Still using the fork, work in the remaining flour to form a manageable dough. Turn this onto a floured surface and knead lightly until smooth. Chill in the refrigerator for 30 minutes.

PREPARING STANDARD PASTRY

1 *Rubbing fat into flour*

3 *Kneading dough lightly*

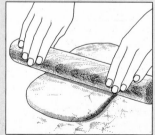

2 *Mixing water into dough*

4 *Rolling out the pastry*

To make one-stage pastry, cream margarine with flour and water.

Oil Pastry

This pastry produces a tender, flaky crumb. It must be mixed quickly and used at once—if left for any length of time, or chilled, it dries out and cannot be rolled.

PREPARATION TIME: *15 minutes*

INGREDIENTS:
5 tablespoons corn oil
5 tablespoons cold water
2 cups all-purpose flour
¼ teaspoon salt

Beat the oil and water together in a large bowl, using a fork. Continue beating until they are evenly blended. Sift the flour and salt together and gradually add it to the oil. Use two knives to incorporate the flour to a dough, then turn it onto a floured surface. Knead the pastry lightly and quickly until it is just smooth and shiny. Roll out the dough and bake like pie pastry.

For oil pastry, use two knives to mix the flour and oil.

Enriched Pastry

PREPARATION TIME: *10 minutes*

INGREDIENTS:
1¼ cups all-purpose flour
Pinch salt
6 tablespoons unsalted butter or margarine
1 egg yolk
1½ teaspoons sugar
3–4 teaspoons water

Sift the flour and salt into a wide bowl. Cut up the butter and rub it into the flour with the fingertips

until the mixture resembles bread crumbs. Beat the egg yolk, sugar, and 2 teaspoons of water in a separate bowl and pour it into the flour mixture. Stir with a round-bladed knife, adding more water as necessary, until the mixture begins to form a dough. Gather this into a ball and turn it onto a floured surface. Knead lightly.

Stirred Pastry

This rather sticky pastry is particularly suited for double-crust fruit pies. The texture of the baked pie is more like cookie dough than pastry.

PREPARATION TIME: *10–15 minutes*

INGREDIENTS:
½ cup plus 2 tablespoons margarine
3 tablespoons butter
2 cups self-rising flour
½ teaspoon salt
3 tablespoons cold water

Beat the margarine and butter in a bowl until soft and well blended. Gradually add the sifted flour and salt, working it in with a wooden spoon. Finally, add the water, blending thoroughly. The mixture will be sticky and difficult to work. Chill the dough in the refrigerator for at least 30 minutes.

Roll out the pastry on a well-floured surface or between sheets of waxed paper dredged with flour.

Cheese Pastry

Ideal for cheese straws, as a crust for vegetable pies, and for flan shells.

PREPARATION TIME: *10 minutes*

INGREDIENTS:
1 cup all-purpose flour
Salt and cayenne pepper
4 tablespoons butter or margarine
½ cup sharp or very sharp grated Cheddar cheese
1 egg yolk
2–3 teaspoons cold water

Sift the flour, a pinch of salt, and a shake of cayenne into a wide bowl.

Cut up the fat into small pieces and rub it quickly into the flour with the fingertips until the mixture resembles fine bread crumbs. Blend in the grated Cheddar cheese and stir in the egg yolk mixed with 1 tablespoon of water to ensure even distribution. Add more water to the mixture to make a stiff dough.

Knead the dough lightly on a floured surface, then place it in the refrigerator to chill.

Covering a pie dish

Roll out the pastry to the required thickness (no more than ¼ inch thick) and 2 inches wider than the pie dish, using the inverted dish as a guide. Cut a 1-inch-wide strip from the outer edge of the pastry and place it on the moistened rim of the pie dish. Seal the strip with water where it joins and then brush the whole strip with water.

Fill the pie dish and set a pie funnel in the center; lift the remaining pastry on the rolling pin and lay it over the pie dish. Press the pastry strip and lid firmly together with the fingers. Trim away any excess pastry with a knife blade held at a slight angle to the pie dish.

To seal the pastry edges firmly so that they do not come apart during baking, hold the knife blade horizontally toward the pie dish and make a series of shallow cuts in the pastry edges.

Use the leftover pastry trimmings to cut decorative shapes, such as leaves or pastry tassels, for the top of the pie. Cut a small slit in the center of the pastry for the steam to escape, and decorate the edges of the pie by fluting or crimping.

Preparing a two-crust pie

Divide the pastry into two portions, one slightly larger than the other. Shape the larger portion into a ball and roll it out on a lightly floured surface to a thickness of ⅛ inch. Rotate the pastry between rolls to keep the edge round; if the edge begins to

COVERING A PIE DISH

Trim the pastry to fit the dish.

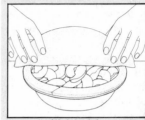
Cover the filled pie dish.

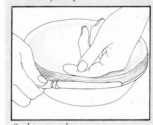
Seal pastry edges.

MAKING A TWO-CRUST PIE

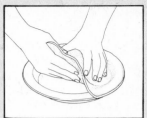
Lift pastry into pie plate.

Place top crust in position.

Fold surplus pastry under.

break, pinch it together with the fingers rather than rerolling it. Roll out the pastry about 1 inch wider than the inverted pie plate.

Fold the pastry in half and lift it onto the pie plate; unfold and loosely ease the pastry into position, being careful not to stretch the pastry. Put the cold filling over the pastry, keeping it slightly domed in the center. Roll out the remaining pastry for the top crust, allowing about a ½-inch extension beyond the rim. Brush the edge of the pastry lining with water, then lift the top crust carefully onto the rolling pin and place in position over the filling.

Seal the edges by either folding the surplus edge of the top crust firmly over the rim of the lining, or by trimming the edges almost level

with the plate and sealing them with a knife or pressing them with a fork. Cut a small slit in the center of the top crust or prick it with a fork in several places to allow the steam to escape while the pie cooks.

Lining a pie plate

For an open-face pie, roll out the pastry ⅛ inch thick and about 1 inch wider than the pie plate. Carefully lift the pastry into the plate and ease it loosely over the bottom and sides. Trim the pastry with scissors or a knife to ½ inch from the plate edge, then fold the pastry under the rim of the plate. Flute the edge (see Finishing and Decorations, page 356) so that the points protrude over the plate rim and thus prevent shrinking during baking.

Pastry

Lining a flan ring

Tart shells are baked in flan rings set on baking sheets, or in a French fluted flan pan with a removable bottom. Roll the pastry out as thinly as possible, $\frac{1}{8}$ inch or less, to a circle 2 inches wider than the ring. With the rolling pin, lift the pastry and lower it into the flan ring, or fold the pastry in half and in half again, and unfold in the flan ring. Lift the edges carefully and press the pastry gently into shape with the fingers, taking care that no air pockets are left between the ring and the pastry. Trim the pastry with a knife or scissors, just above the rim. If a French fluted flan pan is used, press the pastry against the fluted edges, then use the rolling pin to cut off the pastry level with the rim.

Lining tartlet molds

Set the small molds closely together on a baking sheet. Roll out the pastry $\frac{1}{8}$ inch thick to a rectangle or square large enough to cover the whole area of the molds. Roll the dough up on the rolling pin, then unroll the pastry loosely over the molds and press it into them with a small ball of pastry. Run the rolling pin over the molds, first in one direction, then in the other, trimming off any surplus. Press the pastry into shape with the fingers and prick the bottoms (see Baking Blind).

To line a sheet of patty pans, use a plain or fluted pastry cutter $\frac{1}{2}-\frac{3}{4}$ inch wider than the patty to cut out rounds from the pastry. Ease the pastry rounds into the patty pans and prick them with a fork.

Baking blind

Sometimes pastry, especially flan shells and individual tartlets, has to be baked before the filling is put in. This is known as baking blind. Line the pastry shell with aluminum foil or waxed paper cut to shape. Weight down with dried beans. (If kept only for this purpose, the beans can be used again and again.)

Bake the pastry shell in the center of a preheated oven at 400°F for 15 minutes. Remove the beans and aluminum foil and bake for a further 5–10 minutes, or until the pastry is dry and lightly browned.

Alternatively, and especially for tartlets, prick the bottom and sides of the pastry with a fork before lining it with foil.

Flan shells and tartlet molds should be left on a wire rack to cool and shrink slightly before being eased out of their molds.

To bake blind, cover pastry with paper and weigh down with beans.

Finishing and decorations

The sealed edges of a covered pie can be finished in a number of decorative ways. To make a fluted pattern, press the outer edge between thumb and index finger at $\frac{1}{2}-\frac{3}{4}$ inch intervals. Draw the back of a knife between the indentations toward the center of the pie for about $\frac{1}{2}$ inch.

Alternatively, press the edges together with the back of a fork, or use the thumb to make an attractive scalloped pattern.

The top of a covered pie can be decorated with the pastry trimmings.

Roll the pastry out thinly and cut it into small plain or fluted circles, stars, and diamonds. Arrange these in a pattern over the glazed top.

To make leaves, cut the pastry into 1- or 1½-inch-wide strips and cut these into diamond shapes. With the back of a knife, press or trace first the midribs and then the internal veins over each leaf shape.

For a tassel, cut a 1-inch-wide pastry slice about 6 inches long. Make $\frac{3}{4}$-inch-long cuts at intervals of $\frac{1}{4}$ inch. Then roll up the strip, place it on the pie, and open out the cut edges.

Finish the edges of open-face pies and tarts by fluting or crimping. A simple method, using a pair of scissors, is to make cuts just over $\frac{1}{4}$ inch deep and a little over $\frac{1}{4}$ inch apart around the pastry edge. Fold alternate pieces of pastry inward and bend the remaining pieces outward. Or the edges can be decorated with thin pastry strips that have been twisted or braided. Moisten the pastry edge with water before putting on a twisted or braided border.

A lattice pattern is a traditional decoration for many open-face pies and tarts. Cut the rolled-out pastry trimmings into $\frac{1}{2}$-inch-wide strips (a pastry wheel gives an attractive edge) that are long enough to cover the top. Moisten the edges of the shell, then lay half the strips over the filling, 1 inch apart, and lay the remaining strips crisscrossing the first. Trim the strips to shape at the outer edge or fold the pastry lining down over them for a neater finish. For a really professional touch, the pastry strips should be interwoven: Lay them over the filling 1 inch apart, then place a strip of pastry at a right angle across the center. Lift alternate lengths of the first strips of pastry on one half of the tart and place another strip at right angles (shown opposite). Replace the top strips and repeat with the other side of the tart to complete the interwoven effect. The strips may also be twisted before being arranged in the lattice pattern.

Pies can be decorated with pastry flowers. Simple flowers are made by rolling a small piece of pastry to the size and shape of an acorn. Cut out 2 diamond shapes and pinch the edges to round them to a petal shape.

DECORATING PIE EDGES

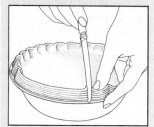

Making a fluted pattern

Making scalloped edges

LINING A FLAN RING

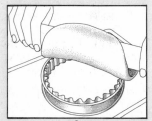

Lay pastry over flan.

Press pastry into fluted ridges.

Roll off surplus pastry.

LINING TARTLET MOLDS

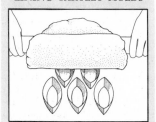

Lay pastry over the molds.

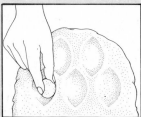

Shape molds with pastry ball.

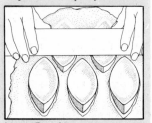

Trim off surplus pastry.

PASTRY DECORATIONS

Pastry leaf shapes

Pastry tassels

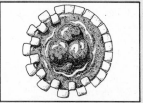

Cut edges on a tart

356

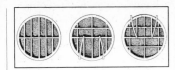

Lattice pattern: Lay pastry strips over top; interleave crossing strips.

Dampen the base of the petals and wrap them around the wide base of the acorn shape. Gently pinch the pastry to seal the pieces together, then bend the tip of each petal slightly outward.

More ornate flowers can be made by making a cross with a knife on a small, flattened round of pastry. Set the round on a square of dampened pastry; set this in turn on another square of dampened pastry, the same size, to form a star pattern. Shape the corners of the squares to resemble petals. Pinch and shape each point of the central round of pastry into a petal to complete the flowers.

Glazing

Glaze the decorated pie before baking to give a shiny golden look: Brush savory pies with beaten whole egg or with egg yolk diluted with a little water or milk and a pinch of salt. Glaze sweet pies by brushing with milk or egg white and dusting with superfine sugar.

Deep-Dish Apple Pie

PREPARATION TIME: *20 minutes*
COOKING TIME: *35 minutes*

INGREDIENTS (*for 4–6*):
1½ pounds cooking apples
4–6 tablespoons sugar
Standard pastry (p.354)
Milk

Peel and core the apples and cut them into chunky slices. Place a pie funnel in the center of a 1½-pint pie dish, arrange half the apple slices in the dish, sprinkle over the sugar, and add the remaining fruit with 3 tablespoons of water.

Cover the pie with the rolled-out pastry, decorate it, and brush the top

with milk. Dust with superfine sugar. Make a slit in the center of the crust for the steam to escape. Set the pie on a baking sheet and bake in the center of a preheated oven at 400°F for 35–40 minutes. If the pastry browns too quickly, cover it loosely with a double layer of moistened waxed paper.

For variation, the water can be replaced with orange juice, and the grated rind of half an orange can be mixed with the sugar.

Alternatively, use 1 pound of apples and ½ pound of blackberries for the filling. Other fruits, such as halved and pitted apricots, plums, peaches, blueberries, and 1-inch pieces of trimmed rhubarb, also make good fruit pies. For rhubarb pie, increase the amount of sugar to ½ cup.

Cheese and Onion Pie

PREPARATION TIME: *30 minutes*
COOKING TIME: *35 minutes*

INGREDIENTS (*for 4–6*):
Standard pastry (p.354)
4 large onions (approximately 1 pound)
1½–2 cups coarsely grated mild cheese
½ teaspoon grated nutmeg
1 teaspoon salt
Black pepper
2 teaspoons Worcestershire sauce
Milk

Peel and quarter the onions. Cook them in boiling water for about 15 minutes or until they are just tender. Drain in a colander, then cool slightly before chopping coarsely.

Divide the prepared pastry in two and roll out each half to fit an 8–9 inch pie plate. Line the plate with half the cheese and the onions. Season with nutmeg, salt, pepper, and Worcestershire sauce. Top with the remaining cheese and cover the pie with pastry. Seal the edges. Brush with milk and make a small slit in the top crust. Bake in a preheated oven at 400°F for 30–35 minutes.

See illustration on page 367.

Lemon Meringue Pie

PREPARATION TIME: *30 minutes*
COOKING TIME: *35–45 minutes*

INGREDIENTS (*for 4–6*)
½ recipe standard pastry (p.354)
1 large thin-skinned lemon
2–3 tablespoons granulated sugar
2 tablespoons cornstarch
2 eggs
1 tablespoon unsalted butter
½ cup superfine sugar

Roll out the pastry and line an 8½-inch pie plate or a 7-inch flan ring. Bake the pastry crust blind in the center of a preheated oven at 400°F for about 15 minutes, or until the pastry is crisp and golden. When cold, remove the pastry from the pie plate or ease away the flan ring.

Meanwhile, peel the rind from the lemon in thin slivers, carefully omitting all white pith. Squeeze the juice from the lemon and set it aside. Put the lemon peel, granulated sugar, and 1 cup of water in a pan; cook over low heat until the sugar has dissolved, then bring this syrup to a boil. Remove the pan from the heat. Blend the cornstarch in a bowl with 3 tablespoons lemon juice, then pour in the syrup through a strainer, stirring thoroughly. Separate the eggs and beat in the egg yolks, one at a time, together with the butter. The mixture should be thick enough to coat the back of a wooden spoon; otherwise, return it to the pan and cook for a few minutes without boiling. Spoon the lemon mixture into the cooked pastry shell set on a baking sheet.

Beat the egg whites until stiff, then add half the superfine sugar and continue beating until the meringue holds its shape and stands in soft peaks. Fold all but 1 teaspoon of the remaining sugar into the meringue, using a rubber spatula.

Pile the meringue over the lemon filling; spread it from the edge toward the center, making sure that it joins the pastry edge; this will prevent the meringue from "weeping."

Sprinkle with the remaining teaspoon of sugar. Reduce the heat to 300°F and bake the pie for 20–30 minutes, or until the meringue is crisp. Serve the pie warm, rather than hot or cold.

See illustration on page 367.

Buttermilk Pie

PREPARATION TIME: *30 minutes*
COOKING TIME: *50 minutes*

INGREDIENTS (*for 4–6*):
½ recipe standard pastry (p.354)
6 tablespoons unsalted butter
1½ cups sugar
2 eggs
3 tablespoons flour
1½ cups buttermilk
3 teaspoons lemon juice, strained
1 teaspoon grated lemon rind
Pinch nutmeg

Roll out the pastry and line an 8½-inch pie plate. Bake the pastry blind* in the center of a preheated oven at 400°F for 10–15 minutes. Allow the pastry to cool completely before adding the filling.

With a wooden spoon, cream the butter and sugar together in a large mixing bowl until pale yellow and fluffy. Separate the eggs and set the whites aside in a clean bowl. Beat the egg yolks into the butter and sugar mixture, one at a time, then gradually beat in the flour.

Add the buttermilk slowly, beating continuously, then stir in the lemon juice and the lemon rind.

In another large bowl beat the egg whites until stiff but not dry. Using a rubber spatula, stir a few tablespoons of the egg whites into the batter to thin it, then fold the batter gently but thoroughly into the remaining egg whites.

Pour this filling into the cooled pie shell and sprinkle a little nutmeg evenly over the top. Preheat the oven to 350°F and bake the pie for 40 minutes or until the filling has set and a knife inserted in the center of the pie comes out clean. Let the pie cool to room temperature and serve.

Duke of Cambridge Tart

PREPARATION TIME: *15 minutes*
COOKING TIME: *40 minutes*

INGREDIENTS (*for 4*):
½ recipe standard pastry (p.354)
⅓ cup candied cherries
¼ cup angelica
½ cup chopped mixed peel
6 tablespoons butter
6 tablespoons sugar
2 egg yolks

Roll out the pastry and line a 7-inch flan ring with it. Chop the cherries and angelica or snip them with scissors. Mix them with the peel and cover the bottom of the pastry crust evenly with the fruit.

Put the butter, sugar, and egg yolks in a small pan over low heat and beat steadily with a wooden spoon. Bring the mixture almost to a boil and pour it over the fruit. Bake the tart in the center of a preheated oven at 375°F for about 40 minutes.

Cheese and Bacon Quiche

PREPARATION TIME: *30 minutes*
COOKING TIME: *40 minutes*

INGREDIENTS (*for 4–6*):
¾ recipe standard pastry (p.354)
1 small onion
1 tablespoon butter or margarine
4 slices lean bacon
1 cup grated Cheddar cheese
2 large eggs
½ cup milk
2 tablespoons light cream or half-and-half
1 tablespoon freshly chopped parsley (optional)
Salt and black pepper

Roll out the pastry and use it to line an 8–8½ inch flan ring. Peel and finely chop the onion and sauté it in the butter over low heat for 5 minutes until soft and transparent. Set aside. Cut the bacon into small pieces. Cook until the fat runs and the bacon begins to crisp. Drain off fat.

Mix the onion and bacon and arrange it in the pastry shell. Cover with the cheese.

Lightly beat the eggs with the milk and cream. Add the chopped parsley, if used, and season to taste. Spoon this mixture over the filling and bake in the center of a preheated oven at 400°F for 30 minutes. Reduce the heat to 350°F and bake for a further 10 minutes until the filling is set and the pastry crisp and golden brown. Serve the quiche warm or cold, with a green salad.

Plum and Cinnamon Pie

PREPARATION TIME: *5 minutes*
COOKING TIME: *40 minutes*
STANDING TIME: *1 hour*

INGREDIENTS (*for 6*):
Stirred pastry (p.355)
2 16-ounce cans yellow plums
1 tablespoon quick-cooking tapioca
¼ teaspoon powdered cinnamon
2 tablespoons butter
1 egg white
Granulated sugar

Drain the plums, reserving the syrup, and remove the pits. Blend the tapioca and powdered cinnamon in a bowl with 6 tablespoons of the plum syrup and leave it to stand for 30 minutes.

Roll out half the pastry and use it to line a 10-inch pie plate. Mix the plums with the tapioca mixture and spoon it over the pastry; dot with butter. Roll out the remaining pastry for the top crust and cover the pie. Seal the edges and make a slit in the top crust. Brush the top with beaten egg white and dust generously with sugar. Chill for 30 minutes.

Set the pie on a heated baking sheet and bake in the center of a preheated oven at 400°F for about 40 minutes. Serve the pie warm, with whipped cream.

See illustration on page 367.

Cheese Straws

PREPARATION TIME: *10 minutes*
COOKING TIME: *35 minutes*

INGREDIENTS:
Cheese pastry (p.355)

Roll out the prepared pastry as thinly as possible to a rectangle. Trim the edges evenly, then cut the pastry into strips ¼ inch wide and 2 inches long, using a floured knife blade. Set the straws on buttered baking sheets. Bake just above the center of a preheated oven at 400°F for 12 minutes or until golden.

Leave the cheese straws to cool on a wire rack.

Rum and Butter Tarts

PREPARATION TIME: *15 minutes*
COOKING TIME: *15–20 minutes*

INGREDIENTS (*for 12–14 tarts*):
½ recipe standard pastry (p.354)
½ cup currants
2 tablespoons butter
½ cup light brown sugar
1 tablespoon light cream or half-and-half
Rum or rum extract
½ egg or 1 egg yolk

Cover the currants with boiling water and leave them to stand until they are plump, about 10 minutes. Drain the currants thoroughly in a colander. Roll out the pastry and use it to line 12–14 patty tins about 2½ inches long. Use a plain or fluted pastry cutter.

Melt the 2 tablespoons of butter in a small pan, remove from the heat, and stir in the light brown sugar, cream, and rum to taste. Add the currants and stir in the thoroughly beaten egg.

Using a teaspoon, divide the currant mixture evenly between the small tarts. Do not let the filling come more than three-quarters up the pastry. Bake just above the center of an oven preheated to 375°F for 15–20 minutes, or until the pastry is crisp to the touch and the filling has turned a golden brown.

CRUMB CRUST

This uncooked crust is ideal for pie shells with fluffy chiffon-type fillings.

PREPARATION TIME: *15 minutes*
CHILLING TIME: *2 hours*

INGREDIENTS:
½ pound graham crackers, zwieback, or ginger snaps
10 tablespoons butter
2–4 tablespoons sugar (optional)

Crush the crackers or cookies a few at a time with a rolling pin between 2 sheets of waxed paper or in a plastic bag. For a fine crumb, break up the crackers coarsely and put them in a blender. Turn the crumbs into a deep bowl. Melt the butter in a small saucepan over low heat. Add the sugar, if used, to the crumbs and mix with the melted butter, stirring with a wooden spoon until they are evenly combined. Spread the crumbly mixture into a 7- or 8-inch-wide shallow

PREPARING CRUMB CRUST

Crush crackers in a plastic bag.

Stir in the melted butter.

Press the mixture into flan ring.

pie plate; or use a flan ring placed on a flat dish or a removable-bottom flan pan. With the back of a spoon, press the crumbs over the bottom and up the sides to form a shell.

Chill the shell in the refrigerator for 2 hours before filling it.

Lime Chiffon Pie

PREPARATION TIME: *1 hour*
CHILLING TIME: *3 hours*

INGREDIENTS (*for 6–8*):
Crumb crust
1 envelope unflavored gelatin
1 cup sugar
¼ teaspoon salt
¼ cup lime juice
½ cup water
4 eggs, separated
2 teaspoons grated lime rind
Green food coloring
Whipped cream

Make the crust from the basic recipe. In the top of a double boiler mix the gelatin, ½ cup of sugar, and salt. Beat in the liquids and egg yolks. Simmer, stirring, until mixture thickens and coats a metal spoon. Add the rind and a few drops of green food coloring. Chill until thickened but not firm. Beat the egg whites until foamy. Add the sugar gradually, beating until stiff. Fold into gelatin mixture and pile this into the crumb crust. Chill for 3 hours. Decorate with whipped cream.

Quick Lemon Cheesecake

PREPARATION TIME: *20 minutes*
CHILLING TIME: *2–3 hours*

INGREDIENTS (*for 4–6*):
Crumb crust
FILLING:
½ cup prepared lemon gelatin dessert
8 ounces soft cream cheese
4 tablespoons sugar
Grated rind of 1 large lemon
TOPPING:
3 tablespoons lemon juice
1½ teaspoons arrowroot
2 tablespoons sugar
Butter

Make the crumb crust from the basic recipe. Shape the crust in an 8-inch flan ring set on a flat plate, or use a fluted removable-bottom flan pan.

Prepare the lemon gelatin as directed on the package. When it has dissolved, chill in the refrigerator until it has the consistency of unbeaten egg white. Beat the cream cheese with the sugar and the lemon rind, then gradually beat in the gelatin. Spoon the smooth filling into the crumb crust and chill until the filling has set.

Add enough water to the lemon juice to make ½ cup. In a small pan, blend the arrowroot to a smooth paste with a little of this liquid, then add the rest of the liquid and the sugar. Bring to a boil, stirring, and keep boiling until the mixture is clear. Remove the pan from the heat and add a piece of butter. Cool the mixture until lukewarm, then spoon it evenly over the filling. Chill for at least 2 hours before serving.

Chocolate Cream Pie

PREPARATION TIME: *20 minutes*
CHILLING TIME: *1 hour*

INGREDIENTS (*for 6*):
Crumb crust
FILLING:
1 cup milk
2 tablespoons sugar
¼ cup flour
1½ teaspoons cornstarch
2 eggs, beaten
2 tablespoons unsalted butter
3–3½ ounces semisweet chocolate, grated
2 teaspoons brandy or rum
Confectioners' sugar
TOPPING:
½ cup heavy cream
1 tablespoon milk
Grated chocolate (optional)

Make the crumb crust according to the basic recipe and line an 8½-inch French fluted flan pan with it.

Heat the milk. Blend the sugar, flour, cornstarch, and beaten eggs together in a bowl, then stir in the milk. Return this mixture to the pan and cook over low heat, stirring continuously, until the mixture thickens and just comes to a boil. Remove the pan from the heat and stir in the butter, cut into small pieces, the chocolate, and brandy. Stir until smooth, then leave to cool slightly. Spoon the filling into the flan shell and dust it with confectioners' sugar to prevent a skin from forming. Chill.

Just before serving, whip the cream with the milk until thick enough to hold its shape. Spoon this in an even layer over the chocolate filling. Dust the cream with coarsely grated chocolate.

See illustration on page 367.

SUET CRUST PASTRY

This type of pastry is used for steamed puddings and for dumplings. For best results, use fresh beef suet.* Correct mixing and handling achieve a pastry with a light, spongy texture. For an even lighter texture, replace ½ cup of the measured flour with 1 cup fresh white bread crumbs.

PREPARATION TIME: *15 minutes*
RESTING TIME: *15 minutes*

INGREDIENTS:
2 cups self-rising flour or 2 cups all-purpose flour and 1 tablespoon baking powder
½ teaspoon salt
1 cup shredded suet
½ cup cold water, approximately

Sift the flour and salt into a bowl (together with baking powder if all-purpose flour is used). Add the suet—remove the skin from fresh suet, then grate or chop it finely with a little of the flour to prevent sticking—and mix thoroughly. Using a round-bladed knife, stir in the water to form a light, elastic dough. Turn the dough onto a lightly floured surface and sprinkle it with a little

flour. Knead the dough lightly with the fingertips and shape it into a ball. Put the dough on a plate and cover with an inverted bowl; let rest 10–15 minutes while filling is prepared.

Lining a pudding mold

Butter a 2½-cup pudding mold. Cut one quarter from the prepared suet pastry and set it aside for the top crust. Roll out the remaining pastry on a floured surface to a circle 2 inches wider than the top of the mold and about ¼ inch thick. Sprinkle pastry with flour; fold in half and then in half again to form a triangle. Roll pastry lightly toward the point.

Place the pastry triangle inside the mold, point downward, and unfold it, molding it to shape. Spoon in the prepared filling. Turn the pastry overhanging the rim of the mold in over the filling and brush with water.

Roll out the remaining pastry to a circle that fits the top of the mold. Lift the pastry on the rolling pin and lay it over the filling. Press the edges firmly together to seal them.

Fold a pleat in a square of aluminum foil or buttered waxed paper—the pleat allows the pudding to rise during cooking. Place the paper over the pudding and twist it under the rim of the mold. Cover the top of the pudding with a clean white napkin or cloth, tie it securely with string below the rim, and tie the ends into a knot.

Dumplings
PREPARATION TIME: *5 minutes*
COOKING TIME: *15 minutes*

INGREDIENTS (*for 8 dumplings*):
Suet crust pastry
Salt and black pepper
Mixed herbs (p.411) or chopped parsley or ¼ cup grated cheese

Half fill a large saucepan with water and put it on to boil. Make the pastry as described in the basic recipe, adding the herbs or cheese to the dry mix. Divide the pastry into 8 equal pieces and shape these into balls.

Put the dumplings into the boiling water, bring it back to a boil, then reduce heat and cover the pan with a tight-fitting lid. Simmer gently for 15 minutes—the dumplings will break up if the water is allowed to boil rapidly. The dumplings can be used as a garnish for soups or stews, or added to casserole dishes for the last 15 minutes.

Beef and Carrot Pudding
PREPARATION TIME: *20 minutes*
COOKING TIME: *2 hours*

INGREDIENTS (*for 4*):
Suet crust pastry
½ pound onions
4 tablespoons drippings
1 pound lean ground beef
½ pound carrots
2 tablespoons ready-made brown sauce
1 teaspoon mixed herbs (p.411)
2 tablespoons flour
1 cup beef stock
Salt and black pepper

Peel and finely chop the onions. Melt the drippings in a pan over moderate heat and sauté the onions until they begin to color. Stir in the ground beef and coarsely grate the peeled carrots straight into the pan. Cook for a further 5 minutes, stirring occasionally. Stir in the brown sauce, mixed herbs, flour, and the stock. Season to taste with salt and freshly ground pepper and remove the pan from the heat. Allow the beef mixture to cool completely.

Line a 4-cup pudding mold with the prepared suet crust and spoon the meat mixture into the mold. Cover with the pastry crust and seal the edges. Cover the pudding with paper and a napkin and set the mold in a large saucepan. Pour boiling water into the pan until the water reaches halfway up sides of mold.

Cover the saucepan with a lid and simmer for 2 hours. Add more boiling water when necessary. Serve the pudding straight from the mold, with boiled potatoes.

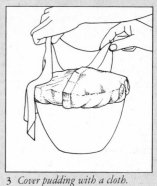

1 *Fold the pastry into a triangle.*

3 *Cover pudding with a cloth.*

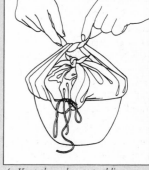

2 *Set pastry point down in mold.*

4 *Knot the ends over pudding.*

Apple and Ginger Roll
PREPARATION TIME: *30 minutes*
COOKING TIME: *1½ hours*

INGREDIENTS (*for 8*):
Suet crust pastry
1 pound cooking apples
½–1 teaspoon ground ginger
¼ cup light brown sugar
⅓ cup white raisins
Superfine sugar

Put a large saucepan half-full of water on to boil. Peel and core the apples, then cut them into even, not too thin slices and put them in a bowl. Mix the ground ginger and sugar together thoroughly, then mix with the sliced apples.

Roll the prepared suet crust pastry into a rectangle about ¼ inch thick. The width of the rectangle must be at least 2 inches smaller than the diameter of the saucepan. Spread the

apple filling over the pastry to within ½ inch of the edges, then sprinkle with the raisins. Turn the edges in over the filling and brush them with water. Roll up the pastry from the longest side and wrap it in aluminum foil, making a pleat in it to allow for expansion during cooking. Leave a short space at each end and twist the foil tightly to seal.

Place a heatproof inverted plate in the pan. Lower the roll into the water and bring it back to a boil. Reduce the heat, cover the pan with a lid, and boil gently for 1½ hours. Add more boiling water, if necessary, to keep the roll covered. Lift the roll from the saucepan with large metal spatulas. Let stand a few minutes. Remove the foil. Put the apple roll on a dish and dredge with superfine sugar. Serve at once with a custard sauce or a butterscotch sauce (p.304).

359

HOT-WATER PASTRY

This crisp, firm pastry has evolved from the original coffer paste. It is used for raised meat and game pies and is usually served cold. The pastry is molded by hand while still warm or fitted into a removable-bottom cake pan or pie mold.

PREPARATION TIME: *15 minutes*
RESTING TIME: *20 minutes*

INGREDIENTS:
3 cups all-purpose flour
½ teaspoon salt
¼ pound lard or margarine
1 egg yolk

Sift the flour and salt into a warmed bowl. Put the fat with ½ cup water into a small saucepan over low heat until the fat has melted, then bring to a boil. Make a well in the flour and drop in the egg yolk. Cover the egg with a little of the flour, then quickly add the hot fat mixture, stirring with a wooden spoon until the mixture is cool enough to handle.

Turn the dough onto a lightly floured surface and knead it quickly until soft and pliable. Shape the dough into a ball, put it on a warm plate, and cover with an inverted bowl. Leave to rest in a warm place for 20 minutes.

To mold the pastry, cut off one-third of the dough and set aside for the top crust; keep it warm. Roll out the pastry thickly and use to line a hinged tin pie mold or a removable-bottom cake pan set on a baking sheet, both thoroughly greased. Alternatively, flour an empty 2-pound jam jar, place the ball of warm dough on the bottom, and carefully mold the dough evenly over the bottom and two-thirds down the sides of the jar. Set the jar aside while the dough cools and settles, then carefully ease out the jar. Spoon the filling into the pastry mold, roll out the remaining pastry for the top, moisten the edges with water or egg glaze, and cover

the filling with the crust. Seal the edges firmly. Cut a slit in the center of the crust and decorate.

Pastry molded around a jar should have a protective band of foil tied around it to prevent the pie from collapsing during baking.

Raised Veal and Bacon Pie

A raised hot-water crust pie takes time and is therefore better made in large quantity. Extra pies should be frozen unbaked. Cook the pie the day before serving to give the jellied stock time to set.

PREPARATION TIME: *1 hour*
COOKING TIME: *about 6 hours*

INGREDIENTS (*for 8*):
PASTRY:
4 cups all-purpose flour
1 teaspoon salt
1 egg yolk
¾ cup lard
JELLIED VEAL STOCK:
2 pounds veal bones, chopped
1 carrot
1 onion
2 bay leaves
6 peppercorns
FILLING:
1 pound lean pork
¾ pound veal shoulder
½ pound lean bacon
1 onion
½ teaspoon salt
¼ teaspoon black pepper
½ teaspoon dried sage
Grated rind of ½ lemon
1 tablespoon chopped parsley
½ pound pork sausage meat
Egg for glazing

Prepare the stock first: Put the chopped veal bones with the cleaned carrot and peeled onion in a large saucepan. Add the bay leaves, peppercorns, and enough water to cover. Bring to a boil, remove the scum from the surface, then cover the pan with a lid. Reduce the heat and simmer the stock for 2½ hours. Strain the stock through cheesecloth, pour it into a clean pan, and reduce* to

MOLDING AND FILLING A RAISED HOT-WATER CRUST PIE

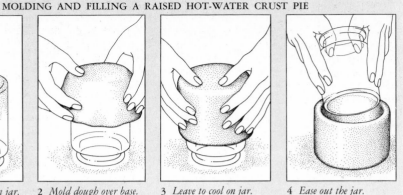

1 *Flour 2-pound jam jar.*   2 *Mold dough over base.*   3 *Leave to cool on jar.*   4 *Ease out the jar.*

5 *Cover the filled pie.*   6 *Cut hole in top.*   7 *Protect with paper.*   8 *Pour in liquid stock.*

about 1 cup by fast boiling. Leave to cool completely.

For the filling, put the pork, veal, half the bacon, and the peeled onion through the coarse blade of a meat grinder. Stir the mixture thoroughly in a large bowl, then add the salt, pepper, sage, lemon rind, and parsley. Moisten the mixture with 3 tablespoons of the veal stock.

Make the pastry as in the basic method for hot-water pastry and leave it to rest. For the pie, use a greased hinged pie or pâté mold 5¾ inches wide by 7½ inches long and 3¼ inches deep, or a 7-inch removable-bottom cake pan that has been lined with aluminum foil.

Roll out two-thirds of the pastry into a circle large enough to line the chosen mold. Fold the pastry in half and lower it into the mold, then unfold the pastry and ease it

smoothly and evenly into the bottom and up the sides. Press the dough well into any indentations in the pie frame.

Line the bottom of the pastry crust with sausage meat. Spoon the ground meat mixture over the top, pressing it down lightly and keeping it slightly domed. Beat the egg with salt and brush over the pastry edge. Roll out the remaining pastry to form the top crust; lift it on the rolling pin over the filling. Press the pastry onto the pie edge and pinch the edges firmly together to seal. Trim the pastry with a sharp knife and save the trimmings.

Glaze the top of the pie by brushing with beaten egg. Roll out the pastry trimmings and cut them into leaf and flower shapes. Arrange these in a pattern on the top and brush with more egg. Make a wide hole in

the center of the top crust to allow the steam to escape.

Set the pie on a baking sheet and bake in the center of a preheated oven at 450°F for 20 minutes. Reduce the heat to 325°F, cover the pie with foil, and continue baking for a further 3 hours. Leave the pie to cool in the mold until quite firm. Remove the mold or cake pan, and when the pie is nearly cold, pour the cool liquid stock slowly through a small funnel into the pie.

Leave the pie to set completely, generally for several hours, when the stock will have set to jelly around the meat. Serve the pie cold, cut into slices or wedges.

See illustration on page 367.

CHOUX PASTRY

This pastry is a French specialty and is used for cream puffs, chocolate eclairs, and profiteroles. During cooking, the pastry should treble in size through the natural lift of air. The resulting featherlight crust surrounds a large cavity that is filled with cream or a sweet custard.

PREPARATION TIME: *20 minutes*

INGREDIENTS (*for about 1 pound*):
½ *cup plus 2 tablespoons all-purpose flour*
Pinch of salt
4 tablespoons butter
½ *cup milk and water, mixed (half of each)*
2 eggs, beaten

Sift the flour and salt onto a sheet of waxed paper. Put the butter and the liquid in a heavy-bottomed pan and cook over low heat until the butter melts. Then raise the heat and rapidly bring the mixture to a boil. Remove the pan from the heat and pour in all the flour. Stir quickly with a wooden spoon until the flour has been absorbed by the liquid, then beat until the dough is smooth and comes away from the sides of the pan. Do not overbeat the dough, or the mixture may separate.

Cool pastry slightly, then beat in the beaten eggs, a little at a time. The pastry should be shiny but not stiff. If the pastry is not going to be used immediately, cover the saucepan tightly with plastic wrap and a lid.

Steamed Cream Puffs

PREPARATION TIME: *20 minutes*
COOKING TIME: *50 minutes*

INGREDIENTS (*for 10 puffs*):
Choux pastry
1 cup heavy cream
Confectioners' sugar

The characteristic light, crisp texture and irregularly cracked tops of these cream puffs are achieved by baking the pastry in its own steam. A large, shallow pan with a tight-fitting lid is necessary, or use a heavy baking sheet and invert a deep roasting pan over it; seal the seam with a flour and water paste after the choux puffs have been placed inside.

Prepare the choux pastry as directed above. While it is still warm, spoon it into a pastry bag fitted with a ½-inch plain tube. Carefully pipe small rounds of the pastry well apart onto the greased sheet. Cover with the roasting pan and bake just above the center of a preheated oven at 400°F for 40–50 minutes.

Leave the puffs undisturbed during cooking, or the steam will escape and cause them to collapse. The end of the cooking time can be estimated by giving the pan a gentle shake—if the puffs are baked they will rattle.

Cool the puffs on a wire rack, then make a slit through the bottoms and fill them with whipped cream. Dust with confectioners' sugar.

Cheese Aigrettes

PREPARATION TIME: *20 minutes*
COOKING TIME: *15–25 minutes*

INGREDIENTS (*for 24 aigrettes*):
Choux pastry
¾ *cup finely grated mild or sharp Cheddar cheese*
Pinch of cayenne pepper
Vegetable oil or vegetable shortening for deep-frying

Make the pastry, following the basic recipe, and beat in the finely grated cheese and cayenne pepper after beating in the eggs. Heat about 2½ inches of corn oil or fat in a deep-fryer, without a basket, to 375°F or until a cube of bread turns golden in 30 seconds. Drop teaspoons of the pastry into the hot fat, about six at a time, and fry for 4–6 minutes until puffed and golden brown. Lift the cheese puffs out with a slotted spoon and leave to drain on paper towels.

Pile the cheese aigrettes onto a hot serving dish and dust with more grated cheese.

Chocolate Eclairs

PREPARATION TIME: *20 minutes*
COOKING TIME: *20–30 minutes*

INGREDIENTS (*for 12–16 eclairs*):
Choux pastry
1 cup heavy cream
1 tablespoon superfine sugar
Chocolate confectioners' frosting from ½ pound confectioners' sugar (p.393)

Make up the choux pastry as directed above and spoon it into a pastry bag fitted with a ½-inch plain tube. Pipe out 3-inch lengths onto a buttered baking sheet, starting with the end of the tube touching the tray and lifting it while pressing the mixture out. Cut off the required lengths neatly with a wet knife.

Bake the eclairs just above the center of a preheated oven at 425°F for about 20 minutes. If the eclairs are not thoroughly dry, reduce the heat to 350°F and continue baking for a further 10 minutes. Remove the eclairs from the oven, slit them down one side to let the steam escape, and leave on a wire rack to cool. Beat the cream and sweeten it with sugar.

When the eclairs are cold, fill them with whipped cream, using a pastry bag and plain tube; cover the tops with the chocolate confectioners' frosting.

Profiteroles

PREPARATION TIME: *1 hour*
COOKING TIME: *15–25 minutes*

INGREDIENTS (*for 20–25 profiteroles*):
Choux pastry
1 cup heavy cream, whipped
Confectioners' sugar
¼ *pound semisweet chocolate squares*
5-ounce can evaporated milk

Make the choux pastry and spoon it into a pastry bag fitted with a plain ½-inch tube. Pipe 20–25 small puffs, well apart, on greased baking sheets and bake in or just above the center of a preheated oven at 425°F for about 15 minutes until well risen, puffed, and crisp. If the profiteroles are not thoroughly dry after 15 minutes, reduce the heat to 350°F and continue baking for 10 minutes longer. Place them on a wire rack and cool completely.

Split the puffs lengthwise, not quite in half. With a spoon fill the hollow centers with whipped cream and dust the tops with sifted confectioners' sugar. To serve, carefully pile the cooled profiteroles into a pyramid on a serving dish and pour a little chocolate sauce over them; serve the rest of the sauce separately in a small bowl.

To make the sauce, melt the chocolate squares in a bowl over a pan of hot but not boiling water. Stir in the evaporated milk and beat thoroughly with a wooden spoon.

Profiteroles are shown in the photograph on page 367.

MAKING CHOUX PASTRY

1 *Heat butter and liquid.*

3 *Beat dough until smooth.*

2 *Pour flour into melted butter.*

4 *Gradually add beaten eggs.*

PIPING OUT CHOCOLATE ECLAIRS

Spoon choux into a pastry bag.

Pipe out 3-inch lengths of dough.

Pastry

FLAKED PASTRIES

Flaked pastries are worth the extra time and effort involved. All three types—flaky pastry, rough puff pastry, and puff pastry—are characterized by fat and air trapped between thin layers of dough. During baking, the trapped air expands and lifts the pastry into several layers.

Certain procedures are common to all flaked pastries to ensure crisp flakes: **1** Handle the pastry lightly and as little as possible. **2** The fat and the dough should have the same consistency and temperature—the fat is therefore made pliable on a plate before use. **3** To prevent the fat from melting out during baking and thus spoiling the texture, the pastry must be chilled during and after making, and before baking. **4** Roll out the pastry evenly. Do not let the rolling pin go over the edges, as this will force out the air. Never stretch the pastry. **5** Before baking, brush the top of the shaped pastry with beaten egg glaze but do not let glaze drip down the sides.

For lining pie plates and flan rings, see instructions and drawings for Pie Pastry on pages 355 and 356.

FLAKY PASTRY

This pastry is used as crusts for savory pies, for Eccles cakes, sausage rolls, cream horns, and other small dessert pastries. It should be made in a cool atmosphere; it is not advisable to make flaky pastry in hot weather.

PREPARATION TIME: *30 minutes*
RESTING TIME: *about 1 hour 10 minutes*

INGREDIENTS (*for 1¼ pounds*):
2 cups all-purpose flour
½ teaspoon salt
6 tablespoons lard
6 tablespoons butter or margarine
7 tablespoons ice water, approximately
1 teaspoon lemon juice

Sift the flour and salt into a wide bowl. Work the lard and butter on a plate until evenly blended and divide it into 4 equal portions. Rub 1 portion of the fat into the flour with the fingertips until the mixture resembles bread crumbs. Add the water and lemon juice and mix the ingredients with a round-bladed knife to make a soft, manageable dough. Turn it out onto a lightly floured surface and knead until all cracks have disappeared. Cover the dough with plastic wrap and leave it to rest in a cool place for 20 minutes. Keep the fat cool as well.

On a lightly floured surface roll out the dough about 24 inches long, 8 inches wide, and ¼ inch thick. Brush off all surplus flour. Cut another quarter of the fat into small flakes and dot them evenly over two-thirds of the pastry and to within ½ inch of the edges. Fold the unbuttered third of the pastry over the fat and fold the buttered top third down. Turn the dough so that the folded edge points to the left and seal all the edges firmly with the side of the little finger.

Cover the pastry with plastic wrap and leave it to rest again in a cool place for about 20 minutes.

Turn the pastry so that the fold points to the right-hand side. Roll the pastry out as before, cover two-thirds with another quarter of fat, and repeat the folding, sealing, and resting as before. Continue with the remaining fat, giving the pastry a half-turn between each rolling. Finally, roll out the pastry to the original rectangle, brush off any surplus flour, fold it up, and wrap it loosely in plastic wrap. Leave it to rest in a cool place for at least 30 minutes before shaping. Bake in the center of a preheated oven at 425°F.

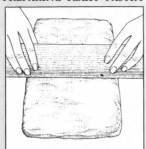

Roll out the cooled dough.

Dot fat over two-thirds of pastry.

Fold unbuttered dough up.

Fold buttered dough over.

Seal pastry edges.

PREPARING FLAKY PASTRY

Eccles Cakes

PREPARATION TIME: *30 minutes*
COOKING TIME: *15 minutes*

INGREDIENTS (*for 10–12 cakes*):
½ recipe flaky pastry
2 tablespoons unsalted butter
2 tablespoons light brown sugar
¼ cup chopped mixed peel
⅓ cup currants
1 egg white
Superfine sugar

Make the filling for these little cakes first: Beat the butter and brown sugar until it is pale and fluffy. Chop the mixed peel into smaller pieces and add to the creamed butter, together with the currants. Roll out the prepared flaky pastry ¼ inch thick. Cut it into rounds with a 3-inch plain cutter.

Put a teaspoon of the filling in the center of each pastry round and draw the edges together to cover the filling completely. Reshape each cake into a round. Turn the cakes over and roll them lightly into flat rounds until the currants just show through the pastry. With the tip of a knife, score the top of the cakes several times in a lattice pattern.

Leave the cakes to rest on buttered baking sheets for 10 minutes in the refrigerator, then brush them with lightly beaten egg white and sprinkle generously with superfine sugar. Bake the cakes near the top of a preheated oven at 425°F for about 15 minutes, or until cakes are golden and puffed.

Eccles cakes are shown in the photograph on page 367.

Cream Horns

PREPARATION TIME: *30 minutes*
COOKING TIME: *10 minutes*

INGREDIENTS (*for 8 horns*):
½ recipe flaky pastry
1 egg
Raspberry or black currant jam
10 tablespoons heavy cream
4 tablespoons light cream
Confectioners' sugar

Roll the prepared flaky pastry out to a strip about 24 inches long and 4 inches wide. Beat the egg and brush it over the pastry. Using a sharp knife, cut the pastry into 8 ribbons 24 inches long and ½ inch wide. Wind each pastry strip around a tin cornet mold, starting at the tip, with the glazed side of the pastry outside; overlap each turn by about ⅛ inch. As it rises during baking, the pastry will reach just short of the metal rim of the mold. Set the moist pastries on a baking sheet with the seam where the strip ends facing downward.

Bake near the top of a preheated oven at 425°F for 8–10 minutes until the horns are a pale golden color. Leave to cool for a few minutes, then with one hand grip the rim of each mold with a clean cloth and carefully twist the mold. Hold the pastry lightly in the other hand and ease it off the mold. Leave the horns to cool completely, then put a teaspoon of jam into the end of each. Just before serving, whip the light and heavy creams together and spoon them into the horns. Dust with confectioners' sugar.

MAKING CREAM HORNS

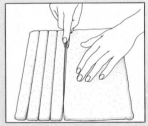

Cut pastry into ribbons.

Shape pastry around cornet molds.

ROUGH PUFF PASTRY

A cross between flaky and puff pastry, rough puff pastry is somewhat easier to make than puff pastry and is as light in texture as flaky pastry, although it becomes heavy when cold. It is ideal for savory pie crusts, sausage rolls, and fruit tarts.

PREPARATION TIME (*including resting*): *1 hour*

INGREDIENTS (*for 1¼ pounds*)
1½ sticks (6 ounces) butter
2 cups all-purpose flour
1 teaspoon salt
1 teaspoon lemon juice
½ cup ice water

Cut the firm but not hard butter into walnut-size pieces. Sift the flour and salt together into a wide bowl and add the butter, the lemon juice, and water. Mix lightly with a round-bladed knife into a soft dough.

Turn the dough onto a floured surface and knead it lightly—as the dough is soft, it needs careful handling. Shape it into a rectangle, then roll it into a strip about ¾ inch thick, 12 inches long, and 4 inches wide, keeping the edges straight. The butter will be seen clearly as yellow streaks in the pastry. Fold the bottom third of the pastry up and the upper third down. Turn the pastry so that the fold points toward the left-hand side; seal the edges lightly with the edge of the little finger. Roll out the pastry again, keeping it ½ inch thick and to a rectangle of 18 inches by 6 inches. Repeat the folding and rolling 4 times, giving the pastry a half-turn each time.

Cover the pastry with plastic wrap and leave in the refrigerator for 20 minutes before every 2 rollings. Rest the finished pastry for 10 minutes before shaping.

This pastry is generally baked in the center of a preheated oven at 425°F or at temperatures and lengths of time given in individual recipes.

ROUGH PUFF PASTRY

Add butter to sifted flour.

Mix in ice water.

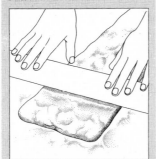
First rolling-out

Fold the dough in thirds.

Sausage Rolls

PREPARATION TIME: *20 minutes*
COOKING TIME: *30 minutes*

INGREDIENTS (*for 18 rolls*):
Rough puff pastry
1 pound sausage meat
Flour
1 egg, beaten

With a sharp knife, cut the prepared rough puff pastry, 18 inches by 6 inches, into 2 strips, each 3 inches wide. Divide the sausage meat in half, shape it into 2 long rolls to fit the pastry strips, and coat the meat lightly with flour. Arrange the sausage meat neatly in the center of the pastry strips. With a pastry brush, paint the edges with beaten egg, then fold over the pastry. Press to seal both of the long edges firmly.

Brush both pastry lengths with beaten egg and cut them into 2-inch-long pieces. Score the top of the pastry lightly, about 1/16 inch deep, with the point of a small knife. Set the sausage rolls on greased baking sheets and bake just above the center of a preheated oven at 425°F for 25–30 minutes, or until rolls are golden brown and puffed.

SAUSAGE ROLLS

Cover sausage meat with pastry.

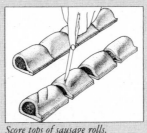
Score tops of sausage rolls.

PUFF PASTRY

This is regarded as the finest and most professional pastry. It is time-consuming but well worth making if a large quantity is required. Puff pastry can also be purchased frozen at some bakeries in large cities. It can be stored uncooked in the freezer for up to 3 or 4 months. Puff pastry, which is used for savory pie crusts, as wrappings for meat and poultry, for vol-au-vents, cream horns, and mille feuilles, must be rolled out six times.

Vol-au-vents, patties, and pastry crusts, which need the greatest rise and flakiness, should always be shaped from the first rolling of the finished dough. The second rolling, including trimmings from the first rolling, can be used for small pastries, such as palmiers.

Prepared uncooked puff pastry can be stored for 2 or 3 days in the refrigerator.

PREPARATION TIME: *30–45 minutes*
RESTING TIME: *2½ hours*

INGREDIENTS:
4 cups all-purpose flour
2 teaspoons salt
1 pound butter
1¼ cups ice water
1 teaspoon lemon juice

Sift the flour and salt into a large bowl. Cut ¼ pound of the butter into small pieces and rub it into the flour with the fingertips. Add the water and lemon juice and, using a round-bladed knife, mix the ingredients to make a firm but pliable dough. Turn the dough onto a lightly floured surface and lightly knead it until smooth. Shape the pastry into a thick round and make 2 cuts through half its depth in the form of a cross.

Open out the four flaps and roll them out until the center is four times as thick as the flaps. Shape the remaining firm butter to fit the center of the dough, leaving a clear ½

MAKING PUFF PASTRY

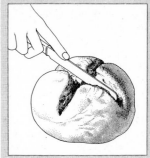
Cut a cross in rounded dough.

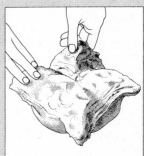
Fold out the four flaps.

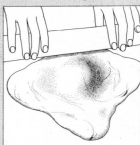
Roll out the flaps.

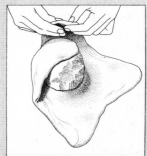
Place remaining butter in center.

363

inch all around. Fold the flaps over the butter, envelope style, and press the edges gently together with a rolling pin. Roll the dough into a rectangle 16 inches by 8 inches, using quick, short strokes. Roll lightly but firmly back and forth so as not to squeeze out the butter. Brush off any surplus flour between rollings. Fold the dough into thirds and press the edges with the edge of the little finger. Wrap the pastry in a cloth or waxed paper, cover with plastic wrap, and leave in the refrigerator for 20 minutes.

Roll out the pastry, seam pointed to the left, to a rectangle as before. Fold and leave to rest for 20 minutes. Repeat rolling, folding, and resting four times, giving the dough a half-turn every time. Leave the dough to rest for 30 minutes in the refrigerator before shaping it. Puff pastry, properly made, should rise about six times in height and should generally be baked in the center or just above the center of a preheated oven at 450°F or at the temperatures and lengths of time that are indicated in the individual recipes.

Steak and Kidney Pie

PREPARATION TIME: *45 minutes*
COOKING TIME: *3 hours*

INGREDIENTS (*for 6*):
½ recipe puff pastry (p.363)
2¼ pounds lean chuck steak
½ pound kidneys
1 large onion
2 cups button mushrooms
2 cloves garlic (optional)
¾ cup seasoned flour (p.412)
3 tablespoons corn oil
7 tablespoons butter
2½ cups beef stock
1 cup dry red wine
Salt and pepper
1 egg

Trim the meat and cut it into 1-inch pieces. Skin, core, and chop the kidneys.* Peel and thinly slice the onion and mushrooms, and peel and crush the garlic, if used. Toss the meat and

kidneys in seasoned flour. Heat the oil with 4 tablespoons of the butter in a skillet and sauté the meat over high heat until evenly browned. Blend in the remaining seasoned flour and spoon the contents of the pan into a large casserole. Melt the remaining butter in another pan and sauté the onion for about 5 minutes; add the mushrooms and garlic and sauté for 2–3 minutes. Pour in the beef stock and red wine, bring to a boil, and pour over the meat.

Cover the casserole with a lid and cook in the center of a preheated oven at 325°F for 1½–2 hours, or until the meat is tender. Lift the meat out with a slotted spoon and put it in a 2-quart pie dish or in a deep baking dish with a pie funnel in the center. Reduce* the casserole juices by fast boiling and pour them over the meat. Let the ingredients cool completely.

Roll out the pastry, ¼ inch thick, to fit the dish. Moisten the rim and lift the pastry over the meat. Seal the edges and brush the pastry with beaten egg. Bake in the center of a preheated oven at 450°F for 20 minutes until the pastry has cooked to a golden brown.

Vol-au-vent

The following quantity makes 1 large 7-inch-wide vol-au-vent shell, 8 3-inch shells for individual servings, or 12–14 small bouchée shells for cocktail snacks.

PREPARATION TIME: *20 minutes*
COOKING TIME: *40 minutes*

INGREDIENTS:
Puff pastry (p.363)
1 egg
1½–2 cups diced, cooked chicken,
*   flaked salmon, or 1 cup shrimp*
1 cup Béchamel sauce (p.301)

For a large crust, roll out the pastry to a 7½-inch square. Using a 7-inch plate or lid as a guide, cut around it with a sharp knife, held at a slightly oblique angle so as to give a bevelled

edge. Place the pastry upside down on a moist baking sheet.

Brush the top of the pastry with beaten egg and mark a 6-inch-wide circle on the pastry with a knife. Cut through half the depth of the pastry, following the mark of the inner circle. Draw a lattice pattern with the knife on the rim of the pastry and leave in a cool place for 15 minutes.

Bake the vol-au-vent shell in the center of a preheated oven at 450°F for about 20 minutes or until risen and brown, then reduce the heat to 350°F for about 20 minutes longer. Cover with aluminum foil if the crust browns too quickly.

Baked vol-au-vent shell. Scoop out the center of half-cooked pastry.

When cooked, carefully ease out the pastry crust and discard any soft pastry from the center. Fill the shell with chicken, salmon, or shrimp blended with the Béchamel sauce. Serve the vol-au-vent hot with hot filling, or cold with a cold filling.

Small vol-au-vent shells are made in a similar way. The pastry should be rolled out ½ inch thick and cut into 3-inch rounds for the shells and 1½-inch rounds for the tops. Bake in a preheated oven at 450°F for 20 minutes. For bouchée shells, roll the pastry out ¼ inch thick and use 2-inch and 1-inch cutters for shells and lids respectively. Bake the shells at 450°F for about 15 minutes.

Crescents Roll the trimmings out ¼ inch thick and cut them into narrow 4–6 inch lengths. Shape these into crescents, set them on a moist

baking sheet, and brush with milk. Bake for barely 10 minutes in a pre-heated oven at 450°F until they are puffed and golden brown. Serve the crescents as a hot garnish with fish dishes and casseroles.

Mille Feuilles

PREPARATION TIME: *40 minutes*
COOKING TIME: *20 minutes*

INGREDIENTS (*for 6 mille feuilles*):
½ recipe puff pastry (p.363)
½ cup raspberry jam
1 cup pastry cream (p.395)
1½ cups confectioners' sugar
Red food coloring

On a lightly floured surface, roll out the pastry approximately ⅛ inch thick into a rectangle 10 inches by 9 inches. Prick it all over at ⅛-inch intervals with a fork. Carefully lift the pastry onto a moist baking sheet that has been sprinkled with water, and bake just above the center of a pre-heated oven at 450°F for 20 minutes or until well risen and golden brown. Cool the pastry on a wire rack, then cut it in half lengthwise. Spread the top of one piece with two-thirds of the raspberry jam. Then cover the jam with pastry cream.

Blend the sifted confectioners' sugar in a bowl with just enough cold water so that the sugar sticks to the spoon. Mix 1 tablespoon of this icing in a cup with a few drops of red food coloring until it becomes pink; spoon into a pastry bag.

Spread the remaining raspberry jam over the second piece of pastry and turn it jam side down onto the pastry cream. Press the pastries together, then cover the top of the pastry with white icing. Pipe thin lines of pink icing at ½-inch intervals lengthwise over the white icing. Draw the tip of a knife quickly back and forth across the width of the pastry at ½-inch intervals to give the icing a feathered effect. Leave the mille feuilles to set, then cut them into 6 equal slices.

Palmiers

PREPARATION TIME: *15 minutes*
COOKING TIME: *14 minutes*

INGREDIENTS (*for 12 palmiers*):
½ recipe puff pastry (p.363)
2 tablespoons superfine sugar
10 tablespoons heavy cream
4 tablespoons light cream
Vanilla sugar

On a lightly floured surface, roll out the pastry to a rectangle 12 inches by 10 inches and approximately ¼ inch thick. Sprinkle the pastry with sugar. Fold the long sides so that they meet in the center. Sprinkle with the remaining sugar and fold the pastry in half lengthwise, hiding the first folds. Press lightly and evenly with the fingertips along the pastry. With a sharp knife, cut the pastry across into 12 slices.

Place the palmiers on a moist baking tray, cut side down and well apart to give them room to spread. Open out the top of each palmier slightly and flatten the whole slice lightly with a round-bladed metal spatula. Bake the palmiers toward the top of a preheated oven at 425°F for 10 minutes, then turn them over and bake for about 4 minutes longer.

Serve the palmiers plain. Alternatively, whip together the heavy and light creams with the vanilla sugar;* sandwich the palmiers in pairs with the cream as filling.

See illustration on page 367.

PALMIERS

Cut folded pastry into slices.

Open and flatten palmier slices.

PÂTE SUCRÉE

This pastry is the French equivalent of enriched pastry. It is crisp yet melting in texture, and neither shrinks nor spreads during baking. Pâte sucrée is usually baked blind.*

PREPARATION TIME: *15 minutes*
RESTING TIME: *1 hour*

INGREDIENTS:
1 cup all-purpose flour
Pinch salt
4 tablespoons sugar
4 tablespoons butter
2 egg yolks

Sift together the flour and salt onto a cool working surface or, preferably, a marble slab. Make a well in the center of the flour and put in the sugar, soft butter, and the egg yolks. Using the fingertips of one hand, pinch and work the sugar, butter, and egg yolks together until well blended. Gradually work in all the flour from the sides and knead the pastry lightly until smooth. Leave the pastry in a cool place or in the refrigerator for at least 1 hour to rest before rolling it out. Bake in the center of a preheated oven at 350°–400°F or at temperatures and lengths of time indicated in the individual recipes.

Bateaux de Miel

PREPARATION TIME: *15 minutes*
COOKING TIME: *7 minutes*
CHILLING TIME: *30 minutes*

INGREDIENTS (*for 6*):
⅓ recipe pâte sucrée
¼ pound unsalted butter
½ cup sugar
¾ cup ground almonds
3 teaspoons thick honey
2 teaspoons strong coffee
Coffee confectioners' frosting
  (p.394)

Roll out the prepared pastry on a lightly floured surface and use it to line 6 boat-shaped molds about 4½ inches long (see Lining Molds under Pie Pastry). Press the pastry lightly into shape. Set the molds on a baking sheet, prick the pastry with a fork, and bake blind* in the center of a preheated oven at 375°F for 5–7 minutes, or until pastry is tinged light brown. Remove from the oven, ease the pastries out of the molds, and cool on a wire rack.

Beat the butter until soft, then add the sugar and beat until light and fluffy. Beat in the almonds, honey, and coffee. Divide the mixture evenly between the cooled pastry boats, piling it up to a peak along the length. Smooth the surface. Chill in the refrigerator for 30 minutes.

When the filling has set, coat the pastries with confectioners' frosting based on 1 cup confectioners' sugar. Leave to set.

Bateaux Saint André

PREPARATION TIME: *20 minutes*
COOKING TIME: *20 minutes*

INGREDIENTS (*for 6 bateaux*):
⅓ recipe pâte sucrée
½ pound cooking apples
2 tablespoons sugar
½ egg white
1 cup confectioners' sugar

Peel, core, and dice the apples and cook them with the sugar and 1 tablespoon water until they have reduced to a thick purée. Cool.

Roll out the pâte sucrée thinly and use it to line 6 boat-shaped molds 4½ inches long. Proceed as described for Bateaux de Miel. Divide the purée equally between the molds.

Beat the egg white lightly in a small bowl, then gradually beat in the sifted confectioners' sugar, using a wooden spoon. Spread a thin layer of this meringue mixture over each boat. Roll out pastry trimmings thinly, cut them into short narrow strips; lay 2 strips across each boat.

Bake the pastry boats in the center of a preheated oven at 375°F for about 10 minutes, or until the pastry has set and the meringue is pale beige. Let the pastries cool slightly, then ease the mold away.

Bateaux aux Fruits

PREPARATION TIME: *20 minutes*
COOKING TIME: *5–7 minutes*

INGREDIENTS (*for 6 bateaux*):
⅓ recipe pâte sucrée
3 tablespoons apricot glaze (p.394)
1½ cups canned fruit (apricot
  halves, pineapple pieces, cherries)
2 tablespoons blanched pistachio
  nuts

Roll out the pastry and line 6 boat-shaped molds as for Bateaux de Miel. Set the lined molds on a baking sheet and bake them blind* in the center of a preheated oven at 375°F for 5–7 minutes, or until the pastry is tinged brown. Cool slightly, then ease out of the molds and cool on a rack.

Brush the inside of the pastry boats with hot apricot glaze. Drain the canned fruit thoroughly, cut the apricot halves in two, and remove the pits from apricots and cherries. Arrange the fruit in the pastry boats, brush fruit and edges of boats with more apricot glaze, and garnish with blanched pistachio nuts.

Bateaux aux Fruits are shown in the photograph on page 367.

Glazed Almond Tart

PREPARATION TIME: *30 minutes*
COOKING TIME: *45–50 minutes*

INGREDIENTS (*for 6–8*):
Pâte sucrée
3 tablespoons apricot or raspberry
  jam
6 tablespoons unsalted butter
6 tablespoons sugar
2 eggs
⅔ cup ground almonds
½ cup confectioners' sugar

Roll out the pâte sucrée thinly and line an 8-inch-diameter removable-bottom fluted flan pan with the pastry. Trim the edges and set the trimmings aside. Spread apricot or raspberry jam evenly over the pastry.

Beat the butter and sugar until fluffy. Beat in the eggs a little at a time, then stir in the almonds. Spoon this mixture over the jam.

Roll out the trimmings and cut them into ¼-inch-wide strips. Lay these in a lattice pattern on top of the filling. Set the pan on a baking sheet and bake above the center of a preheated oven at 350°F for 45–50 minutes or until golden brown.

Brush the baked tart, while still hot, with confectioners' frosting made from the sifted confectioners' sugar and enough water to give a coating consistency (p.393). Return tart to oven for 5 minutes. Cool.

Sugar Cookies

PREPARATION TIME: *about 10*
  minutes
COOKING TIME: *10–15 minutes*

INGREDIENTS:
Leftovers from pâte sucrée
Sugar
Cinnamon
1 egg
1 teaspoon water

Roll out the dough ¼ inch thick and cut into 1¼-inch rounds. Spread a ¼-inch layer of sugar on a pastry board and lay the rounds of dough over it. Pile sugar on top. Roll out rounds into ovals about 2½ inches long. Place on an ungreased cookie sheet. Sprinkle with cinnamon. Beat the egg with the water and brush tops with this mixture. Bake in a preheated 375°F oven for 10–15 minutes until lightly browned.

COMMON FAULTS IN PASTRY MAKING

Pie Pastry
Hard or tough pastry: due to too much liquid, too little fat, overhandling, or too little rubbing in.
Shrunken pastry: excess stretching during rolling out.
Soft and crumbly pastry: too little water or too much fat.
Soggy pastry: filling too moist, or sugar in a sweet pie in contact with pastry. For a double-crust pie, use a metal pie plate and brush bottom crust with egg white, or butter the pie plate before lining.

Toss prepared fruit filling with a mixture of 1 tablespoon flour and ½ cup sugar before covering with crust.
Speckled pastry: undissolved sugar grains in enriched pastry crust.
Sunken pie: oven temperature too low; cold pastry put over hot filling; too much liquid in filling, or too little filling.

Suet Crust Pastry
Heavy pastry: insufficient baking powder; water not kept on the boil during cooking.
Soggy pastry: paper and cloth covering over filled pie too loose; water not kept boiling during cooking.
Tough pastry: dough handled too much and rolled out excessively.

Hot-Water Crust
Cracked pastry: insufficient liquid; too little kneading; liquid not boiling when added to flour.
Dry, difficult-to-mold pastry: liquid not boiling when added to flour; dough not cool enough to shape.
Hard pastry: insufficient amount of fat or liquid.

Choux Pastry
Mixture too soft: insufficient cooling of the flour before adding eggs; eggs added too quickly.
Pastry did not rise: oven too cold; too short baking time.
Sinking after removal from oven: insufficient baking. Further baking sometimes remedies this defect.

Flaky, Rough Puff, and Puff Pastries
Fat running out during baking: oven too cold.
Hard and tough pastry: too much water; overkneading.
Shrinking pastry: insufficient resting; overstretching during rolling.
Too few layers: insufficient resting and chilling; heavy rolling causing fat to break through and intermingle with the pastry; fat too soft.

Baking with Yeast

Home-baked bread has a taste and texture strikingly different from that of commercially baked loaves. Our daily bread is composed of such basic ingredients as flour, yeast, salt, and liquid. Enriched dough mixtures for buns and sweet breads—such as coffee cakes and Sally Lunns—also include butter, spices, dried fruits, and nuts.

Flour

Flour is the most important factor in bread making, and the best loaves are made with hard-wheat flour or bread flour, available in some health food stores. Hard-wheat flour has a high gluten content (from which protein is formed) and aids rising, in combination with yeast; it absorbs liquids easily and produces bread with a light and open texture. All-purpose flour, the most generally available, is a mixture of hard-wheat and soft-wheat flours. For bread making, unbleached all-purpose flour is preferable.

Whole-wheat, or graham, and the coarser stone-ground whole-wheat flour produce yeast doughs of closer texture and with less rise than a white dough. As these flours contain the bran and germ of the wheat, they do not keep well and should be bought as needed. These flours give bread its mealy taste.

Yeast

Fresh or compressed yeast and active dry yeast can be used in bread making. Many small private bakeries will supply fresh yeast, and some supermarkets and health food stores also stock it. Active dry yeast is more concentrated than fresh yeast: $\frac{1}{4}$ ounce (1 package) of active dry yeast is the equivalent of a $\frac{2}{3}$-ounce cake of fresh or compressed yeast.

Fresh yeast should be a creamy beige and have a firm consistency that crumbles easily when broken up. It can be stored in a loosely tied plastic bag in a refrigerator for up to 2 weeks or in the freezer for 6 months.

Fresh yeast is added to flour in three different ways: It is rubbed in, blended with liquid, or added as a batter. Rubbing in is suitable for soft doughs, quick breads, and sweet doughs. Blending with liquid is the basic method and is suitable for all bread recipes. The batter method is best suited for rich yeast doughs and works well with fresh or dry yeast. Do not cream fresh yeast with sugar—this may break down the yeast cells.

Rubbing-in method Crumble the yeast evenly onto the surface of the sifted flour and salt with the tips of the fingers. Add the specified amount of liquid to the flour and yeast mixture to make a soft dough. Work the dough with the fingertips to distribute the yeast evenly.

Blending with liquid Blend the yeast with part of the measured liquid; add this mixture to the flour and salt, together with the remaining liquid.

Batter method Mix one-third of the measured flour with the yeast, blended with all the liquid and 1 teaspoon of sugar. Leave in a warm place until frothy, about 20 minutes, then add the remainder of the flour, the salt, and any other ingredients specified in the recipe.

Active dry yeast This can be stored in a tightly covered container for up to 6 months or until the expiration date marked on the package. Dry yeast is reconstituted in warm water (110°F). (This water should be taken from the amount to be used in the recipe, first dissolved in the proportion of 1 teaspoon sugar to $\frac{1}{2}$ cup water.) Sprinkle the yeast over the water and leave in a warm place until it proofs, or becomes frothy.

Salt

Apart from improving the flavor of bread, salt also affects the gluten in the flour. If salt is omitted, the dough rises too quickly. If there is too much salt, it kills the yeast and gives the bread a heavy or uneven texture. Use only the amount of salt called for in the recipe, and measure it out carefully.

Liquid

This may be milk, water, or a mixture of both. The amount of liquid varies from recipe to recipe, depending on the absorbency of the flour. Milk adds food value and strengthens doughs; it also improves the keeping quality and the color of the crust. For plain bread, however, water alone gives a better texture.

Fat

This is used in enriched yeast doughs for buns, brioches, rolls, croissants, and sweet breads that have a soft outer crust. Fat makes a dough soft and also slows down yeast action, so that the dough rises less than plain bread dough does.

Sugar

Too much sugar added to a dough mixture delays fermentation of the yeast cells; always follow the quantities specified in the recipe and measure the sugar carefully.

Making the dough

Sift the flour and the salt into a mixing bowl, make a well in the center, and add all the liquid at once. Mix it in with one hand, using a wooden spoon, if desired, until the liquid is thoroughly incorporated. Add a little more flour if necessary, and beat the dough against the sides of the bowl until it comes away cleanly. Put the dough on a lightly floured surface. Lightly flour the palms of the hands and knead the dough with the heels of the palms.

Kneading is most important, as it strengthens and develops the dough and enables it to rise. Gather the dough into a ball with the tips of the fingers, then fold the dough toward the body. Press down on the dough and work it away from the body with the palm of the hand. Give the dough a quarter-turn and repeat the kneading.

Knead the dough for about 10 minutes until it feels firm and elastic and no longer sticks to the fingers—it is better to knead the dough too much rather than too little. Bread dough can be kneaded in an electric mixer equipped with a dough hook.

MAKING BREAD DOUGH

Pour the liquid into the flour.

Knead until the dough is elastic.

Let the dough rise in plastic bag.

Rising

After kneading, the dough must be set aside for rising until it has doubled in bulk. A large plastic bag is useful for the rising process. Pour a few drops of corn oil into the bag and swirl it around to distribute it evenly in a thin film. Put the dough in the bag, tie it loosely, and leave the dough until it has doubled in size and springs back when lightly pressed with a finger. The time the dough takes to rise depends on the temperature and the surroundings—it will take about 2 hours at normal room temperature, away from drafts. Dough left to rise in a refrigerator will need 24 hours.

If time is short, the dough can be made to rise in 45–60 minutes in a warm place—over a pan of warm water, for example. However, too much heat may kill the yeast.

After the initial rising, the dough has to be punched down with your fist and then kneaded again to deflate the air bubbles and to ensure a good rise and even texture. Shape the kneaded dough as required and put it into loaf pans or on baking sheets. Cover with plastic wrap or a towel and leave the loaves to rise at room temperature until they have doubled in size.

Baking

Bake the loaves at 400°–450°F, according to the individual recipes. A bowl of hot water placed in the bottom of the oven creates steam, which improves the bread texture.

Storing

Place the baked and cooled loaves in clean plastic bags, leaving the end open. To refresh a crusty loaf, wrap it in aluminum foil and put in the oven at 450°F for about 10 minutes. Let it cool in the foil. If bread is not to be eaten within a day or two, it can be frozen. Seal cooled loaves separately in aluminum foil and store in freezer. To serve, remove foil and heat in a 300°F oven for 30 minutes.

Pastries

ECCLES CAKES
(page 362)

VEAL AND
BACON PIE
(page 360)

PROFITEROLES
(page 361)

CHEESE AND ONION PIE
(page 357)

PLUM AND
CINNAMON PIE
(page 358)

LEMON MERINGUE PIE
(page 357)

BATEAUX AUX FRUITS
(page 365)

PALMIERS
(page 364)

CHOCOLATE CREAM PIE
(page 358)

367

Breads

BACON CORN STICKS
(page 381)

BLUEBERRY MUFFINS
(page 382)

SALLY LUNN
(page 379)

DANISH PASTRIES
(page 378)

WHITE BREAD
(page 375)

BRIOCHES
(page 378)

SODA BREAD
(page 382)

POPPY SEED BRAID
(page 376)

368

CRANBERRY BREAD
(page 382)

BAKING POWDER BISCUITS
(page 381)

FLOWERPOT LOAF
(page 377)

REFRIGERATOR ROLLS
(page 376)

DARK RYE BREAD
(page 377)

SPICY COFFEE CAKE
(page 382)

KUGELHOPF
(page 378)

369

Cakes

RASPBERRY BUNS
(page 385)

LAYER CAKE
(page 385)

JELLY ROLL
(page 388)

ROCK BUNS
(page 385)

COCOA LAYER CAKE
(page 386)

SWISS TARTS
(page 387)

PINEAPPLE AND CHERRY LOAF
(page 386)

GENOISE
(page 388)

GINGERBREAD
(page 389)

DUNDEE CAKE
(page 387)

POUND CAKE
(page 386)

COCONUT CASTLES
(page 387)

371

Cookies

Confectionery

Piccalilli

Tomato Chutney

Pickled Cucumber

Pickled Red Cabbage

Pickled Onions

Apple Mint Chutney

Pickled Beet

PREPARING LOAVES FOR BAKING

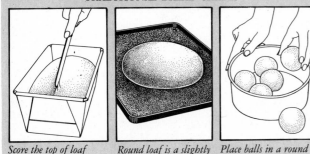

Shape or roll up risen dough to fit buttered loaf pans.

TRADITIONAL BREAD SHAPES

Score the top of loaf with a knife.

Round loaf is a slightly flattened ball of dough.

Place balls in a round pan for a crown loaf.

White Bread

PREPARATION TIME: *25 minutes (plus rising)*
COOKING TIME: *30–40 minutes*

INGREDIENTS (*for 4 loaves*):
12 cups hard-wheat or unbleached all-purpose flour
2 tablespoons salt
2 tablespoons lard
2 packages active dry yeast
3¾ cups warm (110°–115°) water less 3 tablespoons

Sift the flour and salt together into a large bowl and rub in the lard with the fingertips. In a small bowl, blend the yeast with 1 cup of the measured warm water. When the yeast froths and small bubbles appear on the surface, make a well in the center of the flour and pour in the yeast liquid and the remaining water all at once. Work dough with one hand until it leaves the sides of the bowl clean. If necessary, add a little extra flour.

Turn the dough onto a lightly floured surface and knead it with the heels of the palms for about 10 minutes until smooth and elastic. Shape it into a round, then set it aside to rise until it has doubled its size.

Divide the risen dough into 4 equal portions on a lightly floured board. Flatten each piece firmly with the knuckles to knock out any air bubbles, then knead for 2–3 minutes. Stretch each piece of dough into an oblong the same length as the loaf pan, ease it into the greased pan, and score the dough lightly along the top. Alternatively, fold the dough into thirds along the long edges or roll it up like a jelly roll. Tuck the ends under so that the dough, seam downward, fits a 1-pound loaf pan.

Brush the top of the dough with lightly salted water. Cover the pans and leave in a warm place to rise until the dough reaches the top of the pans. Brush the top of the dough

with salted water again and set the pans on baking sheets.

Bake the loaves in the center of a preheated oven at 375°F for about 30 minutes, or until the loaves shrink slightly from the sides of the pans and the upper crust is a deep golden brown. For really crusty bread, turn the loaves out of the pans onto a baking sheet and return them to the oven for a further 5–10 minutes. When done, baked loaves sound hollow when tapped on the bottom with the knuckles. Leave the bread to cool on a wire rack.

See illustration on page 368.

Round Loaf Roll each piece of dough into a ball, flatten it, and place on a floured baking sheet.

Crown Loaf Divide a quarter of the risen dough into 5 or 6 balls. Set these, sides touching, in a buttered, 5-inch-wide cake pan.

Raisin Bread

PREPARATION TIME: *30 minutes (plus rising)*
COOKING TIME: *30 minutes*

INGREDIENTS:
½ cup raisins
⅓ recipe white bread
¼ pound lard or margarine
½ cup sugar
1 teaspoon ground allspice
Cooking oil

Soften the raisins by soaking 10–15 minutes in hot water. Press out excess water with a towel and let raisins dry thoroughly. On a lightly floured surface, roll out the risen dough with a rolling pin to a strip ¼ inch thick. Cut the lard into flakes and put one-third of these over the dough to within ½ inch of the edges. Mix the sugar with the allspice and raisins and sprinkle one-third of the mixture over the fat. Fold the dough up loosely from one of the short sides.

Roll the dough out again into a strip and cover with another third of lard and sugar, together with half the raisins. Roll up again, then roll out into a strip for the third time. Cover

PREPARING RAISIN BREAD

1 *Sprinkle spiced raisins over dough.*

3 *Press dough into corners of pan.*

2 *Fold the dough loosely.*

4 *Score the surface with a knife.*

the dough with the remaining lard, sugar, and raisins.

Roll up the dough, then roll out and shape it to fit a buttered roasting pan 10 inches long by 8 inches wide. Lift the dough into the pan and press it down well, particularly in the corners. Cover the pan with plastic wrap or a towel and leave to rise until the dough has doubled in size. Remove the covering, brush the top of the dough lightly with oil, and sprinkle with a little extra sugar. Score a crisscross pattern across the surface of the dough with the point of a knife.

Bake the raisin bread in the center, or just above, of a preheated oven at 425°F for about 30 minutes. Turn out of the pan and leave to cool on a wire rack. Serve the bread sliced, plain or buttered.

Enriched White Bread

PREPARATION TIME: *35 minutes (plus rising)*
COOKING TIME: *35–45 minutes*

INGREDIENTS:
4 cups hard-wheat or unbleached all-purpose flour
1 teaspoon sugar
1 package active dry yeast
1 cup warm milk
1 teaspoon salt
4 tablespoons margarine
1 egg
GLAZE:
1 egg
1 teaspoon sugar
1 tablespoon water
Poppy seeds (optional)

Mix 1¼ cups flour, the sugar, yeast, and all the milk in a large bowl. Set mixture aside in a warm place for about 20 minutes or until frothy. Sift the remaining flour and the salt into another bowl and rub in the margarine. Make a well in the center of this

375

mixture and add the beaten egg and the frothy yeast mixture all at once. Mix with one hand to make a fairly soft dough that leaves the sides of the bowl clean.

Turn the dough out onto a lightly floured surface, knead it for about 10 minutes until smooth, then place it in an oiled plastic bag and leave to rise and double in size. Knead the risen dough lightly on a floured surface before shaping it.

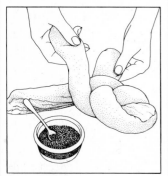

Braided loaf: For a three-strand braid, begin crossing the dough near the top.

Poppy Seed Braid Divide the dough into 3 equal parts and roll each into a 12-inch-long strand. Set the strands side by side on a flat surface and pass the left strand over the center strand, then the right strand over the center strand. Continue until the whole length is braided. Finally, join the short ends of the dough neatly together and tuck them under.

Place the braid on a lightly buttered baking sheet. Beat the egg with the sugar and water to make the glaze. Brush the braid evenly and sprinkle with poppy seeds. Put the braid on the baking sheet, cover, and set aside to rise again until the dough has doubled in size. Bake the loaf in the center of a preheated oven at 375°F for 35–40 minutes. Tap the bottom of the loaf with the knuckles—if it sounds hollow, it is done. Cool on a wire rack.

See illustration on pages 368–369.

Crown Loaf Divide all the risen dough into 12 equal pieces about 2 ounces each. Shape these into balls with the palm of the hand and put them in a buttered 9-inch-diameter cake pan, placing the balls in a circle around the inner edge of the pan, with 3 or 4 balls in the center. Brush with glaze, allow the dough to rise, and bake as already described for 45–60 minutes.

Fancy Rolls Enriched white dough is ideal for light, dinner-type rolls, which can be shaped in a variety of ways. Use about 2 ounces of risen dough for each roll. Roll a piece of dough out about 4 inches long, cut it in half lengthwise, and, holding each strip at both ends, twist it three times. Alternatively, roll each strip into a strand and tie it into a knot in the center.

Another method is to shape 2-ounce pieces of dough into oblong miniature loaves and score the surface with five or six marks, at even intervals. With a scissor point, make triangular cuts between the score

FANCY ROLLS

Twisting strips of dough.

Snipping small cuts in rolls.

Shaping triangular rolls.

marks, through the dough, so that the points are slightly raised.

For triangular rolls, divide a 2-ounce piece of dough into three, shape into balls, and set them on a baking sheet in such a way that all three balls touch each other.

Alternatively, roll a 2-inch piece of dough into a thick strand and shape into a snail or S form.

Brush the rolls with egg glaze and set them aside to rise until doubled in size. Bake the rolls just above the center of a preheated oven at 375°F for 10–15 minutes or until they are golden brown.

Refrigerator Rolls

PREPARATION TIME: *30 minutes (plus rising)*
COOKING TIME: *15 minutes*

INGREDIENTS (*for 36 rolls*):
1½ *cups milk or water*
½ *cup butter*
⅓ *cup sugar*
2 *teaspoons salt*
2 *packages active dry yeast*
½ *cup warm water (105°–115°F)*
2 *eggs, beaten*
5–6 *cups all-purpose flour*

Scald the milk and add the butter, cut into small pieces, the sugar, and salt. Stir until the butter has melted. Cool the mixture until it is lukewarm. Sprinkle the yeast over the warm water. Let stand for 5 minutes, then stir until the yeast is dissolved. Add the eggs and dissolved yeast to the milk mixture. Add 2 cups of the flour and beat well. Add 2 more cups of flour and beat well. Add enough additional flour to make a soft dough just firm enough to handle. Turn the dough out on a floured board and knead until smooth, about 10 minutes.

Place the dough in a buttered bowl, turning the dough over so that its surface is covered with butter. Cover with a clean towel and refrigerate. Remove as much dough as needed at a time.

Turn the dough out on a floured

board and roll it out ¼–½ inch thick. Cut into 2-inch rounds.

Make a crease slightly off center of each round with the back of a knife or a pencil. Invert the rolls and brush with melted butter. Fold the larger half over the smaller half. Press edges down to seal.

Place rolls about ½ inch apart on a lightly buttered baking sheet. Brush with melted butter. Cover with a towel; let rise until double in size.

About 10 minutes before rolls have risen, preheat oven to 425°F. Brush rolls with more melted butter and bake 12–15 minutes until lightly browned.

See illustration on page 369.

Whole Wheat Bread

PREPARATION TIME: *20 minutes (plus rising)*
COOKING TIME: *30–40 minutes*

INGREDIENTS (*for 2 2-pound or 4 1-pound loaves*):
12 *cups whole wheat flour*
2 *tablespoons sugar*
2 *tablespoons salt*
2 *tablespoons lard*
4 *packages active dry yeast*
3¾ *cups warm water*

Sift the flour, sugar, and salt into a large bowl. Cut up the lard and rub it into the flour with the fingertips until the mixture resembles fine bread crumbs. In a small bowl, blend the yeast with 1 cup of the measured warm water and, when frothy, pour it into a well in the center of the flour; add the remaining water. Using one hand, work the mixture together and beat it until the dough leaves the bowl clean. Knead the dough on a lightly floured surface for 10 minutes.

Shape the dough into a large ball and leave it to rise in a lightly oiled plastic bag until it has doubled in size. Turn the dough out on a lightly floured surface and knead again until firm. Divide the dough into 2 or 4 equal pieces and flatten each piece firmly with the knuckles to knock

out any air bubbles. Stretch and roll each piece of dough into an oblong the same length as the pan. Fold it into thirds or roll it up like a jelly roll. Lift the dough into buttered pans, brush with lightly salted water, cover pans, and leave to rise until dough reaches the top of the pans.

Set the pans on baking sheets and bake in the center of a preheated oven at 450°F for about 30 minutes, or until the loaves shrink from the sides of the pans. Cool the loaves on a wire rack and test by tapping them.

For a fancy loaf, divide a quarter of the dough into 4 equal pieces; shape them into rolls the width of a buttered 1-pound loaf pan and fit them, side by side, into the buttered pan. Finish as before. For a round loaf, shape each quarter portion of dough into a round, flatten rounds slightly, then dust with flour and place on a floured baking sheet.

Quick Whole Wheat Loaves

PREPARATION TIME: *20 minutes (plus rising)*
COOKING TIME: *30–40 minutes*

INGREDIENTS (*for 1 1-pound loaf and 8 rolls, or 2 1-pound loaves*):
2 *cups whole wheat flour*
2 *cups all-purpose flour*
2 *teaspoons salt*
2 *teaspoons sugar*
1 *tablespoon lard*
1 *package active dry yeast*
1¼ *cups warm water (110°)*
2–3 *tablespoons cracked wheat or crushed cornflakes*

Sift the two flours, the salt, and sugar into a bowl. Cut up the lard and rub it into the flour with the fingertips. Blend the yeast with all the warm water until the yeast has dissolved and is frothy. Make a well in the center of the flour and pour in the yeast liquid. Mix to a soft, biscuitlike dough, beating until it leaves the sides of the bowl clean (if necessary, add a little more flour).

Divide the dough into 2 equal portions. Shape each piece to half fill a greased 1-pound loaf pan and brush the top of the dough with lightly salted water. Sprinkle with cracked wheat or crushed cornflakes. Place the pans on a baking sheet, cover with plastic wrap or a towel, and leave in a warm place until the dough has doubled in size. Bake the loaves in the center of a preheated oven at 450°F for about 40 minutes. Test for doneness by tapping the bottom of the loaves. If they sound hollow, they are baked. Cool the loaves on a wire rack.

Rolls Divide the whole, risen dough, after rekneading, into 8 equal pieces. Roll each into a round on an unfloured surface, using the palm of one hand. Shake a little flour onto the palm of the hand and press the dough down, hard at first, easing up until the rounds have the shape of a roll. Set the rolls well apart on floured baking sheets, cover them with plastic wrap, and leave them to rise in a warm place until they have doubled in size.

Bake rolls just above the center of a preheated oven at 450°F for about 40 minutes. Cool on a wire rack.

For soft rolls, set the shaped rolls ¾ inch apart on the baking sheets and sprinkle generously with flour. The rolls will spread and bake into contact with each other along the sides, and the flour on top will give them a soft surface.

Flowerpot Loaves Whole wheat bread may also be baked in flowerpots. Use clean clay pots—never plastic. Butter them thoroughly inside and bake them empty in a hot oven several times, allowing a day or two between each baking. This will seal the inner surface and prevent the dough from sticking. A clay flowerpot 4–5 inches wide will hold half a recipe of whole wheat dough. Finish and bake the loaf as already described in the quick whole wheat recipe.

A flowerpot loaf is shown in the photograph on page 369.

Apricot and Walnut Loaf

PREPARATION TIME: *30 minutes (plus rising)*
COOKING TIME: *40–45 minutes*

INGREDIENTS (*for 1 1-pound loaf*):
½ recipe quick whole wheat dough
1 cup dried apricots
2 tablespoons sugar
½ cup chopped walnuts
TOPPING:
2 tablespoons butter or firm margarine
2 tablespoons sugar
⅓ cup flour

Cut up the dried apricots coarsely with scissors and put them in a bowl or on a floured board, with the risen dough, the sugar, and walnuts. Work the mixture together until no streaks can be seen. Line the bottom of a 1-pound loaf pan with buttered waxed paper and butter the sides of the pan. Put the dough in the pan and set in a lightly oiled plastic bag; leave in a warm place for about 1 hour or until the dough has risen to within ½ inch of the rim of the pan.

Meanwhile, make the topping. Rub together the butter, sugar, and flour in a small bowl until the mixture resembles coarse bread crumbs. Cover the risen dough evenly with the crumb mixture and set the pan on a baking sheet. Bake in the center of a preheated oven at 400°F for 40–45 minutes. Leave the baked loaf in the pan for 10 minutes, then turn it out to cool on a wire rack.

Dark Rye Bread

PREPARATION TIME: *1 hour (plus rising)*
COOKING TIME: *35 minutes*

INGREDIENTS (*for 2 loaves*):
½ cup sugar
¾ cup boiling water
3 packages active dry yeast
2 cups warm water (about 110°F)
¼ cup cocoa
2 teaspoons salt
2 tablespoons caraway seeds
2 tablespoons solid shortening or butter, melted
3½ cups all-purpose flour, unsifted
2 cups dark rye flour, unsifted
2 tablespoons cornmeal

Pour the sugar into a heavy 10-inch skillet. Place over medium-high heat until sugar is melted, stirring constantly with a fork. Continue to cook until the sugar is very dark, about 2–3 minutes. Add the boiling water and continue to cook, stirring constantly, until the sugar is dissolved and the liquid is reduced to ½ cup. Remove from the heat; let cool.

In a large bowl of an electric mixer, soften yeast in warm water for 5 minutes; add the cooled caramel liquid, cocoa, salt, caraway seeds, melted shortening, and 2 cups of the all-purpose flour. Beat until smooth. Add the rye flour and beat at medium speed for 4 minutes. With a heavy-duty mixer or by hand, work in 1 more cup all-purpose flour.

Sprinkle ¼ cup of the remaining flour on a board; turn out the dough, cover, and let rest 10 minutes. Then knead until dough is elastic, about 10 minutes, adding only enough flour to prevent sticking. Place dough in a greased bowl; turn over to grease top. Cover and let rise in a warm place until doubled in bulk, about 1 hour. Punch down, turn the dough over in the bowl, cover, and let rise again until doubled, about 1 hour more.

Sprinkle a large baking sheet evenly with the cornmeal. Punch dough down; divide in half. Shape each half into a round ball, flatten slightly, and place on the baking sheet 3–4 inches apart. Cover and let rise until doubled, about 1 hour and 15 minutes.

Bake in a 375°F oven for 35 minutes, or until bread sounds hollow when tapped.

See illustration on page 369.

Babas

PREPARATION TIME: *40 minutes (plus rising)*
COOKING TIME: *15–20 minutes*

INGREDIENTS (*for 16 babas*):
2 cups all-purpose flour
2 packages active dry yeast
6 tablespoons warm (110°F) milk
½ teaspoon salt
2 tablespoons sugar
4 eggs
¼ pound butter
⅔ cup currants
Lard
SYRUP:
4 tablespoons clear honey
4 tablespoons water
3 tablespoons rum, approximately
GARNISH:
1 cup whipped cream

Blend the yeast, milk, and ½ cup of the measured flour together in a large bowl and beat with a wooden spoon until smooth. Leave the yeast in a warm place for about 20 minutes or until frothy. Sift the remaining flour and the salt into the yeast and blend in the sugar, the lightly beaten eggs, softened butter, and the currants. Beat the mixture, which should be fairly soft, with a wooden spoon for 4 minutes.

Grease 16 small ring molds with lard and, using a teaspoon, spoon in the dough until the molds are half-full. Set the ring molds on baking sheets and cover them with sheets of lightly oiled plastic wrap.

Let the babas rise in a warm place until the dough has risen about two-thirds up the sides of the molds.

Bake the babas just above the center of a preheated oven at 400°F

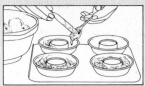

Spoon dough into ring molds.

Pour warm syrup over babas.

Decorate with piped cream.

for 15–20 minutes, or until they have turned golden brown.

Meanwhile, prepare the syrup: Heat the honey and water in a small pan over low heat, then stir in rum to taste. Leave the baked babas to cool for a few minutes in the molds before turning them out onto a plate. While the babas are still hot, spoon the warm syrup over them until it has soaked in. Leave to cool, then transfer the rum-soaked babas to a serving dish and fill the centers with whipped cream.

Serve at once.

377

Kugelhopf

PREPARATION TIME: *25 minutes*
(*plus rising*)
COOKING TIME: *45 minutes*

INGREDIENTS:
3–4 cups all-purpose flour
2 packages active dry yeast
1 cup milk
1 cup raisins
½ cup water
½ cup sugar
½ cup butter
1 teaspoon salt
3 eggs
2 teaspoons rum extract
Butter, softened
⅓ cup ground almonds
GARNISH:
Sifted confectioners' sugar
Candied fruit
Nuts dipped in corn syrup

Stir together 2 cups of the flour and the yeast. Heat the milk, raisins, water, sugar, butter, and salt over low heat until very warm (120°–130°F), stirring to blend. Add to flour-yeast mixture and beat until smooth, about 3 minutes on medium speed of an electric mixer. Blend in the eggs and rum extract; add ½ cup of flour and continue to beat for 2 minutes. Add enough flour to make a thick batter.

Cover and let batter rise in a warm place (80°–85°F) until it is bubbly and has doubled in bulk, after about 1 hour. Stir down.

Spoon into 2 1½-quart or 3 1-quart ram's head or other fancy molds that have been buttered and dusted with ground almonds. Cover. Let batter rise until it has doubled in bulk, about 30 minutes.

Bake in a preheated 325°F oven for 1 hour for 1½-quart loaves or 45 minutes for 1-quart loaves. If necessary to prevent excessive browning, cover during the last 10 minutes of baking. Unmold on wire racks. Dust with confectioners' sugar. Decorate the kugelhopf with candied fruit, and nuts dipped in corn syrup. See illustration on page 369.

Danish Pastries

PREPARATION TIME: *45 minutes*
(*plus rising*)
RESTING TIME: *50 minutes*
COOKING TIME: *10 minutes*

INGREDIENTS:
2 cups all-purpose flour
Pinch salt
2 tablespoons lard
1 tablespoon sugar
1 package active dry yeast
5 tablespoons lukewarm water
2 eggs
¼ pound plus 2 tablespoons unsalted butter
Almond paste
PINWHEEL FILLING:
2 tablespoons butter
2 tablespoons sugar
1 teaspoon ground cinnamon
Currants and chopped mixed peel
GARNISH:
Confectioners' frosting (p.394)
Crushed sugar cube

Sift the flour and salt into a large bowl. Cut up the lard and rub it into the flour with the fingertips; add the sugar and make a well in the center of the flour. Mix the yeast with the water and let stand 5 minutes, then add it to the flour, together with 1 lightly beaten egg. Gradually work in the flour, then beat the soft dough until it leaves the sides of the bowl clean.

Turn the dough out onto a lightly floured surface and knead it until smooth. Put it inside a lightly oiled plastic bag and leave it in the refrigerator for 10 minutes.

Beat the butter with a wooden spoon until soft but not oily, then shape it into a rectangle about 5 inches by 9½ inches. On a floured board, roll out the dough to a 10–11 inch square and place the butter in the center. Fold the two unbuttered sides over so that they just overlap the butter. Seal the open sides with a rolling pin, then roll the dough into an oblong strip, about three times as long as it is wide, and fold the dough in thirds.

DANISH PASTRIES

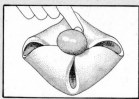
Almond square

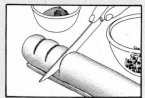
Cutting pinwheels nearly through

Overlapping pinwheels

Place the dough in a lightly oiled plastic bag and leave in the refrigerator for 10 minutes. Remove the bag. Roll out dough, raw edge pointed to the left, to an oblong strip. Fold in thirds. Repeat the resting, rolling, and folding twice more. Finally, rest the dough for 10 minutes in the refrigerator before rolling it out to any of the following shapes:

Almond squares Roll out half the dough to a 10-inch square, then cut it into 4 equal pieces. Fold two corners of each square to meet in the center, envelope style, and repeat with the other two corners. Press down firmly to seal. Place a small round of almond paste in the center of the square.

Crescents Roll out the dough as for almond squares and cut each square diagonally in half. Place a small piece of almond paste at the base of each triangle, then roll it up from the base and curve the dough into a crescent shape.

Cockscombs Roll out half the dough and cut it into 2-inch-wide strips. Cut the strips into 4-inch pieces and make a series of V-shaped indentations through two-thirds of the width.

Open out the pastry piece along the cuts and shape the uncut edge into a slight arch. Brush the pastries with beaten egg and sprinkle with crushed cube sugar.

Pinwheels Roll out half a portion of pastry dough to a rectangle 12 inches by 8 inches. Cream the butter with the sugar and cinnamon and spread over the dough to within ¼ inch of the edges. Scatter a few currants and a little mixed peel over the butter. Cut the dough in half lengthwise and roll each piece from the shorter end into a thick roll. Cut this into 1-inch-thick slices.

Alternatively, make cuts 1 inch apart through three-quarters of the depth of the rolls. Carefully ease the near-cut pinwheels apart so that they overlap slightly. Bake for about 30 minutes or until golden.

Set the pastry shapes well apart on greased baking sheets and cover with sheets of oiled plastic wrap. Leave the pastries to rise in a warm place for 20 minutes. Remove the plastic wrap and brush the pastries with lightly beaten egg. Bake near the top of a preheated oven at 425°F for about 10 minutes or until golden. Place the pastries on a wire rack and, while still warm, brush the almond squares, crescents, and pinwheels with the confectioners' frosting.

Brioches

PREPARATION TIME: *25 minutes*
(*plus rising*)
COOKING TIME: *10 minutes*

INGREDIENTS (*for 12 brioches*):
2 cups all-purpose flour
½ teaspoon salt
1 tablespoon sugar
1 package active dry yeast
¼ cup lukewarm water
2 eggs
¼ cup melted butter

Sift the flour and salt into a bowl and add the sugar. Mix the yeast with the water; let stand 5 minutes. Stir it, with the beaten eggs and the melted butter, into the flour with a wooden spoon. Beat the dough until it leaves the sides of the bowl clean, then turn it out onto a lightly floured surface and knead for about 5 minutes.

Put the dough in an oiled plastic bag and leave it to rise at room temperature for 1–1½ hours, or until it has doubled in size. Turn the risen dough onto a lightly floured surface

BRIOCHES

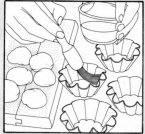
Brush fluted pans with oil.

Insert dough knob in center.

and knead it until smooth. Shape the dough into a sausage and divide it into 12 equal pieces.

Brush 3-inch fluted patty pans with oil and shape three-quarters of each piece of dough into a ball; place it in a patty pan. Using a floured finger, press a hole in the center of the dough as far as the bottom of the pan. Shape the remaining piece of dough into a knob and insert it in the hole. Press lightly with the fingertip to unite the two pieces of dough. When all 12 brioches have been shaped, set the patty pans on a baking sheet and cover them with oiled plastic wrap. Leave to rise until the dough is puffy and reaches just below the tops of the pans.

Remove the wrap and bake the brioches in the center of preheated oven at 450°F for 10 minutes or until golden brown.

See illustration on page 368.

Croissants

PREPARATION TIME: *1–1½ hours* (*plus rising*)
RESTING TIME: *1 hour*
COOKING TIME: *15–20 minutes*

INGREDIENTS (*for 12 croissants*):
4 cups all-purpose flour
2 teaspoons salt
2 tablespoons lard
2 packages active dry yeast
1 cup lukewarm water
1 egg
4–6 ounces butter
GLAZE:
1 egg, beaten
½ teaspoon sugar

Sift the flour and salt into a bowl. Cut up the lard and rub this into the flour with the fingertips until blended to a coarse bread-crumb consistency. Proof the yeast with the water in a small bowl and pour it into a well in the center of the flour, together with the lightly beaten egg. Gradually incorporate the flour with one hand and beat the dough until it leaves the sides of the bowl clean.

Transfer the dough to a lightly floured surface and knead it for about 10 minutes until smooth. Roll out the dough to a strip about 20 inches by 8 inches and ¼ inch thick. If necessary, trim the edges with a knife. Soften the butter with a knife until pliable but not creamy, and divide it into 3 portions. Flake a portion of the butter and dot it over the upper two-thirds of the dough, leaving a ½-inch border unbuttered.

Fold the dough into thirds, bringing up first the unbuttered part of the dough, then folding the opposite part over. Give the dough a half-turn and seal the edges by pressing with the rolling pin. Shape into a long strip again by gently pressing the dough at intervals with the rolling pin; roll out to a rectangle. Dot as before with the second portion of flaked butter, then fold, turn the pastry, and roll again before adding the last of the butter. Fold in thirds again. Work quickly to prevent the dough from becoming warm, thus melting the fat. Keep the edges straight and the corners square.

Put the folded dough in an oiled plastic bag and leave in the refrigerator for 30 minutes. Remove the bag, roll out the dough, and repeat the rolling and folding three times more, but without adding fat. Return the dough to the oiled bag and refrigerate it for another 30 minutes.

To shape the croissants, roll the dough out on a lightly floured surface to a rectangle about 22 inches by 13 inches. Cover with oiled plastic wrap and leave on the table for 10 minutes. Trim the edges with a sharp knife to a rectangle 21 inches by 12 inches; divide the dough in half lengthwise. Cut each strip into 6 triangles, 6 inches wide at the base.

Beat the egg with a few drops of water and the sugar to make a glaze. Brush over the triangles. Roll up each triangle loosely, finishing with the tip underneath, then carefully curve the pastry into a crescent shape. Place the croissants, well spaced, on ungreased baking sheets.

MAKING CROISSANTS

Flake fat over two-thirds of dough.

Fold the dough into thirds.

Seal with a rolling pin.

Roll up dough triangles.

Curve triangle into a crescent.

Brush the tops with a little more egg glaze, cover them with oiled plastic wrap, and leave at room temperature to rise for about 30 minutes or until light and puffy. Brush again with egg glaze before baking the croissants in the center of a preheated oven at 425°F for 15–20 minutes. Use a metal spatula to ease the croissants off the baking sheets. Serve them while still warm.

Anadama Bread

PREPARATION TIME: *20 minutes* (*plus rising*)
COOKING TIME: *55 minutes*

INGREDIENTS (*for 2 loaves*):
2½–3 cups all-purpose flour
1 cup cornmeal
2 packages active dry yeast
1 tablespoon salt
2 cups water
5 tablespoons butter
½ cup molasses

In a large bowl, combine 2½ cups flour, the cornmeal, dry yeast, and salt. Heat the water until warm, then combine with the butter and molasses. Add to the flour mixture. Beat 3 minutes with an electric mixer set at medium speed, or beat by hand—about 150 strokes with a wooden spoon. Add flour as necessary to make a stiff dough.

Turn the dough onto a floured surface and knead for about 10 minutes until it is no longer sticky. Place the dough in a buttered bowl, turning it over in the bowl 2 or 3 times until it is well greased. Set aside to rise in a warm place for 1–1½ hours, or until the dough has doubled in size.

Punch down the dough, divide it into 2 balls, and place each in a buttered 8-inch round cake pan. Allow to rise again until doubled in size, then bake in the center of a preheated oven at 375°F for about 55 minutes or until deep brown. The bread is done if the bottom of the bread sounds hollow when rapped with the knuckles.

Sally Lunn

PREPARATION TIME: *25 minutes* (*plus rising*)
COOKING TIME: *15–20 minutes*

INGREDIENTS (*for 1 loaf*):
1 package active dry yeast
1 teaspoon sugar
1 cup lukewarm milk
4 tablespoons melted butter
2 eggs
4 cups all-purpose flour
1 teaspoon salt
SUGAR TOPPING:
1 tablespoon sugar
1 tablespoon water

Combine the yeast, sugar, and half the milk in a bowl and allow to proof. Add the melted butter and remaining milk. Beat the eggs and add them to the yeast mixture. Sift the flour and salt into a large bowl, make a well in the center, and pour in the milk mixture. Gradually incorporate the flour with the fingers of one hand and beat the dough against the bowl until it leaves the sides clean. Knead on a lightly floured surface until smooth.

Knead the dough into a ball and place it in a 10-by-4-inch tube pan. Cover the pan with a cloth and leave in a warm place for about 1 hour or until the dough has doubled in bulk.

Remove the cloth and set the pan on a baking sheet. Bake just above the center of a preheated oven at 450°F for 15–20 minutes. Meanwhile, make the sugar topping by heating the sugar and water in a small pan over low heat until the sugar has dissolved; then boil it rapidly for 1–2 minutes.

Turn the Sally Lunn out onto a wire rack and, while still warm, brush the top with the sugar water.

See illustration on page 368.

Pumpernickel

PREPARATION TIME: *30 minutes*
  (plus rising)
COOKING TIME: *25 minutes*

INGREDIENTS (*for 3 loaves*):
9 cups all-purpose flour
3 cups rye flour
2 teaspoons salt
1 cup whole bran cereal
¾ cup yellow cornmeal
2 packages active dry yeast
3½ cups water
¼ cup dark molasses
2 ounces unsweetened chocolate
1 tablespoon butter
2 cups mashed potatoes
2 teaspoons caraway seeds

Combine the white and rye flours and place 2 cups of this mixture in a large bowl. Add the salt, bran cereal, cornmeal, and dry yeast; mix well.

Combine the water, molasses, chocolate, and butter in a saucepan. Place over low heat only until the chocolate and butter are almost melted, then gradually add to the flour and yeast mixture, beating very well after each addition. Add the potatoes and 1 cup of the combined all-purpose and rye flours, beating very well. Stir in the caraway seeds and enough of the flour mixture to make a soft dough.

Turn the dough out on a lightly floured board. Cover with a clean cloth and let rise for 15 minutes, then divide into 3 parts. Knead each portion of dough until smooth and elastic, then place in greased bowls and let rise until doubled in bulk, about 1 hour.

Punch down the dough and let it rise again for 30 minutes. Punch it down once more, then shape the dough into balls and place them in 3 greased 8- or 9-inch round cake pans. Cover and let rise in a warm place until doubled, about 45 minutes.

Bake the bread in a preheated 350°F oven for 20–25 minutes, or until the loaves sound hollow when thumped with the knuckles. Cool on wire racks.

SOURDOUGH BAKING

Sourdough bread, long a specialty of cooks on the West Coast, is fairly complicated to prepare because it involves the use of a "starter," a sour yeast, water, and flour mixture that is added to the dough to make it rise. However, once a starter has been established — usually after about 5 days — it can be stored, covered, in the refrigerator almost indefinitely and used as needed.

Sourdough starter

Dissolve ¼ package of granular dry yeast in ¼ cup of lukewarm water. (Test the water on the wrist; if it feels comfortably warm, it is the right temperature. If it is too hot, it will kill the yeast.) Stir in 1 cup of lukewarm water and ¾–1 cup of flour to make a runny batter. Put the mixture in a small crock or fruit jar and cover it with a cloth or plate; do not cover tightly. Store the container in a warm place.

Each day for 5 days, add ½ cup of lukewarm water and enough flour to keep the batter runny. When the batter is quite sour, it is ready for use.

When using sourdough starter, replace the amount used with more water and flour. If the starter is used only occasionally, store it in the refrigerator and add a little flour and water each week.

If the starter is used several times a week, store it in a warm cabinet in the kitchen and add the flour and water every day or every other day.

The water drained from cooked potatoes can be cooled to lukewarm and added to the starter for extra flavor and quicker souring.

Sourdough Bread

PREPARATION TIME: *30 minutes*
  (plus rising)
COOKING TIME: *1 hour*

INGREDIENTS (*for 2 loaves*):
1–2 tablespoons melted butter
½ cup milk
1–2 tablespoons sugar or honey
2 cups sourdough starter
2½ cups all-purpose flour
2 teaspoons salt
1 teaspoon baking soda

Melt the butter in a saucepan and stir in the milk and sugar or honey until just warm. Pour into a mixing bowl. Add the starter, then stir in the flour, salt, and baking soda.

Turn the mixture onto a lightly floured board and knead lightly until the dough is satiny. Place the dough in a buttered bowl and turn dough until it is well greased. Let it rise in a warm place until it has doubled in bulk, about 3 hours.

Punch down the dough and let it rise at least 4 hours more. Shape the dough into 2 loaves.

Place the loaves in a square pan, side by side so that the loaves are touching. Let rise again until they have doubled in bulk, about 2 hours.

Bake in a 350°F oven for 1 hour, or until the loaves pull away from the sides of the pan and sound hollow when tapped lightly on top.

This recipe can also be prepared with whole wheat or rye flours.

Sourdough Rolls

PREPARATION TIME: *20 minutes*
COOKING TIME: *20 minutes*

INGREDIENTS (*for 12 rolls*):
1½ cups all-purpose flour, sifted
2 teaspoons baking powder
¼ teaspoon baking soda
1 teaspoon salt
¼ cup shortening or butter
1 cup sourdough starter
Melted butter

Sift the flour with the baking powder, soda, and salt. Work in the shortening or butter with a fork until the mixture resembles coarse crumbs. Stir in the starter and turn the mixture out onto a lightly floured board. Knead until the dough is satiny.

Pat or roll out the dough about ½ inch thick. Cut into rounds or diamonds with a floured cookie cutter.

Grease a large cake pan well with melted butter. Put in the cut rolls and turn them over to coat both sides with the butter. Let rise 1 hour, or until light, in a warm place.

Bake the rolls in a 425°F oven for 15–20 minutes, or until they are a delicate brown.

Sourdough French Bread

PREPARATION TIME: *30 minutes*
  (plus rising)
COOKING TIME: *45 minutes*

INGREDIENTS (*for 1 large or 2 small loaves*):
2 cups sourdough starter
¾ cup lukewarm water
1 tablespoon sugar
2 teaspoons salt
6 cups all-purpose flour
Cornmeal
Melted butter
GLAZE:
1 tablespoon cornstarch
1 tablespoon sugar
2 tablespoons water

In a large bowl, mix the starter, lukewarm water, sugar, and salt. Sift the flour onto a board, make a hole in the center, and pour in the starter mixture. Stir with the fingers, gradually incorporating more of the flour until it is all mixed in and the dough is smooth and elastic. Place the dough in a greased bowl and brush the top with melted butter. Put the dough in a warm place and let it rise until doubled in bulk. Place it on a lightly floured board and knead lightly for a few minutes, then let it rise again.

Shape the dough into 1 or 2 loaves. The traditional shape is a loaf about 15 inches long, 3 inches wide, and tapered at both ends. Place on a baking sheet that has been sprinkled with cornmeal.

Brush the loaf with melted butter and let it rise until it has doubled in bulk. If desired, make 3 slashes across the top of the loaf with a very sharp, greased knife before baking. Bake in a moderately hot oven (375°F) for about 45 minutes for a large loaf or 35–40 minutes for smaller loaves.

To glaze the bread, remove it from the oven 10 minutes before it is done and brush the top of the bread with a mixture of the cornstarch, sugar, and water. Return the bread to the oven to finish baking.

Sourdough Hot Cakes

PREPARATION TIME: *10 minutes*
COOKING TIME: *15 minutes*

INGREDIENTS (*for 12 hot cakes*):
3 eggs
1 cup milk
2 cups sourdough starter
1¾ cups all-purpose flour, sifted
1 teaspoon baking soda
2 teaspoons baking powder
1½ teaspoons salt
¼ cup sugar

Beat the eggs and add the milk and the starter. Sift together the flour, soda, baking powder, salt, and sugar; blend thoroughly with the egg and milk mixture.

Bake on a greased griddle, turning once when the hot cakes bubble and turn dry at the edges. Serve hot, with butter and jam or syrup.

Quick Breads

Some breads are raised by the quick action of baking powder and self-rising flour, rather than by the lengthy yeast process. These quick breads are one of the delights of the North American table and include such favorites as biscuits, corn bread, muffins, popovers, soda breads, and tea breads.

Not as well known, but equally quick and easy to make, are scones, the British teatime delicacy. Scones are often baked on an iron griddle heated on top of the stove (a cast-iron skillet can also be used). The correct heat is important: If the surface is too hot, the outside crust of the scones becomes too brown, leaving the center uncooked. To test for correct heat, sprinkle a little flour on the surface of the griddle. It should turn light brown in 3 minutes.

Another quick bread, soda bread, is similar to yeast bread in taste and texture; it makes a good substitute for yeast bread when a loaf is required on short notice.

Girdle Scones

PREPARATION TIME: *5 minutes*
COOKING TIME: *10 minutes*

INGREDIENTS (*for 12 scones*):
2 cups all-purpose flour
1 teaspoon baking soda
2 teaspoons cream of tartar
$\frac{1}{2}$ teaspoon salt
2 tablespoons lard or margarine
2 tablespoons sugar
$\frac{1}{2}$–$\frac{3}{4}$ cup milk

Heat a griddle or a heavy-bottomed iron skillet. Sift the flour, baking soda, cream of tartar, and salt into a bowl. Cut up the lard or margarine and rub it into the flour with the fingertips until the mixture resembles fine bread crumbs. Stir in the sugar and gradually add enough milk, mixing with a round-bladed knife, to make a soft dough.

Divide the dough in half. Knead each piece lightly and roll into 2 flat rounds $\frac{1}{4}$–$\frac{1}{2}$ inch thick. Cut each round into 6 even triangles and cook on the greased griddle until evenly brown on one side, then turn and cook on the other side. Allow about 5 minutes for each side. Cool them on a wire rack.

GIRDLE SCONES

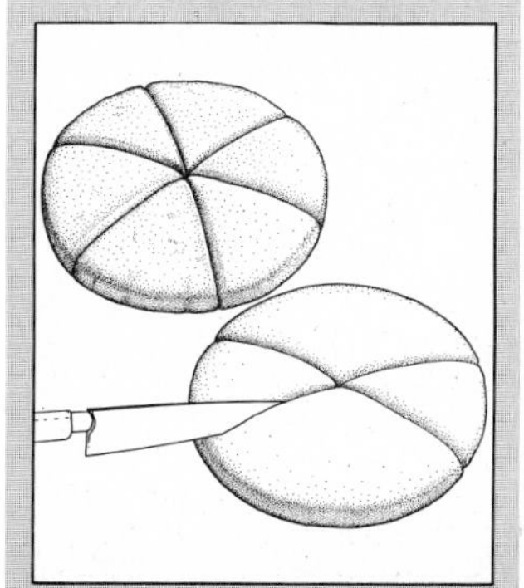

Cut dough rounds into triangles.

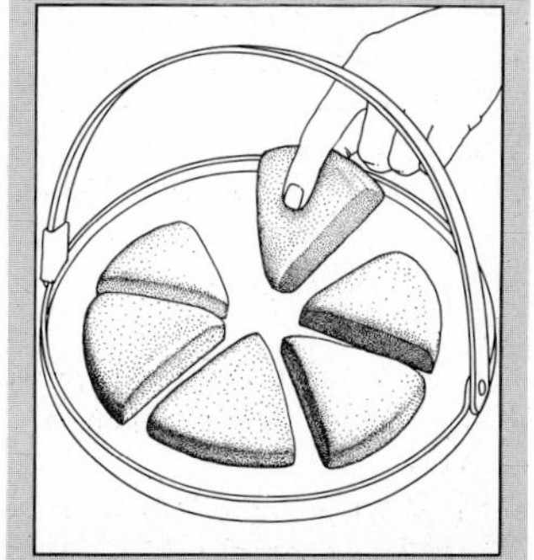

Cook scones on greased griddle.

Oven Scones

PREPARATION TIME: *15 minutes*
COOKING TIME: *10 minutes*

INGREDIENTS (*for 10–12 scones*):
2 cups all-purpose flour
Pinch of salt
$\frac{1}{2}$ teaspoon baking soda
1 teaspoon cream of tartar
3 tablespoons margarine
About 4 tablespoons each milk and water, mixed
Milk for glazing

Sift together the flour, salt, baking soda, and cream of tartar into a wide bowl. Cut up the margarine into small pieces and rub it into the flour with the fingertips. Gradually add the milk and water and mix with a round-bladed knife to give a soft but manageable dough.

Knead the dough quickly on a lightly floured surface to remove all cracks. Roll the dough out $\frac{1}{2}$ inch thick and cut out 2-inch rounds with a plain or fluted pastry cutter. Knead the trimmings together, roll them out, and cut out as many scones as possible. Set the scones on a heated, ungreased baking sheet, brush them with milk, and bake them near the top of a preheated oven at 450°F for about 10 minutes until they are well risen and light golden brown.

Drop Scones

PREPARATION TIME: *5 minutes*
COOKING TIME: *3–5 minutes per batch*

INGREDIENTS (*for 15–18 scones*):
1 cup self-rising flour
Pinch of salt
1 tablespoon sugar
1 egg
About $\frac{1}{2}$ cup milk
Lard for cooking

Set a griddle or heavy-bottomed frying pan over heat. While it is warming, sift the flour and salt into a bowl and stir in the sugar. Make a well in the center and drop in the egg; gradually add the milk, working in the flour with a spoon until a smooth batter is formed.

Grease the heated surface lightly with a little lard or cooking oil. When a slight haze appears after the oil has heated sufficiently, pour on small rounds of batter, well apart, either from a pitcher or dropped off a spoon, to give perfect rounds. As soon as the scones are puffed, bubbling on the surface, and golden on the undersides, turn them over carefully with a metal spatula to brown them on the other side. Serve at once or, if this is not possible, tuck the scones between the folds of a clean dish towel to keep them warm until serving time.

COOKING DROP SCONES

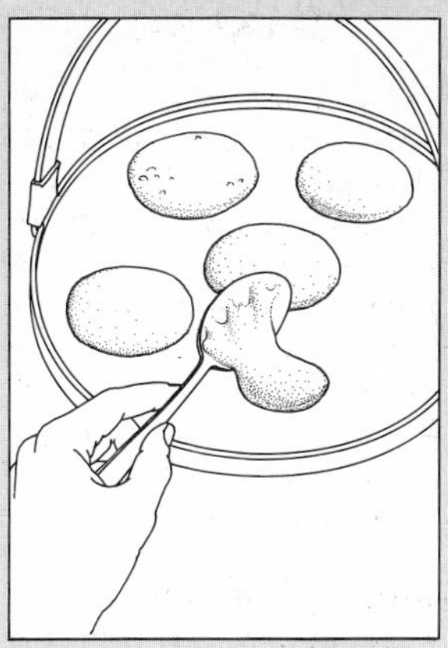

Pour batter onto greased griddle.

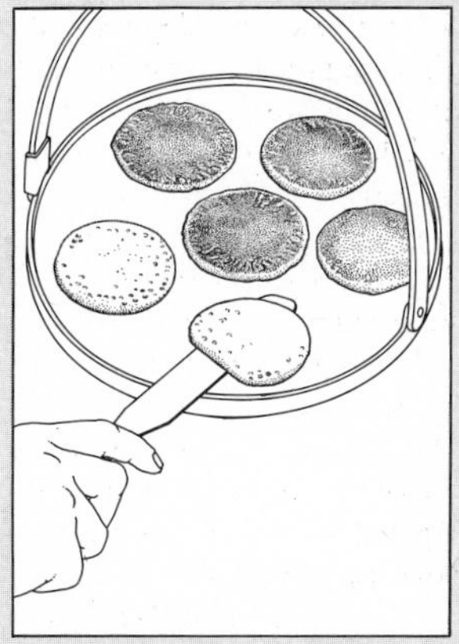

Turn over half-cooked scones.

Baking Powder Biscuits

PREPARATION TIME: *10 minutes*
COOKING TIME: *15 minutes*

INGREDIENTS (*for about 18 2-inch biscuits*):
2 cups sifted all-purpose flour
1 tablespoon double-acting baking powder
$\frac{1}{2}$ teaspoon salt
$\frac{1}{4}$ cup butter or other shortening
$\frac{3}{4}$ cup milk

Sift the flour, baking powder, and salt into a mixing bowl. With a pastry blender or two knives, cut in the butter or other shortening into very fine particles. Add the milk and stir in just enough to make the dough particles cling together. The dough should be very soft. Turn out on a floured surface and knead about ten times, then pat or roll out the dough. The dough should be $\frac{1}{2}$–$\frac{3}{4}$ inch thick for high, fluffy biscuits and about $\frac{1}{4}$ inch thick for thin biscuits. Cut into 2-inch rounds or into squares. Place close together on an ungreased cookie sheet for soft biscuits or far apart for crisper biscuits.

Bake in a preheated 450°F oven for about 12–15 minutes. Serve the biscuits piping hot.

To vary this recipe, add chopped herbs, such as chives, sage, thyme, or oregano, or add grated cheese to the biscuit dough. For drop biscuits, add another $\frac{1}{4}$ cup of milk, drop by spoonfuls onto a buttered baking sheet, and bake the same way.

Bacon Corn Sticks

PREPARATION TIME: *15 minutes*
COOKING TIME: *20 minutes*

INGREDIENTS (*for about 14 corn sticks*):
1 cup sifted all-purpose flour
1 tablespoon double-acting baking powder
1 cup yellow or white cornmeal
1 cup buttermilk
2 tablespoons melted butter
2 eggs
$\frac{3}{4}$ cup crisp bacon bits

Preheat oven to 400°F. Grease corn-stick mold liberally with bacon drippings and heat the mold in the oven while preparing the batter.

Sift the flour and baking powder together. Stir in the cornmeal. In a separate bowl, beat the buttermilk, butter, and eggs lightly. Stir this mixture into the dry ingredients along with the bacon bits. Blend just until the dry ingredients are moistened. Do not overmix.

Spoon the batter into the hot mold until it is about three-quarters full. Bake about 20 minutes until brown and puffy.

Remove the sticks from the mold immediately. Regrease the mold, refill with batter, and bake. Serve the sticks with plenty of butter.

See illustration on page 368.

Soda Bread

PREPARATION TIME: *15 minutes*
COOKING TIME: *30 minutes*

INGREDIENTS:
4 cups all-purpose flour
2 teaspoons baking soda
2 teaspoons cream of tartar
1 teaspoon salt
2 tablespoons lard
1–2 teaspoons sugar (optional)
1¼ cups sour milk, or 1 cup
  buttermilk plus ¼ cup milk
2 cups dark raisins

Sift the flour, baking soda, cream of tartar, and salt into a bowl. Cut up the lard and rub it into the flour with the fingertips until the mixture resembles fine bread crumbs. Mix in the sugar, if used. Make a well in the center of the flour, add the milk (soured with 1 tablespoon of lemon juice) or the buttermilk and milk, and the raisins. Mix to a soft but manageable dough, working the ingredients with a round-bladed knife.

Turn the dough onto a floured surface, knead it lightly, and shape it into a 7-inch round; flatten it slightly. Mark the round into 4 sections with the back of a knife, set it on a floured baking sheet, and bake

in the center of a preheated oven at 400°F for about 30 minutes.

Allow to cool completely on a wire rack and serve fresh, as a breakfast bread or as a quick substitute for yeast-baked bread.

Doughnuts

PREPARATION TIME: *20 minutes*
CHILLING TIME: *1 hour*
COOKING TIME: *20 minutes*

INGREDIENTS (*for 18 doughnuts*):
1 egg
½ cup milk
½ cup sugar
1 tablespoon melted butter
1¾–2 cups flour
2 teaspoons baking powder
¼ teaspoon nutmeg
½ teaspoon salt
Oil for deep-frying
Sugar for coating

In a large mixing bowl, beat the egg and add the milk, sugar, and the melted butter. Sift together 1¾ cups of the flour, the baking powder, nutmeg, and salt; add these to the egg and milk mixture.

Mix thoroughly. If necessary, add more flour to make the dough just firm enough to handle. Chill in the refrigerator for at least 1 hour.

Roll out the dough ⅓ inch thick and cut into doughnut shapes with a floured cutter. Place the doughnuts on floured waxed paper and let stand 5–10 minutes before deep-frying.

Heat the oil to 360°F and deep-fry the doughnuts, three or four at a time, until brown on one side; then turn and brown on the other side. Drain on paper towels.

To sugar-coat the doughnuts, put a few tablespoons of sugar in a paper bag, add 2 or 3 doughnuts at a time, and shake gently until well coated.

Spicy Coffee Cake

PREPARATION TIME: *30 minutes*
COOKING TIME: *40 minutes*

INGREDIENTS (*for 9 large servings*):
½ cup butter
¾ cup sugar
2 eggs
1 teaspoon baking soda
1 cup sour cream
1½ cups all-purpose flour
1½ teaspoons baking powder
¼ teaspoon salt
2 teaspoons cinnamon
¼ teaspoon nutmeg
½ teaspoon ground cloves
4 tablespoons chopped pecans or walnuts
Butter

Cream the butter with ½ cup sugar. Add the eggs, one at a time, beating well after each addition. Mix the baking soda with the sour cream and gradually beat into the butter mixture. Add the flour, sifted with the baking powder and salt.

Prepare the topping by mixing the remaining ¼ cup sugar with the spices and the nuts.

Pour half of the batter into a 9-inch square pan. Sprinkle half of the topping over it, then pour in the rest of the batter and sprinkle the remainder of the topping mixture over it. Dot the top with butter. Bake in a preheated 350°F oven for 40 minutes or until a cake tester inserted in the center of the cake comes out clean.

Bran and Raisin Bread

PREPARATION TIME: *10 minutes*
RESTING TIME: *8 hours*
COOKING TIME: *1¼–1½ hours*

INGREDIENTS:
1 cup flaked bran cereal
1⅓ cups white raisins
1¼ cups light brown sugar
1¼ cups milk
1½ cups self-rising flour
1 teaspoon baking powder

Mix the bran cereal, white raisins, sugar, and milk in a bowl and let the

mixture stand overnight, covered.

Butter and line a loaf pan measuring 9 inches by 5 inches at the top. Sift the flour and baking powder into the soaked ingredients, blend thoroughly, and spoon into the prepared pan. Level off the top of the mixture and bake in the center of a preheated oven at 375°F for about 1¼ hours until the bread is well risen and just firm to the touch. If the loaf browns too quickly, cover it with aluminum foil.

Turn out the loaf, remove the paper, and cool on a wire rack. Serve the loaf sliced and buttered. It is best left for a day or two to mature, and will keep for 1 week in a tin.

Cranberry Bread

PREPARATION TIME: *20 minutes*
COOKING TIME: *1 hour*

INGREDIENTS (*for 2 loaves*):
3 cups all-purpose flour
1 teaspoon baking soda
1 teaspoon baking powder
1 teaspoon salt
2 eggs
1 cup sugar
4 tablespoons melted butter
1¼ cups milk
1 teaspoon rosewater
1¼ cups raw cranberries, halved or coarsely chopped
¾ cup chopped walnuts

Sift together the flour, baking soda, baking powder, and salt. Beat the eggs and sugar in another large mixing bowl until well blended. Stir in the butter, milk, and rosewater. Stir in the flour until it is just moistened, then stir in the cranberries and walnuts and blend together. Do not overwork the dough.

Put the batter in 2 10-by-4-by-5-inch loaf pans and bake in a preheated 350°F oven for 55–60 minutes, or until the center springs back when lightly touched or a cake tester comes out clean when inserted in the center. The top of the loaves will crack, but this is customary with most baking-powder breads.

Cool loaves on a rack, then wrap in plastic wrap or foil, or seal them in a plastic bag. Let stand overnight or a full day before cutting.

Oregon Apple Bread

PREPARATION TIME: *15 minutes*
COOKING TIME: *1 hour*

INGREDIENTS (*for 1 loaf*):
½ cup butter
1¼ cups sugar
2 eggs
2 cups all-purpose flour
2 teaspoons baking powder
1 teaspoon cinnamon
¼ teaspoon nutmeg
1½ cups peeled, grated apple
½ cup chopped walnuts or pecans

Cream the butter and sugar together until fluffy. Add the eggs and beat well. Sift together the dry ingredients; add to the creamed mixture, alternating with the grated apple. Fold in the nuts.

Pour into a buttered and floured loaf pan and bake in a 350°F oven for about 1 hour. Cool in pan for 10 minutes, then turn onto a wire rack.

Blueberry Muffins

PREPARATION TIME: *15 minutes*
COOKING TIME: *25 minutes*

INGREDIENTS (*for about 12 muffins*):
2 cups sifted all-purpose flour
3 teaspoons baking powder
3 tablespoons sugar
¼ teaspoon salt
¾ teaspoon cinnamon
¾ cup milk
1 egg, well beaten
½ cup melted butter
1 cup blueberries

Combine the sifted flour with the baking powder, sugar, salt, and cinnamon, and sift again. Combine the milk, beaten egg, melted butter, and add to the dry ingredients all at once. Stir to moisten. Fold in blueberries.

Butter the muffin tins and fill each two-thirds full. Bake at 400°F about 25 minutes or until brown.

Cake Making

The key to successful cake making lies in following each step of the recipe exactly and in understanding the reaction of the various ingredients to each other. The basic ingredients are fat, flour, leavening agents, eggs, sugar, and often fruit. Correct position in the oven, oven temperature, and the size of the cake pans are also important.

Basically, cakes fall into two categories: those made with fat, and the sponge types made without fat. The génoise, a sponge cake, is the exception; it is made with fat.

In fat-type cakes, the fat is either rubbed in, creamed, or melted. Rubbed-in mixtures are generally used for plain cakes, such as Tyrol cake, while creamed cakes are rich and soft, with a fairly close, even grain and soft crumb.

In melted cakes, such as gingerbread, the fat—often with liquid, sugar, syrup, or molasses added—is poured into the dry ingredients to give a batterlike consistency. Mix cakes by hand or use an electric mixer after incorporating the flour with fat and eggs.

Before starting to mix, make sure the cake pan is the right size. Pans bigger, smaller, or shallower than called for can cause a cake to fail. If the pan is an incorrect size, fill to only half its depth so that the cake will rise to, but not above, the top. Test frequently to see if the cakes are cooked. Prepare the pan either by lining or by greasing with butter and sprinkling with flour. Set the oven to the correct temperature if the cake is to be baked at once after mixing, and assemble the necessary ingredients. Eggs, butter, and stick margarine should be at room temperature.

Fats

Butter, margarine, vegetable shortening, lard, and corn oil are all used in cakes. However, they are not always interchangeable.

Butter gives the best flavor and improves the keeping quality of cakes, but stick margarine can be used in place of butter in most recipes, with only a slight difference in flavor. Soft margarine, sold in tubs, is composed of blended oils; it is particularly suitable for cakes for which all the ingredients are mixed together in one operation.

Vegetable shortening is light and easy to blend with other ingredients. Like lard, this fat contains little or no salt; shortening and lard can be used interchangeably in recipes.

Corn oil is suitable for most recipes using melted fat, but it is advisable to follow the manufacturer's instructions, as the characteristics of oils vary. Corn oil is easy to mix in and gives a soft texture, but the cakes do not keep quite so well.

Flour

Cake flour is made from soft wheat and gives a lighter, crumblier texture. Self-rising flour is all-purpose flour to which baking powder and salt have been added in the proportions of 1½ teaspoons baking powder and ½ teaspoon salt for each cup of flour. All-purpose flour, cake flour, and self-rising flour are used for cakes. All-purpose and cake flours are usually sifted with a pinch of salt. Salt is added not only for flavor but because of its chemical effect in toughening the soft mixture of fat and sugar.

In some melted cakes, flour is mixed with baking soda. These cakes contain molasses, which is slightly acid and must be offset by an alkali to act as a leavening agent.

Leavening agents

Baking powder is a ready-made blend of baking soda and cream of tartar, and these together form carbon dioxide. The rubbery substance in flour known as gluten is capable, when wet, of suspending carbon dioxide in the form of tiny bubbles.

Since all gases expand when they are heated, these bubbles become larger during baking and thus cause a cake to rise.

However, cake mixtures can hold only a certain amount of gas. If too much leavening agent is used, the cake will rise well at first but later collapse, and this results in a heavy, close texture. A combination of cream of tartar and baking soda is sometimes used as an alternative to baking powder, in the proportion of ½ teaspoon cream of tartar to ⅓ teaspoon baking soda.

Eggs

These give lightness to cake mixtures, as they expand on heating and trap the air beaten into the mixture. When whisked egg is used in a cake mixture, air instead of carbon dioxide causes the cake to rise.

Cakes with a high proportion of egg, such as sponge cakes, need little if any leavening agent.

In creamed mixtures, the eggs are beaten in, not whisked, and a little additional leavening is required. In plain cakes, where beaten egg is added with the liquid, the egg helps to bind the mixture but does not act as the main leavening agent.

Sugar

Granulated sugar is the most commonly used sweetener for cakes. Light or dark brown sugar is good for rubbed-in, melted, and fruit cakes. The color and flavor add richness, and the soft, moist quality helps to keep certain cakes in good condition longer.

Syrup, honey, and molasses, often combined with sugar, are used to sweeten, color, and flavor such cakes as gingerbread. They give a close, moist texture.

Fruit and peel

Always choose good-quality dried fruit. Stored white raisins sometimes become hard, but they can be plumped up in hot water and thoroughly drained and dried.

Wash any syrup from candied cherries and dry them thoroughly.

Peel can be bought already chopped, but make sure that it looks soft and moist. Coarsely chopped, thin-cut peel sometimes needs more chopping to make it finer. Large pieces of candied orange, lemon, grapefruit, and citron peel should be stripped of sugar before being shredded, grated, or chopped.

Preparing cake pans

All cakes should be baked in pans that have been buttered, buttered and floured, sugared, or lined with paper. The appearance of a finished cake depends largely on the expert preparation of the cake pan.

Pans for rubbed-in mixtures are often greased only by brushing melted shortening evenly over the inside. But as an extra precaution against sticking and for ease of turning out, a paper liner of buttered waxed paper fitted into the bottom is a good idea. The paper does not necessarily have to reach the edge of the pan, but the center must be covered.

For fatless sponge cakes, flour the greased pan to give an extra crisp crust, or dust it with flour blended with an equal amount of sugar. Shake the dusting mixture around the pan until evenly coated, and remove any excess by gently tapping the inverted pan.

For baking small cupcakes, fluted paper baking cups set in muffin tins are by far the easiest to use; otherwise, butter the tins thoroughly.

Cooking parchment can be used instead of waxed paper to line round or rectangular pans. Pans with a Teflon coating need no greasing or lining, but a paper lining helps to keep a solid crust from forming, especially during long baking. For cakes baked in Teflon-coated pans, the baking time should be reduced by a few minutes, as these pans brown the contents quicker.

Lining a round cake pan

Cut a strip of waxed paper as long as the circumference of the pan and 2 inches wider than the depth of the pan. Make a fold about 1 inch deep along one of the long edges, and cut this at ½-inch intervals up to the fold at a slight angle. Curve the strip around and slip it around the sides of the buttered pan, nicked fold downward so that it lies flat against the bottom of the pan.

Cut a circle of paper slightly smaller than the bottom of the pan and drop it in over the nicked paper. Brush with melted fat. For rich cakes with long cooking times, double-line the pan.

Lining a rectangular pan

Measure the length and width of the pan and add twice the pan's depth to each of these measurements. Cut a rectangle of waxed paper to this size and place the pan squarely in the center. At each corner, make a cut from the angle of the paper as far as the corner of the pan.

Grease the inside of the pan and put in the paper so that it fits closely, overlapping at the corners. Brush again with melted fat.

Oven positions

In gas ovens the hottest shelf is at the top, but in electric ovens the heat is more evenly distributed. A cake is generally baked in or near the center of the oven.

When baking two cakes, place

Cake Making

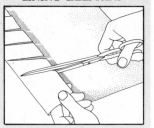

LINING CAKE PANS

Cut folded paper strip.

Cut a circle to fit bottom of pan.

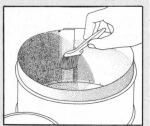

Brush paper with melted butter.

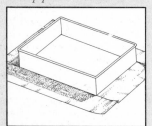

Center rectangular pan over paper.

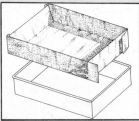

Cut and fold paper to fit pan.

---

them side by side but do not let them touch the sides of the oven or each other. If the pans are too large, bake the cakes on two oven shelves but avoid placing the pans directly over each other. After the cake mixture has set, move the pan on the lower shelf to the upper, and the pan on the upper shelf to the lower.

Small cakes are usually baked above the center but not at the top of the oven. Place the pans or patty pans on baking sheets before putting them in the oven.

Cooling cakes

With only a few exceptions, all cakes should be thoroughly cooled before being cut, frosted, or stored. After baking, most cakes are best left to settle in their pans for 5–10 minutes before being turned out. Large cakes and rich fruitcakes are often left longer so that they are lukewarm when they are turned out.

Run a spatula with a thick blade, or a round-bladed knife around the edge of the cake (do not use metal tools on Teflon-coated pans). Place a wire rack over the cake and invert both the cake and rack, then lift the pan carefully. The lining paper can be peeled off or left on. Turn the cake with the aid of a second rack or the hand so that the top is uppermost. Leave the cake to cool completely on the wire rack. To prevent the wire mesh from marking the surface of a soft-textured cake, place a dish towel over the rack before turning the cake out on it.

Storing cakes

Storage time depends on the type of cake. Generally, frosted cakes stay fresh longer than unfrosted cakes, and the more fat in the cake mixture, the longer it keeps. Fatless sponge cakes should preferably be eaten on the day of baking, since they tend to go stale quickly.

Store plain and frosted cakes in airtight cake tins or similar containers. Cream-filled cakes are best

---

TURNING OUT CAKES

Run knife along inner edge of pan.

Invert cake onto covered rack.

---

kept in the refrigerator. Wrap fruitcakes in aluminum foil with their lining paper left on before storing. If fruitcakes are still slightly warm when wrapped, they will retain moisture better.

Most cakes, properly covered, also store well in the freezer.

RUBBED-IN CAKES

These plain cakes are the easiest of all to make. As the proportion of fat to flour is half or less, rubbed-in mixtures are best eaten when fresh or within 2–3 days of baking. Rubbing in consists of blending flour and fat until they have become a crumblike mixture, using only the tips of the fingers in a gentle, back-and-forth grasping motion.

To keep the mixture cool, raise the hands high when letting the crumbs drop back into the bowl so that the crumbs are cooled by the air.

Shake the bowl occasionally to bring bigger crumbs to the surface of the mixture. Make sure the texture is even, but do not handle more than necessary, or the crumbs will toughen and the fat will become soft and oily.

The amount of liquid added can be critical: too much results in a doughy texture, whereas too little gives a crumbly cake that quickly dries out. For a large cake, the mixture should only just drop off the spoon when gently tapped.

Tyrol Cake

PREPARATION TIME: *25 minutes*
COOKING TIME: *1¾–2 hours*

INGREDIENTS:
2 cups all-purpose flour
Pinch of salt
1 teaspoon ground cinnamon
7 tablespoons margarine
4 tablespoons sugar
⅓ cup currants
⅓ cup white raisins
1 teaspoon baking soda
½ cup plus 2 tablespoons milk
3 level tablespoons clear honey

Butter a 6-inch round cake pan. Sift the flour, salt, and ground cinnamon into a bowl, cut up the margarine, and rub into the flour until the mixture resembles fine bread crumbs. Stir in the sugar, currants, and white raisins and make a well in the center. Add the baking soda to the milk and stir until dissolved. Stir in the honey, and pour this mixture into the well in the flour. Using a wooden spoon, gradually work in the dry ingredients, adding more milk, if necessary, so that the batter acquires a firm dropping consistency.

Spoon the cake mixture into the prepared pan and gently level the top. Bake in the center of a preheated oven at 325°F for 1¾–2 hours, or until the cake is well risen.

Test by inserting a fine skewer into the center of the cake—if the skewer comes away clean, the cake is done. Let the cake cool completely on a wire rack.

Strawberry Shortcake

PREPARATION TIME: *25 minutes*
COOKING TIME: *20 minutes*

INGREDIENTS:
2 cups all-purpose flour
1 teaspoon cream of tartar
½ teaspoon baking soda
Pinch of salt
4 tablespoons butter or margarine
3 tablespoons sugar
1 egg, beaten
3–4 tablespoons milk
FILLING:
2 cups hulled strawberries
1 cup heavy cream
1 tablespoon milk
Superfine sugar
Butter

Sift together the flour, cream of tartar, baking soda, and salt into a bowl. Cut the butter or margarine into small pieces and rub it into the flour until the mixture resembles fine bread crumbs. Blend in the sugar. Make a well in the center and stir in the beaten egg and enough milk to give a soft but manageable dough. Knead lightly on a floured surface, then roll out into a 7-inch circle.

STRAWBERRY SHORTCAKE

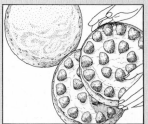

Spread with cream and fruit.

Decorate top with piped cream.

Place on a buttered baking sheet, dust lightly with flour, and bake near the top of a preheated oven at 425°F for about 20 minutes. Cool slightly on a wire rack.

For the filling, slice the strawberries thickly. Beat together the cream and the milk, sweetened with sugar to taste, until it holds its shape. Cut the warm shortcake into 3 layers, horizontally, with a serrated knife. Lightly butter each layer. Spread the cream over all three circles, then top with the sliced strawberries and sandwich the cake together. Decorate the top with piped cream.

Cherry and Coconut Cake

PREPARATION TIME: *30 minutes*
COOKING TIME: *1¼ hours*

INGREDIENTS:
3 cups self-rising flour
Pinch of salt
12 tablespoons (1½ sticks)
 margarine
1⅓ cups candied cherries
⅔ cup shredded coconut
¾ cup sugar
2 large eggs
½ cup plus 2 tablespoons milk
Granulated sugar

Butter a 7½–8 inch round cake pan. Sift the flour and salt into a bowl and rub in the cut-up margarine. Quarter the cherries, toss them in the coconut, and add with the sugar to the flour, stirring lightly to combine. Beat the eggs and stir into the mixture, together with enough milk to give a stiff but dropping consistency.

Turn the mixture into the prepared pan, level the surface, dust with granulated sugar, and bake in the center of a preheated oven at 350°F for about 1¼ hours or until well risen and golden brown. Cool on a wire rack.

Rock Buns

PREPARATION TIME: *15 minutes*
COOKING TIME: *15–20 minutes*

INGREDIENTS (*for 12 buns*):
2 cups all-purpose flour
Pinch of salt
2 teaspoons baking powder
4 tablespoons butter or margarine
4 tablespoons lard or vegetable
 shortening
⅔ cup mixed currants and raisins
½ cup light brown sugar
Grated rind of ½ lemon
1 large egg
1–2 tablespoons milk

Grease 2 baking sheets. Sift together the flour, salt, and baking powder into a bowl. Rub the fats into the flour until the mixture resembles fine bread crumbs. Stir in the currants and raisins, sugar, and lemon rind. Beat the egg with 1 tablespoon of milk. Using a fork, stir the egg mixture into the dry ingredients, adding a little more milk if necessary to give a stiff dough—the mixture should just knit together.

Using 2 forks, place the mixture in 12 small heaps on the greased baking sheets. Keep the mixture rough to give a rocky appearance, which will remain after baking. Bake just above the center of a preheated oven at 400°F for 15–20 minutes or until golden brown. Cool on a wire rack and serve the rock buns fresh.

See illustration on page 370.

Raspberry Buns

PREPARATION TIME: *25 minutes*
COOKING TIME: *10–15 minutes*

INGREDIENTS (*for 10 buns*):
2 cups self-rising flour
Pinch of salt
6 tablespoons sugar
6 tablespoons butter or margarine
1 egg
1 tablespoon milk
Raspberry jam
1 egg, beaten

Grease 2 baking sheets. In a bowl, sift together the flour, salt, and

sugar. Add the butter, cut in small pieces, and rub it quickly into the flour with the fingertips until the mixture resembles fine bread crumbs. With a fork, beat one egg lightly with the milk and mix this into the flour mixture with a round-bladed knife until the mixture has been worked into a light and manageable dough.

Shape the dough between the palms of the hands into 10 uniform balls. Make a hole with a floured finger in the center of each ball and drop in a little raspberry jam. Close up the opening, pinching the edges of the dough together.

Place the buns well apart on the baking sheets, as they double in size when baked. Brush with beaten egg and bake just above the center of a preheated oven at 425°F for 10–15 minutes. Cool on a wire rack.

See illustration on page 370.

Apple Cakes

PREPARATION TIME: *30 minutes*
COOKING TIME: *15 minutes*

INGREDIENTS (*for 16 cakes*):
1 pound cooking apples
Brown sugar
2 cups all-purpose flour
2 teaspoons cream of tartar
1 teaspoon baking soda
Pinch of salt
¼ pound margarine
½ cup granulated sugar
1 egg
Superfine sugar for dusting

Grease 16 shallow muffin tins thoroughly. Peel, core, and slice the apples and cook them, with brown sugar to taste, over low heat until they form a thick purée.

Meanwhile, sift together the flour, cream of tartar, baking soda, and salt. Cut the margarine into small pieces and rub this into the flour until the mixture resembles fine bread crumbs. Stir in sugar and mix in the beaten egg to form a soft but manageable dough. Knead lightly on a floured surface and roll it out ⅛ inch

APPLE CAKES

Roll dough between waxed paper.

Stamp out rounds with cutter.

Put tops over apple filling.

thick. Handle the dough carefully, as it crumbles easily. Cut out 16 bases and 16 tops with a plain 2½-inch-diameter pastry cutter. If necessary, knead the trimmings and roll out more shapes.

Lift the cake bases into the tins with a metal spatula. Cover with a teaspoonful of the apple purée and cover with a pastry top—this seals itself during cooking. Sprinkle the tops with superfine sugar. Bake just above the center of a preheated oven at 400°F for about 15 minutes. Leave to cool slightly in the tins, then ease the cakes out with a metal spatula and cool completely on a wire rack. Serve as soon as cooled.

CREAMED CAKES

Creamed cakes are made from the basic method of blending fat with sugar. Put the cut-up butter or margarine into a bowl large enough to allow the fat and sugar to be beaten vigorously without spilling over. With a wooden spoon, beat the fat against the sides of the bowl until soft; add the sugar and beat the mixture until fluffy and pale yellow. After 7–10 minutes the volume will increase greatly and the mixture will drop easily from the spoon.

If an electric mixer is used, set the dial at the speed suggested in the manufacturer's instructions and allow 3–4 minutes for beating. Switch off the mixer from time to time and scrape the cake mixture down into the bowl.

Layer Cake

PREPARATION TIME: *15 minutes*
COOKING TIME: *25 minutes*

INGREDIENTS:
¼ pound butter or margarine
½ cup sugar
2 large eggs
Vanilla extract or grated lemon
 rind or orange rind
1 cup self-rising flour

Butter 2 7-inch straight-sided layer cake pans and line the bottoms with buttered waxed paper. In a bowl, beat the butter until soft, add the sugar, and cream the ingredients until light and fluffy. Beat in the eggs, one at a time, then add a few drops of vanilla, or lemon or orange rind. Beat in the sifted flour.

Divide this mixture equally between the two pans and level off the surface. Bake the cakes side by side, if possible, in the center of a preheated oven at 350°F for about 25 minutes. Cool on a wire rack.

Layer the two cakes with jam or a butter cream filling and dust the tops with sifted confectioners' sugar. Alternatively, cover with a soft icing.

See illustration on page 370.

CREAMED CAKE MIXTURE

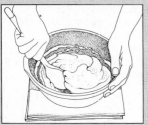

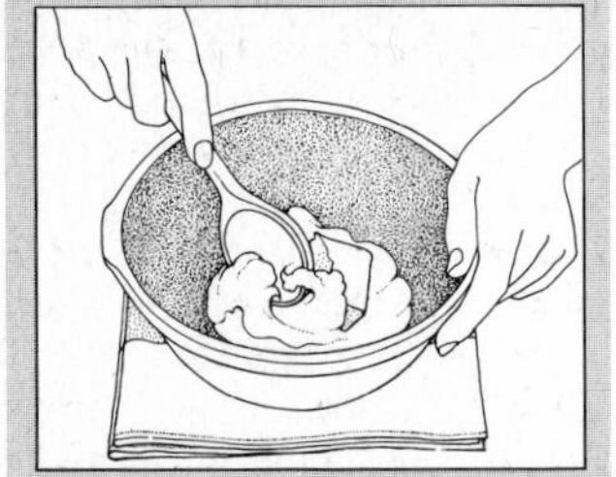

Stand bowl on damp cloth.

Beat butter and sugar until fluffy.

Break egg into mixture and stir.

Alternatively, add beaten egg.

Fold in sifted flour.

Cocoa Layer Cake

PREPARATION TIME: *25 minutes*
COOKING TIME: *30 minutes*

INGREDIENTS:
¼ pound butter or margarine
½ cup sugar
2 large eggs
2 tablespoons cocoa
1 cup self-rising flour
Pinch of salt
FILLING:
3 tablespoons butter or margarine
⅔ cup confectioners' sugar
2 teaspoons coffee extract
1 tablespoon half-and-half

Butter a straight-sided 8-inch layer cake pan and line with paper, cutting the band of paper to come ½ inch above the rim. Butter paper lining.

Beat the butter until soft, add the sugar, and cream the mixture until light and fluffy. Beat the eggs before beating them into the mixture, a little at a time. In a small bowl or cup, blend the cocoa with enough cold water to make a paste. Lightly beat this into the creamed mixture, alternating with the sifted flour and salt. Turn the cake mixture into the prepared pan, level the surface, and bake in the center of a preheated oven at 350°F for about 30 minutes or until the cake is well risen and spongy to the touch.

Meanwhile, make the filling. Beat the butter until soft and creamy; sift the confectioners' sugar and beat it in, a little at a time. Stir in the coffee extract and half-and-half.

Turn the cake onto a wire rack and remove the lining paper. Cut the cold cake in half horizontally and spread the bottom half with the filling; place the top in position and lightly press the two halves together. Dust the top with sifted sugar. Using the back of a knife blade, draw a lattice pattern across the sugar.

See illustration on page 370.

Pound Cake

PREPARATION TIME: *20 minutes*
COOKING TIME: *1–1¼ hours*

INGREDIENTS:
1½ sticks (12 tablespoons) butter or
  margarine
¾ cup sugar
3 large eggs
1¼ cups self-rising flour
1 cup all-purpose flour
Pinch of salt
Grated rind and juice of ½ lemon
Citron peel

Grease a 7-inch round cake pan and line with waxed paper. Beat the butter until soft, add the sugar, and cream until light and fluffy. Add the eggs, one at a time, beating well between each addition. Fold in the sifted flours and salt, alternating with the strained lemon juice and rind. Turn the mixture into the prepared pan and level the surface. Arrange slices of thinly cut citron peel over the top.

Bake in the center of a preheated oven at 325°F for 1–1¼ hours. Leave to cool in the pan for 10 minutes, then turn out onto a wire rack.

See illustration on page 371.

COCOA LAYER CAKE

Sift confectioners' sugar over cake.

Draw lattice pattern across sugar.

Chocolate Pound Cake

PREPARATION TIME: *20 minutes*
COOKING TIME: *1¼–1½ hours*

INGREDIENTS:
3 cups all-purpose flour, sifted
½ cup cocoa
1 teaspoon salt
½ teaspoon baking powder
1 cup butter
½ cup shortening
2½ cups sugar
1 teaspoon vanilla extract
5 eggs
1 cup milk

Sift together the flour, cocoa, salt, and baking powder. Cream the butter and shortening in a mixing bowl and gradually add the sugar, creaming well. Beat in the vanilla extract and the eggs.

Add the dry ingredients to the butter and egg mixture a little at a time, alternating with the milk and ending with the dry ingredients. Blend well and pour the batter into a 10-inch tube pan that has been buttered on the bottom but not on the sides. Bake in the center of a 325°F oven for 1¼–1½ hours.

Pineapple and Cherry Loaf

PREPARATION TIME: *35 minutes*
COOKING TIME: *1½ hours*

INGREDIENTS:
1 cup candied cherries
¼ cup candied pineapple
½ cup ground almonds
Grated rind of ½ lemon
1½ sticks (12 tablespoons) butter or
  margarine
¾ cup sugar
3 eggs
¾ cup self-rising flour
¾ cup all-purpose flour
Pinch of salt

Butter a loaf pan 4½ inches by 9 inches (top measurement); line with buttered waxed paper. Wash and dry the cherries, cut them in half, and set 10 aside. Chop the pineapple and mix with the cherries, ground almonds, and lemon rind.

Beat the butter until soft, add the sugar, then cream the mixture until light and fluffy. Beat the eggs slightly before adding them to the mixture a little at a time. Sift and fold the flours and salt, a third at a time, into the creamed mixture. Lastly, fold in the fruit.

Spoon into the prepared pan, level the surface, and arrange the reserved cherries on top. Cover the pan loosely with aluminum foil, taking care that it does not touch the cake mixture. Bake in the center of a preheated oven at 350°F for about 1½ hours or until well risen and firm to the touch. Cool on a wire rack and remove the lining paper.

See illustration on page 370.

Carrot Cake

PREPARATION TIME: *25 minutes*
COOKING TIME: *35–40 minutes*

INGREDIENTS:
1 cup butter
2 cups sugar
1 teaspoon ground cinnamon
½ teaspoon mace or nutmeg
½–1 teaspoon grated orange rind
4 eggs
1½ cups finely grated or shredded
  carrots
⅔ cup toasted walnuts or filberts,
  finely chopped
2½ cups all-purpose flour, sifted
3 teaspoons baking powder
½ teaspoon salt
⅓ cup warm water

Cream the butter and sugar together until light and fluffy. Beat in the cinnamon, mace or nutmeg, and grated orange rind. Add the eggs one at a time, beating well after each addition. Then gradually stir in the carrots and nuts.

Sift together the flour, baking powder, and salt; add them, with the warm water, to the creamed mixture. Do not beat; fold in the flour just until it is well moistened.

Pour the batter into a buttered 11-by-15-inch cake pan and bake in a preheated 350°F oven for 35–40 minutes, or until the cake springs back when it is pressed lightly in the center.

A few minutes after removing the cake from the oven, loosen it from the sides of the pan and turn out on a rack to cool.

Carrot cake improves in flavor and texture if aged a day or two.

Dundee Cake
PREPARATION TIME: *20 minutes*
COOKING TIME: *3½ hours*

INGREDIENTS:
2 cups all-purpose flour
Pinch of salt
½ pound butter or margarine
1 cup sugar
4 large eggs
2 cups white raisins
2 cups currants
1½ cups chopped mixed peel
⅔ cup small candied cherries
Grated rind of ½ lemon
⅓–½ cup whole almonds

Butter an 8-inch round cake pan and line it with brown paper. Tie a band of paper tightly around the outside of the pan and let it extend about 2 inches above the rim. Set the pan on a double piece of brown paper on a baking sheet.

Sift together the flour and salt. Beat the butter until soft, then beat

BLANCHING ALMONDS

Slide off softened skins.

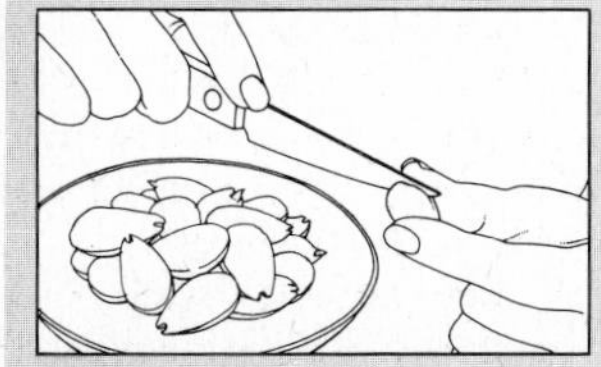

Split almonds in half.

in the sugar; cream the mixture until light and fluffy. Beat in the eggs, a little at a time. Fold in the flour and, when evenly combined, fold in the raisins, currants, peel, cherries, and lemon rind. Blanch* the almonds, slip off the skins, and measure and chop about 3 tablespoons of almonds. Add to the cake mixture and spoon this into the pan.

Split the rest of the almonds lengthwise and arrange them, rounded side up, over the leveled cake surface. Bake just below the center of a preheated oven at 300°F for about 3½ hours. If the cake shows signs of browning too quickly, cover the top with a sheet of damp waxed paper and reduce the heat to 275°F for the last hour. Remove the cake from the oven when a skewer comes away clean from the cake.

Cool in the pan for 30 minutes, then turn out and cool on a wire rack. Wrap the cake in foil, with the lining paper in position. The cake is best kept for at least 1 week and may be kept up to 1 month to bring out the full flavor.

See illustration on page 371.

Orange Butterflies
PREPARATION TIME: *15 minutes*
COOKING TIME: *10 minutes*

INGREDIENTS (*for 12 cakes*):
6 tablespoons butter or margarine
6 tablespoons sugar
1 large egg, beaten
1¼ cups self-rising flour
Pinch of salt
1 teaspoon grated orange rind
1 tablespoon orange juice
Orange-flavored butter cream
Confectioners' sugar

Butter 12 muffin or cupcake pans. Beat the butter until soft, then add the sugar; cream until light and fluffy. Add the beaten egg. Sift the flour and salt, add the orange rind, and fold this into the creamed mixture alternately with the orange juice. Using a teaspoon, fill the pans to half their depth. Bake just above

the center of a preheated oven at 400°F for 10–15 minutes or until well risen and golden. Cool the cupcakes on a wire rack.

Cut a slice from the top of each cupcake and pipe or spoon in a little butter cream. Cut each top slice in half and insert these in the butter cream to resemble the wings of butterflies. Dust with sifted confectioners' sugar and serve.

Coffee Walnut Cake
PREPARATION TIME: *20 minutes*
COOKING TIME: *35–40 minutes*

INGREDIENTS:
½ cup (¼ pound) soft margarine
½ cup sugar
2 large eggs
⅓ cup chopped walnuts
1 tablespoon coffee extract
1 cup self-rising flour
Pinch of salt
1 tablespoon baking powder
FILLING:
⅓ cup soft margarine
1 cup confectioners' sugar
2 teaspoons milk
2 teaspoons coffee extract
Walnut halves

Butter 2 7-inch straight-sided layer cake pans and line the bottoms with buttered waxed paper. Put the margarine, sugar, eggs, chopped walnuts, and coffee extract in a bowl. Sift in the flour with the salt and baking powder. Beat these ingredients with a wooden spoon for 2–3 minutes or until well combined. Divide the mixture between the prepared pans, level the surface, and bake in the center of a preheated oven at 325°F for 35–40 minutes, or until the cakes are well risen and spongy to the touch.

When baked, turn the cakes out on a wire rack to cool before removing the lining paper.

Meanwhile, make the filling: Beat the margarine, sifted confectioners' sugar, milk, and coffee extract in a bowl until smooth. Sandwich the cakes together with two-thirds of the

filling, top with the remaining filling, and mark the surface with the prongs of a fork in a decorative pattern. Place the walnut halves on top of the cake.

Farmhouse Fruitcake
PREPARATION TIME: *10 minutes*
COOKING TIME: *about 1½ hours*

INGREDIENTS:
¾ cup soft margarine
¾ cup sugar
½ cup white raisins
½ cup seedless dark raisins
½ cup candied cherries, chopped
3 cups self-rising flour
Pinch of salt
1 teaspoon mixed spice
3 tablespoons milk
3 eggs

Butter an 8-inch round cake pan and line with buttered waxed paper. Mix the margarine and all the dry ingredients in a bowl, then add the milk and eggs and beat with a wooden spoon until well mixed, about 2–3 minutes. Turn into the prepared pan and level the top.

Bake in the center of a preheated oven at 350°F for about 1½ hours. When a warm skewer comes away clean, the cake is cooked. Leave the cake in the pan for 15 minutes before turning out onto a wire rack to cool.

Swiss Tarts
PREPARATION TIME: *25 minutes*
COOKING TIME: *20 minutes*

INGREDIENTS (*for 6 cakes*):
¼ pound butter
2 tablespoons sugar
Vanilla extract
1 cup all-purpose flour
Confectioners' sugar
Red currant jelly

Place 6 paper muffin cups in a muffin tin and set on a baking sheet. Beat the butter until soft, then add the sugar; cream until light and fluffy. Beat in a few drops of vanilla and gradually add the flour, beating the mixture well between each addition.

Put the mixture in a pastry bag fitted with a large star tube. Pipe the mixture into the muffin cups, starting at the center and piping with a spiral motion around the sides, leaving a shallow depression in the center. Bake in the center of a preheated oven at 350°F for about 20 minutes or until set and tinged with color.

Leave the cakes in their muffin cups to cool on a wire rack. Dredge with confectioners' sugar and top each tart with red currant jelly.

See illustration on page 370.

Coconut Castles
PREPARATION TIME: *20 minutes*
COOKING TIME: *20 minutes*

INGREDIENTS (*for 6–8 small cakes*):
¼ pound butter or margarine
½ cup sugar
2 eggs, beaten
1 cup self-rising flour
Pinch of salt
4 tablespoons red jam or jelly
1 tablespoon water
⅔ cup shredded coconut
6 candied cherries
Angelica

Butter 6 dariole molds.* Beat the butter until soft, add the sugar, and cream until light and fluffy. Beat in the beaten eggs. Gradually fold in the sifted flour and salt. Divide the mixture evenly between the molds, filling them no more than two-thirds full. Set on a baking sheet and bake in the center of a preheated oven at 350°F for 20 minutes or until golden. Cool on a wire rack.

When the castles are cold, bring the jam and water to a boil and cook for 1 minute. Level the wide base of the castles if necessary, brush them all over with the jam, and roll in coconut. Garnish with a cherry and angelica leaves.

See illustration on page 371.

WHISKED CAKES

These are the lightest of all cake mixtures, their texture depending entirely on the incorporated eggs. The fatless cake mixture is used for sponge cakes, which should be baked as soon as they are mixed.

Use a hand-operated rotary beater or balloon whisk; to stabilize the mixture, place the deep bowl of eggs and sugar over hot, not boiling, water. Do not let the mixture become too hot or the sponge will have a tough texture. For a maximum rise, the mixture should be thick enough to leave a trail when the whisk is lifted. If an electric mixer is used, there is no need to heat the bowl.

Blending in the flour is another important step. Sift the flour two or three times, the last time over the whisked egg mixture. Then fold it carefully into the mixture without flattening the bulk. Use a metal spoon or rubber spatula in a figure-of-eight movement.

Strawberry Cream Sponge Cake
PREPARATION TIME: 20 minutes
COOKING TIME: 15 minutes

INGREDIENTS:
¾ cup all-purpose flour
Pinch of salt
3 eggs
⅓ cup sugar
Strawberry jam
½ cup heavy cream
Confectioners' sugar for dusting

Butter and dust with the flour and sugar 2 7-inch-diameter straight-sided cake pans. Sift the flour with the salt twice into a bowl or onto a sheet of waxed paper. Place a deep mixing bowl over a pan of hot water, break the eggs into the bowl, and gradually whisk in the sugar. Continue whisking until the mixture is pale, and thick enough so that when some of it falls from the whisk back into the bowl, it forms a dissolving ribbon over the surface of the mix-

ture. Carefully fold in the sifted flour and salt. Divide the mixture equally between the two pans, putting any scrapings from the bowl at the side of the pans, not in the middle. Bake just above the center of a preheated oven at 375°F for about 15 minutes, or until cakes are pale brown and springy to the touch.

Carefully ease away the edges of the baked cakes with a metal spatula and cool them on a wire rack.

When cold, spread the top of each layer with a thin coating of jam. Cover one layer with whipped cream and place the other, jam side downward, on top. Press lightly together and dust with sifted confectioners' sugar. Keep the cake in the refrigerator until ready to serve.

Jelly Roll
PREPARATION TIME: 15 minutes
COOKING TIME: 10 minutes

INGREDIENTS:
¾ cup all-purpose flour
Pinch of salt
3 large eggs
⅓ cup sugar
1 tablespoon hot water
Jam or cream filling

Sift the flour and salt twice into a bowl or onto waxed paper. Butter a jelly-roll pan measuring 12 inches by 8 inches and line the bottom of the pan with buttered waxed paper or cooking parchment.

Put the eggs and sugar in a large bowl over a pan of hot water and whisk until the mixture is pale and leaves a thick ribbon. Remove from the heat, sift half the flour and salt over the egg mixture, and fold it in carefully, using a rubber spatula. Repeat with the remaining flour and add the hot water. Turn the mixture quickly into the prepared pan, tilting it until evenly covered with the mixture. Bake at once just above the center of a preheated oven at 425°F for about 10 minutes or until the cake is well risen, golden, and springy to the touch.

MAKING A JELLY ROLL

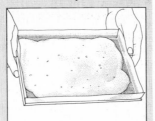

Tilt pan to spread mixture evenly.

Remove lining paper from cake.

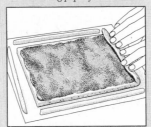

Spread warm jam over cake.

Roll up cake on sugared paper.

Rolling cake for cream filling.

Have ready a sheet of sugar-dredged waxed paper. Turn the soft cake out onto the paper at once, remove the lining paper, and quickly trim off the crisp edges from the cake with a sharp knife. Spread with 4–5 tablespoons of warm jam to within ½ inch of the edges. Roll up the cake at once from the short side, making the first turn firm, then rolling it lightly. Cool on a wire rack covered with a clean dish towel, with the seam of the cake underneath.

The roll may also be spread with a butter-cream filling just before serving. In this case, do not remove the lining paper but roll the cake around it while still warm. When cold, carefully unroll the cake, then spread with whipped cream, butter cream (p.393), or pastry cream (p.395) and roll up again.

Before serving, dust with sifted confectioners' sugar.

See illustration on page 370.

ENRICHED BUTTER SPONGE CAKES

When butter is added to a whisked sponge mixture, it is known as a génoise, a richer variety than other sponges and one that needs slightly longer baking but keeps better. Génoise mixtures are used for gâteaux, layered with cream and fruit, or baked and cut into small individual cakes before being iced and decorated.

Génoise
PREPARATION TIME: 15 minutes
COOKING TIME: 30 minutes

INGREDIENTS:
3 tablespoons unsalted butter
½ cup plus 2 tablespoons all-purpose flour
1 tablespoon cornstarch
3 large eggs
⅓ cup sugar

Butter a 9-inch straight-sided layer cake pan, a deep 8-inch cake pan, or a

7-inch square pan, and line with buttered waxed paper. Heat the butter in a pan over low heat until melted but not hot; remove from the heat and let stand for a few minutes. Sift together the flour and cornstarch three times. Put the eggs in a large deep bowl over a pan of hot water, whisk for a few seconds, then add the sugar and continue whisking until the mixture is quite pale and leaves a thick trail when the whisk is lifted out of the bowl.

Remove the bowl from the heat and whisk for a few minutes longer until the mixture is cool. Using a rubber spatula, carefully fold in half the sifted flour, then pour in the melted butter in a thin stream at the side of the bowl. Fold in the remaining sifted flour. Turn this mixture into the prepared pan and bake near the top of a preheated oven at 375°F for about 30 minutes or until well risen and spongy to the touch. Invert onto a wire rack and leave to cool; remove lining paper.

The génoise, if baked in a deep pan, can be split horizontally into 3 equal layers and sandwiched together with a cream and fruit or butter cream filling (p.393), and the top can be decorated with cream. A shallower cake should be split into 2 layers only and sandwiched together as already described.

A cake baked in a large shallow pan can be cut into fancy individual shapes. Brush these with warm apricot glaze (p.394) and cover with plain or colored confectioners' frosting or fondant icing. Decorate with candied cherries, crystallized violets and roses, silver shot,* or blanched pistachio nuts.

See illustration on page 371.

Iced Petits Fours

PREPARATION TIME: *1¼ hours*
COOKING TIME: *30 minutes*

INGREDIENTS (*for 24–30 cakes*):
3 large eggs
⅓ cup sugar
½ cup plus 2 tablespoons all-purpose flour
1 tablespoon cornstarch
3 tablespoons unsalted butter
Apricot glaze (p.394)
1 pound (1¾ cups) uncooked almond paste (p.395)
Confectioners' frosting from 4 cups confectioners' sugar (p.394)
Food colorings
Flavorings (optional)
Decorations

Butter and line the bottom of a rectangular pan 1 inch deep by 10 inches by 6 inches. Prepare the eggs, sugar, flours, cornstarch, and butter as described for génoise. Turn the mixture into the pan, leveling the top evenly, and bake just above the center of a preheated oven at 375°F for about 30 minutes. Turn out to cool on a covered wire rack and remove the lining paper.

On a flat surface, cut the cake into 24–30 small shapes, such as squares, diamonds, rounds, and crescents. Brush the petits fours with warm apricot glaze and roll out the almond paste thinly. Cut the paste into the same shapes as the petits fours and lay the pieces over the brushed cakes.

Make up the confectioners' frosting into a coating consistency; divide it into 4 portions and color 3 of these green, pink, or lemon. Flavoring may be added to match each color. Set the petits fours on a wire tray over a plate and carefully spoon the frosting over the cakes, using a teaspoon and letting the frosting run down the sides. When the frosting is nearly set, decorate the cakes with, for example, candied cherries, angelica, silver shot,* nuts, or crystallized violets and rose petals.

When dry and set, serve the petits fours in small paper muffin cups.

ICED PETITS FOURS

Stamp out small fancy shapes.

Brush with apricot glaze.

Top with thin almond paste.

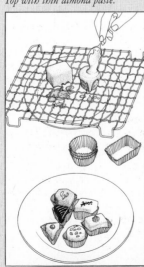

Cover with frosting and decorate.

Almond Petits Fours

PREPARATION TIME: *20 minutes*
COOKING TIME: *20 minutes*

INGREDIENTS (*for 24–30 cakes*):
2 egg whites
⅔ cup ground almonds
¼ cup sugar
Almond extract
Candied cherries
Angelica

Line 2 or 3 baking sheets with cooking parchment. Beat the egg whites in a deep bowl until stiff; lightly fold in the almonds and sugar and add a few drops of almond extract.

Spoon the mixture into a pastry bag fitted with a large rosette tube and pipe it onto the baking sheets in small rosettes and S shapes, leaving about an inch between each. Decorate the petits fours with candied cherries, strips of angelica, silver shot, nuts, or candied violets.

Bake in the center of a preheated oven at 350°F for about 20 minutes or until golden brown.

See illustration on page 373.

ALMOND PETITS FOURS

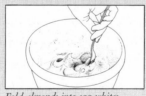

Fold almonds into egg whites.

Pipe out rosettes and S shapes.

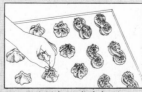

Decorate with candied cherries.

MELTED CAKES

These cakes have a dense, slightly sticky texture and a consistency similar to a thick batter. Molasses or syrup is a major ingredient, and baking powder is used as the main leavening agent.

Gingerbread

PREPARATION TIME: *15 minutes*
COOKING TIME: *1½ hours*

INGREDIENTS:
4 cups all-purpose flour
3 teaspoons ground ginger
3 teaspoons baking powder
1 teaspoon baking soda
1 teaspoon salt
1¼ cups light brown sugar
1½ sticks (12 tablespoons) butter
½ cup molasses
½ cup light corn syrup
1¼ cups milk
1 large egg

Butter a 9-inch square cake pan about 2 inches deep and line it with buttered waxed paper. Sift all the dry ingredients except the sugar into a large bowl. Warm the sugar, butter, molasses, and syrup in a pan over low heat until the butter has just melted. Stir the melted ingredients into the center of the dry mix, together with the milk and beaten egg. Beat thoroughly with a wooden spoon. Pour the mixture into the prepared pan and bake in the center of a preheated oven at 350°F for about 1½ hours or until well risen and just firm to the touch. Leave to cool in the pan for 15 minutes, then turn out to cool on a wire rack. When the gingerbread is cold, wrap in foil without removing the lining paper.

Store gingerbread for 4–7 days before cutting into chunks, to give the flavor time to mellow.

Gingerbread is delicious plain, buttered, or served with a variety of toppings: sweetened whipped cream, hard sauce (p.339), sliced peaches, applesauce, or apple butter.

See illustration on page 371.

Parkin

PREPARATION TIME: *20 minutes*
COOKING TIME: *45 minutes*

INGREDIENTS:
2 cups all-purpose flour
Pinch of salt
2 teaspoons baking powder
2 teaspoons ground ginger
4 tablespoons margarine or butter
4 tablespoons lard
1½ cups oatmeal
½ cup sugar
½ cup light corn syrup
½ cup molasses
4 tablespoons milk

Butter a pan 1½ inches deep by 10 inches by 8 inches and line it with buttered waxed paper. Sift together the flour, salt, baking powder, and ginger into a bowl. Cut the margarine and lard into small pieces and rub into the flour until the mixture resembles fine bread crumbs. Stir in the oatmeal and sugar. Warm the syrup and molasses, pour it into the center of the dry ingredients, together with the milk, and beat lightly with a wooden spoon until thoroughly blended.

Turn the mixture into the prepared pan and bake in the center of a preheated oven at 350°F for about 45 minutes or until the mixture has begun to shrink away from the sides of the pan. It often sinks slightly. Cool on a wire rack. Leave the lining paper in place, wrap the cake in foil, and store for at least a week.

Serve parkin cut into thick slices.

Cookies

Bake cookies at or just above the center of the oven; if two cookie sheets are used, place them above each other in the oven, and halfway through baking switch them over so that all the cookies brown evenly. Cool the baked cookies on a wire rack, lifting them from the sheets as soon as cooked. Some cookies, however, especially those made with syrup or honey, are soft when baking is completed. Leave these on the sheets to settle for a few minutes.

Generally, cookies fall into one of half a dozen main groups: bar types, drop cookies, shaped cookies, piped cookies, refrigerator cookies, and rolled cookies.

SHAPED COOKIES

The dough for shaped cookies is fairly soft and needs quick and light handling. Alternatively, it can be chilled in the refrigerator until stiff, then shaped with the hands.

Ginger Nuts

PREPARATION TIME: *15 minutes*
COOKING TIME: *15 minutes*

INGREDIENTS (*for 24 cookies*):
1 cup self-rising flour
½ teaspoon baking soda
1 teaspoon ground ginger
½ teaspoon ground cinnamon
2 teaspoons sugar
4 tablespoons butter
3 cups light corn syrup

Butter 2 or 3 cookie sheets. Sift the flour, baking soda, ginger, and cinnamon into a bowl; add the sugar. In a small pan, melt the butter without boiling and stir in the syrup. Mix this into the dry ingredients, using a wooden spoon. Shape the dough between the hands into a thick sausage shape before cutting it into 24 even pieces. Roll each piece into a small ball; set the balls well apart on the cookie sheets and flatten slightly.

Bake just above the center of a preheated oven at 375°F for about 15 minutes, or until the tops have cracked and are golden brown. Cool for a few minutes on the sheet before lifting onto a wire rack. Store ginger nuts in an airtight container, as they quickly go soft.

Jumbles

PREPARATION TIME: *40 minutes*
COOKING TIME: *12–15 minutes*

INGREDIENTS (*for 10–15 cookies*):
5 tablespoons butter
5 tablespoons sugar
Half a beaten egg
1¼ cups self-rising flour
1 teaspoon finely grated lemon rind
3 tablespoons ground almonds

Butter 2 cookie sheets. Cream the butter with a wooden spoon until soft but not oily, then add the sugar and continue beating until light and fluffy. Beat in the egg and add the sifted flour, lemon rind, and almonds. Form the mixture into 3 rolls ½–¾ inch wide; cut these into 4-inch-long pieces and form them into S shapes.

Place on the cookie sheets and bake in the center of a preheated oven at 400°F for about 12 minutes, or until the cookies have risen and have turned pale brown. Cool them for a few minutes, then transfer to a wire rack until they have cooled completely. Serve fresh.

See illustration on page 372.

Orange Creams

PREPARATION TIME: *30 minutes*
COOKING TIME: *20 minutes*

INGREDIENTS (*for 18 cookies*):
¼ pound butter
6–8 tablespoons sugar
2 teaspoons light corn syrup
1 egg yolk
Finely grated rind of 1 orange
2¼ cups all-purpose flour
½ teaspoon cream of tartar
1 teaspoon baking powder
FILLING:
4 tablespoons butter
¾ cup confectioners' sugar
Orange juice
Food coloring

Butter 2 or 3 cookie sheets. Using a wooden spoon, cream the butter and sugar until light and fluffy. Beat in the syrup, egg yolk, and orange rind. Sift the flour, cream of tartar, and baking powder over the creamed ingredients and fold in with a rubber spatula to make a soft dough.

Shape the dough into 36 balls about the size of large marbles and set them well apart on the cookie sheets. Bake just above the center of a preheated oven at 375°F for about 20 minutes or until lightly colored and risen. Cool on a wire rack.

For the filling, beat the butter until soft, then gradually beat in the sifted confectioners' sugar with as much orange juice as the filling will take without becoming too soft. Color it pale orange with food coloring. Spread the filling over half the cookies and sandwich them together.

See illustration on page 372.

DROP COOKIES

Baked drop cookies can be soft, with a cakelike texture, or crisp, even brittle. The soft dough is dropped in mounds onto a cookie sheet. If the dough is stiff, one teaspoon can be used to hold the dough, another to scrape the dough from the spoon onto the sheet.

Brandy Snaps

PREPARATION TIME: *15 minutes*
COOKING TIME: *20–30 minutes*

INGREDIENTS (*for 16 cookies*):
4 tablespoons butter
4 tablespoons sugar
2 tablespoons light corn syrup
½ cup all-purpose flour
½ teaspoon ground ginger
1 teaspoon brandy
Finely grated rind of ½ lemon
FILLING:
¾ cup heavy cream
1 tablespoon milk

Butter or line 2 cookie sheets with cooking parchment and butter the handles of a few wooden spoons thoroughly. Melt the butter, sugar, and syrup over low heat. Stir until smooth, then remove.

Sift the flour and ginger, and stir

BRANDY SNAPS

Roll snap around spoon handle.

Remove shaped brandy snap.

Pipe cream into brandy snaps.

it into the melted ingredients. Add the brandy and lemon rind. Mix with a wooden spoon; let cool.

Drop the mixture by teaspoons at 4-inch intervals onto the cookie sheets. Bake near the top of a preheated oven at 350°F for 7–10 minutes, or until the cookies are bubbly, lacy in texture, and golden brown.

Remove the cookies from the oven and quickly roll each snap loosely around a buttered spoon handle, easing them around with a metal spatula. Leave the snaps on the handles until set, then twist them gently off and cool on a wire rack. If the cookies set before they have all been shaped into snaps, return them to the oven for a few minutes until soft and pliable again.

Just before serving, beat together the cream and milk until stiff. Pipe* or spoon the whipped cream into both ends of each snap.

See illustration on page 372.

Tollhouse Cookies

PREPARATION TIME: *15 minutes*
COOKING TIME: *10–12 minutes*

INGREDIENTS (*for 50 cookies*):
1 cup plus 2 tablespoons all-purpose flour, sifted
½ teaspoon baking soda
½ teaspoon salt
½ cup softened butter
¼ cup sugar
½ cup brown sugar, firmly packed
½ teaspoon vanilla extract
¼ teaspoon water
1 egg
1 cup chocolate chips
½ cup chopped pecans

Sift together the flour, baking soda, and salt. In another bowl, combine the butter, sugar, brown sugar, vanilla, and water; beat until creamy. Beat in the egg, add the flour mixture, and blend. Stir in the chocolate chips and nuts.

Drop dough in well-rounded half-teaspoonfuls onto buttered cookie sheets and bake in a 375°F oven for 10–12 minutes.

Coconut Wafers

PREPARATION TIME: *20 minutes*
COOKING TIME: *12 minutes*

INGREDIENTS (*for 18 cookies*):
4 tablespoons butter
4 tablespoons sugar
1 tablespoon light corn syrup
2 teaspoons lemon juice
½ cup all-purpose flour, sifted
⅓ cup fine grated coconut

Butter 2 or 3 cookie sheets. Cream the butter and sugar until light and fluffy, then beat in the syrup. Add the lemon juice, sifted flour, and grated coconut. Drop the dough by teaspoons onto the sheets, setting them well apart because the wafers spread.

Bake just below the center of a preheated oven at 350°F for about 12 minutes; the edges of the wafers should be golden brown and the centers lightly colored. Remove wafers from oven and let them cool slightly before lifting carefully from the sheets onto a wire rack.

See illustration on page 372.

Ginger Drops

PREPARATION TIME: *10 minutes*
COOKING TIME: *15 minutes*

INGREDIENTS (*for 18 cookies*):
1 cup all-purpose flour
½ teaspoon baking soda
1 tablespoon ground ginger
4 teaspoons light corn syrup
4 tablespoons butter or margarine
⅓ cup light brown sugar
¼ cup chopped preserved ginger
2 tablespoons milk

Butter 2 cookie sheets. Sift together the flour, baking soda, and ground ginger. Warm the syrup in a small pan. Cream the butter and sugar until light and fluffy, then stir in the syrup and preserved ginger, half the sifted flour, and 1 tablespoon of the milk. Add the remaining flour and milk and mix ingredients together until they form a soft dough. Drop the mixture in teaspoons, easing it off with the finger onto the cookie

sheets. Set the cookies well apart.

Bake just above the center of a preheated oven at 350°F for about 15 minutes. Cool on a wire rack.

See illustration on page 372.

PIPED COOKIES

The dough for piped cookies is fairly soft and should be piped through a medium-size pastry bag, which is often fitted with a star-shaped tube.

Lemon Meltaways

PREPARATION TIME: *20 minutes*
RESTING TIME: *30 minutes*
COOKING TIME: *30 minutes*

INGREDIENTS (*for about 20 cookies*):
¼ pound butter
¼ cup confectioners' sugar
Finely grated rind of ½ lemon
1 cup all-purpose flour
Sieved apricot jam
GLAZE:
2 tablespoons confectioners' sugar
About 2 teaspoons lemon juice

Butter 2 cookie sheets. In a deep bowl, beat the butter with a wooden spoon until creamy, add the sifted confectioners' sugar, and continue beating until the mixture is pale and fluffy. Stir in the lemon rind and flour to give a soft dough. Spoon the mixture into a pastry bag fitted with a medium star pastry tube, and pipe* out about 20 shell shapes, a little apart from each other. Chill for 30 minutes in the refrigerator.

Bake in the center of a preheated oven at 325°F for about 25 minutes or until lightly browned. For the glaze, blend the sifted confectioners' sugar with enough lemon juice to give a coating consistency.

Leave the baked cookies on the sheets; brush them with sieved jam and then with the lemon glaze. Return the cookies to the oven for a further 5 minutes, then set them on a wire rack to cool and crisp.

See illustration on page 372.

Short Fingers

PREPARATION TIME: *45 minutes*
COOKING TIME: *10–15 minutes*

INGREDIENTS (*for 10–12 cookies*):
9 tablespoons butter
¼ cup confectioners' sugar
1¼ cups all-purpose flour
3 ounces semisweet cooking chocolate
BUTTER CREAM:
2 tablespoons butter
½ cup confectioners' sugar
Vanilla extract

Butter 2 cookie sheets. Cream the butter with a wooden spoon until soft but not oily, then beat in the sifted confectioners' sugar. Stir in the sifted flour. Put the mixture in a pastry bag fitted with a medium star tube and pipe it in 2-inch-long fingers onto the cookie sheets. Bake just above or in the center of a preheated oven at 375°F for 10–15 minutes or until pale golden brown.

Meanwhile, melt the chocolate squares in a bowl over hot water. To make the butter cream, cream the butter until soft, then beat in the sifted confectioners' sugar and a few drops of vanilla extract.

Leave the baked cookies to cool completely on a wire rack. When cold, sandwich them in pairs with the butter cream. Dip one end of each cookie in the melted chocolate and place the cookie on a rack with the chocolate end protruding over the edge. When the chocolate has set, repeat the procedure with the other end. Let the cookies stand for about 1½ hours before serving.

See illustration on page 372.

SHORT FINGERS

Pipe out 2-inch-long fingers.

Sandwich with butter cream.

Coat tips of cookies in chocolate.

Macaroons

PREPARATION TIME: *10 minutes*
COOKING TIME: *15 minutes*

INGREDIENTS (*for 24 cookies*):
¾ cup ground almonds
¾ cup sugar
2 egg whites
1 tablespoon cornstarch
¼ teaspoon vanilla extract
12 blanched almonds

Line 2 or 3 cookie sheets with cooking parchment. Mix the ground almonds with the sugar and add the unbeaten egg whites, setting 1 tablespoon aside. Using a wooden spoon, work the mixture until the ingredients are evenly blended. Stir in the cornstarch, vanilla extract, and 2 teaspoons of water. Spoon the mixture into a pastry bag fitted with a ½-inch plain tube. Pipe the cookies onto the cooking parchment in large round buttons; top each with half an almond. Brush lightly with the remaining egg white.

Bake the macaroons just above or on the center shelf of a preheated oven at 375°F for about 15 minutes or until lightly browned, risen, and slightly cracked. Remove from the sheets and leave the cookies to cool completely on a wire rack. Serve the same day.

See illustration on page 372.

BAR-TYPE COOKIES

With the exception of shortbread, bar-type cookies have a cakelike texture and are baked in one complete piece before being cut up.

Boston Brownies

PREPARATION TIME: *15 minutes*
COOKING TIME: *35 minutes*

INGREDIENTS (*for 16–20 cookies*):
5 tablespoons butter
2 ounces semisweet chocolate
¾ cup sugar
½ cup plus 2 tablespoons self-rising flour
Pinch of salt
2 eggs
½ teaspoon vanilla extract
½ cup shelled walnuts

Butter and flour a shallow 8-inch square pan. Melt the butter and chocolate in a bowl over hot water; add the sugar. Sift the flour and salt into a bowl and stir in the chocolate mixture, beaten eggs, vanilla extract, and chopped walnuts. Beat the mixture until smooth, then spoon it into the prepared pan.

Bake in the center of a preheated oven at 350°F for about 35 minutes, or until the mixture is risen and beginning to leave the sides of the pan. Leave in the pan for a few minutes to cool slightly before cutting the cake into 1½–2 inch squares.

See illustration on page 372.

Shortbread

PREPARATION TIME: *20 minutes*
CHILLING TIME: *1 hour*
COOKING TIME: *1 hour*

INGREDIENTS (*for 8 cookies*):
1¼ cups all-purpose flour
Pinch of salt
¼ cup rice flour
¼ cup sugar
¼ pound butter

Sift the flour, salt, and rice flour into a bowl. Add the sugar and grate the butter, taken straight from the refrigerator, into the dry ingredients. Work the mixture with the fingertips until it resembles bread crumbs. Press the mixture into a 7-inch straight-sided layer cake pan and level off the top. Prick the top all over with a fork and mark the mixture into 8 equal portions, cutting through to the bottom of the pan.

Chill the shortbread in the refrigerator for 1 hour, then bake in the center of a preheated oven at 300°F for about 1 hour or until it is pale yellow. Cool in the pan, then on a wire rack. Break into wedges.

See illustration on page 372.

Spiced Currant Bars

PREPARATION TIME: *25 minutes*
CHILLING TIME: *1 hour*
COOKING TIME: *30 minutes*

INGREDIENTS (*for 16 cookies*):
2 cups all-purpose flour
Pinch of salt
2 teaspoons baking powder
2 teaspoons mixed spices (½ teaspoon
*   each, ground nutmeg, cinnamon,*
*   cloves, ginger)*
¼ pound butter
10 tablespoons sugar
1 tablespoon light corn syrup
1 large egg, beaten
1 cup black currant jam
¾ cup shelled walnuts

Sift together the flour, salt, baking powder, and spices. Cream the butter with the sugar until light and fluffy, then beat in the syrup and beaten egg. Fold in the flour and mix the ingredients thoroughly to a manageable dough. Wrap in foil and chill until firm, about 1 hour.

Butter and line 2 shallow 12-by-4-inch cake pans. Coarsely grate or flake half the chilled dough into the pans and press the top down lightly. Spread the jam over the dough, then grate the remaining dough over the jam and top with the chopped walnuts. Bake just above the center of a preheated oven at 350°F for about 30 minutes. Leave to cool in the pans. Cut into bars about 1½ inches wide.

SHORTBREAD

Grate butter into flour.

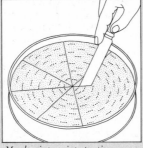

Mark mixture into portions.

SPICED CURRANT BARS

Spread jam over grated dough.

Grate remaining dough over jam.

Pecan Bars

PREPARATION TIME: *10 minutes*
COOKING TIME: *25 minutes*

INGREDIENTS (*for 12 cookies*):
⅔ cup all-purpose flour
1 teaspoon baking powder
⅛ teaspoon salt
¼ cup butter
¾ cup brown sugar, firmly packed
1 egg
1 teaspoon vanilla extract
½ cup chopped pecans

Sift together the flour, baking powder, and salt. Cream the butter with the brown sugar, then beat in the egg and vanilla. Stir in the sifted dry ingredients and the pecans. Spread evenly in a buttered 6-by-9-inch pan and bake in a 350°F oven for 25 minutes. Cool and cut into bars.

ROLLED COOKIES

For rolled cookies the dough must be stiff enough to be rolled to a thickness of ⅛–¼ inch before it is cut into a variety of shapes. Dough that is sticky and difficult to handle is best rolled out between two sheets of waxed paper.

Butter Shorts

PREPARATION TIME: *30 minutes*
COOKING TIME: *25 minutes*

INGREDIENTS (*for 16 cookies*):
¼ pound butter
¼ cup sugar
1½ cups all-purpose flour
Superfine sugar for dredging

Butter 2 cookie sheets. Cream the butter with a wooden spoon until soft but not oily, add the sugar, and beat until pale and fluffy. Work in the sifted flour and knead lightly together with the fingertips to form a ball. Roll this out ⅛ inch thick on a lightly floured surface or between sheets of waxed paper.

Using a 2½–2¾ inch fluted pastry cutter, stamp out rounds and lift them onto the cookie sheets with a

small metal spatula. Prick each cookie twice with a fork and bake just above or on the center shelf of a preheated oven at 300°F until cookies are faintly tinged with brown. Cool on a wire rack and serve the cookies dredged with superfine sugar. These butter shorts will keep fresh in a tightly covered container for about 10 days.

Easter Cookies

PREPARATION TIME: *35 minutes*
COOKING TIME: *15–20 minutes*

INGREDIENTS (*for 24 cookies*):
¼ pound butter
½ cup plus 2 tablespoons sugar
1 egg plus 1 egg yolk
⅓ cup currants
1½ cups all-purpose flour
½ cup rice flour
1 teaspoon mixed spices (equal
*   quantities of ground nutmeg,*
*   cinnamon, cloves, ginger)*
1–2 tablespoons milk

Line 2 or 3 cookie sheets with cooking parchment or buttered waxed paper. Cream the butter with a wooden spoon until soft, add ½ cup of the sugar, and beat thoroughly until pale and fluffy. Separate the egg and beat in the two egg yolks, then stir in the currants. Sift both flours, together with the spices, into the creamed ingredients, a little at a time. Stir to combine, adding a little milk, if necessary, to bind the mixture.

Knead the dough lightly on a floured board, then roll it out ⅛–¼ inch thick. Cut into rounds with a 2½-inch fluted cutter and set the cookies on the cookie sheets. Mark lines about ¼ inch apart with the back of a knife. Bake just above or on the center shelf of a preheated oven at 350°F for 15–20 minutes. After 10 minutes, brush the cookies with the unbeaten egg white and dredge with the remaining sugar. Let the cookies cool on the cookie sheets for a few minutes, then lift them carefully onto a wire rack.

REFRIGERATOR COOKIES

These are usually round and thin, with a crisp texture. The soft dough is shaped into a long roll, wrapped in waxed paper or aluminum foil, and chilled for at least 2 hours. The roll is then cut into thin slices with a sharp knife and baked on buttered cookie sheets. The dough will keep for about a week in the refrigerator, so cookies can be baked as required.

Refrigerator Cookies

PREPARATION TIME: *20 minutes*
CHILLING TIME: *2 hours*
COOKING TIME: *10 minutes*

INGREDIENTS (*for 48 cookies*):
2 cups all-purpose flour
1 teaspoon baking powder
10 tablespoons butter
¾ cup granulated sugar or light
*   brown sugar*
1 teaspoon vanilla extract
1 egg
2 ounces semisweet chocolate
⅓ cup ground hazelnuts, pecans,
*   or walnuts*
Superfine sugar for dusting

Sift together the flour and baking powder. Beat the butter with a wooden spoon until soft, add the sugar, and continue beating until light and fluffy. Beat in the vanilla extract and the beaten egg. Add the flour and grate the chocolate finely into the mixture. Lastly, add the nuts. Stir just enough to combine. Shape the dough on a lightly floured surface into a sausage about 2 inches wide. Wrap in aluminum foil or waxed paper, secure the ends, and chill in the refrigerator.

To bake, slice off thin cookies from the roll. Set them well apart on a greased cookie sheet. Sprinkle with the superfine sugar and bake in the center of a preheated oven at 375°F for about 10 minutes. Remove the cookies to a wire rack to cool.

See illustration on page 372.

Cake Fillings and Toppings

Fillings and toppings make a cake more attractive, but they also have a more practical use. Cakes that have been filled and iced stay moist longer. There are four basic types of fillings: butter cream, cooked fudge frosting, fluffy cooked frosting, and soft sugar icing. For some of these, a candy thermometer is essential.

Butter cream

This is perhaps the most frequently used filling and topping. The sugar, which may be granulated or confectioners' sugar, or a mixture of both, is added in small amounts to creamed butter, then beaten to a light spreading consistency. Whole eggs, egg whites, or egg yolks may also be added.

Cooked fudge frosting

This needs careful attention, as the soft fudge sets quickly and makes spreading difficult. It is used as a topping rather than a filling. A sugar mixture is cooked to a given temperature, cooled, then beaten until creamy. If the frosting sets too quickly, the bowl can be placed over hot water and a teaspoon or two of warm water or milk can be beaten in.

Fluffy cooked frosting

For this type of frosting, sugar, egg whites, water, and flavorings are beaten over boiling water until the mixture stands in stiff peaks. A similar frosting can be made by cooking a syrup from sugar and water, then beating it slowly into beaten egg whites. Both types of frosting spread and swirl easily, but they develop a thin sugar crust after a few days.

Soft sugar icing

This is an uncooked icing based on confectioners' sugar and a liquid, to which flavoring and coloring are added. All soft icings are easy to use and go well with soft-textured cakes, such as sponge cakes. The icing coats the surface smoothly; it is poured over the cake and left to find its own level. A royal icing, used for wedding and birthday cakes, is a cross between a fluffy cooked frosting and a soft sugar icing.

Using fillings and toppings

Numerous variations are possible with a little flair and imagination, but the basic procedure should always be followed.

Always cool a cake completely before filling and icing it, and brush off any loose crumbs that would stick to the icing.

Cut surfaces, such as those produced when a slab cake is cut up into smaller cakes, are often covered with a thin layer of almond confectioners' frosting or fondant icing.

Do not put a firm-textured frosting or filling on a soft, crumbly surface. For crumbly sponge cakes, use a light cream filling that spreads easily.

Make sure that the top of the cake is completely flat if it is to be iced. The cake can be turned upside down and the underside iced if it is more level than the top.

To sandwich two layers of cake, place one layer, top side down, on a plate or flat surface and spread the filling to the edge. Allow the filling to set for a few minutes, then place

Pipe colored frosting in thin lines.

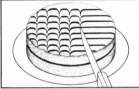

Score across lines with a knife.

Turn cake and score again.

the second layer, top side up, on the filling and lightly press the two layers together.

Before coating a cake with soft icing, put the cake on a wire rack over a plate. Pour the icing over the center of the plain or filled cake and gradually work the icing over the top and down the sides of the cake with a metal spatula.

For a professional touch, spread the icing evenly around the sides of the cake before rolling it in chopped nuts or chocolate shot.* Spread the icing evenly over the top of the cake, then pipe on colored icing in thin lines $\frac{1}{2}$–$\frac{3}{4}$ inch apart, using a pastry bag fitted with a small tube. Before the icing has set, draw lines at right angles over the colored icing with the blunt edge of a knife blade. To complete the pattern, turn the cake 180 degrees and draw the knife between the intersections.

To coat a cake with butter cream, place it on a board and decorate the sides first. Spread the coating evenly

around the sides, using a round-bladed knife, then pile more butter cream on top of the cake. Smooth the cream evenly to the edges with a small metal spatula, then finish the top with a swirled, latticed, or roughed-up pattern, using a fork, knife, or confectioners' comb to achieve the desired effect.

The sides may also be covered with butter cream and then decorated. Cover the sides first, spreading the cream evenly with a spatula. Roll the sides carefully in chocolate sprinkles or shot, or in chopped nuts, then spread butter cream or fondant icing over the top of the cake.

Piped decorations should be applied after the icing has set, but shaped decorations, such as rosebuds, should be applied while the icing is still soft.

To make rosebuds from colored royal icing, fix a small square of waxed paper to an icing nail* with a little of the soft icing. Using a plain or star-shaped small tube fitted to a pastry bag, pipe a center cone onto the paper, then pipe on small petal shapes. Work from right to left and overlap the petals slightly until a rose of the required size is formed. Remove the waxed paper, and when the rosebud has set, place it on the still-soft icing.

ROYAL ICING ROSES

Pipe cone onto waxed paper.

Pipe on overlapping petals.

Butter Cream

PREPARATION TIME: *10 minutes*

INGREDIENTS:
$\frac{1}{4}$ *pound unsalted butter*
1$\frac{1}{2}$–2 cups confectioners' sugar
Vanilla extract (optional)
1–2 tablespoons milk

Beat the softened butter with a wooden spoon or in an electric mixer until creamy. Gradually beat in the sifted confectioners' sugar a spoonful at a time, adding a few drops of vanilla extract, if used, and the milk for a more liquid consistency. This makes enough frosting to coat the sides and top of a 7-inch cake.

To this basic butter cream, a number of different flavors can be added for variety:

Almond: Add 2 tablespoons finely chopped, toasted almonds. Substitute a few drops of almond extract for the vanilla extract.

Chocolate: Add 1–1$\frac{1}{2}$ ounces melted chocolate and omit 1 tablespoon milk. Alternatively, blend 1 tablespoon cocoa with 1 tablespoon hot water. Cool and add to the basic cream, omitting the milk.

Coffee: Omit vanilla extract and milk. Flavor the cream with 2 teaspoons instant coffee blended with 1 teaspoon water.

Ginger: Omit vanilla. Add $\frac{1}{4}$ cup finely chopped preserved ginger.

Lemon: Omit vanilla. Add 1 tablespoon fresh lemon juice and the finely grated rind of 1 lemon.

Liqueur: Omit milk and vanilla. Add 2–3 teaspoons liqueur, such as orange, banana, peppermint, almond, cherry, apricot, blackberry, or pineapple liqueur.

Mocha: Omit vanilla. Mix 2 teaspoons cocoa with 2 teaspoons instant coffee powder to a smooth paste with hot water; cool before adding, and omit milk.

Orange: Omit vanilla and milk. Beat in 2 tablespoons fresh orange juice, the finely grated rind of 1 small orange, and, if desired, 1 teaspoon orange bitters.

Cake Fillings and Toppings

Rich Butter Cream
(Crème au Beurre)
PREPARATION TIME: *20 minutes*

INGREDIENTS:
6 tablespoons sugar
4 tablespoons water
2 egg yolks
4–6 ounces unsalted butter

Put the sugar and water in a heavy-bottomed pan and dissolve over low. heat without boiling. When dissolved, bring the syrup to a boil and boil steadily for 2–3 minutes until a candy thermometer registers 225°F. Beat the egg yolks in a deep bowl and pour in the syrup in a thin, steady stream, beating all the time. Continue to beat until the mixture is thick and cool (the bowl can be placed in ice water). Cream the butter with a wooden spoon. Gradually beat the egg syrup into the butter, a little at a time.

For additional flavor, add 2 ounces semiswect chocolate, melted and cool but still liquid, 1–2 tablespoons coffee extract, or grated orange rind or lemon rind.

Honey-Butter Frosting
PREPARATION TIME: *15 minutes*

INGREDIENTS:
6 tablespoons butter
1½ cups confectioners' sugar
1 tablespoon clear honey
1 tablespoon lemon juice

Beat the butter, which should be at room temperature, until soft but not oily. Gradually sift in the sugar, beating well. Halfway through, beat in the honey and lemon juice.

Caramel Icing
PREPARATION TIME: *20 minutes*

INGREDIENTS:
5 tablespoons half-and-half
6 tablespoons butter
2 tablespoons sugar
3 cups confectioners' sugar

Warm the half-and-half and butter in a small saucepan. In another pan, heat the sugar over medium heat until it turns to a golden caramel. Remove both pans from the heat, pour the half-and-half mixture over the caramel, and return to low heat. Continue heating until the caramel has dissolved, stirring occasionally. Gradually stir in the sifted confectioners' sugar and beat until the icing is smooth and of a spreading consistency. Use fairly soon.

Chocolate Fudge Frosting
PREPARATION TIME: *30 minutes*

INGREDIENTS:
2½ cups granulated sugar
1¼ cups water
2 tablespoons light corn syrup
4 tablespoons unsalted butter
½ cup cocoa

Place all the ingredients in a saucepan and cook, without boiling, until the sugar has dissolved. Bring to a boil and continue boiling over low heat until the candy thermometer registers 238°F.

To prevent sticking, move the thermometer occasionally and draw a wooden spoon across the bottom of the pan, but do not beat. Remove the pan from the heat and let the mixture cool, then beat with a wooden spoon until thick. Coat the cake quickly.

Boiled Frosting
PREPARATION TIME: *30 minutes*

INGREDIENTS:
2 cups sugar
Pinch of cream of tartar
2 egg whites
Vanilla extract (optional)

A candy thermometer is necessary for this frosting; if a thermometer is not available, make the slightly softer seven-minute frosting. Put the sugar and ½ cup of water in a heavy-bottomed pan over low heat and dissolve the sugar without stirring. Blend the cream of tartar with 1 teaspoon of water and add this paste to the syrup. Bring to a boil and continue boiling without stirring until the thermometer registers 240°F (read the thermometer at eye level). Just before this temperature is reached, beat the egg whites in a large bowl until stiff. Remove the syrup from the heat and, when the bubbles subside, pour the hot syrup in a long, thin stream onto the egg whites, beating all the time. Continue beating until the frosting is thick and opaque. Add a few drops of vanilla and spread the frosting quickly over an 8-inch cake.

Seven-Minute Frosting
PREPARATION TIME: *10 minutes*

INGREDIENTS:
1 egg white
¾ cup sugar
Pinch of salt
2 tablespoons water
Pinch of cream of tartar

Put all the ingredients in a deep bowl and, using a rotary or electric hand beater, beat for a few minutes. Place the bowl over a pan of hot water and continue to beat until the mixture is thick enough to stand in peaks, after about 7 minutes. Use at once in the same way as boiled frosting.

Confectioners' Frosting
PREPARATION TIME: *10 minutes*

INGREDIENTS:
1–1½ cups confectioners' sugar
1–2 tablespoons warm water
Food coloring (optional)

Sift the confectioners' sugar into a deep bowl. Add the water, a little at a time, until the mixture is thick enough to coat the back of a wooden spoon. Add a few drops of coloring if required.

A glossier frosting can be obtained by dissolving 2 tablespoons granulated sugar in 4 tablespoons water in a small pan over low heat. Bring to a boil and simmer gently for 5–7 minutes or until the liquid has reduced* by about half. Remove the pan from the heat and cool the pan in cold water until the bottom is lukewarm. Beat in the sifted confectioners' sugar a little at a time. Use at once; the recipe makes enough to cover the top of a 7-inch cake.

The basic frosting may be flavored with, for example, 1 tablespoon of lemon juice to replace 1 tablespoon of the water, or with 1–1½ teaspoons coffee extract as part of the amount of water. Strained orange juice may replace all the water, and a few drops of orange coloring can also be added. Alternatively, blend 2 teaspoons cocoa with 1 tablespoon of the water, or replace 1 tablespoon water with 1 tablespoon liqueur.

Fondant Icing
This traditional icing for petits fours is less brittle than confectioners' frosting. It is practical only when made in large amounts.

PREPARATION TIME: *30 minutes*

INGREDIENTS:
½ cup plus 2 tablespoons water
2 cups sugar
Pinch of cream of tartar or 2 tablespoons glucose

Put the water in a large heavy-bottomed pan, add the sugar, and dissolve to a syrup, without boiling, over low heat. Using a brush dipped in cold water, wipe around the pan at the level of the syrup to prevent crystals from forming. Add the cream of tartar or glucose dissolved in a little water. Bring the syrup to a boil and continue boiling steadily until the syrup registers 240°F (read the thermometer at eye level). Pour the syrup very slowly into a heat-resistant bowl; let stand until a skin forms on top.

Using a wooden spatula, work the icing in a figure-of-eight movement until it becomes opaque and firm. Knead the icing until smooth and store it in an airtight tin until required. Before using, heat the fondant icing in a bowl over hot water, adding a little sugar syrup until the icing has the consistency of heavy cream. Add flavoring and coloring as for confectioners' frosting. Use this icing to cover about 24 petits fours or a 7–8 inch cake.

Royal Icing
PREPARATION TIME: *15 minutes*

INGREDIENTS:
4 egg whites
6–7 cups confectioners' sugar
1 tablespoon lemon juice
2 teaspoons glycerine

Beat the egg whites in a large bowl until frothy. Stir in the sifted confectioners' sugar a little at a time, beating thoroughly with a wooden spoon. When half the sugar has been added, beat in the lemon juice. Continue adding more sugar, beating well after each addition, until the icing forms soft peaks when pulled up with a wooden spoon. For piping purposes the icing should be slightly firmer. Stir in the glycerine, which keeps the icing soft.

Ideally, leave the icing to rest for 24 hours, covered with plastic wrap, and work it through before using. The above amount is enough to coat the top and sides of a 10-inch-wide and 2-inch-deep cake. Let set until firm before decorating.

An electric mixer can be used, but do not overbeat—a fluffy icing results in a rough surface and will break when piped.

Apricot Glaze
PREPARATION TIME: *15 minutes*

INGREDIENTS:
1 pound apricot jam
1 tablespoon lemon juice
4 tablespoons water

Bring all the ingredients slowly to a boil, reduce the heat, and simmer for 5 minutes. Put the mixture through a sieve, return it to the pan, and boil gently for another 5 minutes. Cool the glaze before storing it in a screw-top jar. Use to glaze tarts or to hold almond paste on cakes.

Uncooked Almond Paste

PREPARATION TIME: *10 minutes*

INGREDIENTS:
1 cup confectioners' sugar
½ cup superfine sugar
1⅓ cups ground almonds
1 teaspoon lemon juice
Almond extract
1 egg, beaten

Sift the confectioners' sugar into a bowl and mix in the superfine sugar and almonds. Add the lemon juice and a few drops of almond extract. Gradually stir in the beaten egg, using a wooden spoon or the fingers, until the mixture is a firm but manageable dough. Knead the dough lightly and roll it out.

This quantity makes enough paste to cover a 7-inch cake.

Cooked Almond Paste

This paste resembles marzipan in texture and can be used for making candy as well as for frosting cakes.

PREPARATION TIME: *40 minutes*

INGREDIENTS:
1 pound sugar cubes
½ cup plus 2 tablespoons water
¼ teaspoon cream of tartar
2 cups ground almonds
2 egg whites
½ cup confectioners' sugar
Almond extract (optional)

Dissolve the cube sugar in the water over low heat. Increase the heat and bring the syrup to a boil; stir in the cream of tartar dissolved in a teaspoon of water. Boil until the syrup reaches 240°F (read the candy thermometer at eye level). Remove the pan from the heat and stir rapidly with a wooden spoon until the syrup becomes cloudy. Stir in the ground, almonds and the unbeaten egg whites at once. Return the pan to the heat for a few minutes, stirring the mixture continuously.

Turn the mixture onto a working surface and gradually work in the sifted confectioners' sugar and the almond extract, if desired, with a metal spatula. When cool enough, knead with the fingers until paste has a malleable consistency; add more sugar if needed. Roll out the paste and use to cover a 9-inch cake.

Pastry Cream
(Crème Pâtissière)

PREPARATION TIME: *10 minutes*

INGREDIENTS:
2½ cups milk
½ cup sugar
⅓ cup all-purpose flour
1 tablespoon cornstarch
2 large eggs, beaten
4 tablespoons unsalted butter

Heat the milk in a pan over low heat. In a bowl, blend together the sugar, flour, cornstarch, and beaten eggs; gradually stir in the warm milk. Return the mixture to the pan over low heat and stir continuously until it thickens and just comes to a boil. Remove from the heat and stir in the butter. Cool the cream in the pan; cover the pan closely with waxed paper and a lid to prevent a skin from forming on the surface.

Use the cooled, thick cream on its own or with chopped fruits or nuts between layers of sponge cake.

Coconut Sour Cream Frosting

PREPARATION TIME: *15 minutes*

INGREDIENTS:
2 cups fresh shredded coconut
1 cup sugar
2 cups sour cream

Mix the coconut thoroughly with the remaining ingredients. Cover and refrigerate overnight.

The next day, cut a 2-layer white or yellow cake into 4 layers with a thin, long, sharp-pointed knife, using a sawing motion. Spread each layer with the frosting. Cover and refrigerate the cake for 4 days.

Confectionery

Candy making is an absorbing hobby, and with practice and imagination the finished result looks temptingly professional. Homemade candies, packed in decorative boxes, make ideal presents for Christmas and birthdays. Set the individual candies in paper wrappings and put waxed paper between the layers.

Many traditional candies, such as fudge and toffee, are based on concentrated sugar syrup boiled to high temperatures. A candy thermometer and a large, heavy-bottomed pan are essential. Use a wooden spoon to move the mixture backward and forward while the syrup is reducing. The thermometer should be moved occasionally, as fudge and toffee tend to settle around the bulb and give inaccurate readings.

For chocolate-covered candies, use good-quality sweet baking chocolate. Put it, broken into squares, in a bowl and set this over a pan of hot water. Stir the chocolate continuously with a fork until melted—it should be just warm and must never be allowed to boil. Dip the candies, one at a time, into the chocolate, holding each with sugar tongs, and brush off any excess on the side of the bowl. Leave the candies to set on waxed paper.

See illustration on page 373.

Chocolate Fudge

PREPARATION TIME: *about 1 hour*

INGREDIENTS (*for 1½ pounds*):
2 cups granulated sugar
1 cup water
1 can condensed milk
4½ ounces semisweet cooking chocolate, grated
⅓ cup seedless raisins (optional)

Put the sugar and water in a heavy-bottomed 3-quart pan and dissolve the sugar over low heat. Bring to a boil, add the condensed milk, and boil gently until a candy thermometer registers 240°F. Stir occasionally to prevent sticking. Remove the pan from the heat and add the chocolate; add raisins, if used.

Beat the mixture until thick and creamy, using a wooden spoon. Pour it into a buttered pan measuring 5½ inches by 8 inches by 1 inch.

Leave to cool for several hours, then cut the fudge into 1-inch squares. Wrap in waxed paper.

Collettes

PREPARATION TIME: *1 hour*

INGREDIENTS (*for 18 collettes*):
9 ounces sweet cooking chocolate
4 tablespoons strong black coffee
4 tablespoons butter
2 egg yolks
Rum
Blanched hazelnuts

Melt 4 ounces of the chocolate. Cool slightly, then put a teaspoon of the melted chocolate into a small paper candy case; press another case over the chocolate to squeeze it up the sides. Repeat with the remaining chocolate. Let stand overnight. The next day, peel off paper cases. Melt remaining chocolate and stir in the coffee. When cool, beat in the softened but not oily butter and the egg yolks; add rum to taste. Spoon this mixture into a pastry bag fitted with a large star tube and pipe into the chocolate cases. Top each collette with a hazelnut and leave to set.

Coconut Ice

PREPARATION TIME: *30 minutes*

INGREDIENTS (*for 24–30 squares*):
2 cups sugar
1 cup milk
1⅔ cups shredded coconut
Red food coloring

Oil or butter a shallow pan measuring 8 inches by 6 inches. Dissolve the sugar in the milk over low heat, then bring to a boil and boil gently for about 10 minutes or until the temperature reaches 240°F (read the thermometer at eye level). Remove the pan from the heat and stir in the coconut.

Pour half the mixture quickly into the pan, spreading it evenly. Color the remainder pale pink with a few drops of food coloring and pour quickly over the first layer. Leave until half-set, then mark the coconut into 1-inch squares with a knife. Cut up when quite cold.

Chocolate-Covered Dates

PREPARATION TIME: *20 minutes*

INGREDIENTS:
1 box dates
Almond paste
4 ounces sweet cooking chocolate
Cocktail cherries
Shelled walnuts

Using a small pointed knife, make a small slit in each date and remove the pit. Fill the cavities with uncooked almond paste and close the dates again. Melt the chocolate in a bowl over a pan of hot water and dip the dates in the chocolate, holding them with two forks. Coat evenly and brush off any surplus on the edge of the bowl.

Dry the chocolate-covered dates on sheets of waxed paper. Just before the chocolate has set, decorate the dates with well-drained cocktail cherries cut in half or with pieces of shelled walnuts.

Chocolate-Covered Pineapple
PREPARATION TIME: *20 minutes*

INGREDIENTS:
8-ounce can pineapple rings
6–7 ounces sweet cooking chocolate
Decorations

Drain the pineapple rings thoroughly and cut them into halves or quarters. Break up the chocolate and melt in a bowl over a pan of hot water. Using two forks, carefully dip the pineapple chunks in the chocolate, coating them evenly.

Dry on waxed paper, and before the chocolate sets, decorate with sugar flowers or silver shot.*

Honey Fruit Nut Caramels
PREPARATION TIME: *30 minutes*

INGREDIENTS:
6 tablespoons butter
7 tablespoons light corn syrup
½ cup clear honey
¾ cup walnut halves
½ cup pitted dates

Butter and line with cooking parchment a shallow pan measuring 8 inches by 5 inches. Melt the butter in a large, heavy-bottomed pan set over low heat; add the syrup and honey. Bring the mixture to a boil and continue boiling over gentle heat until the thermometer registers 270°F. Meanwhile, chop the walnuts and dates finely.

Remove the pan from the heat and add the nuts and dates. Beat the mixture vigorously with a wooden spoon until opaque. Pour it into the lined pan and leave to cool. When almost set, cut the caramel with a buttered knife into ¾–1 inch squares. Leave to set for another 24 hours, then break the squares apart; wrap them in waxed paper and store.

Marzipan
INGREDIENTS:
Cooked almond paste
Food coloring
Almonds
Granulated sugar
Dates
Sweet cooking chocolate for melting
Preserved ginger

Cooked almond paste can be colored pink, green, or yellow with a little food coloring, and used as a base or filling for candies.

Stuffed dates: Make a slit in the top of the dates and remove the pits. Fill the cavities with a small piece of plain or colored almond paste; roll the dates in granulated sugar or decorate with blanched split almonds.

Ginger marzipan: Shape pieces of almond paste into marble-sized balls, dip one side in melted chocolate, and top with preserved ginger.

Peanut Brittle
PREPARATION TIME: *1 hour*

INGREDIENTS:
1¾ cups sugar
½ cup plus 2 tablespoons water
¾ cup light corn syrup
2 teaspoons powdered glucose
2 tablespoons butter
½ cup toasted peanuts
½ teaspoon lemon extract
2 teaspoons baking soda

Dissolve the sugar in the water, together with the syrup and glucose, in a large, heavy-bottomed pan set over low heat. Bring to a boil and boil gently until the thermometer registers 300°F (read at eye level).

Add the butter, warmed nuts (rub the skins off first), and lemon extract; heat until the butter is just melted. Stir in the baking soda (the mixture will froth rapidly for a few minutes) and pour it quickly onto an oiled marble slab or large oiled baking sheet.

When cold, break the brittle into pieces. Store in single layers between waxed paper.

Peppermint Creams
PREPARATION TIME: *30 minutes*

INGREDIENTS (*for 25 pieces*):
1¾ cups confectioners' sugar
1 egg white
Oil of peppermint

Sift the sugar into a bowl and blend with enough beaten egg white to form a stiff paste. Add a few drops of oil of peppermint to taste.

Knead the paste lightly in the bowl, using the fingertips. Roll the paste out ¼ inch thick between sheets of waxed paper. Stamp out 1-inch rounds with a plain cutter and leave the mints to dry for about 24 hours.

Rum Truffles
PREPARATION TIME: *35 minutes*
CHILLING TIME: *1 hour*

INGREDIENTS (*for 12 truffles*):
3 ounces sweet cooking chocolate
1 egg yolk
1 tablespoon butter
1 teaspoon rum
1 teaspoon half-and-half or light cream
¼ cup chocolate shot or sprinkles

Melt the chocolate in a small bowl over a pan of hot water. Add the egg yolk, butter, rum, and half-and-half or cream. Beat the mixture until thick, then chill in the refrigerator until it is firm enough to handle.

Shape the mixture into 12 balls and roll them at once in chocolate shot or sprinkles.*

Garnishes

A well-chosen garnish adds texture, color, and flavor to a dish. It should be fresh and simple rather than cluttered, and if the dish is hidden by a sauce, the garnish should give a clue to what is in the sauce. For instance, a dish served *à la véronique*—that is, with a sauce containing white grapes—is always garnished with small bunches of grapes. Many garnishes are classic; lemon and parsley, for example, are traditional with sautéed fish.

Angelica
This large, hardy herb is cultivated commercially for its roots and stalks. Used alone or with cherries to decorate desserts and puddings, it is most easily found in gourmet shops. Buy angelica in strips that are a bright green and are not coated too thickly with sugar. Excess sugar can be removed by placing angelica for a short time in hot water; drain and dry well. Angelica can be chopped, cut into strips, or cut into diamond or leaf shapes.

Aspic
This is used for coating, for holding a garnish in position, or used chopped to garnish a cold dish. The aspic can be made from reduced clarified stock or from stock to which gelatin has been added. To make aspic, first clarify 4 cups (1 quart) of stock, which may be chicken, beef, veal, or fish stock, depending on whether the dish to be coated has a base of poultry, meat, or fish. The cold stock should be free of fat.

Put the stock in a deep saucepan with 3 slightly beaten egg whites. Beat over medium heat with a wire whisk until the mixture comes to a simmer. Remove from the heat and allow to settle for 15 minutes. The egg whites will rise to the surface of the liquid, forming a thick foamy layer in which all the impurities in the stock will be trapped.

Line a sieve with 4 thicknesses of cheesecloth wrung out in cold water.

Push the crust of egg white gently to one side of the pan; ladle the stock into the cheesecloth-lined sieve and let it drip through. When all the strained stock has dripped through and is clear and sparkling, soften 2 packages (2 tablespoons) unflavored gelatin in ¼ cup dry sherry. Stir this into the warm clarified stock until the gelatin dissolves. For coating purposes, stir the aspic over ice until it has the consistency of unbeaten egg white, then place the item to be coated on a wire rack over a plate or tray. Spoon over the aspic until an even layer adheres. Leave until set and repeat if necessary. Decorate by dipping pieces of garnish—tarragon, carrot, olives, or truffle slices—in a little cool but liquid aspic before setting them in position with the point of a skewer. When set, glaze with more aspic. For chopped aspic, turn the aspic onto a piece of wet waxed paper and chop it coarsely.

Bread croûtons:
See Soup Garnishes, page 300.

Bread crumbs
Buttered crumbs are a traditional garnish for game and for dishes served au gratin. Several slices of bread can be put into a blender at a time and quickly made into crumbs. Melt 2 tablespoons butter in a skillet, stir in 2 cups fresh white bread crumbs, and sauté over moderate heat until the crumbs are evenly browned and golden.

Bread triangles

Remove the crusts from ½-inch-thick slices of white bread. Cut each slice into 4 triangles and dip in egg beaten with 1–2 tablespoons milk. Coat the triangles with fresh white bread crumbs and deep-fry in hot oil until crisp and golden. Drain and use to garnish fish dishes.

Candied cherries

These should be washed in warm water to remove the sticky syrup, then dried before being used whole, halved, or chopped.

Carrot curls

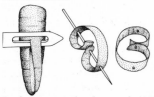

Sandwiches can be decorated with these. Clean and scrape the carrots. With a potato peeler, pare down the length of each carrot to remove a wafer-thin slice. Roll up the slices, fasten with wooden cocktail picks, and put in ice water to curl.

Celery tassels

Edible garnish used with dips. Wash the celery stalks, cut them in 2-inch lengths, then cut down the lengths at narrow intervals almost to the end. Leave the stalks in a bowl of water to curl.

Chantilly cream

Used as a piped or spooned decoration for desserts. Beat 1 cup of chilled heavy cream or whipping cream in a deep chilled bowl, using a hand beater. When the cream thickens, add 3–4 teaspoons sugar and a few drops of vanilla extract and continue to beat slowly until the cream just holds its shape. Whipped cream thickens by the pressure needed to force it through a tube, so it should be light and fluffy to begin with. Pipe the cream through a pastry bag and use a rosette tube.

Chocolate

This takes many forms as a decorative finish to cold desserts, classic gâteaux, and simple cakes. Kept in a cool airtight tin, chocolate shapes will store for about a week.

Squares Put semisweet chocolate into a small bowl, place over a pan of hot water, and allow the chocolate to melt slowly. Line a baking sheet with cooking parchment or waxed paper. Pour the melted chocolate in a thin stream over the paper, and with a small metal spatula spread the chocolate to a thin, smooth layer. Leave to cool until firm, then cut the chocolate into squares with a warm sharp knife. Peel the paper carefully away from the squares.

Leaves Melt the chocolate as for squares and meanwhile clean and dry small rose leaves. Hold the leaves with tweezers and dip the underside of each leaf in the melted chocolate. Leave to dry, chocolate side up. When the chocolate has set, carefully ease the leaves away.

Cucumbers

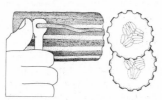

Sliced cucumbers are a traditional garnish for a cold mousse or terrine. Scalloped or ridged cucumbers make a more unusual decoration. Wipe but do not peel a piece of cucumber; score it along the length with a fork or lemon stripper so that it will have a serrated edge when cut into slices. Salt the slices lightly before placing them on the platter.

Eggs

Hard-cooked eggs are sliced or finely chopped to garnish casseroles, vegetable dishes, and salads. Quarter the eggs or slice them crosswise with a very sharp knife, taking care not to crumble the yolk.

Gherkin fans

Drain cocktail gherkins thoroughly, then slice each 3 or 4 times lengthwise almost to the stalk end. Gently ease the slices apart so that they spread out like a fan.

Grapes

These are used frosted, either singly or in small clusters, to garnish sweet mousses, fruit soufflés, and ice creams, or alone as a dessert fruit. Brush single or small clusters of black or white grapes with lightly beaten egg white; dredge heavily with granulated or superfine sugar. Leave on a wire rack to dry.

Lemon and orange spirals

Used to decorate long drinks and the plain surface of desserts, such as cheesecake. Using a potato peeler or lemon stripper, pare off lemon or orange peel, free of white pith, in a continuous spiral. Hang the twisting peel from the rim of the glass.

Mint leaves

Sugared, these are seasonal delicacies with summer fruits. Select firm, small sprigs of leaves, or individual leaves, brush them lightly with egg white, and dredge thoroughly with superfine sugar. Dry and use on the same day.

Mushrooms

Fluted, these are a traditional garnish with broiled meat. Choose large button mushrooms, wipe with a damp cloth, and trim the stem level with the cap. With a sharp knife, make a series of curving cuts ¼ inch apart, following the natural shape of the cap and from the top of the cap to the base. Take out a narrow strip along each indentation. Sauté the mushrooms in a little butter with a squeeze of lemon juice to prevent them from darkening.

Nuts

Almonds are bought whole, halved, chopped, or sliced and slivered. Plain or roasted, all make quick garnishes for gâteaux and sweet soufflés. Whole almonds, bought with or without their skins, can be used whole, split in two along their natural seam, cut into slivers, or chopped. For slivered almonds, blanch whole unskinned almonds in boiling water for 2–3 minutes; rub off the skins and, while still soft, cut the almonds into strips. For toasted almonds, spread the nuts, cut to the required shape, in a shallow pan; brown under a broiler until golden.

Pistachio nuts should always be blanched to remove the skins. Put the nuts in boiling water and soak for about 5 minutes—a pinch of baking soda brightens the green of the nuts. Pour off the water and replace with cold water. Ease off the skins by pinching each nut between thumb and forefinger. Dry the nuts before using them for garnish.

Hazelnuts need to be toasted before the skins can be removed. Place the shelled nuts in a single layer on a shallow pan and toast under the broiler until the skins are dry and the nuts begin to color. Cool slightly, then rub the nuts against each other in a bag to loosen the skins.

Parsley

This is the most versatile and useful of all garnishes, whether in sprigs or chopped. Wash freshly picked parsley as soon as possible, shake well, and remove long stems. Place the parsley in a jar of water reaching to the leaves, or put the parsley stems in a plastic bag, tied at the neck. Parsley will then stay crisp and green for several days. Change the water in the container daily.

Chopped parsley can be used as a garnish arranged in neat lines or at random. Scissors can be used for chopping, but the result is coarser than if parsley is chopped with a knife. Gather the parsley into a tight bunch and with scissors snip off as much as needed directly onto the dish to be garnished.

To chop large quantities of parsley, place the stripped leaves on a chopping board. Use a sharp straight-bladed knife, holding the handle firmly with one hand and the tip of the knife blade with the other. Lift the handle in a seesaw action, gradually chopping the parsley finely or coarsely as required. Alternatively, bunch the parsley leaves in one hand on the chopping board and, using the knife, gradually shred the parsley, moving the fingers back to reveal more parsley. Small wooden chopping bowls equipped with curved-bladed knives are available for chopping parsley, herbs, shallots, and garlic. To preserve the vivid green, put chopped parsley in a piece of cheesecloth, tie loosely, and hold the bag under cold water for a few minutes to rinse thoroughly. Squeeze dry, then shake the parsley out into a bowl. Chopped parsley will keep for a day or two in a covered container in the refrigerator.

Fried parsley makes an attractive garnish for sautéed fish. Allow 4 sprigs of parsley per person and remove the long stems from the perfectly dry parsley. Heat oil to about 375°F, put the parsley in the frying basket, and immerse it in the hot fat. As soon as the hissing ceases, lift out the parsley.

Radish roses

Used to garnish cold entrées, open sandwiches, hors d'oeuvres and salads. Make 6–8 cuts lengthwise through a radish from the base toward the stalk. Put the radishes in a bowl of ice water until they open like flowers. Long radishes look attractive when cut at intervals along the length so that they open out accordion-fashion.

Spun sugar

Used as a decoration for Austrian tortes. Bring 2 cups sugar and 1 cup water to a boil. Boil until the syrup reaches 312°F. Remove from the heat and stir in a pinch of cream of tartar. As the syrup cools, it forms fine threads when dropped from a wooden spoon. Holding an oiled spoon horizontally, pass syrup over the handle, twirling the fine threads.

Tomatoes

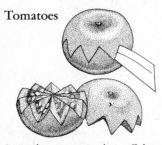

Serrated tomatoes can be stuffed or used as tomato halves as a garnish for salads, sandwiches, and sautéed or broiled fish and meat. Choose firm

tomatoes of even size. Using a small sharp knife, make a series of small V-shaped indentations around the circumference of the tomato. Carefully pull the tomato halves apart. Oranges, grapefruit, and melons may also be separated in this way.

Twists and butterflies

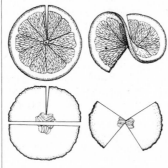

Tomatoes, cucumbers, beets, lemons, and oranges make attractive garnishes for a number of dishes, both savory and sweet. Slice the vegetable or fruit thinly, though not wafer-thin. For twists, cut each slice through to the center, then twist the halves in opposite directions and place in position. For butterflies, make 2 deep V-shaped incisions that meet near the center of each round lemon slice. Remove both wedges to leave a butterfly shape.

Watercress

Another favorite garnish for meat, poultry, and fish dishes. Trim off the stems and wash the watercress leaves. Lift out, rinse, and shake well. Discard any ragged and yellow leaves, and arrange the watercress in small bunches to be added as garnish just before the dish is served. Washed watercress with part of the stem left on will keep for 1 day in the refrigerator if stored in a plastic bag.

Wine with Food

The rules for storing, serving, and drinking wine have grown out of the experience of connoisseurs, who discovered how to treat wine and when to serve it to best advantage. However, these rules are not rigid and they can be changed to suit individual tastes.

Wine is made by crushing grapes to extract the juice, which is then allowed to ferment. During fermentation the grape sugar turns into alcohol and the juice becomes wine.

There are two main categories of wine: table wines and fortified wines. Table wines are drunk with a meal. Fortified wines, to which a spirit, usually brandy, has been added, include aperitifs, which are served before a meal, and dessert wines, such as port.

Table wines may be red, white, or pink (rosé). The variations in color result from different methods of fermentation. In the making of red wine, the grape juice is fermented with the grapes' skins; rosé is made in the same way, but the juice is drawn off after a short time and allowed to ferment without the skins. In the making of white wine, red or white grapes may be used. Only the juice of the grapes is fermented, however, so that the wine is almost colorless.

The extremes of wine flavor are dry or sweet; a dry wine is one in which the sugar has been fermented out.

The label on the wine bottle gives the name of the wine and indicates whether it is dry or sweet. The country of origin will also be given; in the case of expensive wines, the district and the vineyard may be listed. The year of the vintage may also be given.

Buying wine

Most of the wine drunk in Canada is imported from France, Germany, Italy, and, to a lesser extent, Spain, Portugal, Hungary, Switzerland, and Greece. However, Canadian wines from Ontario and British Columbia are gaining in popularity.

The great variety of wine available can be confusing, and the best adviser is a reliable wine merchant.

The price of wine varies according to quality, although other factors also influence prices. For example, wines that are bottled at the famous vineyards where they are produced are at the top end of the price range. At the lower end of the price scale are many palatable wines, often sold in gallon and half-gallon jugs and served as table wines.

Anyone wishing to learn more about wines should read some of the best books on the subject, attend wine tastings and wine-appreciation courses, and sample as many wines as possible. Buying wine by the case can be a sound investment, as there is usually a 10 percent discount on wine sold this way.

Storing and serving wine

Wine should be placed in a dry, dark place, such as a cellar, that has a temperature of 50°–60°F. Table wines should be stored lying down; this keeps the corks moist. A dry cork can allow the entry into the wine of airborne organisms that may spoil it. Most fortified wines are not affected by air in the same way as table wines, so they can be stored upright.

Before serving a red wine, stand it upright and allow it to reach room temperature gradually. A young fruity red wine, such as a Beaujolais or a Canadian Manor St. David, may be served slightly chilled.

A red wine should be opened in order to allow it to breathe; this helps to develop and release the bouquet, or smell, and enhances the taste of the wine. Most young full-bodied wines benefit from being opened a few hours before serving. When an older red wine is served, the cork can be drawn an hour or so before the wine is drunk.

Older red wines sometimes throw a harmless deposit, or sediment, to the bottom of the bottle, so they are best decanted. This involves carefully pouring off the wine through a funnel, leaving the sediment behind. White wine seldom needs decanting because its sediment is colorless, tasteless, and, like the deposit in red wine, harmless.

A white wine should always be served well chilled, although fine old white wine needs only a minimum of chilling. The best way to chill white wine is in a bucket of ice and water. Alternatively, leave the wine in the refrigerator for an hour or so before serving.

Drinking wine

The best kind of glass from which to drink table wine has a large bowl and a stem. With this kind of glass it is possible to admire the color and the clarity of the wine. The glass should be half to two-thirds filled with wine. There should be a space at the top of the glass so that the bouquet of the wine, particularly a red one, can be delicately sniffed. Swirl the wine around in the glass to release the bouquet. When tasting white wine, hold the glass by its stem, rather than under the bowl, to avoid unnecessarily warming the contents. After sipping the first mouthful, allow it to remain for a few seconds on the palate before swallowing.

Wine with the meal

Many meals are improved by wine. If the meal is informal, only one wine is usually served. However, it should be chosen with care to complement all the dishes of the meal.

On a special or formal occasion, when a different wine is drunk with each course, there is a definite order of serving. A white wine should precede a red one except in the case of sweet dessert wines; a dry wine should be served before a sweet one; and a young wine should come before an old one.

Sherry or Madeira can be served with the soup course. Fish should be accompanied by medium-dry or dry white wines, such as Muscadet, Alsace Riesling from France, Moselle from Germany, an American Pinot Chardonnay or Chenin Blanc, or Vino Bianco from Canada. Other French wines–Vouvray, Graves, or white Burgundies such as Meursault, Chassagne-Montrachet, Chablis, or Pouilly-Fuissé–are also appropriately served with fish.

Poultry should be served with a medium-light red wine, but a white wine is also acceptable. For example, a chicken salad goes well with a white Portuguese *vinho verde,* a Riesling, or a Chenin Blanc.

Serve a red Bordeaux or Beaujolais with lamb; and a Rioja Reserva from Spain, a Valpolicella Classico from Italy, or a Canadian Moulin Mouton or Villard Noir with roast veal. A full-bodied red wine is excellent with duck. Pork goes best with a fruity white from Alsace, Germany, or Ontario. Substantial dishes, such as braised beef or steak-and-kidney pudding, can be accompanied by robust French wines, such as Beaune, Pommard, or a Gevrey-Chambertin; a California Barbera or Petite Sirah would also be good.

Spicy dishes tend to overpower wine, but they can be matched by a good dry sherry, a Madeira, or an Alsatian wine like a Gewürztraminer, which has a spicy-sweet taste and a flowery bouquet. In the case of Indian or Mexican food, beer should be served instead of wine, and tea is generally considered to be the best accompaniment to Chinese food.

With the dessert course, serve the heavier, sweeter wines: a good Barsac (from Bordeaux), such as Château Climens or Château Coutet, Seibel or Chanté from Canada, or a sweet sparkling wine from France or Italy. If cheese precedes the dessert, it can be accompanied by any remaining red wine.

Cooking with wine

It is the flavor of wine and not its alcoholic content that improves the taste of food. When wine is added to a dish or a sauce, the cooking evaporates the alcohol.

Never drown a dish in wine; use restraint. When cooking fish, veal, chicken, sweetbreads, and similar delicate foods, use a light dry white wine. Red meats, such as lamb, beef, and game, are prepared with red wines. However, certain classic fish and poultry dishes, such as matelotes and coq au vin, should be prepared with red rather than white wine.

In addition to adding flavor to food, wine can be used to make it moist and tender. Fish marinated in white wine, or meat steeped in red wine, are enhanced in texture as well as taste. Fish need not be marinated for more than an hour; but dry meats, such as venison or beef, can be left for up to 4 days. A useful marinade consists of 1 part olive oil to 3 parts dry red or white wine (depending on the use), to which a bouquet garni, grated onion, and garlic are added.

Wine left over after a meal can be kept for cooking or used as a marinade. Pour the wine into a small bottle and cork it to keep out the air; white wine can be kept in the same way in the refrigerator. If there is no wine left over, cook with some of the wine to be drunk at the meal.

Fortified and dessert wines, such as Madeira, Marsala, port, sherry, and vermouth, can be used to enhance simple dishes. Marsala is an ingredient of the Italian dessert zabaglione, and sherry of lobster Newburg.

Wine is not the only alcoholic drink that improves a dish. Beer and dry cider can also be used in cooking, although they do not have as many uses as wine. Beer is an essential ingredient of classic dishes, such as Welsh rabbit and *Carbonnade à la Flamande* (Belgian beef stew); it also makes an excellent marinade.

Liquor, such as brandy, whiskey, or gin, can be used to flame dishes that do not require long cooking. Before flaming a dish, warm the liquor slightly in a ladle. Then set it alight with a match and pour it over the hot food.

Liquor can be used to flavor dishes. For example, apricot brandy can be used to flame pancakes; calvados, an apple-based brandy from France, can be added to baked apples. Framboise, a French *eau-de-vie,* or clear spirit, can be poured over raspberries, and kirsch is an excellent marinade for pineapple.

Drinks before and after a meal

An aperitif served before a meal should stimulate the appetite without numbing the palate.

A light dry sherry, such as fino or manzanilla, is an excellent aperitif. Serve it slightly chilled, but not so cold that the bouquet is killed.

Another aperitif is vermouth, a drink based on white wine and sharpened with wormwood and various herbs. There are dry and sweet variations.

Champagne can be served at the beginning of a meal. However, if this famous drink is too costly, a dry sparkling wine or a well-chilled white or rosé wine can be served in its place. *Vin blanc cassis,* which is dry white wine flavored with blackcurrant liqueur or syrup, is also a suitable aperitif.

One of the best ways to end a meal that has been accompanied by fine wines is to serve a refreshing glass of mineral water. However, a wide choice of after-dinner wines and spirits is available: brandies, liqueurs, and eaux-de-vie.

Party drinks

A punch is an ideal party refreshment because it can be made in large quantities. It can be prepared by mixing various alcoholic or non-alcoholic drinks to be served hot or cold. Digest Punch and Negus Punch are suitable for festive winter occasions; sangría and fruit cup are suitable for hot summer weather.

Digest Punch

INGREDIENTS:
2 lemons
Cinnamon
Nutmeg
Cloves
Mace
6 tablespoons sugar
1 fifth brandy or rum

Pare the rind from the lemons. Add the rind, cinnamon, nutmeg, cloves, and mace to taste, with the sugar, to 1 cup of water. Bring to a boil and simmer. Strain the mixture into a warmed punch bowl. Add the strained lemon juice and the brandy or rum. Serve at once.

Negus Punch

This punch is named after a famous figure of Queen Anne's day, Colonel Negus, who had a penchant for sweetening wines.

INGREDIENTS:
2 cups port
12 sugar cubes
1 lemon
Pinch of nutmeg

Pour the port into a bowl. Rub the sugar cubes on the lemon rind and float them in the port. Add the nutmeg and the lemon juice. Pour in 4 cups of boiling water and serve.

Sangría

This famous Spanish punch is a rich red and is garnished with fruit. After adding the ice cubes to the bowl, the sangría can be left to cool and dilute itself. Chill the bowl first.

INGREDIENTS:
1 quart Spanish red wine
1 quart club soda
Orange and lemon slices
Sugar syrup

Mix the wine, soda, and fruit in a bowl or glass pitcher and sweeten to taste with sugar syrup. Cool with ice cubes. Serve in wineglasses.

Fruit Cup

Any kind of fruit, such as cherries, peaches, plums, raspberries, or strawberries, can be used to make this summer drink.

INGREDIENTS:
Fresh fruit
⅓ cup sugar
¾ cup brandy
1 bottle white wine
Soda water

Wash and slice the fruit. Put the fruit in a bowl and add sugar and brandy. Let stand 1 day. Add the chilled white wine, which can be diluted with soda water. Serve.

Champagne Punch

INGREDIENTS:
2 bottles champagne
1 bottle dry white wine
1 large bottle soda water
1 cup brandy
Sugar syrup (optional)
1 cup strawberries
1 lemon
Fresh mint

Pour the liquids over a block of ice in a large bowl. Sweeten to taste with sugar syrup, if desired.

Wash, hull, and slice the strawberries in half lengthwise. Wash and thinly slice the lemon and remove the seeds. Add the fruit and fresh mint to the bowl for garnish.

The Cook's Workshop

The cook who prepares meals for a family spends a great deal of time in the kitchen. Therefore, it should be planned carefully so that the homemaker will be able to work with efficiency and comfort. Every detail that is to be changed in an existing kitchen or included in a new kitchen must be noted down before the work is begun. Once the work is in progress, it may be costly to make changes. If the work can be done by one contractor, costs can be kept to a minimum. Employing different workmen to do the plumbing and electrical work and to fit the kitchen units will add to the expense.

PLANNING A KITCHEN

For the greatest efficiency, a kitchen should be laid out so that the storage, preparation, cooking, and serving of food flows smoothly in a logical sequence. If this is not possible, make sure that the food storage, the work areas, the range, and sink are all close together. This arrangement will save the cook time and effort.

Most work surfaces are about 3 feet high, but some manufacturers make other sizes. For a person about 5 feet 3 inches tall, 2 feet 9 inches is usually a convenient height. Taller cooks need the 3-foot size.

If there are young children in the home, their safety should be considered. Child gates should be fitted to stop them from entering the kitchen when no one is there. If detergents and disinfectants are to be kept in a cabinet under the sink, make sure the cabinet has a lock. Switches and outlets should be placed out of the reach of children. Free-standing ranges with drop-door ovens should be anchored. A child can tip one over by standing on the door.

When redesigning an old kitchen, look for ways to save space. Although the dimensions of the room cannot be easily altered, space might be saved and serving made easier by removing an unnecessary door between the kitchen and dining room.

In planning a kitchen, the following basic requirements should be taken into account:

1 There must be a clear space in the kitchen wide enough for the installation of the range. Gas ranges should not be placed under or anywhere near a window where a draft can blow out the flame.

2 Allow two clear spaces for storage or installation of other appliances, one space not less than 2 feet wide, the other not less than 2 feet 8 inches wide. Appliances such as dishwashers can fit under work surfaces.

3 A sink unit should be not less than 24 inches wide.

4 There should be a work surface on each side of the sink and on each side of the range.

When drawing up the plans for do-it-yourself alterations in the kitchen, it is essential to take accurate measurements of the room. Draw a plan of the kitchen on graph paper. Cut out paper models to scale of the kitchen units and slide them around on the plan to get an idea of layout. Use a tape or yardstick to take the following measurements:

1 The wall from floor to ceiling.

2 The positions and widths of the doors and frames and the side on which the doors are hinged.

3 The positions and dimensions of the windows, including the height from the floor to the sill.

4 The dimensions and positions of any wall recesses or protrusions, pipes, gas or electric meters, switches, or outlets.

5 The positions of various service connections, including water, drainage, electricity, and gas.

6 Radiators or heating ducts. The appliances to be included in the plan should be listed on a separate piece of paper, as suggested in the following:

KITCHEN STORAGE UNITS

Storage units should be within easy reach of the work area, and those items used most frequently should be the most easily accessible. One of the commonest mistakes is to place cabinets so high that they cannot be reached with ease, or so low that one is forced to stoop.

Cooking utensils, flatware, dishes, glass, table and kitchen linen, and bowls should be kept on shelves or in drawers. Perishable foods, such as root vegetables, should never be stored in a closed space, but on shelves where air can circulate. Store buckets and cleaning materials, including brooms, floor mops, and vacuum cleaners, in a cleaning closet.

Shelves To allow for the economical storage of different articles, shelving should be of various widths and should be easily adjustable. Shelves for general storage may be either open or enclosed.

Drawers These should be of differing depths to allow for the various gadgets they are to hold. Keep one drawer for flatware.

Cabinets Shallow cabinets no deeper than 9½ inches are useful for storing bulky kitchen equipment in infrequent use, but mixers, blenders, or food processors should be readily available on a work surface. It is an advantage to have everything in the cabinet clearly visible as soon as the doors are opened. Often, shallow cabinets can be built into what would otherwise be wasted space. Sliding doors save space.

Fill-in units Some manufacturers make excellent small fill-in units to utilize the space between wall and base cabinets. Fill-in units with sliding doors that exclude steam can provide suitable storage for spice jars, salad oil, vinegar, and syrups.

Wall mounting There is now a wide range of wall-mounted items, such as can openers, spice racks, and knife racks. Wall-mounted equipment saves storage space and time, and helps to ensure that work surfaces are kept clear.

High-level storage The space at the top of a wall cabinet that reaches to the ceiling can be used for nonperishable items, such as canned foods, soaps, and paper products. Little-used pots and pans can also be transferred to high-level storage. Use a step stool to reach them.

KITCHEN DECORATION

Flooring The kitchen floor should be hard-wearing, resistant to staining, easy to clean, nonslip, and preferably heatproof. The floorings that most meet all the requirements are modern quarry tile and rubber tile, usually coated with liquid wax to give a glossy, dirt-resistant finish.

Cork tile is an attractive flooring that provides warmth underfoot. It should be sealed with clear polyurethane varnish to resist knocks, stains, and grease. Heavy-duty vinyl tile and sheet vinyl are decorative, practical, and reasonably priced.

Wall finishes Kitchen walls should be washable and resistant to steam and grease. Tiles, vinyl wallcoverings, and semigloss or polyurethane paints are all suitable for use either individually or in combination.

KITCHEN EQUIPMENT

Gas ranges

Gas cooking offers advantages not shared by other means of cooking: instant heat, fine adjustment, and, with natural gas, a minimal degree of pollution.

Many gas ranges have inner glass doors for visible oven cooking. Some also have self-cleaning oven linings

CHECKLIST FOR KITCHEN EQUIPMENT

	EXISTING APPLIANCE			TO BE PURCHASED		
	Height	Width	Depth	Height	Width	Depth
Range or cooktops						
Refrigerator-freezer						
Washer						
Dishwasher						
Dryer						
Electric mixer or food processor						
Wall oven						
Ironing equipment						
Microwave oven						
Trash compactor						

Include small electrical appliances, such as toaster, coffee percolator, blender, electric meat grinder, can opener, and knife sharpener.

that keep themselves clean by oxidizing splashes that touch the top and sides of the oven. Although foods spilled on the bottom tray of the range must still be wiped, cleaning is greatly simplified. Other features of gas ranges include:

1 Thermostatic controls; these give accurate time control and ensure greater safety. They are now available on surface burners.

2 Spark ignition that ignites the gas automatically. (The most widely used form of gas burner ignition is the constantly burning pilot light; there is evidence that the pilot light is more efficient, in terms of energy use, than other ignition systems.)

3 Flame-failure device that cuts off the gas flow if the flame is extinguished.

4 Automatic timing that switches on, off, or changes the cooking process at preset times. The timer is usually equipped with a fail-safe device in case of faulty ignition.

5 A rotisserie that rotates food directly under the flame of the broiler.

6 An infrared broiler to cook various kinds of foods faster.

7 Low temperature settings (140°–200°F) to keep foods warm.

8 Control panel placed behind the cooking surface, out of the reach of small children.

Electric ranges and wall ovens
The following features are well worth looking for:
Self-cleaning ovens There are two versions of self-cleaning oven interiors. In the automatic self-cleaner type of interior, the door is latched, the cleaning cycle switched on, and the oven temperature greatly increased. Food splashes are carbonized into a fine dust that can be wiped away with a damp cloth once the oven has cooled.

The stay-clean oven interior is covered with a special coating that also works by oxidation. However, the cleaning process is continuous. **Oven doors** Most models feature inner glass doors and oven lights for visible oven cooking.
Ceramic cooking surfaces Glass ceramic cooking surfaces are available in ranges and in glass ceramic cooktops that are built into the counter. The flat, smooth surface, with its concealed electric heating units, is easy to clean with a damp cloth or with the conditioner-cleaner recommended for these surfaces.
Automatic timing controls Automatic timers on electric ranges and ovens offer great advantages. Dishes are placed in their cooking utensils in the oven and the timer is set to switch itself on and off at predetermined times.

Microwave ovens
Microwave ovens work on an entirely different principle from normal cooking. Very high frequency microwaves are produced and beamed into the food, where they are converted into heat. The food cooks from the inside, and the interior of the oven and the plate on which the food stands remain cool. The special advantage of a microwave oven is the speed with which it can cook food, but since it does not brown foods, there is usually an additional browning unit for this purpose.

Ventilator and exhaust hoods
These remove cooking odors and steam from the kitchen and absorb grease from the air. The built-in hood is fitted with a 2- or 3-speed fan and a duct that takes fumes outdoors. For light cooking smells, it can purify and recirculate air.

One disadvantage of the external duct system is the expense involved in fitting the duct.

Some hoods are also manufactured for installation without ducts.

STORING FOODS IN THE REFRIGERATOR

Food	Storage time	Comments
Bacon	7–10 days	Keep wrapped.
Butter and fats	2–3 weeks	Keep wrapped or covered.
Cheese, soft (except Brie, Camembert)	4–5 days	Keep in covered carton. Remove 1 hour before serving.
Coffee (ground)	3–4 weeks	Keep tightly closed in a glass jar.
Custards	1 day	Cool quickly, cover, and refrigerate immediately.
Fish	1–2 days	Keep tightly covered or wrapped in foil.
Fruit, soft, and green vegetables	1–5 days	Keep covered but allow some air to reach the fruit.
Gravies and sauces	2–3 days	Cool quickly, cover, and refrigerate immediately.
Leftovers (containing meat, sauces, or potatoes)	1 day	Keep meat tightly covered.
Meat and poultry	1–3 days	Store in the meat compartment; keep meat and poultry loosely wrapped in foil. Remove poultry giblets.
Milk and cream	3–5 days	Keep covered.
Nuts (shelled)	3–4 months	Keep in an airtight jar.
Relishes, pickles	2–3 months	After opening, keep airtight.
Roasts, large	4 days	Drain off meat juices; cover loosely.

This type of hood draws fumes and grease into a charcoal filter that acts like a sponge, removing impurities from the air. The filter must be replaced periodically.

Refrigerators
The ideal temperature for short-term storage of perishable foods is just above freezing point. A refrigerator provides this, with a temperature range of between 34°F and 44°F. Most refrigerators have a very low temperature freezing compartment. With a large freezer, food, especially meat, can be bought in quantity, often at a saving. Menu planning is simplified. In many current models, half the storage space is given over to frozen foods and the other half to normal refrigerator storage.

Dishwashers
An automatic dishwasher will wash, rinse, and dry a full load of dishes in 15–90 minutes, depending on the model and the number of cycles. Dishwasher capacity is usually measured by the number of place settings a machine will hold and wash.

Dishwashers are made to fit beneath an existing work surface. They may be the portable type that attaches to the faucet and needs no plumbing, or the built-in type.

With built-ins, space is needed for plumbing at the back of the machine and for opening the door at the front. The level of the machine should be high enough above the outside drain to allow the water to drain away properly. Sink, dishwasher, and waste disposal unit should be close together.

Laundry equipment
Ideally, the washer and dryer should be in a utility room or bathroom, but sometimes this is not possible and they have to go in the kitchen.

There is a choice between machines that have the controls at the front and fit under a counter and those that stand level with the counter and have controls on the top rear of the machine.

Where space is limited, look for the slim stacking units with the dryer mounted over the washer.

Electric mixers
There are two basic types of electric mixer: the hand-held, light-duty mixer, and the heavier, stand-mounted machine with a large range of optional attachments, such as paddles, beaters, and dough hooks.

The hand-held mixer is useful when preparing dishes with several ingredients that require beating in separate bowls. It can also be used for making sauces and puddings that must be beaten while they are cooking. Most mixers have a choice of speeds to deal with different types of mixing, such as beating an egg or mixing a fruitcake. The beaters can be removed for easy cleaning.

Stand-mounted mixers are heavy-duty machines that can do all types of mixing and beating, from whipping cream to kneading bread.

Blenders and food processors
These are useful for making puréed foods, mayonnaise, and soups; for chopping dry ingredients, such as bread crumbs; and, in the case of the food processor, grinding meat or fish and making pastry.

Can openers
Hand-held, wall-mounted, or electric can openers come in many styles.

Coffee grinders
There are some nonelectric coffee grinders, such as copies of the old-fashioned hand-operated coffee grinder. The electrical coffee-grinding devices may be separate units or optional extras on many food mixers and blenders. For maximum coffee flavor, only a small quantity of coffee beans should be ground at one time.

KITCHEN EQUIPMENT

The needs of the family will indicate which kitchen utensils will be essential and which are unnecessary. There is a large range of electrical appliances on the market, such as toasters, coffee percolators, knife sharpeners, can openers, and carving knives.

The following list of kitchen equipment includes all the basic necessities but does not include items for the table (flatware, tableware, and glassware).

BAKING AND ROASTING EQUIPMENT
BAKING DISHES
BAKING SHEETS
BASTING SPOON OR BULB BASTER
CAKE PANS (8- and 9-inch round; 9-inch square)
CASSEROLES WITH COVERS, OVENPROOF AND FLAMEPROOF
COOKIE SHEETS
FLAN RINGS, ROUND AND RECTANGULAR
GRATIN DISHES
JELLY-ROLL PAN
LOAF PANS
MEAT THERMOMETER
MUFFIN PANS
PIE PLATES (2 sizes)
RAMEKINS (1 set)
ROASTING PAN
ROASTING RACK
SOUFFLÉ DISHES
TERRINE

CLEANING UTENSILS
BOTTLE BRUSH
DISH MOPS AND BRUSHES
DISH TOWELS
SCOURING PADS
VEGETABLE BRUSH

CONTAINERS
CANISTERS
PLASTIC STORAGE CONTAINERS

COOKING TOOLS
COOK'S FORK
COOK'S SPOONS, PLAIN, PERFORATED, AND SLOTTED
LADLE
METAL SPATULAS (2 sizes)
PANCAKE TURNER
WOODEN SPATULAS
WOODEN SPOONS

CUTTING TOOLS
APPLE CORER
CHEESE SLICER
CHERRY PITTER
KITCHEN SHEARS
KNIFE SHARPENER, STEEL OR STONE
KNIVES
  BONING KNIFE

BREAD KNIFE
CARVING KNIFE
CHEF'S KNIVES (small and large)
FISH FILLETING KNIFE
GRAPEFRUIT KNIFE
HAM SLICER
PARING KNIFE
SERRATED KNIFE
UTILITY KNIFE
MEAT CLEAVER
PASTRY CUTTERS, PLAIN AND FLUTED
PASTRY WHEEL
POULTRY SHEARS
VEGETABLE PEELER
ZESTER

GENERAL EQUIPMENT
CAKE RACKS
CANDY THERMOMETER
CHEESECLOTH
CHOPPING BOARD
COCKTAIL PICKS OR TOOTHPICKS
COOKIE CUTTERS, ASSORTED SHAPES
COPPER BOWL (for beating egg whites)
DEEP-FAT THERMOMETER
FLOUR SIFTER
FUNNEL
JELLY BAG
LEMON REAMER
MEAT POUNDER
METAL TONGS
NEEDLES, LARDING AND TRUSSING
NUTCRACKER
PASTRY BAG AND TUBES
PASTRY BOARD
PASTRY BRUSH
ROLLING PIN
SKEWERS
TRIVET, ADJUSTABLE

GRINDERS AND GRATERS
COFFEE GRINDER
GARLIC PRESS
GRATER, STAINLESS STEEL
MEAT GRINDER
MORTAR AND PESTLE
PEPPER MILL

KITCHEN STAPLES
ALUMINUM FOIL
FREEZER TAPE
FREEZER WRAP

KITCHEN PARCHMENT
PAPER FRILLS FOR CHOPS AND CROWN ROASTS
PAPER LINERS FOR CUPCAKE PANS
PAPER TOWELS
PLASTIC FOOD BAGS
PLASTIC WRAP
STRING FOR TRUSSING
WAXED PAPER

MEASURING, MIXING, AND WEIGHING EQUIPMENT
MEASURING CUPS, DRY AND LIQUID
MEASURING SPOONS
MIXING BOWLS
ROTARY BEATER
RUBBER SPATULAS
SCALES
WIRE WHISKS (including balloon whisk)

MOLDS
CHARLOTTE MOLD
GELATIN MOLDS
PÂTÉ EN CROÛTE MOLD
RING MOLD

OPENERS
BOTTLE OPENER
CAN OPENER
CORKSCREW
SCREW-TOP JAR OPENER

POTS AND PANS
CRÊPE PAN
DEEP-FRYER
DOUBLE BOILER
EGG POACHER
OMELET PAN
PRESERVING PAN
PRESSURE COOKER
SAUCEPANS (at least 3 sizes)
SAUTÉ PAN
SKILLETS
STEAMER
STOCK POT

STRAINERS AND SIEVES
COLANDER
DRUM SIEVE, NYLON MESH
MOULI FOOD MILL
STRAINER, WIRE OR STAINLESS STEEL
TEA STRAINER

Pots and pans

For the average family, the following pans are useful: 1 1½-quart pan, 2 2½-quart pans, a 6- or 8-quart pot, and a 10- or 12-inch frying pan.

Cast-aluminum pans conduct heat well and evenly. This kind of pan can be used on any type of range.

Enamel cast-iron pans Enamel cast-iron pans are heavy-bottomed and conduct heat evenly. Never subject them to fierce heat. Do not use abrasive scouring pads on them. Before using a new enamel pan, follow the manufacturer's instructions.

Iron pans The old-fashioned black iron skillets and Dutch ovens are excellent for cooking, but they rust easily and must be well seasoned and kept lubricated with oil.

Stainless-steel pans with bottoms made of aluminum or copper, which conduct heat evenly, are durable and easy to clean.

Copper pans lined with tin, nickel, or stainless steel, although expensive, are popular with professional cooks because they are hardwearing and conduct heat well. However, they tarnish quickly. Abrasive cleaners should never be used.

Nonstick coating is popular for use with aluminum and copper pans. Take care not to overheat this type of coating, as overheating harms the surface, and never use metal tools, which scratch nonstick surfaces.

Care of pans

Before using an aluminum pan for the first time, wash it with hot water and detergent, then rinse and dry. After use, avoid abrasives, but use scouring pads if necessary. To remove discoloration, boil a solution of lemon peel and water in the pan.

Wash stainless-steel pans with hot water and detergent. Remove stains with a stainless-steel cleanser. The copper pans lined with tin or nickel should be washed with hot water and detergent. Clean the outside of the pans with copper cleaner or vinegar and salt.

Wash nonstick pans in warm soapy water, using a sponge. Do not use abrasive powders or scouring pads on the nonstick linings.

Casseroles

Flameproof glass can be used over low heat on top of the range as well as in the oven. China, earthenware, and porcelain are generally intended for use only in the oven unless marked flameproof. Cast-iron or steel-coated vitreous enamel can be used either on the range or in the oven. Clean with soapy water.

Measuring spoons, cups, and scales

While the United States has yet to fall into step with the rest of the world in switching over to the metric system of measures, it is expected to do so within the foreseeable future. The first dual measuring cups for liquids are appearing on the market, with fluid ounces marked on one side and deciliters and milliliters on the other.

Eventually, ingredients will be measured not in teaspoons, tablespoons, pints, ounces, fluid ounces, or pounds, but in grams, kilograms, milliliters, deciliters, and liters.

Measuring spoons The leveled metric capacity of a spoon is approximately as follows:

$$15 \text{ ml} = 1 \text{ tablespoon}$$
$$10 \text{ ml} = 2 \text{ teaspoons}$$
$$5 \text{ ml} = 1 \text{ teaspoon}$$
$$2.5 \text{ ml} = \tfrac{1}{2} \text{ teaspoon}$$
$$1.25 \text{ ml} = \tfrac{1}{4} \text{ teaspoon}$$

Liquid cup measures Our standard 8-ounce measuring cup contains approximately $\frac{1}{4}$ liter (actually, 0.236 liter) and $\frac{1}{3}$ cup is approximately $\frac{1}{10}$ liter (1 deciliter or 100 milliliters), but it must be emphasized that these are approximations. The metric markings on the reverse side of the new 8-ounce dual measuring cup are as follows:

$\frac{1}{4}$ liter—250 ml or 2.5 dl
  —200 ml or 2 dl
  —150 ml or 1.5 dl
  —100 ml or 1 dl
  —50 ml or 0.5 dl

The lowest marking, 50 ml, is the equivalent of $3\frac{1}{3}$ tablespoons.

Scales The metric unit for weight is the kilo (kg), which contains 1000 grams, or 2.2 pounds. An ounce is roughly the equivalent of 28 grams. On spring balance scales, each kilo is marked in 500 grams (1.1 pounds), 250 grams (9 ounces), and 125 grams (4⅜ ounces). Each of these is further marked by 25-gram measures.

Metric measures will be easier to use than our present system because they are based on multiples of 10.

COOKING AND BAKING EQUIPMENT

Reading from left to right:

A Clockwise: *jelly bag, drum sieve, timer, plastic storage containers, measuring cup, colander, aspic cutters, metal sieves.* In the center: *tea strainer, bulb baster, rolling pin*

B Above: *fluted pâté en croûte mold, flanked by plain and fluted pastry cut-*
ters. In the center: *set of fluted quiche pans.* On the left: *cream horn molds, boat-shaped mold, and fluted tartlet tin*

C *Set of glass mixing bowls, set of pudding molds, and mortar and pestle*

D *Fancy cookie cutters in front of dariole mold.* At the back: *jelly-roll pans, round layer-cake pans.* At front: *cast-iron griddle, sheets of muffin and tartlet pans*

E *Brioche pans placed on loaf pans.* At front: *savarin mold*

F *Charlotte mold, baking sheet with roasting pans and gelatin molds, kugelhopf mold.* In front: *ring mold*

G *Enameled cast-iron casseroles*

H *Food mill, graters, meat grinder, chopping board, lemon reamer*

I *Set of soufflé dishes, ramekins, pie dishes with pie funnel, gratin dishes*

J Clockwise: *aluminum preserving pan, double boiler, deep-fryer, steamer, asbestos mat, omelet pan, fish poacher.* In the center: *egg poacher*

K *Wire rack, square loose-bottomed cake pans, round loose-bottomed cake pans, nonstick cake pans, waffle iron*

L *Large fabric pastry bag, plain and star vegetable tubes, plain and star-shaped piping tips, plastic decorating bag with decorating tips*

The Cook's Workshop

Reading left to right, first row:

1–3 *Set of chef's knives*
4 *Sharpening steel*
5 *All-purpose knife*
6 *Carving knife*
7 *Ham slicer*
8 *Bread knife*
9 *Grapefruit knife*
10 *Meat tenderizer*
11 *Meat pounder*
12 *Meat cleaver*
13 *Crescent-shaped chopper*
14 *Kitchen shears*
15 *Poultry shears*
16 *Nutcracker*
17 *Cherry pitter*

Second row:

18 *Wooden kitchen fork*
19 *Carving fork*
20 *Metal tongs*
21 & 22 *Ladles*
23 *Three types of metal spatulas*
24 *Rubber spatula*
25 *Wooden spatula*
26 *Pancake turner*
27 *Basting spoon*
28 *Perforated spoon*
29 *Four types of wooden spoons and a wooden spatula*

Third row:

30 *Potato peeler*
31 *Pastry wheel*
32 *Pastry brush*
33 *Melon-ball cutter*
34 *Lemon stripper*
35 *Apple corer*
36 *Bottle opener*
37 *Corkscrew*
38 *Mandoline slicer*
39 *Larding needle*
40 *Trussing needle*
41 *Garlic press*
42 *Potato masher*
43 *Rotary beater*
44 *Balloon whisk*
45 *Skewers*
46 *Deep-fat thermometer*
47 *Manual can opener*
48 *Spiked can opener*
49 *Bottle brush*

General safety procedures

1 Appliances approved by Underwriters' Laboratories are safe.

2 Before cleaning or examining appliances, plugs should be removed from the outlet.

3 If an iron is dropped, it should be examined by a qualified electrician before further use.

4 The kitchen should be provided with enough outlets to avoid trailing cords and overloaded circuits.

5 Cords, which must be kept in good condition, should never be joined together with insulating tape.

6 Never touch plugs or switches with wet hands.

Ranges These should not be positioned near the door, for obvious safety reasons. Gas ranges should not have exhaust fans fitted directly above them.

New gas ranges are fitted with an automatic device that cuts off the gas supply when the pilot light is not igniting. If the pilot light fails on older models and a smell of gas is noticeable, open the windows to create a draft; contact your local utility company. Never attempt to trace a gas leak with a naked flame.

Deep-fryers Never fill more than a third full with oil or fat because the liquids may boil over. If the oil should catch fire, *never* douse the flames with water; cover the pan and turn off the heat.

Fire extinguishers Ideally every kitchen should be equipped with some form of fire extinguisher.

Knives Keep these out of reach of children, preferably on a wall-mounted magnetic knife rack or in wooden cases, apart from other kitchen tools.

Freezing

The freezer is a time and money saver for anyone who cooks for a family. It enables a cook to plan bulk buying and cooking well in advance. And if the rules for the preparation, packaging, and thawing of the raw materials are carefully followed, frozen food loses nothing in freshness and quality. A separate freezer can be housed in a garage or cellar to save valuable kitchen space.

Buying a freezer

Today, most households have a combination refrigerator-freezer. However, if your refrigerator only has the small freezing compartment, it can be supplemented by one of the two basic types of freezer, the upright variety or the top-opening chest type.

The upright variety takes up less floor space and filling it is easy.

The chest type necessitates a list of contents and the use of wire racks and baskets so that you know where everything is and by what date it must be used. The top of a chest freezer can serve as an additional work surface in the kitchen.

Size of freezer

One cubic foot of storage space will contain 20–25 pounds of food. A minimum of 2 cubic feet of freezer space should be allowed for each member of the family—more if the family entertains frequently.

Operating costs

A freezer uses less electricity than a refrigerator. The fuller the freezer is packed, the cheaper it is to operate. To keep electric bills down, the top or door should be opened as infrequently as possible.

Care and maintenance of the freezer

The freezer should be checked yearly by the manufacturer's service representative or by the company that sold the machine. The contents of the freezer should be insured against power failure or breakdowns. Where possible, an arrangement should be made with a frozen food locker plant with emergency generators to store food at short notice.

Unless the freezer is self-defrosting, it should be cleaned out at least once every 6 months, using the following procedure:

1 Remove packages and wrap them in newspaper to prevent thawing.

2 Turn off the electricity and place bowls of boiling water in the cabinet to speed up thawing.

3 Scrape the ice from the sides and scoop it up from the bottom.

4 When the freezer is empty, wipe it with a clean cloth dipped in a solution of baking soda or vinegar and water to remove stale smells.

5 As soon as the freezer is defrosted, turn the control to maximum, then check and return the packages.

If a bag or package breaks in the freezer, the contents should be removed at once to prevent any odor from contaminating the other food in the freezer.

Food should be labeled with the name, weight, and date on which it was frozen and the date by which it should be used. Foods should be stored and used in rotation.

In an emergency

If the power fails, food in a freezer should remain frozen for 48 hours if the door is kept closed. Do not open the door until 6 hours after power has been restored.

Bulk buying for the freezer

The prices of all fresh foods fluctuate according to season. Buy meat and poultry, fruit, and vegetables in peak condition at their lowest prices and in quantities that can easily be wrapped and frozen on the day of purchase. Fish should only be frozen when absolutely fresh.

Bulk suppliers of a wide range of frozen products can be found in most parts of the country.

Equipment for the freezer

Good-quality heavy-duty polyethylene bags, plastic or aluminum-foil containers, and waxed and treated paper containers can be reused if washed after use.

Heatproof glass and metal casseroles and baking dishes save time if they can be used to cook, freeze, and serve a meal. Square or oblong shapes are easier to store in the freezer than round shapes.

Suitable packaging materials

Wrapping: Moistureproof and vaporproof materials such as polyethylene, aluminum foil, and waxed freezer wrap.

Bags: Heavy-duty polyethylene plastic bags, which are usually available in a wide range of sizes.

Cartons and containers: Plastic containers with snap-on lids, waxed cardboard cartons and containers, aluminum trays and stainless-steel bowls with plastic lids. Square and rectangular cartons are easier to store than round ones.

Sealing materials: Sealing iron for sealing polyethylene bags. Rubber bands. Freezer tape.

Labeling materials: Self-adhesive, moistureproof labels. Waterproof felt pen to mark packages.

Successful packaging

If food is improperly wrapped, it will develop "freezer burn"—white spots on the surface. If this occurs, the food must be used immediately. The flavor and texture may be damaged, and food may require a sauce to make it palatable.

Squeeze as much air as possible from the packages before sealing them properly. Solid foods should be packed as closely as possible; liquids should have at least $\frac{1}{2}$ inch headspace to allow for expansion during freezing. Separate items packaged in the same container, such as hamburgers, small steaks, or veal scallops, should be separated by a layer of waxed paper to prevent the foods from sticking together.

GUIDE TO FREEZING PRECOOKED FOOD

Being able to freeze precooked dishes for later use has numerous advantages. Leftovers can be stored for later use. Time can be spent in the kitchen when it is convenient. Quantities of recipes can be doubled to save time, energy, and cooking expense, with one dish eaten at once and the other frozen. People who entertain frequently can do most of the cooking well in advance, and those with large families can stock up for the holidays.

To freeze precooked food successfully, it is important to follow these points carefully:

1 Working surroundings must be scrupulously clean, as freezing does not destroy germs in food.

2 Use top-quality ingredients and season lightly; more seasoning can always be added later.

3 Always slightly undercook dishes that are to be frozen, allowing for the time the food will be in the oven to heat through.

4 When recipes for soups, sauces, and casseroles call for the addition of cream or egg yolks, omit these before freezing and add them when the dishes are being reheated. Do not freeze dishes that contain custard or mayonnaise.

5 Omit garlic before freezing (it can be added later) unless the food is going to remain in the freezer for only a short time.

6 Be generous with sauces so that meat, chicken, fish, and game will not dehydrate when frozen.

7 Cool all cooked and baked dishes quickly and thoroughly before packing and freezing them. Do this by placing the dish, pan, or casserole in a sink of cold water. Ice cubes added to the water will help to cool the dish even faster.

8 Garnish reheated food before serving, not before freezing.

9 Pack and label all precooked foods carefully and note the number of portions. Soups can be frozen in square containers, removed when solid, and then packed in polyethylene bags; casseroles can be frozen in their cooking dishes, turned out, and packed in polyethylene bags to be returned to their dishes for thawing and reheating. Freeze small amounts of vegetable cooking water, broth, and stock in ice-cube trays; then empty the cubes into plastic bags and use as needed in recipes for soups, stews, and sauces.

10 Do not freeze the following, as the results are disappointing: whole cooked roasts or poultry; cold meat without a sauce; gelatin desserts; or sandwiches with mayonnaise, hard-cooked egg, tomato, cucumber, or banana fillings.

GUIDE TO FREEZING FRESH FOOD

Vegetables

Freeze only young, unblemished, freshly picked vegetables.

Most vegetables must be blanched before being frozen. Blanch* the prepared vegetables, 1 pound at a time, in 3 quarts of boiling water. The water should be brought back to a boil within 1 minute of adding the vegetables. Blanching time varies for different vegetables (see chart). Immediately after blanching, the vegetables should be plunged into ice water to cool and to prevent further cooking. Drain the cooled vegetables thoroughly and pack in rigid containers or polyethylene bags.

Vegetables will store for 1 year unless otherwise indicated on chart.

Meat

Only good-quality fresh meat should be frozen. Cut the meat into convenient sizes, such as roasts and chops. Remove as much bone as possible so that the meat will take up less space in the freezer. The bones can be used to make stock.

Meat to be used in stews and casseroles can be cut into cubes and packed in rigid containers.

Remove excess fat, as it can become rancid if exposed to oxygen. For the same reason, pack meat carefully in airtight wrappings. Pad sharp corners or bones with foil or thin self-adhesive plastic wrap to prevent them from perforating the packaging. Wrap the meat in foil first, then overwrap with heavy-duty freezer wrap, excluding as much air as possible.

Weigh the meat before freezing, and label it with weight, description, and date. Chops, steaks, and hamburgers should be interleaved with waxed paper or plastic wrap so that they can be easily separated.

Allow meat to thaw slowly in its wrapping in a cool place or in the

Food (storage time in brackets)	Method	Thawing and serving
COOKIES, unbaked (6 months)	Shape dough into cylinders about 2 inches wide and wrap in foil or plastic wrap. Shape soft mixtures on a paper-lined tray, freeze, then pack carefully in rigid containers, separating layers with paper.	Slightly thaw rolls of uncooked dough, slice, and bake. Shaped cookies can be baked from the frozen state but will need 7–10 minutes more cooking time.
COOKIES, baked	Pack as for shaped soft cookies before freezing.	Baked cookies can be crisped in a warm oven after thawing.
BREAD, baked (4 weeks)	Wrap in polyethylene bags.	Thaw in wrapper at room temperature (3 hours for regular loaves) or overnight in refrigerator. May be thawed in oven at 300°F for about 30 minutes, but this causes bread to go stale quickly. Sliced bread can be toasted from the frozen state.
BREAD AND ROLLS, bought part-baked (4 months)	Freeze immediately after buying; leave loaves in own wrapper, pack rolls in polyethylene bags.	To bake, place frozen unwrapped loaf in oven at 425°F for about 40 minutes. Cool before cutting. Bake unwrapped rolls at 400°F for 15 minutes.
CAKES, (6 months; frosted cakes lose quality after 2 months)	Use less extract and spice than usual. Fill cakes with cream, but not jam, before freezing. Wrap unfilled layer cakes separately or separate with waxed paper or plastic wrap; pack in foil or polyethylene. Freeze frosted cakes unwrapped until frosting has set, then wrap in foil or plastic wrap and pack in boxes to protect frosting.	Cream-filled cakes are best sliced while frozen. Unwrap frosted cakes before thawing so that paper does not stick to frosting. Leave plain cakes in wrapping and thaw at room temperature. Allow 1–2 hours for plain layer cakes and small cakes, 4 hours for frosted cakes.
CASSEROLES: poultry, fish, meat with vegetables, or pasta (2–4 months)	Cool mixture quickly. Turn into a casserole or freezer container. Cover tightly, seal, and label.	If frozen in ovenproof casserole, uncover. Bake at 400°F for 1 hour for pints and 1¾ hours for quarts, or until heated through. Or remove from freezer container and place in top of a double boiler, cover, and heat through.
CROISSANTS AND DANISH PASTRIES, unbaked (6 weeks)	Prepare dough to the stage when all fat has been absorbed, but do not give final rolling. Wrap tightly in polyethylene bag.	Leave in polyethylene bags but unseal and retie loosely to allow dough to rise. Thaw overnight in refrigerator or for about 5 hours at room temperature. Roll and shape before baking.
CROISSANTS AND DANISH PASTRIES, baked (Croissants, 2 months Danish pastries, 1 month)	Wrap in polyethylene bags or foil, or in rigid foil containers.	Thaw in wrapping at room temperature for about 1 hour. If desired, heat in oven, unwrapped, at 350°F for 5 minutes.
ICE CREAM (homemade, 3 months commercial, 1 month)	Wrap bought ice cream in moistureproof bags; freeze homemade ice cream in molds or waxed containers, and overwrap with plastic wrap.	Place in refrigerator for 1–1½ hours to soften.
MEAT DISHES (2 months)	Cook for a slightly shorter time than usual to allow for reheating. Do not season heavily. Make sure meat is completely immersed in gravy or sauce. It is better to add potatoes, rice, noodles, garlic, and celery at time of serving. Pack in rigid foil containers; or freeze in foil-lined casserole, remove, and pack in polyethylene bags.	Turn frozen food out of container into saucepan to reheat. Preformed foil-lined dishes may be reheated in oven in original casserole for 1 hour at 400°F, reducing heat, if necessary, to 350°F for last 40 minutes.

AND PRECOOKED DISHES

Food (storage time in brackets)	Method	Thawing and serving
MEAT LOAVES, PÂTÉS, TERRINES (1 month)	Make in usual way, taking care not to season or spice heavily. When cold, remove from pans or molds and wrap in plastic wrap and also in foil before freezing.	Thaw in wrapping for 6–8 hours, or thaw overnight in refrigerator.
MOUSSES, COLD SOUFFLÉS (2 months)	Freeze in special heatproof and coldproof glassware, or line dishes or molds with foil, freeze, then remove from container and wrap in polyethylene bags to store.	Thaw in refrigerator for 6–8 hours or at room temperature for 2–3 hours.
CRÊPES, unfilled (2 months)	Stack crêpes between layers of waxed paper; wrap them in conveniently sized stacks in foil or plastic wrap.	Thaw in wrapping at room temperature for 2–3 hours, or thaw overnight in refrigerator. To thaw quickly, unwrap, spread out crêpes, and thaw at room temperature for about 20 minutes. Heat individual crêpes in a lightly buttered crêpe pan for 30 seconds each side. Or heat stack of crêpes wrapped in foil in oven at 375°F for 20–30 minutes.
CRÊPES, filled (1–2 months)	Choose fillings that are suitable for freezing. Do not season heavily. Pack filled crêpes in foil containers, seal, and overwrap.	Remove overwrapping, place frozen crêpes in foil container, unopened, in oven at 400°F for about 30 minutes or until thawed.
PASTRY, unbaked (3 months)	Make as usual and roll out to size required. Line foil plates or pie pans, freeze unwrapped, remove from pie pans, and wrap in polyethylene. Roll out top crusts and separate with waxed paper before wrapping in polyethylene. Stack, separating the layers with two sheets of waxed paper, place on cardboard, and wrap. Single- or double-crust fruit pies can be frozen uncooked with the filling in place, ready for baking. Do not make slits in the top crust before freezing. Wrap in foil or polyethylene bags when frozen solid.	Return pie shells to original dishes. Thaw top crusts at room temperature before fitting on filled pies. Pie shells can be baked frozen (ovenproof glassware should be left to stand at room temperature for 10 minutes before baking). Add 5 minutes to baking time. Place unwrapped fruit pies in oven at 425°F for 40–60 minutes. Slit tops of crusts when beginning to thaw.
PASTRY, baked (pastry shells and fruit pies, 6 months meat pies, 3 months)	Bake pies in foil containers and cool quickly. Wrap in foil or polyethylene. Tops can be protected with an inverted foil dish before wrapping.	Thaw at room temperature; pies for 2–4 hours. Reheat in oven.
PIZZAS, unbaked (3 months)	Prepare to baking stage. Wrap in foil or polyethylene. Freeze and overwrap.	Remove wrapping and place frozen pizza in cold oven set at 450°F, bake for 30–35 minutes.
PIZZAS, baked (2 months)	Wrap in foil or polyethylene and freeze as for unbaked pizza.	Remove wrapping and heat in oven at 350°F for about 15 minutes.
SAUCES, SOUPS, STOCKS (2–3 months)	Cool thoroughly and pour into rigid containers; or wrap in polyethylene when frozen solid.	Heat from frozen state until boiling point, or thaw for 1–2 hours at room temperature.
SWEET BREADS, MUFFINS, BISCUITS (6 months)	Wrap in plastic bags in convenient quantities.	Thaw muffins and biscuits for 30–60 minutes at room temperature; warm them in the oven if desired. Thaw sweet breads in wrapping for 2–3 hours at room temperature; or place frozen in oven at 400°F for about 10 minutes or until thawed.

refrigerator. If it is needed in a hurry, the thawing can be speeded up by placing the meat, in its wrapping, in cold water; however, some of the flavor will be lost. Small cuts of meat, such as chops and steaks, can be cooked from the frozen state, but it is advisable to cook them over lower heat than usual.

Poultry and game

Only young, plump birds should be frozen fresh, whole or disjointed. Older birds, whether poultry or game, are best cooked as casseroles before freezing.

Remove giblets and clean and freeze them separately, as they have a shorter storage life. Clean the birds thoroughly; do not stuff them, but truss them ready for cooking. Pad the legs with aluminum foil before wrapping the whole bird in heavy-duty plastic or freezer wrap. Label with weight, description, and date. Pack disjointed birds in portions, interspersed with waxed paper.

Stuffings should be frozen separately, as they should be stored for no longer than a month. Pack livers in plastic bags and freeze for use in pâtés and risottos.

Poultry and game birds should be thawed slowly in their wrappings in the refrigerator. In an emergency, a frozen bird can be thawed in its wrapping in cold water.

Young game birds, well hung, are frozen as poultry. Rabbit is best cut up and frozen in pieces, ready for cooking. Venison should be well hung before it is cut up and frozen.

Fish

Fish should be frozen fresh within 12 hours of being caught. It is not advisable to freeze even fresh shellfish at home, but you can buy frozen crab, clams, and shrimp. These can be stored in the freezer for about 1 month.

Small round fish can be frozen whole after scaling and gutting. Larger round fish should be scaled and gutted, and the heads and tails removed. Flat fish is best frozen in fillets, interleaved with waxed paper. To preserve moisture in the prepared fish, rub with a little olive oil. Wrap in heavy-duty plastic wrap and freezer wrap or aluminum foil, and label as usual.

The delicate flavor of whole salmon and trout can be retained by freezing these fish in a sheet of ice. Dip the fish in cold salted water several times, placing it on a baking sheet in the freezer between immersions so that a layer of ice forms around the fish and seals it from the air. Then pack as for other fish. Salmon and other fatty fish should not be frozen longer than 2 months.

Thaw whole fish slowly in the original wrappings, preferably in the refrigerator. Allow about 8 hours per pound if thawing on the refrigerator shelf, 4 hours per pound at room temperature. If the fish is placed in front of an electric fan, it will take about 2½ hours per pound to thaw out. Cook as soon as the fish is thawed. Steaks and fillets can be cooked from the frozen state.

Fruit

Top-quality fruit in peak condition is suitable for freezing whole; slightly overripe fruit is better puréed.

To prepare fruit for freezing, wash it in chilled water, then drain and dry thoroughly. Soft berries, such as strawberries, blueberries, and raspberries, should be washed only if absolutely necessary.

Keep fruit in a cool place or in the refrigerator until it is prepared for freezing. Pitted fruit can be frozen whole, halved, or sliced. There are three ways of freezing: dry-freezing, sugar-freezing, and syrup-freezing.

Dry-freezing is particularly suitable for small whole berries. Spread the cleaned and dry fruit in a single layer on paper-lined trays. Place in the freezer until firm, then pack the berries in rigid containers or heavy-duty plastic bags.

Freezing

Sugar-freezing is recommended for soft fruits, such as blackberries, raspberries, and strawberries. Pick over the fruit carefully but do not wash it. Layer the fruit with the sugar in rigid containers or mix the two together, allowing ½ cup sugar to 1 pound prepared fruit. Allow about ½ inch headspace.

Syrup-freezing is the best method for nonjuicy fruits and those that discolor during preparation and storage, such as peaches and apricots. The strength of the syrup varies according to the fruit (see chart). Pack the fruit in rigid containers, using enough syrup to cover the fruit well, leaving a ½-inch headspace.

Fruit juices, such as plum, apple, grape, and cherry, freeze well. To each gallon of apple or cherry juice, add 2 teaspoons lemon juice or ½ teaspoon ascorbic acid. Plum, grape, and cherry juice will taste better if fruit is slightly cooked to extract additional flavor from the skins. Extract the juice from the fruits just before freezing it. Fruit for jams and jellies can be frozen without sugar and the juice extracted later without cooking.

Label all packages with the name of the fruit, weight, and the amount of sugar added. Also be sure to indicate the date of freezing.

Whole and sliced frozen fruit will store for as long as 1 year, fruit purées for 6–8 months, and fruit juices for 4–6 months.

All frozen fruits should be thawed slowly in their unopened containers. To serve fruit as a dessert, thaw in the refrigerator for 6 hours or at room temperature for 2–3 hours. Serve the fruit chilled.

If dessert fruit has been frozen in syrup, remove the lid from the container and place a weight over the fruit to keep it immersed in the syrup.

Frozen fruit to be stewed can be cooked without thawing, but fruit for tarts, pies, and puddings should first be thawed.

FREEZING VEGETABLES

Vegetables	Preparation and packing	Cooking
ARTICHOKES, globe	Remove coarse outer leaves and stalks; trim tops and stems, removing chokes. Wash in cold water and blanch in acidulated water* for 7 minutes. Cool and drain. Pack in rigid containers.	Cook frozen in boiling salted water for 8 minutes or until leaves are tender and easily removed.
ASPARAGUS	Remove woody parts, cut into even lengths, and wash well. Grade into thick and thin stems. Blanch thin stems for 2 minutes, thick ones for 4 minutes. Cool and drain. Pack, tips to stalks, in rigid containers or wrap small bundles in waxed paper or foil.	Cook frozen in boiling salted water for 5–8 minutes.
BEANS, green, pole, fava	Wash well. Trim green, slice pole, and shell fava beans. Blanch for 3 minutes, cool, and pack in plastic bags.	Cook frozen in salted water: whole beans and fava beans 7–8 minutes; sliced beans 5 minutes.
BROCCOLI	Trim off woody parts and outer leaves. Wash in salted water; divide into small sprigs and grade in sizes. Blanch for 3–5 minutes, cool, and drain. Pack in rigid containers, stalks to tips.	Cook frozen in boiling salted water for 5–8 minutes.
BRUSSELS SPROUTS	Choose small, compact sprouts. Remove outer leaves. Wash; grade into sizes. Blanch 3 minutes, cool, and drain. Pack in plastic bags.	Cook frozen in boiling salted water for 8 minutes.
CABBAGES, green and red	Choose young, crisp cabbages. Wash thoroughly, shred finely, blanch for 2 minutes, cool, and drain. Pack in plastic bags.	Cook frozen in boiling salted water for 8 minutes.
CARROTS	Choose young carrots. Remove tops, wash, and scrape. Leave whole. Blanch for 5 minutes, cool, and drain. Pack in plastic bags.	Cook frozen in boiling salted water for 8 minutes.
CAULIFLOWER (storage time: 6 months)	Choose firm, white cauliflower. Wash; break into florets. Blanch 3 minutes in acidulated water,* cool, and drain. Pack in plastic bags.	Cook frozen in boiling salted water for 8–10 minutes.
CELERY	Use crisp, young stalks; remove stem bases and leaves. Cut into 1-inch lengths. Blanch 3 minutes, cool, and drain. Pack in plastic bags. Alternatively, pack in rigid containers and cover with blanching liquid.	Thaw at room temperature for 1 hour and add to casseroles and stews. Cook in blanching liquid for about 10 minutes if served as a side dish.
CORN	Freeze fresh young corn only. Remove husks and silk. Blanch 4 minutes, cool, and dry. Pack in foil. Or blanch and cool, cut off kernels, and pack in plastic bags or rigid containers.	Cook frozen corn in boiling salted water for 4–5 minutes.
MUSHROOMS (storage time: 3 months)	Wipe clean; do not peel. Mushrooms more than 1 inch wide should be sliced. Sauté in butter, cool quickly, and pack in containers, leaving ½ inch headspace.	Cook frozen mushrooms in butter, or add to stews and casseroles.
PEAS	Shell young peas. Blanch for 1 minute, shaking basket to distribute heat evenly. Cool, drain, and pack in plastic bags.	Cook frozen in boiling salted water for 7 minutes.
POTATOES	Freeze only small new potatoes whole. Blanch for 4 minutes, cool, drain, and pack in plastic bags. *French fries:* Peel, wash, and dry; cut into even-size strips. Fry in deep fat for 3 minutes. Drain on paper towels and cool quickly. Pack in plastic bags.	Cook frozen in boiling salted water for 15 minutes. Thaw French fries partially at room temperature for 30–60 minutes. Deep-fry for 3 minutes.
SPINACH	Select young leaves; trim off stalks. Wash thoroughly and drain. Blanch in small quantities for 2 minutes. Cool and press out excess moisture. Pack in rigid containers, leaving ½ inch headspace.	Cook frozen spinach in melted butter for 7 minutes.
TOMATOES	*Purée:* Peel, core, and simmer in their own juice for 5 minutes. Purée in blender; cool and pack in rigid containers in quantities suitable for use. *Juice:* Wash, quarter, and core tomatoes. Simmer for 5–10 minutes. Press through a nylon sieve. Add 1 teaspoon salt to 4 cups juice. Cool and pack.	Use frozen purée in sauces, soups, and stews. Thaw juice in container in the refrigerator and serve chilled.
TURNIPS	Trim, peel, and dice young turnips. Blanch for 2½ minutes, cool, and drain. Pack in plastic bags.	Cook frozen diced turnips in boiling salted water for 5–10 minutes. Heat mashed turnips in a double boiler.
ZUCCHINI	Select young zucchini. Wash, trim off ends, and cut into ½-inch slices. Blanch for 1 minute, cool, and drain.	Cook frozen in butter.

FREEZING MEAT

Meat (storage time in brackets)	Preparation and packaging	Thawing
ROASTS (beef, 8 months; lamb, pork, and veal, 6 months)	Wrap in heavy-duty plastic bags, seal well, and label. Can be overwrapped with foil.	Thaw thoroughly before cooking, preferably in the refrigerator. Allow 5 hours per pound in the refrigerator, 2 hours per pound at room temperature.
SCALLOPS, CHOPS, HAMBURGERS, STEAKS, AND CUBED MEAT (3 months)	Pack in suitable quantities. Separate scallops, chops, hamburgers, and steaks with waxed paper. Pack in plastic bags or rigid containers.	These small cuts can be cooked frozen over gentle heat.
GROUND MEAT AND SAUSAGE MEAT (3 months)	Divide into small quantities and pack in bags or rigid containers.	Thaw in a cool place for 1½ hours or in the refrigerator for 3 hours.
VARIETY MEATS AND SAUSAGES (1–3 months)	Clean and trim variety meats. Pack in small quantities in plastic bags.	Thaw in a cool place for 1½ hours or in the refrigerator for 3 hours.

FREEZING POULTRY

Poultry	Preparation and packaging	Thawing
(**CHICKEN** 12 months **DUCK** 4–6 months **GOOSE** 4–6 months **TURKEY** 6 months **GIBLETS** 3 months **LIVERS** 3 months)	Wrap whole birds in heavy-duty polyethylene. Trim bones from joints and wrap individually before packing in heavy-duty polyethylene. Pieces for pies and casseroles can be packed in rigid containers. Pack giblets and livers separately in plastic bags.	Thaw in wrapping in the refrigerator, a whole bird for 8 hours, parts and pieces for 2–3 hours. Thaw livers and giblets in wrapping in the refrigerator for 2 hours.

FREEZING GAME

Game	Preparation and packaging	Thawing
BIRDS (6–8 months)	As poultry	As poultry
RABBIT (6 months)	Wrap each piece in plastic wrap and pack several portions in heavy-duty polyethylene.	Thaw in wrapping in the refrigerator for 2–3 hours.
VENISON (up to 12 months)	Freeze well-hung meat in roasts or chops. Wrap roasts in plastic wrap and polyethylene bags. Pack chops individually.	Thaw in wrapping in the refrigerator for 5 hours.

FREEZING FISH

Fish (storage time in brackets)	Packaging	Thawing
WHOLE FISH (6 months)	Pack tightly in heavy-duty polyethylene.	Thaw large fish in wrapping in the refrigerator for about 6 hours. Small whole fish can be cooked frozen over low heat.
FILLETS, STEAKS (6 months)	Wrap each piece in waxed paper, then pack in suitable portions in heavy-duty polyethylene.	Thaw in wrapping in the refrigerator for about 3 hours.

FREEZING FRUIT

Fruit	Preparation and packing
APPLES	Peel, core, and slice, dropping slices into cold acidulated water. Blanch for 1–2 minutes, then cool in ice water. Drain well. Dry-freeze or sugar-freeze. Pack in polyethylene bags or rigid containers, leaving ½ inch headspace. *Purée:* Prepare as for slices. Cook in a minimum of water and add sugar to taste. Cook until soft, then beat to a smooth pulp. Cool before packing in rigid containers, leaving ½ inch headspace.
APRICOTS	Plunge into boiling water for 30 seconds and peel. Remove pits, and halve or slice. Freeze in syrup made from 2 cups sugar to 4 cups water and add ¼ teaspoon ascorbic acid to every 2 cups syrup. Pack in rigid containers, leaving ½ inch headspace.
BLACKBERRIES, RASPBERRIES, STRAWBERRIES	Dry-freeze or sugar-freeze, then pack in bags or rigid containers. *Purée:* Press through a nylon sieve and sweeten to taste with superfine sugar. Pack in rigid containers.
CHERRIES	Remove stalks, wash and dry cherries, and dry-freeze. Alternatively, remove pits and sugar-freeze until firm. Pack in rigid containers. Freeze pitted cherries in syrup made with 1 cup sugar to 2 cups water; add ½ teaspoon ascorbic acid to every 4 cups syrup. Pack in rigid containers, leaving ½ inch headspace.
CURRANTS, red	Wash, dry, and dry-freeze or sugar-freeze until firm, then pack in rigid containers.
GOOSE-BERRIES	Wash, dry, and trim. Dry-freeze or pack in syrup made with 2 cups sugar to 2 cups water; store in rigid containers.
GRAPEFRUIT	Peel, removing all pith. Divide into segments and sugar-freeze, using 1 cup sugar to 1 pound prepared fruit; when juice starts to run, pack segments in rigid containers.
LEMONS	Squeeze out juice, strain, and freeze in ice-cube trays; pack frozen cubes in plastic bags. Remove all pith from the peel, cut into fine strips, blanch for 1 minute, cool, and pack in small quantities in plastic bags. Or freeze grated peel.
MELONS	Cut in half and remove seeds. Cut flesh into cubes or balls. Freeze in syrup made with 1 cup sugar to 2 cups water. Pack in rigid containers, leaving ½ inch headspace.
ORANGES	Freeze and pack segments as for grapefruit; freeze juice and rind as for lemon.
PEACHES	Peel and pit peaches; cut in half or slice; brush immediately with lemon juice to prevent discoloration. Freeze and pack in syrup as for apricots. Alternatively, purée peeled and pitted peaches. Add 1 tablespoon lemon juice and ½ cup sugar to each pound of prepared fruit. Pack in rigid containers.
PINEAPPLE	Peel and cut into slices or chunks. Pack in rigid containers, separating with double thickness of plastic wrap. Or freeze in syrup made with 1 cup sugar to 2 cups water, including any pineapple juice from the preparation. Pack in rigid containers, leaving ½ inch headspace.
PLUMS	Wash, halve, and remove pits. Freeze as for apricots.
RHUBARB	Wash, trim, and cut into 1-inch lengths. Blanch for 1 minute, drain, and cool. Do not use aluminum containers for packing; sugar-freeze and pack in plastic bags. Alternatively, freeze in syrup made with equal quantities of sugar and water.

A to Z of Cooking Terms

The terms described in this glossary occur throughout the book and are also seen on many restaurant menus. Letters in brackets indicate the country of origin. A stands for Austria; F for France; G for Germany; Gr for Greece; H for Hungary; Hol for Holland; I for Italy; In for India; R for Russia; S for Spain; Sw for Switzerland; and T for Turkey.

A

acidulated water The addition of lemon juice or vinegar to cold water, which prevents discoloration of some fruits and vegetables. To every cup of water, add 1 teaspoon of lemon juice or vinegar
à la (F) In the style of, e.g., *à la Russe* means "in the Russian style"
à la carte (F) 1. Bill of fare from which the diner selects individual dishes. 2. Dishes cooked to order
à la crème (F) Served with cream or with a cream-based sauce
à l'anglaise (F) In the English style, e.g., boiled and served with a sauce
al dente (I) Cooked, but firm to the bite; usually refers to pasta
alla (I) In the style of, e.g., *alla Parmigiano,* means "in Parmesan style"
allumettes (F) 1. A kind of hors d'oeuvre or small entrée made from puff pastry cut into narrow strips and garnished. 2. Small, narrow cakes made from puff pastry and garnished.
amandine (F) Cooking or coating with almonds
amaretti Italian macaroons
antipasti (I) Cold or hot Italian hors d'oeuvres
arrowroot Starch made by grinding the root of a plant of the same name; used mainly for thickening sauces
aspic Clear jelly made from the stock of meat, chicken, or fish
au bleu (F) Blue; fish, especially trout, cooked immediately after being caught in a court bouillon with vinegar will turn blue
au gratin (F) Cooked food sprinkled with crumbs or grated cheese, dotted with butter, and browned under the broiler

B

bain-marie (F) 1. A large pan of hot water, or "bath," in which a smaller pan is placed for cooking contents or to keep foods warm. 2. A double boiler with water in the lower half
barding Covering lean meat, game, and poultry with thin slices of pork fat or bacon to prevent the flesh from drying out during roasting
barquette Small tart baked in an oval pan shaped like a boat. It can be filled with fruit or custard as a dessert, or with cocktail foods, such as cheese, fish, shrimp, or other shellfish
basting Moistening meat or poultry with pan juices during roasting, using a spoon or bulb baster
beating Mixing food to introduce air to make it lighter and fluffier, using a wooden spoon, wire whisk, or electric mixer
binding Adding eggs, cream, or melted fat to a dry mixture to hold it together
bitok (R) Small meat patty made from raw ground beef and bread and bound together with egg
blanching Boiling briefly 1. To loosen the skin from nuts, fruits, and vegetables. 2. To set the color of food and to kill enzymes prior to freezing. 3. To remove strong or bitter flavors
blanquette (F) Veal, chicken, or rabbit stew in a creamy sauce
blending Combining ingredients with a spoon, beater, or electric blender to achieve a uniform mixture
blini, bliny (R) Crêpe made of buckwheat and yeast, traditionally served with caviar and sour cream
boiling Cooking in liquid at a temperature of 212°F
boning Removing bones of meat, poultry, game, or fish
bouchée (F) Small puff-pastry shell, baked blind and filled with a savory or sweet mixture
bouquet garni (F) A combination of parsley, bay leaf, and thyme, tied with string; or a ready-made mixture of herbs in a cloth bag. Used for flavoring soups, stews, sauces, and braised foods. A small bouquet garni should contain 2 sprigs of parsley, $\frac{1}{3}$ bay leaf, and 1 sprig or $\frac{1}{8}$ teaspoon of thyme.
bourguignonne, à la (F) In the style of Burgundy; a method of preparation, usually for large cuts of meat, that includes braising in red wine and garnishing with mushrooms, onions, and bacon
braising Browning in hot fat and then cooking slowly in a covered pot with vegetables and a little liquid
brine Salt and water solution used for pickling and preserving
brioche (F) Soft bread made of rich yeast dough, slightly sweetened
brochette (F) Skewer used for cooking chunks of meat, fish, and vegetables over charcoal or under a broiler
browning Searing the outer surface of meat to seal in the juices
brûlé (F) Finished with a caramelized sugar glaze; applied to dishes such as cream custards
bundt pan A fluted tube pan for baking cakes

C

canapé (F) Appetizer consisting of small pieces of fresh or fried bread, toast, or crackers topped with savory mixtures
cannelloni (I) Pasta stuffed and rolled with savory fillings
capers Pickled flower buds of the Mediterranean caper bush; used to flavor sauces and garnishes
caponata (I) Sicilian dish of fish, eggplant, tomatoes, onions, capers, and olives
caquelon (Sw) Wide, rather shallow earthenware pot often used for cooking cheese fondue
carbonnade (F) Beef stew made with beer
casserole (F) 1. Cooking pot with lid, made of ovenproof or flameproof earthenware, glass, or metal. 2. Slow-cooked stew of meat, fish, or vegetables
cassoulet (F) Stew of dried white beans, pork, lamb, goose or duck, sausage, vegetables, and herbs
champignon (F) Mushroom. *Champignon de Paris:* cultivated button mushroom
Chantilly (F) Served with whipped cream that is slightly sweetened and sometimes flavored with vanilla
Charlotte 1. Hot, molded fruit pudding made of buttered slices of bread and a cooked fruit filling. 2. Cold molded dessert consisting of ladyfingers and a filling of cream and fruit or a cream custard set with gelatin
Charlotte mold Plain mold for charlottes and other desserts, sometimes used for molded salads
chasseur (F) Method of preparing meat, fowl, or eggs with a garnish of mushrooms, shallots, and white wine
chaud-froid (F) Elaborate dish of meat, poultry, game, or fish, masked with a creamy sauce, decorated and glazed with aspic. Served cold
chiffonade (F) Garnish made of shredded lettuce, sorrel, and spinach; used for decorating soups or cold dishes
chilling Cooling food, without freezing it, in the refrigerator
chining Separating the backbone from the ribs in a roast of meat to make carving easier
chinois (F) 1. In the Chinese style. 2. Conical-shaped sieve with a fine mesh
chorizo (S) Smoked spicy pork sausage
civet (F) Game stew with red wine, garnished with onions, bacon, and mushrooms
clarified butter Butter cleared of impurities by slow melting and filtering
clarifying 1. Clearing fats by heating and filtering. 2. Clearing stock for consommés and aspics with beaten egg white
cocotte (F) Small, ovenproof earthenware, porcelain, or metal dish used for baking individual egg dishes, mousses, or soufflés
coddling Cooking slowly in simmering water; usually refers to eggs
colander Perforated metal or plastic basket used for draining away liquids
compote (F) Dessert of fresh or dried fruit cooked whole, or quartered in syrup and served cold
concassé (F) Roughly chopped or broken up by pounding in a mortar
condé (F) 1. Dessert made with rice, e.g., pear condé. 2. Pastry topped with icing and glazed in the oven
conserve Usually a blend of several fruits preserved by boiling with sugar; used like jam
coquille (F) 1. Scallop. 2. Shell-shaped ovenproof dish used to serve fish, shellfish, or poultry
cordon bleu (F) Term applied to highly qualified cooks. According to legend, Louis XV of France once awarded a blue ribbon to a female chef who had prepared an outstanding meal
cornstarch Finely ground flour from corn; used for thickening sauces, puddings, and pie fillings
corn syrup Syrup obtained from corn; used for baking and confectionery
coupe (F) Goblet used for serving ice cream, fruit, and shellfish cocktails
crème (F) French term for fresh cream, butter, or custard cream, and thick creamy soup
crème brûlée (F) Cream custard with caramelized topping
crème caramel (F) Cold molded egg custard with caramel topping
crème fraîche (F) Cream that has been allowed to mature but not to go sour
créole Style of cooking in which peppers, tomatoes, okra, rice, and spicy sauces are used
crêpe (F) Thin pancake
crêpes Suzette (F) Crêpes cooked in orange sauce and flamed in liqueur
crimping Making a decorative border on a pie crust
croquettes (F) Cooked foods molded in small shapes, dipped in egg and crumbs, and deep-fried
croustade (F) Small crispy fried or baked bread or pastry shape that is filled with a savory mixture
croûte (F) 1. Pastry covering for meat, fish, and vegetables. 2. Slice of bread or brioche spread with butter or sauce and baked until crisp
curd Semisolid part of milk, produced by souring
curdle 1. To cause fresh milk or a sauce to separate into solids and liquids by overheating or by adding acid. 2. To cause creamed butter and sugar in a cake recipe to separate by adding the eggs too rapidly
cure To preserve fish or meat by drying, salting, or smoking

D

dariole Small, cup-shaped mold in which pastries or aspics are made
darne (F) Thick slice cut from round fish
daube (F) Stew of braised meat and vegetables
deep fat Hot fat or oil that is deep enough to cover food during frying
deep-frying Frying food by immersing it in hot fat or oil
déglacer (F) To add wine, stock, or cream to loosen browned particles from pan in which food has cooked; this forms the basis for a sauce or gravy
deviling Preparing meat, poultry, or fish with highly seasoned ingredients, for broiling or roasting
dice To cut into small cubes
dough Mixture of flour, water, milk, and sometimes egg and fat, that is firm enough to knead, roll, and shape
dredging Dusting food with flour or sugar
dress 1. To pluck, draw, and truss poultry or game. 2. To arrange or garnish a cooked dish
dressing 1. Sauce for a salad. 2. Stuffing for meat or poultry
drippings Fat that drips from meat, poultry, or game during roasting
dumplings 1. Small balls made of dough, forcemeat, or potato mixture that are steamed or poached; used to garnish soups and stews. 2. Fruit encased in dough and baked
dusting Sprinkling lightly with flour, sugar, spice, or seasoning

E

éclair (F) Light, oblong choux pastry split and filled with cream and usually topped with chocolate icing

en croûte (F) Encased in pastry

en papillote (F) Wrapped, cooked, and served in oiled or buttered paper or foil

entrée (F) 1. Third course in a formal meal, following the fish course. 2. The main course

entremets (F) Dessert

F

fines herbes (F) Mixture of finely chopped fresh parsley, chervil, tarragon, and chives

flake 1. Separating cooked fish into individual flaky slivers. 2. Grating chocolate or cheese into small slivers

flambé (F) Flamed, e.g., food tossed in a pan to which burning brandy or other alcohol has been added

Florentine, à la Served on a bed of buttered spinach and coated with cheese sauce; usually refers to fish or eggs

foie gras (F) The preserved liver of specially fattened goose or duck

folding Enveloping a delicate mixture with a heavier mixture

fondue (Sw) Melted cheese and white wine dish into which diners dunk cubes of bread

fool Cold dessert consisting of fruit purée and whipped cream

freezing Solidifying or preserving food by chilling and storing it at 32°F or lower. A home freezer should maintain a temperature of 0°F or lower

fricadelles (F) Meatballs made with ground pork and veal, spices, white bread crumbs, cream, and egg; they are poached in stock or sautéed

fricassee (F) White stew of chicken, rabbit, veal, and vegetables that are first sautéed in butter, then cooked in stock and finished with cream and egg yolks

frost 1. To coat a cake with an icing of confectioners' sugar. 2. To dip the rim of a glass in egg white and superfine sugar and then chill in a refrigerator until set

fumet (F) Concentrated broth or stock obtained from fish, meat, or vegetables

G

galantine (F) Dish of boned and stuffed poultry, game, or meat, glazed with aspic and served cold

galette (F) 1. Flat pastry cake traditionally baked for Twelfth Night. 2. Flat cake of sliced or mashed potato

garnishing Enhancing a dish with decorations, usually edible

gelatin Transparent protein made from animal bones and tissue that melts in hot liquid and forms a jelly when cold; used for sweet and savory dishes

génoise (F) Rich sponge cake consisting of eggs, sugar, flour, and melted butter; baked in a flat pan

giblets Edible internal organs and trimmings of poultry and game, including the liver, heart, gizzard, neck, and pinions

glacé (F) Glazed, frozen, or iced

glace de viande (F) Meat glaze made from concentrated meat stock

glaze A glossy finish given to food by brushing with beaten egg, milk, sugar syrup, or melted preserves

gnocchi (I) Small dumplings made from semolina, potatoes, or choux pastry

goujon (F) 1. Gudgeons—small fish fried and served as a garnish. 2. Small strips of fried fish, such as sole

goulash (H) Meat and onion stew flavored with paprika

granita (I) Water ice

granité (I) Water ice

gratiné (F) *See* Au Gratin

gravy 1. Juices exuded by roasted meat and poultry. 2. A sauce made from these juices by boiling with stock or wine, sometimes thickened with flour

grèque, à la (F) 1. In the Greek style, i.e., cooked in stock with olive oil. 2. Dishes garnished with savory rice and dressed with oil and vinegar

griddle Flat metal plate used to bake breads and pancakes on the top of the stove. Some stoves are equipped with built-in griddles

grissini (I) Breadsticks

groats Dehusked grain, especially oats, sometimes milled

guiche (F) Alsatian open tart with savory filling made with cream and eggs. Equivalent to quiche

H

hanging Suspending meat or game in a cool, dry place until it is tender

hard sauce Sweet butter sauce flavored with brandy, rum, or whisky; it is chilled until hard and melts when served on hot puddings

haricot (F) Dried white bean

haricot vert (F) Green string bean

hash Dish of chopped food, usually leftover meat, potatoes, or other vegetables, pan-fried together

herbs Plants without woody stems. Commonly used herbs are basil, bay leaf, chervil, marjoram, mint, oregano, parsley, rosemary, sage, savory, tarragon, and thyme; used in fresh or dried form to add flavor to food.

hors d'oeuvre (F) Hot or cold appetizer served at the start of a meal

hulling Removing the calyx from a fruit or vegetable

I

icing Sweet coating for cakes; frosting

icing nails or **flower nails** Metal or plastic nails resembling oversized thumbtacks, with various-shaped heads; used for shaping decorative flowers for cakes

infusing Steeping herbs, tea leaves, or coffee in water or other liquid to extract the flavor

Irish coffee Coffee flavored with Irish whisky and topped with thick cream

J

jus (F) Juices from roasting meat; used as gravy

K

kebab (T) Marinated meat cubes grilled or broiled on a skewer

kedgeree (In) Breakfast or lunch dish of cooked fish or meat, rice, and eggs

kosher Food prepared according to Orthodox Jewish law

kugelhopf Sweetened yeast cake containing dried fruit, baked in a fluted ring mold.

L

langouste (F) Rock or spiny lobster

langue du chat (F) Flat, finger-shaped crisp cookie served with cold desserts

lard Natural or refined pork fat

larding Threading strips of fat through lean meat, using a special needle. This prevents the meat from becoming dry during roasting

lasagne (I) 1. Wide flat noodles, with plain or ruffled edges. 2. A dish consisting of lasagne baked with sauce, cheese, and sometimes sausage or other meat

leaven Substance, such as yeast, that causes dough or batter to rise

legumes (F) 1. Vegetables. 2. Plants with seed pods, such as peas and beans

lentils Seeds of a legume, soaked and used in soups, stews, and purées

Lyonnaise (F) In the Lyons style, usually with onions

M

macaroni (I) Tubular pasta of varying lengths and shapes

macédoine (F) Mixture of fruit or vegetables

macerate To soften food by soaking it in liquid

marinade Blend of oil, wine or vinegar, herbs, and spices; used to flavor or tenderize meat, game, fish, or vegetables

marinate To steep in marinade

marinière (F) 1. Refers to mussels cooked in white wine and herbs and served in their shells. 2. Of fish cooked in white wine and garnished with mussels

marmite (F) Metal or earthenware pot used for making soups

matelote (F) In the sailor's style, e.g., fish stew made with wine or cider

medallions (F) Small circular cuts of meat, fish, or pâté

meringue (F) Beaten egg white blended with sugar; it is spooned or piped on top of sweet pies or into small shapes, then baked crisp at a very low temperature

meunière (F) Literally, "in the style of a miller's wife;" floured, sautéed in butter, seasoned, and sprinkled with parsley and lemon juice

Milanese (I) In the Milan style, e.g., scallops of meat coated in egg, bread crumbs, seasoned with grated Parmesan cheese, and sautéed in butter

mirabelle (F) 1. Small yellow plum used as tart filling. 2. A liqueur made from this fruit

mirepoix (F) Mixture of finely diced vegetables and sometimes ham that, when sautéed in butter, is used as a base for brown sauces and braised dishes

mixed herbs Equal amounts of crumbled aromatic herbs, such as thyme, marjoram, oregano, savory, rosemary, and bay leaf

mocha 1. High-quality coffee. 2. A blend of coffee and chocolate flavors

mouler (F) To grind soft food into a purée, or dry food into a powder

moules (F) Mussels

moussaka Middle Eastern dish of ground meat, eggplant, and tomatoes, topped with cheese sauce or savory custard

mousse 1. Light sweet cold dish made with cream, whipped egg white, and gelatin. 2. A light hot or cold savory dish made with meat, poultry, game, fish, or shellfish

muesli (Sw) Dish of raw rolled oats, coarsely grated apple, nuts, and dried fruit served with cream

N

navarin (F) Stew of lamb and small onions and potatoes

Neapolitan (I) Ice creams and sweet cakes served in layers of different colors and flavors

Niçoise (F) In the Nice style, cooked with tomatoes, onion, garlic, and black olives

noodles Flat ribbon pasta made from flour, water, and egg

Normande, à la (F) In the Normandy style, a method of preparing fish, especially sole, by braising in white wine. 2. A method of preparing meat or chicken by flavoring with cider and a sauce containing calvados

nouilles (F) Noodles

O

osso buco (I) Dish of braised veal marrow bones prepared with tomatoes and wine

P

paella (S) Dish of saffron rice, chicken, and shellfish, named after the large shallow pan in which it is traditionally cooked

panada, panade 1. Thick paste made of flour or bread and used to bind ingredients. 2. a soup made of milk, water, stock, bread, and butter

panettone (I) Cakelike bread with raisins, often served at Christmas

paprika (H) Ground sweet red pepper

parboiling Boiling for a short time to cook food partially

parfait (F) 1. Frozen dessert made of whipped cream and fruit purée. 2. An American dessert in which ice cream in parfait glasses is topped with flavored syrups, sauces, or fruit, and whipped cream

Parmentier (F) Applied to dishes containing potatoes; the term is derived from Antoine Parmentier who introduced the potato to France

pasta (I) Paste made with flour and water, sometimes enriched with egg and oil; used to make macaroni, spaghetti, and the like

pasteurizing Method of sterilizing milk by heating it to 140°–180°F to destroy the bacteria. The term is derived from Louis Pasteur, who developed the method

pastry Dough made with flour, butter, and water and baked or deep-fried until crisp

pastry wheel Small, serrated wooden or metal wheel for cutting and fluting pastry

pâté (F) 1. Savory mixture that is baked in a casserole or terrine and served cold. 2. Savory mixture baked in a pastry shell and served hot or cold

pâte à choux (F) Choux pastry

pâté de foie gras (F) A smooth, seasoned paste made from livers of fattened geese or ducks

patty 1. Small, flat, round or oval cake of food, such as potato cake or fish cake, that is served hot. 2. Small, flat individual pie, such as a chicken patty, that is served hot or cold

paupiette (F) Thin slice of meat rolled around a savory filling

pavé (F) 1. Cold savory mousse set in a square mold coated with aspic. 2. Square sponge cake filled with butter cream and coated with icing

pearl barley Dehusked barley grains; used in soups

pectin Substance extracted from fruit and vegetables; used to set jellies and jams

petits fours (F) 1. Tiny sponge cakes, iced and decorated. 2. Small fruits, e.g., grapes and cherries, coated in sugar glaze. 3. Marzipan colored and shaped to resemble miniature fruits.

petits pois (F) Tiny young green peas

pickle 1. To preserve meat, fish, fruit, or vegetables in brine or vinegar solution. 2. Food preserved in brine or vinegar solution

pilaf, pilau (T) Middle Eastern dish of cooked rice mixed with spiced, cooked meat, chicken, or fish

Cooking Terms

pimiento Green or red bell pepper

pintade (F) Guinea fowl

pipe To force meringue, icing, savory butter, potato purée, or the like, through a pastry bag fitted with a tube, to decorate various dishes

piquante (F) Pleasantly sharp and appetizing

pith In citrus fruit, the white cellular lining of the rind covering the flesh

pizza (I) Open-face pie consisting of a yeast dough topped with tomatoes, cheese, anchovies, and olives

pizzaiola (I) Meat or chicken cooked in red wine and tomato sauce and flavored with garlic

plat du jour (F) Dish of the day, or daily special on a French menu

pluck To remove the feathers from a domesticated or game bird

poaching Cooking food in simmering liquid just below boiling point

polenta (I) Cornmeal made from dried and ground corn

potage (F) Soup

praline (F) Candy consisting of unblanched almonds or pecans caramelized in boiling sugar

preserving Keeping food for long periods of time by treating with refrigeration, freezing, dehydrating, canning, pickling in salt, salting, smoking, or boiling in sugar

printanier (F) Garnish of spring vegetables

prosciutto (I) Raw smoked ham, served finely sliced

Provençale (F) In the Provence style, i.e., cooked with garlic and tomatoes

pudding 1. Baked, boiled, or steamed foods, savory or sweet, served as side or main dishes or desserts. 2. Boiled suet crust that is filled with meat or poultry

pulp 1. Soft, fleshy tissue of fruit or vegetables. 2. To reduce food to a soft mass by crushing or boiling

pulses Seeds of a variety of legumes, such as peas, beans, and lentils

purée (F) 1. Sieved raw or cooked food. 2. Thick vegetable mixture that is passed through a sieve or whirled in an electric blender

Q

quenelles (F) Light savory dumplings made of meat or fish and used as a garnish or in a delicate sauce

quiche (F) Open-face pastry shell filled with a savory custard mixture. *See also* Guiche

R

raclette (Sw) 1. Swiss dish made by holding cheese near a fire until it melts. It is scraped onto a platter and eaten with crusty bread and boiled potatoes. 2. The cheese used to make this dish

ragoût (F) Stew of meat and vegetables

ramekins 1. Individual ovenware dishes. 2. Small pastry shells filled with cream cheese

ratafia 1. Flavoring made from bitter almonds. 2. Liqueur made from fruit kernels. 3. Tiny macaroon

ratatouille (F) Stew made of eggplants, onions, peppers, and tomatoes cooked in olive oil

ravioli (I) Small pasta envelopes filled with a savory stuffing, boiled, and served with a sauce and grated cheese

reducing Concentrating a liquid by boiling and evaporation

relish Sharp or spicy sauce made with fruit or vegetables that adds a piquant flavor to other foods

rendering 1. Slowly cooking meat tissues and trimmings to obtain fat. 2. Clearing frying fat by heating it

rennet Substance extracted from the stomach lining of calves; used to coagulate milk for junket and for making cheese curd

Ricard French licorice-flavored aperitif

rigatoni (I) Ribbed macaroni

risotto (I) Savory rice, sautéed and then cooked in stock, often flavored with cheese

roasting Cooking in the oven with radiant heat, or on a spit over or under an open flame

roe 1. Milt of the male fish, called soft roe. 2. Eggs of the female fish, called hard roe. 3. Eggs of shellfish, also called coral because of their color

Romano (I) 1. In the style of Rome. 2. A dry, sharp Italian cheese similar to Parmesan

rotisserie (F) Rotating spit used for roasting or grilling meat or poultry

roulade (F) Meat, especially beef or veal, rolled around various fillings

roux (F) Mixture of fat and flour that, when cooked, is used as a base for savory sauces

S

saignant (F) Underdone, or very rare; refers to meat

salami (I) Spiced pork sausage, sold fresh or smoked

salmi (F) Stew made by first roasting game and then cooking it in wine sauce

samovar (R) Metal tea urn heated from an inside tube in which charcoal is burned

sauté (F) To cook food rapidly in shallow, hot fat, tossing and turning it until evenly browned

savarin (F) Rich yeast cake that is baked in a ring mold and soaked in liqueur-flavored syrup. Served cold with cream

scald 1. To heat milk or cream to just below boiling point. 2. To plunge fruit or vegetables briefly into boiling water to remove the skins

scallion Young onion with an undeveloped bulb; used for salads and as a garnish

scallop 1. Edible mollusk with white flesh. The deep fluted shell is used for serving the scallops and other foods. 2. Thin slice of meat that is beaten flat and sautéed

scaloppine (I) Small scallops of veal weighing 1–1½ ounces

schnitzel (G) Veal slice; *see* Scallop

scoring 1. Cutting gashes or narrow grooves on the surface of food. 2. Making a pattern of squares or diamonds on pastry crust

searing Browning meat rapidly with high heat to seal in the juices

seasoned flour Flour flavored with salt and pepper. To 1 cup of flour, add 1 teaspoon salt and either ¼ teaspoon black pepper or ½ teaspoon paprika

seasoning Salt, pepper, spices, or herbs that are added to food to improve flavor

shot or **sprinkles** Small candy pellets used for decorating cakes and cookies

sifting Passing through a sieve to remove lumps; usually refers to flour or sugar

simmering Cooking in liquid that is heated to just below boiling point

skewer Metal or wooden pin used to hold meat, poultry, or fish in shape during cooking

skimming Removing floating matter, such as fat or scum, from the surface of broth, jam, or other liquid

smoking Curing food, such as bacon or fish, by exposing it to wood smoke

sorbet (F) Water ice made with fruit juice or purée

soufflé (F) Baked dish consisting of a sauce or purée thickened with egg yolks into which stiffly beaten egg whites are then folded

soufflé dish Straight-sided dish used for cooking and serving soufflés

spaghetti (I) Solid strands of pasta of various thicknesses

spit Revolving skewer or metal rod on which meat, poultry, or game is roasted, usually over a charcoal fire

spring-form mold Baking pan with hinged sides held together by a metal clamp or pin that is opened to release the cake or pie

star anise Star-shaped seed with a licorice flavor; used in oriental cooking

starch 1. Carbohydrate obtained from such foods as rice, corn, and potatoes. 2. A preparation made from such foods; used as a thickening for sauces, soups, and stews

steaming Cooking food in the steam rising from boiling water

steeping 1. Soaking in liquid until saturated with a soluble ingredient. 2. Soaking to remove an ingredient, such as salt, from smoked ham or salt cod

sterilizing Destroying germs by exposing food to heat

stewing To simmer food slowly in a covered pan or casserole

stirring Mixing with a circular movement, using a spoon or fork

straining Separating liquids from solids by passing them through a metal or nylon sieve or through cheesecloth

strudel (A) Thin leaves of pastry dough that are filled with fruit, nuts, or savory mixtures and then rolled and baked

stuffing Savory mixture of bread or rice, herbs, fruit, or ground meat; used to fill poultry, fish, meat, and vegetables

suet Fat around beef or lamb kidneys

syllabub Cold dessert of sweetened thick cream and white wine, often flavored with sherry or brandy

syrup Thick, sweet liquid made by boiling sugar with water, fruit juice, or both

T

table d'hôte (F) Meal of three or more courses at a fixed price

tagliatelle (I) Thin flat egg noodles

terrine (F) 1. Earthenware pot used for cooking and serving pâté. 2. Food cooked in a terrine

timbale (F) 1. Cup-shaped earthenware or metal mold. 2. Food prepared in such a mold

truffles Rare mushroomlike fungus, black or white, with a firm texture and delicate taste. Expensive delicacies, truffles are mainly used as a garnish

trussing Securing a bird or roast of meat in a neat shape with skewers or string before cooking

tube pan Ring-shaped pan for baking cakes

tutti frutti (I) Dried or candied mixed fruits added to ice cream

U

unleavened bread Bread made without a raising agent; when baked, it is thin, flat, and round

V

vanilla sugar Sugar flavored with vanilla by putting it with a vanilla bean in a closed jar

variety meats Edible internal organs of animals, as liver, kidneys, sweetbreads, tripe, brains, tongue, and heart

velouté (F) 1. Basic white sauce made with chicken, veal, or fish stock. 2. Soup with a creamy consistency

vermicelli (I) Very fine strands of pasta

vinaigrette sauce (F) Mixture of oil, vinegar, salt, and pepper, which is sometimes flavored with herbs; used on salads, cold vegetables, meats, and fish

vinegar Clear liquid, primarily acetic acid, obtained by the fermentation of wine, cider, or malt beer

vol-au-vent (F) Light flaky shell of puff pastry

W

wafer Thin cookie made with rice flour; served with ice cream

waffle Batter cooked on a hot greased waffle iron

whey Liquid that separates from the curd when milk curdles; used in making cheese

whipping Beating air into a substance, such as egg whites and cream, with a fork, whisk, rotary beater, or electric mixer to lighten it into a froth and increase its volume

whisk Looped wire utensil used to beat air into eggs, cream, or batters

Wiener Schnitzel (A) Veal slice cooked in the Viennese style, i.e., coated in egg and bread crumbs, sautéed in butter, and sometimes garnished with anchovies and capers

Y

yeast Fungus cells used to produce alcoholic fermentation or to cause dough to rise

yogurt Curdled milk that has been treated with harmless bacteria. In the Middle East it is served as a sauce with meat, fish, and vegetables

Z

zabaglione (I) Dessert consisting of egg yolks, white wine or marsala, and sugar; ingredients are beaten together in the top of a double boiler over boiling water until thick and foamy

zest (F) Colored oily outer skin of citrus fruit; grated or peeled, it is used to flavor foods and liquids

zester Small tool for scraping off zest

Index

Page numbers in regular type refer to the text;
those in *italic* type refer to illustrations.

413

G

Gorgonzola cheese, 44, *45*
and prosciutto sandwich, 189
Gouda cheese, 44
Gougère au fromage, 94
Goujons of sole with tartare sauce, 95
Goulash, Hungarian, 219
Gournay cheese, 43
Granitas. *See* Frozen desserts.
Grape(s)
as garnish, 397
preparation, 345
uses for, 345
varieties of, 16
recipes
chicken livers with. 140
jelly, 351
mold, 340
Grapefruit
freezing, 409
peeling, *346*
preparation, 345
uses for, 345
varieties of, 14
recipes
avocado and citrus salad, 114
in brandy, 125
marmalade, 89
three-fruit marmalade, 89
Gratin of ham, 138
Gravad lax, 133
Gravies, 302–303
storing, 401
thick, 303
thin, 303
See also Sauces, brown.
Greek rice ring, 224
Green beans, 18, *19*
cooking methods for, 329
preparation, 329
serving, 329
recipes
haricots verts au beurre, 69
mimosa, 184
and pears, Westphalian, 245
with sabayon sauce, 206
with sauce vinaigrette, 129
in sour cream, 185
Tuscany style, 266

Green butter, 338
Green peppers. *See* Peppers.
Gruyère cheese, 44
French, 43
recipe
Alpine fondue, 249
Guacamole, 149
Guinea hen, cooking methods for, 324

H

Haddock, 26
filleting, 206
sautéing, 307
smoked, 311
recipes
baked, 117
Barrie, 154
creamed, manicotti with, 162
fisherman's pie, 269
fish mousse with Bercy sauce, 236–237
Mediterranean fish soup, 53
Monte Carlo, 156
pescado a la marina, 217
smoked, mousse, 96
Hake, 26, *27*
sautéing, 307
Halibut, 26
braising, 307
recipes
au gratin, 116
casserole of, 54–55
with corn, 278
Dugléré, 257
plaki, 258
Ham
baking, 315, *316*
boneless, 39
carving, *319*
cooked, 38–39
country-style, 315–316
hocks, 39
roasting, 315
sliced, 39
smoked, 39
steak, 38

whole fresh, 38
recipes
baked, with apricot stuffing, 159
baked glazed, *250,* 251
baked picnic, 200
and chicken loaf, 189
eggplant with, 184–185
glazed, 171
gratin of, 138
jambalaya, 238
jambon à la crème, 201
lample pie, 147
and melon gondolas, 215
omelet, 335
in puff pastry, 119
schinkenfleckerl, 244
slices in Madeira sauce, 220
soufflé, 335
spiced, 107
and veal pie, 240
See also Pork.
Hamburger. *See* Beef.
Hanging poultry, 320
Hangtown fry, 270
Hard-shell clams, 28, *29*
Hare, 31
See also Game.
Haricots verts au beurre, 69
Hash
chicken, 271
red flannel, 289
Havarti cheese, 44, *45*
Hazelnut(s), 11
gantois, 228
torte, Hungarian, 248
Hearts. *See* Variety meats.
Hens, types of, 30
Herb(s)
butters, 338
uses of, 333
See also Names of individual herbs.
Herbed Scotch eggs, 107
Herring
Bismarck, 311
lake, 25
salted, 311
smoked, 311

recipes
marinated, 114
salad, 175
smoked, with horseradish cream, 255
Hollandaise sauce, 303
Homemade green noodles, 81
Homemade marmalade, 88–89
Homemade wines, 352
Honey
-butter frosting, 394
fruit nut caramels, 396
mousse, 340
sauce, 305
Honeyball melons, 17
Honeycomb mold, 340
Honeycomb tripe, 40
Honeydew cups, 236
Honeydew melons, *16,* 17
Hopping John, 251
Hors d'oeuvres. *See* Appetizers.
Horseradish, 20
Horseradish butter, 338
Horseradish sauce, 304
Hot cakes, sourdough, 380
Hot chili fish curry, 158
Hot crab soufflé, 74
Hot cross buns, 129
Hot-water crust, 365
Hot-water pastry, 360
Hubbard squash, 23
Huckleberries, 13
Huevos rancheros, 271
Hungarian goulash, 219
Hungarian hazelnut torte, 248
Hungarian sauce, 302

I

Ice(s)
granita al caffè, 207
strawberry, 166
tomato, 114
Iceberg lettuce, *20,* 21
Icebox cheesecake, 84
Ice cream(s)
freezing, 406
methods of making, 342

pointers to success for, 342
recipes
bread crumb, 210
chocolate, rich, 342–343
coffee, 342
melon, 208
pineapple, 342
praline, 342
strawberry, 166
vanilla, 342
See also Frozen desserts.
Iced petits fours, 389
Iced tangerines, 66
Icing(s)
caramel, 394
fondant, 394
royal, 394
royal, roses, *393*
soft sugar, 393
Imam bayjldi, 124
Individual pizzas, 67
In the midst of winter, 290–293
In-shell clams, 28
Irish stew, 258–259
Italian sausages, chicken with, 60
Italian supplì, 244

J

Jaffa oranges, 15
Jam(s)
fruit for, 349
making, *349*
setting point for, 349
recipes
apple, 350
apricot, 350
blackberry, 350
blueberry, 350
cherry, 350
gooseberry, 350
plum, 350
pudding, steamed, 85
raspberry, 350
rhubarb, 350
strawberry, 350
Jambalaya, 238